T0368403

DEPARTURES *on*
the HOUSE

DEPARTURES *on the* HOUSE

How Retirements, Redistricting and Scandal
Yielded A Near-Postwar Record of House
Members Exiting In 1992

SCOTT CRASS

To order additional copies of this book, contact:
Xlibris
1-888-795-4274
www.Xlibris.com
Orders@Xlibris.com
804319

Table of Contents

Cover Images

Row One

Frank Horton (R-New York); Robert W. Davis (R-Michigan); Donald Pease (D-Ohio); Walter Jones, Sr. (D-North Carolina)

Row Two

Ed Jenkins (D-Georgia); Chalmers Wylie (R-Ohio); Stephen Solarz (D-New York); Jim Jontz (D-Indiana)

Row Three

William Lehman (D-Florida); Edward Roybal (D-California); Howard Wolpe (D-Michigan); John Paul Hammerschmidt (R-Arkansas); Bernard Dwyer (D-New Jersey); David O'B Martin (R-New York)

Row Four

Dante Fascell (R-Florida); Ted Weiss (D-New York); Frank Annunzio (D-Illinois); Clarence Miller (R-Ohio)

PROLOGUE

**Ohio Congresswoman Mary Rose Oakar was arguably the poster
child of the public unrest toward Congress in 1992. When the 103rd
Congress gaveled to order, neither she nor her Cleveland area colleagues
Edward Feighan (left) and Dennis Eckart (right) would be members.
Photo via The Cleveland Plain Dealer**

As the 102nd Congress prepared to adjourn in the fall of 1992, an eight-term Democratic Congresswoman from Cleveland, Ohio named Mary Rose Oakar took part in a special order on the House floor to salute six members of her delegation that would not be returning for the 103rd. "Perhaps no one will ever write a book about these gentlemen and their service," Oakar said, "but I feel very, very strongly that they have achieved notable success in pursuing their respective legislation." At that point, Oakar was locked in a very bitter and ultimately unsuccessful race for a ninth term. Whether she knew she would not return is not known but her challenge for a book to be written was worthy.

Ohio in fact was only a personification of the wild and woolly environment that was 1992 when the largest number of members of the House of Representatives since World War II (110) left Congress with many, including Oakar, doing so involuntarily. Retirements, reapportionment, a wide-reaching check overdraft scandal, and a loophole involving members being permitted to pocket their campaign treasuries contributed to the large turnover. The members who departed encompassed a broad spectrum of the House itself. These included senior Congressmen who served their country in uniform, mid-level members in their legislative prime, rising stars that already proved themselves and backbenchers. They were among the most virtuous individuals whose hearts may have been in the right place, but who simply got caught up with the lure of Washington and the perks of being a member of Congress. All of this made some of the looming departures quite predictable; others came without warning and many of the rest were surprising at the time but not so much in hindsight.

Just as it was for the members of Congress who left office, 1992 was a transformational year for myself as well. At the start of the year I was preparing to complete my senior year at South Brunswick High School in New Jersey, pondering what the next step would be. Post-graduation and summer saw apprehension as I prepared to embark on the next venture, Monmouth University in West Long Branch, New Jersey. Fall of course was getting oriented with classes, new surroundings and making friends. One thing, however, was a constant throughout that year. As a Congressional junkie and then some, I watched with fascination the unfolding events and took glee in trying to predict the unpredictable – which member would be the next to go? Who would next announce their retirement? Who would be redistricted out of office or who would see their careers end by virtue of voter revolt? I was a kid in a candy store. That enjoyment was enhanced by a looming presidential election and razor-tight U.S. Senate races which, in the "Year of the Woman," had its own dynamic (a story for another time and perhaps another book).

The one commonality I heard again and again from nearly everyone I spoke with – members, families and staff, was that "things were different then." Partisanship, while certainly existent, was far from cutthroat and civility governed debates. By the same token, friendships crossed both the partisan aisle and ideological divides. At least one other assumption was debunked through my research. Contrary to how a number of members were portrayed, or even the circumstances for their leaving office, the vast majority were not hacks. They were public servants for the right reasons – because they loved their people and their communities and were willing to fight day and night to see dividends.

Mary Rose Oakar was correct. The departing members from her home state would make fascinating and in some cases inspiring stories, as would members from the rest of the nation. *Departures on the House* portrays biographies of nearly every one of the 110 people who left office that year. Each story is a combination of politics, policy and personality all of which are stories that need to be told.

There are a handful of exclusions from this book. A few members successfully pursued higher office – winning Senate or gubernatorial seats and saw their careers continue well into the next century. The other departures left out are a vocally anti-Semitic Democrat from Chicago and a vocally homophobic Republican from California. Their names need not be mentioned and their stories not be told. What does need to be told is the lay of the land that led to an incredible, unforeseen, (and for junkies like me) exciting year on the House front.

First, however, a few thank yous. To the former members of Congress who assisted me with reading drafts and countless phone conversations and e-mails (even if not everything I had to write about them was positive) I am eternally grateful. I only wish that I had undertaken this project years if not decades earlier when more of your former colleagues were still with us. With that in mind, I want to acknowledge two members – Bob Traxler of Michigan and Liz Patterson of South Carolina, who I was privileged to speak during this arduous process, but who since passed away. I also want to offer profound appreciation to the family members and staffers of my deceased subjects who gave me very valuable information. Finally, to everyone who provided photographs, the quality of this book is greatly enhanced as a result.

To Alexa Marotta, my editor extraordinaire, thank you for meticulous – one might say, punctilious attention you gave my chapters. They say it's the little things, and your ability to spot needles in a haystack is one of your greatest strengths. Finally, to the men and women of the Armed Forces who keep us safe, you are a daily reminder that freedom is not free. As the saying goes, "some gave all but all gave some," and we as Americans would not be able to write books such as this were it not for your sacrifices.

And now, without an overview but no other ado, I give you the men and women who left the House of Representatives in 1992.

CHAPTER ONE

The Lay of the Land – Retirements, Reapportionment and The Mother of All Scandals

The Initial House Landscape

Well before the 1992 cycle began, it was clear that the next Congress was going to see a large turnover for reasons both cyclical and unique. The once-a-decade redistricting was a major circumstance. A number of states, mainly in the Northeast and the Midwest, were losing House seats to the South and West which meant that, while predicting who would draw the short end of the stick was virtually impossible, the size of those delegations had to shrink as the states in the Sunbelt would grow. Members' campaign treasuries were another factor. A debate had long been simmering over whether Congress-people should be able to convert the money in their campaign account - in some cases in the hundreds of thousands, to personal use. In 1989, a decision was reached which essentially was an invitation to take the money and run. It allowed for House members to keep the cash only if they did not serve past January 3, 1993. While the decision only applied to those who had been elected before 1980, that still left dozens for whom quitting in 1992 would make a tempting target.

There were other, more conventional reasons for a large turnover. Retirements occur every cycle and there were a number of sixty and seventy something year olds in the House who were viewed as past their prime. Throughout the course of the cycle, 53 members announced their intention to not seek re-election. The ambition of other members is always prevalent in a chamber of politicians and it was long thought that it was only a matter of time before some aimed for higher office. Sure enough, even before the 102nd Congress convened, certain members were flirting with taking the statewide leap and running for the Senate or their state's governorships. While some opted to stay, about a dozen went forward. There were others who, if not politically vulnerable from the start, would certainly be once their districts were redrawn or they were tagged as insiders or caught up in scandal. That category impacted both the primary and the general election and ultimately forced 43 people to look for new jobs.

The bottom line: when the dust settled and the shouting stopped, 110 House members serving in the 102nd Congress would not return when Speaker Thomas Foley banged the gavel to convene for the 103rd, a post-World War II record.

The span of the departures was awesome. Many congressional classes saw significant reductions in their ranks. Republicans from the class of 1966, which included future President George H.W. Bush, dwindled from five to one. Nine members of the famed Watergate class of 1974 left office, including some of the brightest stars that laid down their seats to defeat.

A number of state delegations were turned upside down. Ohio bade farewell to eight members and the Cleveland delegation was eviscerated with only one member, Louis Stokes returning for the 103. New York State suffered a jolt with the departure of 12 members, more than 1/3 of the delegation. Michigan saw eight of 18 members leave and Arkansas, the Razorback State, delivered a cut of big proportions to its delegation. A small state that relied on seniority to compete with bigger states, Arkansas lost three of its four members and the one who remained returned for a non-consecutive tenure just two years earlier. The "saving grace" for that delegation might have been that, with Bill Clinton's election, a favorite son took over the White House. Georgia did not prove particularly peachy on its incumbents either as six of ten left office, including three who were ousted by voters (to the Democrats chagrin, the man the party most wanted to beat, Minority Whip Newt Gingrich, was not among them – he won his primary by less than 1,000 votes). Other states that saw higher than average turnover: Pennsylvania with eight of 21 having departed and Alabama with three of seven.

A few large delegations bucked the trend. California had 45 House members but only eleven did not return, and four resulted from Senate runs. Some delegations remained almost completely in place. Texas, with all 27 members standing for re-election, saw 26 granted it. North Carolina provided lots of excitement for basketball fans but not so much at the Congressional level as only one of its eleven incumbents did not return. Indiana meanwhile gave nine of its ten members return passes to the 103rd Congress and Tennessee, the "volunteer state," voluntarily sent back all nine. Washington State saw all three of its Republicans return home while Illinois Democrats, reeling by a one-sided GOP remap, were forced to say goodbye to six colleagues who surrendered their seats to retirement or defeat.

Committees were impacted by the turnover as well though, some more than others. The Agriculture committee was one. On the Democratic side, eight of the top ten senior members would return, but eight of the next 10 members (the "middle row") would not. On the GOP side, the top three members departed. Ways and Means saw a similar dynamic. While the top seven most senior Democratic members made their way back for the 103rd, only two members from slot eight to seventeen would. On Foreign Affairs, nine of the top 15 Democrats did not return, including the Chair. On the other hand, the Education and Labor Committee only surrendered three of its twenty-five Democrats.

Nine members of the 1990 House Democratic Basketball Team
Top row: Jim Moody (Wisconsin), Lane Evans (Illinois), Tom McMillen (Maryland), Marty Russo (Illinois) and Robert Mrazek (New York)
Bottom Row: Marty Sabo (Minnesota), Harley Staggers (West Virginia), Tom Downey (New York) and Ben Jones (Georgia)
Seven of the nine members in this photo were among the 1992 departures
Photo via the Library of Congress

The Start of the Cycle

As 1991 got under way, seven aging Congressmen began their last terms: Democrats Glenn Anderson of California, who would turn 79 in 1992, Walter Jones of North Carolina, 79, Frank Annunzio of Illinois, 77, Gus Yatron and Joe Gaydos of Pennsylvania (65 and 66 respectively), Doug Barnard of Georgia, 70 and Republican Bill Dickinson of Alabama, 67. A few strongly intimated during their 1990 campaigns that they would be running for the last time, yet the first and second retirements were none of these folks. They were two Ohioans of whom no one expected to retire. Dennis Eckart was a 41-year old rising star, popular with his colleagues and a favorite of John Dingell, the chair of the Energy and Commerce Committee on which he was active. From the time of his September 30th announcement, Dingell begged him to stay but Eckart decided as early as the previous Christmas that family considerations circumvented his unlimited Congressional potential. Donald Pease, 60, came three days later, not absolutely out of left field but still somewhat unexpected. He cited his desire to "just plain loaf." Third and fourth were more conventional. Barnard quit days later and Anderson, who had actually held a fundraiser months earlier, said he would wrap up his career as well. Jones announced his departure in early November.

Throughout much of this time, members began to declare their intention to seek other office. California was golden for members as Democrats Barbara Boxer and Mel Levine (and for a time, Robert Matsui), planned to mount a bid for the seat of the retiring U.S. Senator Alan Cranston. Tom Campbell was seeking the GOP nod for that seat. A special election to fill the remaining two years of California's other Senate seat that same day and Republican Congressman Bill Dannemeyer (the homophobe) announced that he'd be taking on appointed Senator John Seymour in the primary.

In other states, Washington had two well-respected Republicans – Rod Chandler and Sid Morrison, who were going to try to become U.S. Senator and Governor respectively. In Oregon, nine-term Democrat Les AuCoin was urged to challenge one of Oregon's two U.S. Senators for years and, by the fall of 1991, decided that passing up a race against Bob Packwood was something he could not pass up. Richard Stallings, a very talented and rare Democrat in Idaho, was urged to do the same. He declared his intention to challenge a bombastic and archconservative Republican, Steve Symms, who retired soon after. The retirement of Senator Jake Garn in Utah led Wayne Owens to give up a marginal seat that he demonstrated he could hold to make a very challenging Senate run. Jim Moody of Wisconsin also threw his hat into the ring to take on Senator Bob Kasten, though he first had to navigate his way through a primary. There were only a few gubernatorial races on the ballot but Delaware presented a perfect opportunity for Tom Carper who, as the "First State's" At Large" Congressman, already represented the entire constituency he'd be seeking to govern.

Ohio Congressman Dennis Eckart, 41 in September 1991, shocked colleagues with his retirement, the first among what would be a long, long list. The Capitol Hill newspaper *Roll Call* caught up with him in December 1992 in his almost vacant office
Photo via Getty Images

The obligatory redrawing of the lines began taking shape in early in '91 and one member was eliminated at least a couple of years before. By roughly 1989, it was known that the state of Montana would be surrendering one of its two Congressional seats to reapportionment. Two Congressmen, Democrat Pat Williams and Republican Ron Marlenee, represented the state. Unless one or the other decided to run for Governor, (as many urged) a face-off would be inevitable, long and close which is exactly what transpired.

The first states to compete included ones where only minor tinkering was required – Indiana, Missouri, Oklahoma and Nebraska. This also included Iowa that had to adjust boundaries to drop one seat. Lawmakers did so with relative ease and created a fair fight between a Democrat, Dave Nagle and a Republican, Jim Nussle in what would come to be known as the "Nagle-Nussle tussle." Texas, to the exasperation of the badly outnumbered Republicans, produced a plan that ceded the GOP the seven seats they already held, but nothing else. Democrats held the remaining 20 seats and would draw the lines so that they could continue to be won comfortably. That wasn't all. Texas gained three seats and, confirming the adage that "to the victor goes the spoils," created all three to give lopsided majorities to Democrats. The GOP howled but with Ann Richards as Governor and strong Democratic majorities in the legislature, they were powerless to stop it.

In other large states with divided government, the picture was murkier. California, with seven new seats on the line, had big repercussions for both parties. Some Democrats and Republicans agreed on a plan – Republican Governor Pete Wilson rejected that and gambled with the courts. The gamble was nebulous but on its face, successful. It made a number of districts more competitive, thereby forcing a good six secure Democrats to acquaint themselves with more Republicans than they had been accustomed and vice-versa for a handful in the GOP. Some could use their talent and longevity to absorb this but others had decent hurdles ahead. It was obvious that the political wind would dictate which party would benefit.

Five Republicans elected to the House with future President George H.W. Bush in 1966 were still serving in 1992. Only one, John Myers of Indiana (far left), would remain in the next Congress, Chalmers Wylie of Ohio (third from right), John Paul Hammerschmidt of Arkansas (far right) along with Clarence Miller of Ohio and Guy Vander Jagt of Michigan (not pictured) would become private citizens. Others in the photo include Sonny Montgomery, a Democrat from Mississippi and Michigan Senator Don Riegel. The Gatlin Brothers was the entertainment for the White House barbecue Photo via the George H.W. Bush Presidential Library and Museum

Of the states that completed redrawing in 1991, Illinois was the biggest bonanza and was the GOP that benefitted. With a heavily Democratic legislature, Republican Governor Jim Edgar was content to let a federal court redraw the lines and, in mid-November, the panel accepted the map submitted by the Republicans. Democrats were left scrambling. Not only was Annunzio's seat sacrificed, as both plans called for, but the districts of nine-term suburban Chicago's Marty Russo and two-term downstate's Glen Poshard were dismantled, leaving them with very unattractive options against other Democratic incumbents. On top of that, the district of John Cox, a freshman Democrat who captured his GOP friendly seat in a huge upset, saw the new map try to rectify that going forward. It dropped a few Democratic areas and added parts of Republican-heavy McHenry County, thereby ensuring a re-election campaign that would require not only all of Cox's political skills but also luck against a Republican nominee who would presumably be more credible than the person he upset in 1990. Annunzio initially announced a challenge to a big baron, Ways and Means Chair Dan Rostenkowski, but soon abandoned it and opted to step down. Russo meanwhile opted to challenge Bill Lipinski while Poshard waited until the filing deadline and decided to take on four-termer Terry Bruce in an area that contained only a sliver of Poshard's constituents.

In the same timeframe, a pair of Southeastern states losing a seat managed to reconstruct its lines without much difficulty. Given that the Democratic margins were so big, Kentucky was relatively uncontroversial. Some viewed Republican Larry Hopkins, who had just come across a spectacularly unsuccessful gubernatorial bid, as a prime candidate to have his turf eviscerated but he was surprisingly spared. Legislators instead combined the Sixth and Seventh districts represented by a very secure Republican, Hal Rogers and a formerly secure (until he was nearly obliterated in 1990) Democrat named Chris Perkins. Nevertheless, Hopkins decided to put an end to his career shortly before the new year with Perkins following suit soon after.

Neighboring West Virginia had slightly more drama mostly because there were four Democratic Representatives for a state that would have just three seats after 1992. Many assumed the odd man out would be Nick Joe Rahall, a surprisingly tepid winner in the last election with very few friends in the legislature. The final plan carved up five-termer Harley Staggers and he subsequently decided to take on a fellow five-termer, Alan Mollohan, in a seat where Mollohan had a decided edge.

With full Democratic control, Maryland's redistricting should also have been one-sided but turned out to be anything but. The state was neither gaining nor losing a seat but had to accommodate a second African-American majority district. Different factions of the Democratic Party had conflicting ideas and William Donald Schaefer had his own idea altogether – to protect his friend, Republican Congresswoman Helen Delich Bentley. After months of wrangling, the plan enacted left Tom McMillen, a Democrat from the Eastern Shore, at a severe disadvantage. He decided his best option would be to take on freshman Republican Wayne Gilchrest.

In early January, to no one's surprise whatsoever, Yatron announced plans to quit and Gaydos followed a week later. What was greatly surprising was Lindsay Thomas of Georgia calling it a career as well. Not yet 49, Thomas was as popular as can be with both constituents and colleagues. However, even for a Congressman, when opportunity knocks one has to stare it seriously in the eye. In his case, the opportunity was to run the 1996 Olympics to take place in Atlanta. Also announcing on the same day: a pair of Californians who became trailblazers to their races – Ed Roybal of California (the first Mexican-American to represent his state in 83 years) and Mervyn Dymally who had been an African-American Lieutenant Governor. Andy Ireland of Florida, who roughly midway through his tenure switched to the Republican Party, announced his plans to step down. He was the ranking Republican on the Small Business Committee.

To no one's surprise, Pennsylvania Democrats Gus Yatron and Joe Gaydos both decided to make the 102ⁿᵈ Congress their last. Gaydos's reasoning: "Age they say, is the fire extinguisher of flaming youth. Well, I'm 65. My fires are beginning to burn a little low. I think it's time to think about banking the furnace to conserve some of the heat." Images courtesy of C-SPAN

By the end of February, Florida native Bill Lehman, nearing 79 and the chair of an influential Appropriations subcommittee, announced plans to leave for health reasons. Larry Coughlin, 63, his ranking member and close collaborator surprised many by also deciding to move on. Before the month was out, John Paul Hammerschmidt of Arkansas and ranking member on Public Works yielded to a vow he made early in his career to not run past his 70th birthday. Dickinson, aged 67, made it official simply for the reason that it was time. Walter Jones meanwhile made the befuddling statement that he was pondering reversing his retirement but after a few weeks, he wisely decided to stick with his original plan.

At 49 and with a perpetually safe seat, Georgia Democrat Lindsay Thomas's retirement announcement dazzled colleagues and constituents alike
Photo courtesy of the U.S. House of Representatives Historical Collection

At roughly the same time, a long-running stalemate in Pennsylvania finally broke, producing a plan that was not particularly pleasing for Republicans. The outgoing Gaydos's district was carved up among its neighbors but Yatron's Berks County (Reading) district remained surprisingly in tack, even though it would exist without him. The immediate casualty was Richard Schulze, a nine-term Republican whose district was combined with an overly competitive three-termer named Curt Weldon. Schulze never was keen on serving more than 18 years, and announced his retirement. The district of Rick Santorum, a freshman Republican whose defeat of Democrat Doug Walgren in 1990 was a startling upset, was made significantly more Democratic. This didn't inhibit him, however, from continuing to foil insiders. He filed for re-election and his saving grace was that the leading Democrat in a very fractious field was a former Republican.

Bill Dickinson of Alabama and John Paul Hammerschmidt of Arkansas were just two of the ranking members of House Committees to call it quits (Armed Services and Public Works and Transportation respectively). Others would follow.
Photo via C-SPAN

The Anti-Incumbent Mood

By that point, an increasing distaste for incumbents was percolating. If lawmakers feared a jolt, they faced an earthquake when Maryland held its first primary in the nation on March 10th and seven-term Democratic Congresswoman Beverly Byron was upset by State Delegate Thomas Hattery. Never mind that the primary was more ideologically based (Byron was a conservative Democrat) and that Hattery as an elected official could not claim to be an outsider. The narrative was that Byron was as secure as can be and that is precisely what sent shivers down the spine of incumbents.

**The upset primary defeat of Maryland Congresswoman Beverly Byron
jolted members who feared an anti-incumbent environment.
Photo courtesy of C-SPAN**

Illinois cast its ballots two weeks later on March 17th and it became apparent early that the anti-Semite from Chicago would be trounced. The results were also unambiguous in the two Democratic incumbent matchups necessitated by redistricting. Lipinski roared past Russo while Poshard dwarfed Bruce. In neither instance did the incumbent thought to have the edge at the beginning of the contest prevail. The suspense of the evening was in a South Chicago district where Charlie Hayes, a five-term Democrat with 713 just-revealed overdrafts at the House Bank (see below), narrowly trailed Bobby Rush who was a former member of the Black Panthers and Rush's lead held. That same day, Democratic Senator Alan Dixon was upset by Carol Moseley-Braun which prompted some to call the Illinois primary the St. Patrick's Day Massacre. The news for incumbents wasn't all bad.

That same night, Rostenkowski beat back a challenge from an insurgent Dick Simpson but his 57-43% margin showed faultiness and cracks in his machine. Also noteworthy was the showing of another veteran Congressman who sat on Ways and Means, Republican Phil Crane. He held off Gary Skoien just 55-45%. Skoien used the "out of touch" theme and attacked Crane for his staunchly pro-life stance on abortion.

Enter the impact of most widespread scandal to have hit Congress in generations.

The House Bank Scandal

The euphemistic "House Check Bouncing scandal" came to the forefront in late September 1991 when the Capitol Hill newspaper *Roll Call* reported that 8,331 checks with insufficient balances were written by 269 current members and 56 former. Covering up overdrafts was not primitive. The 101-year-old bank had allegedly taken care of 12,309 overdrafts of members in 1972 alone. To boot, the overdraft penalties were neither waived nor included interest, something that flabbergasted the general public given that this was not a commercial bank standard.

Some points were established at the scandal's inception. One was that no taxpayer money was ever used for the House Bank to pay creditors to whom a problem check was written. Second, members were permitted to draw on their next month's paychecks provided they did not go beyond. Third, the bank delayed crediting deposits at times for days. Fourth, many members could not count on the Bank to religiously notify them (if at all) when their account had insufficient funds on a check coming through.

For critics of the House, all of the explanations in the world could not make this one go away. The scandal had legs and House Minority Leader Robert Michel captured the moment when he called the uproar, "one of those matters that wasn't going to go away." Ironically, Michel along with his counterpart Speaker Tom Foley wanted to make so it did go away.

The first order of business was deciding what to do with the Bank itself and on that there was very little dissension. Foley decided immediately that maintaining the operation, no matter how convenient for members, was a fool's errand. The House agreed, voting 390-8 to close it by the end of the calendar year. This automatically laid the matter to rest, right? Not in a New York minute. Seven freshmen Republicans saw the House Democratic leadership as having feet of clay and intended to pound away until the names of every member who had an overdraft was revealed. They called themselves the "Gang of Seven" and while their quest was guised in reform, the cynicism in Congressional veterans of both parties said that they were looking for partisan gains.

Look no further than their current political positions. Three members of the "Gang of Seven" – Rick Santorum of Pennsylvania, Scott Klug of Wisconsin and Frank Riggs of California had defeated well-regarded incumbents in Democratic-friendly districts against the longest of odds. They were fully aware that they would face Everest-like challenges in order to win second terms. Similarly, Jim Nussle of Iowa won an open seat through one of the slimmest margins of any House race in the nation. This was only because his opponent got caught up in a voter fraud scandal days before. Charles Taylor of North Carolina was in a less politically precarious situation. His seat was marginal also, so much so that it changed partisan hands in four of the previous five elections. Finally, John Boehner of Ohio and John Doolittle of California actually hewed to the part. They were former state legislators whose reputations as hardline conservatives and outcasts within their own ranks dominated their zest for doing things (though Doolittle had barely scraped into the seat). Boehner appeared to be the group's putative leader and once commanded the floor to admonish leadership on the release of the names. "Do this to remove the cloud of suspicion hanging over the heads of those of us who have done nothing wrong," he said. "Do this to restore confidence in this body...."

The signature moment of the "Gang of Seven" arguably came via an October 1st presentation on the House floor by Nussle who opened his remarks with a paper bag over his head—"Mr. Speaker, it's time to take the mask off this institution," he declared as he removed the bag from his head. "It's time to expose the check-bouncing scandal that I like to call 'Rubbergate.' It's time to bring some honor back to this institution."

Some called Nussle's speech a gimmick, others considered it a spectacle, but there was little dispute that "Rubbergate" was now a force to be reckoned with. So was reform for that matter. Indeed, Santorum defended Nussle by pointing to the attention that wearing the bag garnered ("Sometimes banging spoons on a highchair works.") Nussle followed up on the doldrums by lamenting that, "If we don't do something, we're all going to have to wear a paper bag when we go home." The "speech" lasted six seconds and Sonny Montgomery of Mississippi, the Congressman presiding at the Speaker's rostrum, chided Nussle but it came to symbolize the feeling of the American people that Congress seemed impervious to the uproar.

In perhaps the most unmitigated prop ever to be used in a House debate, Iowa Republican Jim Nussle wore a paper bag on the House floor in an attempt to goad leadership into "taking the mask off this institution." Photo courtesy of C-SPAN

At roughly the same time "Rubbergate" fanned the headlines, word came that more than 250 members had $302,000 in outstanding bills from the House restaurant. This led Kansas Republican Pat Roberts, the ranking Republican on the House Administration Committee, to say, "There is no such thing as a free lunch." Roberts ordered his colleagues to pay up noting how, coupled with Rubbergate, the perception "adds to the feeling of people that we're all a bunch of thieves." One easy victim of the perks of Capitol Hill was the practice that allowed the "fixing" of parking tickets, which Foley ordered an end to. Free prescriptions for members at Walter Reed Army Medical Center along with free parking at National Airport were among other things cited as earning the wrath of the general public.

In some cases, the early response to the scandal pit members of state delegations against each other, a case of institution versus change. Klug, part of the "Gang of Seven," rode the winds of change to oust a beloved 32-year veteran, Robert Kastenmeier only a year earlier. This was done in part by calling him "worn, torn and outdated" by hitting him and other senior members for receiving free gasoline. Klug's crusade did not sit well with 22-year House veteran and high- ranking Appropriator David Obey, another Badger State Democrat. Obey sat on many reform committees throughout his tenure and pulled no punches with regard to the Gang of Seven. "Let me be very blunt," he said, "When I see the number of blow-dried boys coming into the Congress these days, in comparison to the number 10, 15 years ago, it absolutely makes me gag - one dimensional, unsophisticated people bent on only one thing: self-promotion at the expense of the institution." Obey, with 64 overdrafts, was among those tarred but was also one of the first to own up. "I will plead fully guilty to the charge that Congress was sloppy, stupid, and shouldn't have allowed it to happen," he said. He was quick to add, there aren't "535 chiselers who are trying to gain a little edge financially."

Klug got an unwelcome distraction at that early date when it was revealed that he was among those who overdrew their account. He had only two bad checks for less than fifty dollars and he pronounced himself, "kind of angry the system was in place that put me and everybody else in this embarrassing situation." He called his involvement "stupid" and said, "I'm embarrassed. But it still doesn't deflect from what we're trying to do." What came out of Klug's mouth next had to have every member of Congress shaking in his or her boots. "It's full steam ahead." Newt Gingrich, the bombastic Minority Whip and longtime Democratic boogeyman, wouldn't allow anything but. He was prepared to go six ways to Sunday to get every name revealed no matter how minimal and he quietly advised the "Gang of Seven" to keep the pressure on.

For the "Gang," full steam ahead meant full release. Foley furiously resisted. His view was, "people don't get their bank records published in the newspaper if they have an overdraft check." He called the push to do so "hysterical." Michel had little desire for that as well, pitting him at odds with many from his party. Foley agreed, however, to refer the matter to the Ethics Committee in order to determine which members were committing "significant, substantial, repeated abuses."

In the meantime, members began gradually coming clean. By the end of the first week in October, 56 members acknowledged overdrawing their account while a whopping 297 denied doing so (the remainder didn't comment). The Wisconsin delegation was ahead of the curve. Of the state's nine members, four of them: Obey, Klug, and Republicans Tom Petri and Steve Gunderson, admitted they overdrew. Petri was evocative of the responses. A staffer said he "typically got the money within an hour" after insufficient funds were indicated.

Another who drew early attention was Pennsylvania's Peter Kostmayer who realized he had 19 overdrafts in one year. He also fought back against reports from the conservative publication *Human Events* that claimed he had overdrawn a check for $23,000. In actuality, it was for a purchase on his dad's home and $29,458.50 was wired within two days. Kostmayer was contrite. "I don't think I or anyone else should get away with it. I made a mistake and it's wrong. We [members of Congress] have to live like everyone else, we have to eat like everyone else, we have to bank like everyone else and we have to park like everyone else."

Other members, particularly those with nominal overdrafts, found it bemusing that they had to share the embarrassment with colleagues with more sizable totals. Democrat Andy Jacobs of Indiana, a man defined by his frugality (he once refused to board a plane because only first class tickets were available and the plane crashed, killing all aboard) had a single overdraft that resulted from an arithmetic error. Jacobs thought he had $122 in his account when it turned out to be $88 (the check he wrote was for $100.) "That's my heinous crime against humanity," he told *The Washington Post*. New Jersey's Marge Roukema (five overdrafts) spoke for those marginally impacted when she acknowledged, "obvious corruption here on the part of some people." She said soon thereafter, "People like me shouldn't be tarred with that brush."

Asked about the imbroglio, President George H.W. Bush refused to comment. He stated, "I'm afraid that anything I say on it would be considered political. You know how I am trying to avoid that."

Neither House Speaker Tom Foley nor his Republican counterpart, Minority Leader Bob Michel (right) had much of an initial appetite to exacerbate the matter of the House Bank. They were challenged and essentially overruled by junior members in both of their caucuses
Photo courtesy of C-SPAN

One certainty was that the House Ethics Committee would investigate the matter but who would lead it was still up for grabs. The panel's chair was Louis Stokes, a Clevelander universally seen as one of the most fair, judicious and competent members of the House. Stokes' realization that he had overdrafts (551 of them) convinced him to recuse himself. This left Matthew McHugh, a nine-term Democrat from Ithaca, at the helm. McHugh's scrupulousness and virtue were regarded among his colleagues as second-to-none so few could question his taking the helm, except perhaps to wonder why he'd do so.

McHugh created four categories. The first two involved members with limited overdrafts that likely were not notified by the bank upon shortage of funds, as was the case on many occasions. Category three centered around "a more serious problem because there was no assurance that they would be covered by the next scheduled salary deposit." The fourth category, which he labeled "very limited," involved members using bad checks at commercial banks to cover a negative balance at the House institution. The top Republican on the panel was Jim Hansen, a six-term Republican from Utah who had a proclivity for doing things by the book. He and McHugh generally worked together in the face of very adverse circumstances.

Releasing The Names

McHugh and his compatriots on the Ethics Committee faced the dilemma of how far to go with the revelations. Beginning in October of 1991, and dangling in the wind for the next five months, the Government Accounting Office investigated the matter. Back home, members were painted with the same broad brush. Kentucky Democrat Romano Mazzoli spoke in February of 1992 in regards to a "dismaying and depressing" atmosphere among constituents. He had zero overdrafts.

For the Ethics Committee, the beginning of March was arguably the beginning of the end. First was the release of the report which explained how such a seemingly docile operation got so out of hand. "When an overdraft was received an employee of the House Bank would generally call the member to advise that the account was overdrawn. However, in some cases the call would not be made, such as in those instances when an overdraft arrived at the bank a day or two before the next net salary deposit. Undoubtedly, there were other times when contacts did not occur as, for example, during a Congressional recess. In those situations, a member might not know that he or she had an overdraft and would appear on the list of overdrafts maintained at the bank. Overdrafts were very seldom returned to their maker. Although calls would generally be made, bad checks were almost always honored, and held until an adequate deposit was made." Charles Hatcher, a Democrat from Georgia and one of the worst offenders, was a rare member to offer confirmation of that practice. He told the AP, "It was not infrequent, but it wasn't every day. You could write the check, and they paid it." The report went on to say that it became the bank's policy to return overdrafts if the account's negative balance exceeded the members' next net salary deposit.

The partisan acrimony was ugly but Democrats and Republicans agreed: New York Democrat Matt McHugh was a natural to conduct the investigation of the House Banking scandal
Photo courtesy of C-SPAN

With that established, a six-member Ethics subcommittee consisting of three members from each party unanimously decided to reveal the names of 24 lawmakers (nineteen current and five former) whom they considered the "worst abusers." That standard had the full endorsement of Foley and Michel. The "worst abusers" were defined as having overdrawn their accounts "routinely and repeatedly." McHugh explained in later years that the definition of "routinely and repeatedly" was "pursuant to a definition of abuser that we developed based upon the processes followed by the Bank personnel, including their advice to members on what was unacceptable use of accounts." This meant going beyond the allowance that the practice of writing checks against their next month's salary was allowed.

The worst abusers were determined by those who exceeded their next paycheck by 20% of the 39 months under scrutiny. Under that standard, Charles Hatcher, a Georgian with 819 checks could be in the same category as Doug Bosco of California, a former member who had a comparably low 124. Conversely, Minnesota Democrat Gerry Sikorski's 697 overdrafts (seventh highest in the House) would spare him from the worst abusers list even though his fellow Democrat from Texas, Charlie Wilson with 81, would at least initially make an appearance. The rationale: while Sikorski only exceeded his following month's paycheck by seven months, Wilson had done so on eight occasions, thus 20%.

There was no dissent on the subcommittee though the full committee debate was not as harmonious. One member, Arizona Republican Jon Kyl expressed his view that, "A person who wrote 850 bad checks…would not be deemed an abuser under the majority's definition, and we don't think that that is defensible." The full committee adopted it by a 10-4 vote with Kyl and three other GOP colleagues – Jim Bunning of Kentucky, David Hobson of Ohio and Nancy Johnson of Connecticut dissenting. McHugh validated the concerns by stating, "Reasonable people can differ and we cannot say that they're wrong and we're right." He also conceded, "I don't know how some of these folks slept at night, given the kind of books that they kept."

The 24-member threshold wouldn't matter in the long run as hardly anyone expected that would be the end of the story. North Carolina Democrat Bill Hefner predicted, "This thing's not going to end with 19. We're all going to have to 'fess up.'" To Hefner's luck, with zero overdrafts, he did not have to fess up. He was in the minority but his prophecy proved spot on and members spent most of March in deep fear. Iowa Republican Fred Grandy who sat on the Ethics Committee answered a reporter's question with, "The mood around here? Abject terror!" It wasn't for naught.

As if on cue, the full House opted on March 12th to release the names of the 24 worst offenders. The vote was 391-36. A vote immediately after authorized the release of the remaining offenders within ten days after the worst abusers, passing unanimously. The overwhelming margins belied the fact that the six hour late-night debate was rancorous, vitriolic and contained at least some unfounded innuendo. Gingrich was at the heart of it. Less than five years earlier, his uncompromising bombast almost singlehandedly sustained the ethics complaints that ultimately led to the resignation of Speaker Jim Wright. Having brought down a big fish and sensed that his party had everything to gain from nationwide discontent, he did not trim his posture.

This time, Gingrich suggested the Democratic leadership "may have been involved in actions stopping Capitol police from investigating cocaine selling in the post office." This was news to the rank-and-file who started booing. Gingrich, however, was undeterred. "Tonight," he continued, "we have a post-office cocaine selling scandal, a House banking scandal, and other scandals are coming – and those responsible for it hiss." (During the Clinton years, Gingrich was forced to admit that he had no evidence to back up his assertion that drug use was rampant among White House staffers, claiming he sometimes said "stupid" things.)

What Gingrich was eluding to in his anything but benign way was that the casualties wouldn't be limited to members of Congress or those affiliated with the House Bank. For starters, it was soon discovered that House Sergeant At Arms Jack Russ was in on the shenanigans. His office was the de-facto supervisor of the Bank and it turned out to have greatly contributed to the laissez faire attitude. How? It turned out that Russ himself had 31 overdrafts at the bank totaling $104,825. More broadly, he was friendly with many members and the Bank gave wide latitude in so far as to look the other way regarding financial issues. Russ resigned the day after the Ethics report was released. Shortly beforehand he was the victim of a bizarre shooting that left him with a face wound, yet accompanied with it were allegations that he staged the attack because the bullet did not do greater damage than grazing his cheek (his wife Susan dumbfoundedly responded by saying, "Jack doesn't have to be explaining why he's not dead.") Eventually, however, he would have to explain why he embezzled and filed false reports that "knowingly and willfully omitted" key transactions. This eventually landed him in jail.

The House Post Office was also becoming increasingly involved and a week after Russ's departure Robert Rota, who headed the Post Office, followed suit. While one person close to the mix said, "I don't think there is any connection with that at all. There's been a plan for him to retire for…many, many months, going back long before the investigation began or even before there was any talk of an investigation," House Administration Chair Charlie Rose of North Carolina cited similar indiscretions as Russ. "Mr. Rota," he said, "was bending so far over backwards to do things for people that he fell over. I'm not going to get into details, but clearly bad judgment was exhibited in many of the things he did." The details would come out soon enough.

The Official Release and Owning Up

**The check saga was poised to combust when the House
voted to release the names of all who had overdrawn
Image via CQ-Roll Call**

After it was decided that the names of those with overdrafts would be made public, Guy Vander Jagt of Michigan responded zealously. He was the head of the National Republican Congressional Committee (NRCC) which was the leadership organization designed to assist House Republican candidates. He sought to make the case that, "The Democrat bank scandal is a metaphor for how they run everything…Just like Watergate was a Republican scandal because the Republicans were in charge," he declared, "Rubbergate is a Democrat scandal because the Democrats are in charge." He pronounced himself, "absolutely overjoyed."

Given that the identity of the members were concealed and only the respected bank accounts could be seen, it was impossible for McHugh and his Ethics Committee colleagues to know who would be singled out. New York Democrat Gary Ackerman allegedly rectified that.

Before the official list was released, a leak occurred and the nation learned that 21 of the 24 names on it were Democrats (16 current and three former members) while three were Republicans, all of whom were currently serving. Many angrily suspected the source of the leak was Ackerman, a New

York Democrat who feared he might be pitted against two colleagues (Jim Scheuer and Bob Mrazek) when the Empire State redrew its lines later in the year. What was the incentive for Ackerman to do so? While Ackerman would hardly come off smelling like a rose (he had 111 overdrafts), Scheuer and Mrazek both occupied spots on the worst abuser list. Meanwhile, a Republican-affiliated group began running ads naming the 21 Democratic abusers while conveniently omitting the names of the three Republicans.

When the official list was released the biggest offender turned out to be a former member – a Democrat turned Republican named Tommy Robinson who wrote 996 bad checks (and disputed that he had any.) The second worst offender had far more to lose. Not only was Mrazek a sitting member but he was also trying to move up to the U.S. Senate. 920 bad checks (initially reported as 972) made that next to impossible and he soon pulled the plug on both his statewide campaign and re-election bid. Third on the list was a well-regarded Michigan Republican named Robert W. Davis whose overdrafts totaled 878.

What about Bob? Bob Mrazek of New York and Bob Davis of Michigan topped the list of current House members who overdrew their accounts. Mrazek's response: "I tried to live within the rules as they were explained to me." Images courtesy of C-SPAN

As it became clear how deep the scandal was, many members started to own up. The responses to allegations ranged from contrite to, "it wasn't my fault," "it wasn't a real bank", to just plain comical. There was even a denial or two.

Wayne Owens of Utah who was seeking a Senate seat conceded, "We've handed our detractors...wonderful political theater" (he committed "no real sin" on his part but acknowledged "sloppiness.") Dana Rohrabacher of California was not as charitable and emphatically stated, "I plead guilty to making one mistake on one check - the rest are the bank's fault."

Connecticut Republican Chris Shays had a relatively low number of overdrafts (18) but not a small figure given that they totaled $46,949.55. He decided a lie would not cut it. "I have an inherent faith that if you tell people the truth they will put it in proper perspective." As in the instance of Rules Committee Chair Joe Moakley of Massachusetts, some resorted to humor. He said of his 90 overdrafts, "I was not a math major at Southie High."

Kansas Democrat Dan Glickman confessed to having 105 overdrafts and his mea culpa was probably harder on himself than even his constituents wanted. "I was pretty damn stupid. I'm a jerk." He even admitted, "I'm thinking about setting up my own bank now. I've learned a lot about how not to operate one." California Democrat Rick Lehman explained his paltry ten overdrafts with, "I don't buy the excuses I've been hearing. We are each responsible for our own behavior." Except in many cases

Minnesota Democrat Tim Penny had a knack for getting under both parties skin when it came to federal spending, but he spoke for many colleagues when he bemoaned the lack of notification by the bank. Only through inquiry did he learn he had three overdrafts and proceeded to alert the Minnesota media. In his book, *Common Cents* Penny detailed his reaction when he learned that there were four more. "Like many members who had already gone public, I called the Ethics Committee to see what the new records showed. They told me I had floated seven checks. That was it. I snapped. I was beyond rage. I was nearly blinded but anger. I knew what it would have to call in the Minnesota reporters a second time and apologized all over again." Kansas Democrat Jim Slattery was another. In October he told the press he "was called one time, five or six years ago, on a small check, and I covered it within the day. One time in nine years." When the full list was released the following April, one had multiplied to 50. Texas Democrat Charlie Stenholm had 88 overdrafts but he had the financial records to prove that nearly half, 42 precisely, should have cleared on time because he put in money to cover them that day.

None other than McHugh validated the lack of notification as he was revealed to have one overdraft. The operation was so discombobulated that Pennsylvania's Tom Foglietta was listed as having an overdraft and he didn't even have an account at the bank.

Some members, such as Hatcher of Georgia, could not attempt to spin the matter and with 819 overdrafts (the sixth highest among both current and former members), honesty and pleas for forgiveness were really the only ways to cut the pie. Hatcher, who exceeded his next month's salary for 35 of the 39 months in question said, "I haven't been a high liver, I don't think. But I've had living and family expenses." Arkansas Democrat Bill Alexander's 487 overdrafts also ranked him among the list of worst abusers and he conceded, "I've basically been broke for the past six years." Oklahoma Republican Mickey Edwards, with 386 checks, was another with severe money woes. Mary Rose Oakar, though, was in a league of her own. Her 213 overdrafts were only the latest in a long-running saga of questionable decisions. Several years back, Oakar's hometown paper reported that she gave a staff member a big raise prior to purchasing a house together. These members lent credence to a Democratic lawmaker who said off the record, "There's a sordid side to it. Almost in everybody's case, it's someone whose life got out of control."

Number four on the list was Doug Walgren of Pennsylvania who was conquered by Santorum in 1990 and was adamant that, "I did not misuse this account." In short because of his 858 overdrafts he went on to say, "There was never a bounced check. There was never any doubt a creditor would be paid." Bill Goodling, a fellow Pennsylvanian and Republican who made the worst offender list with 430 overdrafts, was cited by *Congressional Quarterly* as having suffered, "the indignity of being called a lair by a minister – from Goodling's own denomination no less." Before the list came out Goodling also expressed the fear of other members in stating, "We're all going to be judged by what the press, the public and some members should have been."

Charlie Wilson's public relations strategy was utterly unclassifiable. The well-regarded, irreverent, quip-ready Texas Democrat did not try to pass the blame for his 81 overdrafts that added up to $139,000 ("This is no one's fault but mine") but, if his terminology wasn't eyebrow raising his comparisons certainly made up for it. His justifications were by far among the most creative and entertaining of any member. Wilson initially joked that, "I called in the posse and gave myself up." Citing the fact that no taxpayer money was involved he called the matter "no big deal…not a show-stopper…It's not like molesting young girls or young boys." On potential political repercussions, "It ain't a big deal. I think the people of East Texas know they weren't electing a CPA." In perhaps the most incredulous line of his defense, Wilson said, "If my constituents didn't forgive sloppiness and certain amount of eccentricity, I wouldn't be here in the first place."

There was truth to that. "Good Time Charlie" was known on the Hill for proudly surrounding himself with pretty ladies half his age. They were called "Charlie's Angels." Wilson's fellow Texas Democrat, Ron Coleman, had a similarly nonchalant attitude and labeled the matter "irrelevant." Though Coleman ultimately became one of the few members severely implicated not to get bounced at the polls, he soon discovered that 673 overdrafts would make for a long hard slog to November.

**Texas Democrat Charlie Wilson's explanations of his
bad checks were unclassifiable and priceless
"It's not like molesting young girls or young boys.... If my
constituents didn't forgive sloppiness and certain amount
of eccentricity, I wouldn't be here in the first place"
Photo courtesy of C-SPAN**

As far as elected representatives go, Wilson was one of a kind and non-Charlie Wilson's couldn't have tried to emulate reasoning like his if they wanted to. At best, California Republican Duncan Hunter's strategy was politically tone deaf. At worst, it was refusing to smell the roses. Initially vowing that "nobody has ever had a Duncan Hunter check returned for insufficient funds," it was soon revealed that 407 creditors had a Duncan Hunter check returned adding up to $129,225 (he eventually persuaded the Ethics Committee to shave eight from the total.)

When the scope of his involvement came out, Hunter was defiant. "I won't apologize for it. These overdrafts...occurred in the regular course of business." Hunter could afford to be flippant. The revelations came just after the Golden State's filing deadline and he faced only minimal primary opposition in a heavily Republican district. He also realized that, unlike the total of his checks, talk was cheap. In a year that was shaping up to be virulently anti-incumbent, even apologizing might not cut it so he pulled out all the stops. Appearing on the "Today Show," he sat at a local courthouse for three days giving the public a chance to examine his checks and vowed to pay $4,000 a month until the unemployment rate in his district dropped. "If someone wants to call this a diversionary tactic, it's sure an expensive one."

Then came the restitutions, or at least the public relations campaign of trying to convince their constituents that they were doing so. Stephen Solarz of New York wrote a check to the federal Treasury for $2,349.97, an amount that added up to the charge of an overdraft at his bank plus 20% interest for his 743 bad checks. Massachusetts Democrat Chester Atkins likewise announced he "leveled a penalty on myself of $15 per check plus interest."

By this time, the ubiquity of the scandal was everywhere. A poll conducted by *Newsweek* revealed that 78% of Americans would be less inclined to re-elect a member who floated multiple checks. *The St. Louis Post Dispatch* wrote, "Voters Should Cancel The Check Bouncers In Congress" and *The Greensboro Observer* wrote, "At this Bank, Checks Are On The House." Late Night television, led by Johnny Carson, also got in on the laughs in saying "Folks, you've got to hand it to our House of Representatives. They finally passed something: 5,000 bad checks."

Incidentally, the Bush cabinet was impacted as well as four members who formerly served in Congress with overdrafts (though neither Bush nor Vice-President Dan Quayle were among them.) Then-Secretary of Defense Dick Cheney was one of them and admitted how, "As recently as last Thursday night, I was still telling jokes about the House bank. It doesn't seem quite as funny today." Secretary of Agriculture Ed Madigan and Labor Secretary Lynn Martin were also on the list.

As for the Ethics Committee, the next task was hearing challenges to specific overdrafts, a laborious task given that there were almost 150 members asking for a review on at least one. In some instances it meant the difference between a member being on the board or not. For example, Californians Vic Fazio and Robert Dornan were initially given word of a single overdraft (in Dornan's case, it was for a statue of the Virgin Mary outside of his home.) Yet upon conducting a review the Committee decided to dismiss the overdrafts, leaving each Congressman free to boast of not having had any checks returned. Mrazek saw his total reduced from 972 to 920 but that was hardly a chip at the apple. The results of many other deliberations invited recriminations.

Ultimately, a number of members made their case to be taken off the list and two, Wilson and Scheuer, succeeded (in Scheuer's case, a delay in bank transfers from his own bank was found to be the culprit). Massachusetts Democrat Joe Early's case went the other way on a tie vote and he took to the House floor to blast not only Foley ("he has handled this as a disgrace") but McHugh and Ethics Committee members who, "ran like rats...like rats" when he tried to explain. McHugh later said, "I do think that most members understood that the Committee was simply doing its job, and an unpleasant job it was."

Many members had time on their side. Illinois Democrat Charlie Hayes, although, wasn't one of them. When the Ethics Committee list revealed that he overdrew his account 716 times, thereby ranking him among the worst abusers, he was days away from a tight primary campaign where he was already reeling from a slightly redrawn district. The timing left Hayes a small chance to plot strategy, and he lost his primary. Not surprisingly, he took the House floor shortly after to complain that, "Even before I could adequately respond, I was tried and convicted in the press." That same House floor special order saw another of the worst abusers, Bill Clay of Missouri with 328 checks, deliver arguably the most scholarly, loquacious response for the operation Ethics Committee. His words were, "disgraceful, callous, cavalier, hypocritical and erroneous" (Clay believed at one point that he would be removed as a worst abuser.)

The release of the "Worst Abusers" of the House Bank days before the Illinois primary was likely was the final nail in the coffin for Illinois Democrat Charlie Hayes who was defeated Photo courtesy of C-SPAN

Even other members who faced little political repercussions threw temper-tantrums at leadership. Texas Democrat John Bryant singled out the Speaker. "For Tom Foley," he said, "political leadership is not a responsibility which he relishes. For him, political leadership is painful, and political combat, even when absolutely necessary in order to present the nation with the Democratic alternative, is to be avoided if at all possible. I call on the Speaker to retire at the end of this Congress." Foley called that "an anomaly" which was proved right. Instead, the contention by Minnesota's Jim Oberstar that his measured response was "a mistake of judgment" seemed to take hold and there were no lasting impediments to his Speakership. As freshman the Democrat from New Hampshire, Dick Swett said, the priority ahead was to "de-perk-o-late."

On April 14th, the day before Good Friday, the remainder of the list of offenders was made public. With some exceptions, it revealed the moderately high numbers, such as those who had fewer than 100 but well more than 50. Four Massachusetts members had between 70 and 90 overdrafts, Tom Downey of New York had 151, Carroll Hubbard of Kentucky 152, Agriculture Committee Chair Kika de la Garza 284 and Republican Bill Thomas of California 119). Californians Ron Dellums and Henry Waxman, with 878 and 484 overdrafts respectively, were generally overlooked because they were institutions in such monolithically Democratic districts. 57 overdrafts seemed destined to hurt Don Young, a cantankerous Alaskan already facing a rematch with a Democrat who had held him to 52% in 1990. Another member of the Gang of Seven, Frank Riggs, was found to have three. Among the leaders, Foley had two, Michel had zero, House Majority Leader Dick Gephardt with 28, Majority Whip David Bonior with 76 and Gingrich had 22.

Merrily, Primary Season Rolls Along

As if what *Congressional Quarterly* called the "fear and loathing" among members impacted by the bank scandal wasn't enough, uncertainty reigned in some of the largest states over the state of redistricting leaving many members in a state of flux. Slowly and against the clock, the stalemates ended.

New Jersey's new lines were finalized in mid-March and the court adopted a Republican plan. This was bad news for two-term Democratic Congressman Frank Pallone, who found his Republican Jersey shore turf accustomed to supporting him for arduously fighting ocean dumping, merged with fellow Democrat Bernard Dwyer's gritty Middlesex County base. Dwyer had been pondering wrapping up his career all along and this sealed the deal – he announced his retirement a day later.

A court released their map for Michigan a week later and for incumbents, it was as disruptive as any partisan plan could be. This was because the court rejected both the Democratic and Republican plans as overly partisan even though each pitted one set of Democratic members against the other and one set of Republicans (the Wolverine State was losing two seats.) Howard Wolpe had not been a target of either plan but his district was carved up. The final plan, as long-predicted, combined the turfs of Macomb Democrats

Sander Levin and Dennis Hertel but also dissolved the Ann-Arbor based district of Republican Carl Pursell, a consistent target. Pursell announced his retirement days later. During this time, the plan made the districts of four other Democrats more Republican enough so that, in a bad year which luckily for them 1992 was not shaping up to be, these members would really have to sweat to hold on (which occurred in 1994.)

Next up was Ohio where the Buckeye State's nearly yearlong deadlock had been the most agonizing and climactic for nearly a year, particularly for Republican Clarence Miller. For Democrats, Eckart and Pease's early retirements largely alleviated apprehension among the remaining Northeast Ohio members about their own preservation because it meant an incumbent would not have to be sacrificed. For Republican incumbents, particularly Miller in the southeast part of the state, it was just the opposite. Nearing 75, Miller's district was an obvious target for elimination and other younger Republicans hoped he would simply retire. When Miller made clear he'd do no such thing competing plans were passed, one of which actually spared him. The final plan, however, did indeed carve up the 10th while placing Miller's home in the district of Douglas Applegate, a very secure Democrat. Instead, he decided to challenge a fellow Republican, Bob McEwen, which meant that come January one of those Representatives would not return.

Other protracted struggles. Alabama, where creative Democrats thought they found ways to draw a minority-majority district while not inconveniencing their own members, took a big hit when a Republican court ruled against the plan. Instead, the map they implemented made five-term Democrat Ben Erdreich's district a Republican stronghold while making Claude Harris's district minority-majority.

Georgia also had gone through a lengthy period of uncertainty with multiple maps proposed to accommodate the twin objectives of creating two new African-American seats while dislodging Gingrich, the delegation's loan GOP Congressman. The final map's impact was hard to gage as three Democrats were stepping down. And while Gingrich's suburban Atlanta turf was indeed drawn out from under him, the same was true for Democrats Richard Ray and Ben Jones who were sent scrambling to find a district that would have them. Other Democratic incumbents, Buddy Darden and J. Roy Rowland were forced to surrender African-American enclaves to new minority-majority turf though they emerged less-battered and well positioned to win new terms.

Retirements Galore-They Were Dropping Like Flies

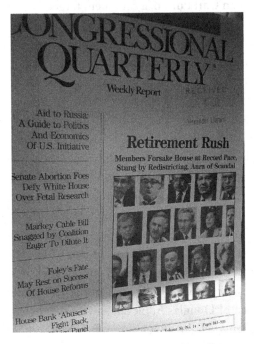

Image courtesy of CQ-Roll Call

The week between March 29th and April 6th was an amalgamation of all the reasons for various departures and a time of complete bedlam for the House and its members as eight House members and a Senator called it quits. March 30th saw three announcements alone. Robert Roe of New Jersey, at the apex of his power as the Chair of the highly coveted Public Works and Transportation Committee shocked all but, after 23 years, he was ready to move on. That same day, Wylie decided he'd had enough of the minority and Wolpe concluded his district was simply unwinnable. Edward Feighan, with 397 overdrafts became a victim of the scandal on April 1st, though unbeknownst to many, he had been thinking about wrapping up his career long before. The following day saw another threesome and with redistricting as the culprit. Hertel, with news of 547 overdrafts looming, decided to forego a challenge to Levin and Harris yielded to the plan for his district to become African-American and stepped aside. Virginia Republican George Allen had just won his seat in a special election that previous November but, when a remap put him in with the much senior Tom Bliley, he decided to concentrate on a bid for governor in 1993 that he won against all expectations.

Ed Feighan of Ohio and Dennis Hertel of Michigan, both Democrats, were among the eight House members who announced their departures in a single week. Feighan's statement: "I have never had to endure such a mean spirited, ugly and dehumanizing atmosphere as the one that now prevails in Washington." Images courtesy of CSPAN

The Senate caused a domino effect as well. North Dakota Senator Kent Conrad promised during his 1986 campaign to retire in '92 if the deficit was not halved. It wasn't, but voters did not seem to care and Conrad still had strong prospects for returning. Instead, his wife was mugged and Conrad announced he was quitting, paving the way for the state's long suffering At-Large Member, Democrat Byron Dorgan, who had been waiting for a Senate seat to open.

The following week was not as bustling on the retirement front but not particularly serene either. The Senate was again responsible for a surprising chip when Colorado freshman Democrat Tim Wirth pulled an absolute stunner when he decided not to stand for a second term. This opened the door for Third District Congressman Ben Nighthorse Campbell, a fellow Democrat, to try to become the first Indian-American to win a Senate seat. That same week, New Jersey's Frank Guarini, 68, opted not to seek re-election as expected. Republican Vin Weber of Minnesota, a telegenic member of the GOP leadership as Conference Secretary and just 41 years old, also decided to move on. While Weber didn't cite his 125 overdrafts as reason for quitting, he eluded to the fact that he had little stomach to salvage the seat.

During the week of Easter, Lowery abandoned his campaign against Cunningham and Bill Broomfield, the ranking member of the Foreign Affairs Committee who had spent 36 years in the House (each one in the minority), decided he had enough as well.

Alabama's Claude Harris (right) was among early April's Spring break-away of members fleeing Capitol Hill. He wouldn't even try to salvage the seat dismantled by the VRA majority-minority requirement. Louisiana's Jerry Huckaby (left), in similar circumstances, ran a brave but uphill race all year but lost by a mile

Other matches were set. Gingrich received a primary challenge from former State Representative, Herman Clark in what promised to be a rough and tumble, insider vs. outsider race. Anticipating discontent over his perks, Gingrich abandoned his Lincoln Continental that was accompanied by a $60,000-a-year driver, George Awkward ("I would be more than happy to take a cab"). His bigger problem was that he had just three months to get acquainted with a constituency that, while Republican, was 100% new and where voters might only know what Clark wanted them to know. Gingrich was preparing to counter with a boatload of money and influence, but those were the two things Clark was using to turn voters away. On cue, Clark spoke of an "imperial Congress" but Gingrich turned the question to who could best deliver. "If you had the choice between the No. 2 ranking Republican in the House," he told a high school civics class, "or you can have a freshman who doesn't have any idea who the Cabinet members are, has never met any of them and has never worked with the President, which one do you think can do more for Cobb County?"

The Pennsylvania primary season kicked off the post-Easter recess with Western Pennsylvania the site of much discontent. Democrat Joe Kolter, reeling from the release of a tape labeling himself "a political whore," lost, taking a humiliating 19% against four rivals. Another Democrat, Austin Murphy, was trailing for much of the night against multiple opponents but finally won re-nomination by just 36-34%. The opposite was true of Bill Coyne. The low-key and highly scrupulous Pittsburgh Democrat was challenged by the prominent lawyer Al Guttman. He implored him to "do something," but 3/4 of voters evidently thought he did plenty. Coyne waltzed to re-nomination with 76%. It was only ten days later that the House Post Office scandal broke and the charges of cash for phony stamp purchases ensnarled Rostenkowski, Murphy and Kolter. The saliency of that scandal would be most dominant in 1993.

The hemorrhaging was less rapid in late April through May, but did not halt. Larry Smith of Florida, a rising five-term Miami Democrat, decided to pull the plug on his campaign amid 161 overdrafts. Michigan's Bob Traxler, a senior Appropriator and one of 13 "College of Cardinals" also announced he was quitting, expressing that "if I don't do it now I never will." On a single day, two central figures in the bank scandal, Bob Davis of Michigan the offender and McHugh the investigator called it a career. Davis had futilely searched for forgiveness while many chalked up McHugh's decision to disgust over the Banking scandal. In actuality, however, he pondered leaving long before and said that had his decision been an election, it would have gone 52-48%. Craig James of Florida, a two-term Republican who appeared safe, announced he was leaving because he didn't want to be associated with the perks of Congress that he had no part of (including the banking scandal and even the House gym.)

By this time, retirements were turning to primaries as the season was now in full swing. The West Virginia incumbent matchup was May 12th and was settled early as Staggers lost to Mollohan by more than a 3-2 margin. A week later was the Oregon Senate primary and Les AuCoin, haunted by his 83 House overdrafts that underdog Harry Lonsdale exploited, saw his lead slowly drip away. It stopped just enough to allow him to eke out a 339-vote win.

Primaries were rapidly approaching involving lawmakers who had many bad checks. If they thought they'd be able to skate through; the month of May certainly cured them of that. May 26th saw three incumbents face the music: senior Democrats Carroll Hubbard of Kentucky and Bill Alexander of Arkansas were bounced outright and Hubbard didn't even see it coming. Another Arkansas

Congressman, Beryl Anthony took just 40%, which meant he'd face a runoff two weeks down the road against Secretary of State Bill McCuen.

Not only were Democrats Carroll Hubbard of Kentucky (second from right) and Joe Kolter of Pennsylvania (far right) ousted in spring primaries, but each suffered the indignity of going to jail. Hubbard's wife Carol (next to her husband) lost her primary for an open seat in Kentucky that same day. Their colleague on the far left, Bruce Vento of Minnesota, never had an iota of scandal and served in the House until his 2000 death
Photo via Getty Images

None of this could be of comfort to Oakar whose own primary with well-known Cuyahoga Commissioner Tim Hagan was just a week away. She faced split opposition as well and, though Ohio didn't have a runoff, her coming in ahead of Hagan wasn't assured. Oakar took 39%, enough to qualify her for November. Meanwhile, the Buckeye State also hosted a member vs. member matchup between Republican incumbents Miller and McEwen. It was a generational fight of sorts and also a cliffhanger. Miller took advantage of McEwen's 166 overdrafts (he conversely had zero) by reminding voters that the score was 0-166. McEwen came out on top by 269 votes.

In California, most incumbents won without difficulty (including Duncan Hunter who took 60% and Thomas with 65%) but Robert Lagomarsino fell to a free-spending Republican millionaire named Michael Huffington. Frank Pallone beat Bob Smith, in part with an ad that said—Little noticed that day was a very weak showing by Jim Ross Lightfoot, an Iowa Republican who had twin problems including 105 overdrafts and a remap that vastly configured his district. Lightfoot faced one opponent, a local businessman named Ronald J. Long but prevailed with just 58%. Long's explanation: "God did it." At any rate, this performance did little to dispel fears among Republicans about Lightfoot's security for November and he catapulted to the top of the vulnerable member list. Meanwhile, Anthony would learn his fate the following week. The runoff was close but McCuen was victorious. Another incumbent had bitten the dust.

Meanwhile, the remap in Louisiana was finally completed and four of the state's eight incumbents would find themselves in two districts. Partisan-wise, the outcome was mixed. Democrats were assured of picking up a newly drawn African-American majority seat but in order to accommodate that the base of eight-term Democrat Jerry Huckaby had to be sacrificed. In attempt to salvage his career, this meant challenging two-term Republican Jim McCrery. Because the state was losing a seat, Republicans had to sacrifice one as well which resulted in three-termer Clyde Holloway having his seat taken away. He wouldn't go quietly, however. A fellow three-termer, Richard Baker was in his sights.

By this point, the retirement boom was turning to New York. Long Island Republican Ray McGrath announced he was quitting in May before the redistricting stalemate ended. He wouldn't be alone. A few members who opted to "pack it in" would have had nary a re-election worry in the world but Buffalo Democrat Henry Nowak and Republican David O.B. Martin of the Northern tier had enough. Later, they were joined by Republican Norman Lent of Long Island. So fast was the delegation dropping (to the consternation of Governor Mario Cuomo who bemoaned the loss of seniority) that one colleague asked McGrath if "something was in the water" in the Empire State. One Congressman would not be joining them, however, even with very large handwriting on the wall. In order to make room for a new Latino-majority district, Stephen Solarz's district had been carved up multiple ways. Solarz desperately wanted to continue his service and, after carefully weighing his very attractive options, he decided to run in the new Latino district.

**Six-term New York Republicans David Martin (left) and Ray McGrath
served in the Legislature together, entered Congress together and surprised
colleagues by leaving together. They were also dear friends til the end –
McGrath hosted Martin weeks before his death. The duo were among
several New Yorkers who announced their departure late in the cycle,
leading one colleague to question if "something was in the water"
Photo courtesy of Tori Duskas**

In an indication that all things must come to an end Charles Bennett,
a Floridian who served 44 years, announced that his time had come and he
would retire (he had planned to make 1992 his last run but the ill health of
his wife led him to reconsider.

June concluded with two late and genuinely unexpected departures. South
Carolina's Sixth District, which was held comfortably by Robin Tallon, had
been transformed into a minority-majority district. Charles Luken was the
real shocker, however. Not only did the freshman Democrat from Cincinnati

win re-nomination, but he was also unopposed in the general election. Family sacrifices made his career unsustainable and Luken pulled the plug.

Democrats Howard Wolpe of Michigan, Beryl Anthony of Arkansas (with his wife Shelia) and Larry Smith of Florida were three additional members who would not hold seats in the 103rd Congress
Photo via Getty Images

And three Republicans – Robert Lagomarsino of California, William Broomfield of Michigan and Carl Pursell of Michigan also closed their careers
Photo via Getty Images

Summer and Beyond

The incumbent horror show seemed to be taking a break for the month of July. With all but a handful of filing deadlines yet to pass, retirements stalled and the only state with a primary on the horizon was Georgia. Clark kept up the pressure on Gingrich's check woes, formulating an ad to the tune of "Old McDonald Had a Farm." The lines were unsparing. "With a bounced check here and a pay raise there, here a check, there a check, everywhere a bounced check. Newt Gingrich wrote a rubber check to the IRS." Gingrich's response: "There's a difference between being embarrassed and being a scandal."

As primary day approached, the race was razor-tight but the odds seemed to favor Gingrich because he was outspending Clark $1 million to $160,000. Early returns bore that out. With 80% reporting, Gingrich trailed 51-49%. Late returns pushed him over by 980 votes (35,699 to 37, 719.) Cobb County opposed him but he mustered together small margins in the other five counties. Adding salt to the wound, it was likely that efforts to beat him may have literally boomeranged by efforts to dislodge him. As one political analyst stated, "Newt would have been beaten in the old district. He must have been born under a lucky star."

Richard Ray hovered short of 50% through the night and a runoff seemed inevitable, though, Ray rallied and got over the top, living to fight another day for a very tough general election. Charlie Hatcher would have to wait a few weeks longer to learn his fate. He took first place in the primary but with just 40% against split opposition, lived to fight another day against Sanford Bishop in a runoff three weeks away. Jones wasn't so fortunate as the "General Lee" couldn't spare him from falling outright to a State Senator named Don Johnson.

Any member with a late primary that hoped voters would be more forgiving as the calendar moved forward was proven wrong by August. Michigan held its primary on August 4th and a novice furniture salesman who saved his vacation time to campaign stunned Vander Jagt. Kansas turned out an incumbent as well but Dick Nichols was hardly in the same boat. The freshman Republican, having watched his Western Kansas district get carved up when the state lost a House seat, decided to challenge Glickman in the 4th district. His immediate problem was that before reaching Glickman, Nichols had to get past Eric Yost, the Senate President whom Republicans were chomping at the bit to face Glickman. Nichols ran a strong race but his respectable 45-34% showing was not enough.

A big "in" was turned "out" in a Michigan shocker as 26-year veteran and Republican Congressional Campaign Chair Guy Vander Jagt was ousted by a furniture salesman in the August primary

Hatcher learned his fate on August 11th and despite his very helpful position on Agriculture, the remap and checks were too much to bear. He fell to Sanford Bishop 53-47%. Another member who long awaited his medicine was Mickey Edwards who failed to advance to the runoff by a decisive margin. Mike Synar, a Sooner State colleague, encountered an increasingly restless electorate in recent cycles but not because of incumbency. Synar was a proud liberal in a constituency that was not. He placed first in the primary with 43% and would face the ultimate test for survival in a runoff three weeks later. Synar's opponent was Drew Edmondson, who had a famous name in Oklahoma politics due to relatives having been in Congress. Many Democrats were not encouraged about Synar's chances.

The first week in September was finally kind to incumbents, though not by breathtaking margins. Don Young of Alaska and Jay Rhodes of Arizona both faced primaries from sitting legislators and while no one expected they would lose, their margins were less than inspiring for fall campaigns that were sure to be cut-throat.

Members got some somber news two days apart. On September 14th, New York Democrat Ted Weiss who had a history of heart trouble died suddenly at the age of 64, leaving his seat open a day before the primary in which he faced a single opponent. The following day, Walter Jones who had been ailing most of the year died of pneumonia.

September 15th was virtually the end of primary season and anti-incumbent activists hoped it would end with a bang. As many as seven incumbents faced realistic losses and while only two ended up biting the dust, most of the others faced rough counts that softened them up for November. Solarz's bold gamble did not pay off as he was narrowly squeezed out by Nydia Valezquez and

Chet Atkins of Massachusetts fell to Marty Meehan by a solid margin. Nick Mavroules, after trailing much of the night, rallied to win by 600 votes and Gerry Sikorski, after being locked in a seesaw battle with Tad Jude, limped to a 49-46%. He survived round one but was in deep trouble with just seven weeks to go to November Joe Early won more comfortably but his 37% in a fractured field put him on serious edge for November. Synar, somewhat against the odds, won re-nomination and Gerry Studds racked up 60%. That same day, Jim Moody decisively lost his Senate primary to Russ Feingold. Meanwhile, Weiss was re-nominated posthumously, leaving the Democratic Committee the sad option of picking a successor (they settled on Jerry Nadler.)

The very tepid primary wins of longtime Massachusetts incumbents Joe Early and Nick Mavroules signified very tough roads for both in the general election
Images courtesy of CSPAN

No election season goes by without late, unconventional retirements and in this case that fell to Mathew Rinaldo. The ten-term New Jersey Republican announced on a Friday in September that he would not seek re-election. What made this so unusual was that he had won re-nomination in June and seemed poised to win in November. Republicans were able to substitute his name with a popular State Senator, Bob Franks.

The last primary was held October 3rd – in the Bayou State. Under Louisiana's system, all candidates run in a single party and if no one gets 50%, the top two advance to a runoff. Naturally, the focus was on the incumbent matchups. Huckaby and McCrery advanced to November but Huckaby's 29% was dreadful (McCrery took 44%) and quickly confirmed that he was a dead man walking. The Eighth district was closer. Holloway took first place with 37% while Baker barely ran ahead of a local businessman, Ned Randolph who sought to appeal to voters' anti-incumbent sentiment by urging them to fire two incumbents at once. Nonetheless, the only Republican incumbent matchup in the nation was now set.

Getting members home to campaign was the next order of business with Congress finally adjourning on October 8th.

The General Election Campaign

By October 1st, *CQ* already had identified Nick Mavroules's race as "Leans Republican" while Jim Ross Lightfoot's was headed in the opposite direction. Both lived by the slogan "never say die" and embraced the metaphor to run as if they were 20 points down. After all, they were.

Following this, the focus turned to members who were seriously endangered. At the top of the Democratic list was five of the top overdrafters (Early, Oakar, Sikorski, Wilson and Coleman) and one member under FBI investigation (Al Bustamante of Texas). House leaders were not high on any returning but while the first three seemed to be running uphill all season, the Texans were viewed as anywhere from slightly behind to up by the hair on their chinny-chin-chin to true tossup status. Most of the dynamics of these races could be found in the individual chapters of the incumbents who left office. Wilson was different, though. He faced an Air Force Vet named Donna Peterson who held him to 56% two years earlier and now, accompanied by a CALF she called "Charlie," she was hoping to finish the job. Bustamante had checks as well (his opponent informed his Spanish audiences of "cheques calientes") but had bigger problems via a federal investigation into racketeering. Still, he was seen as an even bet for prevailing.

Ben Erdreich was running uphill but running hard and few were willing to concede that he could not secure a seat in the 103rd Congress. Peter Kostmayer was also tied down by overdrafts but was facing a very well-known State Senator. His status for most of the season was tossup. George Hochbruechner had never been safe on Long Island Sound and this time 49 overdrafts were complicating his hopes to secure a fourth term in conservative territory. His opponent took 49% against him four years ago and had 50-50 odds of finishing the job. Likewise, Frank McCloskey Indiana's "Bloody Eighth" was in a rematch with the man who held him to 55% in '90, and now had 65 overdrafts to boot. Michigan Democrat Bob Carr, running in substantially more Republican territory, was not safe. His opponent, Dick Chrysler, urged voters to "replace an old Carr with a new Chrysler."

George Brown, a crusty California Democrat was thought to be slightly ahead of his re-election bid although, in an already competitive district made more Republican by redistricting, a loss to pilot Dick Rutan was certainly on the table. First-term Democrat Jim Bacchus, sitting in a Cape Canaveral anchored Florida district that gave Bush 70%, surely had his work cut out for him. As it became clear that 1992 would be a Democratic year, incumbents initially thought to be on the bubble via redistricting. Californians such as Vic Fazio and Anthony Beilenson of California were all but ignored by both parties, who aimed to prioritize other seats they considered competitive.

**Ben Erdreich of Alabama had virtually no chance in salvaging
his House seat following a very adverse redistricting but
still prepared to conduct a world-class campaign
Photo courtesy of C-SPAN**

For Republicans, two senior incumbents Don Young and Tom Coleman topped the list of those most in jeopardy. Young, a riverboat captain with a famously cantankerous disposition was thought to be facing steep odds to return. He trailed behind John Devens, the Valdez Mayor who held him to a 52-48% win in 1990. Some polls showed him trailing by 15 points. Coleman was technically in a tossup but was running against the incumbent wind against a venerable State Senator.

Young was one of three longtime Republican members for whom rematches were on who in 1990 had been nearly unexpectedly jolted into political oblivion. This time, he and his colleagues, Olympia Snowe of Maine and Herb Bateman of Virginia were well prepared but faced an atmosphere that for incumbents was even more uninviting than two years earlier. While Snowe was aided by the presence of a Green Party candidate (Bateman's race was a tossup throughout). To Democrats chagrin, Bill Goodling was moving in the other direction. Though the district was fertilely Republican, 1992 proved that 430 overdrafts could change that. Democrats had a candidate, Paul Kukor but the presence of Tom Humbert, a conservative Republican running as an Independent, increased the odds that Goodling would benefit from split opposition. Sure enough, early October polls bore that out. Democrats still harbored hopes of beating other high check abusers, particularly Duncan Hunter. Opponent Janet Gastil conducted a kite-flying competition and awarded the winner a kite shaped as a bird. The insignia in the middle: "Cancel Duncan Hunter." When Gastil castigated Hunter over the radio for "kiting checks," Hunter saw that as borderline libel but Presidential candidate Ross Perot was on her side. Anemic primary wins for Bob McEwen and Jay Rhodes left Democrats hopeful that voters would boot them out while trying to maintain a sense of realism given the heavy GOP nature of those districts.

There was great uncertainty surrounding the freshmen Gang of Seven. In early October, as many as six of the seven members seemed seriously in danger of not returning, with only Boehner assured of getting another term. Nussle was still considered unlikely to overtake Nagle in the incumbent vs. incumbent matchup. While Democrats desperately wanted to oust Rick Santorum and Scot Klug in favorable districts, the Democratic nominees Frank Pecora and Ada Deer just didn't seem to have the oomph needed to push them over the top. Frank Riggs was in a tossup as was Charlie Taylor who was against the well-known TV reporter Maggie Lauterer. Moving up quickly on the watch list was John Doolittle, the Californian who in 1990, limped to victory in a heavily Republican district against an underfunded Patricia Malberg. This time, Malberg was back and Doolittle was pummeled for calling for more perks while chastising the House as a member of the Gang.

Finally, a major missed opportunity was looming for Democrats in Connecticut. Freshman Gary Franks of Connecticut was the first African-American Republican to win a House seat in 50 years but amassed considerable controversy in his single term. Democrats had hoped for Lynn Taborsak to take him out. However, when she lost the primary to a more conservative Democrat she opted to run on the A Connecticut Party Line (ACP) with the support of Independent Governor Lowell Weicker. In a district that leaned Republican to begin with, diluting the vote was inevitable and Democrats started to fret that the seat was out of reach.

diluting the vote was inevitable and Democrats started to fret that the seat was out of reach.

Democrats still harbored hopes of taking Gingrich down and Tony Center was running a spirited enough race to do so. The limousine took front-and-center as *The Washington Post* wrote, "Center rented a black Lincoln Continental stretch limousine, parked it outside Marshall's Country Kitchen in Marietta and gave lunch customers 150-yard rides, covering the same distance that Gingrich's limo used to travel between his Capitol Hill apartment and his office." The full extent of how Republican that district really was (or how few ticket-splitters remained) wouldn't become evident until after the election.

There was one Republican lawmaker certain to lose It was the Louisiana seat where Baker and Holloway were facing off was close and bitter to the end with mixed views as to who would come out on top (Holloway might have been given the slightest of edges). Given that it was to another Republican, the party was content to sit back and let the fighting go on.

As for reach seats, Democrats were nervously watching Romano Mazzoli, a 22-year pro-lifer from Kentucky. While ahead, he was billed as a possible upset victim against pro-choice State Senator Susan Stokes in an anti-incumbent tide. Republicans guarded against Elton Gallegly, a formerly safe three-termer but one whom redistricting had done few favors. His challenger was Anita Perez-Ferguson who enjoyed heavy funding from Emily's List.

One member whose status on the watch list was dropping was New Jersey's Frank Pallone. Initially pegged as the second most vulnerable Democrat against the very talented State Senator, Joe Kyrillos, Pallone's fortunes rose with the looming Democratic tide. His sincerity and the strong Democratic climate was helping him and though he was hardly home free by mid-October, a loss was not expected. No longer on any watch list was Gene Taylor, a very conservative Democrat who had been tagged for defeat since he voted against the Persian Gulf War.

Incidentally, the most vulnerable member was Joan Kelly Horn of Missouri who seemed to be holding up okay despite the uneven ground due to redistricting. The remap forced her to exchange Democratic precincts for more Republican turf that should have been fatal after just a 54-vote win in 1990. Even so, Horn was giving as good as she got and for most of the race was at least one step ahead of her rival, State House Minority Leader Jim Talent. The same went for Jon Cox in Illinois who was battling against similar dynamics. Both were still limping into November as nervous as a cat on a hot tin roof as both had reason to be in this climate. As it was, 91 new members were assured at this point but Congressional experts speculated that it could top 130.

Election Night

Eight-termers Mary Rose Oakar, a Democrat from Ohio and Tom Coleman, a Missouri Republican, were incumbent losses that by election night were neither close nor surprising Images courtesy of C-SPAN

Election Day was early this year, falling on November 3rd, and for incumbents this was not early enough. Election night would be rough though not brutal and certainly not as brutal as it could have been. In fact, the number of lawmakers unseated (sixteen Democrats and eight Republicans) was actually fewer than predicted. Most of the in-crowd survived, but many did not get off easy by much. While the 24 who fell was a slightly lower amount than analysts and Congressional leaders were expecting, the quality of losses somewhat differed. Some were anti-climactic while others were borderline shockers.

On the Democratic side, the four scandal-tarred incumbents who had long been expected to lose (Early, Oakar, Mavroules and Sikorski) did so mostly without ambiguity. Bustamante, who appeared to be in a true tossup, fell by a whopping 20 points. Huckaby lost to McCrery, a result that was totally anti-climactic though his 26-point deficit was the biggest loss of any incumbent. Tom McMillen lost another redistricting matchup against Gilchrest and Kostmayer whose odds were uncertain, fell to Greenwood. Richard Ray of Georgia appeared to simply get caught in the adverse redistricting and anti-incumbent tide. Hopes that Erdreich, Cox and Horn could convince the many Republicans added to their districts to overlook their party labels were dashed and their perennial status as high-level vulnerables proved to be right all along. On Long Island, it wasn't Hochbruechner who fell but Tom Downey and that was a stunner. The perception, fair or not, that insider status hampered his visibility back home took hold.

Amongst the GOP, Coleman had a pretty early loss and Marlenee, as most thought probable by Election Day, ended up losing to Williams. Baker narrowly prevailed in the all-Republican matchup against Holloway and after midnight McEwen was nudged out by a slim margin. It wasn't until the wee hours of the morning on the East Coast that Riggs and Rhodes, who began the night with decent sized leads, officially lost their seats.

Losses for both parties came almost without warning. South Carolina's Liz Patterson was a shocking second fiddle while Jim Jontz was thought to have had it locked down. In Iowa, it was Nagle who drew the short end of the stick against Nussle in a redistricting matchup, a development that even the most optimistic Republicans saw as unlikely until days before the election. Republicans had a few casualties that weren't out of nowhere but not particularly expected either as senior Republicans Bill Green of New York and Don Ritter of Pennsylvania fell to determined and underrated challengers.

**Jim Jontz of Indiana and Bob McEwen of Ohio could
not swim against the anti-incumbent tide
Photos courtesy of C-SPAN**

Both parties also had incumbents who confounded those who viewed them as dead men walking. Charlie Wilson survived and did so fine, taking 56% of the vote. Young and Lightfoot took far closer wins but won nonetheless, proving the prognosticators wrong (combined with Nussle beating Nagle, Iowa was a true field of disappointment for Democrats.) Ron Coleman trailed early in the evening but came back to edge Ortiz, a beneficiary of the many straight-ticket voters who opted for Clinton.

Among others in close races, Hochbruechner took an 8,000-vote win. This was a landslide given previous close calls and the fact that a loss wouldn't have been a surprise against a repeat opponent (with Downey's loss, Hochbruechner became the sole of his six Long Island colleagues to return to the Hill.) Carr, McCloskey and Mazzoli made it back as did Republicans Franks, Goodling, and by a surprisingly decent margin, Hunter. While Democrats celebrated their ouster of Riggs, they could not rejoice in the results of six of the other "Gang of Seven" members who lived to fight another day.

An anti-incumbent sentiment was not completely non-existent. Beyond defeats, the night was full of veteran lawmakers, mainly Democrats, who became locked in unexpected struggles and trailed slightly with large portions of the vote reported. Six-term Eastern Connecticut Congressman Sam Gejdenson, haunted by 50 overdrafts, ran neck-and-neck with State Senator Ed Muenster. He won by just 4,000 votes in a race so tight that Muenster didn't concede until the next day. In Missouri, nine-term Democrat Harold Volkmer found himself in a horserace he hadn't expected with an energetic but underfunded UMO Professor, Rick Hardy. Two-term Omaha Democrat, Peter Hoagland, was similarly sweating it out with Ron Staskiewicz. Both were down a few hundred votes with close to 90% counted before favorable turf put both on top by 6,000 votes out of the well over 230,000 cast. The Ross Perot phenomenon and his high percentages were viewed as major factors in bringing Gejdenson and Hoagland to near career-enders. A Green party candidate who drained 10,000 votes from his left brought Volkmer to the brink. Another near upset came in Tennessee. Favorite son Al Gore was on the ballot, but that didn't prevent nine-term Democrat Marilyn Lloyd from nearly being dragged under by Zach Wamp. Lloyd saw her healthy lead diminish all evening until her margin solidified to 2,900 votes (105,693 to 102,763.)

Democrat Ron Coleman of Texas (673 overdrafts) and Republican Jim Ross Lightfoot of Iowa (105) survived the check imbroglio. Lightfoot had been left for dead the entire cycle while Coleman was seen as a slight underdog as well Images courtesy of C-SPAN

Austin Murphy's nip'n'tuck race should not have been a surprise, particularly after his near primary defeat with significant new territory from redistricting and adverse publicity from the House Post Office scandal. Ron Townsend hit the Western Pennsylvania Democrat for his scandals and led 51-49% with 68%. When the complete numbers were in, Murphy reversed the 51-49% deficit and secured a place in the 103rd Congress by just 3,000 votes with a total of 114,898 to 111,591.

Other incumbent struggles were less surprising. Richard Lehman had been a perfect fit for his Central Valley, California district before redistricting led him to run in more conservative territory. He seemed to be holding on against paper company executive and first-time candidate Tai Cloud until the weekend before the election when they deadlocked. Lehman finished election night ahead by 888 votes but had to sweat the count of thousands of absentees. The margin increased to 1,030 votes and it wasn't until that Friday that he could say with certainty he won.

Bacchus and another freshman, Collin Peterson, were expected to have tough races mostly because their districts were so politically against them. The counting did not disappoint. Bacchus of Florida was actually declared the loser by some media outlets before late returns gave him a 3,500 win out of 260,000 votes cast, a development Tolley found suspicious enough to contest. On the flip side, Peterson's big lead gradually diminished with the counting until his win was solidified by 3,000 votes at a 50-49% margin.

Republicans were clearly disappointed that redistricting failed to dislodge a single incumbent in either Michigan or North Carolina, where they viewed as many as four Democrats in each delegation as vulnerable to many new GOP-leaning voters. While the seats did not flip, Republicans could take comfort in the fact that many of the margins by which most of the incumbents won dropped substantially from previous cycles. This they only hoped would improve their odds of winning when the climate went south for Democrats, which is exactly what happened in 1994. On the other hand, Democrats came up far short of knocking off Republicans Hal Rogers of Kentucky and Clay Shaw of Florida, whose districts' GOP lean had taken serious hits due to remaps.

Pennsylvania Democrat Austin Murphy was one of a handful of incumbents who won seats in the 103rd Congress, but only after big election night scares Photo courtesy of the U.S. House of Representatives Collection

The GOP also succeeded in capturing open seats. Contests in Colorado, Idaho and Virginia that were considered tossups went their way by double-digit margins as did open seats in Maryland and Georgia that were expected to stay in Democratic hands. Democrats struck back by grabbing newly created seats expected to go the other way in California and by squeezing out wins in Minnesota and Washington State.

Though Republicans had fewer incumbents, they were slightly more successful at preserving those impacted by the bank scandal in November. While McEwen bit the dust (along with Rhodes who had substantially fewer overdrafts), Goodling, Hunter and Lightfoot pulled it out, as did others with noticeably high overdrafts. Among them was Tom Petri of Wisconsin who had 76. Barbara Vucanovich, a Nevada Republican, had an unexpectedly tight call as her mere two checks did not stop her Democratic opponent, Reno Mayor Pete St, from exploiting the issue, tagging her, "Bouncing Barbara." That might have had impact. Vucanavich, a ten-year veteran whose district became more Republican through redistricting, won re-election by four points with under 50% of the vote (48-44%).

The margins of other Republicans were also stunners. Gingrich once again fulminated Democratic hopes and won with 58%. Bateman, who was thought to have had only the slightest edge by Election Day, racked up 60%. Bob Stump of Arizona, Bill McCollum of Florida and Mike Bilirakis flattened their determined foes with 64%, 69%, and 59% respectively. Eleven-term incumbent Bill Young was held to 57%, showing an underperformance on the GOP side (he never fell below that again in his 21 years in Congress to follow.) To compliment that, his neighbor and 30-year Congressional veteran Sam Gibbons also struggled, fending off an insurgent Republican by just 53-41%.

Among the Democrats aiming for Senate seats, Dorgan, Nighthorse-Campbell and Boxer prevailed but AuCoin fell short of Packwood (*The Oregonian's* report on allegations of Packwood's sexual harassment had been held back until after the election.) Stallings and Owens also lost by surprisingly unambiguous margins.

That is a rundown of the House political climate that was 1992. The pages ahead contain in-depth profiles of the lives, achievements and political circumstances of the members whose careers came to an end.

CHAPTER TWO

Brooklynese Solarz Awed Colleagues with International Stature and Imprint of World Affairs

Introductory Quote: "The reason they do not believe sanctions will be sufficient is because they know that Saddam Hussein does not give a whit for the welfare of his own people. All he cares about is the maximization of his own power. However great the economic impact of the sanctions may be, they know, as we know, that Saddam Hussein does not have to run for reelection in 1992. He does not have to worry about a contentious Congress or a critical press. He will hunker down. He will wait. And while he waits, there is a very real possibility that this inherently fractious and fragile coalition will begin to unravel, and the sanctions will erode, and he will prevail." –New York Congressman Stephen J. Solarz as he made his case to a hushed chamber of the U.S. House of Representatives in January 1991 about the need to "fight evil" and pass the Solarz-Michel resolution that would authorize the use of force against Iraq. The body approved the measure.

Photo courtesy of Nina Solarz

1 992 gobbled up the Congressional careers of not just political hacks but
   some of the brightest lights whom, even after having contributing so
much, still had miles to go before they lay down to sleep. Stephen "Steve"
Solarz of New York's Thirteenth Congressional District was among them
and his departure would leave a profound blemish on the fight for dignity
worldwide.

Whip-smart, articulate and distinctly Brooklynese, the apex of Solarz's
grasp was international affairs and his nickname was, "The Marco Polo of
Congress," and boy, did he earn it. Throughout his eighteen years in office,
Solarz's travels around the globe were tireless and his trips often meant meetings
with gems of leaders and odious dictators, including a nine-hour meeting with
a man he referred to in his memoir as, "the most voluble granddaddy of them
all," Fidel Castro of Cuba. Solarz himself expressed his central influence on
foreign soil when he proclaimed, "They might not think I'm important in
Brooklyn but they think I'm pretty important in Mongolia." That boast was
beyond credible. When Solarz visited the district of an Indian member of
Parliament, he was greeted by several hundred fans on a street corner in a poor,
remote area with the banner, "Welcome His Lordship: Congressman Stephen
Solarz." In fact, when Mel Levine, a Foreign Affairs Committee colleague from
California, insisted on traveling to a place that Solarz could not have set foot
in the Middle-East, he opted for a coffee-shop on a boat in Kuwait City and
was asked, "Do you know Congressman Solarz?"

Yet to whom much was given much was expected and Solarz's travels
were far from personal gratification. He had missions that often involved
prodding and cajoled these leaders to at least pretend they had an interest in
advancing human rights in their respective countries. The perception of him
not devoting blood and sweat to parochial affairs was somewhat true, though
not entirely accurate as his Friday night visits to area synagogues and other
local endeavors left him highly popular among his people.

If Solarz wasn't the single greatest freedom warrior the Democratic Party
put forth in the late 20th century, he was certainly the most underrated.
To boot, while far from bombastic but rather soft-spoken, he often had an
illustrious, cultured speaking mechanism for making his points. One example
was in 1984 when South African President P. W. Botha delivered a speech
in Durham that many had cautiously if not futilely hoped would contain
a new call for advancement. Solarz made clear after the fact that he was
unimpressed, saying, "To call it too little too late would be to endow it with
significance, a significance to which it is clearly not entitled."

The high point of Solarz's prominence came in January 1991 when he delivered what conceivably could one day wind up in a book of great Congressional oratory. He passionately spoke in favor of his resolution with House Minority Leader Robert Michel which authorized President George H.W. Bush to use force against Iraqi dictator Saddam Hussein. The passage of Solarz-Michel unleashed a "sky is the limit" talk for Solarz's career that went far beyond Congress and into high-ranking positions including Secretary of State. As evidence of no certainties existing in politics, all of that talk came to an unceremonious end less than two years later as a twin political killing (reapportionment and the House banking scandal) combined to force Solarz out of the job he loved and the public eye.

Solarz was "proof in the pudding" that an unhappy, even traumatic childhood could still result in great things. Born in Manhattan as an only child to parents who divorced while he was young, Solarz wrote in his memoir that, "For reasons I didn't discover until many years later, my mother decided not to keep me and the court awarded custody to my father." When Solarz was ten, his father's second marriage broke up and his father sent him to East 24th Street in Brooklyn where he would be reared by his aunt Beattie. Colleagues of all stripes recognized his leadership abilities early as they chose him president of his sixth-grade class and student government president in high school. Solarz himself did little to dispel that. *The Washington Post* noted that Solarz took a school-trip to Harrisburg, Pennsylvania when Adlai Stevenson was running for president and, "once on the capitol steps, the precocious kid from Brooklyn made an impassioned speech on behalf of the Democratic presidential candidate. Hundreds gathered."

Solarz received his undergrad in Political Science from Brandeis where he edited the student newspaper, *The Justice*. From there, he enrolled in Columbia University with every intention of practicing law but grew instead to find international relations far more scintillating. He graduated in 1967 with an M.A. in Public Law and Government, at which time he was already deeply immersed in the political system. A year earlier, he managed the campaign of Mel Dubin, an anti-Vietnam contender who was seeking the very Congressional seat that Solarz would hold less than a decade later. Dubin was taking on Abe Multer who had been in office for 19 years and Solarz sought a slate of candidates for lower offices, thinking an overflow might increase turnout from the bottom up. "We reasoned that if we could put together a slate and get each candidate to bring in at least a dozen workers, we could field an army of volunteers" (he told the story of promising the Senate nomination to a man named David Falk under the premise that Falk could bring in many volunteers, but soon discovered that he had recruited the wrong David Falk).

Solarz was very nearly successful – Dubin failed to unseat the incumbent by fewer than 1,000 votes, a margin of 51-49%.

1968 was a watershed year for Solarz. Now teaching political science at Brooklyn College, he was strongly anti-war, telling *Open Vault* in 1983 that, "It didn't seem to me at the time that we had any vital national interests at stake there and the price we were paying for our involvement in Vietnam in terms of the blood and treasure we were expending there, without any persuasive justification that as a result of our involvement we were in any significant way enhancing the national interests of our own country seemed to me to be, therefore, utterly unjustified." He backed Bobby Kennedy for president. At the same time, he was again running Dubin's Congressional campaign for Multer's open Congressional seat but lost to Assemblyman Bertram Podell who had the backing of the Brooklyn regular Democratic line. By that time Solarz had made quite an impression, not the least of which was on his new wife Nina, a mother of two and a teacher at Brooklyn College whom he had met during the first Dubin campaign. She encouraged him to run for the State Assembly and, with the help of her parents who contributed generously to the campaign, he won the primary with 58% and 66% in the general. During his six years in the Assembly, Solarz gained a reputation for both accessibility and commitment to fighting for constituent needs. He hosted a program, "Spotlight on Albany," to better inform his constituents of the happenings.

With his bride and trusted confidante, Nina
Photo courtesy of Nina Solarz

By 1974, Congress did not appear to be on Solarz's horizon. If anything, city politics seemed more appealing as he was just coming off a failed but respectable bid for Brooklyn Borough President. Podell's indictment accelerated the timing, although he was quite stubborn in exiting. Podell insisted on standing for re-election and had substantial backing but Solarz challenged him in the primary. While the final margin was not particularly spectacular given Podell's problems, Solarz was victorious by 10% (44-34%) and the general election was a foregone conclusion. The district had the largest concentration of Jews in the nation (2/3) and encompassed Brighton Beach, Coney Island and Sheepshead Bay.

Solarz knew immediately that he would like to serve on the House Foreign Affairs Committee and put on a full-court press to make that goal a reality. He recalled that, in part by courting the panel's chair, "Doc" Morgan of Pennsylvania, "I tried to mobilize some of the friends of Israel in Pennsylvania who knew him through my contacts in the Jewish community to put in a word on my behalf and I spoke to him myself" (then-Majority Leader Tip O'Neill was also helpful). Solarz was awarded the post.

To say Solarz hit the ground running would be a vast understatement as he didn't even need time to find the proverbial men's room. On his death, *The New York Times* called him, "a torrent of activity during his first six months in Congress. According to his office, he made 12 speeches on the House floor, co-sponsored 370 bills, held 11 news conferences, made 24 trips to his district and attended 99 events there, visited 23 subway stations, sent constituents 513,720 pieces of mail and took an 18-day tour of the Middle East."

Though Solarz had seats on the Budget Committee and Merchant Marine and Fisheries throughout his tenure, there was no doubt what was at the core of Solarz's passion: international affairs. A staff member summed up Solarz's philosophy by saying, "Steve's only interested in two things: Brooklyn and the rest of the world." Legislatively and verbally, Solarz did little to dispel that. "To most of the people in my district," he once joked, "Zimbabwe sounds like a new Baskin Robbins flavor." He also was once given a standing ovation on the floor of the Indian Parliament for championing U.S. aid to the nation when others advocated ending it.

By only his third term, Solarz achieved subcommittee chairmanship of the Africa Subcommittee on International Relations and one colleague, Republican Robert Bauman of Maryland, derisively referred to him as "Mr. Africa." Pejorative it may have been but Solarz could hardly have argued the point. From the subcommittee perch, Solarz received money for black South

Africans in the U.S. who were unable to get an adequate education in the mother country due to apartheid. He aimed to maintain the U.S. government policy of sanctions against Rhodesia given they were doing little to improve their odious racial standing.

In the fall of 1980, Solarz strenuously favored providing aid to Ethiopia and Somalia despite the fact that the two were at odds. However, Somalia's attempted annexation of the Ogaden desert in 1980 complicated it. The Somali government agreed to let the U.S. use bases in the Horn of Africa in exchange for $40 million in aid. This sat poorly with Solarz, who grilled Assistant Secretary of State Richard Moose about it at a hearing. "Are you telling us," he asked, "that the Somalis are abandoning one of their major national objectives in exchange for $40 million in foreign military sales?" The Ethiopian government was against it as well calling it, "a dagger poised at the heart" of the nation that Solarz said, "illustrates the potential problem which can be created for us if we proceed in running the risk of involving ourselves in a regional conflict between Ethiopia and Somalia which could escalate to a larger war." Opponents were able to stop the transfer through a rare Congressional prerogative.

That same year, Solarz became the first member of Congress to meet with North Korean Kim Il-Sung and the two discussed possible reunification.

After the 1980 election, Solarz seemed to be as safe as they come. New York State, though, was losing five seats in Congress and the biggest parlor talk was what would happen if Solarz and his very junior colleague, freshman Charles Schumer, were placed in the same district. The alliance between the two men was unmistakable. Schumer had once worked for Solarz as a State Assemblyman, and then succeeded him in that office in '74. With that in mind, Solarz might have expected Schumer to show deference to him if the two had been paired together but Schumer indicated that he would do no such thing. In fact, both men, aware of the high stakes that potentially lay ahead, began stockpiling $1 million dollar war chests. Luckily, the matchup came to pass as Solarz and Schumer were both drawn districts that fit them like gloves and as such, flourished for the next decade (Solarz would continue his devout mastering of foreign affairs while Schumer did the same on judiciary matters). The weary watching would continue. "It wasn't quite like the Hatfields and McCoys," Solarz said. "But neither were we as close as Richard Nixon and Billy Graham."

With Anwar Sadat
Photo courtesy of Nina Solarz

In 1981, Solarz switched to the Subcommittee on Asia and the Pacific Affairs, a panel that encompassed his focuses and defined his remaining time both in Congress and on Earth. At times during that chairmanship, Solarz was an ideological soul mate for liberals that operated under the guise of human rights. Other times, they chafed.

To articulate all of Solarz's international accomplishments would be a lengthy process but there were several highlights, one of which included reigniting U.S. policy toward a more democratic Philippines. Solarz was quite close to Nimoy Aquino, the exiled leader who was murdered – presumably by the Marcos regime, upon his return to his home country. After a number of major newspapers published accounts of lavish spending by the Marcos's, Solarz held hearings on the matter which he would write in his memoir, "resembles the plot of a dimed-store novel more than standard legislative procedure." It exposed the fact that Ferdinand and his wife Imelda invested $350 million into New York real estate. Through the help of Victor Politis, whom Solarz called, "my deep-throat," the Congressman was able to uncover many details about the Marcos's wealth. One of the more jocular, albeit it soon-legendary revelations was that Imelda owned 300 shoes, which invited another Solarzism when he asserted that, "Compared to Imelda Marcos, Marie Antoinette was a bag lady."

Solarz came under great criticism, particularly from Republican lawmakers, for conducting the hearings just prior to the Philippine elections when Nimoy's widow, Corazon, was up against Marcos. His response was that they had been scheduled before Marcos called "snap elections," though he did acknowledge that if they did help swing the election to Aquino, "I wouldn't hang my head in shame." When the election came, cheating was suspected but the Reagan administration said both sides were behind it. This was a charge Solarz later credited to, "smoking hashish in the White House because it was obvious that the overwhelming bulk of the chicanery was the result of the Marcos machine rather than the opposition. I think Marcos is going to laugh all the way to the bank." Solarz and Indiana Republican Senator Richard Lugar began crafting a policy to halt non-humanitarian aid to Manila (which pitted them not only against the administration but Senate Majority Leader Robert Dole). In 1987, Solarz and his New York Republican House colleague Jack Kemp along with Senators Alan Cranston (D-California) and Lugar proposed the Philippine Assistance Program, a ten billion dollar aid package. It was implemented.

With Phillipine President Corazon Aquino
Photo courtesy of Nina Solarz

El Salvador was another hotbed on which Solarz exerted his energy. Like many, he was appalled by El Salvadoran intransigencies against its people and sought to link the aid package being considered in 1983 to improvement. Specifically, he wanted to require the U.S. President to certify that the El Salvadoran government was negotiating with the rebels in order to continue receiving aid. Many balked at that, considering it to be impractical. A compromise, however, was worked out that called for the President to state that an "unconditional dialogue" was taking place. "This way," Solarz reasoned, "the Democratic House, rather than the Republican Senate, would be in the catbird seat." Around the same time, the idea of aiding the Nicaraguan contras was taking center stage but Solarz was not a fan of funding them. "We need to learn the lessons of Vietnam," he said, "but it would be a tragic mistake if we were to be paralyzed from them."

Throughout the 1980s, Solarz displayed little sympathy for Pakistan and by 1990, came to the conclusion that the nation was not making a good faith effort to clamp down on its nuclear activities as they had promised a year earlier (the president had to certify that they were doing so). It was not Solarz's first rendezvous with the issue. In 1985, his panel trimmed aid unless the Reagan administration certified it would not be building a nuclear weapon. After many chances he finally urged the Bush administration to revoke its aid.

In China
Photo courtesy of Nina Solarz

In that vein, Solarz was pro-India to the point that he not only was the key player in the effort to lift the ban on aid to the nation, but he also warded off measures from more conservative lawmakers to cut developmental assistance. Ohio Democrat Ed Feighan was his sponsor and the bill passed.

Aid to Cambodian refugees proved a very tricky road for many members of Congress to navigate because of the specter of Vietnam. Not Solarz. Beginning in 1985, Solarz became the foremost champion of aid. The contentiousness was not so much with the administration but rather other Democrats. Solarz addressed members' concerns by assuring them that, "It will not lead to another American involvement in Indochina. Precisely because of Vietnam, we are not going to send American troops back there." Aid was included in the subcommittee's foreign aid package by a vote of 24-9.

As early as 1985, Solarz wanted to give money to the resistance movement in Cambodia which was composed of at least three groups. In 1990, Solarz was challenged by colleagues from his own party, including Massachusetts Democrat Chet Atkins and a fellow from New York, Robert Mrazek, who fretted that the aid would benefit the Khmer Rouge. Khmer was viewed as the orchestrator of many of the atrocities because it would be aiding Prince Norodom Sihanouk who was close to that regime.

During the debate, Solarz rebuked Mrazek, calling it "flatly untrue" that the Khmer Rouge would get a piece of the pie and vowed to "stake my reputation for integrity on the proposition that there is no credible evidence whatsoever [that] our aid is going to the Khmer Rouge." With the viewpoint that, "Everyone agrees that our goal should be to prevent a Khmer Rouge victory. The disagreements are over how best to achieve the goal," Solarz's contention was that, "Unless the non-communist forces are strengthened, Vietnam may one day withdraw and Pol Pot (the leader of the Khmer Rouge) will return." Furthermore, Solarz buttonholed Atkins whose district contained a large number of Cambodian boat-people by telling him that, "I would provide them with big bucks to strengthen them...if I concluded that was the only way to stop the Khmer Rouge. Frankly, I'm a little bit surprised. I would think you would want to help them." On Hun Sen, "When I first met him in 1981, he was a rustic from the countryside, a Cambodian bumpkin. Now he looks like he was shaped up by media consultants."

Plenty of other times, however, Solarz provided liberals with reassurance that he was still in their company. He was a member of the 47-member Congressional Caucus on Ethiopian Jewry and worked on efforts allowing the remaining Jews in that drought stricken nation to emigrate to Israel.

Solarz was an early and passionate proponent of carrying out sanctions against the government of South Africa and in 1985, called a watered down GOP measure to allow a three-year study, "a classic example of too little, too late. The time for sanctions is now." The following year, when no sanctions were forthcoming, he raised cane with the Reagan administration for unhesitatingly discharging them on other nations (Libya and Honduras), verbalizing, "If we are going to stand up against repression in Central America and terrorism in the Middle East, then I think it is time to stand up against racism in South Africa." Further proof in the pudding was that the "constructive engagement" policy that the Reagan administration had been advocating for getting the government of South Africa to change since it had taken office was not working. "Five years later," he said, "I think the verdict is in. Despite what may have been the best of intentions, the policy has failed."

Solarz was long involved with the Angola situation and had an amendment passed in 1990 (by a vote of 213-200) that would suspend a CIA backed aid package to the rebel group, the National Union for the Total Independence of Angola (UNITA), if the administration certified that the Angolan government was adhering to a cease-fire. Some liberals such as California Democrat Ron Dellums advocated for a more permanent aid moratorium.

With Nelson Mandela
Photo courtesy of Nina Solarz

When it came to Brooklyn, the parochial Solarz was in full bloom and in 1990, introduced a bill that would ban a sports team that abandoned a domicile from using the city's name in their current trademark. Why did Solarz feel the need to take this action some 33 years after the team fled to Los Angeles? Because the Brooklyn Dodgers Sports Bar and Restaurant still existed in Brooklyn. He worked to secure funding for the Ocean Parkway, referred to as the transportation spine of Brooklyn and introduced legislation creating a National Commission on Down Syndrome Act where the Borough had a cluster.

As his prestige advanced, Solarz faced increasing criticism that he was not as committed to local issues as international. One Democratic leader told *New York Magazine* in 1986, "He's animated about Imelda's shoes. He ain't that animated about revitalizing the waterfront...if he could be a foreign policy fellow without being a congressman, he would just as soon be relieved of the nonsense." Former aides rebutted the magazine's characterization, contending that Solarz devotes much time to the "relatively unglamorous problems that plague our urban areas – getting potholes filled, finding money for escalators to the elevated subways in his district (and) promoting anti-arson programs."

Solarz Chief of Staff Michael Lewan acknowledged a "'push/pull' between Brooklyn politics, constituent services and Steve's activity in foreign policy." That said, the district's demographics meant that Brooklyn and the rest of the world were not mutually exclusive. The district, already a melting pot, was diversifying by the day and, "We worked hard to welcome these new Americans while attempting to enhance democracy and human rights back in their home country. Needless to say, these immigrants appreciated his efforts which surely helped the family and friend left behind." Solarz's work on behalf of Israel and against arms sales was obviously fundamental given the substantial Jewish population but, there was an abundance of Italian-American constituents. When a devastating earthquake struck Italy, Solarz worked for an emergency aid package. Lewan's bottom line: "In our district, foreign policy was often the kind of local politics to which Tip O'Neill referred."

Most colleagues on both sides of the aisle were generally awed by Solarz, and that was reflected by who his close friends were – fellow Democrats such as Mo Udall, Barney Frank and Henry Waxman but also Republicans Jim Leach of Iowa and Bob Livingston of Louisiana. Feighan said he "liked working with Steve," calling him, "a hard-working and serious legislator." Lester Wolff, a fellow New York City Democrat and more senior Foreign Affairs Democrat said, "Steve WAS ahead of his time He was a great human rights advocate and brilliant."

With Shimon Peres
Photo courtesy of Nina Solarz

Tom Downey was a fellow Watergate Babyfrom New York who could not overstate the esteem for which he held Solarz and called him, "one of the most remarkable members of the Congress of the United States, someone who was constantly learning, trying to understand." He recalled a New York State delegation meeting where Solarz was asked about a recent trip to India and he launched into a 10-minute prose, which was generally a no-no. Downey recalls there was "not a peep - everybody listened to him talk." He remembers his fellow Suffolk Democrat Otis Pike, a normally curmudgeon fellow, leaning over to him to say, "that was the single best summarization I have ever heard." Downey calls the fact that Solarz was never able to put his credentials to use in a presidential administration "a tragedy." Many of his chief allies were conservative Democrats or Republicans. If Solarz had a trait that could be off-putting, Downey said, "it was that people might accuse him of being a know it all." However, that was a very acceptable rationale because he "knew it all." Still, some colleagues felt Solarz did not always have the tact to essentially show the world that he "knew it all" on foreign affairs and they did not. At one point, a fellow Democrat who lacked expertise on foreign affairs was sponsoring a measure on the House floor when Solarz walked up to him and asked, "Do you know what you're doing?"

Solarz's staff was devoted to him as well and to this day they hold reunions that include Nina. Mary Jane Burt is one such person. A close confidant of Solarz in his Brooklyn office during two separate stints, she called him, "absolutely one of the smartest and most inquisitive people," and stated he was, "so hard working that he was easily inspiring and you wanted to do it yourself." The staff, she said, "had a real deep affection for him." Lewan echoes that. Some staff, he said, "leave swearing never to speak to their boss again. In the Solarz case, we staffers remain friends and family three decades later." In a sign of how inclusive Solarz was, Burt was often included in heavy-policy dinner meetings with important dignitaries regardless of how heavy the topic. He could have a playful sense of humor. He once concluded a business-oriented letter to Zbigniew Brzezinski by telling him to, "practice his tennis. I'm expecting you to put up a stiffer plate the next time we play."

Burt calls him, "a stickler for details, always wanted the exact." He "never had a terrible temper," didn't hold grudges and, "demanded in a humane sort of way the best of everyone." While he loved his car (he and Nina both drove Volkswagon Rabbit's), staff used to drive him because, "it was dangerous for him to be on the road because he was always dictating." To illustrate that, *The Washington Post* wrote in 1990 that Nina prevailed upon him to go swimming with his aides at a work session at his Fire Island home where he continued furiously dictating in the ocean, then incredulously asking, "Why aren't you getting this down?" Certainly down time in what *New York Magazine* called the, "Solarz System," was rare but Solarz would play tennis with anyone (diplomats, staff, interns). He loved reading history/political biographies and went to all kinds of movies which Lewan recalled, "he regularly discussed with any willing listener."

Solarz listened to all viewpoints regardless of his view on the issue. Burt recalls one day lobbying him to vote a certain way on an issue. While he ended up voting contrary, he explained to her in advance why he was doing so and that earned her respect. Nina meanwhile was "the glue that held us all together during some tough times."

Not surprisingly, Solarz was a highly sought after member by the press and did receive attention on high profile endeavors such as Iraq, the Philippines and Turkey. But Lewan says that while his boss certainly enjoyed, "good press...he preferred to pen op-ed pieces where he could explain nuances in diplomacy over sound bites," and, "never ran too hot or cold over media mentions."

Near the end of his career, Solarz was pressing for approval of the Religious Freedom Restoration Act. As it neared passage, he said, "It is perhaps not too hyperbolic to suggest that in the history of the republic, there has rarely been a bill which more closely approximates motherhood and apple pie." Though Solarz was no longer in Congress when the resolution was approved in 1993, his fingerprints were firmly intertwined.

By far, Solarz's biggest moment in the sun came that Saturday afternoon in January 1991 as Congress debated giving the president authority to use force against Iraq. This was against the wishes of a majority of Democrats who wanted to allow time for sanctions to run their course. The moment had been in the making since the previous August when Iraq invaded Kuwait. In fact, to paraphrase Hussein, his stance became the mother of all disagreements with liberals.

In his book, Solarz called supporting the resolution, "the most difficult decision I had to make in my eighteen years in Congress." He lost allies as a result, including Bill Leuchtenburg, a leading historian of 20th century America and *The Village Voice* who called him, "a loathsome benighted incubus whose reptilian visage has darkened the television screens of America" (in his memoir, *Journeys To War and Peace*, Solarz wrote he "had to check the dictionary to find out what 'incubus' meant. I discovered it referred to a demon that had secual intercourse with a sleeping woan"). Solarz did reveal later that he suggested other Democrats be on the resolution but they declined and many wanted it to be bipartisan in any case. So became Solarz-Michel.

As debate prepared to close, Solarz almost forgot to seek recognition but once it was attained, he delivered perhaps the most impassioned speech of his career. He started by noting the irony of his championship of a war-likely resolution: "As we come to the close of this historic debate, I find myself in a somewhat anomalous position. It was almost 25 years ago that I got my start in politics as the campaign manager for one of the first antiwar candidates for Congress in the country. It never occurred to me then that I would be speaking on the floor of the House of Representatives a quarter of a century later in support of a bipartisan resolution that many whom I respect fear could lead to another Vietnam."

Solarz then outlined the attributes of why sanctions would not loosen Hussein's grasp of Kuwait. "Driven by a megalomaniacal lust for power, (Hussein) is determined to dominate the entire Middle East, and if he is not stopped now, we will have to stop him later under circumstances where he will be much more difficult and much more dangerous to contain. None of us wants war." Yet Solarz, noting how the United States waited until December 7, 1941, urged colleagues to heed "the great lesson of our time." He explains this was, "that evil still exists, and when evil is on the march, it must be confronted." His utmost argument: "If we prevail, we will have prevented a brutal dictator from getting his hands on the economic jugular of the world." Colleagues gave him an ovation, then voted to authorize the use of force by a decent-sized vote of 250-183.

With so much of the caucus favoring sanctions, did Solarz surprisingly come under pressure from leadership or colleagues to be less vocal? Not really. Staffers say, "His position was quite clear and his arguments sound." Being Steve Solarz also helped. Lewan recalls, "As often was the case, opponents were a bit timid to argue given Steve's energetic and effective articulation of intellectual and political case to commence military action against Saddam." Over one-third of the Democratic caucus voted with him.

When the war was short and overwhelmingly successful, Solarz became something of a sensation. There was even scant-talk about him running for president and he was invited to address the "cattle show" put on by the Wisconsin Democratic Party in mid-1991. The challenges he would have faced was illustrated when he told the gathering that, "We are witnessing a struggle for the soul of the Democratic Party," a statement that was elicited with a handful of boo's. The fact is Solarz's commitment to ridding America of vicious beasts was not his first rodeo with advocating a muscular foreign policy. As early as 1985, he penned a letter to *The New York Times* in which he wrote, "What Democrats must understand is that our traditional human rights concerns are by no mean incompatible with a realistic and resolute approach to Communism. A new Democratic foreign policy that combined the two would serve our country's interests by facilitating a bipartisan consensus to resist Soviet expansionism and Communist tyranny."

The reception Solarz got on the trail wouldn't make a difference. He had little interest in running for president and would soon be consumed by problems such as retaining his Congressional seat and redistricting. In fact, in describing his luck for 1992, he would resort to using the Jewish term "Schlemazel," which is defined as "a consistently unlucky or accident-prone person."

The culprits surrounding Solarz's defeat were two-fold. One, of course, was redistricting. The Voting Rights Act mandated the creation of a Hispanic majority-district in New York City, a prospect not made easier by the fact that the state was losing three of its House seats. Solarz organized a major campaign to preserve his seat, including enlisting many others on his behalf, including Vice-President Walter Mondale, to make the case for why he should remain in Congress. Then came the House Banking scandal which for Solarz, was more than an incidental.

When the House released the names of those with overdrafts many were stunned to see Solarz's name so high. With 743 overdrafts, he had among the highest amount in the House overall and was on the list of the 24 worst abusers. Solarz was not only apologetic but profuse in his attempt to say that the mistakes were legitimate. "We weren't purchasing stocks. We weren't making speculative investments. We weren't gambling. We weren't playing the horses or using this as some kind of slush fund. There was never any attempt or intent to use the House bank to float a long-term, interest-free loan. It was solely for household expenses." On another occasion, he said, "I was not focusing on the operations of the House Bank. I was trying to be freed up to focus on the problems my constituents sent me here to focus on." However, press accounts noticed that Solarz, "lives in one of Washington's most elegant suburbs and entertains frequently." While he did contend to *The New York Times* that the bank, "was so antiquated," his realism led him to assert that, "I hope I don't become a symbol of everything that's wrong."

The news couldn't have come at a worse time. Solarz had been confident – aides believe "too confident," that a revised district would be offered but, when the new Congressional map was finally produced in June, the district was carved up five different ways. Solarz weighed all of his options carefully, including not running again, but ultimately decided to seek re-election in the new Hispanic majority district. Even a cursory look at the demographics revealed how imposing the odds would be: 58% Latino and just 29% Caucasian. The man who negotiated with dictators was clearly facing his toughest mission yet. Yet Solarz moved forward with his typical gusto and *The Almanac of American Politics* later observed, "It was not a bad strategy. He almost won."

Solarz was joined in the race by six other contenders and as the lone Caucasian, many thought it conceivable that they would split the vote and allow Solarz to pull it out. Indeed, that was his gambit as well. Mayor David Dinkins and Congressman Jose Serrano rallied behind New York City Councilwoman Nydia Velazquez and Serrano even mocked Solarz's heavy media artillery by saying, "How much of the advertising he does is really advertising for his opponent?" Neither was Solarz helped by what *The New York Times* referred to as, "an unusual Election Eve appeal without the approval of the Brooklyn Diocese" when a number of Brooklyn clergy urged voters to opt for a non-Solarz candidate.

Solarz's chief asset was a $2 million war chest. He learned Spanish and hired two prominent aides of Hispanic descent for his campaign, including the well-known Rudy Garcia. He campaigned assiduously to court his new would-be constituents. One ad read, "Cuando cuentan contigo, tienes que actuar" ("When people are counting on you, you have to take action").

Early on primary night, Solarz barely trailed Velazquez, and by 10:30 p.m. it become obvious that he was going to lose. The final margin was 34-28%. "We gave it our all," he told supporters. While later remarking that he was in the "penultimate experience of my political career and I tend to doubt I'll ever be involved in something so significant again," he waxed with introspect and only Solarz-like articulation: "I know there will be other opportunities to serve in my life. Elective office is not the only way to do something constructive." He acknowledged that, "If I made any miscalculations, I did not fully anticipate the firestorm my decision would bring," and said, "my deepest regret is that by the end of the year, when I'm out, Saddam Hussein will still be in. I hope somehow or other that can be corrected — not so much by the miraculous resurrection of your humble servant but by the departure of Saddam from Baghdad."

For a time, there was an indication that Solarz's influence might continue and there was considerable speculation that he might be nominated for the position of Ambassador to India in the Clinton/Gore administration. This came to pass. He instead put together a business model assisting American businesses work with governments allied with the U.S. governments. He wrote opinion pieces for major newspapers, participated in think tank panels, and as Lewan recalled, "settled into life after Congress quite happily." The Republican takeover of the House in 1994, without question, eased some of the pain because serving in the minority would have been, "a political spot he would have hated."

In a 1986 *New York Magazine* interview, Nina was asked how Solarz changed since they first met. Her response: "I think he is much more concerned with using every waking moment for something he sees as constructive." That was his life's mission in a nutshell which he pursued until his untimely death. He passed in 2010 due to esophageal cancer at the far too young age of seventy.

CHAPTER THREE

Elected at 25, Downey Personified Both the Post-Watergate Exuberance and The Perception Of Congress In 1992

Introductory Quote: "I haven't had a date in my district in six months." – New York Congressman Tom Downey, 26, near the end of his first year in Congress. Downey, the youngest member of the House of Representatives, spoke about getting the phone number of a woman who approached him while dining with his parents at a Washington restaurant and giving it to a friend but the gal was uninterested. Downey continued by saying, "I haven't had two days off in six months. I've gotten so now that when I see a two-hour break, I think it's a vacation." He nonetheless told *The New York Times*, "This is something I've always wanted to do. Very few people in life can say that."

Photo courtesy of the Thomas J. Downey Papers #5926, Kheel Center for Labor-Management Documentation and Archives, Cornell University Library.

As 1992 got underway, it was clear that many House members would be caught in an impending avalanche of turnover. New York Democrat Tom Downey wasn't expected to be among them. However, the combination of the House bank and the perception that 18 years in Washington had caused him to lose touch cost him the seat and ended a very unlikely run that began at age 25.

Downey could easily pass for the most idealistic member of Congress profiled in this book. Elected to Congress as a longshot the November following Richard Nixon's surrender of the presidency, he exuded the term "Watergate Baby" literally and figuratively. His sunny disposition, serial do-gooder attitude, and willingness to challenge the system conveyed the reality of his mission: to do more than enjoy the perks and prestige of being a member of Congress. Downey had a genuine concern for serving the people and, throughout his 18 years representing a competitive if not Republican-leaning Long Island district, it showed.

While Downey was born in Ozone Park, Queens, his lifelong identity was with Long Island where he moved with his family as a boy. He graduated from high school in West Islip and enrolled at the New York State School of Industrial Relations at Cornell University and obtained a Bachelor's degree. From there, he started working in the personnel department of Macy's and it was widely noted that, until he left Congress, it would be his only source of income outside the government.

For all of Downey's youth when he ran for Congress, he was not without experience politically. He was elected to the Suffolk County Legislature at the ripe age of 22 by 63 votes and, having been re-elected a year later by roughly 1,900, focused on issues such as sewage. He pursued his law degree at St. John's University School of Law during that time but put this on hiatus to focus on his Congressional campaign (he succeeded in earning it six years into his Congressional stint in 1980).

When Downey indicated that he would run for Congress after waiting in line for gasoline during the energy shortage, many essentially told him to, "settle down, young man." There was no need to rush. Besides, the incumbent he'd be challenging was James Grover who was considered hard working, inoffensive and a genuine nice guy. That aside, there was no reason to think he was vulnerable because in 1972, Nixon took 72% in the district. Downey himself recalls that in looking back, "I didn't really go into the election thinking I was going to win it and so of course I was very surprised that I did. But it became pretty clear early on that we had a shot."

To make that happen, Downey got right to work. The candidate had a phone bank of 35 people and *The New York Times* noted that, "Jeffrey Downey, his 11-year-old brother, delivered campaign literature and made some side bets with classmates who were sons of Republican leaders." On the other hand, Grover was not by any means running an energetic race.

Downey ended with 48.9% to Grover's 45%, a difference of roughly 5,000 votes. The jubilation was so strong that *Newsday* wrote, "It took about five minutes for the storefront office, which was packed with more than 100 young volunteers, to stop ringing with cheers." An ecstatic Downey told them, "[they] have won a great victory," and in referencing Grover's strong '72 margin, claimed they "changed the minds and the souls of almost 30,000 souls in two years." There had been a Conservative Party candidate on the ballot and while it is conceivable that the six percent taken by Neil Greene could have tilted the race to Grover, there is indication that at least some of those voters would have opted for change. Indeed, a reporter asked Downey how it feels to not have taken a majority. His reply: "The nice thing about American system is you don't need one to go to Congress so I'm perfectly fine."

The day after the election, *The Times* famously ran a photo below the fold of Downey and his brother shooting baskets in his driveway and stated, "Everybody wanted to play ball with the new Congressman today. The only problem was that people kept interrupting the basketball game in Tom Downey's driveway."

With the limelight naturally thrust upon Downey as a young newbie (he was profiled in *Rolling Stone*), getting oriented was an adjustment. He was referred to, sometimes mockingly, as "Young Tom Downey," which for him meant two steps forward but at times, one step back. *The Times* in a profile mentioned aides grimacing about being asked what he has "really done besides grabbing headlines about how young he is." Downey himself told the story of a morning when "a Congressman asked if I would go down to the well to get a copy of the amendment. I did, and I brought one back for myself. He asked, 'What do you need that for?' And he told me to give my copy to another Congressman. I said, 'Let him share yours.'"

A far less benign incident occurred shortly after (Downey is not certain when) after a senior and very ornery member, William Barrett of Pennsylvania handed him papers and ordered him to return it to his office. Downey replied by telling him to "go f—k himself." Barrett immediately summoned Donn Anderson, the clerk of the House and told him what "this page" had said and Anderson had to break the news to Barrett that "this page is your

new colleague, Thomas Downey of New York." Barrett was flummoxed and
Downey, not wanting hard feelings, offered to deliver the papers to Barrett's
office after all but Barrett wouldn't have it. The anecdote had one hell of
a postscript. Barrett dropped dead in April of '76 and Anderson joked to
Downey that telling him to "go f—k himself" caused his death.

Downey taking his mock oath a second time
Photo courtesy of Tom Downey

As Downey learned the ropes of Hill life, he was confronted by reality.
One lesson was that in order to be taken seriously, he couldn't get into the
habit of routinely opposing his party's leadership. Downey once referred to
himself as, "a charter member of the Democratic left" but that term wasn't
exclusive for the way he conducted himself. One close confidante said, "Tom
is as comfortable with anti-war groups as he is with the American Legion.
People are pleased when they find out he listens to them. And once he meets
people, he's got their vote, particularly the women." A GOP strategist said of
Downey, "The people on our side who love to hate him know he is prepared."

Downey won a seat on the Armed Services Committee and became
strongly aligned with other infamously rebellious liberals, namely Ron
Dellums of California and Pat Schroeder of Colorado. The trio, along with
three other junior liberals, sought to make their mark during the first budget
Armed Services considered that year and proposed an alternative. The six were
the only members of the committee to support it. That same year, Downey

took aim at the B1 and instead urged that the B52 be fully utilized. Downey's doctrinaire defense views did not come at the expense of his region. Securing military contracts for Grumman Aerospace Company (and later preserving the F14) was high on his priorities.

Schroeder and Michigan Democrat Bob Carr were Downey's partners the following year as they chided the Pentagon's efforts to propagandize ("spook") Americans on Soviet spending on weaponry. It came as Armed Services was to consider its annual military spending bill. The trio authored a minority report that singled out, "a well-orchestrated exercise of careful selection of statistical measures which magnify Soviet capability and minimize our own."

Other highlights marked Downey's first term. When he heard that the Army was conducting hallucinogenic drugs, he called for an investigation. Soon after, the tests ceased. Then there was the matter of Honor code violations at the U.S. Military Academy in West Point of which he became aware when a constituent whose son was at the Academy approached him. "Congressman," she began, "I didn't vote for you and my son was nominated to the Academy by your predecessor but, he's not a cheater and I'd appreciate if you would look into this." That evening, Downey and Fred Kass, his Legislative Director with whom he had roomed in college, drove up to Highland Falls at West Point and "began interviewing all of the jag officers and members of the class who claimed to have been wronged."

Photo courtesy of the Thomas J. Downey Papers #5926, Kheel Center for Labor-Management Documentation and Archives, Cornell University Library

Soon after, Downey issued a report on his findings but couldn't convince his senior Armed Services colleagues to conduct a field hearing on the matter. So "I held my own." Sixty members attended and 267 sent a letter to Army Secretary Martin Hoffman asking him to reconsider how he would respond. The penalty was a relative slap on the wrist - those who cheated would "take a year off but come back if they wanted to." Downey looks back at the investigation with great pride. "It made a big difference in the lives of a number of the cadets," he said, "and over the years I would have a number of officers come up to me and had it not been for your office, I would not have been in the service." For Downey, it was a big shot in the arm as he headed into a potentially tough re-election campaign.

Downey looks back at the investigation with great pride. "It made a big difference in the lives of a number of the cadets," he said, "and over the years I would have a number of officers come up to me and say that, had it not been for your office, I would not have been in the service."

Given Downey's youth and the circumstances of his win, it would not have been out of line to view him on the edge of the precipice headed into 1976. He acknowledged why Republicans wanted to beat him: "If I win in November, the seat will be mine for as long as I want it. If not, I'll be a 27-year-old former Congressman, and the rest of my life will be an anticlimax." He conceded that his 100 percent ADA rating was "not going to help me."

Downey's opponent was Islip Town Supervisor Peter Cohalan who labeled the race "a case of extreme liberalism vs. sanity." Cohalan focused on the issue of busing that he said Downey had not adequately opposed (there had been a local amendment on the ballot.) Unlike Grover, he was able to avoid divisions by securing the Conservative Party endorsement, which essentially didn't matter a great deal. Downey proved his staying power by taking a robust 57%. An even tougher race occurred in 1978. The glow of Watergate was out of the rearview mirror and Downey, like many from his class, was being taken to task for other issues. Downey faced Harold Withers and prevailed with 55%. Prior to 1992, his only other tough race was in 1984 when he was tied down by former Suffolk County prosecutor Paul Aniboli. He also had to contend with a strong showing by Ronald Reagan who racked up 66%. Downey was reduced to 55% but, having persevered, began his second decade in the House.

Photos courtesy of the Thomas J. Downey Papers #5926, Kheel Center for Labor-Management Documentation and Archives, Cornell University Library

The New York Times said Downey, "has used the arsenal of incumbency, in chiding a mobile office, town meetings, weekly columns in local newspapers, weekly radio broadcasts, free blood-pressure checkups, free advice for the elderly and, of course, a Congressional staff that carries a full load of casework." He called voters at night and invited people to drop by his parent's house for tea on Sundays. Another way Downey solidified the district was by pounding the pavement. "I'd like to think if I accomplished anything it's that we showed Democrats would win a very Republican suburbia. There's no substitute for retail politics, standing in the shopping center, going to Eagle Scout courts and knocking on doors." In just a short time, all of Downey's hard work produced impact beyond simply giving him a seat he could hold. It also gave Long Island Democrats a new face they so desperately needed. Former Suffolk County Executive Patrick Halpin whom Downey helped gain a political footing candidly stated, "All our political DNA comes from Tom Downey."

True as that was, Downey the legislator had many facets. One was a serious side that one publication aptly described with regard to weapons: "His ability to organize some fellow liberals into an effective legislative force combines with his solid understanding of the technical complexities of weapons issues has made him one of the most important Pentagon critics and arms control advocates in the House."

Photo courtesy of the Thomas J. Downey Papers #5926, Kheel Center for Labor-Management Documentation and Archives, Cornell University Library

Then there was the Downey who wanted action. A fellow member of the 75-member Democratic class of '74, Stephen Solarz of Brooklyn referred to Downey as "the brash wunderkind from Suffolk whose combative intellectual activism belied the old notion that new members should be seen and not heard." George Miller, another classmate and close friend from California, said as Downey was preparing to leave office, "He would be announcing, 'We're going to do this. We're going to that.' We'd say that the Speaker won't like that and he'd say it didn't matter."

Politics in America 1985 stated Downey's, "irreverent style is not always an asset on the House floor, where his pension for sarcasm sometimes re-enforces the wise guy reputation of his first few terms." At times, his style could often evoke charges of slighting. Don Pease, an Ohio Democrat who served with Downey on Ways and Means once called him "usually so convinced that he is right that he doesn't have a lot of sympathy for people who hold opposing views." At least one other colleague expressed that view in a far more expressive manner.

With his best friend in Congress, Al Gore (left) along with Congressman Joel Pritchard (R-Washington) and Les Aspin (D-Wisconsin)

California Republican Robert "Bob" Dornan, who proudly hewed as far to the right as Downey to the left, once called him "a draft-dodging wimp" while allegedly pulling on his tie. Dornan responded that he didn't actually pull the neckwear. "I just straightened it out for him. It was crooked and needed to be straightened." *The San Diego Union* ran a story with the headline, "Dornan-Downey scuffle ends in tie" and Speaker Tip O'Neill admonished the pair to settle it, "on the street but don't settle it on the House floor."

Even close allies were not exempt. Downey angrily rebutted an assertion by Schroeder that, "everyone here checks our spines in the cloakroom," by standing up during a caucus and declaring, "Life (in Congress) is tough enough without other members dragging it down."

However, making points didn't mean Downey was not liked or respected as he had close friends on both sides of the aisle. Additionally, those who contended that Downey was not serious enough would soon learn otherwise because the issues on which he was most closely aligned during at least his first decade in the House were no laughing matters. They were quite serious. Some may say deadly serious.

Human rights were a paramount concern, particularly the ridding of apartheid in South Africa. Downey, believing it was "the right thing to do," was a prominent member of an ad-hoc organization called the South African Watch Group. In 1977 he and fellow "Watergate Baby" Andy Maguire of New Jersey conducted a special order on the House floor on the one-year anniversary of the murder of Stephen Biko. Expressing the hope that, "Steve's death represents a benchmark here in the United States," Downey authored a letter to South Africa's Ambassador Donald Sole signed by close to 100 colleagues. It chided him for the government's refusal to consent to an independent autopsy of Biko. Another letter he wrote related to the destruction of Crossroads.

Downey was quite interested in issues concerning nuclear arms. He was among the eight Congressmen named as SALT II advisors to the U.S. delegation at the Geneva Arms summit and with Carr, authored a "position paper" that would prohibit submarines from conducting nuclear tests from submarines in "depressed trajectory" (low altitudes). The well-thought out proposal exempted the Soviet Backfire bomber and earned the support of the Carter administration and during a 1979 hearing, Senator Joseph Biden of Delaware took note of Downey of having "dismantled the heavy missile argument a long time ago and did it brilliantly here again today."

In the early 1980s, Downey sat on a SALT II Task Force with the purpose of reigniting it and colleagues, Wisconsin Democrat Les Aspin and Iowa Republican Jim Leach were in the forefront. As Doug Waller noted in the book, *Congress and the Nuclear Freeze:* Downey argued that contrary to longstanding rules, a treaty's approval did not require 2/3 of a Senate vote and thereby could pass both chamber with a majority vote. While this was an iffy proposition given that Republicans controlled the Senate, Downey surmised, "The question then would be whether or not the president would sign it. At this stage, it doesn't look too realistic but it would certainly be something that would be hard pressed to veto given the current compliance that this administration has with the agreement."

Through the years, Downey was active on other weaponry issues. He tried to create a Select Committee on Arms Control but was unable to land the requisite support.and Connecticut Democrat Sam Gejdenson sponsored a resolution to prohibit South Korea from selling 32 American-made howitzers to Uruguay because the nation had a deplorable record on human rights. In

1985, liberals split on the approval of a foreign aid bill but Downey, angered in part by the nixing of the Clark Amendment, opposed it. "What this bill says is that the threat to use force is part and parcel of our diplomacy, and I think that's a mistake."

Downey had no patience for international missions that lacked a purpose. Following the 1983 invasion of Grenada, Downey made clear he was not impressed, telling the Reagan administration, "You have got a lot of questions to answer to allay the fear that this member has that this is an administration that shoots first and asks questions later."

Photo courtesy of the Thomas J. Downey Papers #5926, Kheel Center for Labor-Management Documentation and Archives, Cornell University Library

In the mid-1980s, Downey was a leader against the authorization of the MX missile. During a 1985 debate, he framed his argument around how "the Soviet Union has built a destabilizing missile with the SS-18, and shame on them for building it. The question is whether or not because they have done something stupid we should do something stupid. It is the question of building not what they have built, but building what we need." He went on to assert that, "We did not, every time we wanted a 25-percent increase in accuracy, decide to build a new weapons system; we improved the very fine weapons systems we have." Downey was perturbed when a number of colleagues including Aspin and his best friend in Congress, Albert Gore of Tennessee, were looking for a way to preserve MX and urged Gore in particular to resist Reagan's entreaties. The president and his allies, Downey contended, "believe that real men don't control weapons; real men build them." He was not successful.

Downey also fought against what he viewed as excessive spending on the domestic front and cutting sugar subsidies was high on his plate. In 1985, he and Ohio Republican Bill Gradison proposed an amendment to an Agriculture bill that would reduce the sugar price support system by one percent. Not surprisingly, Southern lawmakers who would be impacted did not take kindly. On the House floor, Downey responded to advocates by stating, "We seek to be fair to the people who are spending more for sugar than they need to, and to force the sugar refiners, the sugar people who are producing this sugar, to be a little more competitive, not a lot more competitive," adding for emphasis, "We could have offered to eliminate this program. We did not." After the effort was defeated 142-263, Downey acknowledged, "I underestimated the enormous protectionist sentiment out there. Also, the farmer at this point is a very sympathetic figure." The duo made attempts in future Congresses but failed with similar results.

The Ways and Means Committee gave Downey his heft of national exposure. Awarded a seat on the prestigious tax-writing panel in 1978, he developed a bond with soon to be Chair Dan Rostenkowski. This, though, hardly meant that the two would universally see eye-to-eye. It did mean, however, that legislatively speaking, Downey had graduated from the junior leagues.

As early as 1979, Norm Lent, a rock-ribbed Nassau Republican told The New York Times his initial opinion of his colleague was shaky. "He may have irritated older members by his rambunctious ways and because he lectured them on the military-industrial complex when he had no experience. But although there initially was some antagonism. it has largely dissipated because he's knowledgeable. I have a high opinion of Tom Downey, frankly. He's highly motivated, ambitious, and he does his homework. I think he's a good man. He's come along quite a bit."

Kathy McLaughlin volunteered on Downey's first re-election campaign and became a receptionist in his office in 1980. She rose to become Administrative Assistant, then Chief of Staff during his last five years in Congress. McLaughlin believes Downey matured as a legislator when he joined that committee. "Through the 80s," she said, "I watched him become a lot more thoughtful about things, a lot more patient, not always chasing things." That became even more true when he took over the Human Services Subcommittee because, "Before, he wasn't settled into a major area."

That role was actually Acting Chair of the Human Services Subcommittee on Ways and Means in mid-1987 when Tennessee Democrat Harold Ford was forced to relinquish the post after indictment on charges of bank fraud. This put him in the midst of some of the most visible policy matters which took shape in the next two successive Congresses; welfare reform in the 100th Congress and landmark child care legislation in the 101st. Like any complex measures, both had near-death setbacks along the way but each made it into law even if it meant that the final product differed from what Downey would have written.

Welfare reform (also known as the 1988 Family Support Act) consisted of education, training to be set up via the states, and an employment requirement for welfare-dependent mothers with children over the age of three. It also contained a mandate for states to crack down on parents who were delinquent in child support. Downey shepherded the bill from its inception.

Downey was exceptionally close to his Ways and Means Chair, Dan Rostenkowski
Photo courtesy of the Thomas J. Downey Papers #5926, Kheel Center for Labor-Management Documentation and Archives, Cornell University Library

Downey's plan, in the words of Colorado Congressman Hank Brown, "involve(s) enormous expenditures" and in order to assuage deficit-hawks of both parties, he persuaded House leaders to tack it onto a deficit reduction package. When the rule governing debate garnered only 117 votes in October 1987, Speaker Jim Wright, in an adroit use of House rules, adjourned the House and reconvened moments later. He dropped the welfare portion, which allowed the rule to pass. It took until December for this to occur under a 213-206 vote along with a bill that not all liberals were on board with. New York Democrat Major Owens was illustrative of the discontent: "There are no day care provisions, there are no places for children to be taken care of. We are going to take away protections that have been provided to children for 50 years and more." Republicans introduced a substitute but in a colloquy with Connecticut GOP Congresswoman Nancy Johnson, Downey shot back by saying that the measure lacked teeth. For one, "the problem is that the transitional day care is not required, because 'desire' does not mean 'require.'"

Downey's Senate counterpart was his senior Senator, Daniel Patrick Moynihan, whose bill was less expensive. As the House-Senate Conference committee planned to iron out the differences, Downey predicted that a strong consensus would take shape. That proved to be anything but.

For starters, the Senate at the last minute tacked on language that mandating "able-bodied" adults in a two-family household spend 16 hours either working or performing community service, the first in the nation of its kind. Downey's response: "I would prefer them to spend 16 hours in job search." He went on to say that "Fathers have a pretty strong attachment to the work force." The Senate bill also contained a $1 billion limit to carry out the training, which Downey didn't like.

Education and Labor Chair Augustus Hawkins called the work requirement "absurd and unrealistic" and Downey was even more candid. "We have to give the conservatives their due. They always have emphasized the importance of work." In the aftermath of this new element, Downey looked to the next election. He vowed, "We're not just going to take the Senate bill. If President Reagan doesn't sign a bill, President Dukakis will. I'd rather come back next year and do a good bill than send a bad bill to the president."

Downey worked with two fellow Watergate Babies – George Miller and Henry Waxman whose jurisdiction on two key subcommittees gave them latitude. Waxman was instrumental in brokering a deal at least as far as working mothers were concerned by introducing Medicaid (though Republicans rejected making it as generous as Waxman wanted). For Downey, welfare reform was proof that the once-brash wunderkind knew when to hold it. When Michigan Democrat William Ford wanted welfare recipients to be paid the same rate as others at that work site, Downey spoke against it. "If we adopt the Ford language, we don't have a conference report. It's not as far as we'd like to go, but it's as far as we're going to get." The conference committees listened to Downey.

The effort to expand childcare was a descendant of welfare reform and also proved Herculean—not just because of Republican presidents. One reason was a public fight among ideological allies both in the House and out. In short, some favored pumping money into programs and others wanted private care and Earned Income Tax Credits (EITC.) Downey was clearly caught in the middle.

Downey began the process by introducing his Act for Better Childcare bill (ABC) that focused more on direct grants but soon came across a culprit otherwise known as the realities of being playing the cards dealt. Similar to the debate over welfare reform, Hawkins wanted a say and was steadfast throughout the entire process on inclusion of ABC. Children's Defense Fund founder Miriam Wright-Edelman also favored this approach and late in the process accused Downey of trying to, "sabotage groundbreaking child care legislation for petty jurisdictional and power reasons," stonewalling and undertaking, "private guerrilla war to kill child-care legislation." Downey blasted this as "immature and inaccurate" and the pair met to smooth things over.

It wasn't that Downey opposed the ABC bill but rather that he knew conservatives and Bush wouldn't accept it. There was also the Congressional schedule ("We have a number of issues that did not lend themselves to overnight negotiations"). On top of that, Downey had to fend off an alternative measure by conservative Democrat Charlie Stenholm of Texas and Republican Clay Shaw of Florida that focused more on childcare settings. Hawkins was not ready to abandon ABC and though he united with Downey just enough to fend off Stenholm-Shaw and get a Democratic version through the House in March of 1990, he was still insisting on ABC when the bill went to conference. Conferees subsequently voted to accept much of what Hawkins wanted over the opposition of Downey. However, in a move that revealed the byzantine nature of Congress, the House voted to instruct conferees to reject language they had already accepted.

Only at the date of adjournment for the session (October 27) did the bill clear. The result was a $22.5 billion package, the first major overhaul since Nixon vetoed a measure in 1971. It contained an amalgamation of EITC ($12.4 billion), a very scaled back version of ABC ($.4.25 billion), Head Start and after school childcare.

Other matters during the Bush administration found Downey less inclined to cooperate. He had choice words for Bush's proposed capital gains, calling it, "a tax holiday for the rich."

His opinion did not change during the early 90s recession. To help combat it, Downey and Gore unveiled a $1,000 tax-cut for families who earned below $50,000 and asked Treasury Secretary Nick Brady what those families would get under a capital gains reduction. At the height of that recession, Downey pushed a proposal through Congress aiding states that used up their Job Opportunities and Basic Skills (JOBS) budget in part by increasing the latitude to states with matching funds. The bill died during a much publicized veto by Bush a month before the 1992 election.

Referred to as "a son of the early-1970s, Downey lived by that creed and expressed it in a 1986 speech on the House floor in which he said, "Let us recognize that freezing or stopping nuclear-weapons testing on this planet is in the U.S. national-security interests. Listen carefully, Hardware freaks, if you want a new MX missile, you better see that SALT 11 is ratified." In 1982, he offered an amendment to nix funding for the Trident submarine but it garnered just 89 votes. In 1985, he chaired an ad-hoc group of fellow members who opposed the MX missile.

There were limits however and being from Long Island removed any ambivalence to Downey's backing of Grumman Corporation. When the Bush administration canceled the F-14 Tomcat fighter Grumman manufactured in the town of Bethpage (where thousands of his constituents worked), he called it, "one of those classic good news, bad news situations. The good news is the Pentagon is going to make some significant budget cuts. The bad news: they want to kill a plane that's based in your district." Still, he was resolved to fight, telling *The New York Times*, "It's going to demand all of my attention all my political skills, but my operational ability and most of my chits. No effort will be spared." Besides, he noted, other prominent liberals including Dellums and Schroeder agreed to continue to fund the project. In 1989, he and South Shore Congressman George Hochbruechner held up the 1990 defense authorization bill until Aspin put money in the budget for production of another 18 F-14Ds, a Grumman produced fighter plane that Defense Secretary Dick Cheney had proposed eliminating.

Downey had a jocular side that was often seen on the House floor, either during debates or the one-minute addresses members delivered prior to the start of sessions.

As the House debated Reagan's tax cut proposals on the day Prince Charles married Diana Spencer in London, Downey called it, "appropriate that we should be debating this bill today, with the royal wedding in the morning, we are debating a bill that will benefit primarily the economically royal in this country in the afternoon. Both bills do not do justice to the vague considerations of fighting inflation, reducing interest rates, or the whole cardinal set of principles of tax justice, equity, simplicity, and neutrality."

A classic example saw an utterly humorless Downey blast Interior Secretary James Watt – no friend of environmentalists, for banning the "Beach Boys" and other rock groups from performing on the Washington Mall during the 1983 4th of July ceremonies (Watt planned to substitute Wayne Newton). Downey took the House floor to inform colleagues that he would be sending the Secretary his worn out album of The Beach Boys Greatest Hits in hopes that Watt would reconsider. "The idea of listening to 'Danke Schoen' over the Mall instead of 'Sail On, Sailor,' 'Good Vibrations,' and 'Heroes and Villains' is deeply troubling to me." He ended by saying, "If Secretary Watt does not recant, it is my hope that he goes on a permanent surfing safari."

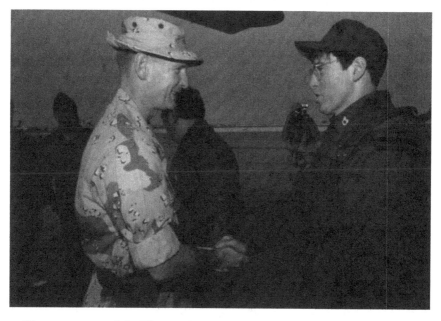

Photo courtesy of the Thomas J. Downey Papers #5926, Kheel Center for Labor-Management Documentation and Archives, Cornell University Library

Another example came the day the House debated the proposed amendment banning flag-desecration: "I have taken a page out of David Letterman's book, and I have prepared for us the top 10 reasons why I think we are here debating the flag amendment. Reason No. 10: If we wrap ourselves in the flag, people won't notice that 37 million Americans don't have health insurance, and there are no plans in this Congress to do anything about it."

Long Island scrappiness was also vintage Downey. During late-1991 Ways and Means testimony with Bush administration economic officials, Downey asked OMB Director Richard Darman about the president's pledge to "restrain personal ambitions at least long enough to get the job done" as far as nursing the economy back to health. "Does that mean," Downey asked, "that the administration is gonna cease and desist from blaming Democrats like the Majority Leader of the Senate...I would assume that when we have a recovery that it will be Mr. Foley and Mr. Mitchell's as well." Darman's response was, "There are some things that may look partisan but are analytically correct."

Off the floor, Downey might have been defined for his love of basketball. He was an integral part of the MBA (Members Basketball Association), a group of members that met at 4 p.m., in the House gym to shoot hoops and unwind, many times before another set of votes. By his final term in Congress, Downey, by virtue of being of the senior member on the team, became the MBA's "Commissioner." One day, as members were playing, a freshman Republican named John Boehner of Ohio, notorious for smoking, lit up a cigarette and Downey had to inform him that there would be no smoking in the gym. The two became friendly and even played from time-to-time.

As an employer, Downey was quite beloved. McLaughlin's opinion was "you couldn't ask for a better boss." Taking bad days out on the staff never occurred because, "he didn't have bad days." Downey was also very hands-off and not a micro-manager. "He left a lot of the day-to-day stuff to staff. Whoever was in charge (of a particular area) was in charge and he respected that." With a young family, Downey wouldn't be bogging down staff by roaming into his office deep into the night nor was he a man about town. Many times, he'd be hosting colleagues at home.

In 1992, Downey joined with Republican Congressman Ron Machtley of Rhode Island to offer an amendment to a Foreign Aid Appropriations measure that would prohibit International Military and Educational Training (IMET) to Indonesia when forces massacred citizens in East Timor. "Because Indonesia is a friend of the United States," Downey explained, "and these events have unfolded thousands of miles away, this tragedy went unnoticed.

But in the past several months, this tragedy has become the focus of the international spotlight...We cannot ignore this tragedy on the other side of the world...It also makes a clear statement that although the world has changed, America's moral responsibility to fight tyranny and oppression remains the same." Floor manager David Obey of Wisconsin accepted the amendment.

For Downey, one thing remained a constant throughout his entire tenure. Government could be a force for good. Near the end of his career as he was championing the Family Leave Act, he said, "talk is a lot cheaper than action." True to form, when Congress failed to enact the proposal in late 1992, Downey compared Congress to, "a very bad Greek chorus to an otherwise interesting Greek drama. The sooner we exit, the happier the whole world will be." Unbeknownst to Downey, he'd be exiting as well.

The anti-incumbent mood had been steadily creeping up on Washington and Rubbergate accelerated it. When the magnitude of the scandal was known, Downey urged members to fess up by saying, "If you stonewall, that's potentially far more damaging than potentially saying, "I screwed up'" and Downey admitted that he had some overdrafts (the Ethics Committee was still compiling the numbers for current and former members). This was not good enough for a small but vocal group of reformers. When seven freshman Republicans went on the rampage regarding the issue of accountability and reform in response to the scandal, Downey replied, "I'd like to think that the Gang of Seven will eventually get serious about the problems of the country." Upon the release of the official list of the members who overdrew, Downey was found to have 151 with a value of $83,000, nowhere near the amount of some of the most egregious abusers but certainly enough to add to the growing perception that Downey was treating Long Island as more of a P.O. Box as opposed to home. Downey vowed to state his case. He expressed to Newsday, "a certain amount of embarrassment for myself and for the House of Representatives...Do I think it will affect me personally? I think it won't help. But I think that people...will weigh my candidacy in a broader context." He said later, "I came here to help people." Any attempt to defray the scandal was complicated by the fact that his wife Chris had worked for the bank's Sergeant-At-Arms.

Downey's Republican rival was Rick Lazio, a 34-year-old member of the Suffolk County Legislature. At first, few thought Downey was in serious trouble of losing the seat. Lazio desperately tried to turn the tables on the issue that had helped Downey 18 years earlier, which started by questioning his rival's Long Island connections.

In a debate during the election season, Downey took aim at the doubters: "I live on Long Island, I have lived here all my life. If you have any doubt, come to 155 Cedar Street, where I have lived for 13 years." While Lazio's goal was to portray Downey as part of the Washington shenanigans, Downey tried to turn the tables by throwing the problems of Suffolk County at him, particularly when it came to a bailout. One ad read, "One day alone Rick Lazio voted to raise Long Island property taxes by $35 million. Just imagine what he could do if we gave him two years as a Congressman." Lazio responded with criticism of Downey that for voters, was far more virulent. One was a flyer entitled, "Tom Downey's Limousine Liberal Guide to Surviving the Recession." The question was, "Tough times on Long Island getting you down? Move to Washington. Rent out your multiple-family Long Island home (one of three homes he owns); put your children in private school in Virginia."

Downey with some of his best friends and allies in Congress, Jim Moody of Wisconsin, (far left), Marty Russo of Illinois and future Speaker Nancy Pelosi of California
Photo courtesy of the Thomas J. Downey Papers #5926, Kheel Center for Labor-Management Documentation and Archives, Cornell University Library

Meanwhile, Downey husbanded his money until late in the campaign. At that point, the race began creeping up and, though many realized it would not land in his lap, he was expected to prevail. Election night began with him down 57-43% and he telephoned Lazio less than 90 minutes after the polls closed to concede. The result was 53-47%, a difference of 13,000 votes out of the 196,000 cast. It was thought that the victory of Republican Senator Alphonse D'Amato hampered Long Islanders from switching back to the Democratic column in local races. A bad aura ensued at Downey's own polling place when few voters would make eye contact with him. One person remarked to him tongue-in-cheek, "I guess it's not true that you're never here."

Downey told supporters, "My hope is that we can help them [the national Democratic ticket] in some way. Even though the outcome was not what we wanted, it was still an extraordinary campaign. We just somehow missed with about eight percent of the voters. Let's just remember that one election does not a life make."

However, deep down Downey was despondent because Gore, his "best friend," had just been elected vice-president. Friends were also bemused. California Congresswoman Nancy Pelosi, among colleagues Downey regularly hosted at his home called him, "masterful at shaping legislation and he was very respected." She added, "It's hard to understand why there wasn't a recognition of his value in his district." Downey also admitted that 1990, when he took a relatively tepid 56%, "didn't feel right" and McLaughlin recalls getting him home more often.

Though out of office, Downey's profile didn't tumble precipitously. Gore was second-in-command and it became common knowledge in Washington that the way to get to Gore was through Downey. Sure enough, Downey was a loyal lieutenant when Gore very nearly went to the top in 2000 and was a footnote in what *The Washington Post* labeled, "one of the more bizarre and titillating episodes of the 2000 campaign." It happened when a George W. Bush campaign volunteer mailed Downey a copy of Bush's own debate prep with the promise to, "call you soon to find out what other materials can be useful to the VP." Downey immediately turned the tape over to the FBI and, to avoid even a perception of a conflict of interest, stepped aside from Gore's debate prep team.

Downey started a lobbying firm with Washington Republican Rod Chandler, Downey/Chandler, which later became Downey/McGrath when Chandler resigned and Ray McGrath, a Long Island Republican took his place. Downey is now married to former EPA Secretary Carol Browner.

CHAPTER FOUR

Despite A Very Politically Adverse District, Wolpe Gave Michigan Constituents Quality and Courage Second-To-None

Introductory Quote: "I have always argued that when people can call you by your first name, that is a way of narrowing distance and improving communications. To hold onto power by putting yourself above the people is ultimately counterproductive." – Howard Wolpe.

Photo Courtesy of Special Collections, Eric V. Hauser Memorial Library, Reed College

The careers of many members of Congress ended in 1992 and the casualties included some of the most energetic, effective and altruistic people. In some instances, the departures were due to circumstances far from their control and Howard Wolpe was at the top of the list. The fact that he would not be standing next to returning colleagues who were taking the oath of office for the 103rd Congress was saddening as Wolpe coud be considered among the most underrated members of the late 20th century.

Redistricting was the culprit that knocked Wolpe out of the Congressional arena. By electing to retire in 1992, the seven-term Michigan Democrat bowed to the reality that winning an eighth term under already hostile political turf would be very unlikely for him.

The fact that Wolpe was able to hold his seat for 14 years was unexpected when he commenced his career but because of his expertise on a wide range of topics and his sincerity, he was successful. Californian Leon Panetta best summed up a prevailing sentiment on the eve of Wolpe's retirement by calling him, "a very good friend of the disenfranchised around the world and particularly in Africa." His friend Wolverine David Bonior, who also served also with Wolpe in the Michigan Legislature, cited Wolpe's true gift as being "one of the more impassioned fighters in this institution on every issue in which justice is at stake, or where championing the oppressed is the issue."

Beyond the very serious missions he took on, Wolpe was known as a wonderful human being, generous boss, and as one confidant noted, a guy with a "brutally self-deprecating sense of humor." He once labeled William Gray, his partner on the most sweeping foreign policy legislation of his generation, a "mensch" but few would argue that the term fit him to a tee.

Photo via The Kalamazoo Gazette

Wolpe had a very worldly and storied pre-Congressional career. It was known that he would be an overachiever at a young age and his professional parents might have been a reason – his father was a pediatrician and mother a clinical psychologist. Wolpe was born in Los Angeles and was accepted to Reed College in Portland, Oregon at the age of sixteen, traveling to the institution by train. He majored in Political Science after which he enrolled at the Massachusetts Institute of Technology (MIT). A course in African studies captured his interest in the region and Wolpe subsequently spent two years near Port Harcourt, Nigeria pursuing his dissertation. He returned home to teach political science and African studies at Western Michigan University and Michigan State University. Wolpe published two of his works on Africa (*Urban Politics in Nigeria: A Study of Port Harcourt* and *Africa: A Post Cold-War Perspective*). The assassination of Dr. Martin Luther King, Jr., enabled him to found a group named Action Now with the focus on moving forward on racial friction and poverty. A year later, he ran for office.

Wolpe's place on a non-partisan but Democratic supported slate for a seat on the Kalamazoo City Commission was not fate accompli. The city was governed by "ultra-conservatives" and Wolpe's team mobilized the support of women, African-Americans and labor. The Chamber of Commerce favored another slate but Wolpe's ticket-mates convinced them of the probability of a fatal split that would return the incumbents to office. For that reason, they backed down. Going forward, the erstwhile Wolpe championed a liberal platform (fair housing in particular) and with help from both labor and the Citizens Action Committee, he placed seventh for seven slots and won the post by 130 votes. He was re-elected two years later and Nancy Crowell, a strategist from that era, called him, "the guy who pulled people from different backgrounds together to talk."

Wolpe won a seat in the Michigan House in 1972, working on the state's landmark bottle law and pushing through right-to-turn on red legislation. Chester Rogers was a close friend and in referring to Wolpe's incessant energy, which included a nearly non-stop door-to-door campaigning, he quipped, "I used to jokingly introduce him as the streetwalker who passed the red light bill."

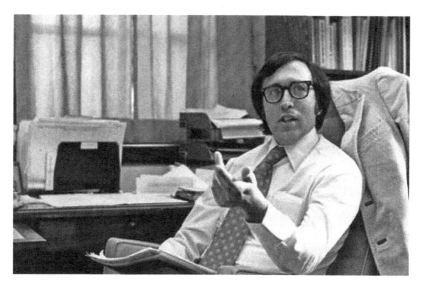

Wolpe as a member of the Michigan Legislature
Photo via the Kalamazoo Gazette

Wolpe's 1978 election to Congress proved that sometimes it took two tries to get the job done, though he very nearly succeeded the first time. When Wolpe announced that he would be taking on incumbent Garry Brown, few gave him much chance of knocking the Republican out. The fact that he had taken 49% was considered amazing, particularly because President Gerald Ford was carrying his home state - and garnering 59% in the district, even as he was losing nationally. Two years later, he tried again. In the interim he accepted an offer from U.S. Senator Don Riegel to run his Lansing office (he resigned in '78 to embark on the campaign as well as to "to serve as a free-lance people helper.") This time it was Democrats who were to benefit from the coattails - Carl Levin was dislodging incumbent Robert Griffin from his Senate seat, and Wolpe reversed the 51-49% loss from two years earlier beating Brown by the same margin. Eaton County made the difference which Wolpe still lost but by less than in '76. He credited the difference to being able to "build on the campaign of two years ago, and we had unprecedented volunteer effort. It gave us an ability to reach out in a personal way." He added that, "I've never seen the extreme kind of commitment and energy that was invested in the campaign by thousands across the district. That made the difference." Brown meanwhile joked that while he believed his constituents "made a horrible mistake," he added that, "in our system, they're entitled to make a mistake."

**With Wisconsin Senator William Proxmire as Wolpe kicked
off his very nearly successful 1976 House campaign
Photo via the Kalamazoo Gazette**

The energy that Wolpe displayed as a candidate continued into his Congressional operation. He would return home every weekend and set up a constituent services organization that colleagues would strive to emulate. Meanwhile, he won a seat on the Foreign Affairs Committee. As Wolpe recounted for the project, every member had dissuaded Wolpe from seeking a seat on the panel because there was so little to gain representing such a strongly GOP electorate. Bill Brodhead, a Democrat from suburban Detroit, was the exception. He urged Wolpe to pursue something to his liking. Congressional leaders evidently had the same thing in mind because they enlarged the committee's membership to accommodate Wolpe (the other committee he settled on was Science, Space and Technology).

If Wolpe's career was nothing short of amazing, there were reasons. One was that he did nothing to temper his liberal voting record and lived to tell about it politically speaking. An example: his ADA ratings in 1979 and 1980 were 100% and 94% respectively. This proved no hindrance in keeping his job 52-47% over James Gilmore as Ronald Reagan was sweeping the district, which Wolpe attributed to "fighting the same sort of battle people want fought right now," and having developed, "a kind of close personal relationship with his constituents." Later in life, he explained that, "I used to insist that my greatest political strength was my fallibility. I have always argued that when people can call you by your first name, that is a way of narrowing distance and improving communications. To hold onto power by putting yourself above the people is ultimately counterproductive."

Whatever issue Wolpe undertook, he talked the talk and walked the walk. No battle was more illustrative than sanctions against the South African government.

His first feel for how difficult progress would be came on the issue of Rhodesia, which he recounted in an oral history discussion at Michigan State University after he left office. Wolpe and other members of the Foreign Affairs Committee were called to an Oval Office meeting with President Carter, who informed members that he wanted to continue sanctions against Rhodesia. At that point, arch-conservative Senator Jesse Helms of North Carolina pleaded with Carter to hold off, calling Bishop Mosarena, "a good Christian gentleman" who would soon be visiting the states. Helms urged them to get to know each other, at which time Wolpe knew that keeping the sanctions would be a tough fight in Congress. As the fight dragged on, Wolpe found himself in the extremely uncomfortable position of having to oppose South Dakota Senator George McGovern, whom he had considered "a hero" and for whom he had campaigned for the presidency in 1972. McGovern was on Wolpe's side when it came to Rhodesia but found the package he had worked out with Helms to be feeble at best and had to tell him when he testified before the House Foreign Affairs Committee. Ultimately, the sanctions remained in place.

Photo via The Kalamazoo Gazette

With Wolpe's 1980 win came a major reward. Many have heard of a "sophomore surge" in politics, but surging to a subcommittee chairmanship is almost unheard of. Wolpe had not been seeking the post nor was he in line for it, but Congressman Toby Moffett of Connecticut had just returned from Africa where there was much apprehension due to the incoming Reagan administration and a GOP Senate and they wanted someone who could articulate a strong counter-balance. Wolpe's close friend and ally, Stephen Solarz of New York, chaired the gavel of the Africa Subcommittee of Foreign Affairs but was moving to another subcommittee and Wolpe, though hesitant to upset the seniority system, began courting other members. Much to his surprise, he learned that a sufficient number of colleagues planned to support him over Dan Mica of Florida. They kept their word and Wolpe got the chairmanship as well as a pulpit from where his legacy would be most firmly established.

First came Zaire where General Mobutu Sese Seko reigned and Wolpe actively sought in his first term to reduce military aid over the opposition to the Reagan administration which wanted to eliminate the Clark Amendment. This amendment prohibited aid to private groups engaging in military operations in Angola. By 1985, the issue was how much aid to provide the nation and the Reagan administration proposed that the $4 million limit be lifted (and in this case raised to $10 million), Wolpe was strongly against it (a $7 million compromise was reached).

In 1982, Wolpe with Pennsylvania Republican Bill Goodling, co-authored a *New York Times* "Letter to the Editor" that urged Shultz to construct a policy on how America would deal with the conflict between Somalia and Ethiopia. "In deciding upon any future reprogramming or supplemental military aid request for Somalia," they wrote, "we will want to look at the extent to which the Administration had developed a comprehensive diplomatic approach to the problem of the Horn and at the responses of Ethiopia, Somalia and Kenya to that approach."

The issue of South Africa was what truly made Wolpe a rock star. His first trip to the nation as a congressman came in 1981 and his delegation included Shirley Chisholm, an African-American from Brooklyn. Wolpe recalled that "when he and Shirley Chisholm saw each other, neither said a word but just embraced each other." Chisholm expressed her gratefulness to Wolpe on the bus with tears rolling down her face. The end of the trip concluded with Wolpe receiving permission for the delegation to visit squawkers outside a crossroads, which the South African police had been trying to destroy in order to force them to leave. At the airport, he conducted an exit press conference. His escort was a man named Howard Walker, a "very fair" African-American whom Wolpe called highly "reserved." At the end of the press conference, he turned to Wolpe and told him that he was "never prouder to be an American."

As the years went on, Wolpe was even more determined to get a sanctions package together. *The Almanac of American Politics* wrote that Wolpe "has been willing to antagonize local interest with facilities in South Africa opposed engines but Wolpe would support no exemption." Kellogg and Upjohn, Co., were both big employers in his district and they made their dissatisfaction with his position known (*The Almanac* noted that Kellogg ended up supporting Wolpe's Republican opponent in 1988).

Still, Wolpe persevered. He had long viewed sanctions as "pillars of America's policy against South Africa's apartheid" and found Reagan's policy of "constructive engagement" with South African officials to be bogus. He explained it might in fact have the opposite effect and "increase the violence because the intransigent [white] elements have been led to believe they can engage in repression without any real cost or American response." Initially, a handful of "bizarre bedfellows," including staunch conservatives Newt Gingrich of Georgia and Bob Walker of Pennsylvania, were part of a group that wanted to form an acceptable package regarding sanctions. However, it soon became clear that a strong bill would have to succeed without them.

Meanwhile, Wolpe went hard to work with Pennsylvania Democrat Bill Gray to impose sanctions on South Africa and the first result was The Anti-Apartheid Act of 1985, a watered down version of what Wolpe and many advocates of throwing the book at South Africa wanted, but it was a bow to political reality. After House passage by a vote of 295-127 and the Senate passing their version, Wolpe confidently predicted the conference committee version would "end up somewhere in between the House and the Senate'" and that Reagan, "in the final analysis will sign any bill passed by the Senate and the House." The Senate never approved the conference repot version and though Reagan did issue an executive order, it was considered to lack teeth.

The following year, Wolpe and Gray were back and bombing gave them new ammunition. This time, they'd stare down Reagan and win – with a little inadvertent help from a GOP Congressman. Mark Siljander represented a neighboring district but his views with Wolpe could not be more different. He was the poster boy of the "Religious Right," who in 1984 had strongly advocated the election of Wolpe's opponent by urging voters to "send another Christian to Congress." He had also been a student of Wolpe's at one point and as Wolpe told it, "had never quite forgiven me for a 'C' I had given him in my class." Not surprisingly, he was opposed to a strong bill and was leading the way for his own substantially watered down measure. Wolpe was not impressed. "The message sent to the South African government is that no matter what they do, there is no cost. This (the alternative) bill would simply delay action; sanctions are the only hope we have of influencing that government."

During this time, Ron Dellums offered an amendment with total divestment that Wolpe personally favored, but knew its inclusion wasn't politically feasible. But posting Dellums's amendment would allow moderates to at least say they voted against it. When Dellums presented his amendment, Siljander was the GOP floor manager and it was up to him to request a vote but he neglected to do so (he might have been distracted by the fact that he had lost re-nomination to Fred Upton and would soon be leaving Congress). Whatever the reason, Dellums' language was now included which enabled Wolpe, Gray and other advocates of the strongest possible language, to enter the House-Senate conference committee in the strongest possible position.

Wolpe staunchly defended the bill on the floor, telling colleagues, "We are saying, by passing this legislation that we do not want America any longer to be an accomplice of apartheid." It passed 308-77. Reagan vetoed it but as Wolpe recalled, "a number of Republicans became increasingly" uncomfortable about Reagan's position. The override took place 313-83 and Wolpe looked back saying, "That single legislative success made all the years I spent in Congress worth the effort."

Wolpe spoke of the ludicrousness of the arguments of the opposition in the years ahead. In a film, he recounted "Those who opposed the effort to impose would use an argument that was really remarkable for its uniqueness. Namely that sanctions were going to hurt the people we most wanted to help, that is the black majority. So there was a really remarkable double standard in the way we thought about and in the way talked about South Africa." Concurrently, Wolpe's success made him a star. After Wolpe's death, Steven McDonald wrote a tribute in which he said, "I can tell story after story of Howard's celebrity - Nelson Mandela calling him on his release from prison or sighting him across a crowded Congressional chamber and waving for Howard and his wife to join him."

Around the same time as the South African issue was making headway, Wolpe was having an impact on an issue that was central to another part of the continent: food aid for Ethiopia. In 1985, he, Mickey Leland of Texas, and

Ted Weiss of New York proposed the African Relief and Recovery Act of 1985 that would authorize $898 million to provide food and its transportation. The Agency for International Development (AID) authorized assistance in 1984 but Wolpe contended that it was, "too late...I think there is a false feeling in the world that the problem of African famine has been solved by the world's relief effort so far. That is a false sense of optimism."

Wolpe was not so quick to support sanctions against Ethiopia because he feared "if imposed, [they] might very well jeopardize the access and network of support that have been created." Liberia, though, was a different story. He and Weiss introduced a resolution questioning Liberia. South African withdrawal from Namibia was also high on Wolpe's plate and he took satisfaction in seeing the nation become independent in 1990. He took aim at the Savimbi group in Africa.

Wolpe's longrunning crusade to sanction the South African government was his finest hour. He is seen with other Democratic soldiers in the cruade, Walter Fauntroy of the District of Columbia, Stephen Solarz of New York and William Gray Photo via Getty Images

In 1990, Wolpe opposed the designation of MFN on China. "I am sure all of us in this body remember sitting glued in front of our television sets that June watching the struggle for freedom in China. We marveled at the stirring sight of millions of people taking to the streets in peaceful protest. They were not throwing rocks. They were not throwing Molotov cocktails.

They carried no weapons. They were armed with the most powerful message of all: That the yearning for freedom is universal and ultimately irresistible."

Though Wolpe had enough on his plate assisting Africa, he still devoted significant resources to domestic affairs. After a tornado devastated Kalamazoo during his first term, Wolpe rolled up his sleeves and got to work as much as anyone. He co-chaired the Northeast-Midwest Coalition where he and another chair, New York Republican Frank Horton, created the concept of making states with large SNL losses pay Federal Deposit Insurance premium to pay for the bill

In response to Reagan Presidential aide Michael Deaver's rendezvous with representing former governments, Wolpe and Ohio Democrat Marcy Kaptur introduced the Foreign Agents Compulsory Ethics in Trade Act (FACE IT). The bill would tighten the "revolving door" by banning officials from lobbying for foreign interests for ten years after leaving the U.S. government. Wolpe explained his rationale as follows: "The fact that Mr. Deaver was using his clout in Congress and his influence in the White House to further the interests of foreign governments and foreign businesses in American policy considerations. While the current ethics in Government law was sufficient to ensnarl Mr. Deaver, it simply offers no protection from the manipulative advantage gained by foreign interests when they hire former high-ranking Federal officials as their lobbyists and representatives."

After the election of 1990, Wolpe traded in his gavel on Foreign Affairs for the Science Committee Investigations on Oversight. Though he passed up previous opportunities to switch, his view was that he accomplished much of his goals – particularly concerning apartheid, on the other panel. Now, Wolpe had other fish to fry and cracking down on waste was chief among them. The Waste Reduction Act was the first of its kind in generating information to states to take measures to eradicate it (New Jersey Senator Frank Lautenberg was the Senate sponsor). The Waste Export Control Act that Wolpe sponsored with Mike Synar of Oklahoma would establish more rigid standards for exporting hazardous waste to foreign nations. Finally, the Taxpayer Right to Know Act mandated pie charts for tax booklets to break down how it was spending money it had collected from taxpayers.

Waste also meant eliminating what he viewed as unnecessary programs and the Superconducting Super Collider, a "project which had very serious problems on its merits," was another thing that incurred Wolpe's wrath. He was concerned about the environment and introduced the Pollution Prevention Act to remedy it. Housing Finance Opportunity Act of 1984 extended for five years the issuance of mortgage revenue bonds as tax exempt.

How was Wolpe behind closed doors? Jim Margolis was a part of his personal and political world since the Kalamazoo Council days. There was no pretense, no heir about him and many, many, laughs, many at Wolpe's instigation. He looked for the best in people," Margolis said. "If you made a mistake, you would acknowledge it. If he made a mistake, he would acknowledge it." He was loyal to a fault – Margolis felt he could be slow to make recommended staff changes because his allegiance was so high.

Wolpe could be clumsy but was far from necessitating a portrayal by actor Chevy Chase. Either way, it became a strength because Margolis said, "Sometimes it was the clumsiness or self-deprecation that made him approachable." Laughter was his only medicine. Margolis recalls one instance during the gubernatorial campaign as Wolpe was proceeding to tape an ad at a local park. Just as he was starting to speak, the park's water sprinklers came on and hit Wolpe from about four different angles. Cleaning himself off was easy - it was resuming the taping that was difficult because Wolpe could not deliver his lines without laughing. The bottom line. He was "an intellectual who didn't make you feel dumb or somehow less worthy. He was wicked smart but had an ability to connect with people."

Except for 1984, when he was held to 53%, Wolpe usually settled for re-election percentages in the mid 50's having only hit 60% once in 1986. In 1990, he defeated Brad Haskins, a 30-year old lawyer the GOP initially had high hopes for, by 58-42%. Two years later, Wolpe ran into another problem: redistricting. The Wolverine State was losing two House seats and with split partisan control, uncertainty reigned as to where the chips would fall and as the logjam continued, a federal court agreed to draw the map.

As March came and various maps were circulating, Wolpe acknowledged, "some very difficult moments." He remained sanguine about the prospects of his district between Kalamazoo and Lansing remaining intact. "The odd man out kept shifting, but I was never the odd man out." When the final product was released, he was indeed the odd man out. He soon decided the new lines were unsalvageable. "For all intents and purposes," he said, "I would be running in what was not only a heavily leaning Republican District, but one in which I would be unknown to all but a few of my perspective constituents. A costly and divisive primary would be almost inevitable if I were to run, and the winner of such a primary would likely emerge with a hollow victory, ill-prepared for the general election fight." Wolpe was out, but hardly down. He told *The Detroit News* shortly after his announcement that, "What I have taken greatest satisfaction from is being able to survive in a district that is overwhelmingly Republican, and have so many people tell me that they feel better about their ability to connect with the political system through my work over the last years." Indeed, one observer of Michigan politics was spot-on when summing up Wolpe's demise by saying redistricting accomplished what Republicans could not. Longtime staffer Marda Robillard called it "sad…real tough the last day he was here."

With his Congressional career over, Wolpe tried to wage a political comeback at the state level. He sought the Democratic nomination for governor and to the surprise of nearly everyone, beat the supposed frontrunner, State Senator and future U.S. Senator Debbie Stabenow in a four-candidate primary 35-30%. Organized labor greatly assisted Wolpe but he was also helped by the presence of East Lansing Mayor Larry Owen who carried everything in the Northern part of the state including the UP. Wolpe won much of Southwestern Michigan as well as pluralities in populous Wayne County (Detroit), Genessee and Saginaw). The primary was for the right to face conservative GOP Governor John Enger and in victory, Wolpe declared, "John Engler has got to go. We're going to pack him up and we're going to move him out." This was wishful thinking. The year 1994 was an immeasurably GOP year and Wolpe was trounced by 62-38% in November. Ever the optimist, Wolpe declared, "When Engler's principles head us down a different path, we're going to be the loyal opposition." For Wolpe, defeat produced a silver lining. The way would soon be paved for him to rekindle his true passion: Africa.

The following year, President Clinton named Wolpe special envoy to Africa's Great Lakes region. His specialty was the unrest in Congo, Rwanda, Burundi and Uganda. He later became director of the Africa program at the Woodrow Wilson International Center for Scholars. Wolpe was confronted by personal tragedy when his second wife Judy drowned in an undercurrent (Wolpe himself was able to escape). He died of a sudden heart attack in 2011 while preparing a memoir at only 72. So vintage was Wolpe's propensity for jocularity that it was written in *The Kalamazoo Gazette* following his memorial service that, "The ceremony ended with a video of Wolpe laughing uncontrollably for a few minutes during the start of an on-camera interview, which brought laughter from the audience." Suitably, Peter Yarrow of the 1960s folk group Peter Paul and Mary sang "Don't Laugh At Me."

Wolpe's apex coincided to some degree with Chicago Bulls Star Michael Jordan. A song about him was written entitled, "Simply the Best." If Wolpe were to have an epitaph, that would be fitting indeed.

CHAPTER FIVE

While Doing Wonders for Cleveland and Breast Cancer Advancements, Oakar Became Poster Child for Negativity Toward Congress in 1992

Introductory Tidbit: During her 1976 primary campaign for a House seat in Cleveland, Mary Rose Oakar distinguished herself from her male rivals by handing out pens with plastic roses to cover them and won. About a decade later, Congresswoman Oakar was attending a meeting with the Congressional leadership at the White House shortly before President Ronald Reagan was to embark on a summit with Soviet Premier Mikhail Gorbachev. Realizing that she happened to have a rose in her purse, Oakar took one out and handed it to Reagan. I'm going to give you this rose pen," she told him. "And rose is a symbol of peace. Try to make peace with them." Reagan thanked her and attached it to his jacket lapel. A few weeks later, Oakar saw pictures of a Reagan/Gorbachev signing ceremony and noticed that Reagan had slipped it into his breast pocket, making the rose visible. She and Reagan rarely agreed on issues of the day but for Oakar, that meant a great deal.

Photo courtesy of C-SPAN

O f the 110 members who did not return to Congress following the election of '92, Mary Rose Oakar was the embodiment. A Democratic Representative from Cleveland who had held office for 16 years, she was a tireless fighter for the "little people," a broad definition in her mind that encompassed women fighting breast cancer, nearly the entire Capitol work force, and ordinary Clevelanders and institutions within. As such, she made a lasting difference for people at the national and community level. On the flip-side, Oakar had a downside that some felt was herself. Bank overdrafts, a series of bad publicity surrounding personnel and other blemishes proved too much for even many of her longtime loyalists as she sought a ninth term in a redrawn district. Be that as it may, Oakar and backers, while conceding mistakes, believe the press, particularly her hometown newspaper, *The Plain Dealer*, embellished the negatives and at least some of that was confirmed following a protracted lawsuit.

Taking a reclusive approach was not in Oakar's DNA. She said her parents instilled her "self-confidence" and even as a source of annoyance to colleagues who called her a "publicity hound," that trait prevailed for her entire career. *Politics in America*, citing Oakar's brief training as an actress via a grant at the Royal Academy of Dramatic Arts in London, opined that "she still seems to be on stage sometimes as she speaks" and she particularly prided herself on taking on the big-boys. She also had a disposition that was unmistakably welcoming and gracious which, along with her distinct Cleveland accent sealed the deal for success.

Oakar's father was a steel worker and a Cleveland Indians fan who would regularly purchase 75 cent a ticket games for the entire family (she is still able to recite the lineup from the 1948 World Series, the last the Indians played prior to 2016). Mary Rose received her primary education from Catholic schools. She made it through in part by working as a long distance telephone operator for Ohio Bell (earning $52.50 a week) and by working the switchboards during the summer. She obtained her Bachelor's from the all-female Ursuline College which she joked about in a 2017 oral history interview saying, "We were not distracted until we went beyond the college campus." She served as student body president.

Oakar went on to earn her M.A. from John Carroll University, then went to London very briefly to study at Royal Academy where she had obtained a grant. Having a passion for education, she first taught at Lourdes Academy, another all-girl facility (a Catholic school), then began teaching English and drama at Cuyahoga Community College. Meanwhile, the performances didn't stop. Oakar and cast members were forced to present one show, "Paint Your Wagon," the night President John F. Kennedy was assassinated because it was sold out and the theater hall was non-refundable (she called doing so incredibly difficult).

The political arena came in 1972 when Oakar was persuaded to seek a seat on the Cleveland Council and her big break came in 1976 when Democratic Congressman Jim Stanton launched a bid for the U.S. Senate. There were eleven candidates in the race and she went about her campaign in two directions. One was conveying her closeness to female voters by reminding them that she was the only candidate of that gender in the field, in part by handing out pens with roses. She did not strictly cater to women, however and heeded the advice of Council President George Forbes, a supporter who told her not to simply focus on women because people knew she was one. Her view was that, "The overriding issue is that people want to feel the person who represents you at the federal level is close to you."

Oakar could not afford a traditional campaign but recalls, "I had more volunteers probably than anybody else." She also benefited from the fact that, "I was a good grader when I was teaching, so my former students both in college and high school were very kind to help me - my former classmates and people from my neighborhood all volunteered" and she used a Model-T Ford to court voters. On primary day, Oakar found that everything did come up roses – she eked out a first place win with 24%, five points ahead of Celebrezze who had 19% (she won the general with 81%). She shared Cleveland with Democratic Congressman Louis Stokes and, at that time, had 12 Cuyahoga suburbs in her district (it increased to 16 following the '82 redistricting). Oakar took seats on the Banking, House Administration, Post Office and Civil Service Committees and eventually, the Select Committee on Aging.

In her first year in office, Oakar took issue with the Carter administration for returning the Crown of St. Stephen to Hungary. A large population of Clevelanders were Hungarian and opposed the return, with the topic also dividing the few Hungarians in Congress.

If colleagues prior to 1982 doubted that Oakar was a force with a canny mind, her role in that year's budget battle undoubtedly fizzled those out. She had proposed an amendment that would shift $5 billion from defense spending to Medicare. Her speech was classic Oakar: "I say to my colleagues that if you want to cut Medicare, it is inhumane, it is indecent, and I say it is immoral; I say we have lost our national conscience for the value of our elderly people and our disabled. I say to my colleagues we have lost a sense of our civilization which we so value and our sense of a democratic decent history and, yes, our sense of morality, when we say that the cost overruns of a submarine are more important, than the health benefits of older Americans." On the topic of older Americans she went on to say, "They are not a strong lobbying group; they are not contributors to campaigns, and so forth. They are just decent people who made this country what it is." Oakar's Democratic colleague, Andy Jacobs of Indiana was even more blunt in saying, "The Oakar amendment essentially provides that we will spend less money killing people in other countries and more money curing people in this country."

By a vote of 228-196, Oakar won the day. Many members waited to vote but centrist Republicans were either taken by Oakar's argument or were concerned about political repercussions if they voted for the cuts. Minority Leader Bob Michel on the other side called it "the margin of difference" as far as adopting the GOP budget.

Photo via The Cleveland Public Library

Oakar became a pro in battling the Reagan administration. While she said multiple times that she liked the President personally, she had no problem calling his record out in uncertain terms. Giving the Saturday morning radio response to his address, she reached back to his tenure as Governor of California to take aim at his civil rights record. "In 1965, Ronald Reagan opposed the Civil Rights Act. Therefore, it is not surprising that the Reagan-Bush Administration has shown such callous disregard and contempt for civil rights both here and abroad."

One person Oakar did not have to play a personal-political game with was Tip O' Neill. She recalled he had often addressed groups of members as "fellas" but "you didn't mind because he was so fair-minded." When Oakar became Vice Chairman of the Democratic Caucus, she prodded O'Neill to convince the White House to let her attend leadership meetings. He agreed but the White House was more reticent and the Speaker told officials that he wouldn't attend unless Oakar was included. They concurred which seemed to settle the matter. In fact, as Oakar walked past White House correspondents such as Sam Donaldson, she received hearty congratulations. She only realized something was amidst when she failed to spot her nametag at the table and learned that because there was no room, she would be relegated to sitting in the corner against the wall. Oakar then informed the chief of protocol that she'd "be holding her first press conference" at which time he switched GOP caucus Chair Jack Kemp's placard. O'Neill, meanwhile might have had minor regret at his success as Reagan began recognizing Oakar at meetings even before him. Incidentally, Oakar's counterpart was future Vice-President Dick Cheney and because both Caucus chairs – Richard Gephardt on the Democratic side and Kemp on the GOP side were running for President, each got to perform the day-to-day functions as chair (Oakar genuinely liked Cheney until he became Vice-President).

When O'Neill announced plans to leave Congress in 1986, she struck gold in having the chance to take his office in the Rayburn House Office Building. O'Neill did not want his office to go to a Republican and when Oakar drew number four in the lottery, O'Neill intervened to make sure she got the office at which point he told her, "I've had such good luck there. I hope, darling, it brings you the same kind of luck." It was smaller than the space she was giving up but she didn't mind a bit.

From her earliest days in Congress, Oakar was fiercely committed to improving conditions of the elderly. Her ceaseless buttonholing eventually prompted O'Neill to give her a seat on the Select Aging Committee, despite the fact that five senior members had their eye on it. Oakar had long been involved in elderly issues and preventing abuse was at its core. She introduced the Older Americans Act which culminated with passage more than a decade later and would, among other results, set up a National Center for Adult Abuses.

House Speaker Tip O'Neill was something of a mentor to Oakar
Photo via The Plain Dealer

The 1981 murder of four American nuns from El Salvador was an example of Oakar going to the mat for her interests. Two of the nuns were from her district which pushed Oakar to fight for answers, viewing the report from the El Salvadoran government as insufficient for getting to the bottom of what transpired. The Reagan administration wasn't coddling her either and Oakar delivered numerous one minute speeches on the House floor rebuking them. Suffice it to say, she was not pleased when less than a year later, the administration (as required by law) certified that the government had been making progress. Oakar called the assertion an "outrage" but a postscript came when she was preparing to travel to El Salvador for the trial of the alleged murderers. The night before the scheduled flight, O'Neill called Oakar to tell her the mission was off? Why? Because, "You're a target."

On the topic of banking, fairness was key. The book *House Rules*, a biography about another member of the Banking Committee, Peter Hoagland of Nebraska, cites her ambivalence about preferential legislation for particular banks. "Exceptions for single institutions…bother me." She pronounced herself, "very concerned about some of the amendments that were passed this morning for individual institutions…" Yet she helped Ameritrust on her home turf by fighting for an amendment in the bill that would permit bank holding companies to turn thrifts into commercial banks. Oakar backed repeal of an amendment passed earlier that would have required financial institutions to obtain federal deposit insurance (taking the side of the Ohio based National Deposit Insurance Corporation). Her general philosophy was, "If the federal government is going to (insure banks) it has a right to expect that these institutions will serve all consumers, no matter how much or how little they have to deposit."

It was on the Post Office and Civil Service Committee that Oakar made quite a mark. She pursued the pay equity issue and her initial goal was a study of "comparable worth." It passed the House twice (Washington Republican Dan Evans was the Senate sponsor). However, North Carolina Senator Jesse Helms put a hold on it due to sponsoring Oakar's opposition to tobacco legislation that he was authoring.

Helms, though, proved not to be Oakar's most ardent foe. This rather proved to be Phyllis Schlafly, founder of the ultra-conservative Eagle Forum that opposed any pay equity and it gave spectators a kerfuffle at one hearing. When Schlafly called "comparable worth…unfair to the traditional family," Oakar shot back, "Phyllis, please don't try to confuse the issue. The issue is not taking a nickel away from a firefighter or an electrician. We don't want to lessen any man's salary in any way, shape or form." She went on to say, "You talk very patriotically. We're all Americans who care. But isn't it unthinkable that we would be such a wealthy country and the greatest rate of poverty is among elderly women?"

Oakar's concern about sex bias extended to studies. Late in 1990, she took the House floor to bemoan a study of 45,000 that concluded that three or four cups of coffee was not hazardous to one's health. "What is disconcerting to me," Oakar said, "is that in this morning's TV news never was it mentioned that men were only studied. This then, becomes very, very dangerous because women who have cystic problems should avoid coffee and other caffeine-containing products.

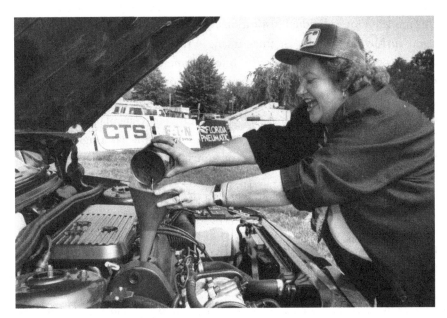

Photo via The Cleveland Plain Dealer

Of all of Oakar's imprints, fast tracking the fight against breast cancer was clearly her Mona Lisa and doing so required a protracted fight against what she once labeled the "cultural prejudices" of the "good ole boys" in Congress. Overcoming it required baby-steps and she was front and center but, for good reason. The disease had killed her mother and her sister had been stricken with it and would succumb a few years later.

In 1989, Oakar put in legislation to increase funding to the National Institute of Health (NIH) by $25 million, with the stipulation that the money had to be allocated for breast cancer research (her argument was that that it was a measly sum compared to what is being spent on defense). It was approved. After the victory, Oakar's Senior Legislative Representative Scott Frey received a call from Rose Kushner, a nationally known breast cancer advocate who asked, "What's next?" Frey was taken aback because he assumed he could simply savor a monumental victory but, there was true urgency to Kushner's question. Kushner had battled the disease since 1974 and unbeknownst to Frey, she was now telephoning him from Georgetown Hospital. Two weeks later, Frey was reading her obituary and at that point, he understood the timeliness of her mission.

That paled in comparison to the struggle over mammography coverage. Oakar first introduced legislation in 1987 that would require coverage as part of Medicare and had success when Congress included it in the Catastrophic Health Act. Senior citizen uproar over the cost, however, forced Congress to repeal the measure. Though Oakar had been trying to include coverage in a reconciliation bill, the Senate had rejected the efforts by the House conference committee to include mammography (along with hospice and respite care). It would be at least another year until another opportunity presented itself. October of 1990 came and it was déjà vu. Congress was on the verge of adjourning when her good friend Brian Donnelly of Massachusetts delivered the news that mammography coverage had again been left out. This was unacceptable to Oakar, and something she made known in the most biting of ways ("I just lost it").

Members of Congress, already kept in session well past the expected adjournment thanks to the budget stalemate, were anxious to leave Washington to campaign for their re-elections. Oakar was relentless to have the provision inserted, to the extent that she had to be escorted to her car by Capitol police as a result. *The Almanac of American Politics* wrote that Oakar argued so vehemently that "Ways and Means Committee Chair Dan Rostenkowski started urging it as strongly as she did" (it helped that Rostenkowski's office received hundreds of calls from women urging him to do so). Surprising even longtime advocates, the measure was included.

By 1991, Oakar was still fighting an uphill slog and she bemoaned the fact that "Only one out of every six grants for breast cancer research recommended for approval gets funded," she said. "I don't buy the argument that we are doing all we can. That is frankly total baloney." She was seeking an increase in the budget still and at one point, she asked colleagues on the floor, "Do we have to bring in the women who are bald from the chemotherapy?" Answering her own question, she did just that.

In May of 1991, advocates were visiting Capitol Hill and one rally was organized. It was dramatized by a 35-year-old mother of four, Ellen Hobbs of California. A new group, "Look Good, Feel Better (LGFG)," had provided Hobbs and other cancer-stricken women wigs and prosthetics but she ripped it off during her speech. "They tell me it's supposed to make me look better," she told the crowd, "but it doesn't." Next, she removed her prosthetic and said, "They told me it's supposed to make me look better but I won't feel better until they find a cure for cancer." When Oakar testified before a House Appropriations Subcommittee on her request for additional funding the following day, she brought Hobbs along and yielded her half of her time. Hobbs repeated the "I won't feel better until" line a number of times and told the all-male panel that she repeatedly had to answer her daughter's questions in the negative by telling her there is no preventative measures she could take to someday prevent getting the disease. This left members, including 81-year-old Chairman William Natcher of Kentucky deeply moved and the money was approved.

By Oakar's last year in office, the breast cancer budget skyrocketed from $158 million to $400 million leading her to say, "I wish this had happened sooner, because we'd be about 10 years closer to finding a cure. Congress is a little Johnny-come-lately on this one. Then again, we've got to go forward, not backward." Incidentally, Oakar's further commitment to eradicating breast cancer was her sponsorship of the National Breast Cancer Strategy Act.

Oakar was also a legendary champion of federal workers and late in her tenure rose to the chairmanship of the House Administration Subcommittee on Personnel and Police. This essentially gave her latitude over many of the concerns relating to the 12,000 employees on the Hill. She opposed a pay freeze for federal retirees and in 1989 passed a bill aiding the Capitol Hill Police. Oakar also introduced legislation tripling the jurisdiction of the House police force and for equal pay for employees – primarily female, of the House Beauty Shop. She indebted herself to colleagues by recommending a House Dining Room Chef, John Saile of Heck's Restaurant in Cleveland, whom the full panel's chair Charlie Rose hired and the quality of the food reportedly improved immensely.

There was also institutional change. First was the Congressional Women's Caucus which she and Colorado Democrat Pat Schroeder helped found. Next was a mission allowing the growing number of female members to use the House gymnasium. There was, as Schroeder put it a, "ladies' health facility" but the members found it inadequate. Oakar, referring to the "mean basketball hook shot," *The Plain Dealer* said she possessed observed, stated that she "probably could have competed with most of the men in Congress, but women weren't allowed to use the gym." For that reason, she and her home state colleague, Marcy Kaptur and Barbara Boxer of California, petitioned members at a Democratic leadership meeting with a rendition of a song "Five-foot-two, Eyes of Blue" composed by Boxer, who was 5'2 to the tune of "Has Anybody Seen My Gal?" The move ultimately worked as members acquiesced.

One rare but notable departure from Oakar's liberal orthodoxy was that she was pro-life, though even on that issue, her limit could be reached. One limit was counseling for women seeking abortions which Oakar sponsored in the form of legislation each Congress. Her reasoning was that, "It would give poor women an option" but women's organizations still shunned her come election time.

Oakar was also not particularly strong on the issue of Israel. She was Lebanese and often succeeded in getting far more aid for the nation than administrations requested. In 1982, she helped push through a $20 million package to Lebanon following an Israeli attack on PLO strongholds in that nation that caused collateral damage. Her comments that, "Since we serve as Israel's weapons supplier, that hostility is extended to us as well," drew a sharp rebuke from supporters of Israel, including Tom Lantos of California who invoked prior incidents where "the whole world watched." While Oakar opposed moving the U.S. embassy from Tel Aviv to Jerusalem, she respects the nation of Israel and has a fond memory of looking out at the city from the King David Hotel and thinking that this is what she read about as a child.

Beyond that, Oakar and her Jewish constituents and colleagues agreed to disagree and she was able to retain much of their backing. When an Israeli family lost their son in a bus explosion, New York Congressman Steve Solarz sent a notice for a memorial service and Oakar was the only member who came. He was grateful and the two became very close friends, as was the case with another Jewish Democrat, Ted Weiss. Oakar proudly cites the Jewish members as being the most avid supporters of her leadership bids. To this day, Oakar believes peace could be achieved if both sides shun the extremists.

"Madam Parochial" is a name that could easily fit Oakar as she was Cleveland's number one backer. She called her constituents "my people" and was on a first-name basis with many of them. Chief of Staff Tom Albert recalls an Oakar meeting with constituents in her office when the President of Wells Fargo walked in and asked to meet with her. Though he had given the maximum allowed to Oakar's campaign, she was going to fulfill her pledge to walk her constituents to the Capitol and delegated Albert to take the meeting. More importantly, she produced for "her people" substantial results.

There was an airport, Navy finance center, senior citizen housing, and the Main Street Bridge linking Cleveland's East and West sides via the Cuyahoga River. Oakar played a crucial role in the revitalization of Tower City and Playhouse Square Center, and obtaining UDAG grants for Cleveland was a priority throughout her tenure. In 1989, her efforts to secure a five-year grant for NASA funding at The Ohio Aerospace Institute paid off as it became one of 17 facilities nationwide to be awarded that distinction. The following year, she received $5 million for the North Coast Harbor. Highway funds poured in during this time, which led Cuyahoga County Engineer Tom Ness to coin her the name: "Our Lady of the Highway." To back up the fact that you can't take drama out of the girl, Oakar in 1989 introduced the Department of Arts and Humanities Organization Act to, among other things, give cabinet status to matters concerning the arts.

That same year, Oakar spearheaded an investigation into the Navy's conclusion that the fatal explosion of the U.S.S. Iowa had been caused by Clayton Hartwig, her constituent. Two years later, the Navy apologized to Hartwig's family. Mike Wallace interviewed Oakar for "60 Minutes" and few doubt Scott Frey's surmisal that, "but for Mary Rose the history of the Iowa disaster would have been written very differently."

On issues regarding the elderly, Oakar was intrepid. This included spearheading surprise inspections of nursing home facilities where it had been accused that drug use was rampant. Reporters accompanied her and uncovered other noxious conditions. She and Banking Committee Democrat Charles Schumer of New York worked on rent control issues because there were abolishment attempts both in that city and in Cleveland.

Oakar was also a leading proponent for building the iconic Rock'n'Roll Hall of Fame in Cleveland and like everything, it was a process-and-a-half. A Herculean challenge appeared to be convincing Jann Wenner, co-founder and Editor of *Rolling Stone* Magazine and Ahmet Ertegun, co-founder and President of Atlantic Records and to abandon the idea of housing the facility in New York City, where Wenner was deadest on housing it (Ertegun was open to Chicago or Detroit but Cleveland was not on his radar). Enter Oakar. She flew to Turkey where Etegun had a home and forged a relationship that sparked a continuing dialogue that included bringing him to Cleveland and visiting a local record store that specialized in old-time rock'n'roll. Eventually, they were won over. In another instance, amid doubts the city could raise $40 million, the Department of Housing and Urban Development rejected an Urban Development Action Grant (Oakar had to clarify to HUD that sponsors were not permitted to solicit funds outside of Ohio). The dedication finally took place in 1995.

Oakar opposed the start of the Gulf War in part because she feared the regional ramifications. "There will be no surgical strike against Saddam Hussein - there will be a world war of untold dimensions." Shortly thereafter, her tenure plodded downhill fast. Oakar bristles at the term "scandals" but admits to unwise decision-making in some cases.

**As a member of the House Banking Committee (Chairman Henry
Gonzalez and fellow Cleveland Congressman Louis Stokes sit to her left)
Photo via The Cleveland Plain Dealer**

Oakar's first ethical woe had hit the surface in 1987 when it came to light that she had kept a longtime aide, Mildred A. Vinicor, on her payroll for two years (at a salary of $24,000 a year) even though Mildred had moved to NYC. Her explanation was that while Vinicor was physically in New York City dealing with health issues, she hard at work on pressing committee matters, including preparing a major report on the effect of homelessness in the Reagan administration. Common Cause asked the Ethics Committee to investigate but Oakar, deciding it would be better to "clean the air," repaid the treasury. Later that year it was revealed that she had increased the salary of another aide, Margaret Mathna, by $10,000. What made it problematic? The two had purchased a condo together. The Ethics Committee didn't recommend punishment, Oakar to this day contends Mathna actually deserved even more money for her work, and the publicity did little to dent Oakar's showing in her district where she won a 73-27% re-election. There was however evidence that the matter impacted her standing with colleagues.

After the election of '88, Oakar entered the race for House Democratic Caucus. Her main rival was the current Budget Committee Chair, Pennsylvania Democrat Bill Gray, though Mike Synar of Oklahoma was also in the race.

Oakar tried to woo colleagues with chocolate replicas of Cleveland's famed Terminal Towers. Members of the Congressional Black Caucus, Boxer and her California colleague, future Speaker Nancy Pelosi were among her core supporters. William Lehman of Florida expressed a conundrum of many colleagues when he wrote in his diary *Mr. Chairman* that while he admired her greatly, he was troubled by the allegations.

Oakar chastised Gray for his PAC committee that aided colleagues and candidates, which she saw as giving him an unfair advantage. Gray called it "an absurdity," claiming, "you don't buy votes in Congress." Interestingly, in 1987 Oakar had criticized fellow Democrat and Banking Committee member Joe Kennedy of Massachusetts for "impugning...the reputation of members," when he suggested that Oakar had shepherded a bill through the committee that would not limit the pay of executives because "we are controlled by special interests." In a slogan not unlike her first run for Congress which read, "She's doing it the old-fashioned way; she's earned it." Oakar predicted she would win on a second ballot. There was no second ballot, however, as Gray dominated with 146 votes as compared to Oakar's 80 and Synar a poor third with 33 votes. Oakar believes a turning point might have come in the midst of a Democratic retreat when Gray brought comedian Bill Cosby who spent much of his time extolling the virtues of Gray.

Oakar was very well revered by her staff whom she called "family." A number were with her the full 16 years and Frey "loved working for her." She could be stern at times and "you'd hear it if something went wrong but you'd hear a thank you when you did right." She never "demeaned" her employees, "understood the value of her staff," and the feeling was mutual. The staff still gathers for reunions nearly three decades after the office closed. In short, "it was a hectic ride but it was a fun ride and we got so much done."

How did Oakar let her hair down? Time often didn't allow that but Chief of Staff Tom Albert said she was naturally into the theater. A lifelong Rodgers and Hammerstein fan, Oakar would often joke that she "played every lead for every musical with young women leading roles back in the day"). Her love for the Indians continues and he recalls catching her at home many a time watching a game.

The career-ending troubles began as early as 1989 when *The Washington Times* reported that Oakar had hired Banking subcommittee aides that were essentially no-shows. She responded by calling it a "sordid, partisan fight" that, by virtue of Republicans claiming committee budgets were exorbitant, "appears to be a smoke screen on the part of certain members of the House

Administration Committee to cover what is nothing more than a naked power grab." Following that was the bank scandal and the extent of Oakar's role was realized when the House Ethics Committee released the names of the 24 "worst abusers." With 213 overdrafts totaling $227,598.09, Oakar's account had been in the red for 21 of the 39 months according to the committee (her highest check was for $18,515.00). Oakar contends that the figure was not nearly that high – that she had actually stopped payment on a number of the checks before they should have cleared. But she said of the matter at the time: "I realize that this was a service that is not available to other citizens, and therefore it was wrong to have it available to a privileged few. I am embarrassed over the way I availed myself of the system and I apologize."

The short term did at least bring ramifications, as Oakar was forced to relinquish her role as chair of the Democratic Platform Committee. Politically, it was clear from the get-go that if Oakar wanted a ninth term, she would be facing the fight of her life. First would come the primary where longtime Cuyahoga County Commissioner Timothy Hagan announced his intention to challenge her. Redistricting had given Oakar the Western Cuyahoga suburbs, which meant that 40% of voters would be hearing about her for the first time. In this area the political leanings were more mixed than in her previous Democratic stronghold.

In the midst of the campaign, Oakar relinquished her role on a Select Committee conducting an investigation of a scandal involving embezzlement and alleged "ghost employees" at the House Post Office. *The Cleveland Plain Dealer* ran a headline, "Oakar Forced From Probe" and insinuated that she had oversight over the "ghost employees." Oakar responded by calling out, "damnable lies" and asserted, "I have news for *The Plain Dealer*. They do not elect me. The people do." In truth, the paper had conducted a drive-by, hours-long investigation to meet a deadline but were relying on two unnamed GOP members of Congress and a Democrat who were providing flimsy accounts. This set the stage for a seven-year libel lawsuit that culminated with a settlement at the expense of the paper.

As the primary approached, Hagan ran ads charging Oakar with "embarrassing us in Washington." Oakar countered with a spot that had an actor who looked like Hagan and a nameplate bearing his name that accused him of being asleep at the wheel during "the largest welfare fraud in state history."

Oakar at her official campaign kickoff for the 1992 election
Photo via The Cleveland Plain Dealer

There were other candidates in the race and accusations existed that Oakar recruited some of them as "stalking horses" to take voters away from Hagan (one was a man named Tom Coyne, not the Mayor of the Cleveland suburb of Brook Park but a carpenter). One alternative candidate in fact was deemed credible enough to garner the backing of *The Plain Dealer*. True or not, it worked to Oakar's benefit as she prevailed 39-30%. In her victory speech, she ticked off a litany of issues and said repeatedly, "and that's why I ran again." She later acknowledged, "This is a tough election for me...The easy way out would have been to say, 'Who needs it? Let me go back to teaching at some community college.'" Her work was not impacted as Frey said "all the troubles that she was facing drover her even more to get things done."

Unfortunately for her, the money she had to spend to hold off Hagan had weakened her and there would be no split field in November. Both parties were initially mixed as to how vulnerable Oakar would be for the fall. Some Republicans even believed that her notoriety, ubiquity, and the heavily Democratic nature of the district would see her to another term. It soon became evident to all, though, that the redrawn district and the scandal left many voters angry.

Republicans nominated businessman Martin Hoke who spent over $100,000 but only prevailed 33-28% in the wide-open primary. He had made his fortune in the previous decade through the founding of, "Red Carpet Cellular."

Oakar was not shy about using the loyalty card. Her slogan was, "She has stood with us through the years. It's now time we stand with her" and she again made her appearances in a convertible that said, "Re-elect Mary Rose." Meanwhile, Hoke bungled his stance on issues – at one point inadvertently calling for a $200 million defense cut and lowering it twice to a $75 billion figure that was high even for Democrats who advocated for a cut. His platform also called for

As pitiful as his issue-oriented campaign was, Hoke's public relations strategy was pretty adroit. Calling Oakar, "the most persuasive advocate for term limits," he diagnosed her as suffering from "a terrible addiction: perkomania." He handed out leaflets that said, "Congress giving you a headache? Take two of these and vote for Martin Hoke." At one point, he accompanied a press conference with a bag that he called, "Oakar's Bag of Dirty Tricks" which he shoved into a garbage can.

Hoke's rationale for running: "What's important to the voters is that she's Mary Rose Oakar. And I'm not." He cited, "a whole bunch of people who can't understand how she could still be around because of the ethical breaches in the past," adding, "This is a bad actor." The two even debated on ABC's "This Week," at which time Hoke had told her, "Miss Oakar, you are still in denial." Oakar was not about to let Hoke have the trump card when it came to calling out scruples. In a local debate, she asked Hoke to explain ten speeding tickets on the record and threw at him, "and while you were speeding you were driving foreign cars." She accused Hoke of paying folks $35 to boo her at various events but, citing her many local accomplishments, told voters her seniority was pivotal for getting that done. *The Plain Dealer*, which backed Oakar in all of her campaigns, agreed and lent a very lukewarm endorsement to Hoke, not exactly shocking given that Oakar's lawsuit was ongoing but she was told she would endorse her if she were to drop the lawsuit. Oakar responded that the only way that would occur is if "you retract all the baloney."

The race was labeled a toss-up throughout, but by October it became clear that Oakar was running uphill. Indeed, any hope supporters had of Oakar hanging onto her job evaporated almost as soon as the polls closed and it became obvious that voters had bounced Oakar. The suburbs reported first and she trailed 64-36%. The existing turf tightened things up but Hoke still ended up winning by a solid 57-43%, carrying everything except for Cleveland, Brooklyn and Newburgh Heights. When she conceded she told backers, "I want to say we have not lost, we have won. We have left ... a lasting legacy on this area." Supporters at Hoke's victory party reportedly sang, "Ding, dong, the witch is dead" and Hoke himself rubbed salt in the wound by saying, "Mary Rose Oakar lost the election because she beat herself."

In 1995, slightly more than two years after leaving office, Oakar was indicted on seven counts, including not reporting both a $50,000 and a $38,000 loan from a Cleveland businessman which was in excess of allowable contributions from a single individual. She and her nephews, who both worked on her campaign, proceeded to put $16,000 of it under ten other names. She was also charged with lying to the FBI and her nephew pled guilty for conspiring with her to circumvent election laws.

Oakar said she, "never, ever profited from my public service..." and vowed that, "at the appropriate time the full truth will speak for itself." Her supports vowed the same and a leader in raising money for Oakar's defense team was none other than Clayton Hartwig's sister. Oakar's truth was that her sister wanted her children to contribute to her campaign but she told them that she didn't want them to do so. In order to satisfy their mother, however, she told them she would write a few checks in their names and they could pay her back years down the road (in actuality she couldn't have cared less if they did repay her). They agreed and Oakar did so. When they re-enforced that was what happened, the prosecutor rebutted that nothing had been in writing. Oakar acknowledged years later that while it wasn't the most thought-out plan, there wasn't anything nefarious about it.

Two charges were subsequently dismissed, one including the failure to disclose the money and the other banking charges, the latter because the House Bank operated within the institution (Oakar's lawyers had argued folks "needed a House Bank scalp"). When the matter went to trial and the verdict came about a year later, Oakar got off with probation, a $32,000 fine and community service. A year later, on the advice of the judge, she and *The Plain Dealer* settled but only after Oakar conditioned it on the paper printing an apology (they did so in very fine print).

With her sister battling breast cancer, Oakar considers losing the election "a blessing" because she was able to spend quality time with her (she died in 1995). By 2000, Oakar was ready for a comeback, seeking a seat in the Ohio Legislature. She declared, "The people have moved on," and was right. In

2008, she was elected to the Ohio Board of Education from District 11 where she served until she was term limited. She also sat on the Advisory Board for the White House Conference on Aging.

As for her own legacy, Oakar once quoted Shakespeare: "To thine own self be true." She then added, "It comes back to what you think of yourself."

Oakar is joined by Vice-President Dan Quayle and his wife Marilyn as well as celebrities Lynda Carter, Willard Scott, Susan G. Komen founder Nancy Brinker and Loni Anderson at a marathon for breast cancer research
Time/Life Photo via Getty Images

CHAPTER SIX

Idealism, Energy and Defying The Odds Was the Story of Jim Jontz

Introductory Quote: "I gave a damn about a dam." – Indiana Congressman Jim Jontz, detailing his reason for launching campaign for the Indiana House in 1974 that was beyond a longshot – stopping construction of the Big Pine Dam in Warren County. He prevailed by two votes against the Majority Leader.

Photo courtesy of Calumet Regional Archives, Indiana University, Northwest

H ad Jim Jontz represented a more politically amenable district, he likely could have had a long and fruitful Congressional career. A youthful Democrat with sheer energy who had won a Statehouse seat against the odds 18 years earlier, Jontz used his hard work and sincerity to persevere despite a philosophy that was well left of his core constituency. When he finally fell victim to that and a general anti-incumbent mood that had been sweeping the nation, the wonder was not that he lost but that he managed to thrive and prosper for as long as he did.

Those in Kokomo, Indiana and the surrounding counties who had the pleasure of being served by Jontz got a wondrous and idealistic representative who casted votes according to his principles, not which way the political winds were blowing. That did not suit everyone fine and dandy, though. *Congressional Quarterly* wrote, "Jontz has acquired a reputation as something of a troublemaker, one who meddles in topics his colleagues would prefer to leave alone." The reason was that much of the time, those areas were germane to areas far away from Indiana's Fifth Congressional District. Aside from causing him to be burned in effigy on at least one occasion, it was a major factor in getting him to lay down his seat at the hands of the voters in 1992. Be that as it may, in fighting for what he believed, Jontz wouldn't have had it any other way.

Jontz was born in Indianapolis, Indiana. In his book, *The People's Choice: Jim Jontz of Indiana*, Ray Boomhower wrote, "From an early age, Jontz displayed a dedication to nature while growing up in the 1960s in the Northern Hill's subdivision of Indianapolis's North side – a 'semi-rural' setting that enabled him to develop his deep love of nature." Appropriately, he majored in Geology at Indiana University in 1973 and led a conservation group, Crisis Biology. He was also getting enchanted with the concept of peaceful protests. Jontz's sister, Mary Lee Turk recalls, "Jim expressed to our parents that he wanted to make changes in the world, for the better. Our parents told him that that was a good goal, but that he needed to work within the system, which he did. This was the time of the Vietnam War when "others were trying to make changes in the world through protests and marches, often violent. Jim liked a good peaceful march and protest, but he spent his life trying to make changes within the system. The year after graduation, he began taking his protest to an elective stage as he took on a highly improbable target: the minority leader of the Indiana House.

Jontz's rendezvous with the legislature could be said to have begun in 1971 as an intern for a newly elected State Representative, Burnett "Pat" Bauer. At the time, Bauer was working on legislation to ban detergents that were 70% phosphate. It passed but opponents didn't retreat - they returned to try to repeal the ban and Jontz would help Bauer foil them. His energy was incessant and Bauer remembers often getting calls from Jontz as late as 11 p.m. and as early as 6 a.m. But there was more than that. Bauer recalls Jontz doing "research all the time," and would sleep in his car so "he wouldn't waste any time" strategizing or working toward achieving his goals.

When Jontz launched his own seemingly hapless bid, he did not do so for the hell of it. He was opposing an Army Corp of Engineers Project to build Big Pine Dam in Warren County and one way to halt it was for the legislature to pass a resolution of disapproval. For whatever reason, the current membership was unwilling to do so and that had local residents feeling forgotten. As Jontz told *The Louisville Courier* as he prepared to take office, "Many are opposed to change. They like the quiet lifestyle and there's a backwoodsy atmosphere in parts of the county...Fifty-some families would be displaced; cemeteries would be flooded; roads cut off; school buses rerouted."

Photo courtesy of Calumet Regional Archives, Indiana University, Northwest

Many viewed Jontz as a fool for thinking he had a chance against John "Jack" Guy but, notwithstanding the favorable nature of the anti-Watergate year, Jontz earned it and the eve of the election embodied why. The person driving him around the district thought that he was taking Jontz home but the candidate knew of a laundromat that was still open which he vowed to visit. It was near midnight yet the decision proved fateful given that he won by two votes. Much as Jontz deserves the credit, Guy also could have prevented his loss had he stumped harder in Warren County but he believed he didn't need to. For Democrats, the year was as big in Indiana as anywhere. The Watergate tide swept up Republican leaders of the Ways and Means Committee and that panel's Taxation Subcommittee, among others.

When Jontz made it to the Legislature (he called it an "unbelievable, fairyland kind of a thing"), Bauer was his mentor and he offered him critical lessons. It wouldn't be uncommon for Jontz to offer amendments to legislation, read them very quickly on the floor and have colleagues vote them down by wide margins. Bauer gave him advice. While understanding that he was trying to give fellow legislators as much information as possible, "you've got to be a salesman...slow it down." To help do so, Bauer agreed to sponsor a few amendments to relieve Jontz of the pressure (he also tried to get Jontz more credit). The bottom line was that Jontz, he said, proved "educable" on how things worked and in the final analysis, he was learning from the best. Bauer eventually became Speaker of the Indiana House and 2020 will mark his golden anniversary as a legislator.

Boomhower said, "he preferred the terms progressive or populist." In 1982, opponent David Diener couldn't understand why "voters kept electing him to office for one reason or another." Diener might not have equated work ethic with getting votes but his colleagues surely did. A fellow Democrat named Sheila Klinker noted that Jontz's desk was nearly always piled higher than any other legislators.

In 1984, Jontz sought a promotion to State Senator. Guy was seeking a comeback but Jontz again had the upper hand. He won and took a salary of $11,600, "plus between $1,000 and $2,500 in interest from a savings and loan account" according to a newspaper report. Shortly thereafter he set his sights on Congress.

Jontz seemed to be mounting a similarly uphill bid for the Kokomo area House seat as in 1974 when the 16-year Republican occupant of the seat, a well-respected moderate named Elwood Hillis, announced his retirement. Jontz won the nomination without opposition and as the campaign went on, *Politics in America* observed that, "Jontz was pressing on with the campaign he began in the fall of 1985." He faced no opposition in the primary, though the general election was infinitely different.

The Republican nominee was State Senator James Butcher and had Republican primary voters nominated their preferred candidate, State Treasurer Julian Ridlen, Jontz's path to Washington would have been far more difficult. Butcher had strong grass roots and conservative support, ultimately resulting in Ridlen's 10% upset. Butcher was a Baptist lay preacher who was staunchly against abortion and pornography, though he was slightly subterranean with those issues following the primary, instead choosing to play-up the economy. This did not work in his favor as *CQ* noted that Jontz "was given unexpected ammunition in May when Rep. Hillis bucked his party's majority and voted for the Democratic trade bill aimed at restricting foreign competition." Butcher opposed the bill and Jontz made sure voters knew it. Butcher didn't help his cause when he labeled Jontz, a divorcee who would never remarry, as a man who, "talks about family values, but he's never had a family." On the other hand, unions such as the UAW in particular, considered Jontz solid as a rock when it came to their issues.

On phone (left) and walking in Washington
Photo courtesy of Calumet Regional Archives, Indiana University, Northwest

As the campaign neared culmination, *CQ* observed that, "It was the full-time person to person effort at all 14 of the district's county's augmented by fundraising that brought in a surprising sum for a Democrat in the district long in GOP hands." Shortly before the election, Republicans counted this seat as a likely hold. On Election Day, Jontz surprised them all by winning with 51%, a mere 5,000 votes among the 156,000 that were cast. Butcher prevailed in the areas at the eastern end of the district but only won Jasper and Porter counties by the barest of margins. Jontz took 53% in Howard County (Kokomo) and captured comfortable if not overwhelming margins in the surrounding counties. A euphoric Jontz credited "the trade and farm issues" for providing the win. "A Democratic win in this district showed that people wanted a change in Washington." This would begin the hard task of serving the very Republican area he called "typical of the Midwest - farms and factories."

The Almanac of American Politics summed up the Jontz enigma stating, "On issues, he has a flair for positions that carry intellectual honesty to impolitic lengths - and for cheap shots-although many will disagree on which is which." No one would disagree with his penchant, for hard work and colleagues soon learned that was Jontz's blood type.

With Speaker Jim Wright
Photo courtesy of Calumet Regional Archives, Indiana University, Northwest

In Washington, Jontz secured seats on the Education and Labor Committee and the Agriculture Committee, though he soon moved to Interior and Insular Affairs, the panel that would one day contribute to his political downfall. Not surprisingly, he was a very involved as an activist legislator with five bills bearing his name having passed in his first term alone. On Education and Labor, he worked toward a six-month amnesty for students who had defaulted on loans.

Much of Jontz's impact was on Agriculture, where he and three other members founded the Congressional Corn Caucus that first year. His reasoning was that, "Events during the 100th Congress, such as budget cuts in the farm program, ethanol legislation, and drought relief legislation, have demonstrated the need for cooperation among members of the Congress from major corn- producing areas." He steered to passage language in a broader agriculture measure that would increase the compensation for farmers and small businesses impacted by the drought. The first bill Jontz introduced was the Farmers Home Loan Buy Back Act which would require the Farmers Home Administration to offer local communities the first chance to buy back FMHA-backed development loans at discounted rates. *The Post Tribune* noted that, "In the 5ᵗʰ District, 43 communities have taken out 67 such loans. Statewide, there are 650 loans."

Jontz with his interns
Photo courtesy of Calumet Regional Archives, Indiana University, Northwest

Shortly before the 1988 election, Jontz sent letters to local grocery store operators urging them to switch to biodegradable plastic bags. He argued that doing so would, "demonstrate to the public the benefits to our environment and our economy of using products made from biodegradable plastics." He also added some local flavor by mentioning, "Corn is Indiana's number one crop, and farmers in our state would benefit immensely from the increased use of biodegradable plastics made from cornstarch."

That campaign gave Jontz an "easy ride", something for which he was hardly accustomed to. As George H.W. Bush was racking up 65% in 1988, Jontz raised his percentage noticeably to 56%, a result that indicated he wouldn't be dislodged anytime in the near future and certainly not in 1990. That year, however, the race turned out closer than expected.

Jontz's tirelessness naturally extended to his committee work, and having a hand in every pot was not unusual. A trivia question among committee staff, not necessarily meant for flattery, was in reference to which of the 17 sections of the 1990 farm bill Jontz did not attach an amendment. The answer was none, and it would be an understatement to say that members were not impressed. Texas Democrat Charlie Stenholm was one of them. He stated, "We are asked to believe that our system of production agriculture is faulty. I don't happen to believe that." Another amendment would strengthen "the family farm system," which led other rural lawmakers to claim that an overzealous federal government could prove detrimental to small farmers. (Kansas Republican Pat Roberts complained that, "Quite frankly, some of my farmers don't have the resources to do that.").

Another area that Jontz took aim at in the 1990 farm bill was U.S. grain, which a number of people questioned the sanity of. Jontz proposed changing the federal standards and said, "I feel we are not meeting the needs of the producer."

In his office (left) and at Lake Bruce in 1987
Photo courtesy of Calumet Regional Archives, Indiana University, Northwest

Since the bill's inception in April, Jontz had arranged five hearings with farmers in the districts to hear their views. Jontz's focus was conservation and, on this topic, Senator Tom Harkin said he was "ahead of his time...is now widely accepted as a fundamental part of our nation's agriculture policy" adding, "although we still have a long way to go to fulfill the vision Jim did so much to instill."

Taking part in a drought conference
From Left to right: Senator Kent Conrad (D-North Dakota),
Congressman Tim Johnson (D-South Dakota), Jontz and Congressman
Steve Gunderson (R-Wisconsin). Senators Robert Dole (R-Kansas)
and "Kit" Bond (R-Missouri) are seated in the next row
Photo courtesy of Calumet Regional Archives, Indiana University, Northwest

Jontz would go on to ruffle colleagues in regards to other issues. One year, for instance, he proposed a measure that would change an umbrella policy for the Unrelated Business Tax, an issue firmly in the hands of the powerful Ways and Means Committee. Jake Pickle, a fellow Democrat who chaired the subcommittee with jurisdiction over that issue, got Jontz's press secretary, Scott Campbell, on the phone to tell him, "you guys really need to call me" before taking such an action.

This all happened before Jontz's national exposure from joining the quest to protect the Northern Spotted Owl to which he conceded, "I always lost those struggles." Calling "the forests of the Northwest (are) as magnificent as the Grand Canyon," Jontz drew up the Ancient Forest Protection Act and wanted Congress to reject lifting a court injunction on the forest. Folks in both parties were far from amused.

Aside from the fact that fellow Democrats from the region felt unnecessary problems were being caused (a colleague from Oregon threw Jontz out of his office), his stance garnered him the attention of Alaska's lone Representative, Republican Don Young. In fact, Young retaliated by introducing a bill granting the Fifth District of Indiana historic preservation status (the "Northwest Indiana Ancient National Forest Act" would designate 1.3 million acres with the rationale to "provide for weekend recreational opportunities for residents of Chicago and Indianapolis"). Boomhower wrote that Jontz "gave Young credit for 'his humorous proposal' and said he kept asking the Alaska legislator if he could have an autographed copy of the bill." And to show he could take the ribbing, Jontz also called Young, "very creative and entertaining" and on another occasion claimed, "Don's a funny guy."

At Mt. Baldy on Earth Day, 1990
Photo courtesy of Calumet Regional Archives, Indiana University, Northwest

Jontz's propensity for wading into matters that had little to do with his district did not go unnoticed. At the height of the timber matter, one sign asked, "How did Oregon get another 5ᵗʰ District?" An Oregon State House member called him, "Congressman Dunce." Jontz's response to them was, "I did not create the division of opinion on this issue within the Northwest. There must be spokespeople for regional interest and national interest. And it's my job to be a spokesperson for national interest."

That didn't mean Jontz neglected regional interests, though. As with everything else, he fulfilled his obligations with gusto. He managed to protect Grissom Air Force Base, fight for construction of the Hoosier Heartland Industrial Corridor from Lafayette to Fort Wayne, and propose the institution of Colfax Township Airport. With Peter Visclosky, he shepherded the Dunes bill through Congress only to have his 1990 opponent, John Johnson contend the legislation was "rushed through Congress."

Jontz was so liberal on social issues that he often acquired as high as a 99% rating from the ADA. In the midst of his 1990 re-election campaign, he filed a bill called the "Commission on Choices in Health Care Reform Act of 1990" which created a 15-member commission used to draw up solutions for the nation's healthcare crisis. One of his rare deviations from liberalism was his support for a Balanced Budget Amendment. He also showed he believed in taking care of the home folks when he said, "I personally believe you would like to see your tax dollars come home to clean up the Grand Calumet than to spend another billion dollars on Star Wars."

Jontz opposed the use of force to remove Iraqi forces from Kuwait and, just as everyone else, was gleeful over the mission's eventual success. He was "concerned that we are not taking the steps that we must to secure the contributions our allies have pledged" and was profuse about the necessity of addressing the needs of the returning troops. He sat on Veterans Affairs and proposed an increase in funding to help veterans deal with PTSD and explained his infatuation for doing so. "The failure of the VA to address PTSD treatment reflects our society's general stigma with mental health problems. We would never ignore a veteran who returned from combat with a physical problem such as a lost limb. PTSD is a similar, combat-related injury. Unfortunately, many veterans with PTSD still find themselves ignored. The VA's existing programs are far from adequate to meet the need which exists for treatment of PTSD." He was aghast when the administration proposed cutting federal impact aid.

Christopher Klose, who managed Jontz's '86 race and later became his chief of staff, said he was "respected for his intellect and what he brought to the conversation even when people disagreed or thought he would hurt their particular interest." What did Klose think inspired Jontz to wade into such hostile territory? Altruism for one. A prominent saying Jontz employed was, "You shouldn't look at issues on the spectrum of left and right, you should look at them from top-to-bottom." More realistically, Klose said he always viewed himself as "on borrowed time" which meant that there was no time to waste, he had to get things done immediately because he felt he might lose the next election.

Jontz's incessant pounding of the pavement and unique personal style clearly accounted for his ability to remain in office despite a very adverse and politically opposite district. While Republicans were frustrated at their inability to beat him, one influential top Republican had the explanation. State GOP Chair Rex Early wistfully noted, "He cuts everybody's lawn. He rides his bicycle backwards and he knows everybody's lost grandson." Sometimes he'd also drive a Chevrolet that he proudly boasted had 192,000 miles. Boomhower wrote that he would show up to parades in "his sister's Rusty-old blue Schwinn bicycle with mismatched tires." Klose recalls how, one year, Jontz managed to cram in seven 4th of July parades that necessitated many convertibles, the handoff of a few pickup trucks, and a short airplane ride. For this, time was on his side. The Fifth encompassed two time zones – Eastern and Central so, to the chagrin of Jontz's staff, there were actually 25 hours in the day. Other techniques included sending potholders to voters accompanied by a letter from his grandmother who lived in the district.

How did Jontz's staff deal with his abundance of energy? By giving as good as he did – voluntarily. Klose describes his former boss as "very energetic, very driven, (he) could sometimes be a taskmaster and expected everyone to work just as hard as he did." Yet, they loved it. Scott Paul spoke of Jontz as being, "demanding but not in an unreasonable way." In the office, he was "not the scolding type but the mentoring type," and he cites word usage suggestions for letters as an example. Jontz's desire to mentor youth benefitted the young and Paul said, "From a Capitol Hill perspective, [Jontz] was a great first boss." Another staffer, Don Kusler, described him as an "interesting character. A bulldog and a sweet person but he was on task."

USA Today also summed up Jontz's image in saying, "He still won't make anyone's best dressed list - and surely would be horrified if he did. He has a cluttered office that looks like someone really works there. On the walls are posters of James Dean, the movie Hoosiers, and the Ancient Forest." *Logansport Pharos-Tribune* reporter Dave Kitchell coined a name for his activity: "Jontzings" and supporters distributed t-shirts that said, "Man on the Move."

Given that he was a "man of the people," Jontz did not accept honoraria but instead gave most of his pay raise to charity and local scholarships. This is not to say, though, that he was totally impervious to using the office to his advantage. He fundraised $48,725 from PACs for his 1988 re-election and became adept at using the office franking privilege for mailings back home. He wasn't a drinker, a schmoozer, nor a back-slapper but he didn't need to be. Klose's context was that, "He could be charming when he needed to be but was a good conversationalist. He could meet people from all walks of life and relate to them."

Furthermore, his friends were members of like-minded interests: Lane Evans of Illinois, Marcy Kaptur of Ohio and even more senior, powerful barons like George Miller of California and David Bonior of Michigan. Jill Long Thompson emulated Jontz in that she captured a Fort Wayne based district in a 1989 special election that was even more lopsidedly Republican than the Fifth. Once she was sworn in, Jontz was always available to be her big-brother on the Hill, "helping me learn the ropes" on Agriculture and even recommending a person from his office to join her staff.

Another admirer, former Congressman David Nagle, an Iowa Democrat whose complete tenure overlapped with Jontz said the word to describe his colleague was, "studious." How? "Jim wanted that job to do something. He didn't want to just be a Congressman. He wanted to be a working Congressman." Obviously, Jontz was not everyone's cup of tea legislatively but Long-Thompson said that never deterred him from collegiality. "It was his nature to be helpful to anyone who he thought would contribute better to public policy and public service....You could not know him and not like him. He had incredible intellectual integrity...He was a principled colleague."

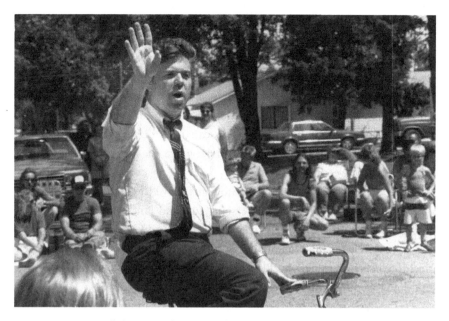

**On a bike at Rochester, Indiana's 1990 Fourth of July
parade, one of the many he crammed in that year**
Photo courtesy of Calumet Regional Archives, Indiana University, Northwest

Until his last race, the formula of pounding the pavement served Jontz exceedingly well come election time. But it hardly insulated him from a serious challenge.

In 1990, Republican John Arthur Johnson spent $600,000 of his own money and hosted a late visit from the most prominent fellow Hoosier at the time, Vice-President Dan Quayle. In a month's time Johnson proposed a four-point plan to address the issue of solid waste, including recycling, and taking aim at the health care crisis with an AmeriCare plan that Jontz hit because it contained a 12% sales tax. Some groups were slow to assist Jontz, and for the first time in his career the Indiana Farm Bureau abandoned him in favor of Johnson, citing the challenger's status as a businessman. Officials acknowledged that Jontz, "has done good things on the farm bill" but referenced his record on other issues when he said, "Farmers are people too. We are not only interested in agriculture issues." Johnson considered giving backing to an opponent of a member of the House Agriculture Committee "a courageous and significant decision."

The campaign was dirty, with a fitting representation described by Johnson when he said, "Before I entered politics I was warned – never get involved in a mud wrestling contest with a pig. You are going to get dirty and the pig is going to enjoy himself." Jontz wrote on his campaign literature that Johnson, "says New Jersey may need to send its waste to Indiana and opposes an import ban." A poll with one month remaining found the two men tied. In short, the budget stalemate in Washington may have helped Jontz, though his margin was still the lowest among Indiana's nine returning members (Republican John Hiler was unseated). But his 53-47% margin was not necessarily a red flag in a tough district given the anti-incumbency that had just begun sweeping the nation.

In as early as March 1991, Republicans vowed to make Jontz pay for opposing the use of force in the Persian Gulf and landed a candidate with the credentials to do so. Steve Buyer (Boo-yer) was a Gulf War veteran and, early on, convened a meeting of each of Jontz's rivals from 1974 onward to get a feel for their experiences and learn from their mistakes. Jontz, meanwhile, kept doing what he did best; serving his district.

As the cycle moved forward, it seems as though Jontz's footing was firm and the likelihood of his removal quickly diminished. Redistricting actually made the district slightly more Democratic but also gave him territory he had not previously served. How did Jontz get to know the people? By bicycle, of course. But some unions, angered by his timber stance, abandoned him. Buyer, meanwhile, slammed franking privileges and other perks associated with House members and asked his would-be constituents to "help [him] recycle Congress."

A week before the election, politicos on both sides predicted that Jontz would win another term. Thus, it was somewhat of a surprise when the votes were counted and Buyer had ousted him by a tiny margin of 51 to 49%, a difference of just under 5,000 votes (112,492 to 107,973). Jontz carried some of the newer areas (Vermillion) but his old base proved suddenly unreliable – he lost Howard County by 2,500 votes. The removal of Lake County from the Fifth proved particularly fatal but was a necessity for Visclosky to pick up given that his Gary oriented First District had lost significant population.

The low ratings of Congress hurt as well and in an anti-incumbent year, Jontz was the only Hoosier to lose their job. Though he was hardly a part of the House Bank scandal (five overdrafts), even tertiary involvement might have been too much for voters who again overlooked his Democratic label. Team Jontz also believes the surge of Ross Perot voters, hire in the fifth than the rest of the state, had impact. Supporters such as Lake County Democratic Chair Robert Pastrick stated the obvious: "He hung from his knuckles for a long time."

At a press conference the next morning, a reporter asked National Republican Congressional Campaign Committee Chair Guy Vander Jagt and his lieutenants why a man who had a reputation for attentiveness to his district was dislodged. The response they gave was simply that Buyer was a stellar candidate.

Always full of energy, Jontz didn't let defeat wear him. He was up early the next morning shaking hands with Kokomo factory workers. In fact Paul, who himself had lost a tight race for the state legislature, saw him that day and said that rather than dwelling on what went wrong, Jontz was looking forward to the next venture. However, there was little on the horizon.

In 1994, Jontz attempted to make a comeback by taking on the most politically uninviting target, venerable Republican Senator Richard Lugar, in what would have been an uphill enough battle in a climate that was favorable to his party. In a year that was an anathema to Democrats nationwide, Jontz knew he was fighting mission impossible the entire time but he called it "a campaign of faith," and said, "I wanted a new challenge." Even faith, though, couldn't guide him through the challenge of toppling Lugar. The incumbent glided toward a fourth term like the marathon runner he that was. At one point, he had well more than a million dollars on hand while Jontz had a mere $60,000 and had an inauspicious start when Democratic voters awarded him the nomination to face Lugar with just 55% against an opponent affiliated with Lyndon LaRouche (the state party attributed that result to low name recognition).

Still, Jontz soldiered on for the fall. He ran a few creative ads, conceding that, "We are not going to get an award for the best-financed campaign, (but) maybe we will for the most creative." One ad reminded voters of the names of many European cities that Lugar had visited which also happened to be towns in Indiana. Another ad featured a chicken to reference the fact that Lugar had labeled one Senate pay raise, "chicken feed." Near the end of the campaign, Jontz used the pick-up to stump in each of the state's 92 counties. The result was predictably lopsided in Lugar's favor and he won re-election 67-31%.

After leaving office, Jontz served as the president of Americans for Democratic Action. He was handcuffed at Siskiyou National Forest in Oregon where he had moved and was now protesting the Sugarloaf Timber Sale which, thanks to a new law signed by President Clinton, expedited logging in this and other forests. While Jontz wasn't happy about it, it was in his true fashion that he told his mortified parents: "I had my suit on." More importantly, the action was consistent with his creed that, "Direct action has helped communicate to the public what this terrible law is all about. It has put a human face on the issue."

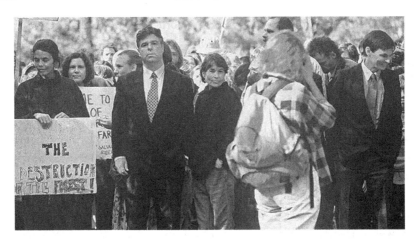

Photo courtesy of Calumet Regional Archives, Indiana University, Northwest

In 2005, Jontz was diagnosed with colon cancer which claimed his life within two years. Among the well wishers who reached out to Jontz in those final days were Lugar and his wife. On his death, Chief of Staff Tom Sugar summed up his greatness by saying, "Jim was always focused on doing the right thing, the good thing, the thing he believed to be right and true. People become very cynical about politics today, but Jim Jontz was the real deal." For nearly his entire run, voters shared that view as well.

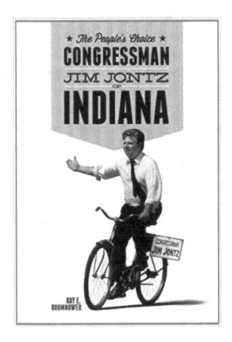

CHAPTER SEVEN

Horton Epitomized the Camaraderie of the Greatest Generation Of Which He Proudly Hailed

Introductory Tidbit: The contra aid package that President Ronald Reagan was promoting was a cliffhanger through the end and when the request reached the House floor, he needed to muster every vote he could get. A call was arranged with New York Congressman Frank Horton but because Reagan would be aboard Air Force One at the time, Horton was told that he should refer to him only by his Secret Service code-name, "Rawhide" and not the President. When Horton accepted the call, he innocently started the conversation by saying, "Mr. President, thanks for calling. I understand I have to call you Rawhide." Horton ultimately opposed the package.

Photo courtesy of the National Institute for the Deaf at Rochester Institute of Technology

W hen Frank Horton was still in Congress, there was a commercial for a product that began with a tune and the words, "Oh, that Rochester man." Horton was the furthest thing from a commercial star but the Republican who represented metro-Rochester in Congress for three decades was as recognizable as can be. Ditto for the respect and admiration he commanded and a style of conciliation that was second-to-none. For decades, Horton's campaign slogan was "the Congressman who cares!" Like doctors who used to make house calls, Horton's greatest love and first priority as a Congressman was visiting his district, and being with and taking care of his constituents. In fact, throughout his entire 30 years in Congress, Horton often boasted that he personally signed every piece of correspondence to his constituents.

For Horton, partisanship was a dirty word. He not only sought compromise but found himself opposing Republican presidents on high profile issues in some years on more occasions than not. *The Almanac of American Politics* called what he espoused, "not all that far from the politics of say, Scoop Jackson," the Washington State Democrat who often found himself taking on his party on matters pertaining to defense. At the end of the day, Horton's legacy was a reputation as an amenable, well-liked member on both sides of the aisle who largely succeeded with his key mission of making government more accessible. In fact, Horton's stature among colleagues was such that in his final two terms, he was selected by his 34-member New York colleagues to be dean of the delegation, an extraordinary gesture given that Republicans were a distinct minority. He would prove the leap of faith to be well-earned as he became a legend for trying to secure coveted assignments for members of both parties of his delegation, and succeeded many times against very steep odds.

Horton's early years were spent in the South. Born in Cuero, Texas, he attended Baton Rouge public schools and received his undergraduate degree from Louisiana State University (LSU) where he was also enrolled in Army ROTC. He graduated and was commissioned as second lieutenant in the Army in 1941 and was on active duty when Pearl Harbor was bombed in December of 1941. He spent the ensuing four years deployed overseas, serving his country in World War II in both North Africa and Italy as an infantry company commander of E Company, 60th Infantry, 9th Division. In October 1942, he recalled the journey in his retirement announcement address from Congress: "We combat loaded and sailed from Hampton Roads, Virginia to participate in Operation Torch, the invasion of North Africa. My company was part of the 60th Regimental Combat Team of Sub-Task Force Goalpost under the command of MG Lucian K. Truscott, Jr. The task force commander of the Allied Forces was Gen. George S. Patton. On November 8 of that year - 1942, I led my company as one of the two assault companies that landed at Green Beach, Mehdia, (and) Port-Lyuatey, French Morocco." He then took part in the Allied campaign across North Africa and in Italy. His life was spared by comrades on three occasions who jumped in front of him to save him. Two died while another had lifelong facial scars. For his service, Horton received the Bronze Star for valor in combat. He also concluded that being spared when others weren't meant service was the only way forward. It was simply a matter of how.

Horton was discharged a Major in 1946 and his introduction to New York State came shortly thereafter when he enrolled at Cornell Law School. In the ensuing years, he built a law practice and became involved with and then President of the community-owned Rochester Red Wings and though he wasn't necessarily salivating at a run for office, he gained notoriety for which aspiring politicians only dream. Horton, would often recount that his second passion in life, after his constituents, was baseball.

Horton's military experience deeply impacted his life and he retained a keen interest in the military and military affairs throughout his tenure in Congress. He believed service. Both his sons served in the military, his oldest son, Frank, served in the Air Force during Vietnam; and his youngest son, Steven, attended the U.S. Naval Academy and served 28 years on active duty retiring as a Rear Admiral in 2001. After the Vietnam War, Horton, with several other members, wrote a book, *How to End the Draft*, in 1967 and was a key member and leader in the Congressional movement to replace the draft with the All-Voluntary Armed Forces which was enacted in 1973.

In high school, Horton had wanted to attend the U.S. Military Academy at West Point but was unable to secure an appointment due to his family not having the political connections necessary, at that time, in Louisiana to be appointed to one of the service academies—this was a lesson that he never forgot. In his 30 years in Congress, in Horton's mind there was not greater responsibility then nominating young men and women to the service academies based on merit. He personally interviewed candidates, held a luncheon each June for new appointees and those currently in the Academies, and then he followed each graduate throughout their military career.

Horton won a seat on the Rochester Council in 1955 and chaired the City Council Public Utilities and Special Services Committee. He lost his seat in 1961 when voters deposed Rochester Republicans of their majority.

What was most extraordinary about Horton's ascension to Congress was that he got it without virtually any resistance. When Kenneth Keating vacated the 38th New York Congressional seat to run for Senate in 1958, Horton was considered to be a major contender for the seat, but would have to face Jessica "Judy" Weis in the Republican primary. Although, Horton believed that he had the grass-roots support to prevail in the primary, he was asked by the party leadership to withdraw ("Frank, this is not your time"). Horton graciously withdrew and supported Weis's candidacy. By 1962, when Weis opted to retire following a cancer diagnosis that would claim her life within a year, the heavily GOP nature of an open seat should have meant that every Republican and their mother would file to seek a once in a lifetime opening. Instead, Horton had the field to himself and with the full support of the party, beat Democrat Robert Bickal with 59%.

Aside from his first race, the only election in which Horton took below 59% was his second when he was held to 56%. Beyond that, his lowest margin of victory was his last campaign – in 1990 when he took 63%. Horton did face a primary in 1984 but dispatched E. Kevin Rowlee 62-38%. He was endorsed by the Democratic Party twice and did not have a Democratic opponent in those elections.

In 1968, when New York Senator Robert Kennedy was assassinated, Governor Nelson Rockefeller called Horton and asked if he would be interested in being appointed to Kennedy's seat for the remainder of Kennedy's Senate term. Rockefeller and Horton were friends and shared similar Republican political philosophies. After much consideration, Horton declined the offer preferring to remain in the House where he felt he could better serve his constituents instead of having to run for election statewide and to be spread thin back home (he told those urging him that serving an entire state would mean they'd only see him back home several times a year). For Horton, serving in the U.S. Congress was always about being a constituent-based representative. Rockefeller appointed another upstate Congressman, Charles Goodell, to Kennedy's Senate seat. In 1970, Goodell lost the Senate seat in a three-way race to Conservative Party candidate James L. Buckley and Horton may well have met the same fate.

**With colleague and fellow World War II veteran Robert J. Dole
Photo courtesy of the Robert J. Dole Archives**

Horton set the stage for his accommodationist style in that first campaign. With a Democrat, John F. Kennedy occupying the White House, he vowed to not, "oppose the President's programs for the opposition sake, but rather, would support them when they are right and oppose them when they are wrong." He hinted at supporting Medicare by backing, "The Social Security approach with coverage for those not under Social Security."

Horton proved early on and in fact throughout his career, that he meant what he said about supporting a president when he agreed with the objective but not when he didn't. Shortly after being sworn in for his first term, Horton was told by the House Republican leadership to vote a certain way on a pending procedural vote to the Civil Rights legislation. Instead, he voted for the Kennedy initiative. Afterwards, an older Republican approached him and said, "Son, you voted the wrong way, you must have made a mistake." Horton assured him that he had not and it had consequences – he would tell others later in life that because of that vote, his name was removed from consideration to assignment to the powerful Judiciary Committee. Instead, he was given an assignment to what many considered a lesser committee - Government Operations (typical Horton, he made the most of it).

Besides supporting sweeping civil rights measures ("the great social drama of the century is the struggle for equality of our fellow citizens who are Negroes"), Horton voted for much of the "Great Society," and opposed GOP attempts to water down Medicare. Horton was on board with the idea of a National Arts and Humanities Foundation in his first Congress and, when it hit the floor in 1965, he was proud to speak of his hometown's contribution. "Rochester, New York, as I am confident my colleagues know, is a truly outstanding community of culture and education. We who are its citizens speak with pride when we discuss our universities, theaters, orchestras and the other elements of education and creative art."

Despite hailing from a part rural and industrial/union district upstate, Horton's time in the nation's capitol made him quite versatile to progress and in 1965, he proposed The Home Rule Act that would give the District of Columbia voting rights. It was enacted eight years later. In the early 1970s, he co-sponsored a measure creating a Consumer Protection Agency. When Ralph Nader charged that the Nixon administration had, "assumed a strong role behind the scenes and disciplining Republican members" into weakening the legislation, Horton called it, "absolutely false." His rationale for a measure was, "I believe that the totality of consumers are not well or fairly represented by the majority of self-anointed and poorly organized consumer spokesman who regularly take potshots at both business and government, in the name of all consumers." He called it "essential if both businessmen and their customers are to have adequate access to the huge complex and heavy-handed federal regulatory process, which affects all of our daily lives."

During the Ford administration, Horton sustained the president on a few override votes (Emergency Housing) but was not with him on bills such as prohibiting strip mining and public service jobs. In the late 1970s, he supported creation of a Department of Education, Department of Energy, the Alaskan Land Act and the Chrysler Aid package while opposing cuts to OSHA and a food stamp cap.

**Horton was a baseball fan but in this case, presented President
Gerald Ford with a Washington Redskins football
Photo courtesy of the Gerald R. Ford Presidential Library and Museum**

Horton did support the Gulf of Tonkin resolution but made clear in 1990 as members deliberated on another resolution authorizing the use of force that he had been had. Tonkin, he said, "was just a statement that U.S. warships had been attacked. I don't think anybody intended that would be a declaration of war. It wasn't debated as such. It was not a vote on the question of giving the president the authority to go to war...I didn't realize it until I was at a briefing with (Defense Secretary Robert) McNamara and Johnson some time later, after we're bombing Haiphong. I asked the question of the secretary, what's the authority? The president jumped up, pulled a rumpled copy of the Gulf of Tonkin resolution out of his pocket and read a few lines of that."

By the late 1980s and nearing the end of his third decade in Congress, Horton's thoughtful pragmatism was still far and wide. His party support score in 1988 was just 28% and he voted with Reagan just 30% of the time. He voted against his party's position 66% of the time in 1990, behind only his close friend, Massachusetts Republican Silvio Conte who had a 71% score. He supported George H.W. Bush with whom he had served just 32%

Specifically, Horton fought to curb acid rain, supported the Democratic minimum wage increase legislation, the Family and Medical Leave Act, the

Civil Rights Act of 1990 (reading the bill would lead opponents to "realize that hiring quotas are specifically prohibited as an unlawful employment practice,") as well as abortion rights without restrictions. In fact, when the Supreme Court in 1989 declared that states had the right to enact their own abortion laws, Horton chided them for not issuing a "firm" ruling, contending it, "could potentially lead to a chaotic situation in the coming months and years" and "an avalanche of legislation."

Horton did oppose the Brady Brady bill and most other gun control measures. And he had no hesitation in supporting the anti-flag-burning amendment and he once explained, "I feel very strongly about the American flag. I was in combat. I've seen people die for their country." He further verbalized his stance on the House floor. "The issue before us has been simply, and perhaps, irresponsibly, framed as one dividing those trying to defend freedom of speech against those trying to weaken this most cherished of American freedoms. Second, it has been framed as one dividing political opportunists seeking to wave the flag in an election year against those acting as courageous guardians of the Constitution." His view was, "the media has contributed largely to the simple framing of this issue."

Horton was very ambivalent about providing aid to the Nicaraguan contras but, that was hardly the case of Don Upson, his chief aide who was pressing him to back it. At one point in the conversation, Horton turned toward Upson and said, "Let me ask you something. Have you ever shot anyone? Have you ever had to shoot someone?" When Upson replied in the negative, Horton made his point. "Because I have (during World War II). "And before I ask someone to shoot something, I want to make sure" all other alternatives had been exercised.

Internal issues were different. Horton opposed term limits ("It's up to the people"), and when members of Congress took enormous heat for proposing a 50% pay increase, Horton was not so quick to condemn it. "We're talking about a level of pay for a job, which is a very important job. That's one of the problems we have. You don't get people who are qualified."

Battling presidents of his own party became routine for Horton. In 1973, Horton was among 12 Republican Congressmen urging President Nixon to enter into negotiations with the then-renegade nation of Cuba by backing a proposal put forth by Peru that would allow the Organization of American States to normalize relations. That same year, Horton was among 14 Republicans who charged the Nixon administration's "bargaining chip" with threatening to unravel future peace agreements.

When Ronald Reagan came into office, Horton was co-chairing the Congressional Northeast and Midwest Coalition. When the new president unveiled his first, fiscally austere budget in 1981, Horton was alarmed that the "safety net" would be gutted by the proposed cuts and met with White House Budget Director David Stockman about reversing them.

Horton had no real feeling either way on the Trident Peacekeeper missile but, when the administration was short votes, he figured he'd use his vote to gain leverage. Horton complained to Budget Director David Stockman that he was having trouble securing relief for a few communities back home. Stockman delivered and Horton announced his support for Trident. About six additional centrists followed suit.

Disagree with the 40th presidents priorities he did but Horton not only liked Reagan personally but admired the skills for which he enabled America to rise up from its malaise. About a week before he was due to leave office, Horton sent the President a letter telling him what he thought his legacy would be. It read, "I know you are proud of the economy, interest rates, employment – all the measurable things, but those are not why future generations will remember you. They will remember you for something far more substantial. You made Americans proud again. You put the country's crises of Watergate and Vietnam to bed and truly made us believe that, indeed, it is Morning in America. That is your legacy to the country, Mr. President." Several days later, Upson recalls being in Horton's office when a call came from the White House. It was the President who told him, "Frank, I am calling to tell you that I think the letter you sent me might be the nicest letter I have ever received, and I thank you for it." Of that call, Upson said, "Mr. Horton was very proud."

In 1988, Horton backed Vice-President George H.W. Bush for president over his fellow New York Republican Jack Kemp with whom he was not particularly close to (Bush and Horton conversely were World war II combat veterans who served together in the House). Bush won the election but that didn't prevent Horton from opposing him on many top initiatives.

How did Horton's Rockefeller style Republicanism go over with GOP colleagues? It was never a problem for Bob Michel, the Illinoisan who was Minority Leader and a good friend. Newt Gingrich was another story. Horton was not a fan of the fire-breathing Georgian and unsurprisingly made phone calls for his opponent, the centrist Ed Madigan of Illinois for the post of Minority Whip in 1989. After Gingrich won by two votes, Horton commented that Gingrich "told me he doesn't want to be a flame-thrower. I have to wait and see." He didn't have to wait long. Gingrich aimed a GOP conference proposal primarily at Horton and Conte requiring them to side with the party on at least 50% of votes in order to keep their posts. It was not enacted.

It was on the Government Operations Committee where Horton truly made his mark. He had long favored giving the Environmental Protection Agency (EPA) cabinet level status though opposed a provision in a House passed bill in 1989 that would create a Bureau of Environmental Statistics. The reason: Congress is "creating an office, the head of which is answerable to no one (and whose) work products – including policy analysis – can be reviewed by no one...even the Inspector General."

Horton likely had two proudest achievements with national ramifications – the Paperwork Reduction Act of 1980 and the Whistleblower Protection Act of 1990 – both of which were likely more difficult getting through than he had initially anticipated.

With the Paperwork Act, Horton saw a need to update the Federal Reports Act of 1942. Horton's first step was to chair a 14-member Commission on Federal Paperwork (New Hampshire Democratic Senator Tom McIntyre co-chaired the panel). Tom Steed, an Oklahoma Democrat who sat on the panel, said that under Horton's leadership, "we made the most impressive analysis yet attempted of this monstrous program. And we were determined to approach it with steps that would be of practical help to the average businessman and the average citizen..."

"By the time the commission concluded its work in September 1977, it had issued 36 reports and had offered 770 recommendations. Among its findings, the commission proffered that 'structural and procedural flaws' in the Federal Reports Act's clearance process 'preclude it from ever being fully successful in controlling the total paperwork burden on the American public.'" *The Washington Post* noted that Horton, "apparently without irony," proposed the Paperwork and Red Tape Reduction Act of 1979. That turned into the Paperwork Reduction Act with Texas Democrat Jack Brooks.

In speaking in favor of the bill on the House floor, Horton said it "provides for the implementation of a very important concept: That the Federal Government should treat information as a resource, not a free good, and manage information as it manages other resources. This concept has been near and dear to me ever since I learned, as chairman of the Commission on Federal Paperwork, how significant it can be. It should become near and dear to all the Members of this House as they realize the substantial economies its implementation can achieve." It cleared the House unanimously in March of 1980 and President Jimmy Carter signed it into law.

Horton was very close to his chairman, Democrat Jack Brooks
Photo courtesy of Steven Horton

Establishing an office of the Inspector General was another crowning achievement. That led to legislation that he sponsored with Brooks and another Democrat, H.L. Fountain of North Carolina. In fact, when Stuart Eizenstat complained of issues, "It was Congressman Horton who tried to calm down Brooks and stress the importance of establishing a good relationship with President Carter and his White House staff." Carter signed the Inspector General Act into law in October of '78.

Horton was not happy when Reagan, on his first day in office, dismissed 15 inspectors generals and confronted him about whether it was political (Reagan assured him that it wasn't). But the vocal disillusionment with the 40th president continued. When the Government Operations Committee examined Reagan's suspension of a federal contracting law in 1985, Horton protested as loudly as anyone on the committee. He asserted he didn't "think that anyone on the Republican side believes the President can appropriately and constitutionally say a provision of a law is not constitutional."

The Whistleblower Protection Act was sponsored with Colorado Democrat Pat Schroeder. Reagan vetoed it in 1988 and Horton did not sugar coat his frustration (it was a "reprehensible act."). By 1990, Bush expressed his willingness to produce a bill and one was molded together and passed without dissent.

Horton's other major committee was on the Postal Service Committee and he established a close rapport with rank and file workers. Specifically, he raised a ruckus when the Postal Service was cut by spending bills and the quality of service declined nationwide. Horton, along with full committee chair Bill Ford of Michigan, were instrumental in passing legislation that returned it to the "off-budget" status where it had been prior to 1973. Calling the Postal Service "unique," Horton said, "These other agencies get their revenues from taxes and user fees."

Override bill requiring confirmation of two management and budget officials

Locally, Horton spent his last decade in Congress futilely trying to get a settlement for Indian tribes in Cayuga and Seneca Counties that been fighting New York State since 1980 to regain land they felt had been illegally seized in 1795. Horton formed a task force to deal with the matter in 1983 but as the issue became intractable, vowed never to "introduce any settlement legislation that is not acceptable to the counties and the Indians. Nothing will be shoved down anyone's throat."

On other matters, Horton won funding for the National Technical Institute for the Deaf and the Microelectronics and Imaging Sciences Center. He worked on St. Lawrence Seaway's Lake Leveling issues, funding for the Women's Rights National Historic Park in Seneca Falls and the National Technical Institute for the Deaf at Rochester Institute of Technology. He fought against downsizing Seneca Army Depot and adding 13,000 acres of the Finger Lakes to his district. The Wine Equity Act was also his. When the Bush administration proposed reducing funding for the Great Lakes Fishery Commission (which administers lamprey control) which monitors the ell population), Horton vowed to fight to restore it).

Many times, Horton used his connections to achieve parochial results. Reagan Commerce Secretary "Mac" Baldridge was a close friend and one Friday afternoon in July of 1987, Horton visited him to advocate for stopping a very substantial disk storage (state of the art at the time) contract that Commerce had awarded to Sony which Kodak was contesting as not in the national interest (Kodak was a major upstate employer). Horton himself called the award biased and suggested the GAO investigate to which Baldridge responded angrily that Kodak would never sharpen their pencil enough to be competitive. Nevertheless, he promised to give an additional seven days. The conversation ended with Horton asking "Mac" about his weekend plans to which he replied that he was going to be taking part in a rodeo. Two days later, Upson was stunned to open the newspaper and read that Baldridge had been killed as the 1,200 pound sorrel on which Baldridge had been riding crushed him.

When it came to serving his constituents, Horton had his own tactics. Griffiss Airforce Base in Rome, New York was on example. Horton met with the general for a briefing at his capitol office, then took him down to the ornate Government Operations Committee room to meet "a couple of people." A couple meant 200, one of whom was the Comptroller General of the U.S. The general was not ecstatic over the tactic but Griffiss was spared. Postscript: A year after Horton left Congress, it closed.

Horton knew how to get a point across. One year, he was irked because a local teacher's union had sent him a letter expressing displeasure over a vote. In the midst of a meeting with them, he'd start filing his nails at which point he'd hold them up and say, "I've been with you my entire career." He also might have thought respect went two ways but found to his chagrin that it wasn't the case. One example was when the Postal Service rejected his advocacy in 1985 of moving a national training postal facility from Norman, Oklahoma to his area. He didn't mince words: "Their economic analysis is a disgrace and full of factual inaccuracies."

Horton was named chair of the Waterloo Memorial Day Committee as the 125th anniversary approached in 1991. When an Auburn constituent suggested a day representing volunteers, Horton proposed a National Volunteer Appreciation Day.

At home, much of Horton's popularity came from tireless pounding of the pavement and a second-to-none constituent service operation. Horton would spend many Saturday's at the Rochester Food Market where he'd know virtually everyone. Horton was so visible at home that even some Democratic challengers questione why they were undertaking their quest to unseat him. William Larson, who haphazardly took him on in 1976 called him "a good guy" and "the best constituent services congressman in the United States." He on the other hand was "naive" for making the race (it begs the question of why he challenged Horton again in 1982). James Vogel, the sacrificial lamb against Horton in 1988, conceded late in the campaign that, "There's probably nobody in here who hasn't received a flag from Congressman Horton, or at least known somebody who has." An Auburn High School Social Studies teacher told *The Post Standard*, "He's been here every year, whether there's an election or not."

Horton was renowned for blanketing his district with the American flag
Photo via Getty Images

Horton was more than happy to undertake seemingly esoteric crusades for his constituents. When an intern informed Horton's legislative director of allergic reactions that fragrance from magazines or mail pieces can bring, Horton wrote to the postal service. "Thousands of Americans suffer adverse health reactions, some of them severe, to samples which arrive in the mail without warning labels. It would seem to me that relatively little expense would be incurred to merely require a warning label on envelopes containing fragrance samples or that a flap be placed over a magazine sample to allow readers the choice of smelling the product."

Horton was proud to be a 24/7 representative of the people and on at least one occasion, was reminded of that via a literal rude awakening. It was 2:30

a.m. when the phone rang. Nancy Horton answered it and on the other end was a man with a distinct Italian accent saying, "she's a no work." What he meant was that his lights were out and, because neighborhood kids tended to throw rocks when it was dark, he needed them back on as a deterrent. Nancy implored the constituent to give them a few minutes and woke Frank who promptly called the CEO of Rochester Gas & Electric. The CEO naturally wondered why the matter couldn't wait until the morning but Horton told him, "if it's important for him to call me, it's important for me to call you." Ten minutes later, the constituent's electricity was back on.

Issues aside, Horton's personal nature was what defined him and he explained his style in early 1989: "I'm not a confrontationalist...Politics is not my bag...On the House Government Operations Committee I worked closely with Jack Brooks. He is one of my best friends" (the two shared an affinity as World War II vets and their Texas births). Upson recalls being appointed as Minority Staff Director of the panel and Brooks admonishing him that he had one challenge: "to get along with me." Upson did so and did it well as he sometimes traveled with Brooks in lieu of Horton. Brooks in fact appeared at a fundraiser for Horton and told donors, "I don't like Rpublicans but you can give money to this guy."

In that same interview, Horton said, "Now John Conyers is chairman, and he said if he had someone to pick as ranking member he would pick me." Conyers confirmed that it was mutual, saying when Horton announced his retirement that, "What was most extraordinary about Frank is his style. Frank prefers accomplishments that will help people rather than insider partisan squabbling that leads nowhere." That's not to say everything from roses between the two as Horton did complain to aides about being "ambushed" by Conyers from time-to-time but the bipartisan bit between the two men was generally stellar.

Horton was indefatigable to the press as well. Louise Hoffman of *The Auburn Citizen* wrote the following on his death: "Frank was easy to reach and he always answered every question. When he didn't know something, he said so. I appreciated his honesty, patience and his humor. He knew he was dealing with a neophyte reporter, but he never made me feel like one. He taught me not to be intimidated by politicians, and to listen hard to what they were, or were not, saying. There were times when I had to hold his feet to the fire on issues, but he always understood the media's responsibility to keep government accountable and the public informed. I don't recall him once being nasty or evasive."

Horton became a mentor to junior Republicans in both advice and aid. Serving on the Steering Committee, he was instrumental in helping a number his fellow New Yorkers of both parties gain prized committee seats – Ray McGrath on Ways and Means in 1981 and Jim Walsh of Syracuse to Agriculture in 1989 – the latter was based on the premise that the Empire State lacked a single member on Agriculture at that time. Fellow Republican David Martin, another recipient of Horton's help said, "A lot of people underestimate the importance and power he has." But it was Syracuse Republican George Wortley who might have most pinpointed to Horton's influence when he observed that he, "holds the power of life and death over the future of every member of the New York delegation."

So highly was Horton thought of that a 1987 testimonial event for him at the Rochester Convention Center drew 1,200 people (the money went to a scholarship in Horton's name). But his visibility among colleagues was different with state legislators. It may be hard to fathom in a time where politics have become downright noxious but the respect that Horton commanded within his home state colleagues that they selected him dean of the delegation, even though Democrats badly outnumbered Republicans. While Horton's congeniality was no doubt one reason, his proclivity to advocate for the state far away from Rochester instilled great respect.

Horton weathered a personally embarrassing incident in 1976 that for other members might have meant self-destruction career-wise. He was tailed by police for six miles on the New York State Thruway in Genesee County when they clocked him at 78 mph (he went up to 105). Two women were in the car – a date named Nancy Richmond and her very good friend and they were returning from dinner in Buffalo. Police immediately recognized Horton upon pulling him over and vowed to simply issue him a warning but Horton would have none of it. He insisted on the full citation because, "I'm not any different than my constituents." He was sentenced to 11 days in jail (released four days early for good behavior), fined $200 and ordered to take a driving class. Horton's attorney had urged him to fight the sentence but he declined. This was election time and local Republicans fretted with one telling *The Rochester Chronicle*, "I think he may be in trouble in Wayne County. The people there are rural, more conservative. I don't think they like this drunken driving business very much."

There were a few postscripts to the incident. Strongly suspecting local Democrats were behind the matter, Horton's family did not feel the newspaper's coverage was fair and balanced. One day, he summoned the reporter and his own lawyer to his office to present his side of the story to clear the record without nuances. A tape recorder was on hand and Horton authorized the now shaking reporter to take copious notes and use anything that was said in that interview for his story, so long as it was factual and presented in context. If not, Horton would take legal action against the paper. Not only did the reporter back off but he subsequently leave town, Frank married Nancy and come Election Day, his re-election was routine – his 66% was just 3% lower than two years earlier. At least some credited his refusal to use his status as a reason.

Horton's nary an election worry could not eradicate a far more precarious matter: redistricting. In 1982, Horton emerged unscathed even though the Empire State had lost an astounding five seats due to the census. For 1992, it became clear that three more seats would be lost. Because it was generally obvious that two of the losses would be absorbed by downstate Democrats, the third seat put Horton in the edge of the sphere. Early in the process, mapmakers envisioned a matchup between Buffalo area Congressmen John LaFalce, a Democrat and Bill Paxon, a Republican. But Paxon allies began making the case that Horton should be the odd man out. One reason was his age – Paxon was half of Horton's. The other was that Horton had been fairly docile when it came to making contributions to New York State legislators, while Paxon, as a former member of the body, had a great deal of recognition.

The final map placed Horton with Democrat Louise Slaughter, a very junior Democrat but a friend and from the very beginning, Horton had no stomach to challenge her. He decided to call it a career and announced his decision on the House floor. After running through his accomplishments and thanking his staff, Horton turned poignant. He cited, 'one more 'thank you' I must make. This one sits at the top of my list. To the thousands of people who went to the ballot box so many times, and who felt it was in their interest for me to serve on their behalf in Congress, you have my lifelong and heartfelt appreciation. You are responsible for the 30-year honor and privilege I have had to serve you in the House of Representatives and I thank you. It has been very gratifying over these years to have had your support. I care deeply about you, your problems and your hopes and dreams for your families and for this great country of ours. I loved my districts and my people and I was thrilled to serve them. It is not easy to say goodbye. His constituents most likely felt the same."

Very few members had been on the floor at the time of Horton's speech but, as it happened, the few that were sat on Foreign Affairs and were among his closest friend. One was Michigan's William Broomfield, himself bolting Congress at the end of the year. His sentiment was that, "It is going to be a great loss not only for your district and for the country, but probably here in the Congress when they are going to need people of your stature and stability to keep things moving in the right direction. Lower Hudson Valley Republican Ben Gilman whose comment, "I know his constituents are going to regret his decision" probably emulated the feelings of everyone.

After his final term ended in 1993 culminating 42 years of public and military service, Horton joined a law firm where he worked for the next 10 years. He died of a stroke in 2004 at age 84. Around the time of his 25th annual testimonial, Horton was asked how he'd like to be remembered. He hedged, then said, "Well, I guess the way to describe it is I hope people will say I knew Frank Horton and he helped me, and he helped my family." For a man whose life was filled with many missions, the one he most aspired to was met head on.

CHAPTER EIGHT

Though Never Banking Chair, Wylie Amassed Influence, Respect and Credibility to Become a Master Legislator

Introductory Tidbit: Not yet a member of Congress, Chalmers Wylie drove to Washington D.C. from Columbus during a blizzard around Christmas of 1966. He was told by Mel Dodge, the Recreation Director for the city of Columbus, that an application for federal funding for the Blackburn Recreation Center had long been languishing. Upon arriving, Wylie found the person with jurisdiction over the area who promptly reviewed the application and stamped it, "okay for funding." Dodge later hired a professional boxer, William "Dynamite" Douglas as a coach and his son, James "Buster" Douglas" would take lessons there that would lead to very hefty dividends (Douglas upset Mike Tyson in a match). Wylie often told the story to students he addressed.

Photo courtesy of Brad Wylie

Calling most politicians bland would probably be unwelcome but, for Chalmers Wylie, he didn't mind a bit. In fact he thrived by it. Wylie is ground zero for the notion that flashiness isn't needed in order to be a powerhouse. While the so-called permanent minority status of House Republicans prevented him from ever chairing the Banking Committee, Wylie's traits caused him to forge strong relations with Democrats on both the committee and the Ohio delegation that he commanded notable respect for.

Wylie's slow, labored voice defined him and for outside observers, his most notorious attribute may have been what one member's biography referred to as "an impressive pompadour." In the halls of Congress, the 6'3" Wylie towered when it came to hammering out intricate compromises – even more impressive given the fact that throughout his entire 26 years, he not only never held a gavel but often sat alongside an autocratic chair who did. It didn't hurt that loyalty was second-nature as former Governor and one-time Wylie campaign manager James Rhodes noted he was, "the most loyal person in public life that I've ever known."

Wylie's non-irritating style might have been at odds with his early character – he was a go-getter who vaulted to the top. A native of Norwich, Ohio, Wylie's family was not wealthy. He picked beans during school, was valedictorian at Pataskala High, and worked on the railroad to pay for his higher education at Otterbein College and Ohio State.

During World War II, Wylie enlisted in the Army in 1943, going overseas even though he lacked a visa. He was part of the 117th Infantry Regiment, became a First Lieutenant and landed at Normandy Beach post D-Day. In the coming months, Wylie would travel to Belgium, Holland, and Germany and was wounded on three separate instances from artillery fire. It was the harrowing missions though that became his true story during the war and yielded him many accolades. One such medal was the Bronze Star and it described his bravery thus: Beginning in August of 1944, "On two occasions, Lieutenant Wylie made reconnaissance under the most hazardous conditions of front-line campaign to select locations for the battalion aid station, and the excellent sites he selected contributed to the quick treatment and evacuation of the wounded."

First Row, Left to Right: Lt. Hunt, Lt. Haluslzak, Lt. Larson, Lt. San Fillippo, Lt. Daniel. Second Row: Chap. Karpinsky, Lt. Cowden, Lt. Col. Frankland, Lt. Melnick, Capt. Davis. Third Row: Capt. Freeman, Lt. Mawpen, Lt. Wylie, Lt. Twiner.

Photo courtesy of Brad Wylie

As if the trauma could not get more grievous, the battles of 1945 were even more chilling. Through this he wound up earning his Silver Star. As a colleague announced on the floor, "When the aid station of which Lieutenant Wylie, assistant battalion surgeon, crossed the Rhine River, the various sections were scattered and disorganized by heavy enemy artillery, mortar, and small arms fire. Lieutenant Wylie courageously moved from one end of the battalion sector to the other, contacting his men. Despite the intense fire, he reorganized his section and set up for operation. Then, under concentrated hostile mortar fire he led the way into a minefield and evacuated wounded men. Lieutenant Wylie's fearless actions and ability to overcome all obstacles saved the lives of a number of wounded men." This occurred in Germany on March 23, 1945.

Forty-five years later, Wylie sought to downplay any claim to heroism. "It was one of those things you don't think about at the time. We had to get them out of there to save their lives." The military had long since acknowledged his actions. In addition to the Bronze and Silver Star, Wylie was presented with the Purple Heart as well as the French Croix de Guerre with Oak Leaf Clusters. Wylie rarely spoke about his war experiences, however. In fact his son Brad recalls only two in-depth conversations, one of which resulted from his jeep driver during the war seeing him on C-Span and seeking him out. The two met and Wylie recalls the driver possessed a knack "for swerving at the right time."

Photo courtesy of Brad Wylie

Returning home, Wylie discovered his niche for law and went on to attain a J.D. from Harvard Law School. He had a quick rise in legal circles, becoming an assistant attorney general for Ohio then an assistant city attorney for Columbus. His election as the city's attorney came in 1953 with the help of Rhodes who served as his campaign manager. A 1956 campaign for Ohio Attorney General ended in a primary defeat at the hands of future U.S. Senator William Saxbe who eked out a 4,000 vote win over Harry Marshall 31-31% (Wylie took 24%). The "Buckeye State" elected Republican governor William O'Neill that year and he had a number of things in mind for Wylie, including heading the Ohio Workman's Compensation Commission. Wylie made the transformation to the legislative body in 1960 when he won a seat in the Ohio House. He would remain a legislator for 32 years.

Photo courtesy of Brad Wylie

In the legislature, Wylie worked on water measures, particularly incentives for industry to install equipment that would enhance the air quality. The bill was vetoed by Democratic Governor Mike DiSalle in 1961 but by '63, an old friend named Jim Rhodes was governor and he signed it into law. When Wylie became a Congressman, *CQ* wrote that "industries in the state have installed hundreds of millions of dollars worth of equipment since passage of the Wylie bill."

Ohio was required to adjust its Congressional boundaries for the 1966 Congressional elections and Wylie just so happened to hold a seat on the committee responsible for drawing them. That resulted in a Columbus-anchored district in territory where he was well-known and he had the extra advantage of the seat being open. He tried to appeal to labor by opposing repeal of Section 14B of Taft-Hartley (largely considered anti-union). He also backed programs such as Head Start, and won the seat with 60% of the votes. One of his classmates was future president George H.W. Bush and the Minority Leader was Gerald Ford. Wylie was assigned to the Banking Committee and Veterans Affairs.

That Wylie's focus near the end of his career was as a moderate who sought compromise belies the fact that early in his career, he was among the most vocal social conservatives in the House. In his first term and repeatedly thereafter, he sponsored an amendment to allow prayer in the schools. Specifically, he believed that state's and local governments should have the freedom to decide whether to implement it. In all likelihood the presence of the measure's Senate sponsor, Minority Leader Everett Dirksen, increased its already high visibility.

Photo courtesy of Brad Wylie

By 1971, Dirksen was deceased but Wylie kept pushing forward. His motivation had come from the Prayer Campaign Committee of Cuyahoga Falls who presented him a petition of 100,000 supporters of the measure. It advanced to a vote by the full House in 1971 after Wylie and other backers of the amendment embarked on a six-month campaign to secure the 218 signatures required to get the bill on the floor (proponents went over the top by three). The 240-162 result of the vote on the House floor was well short of the 2/3 required for passage. Wylie continued introducing the bill in future Congresses but priorities for leaders of both parties were elsewhere and Wylie was content to toil in obscurity and deal with matters within his senior position on the House Banking Committee.

Wylie's next bust with the limelight would come in his last few terms as Congress debated recovery from the Savings and Loan debacle. As Wylie prepared to retire, Iowa Republican Congressman Jim Leach, who would succeed him as ranking member of Banking, said the following: "As early as 1982, before anyone imagined the financial meltdown that would eventually occur within the S&L industry, Chalmers Wylie was fighting to strengthen the capital of savings institutions." That May, the House took up a federal guarantee of the net worths of certain thrifts regardless of the amount of losses in those institutions. Democrat Bruce Vento of Minnesota arduously credited Wylie promoting "closing the regulatory loopholes that had kept brain-dead S&L's open." The Federal Deposit Insurance Corp (FDIC) was losing money at an alarming rate and Wylie and Gonzalez sponsored a measure to replenish its revenue coffers by raising the deposit fee. It was approved within days, something rarely seen in Congress.

In 1987, Congress cleared a bill 382-12 to replenish the S&L coffers and restrict some of their activities, belying the fact that getting to that point wasn't easy. Wylie, calling the bill "a workable compromise" acknowledged that, "Not one of us would have written the bill in the form it is today. But Congress has worked its will. The President has said he will sign the bill."

Some aspects of Wylie's social conservatism lingered through his final years in the institution. In 1984, he opposed an appropriation to the Library of Congress for a braille edition of *Playboy Magazine* because he felt the publication promoted "wanton and illicit sex." He was one of just 38 members to vote to expel Barney Frank, with whom he had worked closely on the Banking Committee. When Frank expressed dissatisfaction to one of Wylie's Banking Committee staffers, he was told that his wife Marjorie's devout Catholic upbringing played a large part (Marjorie meanwhile would often tell friends she didn't believe she had much influence over her husband's general views).

**Left photo via the Ronald Reagan Presidential
Library; right photo courtesy of Brad Wylie**

On other social issues, Wylie was non-ideological. He opposed most gun control measures but had limits; including voting against hunting in several national shrines which was a stance that he was awarded for by The Fund for Animals. Later in his career, he supported the Brady Bill to require a seven-day waiting period prior to the purchase of guns. On the House floor, he explained his decision by pointing to a questionnaire that he sent to his constituents soliciting their views on the matter. Eighty-two percent responded in the affirmative, which Wylie called, "a pretty clear indication to me about how the public stands on this issue." Noting a dramatic spike in Columbus's crime rate, Wylie said, "The people I represent and the people of the Nation have sent a clear message, it seems to me, that they are fed up and they want something done to make the streets safe again."

Wylie almost always voted pro-life, but abortion was in no way central to his background or legislative portfolio. Flag burning, on the other hand, was a different story. When the House debated a proposed amendment to the Constitution making flag burning illegal, Wylie was unusually passionate in his support. While addressing the right to free speech, Wylie said during debate he would "suggest there is some difference between cussing somebody and hitting them in the mouth while you are doing it. That is the difference here. To me, there is a difference between saying something abusive about the flag, although I would object to that too, and an act of physical violence. Burning the flag is not just talk, but a physical assault." Wylie was also not a proponent of term limits which hurt him back home as he was trying to decide whether to seek re-election in 1992.

Wylie was typically quite supportive of Republican presidents but his backing was no blank check. As Watergate was on the verge of bringing down Nixon's presidency, Wylie read Nixon a letter from a constituent and asked, "How do I answer that?" In 1982, he backed President Ronald Reagan by just 56% on all votes, though that changed to 79% the following year.

One of the issues in the administration Wylie had problems with was aiding the Nicaraguan contras, a distinct minority within his party. This was despite Reagan phoning him. Wylie said he "had expressed serious reservations about sending the $100 million to the Nicaraguan opposition movement called the Contras because we've already sent about $100 million down there and I don't see that it's done that much good." After the vote he said, "I just wonder where the money would go. It seems to me as if it might have been throwing good money after bad." When Reagan called again that June, he switched his views and called him "a very persuasive fellow." The key however was that the new language now had, "...very strict accountability provisions. Now for sure we will know where the dollars will go." He voted to sustain Reagan's veto of the 1987 Highway bill.

One area where Wylie did not equivocate was on his longtime support of both a Balanced Budget Amendment and Line-Item Veto. On the former, he told a joint hearing of the Economic Committee, "Had it been in force over the last decade I don't think we would find ourselves in this dilemma where we are today with the huge budget deficit and the huge debt ceiling increase that we need to confront. It's possible that some would like to point the finger at other places, but there is no way that Congress can evade its primary responsibility for taxing and spending decisions under Article I of the Constitution and so we, in these Halls, need to come to grips with the problem."

Wylie's friendship with Bush also gave him unusually close access to the president. One occasion to which he used it to his advantage was enlisting Bush's help in getting China to loan pandas to the city zoo in 1992 for celebration of Christopher Columbus's 500th birthday. The pandas were said to have attracted a million people.

On a more serious note, Wylie recounted calling the White House for information following Iraq's invasion of Kuwait in 1990 and, "The next thing I know, the president's on the phone, saying, 'Hi, Chalmers. What's going on?'" Despite their friendship, Wylie was miffed when the president threatened to veto an intricately written savings and loan bailout that he had helped fashion. The veto threat was "bad timing and it showed bad political judgment on someone's part."

Wylie became ranking member on the House Banking Committee in 1982 and though he was able to work with the panel's chairman, Ferdinand St. Germaine, his abrupt manner was opposite of typical mellowness. This may have been why he embraced the new chair, Henry Gonzalez of Texas, with open arms. It is rare for chairman of a committee and the top member of the opposing party to work in tandem but Wylie and Gonzalez did just that. In fact, the pair worked so well together that Gonzalez came under fire from Democratic caucus members for partaking in an ad for Wylie's 1990 campaign (*Politics in America* cited complaints from younger Democrats that, "the chairman confides more in Wylie than his own party's members").

Gonzalez and Wylie worked together to make the Bush administration's savings and loan bill palatable with members of both sides. This resulted in the Financial Institutions Reform, Recovery and Enforcement Act (FIRREA). Another bill that came in late 1991 through the labors of the two men was the Comprehensive Deposit Insurance Reform and Taxpayer Protection Act. When the bill went to conference, Wylie was instrumental in having Section 151 restored which eliminated a would-be requirement sought by the New York delegation for all financial institutions to obtain federal deposit insurance. Wylie and Gonzalez also passed landmark housing legislation (Wylie told reluctant White House officials he was "determined to see that he gets a housing bill").

On other issues, Wylie in 1978 created the Neighborhood Reinvestment Program and in 1988, the National Services Expansion Act. This led to the National Association of Homebuilders presenting him with its first ever "American Dream Award." He voted for the 1986 legislation that would increase funds for legal advocacy and protective services for the mentally ill. In 1987, Wylie opposed legislation setting an eight percent cap on credit card rates. With Democrat Bruce Vento of Minnesota, he sponsored the Banking Interstate Efficiency Act of 1992 as his term was ending.

Wylie was a steward for downtown Columbus and his achievements for the locals spanned a sundry list of areas. For starters, the city has a very impressive shopping mall – the Columbus City Center, and Wylie worked hard to secure a $17 million grant from the UDAG. The Arthur G. James Cancer Hospital and Research Institute at Ohio State was another example of his assiduous work. He secured funding for the Franklington floodwall in West Columbus that was earmarked in an appropriations bill in the fall of 1992, just as he was preparing to depart Congress. Having already helped bring a Veterans Center to Columbus, a colleague and close friend by the name of Ralph Regula noted in 1992 that Wylie was again "ahead of the curve" by thinking that the best remedy for overcrowding was to have outpatient facilities for vets. Thus, he was able to get the VA to partner with medical facilities to treat veterans. The Blackburn Recreational Center was yet another endeavor of his.

Among colleagues, Wylie was widely respected. In 1989, fellow Ohioans selected him as Dean of the delegation even though Democrats had an 11-10 edge. Republican Bill Gradison of Cincinnati called him "a very outgoing, great man." On a lighter note, Wylie was a devotee of Ohio State football games.

Wylie almost never took digs at critics but one particularly noteworthy instance came at the expense of former Defense Secretary Clark Clifford. The famed advisor to Harry S. Truman in 1981 had called Reagan, "an amiable dunce" and ten years later, was testifying before Banking about his link to the Bank of Credit and Commerce (BCCI) scandal. Wylie posed the question: "Were our witnesses amiable dunces or were they sophisticated financial kingpins?" *The Columbus Dispatch* reported that, "Clifford seems to wince a bit." On a more serious note, Wylie scoffed at Clifford's notion that they were in the dark about BCCI's activities calling it, "very hard for me to swallow, the fact that they were counsel for BCCI, they had financial connections with them and they didn't know that there was a tie between BCCI and First American." Clifford, he said, was a "highly paid front man."

Image via C-SPAN

Though the iteration of Wylie's district changed through several remaps, most of the west side of Columbus endured. Since the 60% Wylie took in his '66 campaign, he routinely went on to win in the 70 percentile. Even in 1986, when he faced a well-funded doctor, Wylie unveiled a group named "Physicians for Wylie" and took 65%. 1990 was different, although. Wylie voted for the final budget summit package that officially broke Bush's "no new taxes" vow and general dismay with Washington was high. Wylie's opponent, a 26-year old guidance counselor named Thomas Emery, displayed great enthusiasm that caused his career-low 59%. Most of Wylie's campaigns were run in his living room, and through the entirety of his career he never bashed an opponent. For one, he felt there was no need to generate name recognition for his foe but more importantly, he saw no virtue in tearing someone down without standing for something.

At the start of 1992 it appeared as though Wylie was making preparations to seek another term. Redistricting was looming and both parties didn't conceal the fact that at least one Republican would have to go. For the most part Wylie appeared safe, but that was before the check bouncing scandal became known. Before the full list of names were released, it was revealed that Wylie had written 515 overdrafts that amounted to $87,049. As such news was emerging, the new map was just being worked out and Wylie said he would reevaluate his plans based on how dramatically his district was redrawn. His spokesman Bill Keesee maintained, "The check issue would not, under any circumstance, keep him from running again. The problem which developed with the operation of the House bank is not an issue with (the) Congressman." Wylie himself predicted that, "Before the year's out this will be a non-issue because it will be ascertained that I did nothing wrong." But local Republicans conducted a poll to test Wylie's standing and he evidently decided it was not worth the fight. He ultimately announced his retirement in late March of 1992.

At the time, Wylie described his announcement as, "a relief... Marjorie has been telling me since the last election she would prefer I not run again." He spoke of going "through some anxious moments about it. I like my job. I had the opportunity to serve the district and the people of Columbus...I thought 26 years was enough." He also conceded, "There is an ugliness in the House now which does not appeal to me" but acknowledged that being in the "permanent minority" was also beginning to faze him. Wylie stated, "the role of ranking Republican on the Banking Committee, with his frustrations and lack of opportunity to make the big difference, does not have that much appeal to me." Yet *Columbus Dispatch* Washington Bureau reporter Roger Lowe wrote on Wylie's death that the emerging tenor might have at least loomed in the back of his mind. "The harsh style of Rep. Newt Gingrich of Georgia, who helped Republicans rise to power in the 1994 elections by attacking the Democratic-majority Congress, was anathema to Wylie.

He didn't like assaults on the institution of Congress, partly because, as a longtime member, he had become part of the institution."

This was evident up until Wylie prepared to depart as colleagues of both parties sung his praises. Mary Rose Oakar, a Democrat from Cleveland, said that, "Rarely has a public servant brought as much thoughtfulness, civility and honor to the sometimes rough-and-tumble political behavior of this body, as has Wylie...the calm voice and constructive views of Chalmers Wylie have helped to temper partisan passions and soften the hard edges of debate while counseling the necessity of bipartisanship in the solution of our country's problems."

Wylie returned to practicing law, and eventually passed away in 1998 at age 77 due to a heart attack. The following year, a Veterans Center in Columbus was renamed the Chalmers P. Wylie VA Ambulatory Care Center in his honor. As he prepared to retire, House Minority Leader Robert Michel credited Wylie with having a singular desire: "to work – not to pose, not to indulge in fancy rhetoric, not to seek the media spotlight, but to do the job for his constituents, his colleagues, and his country."

On his death, Lowe wrote a column entitled, "Wylie Abhored Tactics That Have Transformed Washington Politics." It concluded with the sentence, "No, Chalmers Wylie would not have fit in well in today's Washington." After all, Wylie mutually found the good in everyone. As Indiana Democrat Andy Jacobs once said, "Anybody who does not like Chalmers Wylie does not know Chalmers Wylie."

**Waving goodbye to Capitol Hill with his devoted
staff as his final term came to an end
Photo via the Library of Congress**

CHAPTER NINE

"Five Percent Clarence" Miller a Congressman
of Both Responsibility and Integrity

Introductory Quote: "I can't call the sheriff at 3:00 in the morning on Christmas Eve!" –A constituent's response to Congressman Clarence Miller's query about why he telephoned him rather than the sheriff about barking dogs at 3 a.m. on Christmas Eve. The man rubbed salt in the now fully awake Congressman by adding, "I thought you said that you worked 24 hours a day, so I didn't think it made any difference."

Image via C-SPAN

In a body full of egos and publicity seekers, Clarence Miller was content only to draw attention from his colleagues or the national press when he wanted to make a point. In the late 1970s, that proved fairly often though only for the purpose drawing attention to an issue that he cared about (spending restraint). But before and after, the man who both came to Washington and left with George H.W. Bush was content simply to roll up his sleeves and toil behind the scenes to bring the goods to Southern Ohio. And whether one liked his voting record or not, the feeling toward Miller may have been unanimous that he was an honorable man who rarely if ever took cheap shots and who provided quality and capable representation.

A Republican who represented Ohio's Tenth Congressional District, Miller epitomized the words courtly (for which nearly every publication has labeled him), a true gentleman, and highly principled. And it started during his early years when Miller became a product of his time in the only town in which he'd ever live, Lancaster, Ohio.

Miller typified the American story for a middle-income boy growing up during the Great Depression. The third of six children, his father was an electrician and Miller during high school delivered *The Lancaster Eagle Gazette* and unloaded trucks at the Omar Bakery. Chalmers Wylie, a fellow Ohio Republican from the class of 1966, noted in his farewell for his colleague on the House floor that, "this kept him from often returning home until after midnight, and then rising early the next morning to attend classes." Miller attained his secondary education from the International Correspondence School in Scranton, Pennsylvania, primarily in mathematics and engineering. He married his high-school sweetheart Helen in what became until a true til death do they part story (she passed in 1987 as Miller was beginning his third decade in Congress).

Miller's employment commenced at the Columbia Gas CO. as an electrical engineer. Because he strikes many as kind of a citizen legislator, it was appropriate that at this point, he was awarded two patents – one from the U.S. and another from Canada, which bore his name.

Miller's political career began with an appointment to the Lancaster Council in 1960. Soon after, he became Mayor and proved highly popular. A prime reason: he did not simply pursue that role as mayor of a small town. He tirelessly fought to attract industry and succeeded.

In 1966, Miller embarked on a run for Congress and it was very risky. The thought might never have entered his mind had it not been for a visit from the Democratic incumbent, Walter Moeller at the Mayor's office. Miller's daughter Jackie recalled Moeller "came in dressed in a long western cape, a cowboy hat and boots, and pounded on Dad's desk demanding something." Jackie said he "despised pretense" and recalls him saying, "Right then I decided I'm going to have his job." The President of the Ohio Fuel Gas Company evidently believed in him: he granted Miller a year off with pay.

Though Miller had won a four-way primary with 56%, (34 points ahead of his nearest rival, Fred Berman), his odds against Moeller did not seem bright. The incumbent had been unseated in 1962 but, having regained the seat two years later, appeared to have decent odds of holding again. But Southern Ohio, like the rest of the nation, was moving away from the fervor for which they had embraced the "Great Society" in 1964 and Miller seemed to be articulating balance. One example: "We are not against all federal spending but we are against misguided and reckless giveaways which can be used for political purposes." He spoke of enacting a highway system throughout the communities. On a lighter note, Miller got kicks out of telling the story of a campaign aide who hit a chicken while driving the future Congressman.

Moeller had the backing of organized labor but Miller ousted the incumbent 52-48%, a margin of just under 4,401 votes. He carried eight of the district's 11 counties, including populous Fairfield, his home county by 2,000 votes, half of his margin. Moeller told supporters, "We attempted to fight a good fight. The voters decided otherwise." A classmate of Miller's was a young Texas Congressman named George H.W. Bush. As the term was getting under way, the two men shared adjoining rooms in a building near the Capitol and their wives became so close that when Helen died, Barbara Bush, by this time the wife of the vice-president, delivered the eulogy.

**Holding his granddaughter Amy as Richard Nixon
reaches for the Ohio crowd in 1968
Photo courtesy of Amy Miller-Jackson**

For a part of Ohio that was solidly Republican by the time Miller left office, it was more mixed during his first half and Gerald Ford only carried the district 50-48% as he was losing the Buckeye State in 1976 – even a slightly better showing here could have erased his 11,000 statewide deficit. But Miller's hold was superb and he would never again know a tough general election campaign. In 1968, he was up to 69% and with one exception, would routinely rack up 2/3 until 1990, when he defeated repeat candidate John Buchanan by a margin of 63-37%. He was assigned to the Agriculture and Public Works Committees and in 1973, moved to the big enchilada as committees go, Appropriations. A friend, Illinois Democrat Frank Annunzio said Miller's engineering background enabled him to bring "with him a knack for weighing policy choices in the light of hard realities."

Photo courtesy of Amy Miller-Jackson

In his early years in Congress, Miller would enlighten colleagues with what he called his, "Take Pride in America." Presented via *The Congressional Record*, Miller used this as an opportunity to expose America's greatness to his colleagues. Other endeavors: working with the US Army Corps of Engineers to have them dredge the Hocking River in order to prevent future flooding (the river wrapped around the Ohio University campus in Athens). A lock and dam project at Gallipolis was long in the making to bring about a smooth flow for shipping. And he consistently watched over the air force installations was another priority.

Spending was where Miller's ardent conservatism came out and it began – at least vocally, on 1976 Appropriations measures. As the House began taking up each of the 13 Appropriation bills for Fiscal Year 1977, Miller would regularly introduce his amendment providing for a five percent across the board spending cut. There was the Agriculture Appropriation bill, Interior, Defense, Housing, Labor, etc. Most of Miller's proposals garnered on either side of 100 votes in the 435 member House with one exception: Foreign Aid which saw 187 members vote in the affirmative. While the proposal would still fall short, it would set the stage for surprising passage the following year. Meanwhile, colleagues would bestow on Miller a nickname: "Five Percent Clarence."

Miller stated his logic on the Agriculture Appropriations bill for Fiscal Year 1977, the third such bill on which he attempted to make the cut. Citing the $100 billion federal budget that America operated under in 1962, Miller declared, "it took 186 years to get to that first budget of $100 million. In 9 short years later, in 1971, we had a budget of $200 billion." He then proceeded to tell colleagues that the budget had exploded to $300 for FY1975 and, "Two years later, we come up with a $400 billion budget. Somewhere-somewhere we must find a way to reduce or we will be going the direction of many countries before us."

It was obvious that Miller wasn't preaching rhetoric – but that he was making a case for what he truly believed. "Mr. Speaker," he said in one debate, "I am sincere. I feel that we need to reduce the spending." Miller's view was that all members had an obligation to make tough choices. "Believe me," he said, "I had plenty of items in those bills for my district, just like others have for their districts." Colleagues were rarely insulted. Mississippi Democrat Jamie Whitten who chaired the Agriculture Subcommittee (and later the full Appropriations panel), responded by calling Miller and a few other advocates "good friends," adding, "I appreciate your view."

Photo courtesy of Jackie Williams

In later years, Miller became accustomed to proposing two percent cuts because he knew that was the best he would likely get. In the 1980s, Miller turned to other causes such as reducing the number of yearly Congressional mass mailings from six to three (Miller and his staff were able to make due with two mailings and a survey). Nor did Miller see the logic in the assignment of two aides to members of Appropriations (he had one). The effort to limit the mailings failed but Miller took a fatalistic attitude, as he had with all of his losses: "All we can do is keep working on it." Whether colleagues knew it or not, Miller had credibility on this issue because of his own personal frugality. He and his wife had driven their Pontiac to Washington as he prepared to become a Congressman and, departing Washington for the final time 26-years later, drove a Buick back to Ohio, though Helen Miller had passed by then.

Fiscal issues aside, Miller was conservative but not an ideologue by any means. Though he rarely deviated from Republican orthodoxy, he voted against expelling Massachusetts Democrat Barney Frank when other, more moderate GOP colleagues did not. He took issue with Pat Buchanan's isolationism during his challenge to Bush during the 1992 primary season. "The pledge I intend to make this New Year's, and one I would encourage all of my fellow citizens to make, is to buy American whenever possible. To some, I suspect this will sound trite and simplistic (but) we as consumers will be giving our nation's sluggish economy a much needed shot in the arm." He said he voted against recognizing Jerusalem as the capital of Israel only because he felt it might make the conflict worse.

When it came to courting constituents (even if they weren't voters), Miller was as versatile as they get. Here he is visiting a junk-yard Photo courtesy of Jackie Williams

Miller didn't take to the House floor very often, particularly in later years but, when he did, he surely knew what he was talking about. The 1985 fight over the MX missile was one example. "We have all been deluged with articles and commentary on both sides of this issue. We have heard from our constituents-again, on both sides of this issue. This is all as it should be. That is our free and democratic process in action. We all love and want to pre- serve this free and open society. And that is exactly the point I want to make now. Unfortunately, not all the people of the world have the privilege of living in free societies. Was there a great public debate in the Soviet Union, involving citizens and free media, questioning the production and deployment of over 600 SS-18's and SS-19's, both of which carry multiple war- heads? Are Soviet citizens writing to the bosses in the Kremlin to express their views, and are these views being taken into consideration in determining Soviet policy? Of course not. It is a tragedy, but the fact of the matter is that the Soviet Union is ruled by a few powerful men, who oppress their own people, and seek to dominate other nations. That is what we are up against in dealing with the other superpower."

For years, Miller was ranking Republican on the Treasury/Post Office Subcommittee on Appropriations but, in 1983, he moved to Defense where he'd rank third. But his devotion to his district was unquestioned – he didn't miss a single vote until the first few months of his final term when he was sidelined by a bout with diverticulitis.

Photo courtesy of Linda Roderick

Then there was Miller the public servant. His accessibility was unquestioned. John Carey, who in later years would win election to the Ohio

House said Miller, started with the Congressman in the district. He called him, "a very kind man…was also genuine in that he was the same person whether he was in Waterloo or Washington. I learned many of the values that I use in representing my constituents from Congressman Miller." He was very fond of people and would never shy away from meeting constituents. His daughter Jackie said, "there was no place he wouldn't go to talk to people about what they needed and what they thought." It made no difference if their voting status was in question. "He would tell the driver to stop the car if he saw someone who likely wouldn't go in town to vote."

**George H.W. Bush was a Congressional classmate of
Miller's and Barbara Bush spoke at Helen's funeral
Photo courtesy of Linda Roderick**

Nor would Miller cease serving them at the most seemingly inopportune times. On many occasions, Miller would join his wife at the beach. She was in swim-gear and he a three piece suit. A staffer would invariably bring him letters to sign. So hard at work was Miller on behalf of his district that his granddaughter, Amy Miller-Jackson recalls, "he would wait until the absolute last second to respond to the bells on the clock in his office (signifying a House vote) and then he would fly out of the office and walk-run past the train with me in a full run behind him barely keeping up. He would say 'come on girl - we have to go save the nation!'" Jackson adds, "He never used the word "I.' Instead he used 'We.'" A particularly tough decision on how to vote usually meant he'd be pacing behind his desk. So proud of her grandfather was Miller-Jackson that she was enthralled with "hanging out" with him in his posh Rayburn House office with its view of the Capitol.

Staff appreciation was also a hallmark Miller virtue as he would regularly treat his team to lunch near Christmas time. Linda Roderick was Miller's right-hand assistant for most of her 19 years with Miller. Though she began her employment at the lowest level in his office, she rose to become one of two office managers who was supervising casework from the district office in Lancaster, Ohio. She recalls "no two days were ever the same" and lunch on the run typically was a hamburger with onions. While, "Mr. Miller" could be curt with some employees (more so the male's) if work wasn't being done, he was a joy to work with. The same went for Capitol Hill employees as Roderick recalls many-a-police officer telling her how kind Miller and his wife were to them. Incidentally, Roderick got a unique perspective of Miller post-Congress. He proposed to her at a White House Christmas party and they tied the knot four years later. It's safe to assume she ceased calling him "Mr. Miller."

Miller was not outgoing in the sense that his lack of formal education made it difficult to be gregarious with some of his colleagues who were Ivy Leaguers. Still, he enjoyed deep friendships with senior members of both parties including Charlie Bennett of Florida, Jimmy Quillen of Tennessee, John Paul Hammerschmidt of South Carolina, Willaim Broomfield of Michigan and an Ohioan he would enter and leave the House with, Chalmers Wylie.

Photo courtesy of Linda Roderick

Bob Livingston, a Louisiana Republican served on the Defense Subcommittee with Miller. He recalled in his farewell to his colleague in 1992 that, "Clarence alternatively sat in long and drawn-out hearings, upright and soldierly as always, in his courtly and gentlemanly fashion, asking tough, direct and pertinent questions, always aimed at saving the taxpayer some hard earned money."

Livingston also recalls a trip to Saudi Arabia to visit U.S. troops shortly before the start of Operation Desert Storm." He explained that "a number of members and staff contracted food poisoning," and were sidelined as a result. "But not Clarence. Clarence maintained a vigorous schedule on the trip, only excusing himself periodically for a few minutes each time. Thereafter, he would be impeccably dressed and rigidly composed, and you would never have known Clarence was ill. Clarence knew how ill he was – as the ailment required several hospitalizations for removal of part of his intestine. Still, Livingston made the point, "I realized how tough Clarence Miller really is." Incidentally, Miller had a grandson in the Gulf war, the only member to have that distinction (he supported the use of force).

Miller's effortless re-elections surely meant that he could have continued winning his seat indefinitely if only he would have a seat in which to run. 1992 eviscerated that. The end result was ultimately anti-climactic – Miller had been openly talked of as a probable odd-man out for years prior to the drawing of the lines. Reapportionment would mean that Ohio had to shed two seats, Miller would be turning 75 and, having not served in the legislature unlike some of his younger and more aggressive GOP colleagues in the delegation, he lacked the contacts in Columbus. But the saga itself was quite protracted and Miller came within an eyelash of holding on. Democrats held the Ohio House and Republicans the Senate and they were initially unable to agree on a final product to send GOP Governor George Voinovich into the early months of 1992 (the Senate version would indeed deep-six Miller by putting him in with Democrat Doug Applegate but amazingly, the Senate kept the 10th whole). Meanwhile, the stalemate led to the state's filing deadline being pushed back a month. In late March, a compromise was reached and the district was indeed carved up four different ways. Though Fairfield was placed in the district with freshman Republican Dave Hobson, a fair number of Miller's constituents were in the district of a six-term Republican Bob McEwen. The differences promised to be stark. McEwen was an aggressive 42-year old who aspired to higher office while Miller was a laid back, gentleman not comfortable with slash and burn.

The primary almost didn't go to fruition. After slipping on a bar of soap in the shower just prior to the primary campaign, Miller called a press conference. Many believed he was preparing to announce his retirement. Instead, as *The Almanac of American Politics* noted, he slammed McEwen for the overdrafts, yet also, for denying statements he had made, saying, "Time and time again, Bob looked across the desk at me and either denied saying what was attributed to him by the press, or contended I misunderstood what he had told me," adding, "I had never seen such a performance since Pinocchio." McEwen in turn expressed bemusement as to why Miller was challenging him, claiming, "I tried to be his best friend in the delegation." Meanwhile, Miller joked that, "I'm ready to go, but not as fast as before I went to the hospital."

**Miller attends a celebration for Ernest Petinaud, the
Maitre d' of the Member's Dining Room in the US
Capitol Building who was retiring after 40 years
Photo courtesy of Linda Roderick**

Miller was not shy about raising the bank issue, stating, "I have dealt with that bank for many years. If the bank was so bad and mismanaged, why don't I have a problem?" A Miller commercial noted "the score with bounced checks was 166-0." *The Columbus Dispatch* might have best summed up a key stylistic difference which for Miller, was probably detrimental for such a tight race. "While his ads are tough on McEwen, Miller in person is clearly uncomfortable in attacking McEwen's record." But many issues loomed beyond checks. One was Miller's age which McEwen implicitly raised, saying, in one interview that he was "42 and not ready for a rest home yet."

As the first returns reported, McEwen led Miller by 2,000 votes. But that gradually diminished and when the dust settled, Miller's deficit closed to a mere 269 votes. He refused to concede, claiming irregularities in late-reporting Highland County where McEwen lived and Republican Secretary of State Bob Taft did conduct an informal investigation. By August, Miller was out of money and dropped his challenge, his long tenure sealed by 286 votes (33, 194 to 32,908 votes).

Miller returned to Lancaster where he spent his last two decades. He always made time to advise aspiring GOP candidates for any office. He died in 2011 at age 93. Former Fairfield GOP Chair Steve Davis said, "I think of Clarence Miller as an icon who was a public servant at a time when it was about public service. He was a person who operated on principle and never for personal motivation or personal gain."

Miller in retirement
Photo courtesy of Linda Roderick

CHAPTER TEN

Hammerschmidt had Close Proximity to Presidents Bush, Clinton And Honor

Introductory Quote: "Bill (Clinton) always tells me that had I not defeated him, he would never have become president." – Congressman John Paul Hammerschmidt before adding that, "knowin' Bill, he'd a probably found his way in the White House anyway."

Bill Clinton famously lost his first bid for elective office. It was 1974 and the future president was a 28-year-old professor seeking a U.S. House seat in Northwest Arkansas. His conqueror was John Paul Hammerschmidt, a four-term Republican who deserves as much credit as anyone for making Arkansas a two-party state. That's pretty impressive trivia but for Hammerschmidt, there's more where that came from. Another member of the Class of 1966 from which Hammerschmidt made it to Congress was George H.W. Bush and they became close friends who, even as president, traveled to Capitol Hill for dinner with his colleague and hosted him on his yacht. Hammerschmidt's proximity to both presidents is a part of his story. More consequently, so is his ties to the changing South.

Hammerschmidt explained his early history in an oral interview with the David and Barbara Pryor Center at the University of Arkansas in 2009. "Dad was a boxer and an Army veteran who served on the Mexican border (on boxing, Hammerschmidt said, "I never did care for it myself"). Though his father went to business school, it wouldn't take him long before realizing the lumber business was his passion and he ran the Hammerschmidt Lumber Company. Young John's first memory of a radio in Harrison "was kind of a new deal, and it would play, but it'd have a lotta static, but it did go on and off and on. And people would sit around outside and listen to the World Series in that speaker - in that radio." In high school, Hammerschmidt was a member of the band. He started with the saxophone but ended up playing the French horn.

**Photo courtesy of the David and Barbara Pryor
Center for Oral and Visual History**

For Hammerschmidt, initial higher education was the University of Arkansas and the Citadel but that was put on hold when he enlisted in the U.S. Army Air Corps during World War II. Eventually, he became a pilot with the Third Combat Cargo Group and flew 217 missions, including cargo planes over the famous but treacherous "Burma Hump" in Southeast Asia. So harrowing was the topography that a publication on Hammerschmidt's death wrote that, "the Army Air Corps lost 17 planes and 92 crewmen in one day just because of bad weather. Any mechanical failure or pilot error could mean death in the barren, unforgiving terrain below even if the crew survived a crash." More than once, a landing in rice paddies was required for Hammerschmidt and his crew.

The fear of being shot down also existed. "You'd take quite a bit of fire," he recalled to the Pryor Project, "but those ol' planes were very sturdy. C-47s are marvelous. I mean, they've saved my life many a time." Yet Hammerschmidt was circumspect; "We had it easy compared to D-Day in Europe."

Hammerschmidt recalled that while many of his comrades stopped after the requisite 125 missions, "I kept stayin' on" and was eventually assigned a Traffic Control Officer in Lashio, Burma that had fallen to the Allies. "I lived in an old, bombed-out barracks there next to a [Mitsubishi G4M3 Model 34] Betty [bomber flown by the Japanese] that had been shot down right next to it, and I stayed there in that." One of his tasks was to move mules from Burma to China by airplane and he recounts taking off the doors of the aircraft to accommodate the weight. Hammerschmidt refers to the conflict in China and Burma as "a forgotten war," because, "Europe and Japan were getting all the action."

At war's end, Hammerschmidt was awarded the Distinguished Flying Cross with three oak leaf clusters, the Air Medal with four oak leaf clusters, three Battle Stars, the China War Memorial Medal (by the Republic of China), and the Meritorious Service Award. He retired from the Air Force reserve as a major. He completed his education at Oklahoma State and remained a member of the U.S. Air Force Reserves for 15 years following his discharge.

Photos courtesy of the David and Barbara Pryor Center for Oral and Visual History

For everything that Hammerschmidt put in to building a modern day Republican Party, he never thought of himself as the one to carry its torch. As he explained, he initially was more of a behind the scenes guy but, that didn't last too long. "I began to get involved with friends of mine trying to establish a two-party system. We all came out of a Democrat heritage, basically. But we thought, 'Well, you know, the election's over in Arkansas in June, when the [Democratic] primary is. That's it because there's no need to have any other elections.' So we just tried to establish competition in government. The more I got involved, the more I picked up responsibility." That responsibility soon meant being state committeeman to Harrison County and soon, chair of the state party.

Meanwhile, the Third District had a very capable Congressman named Jim "Judge" Trimble, 72, an eleven-term Democrat who happened to be a friend of the family. Hammerschmidt had nothing against him but he wanted the Republican Party to establish credibility and, he felt the 44% that Trimble's 1964 opponent received could be expanded ("that's almost like a win for a Republican in the third district"). The challenge was trying to recruit local folks to run and the invariable response was, "Well, John Paul, why don't you do that?" He finally obliged and he quickly realized, "this is serious stuff." The fact that his son John was attending prep school in Virginia made a Congressional bid especially convenient, though Hammerschmidt insists he had not been pondering one when he sent him there.

To say Hammerschmidt was a hands-on candidate is an understatement. "I devised my own campaign, and I ran my own campaign, which they tell you never to do," he recalled in the oral history project. "And I wrote all my own ads, which they tell you never to do." He recalls he, "ran a very retail campaign just like Bill Clinton did against me in '74. I went under every grease rack and shook hands...I went to every county fair, and I had a booth in every county fair.... I hauled a - a big ol' trailer that had speakers on it, and it had big signs - 'Hammerschmidt.'" He also had a jingle mimicked from the children's rhyme, "John, Jacob, Jingleheimer Schmidt." It went:

"Let's vote for John Paul Hammerschmidt, that is his name.

Whenever they go out, the people always shout,

'Let's vote for John Paul Hammerschmidt,' da da da da da da da"

One reason for Hammerschmidt's cautiousness might have been that he put $20,000 of his own money into the campaign (his campaign spent $68,000 in total). *The Hope Star* detailed other attributes: "Slender and curly haired, Hammerschmidt is not yet at ease on a speaking platform. He tends to quote others to illustrate his positions." What Hammerschmidt had no trouble enunciating was that Trimble was a "down the line" vote for the Johnson administration or that the engagement in Vietnam was "no-win."

The campaign slowly picked up steam and, "The Friday before the election, a pollster I knew in Little Rock told me it was 45-45 (percent) and I was peaking. He said I'd win with 54 percent. I had a lot of faith in him so I was confident I would win. I wasn't surprised on election day...Everyone always assumed I was just stunned by it because no one except me and that pollster expected it." With coattails from Winthrop Rockefeller who was winning the governorship, Hammerschmidt grabbed 53%, a win of just shy of 10,000 votes.

Hammerschmidt issued a statement on election night in which he pronounced himself "deeply grateful to all of the people of the Third district and of course especially to my friends and neighbors of Harrison and Boone County who gave me such a substantial margin to help elect me as their representative in Congress...The people have spoken their belief in the two party system of government and their conviction that they want a Congressman who puts their best interests above party label. I will be that kind of Congressman." He and Trimble remained friends.

Besides Bush, other classmates and close friends were Sam Steiger of Wisconsin and Tom Kleppe of North Dakota. He also found an ally and close confidante from an unlikely person: Wilbur Mills, the legendary and colorful chair of the Ways and Means Committee. Mills was a Democrat but, more importantly, a fellow Arkansan and that superseded all partisan considerations. Hence, Mills and Hammerschmidt would meet every morning and he recalls Walter Little, the chairman's chauffeur, telling him to "just stand by" if the chairman hadn't yet finished his daily crossword puzzle.

**Photo courtesy of the David and Barbara Pryor
Center for Oral and Visual History**

Hammerschmidt knew he had a tough road to hoe to solidify himself in a historically Democratic area – if that was even possible, but establishing a rapport with his constituents was one way. "I think they liked it that they didn't have to go through anyone to get to me. They could just call up and talk to John Paul." He opted not to buy a home in the nations capital and *The*

Tulsa World noted he, "preferred the coffee shops of places like Bentonville and Siloam Springs to the congressional dining room." He also wore the pride of his people in Washington. Second District Congressman Ed Bethune, the only elected Republican to have served with him from Arkansas, recalls his office wall was decorated with "racks and racks of file folders. It was like looking at a computer, only it was one made out of paper. He marked every sparrow's fall in his district, which was huge at the time."

Another way to build a fortress was landing committee assignments that fit his district like a glove and for Hammerschmidt, that was Public Works and Veterans Affairs (years down the lines, Mills finagled to get him a seat on Ways and Means but he turned it down). In his first term, he began advocating for the Buffalo National River Area. The Buffalo had been a part of Hammerschmidt's life since boyhood and he'd often float down it. The first thing he did was ask for a briefing but the Buffalo River was not in their cards. He waited six years before introducing it to see to it that the votes were there. Other pursuits: a highway bridge across the Norfolk Reservoir in North Central Arkansas (Senators had passed it but conferees agreed to include it), construction of the Northwest Arkansas Regional Airport (XNA), securing $1.9 million in grants for the Little Rock Airport, construction of the two-ton water system that now serves Benton and Washington counties and the widening of U.S. 412 going into Tulsa.

**Photo courtesy of the David and Barbara Pryor
Center for Oral and Visual History**

The Cuban refugee crisis at Fort Chafee tied Hammerschmidt down in the fall of 1980. Besides fretting the fact that people were being housed there, he was "particularly appalled at the reports that the persons being imported are to be paid wages grossly in excess of what is now being paid to local people plus $40 per day per diem." In 1987, Hammerschmidt was thrust back into action again on behalf of Fort Chafee when the Pentagon proposed moving the Joint Readiness Training Center in Arkansas to Fort Polk, Louisiana. He was not successful and the Center relocated to Fort Polk in 1993.

That race against Clinton marked Hammerschmidt's soul tough go in 13 campaigns. Clinton was not only young, hard-working and articulate but, the Third was still Democratic and Hammerschmidt knew early he'd have to fight to win another term.

Clinton tried to gain leverage from the Watergate scandal–Hammerschmidt late during the saga was uncertain that Nixon could be impeached which Clinton said, "puts him out of step with all the Republicans on the Judiciary Committee who voted against impeachment."

With singer Johnny Cash
Photo courtesy of the David and Barbara Pryor
Center for Oral and Visual History

By mid-October, Hammerschmidt knew he was facing the race of his life and, "I had 17 days to turn it around." Clinton, Hammerschmidt told *The Tulsa World*, "had been going around the district distorting my record. He did it very articulately. What I had to do was factually refute those charges."

By Election Day, Hammerschmidt's 19-point lead from an Issue Analysis Reports poll had dropped to just six, 49-43%, and the race moved to tossup status. In keeping with that, the two men traded leads on election night but when the dust settled, Hammerschmidt had held the future president off by 6,294 votes. The home areas of both candidates were counter intuitive: Hammerschmidt barely won Boone County (Harrison) while Clinton lost Washington County (Fayetteville) by nearly 3,000 votes. It was Sebastian County that was key, awarding the incumbent a nearly 2-1 margin.

**Photo courtesy of the David and Barbara Pryor
Center for Oral and Visual History**

Though Hammerschmidt did invoke the truth issue as his friend Bush tried futilely to hold the White House nearly two decades later ("Slick Willie is a good term for him. He is slick enough to make people believe he is something that he isn't"), any lingering wounds from that race healed and

Hammerschmidt often said he liked both Bill and Hillary Clinton. In the years after his defeat, Bush would joke that Hammerschmidt, "did something I could never do. Beat Bill Clinton."

Late in his tenure, Hammerschmidt gave crucial backing to another rising star: a little known Georgian named Newt Gingrich who was trying to become Minority Whip. Even then, Gingrich was known as a verbal bomb thrower and when Hammershmidt nominated him for the position at a closed caucus meeting, he alluded to it ("As you well know, Newt has a style that is distinctive"). But Hammerschmidt added that, "he has tremendous energy and a creative mind that has brought an exciting spirit to our side of the aisle and to the Congress." Gingrich famously prevailed over Ed Madigan of Illinois by a vote of 89-87.

More often than not, Hammerschmidt would win re-election going away. Three times, he was unopposed and in anti-incumbent 1990, he took 71%. In 1982, he polled 64% against Jim McDougal, a Clinton real estate partner who famously landed in jail as a result of fraud in connection with the Whitewater affair.

Hammerschmidt called his district, moderate conservative" and said he tried to compile his voting record as such. Yet when he saw that his constituents might be disadvantaged, no one had to tell him which side to take. One example came early in the Reagan administration when the Budget office put 91 small veteran service centers on the chopping block. Hammerschmidt, by then top Republican on the Veterans Affairs Committee, pledged to reverse it. On that panel, he and his '66 classmate, Mississippi Democrat Sonny Montgomery were exceptionally close and "we went all over everywhere together for veterans," and worked together on a GI Bill.

Beginning in 1984, Hammerschmidt and Democrat Roy Rowland of Georgia began sponsoring what three years later was enacted as the Atomic Veterans Compensation Act of 1987 which would compensate Americans who got sick from exposure to radiation during World War II. "Despite sincere efforts to reconstruct the dosages of radioactivity received by veterans at various nuclear tests," he said on the House floor, "the results of these efforts do not inspire great confidence in many people, and certainly not in me. It simply is not possible, 20 to 40 years after the events, to do much more than guess how high some radiation exposures were."

Throughout his tenure, Hammerschmidt received high ratings from the Conservative Coalition and was generally in the teens or lower among liberal interest groups. One example: Hammerschmidt opposed the creation of a Consumer Protection Agency, maintaining it would, "add yet another layer of bureaucracy to the existing one. It will not answer the regulatory or the consumer problem, but will make things worse, by slowing down the wheels of Government, which already move too slowly. No wonder the ever-increasing bureaucracy seems so estranged from the citizens it should serve."

The start of Hammerschmidt's third decade in the House found him with a new perch: ranking member of Public Works and Transportation. That brought increased responsibility and naturally, more scrutiny from his the Young Turks in his party on spending matters. But if he got too carried away with what has become known as pork-barrel spending, very few complained.

The Almanac of American Politics had written that, "In the time when it is illogical conservatives have the initiative among House Republicans, Hammerschmidt remains a link with the strengths and weaknesses of the Republican past." 1987 was the ultimate test as two high-profile occasions forced him to choose between backing up his president and backing his interests – as well as the overwhelming majority of his constituents.

Hammerschmidt had already supported an override against another president of his party, Richard Nixon on the Federal Water Pollution Control Act just before the 1972 election. Now came enactment of the Clean Water Act which Reagan had vetoed. On the House floor, Hammerschmidt called clean water, "essential to life itself. It is the most precious legacy this Congress can leave to future generations...We cannot afford to go bargain-hunting for clean water." The override was 411-26.

Next was the $87.9 billion Highway bill. Hammerschmidt helped write the bill and urged Reagan to sign it. He didn't listen and Hammerschmidt voted with well above 2/3 of the House to override.

Hammerschmidt worked with Public Works Chair Jim Howard to keep the airport trust fund off budget (and thereby immune to cuts) though House members in 1987 rejected it. He used the 1987 Airport Reauthorization Bill, which Reagan did sign after keeping folks guessing, to push through the House a ten-year extension on a Department of Transportation program that provided airline service to small areas. It passed 385-14.

**Images courtesy of the David and Barbara Pryor
Center for Oral and Visual History**

In 1988, Hammerschmidt opposed a proposal by a fellow Republican, Guy Molinari of New York, to rehire Air Traffic Controllers who had been fired by President Reagan in 1981 for striking. His reasoning: "Putting the strikers and their replacements in the same control tower is sure to create animosity between the two factions." Molinari cited a decrease in existing controllers and their depth of experience. The bill cleared the House 234-180.

Hammerschmidt's last legislative hurrah likely came on the 1991 Transportation Bill which he devised in close consultation with his new chair, Bob Roe of New Jersey. For Arkansas, that meant $1.266 billion and funding for many local highway routes and an electric bus for disabled folks. When Bush's Transportation Secretary, Sam Skinner, labeled many of the bill's goodies unmitigated "pork," Hammerschmidt rejected that notion: "You can call anything pork; I don't think this is pork. Every member that has anything in that bill has been in consultation with their own Department of Transportation. Really what you're doing is just throwing some money in there that gets this thing off to a good start."

Bush obviously listened to Hammerschmidt more than Skinner as he signed the bill into law in his presence. However, getting there was not an easy road. First, Hammerschmidt joined other top leaders of Public Works of both parties who, shortly after the president unveiled his proposal, announced they favored spending 46% more than Bush. Hammerschmidt said their plan, "keeps faith with the American taxpayer by returning trust to the trust fund and by supporting a surface transportation program that will meet our needs for the 21st century." Then came the gas tax.

When Bush became president, he'd travel to the Capitol for Country fried ham complete with grits and redeye gravy (Montgomery, who chaired Veterans Affairs, often joined them and they would argue over who would get stuck with the bill). Bush had offered Hammerschmidt the post of Veterans Affairs Secretary but he declined.

**Photo courtesy of the David and Barbara Pryor
Center for Oral and Visual History**

Hammerschmidt had enormous stature on both sides of the aisle. Democrat Norman Mineta, who would replace Roe as chair in 1993, credited Hammerschmidt's bipartisan bit. "One of the pleasures of being a member of the Public Works Committee is that we try to work out our differences, Democrats and Republicans, to do what is best for America. Few will dispute that it was John Paul, because of his personality and effectiveness, who many times made the difference in ensuring bipartisan support on key infrastructure legislation." Mineta continued, "There is no individual in the House who is more loved and respected than John Paul Hammerschmidt. His honesty, gentleness, decency, and integrity are second to none. Don't be swayed by his quiet manner, because underneath is a man with strong convictions, a sense of purpose, and a keen desire to get things done."

Hammerschmidt was beloved by staff as well. Sante Esposito was counsel for the Democratic side of Public Works and called Hammerschmidt, "first and foremost a gentleman." He "knew what he wanted," but "we all worked together," and even as a member of the opposite partisan staff, Hammerschmidt was always kind to him.

Away from Congress, Hammerschmidt was content hunting, fishing and boating, the latter with his most famous classmate. He had a boat docked in the D.C. area when he was in Congress and John Hammerschmidt, Jr., recalls that, "as freshmen congressmen, my dad and George H.W. Bush would often leave the Capitol at the end of the work day, stop somewhere to pick up some snacks, then go to Bush's motorboat docked nearby and travel down and up the Potomac River."

Hammerschmidt's musical tastes varied – he liked country (Jimmy Rogers), jazz (Pete Fountain) and big-band (Glenn Miller), which came to life in his heyday. So deep was his affection for the latter that John Jr., recalls receiving a cell phone from his dad one time, and the ringtone was the iconic Miller hit, "Chattanooga Choo Choo." John, Jr., was told the Tommy Dorsey Band was performing at a local dance when he was a baby but, his parents couldn't stay because they had to take him to a doctor.

Despite 224 overdrafts at the House bank, Hammerschmidt likely could have kept winning re-election. That same year, he was turning 70 and had vowed not to keep running past his 70th birthday. Therefore, he told constituents, "After very careful consideration and certainly with mixed emotions, I have decided not to seek re-election to the next Congress. Time takes its toll, as does the strain of seemingly constant travel on the 35 to 40 annual weekend trips to Arkansas meetings." Later, he told *The New York Times* that Congress as a whole, "lost a lot of collegiality and comity" while calling the checks, "a bum rap." Guy Vander Jagt, a Michigander and another '66 classmate credited life in the minority. "If John Paul really thought he was going to be chairing Public Works next year, I think that would overcome anything he said about retirement" (the GOP took the House in 1994).

Out of office, Hammerschmidt was still a happy mentor to scores of Republicans. One candidate for office recalled him driving some 95 miles to her fundraiser and back home a year before his death. That passing came in 2015 at age 92. On that occasion, one of his successors in the Third District, Republican Steve Womack said, "If you're an elected official in Arkansas and get mentioned in the same sentence as John Paul Hammerschmidt, you're a success." That is a mighty compliment indeed.

CHAPTER ELEVEN

Bennett of Florida "Mr. Clean"
Throughout His 44-Year Tenure

Introductory Quote: "I was concerned for my life, but I've had guns fired at me before." - Congressman and World War II veteran Charlie Bennett following a mugging by a man with a loaded gun in Jacksonville, Florida. Bennett added, "I told the man I had a wonderful family and friends. I didn't want to die."

Photo courtesy of James Bennett

"Bennett" is a fairly common surname in the United States but there was once a veteran Congressman from Florida whose profile might read more like a "Smith," as in, "Mr. Smith Goes to Washington." Throughout his long career, Representative Charles "Charlie" Bennett of Jacksonville eschewed the characteristics of probity and frugality from Jimmy Stewart's most famous character in a manner that was so persistent and unbending that colleagues on the Hill bestowed on him a nickname: "Mr. Clean." Yet that might have proven a hindrance just as he needed them most in the mid-1980s as he sought to achieve his long elusive goal of securing the Armed Services Committee chairmanship.

The erstwhile Bennett's long career was somewhat paradoxical as he did have an epiphany or two on social and civil rights issues. He was elected as a conservative Democrat in 1948 who opposed Harry Truman and early civil rights measures. But by the time he left office, Bennett was so aligned with national Democrats that, on some issues, it wasn't unusual for him to be championing the causes just as vocally as they. But what remained vintage wine for Bennett was his staunch advocacy of ethics and good government, which led political consultant Mike Tolbert to label Bennett in his winter years, "the epitome of a Southern gentleman." Incidentally, the motto "In God We Trust," that appears on U.S. currency exists because of Bennett.

While Bennett was a native New Yorker, hailing from the small, upstate town of Canton, his family relocated to Tampa, Florida in 1912 (his father moved his family due to his job as a meteorologist).From an early age, Charlie was industrious toward living a life of virtue, becoming an Eagle Scout. At the University of Florida, Bennett display the go-getter skills that served in well in Congress – he was student-body president as well as editor of the student newspaper, *The Florida Alligator* (he worked his way through as a waiter). He continued at UF for law school and entered into practice in Jacksonville. Being politically active helped him win a seat in the Florida House in 1940.

Bennett had planned to seek a seat in Congress as early as two years later, which had he won would have given him a half-century in office come his 1992 retirement. But World War II pre-empted his plans. Bennett could have taken advantage of a provision that exempted sitting legislators from being drafted but he said nothing doing and it was off to the Army. He contacted polio while leading 1,000 gorilla resistance fighters in the Philippines and was forced to rely on crutches and a leg brace for the rest of his life, but not before giving the enemy a true taste of what he was made of. As such, he was awarded the U.S. Silver Star and Bronze Star for combat valor, and the Philippine Medal of honor and Gold Cross for combat valor.

Photo courtesy of James Bennett

Bennett was discharged from Hot Springs, Arkansas where he convalesced for 18 months and, although he was permanently forced to walk with a cane or metal leg brace, he was determined to pick up where he had left off. That meant taking on the Democratic Congressman who had won the seat in Bennett's stead when he was forced into war. Emery Price had literally squeaked into the seat that year in both the primary and general and Bennett spotted vulnerabilities. He mounted a fierce primary challenge and squeaked past Price by 2,500 votes, 52-48%. Price carried most of the district's western counties including populous Alachua (Gainesville). But Bennett was better known in DuVal (Jacksonville) through his law practice and civic involvement (president of the Jacksonville Jaycees and of the Jacksonville UF alumni) and his showing there mirrored the district (he also took the neighboring counties by big margins).

General elections in the solidly Democratic South in those days were all but non-existent and Bennett was off to Congress. Unlike many freshmen, he was able to boast of getting his first committee choice: Armed Services. Price attempted a comeback in 1950 but mustered just 41% in the primary. Only twice in the ensuing 40 yeas did Bennett dip below 75% of the vote, in 1964 and his last election, 1990, when he dropped precipitously, to 73%.

The "In God We Trust" proposal came in 1953 and was referred to the committee on Banking and Currency. Bennett explained his logic for the bill on the floor of the House: "In these days when imperialistic and materialistic communism seeks to attack and destroy freedom, we should continually look for ways to strengthen the foundations of our freedom…Nothing can be more certain than that our country was founded in a spiritual atmosphere and with a firm trust in God. While the sentiment of trust in God is universal and timeless, these particular four words 'In God We Trust' are indigenous to our country.'" Adding "In God We Trust" to currency, Bennett believed, would "serve as a constant reminder" that the nation's political and economic fortunes were tied to its spiritual faith." President Eisenhower signed the measure into law in '55.

Throughout his first decade-and-a-half in Congress, Bennett opposed most major social and civil rights measures. In 1953, he and a new member from West Virginia named Robert Byrd proposed a measure that today would be called a Line Item Veto. When it came to the "Great Society," he opposed the initial creation of Medicare, Elementary and Secondary Education Act, the legislation creating the Department of Housing and Urban Development, repealing Section 14 of Taft-Hartley but did back the National Endowment for the Arts. His "change of conscience" occurred in 1965 when he felt compelled to support the Voting Rights Act. Initially, folks in the district did not take kindly to that vote and vowed a challenge but Bennett emerged unscathed. To be sure, Bennett had always favored progress for his minority constituents. He was an advocate of school construction for defense workers, black and Indian children as early as the mid-1950s.

By that point, Bennett was becoming a senior member on the Armed Services panel and used it to advance and promote Jacksonville's potential. As Bennett prepared to leave office, *The St. Petersburg Times* wrote how, "Thanks to Bennett, Jacksonville enjoys a $500-million annual economic boost from its three naval bases."

Bennett could change on local issues as well. He was at one point so committed to a Cross Florida Barge Canal that in White House recordings that eventually came to light, U.S. Senator George Smathers told President Lyndon Johnson that it was "his baby." He eventually abandoned the idea and became content to let it become a park. Before long, he had become such a strong advocate for the environment that he was receiving multiple awards from organizations such as the Nature Conservancy.

Then there was the Charlie Bennett who epitomized the Congressmen of yore and what really set him apart from his colleagues was his frugality with money that wasn't his. It was not uncommon for him to return office expenses and his veteran disability pension to the U.S. Treasury (he didn't need two sources of income) or to drive home from Congressional recesses rather than fly because it was cheaper. He returned his military pension every year and never voted for a pay raise for a seated Congress, and never accepted a pay raise until he was reelected. As a result of his stewardship on behalf of taxpayers, Bennett earned the, "Watchdog of the Treasury Award" on several occasions which was not a distinction many Democrats could boast of. His ethics were so pronounced that he once returned a cross to a constituent who had made one for him and ordered a staffer who had accepted a box of candy to buy an identical one and mail it back.

If Bennett had never made another contribution to clean government, he would have still been a heavy hitter on the ethical front by doggedly pursuing the creation of an ethics panel. But that wasn't all. One might expect that enactment of a prime proposal would mean a right of first refusal for chairing it. That didn't happen and for years, the assignment evaded him. It wasn't until 1976 that he was appointed, just in time for the Abscam matter and that of Michigan Congressman Charlie Diggs. An early example of his strict penchant for ethics came in 1951 when he proposed "The Ten Commandments of Ethics" for government employees In promoting the legislation, Bennett told a Senate subcommittee how he "was offered cash" to arrange Defense contracts. He declined the offer saying he "did this in the last war." But he also filed a bill that year which would have allowed the purchase of additional furniture for members only with their written request. It would heretofore surprise no one that he had returned $500,000 in addition to declining $120,000 in pay raises throughout the course of his career. Bennett felt if willing, ordinary Americans could do their part also. A bill he sponsored allowed the public to send money to the Treasury to pay down the national debt and by 2010, the fund had taken in roughly $80 million.

Fulfilling his obligation to vote was also notable. As he cast his 15,000[th] vote in 1985, *The Miami Herald* cited, "the time Rep. Charlie Bennett left his wife in labor to go vote. Then there was the day he walked 10 blocks in a blizzard — he cannot walk without a cane — to make a vote. And the time he got stuck in an elevator." This ballooned to over 17,000 by 1991. Bennett could not quite achieve the record set by his friend but junior colleague, William Natcher of Kentucky, who didn't come along until 1953 but who never missed a vote at all until his dying days 40 years later. Bennett might have been able to boast of the same had he not missed several votes in his second term following complications from Polio. He relayed to *The St. Petersburg Times* in 1991 that, "on June 4, 1951, I was given the okay to leave town. I did, and of course a vote dealing with the District of Columbia unexpectedly came up." He said he, "never dreamed that 40 years later, I would be here celebrating this anniversary. I'm thrilled that I am."

As the 1970s turned into the 80s, Bennett opposed ratification of the ERA and supported the Flag Burning Amendment. But as the time went on, Bennett found crucial issues on which to prove liberals that he could pugnaciously be aligned in their camp. Vietnam might have played a role – he had backed the Tonkin Gulf resolution but regretted it as he watched conditions for U.S. troops deteriorate and in the early 1970s, he began speaking out against military operations in Laos and Cambodia. Another area was reducing military spending and SDI research came into his crosshairs (he proposed a $600 million reduction). Another was MX. On using the weapon as leverage with the Soviet's. Bennett's response was, "They could care less." Bennett also was instrumental in creating the U.S. Arms Control and Disarmament Agency.

Bennett cared deeply about the environment and Florida's coast was at the top of the list, specifically preventing beach erosion. He had a major role in preserving the 35,000 acre Timucuan Ecological and Historical Preserve as well as the Key Deer Preserve in the Florida Keys. He sponsored the Fort Caroline National Memorial. Ditto for matters concerning anthropology. The Archaeological and Historic Preservation Act of 1974 and the Native American Burial Site Preservation Act. Other parochial projects he championed: a Jacksonville light rail (which he achieved with the help of fellow Floridian and Appropriations cardinal William Lehman) and an Acosta Bridge Replacement Project.

Bennett co-sponsored the Wilderness Preservation Act and the Land and Water Conservation Act as well as the Americans with Disability Act. In promoting the latter on the House floor, he spoke of his experiences on the battlefield, "But two years later, with the assistance of canes like these, I was able to walk and with these canes, I have walked every step of the past 42 years." And Bennett was ahead of his time on U.S. territories. The District of Columbia Virgin Islands, Guam and American Samoa.

In 1985, Mel Price, who had come to Congress two terms before Bennett, was ousted as chair of Armed Services and Bennett tried to strive toward his long-sought goal of succeeding him. Wisconsin Democrat Les Aspin, whose arrival in Washington lagged behind Bennett by 22 years, prevailed in the full caucus 125-103. Rubbing salt-in-the-wound, Price, proving his infirmity, mistakenly thought Bennett had won the chairmanship and proceeded to congratulate him on the House floor. Bennett replied by "thank(ing) the chairman for his kind tribute, even though it may be premature."

For a time, Bennett saw a chance to prove that Price's statement had indeed been premature. In 1987, the Steering Committee votes Aspin out and Bennett again saw the time as right. But Aspin was determined to plead his case to the full caucus and two other contenders also entered the fray. Fellow Floridian Dante Fascell and Tom Foglietta of Pennsylvania placed his name in nomination. Bennett spoke of his seniority and maintained "it would be an absolute affront to me if they turned me down twice." But as Yogi Bera said, it became, "de-ja vu all over again."

While the Steering Committee voted 16-11 to award the post to Bennett, the endorsement appeared to be perfunctory. House Speaker Jim Wright, who had been believed to be supporting another contender, fellow Texan Marvin Leath, called it a, "traditional thing . . . an act of courtesy." Bennett refused to go for the jugular in twisting his colleagues, simply saying, "I don't want to intrude on their judgement. I'm the most senior and I think I'm qualified." But he received just 44 votes and was eliminated as Aspin defied the odds and hung on. Longtime colleague and fellow Florida Democrat Sam Gibbons attributed Bennett's failure to secure Armed Services to the fact that "other people were more ambitious. He didn't want to turn on people. He'd rather work with them," adding, "He got a raw deal." Bennett conceded as much. "People don't come to me and say, 'If you vote for my canal, I'll vote for yours.'" But he also cited his "appearance of being a very old man." The truth is, Bennett was still mourning the death of his son from a drug overdose and many thought his ability to burst out crying occasionally or to engage in impromptu rambling made him unstable.

Bennett still carried on with good grace. As the House debated whether to authorize President Bush to use force to force Iraq from Kuwait in 1991, Bennett sponsored language with his Illinois colleague, Richard Durbin, which asserted that "the Constitution of the United States vests all power to declare war in the Congress of the United States." Bennett had just taken the oath of office for what would be, unbeknownst to him his final term and cited that as he spoke to his colleagues. "There are those of us who have been to law school, and those of us who took the oath the other day to uphold the Constitution, who feel like we would be abridging or setting aside the Constitution of the United States if we did not comply with the essence of that document where it says that the Congress and not the President would be the people to put our country to war if we were to go to war." While Bennett went on to note that the Founding Fathers did envision exceptions, he laid out their reasoning for advocating Congressional approval. "In history abroad, just prior to the founding of our country, there were many instances of where a king, an emperor, a tyrant of one kind or another, would set about to put his country to war, usually for personal reasons of his own, to strengthen his own hand on the government or something like that. So our Constitution specifically provides that that type of power as far as aggressive offensive war shall be in the hands of Congress, and not in the hands of the President.

Bennett-Durbin passed 302-131. While Congress ultimately granted Bush the power to use force (with Bennett voting "no"), the likelihood is that he would have circumvented Bennett-Durbin even if the body had refused to bestow on him that authority.

Bennett's 1992 retirement was unexpected. Why? Because in early 1991, he sought to shoot down speculation that he might retire when his term ended. "There is no basis for that. I am in good health in every respect, and I plan to run in 1992 because there is Navy business which I feel a new congressional successor would have trouble" looking out for local interests. Moreover, had announced that he would be seeking it but only one last time "because that allows me a couple of decades to spend with my beloved wife and children." But when his wife suffered a stroke, he moved his exit up a term. Congress he said was, "a wonderful place to be," but, "I would not want such personal defects in me to hamper the service that a U.S. representative should render." Redistricting might have been another factor. The new district was not only 50% new to Bennett but no longer containing Democratic friendly and minority neighborhoods (on cue, Republican Tillie Fowler was elected to succeed him in the fall).

As the date of his retirement drew closer, he said, "I don't plan to lower the tempo of my work. I want to be useful in some capacity. I want to live my life as fully as I can." He thought about teaching and would be a natural. For many years, he had taught Sunday School at Jacksonville's Riverside Avenue Christian Church. Bennett's biography at FSU calls him, "a historian of Florida and U.S. colonial history, writing and publishing nine books and several articles." He was awarded an undergraduate degree and Juris Doctorate in Law from University of Florida.

Bennett was given the honor of having a federal office building in Jacksonville named for him but turned it down because he was a sitting member. Meanwhile, he donated $270,835 to the National Park Service. By 1993, his political career behind him, he reconsidered but only grudgingly. He died a decade later at age 92.

In a *Florida Times Union* piece for what would have been Bennett's 100th birthday, reporter Jessie Lynn-Kerr wrote that, for those who "never met Charlie, there is a lifelike statue of him, including his canes, done by sculptor William Duffy in a southeast corner of Hemming Plaza. You'll notice that Charlie is facing in the direction of his two loves - Fort Caroline and Washington."

CHAPTER TWELVE

5'5 Fascell Towered Over Congressional Comity and Human Rights

Introductory Quote: "When Central America sneezes, Miami catches cold." – Dante Fascell on the close link between the region's impact on South Florida.

Fascell's Official Foreign Affairs Committee portrait
Photo courtesy of the U.S. House of Representatives Historical Collection

Dante Fascell was the panorama of several things. A staple of "The Greatest Generation," the Florida Democrat was notorious for embracing brotherhood at every level. Comity was his calling and throughout his 38 years in office, his benevolence, thoughtfulness and stature produced great things both for his career and South Florida. And having presided over the House Foreign Affairs Committee at a time when some of the most boisterous and internationally watched debates took place, Fascell had a soothing presence.

The longtime Congressman's accomplishments spanned all corners of the world. Internationally, he was a founding father of the War Powers Act, the Commission on Security and Cooperation in Europe which monitored the Helsinki Accords, and the Cuban Refugees Assistance Act. His actions also led to the establishment of the Inter-American Foundation, the National Endowment for Democracy and the United States Institute of Peace. Nationally, he was instrumental in the legislation that created the Department of Housing and Urban Development and increasing Congressional and government transparency. Locally, the list is exponential. The Port of Miami, named in Fascell's honor the year he died, the preservation of the Everglades, establishment of Biscayne National Park, getting the Keys declared a marine sanctuary, banning offshore drilling off the Keys as well as countless bridge and beach restoration projects. Shhh! Don't mention this to Fascell – he might be stubborn about taking the credit. Til his dying day, *The Miami Herald* said he "remained a man who seemed little impressed with his own accomplishments, a man cautious about accepting tributes or seeking fame." His character was heralded by none other than Richard Nixon (not exactly an expert on character) who once said he had, "never known anyone, Republican or Democrat, who so consistently put country above party on great issues." And William Broomfield, a Michigan Congressman who served for many years as the top Republican on Foreign Affairs, said of Fascell: "There's been no greater chairman than Dante Fascell."

The Miami Herald summed up vintage Fascell: "Unlike so many telegenic and sound-bite-conscious politicians of today, Fascell believed that he was at his most effective when he operated like a film director, letting others take lead roles and allowing them to bask in the lights." *Politics in America* verbalized it from another angle. Fascell, the publication wrote, was "'a short, aggressive bulldog of a man. He has always been impatient with the slow pace of House business and niceties of floor debate. He likes to cut through the rhetoric, get to the point of an argument, outline a compromise and move on to the next issue." If that was a conscious goal, he did it exceedingly well.

Fascell was born to Italian immigrants, Charles Fascell and Mary Gullotti in Bridgehampton, New York on Long Island. His father was a milkman and the family moved to Coconut Grove, Florida when Dante was a boy. Dante was musically gifted and attended the University of Miami on a music scholarship. He continued at the UM law school and commenced private practice when war came calling. In 1941, he married Jeanne-Marie Pelot and the couple had one son and two daughters.

Fascell gave his soul to World War II. He joined the Florida National Guard and served under General Patton in the Army in Italy and North Africa. As the commander of a truck company, he often recounted how he slept under a jeep he once commanded. He recalled to *Miami New Times* writer Don Lantigua shortly before his death that, the war would become his inspiration for a political career: "Me and my friend Dick Wight crawled under that jeep and the rocks were hard and it was wet. I remember telling him, 'If we ever get out of this thing, I'm going to find out a lot more about how the world works than I know now.... I don't know anything at all now. Wars are started by men, and I ought to be part of the process to help solve these things.'" Half-a-century later when he announced his retirement from Congress, Fascell in part felt he had reached the mountaintop by telling those assembled, "We all should be proud of whatever part we have done to promote the American dream."

Photo courtesy of the Fascell Family

When Fascell returned from war, he resumed his law practice and became active in the Dade County Young Democrats and the Italian-American Club, until he was persuaded to run for a seat in the Florida State House in 1950 and won. His opportunity to run for Congress was unexpected. Democratic incumbent William Lantaff had only won the seat four years earlier and at 41, could have continued in the U.S. House for the foreseeable future. But he abruptly decided to not stand for re-election in 1954 and that created an opening for Fascell in a district that encompassed Dade County (Miami) and Monroe County (the Everglades and the Florida Keys). Using a slogan, "Ring the Bell for Dante Fascell," he won the nomination, narrowly avoiding a runoff against four other candidates. There would be no Republican opposition in November.

While Fascell would rarely sweat electorally over the next 38 years, it was not that hard to hold him below 60% in climates that were not favorable to his party nationally (he took just 57% in both 1966 and '68%. Mostly, however, those were exceptions.

On social issues, Fascell was a solid liberal even in the early days when Dade County wasn't and he would be the only Floridian who refused to sign the Southern manifesto. Nor did he have future qualms about backing forthcoming civil rights legislation. One longtime staffer, Mike Finley said "he knew there were political costs, particularly regarding open housing, but he supported civil rights initiatives despite the probable costs and that took courage."

Fascell shared similar view about Constitutional rights. Near the end of his career, he opposed a flag-burning amendment, his military service notwithstanding not because he had any tolerance for those who were cavalier toward Old Glory but because he believed it was a First Amendment right. "I fought for, and Americans have demonstrated over and over again they will fight and die for what they believe in, the flag of the United States and the values which it represents," he explained. "While I have no use for desecraters and those who want to use some kind of means by which to protest, I think there are a lot of better means and more acceptable, and certainly burning the flag is not acceptable in my eyes and ought to be condemned as strongly as possible."

As a junior Congressman on the Hill
Photo courtesy of the Fascell Family

Beyond civil rights, Fascell had a sense of activism that often led him to take on some very powerful fish in Congress and winning.

One was the 1974 debate over reforming the nation's campaign finance laws. Specifically, he authored an amendment with Minnesota Republican Congressman Bill Frenzel that would create an independent, eight member federal elections board. This saw strenuous opposition from pugnacious House Administration Chairman Wayne Hays which was reported to have led to a shouting match in the House cloakroom. Fascell had been an early riser on the dangers of an unchecked system. He regularly disclosed his personal and campaign finances long before it was fashionable and his philosophy on the matter was, "The whole trouble with campaign finances is the hue and cry that you've been bought? If you need money, are you going to get it from enemy? No. You're going to get it from your friend?"

That same year, Fascell turned to increasing the public's access to Congressional hearings. He sponsored a resolution with Texas Democrat Bob Eckhardt that would open committee hearings to the public, permitting closed sessions only for sensitive national security matters. New York Democrats Sam Stratton amended the act that many advocates viewed as dangerously watering it down to ineffectiveness. Fascell called it, "wrong to have expert witnesses sit in on a markup session of a bill, just as if they were members of Congress, offering their opinions, knocking down ideas, and getting their expertise in the minds of the committee members." It passed on the floor 370-27.

Dante and his bride Jeanne-Marie
Photo courtesy of the Fascell Family

The War Powers Act was another big matter Fascell had his hand in and his introduction of the bill in 1970 occurred three years before final passage (The U.S. invasion of Cambodia was the major motivation). When the chamber took it up in 1973, Fascell contended passage would "assure that the views of Congress are taken into account in the shaping of our national security policies." In a dialogue with Delaware Republican Pete DuPont, he said, "if Congress has the right to declare war by simple majority action, and the country can go to war when the president signs the bill, the Congress should have the right to undeclare war by a simple majority. This should be possible without regard to the fact that we have other tools available to us, either the appropriations process or otherwise. Those other tools are available to us now."

Another titan Fascell ultimately overtook was Government Reform Chair Jack Brooks, a Texas Democrat Fascell liked very much but who was declining to support President Carter's government reorganization plan that Fascell was leading. Brooks believed the proposal "stands the Constitution on its head" and that, "It's our prerogative to legislate and the President's prerogative to veto."

**Fascell (left) with national and Florida heavyweights, Senator George
Smathers, President Kennedy and Governor Farris Bryant
Photo courtesy of the Fascell Family**

As Fascell rose in seniority he began chairing a number of subcommittees. One was the Foreign Affairs Subcommittee on Latin America Inter-American Affairs which went hand-in-hand with his increasingly diverse district. In 1972, Fascell expressed befuddlement when the Nixon administration secretly decided to place ships between Cuba and "friendly" nations, calling it, "the policeman of the world concept. I don't know of any third countries that have asked for our naval protection in the Caribbean."

Foreign affairs were where Fascell greatly deviated from his party. He was virulently anti-Castro and as such, was instrumental in establishing the National Endowment for Democracy. He also resisted attempts by colleagues to abolish funding for Radio Marti, a Miami based media outlet that translates news in Spanish to Cuba. When a delay forced a four-month delay in Radio Marti's debut, Fascell blamed "bureaucratic red tape and snags in the Executive Branch." The response was that the station was tied down by staffing issues.

A decade earlier, he had forged a compromise for continuing to fund Radio Liberty and Radio Free Europe when it was revealed that it had been financed by the CIA. Funding would continue for two years and a commission would study it. The study led to Fascell passing legislation creating the Board for International Broadcasting to operate RFE and RL under a transparent public board appointed by the President.

**Even as a relatively junior member of Congress, Fascell was
a go to person on foreign policy, including by the top brass,
such as Vice-President Hubert Humphrey in 1966
Photo courtesy of the Fascell Family**

After having initially called the Carter administration's response, "less than adequate," to the Mariel Boatlift from Cuba, Fascell in the summer of 1980 urged that aid be expedited to cities with significant numbers of Cuba exiles, of which Miami was at the forefront. "We can argue about status later but right now we have to provide emergency assistance to state and local governments," adding, "the local governments are picking up the tab on what is a national problem." Some members of Congress called the package, "foreign aid for Miami," but it passed.

El Salvador was one area in which local proximity dictated Fascell's support for aid. "People here recognize that a country so close by as El Salvador cannot be allowed to be taken over by Communists but even the very conservative Miamians don't want El Salvador to be turned into another Vietnam." Other Democrats had major qualms but in early 1983, Fascell tried to rectify that by proposing a plan to provide half of the aid immediately and half six months down the road when the nation submitted a plan. Committee members rejected it. Ultimately, an arrangement was worked out that allowed aid to go ahead for three months so long as there was "dialogue, in good faith and without pre-conditions, with all major parties to the conflict in El Salvador for the purpose of achieving an equitable solution to the conflict."

When it came to Russia, Fascell and Broomfield were the first American officials to meet with Mikhail Gorbachev following his declaration of "glastnost" and "perestroika." Before Gorbachev had come on the scene, Fascell had been recognized as a primary critic of Soviet human rights. As chair of the Congressional Helsinki Commission (CSCE) he conducted numerous hearings on Soviet violations of the Helsinki Final Act. When the Soviet Union invaded Afghanistan, Fascell charged that it had "undercut all of the principles," which led to a "bloody, brutal repression instigated and perpetuated by the Soviet Union, depriving Afghanistan and its people of their independence and freedom."

As chair of the Subcommittee on International Operations responsible for authorizing the budgets of the nation's foreign affairs agencies, Fascell oversaw a complete reform of the personnel system through adoption of a new Foreign Service Act. Through the actions of this subcommittee and one he previously chaired, International Organizations and Movements, he promoted budgetary reforms and the strengthening of the U.S. position in the United Nations, the OAS and other international institutions.

If colleagues were bothered that Fascell had to sometimes go his own way with Democratic causes on Foreign Affairs, they didn't show it. In fact, many wanted to reward him. The panel's full chair, Clem Zablocki of Wisconsin was found to be aloof and sometimes in over his head and some members assured Fascell that the votes were there should he challenge him. Citing seniority, he refused to entertain it. Only when Zablocki died suddenly in 1983 did Fascell get the gavel.

Fascell was an unmistakable bread and butter Democrat. So opposed was he to the Reagan tax cuts that he checked himself out of the hospital following a blood clot under his skull to vote against it. He was solidly pro-choice and in the latter portion of his career, was a vocal opponent of drilling off the Florida coast and he worked vigorously with members of both party to ensure that it wouldn't happen.

Fascell chaired initial hearings by the Foreign Affairs Committee on the Iran-Contra affair which he labeled "the president's unfortunate foreign policy initiative." He aspired to chair the ad hoc Iran-Contra committee when it was established but the slot went to Indiana Democrat Lee Hamilton (Fascell nonetheless sat on the panel).

One thing that did bring Fascell fame was his annual Labor Day picnics that became iconic in South Florida. Michael Putney of *The Miami Herald* aptly set the tone for a typical event: "His picnics, at Tropical Crandon Park, were red-white-and-blue family affairs featuring free hot dogs, burgers and soft drinks for all comers, much of it served up by the congressman himself. After lunch there would be an unabashedly patriotic parade led by a military or police color guard, followed by the Congressman, usually holding a grandchild's hand, and a high school marching band playing Stars and Stripes Forever. It may have been a bit corny, but it was genuine, authentic Americana. Like Dante." Another Fascell gift was described by ex-State Senator Ken Myers: "He never forgot a name and he always said hello to you before you said hello to him. He was amazing that way."

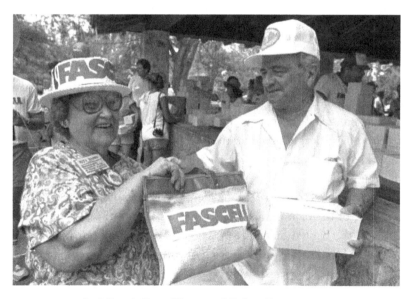

**In Miami, Fascell's annual Labor Day picnics
were as legendary as the man himself
Photo via Getty Images**

By all accounts, Fascell lived a grand life but, it was not without tragedy. In 1984, his 27-year-old son Dante Jon was killed in a car accident. The first person to call him once the news became public was then-Vice-President George H.W. Bush who, having lost a child himself, told him how difficult it was to lose a child.

As a boss and human being, Fascell was second-to-none. How is this certain? Because when he retired in 1992, many of his staffers had been with him for at least twenty years. Barbara van Voorst was his Press Secretary and Special Assistant for 27-years and she recalls staff were part of the family. "You felt you didn't work 'for' him but, rather, 'with' him" and he always made it a point to introduce them. So much a part of their lives was Fascell that he officiated at van Voorst's wedding, even though he didn't have the legal credentials to do so in the Commonwealth of Virginia where it took place (van Voorst had a Justice of the Peace standing by to make it legal but Fascell performed the actual ceremony). That started a movement. "When word got out about this in Miami, others began asking him to do it for them so he became a Notary Public (which makes him legal in Florida) and performed several weddings there. Many of Fascell's staffers who remain in the Beltway area still meet for lunch once a month.

In a 1986 profile, *The Orlando Sentinel* wrote "associates described Fascell affectionately as 'all jowls and eye bags' and 'bulldoggy.'" Fascell could also be self-deprecating. When his campaign team wanted him to do television ads during his 1982 re-election campaign, Fascell called himself, "short and ugly," and was adamant that "you can't put me on television: (they put him on television). Colleagues thought the world of Fascell as well. Lester Wolff of New York, who sat on Foreign Affairs, called him "a gem. A great Chairman - affable but effective."

The close of Fascell's career coincided with great world changes. One was the collapse of the Communist bloc in Eastern Europe and Fascell to some extent gave the United States credit, saying, "Ultimately, our human rights efforts helped lead to the disintegration of the entire eastern empire."

Photo courtesy of the Fascell Family

Fascell's exposure in the national limelight commenced as he began his 19ᵗʰ and final term. It came as a result of Saddam Hussein's invasion of Kuwait. At first, Fascell favored giving President George H.W. Bush wide latitude to try to end the crisis but, by the same token, he wouldn't necessarily mandate that a president be required to negotiate. His view: "I'm not too keen on legislating. You have to preserve the flexibility of the president," while adding, "Nobody wants to give the administration an open-ended commitment." But "in this case, I don't want the appropriating committee's making policy by indirection." Paramount in Fascell's thinking was the responsibility Congress had under the Constitution to act on issues of war. As a champion of Congress' war powers he thought it essential that Congress act to authorize or deny the president's desire to use the armed forces. When the matter finally came for a vote on the floor in January, Fascell again was in the minority of his party and supported the authorization of force despite immense pressure from the Speaker to oppose authorizing the use of force.

With General "Stormin" Norman Schwarzkopf
Photo courtesy of the Fascell Family

In the spring of 1992, *Congressional Quarterly* had called Fascell, "an institution whose career will end only when he says it should." A court-ordered redistricting plan complicated that assessment. It was produced by a Tulane University law professor, M. David Gelfang and ultimately drew a district that, while even more solidly Democratic than before, had stripped him of 75% of his current constituency. Add that to the fact that his 96-year old mother, who had been warning him to slow down, had died a month earlier and Fascell was ready to embrace new ventures.

Fascell's decision was widely seen as surprising but he enumerated his reasoning at a press conference. "I've been in politics for 42 years and have been in the House for 38 of those years. This seems like a good time for a change in my life." He was eligible to pocket thousands in his campaign treasury but vowed to not take a cent.

Fascell announces his retirement under his Foreign Affairs Portrait
Photo courtesy of CQ/Roll Call

Fascell said folks had been "telling me that this district is made-to-order and I believe it is. It's a fine district even though there are people from another county." Broomfield was also stepping down and in fact was invited by Fascell to join him at the podium when he announced his retirement ("Broomfield, you started this"). He urged the incoming Clinton administration to give Fascell a position and in fact Fascell was more than happy to take on assignments but was content to return to Miami where he joined the Miami law firm of Holland & Knight. Unsurprisingly, his primary specialty was International Affairs. A year after leaving office, Fascell was diagnosed with colon cancer. He recovered but in 1997, the cancer returned. When it became clear that Fascell was not going to win his battle, Fascell was awarded the Presidential Medal of Freedom by President Bill Clinton. He died of colon cancer at age 81 just prior to Thanksgiving in 1998.

One obituary succinctly summed up this great man's gifts when he said, "Dante was a towering figure in Congress. He was an American politician of the old school, a survivor from a less partisan, more amiable political era who found no problem in placing the national good above narrow party advantage.

CHAPTER THIRTEEN

"Alabama Bill" Lehman Was a Mighty Auto Dealer and Among the Nicest Men in Congress

Introductory Quote: Storms are "the easiest time to sell cars. Serious buyers only come out in the rain. And the cars all look so shiny." – Car dealer and Florida Congressman Bill Lehman

Photo courtesy of the U.S. House Historical Collection

Could William Lehman have won a best-liked House member contest by unanimous consent? On a personal level, probably although it would be nearly guaranteed if senior members of the Public Works Committee abstained. On a personal level, the Miami Democrat was one of the warmest and most genuine members of the House. He didn't have a crass, curt, or disrespectful bone in his body nor was he involved with any of the mischief or distaste that gave the chamber a bad reputation. Lehman mentored many new members and as chair of a major House Appropriations subcommittee, took pride at accommodating members on their request for projects for their district, albeit with limits ("If you've got a project let me know," was his philosophy in 1983). It was only when Public Works and rank and file members took aim at his authority that he'd KO their projects but Lehman always let them know that it wasn't any malice, it was simply about preserving the integrity of the committee. How was this certain? Well, while Lehman might scoff at being compared to Ronald Reagan, after 6 p.m., they did all become friends again. Not bad for a one-time car dealer.

Lehman was a product of the state of Alabama, part of a vibrant Jewish community of well over 100 families in Selma where he was born in 1913 to candy factory owners. He earned his Business degree at the University of Alabama, then journeyed to New York City to accept a job with a finance company. He was back down south in no time as the company sent him to Miami. Around that time, he married a distant relative, Joan, who was also Jewish and from Alabama.

Lehman then made his entry in the used-car business. He opened his own dealership which Kurt Stone in the book, *The Jews of Capitol Hill* wrote "quickly prospered largely because he was the only used-car dealer who would make financing deals for African-Americans." He purchased his own lot and later, with creative ads (giving away Confederate money while championing "deals as solid as a bale of cotton"), became legendary as "Alabama Bill."

Lehman explained his philosophy to *The Miami Herald* in 1983. "There is nothing like being in the marketplace for knowing what reality is, to separate people from their money, to see how they make a choice." He claimed he, "learned more about people while in the used-car business than I would in 10 years in psychiatry." To wit, Lehman loved rainstorms, for it was when business accelerated. Storms, he said, were, "the easiest time to sell cars. Serious buyers only come out in the rain. And the cars all look so shiny." In the 1960s, Lehman opened a Buick dealership, a move that many might have rightfully viewed as going from used cars to new. In actuality, he was just keeping the lot warm until his son, William, Jr., finished graduate school at which time he'd take it over.

As for the levity surrounding car dealers, David Obey, a longtime colleague on Appropriations and friend, in his book, *Raising Hell For Justice*, called Lehman, "exactly the opposite of the stereotype associated with that profession. He tried every day to measure up to the highest responsibilities of the Judeo-Christian care or Love Thy Neighbor tradition, but that never stopped him from displaying toughness with a situation called for."

For Lehman, mid-life meant not a crisis but a career change and at the age of 49, he received his teaching certificate from the University of Miami and began teaching classic literature at Miami-Norland High School in north Dade. Bill Lehman, Jr., said his father was so smitten with teaching that he could have stuck with it for the duration of his career if only the pay was more sustainable. Realizing teaching full time and running the car business wasn't going to work, he began teaching night classes at Miami Dade Junior College, also going to Oxford.

Lehman proved himself a wonderful human being even then. After Lehman announced his retirement, *Miami Herald* political editor Tom Fiedler authored a column in which he told an anecdote of a nurse who spotted Lehman in an emergency room trauma unit that he was visiting as a Congressman. "One day," the story went, "he came upon her while she was looking quite despondent and he asked what her concern was. She said she told him that she and her boyfriend couldn't go to the senior prom because her boyfriend had no car. Lehman's solution: Lend them one of his."

Eventually, Lehman started getting political. First came election to the Dade County School Board in 1964 which *The Sun Sentinel* credited to, "Lehman's loyal customers - a mix of Crackers, Jews and blacks" in securing his election. He became chairman of the Board in 1970 and didn't hesitate to tackle issues of race because it was right. Longtime Press Secretary John Schelble recalls Lehman telling him how "some of the meetings were so contentious that he had to be escorted to and from." One photo showed him posing beside a bus and when folks asked him why he'd do such a thing, his response was that he wasn't going to defy a court order. Either way, his reputation was such that many who viscerally opposed him on matters of race told him they'd, "never buy a car from anyone else."

In 1972, Lehman entered the Democratic primary for Congress in the newly created district 13th district. In a seven-way primary, Lehman placed second with 20% behind Lee Weissenborn and was generally considered the underdog going into a runoff. Lehman resisted the advice from advisors to run ads condemning Weissenborn's support of forced-busing. So it was the shock of the year when Lehman won with 57%. Weissenborn was forced to admit that he was aware of aides circulating petitions — and that also contributed to Lehman's benefit. Because Lehman had beaten movers and shakers, it took him a while to get his political feet on the ground in the district and in 1974, many regular order Democrats got behind Joyce Goldberg. She did manage to force a runoff but Lehman again proved that was the death-knell to his foes: he took 68%.

Lehman shortly after his election to Congress
Photo courtesy of Florida Memory

In Congress, Lehman was assigned to Education and Labor but, after the election of 1976, Appropriations. He once told a press secretary that "the biggest story you'll ever get is when I die." Lehman didn't look for headlines but on occasion, they could sure find him.

Securing the release of political prisoners, particularly in the Western Hemisphere was high on Lehman's plate throughout his tenure. One was Debora Benchoam, a teenage girl in Argentina. He credited his late daughter Kathy, who had succumbed to a brain tumor two years earlier, with playing a role in the latter. It was 1981 and Benchoam had been jailed four years earlier during Argentina's "dirty war." Out of the blue, Lehman journeyed to Buenos Aires to visit Benchoam in prison, against the recommendations of some in the U.S. Lehman confessed that, "subconsciously I may have been looking for a surrogate daughter," while acknowledging that, "I was also doing something that I think my daughter would have encouraged me to do."

Lehman didn't publicize the mission and even shunned the publicity he received, saying, "I didn't want to do anything that would adversely affect her friends who were still in prison." But he didn't stop there. Once Benchoam was safe on U.S. soil, Lehman helped her land a job on Capitol Hill and gave her away when she was married.

It was smuggling a heart valve into Russia that was perhaps Lehman's most adventurous accomplishment and he recounted the saga in his diary, *Mr. Chairman*. Lehman had been told about a 22-year old woman's need for a valve by a state Department official who knew he had been planning to visit the then-Soviet Union (the woman's relative in New York had purchased the valve but couldn't get anyone to smuggle it in his briefcase). Lehman solved that one.

Accompanied by an aide, Adele Liskov and a State Department interpreter, Lehman recalls "holding on for dear life to a small box contains" the $2,000 valve. The interpreter was told to, "Look for a woman in red standing next to a shot man. They will know who you are. 'Well, what could go wrong did go wrong. The interpreter was given the wrong address.'" As the trio pondered where to go from there, they decided to gamble that their cab driver was not with the KGB. The gamble paid off – the man was Armenian and more than trustworthy and Lehman told how, "sometimes it's the unforeseen elements which lead to either success or failure in the best of plans. In this case, we got lucky." Even if they hadn't, Lehman's philosophy was, "I'm a Congressman. If they catch me, what are they going to do?" In the end, the luck belonged to the recipient and once again, Lehman refrained from publicizing the matter until the operation was a success and her safety from the government was assured.

Lehman also was instrumental in gaining the release of three dissidents who had been jailed for 20 years in Cuba.

Following the unexpected passing of Indiana Democrat Adam Benjamin in the spring of 1982, Lehman took the reins of the Appropriations Subcommittee on Transportation. He was now ne of 13 "College of Cardinals" but as he one explained it, "In my position, I do have some political leverage to get things done." That meant it would be an easy position to make friends – most of the time. While Lehman's proclivity was to build consensus, he had no problems striking members' projects if they did not accede to his or leaderships wishes. But if that wasn't always the exception, it was by no means the rule.

What was the rule was constant bickering with the Public Works Committee that at times bordered on intractable for at least seven years and two chairmen. Leaders of that committee – first Jim Howard of New Jersey and then Glenn Anderson of California as well as Norman Mineta of California who chaired a key subcommittee, believed, contrary to Lehman, that jurisdiction over every Transportation project lay with them and that Lehman's subcommittee had no right to tuck into his appropriation those that hadn't been authorized. Both sides won a little and lost a little. The first year, Anderson prevailed as he convinced the Rules Committee to side with him in eliminating unauthorized projects. After that, things got murkier.

In 1989, the tide seemed to turn in Lehman's favor when the House agreed with him on funding 70 unauthorized projects. The following year, however, Lehman agreed to let Mineta review the projects prior to approval. *Politics in America* noted, "they proceeded to accept virtually every program Lehman sent their way, apparently content not to be ignored." But it wasn't personal – Lehman made sure of that. In fact, when *The Miami Herald* ran a story detailing how a "feud" was taking place between Lehman and Howard, Lehman, who did not have a temper, was visibly upset. He grabbed the paper, called on Howard and made sure he knew that no such feud was ongoing. Rather, "It's just a policy disagreement." In fact, Lehman still attended receptions for Howard and took a member of Mineta's staff, Katherine Karpodf to a Directors Guild of America reception. Lehman and Mineta did work hand-in-hand together in 1985 when, in response to the FAA stating it needed more time to inspect airplanes, the pair asked the GAO to investigate how airline safety inspections were conducted.

Lehman also wasn't shy about cutting the goods of other members who opposed his wants. Lehman did not seek a 1989 Coast Guard increase of five percent (he contended that the current budget was, "not doomsday for the Coast Guard") but, when the full House nonetheless went ahead and backed the extra funding by a vote of 218-198, Lehman was forced to offset the measure by other means. That turned out to be cutting projects from the members who had opposed him (few made that mistake the following year). One was Pat Schroeder, a '72 classmate whom Lehman had even talked up for president (another was the widely respected Lee Hamilton of Indiana). Did she take it personally? Not by a longshot. She called him, "a wonderful soul," and was "never mad at him." The likelihood is that other members felt likewise.

Some Transportation measures, such as 1988, were difficult because of either a lame-duck or recalcitrant president (or both). Lehman supported a provision that would offer compensation to airline workers who lost their jobs due to a merger as did the powerful Air Line Pilots Association (ALPA) but, Reagan didn't so, Lehman reluctantly asked his committee to strike that provision.

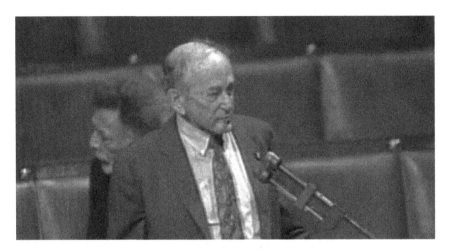

Photo courtesy of C-SPAN

For Dade County, the dividends of Lehman being a "cardinal" were humungous. In 1983, Lehman's first year as a subcommittee chair, $33.8 million of $132.7 million in a jobs bill went to Dade. He worked exceedingly well with ranking member Larry Coughlin of Pennsylvania, even aiding his requests for dollars with some of his own. But when Coughlin asked that the bill be trimmed 4%, Lehman replied while the sum might seem "relatively insignificant...it would mean serious losses for aviation, Coast Guard and railroad projects." Lehman shunned the term, "deals," when it came to securing projects, instead coining the phrase, "mutuality of needs."

Locally, Lehman won funding for an "experimental" rescue unit for Opa-locka, a $500,000 upgrade grant for that city's airport, bridges for Biscayne Bay, a Tri-County Commuter Rail, the Miami Downtown Metromover and an unheard of $1 billion for a Metrorail which Reagan took aim at during a National Conference of Mayors in 1985. Lehman made clear, "the $1 billion subsidy helped build a system that serves less than 10,000 daily riders. That comes to $100,000 per passenger. It would have been a lot cheaper to buy everyone a limousine." Lehman was not amused and spoke of expansions, including to Miami International Airport. He lamented on another occasion when Reagan proposed cutting the budget for mass transit that, "A civilization and the social structure of a nation depends on the well-being of cities, and that depends on fast, efficient transportation."

Lehman's district was solidly Democratic and he never had to worry about re-election difficulties. Thus, his voting record was that of a solid liberal.

Lehman's commitment to equality shined when he blasted Metrorail for not giving a contract to a black firm constructing a route in Liberty City - next to the Martin Luther King, Jr. Station of all places. He supported abortion rights and of course, aid to Israel. The Cuban-American community berated him for opposing arms to other nations in Central America but he was neither flinching nor apologetic. His philosophy: "Liberals too often are trying to do things for the masses, rather than for the individual. That's why I try to help the individual." Those individuals many times included Haitian refugees.

Lehman's firm sense of humanitarianism often meant confronting nations that lacked them. When the House considered aid to Somalia in 1980 Lehman compared it to, "sending a dying man a hand grenade. There has to be a something immoral about this." Three years later, he confronted Secretary of State George Shultz that on U.S. policy in El Salvador, telling him, "We're in a real swamp down there and we ought to get the hell out." With John Porter of Illinois, Lehman tried to tack $1.3 million for Romania but the provision in part fell victim to ire from the Right-To-Life movement and their opposition to Family Planning Amendments (it was worked out). Lehman opposed the repeal of aid to Angola, the Clark amendment which nonetheless passed.

Part of Lehman's reputation was his love of tennis, whether in Washington with colleagues Bob Kastenmeir of Wisconsin, Don Edwards of California or Sonny Montgomery of Mississippi (along with House Chaplain John Ford). At home, he'd play at Miami Shores Country Club. *The Miami Herald* wrote on Lehman's obituary that, "Despite his power, Lehman retained his common touch. He was a breakfast regular for years at Jimmy's restaurant on Northeast 125th Street in North Miami." Lehman also was one of eight members of Congress, including then Senator Al Gore of Tennessee, who purchased an island in the Bahamas.

Then there was Lehman with the big heart. Associates called him a wonderful human being and a generous boss. Mark Olman Ami-El recalled Lehman during his earliest days in Congress. "When he walked into his office and his assembled staff waited for orders, Lehman said, 'We'll work for the good guys.' Everyone knew what that meant." And everyone knew he followed through. Sergio Bendixen, Lehman's one-time press secretary recalled on his death that his boss chose the smallest office — a cubbyhole, really. He was a congressman. He knew he was powerful. He didn't need all the plaques on the wall and the symbols that seemed to make other members of Congress happy. He was secure."

Colleagues on both sides of the aisle liked Lehman as well. Michigan Democrat Bill Brodhead called him, "the nicest man in the House." Maryland Republican Connie Morella said she "found him to be wise, with a sense of humor and humanity." Georgia Democrat Lindsay Thomas came to Congress in 1982 and eventually landed on Appropriations. But his interaction with Lehman began almost immediately in his days in Congress and he called him "a gentleman and a professional who always had time for the younger members who had a lot to learn." Even those who perhaps never encountered Lehman learned the lesson. Ron Klink of Pennsylvania came to Congress just as Lehman departed. "But," he said on the chairman's death, "I must tell you he cast a long shadow. Even after his departure, he was often referred to and talked about because of the respect and admiration he has earned as a serious legislator."

Lehman's constituents evidently felt the same way as staff and other members. Come election time, it was not unusual for him to receive two-thirds of the vote. In fact, by the end of his career, he was running often unopposed altogether.

Lehman underwent surgery for cancer of the salivary gland in 1983 which slurred his speech, leaving some to engage in speculation that he might retire (he joked that he was a rare politician who could "only speak out of one side of his mouth"). But as Geoffrey Tomb in *The Miami Herald* wrote, wrote, "Like a vintage car kept in good tune, Lehman seems to have miles left on his odometer (it was unknown whether Tomb was making reference to Lehman's career as a car dealer). And he is already off and running, humming along, in a 1984 reelection effort."

In mid-1991, Lehman suffered a major stroke while exercising on the treadmill (Californa Democrat Ron Dellums was working out beside him and came to his aid). He eventually resumed work and carried out his full duties but walked with a cane and often relied on a motor scooter. Another challenge was redistricting. In February of 1992, Lehman, who would turn 79 later in the year, decided to call it a career. He made the announcement by leaving the committee hearing that he was chairing and announcing his decision on the House floor. His explanation: "I am no longer sufficiently capable, I no longer have the aggressiveness and physical ability to do the job to meet my own standards and that is why I decided not to seek re-election."

One longtime Capitol Hill staffer and Lehman fan, Tola Thompson summed it up. "Lehman was remarkable gentleman who treated everyone, rich or poor, black or white, the same. He stood up for what was right and just even when it was unpopular for a Southern Congressman to do so."

Lehman had once said he'd like the words, "Nice job, Mr. Chairman," to be on his tombstone. Whether that happened or not, few would quarrel that he truly earned the right to have it.

Photos via Bill Lehman, Jr.

CHAPTER FOURTEEN

Civil Liberties and Personal Decency
Defined New York's Ted Weiss

Introductory Quote: "Whatever room he entered, a living room or the halls of Congress, he was the conscience of that room. There were times I thought he would impeach God, but the fact is, even then you knew he would be intellectually honest. You knew he thought God should be impeached." – New York City Mayor Ed Koch following the death of his late Congressional colleague, Congressman Ted Weiss

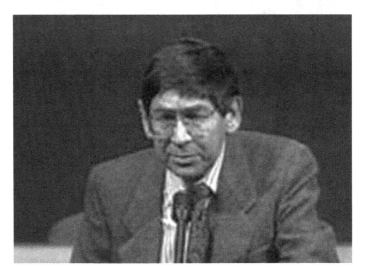

Image via CSPAN

I f any member of Congress who left office in 1992 could have been tasked with authoring the Bill of Rights, that honor without debate would have been given to Ted Weiss of New York. The eight-term Manhattan Democrat was not intended to leave office that year. In fact, facing only token opposition for re-nomination the day before his death, Weiss was not only assured of a winning a new term in Congress but, with the impending election of a Democratic president, of seeing many of his ideals see serious prospects for becoming law. His untimely death from a heart attack led to a vow from allies to continue championing his sunny but indefatigable disposition for progress.

To hear colleagues talk, Weiss was an unusually well-liked member - the "Conscience of the House." For conservatives, he was a bogeyman whose zeal and ubiquity for trying to stymie their causes created resentment that, for them, not Weiss, occasionally bordered on personal.

Weiss was born in Hungary when it was truly the roaring 20's all over the world and he called his school, "remarkably free of anti-Semitism. About the only time you really saw it was on Hungarian Independence Day." Things were rapidly deteriorating in Eastern Europe and the fact that Weiss's parents had divorced when he was seven may well have saved the family's life. His mother, Pearl, arranged to marry a man from New Jersey which allowed him and his sister to emigrate to the United States (his father Joseph was sent to a concentration camp but amazingly survived). The Weiss's settled in South Amboy, New Jersey. After high school, Weiss joined the Armed Forces and then earned both his Bachelor's and J.D. from Syracuse University. He went on to become Assistant District Attorney of Manhattan under the legendary D.A. Frank Hogan.

Weiss was a reformer in the 1950's, opposing the machine of Carmine DeSapio. He became a City Councilman in 1961 and championed the city's first gun control law. He chaired the Committee on Environmental Protection and introduced the first civilian review board. In 1976, when rent control was on the verge of being abolished, Weiss authored a "Letter To The Editor" in *The New York Times* in which he wrote, "Grave social and economic consequences are inherent in removing rental limits and thereby pricing families out of their homes and perhaps out of the city. The people of New York deserve better than to have their elected officials rush into ill-considered decisions based on incomplete information and deliberately misleading conclusions such as are to be found in the Sternlieb Report."

**With future Mayor Ed Koch (far left) and other union
officials around the time of the March on Washington
Photo courtesy of Stephen Weiss**

Noise control was important to Weiss's constituents. At one point, he accused the Lindsay administration of paying "lip service" to the matter (Lindsay eventually signed a less stringent measure in October of 1972). The legislation Weiss proposed to bar discrimination against homosexuals did not make out as well. In fact, it was defeated 7-5 (tactics by the Gay Activist Alliance at a council meeting might have been responsible).

In 1972, Weiss initially backed Lindsay, who had since become a Democrat, for president. He however switched to backing George McGovern after Lindsay's poor showing in the Wisconsin primary.

Shortly before he went to Congress, Weiss and his colleague Henry J. Stern proposed major rule changes. Among the most stringent: tape recordings of full Council and committee meetings, requiring seven days of public notice for hearings, and shortening the process for discharging hearings and committees and Council votes. (bills would have to be taken up by the full body within 60 days absent a hearing). Biannual Reports of counsel employees and seven-days notice before votes on an appointment/nominee would also have been required. Most of the proposals were voted down.

Late in his tenure, Weiss and his colleague Carol Greitzer proposed doubling the fines for people who double-parked without leaving contact information. On a lighter note, Weiss was among the majority of council members who voted to overturn the city's 34-year ban on pinball machines but, as he noted in debate, this did not come without reservations. "I have difficulty working up any real passion for this legislation. I am concerned about the questions raised of mob control of the industry." Yet when he challenged Leon Katz of Brooklyn (the main opponent of the bill) to offer proof that pinball led to organized crime, Katz could not do so.

With New York's junior Senator, Bobby Kennedy
Photo courtesy of Stephen Weiss

Weiss first tried to secure a Congressional seat in 1966 when he challenged the district's Congressman, Leonard Farbstein. Both men were liberal but Farbstein, with ten years seniority, was more of an old-guard member who backed the escalating conflict in Vietnam while Weiss was the reformer who was in staunch opposition.

On primary night, Weiss initially claimed victory when preliminary numbers showed him ahead of Farbstein by 61 votes and called it, "a vote against the President's Vietnam policy." Two days later it was clear that Farbstein had squeaked to re-nomination after all, by 151 votes. Weiss, whose face according to *The New York Times* was "flushed with anger," (not normally a Weiss characteristic) claimed "wholesale fraud perpetrated by Tammany Hall." Weiss wound up suing and the election was re-run, largely on the issue of Vietnam. He called for a "de-facto ceasefire," and asked Farbstein to disavow a letter from a Jewish organization that backed him because Jewish voters had an obligation to back President Johnson's escalation of the conflict. Weiss called that, "the most blatant appeal to ethnic politics I have ever seen." He meanwhile was endorsed by the reform oriented Committee for Democratic Voters. This time, the result was not in doubt as Farbstein won by 1,092 votes. Weiss mounted a return engagement for the seat in 1968 but Farbstein prevailed with 56%.

With then-CIA Director George H.W. Bush. The relationship between the two men was such that after Weiss died, then-President Bush sent Weiss's family a heartfelt letter of condolence
Photo courtesy of Steve Weiss

Weiss finally made it to Congress a decade after he first sought it in 1976 when Bella Abzug gave up the seat to run for the U.S. Senate. He declared his candidacy to replace her and at the filing deadline, the high regard for which he was held was confirmed when no one of stature challenged him for the nomination of the safely Democratic seat, an astonishing occurrence for an open seat. He grabbed 83% in the primary, which was tantamount to winning the actual election. Meanwhile, Abzug lost a tantalizingly close Senate primary to Daniel Patrick Moynihan and, in the days following,

Lieutenant Governor Mary Ann Krupsack suggested that Weiss step aside in order to allow Abzug to regain her place in Congress because, she said, "there was growing concern that women, minorities, the liberal wing might stay home in November because of what had happened to Bella." Weiss resisted her entreaty ("I never wanted to grow up to be a Judge"). He won and in eight ensuing re-elections, never took lower than 80%.

Weiss was initially assigned to the Education and Labor Committee where he focused on education testing as well as Government Operations. In 1983, he stepped down from Education and went to Banking, Finance and Urban Affairs, and later in his tenure a seat on Foreign Affairs.

Weiss's most famous classmate from 1976 was future Vice-President Al Gore, seen with Weiss, his wife Sonya (far left) and Tipper Gore (third from left) Photo courtesy of Stephen Weiss. The man to Sonya's left is believed to be another rising star from that class, future House Majority Leader Richard Gephardt

Politics in America wrote, "There is no question that principle drives Ted Weiss, and often it drives him into Crusades that other members tend to write off as Kamikaze missions."

Civil liberties were high on Weiss's plate and even casting lone "no" votes against legislation with universal support (noticeable in a chamber of 435 members) stood out. The Child Protection Act, an anti-pornography bill that passed 400-1 was an example. He chaired the Americans for Democratic

Action and predictably, his ADA and ACLU score was 100% in 1990 while his NSI was zero. In 1979, he was one of just five members (the others were Yates, Holtzman, Drinan and Ottinger) to receive a perfect rating from the liberal group, Americans for Democratic Action. As colleague Bruce Vento, a fellow '76er from Minnesota said on his passing, Weiss "helped keep that flame of liberalism alive during the 1980s when few wanted to be thought of as a liberal much last appointment of that mission." Weiss's response: "You know you're going to come in for some hassle. But you have to do it."

Locally, Weiss opposed the Westway project along the Hudson River and was dismayed when the Carter administration approved it (Weiss continued leading the opposition and it never did get construction). Still, Carter's reign probably seemed like heaven on earth compared to what Weiss saw when Reagan took office. The new administration's block grant program was labeled, "shift and shaft" and their civil rights priorities were, "derailed civil-rights law enforcement." But Weiss soon had to keep his ear to the ground to ward off a looming problem at home: the 1982 redistricting which created rare potential political perils.

First was the fear that he and Republican colleague Bill Green from the Silk-Stocking district would get thrown into the same district, a theory not unfounded given that New York was losing five House seats. Weiss was initially caught off guard when Mayor Ed Koch, whose re-election Weiss had doggedly championed the previous year, seemed to imply that he would back Green. Weiss's response: "I counted to ten, bit my tongue and decided the Mayor was entitled to have things get away from him once in a while." The plan threw Weiss in with an incumbent New Yorker, but it wasn't Green. It was Jonathan Bingham, a nine-term incumbent from Queens who at sixty-eight years old ultimately decided to retire. Later in the year, Abzug flirted with a comeback but ultimately decided against it. The seat was Weiss's for another decade and he rode it out taking the fight to the Reagan and Bush administrations both on foreign and domestic policy.

As a refugee who himself fled persecution, Weiss had great compassion for others who went through the same. In 1982 he proposed a bill calling for temporary protected status for El Salvadoran citizens (the Reagan administration had classified them as "economic migrants"). He founded the Congressional Working Group on Chile and began a Chinese Political Prisoners Adoption Program. The program consisted of Congress members who adopted a prisoner and subsequently wrote to the Chinese government advocating for the individual's release. However, doling out money to aggressive regimes was not in the plans and Weiss both steadfastly and vocally opposed aid to the governments of El Salvador and Nicaragua to the point that, when direct aid was being considered for the latter, he and Secretary of state George Shultz got into a testy exchange. Weiss accused Shultz of "of twisting facts, distorting facts and misstating facts," but didn't stop there. The tactics, he said, "reminds me of the Army-McCarthy hearings of 1954 in which McCarthy, as a way of getting at the Army, went after a young recent law graduate who asked the senator, 'Have you no decency?'" Shultz called it, "the ultimate perversion to say that an attack on the tactics in Nicaragua is comparable to Sen. McCarthy" and Weiss apologized if the Secretary took the criticism as a direct comparison to McCarthy.

After Reagan launched an invasion of Grenada in 1983, Weiss was aghast that he didn't first seek the approval of Congress. As a result, he filed articles of impeachment. While conceding that removing the president from office would be, "an uphill fight," Weiss justified his actions by saying, "I don't think you put [the resolution] in with the knowledge or expectation of what will happen to it. You put it in because you think it's the right thing to do," adding, "We hope that it generates public discussion." He had six co-sponsors.

With his fellow New York delegation mate and 1984 Vice-Presidential nominee Geraldine Ferraro and with Broadway giant Carol Channing
Photos courtesy of Stephen Weiss

Panama, which occurred late in the decade, was similar. While most Democrats did not want to second-guess the Commander-in-Chief, Weiss's contention was that, "if the Soviet Union were to indict George Bush they would have the right to come in."

Weiss wanted to normalize relations with Cuba to the extent of attempting to get the New York Yankees to play an all-star game there. Three other Congressmen had also met with Cuban officials. When House members wanted to call out Cuba as "injurious to the world community" for promoting drug trafficking, Weiss objected. He labeled it "a misguidedly zealous anti-Cuban, anti-communist anti-whatever kind of paranoia."

On weaponry, Weiss was stunned when he learned that $1 trillion was being spent worldwide. Proposed missile systems did not fare much better. He opposed authorization of the Trident 11 D5 missile and in 1984, introduced an amendment to cut $152 million in funding for the weaponry. It garnered just 93 votes, only four more than a similar amendment by fellow New Yorker Thomas Downey two years earlier.

Occasionally, Weiss's views even caused him to oppose projects for his home turf. A port on Staten Island for the Battleship Iowa was one, and Weiss's conundrum was fear of a catastrophic nuclear accident that might endanger residents. As it was clear that advocates were losing the vote, the Borough's Congressman, Guy Molinari, began twisting arms of other colleagues in a futile effort to save it. Their response: "Look what your own people are doing." Staten Island lost 241-190.

Weiss chaired the Government Operations Subcommittee on Human Resources and Inter Governmental Relations and gave a Special Order speech on the House floor. Frank Horton, his New York Republican colleague who also sat on the panel, observed how, "Pharmaceutical companies trembled at the thought of one of his investigations. So, too, did the FDA officials from time to time he pursued issues ranging from the approval of particular drugs to problems with those drugs from the drug approval process itself to particular efforts for treatment of such a dreaded disease as AIDS."

Weiss was an unsung and most certainly life-saving hero to those afflicted with AIDS. As early as April of 1983, he became the first member of Congress to hold hearings on the new disease that few had ever heard of but which impacted many of his constituents (Henry Waxman of California, whose district encompassed Hollywood, soon did the same by chairing a Commerce Committee hearing). He later worked on AZT research and testing of its effectiveness. When the Department of Education in 1987 released a 28-page handbook that urged schools to stress "appropriate moral and social conduct" (which would be centered on abstinence), Weiss called it, "totally out of touch with reality," because many kids have already engaged in intercourse. Weiss preferred the booklet focus on "the use of condoms, about sanitary needles and so on." He likewise had no tolerance for bureaucrats who seemed to be caught unaware by the crisis. At one hearing, he scolded the witness, telling him, "The problem I have with all of you is that all we get back when we ask for action are words. If the Public Health Service does nothing else, the least you can do is project what the needs will be. Is that too much to ask?"

Another issue on which Weiss had grave concerns was when he got wind of a plan by the Department of Human Services to abolish its Office of Civil Rights. Weiss authored a letter to Secretary Otis Bowen and maintained that, "OCR should be strengthened and supported, not emasculated." The Division stayed put.

Of all of his legislative quests, Weiss's ultimate legacy may be his vigorous, unyielding pursuit on behalf of those with Agent Orange. First, his committee published *The Agent Orange Coverup: A Case of Flawed Science and Political Manipulation*. Chief of Naval Operations Elmo R. Zumwalt Jr., whose son died in Vietnam as a result of exposure to the chemical was an inspiration for this quest.

In 1990, Weiss and Democratic Congressman Lane Evans of Illinois had proposed a bill to provide renumeration. Senate Republicans as well as House Veterans Affairs Chairman Sonny Montgomery refused to support it and Weiss voiced his disapproval in the most noticeable possible way late in 1990. It was the last day of the Congressional session and House members, up for re-election and already kept in Washington far later than usual due to the budget stalemate, were anxious to get home to campaign. Members thought there would be little resistance to a 5% COLA increase for veterans but, when Montgomery asked that it be passed via unanimous consent, Weiss objected. He might have seemed like the Grinch before Christmas but most veterans groups lauded him. Paul Egan, legislative director for the Vietnam Veterans of America said, "What Ted Weiss did was heroic and positive as we look forward to next year. Our hat's off to him."

With Judiciary Chair Jack Brooks of Texas
Photo courtesy of Stephen Weiss

Among other investigations Weiss's subcommittee launched: whether the White House prevented the Office of Management and Budget (OMB) from publishing questionable warning labels on food. He said, "total control over F.D.A's health claims policy is just another example of the neutering" the FDA. The subcommittee published a report detailing as such.

Later in the decade, Weiss virulently opposed both a proposed Constitutional Amendment as well as a law that would prohibit burning of the American flag. "There has been no epidemic of flag burning," he told colleagues as the vote neared. "The best thing we can do is nothing…We don't need a statute. We don't need an amendment. We need more respect for the Constitution of the United States." When proponents of the law dickered over whether the words "physically defile," or "defile," would pass muster from a court point of view, Weiss made clear he was not impressed by the "verbal acrobatics."

Weiss not only resisted attempts to cut funding for the National Endowment for the Arts following two obscene exhibits but uttered perhaps the most illustrative comment about what he thought the consequences would be, and that is that a funding reduction would, "take a piece out of America and what America is all about - and that is freedom of expression." Lawmakers approved the cut 361 to 65. In his last term, Weiss chaired the Congressional Arts Caucus (which he won on his third try) and convinced a number of colleagues, including Marty Russo of Illinois to join, which some labeled a Nobel Prize winning accomplishment. The Arts was even a part of Weiss's personal life. One newspaper reported that, on the rare occasions that he wasn't working, Weiss's passions included music and theater. It was noted that, "in Washington, he regularly attend[ed] movie screenings and art exhibits."

Weiss's sometimes solitary missions did not dent his popularity at home. One reason was that despite stature in the nation's capitol, he always remained true to himself. In 1990 *The New York Times* wrote that, "When Mr. Weiss was a City Councilman in the 1960's, voters often recognized him on the M104 bus, riding down Broadway in a rumpled suit. More recently, his suits looked freshly pressed. But on visits to his district, he still rode the bus."

Hard work was also a hallmark. Jim Gottlieb was Weiss's Chief of Staff for nearly a decade and recalls his boss was profuse in his devotion to the job. Weiss, he said, "never tired of work, of reading, of being prepared, of wanting to know everything he could about an upcoming vote, tomorrow's oversight hearing he would chair, an important constituent meeting - whatever it was." Gottlieb says the staff, "used to joke, no, make fun of, his frequently attending some evening sporting event with the staff, or going to the beach, in his work clothes, tie and jacket always, with briefcase in tow so he could be ready to read between baseball innings or hockey periods."

Acute attentiveness didn't mean he required the same from subordinates and Gottlieb calls him, "respectful of my and other staffers desire to put their families and the needs of children first." Gottlieb adds that Weiss was "not a "boss" or ever in any way demeaning to anyone around him from me to the newest staffer." Stephen Weiss, the Congressman's son said every staffer viewed Weiss as "the boss of a lifetime" and the Capitol Hill publication, Roll Call, concurred. More than once, they bestowed on him their yearly, "Office Angel" Award because of the way he treated his top-notch staff. That's not to say he couldn't be tough but Steve called it similar to his parenting skills. He "gave you as much rope as you needed to hang yourself with but wanted you to work to your potential."

By 1992, another remap was looming and New York was again losing seats. Weiss generally made out okay, though the new district extended to Brooklyn, scooping up neighborhoods such as Coney Island and Brighton Beach. Weiss had a far more pressing problem, however, which was his health.

Weiss's health issues began in 1982 when he underwent bypass surgery. In 1986, after collapsing at a party on Capitol Hill, he underwent a quadruple bypass. On September 13, 1992, the day before he was supposed to face a Libertarian-oriented Democrat, Arthur Block in the primary for a ninth term, Weiss collapsed and died of a heart attack. He was 65 years old. The following day, he won re-nomination with 89%. His funeral was held a day later where future House Speaker Nancy Pelosi was among those who spoke and the "politicking" that a Weiss confidante said went on among potential successors was obscene.

About a week after Weiss's death, New York Democrats held a convention to select the replacement to Weiss on the ballot (publications cited the politicking going on at the funeral). Weiss's widow Sonya threw her name in contention to succeed him as did Abzug and a bevy of state lawmakers including: State Senator Franz Leichter, Representatives Jerry Nadler and Richard Gottfried, Ronnie Eldridge, and Councilwoman Ronnie Eldridge. Sonya told delegates, "Whatever happens tonight, I hope you're getting a good laugh out of it, Ted." The Committee picked Nadler as his successor whose proclivity for upholding civil liberties, no matter how esoteric, fit right in Weiss's mold.

Back in Washington, mourning for Weiss continued well after his funeral. As Congress raced to complete work for the session, the New York delegation organized a Special Order for members to discuss what Weiss meant to them. Fellow New Yorker Jim Scheuer called him "a very mild and friendly and warm-hearted person, never got personal, never got excited, but in his commitment to the causes that seized his imagination, he was absolutely dogged and intrepid and committed with a half degree of determination, and the length and breadth of the issues that galvanized his imagination was really quite remarkable."

Harlem's Charlie Rangel might best have captured his late colleague's contribution. When Rangel entered the House chamber conflicted about how to vote on an issue, he'd gaze up at the board and see which way Weiss had voted. During the special order he said, "If the 435 of us truly represented the United States of America and what that shining Constitution should be, not only to ourselves but a symbol for the entire world that seeks democracy, then

Ted Weiss would not be the exceptional person that he was. We all should have so much of that Ted Weiss in us that we all will be just one of the gang and we all will just be doing the right thing."

Steve Weiss said his father never had any serious aspirations to be anything other than the West Side's Congressman but was enchanted about being a U.S. Supreme Court Justice. Had that ever happened, Steve said, "he would have been a sure Ruth Bader Ginsburg sidekick."

CHAPTER FIFTEEN

Jenkins of Georgia a Rare Southern Powerhouse Among the National Congressional Players

Introductory Quote: "People talk for me. He talks to me." – House Ways on Means Chair Dan Rostenkowski on Congressman Ed Jenkins of Georgia who said on another occasion, "the tougher the issue, the more you want Ed Jenkins in the room."

Photo courtesy of Jo Jenkins

Without question, the legislative and prestige giant of the sextuplet of Georgians who left office in 1992 was Ed Jenkins. Though the

Democrat from Jasper often found himself forced to navigate both ends of the spectrum in order to appeal to his very conservative constituency. He did it well and won a tremendous number of friends who knew no ideological boundaries.

A comment Jenkins made following his 1989 loss for House Majority Leader to Richard Gephardt in June of 1989 essentially sums up his character. Shrugging it off, he declared, "I do not have an ego that needs constant news items." If Jenkins needed a following, he had a knack for finding one simply by walking into a room. As Democratic colleague Marvin Leath put it, he was, "an excellent, excellent political animal." He aimed to negotiate not just to produce deals but rather final products that would have a common sense benefit for Americans and the people of North Georgia. How else can it be explained that more than once, Jenkins outmaneuvered titanic Ways and Means Chair Dan Rostenkowski and yet Rostenkowski would publicly fawn over his colleague for friendship and advice? In fact, the two were often dinner partners at Rosty's favorite hangout, Morton's Steakhouse in Washington D.C).

Referred to as "soft-spoken with hill humor who conducts business in his unassuming, back-country way," Jenkins grew up one of six children to a barber in Young Harris, the same North Georgia town where his very good friend, future Governor Zell Miller, would hail. The two graduated high school together and Miller told Jenkins, "You'll always be my best friend unless you run against me for U.S. Senate," which Jenkins recalled very nearly happened.

Jenkins' grandparents lived in Robbinsville, North Carolina and came to Young Harris on horseback in 1906. His grandfather purchased a store and a boarding house on what is now the campus of Young Harris College. Ed was born in Towns County but eventually moved with his family to Union County directly west. His future wife, Jo Thomasson resided there and following a courtship, they married four days before the dawn of the 1960s. They had two children.

Jenkins and Georgia Governor Zell Miller were close friends growing up
Photo courtesy of Jo Jenkins

The future-Congressman credits a stay at the boarding house by Governor Ed Rivers as what sparked his interest in politics. He graduated first in his class in high school and earned an Associate Arts Degree from Young Harris College (now University) before attending Emory University. The Korean War was ongoing at that time and Jenkins volunteered for the Coast Guard. When he returned, he resumed his education. Qualifying for the GI bill, he earned his law degree from the University of Georgia in 1959 and became a federal prosecutor for three years. From there, he started a practice in his new hometown of Jasper and in 1962 began working as a part-time assistant to Democratic Congressman Phil Landrum, a five-termer who in time became a member of the powerful Ways and Means Committee. It was in that position that Jenkins developed personal relationships with relatively senior members such as Rostenkowski and Tip O'Neill and they proved instrumental in helping him along the corridors of Capitol Hill when he succeeded Landrum 14-years later, a proposition he could not have possibly imagined pursuing at the time.

Landrum gave Jenkins the heads-up before officially calling it quits in 1976, which meant he wanted to give him a head start over other potential candidates. This was a risky proposition. In later years, Jenkins recalled the district as encompassing, "all of Gwinnett County, all of Whitfield County on the west side. We went east to the South Carolina line, north to the North Carolina and Tennessee line, and so we really had everything in north Georgia in the Ninth District." With nine candidates poised to get in for what was then a safely Democratic district, he was not certain he wanted to give up his law practice but after consulting his wife, decided to go for it.

With fellow Georgian Jimmy Carter having won the White House, it was truly an exhilarating time to be in Washington. He supported Jimmy Carter's hospital cost-containment proposal despite misgivings because the president wanted it.

**The men with the best hair (Ed Jenkins) and best smile
(Jimmy Carter) came to Washington in 1977
Photo courtesy of Jo Jenkins**

Jenkins' penchant for outmaneuvering big fish in Washington began with Tip O'Neill. The new House Speaker opposed Jenkins when he mounted a campaign to win a seat on the powerful Ways and Means Committee shortly after coming to Washington. It wasn't personal by any means – O'Neill liked Jenkins very much even though, "he and I fought a great deal because I was too conservative." Jenkins managed to beat the man O'Neill supported, Massachusetts Congressman Robert Drinan (a priest), and they all stayed friends. O'Neill valued Jenkins' counsel and became a trusted member of the "Speaker's Cabinet." Additionally, O'Neill would often seek out Jenkins on legislation of utmost importance "to see how I felt the South would go, and I'd give him a read."

Rostenkowski was another confidante and regional politics made their professional relationship intricate and their personal one as tight as can be.

For starters, Jenkins headed the House Textile Caucus, central to a major economy of his district and the entire Southeastern United States. Pursuant to that, he pushed for the Textile and Apparel Trade Enforcement Act of 1985, a 40% rollback. His reasoning: "There are small communities that are almost totally dependent on this industry for their entire livelihood. If the industry falls, the entire economic base of the town falls." On another occasion: "It's not just a matter of economics. They (opponents) don't see the human element that I see."

On one hand, Jenkins truly accomplished a Houdini. He got it to the floor not just over the opposition of Rostenkowski, but of Trade Subcommittee Chair Sam Gibbons an avid free trader. But those were the limits. At one point, he challenged Reagan's intention to return the bill to Congress without his signature. "He promised five years ago he would not allow imports to exceed the domestic consumptions," Jenkins said, "If he vetoes this bill without offering a plan to cut those imports to consumption levels, then he has broken the promise he made." Reagan did just that.

Three times, the bill cleared Congress and three times it fell to Reagan's veto pen. On one of those override attempts Jenkins, "did something that was a little bit unusual. Instead of having an immediate override vote, which I knew that I could not win, because I couldn't get two-thirds of the House, I checked with a parliamentarian about a specific date for an override, and he said, 'Yes, you can do that.' So, I asked for, and they didn't really realize, I don't think, on the Republican side, what was happening. I asked for an October date, if I remember correctly. At any rate, fairly close to the election in November." Still, the veto was sustained, though in one case the margin was only eight votes and Jenkins took heart that "an overwhelming majority" was against gutting quotas.

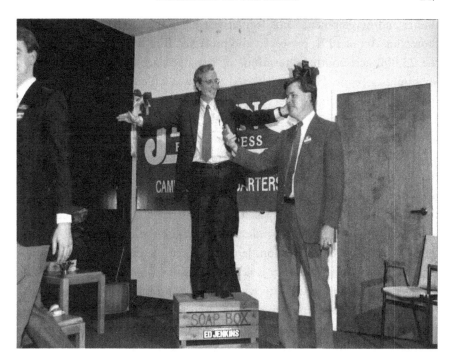

**Sammy Smith was Jenkins's trusted aide and loyal friend
for all but one of his 16 years in Congress
Photo courtesy of Jo Jenkins**

Rostenkowski also kept Jenkins off the House-Senate Conference Committee for the landmark Tax Overhaul Act of 1986. Even so, Jenkins helped persuade Rosty to keep the deduction for state and local taxes and the two men were close pals and dining partners. Others who often attended: Chuck Schumer, Barbara Boxer, Tom Downey, Marty Russo, Charlie Wilson along with Sonny Callahan, a Republican from Alabama.

This was not Jenkins's first rodeo when it came to imports. During his second term, he got the U.S. to negotiate with Hong Kong over crude feathers and down. Textiles were also at the top of Jenkins' mind as Congress considered sanctions against South Africa over Reagan's position. "They are simply ignoring the real facts of life and apparently are committed to eliminating the textile industry in this country."

Another Jenkins initiative was protecting the Chattahoochee National Forest from outside interests, particularly logging and development. "A lot of people are concerned that we are losing our mountains to overharvest of

timber and development." His legislative finale, The Chattahoochee Forest
Protection Act of 1991, preserved and protected this 867,000 acre forest and
the 23,000-acre southern terminus of the Appalachian Trail was named
for him as a result. He also delivered what was called "home-cooking" by
sponsoring the Georgia Reservoir Management Improvement Act of 1988.
The goal was protecting the coveted federal Lake Lanier and Lake Allatoona
in the district from the ever-thirsty metro Atlanta region.

On other matters, Jenkins supported the Gephardt Amendment to a
trade act but voted with the Reagan administration against requiring plants
to give employees two-months notice before closing. While he also supported
the Reagan tax cuts, he opposed the administration's education cuts and
reductions in dairy supports while voting to raise the retirement age to 67.
During the Bush administration, Jenkins backed the Eastern strike board, a
big issue for Gwinnett County residents. He voted to override George H.W.
Bush's veto of both a minimum wage increase and the Family and Medical
Leave Act. He opposed the Civil Rights Act of 1990 (after initially backing
it), sponsored a Balanced Budget Amendment Constitutional amendment to
limit federal spending growth based on prevailing economic factors as early as
1983 and backed the anti-flag-burning amendment. He usually voted pro-life.
On defense related issues, Jenkins voted in favor of aiding the Nicaraguan
contras and SDI research but was in the minority of the Georgia delegation
by opposing the MX missile ("there's no efficiency in spending as fast as we've
been spending in the last five years"). When Congress debated war against
Iraq, Jenkins stuck with the majority of his party in voting to give economic
sanctions time to work.

When Congress was debating whether to authorize a holiday in honor
of the birthday of Dr. Martin Luther King, Jr., Jenkins voted to place it
on the Sunday before to save $500 million. His view as Administrative
Assistant Sammy Smith explained: "He was a preacher, and a Sunday holiday
is appropriate." Yet one characteristic about Jenkins was that he was not afraid
to admit a mistake and in a later oral history project, he recalled he came
to realize that the concept was, "very distasteful to the African American
community," and acknowledged it was one reason he decided not to enter the
Democratic primary for a U.S. Senate seat in 1986 when it "would (likely)
become a real issue."

Photo courtesy of Amy Godfrey

Through witnessing Jenkins's skills and getting to know him, many of his colleagues started urging him to seek a leadership position. In the fall of 1987, the position of Caucus Chair following the '88 elections seemed to top the list. However, Jenkins demurred. Ostensibly, his reason was the time constraints of mounting a leadership position. Those who knew Jenkins wouldn't doubt that it was genuine. He surmised how, "probably unfortunately for me, my early training does not necessarily fit into the 1980s, when you have very aggressive campaigns for leadership post very quickly."

It was not hard to see why Jenkins was hesitant though he did enjoy the backing of some colleagues from across the spectrum including Leath of Texas to his right and Tom Downey of New York to his left. Jenkins was certainly smart enough to know that past votes he casted and opposition to his party's position would come back to hurt him.

Jenkins also took a pass on challenging U.S. Senator Mack Mattingly for a second term in 1986 (that honor went to his junior colleague, Wyche Fowler who, against the odds, knocked off the Republican incumbent.) In a 2008 oral history project Jenkins said his decision not to run was, "the one decision...that I sort of regret, even though I supported Wyche and I thought he did a good job." It clearly was a case of "as one door closes," as the powers that be (Congressional leadership) would soon have for Jenkins a highly sought-after assignment that would send his stock rising in numerous ways.

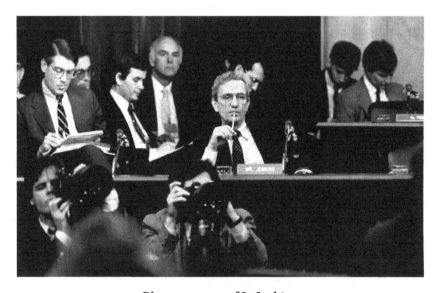

In 1987, O'Neill retired but his successor, Jim Wright, continued consulting him. In one instance, he assisted O'Neill as he prepared to appoint members to the Iran-Contra committee. One seat went to Jenkins himself – and he wasn't even seeking it. Not only was Jenkins the first Congressman to question Oliver North but he was the only member of the committee from the House side who never held a position as Chair. He asked North if it was true that "not a single official elected by the people" knew about the fund. North had to acknowledge that fact but said, "It was my view then, and it continues to be my view now, that we were not breaking the law...that I had assumed that the president...was aware of it." Jenkins said after the testimony that "it wasn't the finest hour of this operation, when they didn't know where the money was deposited. It was sloppy, to say the least." Colleagues nearly unanimously agreed that Jenkins' questioning was the finest hour of the committee. He became the official talk of Washington, flabbergasting for a man who once said "mountain people are more reserved." Alabama Senator Howell Heflin called it "the most pertinent" and Oklahoma Senator David Boren said it "should have been asked several days ago."

How did Jenkins formulate his questions? Smith said he "consulted the special committee's staff who had the extensive expertise and access to all classified documents; secondly, from his own homework and perceptions as a committee member; thirdly, our staff." It helped that he had great admiration for Lee Hamilton, a gellow Democrat from Indiana who led te committee.

Photo courtesy of Jo Jenkins

Jenkins finally decided to take the plunge with a high-level leadership position in 1989 when he challenged Missouri Democrat Richard Gephardt for the position of House Majority Leader. It did not go particularly well. Aside from being a fellow '76er, Gephardt served with Jenkins on Ways and Means and was a friend. Jenkins backed the Missourian during his bid for the 1988 presidential nomination and even stumped for him in Iowa. Thus, it was a contest that began as friends and ended as friends. Jenkins predictably lost by a vote of 76-181 but, in a sign of the overwhelming respect he came to know, spoke of colleagues who would visit him to explain their choice. *The Atlanta Constitution* paraphrased Jenkins as saying, "Sometimes the explanation would stretch to 30 minutes and the members seemed uncomfortable." The lesson he learned: "You should not seek the office where the most popular person in the House is running for the same seat." One vote Jenkins did get was Rostenkowski's.

At the time of his loss Jenkins was determined to dive back in to the Ways and Means arena. Almost immediately, he became a prime player in the debate over President George H.W. Bush's plan to slash the capital gains tax. He and six other Democrats on the Ways and Means Committee came up with an alternative proposal that was embraced by Republicans, including the panel's top Republican, Bill Archer. Jenkins called tax cuts "a long-standing tradition" but Gephardt derided it as the "Bush-Jenkins plan" and tried to peel away some of the six. In part, Gephardt's strategy was to push Ways and Means debate on the bill into the fall and secure a victory by killing it. He didn't succeed, and Jenkins prevailed in committee 19-17. The battle next went to the full House.

With his homespun wit (he was once described by the Atlanta media as "country chic"), Jenkins offered a closing summation of the long debate when it made it to the House floor. "In listening to this debate today, I do not think there is any institution or organization that uses or needs the first amendment more than this institution because every possible statement has been made here today from both sides, not much of it totally accurate." On a substantive note, Jenkins explained that perfect could not be the enemy of the good. The, "well, I am for a little bit of capital gains but I don't like this plan," was not practical for those who liked the idea of a capital gains. "You have to decide whether you are for capital gains or you are against it….I challenge the leadership to explain to us why we do not have a vote on indexing, why we do not have a vote on permanent capital gains reduction if the two-year thing is bad. They need to explain to all of us." He prevailed 190-239 and sixty-four of those in the affirmative were Democrats. The vote also gave new oomph to a party that seemed destined to be shut out of the White House. Jenkins called it, "an opportunity for [the party] to regroup and to take a look at the direction we're going to see if we can't be more positive toward the middle-income class."

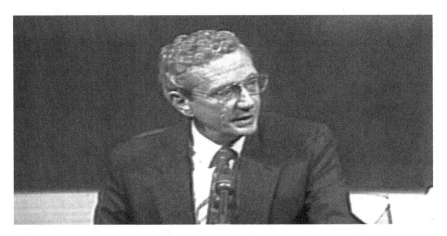

Image courtesy of C-SPAN

Alabama Democrat Ronnie Flippo came to the House with Jenkins in 1976 and they immediately became friends (one common trait was that Jenkins hailed from North Georgia and Flippo North Alabama). Both served on Ways and Means. Flippo describes Jenkins as "a very unusual man. Highly intelligent, unique sense of humor who provided a lot of leadership for a lot of people." One anecdote bears that out. Jenkins would typically arrive on the House floor early in a vote series and cast his vote. The life of a member of Congress was such that it was not unusual for members to know little of the subject matter they were voting on upon entering the chamber, if it didn't pertain to their respective committees. To rectify that, members, particularly Democrats from the Southeast, gazed up at the board to see how Jenkins voted. Of course, Jenkins occasionally could be "mischievous" by switching his vote in the middle of the series. The friendship was so deep that when Ed died, Jo asked Flippo to deliver a eulogy. Staff idolized Jenkins as well. Smith, who spent 15 years with Jenkins, described him as, "in sum, genteel, laid-back, polite, available, and a strategic thinker."

Richard Schulze, a Republican from Pennsylvania was another of Jenkins's closest friends. He calls him, "a wise, kind, generous and thoughtful man who put God, country and family first in his life. While he had a great sense of humor, he endeavored to make things better for those who worked hard to advance themselves and their families. Schulze calls Jenkins, "a good friend, a great legislator and will long be remembered and missed.

For the most part Jenkins's electoral challenges were non-existent. He would nearly always lose fast-growing and suburban Gwinnett County but would prevail in the other counties by such lopsided margins that it wouldn't matter.

In 1988, Jenkins's opponent Joe Hoffman accused him of voting "eight times more liberal" than when he first won the seat. If voters cared, they certainly didn't show it - Jenkins returned to Washington with 63%. Hoffman was back in 1990 and initially, that contest seemed poised to turn out little different than the first. Jenkins did finish double digits ahead but this time, his winning margin slipped to just 12 points, for a 56-44%. He lost Gwinnett, which preferred Hoffman by the reverse 56-44% margin. His other loss interestingly was Cherokee, the district's second most populated countythat is now also suburban.

With a good friend, Joe Sartain, during a re-election campaign
Photos courtesy of Jo Jenkins

1992 was a redistricting year and though Jenkins would have been successful given that Miller was now Governor, he began pondering his future. Shortly before revealing his plans he said, "If you're picking up a lot of new voters and you've got to start all over in an area, that's always time for reflection." He soon after announced his retirement. "That, plus the normal frustrations. You just wake up one morning and say 'Why am I doing this?'" Another reason was that his goal of chairing the committee was now totally elusive. "I looked at the make-up of the committee and tried to determine if I could become chairman in a reasonable amount of time, considering I'll be 60 this year. I came to the conclusion I would not be chairman."

As he prepared to leave office, Democratic Congressman Claude Harris expressed, "All of us who know Ed appreciate his keen with and ready humor, a humor that doesn't spare members, the institution, or Ed himself."

Jenkins retired and in 1994 was named to the University System of Georgia's Board of Regents by his childhood and longtime friend, Governor Zell Miller. He served as member and chairman of the Board while nurturing two grandsons. He died at age 78 in 2012.

The veneration folks have for Jenkins is reflected by Smith who proudly states that, "Even after his retirement from the US Congress and even since his death, I'm still his AA - and proud to be."

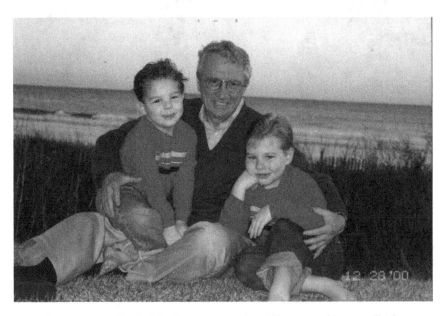

Retirement afforded Jenkins more time to dote over his grandkids
Photo courtesy of Jo Jenkins

CHAPTER SIXTEEN

36 Years in the Beleagured Minority Neither Hampered Broomfield's Effectiveness or Respect from Collegeagues

Introductory Quote: "Yes it would, Mr. Chairman." – Michigan Congressman William Broomfield when his office hall-mate and Ohio colleague, Chalmers Wylie teased him about how nice it would be to serve in the majority. Both retired in 1992 two years before that goal would have been realized.

Photo courtesy of the U.S. House Historical Collection

In 1948, a 26-year old realtor named William Broomfield placed his name on the ballot for the Republican nomination for a State House seat in a Royal Oak, Michigan based legislative district simply to see how many votes he could get. To his surprise, he won and embarked on a career that took him to Congress and didn't sunset until 1992. Along the way, he amazed even himself to have made such strides. "Little did I know when driving to Washington in late 1956 to begin serving in Congress that I would be sitting across the table from hundreds of world leaders such as Chaing-Kai-Shek,

Deng Xiaoping, Mikhail Gorbachev, Queen Elizabeth II, Margaret Thatcher and Anwar Sadat, not to mention eight presidents." Not to mention ten Secretaries of States.

Broomfield's success in life and his 36-year career in the House likely resulted from one word: fidelity. Walking with presidents and kings did not lead him to neglect the needs of his constituents a single iota. In fact, his accessibility was unquestioned and his office fastidious for performing constituent services and answering mail in a timely manner, which Broomfield often took part in himself. If there was one drawback, it was that his relationship with powers came without any in the halls of Congress. Broomfield and his classmate from '56 and close friend, Minority Leader Bob Michel of Illinois, who together held the record for longest service of serving in the House under the rule of the other party.

One could say Broomfield's stint of elected offices began at Royal Oak High School when his classmates tapped him as student body president. After high school, he attended Michigan State University. His service to the nation during World War II came in the U.S. Army Air Corps. When he returned, he went into real estate but local Republicans spotted his talent and tapped him to seek a seat in the State House in 1948 at age 26. He would be challenging an incumbent, George Mathieson, also of Royal Oak (Otto Heber was also in the race). About 5,000 votes were cast Broomfield upset the incumbent by exactly 90 votes with Heber about 500 votes back. But Broomfield didn't have to devote nearly as many resources to the Democratic candidate in the fall because there wasn't one. Once in, Broomfield got acclimated and in 1953, became the youngest Speaker Pro-Tem. He moved to the Senate in 1954.

By 1956, the 18th district's longtime Republican Congressman George Dondero, was retiring and Broomfield decided to undertake what, if unsuccessful, might have been a career-ender. Broomfield went for the seat and faced George Higgins, a fellow State Senator with more seniority. Broomfield edged him 50-46% in the primary (a margin of 1,440 votes) and prepared for what was expected to be a tight race against Paul Sutton, a fellow Royal Oakie. But it wasn't. Broomfield took 57% in a hard-fought as Dwight Eisenhower was winning a second term. In the battle of the favorite sons, Royal Oak went big for Broomfield while Sutton carried Oak Park and little else. Acknowledging that he, "never expected quite the majority I got," Broomfield informed his new constituents that, "I want the people who voted for me to know that I'm going to Washington without any strings attached at all. I'm under no obligation to any pressure groups, corporations or anything. My only debt is to the people of this county. It's a big debt and I hope I can repay it." His constituents obviously felt he did. In 1958, a year of freight for Republicans, Broomfield kept his post hung with 53%.

Only twice through 1972 did Broomfield exceed 60% (the Democratic city of Pontiac was in the district) but after that, his margins never dipped below 60%. That year, his biggest hurdle was the primary and reapportionment again forced Broomfield to take a risk that, like his first run, would almost certainly have meant doomsday for his career had he lost. Broomfield moved his residence to the township of Birmingham to challenge Jack McDonald, a three-term incumbent and fellow Republican who represented much of the new district. He took 59%. Broomfield was aided that year by the issue of busing. It was an emotional issue which had nearly succeeded in ending the careers of a few suburban Detroit colleagues. But Broomfield's sponsorship of an amendment that would prohibit it while appeals were going on. At one point, he had to seek out the assurances of President Richard Nixon "I have no doubt that you secured the best legislation you could under the circumstances." That year, Broomfield got a firsthand taste of the emotions behind that issue when his office was firebombed.

He initially took seats on Public Works and Small Business. The latter, he stayed with throughout his duration but the former, only two terms. His daughter Nancy explained on his death, "Everyone trying to get money and building roads to nowhere. That wasn't his thing. When the opportunity to be on Foreign Affairs came up, he jumped on it." He would make quite a mark, including apparently, on himself. *The Detroit News* in 1992 wrote that, wrote "Throughout his career, he has kept scrapbooks, carefully squirreling away mementos of his attendance at White House state dinners, his many visits to foreign countries and correspondence with foreign leaders."

Broomfield became top Republican on Foreign Affairs in 1975 and held it until his retirement which meant half his career. Broomfield was exceptionally close with his Democratic counterpart on Foreign Affairs, Dante Fascell of Florida, so much so that when Fascell announced his retirement less than a month after Broomfield, he invited his ranking member to join him at the podium ("C'mon Broomfield, you started this"). The secret might have been ego: Fascell, Broomfield said, "doesn't try to pretend he's Secretary of State." Broomfield recommended Fascell for a State Department post when both retired and poke at his Memorial service. Another Democrat who served on Foreign Affairs, Lester Wolff of New York called Broomfield, "a great guy. Great to work with. No politics is his decisions."

Though Broomfield was more supportive than not on Reagan's foreign policy initiatives, rolling over and playing dead was not in his DNA. In Reagan's first year in office, Broomfield opposed the administration's plans to provide $8.5 billion in aircraft to the Saudis in committee Lebanon.

Broomfield was quite active in the fight against Democrats who were staunchly advocating a nuclear freeze. 1982 was the easy part. Broomfield and opponents of the freeze thought they could by time against the opposition with a measure he authored that would call on the U.S. and the Soviet Union decide how and when to implement a freeze. It passed. "We accomplished everything that we could accomplish through that amendment and some 30 others. I was extremely pleased. They freeze supporters can claim anything they want, but the fact is we weren't rolled. We won a clear victory."

Rather than outright oppose Reagan, Broomfield would often formulate the administration's proposals to make them more feasible to Congressional Democrats. Aid to El Salvador was one case. The funding was being considered as a broader Central American aid package and Democrats were bitterly opposed. Broomfield, who contended that the funding Democrats wanted would allow the nation to "bleed to death, proposed a resolution with Pennsylvania Democrat John Murtha that would allow aid to the nation so long as Reagan provided reports to Congress on the nation's progress. The catch, as *The Washington Post* reported was "The funding would be made in two installments, and Congress could veto the second by a joint resolution." Broomfield opened his remarks by admonishing Congress on opposing his measure. "Mr. Chairman, if you want America to pull out completely from El Salvador, then cast your vote for the Studds amendment. If you want to turn that country over to the Marxists, and Cuban-Nicaraguan dominance, vote for this approach. You will be casting a vote for a program which will push El Salvador off the cliff." With Murtha and Majority Leader Jim Wright's backing, the measure bitterly divided House Democrats and it squeaked by 212-208.

Broomfield toured Grenada with other Congressional leaders and made clear from the get-go that the mission was of little use to the U.S. He supported a committee effort, which passed 32-2 to withdraw forces from the island within two months. Given that, he had no problem going along with those who felt it triggered the War Powers Act ("it is clear to me that the war powers act applies in this situation"). It passed 403-23.

Lebanon put Broomfield in a quandary. In autumn of 1983, members of both parties were pressing the Reagan administration to withdraw U.S. forces. Broomfield was more reticent: "What else can you do unless you want to write off the Middle East and chances for a peace settlement there?" But in October, the bombing of a barrack housing U.S. troops killed 249 Marines and Broomfield the following February told Secretary of State George Shultz that, "We are wondering whether or not our policy is dramatically changing. We were relieved, frankly, when the President made the move to gradually remove our marines, but I have to say that I'm one who is beginning to wonder whether we're going beyond a reasonable amount of shelling."

Through thick and thin, Broomfield labored on behalf of the administration's quest to aid the Nicaraguan contras. Lawmakers had consistently granted the aid by razor-thin margins after acrimonious and emotional debates, in 1987, the issue was up for a vote again and Broomfield was not ecstatic. Referring to "stop and start policies," Broomfield asked colleagues, "Do we stand with the forces of freedom or cave in to the forces of Communism?" The vote was 230 to 196 against the aid.

When Congress took up Iran Contra, Broomfield displayed little inclination to make nice. He opposed the investigation of the Iran-Contra in its current form, which he called, "an outlandishly broad scope. The nation cannot afford another…committee exercise in which leaks damaging to our nation's diplomatic and intelligence efforts."

**Broomfield, who by virtue of being in the minority during his entire career, never held a gavel, jokingly takes aim at Hawaii Democrat Daniel Inouye of Hawaii during the Iran Contra Committee hearings
Photo via Getty Images**

While Broomfield chided Reagan for getting himself into the Iran-Contra imbroglio, he genuinely believed he was putting his best foot forward with regard to getting to the bottom of it. At one hearing, he expressed his view that Congress as much as anyone was derelict. "I am not even a lawyer, but I have got some common sense, and I am not one of those who is predicting who should or who shouldn't be indicted…Since Vietnam, Congress likes to boast that it has been an equal partner with the President in shaping foreign policy. I think Congress ought to shoulder the blame for an on-again/off-again foreign policy in Nicaragua. President Reagan, who still carries the burden of making foreign policy, must deal almost daily with the 535 Secretaries of State in the House and Senate who seldom can form a simple majority around a single issue."

One defense of Reagan that was a bridge to far was his unwillingness to accept sanctions against South Africa and Broomfield had no problem voting to override his veto in 1986. On it getting to that point, "The administration must share some blame for dragging its feet." He did take issue with the administration's plan to redo the U.S. Embassy in Moscow.

Where Broomfield's backing was unrequited was Israel and Greece. He viewed Greece as entitled to the same monetary aid as Turkey and in 1982, co-sponsored a resolution calling on the U.S. government to fight for Turkey's withdrawal from Cyprus. "Passage will be sending a clear signal to Turkey that the continued occupation of Cyprus is not acceptable and that the rights of the people of Cyprus must be restored."

One foreign affairs matter Broomfield championed that was out of the limelight was revoking the security status of the nation of New Zealand because of its prohibition of nuclear weapons in its ports. His rationale: "New Zealand cannot expect to enjoy the benefits of a close defense alliance with the United States without accepting the burdens that go with it,"

When George H.W. Bush was in the White House (the two had served in Congress for four years), Broomfield still tried to lend support but felt the administration still gave him ammunition not to. Tiananmen Square was one example and Broomfield and New York Democrat Stephen Solarz proposed a measure following the Chinese government sending in the tanks that contained stronger sanctions than the administration wanted. The House passed it unanimously. Broomfield's response: "I regret that we were not able to get the backing of the Administration. The Chinese leadership should realize that there is a very deep-seated revulsion in Congress about the barbarian tactics they have employed."

The following January, when Bush vetoed a measure that would allow Chinese dissidents to remain in the U.S. until the crisis had passed, Broomfield led the way for an override calling the vote, "a referendum on human rights that will be heard around the world" (it cleared the House but died in the Senate). And when Saddam Hussein invaded Kuwait, Broomfield, along with Fascell, were in symmetry that the president had a duty to consult Congress in every step of the way. Specifically, when Bush drastically increased the number of U.S. troops going to the Persian Gulf shortly after the '90 elections, Broomfield called it, "the main reason support for the policy is eroding."

Broomfield with some of his closest friends in Congress, including Minority Leader and 1956 classmate Bob Michel, President George H.W. Bush, and House Foreign Affairs Chair Dante Fascell Official White House Photo

On domestic issues, particularly when his friend Gerry Ford was in the White House, Broomfield could be more partisan. He opposed the creation of a Consumer Affairs branch, aid to New York City and voted to sustain nearly every one of Ford's vetoes, including a bill banning strip mining on which he had originally had voted in favor. But Broomfield was no lackey for any president. In 1982, he was one of 32 GOP House members who traveled to Camp David to hear the president out as he sought passage of his tax package. He did often sustain Bush's vetoes but opposed the 1990 budget summit agreement because he could not support his abandonment of his "no new taxes" pledge. Other issues Broomfield pursued. Advocating for the Maritime Administration to sell ships built before 1946 in the National Defense Reserve fleet.

In 1990, Broomfield beat Walter Briggs, nephew of Senator Phil Hart whom *The Almanac of American Politics* noted was not even born when Broomfield entered Congress, 66-34%.

Broomfield's retirement announcement in April of 1992 was not particularly expected. He had made it through redistricting and, though he did face a primary opponent, was not expected to be seriously threatened. But frustration and minority status appeared to be take its toll and he announced just after Easter that he was joining the scores of lawmakers who were leaving. Calling it, my most difficult political decision," he cited "gridlock between the administration and Congress," but also the recent scandals that had plagued the institution (Broomfield had zero overdrafts at the House Bank). He explained, "I just have got to the point where I have been very, very disgusted . . . that nothing is getting done down there," "And as upsetting as the recent scandals in the House have been, I am even more disturbed by Congress's inability to address the really important national issues affecting our country, such as balancing the federal budget and resolving the inequities in the health system." Most important though, Broomfield said he wanted to, "step out and enjoy life a little bit...I didn't want to stay and be carried out. ... I wanted to leave when I was feeling good...There is life after politics, at least I hope there is." Meanwhile, Michel would continue to serve and *CQ* noted he issued a panegyric statement, "His retirement left him eligible to convert $655,652 into his personal use but Broomfield vowed to, "not take that money and run." True to his word, he gave every penny to charity or scholarships.

As members saluted Broomfield on the House floor as his term was winding down, one word that was used repeatedly to describe him was "counsel." Robert Lagomarsino, a fellow Republican on Foreign Affairs, called him, "the kind of friend everyone needs – intelligent, thoughtful, experienced, always ready to help with good counsel and advice whenever you need it." Broomfield's longevity often meant wisdom that served as counsel to his younger colleagues. Republican Bob Livingston of Louisiana commented on his death that, "There was never a more kind, considerate, and truly gentle man to have served in Congress. Anyone who knew Bill considered himself to be his friend and was the better for it."

Broomfield and House Minority Leader Bob Michel came
to the House in 1956 and were friends for life (Broomfield
proceded Michel into retirement by two years)
Photo via Getty Images

Broomfield escorts ex-President Richard Nixon into
his Capitol Hill office on September 3, 1992
Photo via Getty images

After an Upset Win, Dickinson Proved No Fluke and Rose To Top Armed Services Position

Introductory Quote: "When so few politicians do all the final horse trading behind closed doors, you can never be certain that what they bring home is a nag or a filly." - Alabama Congressman Bill Dickinson

Photo courtesy of the Collection of the U.S. House of Representatives

U ntil 1964, Alabama epitomized the "Solid South" for Democrats as even the slightest GOP breakthrough seemed impenetrable. But backlash over that year's Civil Rights Act propelled William "Bill" Dickinson and four other Alabama Republicans to win Democratic House seats in unmitigated upsets that year. Even before they took office, many might have rightfully assumed these new members were already lame-ducks and some of them were. Yet Dickinson proved durable. He kept his seat for 28 years and, with a senior position on the House Armed services Committee, became a go-to person for beefing up military installations.

Dickinson was the epitome of a Southern Congressman: increasingly graying, burly, sometimes reticent to shed anachronistic if not ethnocentric views while arduously championing local defense needs and a muscular national budget. Philosophically however, particularly as his career wound down, Dickinson went from an inveterate display of rhetoric when it came to social issues to at least some degree of evolving with the times.

Dickinson's life aside from Washington was spent in the Lee County town of Opelika. He served in the U.S. Navy during World War II in the European Theater and later a Major in the U.S. Air Force Reserves. After the war, Dickinson earned his J.D. degree from the University of Alabama Law School and after had a thriving career. A resident of Opelika, he was judge of Lee County Court of Common Pleas and of Juvenile Court and finally a Judge on the Fifth Judicial Circuit.

By 1964, as Vice-President of Southern Railway, Dickinson was high on a hog. He was also Democrat? What prompted him to switch parties and run for Congress – a mission he himself must have expected would be a kamikaze run, especially given the fact that the man he was seeking to unseat, George Grant, had been around since 1938. Mindful of the fact that many voters were accustomed to voting straight Democratic ticket, Dickinson's slogan was, "First for Bill, and then as you will." He took an astounding 62%.

Photo courtesy of the Alabama Department of Archives and History

Dickinson made his presence known almost as soon as he arrived and it wasn't altogether positive. The 1965 march from Montgomery to Selma had taken place just three months after he had taken office and he made his opinion known to all in two separate speeches. One speech, which he titled, "March on Montgomery: The Untold Story," he claimed "Drunkenness and sex orgies were the order of the day in Selma, on the road to Montgomery, and in Montgomery...News reporters saw this, law enforcement saw this, and Mr. Speaker, photographs were taken of this, I am told." It continued: "The Communist Party and the Communist apparatus is the undergirding structure for all of the racial troubles in Alabama for the last three months."

The response was as strong an uproar as can be. Colleagues walked off the floor and New York Democrat William Ryan said, "I am sure that the gentleman from Alabama remembered the old legal adage: When you do not have the facts on your side, try the opposition." Members of the clergy joined the fray with Charles Blackwell, who led the March alongside Martin Luther King, Jr., called the accusations "garbage," the Reverend Dom Orsini accusing Dickinson of "trying to defame and debunk the whole civil rights movement with a new type of McCarthyism." Another, Reverend, Richard F. Dickinson, of the United Church of Christ said, "You would find more friendly conversations between boys and girls at a church camp than on the march," adding, "These people were deeply conscious of the high purpose of their undertaking." Dickinson later had to concede that he had no proof for the allegations but not before arranging a second, 60-minute special order on the House floor in which he used sworn affidavits to back up his earlier contentions.

Beyond his misstatement, the initial record Dickinson compiled was staunchly conservative as he opposed forthcoming civil rights and Great Society legislation. In 1973, he sponsored an amendment that would prohibit food stamps for striking workers. When House Democrats advanced federal funding of political conventions, Dickinson called it the "most repugnant and objectionable" part...We can find through the whole thread of this bill the partisanship, I suppose, which is part of this ball game. But let me remind all of us that with the purse strings goes control."

Dickinson could be snippy on matters substantive or small. When the House in 1971 took up Nedzi-Whalen, which would mandate that operations in Southeast Asia cease by years end, Dickinson called it a charade. "Anyone who says this is a vote for peace and a vote against it is a vote to prologue the war is either being a demagogue or is totally ignorant of what this amendment will do." Later, he said, "If the Soviets start to roll and use their chemical agents, we will hit them with an opinion poll. That will stop them in their tracks." In 1988, when asked why he routinely opposed procedural votes approving the House journal, Dickinson called it, "a throw away vote that doesn't make a tinker's Damn. So rather than approving something I haven't read and don't know what's in it and don't know anything about it, I just vote no." And when Connecticut Democrat Sam Gejdenson unveiled legislation in 1990 that would speed the process for common exports, Dickinson replied that he, "share(d) the view of one writer who recently termed HR 4653 the, 'Soviet Military Relief Act."

Photo courtesy of the Alabama Department of Archives and History

Dickinson could be biting with presidents as well. He had little use for President Jimmy Carter, implying that the peanut farmer from Plains, Georgia had little more than peanuts for brains. He called Carter, "far and away the poorest, sorriest," president whom he served under. Ronald Reagan was a much different story. Aside from championing his military buildup, Dickinson was Reagan's man on a number of fronts. In 1985, he sponsored four amendments the administration wanted stricken. But he refused to be a rubber-stamp and could be critical when he thought Reagan blew it, such as his contention that the administration was "stonewalling" an MX missile funding deal Dickinson had helped produce. Reagan didn't seem to mind. In a 1986 visit to Alabama, Reagan recognized it, telling the crowd that, "no member of the House has done more in rebuilding the nation's defense than you have, Bill."

One way Dickinson might have supplemented his earlier opposition was by shepherding approval of the MX missile, a battle royal if there ever was one in the House. Congress's effort to kill the MX missile, which Dickinson strenuously opposed, coincide with the beginning of the Geneva Convention. "This Congress serves notice on the Soviets that we are not going to build and deploy the system anyway there is very little for them to negotiate about." The debate had been going on since the war of the roses and Dickinson implored colleagues: "Let us make a final decision today. We have rehashed this thing so many times. He wanted as many as 12 missiles approved which the House adopted.

Photo via the U.S. National Archives

In the 1980s, Dickinson took a hard-line position on the Soviet Union as he had on Vietnam. El Salvador was another.

When Congress and the president agreed to $33 billion in military cost reductions in late 1987, the Navy would inevitably bear at least some of the brunt, which was codified by the retirement of 16 frigates. That was apparently too much for Navy Secretary (and future U.S. Senator) James Webb. But Dickinson was unmoved. "If anybody's living in fat city, it's been the Navy for the past few years."

Dickinson was among many who did see the necessity in 1988 of closing 20 bases nationwide and he called enacting it "a small window of opportunity." Reminding colleagues that, "We have a lame-duck Congress, we have a lame-duck administration, we have a lame-duck Secretary of Defense, all of whom support this legislation. If we do not pass this bill and allow these base closures to be named this year, it will be another 10 years before such an opportunity comes again."

First and foremost, Dickinson looked out for his home state's defense industry. He was instrumental in securing projects for Maxwell and Gunter Air Force Base and Fort Rucker, all in his district. In 1973, Dickinson was instrumental in getting U.S. training and retraining to Fort Rucker and helping it become the Army Aviation home. 16 years later, Dickinson was able to match the private funding raised to secure a grant for a new U.S. Army Aviation Museum. It is partly for this reason that the nickname, "The Godfather of Army Aviation" was bestowed on Dickinson. In fact, his championship of the use of the Apache helicopter during the Persian Gulf War enabled it to become the first aircraft to open fire at war's commencement.

The Encyclopedia of Alabama noted Dickinson, "fought to maintain funding for the M1 Abrams tank, the M3 Bradley troop carrier, and the AH-64 Apache and UH-60 Blackhawk helicopters, all of which have become mainstays in the arsenal of the U.S. military." In fact, his championship of the use of the Apache helicopter during the Persian Gulf War enabled it to become the first aircraft to open fire at war's commencement.

Dickinson put in his two cents on the war against drugs. Convinced that "the Democrats began making a partisan issue" of it, he introduced an amendment that he conceded was "not thought through sufficiently" but that he nonetheless wanted to put on the table. It would allow the president to use the military to intercept aircraft and ships suspected to be holding drugs at the border and would be carried out in part by radar planes. One reason Dickinson had reservations was the potential using the military in this manner had to prevent service members "basic assignment to defend the nation." It passed 385-23.

For the state, he was instrumental in getting funding for the Outer Loop Interstate.

The peak of Dickinson's influence was in the early 1980s. Republicans were in the minority in the House but the Democratic chair of the Armed Services Committee, Mel Price of Illinois, was elderly and losing his grip. Rather than make partisan hey out of Price's woes, Dickinson publicly came to his aid. A sign of their mutual trust came one day when Price had to step away from the podium. Rather than pass the gavel to the next Democrat in line, he turned it over to Dickinson, somewhat annoying the majority side of the aisle, but not out of disrespect for Dickinson. Michigan Democrat Dennis Hertel served on Armed Services for twelve years and calls him "well liked and respected by Democratic members. More importantly we trusted him I actually think he had more influence than most ranking Members." Also, both parties shared a single staff.

In 1984, the Democratic caucus dumped Price in favor of Les Aspin, an energetic liberal from Wisconsin. For the first few year of Aspin's reign, Dickinson's rapport with him was strong. But in 1988, he felt cut out from the negotiations on the '89 defense authorization bill that were taking place between Aspin and his Senate counterparts, Democrat Sam Nunn of Georgia and Republican John Warner of Virginia, so much so that he refused to sign the conference report ("I don't want my handprints on it"). Aspin replied that he had addressed at least some of Dickinson's concerns and wondered whether, "Next year, maybe we should have a 'gang of two' instead of a 'gang of four.'" Apparently, Aspin meant what he had said because Dickinson felt similarly alienated in 1990.

The pair argued on other issues.

When members couldn't agree on how much to fund the MX (also known as the LGM-118a Peacekeeper) and the Midgetman (which he had little use for), Dickinson sought to propose a compromise of $650 million and $350 million respectively but the full House rejected it, leading Dickinson to observe, "Sometimes people get too cute." But late in 1988, things changed. Aspin brokered a historic deal with Ron Dellums, one of the most liberal members of the House and John Kasich, a conservative budget-buster from Ohio to eliminate funding for the B-2 bomber. *CQ* noted, Dickinson "complained that Aspin had used the savings reaped from elimination of the B-2 to provide pork-barrel benefits to committee members in exchange for their support for the authorization measure." His assertion: "When he canceled the B-2, he automatically got $2.7 billion worth of chits. He and his staff have been all over working on my guys."

As his years in Washington moved forward, so did at least some of Dickinson's views. In 1992, Dickinson he one of seven members who switched his vote to support overturning allowing abortions in military facilities. Earlier, he had voted for Family Planning. He even was supportive of women in combat, contending that, "If a service member has what it takes to perform competently in a combat support role, he or she should have the same chance to compete for that position regardless of gender." Dickinson made clear that he wasn't "talking about eliminating the combat exclusion laws. I'm merely suggesting that women should be able, if they choose, to compete with men for positions outside of combat itself." And as he left office, he displayed very early fortitude by questioning the wisdom of continuing to display the Confederate flag over the state capitol. "Getting industry to come to Alabama with the public perception of Alabama is very difficult. People who have never been there still have a picture of Alabama with (former Birmingham Public Safety Commissioner) Bull Connor setting the dogs loose on demonstrators, and little George (Wallace) standing in the schoolhouse door."

That's not to say Dickinson's ideological pendulum swung completely in the other direction. His voting record remained solidly conservative. He was beyond leery of allowing women in combat. "Speaking from a Southern exposure, I tell you it would not be popular at all to mandate that women be in combat roles, particularly...in infantry or special forces combat." He introduced Constitutional amendments making English the official language of the United States as well as one calling for the reconfirmation of federal judges every six years, arguing that doing so would be, "bound to keep them a little more honest."

People who did not find Dickinson sniping and biting were his staff. Clay Swanzy ran his office for many years and he called his boss, "very easy going, (a) wonderful sense of humor, very compassionate." Dickinson, he said, "did not curse nor did he lose his temper very often." He loved to entertain.

Dickinson made no bones about enjoying the many perks of being a Congressman. He traveled around the world wildly and initially, was the only Alabaman to back the 1989 pay-raise President Bush was advocating for members of Congress though he reversed that within a month.

Prior to 1982, Dickinson won re-election more often than not in the mid-50s, occasionally topping 60%. Swanzy credited, "the secret of his success" to "campaign(ing) all the time." He still had two very near-career-enders during his last decade in office.

In 1982, State Public Service Commission head Billy Joe Camp was his Democratic opponent and he wrapped himself around his former boss, Governor George Wallace who was making a comeback. He accused Dickinson of being unresponsive to the interests of agriculture in the district. But Camp struggled with fundraising, and at one point had just $10,000 on hand compared with $150,000 for the incumbent. Camp smashed in many of the rural areas but Montgomery and Dothan delivered big for Dickinson, who held his seat by 1,386 votes.

Bamberg came on board shortly after and he did admit to walking into a "feeling of a sinking ship." He confirmed that the farmers, particularly the peanut producers, felt neglected and, "we worked very hard to bring them back into the fold." They formed the Agriculture Advisory Commission so Dickinson could be kept abreast of issues of importance.

Dickinson had long been talking about calling it a career in 1992 but the end almost came involuntarily sooner. He was actually taking a big risk standing for re-election in '90 following influence peddling allegations that made its way to *The New York Times* but, more ominously, to the House Ethics Committee. A longtime hometown companion, Ben Collier, had given Dickinson 1/3 of profits that resulted from a $300,000 contract for a military uniform company that Dickinson steered to Collier (the expectation as outlined by Collier was that, the Congressman "will use his capabilities to cause the capital to be invested in as profitable a way as possible"). Profits or losses were to be shared, two-thirds for Collier and one-third for Dickinson, who apparently boasted how he "got a good deal. You put up the money and I'll put up the know-how." Dickinson's response: "I have been trying to promote his company, the largest private employer in my district. There was no relationship between the two facts...So far as I can ascertain, there was nothing illegal, unethical or immoral in my entering a business venture which is not in any way connected to my job or legislation."

As the 1990 campaign season opened, Dickinson was on the receiving end of mountains of bad publicity. His Democratic foe, Faye Baggiano, was very well connected, having served the last two Democratic governors of Alabama, Wallace and Fob James. It was therefore no surprise that Baggiano made the theme of her race Dickinson's, "pattern of ethical problems" and there was more where that came from. Baggiano charged Dickinson with accepting money from oil companies even as he looked into allegations of price gouging. Dickinson's response was, "If it shows anything, it shows I'm certainly not influenced by political contributions from any PAC. I'm not influenced by political contributions. If the oil companies are gouging, I'm going to say so. If they want to continue to support me, I'll give them my address." She ran an ad criticizing his frequent travel to France ('Masseur Dickinson, your usual table." The entire staff, including Dickinson, got a kick out of that. Baggiano tried to get Dickinson to debate but his response was, "I've voted on everything three times."

The incumbent's slogan was, "Dickinson: Now...More than Ever" and voters agreed. Dickinson squeaked by with a margin of 4,406 votes out of 171,000 cast, 51-49%. The margin was generally geographical. Baggiano carried Montgomery and most of the counties big and small in the Northern end of the district. Dickinson conversely carried almost all of the Southern terrain (with the exception of Dale County). Many believed his vocal support of the military buildup in the Persian Gulf following Saddam Hussein's invasion of Kuwait tipped the scales. He said on election night that, "I think I really paid a price by being in Washington in the first four or five weeks of the campaign."

As 1992 opened, Dickinson seemed genuinely undecided about his re-election plans but, in early March, he announced his retirement. His impending departure was felt in circles both his personal circles and interests pertaining to Alabama. Montgomery County Republican Chair Roxanne Lancaster conceded going, "all female when he tried to talk to me and I just started crying. I have been his campaign director since 1964 - I've grown old in this job." Dickinson himself was circumspect: "I've always said, as those who have been around me much know, when I no longer felt it was fun and I wasn't enjoying the job and couldn't get any satisfaction out of it, then it would be time to hang it up. We've reached that point." He also added the current defense cutback played a role: "I'm not anxious to take part in the dismantling of our defense establishment. It's shortsighted." Dickinson also said it was "time for me to turn over the position and responsibilities to another, younger person. I have held an elected office for over 40 years, the last 28 of which have been in Congress...." Yet that didn't stop him from joking about throwing his hat into the ring for governor of Alabama in 1994. 1992 was the last year that members could pocket their campaign treasuries and Dickinson still had $317,000 on hand (within several months he had used the money to purchase a car and a computer).

CHAPTER EIGHTEEN

Machine-Oriented Annunzio Didn't Take Himself Too Seriously, but Took Protecting Consumers Darned Seriously

Introductory Quote: "You can tell the American people they just got f-ck-d." – Illinois Congressman Frank Annunzio to columnist Al Hunt the day the House overturned an Annunzio amendment on wage and price controls they had passed only a day before. When Hunt replied that he couldn't print the statement because it would be appearing in a "family newspaper," Annunzio replied, "All right, tell them the American family just got f-ck-d."

Annunzio with colleagues Peter Rodino (D-New Jersey) and John LaFalce (D-New York)
Photo courtesy of John LaFalce

There is that old saying from that movie, "Forrest Gump," that, "Life is like a box of chocolates. You never know what you'll get inside." With Frank Annunzio, you nearly always knew what you'd get inside. Widely known as among the chamber's most colorful, profane members with a knack for expressing himself prolifically, Annunzio was throughout his 28-years in Congress a caricature of a stereotypical, machine-pol which, imagewise at least, was not always drawn in his favor. But he was viewed as a genuinely nice man with some stern convictions and viewpoints that were fairly representative of what at the time was his very non-gentrified district. His desire for consumer fairness saw him pressing the issue of reforms in the credit-card industry long before it was conventional among colleagues and it eventually yielded serious results

Chairing a prominent Banking Subcommittee and the full House Administration Committee, Annunzio at one point was cited by noted columnist Jack Anderson as one of the best and most popular, "backroom operators." Jim Leach, a Republican Congressman from Iowa who sat with Annunzio on the Banking and Urban Affairs Committee, might have summed up his repertoire. "Congress is a body of more homogeneity than one should expect, and Frank stands out as one of the real characters - an individual who spoke his piece in his own way, which generally involved a greater twinkle than a reading of any script would seem possible."

Annunzio was also among the proudest of Italian-Americans to have ever served in Congress. John LaFalce was a Democratic Congressman from Buffalo, New York who sat with Annunzio on Banking. He called him, "first, foremost and always an Italian-American" and *The Chicago Tribune* noted on Annunzio's death that he often used it to combat "what he considered to be negative portrayals of Italian-Americans." His parents came to the Little Italy section of Chicago from the Italian town of Calabria and Frank was their first of four children. His hero was baseball great Joe DiMaggio and he shined shoes at the Hull House which was founded by social reformer Jane Addams to help women and immigrants advance. Annunzio's wife, Angeline Alesia, though born in Indiana, was one of ten children whose family also hailed from Calabria. His high school classmates voted him "Most Likely to Succeed" and his daughter Lucia notes that occurred early – "he married the prettiest girl on the block."

Annunzio graduated from Crane Technical High School and after securing his degree from DePaul University in Chicago, taught history and civics in the Chicago Public School system, and arguably lived a little of it. He helped organize the infamous and bloody Republic Steel strike that killed ten on Memorial Day of 1937, then returned to DePaul to attain his M.A. (his preparation for obtaing a Ph.D was thwarted by World War II). In the ensuing years, Annunzio was an assistant supervisor of the National Defense Program at Austin High School and an educational representative of the United Steelworkers. During the war, Annunzio had two stints as chair of the War Ration Board.

In 1949, Annunzio became Illinois Secretary of Labor and his boss was the fabled governor, Adlai Stevenson who had won the Democratic nomination for president at the time he was serving him. If anyone doubted in those pre-civil rights days that Annunzio would be committed to the movement, that came to pass at that time when he mandated that "white" or "color" signs be removed. Martin Luther King, Jr., was one of his heroes.

Annunzio made it to Congress in 1964 when three-term Democrat Roland Libonati declined to seek re-election and, himself a man with a colorful background, proved to be Annunzio's predecessor in more ways than one. At one point Al Capone's lawyer, Libonati said, "I liked him because he respected me." The Daley machine tapped Annunzio to succeed him and he won the primary unopposed and took 85% in the general. This would be the "Great Society" Congress and Annunzio was a firm supporter of President Lyndon B. Johnson's programs. With a seat on the Banking Committee, he was active in the 1970 debate to impose crime insurance legislation. Calling the concept, "long overdue," he contended that victims, "might still be alive had they not sought to protect their property, which was uninsured because of the cost of that insurance."

**Photo courtesy of the Special Collections and University
Archives, University of Illinois at Chicago Library**

This district was quintessential Chicago which *CQ* noted was the Loop,
the downtown waterfront, West Madison, Skid Row, and many slum rooming
houses plus urban renewals." Annuzio, with his pulse close to the people,
became firmly ensconced in the new district prior to the 1972 redistricting.
That year, a map that fairly closely (but not monolithically) resembled the
Republican plan was adopted 2-1 by a judicial panel and it carved Annunzio
into a district held by George Collins, an African-American freshman in a
district that was 55% black. Annunzio's comment was that "the only thing I
could say about the Illinois redistricting is that it's terrible." But in reality, he
didn't make out terribly at all.

Party leaders backed Collins for the seat but a fellow Democrat, Roman
Pucinski held the heavily Polish/German 11ᵗʰ Congressional District that
he would be leaving to challenge incumbent Republican Senator Charles
Percy (he lost). The Daley machine prevailed on Annunzio to run there. The
campaign was not easy. *CQ* had noted that "it probably favors Democrats
except in strong Republican years" and 1972 just happened to be such a
year as Richard Nixon was expected to romp the very unpopular George
McGovern. Annunzio did face a very formidable opponent in City Alderman
John Hoellen who tried his darndest to tie him to the Daley machine. At
one point, Hoellen even filed a suit against Annunzio's campaign for sending
franked mailings to parts of the district he was not yet representing but

Annunzio responded that he was acting, "upon official business. He prevailed 53-47% and until 1990, was never again hard pressed.

If Annunzio had two areas of specialty while in Congress, it was credit fairness and coinage. The credit issue had many incarnations and spanned much of Annunzio's time on the Banking panel.

**Marching in a parade with Illinois Governor Dan Walker (far left),
Mayor Richard Daley (third from left) and other officials
Photo courtesy of the Special Collections and University
Archives, University of Illinois at Chicago Library**

In 1980, Annunzio tussled with Wisconsin Senator William Proxmire over the repeal of certain provisions from the 1968 Truth-in lending Act that Proxmire himself had issued (one was notifying the consumer of all forthcoming charges). Annunzio resisted, initially refusing to even consider the Senate bill, but was forced to accept concessions when the two measures went to a conference committee.

In 1984, Annunzio proposed permanent prohibitions on surcharges, calling them, "loan shark interest rates" In 1986, he sought to lower interest rates for banks and retail stores but that proposal failed to make it out of committee when two Democrats declined to back it. That same year, he proposed legislative action when credit card companies kept interest race at exorbitant levels. This proved necessary, he said, "because a majority of credit card issuers have not cut their rates. It now appears that voluntary action will not work and it is time to vote on legislative cuts."

In 1987, Annunzio was back with a credit card rate cap. It was an amendment to a disclosure bill and when opponents said it would stifle competition, Annunzio replied, "There is about as much competition in credit card rates as there would be in a wrestling match between Gorilla Monsoon and Tiny Tim. Before banks lower their interest rates, Hulk Hogan will be chosen Miss America." That very poignant warning failed to heed colleagues who rejected his amendment 356-56.

Seeking to get a handle on lending abuses was another cause and Annunzio in 1988 sponsored the Home Equity Loan Consumer Protection Act. Among other things, the law would increase disclosure requirements and misleading advertising for the industry which Annunzio viewed as a necessity because "there was a time when only termites could do more damage to a homeowner than a home-equity loan." He wanted women to have the same credit opportunities as men without regard of their marital status.

With Illinois Democratic Women's Caucus Members
Photo courtesy of the Special Collections and University
Archives, University of Illinois at Chicago Library

Annunzio also held banks feet to the fire on the issue of red-lining. Leach, a member of the panel, recalls, "sitting there and all the sudden Frank is screaming at Burns, 'You're guilty of red-lining! Stop red-lining Italy!' I didn't know Frank Annunzio at the time and I didn't know he wasn't serious.'" *The New York Times* also noted that he had an aide play "Stars and Stripes Forever" as another amendment was being considered and proudly justified it by saying, "It passed."

By the end of the decade, Annunzio was still on the warpath against those who were up to no-good. One amendment he pushed through on a 382-41 vote would impose civil penalties of up to $1 million a day on financial institutions that took part in criminal offenses.

Annunzio's imprint on the coinage issue was noteworthy particularly when it came to events of international pride. For instance, he passed a bill prior to the 1984 Summer Olympics that the mint would be government funded as opposed to private and as a result, many believe Annunzio's attentiveness singlehandedly saved the Olympics that year. He presided over the coinage for The Statue of Liberty's 100th anniversary, complete with a $5 gold piece. He tried to do the same for the bicentennial of the U.S. Constitution but was hampered. And as the Congressional bicentennial approached, Annunzio, under Prins urging, also tried to use coinage profits to go toward an overhaul of the U.S. Capitol. Prins called the building, "in bad need of refurbishing," and said, "This coin program gives us a way to make some improvements."

Annunzio staunchly opposed proposals that would replace the $1 bill with coins. Declaring the Susan B. Anthony dollar, "a flop," Annunzio said, "there's just no public sentiment for a dollar coin at this time." In 1987, Annunzio took issue with the Mint for having American Eagle bullion coins made overseas, saying, "Americans wanted to buy American gold, and if the treasury is not going to sell American gold, they should tell people that." Gene Essner, deputy director of the Mint, replied that there was not enough gold. In 1988, Annunzio was exasperated when dies of the Gold Eagle disappeared while going cross country from West Point, New York to San Francisco. This was the second such incident as 44 dies for the Statue of Liberty coins went missing in 1986 which prompted Annunzio to declare them, "shipped as ordinary freight, as if they were a crate of oranges."

On labor issues, Annunzio was firmly in the corner of the little guy. But on cultural issues, he usually leaned toward the right side of the spectrum. He was pro-life and joined a number of other Illinois Democrats in opposing the Civil Rights Act of 1991. In the run-up to the Gulf War, Annunzio sided with the majority of Democrats who wanted to give sanctions the opportunity to run their course, arguing that, "Toughness, patience, and persistence pay off when economic sanctions are imposed. Five months are not enough. It will take until at least spring or early summer to weaken Saddam militarily and destroy his ability to effectively wage war." And that same year, Annunzio abandoned his opposition to gun control and backed the proposed seven day waiting period known as the Brady Bill. On the House floor, he said, "we've all heard the old saying that an ounce of prevention is worth a pound of cure. By the same token, the Brady Handgun Violence Protection Act won't eliminate firearm abuse-but it will provide a simple, effective way for us to begin saving the lives of innocent people across this country." He co-sponsored the Balanced Budget Amendment but switched.

**Annunzio at Carl Schurz High School with Principal
Maloney and the school's mascot, the Bulldog
Photo courtesy of the Special Collections and University
Archives, University of Illinois at Chicago Library**

Taking care of the mortgage industry was central to his effectiveness. "Whatever it takes to save the industry we have to be prepared to do," he said at one point. That came back to haunt him in the late 1980s when thrift after thrift folded. Annunzio had little to do with it but he was portrayed, whether fairly or not, as having his hand in the cookie jar by virtue of supporting them. This gave him the race of his life as he sought his final term in 1990.

Kathleen Day in *S & L Hell: The People and the Politics Behind the $1 Trillion Savings and Loan* wrote, "When he attended hearings, he sat on Chairman St. Germaine's right, motionless, wearing thick-black glasses and a suit that seemed too big for him. He asked questions fed to him, either in written form or through whispers in his ear, by Prins. Even then, he often bungled questions." Prins would be Curtis Prins, staff director of the Consumer Affairs and Coinage subcommittee and later Financial Institutions. But he was not just any staff director - he was often called "Congressman Prins." In recent years, Prins didn't dispute this and Annunzio, while in Congress, was proud to let everyone from Wall Street to the Treasury Secretary know that it was indeed the case.

When Annunzio became chair of the Regulation and Insurance Subcommittee on Banking, his attitude as Prins relayed it was, "I really don't want to get into this. I don't have the time" (he was instead occupied by House Administration). His solution. "I want you to run it" and the only admonishment was, "Don't get me onto trouble." In order to accept that arrangement, Prins told Annunzio that he needed his full backing not only when times were good but when they were rocky. Annunzio gave him his word and delivered. Prins said he, "never interfered with anything we did. He never criticized anything." And he backed him 100%. Prin's assignment meant that he would often vote in Annunzio's stead (permitted in committees, though not on the House floor), which made him subject to lobbying from other members during close votes. It also almost certainly made him the most powerful aide on the Hill. While Annunzio family members dispute the fact that Annunzio was a lackey, they acknowledge the outsized role Prins played in his life. After all, Prins viewed Annunzio and his wife as second parents, traveled extensively with them and delivered a eulogy at his funeral.

On the Hill, Annunzio was popular. His daughter Lucia recalled "there wasn't a waitor who didn't know his name," nor a police officer. He was a common man who drove a '72 Chevy Ventura. Frank Guarini, a colleague of Annunzio's from New Jersey, expressed a common sentiment about him. "He was colorful, down to earth, blessed with good personality and helpful to everyone." The colorful, down-to-earth aspect was crystal clear and for aides, sometimes in the most blushingly public of ways.

For starters, Annunzio was notorious for butchering colleague's names. One day, while introducing Wisconsin colleague Jerry Klezca, he did it one time too many to which Klezca replied, "Thank you Chairman Annunciation."

Maryland Democrat Kwesi Mfume was also on the receiving end of the mispronunciation.

Pronunciation aside, so much as even remembering names could prove challenging and Mike Lowry of Washington State learned that the hard way. Annunzio could never recall his name when he had a shaven-face but on one occasion, he sported his recently grown beard and at one point, he was seeking recognition from Annunzio during a hearing. As Lowry's turn came, Annunzio turned to Prim and said, "Curt, whose the c—ks——r with the beard." The line was picked up audibly by the microphone. After that, Prim put a kickswitch on the microphone and stood over his boss.

A sense of humor Annunzio did not have but a generous heart he did and unbeknownst to many, he wasn't afraid to show it. In her memoir, *Bella*, New York Congresswoman Bella Abzug had written how she had nearly been struck by a motorist at a capitol intersection and telling the police office, "nobody would miss me." Shortly after, Annunzio very nearly had the same encounter and the officer explained to him Abzug's comment. "What do you mean telling the cop nobody would miss you," Annunzio asked Abzug? "I had to tell him, 'She's absolutely wrong. We would all miss her and her passion and her concern and her smile, and her carrying on, and her joking, especially when she doesn't win a vote.'" Neither was Annunzio a publicity hound. He'd often turn down television requests and interviews, instead having Prins do it.

Annunzio's Italian heritage was a matter of extreme pride. He and another proud Italian, Peter Rodino of New Jersey, sponsored legislation making Columbus Day a legal holiday and Annunzio vigorously tamped down critics who questioned the explorer's role in discovery America. LaFalce recalls a hearing where the witness casually contested Columbus's role and Annunzio shot back, "When Christopher Columbus discovered America, it stayed discovered." Annunzio also fought for the National Italian American Foundation (NIAF) and for much of his life, was involved with the planning and fundraising for Chicago's annual parade. Being close to Rev. Armando Pierini of Northlake also gave him access to singer Frank Sinatra and when the two wrote to Sinatra asking him to headline a benefit, the singer replied, "You print the tickets and I'll be happy to pay for the rest." What can't be overstated, however was that Annunzio was beloved by all ethnic groups. He had a great affinity for the Jewish-community and counted members of that faith as among his closest friends.

Annunzio's later years in Congress, and ultimately, the circumstances for his departure, were not particularly auspicious. First there was the grueling 1990 re-election campaign, the likes of which Annunzio was totally unaccustomed. It resulted from the attempt to tar Annunzio with the stint of the virulently incoming savings and loan (S&L crisis).

Annunzio with New York Senator Al D'Amato and New Jersey Congressman Frank Guarini at an event honoring Lee Iacocca Photo courtesy of the Saint Peter's University Archives: Frank J. Guarini Special Collection (SC04): Accession SC04-2010-0006, Box 9, Folder

Financial institutions knew they had a friend in Annunzio - more than a third of his contributions came from financial institutions. In addition, two of Annunzio's son-in-laws were employed by Skokie Federal, Charles Keating visited Annunzio's office on numerous occasions and Prins was regularly feted by the industry to the point that Dey wrote that Prins had "accepted legislative seminars" from the industry and "was wined and dined during that visit to Keating's home and took in a little golf." Annunzio's response: "In my heart of hearts, I knew there would be a bad interpretation. I am very proud of both boys. I didn't tell them who to work for." But undeniably, Annunzio along with then-House Speaker Jim Wright wanted the bailout limit for S&Ls to be substantially higher than $5 billion and as high as $15 billion.

Dante Fascell, a Florida colleague, might have inadvertently referenced his colleague's conundrum in his farewell speech to his colleague in 1992. "In Frank's role as chairman, he wanted to ensure the financial soundness of the S&L industry but also guarantee that S&L's would continue to serve average Americans."

When S&L's became as popular as the plague, Annunzio's status as a friend provoked a he said/she said. When the Bush administration proposed legislation cracking down on S&L's, the U.S. League of Savings Institutions approached Annunzio. *The Washington Post* quoted League President Fred Webber as Annunzio telling him to not, "overreact to the Bush plan. Remember the plan is, the president sends up a bill and we rewrite it…we will take care of these issues.'" Annunzio later called that account, "a rotten lie," and contends "I told them they were in deep trouble."

But career-wise, it was Annunzio who was in deep-trouble. As he sought a 19th term in 1990, Republicans made clear quite early that he would be at the top of their target list and though he had taken 65% in his 1988 re-election, they saw the fact that Bush had received 53% in the district as encouragement. They landed Walter Dudycz, a State Senator and police officer whose Ukranian lineage was well in line with a number of would-be constituents.

Annunzio's campaign got the assistance of a young consultant named David Axelrod who did not mince words about Dudycz's shtick: "Walter Dudycz is a phony - to present himself as the champion of taxpayers, and then be on two public [payrolls] and vote for the Sears bailout. I think Dudycz is basically a guy who's found himself a hook, whether it's taxes or the flag thing. I think he's basically an opportunist. The only thing that distinguishes him from a Newt Gingrich or a Jesse Helms is that he's less intelligent." He was very conservative, the only legislator to vote against the Build Illinois Legislation. They dubbed-him "Double-dipping Dudycz" for what Democrats contended was 87 days on multiple payrolls. Ways and Means Chair Dan Rostenkowski hosted a $500 a fund-raiser for Annunzio who at one point late in the campaign, Annunzio asserted, "They thought I would go without a fight. Well, they don't know Frank Annunzio." Fortunately for him, however, enough of his constituents did know Frank Annunzio.

The Tribune came through for Annunzio in a half-hearted way. They opined that he, "could make better use of his influence than serving as a placement agency for his in-laws," adding, "Sometimes he has." But the paper made clear that Dudycz wasn't an option. "If the Republicans offered a strong alternative, they would have a good case for defeating Annunzio.

But (Dudycz) doesn't understand details of the federal budget crisis. He offers no depth of thinking on other federal problems. His greatest political success has been grandstanding on the flag-burning issue. In short, he's not prepared for Congress." Voters evidently agreed and gave Annunzio a lukewarm endorsement of his own: he prevailed over Dudycz 54-45%. His election night contention: "I never had any fear. I always felt I was going to win," adding, "the voters proved you can't buy a seat in Congress in the 11th District." The challenger offered a different spin. "He had the politicians, the precinct captains and the mayor of Chicago along with 26 years of incumbency," while also gratuitously throwing in, "People reread George Bush's lips and that didn't help."

After the election, the only thing that seemed safe for Annunzio was his seat itself. The full caucus had the power to ratify the election of its committee chairs and initially, Annunzio seemed secure at House Administration. But when the votes were ratified, he had been deposed by a vote of 127-125 (Charlie Rose of North Carolina was voted the new chair). Congressman Gary Ackerman of New York might have summed up the prevailing sentiment when he said, "People were talking about effectiveness."

Then there was redistricting. Democrats controlled the legislature but the governor was a Republican, Jim Edgar. Not only was the state losing two House seats to reapportionment but a new majority-Latino district in the Chicago area was required. Approaching 77 and with obvious electoral vulnerability, Annunzio was a prime target but was doing little to help his cause by not attending meetings with the delegation, which was reflected when even Democratic circulated remap plans displaced him. Ultimately, the map that was used was adopted by a court and it sliced his district a number of ways.

Initially, Annunzio vowed to run in the seat of one of the most powerful House barons, Rostenkowski, despite the fact that Rostenkowski hadn't yet indicated if he would run (despite their nearly three decades as colleagues, the two were acquaintances but not particularly close). Constituent wise, Annunzio's disadvantage wasn't that bad: 43 percent of the residents of the new district were in Rostenkowski's district while 40 percent were from the current 11th. But 20% would be new to both men and one would have to assume that Rostenkowski's power would entice many of those people into opting for him in a primary and that was illustrated by a call from Chicago Mayor Richard Daley, Jr., shortly after the map was released. "Frank," the Mayor told him, "I really hate Rostenkowski but I love the chair of the Ways and Means Committee."

For this reason, many were sanguine about Annunzio's chances of beating Rostenkowski. Prins wasn't one of them. He remembered Rostenkowski being forced to flee angry senior citizens following enactment of the catastrophic health legislation and he had envisioned running a contrast ad showing Annunzio meeting with his constituents (which likely would have featured him speaking to people assembled in a room). The screen would cut to Rostenkowski running and the narrator would say, "And this is Dan Rostenkowski meeting with his constituents."

The Monday after Thanksgiving, Annunzio was running as if he was ten points down. But a few hours after saying, "I don't intend to get out at this time or any other time," Annunzio withdrew. His official reason: After spending Thanksgiving with my family in Chicago, I realized that it is time for me to come home....I want to spend as much time as possible with my family so as not to miss any more important moments." In retrospect, Annunzio was in the early stages of Parkinson's Disease and Prins had urged him to hold out so that he could get something from Daley in return.

In later years, he became particularly angry about the television series, "The Sopranos" for the way it portrayed Italian-Americans. In fact, after his death, spokesman Dominic DiFrisco said Annunzio, "tried to make everyone aware of the positive aspects of the Italian American community and was puzzled and chagrined by the ceaseless efforts to depict us as wanton criminals."

Annunzio died at age 86 in 2001 and his family was stunned by the more than 2,000 mourners of all faiths who came to express condolences. His wisdom and common-sense means of expressing it could have been sorely used over the years. LaFalce for one feels that "had Frank remained in Congress, we would not have had the recession in 2008. Frank would have been all over the predatory lending practices."

CHAPTER NINETEEN

Chairman Jones a Special Congressman With a Heart as Large as the Outer Banks He Championed

Introductory Tidbit: Walter B. Jones, Sr., represented North Carolina tobacco country so, when a reporter randomly called each member of the Tarheel State delegation to inquire about their smoking habits, Jones was forced to think fast. He had quit cold turkey several years back but, as *The Charlotte Observer* **wrote, before returning the reporter's call he, "quickly bummed a cigarette" and told the fella that he was smoking as we speak. The reporter told Jones "You've killed my story," at which point Jones replied, "Good." In relaying that story, Jones credited the reporter with, "forc(ing) me back to smoking."**

Image courtesy of the Walter Jones, Sr., Papers,
Joyner Library, East Carolina University

Walter B. Jones, Sr., was the only one of eleven North Carolinians to not return to the House following the conclusion of the 102nd Congress. The 13-term Democrat had announced his retirement in October of 1991 but died four months before the term concluded. At the time of his passing,

Jones was the senior member of the delegation and a mentor to many younger colleagues both in Carolina and the committee he chaired, Merchant Marine and Fisheries. A man of warmth and Southern genteel, his quiet tenacity reinvigorated the panel's semi-dormant standing and took on many nationally sensitive issues when he was at its helm.

If any irony exists about Jones, it's that because he ruffled almost no feathers and sought so few headlines outside of his perch, the national fame linked to his name undoubtedly resulted from his son, Walter B. Jones, Jr., who won election to another seat in Congress as a Republican in 1994. The younger Jones, prior to his own death in office in 2019, was notorious for iconoclastic views that puts him counter to his party right to his last breath.

The Almanac of American Politics once said Jones took "an aging and often ailing committee and pumped some life and verve into it." Well before he had announced his retirement from Congress – in a manner so unwanted that he briefly reconsidered, Jones was confined to a wheelchair and his vitality was noticeably faltering. Yet in a district that contained an agricultural abundance and the treasured outer banks, Jones fulfilled his chief mission of championing issues in that area and did so with utmost zeal.

The Raleigh News and Observer said the following: Jones "wasn't a flamboyant orator, and he didn't do the kind of flashy deeds guaranteed to make headlines. He was steadily conservative in style, although his voting record in recent years had a liberal strain. What mattered most to Jones, and to the people of the First District, was that he knew how to get things done for the folks back home." Rob Christensen of *The Charlotte Observer* wrote that Jones "has been known for a down-home, plain-shoe style frequently punctuated by earthy wit" as his colleague Jack Betts called him puckish (and) fun-loving."

New York Democrat Nita Lowey, a very junior Democrat to Jones, backed that assertion up, noting he "could break up a tense committee meeting with humorous remarks." Michigan Democrat Dennis Hertel came to Congress in 1980 and was placed on Merchant Marine. He recalls Transportation Secretary Elizabeth Dole – a native of North Carolina, testifying and Jones reminding her how the Secretary shared the name of his first wife and how much affection he 667-0877had for her. He also recalls Jones's office being stocked with cartons of cigarettes and liquor and being asked what he drinks? And Patsy Mink, a colleague from Hawaii who served with Jones on Merchant Marine, spoke on his death of "a calm, persisting style that would become his trademark."

Jones's knack for understanding his own people extended to the literal sense. Hertel recalls a meeting in which a group of fisherman from the district traveled to Washington for a hearing and presented their testimony in a Carolina dialect so distinct that neither other committee members or staff could unravel. Jones didn't had that problem. When the testimony concluded, he called it "the most concise, accurate statement about this problem after all these years."

Jones grew up in Fayetteville and as a boy, delivered newspapers for *The Fayetteville Observer*. Life changed at age 13 when his father, Walter G. Jones, succumbed to an ailment that he had contracted during World War 1 nearly a decade earlier, leaving his mother to support the family as a stenographer for the Cumberland County Health Department. Jones excelled at football in high school which landed him a scholarship at North Carolina State after which he dabbled in the office supply business. Yet he found himself lacking for zest and decided further opportunity awaited as a traveling salesman in the Pitt County town of Farmville. During much of this time, Jones was a referee at local college sporting events and that produced the regard and acquaintanship among locals to move into the political arena. Once he took the plunge, his years of holding office would span more than half his life and til his dying day.

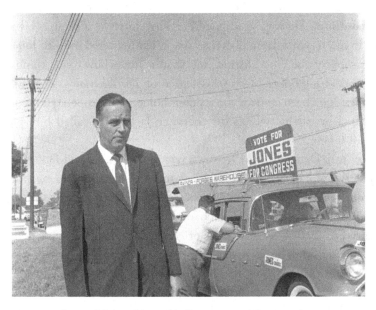

Jones during his 1960 Congressional campaign
Photo courtesy of the Walter Jones, Sr., Papers,
Joyner Library, East Carolina University

The first office Jones sought was a seat on the Farmville Commission in 1946. He won and became Mayor soon after. In 1954, a seat opened in the North Carolina House and Jones went for it. He first got the Congressional bug in 1960 when he mounted a challenge to ten-term Congressman Herb Bonner. The incumbent himself chaired Merchant Marine so, the race was naturally viewed as uphill but Jones did hold Bonner to 58% and carried three counties. Far from dejected, he returned to the legislature and in 1964, moved up a spot, winning a seat in the State Senate. Less than a year later, Bonner died and Jones pursued the vacancy.

With the First District a solidly Democratic bastion, Jones knew that the action would be in the late 1965 primary. So did everyone else as the field to succeed him included Bonner's longtime assistant, Henry Oglesbe as well as Don Langston, a friend and Roger Jackson, a colleague in the legislature. A noticeable presence was Sarah Small, an African-American and activist with the Williamson chapter of Southern Christian Leadership Conference and her candidacy was laudable given the infancy of the civil rights movement in the South. One of Small's campaign managers was Floyd McKissick, the national chairman of the Congress of Racial Equality. Many had hoped her fairly decent sized backing at a time when African-Americans were just becoming active in politics could propel her into a runoff. As it happened, Small did earn a solid 15% but Jones got 60%, which was more than enough to win the primary outright.

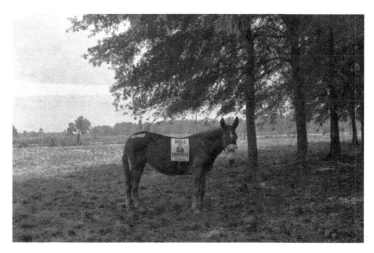

**Keeping up with the Jones's supporters: they
came in all shapes and sizes Jones had
Photo courtesy of the Walter Jones, Sr., Papers,
Joyner Library, East Carolina University**

The general election was an energetic contest with future U.S. Senator John East, a Republican who also hailed from Pitt County. Jones took every county but Beaufort and Washington, again getting 60%. A new remap was in affect for the fall and the GOP was investing in the district but Jones notched it up slightly against East, this time carrying every county.

Late in his career, *Politics in America* wrote, "The First begins at the ocean, passes through fishing ports and coastal swamps, and ends in flat fields of soybeans, corn, peanuts and tobacco" and Jones compiled a record that was beyond sufficient. He was assigned to the Agriculture Committee and Merchant Marine, assignments that put him a position to pay major dividends for the district.

Jones (far right) and his Republican opponent,
John East, meet during the campaign
Photo courtesy of the Walter Jones, Sr., Papers,
Joyner Library, East Carolina University

Jones's first subcommittee chairmanship was Agriculture's Oilseeds and Rice but if was after the election of 1974 that he took the much more meaningful (for the First District) Subcommittee of Peanuts and Tobacco. There, supporters and opponents alike learned of his commitment to protecting the tobacco price support program, some via baptism by fire. He had long been a tireless defender of maintaining a rigorous tobacco support system as Clayton Yeutter, Assistant Secretary of Affairs for International Affairs and Commodity Programs, realized during a 1974 hearing. When Jones thanked him for saying in an earlier statement "that the administration is satisfied with the very effective tobacco program now in effort," Yeutter mildly protested ("I don't think I used quite those words"). Jones's response was, "I am just trying to help you through." A year later, Jones was among the Congressmen instrumental in urging President Gerald Ford to allow an ambitious price support measure become law even with reservations about one provision.

Though no longer chair of the subcommittee in 1982, Jones's comments at a field hearing in the town of Kingston in his district illustrated the program's perpetual challenges. "Need I remind you of the constant attack on this program in the halls of Congress almost from day to day and it takes a unified effort of the farmers, manufacturers, shippers, buyers, Congressmen and everybody concerned to save the program." So far we've been successful."

Jones on the Hill
Photo courtesy of the Walter Jones, Sr., Papers,
Joyner Library, East Carolina University

By 1981, Jones suffered from diabetes which caused circulatory issues in his legs and the physical frailties showed. Consequently, few expected that he would seek to move to a position of power. Those people were proven wrong in a big way and Jones got a second act in Congress which he essentially used to reinvent his image. The new gig was the chairmanship of Merchant Marine which resulted from the defeat of scandal-tarred John Murphy of New York (the Peanuts and Tobacco Chairmanship would stay in capable local hands as Jones simply passed it off the Charlie Rose of the Seventh District).

One reason for Jones's newly invigorated reputation was his staff as he replaced many of Murphy's cronies and installed his own people. Mink, who served with Jones on Merchant Marine during her first, non-consecutive stint in the House, said the reputation was that "his committee functions the best on Capitol Hill and how responsive and helpful his staff always is. There is not one that is surly and arrogant as so many are on other committees."

1981 was the year Ronald Reagan came to office and Jones's desire to have a hefty maritime meant that he would often find himself on the defensive against administration's attempts to cut the Coast Guard budget (his metaphor was that the cuts "would never sail."). The same went for oceanographic research programs.

If Jones were to acquire any nickname, "Mr. Ocean," would be appropriate. Early legislation he championed: the National Sea Grant College Program and the National Marine Sanctuaries Program and modernization of ocean liner cartels. The Foreign Shipping Practices Act increased both the outflow and imports of U.S. goods on American ships while The Coastal Zone Management Act returned jurisdiction of their coasts to states. Jones successfully authored a delay in forcing fishermen to use Sea Turtle Excluded Devices on their trawlers. And as a proponent of gutting most boat user fees, Jones opposed attempts by the Reagan administration to impose a $10 license fee on oceanic fishermen as a

On matters when ocean and land would collide, Jones in 1987 tucked into a national flood insurance language to help beachfront homeowners confronted by the threat of natural disasters and a separate measure requiring the Small Business Administration to provide low interest loans to people who might be impacted by the red tide.

It's not an exaggeration to say that Jones's advocacy involved every increment of issues concerning merchants. Or excrements as the case may be. One Jones cause was to increase money for pump-out facilities for boaters to dispose of their business. One Jones press release set the tone by asking, "What happens when the call to Nature and the call of nature collide? It's not very pretty."

Image via C-SPAN

A rare moment in the national spotlight resulted through Jones's sponsorship of The RMS Titanic Maritime Memorial Act of 1986 that placed limitations on commercial exploration of the Titanic, which had been discovered a year earlier. Reagan signed the bill but as John P. Easton and Charles Haas wrote in a book, *Titanic: Destination Disaster* that, "It might well be a moot gesture. Titanic lies in international waters beyond any legal jurisdiction…" Indeed, a year later, when a French expedition team began plotting missions to retrieve artifacts from the Titanic, Jones was forced to act "to protect the integrity of the Titanic" from those who would "rifle the wreck." The bill he drafted would make it illegal to seize material from the ocean floor, which in many cases was the final resting place of victims of the 1912 accident.

Considering a few of his district predecessors had chaired Merchant Marine, it was no surprise that Jones was the fiercest fighter of parochialism the region had ever seen. He obtained a National Marine Fisheries Services bill for a lab and help shepherd the Fort Raleigh National Historic Site on Roanoke Island. He proposed an amendment to the Clean Water Act that established the Albermaric Sound-Pamlico Estuarine System to study sound ways to manage it.

The idea of drilling in Alaska proved Jones could be malleable when circumstances demanded. Over a brief period prior to 1989, he had been favorable to limited drilling in ANWR with extensive safeguards (a "protective management zone"). Then the Exxon-Valdez oil spill occurred and that prospect lost feasibility. "We had hoped before the oil spill to come out with a bill in July," he said, "but due to the emotional crisis the spill has created, we think it is best to put it on the back-burner until the emotionalism has subsided." Instead, the trajectory of oil drilling would be turned inside out and Jones would be at least one of the players at the forefront.

Declaring that, "It took a tragedy like the Exxon Valdez to cause the entire Congress to focus on this issue," Jones immediately went to work on the Oil Pollution Act of 1989, legislation with a span so awesome that five standing committees held hearings, and 16-months came and went before enactment. Jones's first task was to keep a majority of his committee together and that was severely put to the test when California Republican Norm Shumway proposed pre-empting state liability limits with a federal one. That seemed certain to cause a logjam with Senators and put members on both sides of the debate. Jones's philosophy was that, "Compromises should only be made when needed, and then only at the conference table." Polar opposites such as Gerry Studds of Massachusetts who supported it and Billy Tauzin of Louisiana, who opposed it, agreed. Eventually, the committee adopted compromise language that Jones put forth.

The chairman had to give ground on other matters. California's George Miller, who chaired an influential House subcommittee, had his own view of what he wanted to see in the bill, and a five-cent-per-barrel tax for the cleanup was what they had in mind. Eventually, Jones amalgamated the versions from the respective committees and put forth what he viewed as a compromise, even though one Interior staffer called it a "sham."

**Photo courtesy of the Walter Jones, Sr., Papers,
Joyner Library, East Carolina University**

When the bill went before the full House, Jones opposed Miller's amendment. "Some people say that the state laws with unlimited liability for spillers will serve to prevent future spills. This is a silly argument. There are existing state laws with unlimited liability and they sure did not prevent the spills we saw this summer." He did argue in favor an amendment offered by New Jersey Democrat William J. Hughes to prohibit state liability limits from exceeding those about to be passed by the federal legislation. He called the amendment, "one which strikes a careful balance between two concerns. Many states have expressed their feelings that they must be able to enact laws to protect their citizens from the potential harm of oil spills. On the other hand, in order to ensure that those who engage in the transportation of oil are able to insure themselves, and therefore, that they will stay in the business of transporting oil in a responsible manner, they must not be unduly subjected to unlimited liability. The amendment achieves both of these goals."

Ultimately, the Oil Protection Act of 1989 became the Oil Protection Act of 1990 when President George H.W. Bush signed it into law 16 months after its inception and it contained Jones's fingerprints in more ways than one. He had been able to secure a last minute parochial victory when he inserted a provision into the bill prohibiting drilling in Cape Hatteras in the Outer Banks off the Carolina coast until October of the following year (Mobil Oil had been plotting to do exploration). The bill had been introduced that January and was called the Outer Banks Protection Act but, got tied up in the process and the win did not come from House Appropriators. When Jones made his request, the Committee would not accommodate him for the sheer reason that they feared it could open a Pandora's Box. But Jones warded off an amendment by Ohio Republican Ralph Regula on the House floor, then convinced House-Senate negotiators to leave the measure in the final bill. Some legitimately worried that the Bush administration might veto the measure with the provision attached but, he was anxious to sign something and wasn't going to hold it up over one line.

East Carolina University Political Science professor Carmine Scavo labeled Jones, "kind of a liberal Democrat, but he disguised it in populist rhetoric." Ike Andrews, elected to Congress from North Carolina in 1972, recalled walking onto the House floor as a new member in 1973 and asking Jones how he should vote on the issue at hand. When Jones replied that Andrews should vote "yes," but he would vote "no," Andrews queried him but the response was that a "no" vote was the only way to go for Jones because it wouldn't be popular in his rural cicles.

Early in his career, Jones opposed busing and federal funding for abortion but gradually became more outwardly progressive. His ADA score fluctuated - as low as 22% in 1980 but proportionally higher toward the end of his career (80% in 1988 for example). By that time, he was backing much of the Democratic economic and social agenda but not without an occasional departure, such as supporting the flag burning amendment.

After 1966, Jones didn't dip below 69% in a general election until 1984 though he did have to stare down a semi-tough primary as he entered his 70s. 1984 saw John Gilliam, a peanut farmer and state representative, mount the opposition but Jones took 61%, losing only two counties near the Virginia line. In 1988 and '90, concerns about Jones's health were mounting but that didn't deter 65% of constituents from voting to return him to Washington. In both instances, he beat realtor Howard Moye who campaigned on "moral and fiscal conservatism." Even before 1990, it was evident for a variety of reasons that it would likely be his last hurrah.

One was that Jones's frailties were becoming more obvious which was reflected by the fact that 46 members of the Democratic caucus voted against reappointing him as chair of Merchant Marine (two other aging committee chairs were deposed outright). One colleague even said of Jones: "He retired years ago and didn't tell anyone." Jones did little to dispel that impression by reading "verbatim…and rarely lifting his head" while making a statement on the floor.

The more dominant reason was that the Voting Rights Act required the creation of at least one African-American majority district in North Carolina and the First District was an obvious candidate. Indeed, when the maps were finalized in mid-1991, the percentage of black residents increased from 32% to 57%. In October, Jones made official his plans to retire.

Confessing, "it has been hard to make this decision," Jones acknowledged that the demographic makeover of the district "has made it impossible for many of my friends and neighbors to continue vote for me." His appreciation to district residents was high as he declared that, "Many seek the privilege of public office. Few, such as myself, have been so honored." Jones's impending departure made him eligible to convert his federal campaign treasury to personal use and, while other members declined to do so, Jones vowed that refunding all of his contributors over such a long period of time would be next to impossible. Sadly, he never got the opportunity to enjoy either his retirement or the money.

Late in August of 1992, Jones was hospitalized for a "tenacious" pneumonia which caused multiple organ failure. He rallied somewhat but his weakened body could not sustain the ailment and he died on September 15 at age 79. The characteristics that made him a giant was noted by colleagues. Glenn Anderson of California, himself 79 and finishing his last term, gave a panegyric statement on the House floor in which he said, "In every man's life, he encounters a few people who are far from ordinary - men whom he feels a great sense of privilege to have the opportunity to know and to work with. Walter Jones was one of those men." Anderson went on to note how, "Friendships can be hard to hold in the House. I was lucky to have an enduring one with Walter Jones." Many members of both parties traveled to North Carolina for the funeral.

As *The Goldsboro News Argus* observed on his passing: Jones "gave heart service, not lip service."

**Photo courtesy of the Walter Jones, Sr., Papers,
Joyner Library, East Carolina University**

CHAPTER TWENTY

Anderson's Legacy Was Hard Work, Quiet Tenacity and Transcendency in Putting Long Beach on the Map

Introductory Quote: "I am not sure that if he stayed here much longer we would be able to get any more programs into the State of California—it is about ready to sink into the Pacific Ocean." - New Jersey Congressman Robert Roe on the legacy of his predecessor as chair of the Public Works and Transportation Committee, Glenn Anderson as he prepared to retire in 1992.

Photo courtesy of the U.S. House of Representatives Historical Collection

During his 1966 re-election campaign as California's Lieutenant Governor, Glenn Anderson put up a billboard proclaiming himself, "The Quiet Fighter," and few would think of disparaging that slogan. Throughout his 52-year political career, Anderson epitomized the highs and lows of Southern California's mid-20th century. From organizing a sleepy town, being associated with the infamous Watts riots, battling separate statewide tickets of two future presidents from California, securing countless transportation and infrastructure improvements and finally, helping the sleepy port city of Long Beach realize its international greatness, Anderson did it all. And like the Golden State itself, he endured setbacks along the way.

Anderson was not the oldest of the 1992 House retirees (Charlie Bennett of Florida had more than two years on him) but he, and Walter Jones, his colleague from the Merchant Marine Committee were certainly the least surprising. At 79, he had long slowed down and, having been removed from the helm of the Public Works and Transportation Committee by fellow Democrats, his best days were clearly behind. But boy, were those glory days. In Congress, transportation was Anderson's niche and the goodies with which he showered the region made him the envy of all of his colleagues. In California politics, Anderson's knack was long-term planning and that was reflected in areas from growth to education.

Long Beach lobbyist Larry Taub credited Anderson for, "basically put(ting) Long Beach on the map" while *LA Times* writer Ted Johnson even more succinctly summed up his mantra following his death. Anderson "rarely took the forefront of partisan turf wars, social controversies or foreign policy. But when it came to lining up federal support for tunnels or rail lines, he was a master." All the while, he was viewed as "nice and quiet" which he once admitted he "liked" because that implied he was underestimated. House Speaker Jim Wright publicly called Anderson "one of the finest writers of legislation I have ever seen."

Anderson had an eclectic background. His parents were Chicagoans who had settled the town of Hawthorne, California seven years before Glenn was born. His father died when Glenn was 12 and his brother, the equivalent to a minor league baseball player in those days, vanished three years later. There was suspicion that the disappearance was connected to a major game that same day and in ensuing years, Glenn and his mother would journey to locations on tips that he might be found (he never was). At any rate, Glenn's early manhood was a combination of hardscrabble and glamour in what was still small-town, somewhat desolate, southern California.

At that time, Glenn went to work delivering newsreel film and was forced to use his bicycle to get to and from work because they weren't permitted on the streetcar. Anderson was also a banjo-singer in an all-girls group and a motorcycle racer in his late teens who electrified spectators as he rode into the 1932 Summer Olympics in Los Angeles to gather newsreel from the finish line and deliver it to its destination. One instance involved Ralph Metcalf's photo finish in the 100 meter dash. Nearly 40 years later, Metcalf was elected to Congress from Illinois. Anderson had arrived two years earlier and the story goes that both claimed to remember one another from the finish line.

Anderson's stage name was "Kid Malcolm." "Malcolm was his middle name and Anderson's reason for not using Glenn was that he feared motorcycling might be seen as unbecoming. But he really began earning money when he offered to use the motorcycle to perform stunts with the bike in Hollywood films. This led to Anderson being hired as a courier for publicity photos and the many forms of his delivery methods led Anderson to quip that he had been "foot messenger, bicycle messenger, and motorcycle messenger."

Myron Roberts and Harold Garvin wrote in their book, *Glenn M. Anderson: Conscience of California* wrote, "With the money he earned from races and motion pictures, Anderson opened a small garage in Hawthorne, one which soon grew to be one of the few thriving businesses in the Depression-hit town," in part because local police hired him to service their vehicles. He opened a construction business and attended UCLA.

Anderson's hardscrabble was illuminated by a scholarship to UC-Berkley that he was forced to turn down due to his status as the breadwinner of the family. Instead, he attended UCLA part-time though did not obtain his degree until he was Lieutenant Governor. His interest in politics came in 1936 This was a period of a long drought for California Democrats and Anderson organized a Young Democrats chapter to begin righting that. His own first run for elective office came in 1940 when he was elected Mayor of the L.A. suburb of Hawthorne, which *The Almanac of American Politics* tells readers is the "home town of the not-yet-born Beach Boys." Anderson was essentially drafted into the race by reformers who, as his bio cites, "were growing increasingly restless about what they believed to be an ineffective and possibly corrupt city council" and when elected, the man believed to be the youngest mayor in the nation at the time didn't disappoint.

Progress was the name of Anderson's game and he managed to build a water filtration system and prevent the legalization of gambling (which led the police chief to later confess that, "I could have had you killed for $50"). As it became clear that World War II was on the horizon, Anderson, who had forged strong relations with the Chinese community who used his garage, combined prescience and his entrepreneurial mind by coming up with a plan for the city to build a municipal airport that would soon be used by Northrop Aircraft to fly their aircraft into war.

In 1942, Anderson was elected to the State Assembly. War was ongoing at this point but Anderson felt strongly that it was his duty to serve and enlisted in the Army even though he was exempt as a sitting legislator. He attended Officer Training School but missed out on attaining the status because of a rule that prohibited candidates from not missing a day. Anderson pushed himself hard to meet that requirement, showing up even with a temperature well over 100. The result was that he nearly collapsed and did miss a day. Instead, Anderson had to settle for the rank of Sergeant. After the war, Anderson returned to the Assembly where he chaired the Lighting, Streets and Bridges Committee. His greatest accomplishment there was probably pushing through the establishment of El Camino College.

For several years, Anderson's career languished. A 1950 attempt to unseat State Senator Jack Tenney, a fellow Democrat, fell flat by a razor-tight margin while his challenge to incumbent Raymond V. Darby for an L.A. County Board of Supervisors seat two years later failed more spectacularly. After, Anderson went behind the scenes and was tapped again to rebuild as chair of the California Democratic Party. One person active in party affairs, Goldie Kennedy recalled how, "At that time, the state Democratic Party had nothing – no office, furniture or even a telephone. Glenn got them for us and set up a functioning office." Anderson began to rebuild the party via what his biography labeled, "grassroots" which led to the formation of "over 100 Democratic clubs in Southern California alone." Future U.S. Senator and ticket-mate Alan Cranston was another brother in comrade and as Anderson was elected LG, he would become the first Democratic Comptroller since 1886.

Those wins did not come easy. In 1958, Anderson's victory was a surprise and his margin over incumbent Harold Powers was 90,000 votes out of more than 5 million cast while his 1962 re-election over San Francisco Mayor George Christopher was almost equally tight -163,000 votes. Anderson played a large role in organizing the state's Master Plan for Higher Education, a visionary but time-sensitive plan to accommodate the expected enrollment in California's higher education facilities. Most of the time, however, the job was no-man's land. Anderson had few responsibilities and one story goes that he was so bored wandering around the capital one day that he asked the press corps if he could empty their wastepaper basket.

Photo courtesy of Evan Anderson Braude

The events of mid-1965 more than made up for it. Brown had frequently traveled out of state and Anderson performed the typical mundane duties of governor. Brown was in Greece that April when riots in Watts broke out, fueled by erroneous reports of police brutality when a black motorist, Marquette Frye, was pulled over by police. Tensions escalated and before long, one sergeant compared "the streets of Watts (to) all-out war zone in some far-off foreign country." Over a five-day period, 35 people were dead. Because the matter quickly went over the heads of the L.A. Police, Chief William Parker at 10:30 a.m. requested that Anderson call out the National Guard but he hesitated until 5:05 p.m. In that time, he consulted African-American clergy seeking their advice. As Watts burned, Parker criticized Anderson and "red-tape" delay. The LG responded: "This man apparently thinks his hourly appearances on television will stop the riots."

While Parker was drawing fire from black leaders, it was Anderson who became the face of the crisis and he soon was labeled, "the man who fiddled while Watts burned." In subsequent days, at least one formal investigation bore that out. The Brown-formed McCone Commission investigated the situation which upon conclusion chided Anderson for, "hesitating when he should have acted."

Photos courtesy of Evan Anderson-Braude

This conclusion may not have been entirely fair. In their book, *Glenn Anderson: Conscience of California* Roberts and Garvin wrote, "Guardsman are civilians who serve on a part-time basis. It takes time for troops to be assembled, orders and weapons distributed, transport arranged, plans to be made for the most effective distribution of troops. Most of the public does not understand this." Additionally, it was thought that Brown's team was using Anderson as a scapegoat to sugarcoat their own inadequate response.

There was a method for the madness. Brown and local officials had long suspected conditions would degenerate to this magnitude and had an agreement that the National Guard would be called. The problem was that Anderson was not part of those discussions nor did anyone bother to inform him. All of this is speculation. What is not speculation is that as Anderson came up for re-election in 1966, he was in deep political trouble.

Republicans nominated Ronald Reagan to face Brown and Robert Finch, campaign manager for Richard Nixon during the razor-tight 1960 Presidential campaign, to take on Anderson. Finch would often tell voters, "My opponent has been as hard to find in this campaign as he was during a crisis." Naturally, Nixon took tremendous interest in the race and he told strategists, "I want everyone in California to believe that Glenn Anderson was responsible for Watts." A sufficient enough number did and Anderson garnered just 40% against Finch. Brown hardly did better, losing to Reagan 57-42%. This proved another example of Anderson's sound political inclinations. Brown had maneuvered early in the campaign to try to make sure Reagan won the GOP nod, believing him to be the weaker opponent. Anderson by contrast recognized that Reagan would be formidable and advised against it.

It seemed there was little place to go after that but, two years later, Anderson found himself in the right time at the right place: the 17ᵗʰ Congressional District. Thirteen-term Congressman Cecil King retired and Anderson won the race to succeed him. But he had to battle every square mile to win. In the primary, Anderson's main opponents were LA Councilman John Gibson, Jr., and Walter Tucker, Sr., whose son would be winning a district that encompassed much of the 17ᵗʰ the year Anderson retired. Anderson won the primary with just 35% which makes it doubtful that he could have survived a runoff or prevailed if the field was less convoluted. The general was against Joe Blatchford, an attorney leader of an L.A. based Peace Corps operation, and Anderson was considered the distinct underdog. But he squeaked to victory by a mere 4,000 votes.

Anderson was assigned to the Merchant Marine Committee and Public Works and Transportation, two posts which suited his district like a glove. In 1975, he became chair of the Public Works Aviation Subcommittee after a reorganization that moved that issue to that committee. Reducing airplane noise reduction was on Anderson's agenda for two years and for much of the 95ᵗʰ Congress, it was touch and go. The subcommittee also oversaw sweeping deregulation of the trucking industry legislation. Anderson was not particularly enamored with the legislation but President Carter and Massachusetts Senator Ted Kennedy were strong proponents. Setbacks ensued on both issues but they were in character with what Anderson was accustomed.

On the noise issue, Anderson's own subcommittee in March of 1979 adopted language by Elliot Levitas, a fellow Democrat from Georgia that was counter to what he had been proposing (Levitas's motive was likely protecting Delta Airlines which was based in Atlanta) and Anderson adjourned the committee until after the Easter recess in order to regroup. That regrouping appeared to come in various peaks and valleys throughout the year. In May, Anderson opposed language the full committee produced because it was, "at the behest of the airline industry and the airframe and engine manufacturers would tie the FAA's hands and leave it helpless in the face of critical noise and safety problems." It still cleared 29-14.

By November, airport operators, under the auspices of the Port Authority of New York and New Jersey, were lobbying the House to codify Senate backed language allowing prior agreed noise control to exceed the previously agreed to 1985. This did not sit well with Anderson and other members in districts near airports, including Newt Gingrich, a freshman Republican from Georgia. Much of the dispute involved which aircraft to exempt from the requirement – some wanted to water it down to allow two and three engine planes to bypass the regulations but advocates contended these aircraft encompass the overwhelming number of the complaints.

An initial compromise was worked out in December and it was agreed that only two engine planes would be exempt but Anderson refused to sign on. Another compromise was hastily hammered out a week later which Anderson this time called "a real plus." The Airport Operators Council International (AOCI) felt otherwise and confusion over what was in and out of the final bill reigned among members who were trying to beat town for Christmas. Anderson urged action; "If we pass this conference report, today's noisy airplanes will be replaced by stage 3 planes which are much quieter than stage 2; so, when somebody says the conference report is a step backward, I question that. I think it's just the opposite." While lawmakers did clear the rule to consider the legislation, the 195-192 vote left proponents worried that the bill itself might fail and they withdrew it.

Trucking was on a similar path in that Anderson had problems with the version offered but again, language satisfactory to all sides was worked out. Ultimately, The Motor Carrier Bill of 1980 cleared as did the trucking deregulation bill passed 367-13 in 1980.

Three years later, it was the bus industry's turn. Anderson sponsored the Bus Regulatory Reform Act of 1982 which he felt would offer smaller bus lines potential for competition. When the law passed and Greyhound abandoned many routes, Anderson took his share of the blame. His aide Bob Freeland responded that it was "the same fear" naysayers used during the trucking battle. "If there's enough business, then you have small truckers picking up the little loads and bringing them to big centers." Greyhound's CEO was even more pronounced: Making clear that it was low usage routes that were abandoned first, "I don't think a person on Podunk Junction is going to feel inconvenienced about traveling to a center five or 10 miles away to catch a bus."

Other issues loomed at Transportation. In 1979, Anderson sponsored legislation that raised the retirement age for airline pilots from 60 to 61 ½. In '84, he got through the requirement of child safety seats. That same year, he attached an amendment to a gasoline tax that would ban the disposal of decommissioned submarines at sea, which Anderson called a necessity for making sure, "our coastal waters are safe for fishing and recreation."

A 1984 amending of the Surface Transportation Assistance Act of 1982 brought Anderson national publicity for which he was rarely accustomed as a Congressman. The legislation dealt with highway safety and two provisions in particular would change the face of driving.

One required states to put at least eight percent of their highway safety funds to "the use of child restraint systems in motor vehicles" and that meant adoption of child safety seats. Anderson explained his reasoning on the House floor by referring to a Surgeon General report that states, "no other preventable cause poses such a major threat as (automobile) accidents which account for 45 percent of total childhood mortality. 'That is right. More infants and small children under 5 years old are killed or crippled while riding in motor vehicles than the totals killed or crippled by the seven common childhood diseases that youngsters are routinely immunized against.'"

The second provision in the legislation would raise the drinking age from 18 to 21. It passed by voice vote and 81-16 in the Senate, remarkably few defections for an issue that would impact a significant portion of the voting population nationwide. In 1987, Anderson again presided over a major highway bill – this one worth $92 billion which Anderson vowed, "will assure the completion of the greatest public-works project this country has ever undertaken." Most of the contention centered around pleas by rural lawmakers to allow states to increase the speed limit to 65 mph but Anderson and the full panel's chair, Jim Howard of New Jersey, the principle sponsor, held firm that it should stay at 55. Lawmakers sided with him, but by only 20 votes and Senators opted for a demonstration project raising it. That left the momentum firmly with higher speed advocates as the bill went to conference and the final package left the provision in tact (the bill became law over Reagan's veto due to cost). Significantly, Anderson was the first member of Congress to successfully break open the highway trust fund for spending on public transit and this was done before he was even a subcommittee chair.

Photos courtesy of Evan Anderson Braude

Socially, Anderson was a solid liberal. He was pro-choice, anti-death penalty, co-sponsor of the ERA, and almost a firm environmentalist (unless the other side was the tuna industry). He sponsored union status for postal service employers, financial assistance for urban schools and coordination of a committee to confront the disease, Lupus. On defense issues, Anderson could depart from the liberal orthodoxy, particularly supporting weapon systems such as the B-1 bomber. His fights for equality and inclusiveness in state government accompanied him to Washington. Paul Schlesinger recalls Cesar Chavez attending a small campaign event for Anderson and when he asked what brought him there, Chavez told him that as Lieutenant Governor, Anderson attended a big UFW march in Sacramento that Brown was afraid to. Not only did Anderson march but he also met with them. As a result, Chavez told Schlesinger "he would do anything" for Anderson, which left him both moved and proud.

Whether Anderson was meant to attain a chairmanship will never be known. In March 1988, Anderson was 75 while Howard of New Jersey was an energetic 60 and showing no signs of retirement when he was felled by a sudden heart attack and Anderson got the post. While the two men's styles could hardly be more distinct – Howard was boisterous while Anderson more laid back, the priorities were the same and that meant warding off what they viewed as overeager and encroaching Appropriators. Specifically, the Public Works leaders frowned on Appropriators tacking on projects that they hadn't authorized.

Anderson took his case to the Rules Committee and told them, "I believe it is time to stop this deliberate evasion of the proper way to legislate." He also believed, "We're supposed to know a little bit more about these things than a general committee like Appropriations does. They can't be experts on everything." Rules rarely sided with him but Anderson never took it personally. Paul Schlesinger, who worked for him for 14 years both in his personal office and as Staff Director of Public Works, cannot recall Anderson expressing a negative feeling about almost anyone. Neither can even his own wife. In her intro to the bio, Lee wrote that when she became angry, Glenn would remind her that, there are always two sides to every story," and "damn" would be the biggest foul language he'd ever use.

What Anderson was an expert on was Long Beach and its surroundings. He got the Harbor Freeway, and the Long Beach Freeway designated as interstates. He fought hard for a 17.3 mile Norwalk-El Segundo Freeway, insisted that it include rail in the median, and the I-105 eventually, it came to bear his name (the battle went on so long that one local Mayor proposed naming it the, "Second Century Freeway)." His impact on the Ports in both Los Angeles and Long Beach was such that it is not known where either ends. The main channel into the Port of L.A. in fact bears Anderson's name – "The Glenn M. Anderson Deep Ship Channel. In a rare interview, Anderson boasted how, "In the history of our country, there are but two congressmen after whom ports have been named. Sam Houston of Houston and Glenn Anderson of Los Angeles. He also obtained crucial funds for the metrorail subway system. Anderson's shining city on the hill was San Pedro where he could look out the window of his condominium with a telescope and see ships going in and out of the Port.

Photos courtesy of Evan Anderson Braude

In every endeavor, Anderson was far from a media hound. He was suspicious of the press and usually shunned interviews and the Torrance, California based *Daily Breeze* wrote he, "often appears stiff and uncomfortable on the few occasions he deals with the media. He rarely speaks on the House floor and never without notes or a full text. He studiously avoids the limelight." Howard defended him. "I've sat next to him for years. He's got a hell of a sense of humor, which an awful lot of people would say, 'Boy, that's a surprise.'"

Having often stayed with Anderson in the office until 9 p.m., Schlesinger concedes that his boss "was not somebody who would put his feet up on the table and have a beer. He wasn't a back-slapper, stereotypical kidding-around Congressman. But he was a straight-arrow." And Schlesinger was profuse that, "nobody's done more for me in my career than Glenn Anderson. He showed me the right way to do things and there will never be anybody outside of my family" that had the influence that the Congressman did.

One person Anderson did run foul of was his fellow Californian, Phil Burton. Though Anderson and Burton had once been neighbors in Washington, Anderson had supported Texas Congressman Jim Wright, who was a senior member of Public Works, in the down-to-the-wire 1976 battle for Majority Leader that Wright won by a vote and Burton was not the forgetting type, even years down the road.

A column had been written in the months after the vote speculating that Burton might extract revenge against those who opposed him and Anderson kept it in his office. Fast forward. Burton had a major hand in the 1982 remap ("my contribution to modern art") and Anderson was given a district that not only stripped him of some of his Long Beach jewels, but made it substantially more Republican so that he had to fight to hold it. The GOP put up Brian Lungren, whose brother Dan represented a neighboring district in Congress. Through Dan, Brian had fundraising help and referred to Anderson as "tax and spend Glenn," but 1982 was a Democratic year and Anderson held him off by 18%, 58-40%.

By 1990, Anderson's seat was safe as can be – he won his 12th term with 62%. The Public Works chairmanship was another matter, for a variety of reasons.

Committee Democrats had long been concerned about Anderson's energy – that he often forgot certain names (his wife claimed that was nothing new) and that he relied too much on his staff (during one Rules Committee hearing, Schlesinger at one point began answering members' questions before he was cut off as a matter of protocol). There was his staunch parochialism which led members in the rest of the nation to think he forgot about them (He once said, "I think I know my district as well if not better than any congressman. I know where every water line is, where every earthquake fault is...").

Another gripe was that Anderson consulted Republicans more than their own side, which bore fruit when he agreed to allow a portrait of the committee's ranking Republican, John Paul Hammerschmidt in a small committee room even though as a Republican, he had never been chair. In truth, Anderson did bend over backwards to include Republicans in policy, including them on official trips and allowing them to offer amendments even those he wasn't supporting). But stamina was the overriding issue – Anderson had undergone quadruple bypass surgery in 1988 and while he had made a full recovery, many simply viewed him as no longer being up to the job.

After the election, Democrats fired a shot across the bow at Anderson in a closed-meeting when only two of the panel's 34 members - Bob Roe of New Jersey and Doug Applegate of Ohio, voted to keep him as chair. The full caucus codified that the following day by a vote of 152-100 and Roe was subsequently elected chairman over Norman Mineta of California. Peter DeFazio, an Oregon Congressman who sat on the panel, expressed the prevailing view of many of his colleagues when he said, "We want people to represent us who seem to be dynamic, to be getting things done nationally." Anderson was courteous but clearly hurt. The day after the vote, he graciously met with Roe but his own influence was continuing downhill.

In the months ahead, colleagues noticed that Anderson had nodded off during at least some important debates on the House floor (which was common for Congressmen in the days of yore). His response: "I'm not saying I'm the best guy but, I do some things on the floor that are good." Still, Anderson held a series of fundraisers and retirement was not a sure thing, until it was. His departure announcement came in mid-December: "After more than 50 great years of public service to the people in the state of California, it is difficult to think of not continuing in that service." Shortly after, he said, "I know a lot of younger people who are probably a bit more aggressive than I am who probably felt like I did 30 or 40 years ago. I'll be 79 in six weeks. If anyone would be considered an old duffer, I think I'd probably qualify."

By that time, Anderson was in the early stages of Alzheimer's Disease, a fact his family kept to themselves until the waning days of 1992. Anderson tried to keep the seat in the family and his step-son, Evan Anderson-Braude won the Democratic primary to succeed him but lost the November election to Republican Stephen Horn 49-43%. As his term prepared to wind down, Anderson offered a sentiment no one would dare dispute. "I'll miss it. But I love California."

During that final year in office, House colleagues approved the renaming of the Long Beach Federal Building in Anderson's honor. It was a block away from the district he represented. For roughly the last decade of his life, Anderson lived in a condo on a hill in San Pedro where he could look with a telescope and see the ships coming in and out of the Port of the LA, through the GMA Deep Ship Channel.

Anderson succumbed to Alzheimer's in December of 1994 at age 81.

CHAPTER TWENTY-ONE

Roybal a True Hispanic Trailblazer and Hell of a Fella

Introductory Quote: "I'm not Mexican. I am a Mexican American. And I don't speak a word of Mexican. I speak Spanish." –Edward Roybal at his first meeting as a Los Angeles Councilman in 1949 in response to his introduction by a colleague as "our new Mexican-speaking councilman, representing the Mexican people in his district." Roybal trashed the text of his prepared remarks in order to respond to that assertion.

Photo courtesy of the U.S. House of Representatives Historical Collection

E dward Roybal was a true trailblazer for the Latino community. His 1962 election to the U.S. House made him the first Latino to win a seat in Congress from California in 83 years. That mirrored his earlier history – his 1949 win of a Los Angeles Council seat came 68 years since a prior Latino had served in that body. Roybal would also become the first Latino to win a major party nomination statewide as he was the Democratic standard bearer for Lieutenant Governor in 1954. Win or lose, his influence was profound.

Stately and reverent, Roybal was labeled, "a reserved if almost dour figure," but also a man with "quiet energy." He generated few headlines beyond his district yet fought like a bulldog for matters closer to his heart. These included mobilizing against unfair immigration law revision attempts and addressing increasing social epidemics such as bilingual education, AIDS and Alzheimers. Personally, he was very generous with his time and was called by *The LA Times* "a mentor to scores of other lawmakers."

The Roybal's went so far back in present day New Mexico that Edward's ancestor helped found Santa Fe in 1610, 306 years before he was born in Albuquerque. Edward, an eighth generation American, traveled west with his family at age six when his father was in search of employment. They settled in the city's Eastside where his father found work as a carpenter. But young Eddie experienced discrimination early on. Pre-dark sirens indicated that Mexican-Americans must return to their homes and at the age of 14, he and other playmates were told that they could not use the Evergreen swim pool unless it was the day before cleaning was scheduled. Roybal fought the policy and prevailed and the incident shaped his thinking. It also prompted his Republican colleague, David Dreier to note on Roybal's death how, "Twenty-five years before Rosa Parks refused to give up her seat on that bus in Montgomery, Alabama, a young Ed Roybal was in the vanguard of the struggle for equality here in Los Angeles."

Academically, Royal was strong in both math and reading and *The L.A. Times* wrote in 1999 that his mother Eloise "expected her nine younger children to copy him." Coming of age during the Great Depression, Roybal joined the Civilian Conservation Corps (CCC) but was still able to earn an education – his degree in Business Administration came from the University of California at Los Angeles and Kaiser College. In the meantime, discrimination didn't dissipate. On his first date with his future wife Lucille, *The Times* wrote, "a white officer came up, rifled through Roybal's pockets, then dumped their dinner on the sidewalk."

After serving in the Army during World War 11, Roybal briefly worked for 20th Century Fox, the became Director of Health Education at the Los Angeles County Tuberculosis and Health Association. He organized a mobile x-ray clinic to serve the poor and seemed content with life in Boyle Heights.

To call Roybal reticent about entering politics is an understatement. "I didn't want to do it," he recalled in 1999, "but I had no other choice." By "no choice," he was referring to what was essentially blackmail by an ally. Frank

Foyce, a Spanish movie theater chain owner who provided critical financing for the x-ray unit. In 1947, he, along with area doctors, was among those pressing Roybal to seek a seat on Council. When Roybal declined, Foyce vowed to halt the money which would have been devastating to the needy children. Roybal had no choice but to capitulate.

That run for council was in the Ninth District against six-term council member Parley P. Christensen but garnered just 27%. The defeat convinced him that Latino candidates needed structure to help ensure wins and he founded the Community Services Organization (CSO). One of CSO's goals was registering Mexican-Americans to vote and legendary community organizer Saul Alinsky's affiliate helped put 17,000 new voters on the rolls. That made all the difference in the world come 1949 when Roybal tried again.

This time, Roybal put together a coalition that included Jews, African-Americans and Japanese Americans. His message was, "Our skin is brown and our battle is the same. Our victory cannot but be a victory for you too." Christensen was one month shy of his 80th birthday which perhaps impacted his energy. He took first place and forced a runoff. As the campaign continued, Tom Sitton in the book, *Los Angeles Transformed: Fletcher Bowron's Urban Reform Revival, 1938-1953* wrote, "a freightened Christensen resorted to red-baiting and racism to defeat the challenger, but the incumbent could only carry the downtown portion of the district in the general election." His margin was 8,500 votes.

In office, Roybal had shattered a racial ceiling but still had plenty of doubters. Of his colleagues: "They thought I would fall flat on my face," he said later. "They felt right along that I was not their equal." But he wasn't about to back down. Katherine Underwood in, *Pioneering Minority Representation: Edward Roybal and the Los Angeles City Council, 1949-1962* wrote that "compared to the city as a whole, the ninth district was a demographic smorgasbord," and Roybal "emerged as the only city council member who consistently spoke on behalf of minority and low-income groups." One example was rent control and Roybal was the sole councilman to oppose gutting it. The same went for the Subversive Registration Bill which mandated loyalty to the U.S. government. He fought against the creation of Dodger Stadium which he viewed as deleterious to Mexican residents but to no avail (daughter Lucille recalls a man calling his home saying, "my father was un-American because he was against baseball and the Dodgers"). Mostly though, Roybal's interests were parochial and improving the district's infrastructure (sewers, traffic lights) dominated his agenda. He chaired the Public Health and Welfare Committee.

Taking the oath as L.A's first Mexican-American Councilman since 1949
Photo courtesy of the Library Special Collections,
Charles E. Young Research Library, UCLA

Once his foot was in the door, Roybal rose fast. Within five years, California Democrats tapped him as their standard bearer for lieutenant governor, facing incumbent Howard J. Powers. Kenneth Burt wrote on his blog that, "Roybal traversed the state by automobile, campaigning before a variety of audiences... Many of those hearing about Roybal over the radio were newly registered voters. This was particularly true in places like San Jose where Eduardo Quevedo introduced Roybal to a bilingual crowd at a rally at the Civic Auditorium. The excitement over having a Mexican American on the ballot likewise reached into the Central Valley, according to Richard Chávez, who helped organize CSO in Kern County." But Republican Governor

Goodwin Knight was winning re-election resoundingly and Californians stayed with the ticket. Still, Roybal's 45% was considered respectable.

In 1958, Roybal tried to break one more hurdle by aiming for a seat on the L.A. County Supervisors Board of Supervisors and his opponent was Ernest Debs. Though the count ended with Roybal 390 votes ahead, a 12,000 vote tabulation error swung the seat to Debs by roughly 10,000 votes out of 273,000 cast. Some supporters cried fraud but Roybal was more inclined to look toward the future and the way around that happening again was Latino empowerment. Accordingly, he and a prominent attorney, Henry Lopez, formed the Mexican American Political Action Committee to register new Latino voters.

Much of that time saw Roybal tangling with L.A. Police Chief William Parker, a noted hardliner on criminal matters especially as it involved minorities and at one point, he formed a citizen/community committee to investigate their practices. His outspokenness led him to fear for his children's safety and he warned them never to enter a police car, "even if the guy said I'd been taken to the hospital and that he would take them to my bedside." The hostilities continued into the 1960s, when Parker referred to Mexicans as "the wild-tribe of the inter-mountains of Mexico," Roybal demanded an apology. Parker's response: "I meant no disrespect except as you desire to interpret it as such."

The Roybal's on Election Night, 1954 (you'd never know he was losing by the smile)and with visiting dignitaries Photo courtesy of the Library Special Collections, Charles E. Young Research Library, UCLA

1962 brought more opportunities. Redistricting moved the district of Republican Congressman Gordon McDonough into heavily Hispanic Democratic enclaves of East L.A. which made the 30th district substantially more Democratic.

Roybal tossed his hat into the ring and faced Loyola University government professor William Fitzgerald and Greg "Pappy" Boyington in the primary. Boyington whose autobiography, "Baa Baa Black Sheep" inspired a brief television series, was a clear frontrunner when it came to flamboyance. A retired Marine, Boyington had shot down 28 Japanese aircraft during World War II before he himself was fired upon in the sky and presumed dead (he had been sent to a Japanese POW camp).

Roybal was endorsed by the Committee for a Sane Nuclear Policy which his more centrist rivals had hoped would generate backlash in their favor. It didn't and the surprise on primary day was that Roybal came in 40 points ahead of Fitzgerald with a whopping 63%. For the general election, McDonough did not go down without a fight but still saw his hopes to hang on to his seat extinguished by nearly 14% as Roybal won 57-43%.

Denied his first opportunity to sit on the Foreign Affairs Committee, Roybal was assigned to Veterans Affairs and Interior. He did get the Foreign Affairs post in 1965 and Appropriations six years later where he'd remain for the next 22 years. In 1966, Royal traveled to Tucson for what was billed as an informal hearing with Mo Udall on the Vietnam War. His earliest major accomplishment was bilingual education. Now as common as apple pie in America, Roybal, by steering to passage the National Bilingual Education Act in 1968, helped ensure that language barriers would leave no student behind.

By the mid-1970s, Roybal was looking to broaden the scope of knowledge and needs of the Hispanic community. He founded the Congressional Hispanic Caucus (its motto was, "Each one, teach one"), and the National Association of Latino Elected Officials (NALEO).

Photo courtesy of the Roybal Foundation

During the 1980 Appropriations season, Roybal wanted to see the funding formula reflected for fairness to warmer states and proposed a measure that would shift the heating funds for the Frost Belt to cooling funds for the sunbelt. House members sided with the Northeast/Midwest by a vote of 215-199.

The advent of the Reagan administration brought new opportunities for Roybal and seemingly unlimited reasons for disgust. In Congress, retirements and defeats would mean he'd inherit the chair of the Treasury, Postal Service, General Government Subcommittee. One purview of the subcommittee was the Secret Service and when the assassination attempt on Reagan occurred, Roybal suggested president's wear bullet-proof vests in public. "If he had one this time," he surmised, "nothing would have happened." Bickering with the administration over appropriations was not uncommon – as Roybal considered the austere FY 84 budget request, he made clear that postal rates could double if the proposed cuts went through (ultimately, funding was cut but not by nearly as much as Mr. Reagan had proposed).

Early on, the administration's immigration policies made it clear that Roybal would be mounting an angry game of defense. Within two weeks, Education Secretary Bell revoked a regulation that students be taught in their native languages.

When the House debated a major immigration overhaul well into the night near the close of the 1982 session, Roybal was angered. "We took time during the day to debate a bill that deals only with dirt and wild animals and the wilderness of this nation, but late at night we debate a bill that affects millions of individuals." Substantively, Roybal wanted amnesty and welfare and opposed the bill's provision for criminal penalties for employers who knowingly hired illegal aliens. He helped kill the bill in part by filing a number of amendments. In actuality, the only thing that ended was the session itself – proponents were back next time and even further in the trenches.

Throughout the 98th Congress, House Speaker Thomas P. "Tip" O'Neill punted on considering the measure, which he did not support but, by early 1984, against Roybal's wishes, vowed to eventually bring it to the floor. To say O'Neill was irked by Roybal might be an understatement – one person said, "The Speaker feels he's been misled." Roybal's response: "Were both professional politicians. We'll have a drink when it's over and forget about it."

Proponents, which included unions anxious about protecting American jobs, said Roybal was misrepresenting the bill's employee sanction provisions. That language, Roybal predicted would see widespread consequences. Besides having the potential of creating, "a police state," he expressed fears that it would mean, "the indignity of having to carry with us a dog tag using that dog tag throughout the 24 hours of the day." He further felt, "The employer who does not want to get involved will just say to himself, "I will not interview anyone who may look Hispanic or who may have a foreign accent, or who may not be blond and blue-eyed." This time, legislation actually passed the House but stalled in a House/Senate conference committee.

By 1986, stalling was no longer realistic. Momentum was with a compromise and a bill not only passed but got the votes of a few Mexican-American members of Congress such as Esteban Torres of California and Albert Bustamante of Texas.

On another immigration matter, Roybal combined a disparate coalition on legislation reversing the administration's plan to evict families from public housing if even one person was found to be an illegal alien. Roybal had filed legislation prohibiting the removal of any family but Robert Dornan, a very conservative California Republican, made the proposal more palatable by proposing language that made it applicable to either those over age 61 or if one resident had legal residency (*The New York Times* cited, "No documentary evidence would be required to support such a claim").

In 1990, yet another measure was up and contained provisions Roybal liked but, theoretical forgery-proof driver's licenses tucked in during conference by the measure's Senate sponsor, Wyoming Republican Alan Simpson wasn't one of them. His view: "It is ironic that South Africa has just abandoned is notorious pass-card identification program that has been an essential element of apartheid." The House was rushing to adjourn for elections but Roybal and his L.A. colleague, Esteban Torres, killed a House rule that would have brought the bill up with the language for final passage. When Simpson removed the measure, Roybal relented and the legislation cleared.

Overall, Roybal's opinion of Immigration and Natural Service (INS) was not high. The agency was, "Next to the IRS...the most discourteous arm of the federal government."

Roybal became chairman of the Select Committee on Aging in 1983 and the challenges were right on his plate. One example was when the administration proposed lower than expected rate increases for hospice care patients. As the 80s went on, two new epidemics struck the nation: AIDS and Alzheimer's. On AIDS, Roybal told *The Times* colleagues were not moved by his call to action. "They saw it as a 'gay disease' and to hell with them. When I proposed research, one of the congressmen blew a kiss toward me." On the latter, he introduced the Comprehensive Alzheimers Assistance, Research and

Education Act (CARE). Provisions from other bills were amalgamated and it was enacted. Roybal also introduced the "Homecare Quality Assurance Act," and legislation that he felt would put the nation on the path to universal coverage. Medigap and Meals on Wheels were other priorities. In 1989, he convened a hearing on insurance companies that were raising Medigap premiums in some cases by as much as 133%.

With actor Anthony Quinn
Los Angeles Times Photographic Archives (Collection 1429), Library
Special Collections, Charles E. Young Research Library, UCLA

Roybal was the only "Cardinal" west of Iowa and Henry Lozano was his longtime chief of staff. It was often said that Henry, "ran the West Coast. Everything went through Henry." Whoeverf ran the west coast, it was no surprise that Roybal's Appropriation bills contained many goodies, such as $140 million for an L.A. Metro Rail. Roybal was also known as a generous boss. When conferees returned with a new Treasury bill, he noted "the language is not acceptable to the staff, and I can't work with a staff that's not happy."

The one blemish on Roybal's long tenure was a 1978 reprimand by his colleagues for his acceptance, and lying about a $1,000 gift from South Korean businessman Tongsun Park on four occasions and for failing to report it. The Ethics Committee was investigating Roybal and two other California Democrats – John McFall and Charles Wilson and when the panel issued its recommendation that Roybal be censured, minority members made their displeasure known. Ethics Chair John Flynt of Georgia responded that the panel actually considered expulsion before deciding on the lesser penalty but that was not appeasement when they believed that different standards were in play.

As the vote neared, colleagues defended Roybal. Long Beach Democrat Glenn Anderson of Long Beach said on the floor, "I am in my 38th year of public life. If I had to name one person in public life whom I felt had the greatest integrity, I would consider Ed Roybal a top candidate for that particular choice...There is not, in my opinion, a dishonest bone in Ed Roybal." Phil Burton expressed, "an uneasy feeling that my dear friend and our great colleague, Ed Roybal, would be the last person whose conduct should be measured here in the proposed action of other members." Ron Dellums of Oakland was even more blunt. Asserting that "the whole thing stinks to high heaven," he was furious that "two of our white colleagues are brought down here to be slapped on the wrist and one of my brown brothers is down here to be totally wiped out in the process."

Roybal in his Capitol Hill office
Photo courtesy of Library Special Collections,
Charles E. Young Research Library, UCLA

Roybal himself took the floor. He began by sharing his opinion that, history is being made on a daily basis in the Halls of Congress, but the history that is being made on this Friday, the 13th of October of 1978, will long be remembered by Americans who place high value on justice, fairness, and equality." He first cited the "undisputed" fact that Ethics Committee aides told him he did not need an attorney to testify before ethics and that the committee exonerated him of making a false statement. He then explained the Tongsun Park connection, telling colleagues he, "went to Mr. (Otto) Passman's office at his request and received a contribution from a friend of his, and after that was over, it never dawned on me that the man there was someday going to be the much-publicized Tongsun park that we now know as a rich playboy socialite..."

At that point, Roybal's allies went to work convincing colleagues to simply reprimand him and which led to a debate on the House floor. At one point, Roybal argued his own case.

House members voted to recommit the censure by a vote of 210-170 and the reprimand of Roybal was adopted unanimously (every Californian save Republican Charlie Wiggins voted for the lesser penalty). Roybal labeled the outcome, "certainly a victory for me, for the civil rights of all congressmen, and for all Americans who believe in the constitutional rights to equal justice for all Americans." That fall, Roybal took his usual, albeit slightly reduced large election margin and moved forward completely unscarred.

Roybal's cerebral style led to second-guessing late in his career when his long attempts to steer $1.1 billion in reimbursement funding to help California deal with its increasing immigration population fell flat. He was dean of the delegation at that point and one California Democrat who wouldn't be named said, "You have to question why he didn't produce something given his longtime loyalties. He wasn't forceful, he wasn't aggressive and he didn't seem to know how to work the system." Roybal responded, "there's a little blame to be spread around widely." Once in a blue moon, Roybal could be unpredictable. At one point, he asked a nude statue to be removed from an office building that would bear his name which prompted Oregon Democrat Les AuCoin to question, "Who in the hell elected Ed Roybal our Minister of Culture?"

Photo courtesy of C-SPAN

In 1992, Roybal was approaching his 30th anniversary in Congress and retirement was thought to be on the horizon. In fact, with the unveiling of a redistricting plan that seemed to guarantee a seat for Roybal's daughter, State Assemblywoman Lucille Roybal-Allard in a neighboring district, Congressional watchers were gleeful that a father and daughter serving together would result. In January of 1992, however, Roybal announced his retirement. The ill health of his wife – cross-country flights in particular impacted her, contributed to his decision as he refused to leave her.

Though Roybal endorsed Lozano for the seat, he opted not to run and the Democratic nomination went to State Assemblyman Xavier Becerra, who prevailed in November with ease. Roybal-Allard won the neighboring seat which she holds to this day. Roybal died at age 89 in 2005.

House members paid tribute to Roybal on the floor following his passing, Texas Democrat Solomon Ortiz noted that he was one of many newcomers mentored by him. He said thus: "Paying tribute to Ed Roybal is to remember that, to see the future, you must stand on the shoulders of a giant. And this Hispanic pioneer had giant shoulders on which we all stand today."

In 2014, Roybal was posthumously awarded the Presidential Medal of Freedom. Other honorees included actress Meryl Streep, singer Stevie Wonder, Tom Brokaw and three civil rights workers who were murdered in Mississippi during the "Freedom Summer" of 1964. Lucille accepted it in his stead.

CHAPTER TWENTY-TWO

A Great Guy: Gifted Orator Vander Jagt Had a Partisan Streak as Longtime Head of NRCC but Never Allowed it to Impact Civility

Introductory Tidbit: "(John) Ehrlichman is one of the better people in the White House. His soul is not always torn by fear that the President might not be re-elected and he can consider the issue on its merits." – John Corry in a 1971 *Harper's Magazine* profile on Vander Jagt entitled, *The Day in the Life of a Congressman*. Ehrlichman, who was Nixon's domestic policy chief, went to prison for his role in Watergate. Corry went on to write that Ehrlichman was a neighbor of Vander Jagt and Ehrlichman's daughter was their babysitter.

Photo courtesy of the U.S. House of Representatives Collection

Michigan Congressman Guy Vander Jagt had such a spellbinding speaking ability that one might think he was the member of the class of 1966 to capture the presidency, rather than George H.W. Bush. Instead, the thirteen-term Republican from Cadillac, a classmate of Bush, a delegation-mate of Gerald Ford, and the person who placed Ronald Reagan's name in nomination was content working behind the scenes to promote GOP dominance. Such impact did Vander Jagt have that at one tribute after his passing, the man who would be the first GOP House Speaker in 40 years, Newt Gingrich, credited two people for being responsible for the advent of the modern Republican party: Reagan and Vander Jagt.

Vander Jagt's speaking ability garnered him compliments from some of the best in America. Nixon called him "the best public speaker in America." And Reagan, who selected him to deliver the keynote at the 1980 Republican National Convention once said, "Some call me 'The Great Communicator,' but if there was one thing I dreaded during my eight years in Washington, it was having to follow Guy Vander Jagt to the podium." He was also a man of ebullience, notorious during his time in Congress for not wanting to waste a moment gladhandling colleagues with his sunny disposition.

One could say Vander Jagt (VAN der jack) went Dutch his whole life. Both of his parents were immigrants and Vander Jagt was so proud of his heritage that he introduced a resolution designating November 16 as "Dutch American Heritage Day." Born in Cadillac to a farmer/livestock dealer, he enrolled in Hope College and won the office of student body president under the slogan, "Fly High With Guy." Vander Jagt often practiced his speeches in the woods and *The Grand Rapids Press* said he "memorized and rehearsed every speech" ("If you were trying to talk some girl into marrying you, you wouldn't need notes"). A good friend, Republican Congressman Richard Schulze of Pennsylvania once credited Vander Jagt with having "learned how to put the fear of GOD into his listeners." He certainly succeeded putting a fear of GOD into the judges. Not only was he a state champion three years in a row (he was also a disc jockey) but in his senior year he won the National Oratorical Championship.

For a time, Vander Jagt considered using his speaking skills for the ministry and he attended Yale Divinity School. Eventually, however, he decided that the law was his forte and he enrolled in Michigan State Law School, after which he was picked up by the large firm, Warner, Norcross and Judd. He also gained fame as news director of a local tv station, WWTV-Cadillac. Vander Jagt won a seat in the Michigan Senate in 1964 by beating a well-regarded doctor in a campaign that saw both candidates regularly meet for drinks and served on the Appropriations and Tourist Relations Committees and made ethics legislation a big project. At the end of his first year, the press gallery named him the body's outstanding freshman.

When Robert Griffin was appointed to fill a U.S. Senate vacancy in 1966, Vander Jagt entered the primary to succeed him. He faced two opponents but prevailed with 65%. Vander Jagt would be seeking the special election and the general simultaneously and neither was a contest. He beat Democrat Henry Dongvillo 67-33% in both (carrying every county but Lake which he lost by a hair). When Vander Jagt came to Congress, he was assigned to the Government Operations Committee and Science and Aeuroneautics. He won a seat on Foreign Affairs as he began his second term and Ways and Means in 1975. Ford was Minority Leader and mentor.

The economic stimulus package that passed by a narrow vote set this country on the path to its current economic prosperity."

House Minority Leader Gerald Ford had a big
impact on Vander Jagt's rise in Congress
Photo courtesy of the Gerald R. Ford Presidential Library and Museum

Vander Jagt worked hard for his district and in 1971, broke a stalemate between the Nixon Administration Michigan and Governor William Milliken to (guided in part by John Ehrlichman) to get a $2 billion grant for the Muskegon Sewer system. The Sleeping Bear Dunes National Lakeshore Act of 1972 and The National Diabetes Act 1974 were the two major legislative endeavors that Vander Jagt worked on that became law and critics have noted that as his career advanced, little else was associated with his name. Sleeping Bear was the creation of a 61,000 park on Lake Michigan.

Diabetes was of particular importance to Vander Jagt. When Congress in 1972 passed legislation renaming the National Institute of Arthritis and Metabolic Diseases as the National Institute of Arthritis, Metabolism and Digestive Diseases, he proposed putting diabetes in the title. His reasoning: "Despite the fact that the disease is increasing at a tremendous rate, increasing three times as fast as our population—the incidence of diabetes has more than doubled within the last 20 years - the federal government in terms of research on this dread disease has not increased its efforts. In fact it is spending today less on research into this disease than it spent four years ago."

With Vice President Nelson Rockefeller and
Tennessee Congressman Jimmy Quillen
Photo courtesy of the Gerald R. Ford Presidential Library and Museum

Save for a few of those environmental bills with a home state tinge, Vander Jagt could never have been viewed as particularly moderate. He was one of three members of the Government Operations Committee to oppose the Consumer Protection Act of 1974. His ACA and ACLU scores were sometimes zero while his NSI score was 100% in 1990. His economic liberal score was actually is zero in 1989 as was his social score in 1990. But he did back Cooper-Church, oppose the Super Conducter SuperCollider and was the only Republican among 18 signatorees on a 1973 letter urging the Master's Tournament in Augusta, Georgia to allow Lee Elder, an African-American golfer, to play (not since 1934 had an African-American took part). At one point in the midst of a campaign, he even was commended by a union man during a debate who publicly called Vander Jagt a friend of whom he could say nothing negative.

Many of Vander Jagt's other initiatives were pursued through Ways and Means and international trade legislation was at the top of the heap. It was in 1975 that he captured that seat and he led the opposition to an amendment by his New York colleague, Democrat Charlie Rangel, to increase by $50 Supplemental Security Income (SSI) The cost, Vander Jagt said, would be astronomical. He was an original sponsor of the ESOP (Employee Stock ownership plans). Vander Jagt once summed up his philosophy on taxes: "You know, there is a difference between Republicans and Democrats. By and large, Democrats really do believe in more spending so government can do more good things for people. Republicans really do believe in less spending so the taxpayer can keep more."

A pet cause of Vander Jagt's late in his tenure was to get cities below $250,000 exempted from the mandatory reformulated gasoline program to clean area. He introduced and successfully adopted legislation to provide relief from unfair retroactive tax assessments on Michigan's 39 private workers compensation. It's a fact that more than 7,000 companies and tens of thousands of Michigan workers benefited through that legislation. He worked on the widening of US 31.

Vander Jagt was a splendid politicker. In an in-depth 1971 profile for *Harper's Magazine*, John Corry wrote, "If he bends too quickly to tie his shoelaces when he is on the up escalator, he might pass without seeing someone on the down escalator to whom he might want to nod" ("I used six seconds I might have otherwise wasted," he said as he tied his shoes after greeting a colleague going down). While not absent-minded by any means, Vander Jagt could be notoriously forgetful and the profile noted his staff often had to remind him to take his keys, wallet, airline tickets, etc.

Among colleagues, Vander Jagt might have earned his political chits by being named "Bullshot of the Year," betowed on him by colleagues for raising the biggest ruckus during paddle ball in the House gym. It probably helped him win the chairmanship of the Republican Congressional Campaign Committee after the party's shellacking in the anti-Watergate year, though the man he beat was the ideological and not well-regarded John Rousselat of California. The GOP had lost 42 seats and would enter the new Congress holding just 144 seats out of 435. Vander Jagt's start wasn't too auspicious. His drive for "76 in '76 went nowhere and even a 15-seat House gain in '78 was a little lower than some had expected in a Democratic midterm (Vander Jagt began the year hoping for 30). 1980 would yield far more successes on a number of fronts.

Vander Jagt was so devoted to Reagan that, in the run-up to the convention, he even seemed to be approaching it like a Republican Congressional cycle. When NBCs "Today" vowed to give John Anderson free interviews, Vander Jagt compared it to "allowing one of the three candidates to make free commercials during the convention" (Vander Jagt had supported Anderson, a good friend, in a leadership bid against Ohio's Sam DeVine ten years earlier).

As the convention opened, Vander Jagt was receiving mention for the vice-presidential slot (one admirer had even ordered buttons that said, "VVP"). Reagan was impressed as well and his choice was difficulty as a result. What was clear was that he'd be delivering the keynote address and that would give him an opportunity to make his oratory shine. He took a jab at Morris K. "Mo" Udall keynoting the Democratic National Convention by saying, "Poor old Mo has to make Jimmy Carter look go. Now that is not a hard job. It's an impossibility." On a more serious note, Vander Jagt charged the Carter administration with "deliberately" bringing economic heartaches, "rally on purpose. They increased interest rates on purpose," he explained, "they tightened credit and on purpose last fall, the Carter Congress adopted the Carter budget of despair which their chairmen said was deliberately declined to slow the economy down." He noted that what this really had the impact of doing was producing, "one million more fathers into the heartache of saying, 'Daddy doesn't have a job anymore.'"

That November proved Vander Jagt's most triumphant as NRCC head. Not only did Reagan win the White House and the GOP take the Senate but he led House Republicans to a 35-seat pickup, defeating Democrats both junior and senior that almost no one even viewed as vulnerable. While that was not enough to put the GOP in charge of the House, it was enough to ensure Reagan a "working majority" which would prove so essential for enactment of much of the new President's agenda (his first budget, tax cuts, etc.). Vander Jagt tried to exploit it. The Republican Minority Leader slot was open and Vander Jagt pursued it. But he was facing Bob Michel of Illinois, a more senior colleague whom many felt had worked his way through the ranks. Congressman Ed Bethune, an Arkansas Republican who supported Vander Jagt, said, "the issue implicit in this race is whether Republicans will increasingly engage in the politics of confrontation that younger members follow or the politics of compromise." Newer, younger members, many of whose district's Vander Jagt visited during their initial runs for Congress (the "Turks") clearly gravitated toward the latter and that benefitted him. Despite his smashing performance, many members felt he just wasn't ready for prime time. Fairly or not, others viewed him as at least something of a showhorse.

One initiative Vander Jagt took on was building up the party. In 1991, as New York Governor Mario Cuomo was pondering a run for the White House, he told New York donors, "I hope your governor runs, because I think George Bush will clobber him. I don't think he'll get a vote in the west, or the south."

Voters gave Vander Jagt a shot across the bow in 1990 which he did not heed for the future. He outspent a Traverse City businesswoman, Geraldine Greene $452,000 to $22,000 yet still managed to beat her by just ten points, 55-45% while losing several counties. This was a stinging rebuke for a longterm incumbent in a district Bush had taken 62%. Only in the Watergate year of 1974 had Vander Jagt even polled below 60%. Vander Jagt was likely hurt by an ABC News "Prime Time Live" profile which showed he and other members in Barbados. He was also, like most members, tied down by the protracted budget negotiations, the final result which proved unpopular and contributed to an already prevalent anti-incumbent feeling.

On election night, Greene said, "We've sent Guy Vander Jagt back to Washington very humiliated and perhaps a little humble." Meanwhile, Vander Jagt also found the winds of change hunting around the Capitol front. For years, he had routinely won the races to continue leading the NRCC but had never been challenged. This time was different and a four-term Congressman named Don Sundquist of Tennessee jumped into the race to face him. Vander Jagt compared himself to Egyptiona President Hosni Mubarek "after Saddam Hussein looked him in the eye and said, 'Oh, I would never attack Kuwait.' I do not feel comfortable that someone has launched a campaign against me in the last 10 days of this election when every fiber of my energy is devoted on trying to elect Republicans." Sundquist raised the issue of finances and as *Politics in America* noted, airing such issues in public made Sundquist's colleagues more than a little uncomfortable." With Gingrich's backing, Vander Jagt kept his job 98-66.

As 1992 opened, it's not clear Vander Jagt was girding up for a potentially tight general election but he certainly wasn't expecting any trouble in the primary. Yet that's where it found him.

The beginning of the year found Vander Jagt giddy. The House Banking scandal had just come to the forefront and Vander Jagt pronounced himself "absolutely overjoyed." The number of overdrafts he had was zero but he vowed, "There will be many, many members who will be taken out, lose their re-election because of their record of bounced checks." His spin was that "it was a Democratic scandal because the Democrats were clearly in charge." Yet discontent with Vander Jagt that had begun creeping up on election night 1990 was now brewing with a vengeance. and the perception of a loyal Republican on primary night that, "Guy was spending too much time on national business and not enough at home," was creeping up. Another said,

"Voters were looking for real people at the doors and not just glitzy campaigns."

For starters, State Senator William Van Regenmorter had made serious outreach about challenging Vander Jagt and even the calls from national Republican leaders urging him to not do so didn't dissuade him. Ultimately, Van Regenmorter decided against running because of the burden he feared it would place on his family. A colleague, Mel DeStigter, was not deterred, "because Guy no longer represents the interests" of the district. A little-known furniture executive named Peter Hoekstra also entered the race.

At first, the entrance of three candidates in the race seemed to create a perception that Vander Jagt was out of the woods. Not only could neither of the two come close to matching Vander Jagt's name recognition but they were expected to split the anti-Vander Jagt vote. One of the candidates proved them wrong.

Hoekstra could not possibly match Vander Jagt with money – the incumbent spent $725,000 vs. just $55,000 for Hoekstra (his campaign staff consisted of two paid aides working in his basement). But he did have other techniques, chief among them visibility. Famously saving his two weeks of vacation time for campaigning, Hoekstra embarked on a 250-mile bicycle tour of the district. Vander Jagt's slogan was, "He's there for us," but as *CQ* noted, it wasn't clear who the "there" was.

Vander Jagt carried the Northern six counties in the district with above or near 50% of the vote but they were relatively small population-wise. Hoekstra took Allegan which was a fairly decent size as well as much bigger Ottawa, where he outdistanced the incumbent by nearly 2-1 and a majority of the vote (he had 52%, Vander Jagt just 29% and De Stigter 17%. The final margin gave Hoekstra 46%, Vander Jagt 40% and De Stigter just under 14%. In conceding, Vander Jagt said, "There is a ferocious tide against incumbents running across the country and I could not swim strongly enough to offset it." Hoekstra meanwhile predicted that, "Sooner or later, my guess is it'll end up as a case study in the political science textbooks."

Even defeat gave Vander Jagt a way of creating a partisan spin. "This was not Democrat or Republican. It was 100 percent anti-incumbent. There is no solace there for the Democrats in the House. Any Democratic incumbent should learn from my defeat that any incumbent is vulnerable, and there are more Democratic incumbents than there are Republican incumbents." Yet he acknowledged, "The forest fire I started burned down my own little patch of trees."

Despite his pit-bull like approach to hammering Democrats, Vander Jagt generally enjoyed strong relations with those from Michigan. Bob Carr of Pontiac was one example. While joking that he was "glad" to see Vander Jagt retire" as NRCC head in October of '92, he was quick to add that he was "sad to see him go from the Congress...Guy is one of those rare individuals who, despite a role that requires him to work as an adversary and despite disagreements occasionally on a partisan matter, Guy is a tremendous individual who graced this body with an oratorical style, a personable manner that made it fun to even work with someone who was on the other side of you from time to time." Dennis Hertel was another admirer. Dennis Hertel proved evocative of this. A Democratic Congressman from the Detroit suburbs for 12 years, he made clear that party was no impediment to friendship. Though, "Guy and I probably didn't agree on anything, I liked him as a person." While Hertel didn't have particularly tough races, it was still noteworthy that Vander Jagt "would drop by my fundraisers, even at the National Democratic Club. This surprised some guests." Hertel recalls taking his son to Vander Jagt's house to watch Detroit Lions football games and co-chairing the Michigan State Society and choosing his daughter to be National Cherry Blossom Festival Princess.

The general election was in November and while Vander Jagt was no longer a candidate, he continued at the helm of the NRCC. At around midnight on election night, he saw it as extraordinary that as Bush was losing the White House, the GOP was adding to its ranks and boasted that House Republicans were in a position to gain at least 20 seats (the final number was ten). Vander Jagt meanwhile left Congress and joined the lucrative lobbying firm Baker Hostetler.

Republicans took control of the House in 1994 and Vander Jagt succumbed to a two-year battle with pancreatic cancer in 2007. Michigan Governor John Engler, delivering the eulogy at Vander Jagt's funeral, credited him for "a sort of Moses-type role. He got all the way to the river but couldn't get across the water."

CHAPTER TWENTY-THREE

From Left to Right, Lent was Long Island's Own

Introductory Quote: "Let's vote out Lowenstein for Lent." – The slogan of New York State Senator Norman Lent in his 1970 Congressional campaign against freshman Congressman Allard Lowenstein. Voters did just that as Lent was elected.

Photo courtesy of the U.S. House of Representatives Historical Collection

To paraphrase the motto of the giant New York metro King Cullen grocery chain, New York Republican Congressman Norman Lent was Long Island's own. He resided on the Island through the conclusion of his professional career and his distinct accent made clear that his alliance was authentic. More importantly, his entire agenda in Congress was one of fierce parochialism and while, not flashy in any sense of the word, he used his powers and negotiating style to score the best deal possible for the working-class men and women he represented for 22-years.

Lent was another one of those lawmakers who combined conviviality, realism, and according to *The New York Times* an, "earnest," style of legislating. That resulted in strong partnerships in Washington which left an indelible mark on policy matters of the utmost importance, particularly clean air.

If any name could aptly describe Lent's contributions, it would certainly be, "Mr. Negotiator." From his days in the New York State legislature where he sought a compromise on the not-universally accepted issue of abortion rights to his Congressional days when he was a major player on the Superfund law, a landmark Clean Air Act and other delicate policy matters, Lent combined legislative realism with compromise. Embracing the term that "politics makes strange bedfellows," gave Lent carte blanche to form political alliances with people not always with whom he'd normally be expected and he often served as a go-between for House Republicans and the titanic Energy and Commerce Committee Chair, John Dingell, with whom he was often aligned even as leader of the loyal opposition as top Repulican on the panel.

Michael Scrivner, Lent's Administrative Assistant recalls that, "on most bills Norman thought it was preferable to negotiate a better product even if it meant voting "yes" than just vote "no" and let a bad bill pass with just Democrat votes." While that sometimes resulted in losing the support of some of the more conservative Republicans, he, "generally held his troops together quite well and had a positive influence on legislation." Yet also had stern guiding principles and wouldn't abandon them if it meant anything less than a fair deal for his region.

Lent was no liberal. He won his seat in a slash and burn (some say over-the-top) campaign against an incumbent Democrat who epitomized the anti-Vietnam peace movement and often delighted in the role of Republican boogeyman against national figures. Fellow Long Islander Lester Wolff, a Democrat, labeled him, "very effective but political." But as Lawrence Levy noted on Lent's death, he was "one of the first green Republicans, one of those people who did not see the environment as an enemy," and in the end, his down-the-line conservatism on most other issues notwithstanding, he will be remembered for his fight for clean air.

The initials of Norman Frederick Lent – NFL, could on occasion be a source of levity. John Hambel served Lent in a number of capacities for 36 years starting at age 15. As a campaign volunteer, he recalls, "all of the phone books had 'Property of NFL' on them. I couldn't figure out why the National Football League was involved." Metaphorically speaking, Lent himself took the ball and ran with it. Administrative Assistant Michael Scrivner recalls "Norman wore a ring with his initials and liked to have fun with people who asked about it, saying with a straight face that it was his league championship ring from his playing days as 'Crazy Legs Lent.' More than a few fell for it - at least for a minute."

Besides being Long Island's own, Lent arguably could be a New York original. His ancestor, Abraham de Ryck, was among the earliest to descend on what was then New Netherland in 1637. It might have been appropriate that Lent's birthplace was the town of Oceanside because throughout his career, he was ferocious about protecting area beaches and waterways from pollution. Lent was raised in East Rockaway and attended school in Malverne and Lynbrook. He served in the Navy and during the Korean War was a codebreaker, then attended law school at Cornell which led to commencement of a practice in East Rockaway where he in time became an associate justice. All the while, Lent was becoming a favorite of the legendary Nassau County Republican machine, particularly its future chair, Joseph Margiotta and was awarded the nomination for a State Senate seat in 1962 (Joe Carlino was chairing the party at that time).

Lent prevailed in the general with an astounding 62% but afterwards, had three semi-close calls in a row. 1964 was the Lyndon Johnson stampede which impacted even Republican Long Island and Lent held his seat with 52%. The next two cycles were more favorable but Lent was still tied down by local factors (a Conservative candidate on the ballot in '66 drew 5%) and escaped defeat with 51% each time. Redistricting also played a role. The districts were redrawn twice to comply with the U.S. Supreme Court decision, Baker vs. Carr and in eight years, Lent ran in three districts (the 2nd, 6th and 7th).

Lent's chairmanship of the Joint Legislative Committee on Public Health and Medicare forced him to plunge deep into the fat of thorny issues that were in the middle of the plate. One was the sharp rise of New Yorkers on welfare which critics were arguing was a result of advertising. Lent convened a hearing and rebutted Manhattan Assemblyman Albert Blumenthal's contention that "the poor man must rely on government" by saying, "There are many responsible people in the state, Mr. Blumenthal, who do not feel that people should be encouraged to go on welfare. They feel that people should be encouraged to go to work." Three weeks later, Lent and Buffalo Republican William Adams pushed through a $300 million cut to the state's Medicaid program Lent contended that the cuts would still leave the state with "the most liberal of any in the country" and mimicked a chief antagonist on this issue, Queens Democratic State Senator Seymour Thaler by asking if he was prepared, "to introduce a bill for food-a-caid...for shelter-a-caid," a question that elicited a great deal of laughter.

Lent was not a supporter of abortion rights and would oppose federal funding of the procedure in Congress but did cave to reality and focus on influencing consideration of legislation that would liberalize the procedure as it made its way through the legislature. "It is not a question of whether a law will be passed," Lent explained. "It is a question of what form it should take. There is a climate in the Legislature for a change in the law."

One area on which Lent was not ambivalent in his opposition was busing. Calling Malverne, "the unwilling," guinea pig on this issue, Lent pushed through legislation prohibiting busing on the basis of race. His reasoning: "Other communities have been clobbered by this directive" (it was later ruled unconstitutional). He also looked into abuses by municipal hospitals.

By 1968, the political winds were firmly on Lent's side and his opposition to busing had endeared him to the suburbs, which pushed him to 59%. At that point, his standing was clearly solidified but local leaders convinced Lent that the area's Democratic Congressman, Allard Lowenstein was vulnerable in the next election and Lent found the opportunity too inviting to pass up. Joe Margiotta wished he had. Concerned that the Senate seat would be lost without him, he wanted Lent to stay put. So adamant was he about preventing Lent from running that several Executive Leaders in each village invited Lynbrook attorney Francis Becker, son of Congressman Frank Becker and friend of Lent's, to speak to their clubs while declining to invite Lent. But Lent made clear that he wouldn't stand for the Senate seat regardless of the Congressional race so, when he crashed the Republican meetings, committeemen voted their conscience and Lent was their choice.

Lowenstein had seemed a fluke Congressman from the start. An upset winner in 1968, his vocal identification with the anti-war movement did not seem fitting for this part of the Island, a portion that had been made more Republican by the removal of five Democratic towns. In rhetoric that was seen as slightly over-the-top, Lent charged Lowenstein with apologist invective, labeling him "the voice from Hanoi" and the "chief apologist for the Black Panthers." While he had to contend with a Right-to-Life candidate, he still prevailed 51-46%. Other than post-Watergate 1974 when Lent was held to an unexpectedly low 53% and '76 when he took 55%, Lent never dipped below 60% for the remainder of his tenure.

Much of Lent's early energy was on the Merchant Marine and Fisheries Committee. A hallmark of his philosophy was local control and one amendment he sponsored would amend the Coastal Zone Management Act to give localities control. This meant increasing coastal fishing jurisdiction from 12 to 200 miles. Eradicating the sewage problem on Long Island beaches was also high on his plate and, in the summer of 1974, it resulted in Lent undertaking a rare colorful stunt to prove a point. He had called a hearing at the iconic Jones Beach but just prior to its commencement, embarked on a boat owned by New Year's Eve legend Guy Lombardo and piloted by his brother. Hambel recalls Lent jumping off the boat, "swimming 100 yards to shore, dried off, got dressed and convened the hearing." The busing issue had some spillover and Lent in his first term proposed a Constitutional amendment to prohibit it. This he said, "seems to be the only recourse the people have."

As he gained a reputation, Lent proved himself no lackey for Republican presidents. During the infancy of the Reagan presidency, he tried to give the administration latitude when he unveiled his first, fiscally austere (some say draconian) budget. "The risk is in not voting for it," Lent said. But, he added, "There are things I regard as too severe…I reassured my elderly constituents that there was nothing in the Reagan proposals that would detract from the current levels of what they are receiving." One area Lent worked on softening was preserving Amtrak funding for routes outside the Northeast that the Reagan administration proposed cutting.

Photo courtesy of John Hambel

On the Energy and Commerce Committee, Lent was a member of the Subcommittee on Commerce, Transportation and Tourism where the panel's chair, Democrat Jim Florio of New Jersey, was often his nemesis, albeit a productive one. One example was 1984 when Lent, citing cost, watered down pension legislation that called for women to be given the same preference as men (The Nondiscrimination in Insurance Act"). Arguing that women would actually see an 11 percent increase in premiums (versus a three percent decrease for men), Lent and Mississippi Democrat Wayne Dowdy instead proposed a substitute that would require the equality clause to apply only to perspective pensions, not those of current retirees. Lent convinced a majority of the full committee members to back his proposal.

Lent and Florio were forced into action on another pension issue – the elimination of the Railroad Retirement System and even after negotiations between union and railroad officials, Lent was not enamored, claiming "it foists most of the cost of the agreement on the taxpayers. It fails to address the underlying structural problems of the system which causes these problems to recur all the time."

Lent and Florio battled again on the sale on Conrail. He supported Conrail and as *Politics in America* noted, insisted on giving the railroad a little more time to make a profit. He wanted a clean bill, calling anything less, "an invitation to every special interest group in the nation to come running to pressure contrast for special provisions or other changes in any purchase agreement." But this time, it was Republicans, including the panel's ranking Republican, Jim Broyhill, who said Lent's proposal would go, "too far and tying the hands of administration in attempts to achieve their purpose to sell all or parts of Conrail as soon as possible

Conrail moved back to the forefront in 1986 when the Reagan administration advocated selling the railroad. When other members proposed combining the sale with revisions to a sweeping deregulation law known as the Staggers Act, Lent agreed with the administration's desire to avoid "extraneous" issue. When that was poised to fail, he put together a compromise which earned the backing of Florio and Waxman, though not Dingell. It was approved 22-20.

Florio was in no mood to contest Lent when he unveiled a proposal retaining federal noise control standards, despite the Reagan administration's plan to phase them out. Lent contended that it was "only logical that there be a single uniform federal standard nationwide. There would be great confusion and chaos if carriers were subjected to a variety of standards." Lent could also take issue with fellow New Yorkers, including Queens Democrat Geraldine Ferraro who proposed transporting radioactive material through New York City. Lent, noting that many traveled through Long Island, said the bill, "prematurely and arbitrarily" would circumvent measures that, "seeks to balance national and local interests by providing a uniform national highway routing program."

There was also the issue of ocean dumping in the 1980s. To hear Lent tell it, one could get the impression that it was New York against New Jersey. Lent initially had a problem with the potential for $5,000 penalties for ocean dumping, calling it a "screw New York" provision. The matter was largely instigated by New Jerseyans angry about the crisis on their shores but Lent and other New Yorkers noted that they were in a box because, "the waste can't be burned because of clean air and we can't bury it because of groundwater concerns." This, he said, "would amount to environmental gridlock."

Enacting a Superfund Law was a herculean battle. At the outset of its 1980 creation (the acronym was CERCLA), Lent authored an amendment that sunsetted the cleanup program five years after enactment, which certainly though inadvertently led to contentious struggles as the renewal portion got underway. One came in 1984 when the House adopted by a vote of 208-200 an amendment by Michigan Republican Harold Sawyer that would weaken the bill by removing the ability of victims to file federal lawsuits against polluters and Lent might not have wanted a similar mistake to kill the bill (he was also genuinely concerned with cost). Lent was not happy with Democrats plans to consolidate the package with a hazardous waste package, calling it "a politically motivated election year strategy" because it would force the Senate into "a take it or leave it package." More ominously, he professed, "By sending RCRA and superfund over as one, we would be trying to force the Senate to act on a legislative package, the major portion of which has not been reviewed by the appropriate Senate committees," he said. Lent sought recognition to amend the measure in committee but Florio ruled him out of order and it died for that Congress.

By 1985, 14 Superfund sites on Long Island alone were either on the "high priority" or seeking inclusion or updated list, the most polluted of which were at Grumman (the pollution came about when Grumman was mass-producing planes for U.S. soldiers during World War II). Lent wanted to cut down on the cost by limiting the legislation to site cleanup rather than including personal compensation, arguing, "We could start to make a Christmas tree out of this." But after the subcommittee rejected a more stringent Superfund law that Florio had negotiated, Lent and Ohio Democrat Dennis Eckart put together a compromise that cleared the committee 31-10. He wrote in *The New York Times*, "Superfund encompasses a great number of complex issues. Interested parties from all sides have participated in the debate. As legislators, my colleagues and I must look at the entire spectrum of possible solutions and consider what is legislatively possible."

Lent's support was not impervious to the politics of the process and he specifically blasted Democrats for "a partisan strategy" and "a politically motivated crapshoot which will result in no hazardous-waste legislation being enacted this year." But once stated, his support was unshakable and in 1986, as was Reagan flirted with vetoing the measure that had cleared 391-33, Lent urged him to "think twice...The consensus among the leadership on both sides of the aisle is we are prepared to go to the wall."

Finally, Lent and Florio did battle one more time on a Lent sponsor bill to overturn the "window sticker" that delineated defects on used automobile. Lent called the Federal Trade Commission regulations "both ambiguous and ineffective" and members agreed 286-133.

On other measures, Lent, Florio and other Democrats were fairly harmonious. The Resource Conservation and Recovery Act of 1976, which Lent worked on, was an extension of the 1965 Act that provided management of hazardous waste sites and he and Florio worked on the 1982 renewal legislation that died in the Senate that year, though one was initially enacted. Lent also supported 1988 acid rain legislation put forth by Waxman and Gerry Sikorski though did back an amendment by Virginia Republican Tom Bliley to leave the default. The vote was 11-9.

The relationship between Lent and the jurisdictionally autocratic Dingell was evocative of how legislation is produced. Much of the time, Scrivner said Lent "saw his role and that of committee Republicans to temper those efforts and push back against (regulatory) overreach by the Democrats," which often included Dingell. But not always. *The Almanac of American Politics* wrote how, "Interestingly, on clean air, Lent, with his white collar district, favors tougher regulation than Dingell, who represents the smokestacks of Dearborn and downriver Detroit." In actuality, the goal of both Lent and Dingell was to thwart the imposing agenda of Health Subcommittee Chair Henry Waxman whose ambition was to nationalize the stringent California standards. On the issue of vehicles and alternative fuels, Lent found himself seeking less regulation than even the Bush administration.

In one instance in 1989, Lent and Dingell were backing a "fuel neutrality" amendment to the Clean Air At put forth by Texas Republican Jack Fields that was actually weaker than what Bush favored because, as White House spokesman Stephen Hart said, "something got lost in the translation" and that was whether the president actually favored it. The amendment was adopted. Lent, Dingell, Waxman and others hammered out arduous details one Saturday night.

Photo courtesy of John Hambel

One area on which Lent might have gone counter to at least some of his constituent wishes was advocating operation of the Shoreham Nuclear Power Plant. Speaking against an amendment by Massachusetts Democrat Ed Markey to prevent a start-up license of both Shoreham and Seabrook in New Hampshire, Lent asked, "How many more young men, how many more American vessels do we have to put at rest in the Persian Gulf so we can continue this obscene policy of attempting to close down nuclear power plants?" Lent's vote was decisive as Markey's amendment failed 21-21.

Lent was an arduous champion of recycling. In 1989, he authored a piece in *EPA Journal* in which he noted how, "Sadly, political paranoia and the NIMBY (Not in My Backyard Syndrome) have paralyzed responsible efforts to deal with the nation's waste disposal crisis in a realistic manner. It's time to recognize that there is no magic cure-all and citizens must be willing to make the hard choices to stop the trashing of America now, before it's too late."

Lent played a big role in the Resources Conservation and Recovery Act, the Toxic Substances Control Act and legislation raising the age of alcohol consumption to 21, the latter on which he was an early backer. With Senator Ron Wyden, he sponsored a bill to ease the insurance liability risk coverage.

On foreign affairs, Lent was unabashedly pro-Israel and was awarded the Prime Minister's Medal as early as 1977. In 1981, he and Maryland Democrat Clarence Long sponsored a resolution disapproving of Reagan's plan to sell AWAC missiles to Saudi Arabia. Lent proudly noted it was the first time a disapproval resolution drew 200 co-sponsors and when it finally reached the floor at the end of the year following unsuccessful attempts to get the administration to pull back, it passed with 243 votes.

Parochially, Lent led the fight to save the F-14 which of course was manufactured at Long Island's, Northrup-Grumman. He initially had hope that the F-14 could be salvaged but when it came to pass, he was still sanguine that other doors would open. "Despite the decision to terminate the F-14, it is likely that the Navy will come back to Grumman for more before they allow the assembly line to close. The F-14, in my opinion, is looking better and better all the time.'" Lent even delighted in pointing out that the F-14 was used in the mega-hit movie, "Top Gun," and he and his Long Island comrades facilitated copies of the film for members of the Armed Services Committee. Lent conceded that doing so, "may be a little hokey but we think it's called for. We feel it tells the story of the F-14." That bought the weapon time as did the commencement of the Persian Gulf War and Lent was only to eager to illustrate the tone: "American carriers steaming to the Middle East carry Grumman F-14 squadrons, which will once again be the workhorses of the air." But in the end, it could not be saved in perpetuity.

Fairchild, Long Island's other major defense company, was not left out of Lent's advocacy. It manufactured the A-10 but at one point, the Pentagon had tried to end its production. Scrivner recalls Lent "made it clear to the White House that he would have a hard time voting for something that hurt jobs on Long Island."

On another matter, Lent in 1987 filed a bill requiring striking Long Island Railroad (LIRR) workers to return to work with a 60 day "cooling-off" period. The House passed the measure on a voice vote.

While Lent loved brokering deals, his loyalty as a Republican was unquestioned. He usually sided with his party on contentious domestic roll calls but not always. As the Voting Rights Amendment came up for renewal in 1981, Lent voted against most Republican authored provisions weakening the law though did back an amendment by Illinois Republican Robert McClory eliminating the bilingual requirement. Later in the decade, He voted to override Reagan's veto of the 1988 Civil Rights Restoration Act though opted to sustain Bush's veto of the Civil Rights Act of 1990. He opposed federal funding of abortion.

Photo courtesy of C-SPAN

Similarly, Lent's conviviality with liberals from the days of his first campaign did not inoculate him from throwing partisan punches. During the 1988 presidential campaign, he and other GOP Congressmen held a press conference criticizing Democratic Presidential nominee Michael Dukakis for appointing three people to the Democratic National Committee that were anti-Semitic as a favor to the Rev. Jesse Jackson. Doing so, he said, "raises questions about Michael Dukakis's judgment and his submission" to Mr. Jackson. "Obviously, Governor Dukakis has failed to grasp the message his appointments send."

Despite a penchant for what some amounted to taking cheap shots at the other side, Lent's relationship with the other side was usually as sound as Long Island itself. North Shore Congressman George Hochbruechner, a Democrat with whom Lent served six years, called him, "a true gentlemen, a credit to the Republican Party and a colleague who worked in a bipartisan and effective way for the people of Long Island. He played a major role with Billy Joel and me in protecting Peconic Bay by helping to pass the law that placed it into the National Estuary Program."

Lent also had a way with phrases. During his days in the Senate, he referred to Medicaid as, "a scapegoat to cover up increased taxes." In 1981, when New York State was trying to reach a settlement with Hooker Chemicals and Plastic Corporation, Lent cited a "delicatessen of chemicals" they had dumped. And on the environment, he spoke of how, "We continue to play a game of chemical roulette with man's biological future. We've got to stop this."

In 1986, Lent ascended to the position of top Republican on Energy and Commerce, which on many other committees would be a worthless title given that the GOP was in the minority. Lnly Lent knew how to deal and that made him a, "valued ally or respected adversary" of Dingell. This was most on display as the committee considered the Clean Air Act that the Bush administration had submitted and Lent joined with Dingell in producing a compromise. They also opposed amendments together such as the one million alternative fuels for cars mandate by 1997 which came up in 1989. Lent was also in favor of a national energy policy and put together his own package – the National Energy Policy Act of 1992.

The regulation of phone and cable rates was the meat of Energy and Commerce's existence and Lent played integral roles in both. took up When Commerce took up universal phone service legislation in 1983, Lent resisted efforts by legislators from rural and lower populated areas to reduce local rates because he feared it would come from the expense of larger areas. "The only thing understandable about the bill," he said, "is its politics. Members supporting the bill can go back to their districts and claim, tongue and cheek that they voted to save their constituents $24 a year."

Lent was active on the Cable Television Act and in mid-1992, sponsored the Bush administration's alternative. That proposal was defeated by a vote of 266-144 and lawmakers went on to adopt broader legislation 340-73, with Lent in the opposition. When Bush vetoed the measure, Lent voted to sustain it but the full House did not. Another issue Lent took on: the Inside Trading and Securities Fraud Enforcement Act.

No colleague agreed with Lent 100% of the time but he was very amenable. He was even one of four New York Republicans who supported

Bronx Democrat Robert Garcia in 1988 when he was under indictment for his role in the Wedtech scandal. Scrivner said that his boss "enjoyed the cut and thrust of politics, was not shy about mixing it up with opponents to advocate political positions, defend policy differences and friends (regardless of party)." By the same token, he "was courteous, considerate, popular with colleagues and a pleasure to spend time with."

Hambel calls Lent "the best boss I ever worked for," and he went on to work for Republican politicians in high places. "Despite our personal relationship," Hambel adds, "he never treated me like a kid - he treated me as a political equal, so our discussions could be wide-ranging and I wouldn't hold anything back...He didn't suffer fools gladly, but he treated others with respect." Lent also "led by example" and that showed every two years as the campaign got underway. The headquarters was an empty bank building that essentially sat desolate during the roughly 20 months that it was vacant and was filthy. How did Lent rectify that? "Without saying a word to anyone," Hambel remembers, "NFL got a mop and bucket and descended the cramped stairs to clean the toilets. I knew from that moment that he would never ask me to do something that he wasn't willing to do himself."

Lent rarely invited personal scrutiny but on occasion was forced to preempt criticism. One was his wife, Barbara Morris's employment with Nynex which he considered a "tempest in a teapot." But he nevertheless acquiesced to vocal government watchers and asked the Ethics Committee about a potential conflict of interest when Lent cast votes on issues relating to the utility. Ethics Committee found no conflict of interest. Lent was also a fervent supporter of the Wounded Warriors Project and the Salvation Army.

Like so many members in the Spring of 1992, Lent had inherent frustration. Yet, with zero bounced checks and a continued Republican leaning constituency, he could have continued to be granted new terms by voters had he asked them. But on June 23, 1992, he chose not to. One reason was redistricting, which gave him much new territory. But it wasn't everything. "The redistricting process," he said, "may have stimulated the decision, but I've concluded the time is right to move on to new challenges. I've been doing this for 22 years, offering Republican alternatives, and after a while, you feel it's time to move." A "sense of paralysis and gridlock" also played a role.

Lent remained in the Washington area and formed a government relations firm, Lent and Scrivner which focused on telecommunications. He died of cancer in 2012 at age 81.

CHAPTER TWENTY-FOUR

Independent "Jersey First" Style
Allowed Rinaldo to Thrive

Introductory Quote: "What it proves that the only label people really care about is performance. Any Republican in New Jersey would give his right arm to the kind of support and vote I've received." – New Jersey Congressman Matthew Rinaldo following his 1980 re-election in which he garnered 77%.

**Photo courtesy of the Seton Hall University Library
Archives and Special Collections Center**

From dealing with the elderly to children and families, Matthew Rinaldo was without question one of the most compassionate legislators the Garden State sent to Congress. A Republican who represented a Union County anchored district for 20 years, Rinaldo not only wasn't shy about abandoning his fellow Republican presidents on high-profile legislative matters – but was often among a nearly invisible handful to do so. While much of that was for political necessity – the Seventh Congressional district leaned Republican but had ideological limits, few who watched Rinaldo make the rounds could imagine that it was anything but altruistic.

The Star-Ledger on Rinaldo's death delineated what was so special about him. "Rinaldo, who never married, frequently made the rounds of community and senior citizen organizations, testimonial dinners and labor functions in his district, and spent many an evening in his Capitol Hill office calling constituents to personally address their concerns..." He also took pride in making sure his voting-record was tailored to a single component: "Jersey First."

Known to his friends and colleagues as, "Matty," was a life-blood of Central Jersey. He was born in what was the then thriving town of Elizabeth, received his Bachelor's at Rutgers and his Master's at Seton Hall. A Ph.D in Public Policy was attained at the end of his first year in Congress.

Rinaldo was the only Republican in his family but his political rise came in GOP circles. It started with his appointment to the Union County Zoning Board of Adjustment in 1963. Four years later, he was a Freeholder from the County before heading to Trenton as a State Senator in 1967. The entire ticket resoundingly beat the Democrats, including an incumbent, Mildred Barry Hughes. He was one of two Senate Republicans – his seat-mate Francis McDermott was the other, who voted against Governor William Cahill's proposal to increase New Jersey's sales tax from three to five percent. In 1971, the ticket was again victorious but this time, Rinaldo roared to first-place, far outdistancing his running-mates.

The interest in industry regulation that Rinaldo so cogently pursued in Congress dated back to his legislative days and he introduced a number of esoteric initiatives in that area. In 1972, he sponsored a measure requiring that new cable lines be placed underground. When Public Service Gas and Electric opposed the bill, Rinaldo called it, "a battle between one giant utility against the people of New Jersey." The bill was defeated. Another bill that he introduced would require vehicles to be off the premises of drive-in movie theaters within an hour after the last film ended. The purpose was to prevent asphyxiation which had claimed the lives of two teen-agers in New York. Another bill would prevent clips of "x" rated films being shown before GP (since renamed PG) related movies.

Rinaldo would not be in Trenton much longer. An aging eight-term incumbent, Ruth Dwyer decided to quit that year and endorsed Rinaldo to succeed her in a district that encompassed all but three towns in Union.

He faced Jerry Fitzgerald English but, even in the most Democratic friendly towns such as Elizabeth, Rinaldo was able to count on Democratic support, particularly within the Italian-American community. He won with 63%. While he lived with his parents in Jersey, in Washington, he took a room at the Watergate apartment complex, a building that would make unmitigated history during that very first term.

Photos courtesy of the Seton Hall University Library
Archives and Special Collections Center

In a profile series with *The New York Times*, Rinaldo noted the enormity of the events in Congress. "Since I've been in Washington—and that's only 10 months now—a President has been sworn into office, a war (Vietnam) has ended, another has begun and Watergate and this most recent affair have taken place. Throughout it all, the Congress has played a major role. It's been quite a year." His proximity to a Minority Leader named Gerry Ford helped Rinaldo play a major role. Rinaldo was named an assistant to the House Minority and was sitting beside him when news of Spiro Agnews' resignation hit. "It just happened to be my week to work with the Minority Leader, and I was sitting next to him when Representative [Elford A.] Cederberg [of Michigan] rushed over to us with his face flushed and reported the news. A minute later, a 'Dear Gerry' note announcing the decision arrived from Mr. Agnew."

The moderate niche that made Rinaldo so renowned may have caught the eye of many because during his first term – one where it was understandable that a freshman member in the midst of Watergate would be overshadowed by other matters in his first term, Rinaldo took aim at inflation. He spoke of spending madness and asked for a re-evaluation of 650 government programs he said was costing the taxpayers. Among the examples cited by *The Courier*: $117,250 for the U.S. board of Tea-Tasters, $468,000 a year to England's Queen Elizabeth for not planting cotton on her Mississippi plantation, a $5,000 study of Polish chins B.C., and $205,000 to the International Screw Thread Committee which was established at the end of World War 1 as a "temporary agency." The respect Rinaldo had earned was such that in 1974, as a number of Republicans were abandoning their party due to Watergate, Rinaldo was inching up to 65% over a 25-year old building developer named Adam Levin.

Photos courtesy of the Seton Hall University Library
Archives and Special Collections Center

Rinaldo voted to provide emergency mortgage interest subsidies for low income families in 1975. He was one of only two Republicans to oppose a fellow Republican, Jim Broyhill's bill killing residency training programs. He pushed through an amendment to a housing bill that would prohibit elderly Social Security recipients from being subject to rent increases by getting Social Security increases. It passed on a vote of 260-199. He also supported overrides of Ford vetoes of Emergency jobs, housing, strip mining standards as well as an independent consumer protection agency. At times, the Ford administration (and occasionally the president himself), would seek out Rinaldo's help and he did promise to keep an open mind were he the deciding vote. If not, however, he was not going to abandon his constituents and they understood. Less understanding was Minority Leader John Rhodes when Rinaldo was among the only Republicans to oppose it in the late 1970s Rhodes told him "you should be voting with us," but Rinaldo replied, "I'm going to vote my district," and he believed it would not be beneficial.

In 1976, Rinaldo was the only member of the New Jersey delegation to support production of the B-1 bomber. In the 1979-'81 Congress, he voted against a cap on food stamps, for the creation of the Department of Education and for the Alaska Land bill. In some cases, Rinaldo had a 100% score from the AFL-CIO. By the same token, his ratings from the conservative ACU diminished as the years went on.

**Photo courtesy of the Seton Hall University Library
Archives and Special Collections Center**

Rinaldo had no problems being a thorn in the spine to the Reagan administration. As the House debated whether to approve funding for the

MX missile in 1985, he expressed concerns. He opposed the administration's plans to pay reparations to the families of Iranians killed in the Navy's downing of a civilian plane over the Persian Gulf in 1987. While the president cited "compassion," and promised that not a single penny would go toward the Iranian government, Rinaldo was unmoved. He called the action "precipitous...We don't know all the facts surrounding this incident, nor do we know to what degree the government of Iran shares responsibility for this tragedy...There has never been one iota of remorse or regret on the part of Iran for the tragedy it has inflicted on Americans for the last nine years." Rinaldo sponsored a sense of Congress resolution stating that the reparations should not go forward. He voted to override his veto of a trade bill which contained the two-month requirement for notification before plants could shut their doors.

When George H.W. Bush became President, Rinaldo's brush with moderation continued. Though he dutifully introduced the president when he visited a Union County elementary school in 1989, he rarely provided him cover if he thought he was wrong. He voted for the Democratic proposal to increase the minimum wage, voted to override Bush's veto of the Family and Medical Leave Act. Rinaldo did back the 1989 Constitutional amendment prohibiting desecration of the flag.

With a seat on the Energy and Commerce Committee, Rinaldo's niche was public utilities.

In 1983, Rinaldo proposed an amendment to the Universal Telephone Service Preservation Act that would suspend for one-year an access charge on business and residential customers that the FCC was seeking. But Commerce Chair John Dingell charged the measure would benefit AT&T which strongly backed it and the amendment was rejected. In the advent of the fax, he took aim at unsolicited transactions.

Eventually, Rinaldo became the top Republican on the Subcommittee on Telecommunications and Finance and his relationship with Chairman Ed Markey of Massachusetts was among the most amicable on Capitol Hill. The two worked long and hard to draft a bill designed to curb insider trading. Another area on which Rinaldo and Markey partnered took aim at "renegade" cable operators. But consumer advocates and several members of the committee – Rick Boucher of Virginia and Jim Cooper of Tennessee, complained that the measure lacked teeth.

**Photo courtesy of the Seton Hall University Library
Archives and Special Collections Center**

Rinaldo's lasting legacy was probably children's programming. He was part of the Television Decency Act of 1987. One issue that sponsors tried to take aim at was Dial-A-Porn to which Rinaldo said the following at a hearing: "Two issues should be made clear: First, what is or is not obscene is not changed by this bill; that is a judicial responsibility. Second, whether obscene calls are legal or illegal has already been answered. Obscenity and indecency in telephone communications have been illegal at least since the Communications Act was passed in 1934. Our 1983 amendments explicitly clarified that automated dial-a-porn services were prohibited by law as well. Where things went astray was when the law tried to come up with different rules for children than adults." He was also appalled by the violence on cable television and in 1988 put together a bill which linked educational programs to license renewal. The House had approved the measure 328-78. But when

Reagan vetoed it the day before the election, Rinaldo was dumbfounded. The president had eluded to freedom issues in his veto, contending that, "the Constitution simply does not empower the federal government to oversee the programming decisions of broadcasters in the manner prescribed by this bill." Rinaldo shot back that it was, "a conservative piece of legislation with a minimal amount" of regulation. But Reagan was preparing to depart and Rinaldo and allies were back just months later with an even stronger bill.

With Democrats John Bryant of Texas and Terry Bruce of Illinois, "The Children's Television Act of 1989" was back the following year and its mission was "to reinstate restrictions on advertising during children's television, to enforce the obligation of broadcasters to meet the educational and informational needs of the child audience," One provision was to cap commercials during children's television. Rinaldo called certain children's programs, "little more than long, animated commercials for toys, breakfast foods, games and other products promoted by cartoon heroes" and again proposed the requirement. But the broadcast industry objected and the provision was dropped. Still, a strong bill emerged and one provision called for closed captioning television for the deaf.

**Photo courtesy of the Seton Hall University Library
Archives and Special Collections Center**

Rinaldo was appointed to the Select Committee on Aging in 1978 and by the next term, was the top Republican on the panel. He scolded the Reagan administration and said, "We shouldn't be afraid or skittish about providing an expansion of Medicare." He advocated for the Older Americans Act to provide home care to the elderly and in later years, urged George H.W. Bush to end the senior citizen surtax, which he labeled "unfair and onerous" (the whole law was repealed by year's end).

Locally, Rinaldo addressed concerns about postal-delivery and flooding and airport noise from Newark Airport. Acid rain, stopping ocean dumping of medical waste and making sure the Superfund was as strong as can be were also priorities.

If any criticism arose about Rinaldo, it was that he could at times be self-centered. In particular, he could drive colleagues crazy by keeping an open mind on an issue even if he had little or no intention of abandoning the position that he was ultimately expected to take. Teti recalls the MX missile as one such issue. Rinaldo had always been strong on defense matters but, he did make serious overture to both sides. "Consequently," Teti recalls, "he'd be getting a lot of people on the left pushing and pushing," but sided with defense hawks. While Teti did not believe Rinaldo had been seriously considering voting against MX, he believes he wanted to show flexibility and his straddling was not confined to this issue. Teti called his boss, "a traditional guy. If you talked to him about ideas that were dramatic and bold, that was not him."

When late night votes were ongoing, Rinaldo would expect his legislative staff to remain at work. Yet he would also call his staff in the district office and tell them that if his DC staff had to stay, it wouldn't be fair for them to leave while their comrades were still working. Another pet-peeve Rinaldo had was proofing each of the responses to letters that would be mailed to constituents. The tiniest typo would result in the entire letter being re-written. Paul Schlegel was with Rinaldo for most of his 20 years in office and concedes that he was "fairly demanding," and "always wanted to avoid a mistake." That said, "he didn't blow up and fire people because they made mistakes." By and large, the staff liked Rinaldo and unlike other offices, the staff as generally close-knit devoid of any backstabbing, etc.

**Photo courtesy of the Seton Hall University Library
Archives and Special Collections Center**

After the election of 1980, Rinaldo was pressed hard to consider seeking either the following year's governor's contest or the U.S. senate seat in '82. While Rinaldo said he was, keeping my options open," he ultimately decided not to give up his seat. But to stay in Congress, he had to fight and a selfless decision contributed to his only genuinely tough re-election bid in his twenty years in Congress. That year, Rinaldo took one for the team and ran in a competitive district to spare two fellow Republicans, Marge Roukema and Jim Courter, who had been impacted by redistricting (Courter did not exactly show ever-lasting appreciation. When Rinaldo expressed interest in an opening for the Committee on Committees, Courter went for it and edged Rinaldo out).

The new district was monstrously drawn territory which stretched from Elizabeth in Union County to Princeton in Mercer County to just short of the Jersey Shore. It was labeled the "Fish Hook District." His opponent was a familiar one – Levin who in the interim of his '74 loss had become the State's Consumer Affairs Director. Having contributed to many Jersey Democrats, Levin was in a position to have a district drawn to his liking and the new 7th was the result. Levin may not have expected to face Rinaldo but, nearly 2/3 of the voters were Rinaldo's current constituents, and, after consultation with his friend, NRCC Chair Guy Vander Jagt of Michigan, Rinaldo decided to run. Levin spent a record on a House race for that point but Rinaldo won with 56%, at which point he told supporters, "We overcame a national trend, a new district and a $2 million campaign by my opponent. I hope that this is the last time that money dominates an election campaign as much as it did in this one." In that district at least, it would be. A new Congressional map was enacted for the next cycle and Rinaldo's ensuing four re-elections were afterthoughts.

Photo courtesy of the Seton Hall University Library Archives and Special Collections Center

Though the 1992 remap meant another seat loss for the Garden State, that year's election was looking to be much different. Attorney Leonard Sendelsky was in the race but the district was hardly on the radar screen of either party. What was on the radar screen was Rinaldo's growing distaste for Congress. Still, all was a go for another term until September 11 when he abruptly pulled the plug on his re-election campaign. "Even though I had every intention of continuing to serve in Congress," he said, "I felt compelled to explore challenging opportunities to do something new and different." In an interview with *The Courier-News* the Friday night he announced, Rinaldo said he made the decision that morning after a sleepless night. "It wasn't an easy decision," he conceded. "I couldn't sleep last night thinking about it.

When you've been in the House for 20 years, it's something that you know you'll really miss." At the end of the day, "I decided that realistically 20 years was a long time, and it was time to turn it over to someone else. If you want to go into the private sector and start a second career, you can't wait until you're too old."

The announcement was met with panegyric head-scratching from local Republicans who had mere days to find someone to take his slot on the ballot. His New Jersey Republican colleague in Congress, Chris Smith remarked that Rinaldo "said he was losing interest, but I didn't think he was losing this much interest." Senate President Donald DiFrancesco said, "Knowing Matty, I'm sure he thought this through. But this is late, very late." Fortunately for Republicans, they had a ready contender in State Assemblyman Bob Franks who had nothing to lose – New Jersey legislative elections are held in odd-numbered years and his running would not require him to give up his seat. Franks defeated Sendelsky in November.

If supporters had it their way, Rinaldo wouldn't have been out of office for long as a governor's race loomed in New Jersey and many Republicans wanted to see Rinaldo give it a go. Just before Easter, however, he decided against making a bid, believing that while he had, "an excellent chance" to win... After 27 years in public service...I simply decided that serving as governor is not something I wanted to do at this time in my life," He died at age 77 from complications of Parkinson's Disease in 2008. His service was held at the church he had attended his entire life.

CHAPTER TWENTY-FIVE

Gentleman Lagomarsino a Dogged Advocate for Human Rights and Santa Barbara Coast

Introductory Quote: "When I say Murphy, you say 'here.'" – Robert Lagomarsino's chief petty officer in the Navy during World War II. The superior could not pronounce "Lagomarsino" nor did he try.

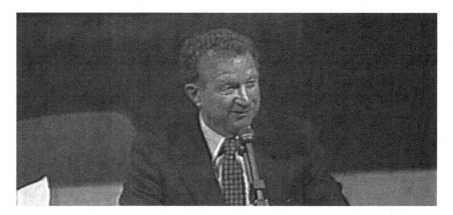

Image via C-Span

Nationally, the name of Robert Lagomarsino would mean very little but residents of Santa Barbara and its surrounding counties might greet it with reverence. As well it should.

Throughout a 34-year political career and nearly 19 years in Congress, Lagomarsino displayed an inveterate interest in human rights and protection for his coastal district that, while often putting him at odds with fellow Republicans – including a president who was his constituent, ensured his philosophy that nothing should detract the California coast from the pristine, tourist destination for which it is renowned. On that and other issues, he gained a reputation as a politically pragmatic and personally decent man, revered by many colleagues and a staff who called him, "Lago."

In an area with many transplants, Lagomarsino was a Ventura County lifer. Actually, his family's association went back well before that – his grandfather John had settled there from Genoa, Italy in the early 1890s a few years after ending up in San Francisco and operated several saloons before founding Ventura's Lima Bean Bank. His father Emilio was a banker, the youngest of five and Catholic while mother Maquone Gates was Protestant which caused some members of her family to frown (she did convert to Catholicism but Lagomarsino jokes that, "she was never really as religious as most people who were married to Italians are").

One thing the couple did have in common was their partisan lineage: both were Republicans. However, the Lagomarsino's lost their home during the Depression and his father switched parties to vote for FDR in 1936 though the Congressman in an oral history interview for the California State Archives did say he was fairly certain that was the only time he voted Democratic. Young Robert attended Catholic school for all but one year of his grammar education but went through the Ventura middle and high schools. His hobbies were few because "I worked all the time after school at our warehouse."

Lagomarsino was 15 when the Japanese attacked Pearl Harbor and he was a very young air raid warden. By the time he turned 18, America was three years into the war and Lagomarsino's desire to serve in the Marine Corps was vetoed by his parents. They were willing to authorize his joining the Navy but threw in another roadblock: he could not do so until he completed high school and he obliged. What Lagomarsino really aspired to was aviation but his vision wasn't up to military standards. Neither was his driving ability apparently – when military officers at San Diego Naval Training Center learned that he had been ticketed for speeding, they assigned him to the prisoner-at-large shack.

After basic training concluded, Lagomarsino attended hospital corps school at San Diego's Naval hospital and dental technician school followed at Terminal Island in Long Beach. With his preparation out of the way, Lagomarsino found himself a pharmacist mate (in his oral history project he said he, "didn't know what a pharmacist's mate was but it sounded pretty good to me"). Near the end of his service, he was assigned to the U.S.S. William Mitchell (AP-114) and the Rock Rogue. He "made one stop to Japan to bring a load of troops back," a mission he said, "had a big impact. (It) made me certainly very patriotic and very appreciative of the armed services. And certainly it gives you a lot of discipline."

When the war concluded, Lagomarsino continued assisting sailors with their dental needs. He also pursued his education – the University of California of Santa Barbara followed by the Santa Clara University School of Law and started the firm, Danch, Farrell & Lagomarsino. By 1958, Lagomarsino had been married and divorced when an an aunt of Norma Jean Mabrey suggested she meet him. She obliged and the pair fell in love and married.

Lagomarsino's political career commenced almost by accident. His ambition for public office was non-existent (he had attempted to be appointed to the Ojai Planning Board) but one night when he was complaining to his wife about an issue, she told him to seek a council seat. He obliged and won. By the end of the year, the incumbent Mayor resigned and colleagues tapped Lahomarsino to replace him.

At that time, Lagomarsino had been practicing law but the 1961 death of longtime State Senator James McBride, a Democrat and friend of his dad's, prompted him to seek the seat and he took advantage of a split among two Democrats to capture the seat with 38%. Both of his rivals took 31%. His win was no fluke. The next time Lagomarsino had to stand for re-election, it was as Lyndon Johnson was swamping Barry Goldwater in California. While Lagomarsino took heat from some members of the party for not printing the word "Republican" on his literature, he held his seat with 55% and with ease for his next decade, despite the fact that the district leaned Democratic.

At the outset of his service, Lagomarsino had learned from a colleague that "the duty" of the State Senate is, "to protect the people against the state assembly." In fact, he recalled later that, "the competition was intense - much more so than Democrat/Republican." For his part, Lagomarsino focused on local issues.

At that time, Ventura County was not yet the exurban area of activity that it has since become but Lagomarsino would do his part to change that. In 1965, he proposed legislation authorizing a state study to bring a UC campus to Ventura and shepherded a bill - the Garrigus-Lagomarsino Act that created a vocational school in each of the Golden State's counties.

That year, Lagomarsino became chairman of the Senate Committee on Natural Resources and Wildlife and won the first ever Legislative Conservationist of the Year award from the California Wildlife Federation. California's Attorney General, Evelle Younger, called him, "Law Enforcement's best friend in Sacramento." Other committees he served on: Institutions and Government Efficiency, the Commission for Economic Development and Rules.

**Photo courtesy of California State University Channel Islands,
John Spoor Broome Library, Robert J. Lagomarsino Archives**

Accomplishments-wise in his latter tenure included the Consumer Protection Act which preceded passage of a federal law. California's Wild and Scenic Legislation came several years after President Lyndon Johnson put his signature on national legislation. Other Lagomarsino legislative victories: the California Child Anti-Pornography Act (1969); the Marine Resources Protection Act (1970); the Jury Reform Act (1972); the Welfare Reform Act (1973) and increasing the fines for killing a California condor.

In 1969, there was a massive oil spill off the coast of Santa Barbara and President Nixon came to inspect the damage. The sand had rendered the oil invisible and Nixon was asking where it was. "About that time," Lagomarsino recalls, "I looked back and I saw a wave running in and I reached out and grabbed him and pulled him back so his feet wouldn't get wet. And as soon as I touched him I thought, 'I'm going to get shot.' You're not supposed to put your hands on the president of the United States." Substantively, Lagomarsino recalled in his oral history project that he worked on future safeguards to prevent future spills. Among them: "I was able to talk to six major oil companies to stop shipping Alaskan oil through the Santa Barbara Channel but to go outside. We also convinced the Coast Guard to establish a NAVTEX radio navigation system."

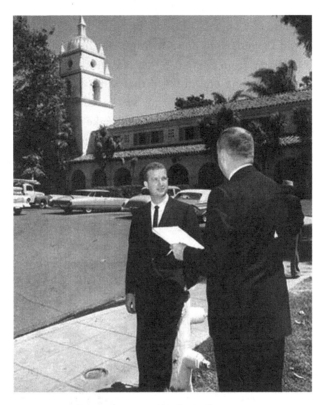

Lagomarsino as a State Senator
Photo courtesy of California State University Channel Islands,
John Spoor Broome Library, Robert J. Lagomarsino Archives

The bulf of Lagomarsino's tenure in the legislature coincided with Ronald Reagan's governorship and his door was always open. He recalls the only time seeing the future-President angry was when Lagomarsino was shepherding Reagan's tax bill through the Senate. He brought a recalcitrant colleague to see Reagan in hopes of convincing him to support the bill. He wouldn't and the Gipper threw his glasses on the table.

Lagomarsino's opportunity to run for Congress came earlier than he had anticipated when longtime Congressman Charles Teague, a Republican, died suddenly in January of 1974. He entered the race to succeed him and at a time when the Watergate scandal was anathema to Republicans of all stripes, he shifted the focus to his efforts to make stricter laws following the Santa Barbara oil spill five years earlier. The frontrunners in the all-party election were two Ojians – Lagomarsino and one of his successors as Mayor, James Loebl. The chief argument of Loebl was, "Don't vote Republican and send Nixon another vote in Congress." But voters didn't heed that.

Not only did Lagomarsino prevail with 54% and avoiding a runoff but he prevented his party from going 0-5 that season: the GOP lost four other special elections, including one in Ohio that same day. Lagomarsino, who as the returns came in confessed that he was "sweating bullets," predicted that "the Republican National Committee will take heart from my election as a sign that Republicans can still be elected under the right conditions." Norma said Nixon "thought that because my husband got elected that that would do something good for him...But it wasn't that at all. It was [that] the constituents knew him and it was pretty much the same congressional district as had been the senate district for the California State Senate so that the people knew and went for him."

Photo courtesy of California State University Channel Islands, John Spoor Broome Library, Robert J. Lagomarsino Archives

If Lagomarsino's win made national Republicans feel better, it was a short lived as it was the four losses in the other specials, not his victory that portended the party's catastrophic 40 seat loss in November. Lagomarsino again avoided being among those casualties. Loebl was back for the regular cycle but Lagomarsino's margin rose to 56%. Two years later, he was up to 64% and never dipped below 61% until 1988.

President Reagan and his Congressman
Photos courtesy of California State University Channel Islands,
John Spoor Broome Library, Robert J. Lagomarsino Archives

Appropriate for his interests, Lagomarsino took seats on Foreign Affairs and the Interior and Insular Affairs Committee. He became the top Republican on the Foreign Affairs Subcommittee on Western Hemisphere Affairs in 1989. One endeavor was successfully adding $75 million to Reagan's aid request for the Dominican Republic.

In his first full term, Lagomarsino got more than $20 million in an appropriation for a space program. A sizable portion of that would go toward Vandenberg Air Force Base near the district that Lagomarsino championed throughout his career. He had little use for gun control measures but did support the Brady Bill near the end of his career. He sponsored legislation with Michigan Senator Donald Riegel that would gut withholding taxes for first-time home-buyers.

In 1979, Lagomarsino proposed an amendment requiring the president to withdraw recognition from Peking if it was deemed a security threat to Taiwan. He had more luck with another amendment that required the president to notify Congress of threats to peace in the region should Taiwan be threatened. Yet another required the State Department to submit the human rights records of all nations that were participants in the United Nations. He had told Deputy Secretary of State Warren Christopher in no uncertain terms that, "this body and specifically this committee take a direct interest in the nature and quantity of arms sold to Taiwan and intend to be a full partner in any decision made on this matter." Around that time, he called China, "the world's largest concentration camp."

Throughout his career, Lagomarsino was active in matters concerning the Soviet Union, particularly that the nation comply with international agreements. One such area was Soviet Jewry which, in 1983, he accused the government of having "virtually choked off." He called, "the growing official harassment and denial of basic rights to Jewish citizens (a) sobering reality." That year, he sponsored a resolutions with several other colleagues supporting the Contadora group's effortorts to secure peace in Central America.

Lagomarsino supported priorities of his most famous constituent and one on which he was the most vocal was Reagan's advocacy of the Nicaraguan contras. After the pro-contra forces prevailed on the House floor in 1986 by a vote of 221-209, Lagomarsino expressed relief. "Had we lost, it would have been not only a defeat for the President, but as a practical matter it would have doomed the contras and put the Central American democracies in a terrible position. Passage doesn't guarantee anything, it just provides a chance for the problems to be solved."

The battle over aid to El Salvador proceeded along similar lines. In 1983, Lagomarsino resisted calls to cut aid to El Salvador that others had begun to promote since the murder of four nuns in 1980. During Foreign Affairs Committee debate, he said, "One person who would be very happy to see this amendment passed is Fidel Castro?" He asked, "Do we wash our hands of the situation and walk away? If the United States did that, I think there would be tragic results for all of the things that I think we are all concerned about." A compromise was worked out.

The 1984 election of Jose Napoleon Duarte made the issue temporarily moot as Duarte was a member of the resistance movement. By 1989, Duerte was no longer in power and supporters of democracy were getting mixed signals over the new rein. New President Alfredo Cristiani got a nice rapport from Capitol Hill but many were unconvinced of his ultimate commitment to human rights and still wanted to cut the aid. The election of a new American president, George H.W. Bush, complicated this debate and Lagomarsino argued that cut backs would not be prudent, "even before they have had a chance to prove themselves."

Lagomarsino was not always alongside the Gipper. Initially, he opposed the South African sanctions legislation, one of just 127 members to do so. However, the following year, he successfully opted to override Reagan's veto of similar legislation.

During the Bush administration, Lagomarsino wanted to give a chance to the emerging Polish democracy and as the House Foreign Affairs Committee was considering an aid package in 1989, called the "opportunity one that may not come along again for a long, long time and I think we should grab it and run." Only one dissension was recorded.

On the domestic front, Lagomarsino's crown jewel was undoubtedly the establishment of Channel Islands as a national park. Testifying in favor of the bill, he said, "The islands, which lie at a distance of 11 to 60 miles off the coast of Santa Barbara and Ventura counties in my district, contain nationally significant scenic, ecological, cultural and scientific features which deserve to be protected as a national park for the benefit of generations to come." Defining the driving doctrine for the park Lagomarsino stated, "Because of the singular vulnerability of the islands' resources, some of which exist nowhere else on earth, this legislation specifies that the proposed park would be administered on a low-intensity, limited entry basis, so that visitor use within the park is restricted to levels which would not threaten to destroy the delicately balanced environment found there."

After a previous effort had failed, the National Park Service (NPS) offered a description of a final product. "The new national park would include Santa Barbara and Anacapa Islands (the former Channel Islands National Monument) and add Santa Rosa, Santa Cruz, and San Miguel Islands, the latter to remain under the ownership of the U. S. Navy but managed by the NPS." Lagomarsino fought to secure new appropriations for the park each year he remained in office. In appreciation, the park houses the Channel Islands National Park Robert J. Lagomarsino Visitor Center.

Coming from a district with numerous Coast Guard interests, Lagomarsino bemoaned possible cuts. During one 1989 debate, he stated, "We can hardly stand in the well of this House and protest against the flood of drugs streaming into our country and our cities and our schools without also standing up on the floor and voting to providing the Coast Guard with the necessary resources to act."

Lagomarsino was at the helm of the POW/MIA Task Force which his biography points out was "the only official body of Congress that was chaired by a Republican." In 1985, after a number of failed attempts by other members of Congress, his legislation authorizing a Prisoner of War Medal was enacted.

Another area that garnered much of Lagomarsino's initiative was pay raises for government officials including members of Congress. He wanted them to take affect after the close of the Congressional sessions on which it was enacted saying, "Part of this is not new. James Madison submitted the idea that no pay raise should go into affect until the next election as far as the original Bill of Rights." Lagomarsino also made clear he had little patience for members approving them in secret and advocated for a roll call vote anytime one was voted on. He was also a big proponent of the federal government paying its bills on time or facing default.

CQ's *Politics in America* noted that Lagomarsino had "an unusually blithe moment in 1990" when Bush cited his aversion to broccoli. The Congressman's reasoning: "even the president can be wrong about some things – especially vegetables."

With House Minority Leader Bob Michel (R-Illinois)
Image courtesy of C-Span

Lagomarsino was not impervious to partisanship when it came to presidential politics. During the 1980 campaign, he delivered a floor speech, "What is going on with the Carter administration? Can they not get their act together? First, they decide to vote for a U.N. resolution criticizing Israel's settlement policy, then they say that was a mistake resulting from a 'failure in communications.' No wonder they cannot deal with Iran. They cannot even get their signals straight between the White House." And U.S. prestige is suffering home and abroad thanks to the continuing saga of a president who is flunking his on-the-job training." During the 1992 Presidential election, Lagomarsino delivered a number of "one-minute's" on the House floor critical of Democratic presidential nominee, Bill Clinton.

Lagomarsino's respect among his colleagues was such that he was Secretary of the Republican Conference, a position that made him fourth in the Republican leadership. As that came to an end in 1988, he failed in his attempt to move up to the slot of vice-chair, a position he lost to the far more combative Bill McCollum of Florida.

Across the aisle, Lagomarsino established strong working relations with fellow Californians Phil Burton and Ron Dellums – two of the most liberal members of Congress (Dellums in fact was instrumental in securing funding for the Western Space Museum and Science Center). He liked Arizona Congressman Morris K. "Mo" Udall very much and in fact he supported his Alaska Land bill.

Lagomarsino's one tough race for re-election came in 1988 when he faced a State Senator named Gary Hart. While Hart was of no relation to the former Colorado Senator who had launched a White House bid that same year, he did enjoy heavy backing and recruitment from Los Angeles area Congressmen Henry Waxman, Howard Berman and Mel Levine. Lagomarsino was incredulous when the League of Conservation Voters included him on its list of "Dirty Dozen" given his record against offshore drilling and establishing the Channel Islands. Both contenders raised $1.5 million and Hart actually outspent Lagomarsino by a nominal margin. The results were almost as neck and neck. A poll released a week before the election gave Lagomarsino a six point lead. The race ended much closer and on election night, he led by fewer than 2,500 votes. Hart eked out a victory by 1.5% in Ventura but Lagomarsino doubled that in Santa Barbara. Only after the absentees had been tabulated did it become clear that Lagomarsino had hung onto his seat by a margin of 3,993 votes, 50-49%.

With Hart passing on a rematch, 1990 was generally easy-going though Lagomarsino was briefly put on the defensive by Bush's decision to exempt the California coast from offshore drilling – with the exception of Santa Barbara and Ventura. His opponent, former Hart aide Anita Perez-Ferguson, seized on that and hit Lagomarsino for failing to use his influence. In truth, Lagomarsino as early as 1987 had made sure the Santa Barbara channel was seen on maps as "an area to be avoided." He prevailed 55-44% and said as the votes were being counted, "She shouldn't have attacked my integrity and claimed that I have a bad environmental record when I don't."

By January 1992, Lagomarsino was in trouble. A new redistricting plan had merged much of his turf with a fellow Republican and much junior member named Elton Gallegly. Republican Governor Pete Wilson wanted to keep both men in Congress and successfully prevailed on Lagomarsino to move from Ventura to Santa Barbara, which he called his "hardest political decision." He rented a condo in order to establish residence. As a longtime incumbent, that normally would have been enough for Lagomarsino to salvage his seat but Michael Huffington, a fellow Republican, had other ideas. The wealthy Santa Barbara businessman had two necessary assets in his corner: oodles of money and discontent over incumbents, not to mention the fact that Lagomarsino, while not unknown, had represented little of the territory prior. GOP luminaries from Vice-President Dan Quayle to Republican locals and scores of Congressional colleagues tried to convince Huffington not to force a primary but to no avail.

The race was a slugfest to the end. The incumbent portrayed his challenger as a Texan who only recently began paying California taxes. Huffington replied that Lagomarsino could "play dirty or play clean." Huffington outspent Lagomarsino 5-1 (so much that Lagomarsino loaned his campaign $300,000 and decided to stop watching TV out of frustration). He gained traction over the incumbent's eight overdrafts – a very low amount compared to other incumbents, but also, the fact that he was pro-choice while Lagomarsino opposed to abortion. Meanwhile, Lagomarsino compared it to, "running a clean race against an opponent on steroids."

The incumbent's years of service to Santa Barbara served him well as he carried it by 13%. His downfall was in San Luis Obispo which opted for Huffington by more than thirty points. The final margin was 49-43% in favor of the challenger.

The next day, a despondent Lagomarsino said, "I never planned to stay until I was carried out. I wanted to walk out when I was ready to leave, and when I felt there was someone good to replace me. It was not to be, I guess… It hurts." His wife was less charitable toward the voters decision. "We love it here. It's too bad the people here don't love us." Gallegly was distraught, telling reporters the morning after that he had "survivor guilt." But he added, "I still feel that Bob Lagomarsino is my mentor." *Politics in America* wrote that in the aftermath of the defeat, "Lagomarsino, angered at seeing his Congressional career come to an end, considered a write-in bid but didn't."

As he prepared to depart Congress, Lagomarsino was saluted by members from both parties. Long Beach Democrat Glenn Anderson, who served as lieutenant Governor when Lagomarsino was in the Senate, noted that, "Too often in Congress, partisan bickering and political posturing overshadow the working relationships and friendships that extend across the aisle. I was lucky enough to have forged such a relationship with Bob Lagomarsino."

In 1993, Lagomarsino did not hold an office but the word retirement was non-existent. He lobbied to save Point Mugu and Port Hueneme Navy stations and directed several preservation groups including Friends of the Chanel Island. He continues to be held in high esteem both at home and by his former colleagues in the nation's capitol.

CHAPTER TWENTY-SIX

Quiet Jersey Appropriator Dwyer Believed the Only Member of Congress at Pearl Harbor

Introductory Quote: "Being here at the time of the attack has given me insight into the futility of war and how wasteful war is. The experience gave me some perspective about life, family and service to your country that have always remained with me." – New Jersey Congressman Bernard Dwyer's remarks at Pearl Harbor on the 50th anniversary of the attack. Dwyer is believed to have been the only future member of Congress present on that day that would live in infamy.

Photo courtesy of Pamela Dwyer Stockton

Imagine a Congressman never seeking out the flair of a camera, rarely making a speech on the House floor and seldom being mesmerized by the perks that accompany being a member of Congress. While it might be impossible to imagine, for residents of what in his second term became the

Sixth Congressional District of New Jersey (it had been the 15th beforehand), this was the man who represented them in Washington for six terms. His name was Bernard Dwyer and seeing that his state and Middlesex County-oriented district got their fair share was his singular concern.

Throughout his career, "Bernie" Dwyer was a man who accomplished an abundance for his people but he was content to do it in the most nonchalant of ways. He is believed to be the only person serving at Pearl Harbor when it was attacked who later served in the United States Congress and later, when confronted with the choice of loyalty to his party versus making a sound judgement on the facts, he opted for the facts every time. While that left him devoid of winning a popularity contest with his fellow Democrats on at least one high profile occasion, an occasion that saw some calling for his head, the generally outstanding Democrat proved that conscience and Dwyer went hand-in-hand.

Dwyer's aversion to publicity was especially unusual because he had held elective office for much of his adult life. Though 59 when he made it to Congress in 1980, Dwyer was no political rookie in the least. He first was elected to office as a member of the Edison Council in 1958, eventually becoming Mayor. In 1973, he became a State Senator and was that chamber's Majority Leader when he mounted his bid for Congress.

One thing Dwyer did not have an aversion to was Middlesex County – he was a lifer. He was born in the industrial city of Perth Amboy and spent most of his years in Edison 20 minutes away. After graduation from high school, he joined the Civilian Conservation Corps (CCC) and was sent to Idaho. He returned home, joined the Naval Reserve and got called up pretty quickly. He was sent to the Navy's radio school in Noroton, Connecticut.

On December 7, 1941, Dwyer was a 20-year old radio man on the destroyer, the USS Dale. As Chief of Staff Lyle Dennis recalls, Dwyer would joke in future years that as "a 20-year old, single guy in Hawaii, he viewed himself as on top of the world." That changed on the day that would live in infamy. When the bombs started going off, the Dale turned on its engine and safely vacated the area. As the 50th anniversary approached, an NBC News reporter named Marjorie Margolies-Mezvinsky contacted Dwyer's office hoping to do a story. Dennis was thrilled at the idea but Dwyer, who rarely spoke about his experiences, had no interest (the following year, Margolies-Mezvinsky became a member of Congress from Pennsylvania).

In war time and with Lilyan, his bride of 49 years
Photos courtesy of Pamela Dwyer Stockton

Dwyer did agree to serve as Grand-Marshall of Honolulu's remembrance ceremony that year and proudly brought along his grandson. On the military plane transporting members of Congress, a bombastic conservative colleague from California named Bob Dornan was surprised that Dwyer was on board. When told that Dwyer was a part of Pearl Harbor, Dornan approached his colleague and said, "Mr. Dwyer, I salute you." Dwyer was humble as usual but gracious. A postscript: When Dwyer was being saluted in a Special Order speech as he prepared to retire, Dornan was the first person to bring up Pearl Harbor.

Dwyer remained in the Navy until the war ended and upon returning, took insurance classes at Rutgers University-Newark. He married Lilyan Sudzina and made the insurance business his profession, becoming a partner at Fraser Brothers Insurance.

In 1957, Dwyer ran for Council in Edison on the Democratic slate. A Mayor-Council form of government had recently been approved by voters but now Republicans who controlled the town seemed to be backing away from implementing it (their standard-bearer for Mayor had opposed it). Democrats published a long ad in *The Courier-News* which began by telling voters of some "downright malicious whispering not fit for publication." They went on to tell voters they were not "obligated to anyone. You can be sure the Business Administrator will be a qualified expert and not a political hack. So here's your campaign in a nutshell. Who are you going to choose as the custodians of your new government? Republicans who only last year sought to destroy mayor-council before it was born? Or would you rather trust its avowed friends - the Democratic candidates who fought for Mayor-Council and made it a reality." Voters chose the latter.

Dwyer became a councilman, council president, and then mayor of Edison. His successor as mayor credited him with making significant infrastructure improvements in the township, as well as "providing funds for the town's public schools and developing parks throughout the community." Among his other accomplishments: appointing Harry Russell the first African-American member of the Edison Township Board of Education.

In 1973, Dwyer went to the legislature, winning a seat in the New Jersey Senate with 2/3 of the vote. There, he sided with Jim Duggan over Governor Brendan Byrne in the battle for Senate president (the governor favored Bergen's Mathew Feldman for the post while the Democratic chairman James Duggan favored Frank Dodd of Essex). Byrne didn't hold that against Dwyer when it came to signing his bills into law. In 1977, Byrne signed legislation Dwyer proposed that would exempt gold and silver from the sales tax that Byrne had famously championed a year earlier. The law mandated the dealer to be registered with the Securities and Exchange Commission. For four years, he was the Chairman of the Legislature's Joint Appropriations Committee followed by Majority Leader.

Even in the midst of his Congressional campaign, Dwyer looked out for his people. He had been alarmed to learn that a Japanese automobile company, then called Datsun, had submitted the lowest bid to sell vehicles to the state at a time when a Ford plant in Edison and the General Motors plant in Linden were struggling under the pressure of cheap foreign imports, which potentially meant a loss of thousands of jobs. Dwyer sponsored a bill mandating that all state agencies use American fleet. Doing so, he said, would give plants "the respite to meet the competition."

When the longtime Congressman for whom the then-15th district was created in 1962 decided to retire in 1980, Dwyer aimed for the job. The field was distinguished of presents and futures. It would include Assemblyman David Schwartz, future Assemblyman and Edison Mayor George Spadoro and Richard Pucci who would go on to serve nearly three decades as mayor of Monroe Township. Dwyer won the bulk of the newspaper endorsements including *The New York Times* and had the powerful Middlesex County Democratic Organization in his corner. Spadoro did manage to capture Woodbridge, Sayreville and Linden but Dwyer won big in Edison and took 32% for 25% for Schwartz. He vowed that while the primary was based "primarily on personality," November would be based on "national issues." However, he was mistaken as few could have predicted how far the fortunes of Jimmy Carter and the Democratic Party would tank. Dwyer took 53% in November over William O'Sullivan, Jr., who had campaigned on change. Dwyer meanwhile called it imperative for both parties to address the economy on a "non-adversary basis."

Dwyer was assigned to the Appropriations Committee and throughout his first ten years, he served on the Labor-HHS-Education Subcommittee along with Commerce-Justice-State and, in his final term, the Energy and Water Subcommittee and Defense. Beach preservation and restoration were high on his plate. He fought for the development of nationwide undersea research centers and one would be housed at Rutgers. He and Morris County Republican Dean Gallo worked on a drainage tunnel for the Passaic River to reduce flooding.

In 1989, Dwyer joined with seven other members of the delegation that would block the sale of plutonium for nuclear weapons. Days earlier, he was among another quartet of Jerseyans who signed a letter spearheaded by fellow Democrat William J. Hughes to prevent sewage sludge from being dumped offshore into the ocean from where it could potentially migrate onto the beaches. He fought for sewage projects for his communities, funding for Amtrak (and a stop at New Brunswick's station), an alcohol abuse program at Rutgers, as well as a Red Cross AIDS program. Another area he advanced: tax credits for the handicapped who owned homes.

On social issues, Dwyer was solidly aligned with his party. He was pro-choice, the only one of the Catholic quartet of Jersey departures from Congress in '92 who were (he was also the only one married as Bob Roe, Frank Guarini and Republican Matt Rinaldo were all lifelong bachelors). He also opposed the Constitutional amendment banning flag burning. Dwyer could deviate occasionally from the liberal orthodoxy on defense matters (refusing to end production of the B-2 stealth bombers) but by and large believed that a strong defense did not mean, "a bloated defense."

Photo courtesy of Pamela Dwyer Stockton

In 1987, Dwyer put a novel idea for housing into legislation: "granny flats." It emanated from Australia and the concept was that people could the result was the "Elderly Cottage Housing Opportunity Act" (ECHO) that he proposed which would offer tax credits to those who took advantage of it, as several states already were.

Because Dwyer came to Congress just as the Iran hostage standoff had ended, embassy security was a big concern and he and other members frequently joined Commerce chair Neal Smith of Iowa in traveling to different nations to inspect various posts worldwide. In 1986, Dwyer was one of 19 members of a bipartisan delegation that traveled to the Philippines to witness that nation's presidential election.

Dennis, who served as Dwyer's Chief of Staff throughout his entire tenure, called him, "a very good boss." While "Congress is a very tough place," Dwyer was not like that. "He was very fair, very honest with staff," even as he "kind of did things his own way." He was also sensitive to their needs. Dennis usually believed that staff should remain in the office when the House had late votes if Dwyer had to cast a vote on matters that pertained to their specific areas of expertise. Dwyer, on the other hand, would tell them to go home to their families saying, "I know how I'm supposed to vote."

Many of those same attributes defined Dwyer as a colleague. He was truly a man of see no evil, hear no evil. He rarely had a discourteous word about anyone and vice-versa. Former Governor Jim Florio on Dwyer's death said "even his political opponents conceded he was a very trustworthy person." The opponent Florio might have been referring to was Peter Sica, who challenged Dwyer in 1988 but who "Of all the people I've ever run against, Dwyer was a real gentleman. Our positions on all the issues were quite different but he was probably the most sincere person I've ever met in politics." He had a dry sense of humor.

Dwyer's penchant for taking credit was the antithesis of a politician – it was simply non-existent. A New York colleague and fellow Appropriator, Democrat Matthew McHugh, summed up Dwyer's style: He is "thoughtful but doesn't necessarily think out loud. He's not stupid. He's quiet." His friends were like-minded Northeastern Appropriators: Pennsylvania Democrats Tom Foglietta and Jack Murtha, Steny Hoyer of Maryland and Joe Early of Massachusetts, along with Hughes who did not serve on the panel.

There was also Dwyer the public servant. Pamela Dwyer Stockman, the Congressman's daughter, recalls that he was always available to his constituents. "We NEVER had an unlisted phone number. When he would say to someone 'give me a call' he/she often asked how to get the number. And he would say 'look in the telephone directory, my home and business numbers are in there.'" His dedication went further. "If he was working outside the house raking leaves, etc., and someone stopped to talk he always listened. And he usually had a piece of scrap paper in his pocket to jot down a request, a question, whatever, so he could get back to people."

In 1985, Speaker Tip O'Neill named Dwyer (and Roe) to the Select Committee on Intelligence. *The Star-Ledger* observed, "Two key attributes were needed to be named to the House panel: loyalty to House Speaker Tip O'Neill and unswerving opposition to more aid to the (Nicaraguan) contras." O'Neill also had named Dwyer to the Standards of Official Conduct (Ethics) which would have some irony four years later when the panel investigated O'Neill's successor as Speaker, Jim Wright.

Photo courtesy of Pamela Dwyer Stockton

Dwyer achieved more notoriety through his seat on the Ethics Committee and that encapsulated his known ability to call them as he saw them. In fact, when O'Neill appointed him to serve, a key reason was that he had said he has "no reservation about saying 'no comment' to the press." Dwyer had in fact made so few waves in his first eight years that, it came as a genuine earthquake when he cast a decisive vote to charge O'Neill's successor as Speaker, Jim Wright with accepting $145,000 in gifts over a ten-year period from George Mallick, operator of a prominent Fort Worth business. The catch was that Mallick, that was taking part in an ongoing rebuilding the Fort Worth landscape. Less controversial but still not unanimous (the vote was 10-2) was that the Speaker's income from his book, *Reflections of a Public Man* exceeded what was permitted under House rules.

Dwyer's newfound fame was accompanied by the ire of at least some very vocal and prominent members in the democratic caucus, some of whom quite overtly hinted at repercussions. Texas Democrat Charlie Wilson, a fellow appropriator and staunch Wright defender remarked, "I don't know what happened to Bernie," before accusing he and Atkins of having "jumped ship."

He added: "When the fight is over, the sun is going to shine on everybody but Atkins and Dwyer." Another Texan, Jack Brooks, when asked what Dwyer and Atkins should do, simply replied, "pray." Dwyer's philosophy, as Dennis explained it was that, "I liked Jim, he's been good to me but, he broke the rules." Meanwhile, many other fellow Democrats approached Dwyer and essentially told him, "I'm glad it wasn't me."

In the end, the talk about ramifications proved just that and Dwyer went about quietly serving New Jersey, which he appeared content to do at voters' pleasure for the foreseeable future. That slowly began changing and ultimately concluded due to circumstances entirely out of his control.

Photos courtesy of Pamela Dwyer Stockton

First came Dwyer's 1990 re-election campaign which, almost approaching election night, he appeared poised to win without much resistance. But the state's new governor and Dwyer's former House colleague, Jim Florio, had put forth a $2.8 billion tax increase that summer and voters were revolting against everything Democratic. The budget stalemate at the federal level between President George H.W. Bush and Congressional Democrats proved little easier as an agreement enacted literally ten days before Election Day – which Dwyer opposed on the basis of "fairness," nevertheless tarnished all incumbents. Dwyer's Republican challenger Paul Danielczyk opposed the agreement, instead backing a package put together by Minority Whip Newt Gingrich that didn't increase taxes. He hit Dwyer for his frequent foreign travel, calling him, "one of the Marco Polos of Congress" (Dwyer replied that he was in the district every weekend).

Danielczyk had spent just $8,000 on his campaign but early on election night, Danielczyk stunned many by taking a 24 vote lead over the incumbent. When the final votes were tallied, Dwyer had held on to his job, but only by a margin of 5,604 votes for a 51-46% win. He actually lost Middlesex by 43 votes and his entire margin came from a 62% showing in Union, which Danielczyk actually lambasted for even being in the district. While calling it the, most difficult congressional race by far," Dwyer accepting his win said, "I hope to serve the district well as we've done in the past."

He would hardly get the chance. Redistricting was around the corner and the Garden State was losing a seat. It seems highly unlikely that Democrats, nor Republicans for that matter, wanted Dwyer to be the odd man out and, though 71, he had no intention of being the sacrificial lamb. But when Alan Rosenthal voted to break a tie between the two parties by choosing the plan state Republicans had offered, Dwyer found most of his Middlesex turf merged with fellow Democrat Frank Pallone whose base covered much more conservative terrain in Monmouth County. He announced his departure a day later. While Dwyer contended that he had at least been thinking about retirement before the remap, a statement he issued noted "a district in which nearly half the residents would be new to me, and I to them, certainly helped me to finalize my decision."

Photo courtesy of Pamela Dwyer Stockton

Incidentally, days after the plan was released, Roe, whose district had to be preserved, announced his retirement and Democrats, fearful of losing that seat as well (they didn't) engaged in recriminations that Dwyer could have been spared had Roe not waited until after the map had been in place before revealing his decision (Dennis said that Dwyer, as typical, was not angry).

Dwyer returned to Edison but relocated to nearby Metuchen a few years later. That is where he died in 1998 of a heart attack at age 77 while behind the wheel.

In closing, Dwyer had much to be proud of but tooting his horn was not his style and that probably lasted until his final days. As Pamela told mourners at his funereal, "He would be embarrassed that I got up here today and embarrassed at the many kind things people have said and thought about him in the past few days." *The Home News Tribune* was even more cogent writing that "in politics, there are few real gentlemen. Now there are even fewer."

CHAPTER TWENTY-SEVEN

Bank Probe Chair McHugh Recognized by Colleagues for Scrupulousness in Both Work and Life

Introductory Quote: "I always kid him and tell him he is what every Catholic mother wants her son to grow up to be." -Wisconsin Democratic Congressman David Obey, a longtime colleague of the subject at hand.

Photo courtesy of Matthew McHugh

F ew would argue that the mass exodus of members of Congress in 1992 included folks that were both good and bad but one would be hard pressed to find anyone who would define New York Democrat Matthew

McHugh as remotely negative. The upstate Democrat's model for probity was as sprawling as the large, tri-regional district that he represented for 18 years. It was a reason colleagues routinely sought his counsel and why the Congressional leadership tapped him to take on a very high profile assignment he could easily have done without; leading the investigation of the House overdraft scandal that engulfed more than half the chamber's members and ended many careers.

A former colleague from Wisconsin by the name of Robert Cornell said, "I often say Matt would have made a wonderful priest," an assertion Cornell could credibly make because in another life he was one. Stephen Solarz, a fellow New Yorker whose entire tenure overlapped with McHugh's would write in his memoir that his colleague, "more than most, was always inclined to do what was right rather than what was expedient." It was largely because of those qualities or perhaps in spite of them that McHugh didn't, at least until he undertook the check bouncing scandal, have an enemy in the House. And even then they were sparse.

The Almanac of American Politics cited McHugh's, "accent that shows traces of his upbringing in Philadelphia and Brooklyn," and his link to both was unmistakable. He was born in the City of Brotherly Love, the grandson of an Irish immigrant from County Donegal. His father was the eldest of five children whom McHugh describes as "a simple, decent man," who left high school to begin working and never graduated. One of those jobs was a prison guard at the penitentiary operated by the City of Philadelphia. The McHughs moved to Brooklyn after Matt finished first grade in parochial school when his father was offered a job as a salesman for Gulf Oil in Westchester County, New York. Matt then went on to attend Brooklyn Technical High School and for his higher education, Mount Saint Mary College followed by the Villanova University School of Law. McHugh had good fortunes on the latter. Lacking the resources to pay, McHugh was toying with joining the Air Force until he landed a resident counselor position which covered his room and board and a scholarship that covered his tuition. A fellow student who started a year after McHugh was John LaFalce of Buffalo. They became friends and a decade later were elected to Congress together as Democrats.

McHugh's three years in law school coincided with John F. Kennedy's time in the White House and being part of a large, Irish-Catholic family, he was both captivated and motivated. "For many of us," he explained, "Kennedy was not only young and attractive, but an intelligent, articulate leader who could bring new energy and idealism to the country. His sudden death by assassination was a truly traumatic event for many people here and abroad."

At the time, McHugh had little intention of pursuing a political career and not only was he not destined to be an upstate politician but was not even destined to be upstate. He and his bride settled in Queens and McHugh went to work at a Wall Street law firm by the name of Donovan, Leisure, Newton and Irvine. The "congestion" of the city, though, convinced the couple to seek a quality of life elsewhere. Upon falling in love with the lake in Ithaca, they chose to relocate and eventually had three children. He started a law practice and became a prosecutor, but his interest in public service "never waned and when the opportunity later presented itself to run for political office, it was thoroughly consistent with my interests and values." That opportunity was intended to be a "sacrificial lamb" attempt to become Tompkins County D.A., but something happened on the way to his defeat: he was elected.

It was not a dormant period by any means. The Vietnam War was still raging and Cornell, like other campuses, had its share of divisions. The most widespread was in 1969 when 100 members of the Afro-American Society (AAS) took control of the Willard Straight Hall on campus. A number of faculty subsequently joined them and shut down the campus. Locals proceeded to grab their weapons and descended on the campus. McHugh wound up charging the students with misdemeanor trespassing. Years later he recalled, "It was one of those cases in my life where I realized that restraint under pressure is important." Other matters McHugh worked on as D.A.: putting together a drug treatment facility.

Congress may never have been on McHugh's horizon, but in 1974 the opportunity to serve presented itself when Republican incumbent Howard W. Robison of the 27th Congressional district announced his retirement and McHugh took the reins. The territory of the district was the size of Connecticut, and Republicans outnumbered Democrats 2-1 with no Democrat having represented the majority of the counties throughout the 20th century. Furthermore, McHugh was hardly known outside of Ithaca. He still managed to capture the Democratic nomination in a four-person field, outdistancing his nearest rival Robert Kropp 46-27%.

With New York Governor Hugh Carey
Photo courtesy of Matt McHugh

Binghamton Mayor Alfred Libous won the GOP primary and contended McHugh "...was even more liberal than we originally believed." The Conservative Party meanwhile nominated Franklin B. Resseguie, a "moderate conservative Republican" who was also trying to appeal to centrist Democrats. McHugh tried to blunt the ideological attacks by vowing to conduct himself "in the tradition of reason and balance" of Robison. That proved the right formula in the post-Watergate election and he won by a margin of 15,000 votes, 53-43% (Resseguie took 4%). He carried every county except for Delaware (explaining that "Delaware is 75% Republican after all"), and racked up ¾ in Tompkins. He even carried Broome County where Binghamton was located.

In the days following his win, McHugh had said, "If I am going to be re-elected, I am going to have to make myself known in the district and I am going to have to make myself available." Securing suitable committee assignments was a necessary start and McHugh made it loud and clear that his first, second, and third committee preference was a seat on the House Agriculture Committee (Judiciary was an option as well). McHugh confessed that he had given the idea nary a thought while campaigning but that, in talking with would-be constituents, he learned that, contrary to what many believed, agriculture is central to many parts of New York State. The 27th in fact contained a fair number of dairy farmers as well as the State School of Agriculture and the dairy farmers, he said, "gave me a way of relating" to the people. He ultimately ended up on Ag along with Interior and for someone who knew next to nothing on the subject, became a go-to person for urban colleagues. LaFalce was among them and he joked that, "Boy, I'd have to have to have a good reason," to oppose him. Meanwhile, McHugh opened offices in Binghamton, Monticello and Ithaca.

One of McHugh's first major legislative endeavors involved emergency aid for railroads and the requirement of the Rail Service Planning Office to hold hearings on reorganization plans. Another accomplishment he took pride in was passing a bill granting the Upper Delaware River a wild and scenic status. Much of that waterway separates the New York and Pennsylvania border and roughly 70 miles went through the 27th. Unlike other preservations, a good deal of development took place in this part of the Delaware and "there were communities that had a real interest in how that management took place." In short, local officials were leery about the feds ordering them around so McHugh sponsored a unique mechanism to allow local communities to participate in management of the river corridor in conjunction with the National Park Service.

Photo courtesy of Matthew McHugh

As a Representative, McHugh worked the district hard and as he geared up for what he anticipated to be a strenuous 1976 re-election campaign, spoke of the grueling elements of the life of a Congressman. He confessed that, "If I lost, my wife wouldn't be heartbroken. Sometimes I wonder if I'm being too selfish. I rarely see my children. It's hard to develop deep friendships as you do in your hometown. While you see a lot of people every day, you often don't have quality time to spend with them."

Within that particular cycle, McHugh didn't need to work as hard as he did given that Republicans essentially gave him a pass by nominating William Harter. In any case, he would joke, "I haven't been campaigning. I've been working for my constituents." McHugh won the election 2-1. For the rest of that first decade in Congress, however, that became the exception rather than the rule. In fact, until 1984 his clockwork-like 55.5 and 56.6% margin would become almost obligatory. His opponent in 1978 and '80 was Ithaca businessman Neil Wallace. In '78, the glow of Watergate had somewhat faded and he held Wallace off 55-45%. This was slightly lower than anticipated, perhaps due to the fact that he did not campaign as hard as he should have. In '80, *Congressional Quarterly* wrote that despite his intense door-knocking, Wallace's "personality is described as too aggressive and abrasive for the taste of many voters." Reagan took a ten-point plurality in the district but McHugh kept his job by nearly the same margin, 55-44%.

Conducting a town meeting
Photo courtesy of Matthew McHugh

When Ed Koch left the House to become Mayor of New York City in 1977, McHugh sought to replace him as member on the Appropriations Committee. He edged downstate's Jim Scheuer 14-11 for the slot and immediately began pursuing parochial and international needs on the Rural Development and Agriculture Subcommittee and the Foreign Operations Subcommittee.

On Agriculture, McHugh made nutrition programs his niche. One reason was that, "there was really no one else on the committee that really focused on this. Most focused on commodities, etc." That meant championing funding for the WIC program and taking part in a lawsuit initiated by California Democrat George Miller in 1985 over not adequately funding the food stamps program.

Until the Ethics Committee and the bank matter, McHugh's time on Foreign Ops was where he made a name for himself. By and large, he was a strong proponent of foreign aid and in a 1978 *New York Times* op/ed piece, he explained why its popularity has declined. One was ethnocentrism. "Today," he wrote, "many of those we help differ from us in their values and cultures. They often lack democratic traditions and criticize us in public forums. Still, we are capable of understanding a changing world if our leaders frame the issue in perspective." In response to those who griped that American dollars were ending up in the hands of unsavory nations, McHugh wrote, "foreign aid should not be tested solely by our feelings about Idi Amin, Vietnam or Laos. It must be judged against the broader realities of our economic and political interests, as well as our traditional humanitarian values." McHugh's bottom line: "The foreign aid program serves our interests. If political leaders, including those of us in Congress, present the case more effectively, there will be constituency in the country to support it."

When the Reagan administration came to power, McHugh was even less shy about battling his foreign aid priorities. El Salvador was one. McHugh had long been a foe of aid to the Central American nation and wanted to scrap it entirely in 1983 contending that, "Without a clear promise of negotiations and some specific steps as to how they could be arranged," it would essentially be akin to throwing money down a rabbit hole. Although that effort went nowhere, he did cast the deciding vote in the Foreign Operations Subcommittee in support of an amendment by Long that would authorize $30 million in military aid for the nation, half of what Reagan was seeking. The reason: committee members would be surrendering their leverage if they granted Reagan the full amount.

The quest continued throughout the decade. McHugh seemed briefly sympathetic to the nation's potential when its new leader, Napolean Duarte, was installed. He referred to it as "a changing, evolving situation." When six Jesuit priests were murdered in the nation in 1989, McHugh led the fight on the House floor to eradicate an amendment by Michigan Democrat George Crockett that kept military aid flowing. Meanwhile, McHugh was appointed to serve on a special Congressional committee investigating the matter.

McHugh opposed aid to Nicaragua as well. His view was, "Aid to the Contras should be terminated if for no other reason than it is a polarizing issue that is poisoning the rest of our Central American policy." His view toward the warring Contras and Sandinistas was, "I don't know relatively speaking whose worse...They're both bad." Instead, he favored diplomacy.

McHugh also opposed administration weaponry proposals such as the ASAT (anti-satellite missile) and in 1984 proposed an amendment that, at the very least, would postpone the system's testing pending negotiations. To him, the ball seemed to be in the Russians court. "I don't know if (they) are serious or not but we have not taken up that expression of interest. The question is, what are the plans and is there any prospect for entering into meaningful negotiations." McHugh also opposed the procurement of 21 MX missiles in 1985 but four years later, refused to halt production of the B-2 stealth bomber, as they were manufactured in New York.

Photo courtesy of Matthew McHugh

When Reagan proposed significantly trimming the World Bank's International Development Association (IDA) budget in FY 1986, McHugh said the cost in "economic and political terms" would be "much more than we save." McHugh's upstate New York colleague and fellow appropriator, Jack Kemp, agreed with Reagan as did California Congressman Jerry Lewis and Senate conservatives. Obey, however, had the gavel and gave McHugh what he wanted. McHugh had steadfastly argued against an attempt to cut funding for the Import/Export Bank.

Aid to Angola was another matter that divided the Democratic caucus. Florida's venerable Claude Pepper backed it, but only because Cuban-American troops were in Angola and Pepper felt U.S. aid would negate the need for them (Kemp advocated for it as well). McHugh was initially vocal in his opposition to aid the National Union for the Total Independence of Angola forces (UNITA). The aid was something California Democrat Ron Dellums called "morally indefensible" and McHugh, along with Michigan Democrat Harold Wolpe, proposed cutting it off. McHugh even went so far as to contact Shultz urging him to end it and circulated a letter among his colleagues arguing aid "would damage our relations with governments throughout Africa." The document garnered 100 signatories. By 1988, McHugh seemed to somewhat relax his opposition having sensed progress. Two years later, however, he was questioning the need for aid given that the Soviet Union was putting a moratorium on its own aid to Angola (it was referred to as the "zero-zero"). McHugh contended, "It becomes more of a civil war, rather than Soviet expansionism."

Occasionally, McHugh found himself in the unlikely and paradoxical position of arguing the administration's cause as Republican allies went in the opposite direction. In 1984, for example, McHugh was in favor of the administration's plan to create an Inter-American Investment Corporation to assist businesses. Kemp argued strenuously against the proposal but McHugh prevailed. He also advocated for passage of Reagan's Caribbean Basin initiative that Reagan wound up vetoing.

McHugh prided himself on strongly backing Israel and was considered a mensch by Jewish interest groups and constituents. This commitment was demonstrated during his first year in the House when he and 25 other members of Congress protested the Arab boycott. The contention of the Congressmen was that it was in violation of the 1965 Export Administration Act. McHugh again stood with Israel in 1978 during a standoff between Long and Secretary of State Cyrus Vance over sale of weaponry to Israel, Egypt and Saudi Arabia.

Vance insisted on all or nothing, Long wanted nothing at all but McHugh favored providing Israel the weapons. McHugh was not impervious to criticizing the Jewish State. He felt that Israel's government should negotiate with the Palestinian Liberation Authority, a stance not always pleasing to pro-Israel backers. McHugh wasn't bothered, contending that not even the most fervent of Israel backers "have to accept every policy position the Israeli government takes."

One continent that had no ambivalence when it came to aid was Africa. McHugh had long pressed for increasing food aid and in 1984, wrote an amendment in Appropriations to increase Africa's food budget by $90 million.

McHugh proudly wears a lei given to him by Pakistanis he met in the Kyber Pass on the Pakistan and Afghan border during the Soviets occupied of Afghanistan Photo courtesy of Matthew McHugh

The Almanac of American Politics' characterization of McHugh being "slow (perhaps impossible) to anger" was put to the test in 1981 when McHugh was uncharacteristically upset by Ohio Republican John Ashbrook's proposal to add the words "or indirectly" to a carefully crafted Appropriations measure that contained a provision banning "direct" aid to certain nations. McHugh's comeback: "We have spent...literally months to put together a compromise bill. At literally the eleventh and a half hour, this amendment comes forward which will, in effect, destroy that compromise."

With New York Governor Mario Cuomo
Photo courtesy of Matthew McHugh

One person McHugh was close to was Obey who replaced Long as head of Foreign Ops following Long's re-election defeat in 1984. Obey was often a travel partner and leader of delegations for which he traveled to refugee camps in Guatemala and Poland where they were denied access to jailed dissident Lech Walesa (that would surely not be the case when they went again in 1989 following the collapse of the Eastern Bloc, as Walesa was now President). There was also a trip to Palestine in attempt to pressure Yasser Arafat to talk peace.

It was not always kinder and gentler under Reagan's successor, George H.W. Bush. In 1985 McHugh had been appointed to the House Intelligence Committee (HPSCI) but five years later, became apoplectic when Bush vetoed the Intelligence Reauthorization bill which he considered, "totally unjustified (McHugh had spent years laboring on a provision that would mandate the administration to notify Congress when covert operations were conducted). A compromise was reached.

McHugh opposed the Gulf War, believing sanctions on Iraq should be given more time. After the war ended, he was appointed by the House Speaker to lead a delegation to the Turkish-Iraqi border where thousands of Kurds had fled to escape Saddam Hussein's military. The condition of the Kurd civilians was perilous. American military forces were providing essential food and shelter, as well as protection. The delegation supported that effort, but expressed the hope that the relief effort would eventually be picked up by an international force ("Now that we have gotten in," he told *The Post Journal*, "there is a real question of how we get out...I won't be happy to see U.S. forces remaining there two months from now." McHugh also pursued forgiving the debts of nations such as Poland, which was in the midst of abandoning its Communist bent. McHugh said that while he had differences with President George H.W. Bush, "I respected him and found more common ground with him than I had with President Reagan (whom he liked on a personal level). Bush was more pragmatic and among the Republicans I served with, I liked him the best."

McHugh did make one attempt to secure a place in leadership. He vied for the position of Caucus Chair following the 1980 election but he managed just 41 votes to Gillis Long's 146 and Charlie Rose's 53. Leadership recognized the value McHugh brought and in future

Congresses he was put on the Democratic Steering Committee and assigned to work his colleagues on important votes. In late 1980 he was active in the debate over riders. While he did not have a problem with riders if they were offered in the committee that had jurisdiction over the specific area, as a number of his colleagues did, he favored a moratorium on them if they did not.

With the beloved Speaker, Tip O'Neill
Photo courtesy of Matthew McHugh

McHugh also chaired the Democratic Study Group that, in 1984, put a budget on the floor of the House. When he presented the budget on the House floor, he told colleagues it "would reduce budget deficits more than any other budget proposal now pending...In short, Mr. Chairman, this resolution offers us the best opportunity to take a significant step in reducing budget deficits. And make no mistake about it, that is the standard by which our action will be judged. Deficits, as we all know, are the greatest threat to our economy and to our security and we must act today to reduce those deficits significantly." The proposal ultimately failed but garnered 132 votes, including from five Republicans.

When it came to domestic affairs, McHugh was one of 20 signatories, including both liberals (Barbara Boxer of California and Marty Sabo of Minnesota) and moderates (Dan Glickman of Kansas and Ronnie Flippo of Alabama) on a letter urging President Reagan to create a deficit reduction task force "drive to stem the flood of red ink." At one point, he even proposed a spending freeze. When the 1990 budget summit produced a compromise few could proudly advocate for, McHugh urged his colleagues to back it. "Like many others, I have heartburn over specifics of the budget summit agreement. At the same time, I don't think it is responsible to say I don't like it and vote no on the budget resolution. We simply have to have a serious deficit reduction program." McHugh reserved the right to oppose it if it was rejected and cuts were trimmed even further.

McHugh was pro-life but not rigidly so. He was a realist, believing in exceptions that the Hyde Amendment did not grant and also took the position that supporting a Constitutional amendment prohibiting abortion was not a viable option." Therefore, he called votes as he saw them and while he was initially a "nay" on a 1989 vote providing federal funds of the procedure in cases of rape and incest, he did switch his vote when Bush vetoed the entire Appropriation measure that contained the language. His explanation: "While I would have preferred different language on abortion, and indeed voted for more limited funding when the issue was presented separately, abortion was only one item in this much larger bill." McHugh was also willing to vote to remove the Bush administration's "gag rule" which offered counseling to women about abortions at federally funded clinics. On other social issues, McHugh was a dependable liberal. In 1989, he voted to reject the pay raise as well as the proposed anti-flag desecration amendment.

McHugh's choice for President in 1988 was his '74 classmate, Senator Paul Simon of Illinois, another member widely respected for his personal integrity whom he praised as "an able and dedicated leader, a scholar and a pragmatist, a thinker who is able to translate great ideas..."

He praised Simon as "the person with the right priorities." McHugh co-chaired Simon's New York State campaign which interestingly ended just before the state's primary approached that April as Simon suspended his campaign due to lack of support.

Testifying on the necessity of campaign reform (the legendary Morris K. "Mo" Udall sits on the far left) Photo courtesy of Matthew McHugh

For the most part, McHugh was content to toil quietly on behalf of his beliefs without seeking publicity. That was one reason editors of the bi-annual publication, *Politics in America*, in 1986 named him one of the "12 Most Underrated Members of Congress." In 1990, McHugh made rare national headlines when he, along with Democratic colleagues Pat Schroeder and Barney Frank, took the rare step of calling for an Ethics Committee investigation of Gus Savage. He was a hate-spewing, truculent African-American colleague from Illinois who had been accused of making sexual advances to a Peace Corp volunteer during a trip to Zaire. In a letter to Chairman Julian Dixon, the three lawmakers wrote, "We have no independent knowledge of the facts in this matter. But we believe that the accusation is sufficiently serious to justify your looking into it." The panel eventually concluded that Savage did indeed make "sexual advances" and Savage responded by charging "widespread racism" (somewhat befuddling because the Chairman of Ethics, Julian Dixon of California, also happened to be African-American). As for whether a proper penalty resulted, McHugh replied, "Well, let's put it this way – I think the Ethics Committee looked into (it) and reached the best judgment they could."

Little did McHugh know that he himself would soon be sitting in judgment of his colleagues – many, many of them. The narrative was the most visible and wide-reaching scandal to hit Congress collectively, perhaps in history, when the Capitol Hill newspaper *Roll Call* reported that 8,331 checks of members of Congress through June 30, 1991 had insufficient balances. This was by no means a new practice. For example, 12,309 checks had been stalled for insufficient funds in 1972). Not only were the creditors paid, but overdraft fees and interest were waived which would never have happened at a commercial bank. That got the ire of Americans and nothing that was done in the days that followed, including the subsequent closure of the bank by Speaker Tom Foley, quelled it. This led to the formation of a "Gang of Seven," a group of seven freshman Republicans (including future Speaker John Boehner) demanding "reform" in the House. One member, Jim Nussle of Iowa, wore a paper bag on the House floor to signify the necessity of "taking the masks off."

Leaders persuaded McHugh to take on the assignment when the panel's current chair, Louis Stokes of Ohio, recused himself when he discovered that he had a high number of overdrafts (which turned out to be 551).

McHugh's first priority was to ensure that he was not among the members who had overdrawn their account. A letter was produced declaring him to be overdraft free. It was later brought to his attention that he did have a single overdraft of $251.00 for a mortgage that was covered the next day, and was something he expressed profound embarrassment for.

No one thought McHugh's relationship with other colleagues would impair his ability to discharge his duties with the utmost impartiality. Early in the process, Frank extolled McHugh's virtues: "We're lucky that he was around to do it because he's got absolute integrity. He will not be influenced, I think, by personalities to go too softly on people. Nor will he play that kind of political game and decide, 'Well, I'd better mete out some harsh penalties even if they're not deserved because otherwise, the public will not like me'" (this was easy for Frank to say – he had zero overdrafts). In his early days on the job, McHugh himself viewed pressure as unlikely because, "until the inquiry is concluded, there are hundreds of members who could potentially be targets." This turned out to be a rare misjudgment.

McHugh's first step in formulating the investigation was to create four categories. The first two involved members with limited overdrafts that likely were not notified by the bank upon shortage of funds, as was the case on innumerable occasions. Category three centered around "a more serious problem because there was no assurance that they would be covered by the next scheduled salary deposit." McHugh called that one "very limited." He also learned that "the Bank would visit the member individually and tell them that it was not appropriate to draw down your next month's salary plus another month. They kind of came up with that standard and we adopted that as what an abuse would be...simply because members had been advised" about the hurdles of doing that.

After a five-month investigation, the Government Accounting Office (GAO) released a report. Jack Russ was the House Sergeant at Arms who oversaw the bank and after the report was made public, he resigned. At the time McHugh took charge, publicizing the names of those with overdrafts was not in the cards – the committee didn't even know who the offenders were because it was done anonymously until the very end when the GAO would identify those people that drafted more than they were supposed to. McHugh simply wanted to separate the good from the bad – the genuine abusers from those who were minimally careless. Public outcry and constant rebukes on the Democratic leadership from Minority Whip Newt Gingrich made that goal impossible to stick to. Still, McHugh's place at that point was unblemished. As one Republican said, "I don't know anybody who's had a more difficult job in Congress and handled it better. Panic has set in. A lot of people feel we're out to get them."

First, the Ethics Committee in consultation with Speaker Foley and Minority Leader Michel decided to reveal the names of 24 lawmakers (19 current and five former) whom they considered to be the "worst abusers" who had overdrawn "routinely and repeatedly." McHugh recently said the definition of "routinely and repeatedly," everyone settled on was "pursuant to a definition of abuser that we developed based upon the processes followed by the bank personnel, including their advice to members on what was unacceptable use of accounts."

Because the identity of the members were concealed and only the bank account numbers of the respected members could be seen, it was impossible for McHugh and his Ethics colleagues to know who would be singled out. Panel members thus adopted the plan by a 10-4 vote and the names were made public.

Ultimately, a number of members made their case to be taken off the list and two, Jim Scheuer of New York and Charlie Wilson of Texas, succeeded.

Massachusetts Democrat Joe Early, though, did not and took to the House floor to blast not only Foley ("[who] handled this as a disgrace") but also McHugh and the committee who, "ran like rats...like rats."

Leadership of both parties attempted to put the matter behind them but some lawmakers still wanted more. In March, members voted 426-0 to reveal the names of every member whose name had appeared on the list and on April 15, 1992, members took their medicine as the names of every member with an overdraft was made public. McHugh said later, "I do think that most members understood that the Committee was simply doing its job, and an unpleasant job it was." But he came through it with his reputation and dignity in tact (Grandy called McHugh, "what Republicans feel everybody should be like"). Regardless, the emotional exhaustion was evident.

At a town meeting shortly after the names were revealed, McHugh repeated a question from an audience member. "I'm being asked, how do I feel Congress is working these days ... or not working." He then answered the questioner and said, "You were being kind." A short time later, he announced that he would not be seeking re-election to a tenth term that fall.

McHugh's decision to leave Congress after being the face of the Ethics Committee investigation involving the most widespread scandal to hit Capitol Hill in decades was what *The New York Times* called, "a surprise even bigger than his election 18 years ago in an upstate New York bastion of Republicanism." The rancor from the scandal might have been a bit too much for a legislator whose docile nature and collegiality were a trademark. He lamented as much: "I will admit to some pain and frustration when I find myself frequently put in the position of defending my character for simply being a member of Congress. There is now too great a gulf between my hopeful belief in what our institutions can be and the public perceptions of them...The political dialogue has been diminished. It has been reduced to 30-second commercials. Couple that with the perception that politics is dominated by powerful interest groups and you have a system which does not ennoble politics and government."

Obey added context to the decision by saying, "It's not the bank investigation, it's getting devoured by a feeding frenzy that makes no distinction between the best and the worst in the House."

In Washington and at home, McHugh's departure was mourned like a death in the family. Tompkins County Democratic Chair Irene Stein captured the sentiments of many when she said, "I know no one is unique but Matt McHugh's don't grow on trees. And they do not grow on trees in

Congress." Jim Hansen of Utah, McHugh's Republican counterpart on Ethics issued a panegyric statement saying, "We need more people of his stature and responsibility."

McHugh later stated regarding his retirement that, "I am sure that some of my colleagues thought that it was because of my experience chairing the Bank investigation. That was understandable, but not true. My reasons were more personal and family related and had nothing to do with the investigation." Days later in fact, McHugh told *The New York Times*, "Its been running through my mind for a few years. The main reason is we're not getting enough done. The job takes a terrible toll on a family. The question is whether it's justified. My judgment was that it wasn't any longer." He added, "This country was sold a bill of goods in the 1980's. Now people are hurting. They're angry and frustrated. But the President is not willing or able to communicate the importance of rising above our parochial interests." Still, it was not an easy call. He said that if it had been an election, his decision to not run would be 52-48%. But until I sat down with my staff, there was a chance I might go forward."

In March 1993, McHugh became General Counsel to Cornell University and counselor to the president of the World Bank. He declared that his goals were to, "make sure that the World Bank continually focuses on projects for the truly needy people in the world and that those projects are environmentally sensitive." He remains active with the Association of Former Members of Congress.

In closing, LaFalce, who along with Henry Nowak, another Buffalo Democrat from the class of 1974 keep in close touch with McHugh, said there is "no finer human being, no finer Congressman than Matt McHugh." That's a sentiment that could almost certainly garner unanimous consent.

CHAPTER TWENTY-EIGHT

Never Boastful, Pease Achieved
Lasting Results on Sundry Issues

Introductory Tidbit: Ohio Congressman Donald J. Pease was notorious for making sure his constituents knew how, unlike a number of colleagues, his assets were limited to his Congressional salary. One day in 1986 while addressing the Ashland County Democrats, Pease amplified the extent to which that was true. "A little boy came to our home in Oberlin this week," he told the crowd, "and he had his piggy bank with him. Jeanne (his wife) went to the door. The boy said he wanted to give his pennies to Congressman Pease. Jeanne asked him why, and he said, 'Oh, my mom and dad said Congressman Pease is the poorest politician they know.'"

Photo courtesy of the U.S. House of Representatives Historical Collection

One of the most important and effective lawmakers for much of his 16-year Congressional career was Donald J. Pease of Ohio. Who, you might ask? Exactly. Pease (PEAZ) was not someone who sought the spotlight, focusing instead on personal, common sense persuasion, stressing fairness, and getting results. He liked it that way, in fact, using that demeanor to leave indelible legislative fingerprints on tax policy, human rights, trade and helping the working-class Americans in his 13th District of Ohio and across the country. All the while and more importantly, Pease epitomized the term "a gentleman and a scholar" and, it was not surprising that when colleagues lauded him as the 102nd Congress drew to a close and he prepared to depart, people on both sides of the aisle profusely made it known that his absence would be sorely felt.

The Columbus Dispatch once described Pease as "bland (and) soft-spoken with little flair for self-promotion, (who) often appears more at home with the pen than at the podium." *The Washington Post* said he "shunned the party circuit and talk shows." Pease himself pegged himself as a "common-sense, workman like Congressman concerned with facts and logic" while a fellow Democrat from Ohio, John Seiberling of Ohio, himself a model of probity and integrity, was more succinct. "I always noticed that when he got up to speak, he wasn't one of those spellbinders. But everyone stopped and listened. They thought he had something to say."

Accurate a portrayal as those may be, Pease had two guiding principles in politics and life – acting with the courage of his convictions and fairness. When Ronald Reagan was elected President in 1980 and sent his first budget to Congress, he said "if Members of Congress didn't like it, then they should come up with their own." Not one to pass up a challenge, Pease rolled up his sleeves, sweated the details, and offered up his own alternative federal budget plan. That wasn't all. Through his posts on the International Relations and Ways and Means Committees, Pease fought doggedly against unfair trade practices, for fairness for workers overseas and at home, and fairness for all taxpayers within the U.S. tax code. While it could cause him frustration, his unflinching resolve in showing up for the fights often yielded dividends.

Growing up in Toledo, Pease could have passed for the boy next door. An Eagle Scout, president of his high school and college classes, Pease married his high school sweetheart, Jeanne, with whom he had one child, Jennifer. He got his education – a Bachelor's degree in Journalism and a Master's degree in Government from Ohio University, where he edited the school newspaper. From there, he attended King's College at the University of Durham in England as a Fulbright Scholar. Following a two-year period in the U.S. Army, Pease bought into *The Oberlin News-Tribune* and put it on the international map. *The Plain Dealer* noted that under his leadership, "the weekly paper won more than 85 state and national prizes, including several as best among its circulation size of 2,300." His partners were Brad Williams and Charles Mosher, the latter a Republican who just happened to proceed

Pease in Congress. He sold his share when he entered politics. Pease had been a Republican in those days but not for much longer.

It was in the town of Oberlin, Ohio that Pease found the launching pad for public service. His first post was serving as Chairman of the Oberlin Public Utilities Commission in 1960. Within two years, he was on the City Council. In 1964, Pease joined the Ohio Senate where he would ricochet from chamber to chamber over the ensuing dozen years – he lost his seat in 1966 but made it to the Ohio House two years later, staying there six years before returning to the Senate. In the legislature, Pease chaired the Education Review Funding Committee and championed issues of importance to teachers. He also spearheaded an in-depth investigation and overhaul of Ohio's Workmen's Compensation System. A bigger opportunity, however, was in the offing.

Pease announced his intention to run for Congress, after Mosher called it quits in 1976. Though the men were of different parties, they were close personal friends and Mosher was not afraid to back him. So did most voters. Pease prevailed in a three-way primary with 63% and in the general with 66%, thus ensuring the district would remain with Congressional continuity in one sense: Mosher ironically had been editor of *The Oberlin News-Tribune* before himself heading to Congress. Pease polled in the 60s in each of his subsequent re-elections prior to 1990.

With his lady for life, Jeanne, his high school sweetheart and bride
Photo courtesy of Jennifer Pease

The part of Northeast Ohio Pease was serving was home to many blue-collar workers and his primary interest in Congress was indeed issues central to the quality of life of the American worker. It's population center – Lorain was so diverse that *Congressional Districts in the 1980s* wrote, "56 different ethnic groups have been counted within its borders." Oberlin was working-class as well and while the 1980s remap removed a handful of urban areas from the district and replaced them with communities that were fertilely GOP, it did not alter the union-dominated character. Not surprisingly, his ADA and COPE ratings were regularly above 80%.

Pease was initially assigned to the House International Relations and Science and Technology Committees. Not surprisingly, for a man with Pease's convictions, he got right to work on international human rights issues and standing up for working people and this quiet, unassuming Ohio congressman first set his sights on Idi Amin and his genocidal regime in Uganda.

In 1977, Pease had barely settled in Congress when he introduced legislation to cut off U.S. trade with that East African regime, thus severing a crucial source of hard currency that Amin used to enrich himself (e.g. liquor, Gulfstream jets) and buy the loyalties of his mercenary army (Bell helicopters and munitions). Also, at that time, Pease disclosed that a handful of brand name U.S.-based coffee companies (e.g. Maxwell House, Chock Full of Nuts, Folgers) were leading importers of Ugandan coffee, thus highlighting that American coffee drinkers were unwittingly playing a vital role in bankrolling Amin's bloody reign of terror.

Furthermore, Pease called for a consumer boycott of the nefarious coffee companies and enlisted U.S. Representative Jim Mattox, a Texas colleague, to join him in writing and demanding that Pentagon and U.S. State Department officials immediately ban the sale of helicopters to the Ugandan military. Remarkably, over the opposition of the Carter administration and the furious lobbying of the coffee companies, Pease won congressional approval and President Jimmy Carter's grudging acceptance of his ground-breaking human rights bill – a truly rare feat for a freshman legislator and one which Pease called "a good first step" toward making the promotion of respect for international human rights a hallmark of U.S. foreign policy.

It was Pease's Chief of Staff, William Goold who brought the matter to his attention because, "It became obvious to me the more I investigated how exceptional Amin's dependency was on this coffee lifeline." As a result, *The Beacon*, in an almost unheard of front-page profile of Pease, wrote that he "allowed him to devote all his time to investigating the hunch." *The Beacon* reporter asked

Pease if he faced complaints over his pursuit of a matter half a world away, he replied, "I felt a sense of moral outrage over what was going on in Uganda – and when it became apparent that I could do something about it, I did."

Pease's colleagues witnessed both his tenacity and persuasive style. His colleague and classmate, Bruce Vento of Minnesota observed, "He played a very important role as the conscience of the House and, finally, the country."

**Bill Goold (seen in retirement in Montana) was Pease's
longtime confidante and devoted top aide
Photo courtesy of Bill Goold**

That tenacity and persuasive style was on display in 1981 when Pease managed to snag a seat on the Ways and Means Committee and became a close ally of titanic chairman, Dan Rostenkowski, an unlikely alliance to be sure. 'Rosty' was the barrel-shaped, consummate machine-pol from Chicago who hammered out his differences on the golf course and in smoke-filled rooms. In other words, he was nearly the opposite of Pease. Nevertheless, he often turned to Pease for help when crafting progressive tax legislation and explaining it to his colleagues.

Throughout the remainder of his congressional service, Pease worked tirelessly for a more progressive tax system. His greatest achievement in this regard came with the provision included in the Omnibus Budget Reconciliation Act of 1990 enactment, became known as 'the Pease rule' or 'the 'Love Boat tax' in IRS jargon.

It had become clear that the Reagan tax cuts had skewed very favorably to the benefit of wealthy taxpayers and resulted in record budget deficits for as far as the eye could see. In response and to require that all wealthy income taxpayers kick in more, Pease authored an ingenious provision limiting the amount of itemized deductions that high income taxpayers could claim in any given year (i.e. adjusted gross income over $100,000 for individuals or $50,000 for married couples filing separate returns.) It effectively raised the marginal income tax rate of affected taxpayers by an estimated 1%, raised tens of billions in much-needed revenue. As Pease explained, "Ordinary citizens believe that our tax system is not fair, that people are getting away with something that the ordinary cannot. This is the cleanest way to make the tax system more progressive."

In 1991, Pease was one member with the foresight to publicly question then high-rolling New York business tycoon Donald Trump, when he testified before the House Budget Committee to discuss the effects of that law.

Pease's commitment to integrity in office and good government was standard operating procedure. That is why, for example, he routinely voted on principle against closing Ways and Means committee proceedings and conferences. "I hate to say it, but members are more willing to make tough decisions on controversial bills in closed meetings. After a closed meeting, anybody can come out and say before the cameras and to his or her supporters, 'I fought like a tiger for you in there, but I lost."

Compromise was one thing – priorities were another. While both House Democrats and Senate Republicans were drafting deficit reduction plans in 1984, the devil did prove to be in the details. In that vein, Pease opposed spending caps that Republicans were pushing in exchange for tax cuts. He boldly stated, "I for one, do not want to increase medical costs to senior citizens in order to reduce taxes even further for wealthy individuals and some of the largest corporations in America."

During the next session of Congress, Pease was one of eleven House conferees (seven Democrats and four Republicans) who negotiated the landmark 1986 tax law. His appointment came as a genuine surprise to even himself, calling it "the best thing that's ever happened to me since I came to Congress." By tapping Pease, Rostenkowski was leapfrogging seven colleagues with more seniority, but 'Rosty' clearly knew that Pease had both the smarts and the principled resolve to deliver a final legislative product that would be more fair and balanced for all taxpayers.

Photo courtesy of Jennifer Pease

The reconciliation of the competing House and Senate tax bills began once Congress returned from its 4th of July recess. From the outset, Pease recognized, "Both bills have a lot of strengths. If we pick the best parts of each bill, we'll have a great tax bill." Its culmination was Reagan's signature on a long and messy, year-long dispute practice that began when Ways and Means first commenced hearings. True to form, Pease delivered on comprehensive tax reform, while also including provisions to help finance a new sports complex in Cleveland and the New World Center in Columbus, which any conscientious legislator would do in service to his district, state, and region.

Turning to consideration of a comprehensive trade bill in 1987-1988, Pease was in no mood to accommodate the Reagan administration's doctrinaire free trade bias and especially when the hollowing out of America's industrial base was in full swing. Once again, when the sweeping Omnibus Trade and Competitiveness Act of 1988 was finally signed into law, it included several Pease provisions which the Reagan administration certainly would have preferred to have done without. One noteworthy amendment required trade impact statements to accompany future budget proposals, "not after they have been passed, and the damage has been done," Pease explained.

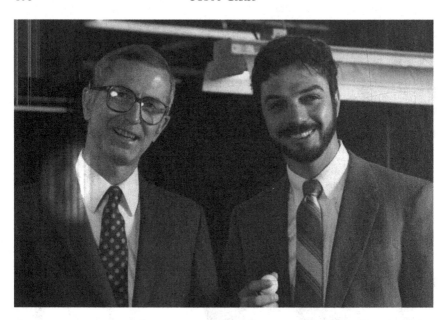

Photo courtesy of William Goold

In 1988, and throughout his time in Congress, Pease was in the vanguard advocating for hard-pressed American workers and their besieged families– many of whom were losing their jobs and being adversely affected by unfair trade in other ways. For instance, he routinely fought for the extension of unemployment benefits for laid-off workers who had lost their jobs to imports dumped into the U.S. marketplace. One time, in fact and with encouragement from Rostenkowski, Pease crafted legislation unsuccessfully that not only extended much-need unemployment compensation benefits (to which Reagan was opposed), but allowed displaced workers to receive wage vouchers up to $4,000/year, if they were reassigned or forced to accept other jobs at lower pay. While Pease was unable to single-handedly stem the decline of U.S. manufacturing and the loss of good-paying, stable jobs that accompanied it, he certainly never gave up the fight. The comprehensive Trade Worker Adjustment Assistance Act was one of the last bills he sponsored, as he headed out the door in 1992 into retirement.

Pease truly was an extraordinary champion for fair play and the rights of working people at home and abroad. Just when economic globalization was taking off, .he won enactment of a ground-breaking provision that defined as an actionable unfair trade practice for the first time, any government's systematic denial of internationally recognized worker rights (e.g. freedom of association, the right to organize and bargain collectively, and the prohibition of forced labor and exploitative child labor) as a means to gain competitive advantage in the manufacture of products for export. Whether in GATT negotiations in Geneva, Switzerland or on the House floor, he pointedly argued, "Just because enforceable global rules have yet to be designed to cope with certain egregious unfair trade practices doesn't mean that the U.S. government should stand by idly while American firms and workers are injured." The Multinational Monitor reported, "The Pease amendment is designed to ensure that U.S. workers will not be forced to compete with workers in countries which do not enforce basic labor rights."

In June, 1989, when the pro-democracy movement was crushed in Tiananmen Square, Pease was the first member of Congress to step forward and sponsor legislation to condition China's application for most-favored-nation status upon respect for internationally-recognized worker human rights and worker rights. Soon after, he teamed up with a fairly recently elected colleague, California Congresswoman Representative Nancy Pelosi, to press that case relentlessly. Before Pease was finished legislating, he secured the enactment of a dozen measures linking respect for internationally-recognized worker rights and basic labor standards to U.S. trade, aid and investment policies.

Photos courtesy of William Goold

At home, Pease's popularity was cemented by that he loved meeting his constituents. He once told *The Morning-Journal* that "I never feel a campaign is really complete until I campaign door-to-door" (he was legendary for his love of walking). Among colleagues of all partisan stripes, his likability was unmatched, in large part, because he knew how to debate and not debase. Canton, Ohio Republican Ralph Regula called him, "absolutely 100 percent integrity. He's thoughtful, intelligent and hard-working." Cincinnati's Bill Gradison, who served with Pease on Ways and Means, referred to him as "a fine gentleman (who worked well with every member of the committee and was highly respected."

Pease provided *The Morning Journal* an account of how in part he fostered these abilities. It was in 1962, "when I first started serving on City Council in Oberlin, I served with another man, Homer Blanchard. I was as liberal then, as I am now. He was quite conservative. We almost always voted alike on issues. We worked out an arrangement early on to discuss or argue issues with each other." But Pease was not immune to expressing his frustration with a colleague. In 1989, frustrated by the backing that his Ways and Means colleague, Democrat Ed Jenkins of Georgia was extending for a capital gains tax cut that the Bush administration was advocating, Pease told CQ that, "Given the opposition of the Speaker, the Majority Leader and the Majority Whip, he has the responsibility to join the team."

Pease was an immensely loyal person, both to his constituents and employees. Goold came on board in the first-wave of full time hires by the General Assembly in 1975 and was his Chief of Staff throughout his 16 years in Congress. Calling his boss, "self-effacing" and just "Don," he recalls folks in Oberlin commenting on "Don Pease, that great guy who lives down the street and who also happens to represent us in Congress." Goold calls it "one of the greatest privileges in my lifetime to befriend" and serve him. His style proved a winning formula at election time.

Like many incumbents, Pease saw his 1990 percentage drop a little more than slightly from two years earlier when he won re-election with 70% (his margin was 57-37%) with an Independent grabbing the remainder. But aside from the looming perils of redistricting, he wasn't in any danger and so it came as a big surprise when he announced in early October of 1991 that he would not seek re-election when his term expired the following year.

Pease's retirement announcement made him the second member of the Ohio Congressional Delegation to declare plans to head for the door. It just so happened that the first member was his neighbor, Dennis Eckart of

Mentor, Ohio, who had shocked folks by calling it quits two weeks earlier. That wasn't entirely a coincidence. Pease had been contemplating leaving for some time but held off in order to protect his seat from being carved up. But Eckart leaving freed up territory (his seat was the one that ended up getting divided up). Still, fatigue and minor health issues - he had undergone two heart operations including quintuple bypass in 1981, obviously factored in. "After three decades of 60-plus hour weeks in public life at local, state and federal levels," he explained, "I want to lead a more normal life and pursue a multitude of other interests." He spoke of wanting to give something back to his wife who had put up with the demands of public service but also said he simply looked forward to "plain-loafing," and for that, he probably got unanimous consent that it would be well deserved. Despite an obvious physical toll, Vento said, "I think Don looks the same and has maintained his demeanor throughout these 16 years." Perhaps most fittingly, Congressman Jim Oberstar (D-Minnesota) noted that Pease "rose from a typical American background to do uncommon things for his fellow Americans."

Like many colleagues, Pease was eligible to pocket his remaining campaign treasury. But he vowed to do no such thing. Instead, he donating the bulk of his leftover campaign funds to local charities and student in need.....a straight arrow in public office who always honored the public trust placed in him.

Pease's desire to "plain-loaf", however, did mean idle time in retirement. In 1993, President Clinton appointed him to serve on Amtrak's Board of Directors. Thereafter, he was a much beloved Visiting Distinguished Professor in Government Studies at Oberlin College.

Following his retirement announcement, 'Given my history of heart disease, I can't count on reaching 70 and having another 10 years." Sadly, this very wise man proved all too prophetic as a heart attack indeed claimed his life in 2002 at the age of 70 and Marcy Kaptur, who represented the Toledo district in which Pease was born was, "convinced that one of the reasons for his early death was that he worked so hard." The Medina Post Office was named in his honor as was the bike path in Oberlin him due to his fondness for cycling.

Going through his drawers in the waning days of his term
Photo via The Library of Congress

Byron's First in Nation Primary Loss Jolted Incumbents: Maryland Democrat Carved Strong Niche with Presidents and Voters

Introductory Tidbit: After the successful conclusion of the Gulf War, Maryland Congresswoman Beverly Byron visited Saudi Arabia with her Democratic colleague, fellow Marylander Steny Hoyer and, as *The Baltimore Sun* observed, "She ran afoul of the morality police." Saudi police in the capital of Riyadh objected to the fact that she was wearing pants and detained her for interrogation. Byron was released within hours and permitted to finish the duration of her trip.

Photo courtesy of Beverly Byron

In a year that saw a number of House incumbents lose, Maryland Democrat Beverly Byron's primary defeat was a shot heard round the nation. Not only was Byron the first to fall in the earliest Congressional primary in the country - March 10, but her upset by a solid 12 point made colleagues take note that the long-rumored anti-incumbent trend was no longer a pebble, but a ripple that would soon be felt by many members.

Because Byron had generally represented her suburban/rural Maryland turf without national headlines and had no scandal or bank overdrafts, her upset was a true stunner. Yet a closer analysis of the Sixth Congressional District primary that sent her packing after 14 years revealed that incumbency had little or nothing to do with it. Byron in fact lost because of ideology - she was a fairly conservative Democrat in a district that, while right leaning as a whole, was liberalizing among the party activists who dominated the primary. She had in fact been given a soft warning of the unrest two years earlier when she held off a primary challenger with 64% of the vote but actually lost the small portion of Montgomery County in the Washington suburbs. For '92, Thomas Hattery, the Maryland Delegate running to her left, had a record and name recognition that could easily reinforce the base.

By the time of her first election in 1978, Maryland's Sixth Congressional District had turned into a Byron family tradition. Her husband Goodloe held the seat for eight years prior to his sudden death a month before the election and not one but both of his parents had served in the House. Goodloe's father William was killed in 1941 en route to Mexico as a member of the Military Affairs Committee when the plane that was carrying both he and famed World War 1 pilot Eddie Rickenbacker crashed into Mount Story outside of Atlanta (Rickenbacker survived) and his wife Katharine Edgar Byron won the special election to fill the remainder of his term. In fact, even his great-grandfather, a Republican named Louis McComas had once been both a Congressman and a Senator from Maryland. On his death, one of Goodloe's employees said that "all he wanted was to be what his father was, a congressman and nothing more."

It might surprise some to learn that the generally unassuming Beverly Byron grew up in unusual circumstances and had exposure to some of the leading players on both the political and military stage. Byron's father, Harry Butcher had become vice-president of CBS in 1934, several years after he had help establish the CBS Washington affiliate, WJSV.

Naturally, the stature of young Beverly's family meant that her contemporaries would come from similar upbringings and one of her friends was Diana Hopkins, the daughter of President Franklin Roosevelt's trusted aide, Harry Hopkins. That gave her access to the White House grounds and Byron recalled to *The Frederick News Post* in 2017, "We would swim in the pool and duck our heads under water when the Secret Service came through as if they wouldn't know we were out there." That even sometimes meant lunch with the president and she recalled to the House Oral History project that one night when she was five, "it was FDR, and Eleanor, and Diana Hopkins, and myself."

During World War II, Beverly and her mother lived in the Wardman Park Hotel in Washington D.C., along with other prominent folks (more on her father below). Thus, she recalls, "it wasn't at all unusual for the house to be filled with people that were just friends but they happened to be working at the White House, or they happened to be in the center of government, or they happened to be in Congress."

The Frederick News Post also reported Byron catching glimpses of President Harry S. Truman from time to time as he entered the elevator of the complex where her parents lived during the war to play cards with, among others, George Allen, a member of the Board of Commissioners for Washington D.C. (she was also a fudge taster from Supreme Court Justice Fred Vinson who lived nearby). But it was President Dwight D. Eisenhower who truly stands out. Byron's parents had become close personal friends of Ike and Mamie in the 1930s and at the outbreak of World War II, Ike asked Harry to go overseas with him to keep a diary of his war experiences. During that time, Mamie lived with the Butchers. After the war ended, Harry published, *My Three Years With Eisenhower* and the friendship lasted a lifetime. The Eisenhowers even showed up at the Byron home on the way back from Camp David to help her observe her 26th birthday, a very big deal for a sitting president.

With Naval Medical unit aboard the USS Kentucky
Photo courtesy of Beverly Byron

Beverly and Goodloe met in Washington in 1948 when her mother was attending the Democratic National Convention in Philadelphia. A friend was going out on a date and her mother told Beverly she had to go along. Goodloe was there. The prominence of both families meant the 1952 engagement would be featured in *The New York Times*. The pair had two children and spent two years in Germany when he was in the Army. Beverly eventually became Treasurer of the Maryland Young Democrats and Goodloe was elected to the Maryland House of Delegates. In 1970, he won the same House seat his parents held, after promising his wife in '68 that he would be getting out of politics. Goodloe forged strong relations with his district and one campaign literature featured the headline, "Dine with the Byrons" and offered voters recipes galore.

Goodloe's likability ran across the spectrum in Washington as well. Baltimore Congressman Parren Mitchell, an unapologetic liberal, said that, "quite apart from his legislative accomplishments, I think that he will be best known for that kind of fine attention to detail and service that he gave to his constituents." New York Senator Jacob Javits called him, "a thorough-going, delightful gentleman, a high-spirited, patriotic gentleman."

Though Goodloe suffered from heart problems, his death of a heart attack in 1978 at age 49 was a genuine shock. It was now exactly four weeks before Election Day and Maryland's governor prevailed on a very reluctant Byron to allow him to submit her name to the Central Committee to fill the seat (her kids conversely were eager for her to do it). The Committee ratified Byron and she won the general election over a man who had assaulted a bus driver with 92%. The abbreviated campaign meant she would receive a single contribution of $100 from a longtime friend (which she used to pay her filing fee) and joke years later that she was probably "the only member that has ever been elected that never took a stand on an issue." Harry Butcher, still living, had the pride of seeing his daughter win a seat on Congress.

In a rarity for House freshman, Byron was successful at obtaining her committee requests. Armed Services, on which Goodloe had sat, was a natural but she also wanted Interior which she justified by the fact that her district contained six national parks. The jurisdiction of those two committees generally encompassed Byron's congressional scope and throughout her 14-years in Congress, she made few headlines beyond them.

Representing a conservative district usually meant that Byron was against burdensome regulation and in 1980, when the House was debating an OSHA renewal bill, Byron proposed an amendment to "exempt small businesses in safe industries from routine OSHA safety inspections," assuring OSHA backers that, "it would not exempt any firms from compliance with OSHA health requirements." It was similar to an amendment offered by Oklahoma Senator David Boren in that body. She cites a constituent who was visited by eight government inspectors in a single day.

On most issues up and down the spectrum (abortion, gun control, the nuclear freeze and gun control), Byron voted a conservative line. She was an almost non-existent northern Democratic vote for Ronald Reagan's budget and in fact the only other person in this category to back it, Ronald Mottl of Ohio, was unseated in his next primary. But Byron verbalized that, "The system we've been working under has not worked. I'm willing to give the President's proposals a chance." She sided with President George H.W. Bush on his veto of both the minimum wage increase and the Family and Medical Leave Act.

With Mother Theresa
Photo courtesy of Beverly Byron

One issue on which Byron voted with the left at least partially was funding for the MX missile and the first attempt, with Massachusetts Democrat Nick Mavroules in 1982, was very nearly successful. It would have trimmed $1.14 billion for production and failed just 212-209. It's not that Byron wanted to deep-six the MX as much as she was concerned about the inadequate long-term planning. When the amendment lost, Byron did vote for the system and when the same battle-lines were drawn in 1984, she was fully on board, pleading the case that, "I think for this nation, at this time, to decide not to go ahead with the MX, to let down our NATO allies, to not support the continuation of the modernization of our missile program is a wrong signal." Byron also attempted to forge a compromise on the anti-satellite missile (ASAT) which would have permitted the U.S. to conduct the same number of tests as the Soviet Union.

It's an understatement to say that for much of Byron's career, she was not enamored with the concept of women taking on active duty roles. The Gulf War was an evolvement. The Congresswoman had in the past opposed attempts by her sometimes nemesis on Armed Services, Pat Schroeder of Colorado to allow women in the Air Force to undertake combat related missions and she even held a hearing to examine the issue.

Once the war concluded, Byron soon began advocating for the Navy and Marines to do the same. "We had women flying in tanker...and C'5's (and) helicopters that were in a threatened environment, that were in a hostile environment, in a front-line environment." She added that it wasn't particularly "monumental. For me, it was just the next logical step."

One person who did not see that as the next logical step was Donald Rice, the Secretary of the Air Force who just happened to be from Fredrick, Maryland. He contacted Byron and asked why she was "picking" on the Air Force. She replied that it was not the case and her amendment was to have gender neutral aviators."

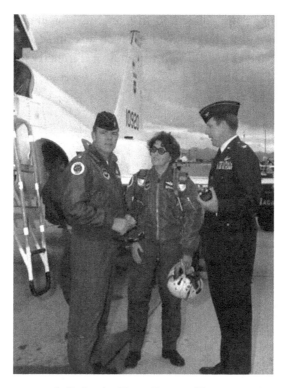

At Luke Air Force Base in Tuscon
Photo courtesy of Beverly Byron

As it reached the floor of the full House, neither Schroeder nor bombastic Republican Robert Dornan of California felt they could support the amendment (Schroeder didn't think it went far enough as Dornan felt it went too far) but Byron "suggested you rethink that," reminding them they were on record of having voted for the measure not only in committee but the subcommittee as well. They relented and the House cleared it 268 to 161. Byron did however, say she had been, "historically opposed to throwing the whole thing out at once" and she and Schroeder sponsored the amendment to gut the 1948 Combat Exclusion Act which cleared the committee.

Byron was not opposed to the concept of military advancement. The philosophy that governed much of her Congressional career was, "I think women are perfectly capable of handling many roles. I'm just not ready to see us send them into combat units." As early as 1987, she in fact had introduced what would be two-year pilot program to offer women advancement and ''the opportunity to air all of the potential pitfalls and to develop a firm consensus - among the public and in Congress - on the role of military women" (Byron was candid that her legislation was aimed at putting pressure on the military and that she would withdraw it if military brass took action on their own which they did).

**At an Afghan refugee camp in Pakistan and
getting ready to tour with the contras
Photos courtesy of Beverly Byron**

One area on which Byron did not need gradual enrichment was anger over harassment of women in the military. The Acadia in San Diego saw 36 female veterans become pregnant and the Tailhook scandal distressed her as well. Increasing child care and health care opportunities for servicewoman were priorities as well.

The outdoors had long been a passion for Byron and that reflected legislatively. For starters, she proposed a bill that would establish a "National Physical Fitness and Sports Month." She also took an interest in issues pertaining to the Chesapeake & Ohio (C & O) Canal) on matters big and small. One smaller matter was asking local police in 1987 to assist the limited National Park Service in patrolling the towpath where rowdy partygoers wreaked havoc. Others were Evitts Creek Aqueduct and obtaining funds for flood control projects.

Monuments were other endeavors and Antietam Battlefield was a priority. Byron passed a measure that not only allowed the federal government to purchase more of the deadly Civil War site but also secured money for the park service to do so as well. As she saw it, "I think it's a good idea for preservation. Especially in the case of my grandchildren, it brings an awareness of heritage and preservation. We plan to go up {on the mountain} and have a picnic. We figure we've got six square feet." The Monocacy Civil War Battlefield also piqued her interest.

In literally her last moments on the House floor as a member, Byron saw the American Discovery Trail, a designation of a 5,500 mile hiking trail across the nation, to passage. The second prime sponsor was a classmate, Republican Doug Bereuter of Nebraska who, as Congress was preparing to adjourn for the '92 elections, informed her that he had a problem with a specific amendment. Byron had lost the election but very much wanted to work out all remaining kinks. "So I stood at the desk at 3:00 in the morning with scissors and scotch tape and put together the changes" and the House passed the measure. But the coast still was not entirely clear. Texas Senator Phil Gramm, who had entered the House as a Democrat with Byron in '78, had placed a hold on most legislation in his chamber but Byron, after moments of pleading from a pay-phone en route to Detroit, impressed upon him that she was a lame-duck Congresswoman and Gramm agreed to drop his hold.

In India (top) and in China, including with the military (bottom)
Photo courtesy of Beverly Byron

Maryland's Sixth Congressional District was 320-miles long and covered six media markets: Washington, Baltimore, Hagerstown, Cumberland, Pittsburgh, and Harrisburg. But Byron's energy was bountiful. Then-Congressman Ben Cardin recalled "many evenings when Bev would finish a late session of Congress, only to leave for a two-hour drive to attend an event in her district."

On the fun side, Byron led her team to victory in the Capital Challenge, a three-mile race involving other departments. She was also quite generous toward others. Cardin recalls shortly after her initial election to Congress, "Bev and her longtime Chief of Staff, Brent Ayer, showed up in work clothes to help my staff and me move into our new offices in the Cannon attic." Fellow Marylander Steny Hoyer, who served with Goodloe in the legislature, was also a good friend.

Female House members were few-and-far-between in Congress (16) but with four of them hailing from Maryland, they made up literally half the House delegation and a quarter of the membership of the House. Byron proudly notes that Howard County, which fell into three Congressional districts, was represented entirely by women.

Ideology in no way inhibited Byron's ability to work with opposites. She was close for example with California Democrat Ron Dellums who sat on Armed Services and was among the most vocally progressive members of the House and also Barney Frank of Massachusetts. As the 1980s turned to the 90s, however, Byron's more liberal constituents were becoming antsy and Hattery launched his run believing that there were enough voters who were ready to change.

At the Berlin War
Photo courtesy of Beverly Byron

It wasn't just ideology. Hattery attacked Byron for backing a $35,000 pay raise and for taxpayer-financed trips (junkets). As about half the vote was counted, Hattery had opened a solid lead and Byron's campaign manager, Beau Wright, while concerned said, "We've still got a long way to go. You know what Yogi said." But in fact it was over and the final margin was a thumping – a 56-44% win for Hattery. Even the Western Maryland counties in the Panhandle, Allegany and Garrett abandoned Byron. After her loss, Byron took aim at Democratic Senator Barbara Mikulski (her mentor in the house with whom she traveled extensively), for nor sufficiently helping her. Byron had wanted to keep the Montgomery County portion of the seat in her new district but was rebuffed and it went to Republican Connie Morella.

At the end of the day, Byron got the last laugh as Hattery himself was upset in the general election by Roscoe Bartlett, a 66-year old who himself had lost to Byron 74-26% in 1982. Bartlett payed a visit to Byron before addressing his supporters. Byron's reaction: "After the primary, I thought I understood this district to be much more conservative than Mr. Hattery's views. And today's results proved that."

Come January of '93, Byron was out of office but hardly retired. She was however, determined to set her own pace. "I'm not looking for a full-time job," she told *The Baltimore Sun* after nearly a year out of office. "I don't want to be tied down to a 40-hour-a-week job or have somebody with a time clock say 'It's five minutes after nine, you're late.'" Instead, she worked at her own leisure. She was a Commissioner on the Defense Base Closure and Realignment Commission which recommended which military bases around the nation would close. It was a post that required approval from Senators and at her confirmation hearing, Armed Services Committee Chair Sam Nunn (D-Georgia) asked Byron if she'd be willing to close a base in the Sixth district to which she replied in the affirmative "if it met the criteria." Byron also undertook consulting work that involved seeking to upgrade the flow of basic supplies to Russia ("Part of the problem in Russia is that nobody knows who to talk to"). There was the Naval Academy Board of Visitors and the task force that investigated widespread cheating. Meanwhile, she married again, to Kirk Walsh.

For a career that was completely unsought, it's a record of accomplishments that would make anyone proud.

CHAPTER THIRTY

Guarini the Quintessential Hudson County Resident – and Italian Man

Introductory Tidbit: It's a small world after all – even as far away as Nicaragua. When newly democratically elected Nicaraguan President Violeta Chomorro visited Washington D.C., in 1990, she noticed the Guarini sign on the New Jersey lawmaker's office. The Guarini name immediately sounded familiar and Chamorro recalled that her college roommate had the same last name. It turned out to be the Congressman's sister, Marie Guarini Mangin and they had attended Blackstone College for the Girls in Virginia (Chomorro, then Violeta Barrios, was forced to abandon school in order to tend to her father's ill health). They immediately became reacquainted.

Guarini (left) and his New York colleague, John LaFalce, engaged in a weekly weight check competition in 1992
Photo via Getty Images

I n life, everyone has a pride and joy. For Frank Guarini, it was his native city and the only place he ever called home, Jersey City, New Jersey. Guarini has a photo with legendary songwriter Tony Bennett in his office and from rags to riches and a life now in its 95th year, Guarini has lived the good life, and has tried to give much of it back to his city.

Erudite yet empathetic, Guarini (Gwar-ee-nee) was born in the city in 1924. The Guarini's were not a family of wealth but was certainly a product of prosperity (his father, Frank Guarini, Sr., was Jersey City's Corporation Counsel). Young Frank attended St. Aloysius and St. Paul. During World War 11, Guarini served as a lieutenant in the Navy aboard the U.S.S. mount McKinley. The Hague Academy of international law in the Netherlands. When he returned, he attained his B.A. from Dartmouth College followed by his law degree at New York University and established a practice in Jersey City.

As Guarini's clientele began increasing, he began purchasing mid-sized real estate. That increased his net worth so that he became a millionaire which fueled his generosity in later years. It was in 1965 that Guarini sought elective office and he won a seat in the New Jersey State Senate in 1965 and concentrated on air and water pollution control issues, eventually ascending to the chairmanship of the committee with jurisdiction over those issues.

In 1970, Guarini acquired the U.S. Senate bug and it took most of the decade to shed. That year, he undertook what would seem to have been a career-ending move by challenging U.S. Senator Harrison Williams for re-nomination. In running, Guarini lamented the "sad disarray" of the Democratic Party following the bitter divisions that led to the party's narrow defeat in 1968. He accused Williams of focusing on national Democratic constituencies at the expense of New Jersey and pledged to fight for the "invisible American." At a Somerset County Democratic event at which Williams was not present, Guarini portrayed him as lacking "the spunk"… he has stayed away for five years and now makes asinine statements." Guarini drew 35% but carried only Hudson where he had the party-line.

Guarini seriously flirted with seeking the Democratic nomination to challenge U.S. Senator Cliff Case in 1978 but local leaders prevailed on him for a more sure-fire opportunity: New Jersey's Fourteenth Congressional District. Incumbent Joe LeFante had struggled with the powers of Hudson County before even winning his single term in '76 (by a tepid 50-45%, a beyond dreadful margin for these ancestrally Democratic margin for these parts). Guarini faced token opposition in the primary, then restored the 14th to its Democratic norms by grabbing 64% in the general.

After lobbying by fellow Jersey Democrat Robert Roe, Guarini scored a major feat by landing a seat on the Ways and Means Committee in his freshman year. This was not just important because of the committee's prestige – it was

right up Guarini's alley as a tax attorney. He was not particularly close to the
panel's storied chair, Dan Rostenkowski and the two tussled on more than
one occasion (one of Guarini's closest pals to this day is another committee
member who later became chair, Charlie Rangel of New York).

Sometimes, battling the titanic chairman did not end well. One instance
neither he nor most of his colleagues will forget is Guarini's quest to provide
tax benefits for workers who returned to school. Many of the powers that
be, including Rostenkowski, had a long standing policy of finding offsetting
revenue to pay for it and it was Guarini's intention to limit the income class
that could take advantage of it (a cosmopolitan term is "pay as you go").
Guarini did just that but Rostenkowski ended up using the new found money
for something else. He compared it to, "the great train robbery." This led
colleagues to coin the term, "getting Guarinied," which resonates in Ways
and Means circles to this day.

With Lee Iacocca
Saint Peter's University Archives: Frank J. Guarini Special Collection (SC04):
Accession SC04-2010-0006, Box 9

Other times, Guarini could take aim at King Rostenkowski and leave
him mortally wounded. In 1988, as the Ways and Means Committee was
considering the Technical Corrections and Miscellaneous Revenue Act
of 1988 to correct the minor deficiencies that resulted from the '86 tax

package, he and Connecticut Democrat Barbara Kennelly deviated from Rostenkowski's plan to tax the life insurance industry at a high rate by introducing an alternative plan (Rostenkowski's contention was that, "Life insurance was the only industry that received a pass in 1986"). But Ways and Means members sided with Guarini and Kennelly. At the end of the day, Guarini was among just three members of Ways and Means – and the only Democrat, who opposed the corrections measure.

Either way, the sparring didn't inhibit Rostenkowski from nominating Guarini for one of the Budget Committee spots reserved for Ways and Means members in 1987. Guarini would chair that Budget Committee's Task Force on Urgent Fiscal Matters and also the board of the CLAA. And in 1985, the chairman had approved a tax break Guarini had been seeking for the Meadowlands stadium in his district.

Initially, as the House was nearing passage of the landmark tax overhaul in 1986, Guarini told colleagues that, "Fairness is the hallmark of this bill. We have strengthened the minimum tax for corporations and individuals. No longer will we hear about those who escape their responsibility. Taxpayers and corporations alike will pay their fair share." But one person who in time said the wealthy got off too easy was a New York businessman named Donald Trump. Guarini and California Republican Bill Thomas introduced a bill that called for people in Trump's position to give back the benefits.

With Ol' Blue Eyes, a District 14 (Hoboken) native
Photo courtesy of Frank Guarini

Guarini was the House sponsor of New York Senator Daniel Patrick Moynihan's "Moyniplan," that would cut the Social Security payroll tax. "Until we get the government's hands out of the Social Security cookie jar," he said, "we won't be able to develop the discipline to consider the many alternatives that are available." But with President George H.W. Bush calling the measure "a charade" that he suspected would force him to abandon his famous "no new taxes," pledge, little movement resulted.

Guarini expended a tremendous amount of energy on shaping trade policies and his creed could essentially be summed up as free but fair. In 1986, after returning from a trade conference Guarini told members and witnesses at a Ways and Means hearing that "many of the discussions and some of the advice we got that macroeconomics will take care of the whole problem, that there may not be any need for any trade reform laws. I don't share that opinion and I think that we must go beyond microeconomics if we are really to send the right signals out to the rest of the world, and we must reform our trade laws."

Japan was the nation most in the path of his fury. Angered by the Bush administration's stalling and obfuscating when it came to getting tough with Japan, Guarini in 1989 introduced a number of measures expanding U.S. options when it came to U.S. prerogatives as far as potential retaliation. "What it gets down to is that no matter what we do in negotiating or no matter what we do in passing laws, as long as the attitude of Japan is as it is, and the spirit of our trade law is not adhered to, they can get around anything. So, the laws we passed or do not pass may not be sufficient if they do not have the proper attitude or spirit in following through a system of fair trade with the United States." He authored the Automotive Trade Equity Act of 1992 to help remedy that.

Guarini's free but fair trade mantra extended to protectionism. *The Almanac of American Politics* noted that "Hudson County...has 700 textile and apparel plants with 16,000 workers" and in 1989, Guarini supported the protectionist measure offered by Georgia Democrat Ed Jenkins (later that year, he opposed a capital gains tax increase that Jenkins had authored). One issue that put Guarini in a complicated position was trade.

With the legendary Tony Bennett
Photo courtesy of Frank Guarini

Guarini wasn't immune to fighting for fairness for consumers. He introduced legislation limiting the linkage of loans for the purchase of cars with home equity. It was primarily aimed at Tax Smart. And he sponsored legislation in 1992 reauthorizing the Low-Income Housing Tax Credit (LIHTC). Another issue: increasing the accountability of Savings and loan thrifts by reining in the loophole by which they could recover their losses. It was just after the S & L crisis and it was explained thus: "If an investor sells a thrift for $50 that has a book value of $100, the government makes up the $50 loss but the investor can claim the loss as a tax write-off." He said, "The taxpayer is sick and tired of paying for the S&L bailout. It's time Congress took some action to save the taxpayer some money." And when he realized that Exxon Corp.would only end up paying $8 million as opposed to the $15 million of the initial settlement, Guarini called for tax deductions to be reformed.

Another prominent initiative for Guarini was combating drugs and in 1987, he proposed a series of anti-narcotic initiatives. One was the National Narcotics Act. Another would establish the Office of Director of National and International Drug Operations and Policy to plan and coordinate drug enforcement efforts of the Federal Government. It also required the Director to report to the Congress on U.S. policy with respect to illegal drugs. He was co-chair of the Congressional Friends of the Caribbean Basin.

Among colleagues, Guarini was known for his impeccable dressing ability and sense of humor. Fellow New Jersey Democrat Rob Andrews told a story as Guarini prepared to depart Congress of a rare vote on the House floor when the teller actually called members names (as opposed to members inserting electronic cards). Andrews and Guarini cast their votes and sat down when Guarini got up to again vote. Andrews asked what he was doing and he replied, "I'm from Jersey City. I'm going to get counted again."

An unusually public incident in Guarini's career came in 1991 following events at an Arkansas retreat at a Democratic Congressional Committee fundraiser hosted by its former chair, Beryl Anthony (who hailed from that state). It was a quail hunting trip and Guarini aimed his rifle a little low, thereby grazing a dog. *Washington Post* reporter Tom Kenworthy, describing Guarini as "hailing from the wilds of Jersey City," wrote "the tale got better and better as it was told and retold and embellished on the floor of the House. By Wednesday, House members were saying that Guarini had fired at a covey of quail that was still on the ground -- and had shot off the dog's tail and transformed the pointer from a basso profundo to a contralto." The article also quoted Guarini as saying that despite the incident, "he and the dog have remained the best of friends."

Guarini's pride in his home area was such that he even led a lawsuit to expand it, in a sense. Seeking clarity on whether Ellis Island and the Statue of Liberty was part of New York or New Jersey, Guarini wanted the question settled to whether, as one newspaper said it, "Miss Liberty is a New Jersey resident." Guarini argued that "money and jobs are part of the issue. But pride is also an issue. New Jersey has been put upon by New York for years." The litigation dragged on for 14 years before the U.S. Supreme Court finally ruled that Ellis Island is a part of the Garden State. Guarini displayed similar sentiments on the House floor when arguing for including "New Jersey" in the title of the International and Bulk Mail Center. "We must allow New Jerseyites to be proud of being home to the largest bulk mail facility in the nation."

Guarini opposed a Congressional attempt to revoke the United States Most Favored Nation status (MFN) for China. Doing so, he argued, "would not hurt the conservative elements of the Communist Party that are responsible for the human rights atrocities at Tiananmen Square. Rather, it would strengthen the repressive factions who have not supported an open door policy. It would hurt the very elements in China's society that have embraced economic reform." Speaking on the House floor, Guarini compared the situation to the recent fall of the Communist bloc in Eastern Europe. "Poland, Hungary, Czechoslovakia which had the strongest ties with the West. (They) were the first countries to shed their Communist shackles and embrace economic reforms. China will do likewise if we are patient. We cannot dismiss lightly." Incidentally, Guarini was part of a Congressional delegation that visited some of those newly democratic nations in February 1990.

Photo courtesy of C-SPAN

For Guarini, supporting the liberal orthodoxy did have its limits. One was the issue of flag-burning and he was not skimpy about expressing his opposition to the Supreme Court decision permitting flag burning. He said the "decision did nothing but divide the country. If everything else fails, I certainly would agree with the president...Amending the Constitution is a fallback position." Guarini noted that the decision was all the more stinging because it was authored by New Jersey native William Brennan and some residents advocated removing Brennan's name from the Hudson County courthouse.

In later years, Guarini spoke of an incident at the White House just before the start of Persian Gulf War. He and a number of other members had been meeting with bush as Congress deliberated authorizing the use of force against Iraq. Guarini asked Bush what would happen after Iraq left Kuwait. The president replied testily that he had no idea. An hour later, Guarini was back at his office when the phone rang. It was the president and he wanted to apologize for his rudeness in tone. He still didn't have an answer to the question but it wasn't his forte to be discourteous.

By the start of 1992, Guarini's name was prominently making the rounds as a potential retiree but as late as mid-March, he himself did little to tip his hand. It was no secret that redistricting required a majority-minority district which would necessitate expanding the district lines from beyond the comforting confines of Hudson and into minority areas of Essex, Union and Middlesex which would continue to be safely Democratic but inviting for a potential primary opponent such as State Senator Robert Menendez. The redraw was exactly what happened but in the days ahead, even with an April filing deadline looming, Guarini seemed genuinely undecided about running again. One rumor was that Guarini would retire in Governor Jim Florio would appoint him to a seat on the exclusive New Jersey Sports and exposition Authority. Ultimately, he decided to call it a career. Guarini put a perspective on things" "It's time to go home," he said. "It's time to resume my private life. The job satisfaction hasn't been the greatest, but it's not the work itself. It's just that deep down in your guts you know when it's time to go home to friends and family" (he later said he had a life before Congress and I'll have a life after it"). After Guarini's announcement, Menendez said he would not have challenged him should he had decided to stay on.

Guarini promptly returned to real estate but several times thought he had one last act on the political stage: Ambassador to Italy. In October 1993, word got out that President Clinton was about to tap Guarini for the position. It so happened that President Clinton was coming to New Jersey for a fundraiser for Florio and the governor asked if he could announce it to the crowd. The White House said yes. But the appointment fell through. Four years later, there was another opening. The jockeying was between Guarini and a very good friend and former colleague, Congressman Tom Foglietta of Pennsylvania. The irony is that not only was Foglietta succeeded by a Caucasian but one continues to represent that district to this day.

When he left office, Guarini was eligible to pocket $245,219 from his campaign treasury but he gave every penny to charity – and much, much more. In recent years, Guarini has donated $100,000 to the Hudson County

Chamber of Commerce, $10 million to Dartmouth and $20 million to NYU Law School. There is a Guarini Institute of Government and Leadership at Saint Peter's University. "Life has gone by very quickly and has been very good to me," he said. "I kind of feel like I'm the luckiest guy in the world." And Jersey City can undoubtedly say the same of Frank Guarini.

CHAPTER THIRTY-ONE

Russo's Tough Chicago Streak Belied
Legislative Talents and a Heart of Gold

Introductory Tidbit: As Marty Russo prepared to take the mock of oath of office shortly after being formally sworn in on the House floor, he received word of what he initially viewed as friendly advice from his fellow and much senior Chicagoan, Dan Rostenkowski. Russo stood at 6'3" while House Speaker Carl Albert was a foot below. It might embarrass Albert "Rosty" surmised, if Russo towered over him during the oath and he encouraged his new colleague to simply raise his hand while sitting down. Russo readily agreed. When Albert reached Russo and his assembled family, Russo dutifully followed "Rosty's" instructions and the pair exchanged pleasantries for 3-4 minutes as other anxious members waited. Finally, Albert posed the question. "Marty, are you interested in having this picture taken?" When Russo responded in the affirmative, the Speaker asked, "Well when are you going to stand up?" Russo never got around to asking "Rosty," who would become a future friend and collaborator, if he had set him up.

Photo courtesy of Marty Russo

M arty Russo was another one of those many Watergate Babies who until the last minute really wasn't supposed to be one. His capture of a suburban Chicago House seat was a major upset and in Congress, Russo didn't ingratiate the reform or hard left mantra of some of his other brethren. Yet his youth, athleticism, salt and pepper hair, and wily political disposition made him a prototype of the class. Had it not been for an adverse redistricting, Russo may have had a major impact on public policy (specifically healthcare) throughout the 1990's and beyond.

The Chicago Reader once said Russo displays the attributes of "a self-confident, engaging figure…the brusque, no-nonsense mannerisms of his Taylor Street childhood still clearly show through a social patina acquired over the years in Congress, where he has developed a reputation as an effective party whip and as possibly the body's best golfer."

Martin Anthony Russo was a first-generation Italian who hailed from Chicago and his heritage and upbringing proudly defines him. He grew up in an all-Italian neighborhood and his grandmother insisted that he and his three siblings learn the language. After she passed, he said, "I didn't have a reason to keep using it." What Russo continued using were his Italian smarts. "You grew up faster because it was a little bit of a rough neighborhood." He obtained his Bachelor's and J.D. from DePaul University and resided in the city's Little Italy section.

In late 1973, Russo was a 29-year-old Cook County Assistant Attorney and Democratic loyalist. This garnered him the attention of Chicago Mayor Richard Daley's machine that tapped him to mount what seemed like a kamikaze run – a challenge to Republican Congressman Robert Hanrahan the following year. Though only in his first term, Hanrahan seemed as secure as they come. He captured 66% in the '72 election as Richard Nixon took 70% in the district. Still, Russo saw an opportunity and went for it with all of his might.

With his friend Bob Macari as the campaign manager, Russo's strategy was to essentially tag Hanrahan as a "nothingburger." At the grand opening of his campaign headquarters, he framed the campaign as between a championing of aspirations and a political hack. He questioned the incumbent's "performance, sincerity, priorities and actions," and said he displayed, "a total disregard for the hopes and expectations of working Americans." One example was to rationalize several projects that Hanrahan promoted during his freshman term in Congress. "I don't question that overpasses are important," he said, "that the Little Cal needs help and that the plight of the oppressed people of Eastern Europe as symbolized by Seaman Kidurka (an attempted U.S. defector from Lithuania) is very real. I only question the priorities of a man who seems to spend too much of his time getting publicity for these activities while doing nothing about more important problems facing the nation today."

Russo can barely be seen in back of his abundance of volunteers during his first race for Congress
Photo courtesy of Marty Russo

Still, gaining traction was tough. On the 40th anniversary of his election, Russo wrote how he struggled to be seen as a credible threat for flipping the seat. "From Washington, although at first I could not attract much attention, eventually I received help from a young Senator from Delaware, Joe Biden, as well as garnering visits from future President Jimmy Carter and future Vice President Walter Mondale." Even Daley asked if Russo is "the best we have." Despite some election night drama, voters responded in the affirmative.

With slow counting and contradictory figures reported from Chicago, the vote counting was cacophonous. Hanrahan consistently trailed Russo, though expected the many outstanding suburban areas to eventually put him over the top. When the count reached 75%, the incumbent still vowed to "stick to his guns" and held out hope that the remaining suburbia would come through. Daley called Russo to congratulate him at 10:30 p.m. and Russo, while not making an outright declaration of victory, expressed confidence that the win would hold. He credited "a grass roots oriented campaign," adding, "Bob Hanrahan was a formidable opponent and I am sure he is as proud of his people as I am of mine." In the end, Russo's winning margin was 5,000 votes, 53-47%.

By working the district hard and hosting sessions with voters nearly every Saturday, Russo became politically situated very quickly. He enjoyed a big sophomore surge in 1976, vaulting to 59% and wouldn't again fall below 60% until his final primary 16 years later. He took 71% in 1990 when Republicans were forced to install a candidate after the primary because no one even tried to take him on.

Photos courtesy of Marty Russo

In his second term, Russo won a seat on the Commerce Committee where amid lobbying from Michigan Democrat John Dingell who praised his political skills, he voted against the more stringent committee version of the Clean Air Act in committee. In 1979, when the committee considered Connecticut Democrat Toby Moffett's measure continuing price controls, Russo was again the recipient of heavily lobbying from the Carter administration. He was, however, more motivated by the insecurity among his constituents. "People at home ask me, 'What's it doing for me, Marty?' And I have to tell them it really doesn't give us a return." Undecided until the last minute, Russo voted in favor but it failed 21-21.

Later that year, Russo was again on the opposing camp of Carter's carefully weaved together hospital cost containment. He revealed his position at the last moment to send it to a 21-21 defeat in Commerce, ostensibly because he felt it gave preference to hospitals in the Northeast as opposed to the Midwest. To say he was raked over the coals was an understatement. Carter's Chief Domestic Policy Adviser Stuart Eizenstat wrote in his book *President Carter: The White House Years* that, "This turned out to be one of the few times Carter retaliated. He pointedly singled out Russo at a White House briefing for Democratic Congressmen and at the next Democratic breakfast. Commerce Secretary (Juanita) Kreps cancelled her appearance in his district for a small business meeting Russo had publicized. And when two Pope's passed in 1978, Russo twice became the House's only Italian-Catholic to be omitted from the White House delegation to the Vatican for the installation of the new Pope."

On another matter, Russo and Republican Congresswoman Millicent Fenwick of New Jersey fought the Federal Trade Commission's proposal to regulate funeral homes. He contended that the new directives would be especially burdensome for small businesses, many of whom he represented.

Russo was on the basketball court early and, along with a fellow member of the class of '74, Andy Maguire of New Jersey, was labeled part of the "Wet Hair Caucus" for jumping in the gym shower as it came time to cast late-day votes. Maguire jokes that Russo, "always thought I was hacking him under the basket. And I was," conceding there was, "no way to stop him from banking the ball in." It's not like Russo required help. On one occasion, he caught a pass from NBA great Magic Johnson.

It was Russo's association with the baseball diamond that made him a legend. He learned about the great Congressional extracurricular at orientation when Mendel Davis of South Carolina asked him if he played baseball. When Russo told him his position was third base, Davis replied, "Great, we need a third baseman." Russo didn't know it but a Congressional baseball team existed since 1909 though Democrats were in a drought, having not won in twelve seasons. This changed in 1975 when they prevailed 2-1. Russo loved it for the "lasting friendships you make on both sides of the aisle. This is something you have in common. It's not about politics. It's all about sports and competing." Decades after he left Congress he would often emcee the Congressional Baseball games.

Photo courtesy of Marty Russo

Russo's athleticism was not limited to those two sports. He played paddleball with George H.W. Bush even into his presidential years and golfed with the Ways and Means Chair and fellow Chicagoan Dan Rostenkowski.

During his last decade in Congress, Russo was part of a quartet of a storied household that become the subject of national parody. Frustrated by attempts to get home to Virginia during a snowstorm, Russo spent the night at a townhouse owned by his California colleague, George Miller and later shared by Schumer and Leon Panetta of California. Russo moved in shortly thereafter and the humble abode developed a reputation as Capitol Hill's "Animal House" (Downey referred to the House as "Washington's Algonquin table.") In 1987 Janis Berman, wife of the quartet's colleague Howard Berman of California, wrote a script that resembled the household, though with slightly different demographics (one Congressman was African-American and the other a woman.) Russo calls it "the best ten years ever spent."

**Exulting in the thrill of victory with Republican Don Clausen of California
Photo courtesy of Marty Russo**

In 1981, Russo's legislative focus changed directions but essentially was just a rare case of moving from one prestigious panel to another. "Rosty" was no doubt a key reason. He was there for him since day one and provided critical advice on being an effective legislator. "You don't always have to throw a touchdown pass every time you move legislation. You've just got to move it down the field and eventually get it in the end zone." "Rosty" would become a legend for heeding his own advice as Chair of Ways and Means and, having just assumed the chairmanship, he wanted Russo on his team. He provided him key assistance in outmaneuvering another member to win a seat on the Committee. "Rosty" implored Russo to, "Get here on your own and then I'll help you." He lived up to that vow. Russo held him so strongly in regard that he named a son after him. That didn't mean they were always on the same page but most of the time, they tended to read from the same book and be in agreement.

One example was the famous tax reform package of 1986. Russo and Schumer advocated a 25 percent minimum tax for taxpayers who earned more than $100,000 per year. "If we do nothing else in reform," Russo said, "we should make sure that corporations and individuals pay their fair share." Rostenkowski was not initially enamored with the bill, calling it a "cop-out" if nothing else was done. He pledged to support it, however, and in the end not only embraced the provision but also put Russo on the House-Senate conference committee. This was a big leap considering other members ranked well ahead of him seniority-wise. As a result, Russo became a loyal lieutenant which *Congressional Quarterly* summed up in a profile of the tax bill's conferees by stating, "Russo's Priorities: whatever Rostenkowski wants."

From Ways and Means, Russo tried to get more money to industrial hospitals. He sponsored a $25,000 tax deduction for small businesses seeking to purchase new equipment. As the 1991 recession deepened, Russo and New Jersey Senator Bill Bradley sponsored the Families Tax Relief Act, the main component being a $350 refundable tax credit for every child in a household under age 18. Its beauty was that because the savings would come from wasteful defense and domestic spending, it wouldn't require a single tax increase.

Photo courtesy of Marty Russo

Russo knew the key to appealing to his middle-income district was to vote their interests. He often walked a fine line on social issues even as a member of the Democratic Whip team and the Steering Committee. While he supported the Minimum Wage Act and the Family and Medical Leave Act, he opposed abortion, the 1990 budget summit package that contained tax increases, and surprised many by also opting against the Civil Rights Act of 1990. On the latter, Texas Judiciary Committee Chair Jack Brooks and one of the sponsors responded, "I think he can vote any way he wants to. As long as he could survive voting against white women in Chicago."

Outliers aside, Russo helped advance leadership priorities considerably. A vivid example came during a cliffhanger vote on the MX missile when Russo spotted the short, portly Congressman from Hawaii, Daniel Akaka and carried him into the chamber to cast the deciding vote. In 1988, Russo along with Miller and Butler Derrick of South Carolina helped sink a budget resolution because they felt defense spending was too weighty. Neither was there ambiguity in his Democratic loyalty when he opposed the Bush administration's attempt to limit the capital gains and his stance was evocative of his commitment to the working class. "Mr. Chairman," he said on the House floor, "This is not a question of productivity. It is not a question of jobs. This is not a question of competition. This is a question of outright greed."

Beyond that, Russo opposed a flag-burning amendment, a Balanced Budget Amendment and the Persian Gulf War. He was a proponent of gun control since his earliest days in office.

Foreign affairs wasn't high on Russo's priorities though he teamed up with future House Speaker Nancy Pelosi and his Watergate classmate and close friend, Tom Downey of New York, in sponsoring legislation stripping Most Favored Nation Status (MFM) from China until the nation improved its pitiful record on human rights.

Russo was notorious for displaying a mildly truculent side. *Politics in America, 1992* wrote that, "In a moment of late-night raw nerves late in 1989, Russo took a swing He once swung at a colleague, Dennis Eckart of Ohio, on the House floor. He missed." On another occasion as New Jersey Democrat Frank Guarini was delivering remarks, Russo grew impatient and exclaimed, "Look Frank, I've listened to your idiotic comments for a half hour." But

Guarini was a dear friend and Eckart hardly remembered the incident, calling it "a passing spark in life." What he does remember is Russo as a layperson and legislator to which he offers effusive praise. Labeling him "colorful, charismatic, [and a] hard not to like, Midwestern, Chicago, street-smart, ethnic pol," Eckart, a fellow Whip, said Russo "understood the interaction between good policy and good politics...his word was good and he really did know how to count." Russo was "the kind of guy I wanted on my side," and adds, "I liked and trusted him and remember him fondly."

Could Russo be a little short-tempered? He concedes that when it was his mission to round up votes as a Whip and "members would give me all kinds of grief" for very little political reason, his agitation would show. Yet to know Russo is to love him as Ray McGrath, a former GOP colleague attests. The two men served together on Ways and Means and McGrath calls Russo "one of my closest friends. A lot of people think he's tough and gruff but he's just a decent guy." McGrath recalls undergoing ankle surgery that would end his days on the links with Russo, but his partner still constantly called to check up on him.

At times Russo could be quite animated. One instance was in the summer of 1992 when both parties released a report on the much-maligned House Post Office. Republicans were using the operation to prove their contention that the House had fallen into a state of disrepair under Democratic rule but Russo wasn't having it. He took the floor and started off by asking, "What corruption are we trying to cover up? First of all, we are sending all documents and all transcripts to the Ethics Committee and the Justice Department so there is no cover-up." His voice rising, he went on to say, "We have an economy that sick, we have high unemployment, we have crack babies born every day, we have an educational system that can't survive – nothing's being done about it. We have the AIDS epidemic, everybody wants to sweep it under the table. We have all these huge, enormous problems. And what are the people on C-Span watching? Are they watching us solve these problems? No, we don't want to solve those problems. God-forbid, we should ever take a tough vote in the House of Representatives....That's why they're going to kick a lot of us out of here because they don't see us addressing the problems that they face everyday day in and day out."

**With his Capitol Hill "Alpha" housemates, Leon Panetta of California,
Charles Schumer of New York and George Miller of California
Photo courtesy of Marty Russo**

Russo's last term might have been his grandest and certainly gave him his moment in the sun. It came in the form of a single-payer healthcare bill he introduced in 1991. As he unveiled the proposal on the House floor, he said, "Surveys show that Americans want national health insurance, but fear the cost would be too high. In fact, under this single-payer system, 95 percent of Americans would pay less for health care than they do now. Senior citizens would not only save $33 billion a year over what they now spend on health care but would also receive long-term care in addition to many other benefits. The nonelderly would save $25 billion a year and gain permanent access to quality health care." For that Congress, the euphemism for single-payer was, "the Russo bill" and its original co-sponsors included Pelosi and Schumer, two future Democratic leaders of the House and Senate chambers.

Russo was not naive enough to think single payer would pass on the spot. His real motive was to "spur debate . . . and move us closer to solving our health-care crisis." *The Chicago Tribune* noted, "Russo has lined up support from the United Automobile Workers; the American Federation of State, County and Municipal Employees; the United Electrical Workers; and the American Postal Workers Union." Every Chicago Democrat co-sponsored the bill except for Rostenkowski who likely had to keep his options open as head of the panel that would be considering it.

The pros and cons of single-payer were illustrated during a 1991 Ways and Means Committee hearing where Dr. Robert Reischauer, Director of the Congressional Budget Office, testified. Russo told him, "I fully agree with the assertion that a single-payer system would actually slow growth in health spending but I disagree that consumers would probably face increased constraints on their freedom to choose health care providers and health insurance coverage. If you look at the Canadian system, the consumers choose their own providers. If you look at my bill, H.R. 1300 consumers would still be free to choose their own providers." He asked Reischauer, "What makes you think a single-payer system would prevent consumers from choosing their own providers?" The Director replied, "I don't think it's inevitable that you would eliminate freedom of choice but you would have less choice than you have under our system right now is really lets 1,000 flowers bloom with respect to providers." Reischauer elaborated by saying, "People could choose doctors but many doctors don't practice out of certain hospitals." This essentially meant folks would have to settle for being treated by staff members of the facility. Russo retorted that, "All you're changing in a single-payer system is who the ultimate 'payer' is. Why would that eliminate the ability to pick who you go see?" When Reischauer replied that the number of hospitals would be limited, Russo's answer was, "We wouldn't face those shortages for 20 years to come."

Russo spent the ensuing one and a half years stumping the country for his proposal but, as electoral politics brought to light, he didn't have 20 years on his side.

As this was going on, Republicans were plotting to end the Congressional careers of at least three Illinois Democrats and Russo would wind up among them. The state was losing two Congressional seats while also having to accommodate a new Latino-Majority district but the Democratic-controlled Illinois legislature and Republican Governor Jim Edgar were unable to agree on a new map. The Democratic plan would have spared much of Russo's turf but a federal court adopted the Republican plan which did anything but. The new map placed Russo's home with that of fellow Democrat

George Sangmeister, a sophomore. At the end of the day however he viewed challenging another Democrat, five-termer Bill Lipinski, as a better option even though the constituents in the new Third District were 65% Lipinski's. Predictably, Lipinski was not happy. "If we were such good friends," he said, "why does he challenge me?" The two were not steadfastly close but any cordiality from many flights home together would quickly unravel as the campaign proceeded to escalate into what *The Chicago Sun Times* called, "blood-and-guts campaigns" by both men. Russo did not want it to be that way but when he approached Lipinski about conducting a civil campaign the response was, "Marty, you run your campaign. I'll run mine."

Russo began the campaign with several advantages, notably his seniority and position on Ways and Means. Lipinski sought to capitalize on both. Presenting himself as "one of you," he labeled Russo "the creature of special interests, Washington insiders, and lobbyists." He on the other hand was "Bungalow Bill" which was coincidental in that he lived in a large home. Russo's response: "I ought to smack him...It's another negative attack from a desperate, sleazy campaign." *The Chicago Reader* noted that Russo said, "his house and garage are larger because his sister-in-law, mother-in-law, and two sons live there with his wife and him."

Russo countered that Lipinski drove an Italian-manufactured Fiat while calling for restrictions on foreign imports (Lipinski said his call for fewer Japanese imports did not necessarily translate to worldwide.) Lipinski argued that Russo's agenda lacked a local focus but Russo had a ready-made answer for that: "Everything I do has an effect locally. You give somebody better health care, you affect everyone in your district. You make the tax code fairer, you affected everybody in your district."

On healthcare, Russo questioned Lipinski for his lukewarm backing of his bill proposal, saying, "If he were sincere, he'd spend more time helping me than criticizing me." Lipinski said he was ambivalent about supporting any specific bill because healthcare reform was still in its infancy and, "I don't know what I want till the people know what they want."

Ethics also made its way into the mix. Russo accused Lipinski of forcing his employees to make $45,000 contributions to his campaign over the years. While much of that money went to the 23rd Ward where Lipinski served as Chair, Russo said, 'I believe this evidence demonstrates that Mr. Lipinski is requiring his congressional staff to make these contributions so that he may benefit personally...I don't mind losing to Bill Lipinski straight up, but I'm not going to let him cheat to win an election."

New Jersey Senator Bill Bradley came to stump for Russo (Lipinski evidently held no hard feelings – he was one of just six House Democrats to back Bradley's 2000 Presidential bid over Al Gore.)

With weeks to go before the mid-March face-off, polls showed Lipinski leading with nearly half the vote. The remap removed a few comfortably pro-Lipinski Chicago enclaves from the Third and the Southwest side were viewed as genuinely up for grabs. Lipinski's alliance with legendary House Speaker Mike Madigan paid off as he circled the wagons for his friend and the pro-life community gave him tactic backing.

Primary night was a bloodbath as Russo lost 58-37%. The suburbs came through for him by a microscopic margin but he was buried in Chicago, trailing Lipinski by 25,000 votes. He put a good face on the outcome though. "Even though my career will come to an end shortly…I wish Bill Lipinski the best. I certainly hope a Democrat wins this district." Even in victory, Lipinski tried to get in a last swipe saying, "the neighborhood was more than a match for the inside-the-beltway PACman."

With nearly a year remaining before his term expired, Russo was not to make himself a lame duck and continued stumping hard for single-payer. He told *The Wall Street Journal* a decade later that he believed, "it helped the Democrats take back the White House that year."

Some might say that despite his defeat, Russo moved on to bigger things. He became CEO of Cassidy and Associates, one of the most prestigious lobbying firms in Washington. He had a cameo that appeared on "Alpha House," the show that was based off of his fraternity-like living arrangements with his three colleagues. He now lectures nationwide on politics, the U.S. Government and motivation.

CHAPTER THIRTY-TWO

McGrath a Master of Collegiality, Moderation and Working Across Party Lines

Introductory Tidbit: "Anybody who wants a story about a fight should go see 'Rocky IV.'" - John Buckley, spokesman for New York Congressman Ray McGrath following a 1985 shouting match that nearly came to blows with fellow New York Republican Jack Kemp over the forthcoming tax overhaul. The dispute occurred in a meeting with leading White House officials but McGrath later called the episode, "just a little heated exchange that got a little out of hand, and I regret that it ever happened."

Photo courtesy of the Collection of the U.S. House of Representatives

Ray McGrath possesses all of the traits one would expect of a product of the Nassau County Republican organization: loyalty, friendliness, and an open-mindedness to vote as he thinks his constituents would be pleased. And throughout his twelve years in Congress, his re-election margins indicated that they sure were.

DEPARTURES ON THE HOUSE 451

The word gregarious rarely escapes profiles of McGrath, a six-term centrist Republican Congressman who is as Long Island as it comes. Born in Corona, Queens, McGrath and his family moved to Valley Stream on Long Island when he was four. He attended private school through eighth grade and, in high school, was active in a number of sports. McGrath earned his Bachelor's from State University and his Master's from New York University but initially, didn't go very far. He taught at the University and lectured at Hunter College before starting his career as deputy director of the Hempstead Township Parks and Recreation. He also epitomized the Fighting Irish. Brad Johnson of New York Governor Mario Cuomo's Washington D.C. staff said, McGrath "picked his fights," and that, "I always felt reassured when I was on Ray's list."

McGrath won a State House seat in 1976 and focused on issues pertaining to Medicaid but also elephant protection legislation which led to ribbing from colleagues, particularly Democrats. *The New York Times* showcased Assemblywoman May Newburger who in 1979 joked, "We believe you can substitute the word Republican wherever you see the word elephant, as the elephant is the symbol of the Republican party. We agree with Mr. McGrath that the Republican Party is an endangered species."

In Albany, McGrath had three roommates. Like him, all were Irish-Catholic with one key difference: they were Democrats. They were Tom Culhane and John Darie of the Bronx and Dan Walyn, the Majority Leader from the Southern Tier. They were referred to as the "Four Horsemen." That increased McGrath's proximity to House Speaker Stanley Fink.

McGrath easily won a second term but, the retirement of longtime Congressman John Wydler in 1980 gave him an opening to strive for Washington D.C. One might expect that the solid GOP nature of the Fifth Congressional District might mean a crowded primary for a rare open seat but McGrath captured the nomination unopposed. Why? He was a loyalist of Nassau County GOP Chair Joseph Margiotta who cleared the field for him. The general election was a tad closer than expected against former State Senator Karen Burstein, who in recent years had been serving on the state's Public Service Commission. But 1980, with Ronald Reagan's romp at the national level, proved the worst year for Democrats to be making inroads and McGrath ended up cruising 58-42%. He was assigned to the Government Operations and Science and Technology Committees.

In the days following the election, McGrath received an outreach from a man in very high places. It was Congressional orientation and McGrath was assigned a gym locker two down from George H.W. Bush who as a former member of congress continued to enjoy gym privileges. Bush also happened to be Vice-President-elect and he struck up small talk with McGrath. Bush first asked McGrath if he had an office or staff to which he replied "no." Bush's next question was whether he had a campaign debt to which he replied in the affirmative. When he promised to help pay it off, McGrath doubted it would happen. But one of Bush's aides was Rich Bond, a Valley Stream native whom McGrath once babysat and in May of '81, he telephoned McGrath at the Capitol and asked him to be at the airstrip at 4 p.m. The Vice-President would be addressing the New York State Conservative Party dinner and wanted McGrath to accompany him. When they landed, the Grand Concourse Parkway was closed to motorists and Bush exclaimed, "Ray, look at all the people waving," to which McGrath replied, "they're waving with one finger." When they finally arrived, Bush introduced him to wealthy donors who promptly agreed to help. On the return trip, McGrath profusely thanked Bush and zealously proclaimed, "I'm for Bush. Any Bush."

McGrath was proud to be a centrist but, like many Republicans on Long Island, was thrown on the defensive in 1982 not just by Reaganomics, but by Margiotta who was in the process of being convicted for federal mail and extortion charges. Before getting to his re-election, McGrath had to get through redistricting. New York was losing five seats as a result of reapportionment but in a true human relations story, that proved a testament to how beloved McGrath was across the spectrum made that no problem whatsoever. came in 1982 from the very top. With so much at stake, it was uncertain from start to finish which members would be the odd men out. Jeff Wice was drawing up various maps and when he presented the final proposed map to the Assembly leadership, the first question Speaker Saul Fink asked Wice was, "Is Ray McGrath safe?" Why was that extraordinary? Because Fink was a Democrat, and the most powerful one at that. So strong was their bond that when Fink was dying of cancer in 1997, McGrath was among the last to speak with him.

McGrath's opponent that year, Arnold Miller, had worked for Allard Lowenstein, the former Congressman and ferocious anti-war activist whom many Republicans viewed as a radical. McGrath cited Social Security as the "number one on the hit parade of concerns in my district," and he told *The New York Times* a forum that he scheduled drew more than 1,000 (he had expected around 200). He opposed Budget Committee Chair Jim Jones's plans for "revenue enhancements," because, "that would do away with a third year of tax cuts and I'm not for that." McGrath won re-election that year with 56%.

McGrath was not always copasetic with the priorities of the Democratic controlled House. When the chamber cleared a jobs relief bill in early 1983, he complained that it "did virtually nothing for my district at all. The fact simply is this - left on its own, the bill is five cents short and five months too late." Their Social Security plan was, "pie-in-the-sky. They assumed there would be a 5 percent unemployment rate for 65 years and a 4 percent inflation rate until the end of the century."

In 1985, McGrath prevailed over two other New York Republicans to win a seat on the Ways and Means Committee (a senior upstate colleague, Frank Horton of Rochester, gave him critical backing as the two had been colleagues on Government Operations). McGrath developed a notably amicable relationship with panel's gargantuan chair, Dan Rostenkowski. *Politics in America, 1986* said the two men's affinity should not come as a surprise. "Both men were products of political machines and both are given to skillfully winning political fights than to taking part in ideological debates."

One example was the famous 1986 tax overhaul. When Rostenkowski unveiled a compromise in the fall of 1985, McGrath called the state and local tax provisions "totally unacceptable and inadequate for most middle-class Americans. New York has one of the highest tax rates in the nation." It was a long, long process and by 1986, McGrath was determined that Rostenkowski would get a bill, even pushing back against early reviews by a reluctant Reagan team who "won't say they love it." In fact, McGrath recalls that while the administration wasn't embracing making the state and local deduction more palatable, they simply wanted a bill and essentially didn't care what was in it. McGrath on the other hand was adamant, so much so that he drafted a resolution calling them, "essential to the well-being of moderate-income Americans, state, and local governments and the housing industry."

As Sarah Liebschulz wrote in the book, *Bargaining Under Federalism: Contemporary New York,* the issue united the state's fragmented delegation but it opened McGrath to mild-ribbing from members of his own party. In fact, when Rostenkowski made an announcement summing Democrats to a caucus on the House floor, a GOP colleague shouted, "Ray, you better go too."

McGrath's explained that his bedrock philosophy was, "I'm an old fashioned guy. When you make a deal, you stick with it" and at one point, pronounced himself "outraged" by mailings targeting his vote. The chairman wooed McGrath and other New York State Republicans with water, waste treatment projects. *The New York Times* cited how McGrath, "even managed to get a special exemption from an obscure tax rule on foreign income for the Esselte Pendaflex Corporation, an office products company based in Garden City, L.I., most of whose stockholders are abroad." A package cleared Congress in September of '86.

During debate on the 1987 Catastrophic Health legislation, McGrath was the only Republican on Ways and Means to join Democrats in voting for a prescription-drug benefit for outpatient and he, Bill Gradison of Ohio and Nancy Johnson of Connecticut sided with them on child care legislation.

McGrath's parochialism extended to seemingly every sector of Long Island. He was a tireless booster of Northrup Grumman, the space program (of which success means positive ramifications for the Island) and noise control. He opposed the taxing of public employees and pressed for fair tax treatment of foreign subsidiaries. He introduced a bill calling for tax-exempt status to non-profits providing health benefits, a duty suspension on glass that packaged flowers and got substantial funding for dredging at the landmark Jones Beach. He sponsored a resolution creating Student Awareness of Drunk Driving Month.

Voting wise, McGrath had a few notable openings but mostly opted conservative. Still, his support scores for his fellow Republicans in the White House were not spectacular. His backing of Reagan was in the 60s throughout his first three years (though he did vote to override his veto of the 1982 supplemental), then dwindled to just 49% in 1984. It was 46% in 1988, Reagan's final year in office. He opposed abortion and early in his tenure, ratification for the Equal Rights Amendment (ERA) but backed the 1987 Highway bill, the two-month plant closing notification legislation and the Civil Rights Restoration Act over Reagan's veto. While he declined to support the Civil Rights Act of 1990 which many viewed as a "quota bill," or the Democrats higher minimum wage package, he did override President George H.W. Bush on the Family and Medical Leave Act that year. For much of that time, he counted himself among those who wanted more stringent clean air legislation than the Bush administration wanted.

McGrath was generally supportive of both presidents foreign policy initiatives but early in 1987 ceased temporarily on providing aid to the Nicaraguan contras because "people at home want to know where the money went." He also voted to freeze aid to El Salvador. On other matters, McGrath was among the members urging the Vatican to recognize Israel and was among the 24 Catholic House members who signed a letter to the Catholic

Church urging — A sense of Congress resolution that bore his name would rebuke France for not detaining Palestinian terrorist George Habash during his visit to that nation. Another urged Austria to dispense with video-games that promote neo-Nazism.

With Chairman Dan Rostenkowski on the 200th
anniversary of the Committee on Ways and Means
Photo courtesy of Ray McGrath

A jovial and garrulous fellow, McGrath liked the Washington social scene and was immensely popular with his colleagues, particularly his fellow New Yorkers and had long eyed romance and marriage for two of them, Republicans Susan Molinari of Staten Island and Bill Paxon from Western New York. Molinari wrote in her memoir, *Representative Mom*, "Whenever he saw us together on the floor of the House, he'd grab our hands and start sermonizing, 'Dearly beloved...' and offering to marry us right there in the midst of the debate." Molinari and Paxon became engaged on the House floor in August of 1993 and married soon after.

Illinois Democrat Marty Russo of Illinois is another McGrath fan. The two got to know each other during the 1986 Tax Act when both were serving on Ways and Means and Russo calls him, "always easy to work with and a great legislator who knows the issues. But most of all he is a man of integrity who you know will always keep his word. Our families became close over the years and I am honored to have him as a friend." The two in fact golfed regularly together over the years until McGrath's ankle forced him to quit.

Images via C-Span

McGrath's electoral security was never in question though his 1990 margin over Environment Defense Fund attorney Mark Epstein 55-41%, while still comfortable, was his lowest since winning the seat. A few factors contributed to that drop-off including a Right-To-Life candidate siphoning off more than 4% and McGrath being one of nine House members secretly videotaped by ABC's "Prime Time Live" vacationing in Barbados on a government funded trip with their spouses and military escorts (there was a fair amount of business conducted as well). Two weeks before the election, McGrath had been hospitalized briefly for chest pains (his blood pressure was found to be 150 over 100).

As 1992 moved forward, there were few signs that McGrath was even flirting with retirement. Frustration and the House Banking scandal might have been the last straw. McGrath had the most tertiary involvement possible – two overdrafts, but like other members, he was irked by the process for which he was notified (he basically wasn't). It was only when asking an aide to track down his letter stating that he had no overdrafts to learn otherwise, to which he exclaimed, "You've got to be kidding me!"

Still, it wasn't until June 1992 that McGrath seemingly suddenly announced that he wouldn't stand for a seventh term. In fact, a series of incidences had forced him to ponder it weeks earlier. The first came a few weeks after McGrath had slammed his car door into his leg when he ended up in the hospital with a blood clot. The second came when he missed his son's first birthday party and not by choice. McGrath had arranged to take the 2:30 p.m. Delta express from Washington to New York. His plane was taxiing and about to take off when the inadvertent landing of another aircraft closed the airport. In the weeks that followed, McGrath was kept awake thinking, "This will never end. I've been doing this for a long time and I can't even get to my son's birthday." Shortly thereafter, he decided to leave the arena.

McGrath's statement cited family obligations ("I desperately want to become the type of father my father was to me"). He said the epiphany came gradually as he was being forced to communicate with his year-old child by phone. "I thought, 'There has to be a better way! It's become very difficult to talk to a 13-month-old on the phone. I'd rather watch my son's Little League game than toss out the first ball at 21 Little League games in my district."

Shortly after his retirement, McGrath became the first alumnus of Valley Stream High School South to be given a Distinguished Alumni Award. Professionally, he became president of the Beer Institute., then partnered with his former Long Island and Ways and Means colleague, Tom Downey to form one of Washington's most well-versed lobbying firms, Downey/McGrath.

CHAPTER THIRTY-THREE

Highly Respected Martin was the North Country's Number One Advocate who Oversaw Major Dividends

Introductory Quote: "Semper paratus (always be prepared) is the name of the game." – A saying of proud Marine and Congressman David Martin

Photo courtesy of Tori Duskas

If New York Congressman David Martin had a slogan for his work on behalf of his district, it might be, "Nobody's man but yours." Obscure, hard-working and well-liked by colleagues on both sides of the aisle, Martin had a local touch. This made him inherently popular and led to a winning span that could have gone well beyond the dozen years that he held his House seat. But Martin decided to join the illustrious list of retirees in June of 1992, announcing late in the filing cycle that at 48, he was ready to bring his tenure to a close.

New York's Twenty-Sixth Congressional District encompassed the North Country. The area was cold, bucolic and somewhat sleepy with major economic hardships but Martin's hard-work made it a military force to be reckoned with. It was also solidly Republican and that reflected come election time.

David O'Brien Martin lived his entire life in St. Lawrence County (he was born in Ogdensburg but lived in Canton through grade school and his Congressional years). A Catholic, he graduated from Notre Dame where he was commissioned as an officer in the Marine Corps. Vietnam was soon awaiting and Martin would soon find himself a radar intercept officer on the F-4 Phantom jet in Chu Lai. Eventually, he earned his law degree from Albany and pursued elective office for which he became a natural. His obituary credited him as "the consummate politician who had a warm handshake, a quick smile and an ability to tell a story like few others."

Martin won a seat on the St. Lawrence Legislature in 1973 and the New York State Legislature three years later. In 1980, the retirement of mega-popular Republican Congressman Robert McEwen made it possible for Martin to run for Congress.

In every election save his first primary, Martin was utterly safe. Even his initial general election campaign against a former Lieutenant Governor of the State of New York, Mary Ann Krupsack, proved a walk in the park as Martin took 64% (a Right To Life candidate grabbed 5%). The primary on the other hand had some life to it but Martin, with backing from four of the district's five county chairs, defeated a colleague in the Assembly, John Zagame with 70%. In his five subsequent re-elections, Martin surpassed 70% three times and was twice unopposed altogether. For someone with such non-existent worries, Martin often fundraised like he was in the race of his life, often collecting money from defense-related PACs.

Photo courtesy of Tori Duskas

Naturally, Martin was placed on the Armed Services Committee and early on, served on the committee that investigated the bombing of the American barracks in Beirut that claimed the lives of 241 Marines. Martin was one of two members (Bob Stump of Arizona the other) who refused to sign the majority report following the investigation. "We agree that all in the chain of command must be held responsible...to assign culpability for not defending against this specific type of attack to those who did not have the benefit of 20-20 hindsight . . . is unfair."

Mostly, Martin would use it to promote his area's interest. Just as McEwen had given the North Country region life through his steadfast attempts to land the 1980 Winter Olympics in Plattsburg, Martin decided to pursue military benefits. One was the reactivation of the 10th Mountain Division to Fort Drum in Watertown. This was the first Army expansion since 1975 and former Congressman Sam Stratton of Albany, a Democrat who and Dean of the delegation as the effort was ongoing, called Martin its, "undisputed captain."

From the get-go, landing the expansion seemed like a longshot and Martin told local interests, "The odds are long; I'll be candid with you," Adequate housing was one challenge but so was modernization – the barracks on the premise were mostly from World War II. One factor that Martin felt was in Drum's favor was the need for European-bound troops to train in cold weather. Township officials raced to address the deficiencies and New York State government, led by Governor Mario Cuomo, made clear that no stone would be left unturned.

Photo courtesy of Tori Duskas

Fort Drum was competing with six other locations and the U.S. Army said, "New York was considered the alternate location, with Fort Benning, Georgia the front runner." But when the news came in September of 1984 that Drum had indeed been chosen, a jubilant Martin declared, "The Department of Defense's decision makes everyone a winner."

And for good reason.

The 10th Division soon became the largest employer in upstate New York and as its presence at Fort Drum hit 30 in 2014, *The Watertown Daily News* said it, "accounted for an economic impact of $19.72 billion on the region over the past quarter century." Additionally, "the number of jobs in Jefferson County surged by more than 50 percent." Martin recognized early after the decision had been announced that if they built it they'll come and he was instrumental in the allocation of $1.3 billion in construction upgrade money for Drum. In 1990, dignitaries and common folk of all stripes held a dinner recognizing Martin for his efforts and it turned into what *The Waterville Daily News* called, "gratitude and gag gifts."

Though Martin and Defense Secretary Dick Cheney had served together in Congress, their priorities were not of total symmetry. Martin opposed the Pentagon's planned cancellation of both the Osprey Aircraft (Marines) or the F-14 fighter (Navy), worried that it would eventually run the risk of having only antiquated systems in Europe. But when Cheney in 1990 spoke of a forthcoming round of base closings, Martin was not initially worried about Drum. "He can't say any base is exempt," he told *The Watertown Daily News*, "There is nothing surprising in what he said. He could not set aside any base or bases…I can understand why he can't rule anything out. It would make Capitol Hill look like Anzio beachhead."

Martin also believed that NATO should meet its obligation of "burden-sharing." In 1990, he offered an amendment that would prevent the removal of certain overseas troops, referred to as a "dual basing." Also prohibited in the language would be government funds relocating the U.S. Air Force First Tactical Wing of F-16S to Italy from Spain. It was rejected 174-249.

Photo courtesy of Tori Duskas

On political issues, Martin could be unclassifiable. He sustained the Democrats veto of a minimum wage increase in 1989, instead opting for a smaller increase the Bush administration had proposed, but backed the Family and Medical Leave Act as well as legislation granting the EPA cabinet level status. He was one of just three members from the New York delegation to back limiting National Endowment of the Arts (NEA) grants. He backed extra unemployment benefits in recession-heavy 1991. But Martin did favor more taxes on the wealthy and made that known during the 1990 budget summit package which he did end up supporting. He wanted higher penalties for those who caused oil spill and devoted significant energy to the reduction of acid rain. He generally voted pro-life but in 1992 voted to allow family planning clinics to advise women about abortion availability. Martin also opposed the two-term limit on the presidency and his quest to repeal the Constitutional amendment drew well over 100 sponsors. So concerned was Martin about a possible conflict of interest that he abstained on S&L legislation even though he had received an all-clear from Ethics because he sat on the board of the Key Bank of Central New York.

As a colleague, Martin was exceptionally respected by partisans on both sides of the aisle. At the time of his retirement, Schroeder called him, "a really decent person. We certainly understood each other and treated each other very fairly and didn't try to make our philosophical differences into ideological wars. And we are good friends beyond that." She was "very, very saddened" that he chose to not stay on. Ithaca Democrat Matthew McHugh called Martin, "a decent, congenial colleague willing to work on a bipartisan basis." While pointing out that, "we did not share any committee assignments, since we both were members of the New York delegation, I knew him well and liked and respected him."

Photo courtesy of Tori Duskas

More than one colleague, including New York's Gerry Solomon and Kentucky's Hal Rogers, both Republicans, told *The Watertown Daily News* that they considered Martin their best friend while Jim Walsh of Syracuse called him a close advisor. Kentucky Republican Jim Bunning might have best summed up the impact he brought when he told the paper, "It is sad to see a person of quality like Dave Martin leave because of the unrest in the House of Representatives." And Frank Horton relayed that the cantankerous Alaska Republican Don Young, who was a little leery about having Martin join the Interior Committee initially, later told him, "That Dave Martin is one of the best I have ever had on my committee, and I'd like to have him back."

Martin's decision to retire – which he made public on the 12ᵗʰ anniversary of his announcement for the seat, was generally viewed as a shock but, the incumbent was circumspect. For one, he had vowed early in his career, "not to attempt to perpetuate myself in this office forever." The Congressional lifestyle was another consideration. "Living a couple of hundred days a year out of a suitcase is not something you want to do. You have to work with the zeal of a crusader, which I think I've done. The only promise I made my constituents is to work 60 seconds every minute, which I think I've done." Most importantly, it became a question of, "What do I do next? There is nothing hot on the burner. I don't want to be a lame duck any longer than I have to." What he did next was continue his commitment to his people and in that vein, Martin's attempt to return to private life was not successful, at least at first.

Plattsburgh Air Force Base in particular was on the bubble (the district was also home to Drum and Griffiss) and his successor, State Senator John McHugh, hired him to help lead the effort to spare Plattsburgh from being closed. McHugh, who made his decision known to cheering supporters on Capitol Hill the day he was sworn in, said, "The best person in America for that job is Dave Martin. No one knows more about the legislative process, more about the closure commission or more about creating legislation." Calling it, "a hell of an idea, frankly," Martin responded that he wanted McHugh "to meet everybody it took me 12 years to know, starting with Colin Powell and everybody else he will be dealing with on the Armed Services Committee."

After efforts to save Plattsburgh fizzled, Martin became a professor at the Naval War College in Newport, R.I., and later a soft-drink company executive (another New York Republican who had overlapped with Martin in Congress and the Assembly, Ray McGrath, became a beer company executive in his post-Congressional life). In 2000, Martin went back to Washington as a lobbyist.

In his down time, Martin's obituary noted, "He was an avid student of history, especially as it pertained to the Civil War. As an aficionado of poetry, he enjoyed reciting the classics, especially with his granddaughter."

At the testimonial recognizing Martin's accomplishments, McEwen, the ex-Congressman expressed his view that, "you're a better congressman than I was, and I probably wasn't half as good as I thought I was." While some might take issue with McEwen's modesty - he also had a reputation as an inherently responsive Congressman, a statement by ex-State Senator H. Douglas Barclay likely better captures the mark about Martin. His sentiment: "He probably did more for the North Country than anyone has."

Photo courtesy of Tori Duskas

CHAPTER THIRTY-FOUR

Davis's Notoriety with House Bank Belied Accomplishments and Bipartisan Nature

Introductory Quote: "The American Indian did not know the meaning of the word 'exploitation' until he learned it at the white man's knee." -Michigan Congressman Robert W. Davis, who throughout his career was an ardent proponent of Native American fishing rights.

Photo courtesy of the U.S. House of Representatives Collections

Had it not been for a fusillade of bad publicity and involvement in the most wide reaching Congressional scandal in decades, Robert "Bob" W. Davis might have served in Congress until the day he died, as he once told a reporter he'd hope to. Even before the House banking scandal, however, the intensely parochial Michigan Republican had been confronted by publicity that while not nefarious, was certainly cringeworthy from a public relations standpoint. None of this could change the fact, however, that among colleagues and staff, Davis was an even-keeled, garrulous and honorable man who had just as many dear friends on the Democratic side as his own. His endless devotion to his constituents earned him both appreciation and big re-election margins until his career culminated.

Davis represented the UP – Michigan's the Upper Peninsula and *The Almanac of American Politics* labeled the "vast geography" of the district, "unique. More shoreline than any other district in the continental United States: 22, 561 square miles of land; 28 counties; a border with Canada; two time zones." It was also politically mixed. Gerry Ford, Michigan's favorite son, barely hung onto it in his 1976 election campaign and Ronald Reagan and George H.W. Bush both underperformed their statewide showings. But Davis compiled a something for everyone record and that showed come election time.

Davis was born in Marquette, Michigan. He attended Northern Michigan University and Hillsdale College before receiving his B.A. in Mortuary Science from Wayne State University and opened a funeral home with his father. He won political office on the St. Ignace Council, then advanced to the Michigan House and Senate. One of his most meaningful mechanisms for increasing economic activity into his district was working with Governor George Romney to lower the toll on the Mackinac Bridge that connects the Upper Peninsula and lower Michigan from $7.50 to $1.50. Davis knew better than anyone how the expense of the bridge could take its toll on motorists (no pun intended), so much so that he'd keep one old car on either side.

Before heading to Washington as a Congressman, Davis testified before the Interior and Insular Affairs Subcommittee on Energy and the Environment in 1976 when the U.S. Energy Research and Development Administration (ERDA) was examining storing nuclear waste near the Northern Michigan town of Wilson in Alpina County. Noting the area was "not uninhabited barren land," Davis homed in on the risks stating, "If there is a disposal system chosen, there will always be the problem of human error. We understand that. Site selection could be poor. Containment structure could be faulty. It is extraordinarily difficult to see ahead 250,000 years." In bad years, Davis's hold on his seat was tenuous, as he escaped defeat by just 1,200 votes but, by and large, the respect he garnered was through the roof.

By 1978, Davis was Republican leader in the Michigan State Senate but, when Republican Congressman Phil Ruppe wouldn't abandon his bid for the U.S. Senate (even though the incumbent Republican, Bob Griffin reversed his plans to retire), Davis entered the race to succeed him. Facing Michigan Board of Education President Edmund Vandette, Davis had to contend with being tarred with the indignity of living "below the bridge" (he was from Gaylord) and most residents were Yoopers but he still prevailed 58-42%. In the fall, he won 55-45% over savings and loan executive Keith McLeod.

In his very first year in office, Davis was able to help his constituents deal legislation with international ramifications: the Panama Canal Treaty. The Treaty called for the cancellation of international fish nets and that would have a detrimental economic impact on the lake-heavy 11th district. When the Merchant Marine Committee took up the Treaty, Davis voted against it. When it hit the floor, he sprang into action to try to gain some concessions though still wasn't comfortable enough to back either conference report.

Photo courtesy of Mark Ruge

In office, Davis had perhaps the most liberal voting record of any Republican outside the Northeast. He supported creation of a Department of Education and opposed cutting back on food stamps while supporting both the Reagan budget and tax cut. In 1982, he actually opposed the Reagan administration on more House roll calls (47%) then supported him (45%). He was pro-life but opposed raising the Social Security retirement age to

67 and was firmly supportive of the failed effort to require a two-month plant notification rule prior to a plant closing. He was also indignant "On the day of the president's announcement, the single remaining copper mine in my district – which used to employ over 3,000 people, shut down all operation." Davis thereby prioritized finding aid for those unemployed and also focused on copper tariffs. When George W. Bush was president, he voted to override his veto of the minimum wage increase, Family Leave Act and civil rights legislation. He voted for the controversial pay raise and by 1992, many realized why.

Davis's ability to call balls and strikes on issues naturally meant many friends across the aisle. Dennis Hertel, a Democratic Representative from suburban Detroit, considered Davis his best friend in the chamber. Davis and Hertel had served together in the Michigan House but hardly knew each other. That changed when they came to Congress two years apart. The duo both served on Merchant Marine and accordingly, worked closely together for their region. That extended to socializing and after Congress, Davis taught Hertel to boat. That's not to say they agreed on everything – in the run-up of the Gulf War they appeared on radio shows together arguing opposite stands. But Hertel viewed Davis as "the greatest guy." Another Michigan Democrat David Bonior, who by the end of Davis's final term was House Majority Whip, called his colleagues, "one of my best votes on labor issues. When I needed Republican votes, he was most often there. And he was a very nice, interesting guy - I liked him. We traveled together."

Locally, Davis fought to keep the U.S. Coast Guard cutter Mackinaw in the district, a staff library for K.I. Sawyer Air Force Base near Marquette and a 250-person refueling squadron when a 500-person fighter-interceptor squadron was pulled from the base. He wanted a national park Calumet. He also played a vital role in the creation of The Thunder Bay National Marine Sanctuary and Keweenaw National Historic Parks. An expansion of the Hammond Bay Biological Laboratory which studied sea lamprey control was another.

By 1989, Davis was ranking member of the Merchant Marine and Fisheries. In a rare departure from his usual environmental activism, he generally sided with the Bush administration and oil companies following the Exxon-Valdez oil spill (he said of environmentalists, "On issues like this, they asked for the Sun, and if they end up with the moon, they're still not satisfied"). He introduced the Non-Indigenous Aquatic Nuisance Prevention and Control Act in 1990. Zebra mussel.

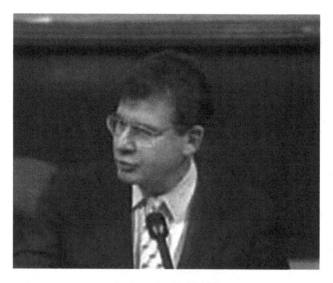

Image via C-SPAN

Representing a district that was by no means affluent led Davis to devote all of his resources to championing his constituents needs. He operated eleven district offices (far more than many sprawling districts in the western states) and sent his staff to senior citizen centers almost daily. Davis's deftness at serving such vast territory was noted in a special order as he prepared to leave Congress. Grand Rapids Republican Congressman Paul Henry said, "If you stop in the small towns in the tip of Michigan's mitten, or drive through the Upper Peninsula along Highway 28 or U.S. 2, chances are the folks you meet can tell you the last time they had a chat with Bob."

Davis's loyalty to the district meant immense loyalty from his staff, some of whom were with him throughout his entire tenure. Mark Ruge (ROO-GEE) had a small gap in his service but was as close to Davis as anyone. He was a legislative aide, press secretary, Merchant Marine aide and Chief of Staff on two separate stints (he left to attend law school and resumed the position). Ruge calls Davis "a second father to me," and "the best boss I could ever hope for."

In his spare time, Davis's "passion," as cited by his obituary meant, "spending weekends at his Northern Neck home where he enjoyed gardening, boating, and time spent with family and friends."

The latter part of Davis's Congressional career found him dealing with sensationalism. The first incident came when his third wife Marty made public a very revealing photo. Her objective was to respond to an article in *The*

Washington Dossier that expressed surprise at the notion that Congressional wives were attractive (she was a one-time television news anchor) and she succeeded. It was a myth, she said, that all wives were "cloying Barbie dolls swathed in Ultrasuede" or "stuck in a 1950s Donna Reed time warp." What was Marty's method for dispelling this? Publishing a photo that was once intended for her husband. The Downfall Dictionary described the photo: "Marty is bending over and shooting the camera an alluring look while wearing a cutaway black exercise leotard and high heels." At the time, she was 36 and he was 52. She called the matter, "ridiculous, absurd, and overblown," while adding, "I'm waiting for *The National Enquirer* to start sifting through my garbage." On another occasion she said, "Can't we just start talking about Geneva or something?"

Bob Davis said he, "just chuckled when I found out," and acknowledged being on the receiving end of ribbing from his colleagues but the incident took on a life of its own. Some Congressional wives backed her up while others said she should have kept her thoughts private. Marty meanwhile turned down all national media request as well her husband's invitation to attend the State of the Union (she said, "I did not want to upstage Ronnie Reagan"). The matter eventually died down but Marty caused more hoopla in 1989 when Congress debated granting itself a pay raise. Marty's position was absolutely. The Davis's later divorced.

Then, Davis was forced to explain why he put Brook Ball, a 28-year old woman with whom he was living, was put on the committee's payroll for $28,000 a year. Davis accused Marty of being behind the leak and contended that an opinion he sought from the House Ethics Committee came back in his favor. Furthermore, he said, her salary was less than most other committee aides. "People base their opinions of me on how I do my job, and I do a good job...I made no mistake here." As evidence of no intended nefariousness, Davis and Ball eventually married.

Davis intended to continue in Congress indefinitely. When a reporter questioned whether he would retire in 1992 to exploit a loophole that allowed him to pocket campaign cash (1992 was the latest members could retire to do so), Davis vowed would not impact him "Bob Davis will be here long after that time," he said. "I don't intend to retire. Never." Having won with 60% and 61% in '88 and '90, there seemed little reason to believe voters would retire him.

In early 1992, Davis appeared headed for a fairly routine re-election when the House bank scandal broke and members voted to release the names of the 24 worst abusers of the bank. Unlike the contention of many members, Davis knew that his financial affairs were poor and braced constituents that he would be very high on the list (he was in the midst of, "the worst period in my financial life"). He was not mistaken. When the list came out, Davis found himself the third worst abuser, only behind former Arkansas Republican Tommy Robinson and New York Democrat Robert Mrazek. Having overdrawn his account 878 times in the 39 months, Davis had compiled $344,000 in bad checks and had exceeded the paycheck of his next salary for eight of those months.

Davis was nonetheless adamant that "No taxpayer's money was ever on the line. When I overdrew I was covered by other congressmen's money, not public money. No laws or rules were broken because it really wasn't a bank but a cooperative check-cashing fund."

At first, Davis was determined to petition his constituents for forgiveness. Other Republicans were not feeling so charitable and a number of elected officials openly pondered challenging him in a primary. One, businessman Bob Kurz, referred to Davis as "Bob 'will you take my check?' Davis." Michigan's Republican chairman, Chuck Yob sent a letter to local Republican committeemen warning that if Davis was re-nominated, "you can kiss your Congressional seat goodbye." Davis did have the backing of his Wolverine colleague, Guy Vander Jagt, who chaired the Republican Congressional Campaign Committee and who would ironically lose his own seat in the August. As a result of the backlash, Davis was also encountering enormous difficulty raising money and had only $82,000 on hand. In early May, Davis was lamenting how before he came to Congress he was operating a funeral home. "I can't go back to doing that," he said. A week later, he announced that he would not stand for re-election, maintaining any race would be dirty and, "ultimately I decided that I was not interested in that kind of campaign."

In that special order as Davis was leaving Congress, Wisconsin Republican Toby Roth summed up the essence of Bob Davis. Recalling his help for his state's shipbuilders, Roth invoked Davis's willingness to help. "He has not always been dynamic," Roth said, "but he is a person that always gets the job done." That was the heart of Bob Davis.

Davis died in 2009 at age 77.

CHAPTER THIRTY-FIVE

Hertel's Mission was a Fair Deal for His Working-Class Suburban Detroit Constituency

Introductory Quote: "Earliest evidence of this sport was found buried with a child in ancient Egypt around 5200 B.C...now played in more than 79 countries world-wide . . . in the United States alone, over 69 million Americans participate." – A 1985 "Dear Colleague" letter from Michigan Congressman Dennis Hertel to his colleague as picked up by *The New York Times*. **It asked them to "solve this mystery.' The answer: bowling.**

Photo courtesy of the Collection of the U.S. House of Representatives

T he term, "waste, fraud and abuse" has a prominent place in today's government lexicon but if anyone can be given credit for putting it there, it would be tenacious former Member of the House of Representatives, Dennis Hertel of Michigan. Throughout his twelve years (six terms) in Congress and as a member of the Armed Services Committee, he undertook numerous measures to combat what he viewed as a wasteful if not heinous display of government misuse.

Hertel (Her-TELL) was another of those talented politicians whose ability to deliver such capable and quality representation to his people was enhanced because he was one of them and held his suburban Detroit seat with ease before becoming a casualty of reapportionment.

Born in Detroit, Michigan, Hertel attended Eastern Michigan State University. There he was elected president of the student government. He later received his law degree from Wayne State University, which he paid for by teaching in the Detroit Public school system, the same school system he attended as a child. Before graduating, Hertel co-chaired future U.S. Senator Carl Levin's Detroit Council race. The outcome was so spectacular that Levin earned the largest citywide total and became Council President, a position that proved a launching pad for his successful U.S. Senate run five years later. In 1974, just two weeks after graduating from law school, Hertel won a seat in the Michigan House where he co-chaired the Judiciary Committee and had a profound impact on the Michigan courts, chairing a reorganization of the Michigan court system working closely with Governor William Milliken and Michigan Chief Justice G. Mennen "Soapy" Williams.

Hertel supervised major revisions of the State's Juvenile, Probate, and Condemnation Codes, and pursued legislation requiring mandatory sentences for criminals using handguns, as well as outlawing dangerous double-barreled oil tankers on state highways. During his time in the Michigan House, he also chaired the Michigan Port Development Joint Committee that authored the Hertel Michigan Port Authority Act, creating the Detroit Wayne County Port Authority, resulting in a modernized and improved Port that now handles over 14 million tons of cargo annually. He also chaired the Special Committee on Child Abuse Prevention and the Michigan Crime Prevention Task Force.

During that period, the Hertel name was becoming one of dynastic proportions in the Detroit area. When Dennis was in the State House, his brother John was elected a State Senator, and when Dennis gave up the seat to run for Congress, another brother, Curtis, ran to succeed him and won. (CQ observed that voters would only have to remember the name "Hertel" for their Congressman, State Senator, and State Representative.) Curtis would ultimately rise to the position of Speaker of the Michigan House, while John would go on to become the Chairman of both the Wayne, and later Macomb County Board of Commissioners.

Republican Governor Bill Milliken signed a Hertel bill into law
requiring mandatory sentences for crimes committed with guns
Photo courtesy of Dennis Hertel

In 1980, the 14th district's longtime Democratic incumbent, Lucien Nedzi, announced his retirement and Hertel went for the seat. The district included Hamtramck, Warren, the Grosse Pointes and portions of Macomb County where the proverbial Reagan Democrats would be getting their names. The primary was not Hertel's for the taking. A colleague in the State Legislature, Senator John Kelly, was seeking the seat and was similar to Hertel in many ways. That's where Hertel's connections were critical. He had backing from the United Auto Workers Union (UAW), and as *CQ* wrote, "the mayors of the three major suburbs in Macomb County, which contributes about a third of the district's Democratic vote." To boot, Kelly suffered from likability issues. "He has not been liked by his legislative colleagues, who consider him a maverick with a sharp tongue." On primary day, Kelly aides were optimistic that low turnout would favor their candidate, with a spokesman calling Hertel supporters, "sunshine voters. Our voters are more committed." To their chagrin, Hertel's people displayed commitment as well and he took home a whopping 62 percent of the vote cast that day.

Despite Nedzi's longtime hold on the district, the general election was not anti-climactic. Longtime political reporter John Caputo of Detroit's CBS affiliate decided to make the race for the GOP, and labeled Hertel, "a political hack." As Election Day approached, *CQ* labeled the contest one with, "No Clear Favorite." However, as *Politics in America 1986* noted, Hertel "wore out four pairs of shoes walking through the precincts" and one slogan was, "He's accessible not just at election time." Ultimately, the 14th's Democratic bent was enough to leave him breathing room and he prevailed 53 to 46 percent, a margin of roughly 12,000 votes. He credited the victory to, "three thousand personal volunteers, a lot of hard work and a lot of sweat."

**Hertel with his wife Cindy and three daughters during the
1980 campaign. A fourth child would soon follow
Photo courtesy of Dennis Hertel**

Though Hertel would never have a tough re-election contest during his six terms, John Lauve, his 1984 opponent and the main proponent of a recall initiative against Democratic Governor Jim Blanchard a year earlier, held him to 59 percent. In 1990, which would ultimately be Hertel's last re-election contest, he racked up 64 percent.

Hertel represented the heart of the nation's auto producing territory - 54,000 auto workers were based in the district which UPI in 1991 called, "the most of any district in the nation." As such, his energy went into promoting their interests and he did so indefatigably and passionately. As a plethora of plants closed, he firmly supported the Gephardt Amendment that would retaliate against Japan asserting, "There's a trade war and we're losing it. There are those who say (the Gephardt amendment is) too tough, too strong. I say to you it can't be. Don't be afraid to protect our American way of life."

In September 1982, Hertel gave the Democratic response to President Reagan's Saturday radio address and called for a return of the Depression-era Reconstruction Finance Corporation, which he labeled "a new Reindustrialization Finance Corporation to help Americans do what they do best: To expand opportunities, to create goods and to create jobs." As Chair of an Armed Services panel on preserving the defense industrial base, he sponsored an amendment to promote advanced forms of flexible manufacturing and worked with Michigan members of the Appropriations Committee to secure funding for the program at Focus Hope in Detroit.

Besides its abundance of car manufacturing plants, Hertel's district also contained military installations and his seat on Armed Services made him a dogged advocate for its needs. The Tank-Automotive Command (TACOM) was located in his district, and Hertel didn't mince words when the Department of Defense proposed moving it to Huntsville, Alabama in early 1991. Even though TACOM was salvaged, Hertel had no qualms at ridiculing the proposal. "Some idiot came up with this idea of consolidating the commands without looking at the numbers. It didn't make any sense to move all those people to Alabama. It would have cost a billion dollars to build a place for them." He then took aim at the proposed Vision 2000 plan, which would have ended tank production in the middle of the Gulf War and said, "if the plan costs more than it would save in a reasonable time, then it's not really a savings."

Dennis Hertel

Democrat for U.S. Congress

is walking door to door
to talk with you

Images courtesy of Dennis Hertel

Concerned about excessive spending, Hertel stood out by casting the sole vote against the Armed Services Authorization in 1981, and routinely opposed the funding of a number of weapons systems. Following the uproar over a Pentagon toilet seat costing in the hundreds, Hertel called it necessary to "serve notice" on overspending and was asked by Speaker O'Neill to chair a Democratic Task Force on Waste, Fraud, and Abuse in Defense. This group succeeded in passing numerous reforms including, business -government revolving-door prohibitions, and independent operational testing requirements in the face of Reagan Administration opposition.

Hertel authored a provision to a Pentagon purchasing reform bill that would penalize companies up to $500,000 for submitting reimbursement for prohibited items. Another amendment that would have given latitude to the inspector general to put the kibosh on requests was defeated by a vote of 240-176. Hertel was not a fan of the Strategic Defense Initiative Program (SDI) either and in 1987, an amendment he proposed required Congress to approve future deployments, but it was defeated in Committee. Never afraid to lose a vote in a good cause, Hertel was annually defeated in floor amendments five times in opposing the rail-basing mode of the MX missile, which would have sent atomic weapons onto the civilian railway system. Although he lost those votes, the issues he raised ultimately lead to the scrapping of the program.

A more successful effort to block wasteful spending was Hertel's 1986 effort to block Strategic Homeporting. This blatantly political pork barrel project by then Navy Secretary John Lehman would have increased the number of naval homeports in the states of Republican Senators up for election that year. Hertel succeeded in blocking four of the six proposed in committee. In a possibly illegal lobbying effort, Lehman lobbied aggressively to reverse this action on the House floor. In what was described by his colleagues as the slickest parliamentary move ever seen, Hertel's withdrawing of his own amendment foiled Lehman's effort and denied him his vote. Hertel also enlisted conservative icon Barry Goldwater to block Homeporting on the Senate side. Having seen the political shenanigans of military base movements, Hertel blocked Chairman Les Aspin's effort to advance Defense Secretary Dick Cheney's Base Closure Commission plans. While it ultimately passed, Hertel was able to make important changes that helped reduce the adverse impact on communities. Hertel's warnings that those closures "would never save one dime" have been repeatedly echoed in GAO reports.

Photo courtesy of Dennis Hertel

The one area of military spending where Hertel was generous was pay raises for personnel and he fought for an amendment to put them into effect sooner. Although he opposed the first Gulf War, Hertel supported the troops and was horrified to learn that U.S. Marines were planning on assaulting Kuwait City using old model M60 tanks and he quietly worked behind the scenes to ensure the Marines had new M1 Abrams Main Battle Tanks (produced in his district). At the end of his tenure, Hertel Chaired the Armed Services Subcommittee on Oversight and Investigations, upon the resignation of Nicholas Mavroules.

Hertel's other committee assignment was Merchant Marine and Fisheries, and in his first term he took issue with Martin Belsky, assistant administrator of the National Oceanic and Atmospheric Administration (NOAA) who during renewal of the National Oceanic Pollution Planning Act of 1978 argued that an office devoting its resources entirely to the Great Lakes was not necessary. Hertel declared otherwise. In a letter with colleague (and future Michigan Governor Jim Blanchard), Hertel cited the lack of "administrative oversight... There are seven federal departments, three federal agencies, 20 universities, and numerous state governmental agencies and programs currently responsible for research regarding the use and quality of water in the Great Lakes. Their actions overlap, yet, they do not necessarily sufficiently analyze the problems created by the vast multiple usage of the Great Lakes."

Even historical aspects of the Great Lakes were not immune from Hertel's perspective. In 1988, Hertel co-sponsored a bill authored by Nebraska Republican Doug Bereuter that would preserve shipwrecks, of which the Great Lakes has many.

Then, there were also zebra mussels. When they were discovered on the floor of the Great Lakes in the 1990s, fears of water contamination resulted, as did other complications such as the clogging of water systems, etc. Hertel co-sponsored the Nonindigenous Aquatic Nuisance Prevention and Control Act (NANPCA) to combat them. "You remember the killer bees. Well, this scenario could easily be read as the attack of the killer mussels."

Photo courtesy of C-SPAN

By the end of his tenure, Hertel had a perch that could give heft to addressing matters such as these. He Chaired the Oceanography and Great Lakes Subcommittee and sponsored the National Oceanic and Administration Authorization Act of 1992. One purpose was to improve the efficiency of coordination between local and federal governmental agencies. Another was to measure the toxins in lakes and its impact on fish. He said, "At a time when threats to our Great Lakes are large and funds for scientific research are small, we must do our utmost to ensure that the science is focused, well-coordinated and cost-effective." Hertel also sponsored the NOAA Fleet Modernization Act, and greatly expanded the Marine Sanctuary program which lead to the naming of a Great Lakes sanctuary after his Michigan colleague and dear friend, Republican, Bob Davis.

Hertel sometimes made contributions to legislation far away from his district, such as the preservation of the Florida Keys. An amendment he offered permanently prohibiting drilling in the sanctuary was signed into law. At one point in 1987, Hertel found himself in a battle with officials from New England over their quest to acquire more federal dollars to purchase shoreline for vacationers, only to have developers swoop in and make that impossible. Hertel convened a hearing in Rhode Island but was unpersuaded by the local officials. "You don't have five year's left," he exclaimed. "There isn't any time left. It just is incredible to me that more hasn't been done at the state level in all these decades."

Perhaps Hertel's most enduring and understated effort was a cross-over between his roles on the Armed Services Research and Development Subcommittee and his Chair of the Oceanography Subcommittee. Realizing there was a profound problem facing the submarine forces, Hertel worked with the first Bush Administration and the Oceanographer of the Navy to provide the first resources to study climate change and its effect on naval operations. President Bush released the first $70 million for research that showed the profound effects of climate change.

Hertel was vocal about supporting the quickly collapsing Eastern bloc. He sponsored a resolution establishing "Baltic Freedom Day" and actively pressed for the use of the Agency for International Development to provide medical supplies for distribution in Poland by private and voluntary organizations.

On a jocular note, and one that his working-class constituency likely appreciated, Hertel in 1985 introduced a resolution designating January 5th as National Bowling Week and circulated a "Dear Colleague" letter dropping tidbits about the sport and posing the question, "Can You Solve This Mystery?"

Internally, Hertel was a member of the Democratic Task Force and was held in high regard by colleagues. On the other hand, serving under Republican presidents, his administration support score could be described as anemic – just 14 percent in 1986 and 18 percent in 1990. Conversely, his ADA score routinely hovered around 90 percent and his AFL-CIO rating was often 100 percent.

Hertel was close to Tip O'Neill, so much so that he would often go to where the Speaker was doing his daily press gaggles, if only to find out what time of the week the House would be adjourning. One day, O'Neill invited Hertel to an event at the Gerald Ford Presidential Library in Grand Rapids where the ex-President would be. Hertel hedged but grudgingly accepted not because of any ill will toward Ford but, because Grand Rapids was far outside of his district. O'Neill pressed him simply because he Ford was from Michigan and he felt someone from the state should be there. There was one caveat. Hertel told O'Neill that he wanted to stay in Washington long enough to cast a vote on a Philippine aid package and O'Neill told him to not be late. Hertel made it but barely and only because the car he was traveling in was driving 80 mph. O'Neill was curt but that changed when O'Neill learned the aid package had passed by one vote, at which time he loosened up and told Hertel he was "glad you stayed." Upon landing, he and the Speaker hailed a cab and checked into a hotel unaccompanied (Hertel chafed that the room they gave the Speaker was flimsy at best), then attended the event that featured Chevy Chase, the "Saturday Night Live" icon who had made his career in part by mimicking Ford's clumsiness, stumbling into the room.

Nationally, Hertel in 1988, endorsed Massachusetts Governor Michael Dukakis, bypassing a trio of current and former House colleagues running for president, though he did wait until mid-March following Super Tuesday when it became obvious to everyone except for the candidates that Dukakis would be the nominee. His rationale was, "As industrial states, Massachusetts and Michigan face many of the same problems. Mike Dukakis has dealt with these problems as governor of Massachusetts and has successfully implemented innovative solutions to turn the Massachusetts economy into one of the most productive and admired in the country."

As it became clear that Michigan was going to lose two House seats, the one thing that was evident early on was that the districts of Hertel and fellow Democrat Sander Levin, Carl's brother, would get combined, due to the fact that the Voting Rights Act mandated that the districts of Detroit's two African-American members of Congress had to pick up population. Indeed, both the Democratic and Republican plans paired Hertel and Levin, though where the loss of the second seat would come from proved a point of contention that resulted in a stalemate.

Even after the lines became a reality, Hertel initially had no intention of backing down. sixty percent of the new district contained constituents from Hertel's, while 31 percent came from Levin's. However, Levin, having nearly been elected Governor on two separate occasions had plenty of name recognition, and was further enhanced by the fact that his brother Carl was Michigan's junior Senator. To complicate matters even more, Hertel and Levin went way back – Hertel had cut his teeth on Levin's failed campaigns for governor and encouraged him to run for the House in 1982. The Hertels and Levins were the only brothers in Michigan politics and thus shared a special affinity and Hertel alluded to his distaste with having to take him on ("How do you run against a friend and his brother? How do you get angry at a friend?"). The answer was that he wouldn't, and one reason was that he had a bigger problem.

As March came to a close, it became obvious that Hertel would have a prominent place on the list of House members who overdrew their House bank accounts and the total was 547. In the frenzy whipped up to stigmatize the Democratic leadership, Hertel never got the chance to tell his side of the story.

Distaste for the institution was one reason. "I'm angry and frustrated with Congress. The work here is no longer satisfying...There's gridlock between Capitol Hill and the administration. Nothing is getting done and it's the American people who are paying the price." The reaction from local officials was one of profound regret. Macomb County Board of Commissioners Chairman Patrick Johnson called Hertel's decision a "political tragedy" while the county's Democratic Chairman Leo Lalonde called him, "a damned good congressman." *The Detroit Free Press* wrote how Hertel and close friend, Democrat Brian Donnelly of Massachusetts, had often commiserated on the failures of Congress, with Donnelly himself announcing his retirement just weeks prior.

**After Hertel announced that he would forego a primary against
his colleague, Sander Levin (left), Hertel invited "Sandy" and
his brother, U.S. Senator Carl Levin, to his office. The Levins
had been a part of Hertel's political world since law school
Photo via Getty Images**

After leaving Congress, Hertel became the Founder/Vice President
of the Global Democracy Initiative which provides election oversight and
democracy-building across the world with former legislators from the U.S.,
Canada, and the European Union. Hertel was later appointed a Distinguished
Professor at the United States National Defense University, Near East South
Asia Center for Strategic Studies, educating state and defense personnel from
28 nations about the U.S. Congress. Active with the Former Members of
Congress Association, he gives talks and lectures at universities and colleges
throughout North America and in Europe, and has served as its President.

Hertel also serves on the boards of the Congressional Hunger Center and
as Vice-President of the National Environmental Policy Institute bringing
together state, local, and federal officials along with the private sector to
improve environmental cooperation. He uses his extensive experience in
Congress combined with law practice to serve clients and to support his own
interests. These included the Samaritan Center, with Director Brother Francis,

where he helped transform a vacant hospital in Hertel's old neighborhood into a community center serving over 40,000 lower-income Detroiters each month. He is also a board member of the Northern Virginia Conservation Trust.

For five years Hertel was a partner in the Livingston Group, a government consulting and lobbying firm in Washington, D.C. He later joined as, Of Counsel, the Franklin Partnership with his great friend Pete Rose. Hertel and Cindy, his wife of 48 years, have four children and six grandchildren. Having grown up in Detroit, Hertel remains a big fan of Motown (he's met Smokey Robinson and Stevie Wonder) as well as the Beatles and Rolling Stones. He still rides horses weekly, can be found frequently on his power boat on the Potomac, and roots for Michigan sports teams.

Hertel was a devoted Congressman, as well as a devoted dad, and not in that order
Photo courtesy of Dennis Hertel

CHAPTER THIRTY-SIX

First To Depart: Talented Eckart's Early Retirement Stunned Colleagues

Introductory Quote: "You know Dan Quayle and I know Dan Quayle and you are no Dan Quayle." – Democratic Vice Presidential nominee Lloyd Bentsen to Ohio Congressman Dennis Eckart during a meeting with House Democrats shortly after Bentsen unleashed his famous, "You're no Jack Kennedy" zinger at his Republican counterpart, Dan Quayle. Eckart had played Quayle in mock debates with Bentsen.

Photo courtesy of Dennis Eckart

Of all the members who called it quits in 1992, Dennis Eckert was the first to announce. He was also one of the most shocking. At that early date in September of 1991, few members could have envisioned their youthful colleague's departure as a precursor for the turmoil that would follow among their own 14 months before Election Day. But if the well respected and scandal- free Eckart's departure would ultimately prove one thing, it was that the first cut was the deepest.

Eckart's retirement was especially noteworthy because at age 41, he hadn't known anything but politics as an adult. Elected to the Ohio House at 24, he had become a Congressman at 30. Moreover, with a seat on the powerful Energy and Commerce Committee in the U.S. House, he already had impacted many issues. That was helped by the panel's carnivorous chair, John Dingell, a friend and hunting partner and who following Eckart's departure announcement poignantly begged him to reconsider. He was after all a natural and if one needed evidence of that, consider this. Eckart was instrumental in the override of the only veto of George H.W. Bush's presidency. It was the cable Reauthorization Act and most remarkably, it occurred one month before Bush faced re-election.

Politics in America called Eckart "rarely at a loss for a pithy quote" and his ability to throw out words and catch phrases for an issue – whether seriously, flippantly, or both made him a highly effective person for causes or legislative matters he undertook. Another Congressional publication said, "His standing also reflects colleagues' respect for his ability to master the details of highly technical issues that have come before his committee." That undoubtedly ranked among the top reasons that Eckart in 1988 was tapped by national Democrats to coach the party's vice-presidential nominee, Lloyd Bentsen prior to his debate with his Republican counterpart, Dan Quayle. By the early 1990s, Eckart's prospects in the House were indeed unlimited but, apparently he realized his time with his family was as well, and that ultimately proved the dominant driving factor in his decision.

Eckart's decision to leave wasn't the first time he had been near the apex of power before moving on to what he considered to be greener pastures. When he left the Ohio House, he was on the verge of chairing that body's Ways and Means Committee but, the retirement of the local Congressman, fellow Democrat Charlie Vanik made the chance to leap to Washington far more enticing. It was a risky move.

The issue wasn't so much the election to succeed Vanik – a fellow member of the Legislature, Eckart's Democratic rival, Tim McCormack, had angered many with his presence in the race even before Vanik got out and Eckart had little trouble dispatching him and winning the general election even as Ronald Reagan was sweeping the district. But Ohio would be losing two House seats in 1982 and as a freshman, Eckart faced dicey prospects. Electorally, he came out fine though he was forced to run in a district that only contained 15% of his constituents.

Eckart has been a faithful son of greater Cleveland his entire life (his family was of Slovenian orgin just near the Austrian border). He was born in Euclid, an immediate suburb of the city, earned his undergraduate from

Xavier University in just three years and followed by taking his law degree at Cleveland State's Marshall College of Law. He won a seat in the legislature at age 24 in 1974 and focused on consumer affairs and senior issues. In fact, one might say he became a hero to the latter demographic by pushing through tax credits to assist with energy bills. In his campaign for what was then Ohio's 22nd Congressional District, Eckart benefitted from his endorsement by Vanik and for his attempt to woo the district's sizable Jewish community. He beat McCormack 41-24% (to 17% for Anthony Calabrese, Jr.) then prevailed over former Judge Joseph Nahra 55-41%.

**The man from Mentor, Ohio had two of his own – his
predecessor Charlie Vanik and his chairman, John Dingell
Photo courtesy of Dennis Eckart**

In Congress, Eckart's undisputed mentor was Dingell. Eckart explained that connection when Dingell died in 20119. "Although 25 years his junior we both came from similar ethnic stock and states in the industrial Great Lakes Midwest." Eckart in fact was on a European CODEL with Dingell bound for Poland in 1989 when word came that Polish Communist leader General Jarazelski had "abruptly left office under pressure from the Polish labor Solidarity movement. Within hours we landed in Poland and went to the HQ for Solidarity and thus became the first Americans to meet with the de facto Polish leader of Solidarity Lech Walensa" (Dingell of curse was legendary for his Polish pride).

Eckart was named a Democratic whip as a freshman. Coming from a state that was heavy with industry, and at times unemployment, he knew that his constituents were not giving him a blank check to protect the environment, even though he exerted much energy during his career toward doing so. While he often did ring the praise of the environmental community, such as when he undertook a five-year quest to require "federal facility and defense department facilities cleanups" to comply with national environmental laws, he often was forced to oppose them when he felt parochial interests were at stake. On occasion, that drew a heated response (he once accused one group of "character besmirchment" as a result).

One highly public instance came in 1984, Eckart perhaps inadvertently dealt a deadly blow (at least until 1990) to Health Subcommittee Chair Henry Waxman's efforts to reauthorize the Clean Air Act because he refused to vote for stringent anti-acid rain provisions that had been tied 9-9 prior to his vote (Eckart was concerned about the impact on Ohio).

Initially, Eckart had offered Waxman and the other sponsor of the legislation, Gerry Sikorski of Minnesota, at least a hefty verbal bone on which to chew. "There are a lot of folks who won't say what I say - that acid rain is a problem. But I'm not about to take a point position on the issue. I don't like to fry myself in the voting griddle unless I have to." But in truth, that statement summed up his reservations in a nutshell. He wanted to back the standards of Waxman-Sikorski but coal miners fretted about the loss of jobs and as, David Maraniss wrote in a lengthy *Washington Post* series on the workings of the Energy and Commerce Committee, "The utilities have told him that it will raise consumer electricity rates by 18 percent. On the other hand, he likes the fact that HR-3400 makes it a national, not just a predominantly Midwestern, issue."

When Waxman criticized Eckart after the vote, he replied, "This bill did not come down from Mt. Sinai carved on two tablets of stone" (Waxman, who pulled the bill rather than pass a watered-down version, later singled Eckart out in his memoir though the two did enjoy a collegial relationship in later years). But it wasn't just Waxman who was exerting pressure – Eckart revealed that his father-in-law had urged him to back the tough provisions and Eckart himself cited "the agony." He told *The New York Times*, "This is how Representatives get whipsawed. I vote one way and people say, 'Aren't you supposed to represent the national interest?' I vote the other way and people say, 'We sent you there to represent us'" (*The Times* introduced that piece with the headline, "Congress: A Lesson From Whipsawing 101").

With "Roots" author Alex Haley
Photo courtesy of Dennis Eckart

Another instance of Eckart getting caught in the middle was the Superfund legislation. In 1985, he seemed to have scored an improbable victory when a subcommittee approved a bill that he crafted over a version put together by New Jersey Democrat Jim Florio – an accomplishment all the more jarring because Florio was head of the subcommittee. *The New York Times* noted one hearing that Florio "ended early and staff members doused the lights on Mr. Eckart." As the process went on, it turned into a rollercoaster where both sides could claim victory in winning battles though not necessarily the war. A week later, the committee partly reversed Eckart's victory (which made neither man happy) but he acknowledged, "I don't view this as ending today." In truth, however, it was an ending for the session as the House codified Florio's product.

When it came to clean air matters, Eckart's work carried through to the final authorization in 1990 – and his ever-present quips were on full display. In 1988, he was a member of the "group of nine" Commerce Committee Democrats who tried to find agreement between Dingell and his arch-nemesis on the panel, Waxman. That proved elusive for the session but it did materialize in 1990 at which time, Eckart quipped, "If anybody had ever told me that a John-Henry agreement could be struck on tailpipe emissions, I would have said that the heavens would have had to have parted the skies, the earth would have rolled and the clouds would have rumbled. But in fact they did." Eckart played a pivotal role later in the year when the House/Senate conference committee ironed out the differences, an agreement that began to take shape when he approached Senate Majority Leader George Mitchell.

Eckart's devotion to doing what he felt was right for his people could occasionally take him in the other direction, which sometimes meant opposing Dingell. One amendment he vociferously pushed involved citizens right-to-know about toxic substances and providing them additional mechanisms to sue polluters. This was in part a reaction to the 1970s construction of the Perry Nuclear Power Plant which Eckart had adamantly opposed as a state legislator. He was equally vehement about cancelling the Unit Two reactor, saying it was necessary to save them "from their own folly." They, "have been spending money like drunken sailors."

Finally in 1992, Eckart chastised the Bush administration for easing regulations on production increases which Eckart contended, "allows (industry) an automatic increase in emissions for up to 90 days with no authority for public review or comment…We should not be making indiscriminate changes without the public having" a say.

With President Lech Walensa
Photo courtesy of Dennis Eckart

On other issues, Eckart was such a hero to environmentalists that one might think everything was universally hunky-dory. At the same time that he had been politely declining to push acid rain over the top, Eckart displayed little affinity for compromise in 1985 when it came to drinking water. "You can lead the EPA to water but you can't make them regulate." He authored clean water with Illinois Republican Ed Madigan and authored a sweeping reauthorization of the Safe Drinking Water Act that called for limiting 83 contaminants. His navigation of thorny issues such as groundwater provisions resulted in a mere 21 dissensions on final passage.

Determination continued til the end. In his final year in Congress, Eckart championed minimum standards for cleanup. "How do we make them realize that if these same substances were found anywhere else they would be regulated? They feel they are entitled to this free ride, when in fact the days of entitlements for the oil industry are over."

Eckart's position on the Small Business Committee complimented Energy and Commerce and as chair of the Small Business Committee's Anti-Trust, Impact of Deregulation and Ecology Subcommittee, he pursued a few endeavors that were more than a little bit esoteric. After conducting hearings that delved into the mega-popular Nintendo's "significant intimidation in the retail market," Eckart sought to limit its anti-trust status. And following a four-day pollution oriented fact-finding trip to Antarctica with Colorado Republican Dan Schaeffer, he commented on the outdated facilities, saying, "It doesn't make sense to spend millions on research and science if you can't support them" (Eckart and Schaefer bet a shower on a Cleveland Browns-Denver Bronco's game and emerged on the high end of the stick, which led Eckart to quip to the *Akron Beacon Journal*, "I got three and he got one." On another note, the trip produced a number of unsettling moments, including one where a whale breached just 35 feet from he and his Congressional party which led Eckart to later express, "This wasn't Sea World. I was scared to death."

On most other matters, Eckart generally aligned with the liberal camp (support for the Balanced Budget Amendment and a Constitutional amendment banning flag burning were rare exceptions). In 1992, he sponsored a measure that would cancel funding for the Superconducting Super Collider. "We have heard the proponents tell us that the Superconducting Supercollider will cure everything except the heartbreak of psoriasis. The fact of the matter is that it will not make one person well in this country." Despite the fact that one billion dollars had already been allocated for the project, Eckart adroitly reminded his colleagues of the vote on Balanced Budget just a week earlier and said lawmakers who had supported it now had, "an opportunity to put our votes where our voices were...." It was adopted by a vote of 232-181. He was also active in nuclear accident-insurance legislation to increase compensation. "To take the training wheels off the K-Mart, blue light special for the nuclear power industry" and a "raw deal for the taxpayers."

With a national and Ohio hero, Senator John Glenn
Photo courtesy of Dennis Eckart

Eckart's displayed his idealistic streak during the 1984 holiday season when he was furiously contacting colleagues urging them to dump aging and increasingly infirm Armed Services Chair Mel Price in favor of the much younger Les Aspin of Wisconsin. Aspin prevailed on a vote by the full caucus. "If we had lost," Eckart said, "we all would have been in trouble." Locally, he secured $5 million for Coast Guard Stations on Lake Erie.

Levity was something that was easy for Eckart. A case in point was when Massachusetts Democrat Barney Frank compared the U.S. Senate to jello before subsequently issuing an apology. Eckart raise a point of order and asked if "the gentleman had apologized to (jello manufacturer) General Mills." "Silly" was often a part of his political vocabulary. The EPA's 1984 policy was silly," and when his Youngstown, Ohio colleague James Traficant proposed putting missiles on barges to deter a Soviet invasion, Eckart lambasted it as, "the silliest thing he's ever heard of...It just puts us right in the middle of the

Soviet bull's-eye" (Eckart had little patience for his colleague's zaniness. On another occasion, as Traficant pursued a Ways and Means Committee seat, Eckart said it would be "a joke").

Another trait that came easy for Eckart was political smarts and that's a main reason he was selected to coach Lloyd Bentsen. In fact, he had done work in the debate area for some years before Dukakis/Bentsen and also had closely examined tape of Quayle made by local tv stations at his local appearances (pointing out "this was way before trackers"). He also recounted that Bentsen, who as the nation now knows following that debate, had been a longstanding friend of JFK and was "incredulous" that Quayle would equate himself to him.

One place trouble rarely found Eckart was the electoral battlefield. 1982 was dicey – his district was the one targeted for elimination and consequently, Eckart was planning to target a fairly conservative four-term Democratic incumbent Ron Mottl. But when Republican William Stanton retired, Eckart made a surprise decision to move (his former Ohio House colleague Edward Feighan challenged Mottl and beat him). He won with 61% and never again had a tough race (in 1990, as many incumbents dipped, Eckart increased his percentage from 62% over Margaret Mueller to 66%).

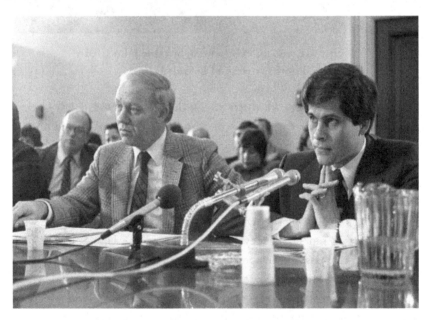

Testifying with colleague Jim Oberstar of Minnesota
Photo courtesy of Dennis Eckart

As shocking as Eckart's retirement announcement was to his colleagues, it was not a decision he and his family came to lightly. As early as Christmas Day, 1990, he left a note for his wife under the tree that the term he had just won would be his last. Still, Eckart had at least initially began acting like a candidate. 1992 was a redistricting year and Ohio would again be losing two seats. Thus, Eckart stepped up his donations to the powers that be, giving $1,000 to House Speaker Vern Riffe. As he announced his plans to step down, Eckart said, "For 18 years I have placed my passion for politics and public service above the rest of my family and friends. At a very early age our son, Eddy, used to say that his dad 'shakes hands for a living.' One year I was on airplanes more than 90 times. That's more than the total number of soccer games and swim meets I've been able to attend." He added, "I've found myself making more decisions over the phone than over the kitchen table." Early in his career, he called himself a "guided missile," with zero control over his schedule and his retirement did not make him a Johnny-Come-Lately on that score. In a *New York Times* profile early in Eckart's tenure, he noted that he had visited a bowling alley one night only to have three constituents recognize him and tell him their problems.

Eckart did acknowledge apprehensiveness over the forthcoming ventures out of office and compared it to, "someone who is standing on top of a diving board. I know there's water in the pool below and I'm 10 feet above it. I don't know if it's going to be a '10' or a belly flop." He did just fine. He delivered commentary for Cleveland TV and began specializing in international law. Incidentally, Eckart's decision to retire inspired other forty-something colleagues to do the same. Close friend Brian Donnelly of Massachusetts announced his retirement that same cycle while Tim Penny of Minnesota and Jim Slattery of Kansas did the same two years later. But all said they were motivated by Eckart.

Eckart's respect loomed large enough that in 2006, a decade and a half after he left office, a number of Senators who had served with him in the House tried to talk him into making a comeback by seeking a U.S. Senate seat but by that time, Eckart was firmly entrenched in private life. These days, Eddie seems to be the man on the move in that family as he too has been courted to run for a U.S. House seat.

Discussing a gas tax with Ways and Means Chair Dan
Rostenkowski and Ohio's Governor, George Voinovich
Photo courtesy of Dennis Eckart

CHAPTER THIRTY-SEVEN

Feighan's Legacy is The Brady Bill, Decency and Stephanopoulos

Introductory Quote: "Did I discover George Stephanopoulos? I would prefer to say that George Stephanopoulos discovered me." – Edward Feighan on his one-time employee and future journalist and communication star.

Photo courtesy of the U.S. House of Representatives Historical Collection

E dward Feighan served ten years in Congress, a relatively short time in comparison to other members. Yet being what *Congressional Quarterly* called, "a persistent but low-key lawmaker," the attention he brought to matters on both on the international and domestic front gave them gravitas that were giant steps toward ultimately making them become law. The inauspicious manner by which his tenure ended notwithstanding, Feighan's record is one of great satisfaction from which many citizens benefit. On another note, the personal decency attributed to Feighan is apropos of someone who early in life seriously toyed with the priesthood.

Feighan hails from a celebrated Irish-Catholic family in the Greater Cleveland area that took great pride in the president of their heritage, John F. Kennedy. His grandfather manufactured Erin Brew beer while his uncle, Michael Feighan, was a respected Congressman at the heart of a number of social battles. Unlike his nephew, the elder Feighan's standing with other Democrats was not always grand. He was reported to have called Kennedy "a nigger lover" and did not get along with Lyndon Johnson. One interesting tidbit: While Feighan's mother wanted to name him, David, his Irish paternal grandfather scoffed at that, believing it was too Jewish sounding. Yet Feighan from his earliest years became friendly with the Jewish community and vowed to name his first-born son, David. He fulfilled that vow.

Feighan's dad was a prominent attorney and another uncle a municipal court judge. Edward attended high school at an all-boys school and after graduation, enrolled at Borromeo Seminary that was part of the Cleveland Diocese. He recalled "the effects of Vatican Council II hadn't quite begun to infiltrate the American Catholic experience yet. We sang Gregorian Chant each morning, kept Grand Silence until after breakfast, wore cassocks and collars and were allowed to leave our campus for a couple of hours on Saturday mornings. Yet I really liked the experience." For whatever reason, Feighan decided that a life in the seminary was not for him and he married and had children (later becoming agnostic altogether). Instead, serving people via politics became more his forte.

Though Feighan had lived in a political home, he had not really entertained the idea of running for office. The motivation came after college when he was teaching high-school English and living in Cleveland. To prepare, Feighan became involved in other campaigns and in 1972, when a retiring State House member decided not to seek re-election and turned to Feighan. He was just 25 but decided to take on the challenge and won, becoming the youngest member of the chamber until he surrendered the title in 1974 when, "a young upstart named (future U.S. Senator) Sherrod Brown" was elected at age 22 (his future U.S. House colleague Dennis Eckart also joined the chamber that year at age 24).

As a House member, Feighan focused on handgun control though acknowledges he didn't get far. Juvenile justice encompassed much of his energy as did an overhaul of the Buckeye State's criminal statutes, which he worked on with fellow Clevelander Harry Lehman.

In 1977, longtime Cleveland Mayor Ralph Perk, a Republican was seeking re-election but the general feeling was that he had lost touch with his base, particularly the West Side. The city's electric company, Municipal Light

(MUNY Light) was also a galvanizing issue as many viewed it as a source of Cleveland's increasingly dire fiscal situation. The Democratic establishment openly courted a number of seasoned figures to challenge Perk but most passed. Feighan, just turning 30 and still in law school, proved the exception though it was a decision he made "on very short notice." So did Dennis Kucinich, only a year older who had been the clerk of the Municipal Court in Cleveland and had been seeking elected office as long as Feighan had held it (he was losing his bid for a House seat in '72 as Feighan was winning his). Feighan recalls, "there was a sentiment that we wanted a more conventional candidate" and while a number of Democrats entered the convention to obtain the party's endorsement, they all consolidated around Feighan when he earned it. All that is except Kucinich who had bypassed the process.

1977 was a year that, unlike when Perk first became Mayor, all candidates ran in a blanket primary and the top two finishers would meet in a November runoff. On primary night, the jolt was that not only did Feighan and Kucinich run ahead of Perk, but Feighan came within 300 votes of Kucinich. He was helped by racking up 60% on the West Side. Either way, the two were now locked in a runoff. As early as primary night, Feighan tried to turn the tables on Kucinich, who had said in announcement that, "everybody knows I'm the only one who can beat Ralph Perk," to which Feighan responded, "Everyone knows I'm the only one who can beat Dennis Kucinich." One month later, he very nearly did.

During the 1977 Mayoral election
Photo via The Plain Dealer

Kucinich challenged his rival to two debates a week, "one on the East Side, one on the West Side." He hit Feighan, whom he derided as, "The Missionary" for chairing a tax abatement committee, labeled him a "tool," and, "not really one of us." Feighan would not resort to negative campaigning but did press the maturity issue even though ironically, he was actually a year younger than Kucinich.

Kucinich cut into at least some establishment support as influential African-American Congressman Lou Stokes and U.S. Senator Howard Metzenbaum backed him. City Council President George Forbes, however, was squarely in Feighan's corner as was Ohio's other Senator, John Glenn, a move Feighan called, "bold." While Feighan jokes that Glenn was "overwhelmed by the wonderful presence I had," he knew that in actuality, part of it stemmed from a well-known feud with Metzenbaum.

The election was a nail-biter but Kucinich finished on top by 2,973 votes (93,047 to 90,074). Feighan was gracious in defeat and made clear that, "I hope he becomes the best mayor Cleveland has ever had" (Kucinich had a stormy tenure that included firing his police commissioner on Good Friday. His high point might have been beating back a recall effort by 236 votes).

For Feighan, losing was merely a minor electoral blemish. He was still firmly entrenched in his State House seat where he would chair the Subcommittee on Housing but higher callings were evident. The following year, he gave up his House seat in order to try to become a Cuyahoga County Commissioner and with incumbent Seth Taft having himself nearly won the Cleveland Mayoralty in 1967 over Stokes's brother Carl, it could easily have been known as the race between also-rans. Feighan eked out a 51% win which was accompanied by news that he had passed the bar exam. Before learning the results of either, Feighan recalls telling his new wife Nadine that it would be either feast or famine.

By early 1982, Northeast Ohio was getting battered by Reaganomics and liberals found little to like in the voting record of the area's Congressman, Ronald Mottl, a fellow Democrat. A four-term incumbent, Mottl had the most conservative voting record of any Democrat North of the Mason-Dixon Line. He had supported the Reagan economic and tax proposals and opposed busing. Much like the '77 Mayoral race, some of Mottl's Democratic constituents were restless.

1982 was also a redistricting year and Mottl would face the misfortune of having to introduce himself to a district 55% new, including thousands of bread-and-butter Democrats who had never voted for him. Support for the Reagan agenda wouldn't be a quality that would have them at hello, particularly when one union headlined their newsletter with, "Ohio Republicans and Mottl

Betray Ohio." Meanwhile, Feighan's Mayoral bid and county seat overlap made him a natural to undertake the bid and powerful leaders, including his lifelong friend, Cuyahoga Democratic Chair Tim Hagan, urged him to run. Initially, he hesitated but shortly before the filing deadline decided to take the plunge.

Once again, Feighan found himself under attack as the establishment candidate, an ironic charge given that Mottl was the incumbent. He framed the debate as between, "a person who has guts and courage or someone who is the puppet of Boss Hagan" and called Feighan "well-greased (who) has the party bosses." Because Feighan lived slightly outside the district, Mottl labeled him, "Inner City Ed." Mottl had establishment support of his own, from Washington D.C., including from a number of prominent colleagues who sent donations.

In a nationally watched debate at City Club, Feighan accused Mottl of, "throw(ing) the poor through the window of vulnerability," charges he was able to back up with heavy artillery. The mighty AFL-CIO was on his side which was one reason he was able to post more money on hand. That was enough to unseat the incumbent by the slimmest of margins, 1,213 votes or 49-47%, and he told jubilant supporters that, "I think the election serves as a message to Reagan and his supporters that what is needed is a bold, new economic policy." In a Democratic district like the 19th, that was music to voters' ears and Feighan took 59% in the general against Richard Anter II.

From the moment Feighan took his seat in Congress, it was evident that he'd be a Congressional rarity. He was given a gavel on the spot, albeit a minor one: the chairmanship of the House Task Force on International Narcotics Control and he pushed for increased penalties against countries that illegally export drugs to the United States. Feighan was also assigned to the Judiciary Committee and Foreign Affairs. Acquiring a seat on the latter posed a slight challenge, but only because his uncle and Chairman Peter Rodino had a history from their years in Congress together (besides the fact that Mike Feighan was more conservative than Rodino, the two butted heads over roles on the committee). Rodino in fact told Feighan, "I hope you're not like your uncle." Feighan got the seat and he and Rodino had a beautiful relationship. In fact, in Feighan's first year in office he named Feighan one of five Congressional positions to the Commission on Migration. Feighan had no idea what that was but it involved a trip to Geneva.

Despite his Catholic upbringing, Feighan was solidly pro-choice and opposed capital punishment and, with one or two exceptions, was fairly liberal on most domestic matters. That led his uncle to berate him and one day tell him he had "pro-communist" views for his refusal to support arms to Nicaraguan contras.

Accompanying Robert Redford around Capitol Hill
Photo courtesy of Edward Feighan

Much of Feighan's legislative portfolio centered around his deep commitment to human rights around the world. In 1984, he introduced an amendment that would withdraw $21 million in aid to Turkey unless it recognized Cyprus. A few months later, he introduced an amendment limiting aid to Turkey while also helping Cyprus. He called the, "modest cap...a clear frustration over the deadlock on Cyprus." With Steve Solarz, he proposed an amendment to maintain assistance to India while going after them for Kashmiris. Feighan-Solarz passed.

After a trip to China the winter following Tiananmen Square, Feighan criticized the Bush administration for meeting with leaders of that regime. "The repression of the Chinese government has gotten worse over the last six months, not better...They are prepared to resume business as usual with the Chinese."

As one of ten members of Congress who served on the Helsinki Commission, Feighan was a staunch champion of Jewish interests and fought for the release of a number of people from both Eastern Europe (particularly Lithuanians who were being held by the Soviet Union) as well as the Soviet Union itself. When the Soviet government began allowing a record number of Jews to emigrate, Feighan advocated a one-year hold on the Jackson-Vanik amendment for that nation. In a 1989 editorial in *The*

Christian Science Monitor, Feighan explained, "The amendment has largely accomplished its purpose. The Soviet government, which badly wants, and needs, expanded trade with the U.S., is responding to the pressure exerted by Jackson-Vanik when it allows 4,000 Jews a month to leave." He note that, "Former Congressman Charles Vanik, who co-wrote the Jackson-Vanik law with then-Sen. Henry Jackson, says that today's climate is, "precisely the climate we anticipated when we wrote our law."

Feighan made news on the international front in early 1985 when he, Pennsylvania colleague Tom Foglietta and two others were "handled roughly" when they were accompanying dissident Kim Dae Jung at South Korea's airport in Seoul (Jung had been returning to Korea for the first time in two years).

**With two distinguished Irish gentlemen from Massachusetts
Photos courtesy of Edward Feighan**

Feighan's biggest legacy came on the domestic front - the Brady Bill and, though it wasn't enacted until after he had left office and a Democratic president was installed, his work on the matter illustrated the long, tough slog and the virtue of patience that is required of any even seemingly minor change in social policy. The issue was a waiting period for handgun purchases that would therein become known for White House Press Secretary Jim Brady who sustained life-changing injuries during the 1981 assassination attempt on Reagan.

Today, the Brady Bill is among the most well-known laws on the books but the name is not a euphemism and like everything, there is a story as to how it came to be. The House Judiciary Committee was hearing a bill put forth by Feighan for mandatory waiting periods before the purchase of a handgun. Jim Brady, mortally wounded during the assassination attempt of President Ronald Reagan, was testifying. During the hearing, the committee's chair, Peter Rodino of New Jersey, signaled Feighan to approach the rostrum. The bill would stand a better chance of enactment, Rodino said, if "you make a motion to call this the Brady Bill." Feighan thought for a moment and decided to do so. "I'll sacrifice a little ego," he thought, "because it would give us the visibility it wouldn't have had otherwise." With that, Brady took on a life of its own.

Feighan's impetus at advancing the Brady Bill was local. In 1984, a shooting at a Cleveland library that left a 19-year-old dead made national headlines. When he had been approached by Hoffman, whose group proceeded Brady's, the two decided to work together. Feighan acknowledged the bill was certainly, "far from a perfect system. It will not identify every felon who is otherwise barred from owning a gun." It was, however, a start. And a finish if the NRA had its way. In 1987, Feighan wrote in *The New York Times*, "Who would argue against legislation that could keep criminals and crazies from buying a handgun…not surprisingly, the National Rifle Association (NRA) is preparing to fight such legislation with all the high-powered political ammunition it can muster."

**Unlike his famous Senator, Feighan was content
making a difference on the ground
Photo courtesy of Edward Feighan**

Feighan thus found that efforts to mandate a seven-day waiting period prior to the purchase of a handgun encompassed three different Congresses. In 1988, it was done in by a poison pill of sorts on the House floor and, being grouped into a drug bill, was voted down 228-182. Feighan pronounced gun control proponents, "outgunned by the forces of the National Rifle Association because of their campaign of deception and distortion."

The bill next went before the Judiciary Committee in 1990 and passed by a vote of 27 to 9. It not only called for background checks but for authorities to give sworn statements to authorities if they suspected a potential buyer to have either a criminal record or be mentally unfit for purchase. Prior to passage, Feighan and Brady supporters fended off a proposal from Florida Republican Bill McCollum that would require states to conduct instant background checks in part by updating their databases, partly by involving the argument that an endeavor of this magnitude would take years to develop. Support among Republicans jumped from one Republican in 1988 to six this time. Congressional leaders never put the bill to a vote and it died for the Congress.

In his "persistent and low-key style," Feighan would try, try again and early in the next Congress, he got help from a very unlikely person: Ronald Reagan. The now 80-year old ex-president unequivocally stated support for the Brady Bill.

That time, it fell on a Democrat, Harley Staggers of West Virginia, to offer the counter-proposal and Feighan's partner on the effort, then-Congressman Chuck Schumer of New York called Staggers' effort, "a ruse, a sham, a fake." Feighan's sympathy for Staggers was non-existent as well and his measure was defeated (Feighan liked Staggers personally very much). McCollum was also back with a substitute but lawmakers rejected that one as well.

As the House debated the "Brady Bill," Feighan hearkened back to the January authorization of the Gulf War in instructing colleagues on the essentials of reaching a decision through clear thinking. Noting lawmakers, "cast what clearly was the most controversial vote of this year and certainly of the entire Congress...for each one of us in the decision leading up to that vote, we went through a period of soul-searching and looking into each of our own consciences. We all strove to do the right thing. We did not consult with lobbies, we did not focus on the next election, but our prime consideration was the young Americans who might lose their lives in any ensuing conflict," adding, "I think will be, on our minds today."

The final speaker for opponents of the Brady Bill was John Dingell, the very powerful Michigan Democrat who had been on the Board of the NRA.

Feighan was somewhat intimidated by having to follow him as a closing speaker for his own side but did so – and got a standing ovation. He knows "it wasn't because of my oratory," but because he took on Dingell. The bill finally cleared the House by a vote of 239-186 after which Feighan conceded, "The Senate is a major hurdle." That proved to be true and no action was taken for the remainder of that session of Congress. The bill finally passed in 1993 when Bill Clinton became president and though Feighan was no longer a member of Congress, he was at the White House for the bill signing.

Photos courtesy of Edward Feighan

The Brady Bill was not only Feighan's pursuit on the gun front. He tried to ban plastic gun, semi-automatic weapons and introduced the Felon Gun Prohibition Act.

On some issues, Feighan was open to conversion. Longtime Chief of Staff Mike Rosenberg noted that he had initially opposed a "single-payer," health system, believing it to be political suicide before one day strolling in the office and declaring that it was the only way to go.

Occasionally, Feighan did not fall in line with his party. In 1989, he confounded Democrats when he signed, then withdrew his name from a letter prepared by Congresswoman Pat Schroeder that would have required Attorney General Richard Thornburgh to appoint an independent counsel to investigate the collapse of the Silverado Savings and Loan, which had been run by Bush's son Neil. Feighan's withdrawal left proponents one signature shy of the required twelve and Thornburgh subsequently rejected Democrats requests for the special prosecutor. Rosenberg cited the reason. His boss had simply felt it was, "too personal an attack on a president" and he recalls Bush was grateful. Feighan's press secretary John Sweeney, on the other hand, might not have been as appreciative. Sweeney, literally stayed at the office all night on a Friday fielding calls from the national press.

Among colleagues and staff, who called him, "Edward," Feighan was viewed as a man of utmost decency. Rosenberg recalls that while Feighan could sometimes be in a sore mood if a certain job wasn't being fulfilled, he was an absolute joy to work with, "a true man of principle." He recalled one day joking that Feighan as boss had all of the leverage in their relationship. When Feighan replied that it wasn't the case, that he could always quit, Rosenberg was honored because the Congressman was putting the two of them on equal footing. Others shared a similar view. As he was vacating his office, *The Plain Dealer* observed that he "genuinely seems unaffected by a decade of being treated like royalty."

Dan Clarke ran Feighan's district office for eight years. Not only was Feighan "not egotistical," but he was "as even-keeled a human being as I have ever known." In fact, many times he recalls his boss calming him down and assuring him that everything would be fine. He cites "a real camaraderie in the staff which he fostered." Feighan, he said, was "a very, very good politician but he's also intellectually honest and very intellectually smart."

George Stephanopoulos is another proud Feighan alumnus. Congressman-elect Feighan had offered Stephanopoulos, 21, an entry-level position in his office in late 1982, just a day after watching him on ABC's "Nightline" following the shooting death of anti-nuclear advocate Norman Mayer as he threatened to blow up the Washington Monument. Stephanopoulos, who had submitted his application to Feighan only a day earlier, had been working at the Arms Control Association where Mayer would regularly walk into its Washington D.C. headquarters and it became his responsibility to, if not reason with Mayer, than to certainly befriend him. Feighan told Stephanopoulos, "If you can get yourself on Nightline, maybe you can do some good for me." Stephanopoulos in turn said I'll always be grateful for my seminal work experiences with Ed."

In his book, *All Too Human*, Stephanopoulos detailed an early blunder, preparing a floor speech for his boss criticizing President Reagan for the attack on Grenada. Stephanopoulos wrote, "Feighan questioned the invasion from the House floor - and he never let me forget it" as few colleagues joined him. Asked to elaborate, Stephanopoulos said Feighan was hardly angry but did give him "more good natured but pointed ribbing."

Feighan served ten years in Congress and often took pains to explain the gerrymandered "u" shaped district. Electorally, it treated him well, albeit after two hard-fought re-election campaigns. The first was in 1984 when Reagan topped the ballot. Feighan's opponent, Matthew Hatchadorian, was a Senator and Cuyahoga County Auditor and one *CQ* called "an experienced, aggressive campaigner." Hatchadorian presented himself as a moderate, particularly noting his support for the ERA and Republicans hoped residual distaste about Feighan from the Mottl primary still lingered among conservative Mottl supporters. But Feighan appealed to conservatives through his anti-drug effort and won with 56%. 1986 found him forced to hustle as well. He was challenged by Gary Suhadolnik, a two-term State Senator who, as *The Akron Beacon Journal* wrote it, portrayed Feighan "as a left-wing liberal, hell-bent on raising taxes, globe-trotting, squandering money on worthless programs and avoiding tough votes, to name just a few alleged indiscretions." He prevailed 55-45% and won his fourth and fifth terms with 70% and 65% respectively. Voters' seemed to echo opinions about Feighan similar to *The Akron Beacon Journal* which, in endorsing him for re-election in 1990, called him, "well-informed and, while we do not always agree with his approach on specific issues, his positions have been arrived at honestly and thoughtfully."

With the man he, "discovered," George Stephanopoulos
Photo courtesy of Edward Feighan

Around the time Feighan was basking in the glow of the "Brady Bill," he was confronted by a pair of other hurdles that, careerwise, would prove insurmountable. First came redistricting. Ohio was slated to lose two seats and one was without question going to come at the expense of population losing Northeast Ohio. Aware that this might prove a predicament, Feighan had flirted with both running for governor in 1990 and taking the number two position with House Speaker Vern Riffe (RIFE) who contemplated running. Both came to pass.

Riffe still held the Speaker's gavel and with "Riffe Insurance" as it was called, Feighan seemed likely to fair fine from redistricting and the Speaker told allies as much. Another boon came with the autumn 1991 retirement announcements by his two colleagues, Eckart and Donald Pease, which made it obvious that Feighan would at least have a district in which to run. Legislative negotiations went so down to the wire that boundaries weren't settled upon until March of '92, just weeks before a new filing deadline (the original had to be postponed for lack of agreement) and after news about Feighan's bank woes made headlines. The final product did make Feighan's would be new territory more Republican (he picked up Ashtabula and Lake Counties) but certainly winnable. But he soon found himself stuck with another whammy.

When revelations of member overdrafts at the House bank reached the public, Feighan denied he had any. But when members of the House Ethics Committee decided to release the names of the 24 worst abusers, Feighan found himself on the list with 397 overdrafts and that his negative balance exceeded his paycheck for eight of the 39 months scrutinized. He pronounced himself "stunned."

Eckart while acknowledging that, "Ed Feighan just bought himself an election contest," was quick to add, "But anybody who thinks this single issue will sweep him out of office doesn't know Ed Feighan." Unbeknownst to many was that Feighan had been thinking of packing it in even before the scandal unfolded and on April 1, he announced his departure. In his announcement, he said, "The most important influence was my family. My family was second. And my family was third. I say that genuinely." He was also candid. "I have never had to endure such a mean-spirited, ugly and dehumanizing atmosphere as the one which now prevails in Washington. For the first time in memory, there is a small group of partisan extremists in the House who have sent out to destroy the institution in the name of reform." He bemoaned the obsession with the scandals of the day, calling "the public debate...more on the House bank, the House gym, the House restaurant, than it is on a devastated economy..." Nadine conceded, "Its down sides were starting to outweigh the good sides." As his term winded down, Feighan said he loved being a Congressman and that he doubted "a comparable period in my life that approaches the satisfaction of this" would come along.

In his immediate aftermath, Feighan was reportedly in serious contention to be assistant secretary for human rights but wasn't picked.

As Feighan prepared to leave office, Mike Oxley, a Republican colleague in both the legislature and Congress lauded him by saying he, "has made a career out of making Ohio and the nation better places." In the quarter-of-a-century since he has left office, the fruits of his efforts have long been on full display.

CHAPTER THIRTY-EIGHT

Mrazek's Quest for Higher Office Cut Short by His Second Highest Number of Overdrafts at House Bank

Introductory Quote: I'm well prepared to do the job. The only question in my mind is whether I can win. When you get past votes I can count on from my family and my Czeck base, I still need about three million more." – New York Congressman Robert Mrazek as he was nearing a decision on entering the 1992 U.S. Senate race.

Photo courtesy of the U.S. House of Representatives Collection

During his decade in Congress, Robert Mrazek proved himself to be a very talented member of Congress, whose compassion could not be understated. However, his 920 overdrafts at the House Bank not only obscured that reputation, but extinguished any chance he had at the higher office, of which he had been vigorously pursuing. His arguably voluntary retirement did, however, give way to a second, equally meaningful career: authoring Civil War related novels (Mrazek is a profound buff on that subject).

To this date, Mrazek (Muh-RA-ZIK) is the only legislator of Czeck descent to serve in Congress, and that distinction was a tremendous source of pride. He was born in Newport, Rhode Island and obtained his education at Cornell University, serving in the Navy during the Vietnam War where he lost the site of part of his left eye due to a training accident.

Mrazek did attend the London Film School after the service, but got the political bug early. He started as an aide to U.S. Senator Vance Hartke, a Democrat from Indiana, and in 1972, decided he wanted to be in Congress in his own right, an audacious move, but one that didn't result in many votes – he garnered just 24% in the primary against Carlton Bales. In 1976, however, Mrazek lowered his sites and was elected to the Suffolk County Legislature. He became Minority Leader several years later. In 1982, Mrazek spotted a more realistic opportunity to aim for Congress, and once safely through the primary, had the Democratic leadership publicly cheering for him. Why? Because of the person he was running against, a combative freshman named John LeBoutillier.

LeBoutillier had been one of those shocking "Reagan Robots" pulled into Congress in 1980 by the then-winning GOP Presidential candidate's coattails. Merely 27, he had unseated the hard-working and well thought of eight-term Democratic incumbent Lester Wolff in a Nassau County centered district, which at the time included a portion of Queens. The '82 redistricting had excised Queens from the district and added Suffolk County, where Mrazek's tenure in the county legislature had made him exceedingly popular. That made 2/3 of the district new for LeBoutillier. But that wasn't the incumbent's biggest problem.

To call LeBoutillier brash was a big understatement. He had referred to Reagan's cabinet as "boring," Senate Foreign Affairs Chairman Charles Percy, a fellow Republican as a "wimp," and House Speaker Tip O'Neill as, "big, fat and out of control, just like the federal deficit."

The surprising thing about the fall campaign was that, despite LeBoutillier having earned the enmity of O'Neill and others for his name-calling, the race wasn't particularly targeted by national Democrats until almost the campaign's final days. In fact, *The New York Times*, on October 21, wrote that Mrazek was "not on a list of six Democratic challengers the committee believes can unseat freshman Republicans in Congress." Mrazek himself recognized that the district was rough-sledding for his party and hoped to branch out beyond outnumbered Democrats by declaring himself, "not a company boy. ...My philosophy is not a party philosophy."

Given the expensive nature of New York City television, Mrazek was content to air most of his media campaign on radio. He spoke of LeBoutillier's "eccentricities," of which the incumbent provided plenty of ammunition. In the closing days of the campaign, LeBoutillier traveled to Massachusetts to participate in the quixotic endeavor of unseating O'Neill in a Democratic-heavy district, taking valuable time away from a district he acknowledged he needed to do better at getting to know. Mrazek also mocked his rival for his suggestion that violent prisoners be sent to a polar prison in Alaska ("Fantasy Island"). When the dust settled, Mrazek ousted the incumbent 52-46%, a margin of nearly 11,000 votes. With a grateful O'Neill's help, he became the only freshman in a class of a fair number of Democrats to be assigned to the powerful Appropriations Committee.

It took Mrazek two cycles to get his feet on the ground. In 1984, Republicans thought they had a winner with Reagan's popularity and the candidacy of Robert Quinn. Mrazek's 6,500 win in Suffolk was almost his entire margin districtwide as Mrazek hung on by 7,292 votes (he even squeezed out an 800 vote win in Nassau). He cruised the next two cycles and, while not particularly endangered in 1990, might have become caught up in the anti-incumbent mood that blossomed late in the year. He held off businessman Robert Previdi, whom *Politics in America* notes referred to The Clean Air Act as "some cockamamie bill," by ten points, 53-43%, a difference of just 14,000 votes.

In Congress, Mrazek pursued causes that were both meaningful and sundry. In 1989, he led to passage, by a vote of 356-60, a ban on logging and a preservation of the historic forests in Alaska's Tongass National Forest. An attempt a year earlier to limit the logging had failed when the Senate didn't act, although the House had passed watered down language that year sponsored by California Democrat George Miller. Enactment in 1989 came in the face of a plea by Alaska's Republican member of Congress, Don Young, who warned of potentially devastating job losses. Mrazek's response was, "We're giving them those trees for the price of cheeseburgers." His efforts gained some appreciation with the home folks. In that year's Congressional election, 300 voters wrote Mrazek's name in against Young, though it's unclear how they spelled it.

Next, Mrazek was a Civil War buff and he scored a big win by preserving the Manassas Battlefield (he posed the question, "What is the price of our national historical heritage?"). And when it came to preservation, Mrazek had other causes.

Photo via C-SPAN

Preservation of black and white films was a major undertaking during Mrazek's ten years in Congress and he sponsored the National Film Preservation Act of 1988. His impetus was the uproar within Hollywood following the colorization of the film, "The Maltese Falcon" and enlisting gargantuan film maker Steven Spielberg was central to getting the cause off the ground (he raised over $100,000). So were Jimmy Stewart and Lauren Bacall, the latter who appeared on Capitol Hill and told lawmakers it was "an obscenity that they're colorizing those films." Mrazek called his proposal, "a significant first step toward the ultimate recognition of artists' moral rights" and recalled later, "it was about determining for the first time that film was an art form, and worthy of protection like Stephen Decatur's home or John Philip Sousa's music."

Despite initial resistance from fellow Appropriators, Mrazek had the measure attached to a rider with help from the panel's Interior subcommittee chair, Sid Yates, who as a near octogenarian, likely remembered those films in their original form as a young adult. A conference committee compromise was that the Library of Congress would pick 25, "culturally, historically or esthetically significant," films to preserve, not exactly an overjoyment for film activists, but something they could use as a starting point for the future. As a result of their efforts, Mrazek and Yates were presented awards at the 1989 Directors Guild of America ceremony.

Another effort: increasing the number of Armerasian's who could emigrate to the U.S. This undertaking began when high school students from the district circulated a petition that garnered 28,000 signatures for Le Van Minh, 15, to be allowed to come to the U.S. The matter culminated with Mrazek's journeying to Vietnam, meeting with officials and ultimately bringing Le Van to the U.S. He didn't stop there. The Mrazek-Van Minh journey had been made possible by the Congressman's sponsorship of the Amerasian Homecoming Act, which would allow children of Asian born service members to emigrate to the U.S. The Asylumnist wrote in 2017 that "approximately 25,000 Amerasians and about 70,000 of their family members immigrated to the United States."

Not everything Mrazek did was warmly received. In 1990, he tangled with his fellow New York Democrat, Stephen Solarz, on the issue of aiding non-communist resistance in Cambodia. The amount was $7 million and Mrazek and other Democrats were convinced that, despite intentions to the contrary, the money was ending up in the hands of the Khmer Rouge, which *The Washington Post* quoted Wisconsin Democrat David Obey as "hav(ing) more blood on their hands than anyone since Hitler and Stalin." While Solarz, who was advocating the aid to Cambodia, angrily disputed the fact that Khmer Rouge was thwarting the aid, Mrazek stood firm. "The U.S. is living a lie," he bellowed. "The lie is that U.S. aid contributes to a peaceful solution." Even with this, Solarz won the day, as the House codified the aid by a vote of 260 to 163.

By and large, Mrazek was a strong bread and butter Democrat - pro-choice, anti-flag burning amendment. He opposed aid to the contras and sided with liberals in most of their attempts to cut back on weapon systems. On a lighter note, he was managing partner in a business venture with seven other fellow Democratic members of Congress, including then-Senator Al Gore, who purchased Pierre's Island, a small portion of the Bahamas. The venture fell apart a few years later when its cost outweighed the pleasures, and Mrazrek acceded to his partner's requests to sell it.

If Mrazek liked challenges, winning the Senate nomination would have been a formidable one. His rivals were both nationally-known and statewide veterans – former Vice-Presidential nominee Geraldine Ferraro, New York State Attorney General Robert Abrams, New York City Comptroller and former Congresswoman Elizabeth Holtzman, and the Rev. Al Sharpton. Mrazek asserted that his name could serve as an asset by saying, "I'm not totally a desperation candidate. I'm trying to convince people that they should take a leap of faith that a guy with a name that they can't pronounce has the stuff" (he joked that he "accept[ed] five different pronunciations of my name").

Several factors made Mrazek decide to go for all or nothing at all. One was that New York State would be losing three House seats via reapportionment, and it was a near given that one of those would come out of Long Island. Two was what he viewed as a relatively long wait before he would graduate to real influence: "Twenty-seven Democrats separate me from the chairmanship of the Appropriations Committee," he said, "and the issues I want to address are beyond the realm of a junior congressman."

Initially, some rival candidates, notably Abrams, seemed unconcerned by Mrazek's candidacy. This prompted his Long Island colleague, Democrat Tom Downey, to issue a warning: "If I were Bob Abrams, I'd be a lot more concerned about Bob Mrazek than they probably are."

Mrazek knew that his first test was to demonstrate that he could raise money. He invested a great deal of time upstate, where he viewed the other three candidates' liberal orthodoxy as a possible impediment, and *The New York Times* in early 1992 noted that "he crawled from town-to-town with only a rental car, a driver and a map." He did succeed in raising $1.2 million.

By March 1992, his campaign seemed to be gaining momentum, though far from the amount likely to topple three Democratic titans. Then came Rubbergate. When the official list of members who had overdrafts was released, Mrazek didn't just figure prominently on it – he literally topped the list. With 920 overdrafts, no current member had a higher amount of bad checks than Mrazek (only retired Arkansas Congressman Tommy Robinson, with 996 overdrafts, had more). At first, the official list revealed that he actually had overdrawn his account 972 times, but the final number brought it down to a still staggering 920, an amount of $351,608.62. He had been overdrawn by more than his monthly salary for 23 of the 39 months within the investigation.

Mrazek responded to his political problems with levity: "My campaign has taken off like a rocket ship. Hundreds of people have called my district office saying, 'Run, Bob. Run.' Unfortunately, most of them meant that I should run for Brazil." He referred to the episode as a "surrealistic, Kafkaesque nightmare." But in truth, his kids were bearing out the brunt of the abuse. Mrazek told reporters of his son's bus driver joking that "super balls don't bounce as high as your dad's checks."

On a more serious note, Mrazek claimed he was being tried in the media with incorrect facts. I never had a check returned, never cost the taxpayers a dime, never broke a law or a House rule, consistently deposited in that bank far more than I withdrew, and made certain that my account was in balance or better at the start of each month…I now find to my horror and regret that, contrary to what my office had always been told, being in balance at the start of each month was not enough." Mrazek ultimately bowed out of the Senate race and declined to re-enter the contest for his House seat. In the period of having left office, he returned $218,000 to PACs.

After what he calls, "A 30-year detour," Mrazek was able to pursue his dream with the arts. He has published at least seven books relating to the Civil War, including *Valhalla*, *A Dawn Like Thunder*, *To Kingdom Come*, and *Unholy Fire*. 2016, debuted the film, "The Congressman." It featured actor Treat Williams and was the story of a fictitious Congressman from Maine, Charlie Winship (Mrazek spends part of his year in New York and the other half on a remote island in the state of Maine).

CHAPTER THIRTY-NINE

Smith of Florida Productively Pugnacious: Congressman Lacked Subtlety but Not Results

Introductory Tidbit: "The Fiddler on the Roof" song, "Matchmaker" is intertwined in American and Jewish culture but for a time, it was intertwined in Capitol Hill culture as well. The man who partially presided over this was Congressman Larry Smith of Florida but, don't mention the term Matchmaker to him. For Smith, it was simply a Jewish social group and he frowns on the idea that he was fixing Jewish singles up ("I do not consider myself a rabbi or a shadchen" - Yiddish for matchmaker). The person who did consider himself a shadchen was Minnesota Republican Senator Rudy Boschwitz who famously tried to fix up Jewish singles and discourage cross marriages, even to the couple's faces. Smith took the group over when Boschwitz lost re-election to Paul Wellstone in 1990. Smith's mission statement was easy. "I am trying to provide a forum where young people can get together. I am not trying to put individual together. There's a difference." He scoffed at "meddling." Semantics aside, the group was a success and the events often drew as many as 800 Jewish singles.

Photo via Florida Memory

If people make the observation that the name "Smith" is not distinctly Jewish, it is for good reason. Florida Democratic Congressman Lawrence J. "Larry" Smith's family's surname was actually "Schmidt," but his father changed it to "Smith" before entering the U.S. Army, changed it to "Smith." Regardless, Smith's link to the Jewish community in both his native Empire State and his adopted state of Florida is as unambiguous as can be. Beyond the fact that his family (starting with his grandfather, Gerson Schmidt), were kosher caterers from New York City, the effervescence and flamboyance with which he promoted Israel and other Jewish causes was a hallmark of his ten-years in the U.S. House. It also produced what became among the most widely aired exchanges between a member of Congress and an administration of U.S.-Israel policy when Smith sparred with Secretary of State James Baker on the issue of loan guarantees.

A good way of describing Smith might be to call him productively pugnacious. *The Almanac of American Politics* observed that the Brooklyn born Smith was, "possessed of a zest for argument and a brash New York style" and *The Washington Post* in 1991 called him, "a large man with a large voice and big gestures…and has a reputation as a blustering, table-pounding legislator with big opinions on everything."

Smith would probably take issue with the term "bluster." The term alludes to ineffectiveness whereas he had indelible accomplishments. Still, he was forced to concede in his first term that, "Maybe I have to learn to be a little humble, a little more reticent." Smith was not sardonic by any means – he meant what he said and how he said it and as a result, he fit in fine in his Broward-Dade based district, many of whom were themselves Northeastern transplants and "snowbirders."

Eventually, colleagues grew to appreciate that as well. Wisconsin Democrat David Obey, no shrinking violet himself, chaired the Appropriations Foreign Operations Subcommittee on which Smith sat. As Smith's career neared an end Obey said, "You always know where Larry Smith stands. I like to deal with people like that, because there is absolutely no guile to him, and as a consequence you always know that you are dealing with a straight shooter, and I do not think you can say anything better about any person in this institution."

In manner and in diction, Larry Smith was distinctly New York and his Brooklynese dialect remains to this day. He was born in the Borough and educated in the East Meadow School System on Long Island where his father Martin had moved the family to operate yet another business that his own father Gerson had started. So central was Gerson Smith to the Jewish community in New York City that *The Miami Herald* cited the catering business he operated, Stuyvesant Casino, as "one of the first in America not associated with a synagogue." Martin continued the business and in later years, expanded it to areas that included beach and nightclubs. The establishments saw a number of celebrities discovered, including opera star Jan Pierce. For Larry Smith, it was also a path to the rest of his life. He met his future wife Shelia there one summer while running the concession stand (she and her mother asked their hot dog be cut in two).

Smith attended New York University and obtained his law degree from Brooklyn Law School. Citing the desire to raise a family in, "what was then, a more tranquil and beautiful place," Smith relocated to Hollywood, Florida in 1970. Among the gripes he had with New York City: the snow and traffic, and "the somewhat disorderliness of the court and justice system." He immediately jumped into the local political fray and very soon thereafter was President of the PTA of the local elementary school where his children attended. He also chaired the South Broward Bar Association, the Hollywood Planning and Zoning Board and helped found a synagogue, Temple Solel.

By 1978, Smith was elected to the Florida State House where in his last term, he chaired the House Criminal Justice Committee. *Congressional Quarterly*, noting Smith's emphasis on criminal justice issues wrote how, "responding to Florida's recent preoccupation with crime problems…(he) kept his committee busy passing a variety of law to crack down on criminals." He sponsored anti-drunk-driving legislation and secured new judgeships for a booming area. That proved a feather in his cap when he sought higher office.

Florida was the beneficiary of four new House districts as a result of the 1982 reapportionment and Smith pursued one of the safely Democratic House seats that was centered on South Broward County and a small portion of Dade. The primary was a friends, neighbors and what some called a "battle of the condominiums" contest between Smith and ex-State Representative Alan Becker who, after losing a race for Attorney General in 1978 and a Congressional seat to Clay Shaw two years later, was hoping to make the third time a charm. Smith had other ideas.

For starters, Becker had moved from Miami Beach to Plantation only three years earlier, leading Smith to say, "I don't think you should be able to go to Congress and represent the community unless you have proven that you have worked in the community in the past." Becker contended that his law firm had served many of the district's condominiums on legal matters (they are about as common here as skyscrapers in New York City) and earned gratification for his work in the legislature when it came to bills on safety violations. Yet Smith had far more establishment backing, particularly from unions and while his distinct Brooklyn accent might have been a liability in other portions of Florida, it was likely an asset in territory with so many Northern transplants. To remind voters that he was indeed a member of the tribe, he referenced the fact that his wife's maiden name was "Cohen." Plus, he had plenty of energy, telling *The Miami Herald*, "My problem is that there aren't more of me. My goal would be to meet everybody. I can't. That's more frustrating than anything else." Smith also dwarfed Becker in finances, spending nearly double that of his foe (campaign staff did prevail on him to part with his red Corvette, surmising it might be an impediment).

The race was largely considered a tossup in its final days but Smith put it away rather comfortably. He carried Broward 58-42% while Becker took Dade 57-43%. But Broward was 2/3 of the district which was enough for a 55-45% win for Smith (Becker responded to the returns with puzzlement telling a reporter it "beats the hell out of me"). Yet when Smith needed professional rehabilitation after a low period in life (see later in the chapter), Becker was among the first to reach out to him and land on his feet. The general election was no contest as Smith racked up 68% (though a mere 52% in Dade) against Maurice Berkowitz, the vice-chairman of the Commission of Port Everglades.

Smith faced a more formidable challenge against State Representative Tom Bush in 1984 and lost Dade 2-1, but took 64% in Broward for a 56% win. His general elections were easy after that though, given that one opponent shared the same last name – Joseph Smith in 1988, he joked that, "even I had to be very careful when I went into the booth to vote for myself" (voters were not confused and Smith took 69%).

In Congress, Smith was assigned to the Foreign Affairs and Judiciary Committees, posts that were right up his alley. He won a coveted seat on Appropriations at the start of his fifth and final term.

Smith's mission of fighting for Israel's interests began in his very first term. In 1984, he introduced a bill prohibiting the sales by the Reagan administration of Stinger air defense guided missile systems to Jordan and Saudi Arabia which garnered 91 co-sponsors. The administration backed down – but only for that year.

The following year, the administration wanted to sell F-16 and F-20 planes to the nation and Smith and other Israel supporters were not assuaged when Secretary of State George Shultz proposed the idea of the president simply certifying that their intentions were sound. They called that impractical. In 1985, he sponsored an amendment to the FY 1986 Foreign Assistance Authorization Act requiring the president to certify that Jordan supports Israel's right to exist "and has agreed to enter into prompt and direct peace negotiations before allowing a major arms sale." Jordan protested but Smith told *The Christian Science Monitor* that while he, "commends (Jordan) for trying to take steps toward peace, we have to say, 'Until you give us something we can utilize in the peace process, you can't expect us to give you everything you want.'" He also contended that additional arms would "upset the qualitative arms balance" in the region. Ted Kennedy and John Heinz were the Senate sponsors and Joint Resolution 228 convincingly passed both chambers.

This was not the first time Smith got on the wrong side of Jordan's King Hussein. Another Congressman with the surname Smith, Democratic Representative Neal Smith of Iowa, recalls a trip to Jordan with Smith and his fellow Florida Democrat, Bill Lehman when Smith expressed displeasure with King Hussein over his treatment of the Israelis following the Six Day War. The King responded testily and told Smith that Israeli Defense Minister Moshe Dayan had come in and began occupying a big part of the country. "As long as they are here occupying my country," Hussein said, "we are at war."

Smith and his staff
Photo courtesy of Larry Smith

In 1988, Smith, along with New York Democrat Charles Schumer and Maryland Republican Connie Morella authored a letter to Shultz urging him to cancel "Bradley fighting vehicles, TOW missiles and AWACKS support system" that had been planned for Saudi Arabia. And in 1990, Smith protested when the Bush administration included M-1 tanks in its sale to Saudi Arabia. "I am disappointed that what they have put in this package does not accord with my understanding of what would be done in the short term and the long term."

Smith also had a message for President George H.W. Bush for any negotiations he might enter into with PLO leader Yasser Arafat. The United States, he said, should draw a "line in the sand. If there are any more terrorist incidents by anyone close to you, we will hold you responsible."

Smith took on other matters important to the Jewish community. In 1986, he circulated a petition among Floridians calling for the Soviet Union to allow Jews to emigrate. In an interview with *The Jewish Floridian*, Smith said he wanted it to coincide with Reagan's upcoming summit with Mikhail Gorbachev. The goal was to get Reagan to, "bring up as an integral part of any summit…or any Soviet-U.S. discussion, the issue of human rights and Soviet Jewry and Soviet emigration."

Shelia Smith was a founding member of the Congressional Wives for Soviet Jewry and traveled to Europe with other members wives to further the attempts to get emigration for the Jewish community in the Soviet Union. Smith himself was with Natan Sharansky and traveled to the Soviet Union to meet with political leaders on the issue.

It wasn't simply Israel on which Smith could be perturbed with Reagan/ Bush. He once pronounced himself, "personally cheated" by administration promises vs. reality involving Lebanon.

Smith was also member of The House Select Committee on Narcotics Abuse and Control and worked closely with the panel's chair, Edward Feighan of Ohio. That gave him many opportunities to display his acerbic streak. One instance was in 1984 when the Reagan administration testified that jurisdictional disputes were largely a thing of the past. Smith verbalized to reporters that, "A good game is being talked, but that's all." On another occasion, he questioned, "How can I tell other countries that the United States disapproves their anti-drug efforts when the United States government itself is neglecting to deal with its own failed policies?" One tangible result of Smith's crusade against the abuse of drugs came when he succeeded in outlawing Quaaludes after having done the same in the state of Florida.

One perhaps classic example of Smith's productive pugnacity. He made it known to Dade County officials that he was not happy about not being sufficiently recognized as a member of the delegation. His district only contained 20% of the county but he was very popular in the Cuban community in Dade and always won a majority of their votes in his district. While Smith disputed *Sun Sentinel* claims that he was yelling at that particular meeting, he did respond that what he was trying to communicate his message, which was, "I thought it was incumbent on them to understand I represent a significant part of the county. I think most of the Dade County elective officials forget there is a Congressman who represents the district west of the Palmetto Expressway from the Dade County line to Bird Road, and I happen to be that Congressman."

In 1991, Smith interjected himself into a dispute between proponents of the space station and those that wanted a moratorium in order for housing programs to be funded. An amendment he proposed would require funding of the space station to come from NASA but it was defeated. "This is another one of those votes we are being asked to take against people, against American citizens who somehow become, for at least some members on the other side, the lowest priority in this country. This is not for projects, it is not for programs, it is not for a space station; it is not for anything but people." He went on to assert that "guns for butter is no longer an economic theory with any relevance with regard to the budget process in this country. You can no longer decide to reduce guns and increase butter."

Photo courtesy of Larry Smith

Smith's ardent defense of Israel might have produced among the most memorable exchanges between a member of Congress and the administration on U.S.-Israel policy. Secretary of State James Baker was testifying before the Appropriations Foreign Operations Subcommittee on Israel's request for loan guarantees. Some backers of the Jewish State viewed the administration's response as ambiguous and others simply hostile. Smith fell firmly in the latter camp, particularly when the conditions Baker delineated was not using money to build additional settlements. Smith saliently told Baker he found that attitude "extremely offensive." The secretary responded, "Larry, I will determine when I finish my answers, not you." An angry Smith responded by throwing his glasses on the table and saying, "I hope that someday the American public is going to determine whether you finish your answers. It's disgraceful." The clip was widely circulated on nightly news outlets and, in spite of Smith's forthcoming problems, might have marked his 15-minutes of fame. The gesture was not impulsive. Unlike George and Barbara Bush, whom Smith always found to be most-welcoming regardless of strong political differences, Smith never found himself able to have a substantive conversation with Baker on virtually anything.

When Saddam Hussein invaded Kuwait in 1990, Smith spoke of punishing nations, particularly Brazil and China that sold nuclear weapon technology to Iraq. The following January, however, he opposed the Congressional resolution authorizing President Bush to use force against Iraq. One reason was not knowing its cost, which he said the administration was not providing. On the House floor, he asked colleagues, "Is that fair for you to make the most important decision of your careers, your lives, affecting your neighbor's children, husbands, and wives, based on no information? Third of all, it is premature."

Locally, Smith was a big opponent of drilling off the Florida Keys and in 1990, he tried to prevent a future tug of war over whether the federal government or Florida should pay for the repurchase of the 73 leases. Legislation he introduced would give oil companies a credit. In the summer of 1990, Bush ultimately cancelled new leases until the year 2000. Smith was solidly anti-Castro and resisted efforts to disband Radio Marti. In 1990, signed a letter urging Mikhail Gorbachev to end aid to Cuba. But he switched to support aid to the Nicaraguan contras in 1985. Explaining his change of heart, Smith said, "You have to monitor and watch the facts as they change and change with them," calling some of Ortega's policy, "a slap in the face. I'm opposed to intervention. I don't want to see one American serviceman fighting in Central America. But I think the way you avoid it is to keep the pressure up on the Sandinistas." Smith at one point co-chaired a task force on the matter with Pennsylvania Democrat Peter Kostmayer.

Smith was also prescient. As early as the late 1980s, he had been the first member of Congress to predict that there would one day be a terrorist attack in the United States. He chaired the Congressional Affairs Committee Task Force on International Narcotics and Terrorism.

On other issues, Smith was a solid liberal. He was vehemently pro-choice and usually voted with labor. He undertook an effort to ban Saturday Night Specials and sponsored a bill with New Jersey Democrat William J. Hughes banning the sale of machine guns. When the chamber debated an amendment banning flag burning, Smith questioned where it would end. "If you took a copy of the Constitution out you could burn it with impunity...The flag is just a piece of cloth. Pay tribute to what the country is, not the flag."

How did Smith's productive pugnacity play with his staff. To hear Bernie Friedman, his 1982 campaign manager and Chief of Staff tell it, the quality was pretty refreshing. For one, "you always knew where you stood and what was on his mind. He did have strong opinions." Among other things, this applied to drafts and whether he liked them or didn't. Friedman is clear that if Smith had to "get something off his chest, five-minutes later he was wonderful."

Smith was also not self-centered. Staff called him "Larry," interns were treated in the Members Dining Room and he insisted on sharing the credit. Smith was "incredibly proud of his staff when there was good in the office." Smith was also more "self-sufficient" than many members and often drove himself both as a Congressman and during campaigns. While Friedman was entrusted with making staff-level decisions, there was one requirement that he deferred to Smith: advice on who to use for catering events (hosting groups or constituents). Why? Smith's family background made that critical.

After U.S. Senator Lawton Chiles upended the political world by announcing his retirement in 1988, Smith flirted with the idea of running to succeed him but ultimately declared himself, "very happy and comfortable in the House. I believe that I will be in positions of leadership and importance in the very near future, and I think it's important for people of seniority to stay in the House and do the job that needs to be done."

Smith was unopposed for re-election in 1990 and, even with the uncertainties of redistricting looming, could probably have held the seat indefinitely. Even the unwelcome distraction of having 161 overdrafts at the so-called House bank might not have been enough to dislodge him given the relative compactness of his district (Smith, like so many members, lived by the rules explained to him that checks could be drawn within the next month's salary). By May 1992, however, he decided it was not worth the price.

**With former colleague and friend, Steny Hoyer of Maryland
Photo courtesy of Larry Smith**

In what *Roll Call* labeled, "one of the more unusual of the dozens of retirement announcements this year," Smith taped a two-minute speech telling his constituents why he wouldn't stand for a sixth term, at the top of which was, "Washington doesn't work anymore." In the days following his announcement, Smith shared some of those reasons more in-depth. To *The Sun-Sentinal*, he spoke of the financial toll. "I gave the best, most productive years of my life — ages 37 to 51 — and I have nothing to show for it," he said. "I really do need to turn my attention now to making my financial situation a little better so I can fulfill my obligations as a husband and as a father." Citing a potential list of successors – none of whom actually won, Smith said, "These are people who believe in the same things I do. There may be others. I've never considered myself so important that I couldn't be replaced by someone else."

A lame duck he was but Smith was not about to render himself moot for the rest of his term. He stumped all over the country for Democratic Presidential candidate Bill Clinton, saying Bush, "poisoned the well" against Israel "for domestic reasons by singling out Jews."

The immediate transition from statesmen to private citizen was marked by insult and injury. Reports had come to the surface before he left office that he had used $4,000 from his campaign fund to pay a gambling debt in the Bahamas and took illegal contributions from his former law partner, which was given back. Smith said he's "not a gambler," and called it, "a spur-of-the-moment decision that was a mistake." All moneys were repaid but Smith ultimately was forced to plead guilty to failing to report income and improper use of the campaign fund and was sentenced to three months in a minimum security prison. His lawyer called it "an isolated incident," and said Smith, "recognizes it was poor judgment on his part." As he addressed the jury as he was about to be sentenced, Smith pronounced himself, "ashamed and small" but contended he "never stole a dime."

The episode cost Smith his bar license for three years and it would not be retroactive to the date of conviction (a slight cry from the two-year retroactive sentence the judge wanted). Smith nevertheless landed on his feet and would become big again. In the years since, he has rehabilitated himself as a successful lobbyist in the nation's capitol and an attorney in Florida. His son Grant has aided him as well. He remains appreciative by the people of Israel for all that he accomplished on her behalf. And for his attitude on this and other things he cared about, he apologizes to no one.

CHAPTER FORTY

Levine's Gravitas Led to Many Accomplishments but Not a Senate Seat

Introductory Quote: "I've been told to take half a loaf; it's better than none. I find that unacceptable in the area of human needs." – Mel Levine during his commencement address at Harvard University

Levine with his kids, son Adam (8) and twins, Cara and Jake (5) at a Congressional Baseball Game
Photo via Getty Images

California Congressman Mel Levine was an immensely talented Representative who had his finger on the pulse of issues of his socially liberal, Jewish and trade-minded district. His intelligence and easygoing manner made the coastal Los Angeles Democrat a serious player on a wide variety of issues and could easily have made him a national player had he not been stymied by a quest for higher office (in his case the U.S. Senate) in 1992.

Levine (La-VINE) was a former marathon runner and a product of the legendary Henry Waxman-Howard Berman machine. While the term "machine" to him is "overused and inaccurate," as members of Congress, the trio did share a treasurer and collaborated over how to distribute the wealth among candidates they supported. But unlike his two colleagues who were able to keep going in Congress literally for decades, Levine saw an opportunity for a promotion, took it, only to fall flat and fade into political oblivion.

The observation of a publication that Levine was, "articulate and wealthy, pleasant but hard-driving" is a pretty accurate summation of this lawyer/legislator's career. Though Levine successfully appealed to most segments of his district, he did hail from a well-to-do family which prompted *The LA Times* to quip that he was "no pampered prep-schooler." In fact, Levine's background spanned coast to coast and encompassed at least some financial modesty early on.

Levine's paternal grandparents emigrated from Russia to New York City around the beginning of the century but moved to L.A. when his grandpa couldn't find anyone to hire him and not work on the Sabbath. His maternal grandparents had settled in San Francisco from Romania and Canada and met when they were dealing with the after effects of the epic 1906 earthquake.

Levine was born in the Los Feliz section of L.A., but was raised in Hancock Park until his family moved to Beverly Hills when he was 15. For no reason other than the fact that he hailed from L.A., Levine was forced to repeat ninth grade, but "then they skipped me from the ninth to the eleventh grade so I actually ended up only going to Beverly High a little more than two years…and compressed my high school education into two years and three months." Levine's father was a Republican and close to legendary moderate Senator Tom Kuchel (his mother was a Democrat which proved the axiom, "politics makes strange bedfellows") and Mel admits that, "much to my retrospective embarrassment," he was for Richard Nixon against John F. Kennedy during the 1960 presidential campaign. By 1967, he was backing Bobby Kennedy for a race against President Lyndon B. Johnson that the New York Senator had yet to undertake. Levine credits attending school at UC-Berkeley for his political metamorphosis.

When it came time for higher education, Levine came "within a hairsbreath" of attending West Point University but his mother vetoed it. Instead, he pursued his undergrad at Berkeley and as he recalled during a 2004 oral history interview for the State Archives, "it exposed me to a diversity and a breadth and series of experiences and people and issues and ideas that I had no knowledge of and it also exposed me to an interest in politics, if not a passion about politics that I didn't have before." Levine apparently also became confident in his own abilities because he started running for office at Berkeley "the moment I got there because I just loved the place and thought it would be fun." His first win was freshman class president and his last was student body president (he delivered the commencement address to boot).

After Berkeley, Levine attended Princeton University to earn his Master's in Public Administration at the Woodrow Wilson School of Public and International Affairs. One might say Princeton was most valuable for Levine's future world because with only 29 students in the program, "I learned how to write and I learned how to think more analytically." From there, he landed at Harvard University where he pursued his law degree and delivered the commencement address. He told fellow graduates how, "We are told to follow 'the system.' But when I look at that 'system,' I see...standards but not compassion." Levine then began practicing law at the firm of Wyman, Bautzer, Rothman and Kuchel.

Levine's political involvement began as a legislative assistant to California Democratic Senator John Tunney which he called, "doing the legislative work without having to do the politics." That would soon change. When West Side Assemblyman Alan Sieroty moved to the Senate in late 1976, Levine, who was partnering in a law firm, Levine, Krom and Unger went for his 44th District seat (primarily based in Santa Monica, Venice and Century City). Despite poor odds in the beginning, he assembled a cadre of supporters nearly any first-time contenders would die for: Hubert Humphrey and Alan Cranston on the left and Kuchel and moderate former Congressman Al Bell on the right. The first round was an all-party primary of ten Democrats, two Republicans and a Libertarian. Levine advanced to the runoff, prevailing against Ruth Yannatta, who had been affiliated with liberal activist Tom Hayden by roughly 1,700 votes. He won the general a month later over attorney Dana Reed 56-44%. By 1978, Levine was up to 69%, a margin he came close to matching two years later.

Levine's niche was energy issues and he would quickly rise to the chairmanship of the Energy subcommittee. He opposed a liquefied natural gas terminal (lng) in Southern California and was one of two votes against it on Resources, angering Kuchel who served on an influential board that wanted the project.

The late 1970s was a time "solar was in its infancy," and Levine proposed the Solar Rights Act of 1978. It authorized the right of people to create Solar Access easements and Levine proudly notes it is still on the books today. One law that never made it to the books to Levine's profound frustration was one that he spent most of his time in Sacramento pursuing. It would have allowed property owners to contract with owners for access to the sun and require homes and apartments to be retrofitted for energy conservation before selling. Real estate, builders and utility interests initially opposed it and Levine spent four years carefully weaving together language that satisfied all parties. It finally passed the Assembly in 1982 but died in the Senate one vote short at midnight on the last day of the session. Levine also authored the Conservation Tax Credit legislation. Beyond that, Kurt Stone in *The Jews of Capitol Hill* wrote that 61 bills bearing Levine's name became law and that the job was ideal because, "it was doing the legislative work without having to do the politics."

Speaker Willie Brown wanted Levine to chair the Criminal Justice Committee but his interest was limited and by that point, he had Congress in his sites. As he recalled to the oral history project, "I didn't want to be the point person as the chairman on issues that were as controversial as that at that time where I knew my positions would be lightning rod positions."

In the Assembly, Levine was one of Berman's best friends and biggest supporters as he sought the Speakership but Willie Brown ultimately won the post as a compromise choice. At that time, the duo "both concluded our future was probably brighter if we went to Washington." With friends in high places, that actually went according to plan. The architect of the 1982 remap was powerful Democratic Congressman Phil Burton who labeled it, "my contribution to modern art" and Levine and Berman were prime benefactors.

The coast saw the removal of a number of heavy Republican enclaves from a district that was already a marginal district, albeit one where Republicans usually prevailed, including Palos Verdes Peninsula. It compensated by adding Democratic Santa Monica and Jewish areas. Another thing that added appeal to Levine: 40% of his legislative constituents fell into the boundaries of this district. Add that to the fact that the current Congressman, arch-conservative Republican Robert "Bob" Dornan had already announced that he'd be leaving the seat behind to pursue a Senate bid and it was practically made for his taking, which was confirmed near the filing deadline as no Democrat file to challenge Levine. He won the general over country club owner Bart Christensen with 59%.

Waxman viewed Levine as a natural for a seat on the Energy and Commerce Committee but titanic chair John Dingell, a longtime Waxman nemesis, saw Levine as another Waxman vote on clean air matters and vetoed the choice. It mattered little – Levine could utilize his talents on whatever legislative endeavors he would undertake, which Waxman and Berman attested to. Waxman said, "People looked up to Mel as a serious legislator, a man who understands policy and who can give a thoughtful answer to anything that's asked of him." Berman called Levine, "a creative smart legislator with a winning personality that allowed him to work with colleagues effectively, regardless of party or ideology."

Swearing-in Day
Photo courtesy of Mel Levine

In office, Levine had a broad array of legislative interests but foreign policy and environmental protection topped his portfolio, and his seats on the Foreign Affairs Committee and Interior were central for pursuing these interests. The War on Drugs was another passion and Levine's 1989 assignment to the Judiciary Committee was important for that area.

Articulating the interests of Israel was a ritual that Levine eagerly and devotedly fulfilled throughout his entire tenure. His first term saw an unusual number of high-profile successes on that front, one of which was pushing through language requiring "standards" for negotiations with the Palestinian Liberation Authority (PLO). The 1984 Summer Olympics were in Los Angeles and Levine signed a letter criticizing the attempt by the PLO to establish an Olympic team as, "morally repugnant and inconsistent with the international organization's charter. We would think that recognition of the PLO by the IOC (International Olympics Committee) would be unthinkable in light of the massacre of Israeli athletes in the 1972 Munich Games by an affiliate of the PLO." In 1988, Levine circulated a letter with Republican John Miller of Washington taking Secretary of State George Shultz to task for meeting with people with ties to the PLO. He spoke heavily against the Reagan administration's proposed $200 million cut in aid to Israel.

Photo courtesy of Mel Levine

In later years, when the Reagan and Bush administrations wanted to provide infrastructure to nations that had uncertain records or intentions, the focus of Levine and other allies of Israel were concentrated on trying to get the best possible deal for the Jewish State. One instance was Reagan's desire to sell planes to Saudi Arabia which Levine, citing, "an atrocious Saudi track record regarding U.S. interests" found inconceivable. Hence, he led the effort to remove Stinger missiles from that sale. Two years later, Levine worked with his Foreign Affairs Committee colleague, Larry Smith of Florida, to make the administration's proposed Kuwait arm sale more favorable to Israel.

Levine also chided the Japanese for both not being more supportive of Israel during the Persian Gulf War and for participating in the Arab boycott. It was perhaps with the idea of preventing future deals that in 1987, he sponsored the Arms Export Reform Act. The Senate sponsor was Joseph R. Biden of Delaware. A similar bill had been proposed by Levine and Democratic Senator Claiborne Pell of Rhode Island the previous year and Levine contended it "takes on an additional timeliness" because the Iran-Contra arms scandal was starting to percolate. Finally, he worked on mechanisms allowing Syrian Jews to emigrate.

Levine worked on other foreign policy initiatives. Condemning Reagan's, "Gunboat diplomacy," he advocated placing limits on America's presence in Central America. Amid rejections by the Pakistani government to open investigations, Levine in 1987 sponsored a resolution pending "verifiable" proof that it is not conducting nuclear tests. He accused the government of doing, "arrogant violations of our laws and trust" due to "obvious and repeated attempts to acquire a nuclear weapons capability."

After the Chinese massacre at Tiananmen Square, Levine proposed a six-month export expansion suspension and in October 1990, voiced disapproval with Bush's plan to bestow Most-Favored Nation Status on China. "President Bush's kow-towing to the Chinese leadership has failed to deliver any meaningful improvements in the People's Republic of China," he said on the House floor. "The human rights crisis has grown worse, not better…And then, just in case the Beijing leadership didn't get the message that the United States would ignore the killings, repression and continued persecution of dissenters, the administration called for renewal of Most Favored Nation Status for the People's Republic of China in June…. Emigration and travel outside of China have always been tightly restricted by the Chinese authorities, and exit permits are routinely denied, particularly if there is any evidence, even a false confession extracted under duress, of participation under the democracy movement."

Representing a trade-heavy district, Levine chaired the House Task Force on Exports and once said the U.S. must "sink and swim" with Japan." He wasn't always that magnanimous when he saw U.S. interests threatened. When a Japanese company, Fanuc Ltd, wanted to invest 40% in Moore Special Tool Co., Levine spearheaded a letter to the administration to nix approval, arguing that, "No case could be a clearer candidate for CFIUS rejection." It would allow "a vital component of our domestically owned defense industrial base to be controlled by foreign owners who do not share American national security interests." Fanuc withdrew the offer.

Levine, along with Berman (though not Waxman) supported the Gulf War. His reasoning: "What cannot be achieved by diplomacy or sanctions alone is our ability to defeat Saddam's increased ability to utilize chemical, biological and nuclear weapons. We must be willing to act now or face the grave risk of Saddam's nuclear weapons to the nation into the world."

Closer to home, environmental issues were quite pressing in this district and in Levine's first term, he and several other California legislators blocked Interior Secretary James Watt and EPA Administrator Ann Burford Gorsuch (mother of the current U.S. Supreme Court Justice Neil Gorsuch) form sinking oil wells in environmentally sensitive coastal waters. One of these waters was the Santa Monica Bay, much of which touched his district. He fought against offshore drilling and led the fight against Occidental Petroleum's proposed Proposition O. And he sponsored a resolution to establish the Manzanar National Historic Site in the Sierra Nevada's Owens Valley and a Japanese American National Historic Landmark Theme Study Act.

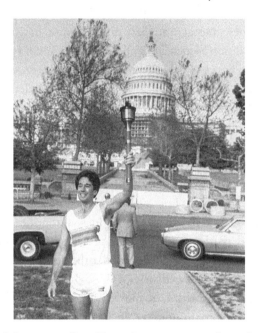

Levine didn't just run for office – he ran in a number of marathons
Photo via Getty Images

Beginning in 1986, he began sponsoring the California Desert Protection Act which contained the creation of national parks for, among others, Death Valley, Joshua Tree, and the Mojave Desert. Although popular with environmentalists, the Act met resistance from other segments for its prohibitions on recreational vehicles. Duncan Hunter of San Diego captured the discontent when he said, "Conditions in the desert are hard and vehicles are a must" and another California Republican, Jerry Lewis of Redlands, proposed an alternative that critics actually said would be a step back (it did not contain much national park protection). Even some Democrats were not on board. Senator Dale Bumpers of Arkansas cited, "significant detrimental effects on mining and grazing interests and to recreational users" In late 1991, the measure did pass the House 297-136 but, Republican Senator John

Seymour resorted to dilatory tactics and it took the 103rd Congress, when Levine was out of office to gain enactment.

Levine was a persistent advocate for seeing that the HDTV (high-definition television) realized its maximal potential. As co-chair of the HDTV task force, he argued that the headway the Japanese had made with the device was an overriding reason for the U.S. to invest in its success. "If ceding HDTV development helps foreigners monopolize the next generation of electronic components," he wrote in *The New York Times*, "it will not be long before America becomes a second-rate manufacturing power." Government aid was a necessity and he viewed a consortium as the way to go.

Photo courtesy of C-SPAN

Levine was one of four Congressional leaders of the Military Reform Caucus (his co-chairs were Republican Congressman Denny Smith of Oregon, Democratic Senator David Pryor of Arkansas and Republican Charles Grassley of Iowa). According to Levine Chief of Staff Bill Andresen, its goal was to investigate the purchasing of weapons "that were too sophisticated, not reliable and weren't being adequately tested."

The tobacco industry and Levine were anything but two peas in a pod. He wanted tobacco exports to be substantially regulated, contending that as it currently stood, "the message we are sending is that Asian lungs are more expendable than American lungs." To accomplish that, Levine filed a bill with Massachusetts Democrat Chet Atkins requiring warning labels for cigarette cartons sold overseas. He was a stalwart supporter of gun control. In 1988, he proposed the Toy Gun Safety and Child Protection Act and as the Brady Bill came up for discussion, he tried to convince colleagues that a counter proposal by Democrat Harley Staggers of West Virginia was far weaker. The Staggers bill, he said, led to a, "a particular misunderstanding that seems to be going around on the floor today by simply emphasizing that it is utterly inconsistent to believe that one can vote both for the Staggers amendment and the Brady bill. A vote for Staggers is purely and simply a vote to kill the Brady bill. Passage of the Staggers amendment would be a cruel hoax on the American people. They would be urged to believe they were getting safer streets legislation, but what we would really be giving them is a whopping tax bill and a vague background check sometime in the 21st century."

Levine was both popular and respected with his colleagues. He was the pitcher on the Democratic baseball team and forged strong relationships with far more conservative colleagues by getting to know them on the mound, the House gym, etc. He was beloved among his staff as well. Andresen started with Levine in his earliest days in the Assembly and served as his Chief of Staff throughout his entire decade in Congress. He calls his boss "very gracious and appreciative toward the staff" (holiday parties, etc.) and "a hard guy not to like."

Come election time, Levine was fairly secure but his percentage dipped noticeably in 1984 as he sought a second term. Though Levine found himself a surprising target from former Rams running back Robert Scribner, it was he who had his eye off the ball (he was busy campaigning against a statewide proposition that would roll back the Burton remap). Scribner was a member of the evangelical Foursquare Gospel Church and he asked voters to, "link arms with us as we literally take territory for our Lord Jesus Christ." Reagan was carrying the district and Levine hung on by a modest 55-42%. Scribner was back two years later but Levine got the message and won by a touchdown - 64% and easily in his subsequent two races.

In 1992, Levine saw circumstances and his own ambitions for statewide office intersect. One was his longstanding desire to seek higher office, as he had flirted with the idea of making a Senate run in '88 (ironically, it was Leo McCarthy who became the Democratic standard bearer). By 1992, the decision was almost made for him. The state's new redistricting plan placed Levine in a district with Waxman and another Democrat, Anthony Beilenson. Waxman never intended to run there but Levine's dilemma should he wished to remain in the House was to challenge Beilenson or run in a newly created, more Republican leaning district. Levine decided he might as well put it all on the line and run for the Senate (ironically, Jane Harman did manage to hold the new district for Democrats).

Taking this route was as risky as can be. Levine would be facing two opponents in the primary – the state's Lieutenant Governor, Leo McCarthy and his much more liberal colleague to the north, Barbara Boxer of San Francisco. On top of that, his name recognition was low and California is both expansive and expensive which means getting acquainted with voters would require big moolah.

McCarthy as a statewide official was perceived as the front-runner and polls in both the beginning and middle of the campaign bore that out. This was not the first time Levine and McCarthy had at least indirectly butted heads. In 1980, it was McCarthy whom Berman was trying to depose as Speaker and Levine, in part because, as Levine would later recall, "There was a sense that Leo was focused more on Leo than he was on the caucus."

Levine, whom *The Los Angeles Times'* observed, "is such a boyish-looking 48 that he still looks like everyone's younger brother," seemed to gain a little momentum toward the close of 1991 and for a time, it turned out to be anyone's race. But he had the misfortune of making the race just after the Anita Hill accusations against Clarence Thomas and it was clear that the "Year of the Woman" was upon the nation. How powerful was it? Just before it made the headlines, Boxer was having such fundraising woes that she was reportedly ready to hang up shop. After, she was all but unstoppable.

Levine had other hurdles for which he did little to overcome. One was his lack of press-the-flesh campaigning. Instead, he put most of his eggs in the advertisement basket, spending $4 million (his consultant was BAD Campaign, which was run by Berman's brother and his partner, Carl D'Agostino). It required much time on the phone dialing for dollars, which the book, *Running as a Woman: Gender and Power in American Politics* noted caused his phone bill to swell to $61,229. Raising money proved no problem but the lack of time on the trail garnered him the nickname, the "stealth candidate." That prompted *The LA Times* to run a headline, "Levine Meet's The People – In Sister's Back Yard." The paper cited one fundraiser, as containing, "extended family. You know...Steven Spielberg, Sally Field, Billy Crystal and a few others from show biz, the law, business and politics." Levine responded to the naysayers by promising a repeat of his first election to the legislature when he surprised the pundits and establishment. "It's not early name recognition that wins elections. It's the ability to inspire the electorate between now and Election Day."

With roughly ten weeks before the June primary, Levine began unleashing his war chest. A Star Wars theme and a James Earl Jones voiceover were two highlights (every commercial would end with the Jones words, "wisdom, courage, one of a kind, Democrat for Senate, Mel Levine," and his support increased from single digits to 20%. He emphasized his support for the death penalty. The House bank scandal gave him a mechanism to highlight to his zero overdrafts – Boxer conversely had 143, and he told voters, "My account's at a local bank, like yours" (he did have a House bank account at one point but gave it up). In one of the most virulently anti-incumbent years, Levine did not disparage the fact that he was an officeholder. "My ads make very clear that I am Congressman Mel Levine running for Senate. I am certainly not trying to define myself as an outsider because I am not one."

At that time, he was polling just 7% and many questioned the wisdom of waiting so long to advertise. Levine also saw an opening with the Los Angeles riots six weeks before primary day and one of his ads cited "a failure of political leadership. A democratic society can't tolerate mob rule." He even went after his own leadership on the issue of urban unrest, verbalizing how, "You have Republicans who basically talk very tough law-and-order talk and aren't prepared to provide the resources to do anything about it, and you have Democrats who sweep it under the rug, who won't deal with it, who won't even talk about it." He also said, "We have people terrified to go out their front door." Some ads that Levine's campaign team aired were done without his knowledge and he would not have approved them.

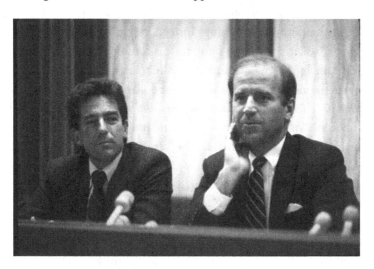

Two very respected voices on foreign affairs – Levine and
future Vice-President Joe Biden of Delaware
Photo via Getty Images

By primary day, Boxer had vaulted into the lead and the come from behind win Levine had talked about did not materialize. He took just 21% as Boxer won 43% with McCarthy earning 30%. Levine was shut out from the map altogether as he failed to carry a single county and in fact was consigned to just 26% even in L.A (he does proudly point out that he carried the most heavily African-American Congressional district in L.A.). As his term neared an end, Levine offered a rationale for doing so poorly: "I happened to run in the year of the woman. I didn't represent change the way Barbara did because of her gender and her message." Still, the race both began and ended between two allies and Levine assisted Boxer in the general election, which she narrowly won. He also lamented about how proud he is of nearly every aspect of his career, except for the Senate race.

Photo courtesy of Mel Levine

Levine finished his term in Congress and embraced the world of both law and boards. He is President of the Los Angeles Board of Water and Power Commissioners, on the Advisory Board of the Goldman School of Public Policy at the University of California (Berkeley), and a Director of the Pacific Council on International Policy. He takes pride in pointing out that all of these boards are non-profits. Not neglecting Jewish affairs, Vice-President Al Gore asked him to get involved with co-President of Builders for Peace, which was the private sectors commitment to the peace process (Levine became its co-chairman). He later became the U.S. Chair of the U.S.-Israel-Palestinian "Anti-Incitement" Committee. Named one of the 100 Most Influential Lawyers" in California, he has repeatedly made the list of one of the "Best Lawyers in America." He practices international law at Gibson, Dunn & Crutcher.

CHAPTER FORTY-ONE

Yatron and Gaydos Old School, Ethnic
Democrats Who Tended to Home Folks Needs

Introductory Quote: For four years in his early days, Pennsylvania Gus Yatron was a famed boxer so, when he thought he would have an opportunity to box legends Jimmy Ellis and Joe Frazier on Capitol Hill in 1970, he was ecstatic (another Congressman, Jim Wright of Texas, was also supposed to take part). But House Speaker John McCormack was an old-fashioned, 79-year old who was worried about the propriety of using a House building for a money-making event and he canceled it. Yatron had been practicing for months and called himself, "tense and up for it." Wright was less diplomatic. He told The New York Times he was "mortified," calling it, "the most glaring example of bad manners I've seen in 16 years in Congress. We invited the two best boxers in the nation here, and then we withdrew the invitation at the last minute think it's atrocious."

Gus Yatron and Joe Gaydos
Photos courtesy of George Yatron (left) and Joe Gaydos Jr. (right)

1992 saw the retirement of two Democratic Congressmen from the Keystone State who were both elected in 1968 – Gus Yatron and Joe Gaydos. The two had different backgrounds –Yatron, a 6'1, 250 pound boxer, took the business route as an ice cream proprietor (Yatron's Ice Cream) while Gaydos took the more traditional route - an assistant attorney general and labor lawyer. But both were State Senators directly before headed to Congress, though Yatron's service in the legislature was a dozen years and Gaydos's briefer – just under two years.

Each was indicative of the old school, ethnic politicians that was predominant in a large segment of Congress in their day (Yatron was proudly Greek-American while Gaydos was the first Slovick ever elected to Congress). This meant generally shunning the limelight and toying behind the scenes, while showing up dutifully to vote. It also made them traditional Democrats – for example, opposing abortion, not supporting every attempt to ratify the ERA but backing the amendment prohibiting the desecration of the flag. But their "for the people" credentials were solid and their advocacy on behalf of their districts was always among their most admirable attributes and, throughout their durations in Congress, they never forgot their humble roots.

Gus Yatron

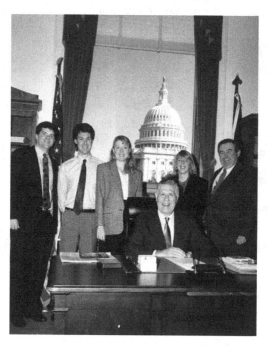

Yatron and his staff
Photo courtesy of George Yatron

The Sixth Congressional District was far enough from Philly that it was not the suburbs but close enough to Lancaster and Harrisburg to be considered central Pennsylvania. Blue-collar, working class Reading was the main ingredient but Schuylkill (Skoo-kie) and Carbon encompassed prominent portions.

Throughout his entire life, Yatron was a faithful son of Reading. His parents, however, were Greek immigrants from Mytilene on the island of Lesbos. Born Constantine Yatron, "Gus" drove a delivery truck for his father, the original owner of Yatron's Ice Cream. A tackle on his high school football team, he earned his degree from Kutztown State Teachers College where he met his future wife Millie. Yatron had another passion in those days – boxing. He was a professional heavyweight who became something of a mini-celebrity with a 13-2-1 record. Heavyweight sports were not uncommon to Yatron who played football for the Golden Bears and by the time he made it to Congress, had his colleagues marveling at his ability to hit the speed bag in the gym.

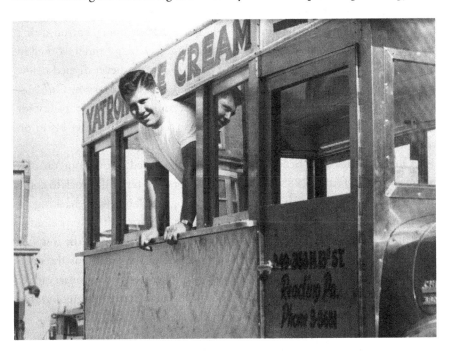

Yatron the ice cream man
Photo courtesy of Gus Yatron

Public service began with a stint on the Reading School Board. In 1956, a State House seat was open and Yatron went for it. He was elected and so began a legislative career that would last 36 years. He moved to the Senate four years later. In the legislature, Yatron worked on improving conditions of the mental institutions and addressing silicosis. He was an active, albeit not necessarily successful legislator, as *CQ* noted he "introduced scores of bills only to see a small fraction approved." legislator

In 1968, Democratic incumbent George Rhodes decided to retire and Yatron went for it. He vowed to increase tourism for the district. With a comfortable margin in Berks County (Reading), Yatron offset Yonavik's win in Schulykill and won over Peter Yonavick 51% - 48%.

Yatron's existence throughout his entire tenure was against the political grain. Jimmy Carter carried the district by a mere 1,100 votes despite carrying Pennsylvania but four years later, Ronald Reagan took 59% and George H.W. Bush won 61%, far more than their statewide showings. In fact, while Yatron only held a small portion of Lancaster County, he was the first Democrat to do so since James Buchanan in 1830. With that in mind, Yatron didn't automatically feel the need to embrace any political ideology and it worked in his favor. For the ensuing 20 years prior to 1990, Yatron never dipped below 63%. One reason was he did the seemingly impressive. *The Morning Call* said, "Yatron amazes friends and foes alike with a seemingly limitless capacity for remembering names and faces." Another was focusing like a laser beam on constituent service and issues of importance to the region.

One was black-lung benefits and the issue remained throughout Yatron's entire tenure. In fact, in 1985, he pressured Labor Secretary Bill Brock to come up with a plan to adequately address the backlogs of claims (even backing an amendment to allow all 90 judges in the Labor Department to hear claims. Another accomplishment was the location of a federal prison to the town of Minerville. Rejuvenating his home-town also took high energy as the once vibrant Reading had deteriorated. On cultural issues, he was conservative, opposing abortion and Mo Udall's Alaska Wilderness Protection Act but, his pulse was firmly viewed on the side of the people.

As a Greek-American, Yatron was naturally upset over the Turkish invasion of the island of Cyprus.

There were some, particularly vocal liberals who claimed Yatron was not confrontational enough. Following the 1980 elections, Yatron was stripped of his gavel by Michael Barnes of Maryland, who was ten years Yatron's junior in Congress, as chair of the Western Hemisphere Affairs subcommittee. One under the radar reason given was that Yatron was not viewed as intellectually or aggressive strong enough to go head-to-head with incoming Secretary of State Alexander Haig. A Yatron spokesman said he was not "giving much credence to it."

enough. But Yatron regained a footing – and a gavel, two years later by taking the Foreign Affairs Subcommittee on Human Rights and International Organizations which culminated with the end of his Congressional tenure.

One hearing Yatron chaired was in 1986 and he expressed his displeasure in uncertain terms over the lax approach to processing applications for Cubans who wanted to emigrate to the U.S. When Immigration and Naturalization refused to send a witness to the hearing, Yatron said they were "stonewalling" and displaying "a total disregard of legitimate Congressional concern on these human rights issues."

Throughout his long career, Yatron was a steadfast backer of Israel but was forced to reassure supporters of the Jewish State when he held hearings on alleged Israeli violence against Palestinians which he called, "unacceptable by any standard." The beef among supporters was that Yatron didn't have any pro-Israel officials rebutting the testimony which Yatron attributed to not wanting "a policy which places America's commitment to human rights and democratic institutions above offending ruthless regimes, with which the administration is currently seeking to curry favor."

In 1989, no one could doubt his commitment. Yatron frowned on the Palestinian Liberation Organization's (PLO) efforts to obtain recognition by the United Nations at the World Health Organization. He called it "ill-conceived for a number of reasons," one being that "it would seriously undermine efforts to achieve a comprehensive peace in the Middle East." "In his communication to the WHO, Yasser Arafat's letterhead includes the symbol of his Palestine. This letterhead includes the entirety of the State of Israel."

Years earlier, Yatron criticized both Pinochet of Chile and Marcos of the Philippines. He opposed Contra aid to rebels in Nicaragua, but also pointed out human rights violations within the Sandinista regime.

**Yatron's personal style made him exceedingly popular
in Republican territory campaigning
Photo courtesy of George Yatron**

In many ways, Yatron was far-sighted. Had President George H.W. Bush heeded the advice of Yatron, a fair amount of conflict that was the Persian Gulf War could have been heeded off as Yatron had actually been a champion of sanctions against the Hussein regime since the Iraqi dictator launched poison gas against the Kurds in 1988. But the Bush administration opposed them. The same went for China following the massacre at Tienanmen Square in 1989. As a result, Yatron found himself opposing the administration on initiatives concerning both nations that went before Congress in far more high profile settings.

In the run-up to the Persian Gulf War, Yatron voted with his colleagues who wanted to give more time for sanctions to work against Iraq. "The policy of sanctions has the broad-based support of the American public," he told colleagues. "History has demonstrated time and time again that strong support at home for major action abroad has long been the formula for success in American foreign policy. It is in keeping with this democratic tradition that I support the Hamilton-Gephardt resolution."

Yatron was similarly passionate about putting pressure on China for their human rights record. "For those who contend that denying most-favored-nation status will cause China to retreat into isolation, thereby making it difficult to promote reforms, I submit that our current policy of economic engagement has not deterred China from being one of the worst human rights violators in the world."

When the Iraq War culminated, Yatron wanted the administration to delve further into the Human Rights side. "The Gulf crisis has brought the U.S. into political and military alliances with several ruthlessly repressive regimes, including Syria and China," Yatron said. While "important to the success of our current efforts in the gulf, it is also very important that we use these new alliances as opportunities to press these regimes to improve human rights," and he explicitly mentioned Syria.

Paul Kanjorski, who would later come to represent a neighboring district, referred to his colleague as, "Gentleman Gus." Bill Clinger, a Republican who represented western Pennsylvania noted that for an ex-boxer, Yatron is "a surprisingly gentle and engaging person." John Murtha echoed that, with a caveat. He called Yatron, "without a doubt one of the toughest people I have ever met. He did not complain and he did not get riled up very often, but if he did, you knew it. He took a very firm position, as much of a gentleman as he was." As Capitol Hill employees would attest, Yatron was also an affable people-person. He was on a first-name basis with many of the personnel and had knowledge of their lives. One colleague told Yatron "they can't vote for you," but he was a people person. On down time, Yatron enjoyed exercising, watching sports, and automobiles. His musical taste included big band, Rod Stewart, Sting, and Dionne Warwick.

Gus and Millie Yatron
Photo courtesy of George Yatron

Fairly or not, Yatron was plagued from time to time by questions about his intelligence. *Spy Magazine* in 1989 published a piece that detailed Yatron struggling to answer a question about his opposition to federally funded abortions, contending that he couldn't find the paper where he had written his notes.

Yatron began thinking of wrapping up his Congressional career at or near the 1990 election. He dispatched his foe, John Hicks, with 57% which The Almanac of American Politics, noting the rather substantial drop from previous elections, cited as "not disaster but certainly a warning sign."

Even before 1990, however, with redistricting costing the Keystone State two seats in Congress, Yatron began thinking the term at hand would be his final. He had already undergone a double hip replacement operation but a five-hour heart bypass surgery in the summer of '91 probably exacerbated the decision. Yatron himself lent fuel to the fire when he told The Morning Call on the occasion of his swearing-in that he "probably" would retire, wanting to keep it to a dozen terms. Yet Yatron continued to fundraise throughout 1991 and contributed to money to committees that would hold sway over how boundaries would be affected. Finally, he announced shortly after the New Year that he would not be a candidate for another term. His retirement statement called his Congressional years, "challenging and rewarding and I have tried to be conscientious in my duties and responsive to my constituency."

For Sixth district politicos, that turned out to be the most anti-climactic news of the season. What was a genuine surprise was that when a new map was finally issued (it was drawn up by a court), the district was largely preserved and even more befuddling, the man for whom it was drawn, State Senator Michael O'Pake, who had been quietly trying to nudge Yatron into retirement, ultimately decided not to run. His seat did stay in Democratic hands, however as his successor was the sheriff of Schuylkill, Tim Holden.

Yatron had $165,969 left in his campaign treasury at the time of his departure but used it to set up a scholarship. Retirement was generally fulfilling though Yatron was plagued throughout by bad knees. He died of a heart attack at age 75 in 2003.

Photo courtesy of George Yatron

Joe Gaydos

Yatron was the boxer but when Gaydos was asked about a possible 1992 retirement, it was he who unleashed the metaphor by stating, "That may happen. There comes a time when you have to throw in the gloves."

If the term backbencher can sometimes have a negative connotation, it might be the way Joe Gaydos liked it. In 24 years, he rarely commented to reporters ("Many times I have nothing to say"). He did tell *The Post Gazette* in one of the few interviews he granted that, "The persons that want the more glamorous type of committees and seeks them are the ones that have ambition, that want to be governor, or senator or president. I had no ambitions and still have no ambitions now." Jon Delano was a staffer on Capitol Hill and he described Gaydos thus: "How a member of Congress treated others on the Hill was always my test of decency, and Joe Gaydos passed with flying colors. During my 14 years in the Congress, he was great fun to be with - caustic and irreverent at times, but never fake - an old-school politician who preferred to work hard quietly behind the scenes than in some flamboyant public way."

Gaydos was a true man of Southwestern Pennsylvania. Born in Braddock, the town that he was most associated with was McKeesport where he resided during his career and through his retirement. This is an area *Politics in America* calls "a vanishing breed" for steel and manufacturing interests and his father in fact had been a miner until his grandmother made him quit following an explosion (he was able to find refuge above ground in a steel mill).

Gaydos and his mother during World War II
Photos courtesy of Joe Gaydos, Jr.

Gaydos lied about his age to enlist in the Navy during World War II and was sent to the Pacific as a signalman, then returned to attend Notre Dame Law School on the GI Bill. In time, Gaydos became an assistant county solicitor and a deputy state attorney general and while clerking for a local judge, he was introduced to the woman who would become his bride, Alice. Eventually, Gaydos wound up as general counsel to District 5 of the United Mine Workers of America.

When Gaydos secured a State Senate seat in 1967, he might have expected to remain there for some time. Local Democrats had other ideas. Incumbent Elmer Holland was aging and they were trying to nudge Gaydos into challenging him. Holland took the hint and announced his retirement, though he died prior to the end of the term. That necessitated a special election that was held concurrently with the November general. Gaydos won both handily and for the next quarter-of-a-century had nary a re-election worry in the world.

Photos courtesy of Joe Gaydos, Jr.

What was at the heart of Gaydos's legislative portfolio? Basically anything labor. For that reason, the Education and Labor Committee was the only one for which he could possibly be suited. Gaydos called it, "non-sexy but of extreme, fundamental importance touching practically everybody in your constituency…down and dirty types of things that have to be done." He did it – and almost everyone around him said he did it well. In fact, early in his tenure, the delegation's dean, "Doc" Morgan, who held a district nearby, secured a seat for him on Appropriations but Gaydos preferred to stay where he was. And though his name is nary the first to come up when mentioning ERISA and OSHA, omitting Gaydos as a founding father of those two sweeping laws would be a grievous error indeed.

The Employee Retirement Income Security Act (ERISA) was a major part of Gaydos's legislative portfolio. This, he said, proved a "life raft," given the hardships that those arose for those in his area laid off by closings, etc., and Gaydos said without it, it would be "a complete catastrophe." That was precisely why he said, "If I spent all of my time in Congress and didn't do anything else, ERISA would probably be the crowning glory, along with OSHA." That would be the Occupational Health and Safety Administration. Throughout much of his remaining tenure, Gaydos fought against attempts – some by fellow Democrats, to weaken the law. When Maryland Democrat Beverly Byron proposed an amendment exempting in 1980 that, as she told it, "would exempt small businesses in safe industries from routine OSHA safety inspections," while not touching more hazardous industries. Gaydos protested. "It seems fundamental," he said on the House floor, "that workers in small businesses are entitled to the same protection as workers in large enterprises. This amendment creates two classes of employees, one class entitled to the full protection of the law, and another class of substantially less than fully protected workers."

Photos courtesy of Joe Gaydos, Jr.

When Ronald Reagan captured the White House, *The Pittsburgh Post Gazette* said the change in guard "saw him fighting many an unsuccessful rear-guard action against President Reagan's attempts to decimate OSHA."

Gaydos chaired Education and Labor's Health and Safety subcommittee for 16 years prior to his retirement. Many times, he would say, "Lost companies, lost jobs, lost manufacturing capabilities inevitably results from the one-sided and so-called-free-trade policy." One solution for addressing "dumping" that was costing U.S. workers their jobs was requiring quotas on imports to the U.S. The Congressional Steel Caucus was another means of proactiveness when it came to jobs and Gaydos proposed the Fair Trade In Steel Act of 1984. One of the rare occasions Gaydos caught flak from steelers was when he supported a merger. "The move will allow the company to concentrate on its steel production while it makes a steady return on oil drilling. It's an economic fact of life. These days a large company must diversify or die."

In that vein, fiery is a word few if anyone would use to describe Gaydos but, when it came to his own people, he could show a sparkle or two. On the lack of reciprocity, he said, "Our trade partners are using every cunning trick of trade War. Bluff and Bluster and subsidy and thumping and state capitalism...People are tired of New Testament trade based on meekness and turning the other cheek. They are ready for some Old Testament Justice."

In coal mining country, mine safety was of importance and he made clear his loyalty was with miners when he delivered remarks on the House floor near the end of Reagan's first year in office by blasting cuts to the Mine Safety and Health Administration (MSHA) in the wake of the deaths of 24 miners in three separate incidents. Explaining that MSHA was "fully funded in 1980," Gaydos told the chamber "we should have been discussing ways to make MSHA more effective, and making judgements based on effectiveness, rather than responding to untried economic theory."

On more than one occasion, Gaydos commenced hearings on minre safety. When United Mine Workers President Richard L. Trumka accused the Reagan administration of undermining mine safety, Gaydos vowed to conduct his own investigation. He also held mine executives feet to the fire. At one hearing in 1987, he told operators of Wilberg, a mine in Utah where 27 miners died while trapped underground that "there are criminal sanctions (in the industry)...this comes very close to that in my estimation." At the time of his retirement, Gaydos had a workplace disclosure bill in the hopper for mine safety. He also took aim at ridding society of hazardous chemicals.

Gaydos in 1986 sponsored a bill that he called, "a giant step toward eliminating cancer." Its primary component would be the establishment of a Risk Assessment Board to determine and thereby notify risks groups of workers in various fields for contacting the disease. Education and Labor approved the measure but with the Reagan administration in opposition, little came out of it.

Reagan fared a little better with Gaydos on matters pertaining to defense. In 1986, he and Jack Murtha were the only Pennsylvania Democrats to back Reagan's request for aid to the Nicaraguan contras. He also backed SDI research. On the question of war in Iraq, Gaydos sided with the majority in his party and against President George H.W. Bush by preferring the continuation of sanctions. He went on to explain why. "When we entered World War II, it was because we had a sense of purpose. We knew our enemy, we knew why we fighting. That has not been the case in recent military actions involving American troops."

On domestic issues beyond labor, Gaydos was truly aligned with labor but more conservative on cultural issues. In the 1970s, he supported Mo Udall's Alaska Wilderness Protection Act (which Yatron had opposed) but generally opposed busing except for, as one amendment stated, to the student's "closest or next closest" school district." He voted against public financing of campaigns in committee. He was for the anti-flag burning amendment. "Voters here know I love the flag and that I love this country. What we have to do is ask what is more dangerous: a handful of malcontents who want to desecrate the flag; or overreacting to them and amending the very principles on which this country was founded."

The other committee on which Gaydos served was House Administration and his perch as chair of the Accounts Subcommittee gave him some leverage with other members, one of whom called it, "a hell of a hammer over other people," adding, "Joe can be tough as hell." Near the end of his career, Gaydos was forced to resist other members requests for higher budgets, including freezing his own, which may have contributed (though was by no means decisive) in his 158-64 loss to Charlie Rose for the chairmanship of the full committee following the 1990 elections when the caucus rejected the bid of Frank Annunzio of Illinois to remain chair.

Gaydos was as old-school as one could get and that counted both ways reputation-wise. No one ever accused Gaydos of being unscrupulous or of having his hand in the cookie-jar about anything but one House aide mentioned he "hailed from an era where ethics mattered less." That was arguably put to the test when Gaydos was given one high-profile assignment: sitting on the House Ethics Committee at a time when the panel was reviewing possible indiscretions against House Speaker Jim Wright for his book deal, *Reflections of a Public Man*. While Gaydos called the appointment, "an indication of leaders' faith that you have some integrity," he was one of only two members of the twelve-person committee who routinely voted against sanctioning Wright (Alan Mollohan of West Virginia was the other). Though he did back the final April 1989 report that basically signaled that Wright's grave was dug, *CQ* noted that Gaydos was the only member absent at a press conference to announce the findings. On another matter, Gaydos and 11 other colleagues, mostly old bulls, voted against legislation in 1988 that would make most civil rights laws applicable to Congress.

For Gaydos, achieving his goals meant working well with others. Bill Goodling, a fellow member of the Education and Labor Committee and a senior, explained Gaydos's style. "If his legislation or my legislation did not quite suit each other, we could always sit down and work those problems out." One Pennsylvanian called him "the granddaddy of our delegation," while Bob Borski noted the advice Gaydos provided as a new member: "He taught me to be bipartisan, to work hard for the people you represent, (and) to stay in close contact with the people you represent." Gaydos hailed the cohesiveness of the delegation which he promoted: "We not only as Republicans and Democrats but as a delegation utilized our collective abilities to work with each successive administration and the House and Senate leadership to achieve many initiatives to help our State and the citizens of Pennsylvania. As the Members know, Pennsylvania is one of the States hardest hit by the recession of 1980, and many of our efforts focused on attempts to revitalize the State's distressed areas."

One area Gaydos successfully worked on that Pennsylvania colleagues no-doubt appreciated: fighting the efforts of the Department of Commerce to adjust the census, which would have caused the Keystone State to lose a third Congressional seat rather than two. As it happened, his own seat was thought to be at serious risk of falling victim to reapportionment but Gaydos showed little signs of caring.

By 1991, Gaydos had reached his penultimate status in Congress. He was dean of Pennsylvania's 23 member delegation (Republican Joe McDade was more senior but Democrats had more members) and prided himself on his ability to foster bipartisan cooperation. But that was about his only leadership. He had been bypassed for the position of the House Administration

Committee chairmanship and though he was number two on Education and Labor, the prospect of him getting the slot even if Bill Ford were to retire was very unlikely given his status as a backbencher and the fact that chairs of this committee tend to be vocal. His top aide, Bernie Mandella, had quit. Plus, Gaydos had only taken 66% in his '90 primary, a sign that some restless voters wanted him to begin wrapping up his career.

But the deciding factor, as in Yatron's case, might have been redistricting. The state had to lose two districts and population-wise, the 20th had shed nine percent of its population which *The Pittsburgh Post Gazette* noted was "the second biggest loser in the state." When Gaydos made his retirement official in January of '92, he gave the following explanation: "Age they say is the fire extinguisher for flaming youth. Well, I'm 65. My fires are beginning to burn a little low. It's time to think about banking the furnace to conserve some of the heat" (he also talked of "taking in sail"). Gaydos's decision may have been instrumental in causing the district to disappear and it was gobbled up by others around metro-Pittsburgh.

Gaydos resumed practicing law in McKeesport with his son, which was promptly renamed, "Gaydos, Gaydos & Associates." He died of leukemia at age 88 in 2015.

To sum up Gaydos's legacy, Bud Shuster was a conservative Republican from Altoona, Pennsylvania who served alongside Gaydos for 20 years but, as he fondly told colleagues in a farewell speech to Gaydos as he prepared to retire, the two grew up in the same town and even once lived in the same home. Shuster recalled, "Some years ago when I returned to the steel valley, a reporter observed that had I continued to live there, I might have been running against Congressman Gaydos. I quickly replied that had I still been living there, in all probability I would have been voting for Congressman Gaydos." Shuster added that he heard an earful from local Republicans but "facts are facts."

CHAPTER FORTY-TWO

The Bow-Tie Says It All: Coughlin Capably Served Upper-Class Montgomery County, PA

Introductory Quote: "I do not think the repository of all wisdom is in the Executive Branch." –Congressman Larry Coughlin

Some House members who voluntarily left office at the end of in 1992 were remarkably unsurprising while others were genuine shockers. Larry Coughlin of Pennsylvania without question fell into the latter group, and that was confirmed by many of his colleagues. In a special order speech on the floor of the House as the 102nd Congress neared an end, fellow Pennsylvanian and Appropriator John Murtha called Coughlin, "one of the few people that surprised many of us by his retiring from Congress…he is in the prime of life, he is at the height of his seniority and his experience and his influence." That is, at least as far as being in the minority was concerned.

It was easy to see why Coughlin was so respected. With a moderate voting record and an Appropriations perch that funneled goods to suburban Philadelphia's interests, he seemed in grand shape for the foreseeable future. Plus, he was one of a few members whose daily bowtie was a trademark. A story was told on Coughlin's death of a reporter asking how a person with a bow-tie can be trusted. Coughlin's reply: "I've never known one who wasn't trustworthy."

Lawrence "Larry" Coughlin (Coff-lin) is a microcosm of his Philadelphia Main Line/Montgomery County district – the most prosperous and educated in the state at the time, and his education as much as anything bears that out. Having grown up wealthy in Wilkes-Barre in 1929, he attended private school in Connecticut, received his undergraduate degree from Yale, his MBA from Harvard Business School and his law degree from Temple at night (he worked on a steel line as a foreman by day). He had served in the Marines during the Korean War under Lt. Gen. Lewis "Chesty" Puller.

After finishing law school, Coughlin began practicing in Philly but also garnered the attention of GOP Gubernatorial candidate William Scranton by cutting his teeth on his successful 1962 campaign. Two years later, Coughlin was elected to the Pennsylvania House, then received a promotion before possibly even discovering where the men's room was because two years later, he was winning a Senate seat. The seemingly cyclical-job switching came in 1968 when the Main Line's current U.S. House occupant, Richard Schweikert, decided to challenge Democrat Joe Clark for the U.S. Senate (and won). Coughlin won the primary to succeed Schweikert with 71% and the general with 62%. "will ease the intolerable and unfair burden of people raising families and people living on limited incomes who have borne a disproportionate share of the staggering tax bill at all governmental levels over the past quarter century." He spoke of, "a new order of national priorities that humanizes programs in terms of what they do for people."

Coughlin tried to strike a balance early on. In 1971, he joined four other Republicans in sending a "Dear Colleague" letter that expressed their view that the U.S. should cease operations in Southeast Asia by the end of the year. Two years later, he was among 14 signatories on a letter that urged the Nixon administration to approach forthcoming negotiations on progress from previous forums as opposed to threat of potentially new weapons.

Coughlin's years in office was emblematic of the clear GOP lean of the district, and his re-elections were almost always above the 60%. His one spirited race – which didn't end up all that close, came in 1984 from Montgomery County Commissioner Joe Hoeffel, a photogenic pol who had won a predominantly GOP district, and who at 34, was nearly a generation younger than the incumbent. Touting Coughlin's philosophy as, "a middle course going nowhere," he called the incumbent "a nice guy in a bowtie with a mediocre record and little political courage." Hoeffel laid out his path to victory by citing statistics that showed the 13th's Republican edge had dwindled since 1968, and vowed to clean up in the Philly portion of the district while gaining ticket splitters elsewhere. Coughlin scoffed at that notion but Hoeffel did penetrate somewhat – he held Coughlin to 56%.

Image courtesy of C-SPAN

Hoeffel was back in 1986 and accused Coughlin of "flip-flopping." Bush stumped for his old friend in Norristown. At one point, SEPTA Chief Lewis Gould Jr., was criticized for penning a letter that called Coughlin, "a champion of mass transit," politicking that Hoeffel called, "really outrageous." But constituents agreed and Coughlin found himself back up to 59%.

It was somewhat legendary in the halls of Congress that Coughlin traded a seat on Judiciary for Appropriations in 1973 just as the former was about to begin nationally riveting hearings that would culminate with the resignation of President Richard Nixon. But being spared of national exposure only allowed Coughlin to focus more on his district. Coughlin was ranking Republican on the Transportation Subcommittee on Appropriations and worked harmoniously with his Democratic counterpart, Bill Lehman of Florida. Though the two were certainly never in full agreement, the relationship between the two men and their staffs was so strong that on at least one occasion, Lehman parted with some of his own district funding when Coughlin told him he was going to come up short for his own.

Mass-transit above all was how Coughlin delivered. In 1988, he and inner-city Democrat Bill Gray got $7.2 million for the city's commuter rail. Beyond mass-transit, Coughlin delivered Philly plenty of other goods. One was a $2 million allocation for the renovation of Pennsylvania's oldest African-American theater, the New Freedom Theater on Broad Street.

Photo courtesy of the Gerald R. Ford Presidential Library and Museum

Much of Coughlin's mid-tenure found him taking aim at funding for the Clinch River Nuclear reactor in Oak Ridge, Tennessee. His first efforts came in 1975 when he proposed an amendment to an Energy Research bill to prohibit money for a breeder reactor plant on the River. Coughlin called his amendment, "a major crossroad in the program which, if we take it now we'll irretrievably commit us to this program in the long run he called it a disaster today in terms of cost overruns...schedule delays...and maladministration." It was rejected 136-227.

By 1981, the tide was turning which Coughlin helped along by likening the project to, "a nuclear white elephant that will consumer massive amounts of taxpayers' dollars and be outdated and inadequate before it's even finished." Proponents were not successful that year but at the end of '82, funding was deleted by a vote of 217-196, despite the vociferous support of powerful Senate Majority Leader Howard Baker who represented the Volunteer State. Coughlin stood firm: "If the studies are something other than cosmetic it would seem prudent to await their conclusions before authorizing construction at Clinch River."

The proposed Westway Highway in New York City was another proposal that earned Coughlin's wrath and he made that clear by labeling it, "wasteful, environmentally questionable boondoggles." It survived Coughlin's attempts to kill it in Appropriations because his fellow Republican, Manhattan's Bill Green wanted it though eventually, that fell by the wayside as well.

Photo courtesy of the Collection of U.S. House of Representatives

Coughlin also opposed Reagan's request for testing of a 17-foot-long anti-satellite weapon and California Democrat George Brown was his partner on that endeavor and in 1984, the pair successfully convinced colleagues to prohibit its testing. The then-Congressman who spoke on behalf of and moved the bill was a Tennessee Democrat named Al Gore. The vote was 238 to 181 and 58 Republicans backed Coughlin against the President. Coughlin was also one of only three Appropriations Committee Republicans to back a test ban treaty. This time, however, Coughlin was on the losing side.

Coughlin was an early supporter of Bush's for the 1988 Presidential election and once elected, Bush made him a point-man for his goal to combat the 1989 drug epidemic. When many complained that the spending the president proposed was insufficient, Coughlin replied, "This isn't chicken feed. We need to implement the president's plan and give it a chance before we criticize it."

When it came to voting with Presidents, Coughlin was never monolithic – his highest was 69% in 1989, the first year of the Bush presidency (his highest before that was 66% the first year of Reagan's). But he could go as low as 48% (1986) and just 58% in 1990. In no Congress was Coughlin's classification as a quintessential moderate more provable than the 101st. Though he sustained Bush's veto of a higher minimum wage law, he overrode him on the Civil

Rights Act, the Family and Medical Leave Act, while also voting a solid pro-choice line. And opting to reduce SDI funding. But it might have been somewhat paradoxical that he backed the firebrand Newt Gingrich for Minority Whip as opposed to the more accommodating Ed Madigan of Illinois (Gingrich famously eked out a two-vote win).

Coughlin the colleague always lent a hand. Republican Bill Clinger won a seat in Congress from Western Pennsylvania in 1978 and said Coughlin "helped me from the get-go" with the committee process and "told me how to get to the bathroom." The pair stayed in touch when Coughlin retired.

Coughlin's mellow style by no means inoculated him from taking firing a shot across the bow. One example was when he bemoaned the process by which House Democrats were debating a campaign finance measure which he expressed on the House floor in 1976. "Mr. Speaker, here we go again, precipitately another travesty. Here We Go Again, considering reform under a gag rule. Here we go again, not being permitted to work the wheel of his house. Here we go again, being dictated to by the majority leadership. What are we afraid of? The only excuse for a gag rule is fear of what the people's elected representatives might do."

Coughlin with colleagues Andy Ireland of Florida, (far left), Sonny Montgomery of Mississippi and House Speaker Tip O'Neill Photo courtesy of Andy Ireland

Shortly after the Gulf War began, Coughlin drew eyebrows by comparing CNN reporter Peter Arnett to Joseph Goebbels, and calling his coverage on the House floor, "disgusting if not treasonous," and contending he was "being used as a propaganda tool by Iraqi dictator Saddam Hussein..."

Mostly though, Coughlin was content fighting for his district, which included securing funding for SEPTA, housing and drug programs. He fought for approval of a Blue Route in Delaware County which was intended to link access to the Pennsylvania Turnpike. On the sometimes animosity between suburban Montgomery County and the City of Brotherly Love, Coughlin made clear that, "We can't get along without Philadelphia and Philadelphia can't exist about us." In late-1991, there was talk that Bush might tap Coughlin to be his Secretary of Transportation but, the post instead went to another family loyalist, Andy Card. Meanwhile, Coughlin chaired the Capitol Hill Marines which was composed of other colleagues who had served in the branch.

Around that time, Coughlin began pondering his own political future. 1992 was a redistricting year and he refused to entertain whether to seek re-election until new district lines were finalized. Having won 60-40% in 1990, his seat itself was in no imminent danger, though his support was far from unanimous on the right. Nurse Susan Boyer announced a bid to unseat him, saying the Congressman "talks like Ronald Reagan at home but votes like Pete Kostmayer (a liberal Democrat from Bucks County) in Congress," a real insult in these parts. He does not represent the views of most people in this district."

Instead, Coughlin spared her the challenge. Declaring, "It's time to move on to new challenges," he announced his departure roughly three weeks before Pennsylvania's filing deadline. Unleashing on the system was an official reason: "Forty years of Democratic control by a now-tired majority has led to constant carping with worn-out phrases and recycling of the same one-shot giveaways and welfare make-work programs. It has also led to an arrogance of power that begets practices which have demeaned the institution."

Coughlin died of cancer at age 72 in 2001.

CHAPTER FORTY-THREE

Schulze Thrived on Bipartisanship in Congress

Introductory Tidbit: Richard Schulze was a rare Republican to win a House seat in the post-Watergate class of 1974 – one of just 17 versus 75 Democrats. Two other members were Charles Grassley of Iowa and Jim Jeffords of Vermont, each of whom approached the chamber with casts from injuries. As they approached the well, one over-exuberant Democrat shouted "There's two more we almost got."

Photo courtesy of the U.S. House of Representatives Collection

Richard Schulze was another of those fairly senior members of Congress who left office in 1992 but, in talking to him, that was basically the Pennsylvania Republican's plan all along. Schulze, a well-liked member whose legacy may be going to bat to ensure that American workers impacted by trade agreements got a fair deal, knew the necessity of forging strong relations with the majority party in order to accomplish his legislative goals. And even talking about it close to three decades later makes him proud.

With the exception of his brief attendance at the University of Houston and his time in the Army, Schulze was a lifer in Philadelphia and its collar counties through the culmination of his Congressional career. He was born in the city and, following Houston, attended Villanova University and Temple University. He then married Anne "Nancy" Lockwood and had four children.

The owner of an appliance business, and later what became a successful home construction and land development company in the town of Paoli, Schulze joked that every time a new child came along, "I had to start another business." But he's immensely proud of all that he accomplished. "200 years from now," he said, "I thought being a small businessman in a small town and giving people opportunities for employment" would be a symbol of leadership with opportunities for upward mobility was an important aspect of the glue which forms a strong society."

Schulze's political career began in 1960 with a stint on the Tredyffrin Township Republican Committee. Beforehand, Schulze was "not very political," as his involvement had been limited to attending local committee meetings. As a Scout Master Schulze was at meetings due to his concern over the loss of open space in the rapidly developing area. Finally, another regular admonished him saying, "You're always shooting your mouth off at these meetings. It's now time for you to either put up or shut up." He'd get his chance soon enough and putting up meant to run for Republican Committeeman.

In an ironic adherence to the fact that all politics is local, Schulze's opportunity to get a foot in the door came when a Republican Committeeman who happened to be Catholic informed colleagues that he would be stepping down. The reason: he was planning on casting his vote for John F. Kennedy for president. That created an opening for Schulze. Four years later, Schulze led a local effort for the GOP standard beater, Barry Goldwater. Though the Arizona Senator was swamped by incumbent President Lyndon B. Johnson statewide, Schulze proudly notes that he delivered his own precinct.

Schulze was soon tapped for the post of Chester County Registar of Wills and Clerk of Orphans Court which is a fancy name for county surrogate. He won a Pennsylvania House seat in 1968 and held it for three terms prior to heading to Congress. In that role, he focused on campaign finance, environmental and tax legislation. His opening for Congress came in 1974 when fellow Republican John Ware announced his retirement. It didn't take Schulze long to garner the support of the powerful Delaware County Republican Organization, also known as the War Board. In order to win the nomination, however, Schulze had to fend off a challenge from a wealthy, 27-year old attorney from Chester, John West in the primary. But West was hurt by charges of embellishing his position with the Nixon White House. Meanwhile. Professor James Mline tried to appeal to the more liberal end of the spectrum. But Schulze was aided by the fact that six generations of his family had resided in the area and that the Del Co. organization is among the most organized in the nation. Telling voters he doesn't, "drive a Ferrari," he won the primary with 45% while West garnered 29%.

In a year when Republicans were losing more than forty seats nationwide, Schulze won the general election with 60%, a figure he dipped below only once in his eight subsequent re-election bids. Because the GOP class was dwarfed by the 75-member "Watergate Babies," on the Democratic side, the opportunity for plum assignments were non-existent and Schulze was assigned to Armed Services and Banking.

Almost immediately, Schulze introduced a Constitutional amendment limiting the terms of members. "I didn't have to spend a lot of time campaigning as many members do," noting that if terms were longer, "members might actually have more freedom to legislate for a year rather than immediately gearing up for the campaign." But members are loath to place limits on their own powers and the proposal went nowhere. Schulze still was able to bask in the fruit of great publicity in that first term when President Gerald Ford traveled to Valley Forge on the day of the bicentennial to sign legislation Schulze had sponsored making it a historic site, now named Valley Forge National Historic Park.

It was at the beginning of his second term that Schulze captured a seat on the prestigious Ways and Means Committee. The position seemed a natural. Aside from the fact that he had served on Ways and Means in the State House, he "enjoyed taxes and taxation and its nitty-grittiness" and, having spoken to leadership about it, was "somewhat assured" that he'd win the post. In later years, there became a running joke with his Republican colleague from the Keystone State, Bill Goodling over whether the coin flip to determine who would get the seat was actually one-sided. Schulze had heard that later but Goodling was a friend who, having remained in Congress for the GOP takeover in 1994, arguably went on to even bigger things: he won a committee chairmanship.

Schulze put his fiscal conservatism and fascination with fiscal matters to work by sponsoring an early version of a Taxpayers Bill of Rights. With Senator Bill Roth, he proposed "a subtraction method" value added tax. The following year, he proposed BAMT – the Business Alternative Minimum Tax and repeatedly introduced a uniform business tax. He furiously opposed President Jimmy Carter's proposed limits on deductions for entertainment expenses, saying it amounted to, "putting the screws to a sector of the economy that can't afford it" to give it "a little sex appeal" (his affluent district would have felt its impact). Schulze did back Carter on another matter. Along with South Carolina Democrat Butler Derrick, he provided a last minute switch that allowed the Carter administration to prevail on a vote dropping the Turkish arms embargo.

When Ronald Reagan won the presidency, Schulze saw an opportunity for some of his proposals to advance. Schulze liked Reagan personally. He had first met the future president in 1978 when he traveled to the Valley Forge Military Academy for a Schulze campaign event. The media had portrayed Reagan as a lightweight who needed 3'5 cards to enunciate his thoughts. Yet after 20 minutes of talking to the Gipper, Schulze came away "deeply impressed." He labeled Reagan, "an intellect with a firm grounding in conservative philosophy. He captured me." But by 1982, he was at least temporarily, singing a slightly different tune.

Photo courtesy of Richard Schulze

At one point, Mississippi Republican Trent Lott teased Schulze about having the most pro-Reagan voting record in the entire House. Schulze responded by saying he might have to stop. He had been trying to get a constituent a position as a driver in the White House without success, and was told he already had three Cabinet members from his district (Drew Lewis, Dick Schweiker and General Al Haig.) Schulze's voting record was decidedly pro-Reagan on most non-trade measures, though his presidential support score did dip noticeably at times (57% in 1982 vs. 70% a year earlier and 72% in 1983).

Ironically, some discontent toward the administration started after the awarding of the restoration of the battleship Iowa not to Chester County, Pennsylvania but to Pascagoula, Mississippi, which was located firmly in the heart of Lott's district (worth noting was that Lott was the House Minority

Whip). Schulze put out a statement lambasting the priorities of the president's team: "I am finally convinced that the Reagan Administration is increasingly insensitive to the unemployment problems facing this nation and especially the economic problems plaguing the distressed cities of this nation such as Chester. The administration just doesn't seem to have any common sense in the way it does things and the Iowa decision was a perfect example. Here's the port city of Chester, one of the two or three most distressed in the nation with a significant minority population. It has the facilities that could do the job but instead they send the ship to Pascagoula, Mississippi which has a huge backlog of work."

Schulze made clear that his criticism was in part designed to wake the White House up going forward. "The pot is bubbling. The White House has got to be aware of that or they will have trouble. The whole Pennsylvania delegation feels increasingly disenchanted…All White Houses are on a four-year cycle. I don't think they care two cents about what happens in the midterm elections. I'm an optimist I keep thinking things are going to work out that we are going to provide more job opportunities but I wish they wouldn't make it so difficult to be an optimist." This discontent did not stop Reagan from naming Schulze to the Presidential Advisory Committee on Federalism.

With Speaker Tip O'Neill and Anwar Sadat
Photo courtesy of Richard Schulze

The episode revealed Schulze's insatiable appetite to go to bat for his constituents. The Congressional Mushroom Caucus was another. Its inception "stemmed" from the fact that canned mushrooms in particular were being imported from other regions of the world (the Orient stood out). *The Washington Post* noted that Schulze, "whose district considers itself the mushroom capital of the world, went into action: He formed a congressional mushroom caucus." The paper noted that the "fungus forum" soon had 61 members (Schulze also pushed legislation to require country of orgin labels for mushrooms).

Other accomplishments: major small business legislation.

Schulze, with House Minority Leader Bob Michel,
founded The Congressional Mushroom Caucus
Photo via Getty Images

Schulze's biggest impact came on trade policy. His biggest beef was that, "We're viewed around the world as being Mr. Nice Guy. We talk tough but we don't usually deliver." Schulze thought up a number of ways to change that. For starters, he proposed a 20 percent surcharge on imports. He made clear that he was not happy with "dumping" and when the Ways and Means Committee endorsed the Trade Remedies Reform Act, it adopted a Schulze sponsored measure to keep the stringent provisions for communist nations in place (some colleagues proposed relaxing the measure). And he again took aim at the acuity of the Reagan administration during the trade bill. "I'm concerned that the administration doesn't know what's going on. We're not only going to pass this legislation, we're going to override." When the markup did take place, he proposed an amendment exempting textiles and toys from limits but was defeated.

Schulze loved dangling free trade not only before the eyes of other nations, but also administrations of his own party that he didn't think were doing his constituents well. He made that clear with a resolution to allow Congress to get back in the business of regulating trade deals, an area it had abdicated in 1934. "Do I really mean we should take it all back," he asked? "Of course not. But every now and then I like to remind them." Another time, when the Supreme Court declared unconstitutional the portion of the Trade Act of 1974 that gave Congressional veto to presidential appointments, Schulze tried to mend the difference by proposing legislation that address the court's concerns. It passed.

Schulze was not shy about wanting to restrict the bestowing of Most Favored Nation Status to countries with those that conducted either unfair trade practices or had poor human rights records and Romania was at the top of his list. He opposed Reagan's move to grant MFN to that nation, specifically citing their restrictive emigration policies which he considered in violation of the Jackson-Vanik law. When Ways and Means colleagues rejected his efforts to gut that distinction, Schulze pronounced himself, "appalled that we are so gullible as to believe that this government in Romania will keep its promises when in the past, they have responded with only short-term improvements in their policies on emigration."

China incurred similar wrath as Schulze felt bestowing the distinction of MFN would hurt American workers. Nor did he have much patience on China with Reagan's successor, George H.W. Bush. On a vote imposing trade conditions on China, Schulze said "the policy of appeasement has failed." The issue came before the House again in 1990, after the Tiananmen Square massacre and Schulze pointed out a new requirement instituted by the Chinese government forcing those seeking to leave the nation from stating their whereabouts when the massacre occurred (citing electrocution as a consequence of giving a wrong answer). Schulze told members, "You will hear some people credit China for filling its annual United States immigration quota allotment. However, given that China has 1.1 billion inhabitants, filling a 20,000 immigrant visa quota is hardly proof of a free and open emigration policy." When the matter of sanctions on South Africa was debated, Schulze tried to get the importation of diamonds banned. He subsequently voted to override Reagan's veto of the measure.

Schulze was active on the Trade Act. Schulze expressed "disappointment that it took a $170 billion trade deficit to finally remove our rose-tinted glasses." He sponsored an import tax bill in 1985 and a border tax in 1992. "If this creates an incentive for Canada to negotiate, then I'm all for it."

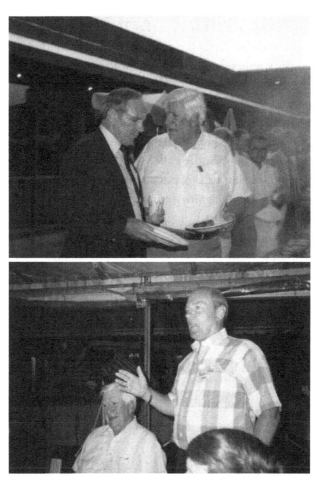

**Despite the obvious partisan differences, Schulze
and Tip O'Neill were genuine friends
Photos courtesy of Dick Schulze**

When it came to legislating with success, Schulze knew that Democrats were firmly in control of the House and that, were he going to accomplish something substantive, it usually had to involve seeking out a member of the majority party. He was seated on Ways and Means and had a strong relationship with the titanic chairman, Dan Rostenkowski, so much so that when Schulze announced his retirement, the chairman called him the night before his own tight primary for re-election to congratulate him. Other Democrats he was

SCOTT CRASS

close to: fellow Ways and Means Committee members Beryl Anthony of Arkansas and Ed Jenkins of Georgia. He would go hunting with Democratic committee barons John Dingell of Michigan and Jack Brooks of Texas. Schulze even considered Democratic House Speaker Tip O'Neill to be a friend and the two used to golf together (after 6 p.m., of course). The bottom line: Schulze takes pride in the strong relations he forged with Democrats.

The fall of 1989 was busy for Schulze. He played a role in the effort to repeal the catastrophic health insurance that was causing many seniors premiums to skyrocket (the video of Rostenkowski being chased to his car by constituents went viral). House Democrats were not happy with what the Senate was advancing but Schulze called it, "the best we are going to be able to get." In the end, the law was repealed.

That year, Schulze took significant interest in shaping child care legislation. While he supported a bill that would adequately address needs, he took issue with mandatory training for workers that would be given on the taxpayers time. "Imagine spending government money to train a grandmother how to change a diaper." Instead, he and New Mexico Republican Senator Pete Domenici authored the "Toddler Tax Credit," to give families more to work with as they sought care. Home buyers were not exempt either as Schulze was proposing giving first time purchaser a slice of the American dream by eliminating federal taxes.

Photo courtesy of Dick Schulze

Schulze leaned conservative on social issues but was never ideologically beholden to one side or the other. He voted to override Reagan's veto of landmark highway legislation in 1987. On gun control, he said, "Let's not fall into the politically expedient device of blaming an inanimate object for the behavior of human beings." He opposed passage of the Brady Bill and was one of just 22 Republicans to support the Civil Rights Act of 1991 at a time Bush was threatening a veto (both sides compromised in the fall). In 1991, he co-sponsored an amendment to prevent "double-dipping," which garnered the backing of Treasury Secretary Nick Brady, a proposal that was important to the pensions of workers in companies that filed for bankruptcy. And Schulze gave environmentalists much to like. These included tax incentives for decommissioning nuclear plants, newspapers using recycled newsprint, historic rehabilitation tax breaks, wetlands.

Another major initiative was Schulze's founding of the Congressional Sportsman's caucus. Starting at a young age fishing and hunting with his father, he had a lifetime devotion to outdoor activities. As a member of congress, when he suggested to others that they start a Sportsmen's Caucus, he invariably was told that they were too busy. Finally, while conversing with Congressman Bill Dickinson of Alabama, Dickinson said, "Why don't you do it?" Schulze then assigned staff member Brian Stangland (son of Minnesota Republican Congressman Arlen Stangland) to lay the groundwork for the Sportsmen's Caucus. There followed several months of legal preparation and the garnering of support. Since partisan ventures tend to come and go over time, Schulze believed it was important to establish the Caucus as bipartisan. During votes on the house floor, he spoke to several Democrats about the Caucus. He was told to go to Lindsey Thomas of Georgia, who was known as "the best turkey caller in the South." Thomas agreed to participate and became an active member of the Caucus. With powerful influence over conservation and wildlife issues, the Sportsmen's Caucus has become the largest caucus in Congress. The Caucus has spawned a Governor's Sportsmen's Caucus as well as Sportsmen's Caucuses in State Legislatures throughout the country.

Images via C-SPAN

How was Schulze as a boss? Rob Hartwell was one of his Chiefs of Staff and calls it "the greatest learning experience of my life." While Schulze was "tough and demanding," Hartwell is quick to add "fair." He asked many policy questions and expected staff to be prepared. That said, he was not a screamer. Hartwell recalls an incident where he and another aide were being quizzed on an issue. While Hartwell didn't have a complete answer, he told Schulze he could find it and that was okay. The other person "fudged" the answer and Schulze knew it and got a very stern warning. Schulze was also appreciative. Staff would be treated to Christmas gatherings at his home and occasionally, a nice restaurant in the country.

Schulze's re-election campaigns would almost always be snoozers as he'd routinely top 70%. In one election cycle Schulze had a plurality of over 100,000. In 1990, Rostenkowski took a bipartisan delegation to the Caribbean to negotiate the Caribbean Basin Initiative trade agreement. The trip was exposed by Barbara Walters as nefarious and profiled on ABC's "Prime Time Live." That may have contributed to his precipitous drop that fall. His 78%-22% margin in 1988 dipped to just 57-35% in 1990, clearly evidence that fences needed tending. But Schulze had a far deeper problem: redistricting. Pennsylvania was set to lose two Congressional districts in 1992 and Democrats, though one seat shy of a majority in the State Senate, had the upper hand.

Indeed, when the parties were unable to compromise on which members would get the ax, a court issued a new map and Schulze's worst fears were realized. The new map merged much of his turf with the Delaware County base of his three-term GOP colleague, Curt Weldon. At first, Schulze vowed to wait for a federal court to rule on the matter, saying, "I'm not only a Presbyterian, I'm getting to be a good Presbyterian. They believe in predestination, and I've never been such a good a Presbyterian that I believed in that, but I'm rapidly becoming one." Nor would he publicly rule out challenging Weldon, adding, "I grew up in that area and have deep and historical and emotional ties to that area." Yet when the plan was finalized, he decided to call it a career. One player instrumental in the redistricting matter claimed Schulze, "had no one speaking for him. Every other congressman had some powerful support" as far as allies in the legislature.

Still, Schulze's decision had also been impacted by the death of his wife Nancy in 1990. She was a woman who was praised by one admirer as "having electrified the room," and he conceded, "I feel less whole." But he was also guided in part by his 18-year rule. As he prepared to leave Congress, Schulze was lauded by his colleagues. Republican Congressman and future Governor Tom Ridge said, "You never left a conversation with Dick Schulze not understanding completely how he felt about this matter and why he felt the way he did."

Meanwhile, Schulze remarried another person impacted by tragedy – Nancy Waltermire whose husband Jim, Montana's Secretary of State and Republican frontrunner for governor, had perished in a plane crash while campaigning in 1988. Nancy founded the Republican Congressional Wives Speakers and during the 1996 presidential campaign, was Director of Celebrities for the Dole/Kemp Campaign with a production rate that had the top brass referring to her as "The 800 Pound Gorilla."

As for Schulze, at first he openly pondered the idea of teaching ("I'd love to have rowdy college kids. It's the opportunity to take a mind and blow it up like a balloon." Instead, he began lobbying, including becoming a partner of a firm with a bipartisan group of former members. For a man whose trademark was bipartisanship, Schulze couldn't have it any other way.

CHAPTER FORTY-FOUR

Coach Pursell a Thoughtful Centrist in the Mold of His Michigan District

Introductory Quote: "They've got more players, but we're better. It's like Democrats and Republicans: They've got the numbers but we've got the quality." –Carl Pursell following a 1987 Congressional basketball game. Despite Pursell's proclamation, the "Fighting Elephants" fell to the Dunkin' Donkeys 53-47.

Photo courtesy of Roll Call

O f all the members of Congress who did not return for the 103rd, Michigan's Carl Pursell could be considered among the most altruistic. He was a true moderate who had no qualms about saying "no" to his party or president, particularly on the domestic front. He was a visionary who throughout his 16-years in Congress led a number of caucuses designed to achieve sundry goals. On at least one occasion he took on a rarity at his own district's expense: sacred cows. Pursell was so concerned about the mounting federal deficit that he voluntarily did away with an Army Corps of Engineer Project that would have allocated $3 million for cleaning the Rogue River in his district. Pursell in fact implored other members to follow his lead though

578

the number who actually did oblige probably could have been squeezed into a phone booth.

Pursell grew up in Inlay City, Michigan, where his family moved to from Detroit. His father was in the printing business and later became a publisher. During college at Eastern Michigan University, Pursell followed in his father's footsteps in the printing arena and got a job working for a local printer for $1.35/hour at a time when, "most of the students were waiting tables in the dorms for $.50 an hour. So I was making three times their amount in 1/3 of the time." Pursell also played sports but an ankle break on the basketball court unfortunately ended that career. Meanwhile, he met his wife Peggy on a blind date.

Pursell also served in the Army as an Advanced Officer in Fort Benning, Georgia. "The reason I wanted that," he said was because, "I wanted to be at least in my career, a Field Officer, not a Staff Officer like Eisenhower and MacArthur. I wanted to be the Patton kind, cause I think you're in the real world. The staff people sit behind a desk and the Field Officer's out in front. So I took that training." He was later sent to Ft. Leonardwood, Missouri. It was during his time in the Army that he got experience doing what he became so renowned for in Congress: coaching softball (and basketball.) Some of his team included Tony Cubak who would one day play for the New York Yankees and Abe Woodson, Carl Kane and Casey Jones who joined the Boston Celtics. He continued in the Army Reserves after his service ended and established an eclectic professional field.

Pursell dabbled in real estate, operating an office supply business, and teaching before winning a seat on the Wayne County Board of Commissioners. This soon led to the Michigan Senate where he sponsored the Gifted and Talented Act and school aid legislation with Dale Kildee, a Democrat from Flint with whom he came to Congress in 1976. As Pursell's tenure drew on, his stature increased so that his name was dropped as a potential running mate for GOP Governor William Milliken in 1974.

The impetus for Pursell's ticket to Congress came in late 1975 when he received a tip from his Congressman, Republican Marvin Esch. He was going to give up his seat to run for the U.S. Senate and he wanted Pursell to succeed him. Esch got his wish but just barely. Pursell faced Edward C. Pierce, an Ann Arbor doctor and the final margin of 344 votes took weeks to certify. He was a clear beneficiary from incumbent President Gerald Ford who was winning his home state of Michigan while narrowly losing the White House. Pursell became only the second member of Congress from Plymouth in its history – Ebeneezer Pennimon served as a Whig in the early 1850s.

On his retirement, *The Detroit Free Press* noted that despite 16 years in the nation's capital, Pursell hardly went Washington. The article cited how his, "roots in Plymouth, where he maintains a home on six acres, run deep. He has never moved his family to Washington, unlike most members of Congress. His wife, Peggy, is a teacher in Livonia. Pursell commuted home every weekend."

Pursell's biggest secret for cultivating his decidedly centrist district was his own knee-jerk moderate inclinations. He was pro-choice and voted for creation of a U.S. Department of Education as well as the Alaska Land Act, a nuclear moratorium, fair housing enforcement, and the Chrysler Loan Package. He cast votes against OSHA money and a cap on food stamps.

Legendary ex-Michigan Governor George Romney taught Pursell the importance of courting unions. His advice: "you start going to plant gates and you gotta listen." He evidently listened and acted. Pursell's COPE score in 1980 was 71% and his ADA rating an astounding 89, though it had been closer to earth for a Republican in the previous two years - 53 and 60% respectively. Nonetheless, this paid off come election time as the United Auto Workers backed Pursell during at least one re-election campaign.

After the 1978 elections, Pursell was assigned to the House Appropriations Committee, "over the objections of more conservative republicans," according to a 1986 publication of *Politics in America*. By his final term, he was ranking Republican on the subcommittee on Labor, Health and Education where he strived to bring home programs and research money that would benefit the University of Michigan and other area schools. Nursing research also topped his agenda. Pursell's position was valuable to others in the delegation. In 1983, he landed money for a "people-mover" in Detroit and renovation of an Amtrak station in Jackson.

When Ronald Reagan became president, Pursell suddenly found himself with more visibility. Many Republicans from the Northeast and Midwest were disturbed if not aghast at the new administration's massive budget cuts, particularly to interests that were central to their constituencies. As he recounted in an oral history project years after leaving Congress, Pursell's philosophy was, "Okay, we're going to organize or Reagan's all finished." In response (White House Chief of Staff) Jim Baker said, "Carl you're absolutely right so I want you at the White House with your steering Committee every Thursday at 4:00 o'clock."

Pursell had long been interested in bringing together various sections of both parties and Baker's decree gave him the impetus to organize the "Gypsy Moths." This was a counter in part to the conservative "Boll Weevils" on the Democratic side who joined Republicans to hand Reagan key wins on budget issues. *The New York Times* explained, "The Gypsy Moths were named for an insect that has been ravaging New England foliage, and most of them represent regions of the Northeast and Middle West that are suffering severely from the recession." Pursell in that role was like a kid at Christmas ("I started to negotiate. I had a power position"). He explained, "Some Republicans want to limit the party. We want a broader-based party along the lines of Lincoln."

Pursell's position often required him to take on his former Michigan colleague and '76 classmate, White House Budget Director David Stockman. His argument was "the proposed cuts, in effect, leave declining regions to their own fate, a policy that in the end will spell economic disaster for the entire country." He explained that, "We expressed our concern that all the bargaining seemed to be taking place with the southern Democrats and we said the RepublicanS cannot afford to write off the Northeast and Midwest just because we have urban constituents."

That November, Pursell and two like-minded Republicans, Jim Leach of Iowa and Bill Green of New York, sat down with *The New York Times* and were asked whether they felt out of step with the increasingly conservative segments of their caucus. Pursell responded: "I'm not sure it's totally a matter of being out of step. I think many of us from the Middle West or the Northeast have thought for years that Federal policy has somewhat favored the Sunbelt. I think we've seen a Southern strategy for a long, long time and I think we have really not disciplined ourselves in a cohesive team effort to set priorities, to overcome that favoritism."

The "Gypsy Moths" first success came in October of '81 when the House, aided by 39 Republicans, rejected an attempt to recommit a Health and Labor Appropriations bill to make further cuts. His reasoning: "I don't think we can make the balancing act by just touching this bill. If we send this bill back to committee, to cut only it, without looking at the defense budget and the water projects, it's unfair." In 1982, Pursell was one of 13 moderates who voted against the Republican budget on the House floor.

Pursell saw some of his leverage lost following the '82 elections when Democrats recaptured twenty-six seats. Most of these newcomers were liberal Democrats who canceled out the Boll Weevils, which meant the leverage of the Gypsy Moths was now almost non-existent. Pursell recalls fellow moths asking him, "Carl what do we do now? 'I said, well let's write a Federal budget.'" Pursell called that a, "Helluva challenge," but proudly adds, "We did. We spent a thousand hours doing it, I introduced it on time, it was a whole budget freeze for five years."

In the latter part of the 1980s Pursell's claim to being a genuine centrist proved mixed. He abandoned Reagan on his veto of a 60-day plant notification bill but sided with him on a massive highway spending bill that Congress subsequently overrode. He backed George H.W. Bush on his vetoes of the minimum wage increase and the Family and Medical Leave Act. For the most part, he sided with abortion rights and gun control supporters. Around that time, Pursell's power was increasing by virtue of his vision and other Republicans, likeminded or not, began taking notice.

Arms control was another issue where Pursell's moderate proclivities often took center field and in 1983, he delineated his distaste for chemical weapons. "Try to imagine," he told his colleagues, "a situation in which grown men were lying on the ground vomiting, choking, gasping for air. The only purpose of chemical weapons is to inflict death and destruction in the most horrible ways." Pursell was not a fan of the Star Wars missile system and in 1987, was one of three Republicans including Silvio Conte of Massachusetts and Bill Green of New York who voted with Democrats on a Norm Dicks amendment to SALT 11.

In 1990, Pursell introduced legislation to repeal the 1970 Newspaper Preservation Act. His motivation was watching the rival *Detroit News* and *The Detroit Free Press* form joint operating agreements (JOAs) which required exceptions from the U.S. Attorney General. Pursell's rationale was that it "seems ironic that some of the very voices which call for free market forces to work in other industries seek government protection for creating monopolies in their own." Additionally, "Newspapers which seek JOAs are put in a compromising position of being dependent on the federal government for their survival? How can such newspapers truly fulfill their watchdog role?"

As the 80s were drawing to a close, Pursell saw an opportunity to form another caucus known as the "92 Group." This was a collaborative Congressional effort to try to get a Republican House majority by 1992. Still, he was emphatic after his career closed that, "I did everything bipartisan - never party line." In 1990, Pursell became known for another crusade: a sincere attempt at deficit reduction that caused an affinity with conservatives. It started earlier in the year with the Rogue River in Michigan. Pursell had been pressed to put in an authorization to clean the River, which the Corps of

Engineers very much wanted, but declined to do so because of what he viewed as a burden on the deficit. He asked colleagues to sacrifice some of their pet projects but got very few takers.

That said, "soul mating" with the right, at least on fiscal issues, continued. By October, Pursell was deeply unhappy about what the budget package negotiated by Bush and Democratic leaders would do to the deficit. At one point during that stalemate, Pursell was telephoned by Ford who urged him to stick with Bush as the leader of the party. Pursell in turn reminded Ford that as president he had issued vetoes on 22 spending bills and Ford replied, "you were gutsy, you did what had to be done." Pursell recalled in the oral history project asking Ford to "call Bush back and tell him to veto some damn bills up there and then we get some clout here and our minority becomes a majority." Deciding to walk the walk, Pursell joined with Ohio Republican John Kasich, an unabashed conservative with a budget-cutting zeal, and put together an alternative package. However, Democratic leaders failed to put it up for a vote.

While getting personal was not Pursell's style, he increasingly found himself using the process as a means of extrapolating differences between the partisan rule of the House. One example came during the protracted budget summit negotiations in October 1990 and Pursell took the opportunity to bemoan the Democratic process for passing it. "Mr. Speaker," his floor speech began. "It was a night of infamy last Thursday, October 4, when the budget summit resolution came to this House at 1:15 a.m., in the middle of the night. The Democratic budget resolution followed on October 7, 2:30 a.m., in the middle of the night. The rule that would not allow consideration of the Pursell-Kasich Republican budget plan was voted out of the Committee on Rules on October 15, at 1 a.m. in the middle of the night. The Democrats passed their own rule for their own plan, in the middle of the night. So we have a World Series going on here in which we play only by the Democratic rules, in which they have waived the rules for the Budget Act 62 times in the 101st Congress. We demand the same rules as the Democrats, just like the Cincinnati Reds and the Oakland A's must use in the World Series. The Democrats cannot even play fair and square on the same day that the civil rights bill is debated on the floor of the House. Can you believe that, America?"

If that speech was not vintage Pursell, it was not exactly a once in a lifetime manifestation either. *The Almanac of American Politics* called Pursell, "rumpled, chatty, usually inclined to seek consensus but ready to speak out when aroused." He evidently felt aroused in the midst of that same budget cacophony when he made it clear to Bush Chief of Staff John Sununu, who was trying to get Republican lawmakers to fall in line that, "We don't appreciate your staff coming up here to threaten us." Fellow Republicans at the caucus meeting cheered. In that regard Pursell's Michigan Republican colleague, Fred Upton, told a story that in Washington D.C. could only be regards as the grandest compliment. It came from former Reagan Chief of Staff Ken Duberstein and as Upton told it, "No member of the House commanded more respect when he came down to meet with the President than Carl Pursell because he was a straight shooter, not a rubber stamp. He called them as he saw them, and that is terrific respect, certainly from everyone in his district as well as those downtown in the White House.'"

Another event came after the 1990 elections when he tried to move into leadership by challenging incumbent and fellow appropriator Jerry Lewis for the position of Republican Conference Chair. Pursell explained, "I see my role as offering a higher level of leadership than what I call business as usual. We can be major players in giving the country two major strategies." A major beef was, "We're on the defensive all the time."

Despite his relative moderate proclivities, Pursell garnered the backing of House Minority Whip Newt Gingrich whose theme was also bold ideas which was notable because Pursell despised the style of personal debasing for which Gingrich was becoming legendary for promoting. Lewis prevailed 98-64 and Pursell later acknowledged that Gingrich's "purpose was not to help Carl Pursell but to dump Jerry Lewis."

In a post-Congress oral history project, Pursell admitted as much. "I wasn't a great lover of Newt Gingrich," he said, "I didn't like his style. I didn't like his philosophy. I couldn't agree so I was never part of the COS that (was) called the Conservative Opportunity Society. So I was going in a different direction. My party of Lincoln vs. the narrow focus of the Christian Right and all the rest that makes up that party. Not that I'm not moral and religious and that but they have a litmus test for everything. You're either Right to Life or you're not part of the party."

In Congress, Pursell was known for a leader in another area: baseball. A lefty, he proudly coached the House Republicans in their games on the diamond. While lauding his colleague on the House floor as he prepared to retire, fellow Michigan Republican Dave Camp said "Carl's six-game record of four wins and only two losses shows that while winning battles on that floor of the House is sometimes a field of dreams, we are to be taken seriously at America's other favorite pastime of baseball."

After his '76 squeaker, the only time Pursell was remotely threatened as he sought new terms was in 1988 when an Ann Arbor State Senator named Lana Pollack tried to make a case against him. The League of Conservation Voters had named Pursell to its Dirty Dozen (they also did the same to another incumbent that year, Robert Lagomarsino in California who had made a career of opposing offshore drilling.) Pollack led Pursell slightly as the count neared the half-way point but, as returns reported from Western Wayne and other rural areas, the incumbent leapt to a ten-point lead and kept his job with 55%. Pursell ran behind Bush who was taking 58% in the district but explained, "Some years, I run ahead of the President. Other years, I don't. It's really hard to tell"). In 1990, Pursell won with 64% but problems relating to his tenure were looming.

From the time it became clear that Michigan would be losing two Congressional seats, it was the least kept secret in political circles that Pursell might be the odd man out. Control of the legislature was split between the two parties but many of Pursell's old colleagues had left office, so unlike other, younger members, he had few friends to lobby to preserve his district.

By early 1992, it was decided that a judicial panel would determine the plan. Democrats proposed throwing Pursell into a district with William Broomfield, a fellow Republican who was in his 36th year in Congress and immensely popular. Ironically, Pursell was aided by a plan submitted by Lansing-area Democrat Bob Carr who, in an effort to protect his own base, submitted a map that preserved 70% of his district. When the panel issued its ruling, Pursell's worst fears surfaced. Plymouth was moved to the Democratic friendly district held by powerful Democratic baron William Ford (ironically, Ford retired two years later and in Republican-friendly 1994, Pursell might very well have won the seat had he gone for it). Nevertheless, that was a pipe's dream in March of '92 and Pursell recognized that.

After the plans were released, Pursell's predicament was illustrated by the Dean of the Michigan delegation, the powerful John Dingell. He said he would "have had to leave a home he loves or face three quick rounds with a bengal tiger." Pursell evidently reached that same conclusion and he announced his retirement a day later. Curiously, the coach on the Democratic side, Marty Russo of Illinois, was also a casualty of redistricting that year. Shortly after he announced his retirement, Pursell joked that he'd like to "win one going-away.

Many mourned their colleague's looming departure and Michigan GOP colleague Guy Vander Jagt said in a statement, "I thought it was quite apparent

that he would run in the new district. It is truly a shock followed by sadness"
(there were evidently no hard feelings from 1980 when Pursell did not back
his fellow Michigander's bid to become Minority Leader. Vander Jagt, he said,
was "a nice guy but he wasn't ready for floor leadership.")

As Pursell prepared to depart, Illinois Republican and fellow Appropriator
John Porter paid tribute to him: "There are many people here who are part of
the problem but the gentleman from Michigan has been part of the solution.
He has come here to govern not just to express his philosophy over and over
again at the opposite side, but to take responsibility for the bottom line, to
make the tough decisions that it takes to make this country work. We need
more people like the gentleman from Michigan in this chamber."

After leaving office, Pursell coached soccer and served as an Eastern
Michigan University regent, retiring in 1999. When he died in 2009 after a
long illness at age 76, the House of Representatives paused for a moment of
silence. His son Philip said his father, "accomplished in death what he could
not in life - a moment of silence in the House of Representatives."

CHAPTER FORTY-FIVE

Rubbergate Bounced Hubbard from a Seat He Could Have Held Many More Years – At Least Before Prison

Introductory Quote: "You're not going to pay by check are you?" – The barber of Michigan Congressman Paul Henry following the revelation of the many members of Congress who had written overdrafts.

Photo via the Kenton County Library

The phrase, "Sometimes you're the windshield, sometimes you're the bug," may eminently exemplify the career of Carroll Hubbard though, many times, winding up as the bug was self-destructive. With the exception of a failed gubernatorial bid five years into his tenure, Hubbard glided through every election save two: his first in which he prevailed and his last in which he did not. The first was achieved by narrowly bouncing a 16-year incumbent in the Democratic primary while 18 years later he found the shoe on the other foot when he himself was bounced as a result of the House check overdraft scandal (evidently, dislodging longtime incumbents in primaries was seemingly obligatory for voters in Kentucky's First Congressional District as the man Hubbard beat had himself made it to Congress by wresting away an incumbent who had served 22 years). But he was on the outs with more than one leading Democrat in the Bluegrass State and engaged in a venomous, protracted feud with his state's largest newspaper that he found to be malicious.

Hubbard might not ever have achieved his goal to become governor of Kentucky but he represented his middle-of-the-road but conservative leaning constituency fairly well. As not only a Watergate baby but president of his freshman class, one might have expected Hubbard to have been right in the midst of the reformist idealism that encapsulated the class. He was not though he was well-liked and did provide the class critical votes on roll calls. But late-breaking scandals meant he would be one of those politicians who what could have been.

Hubbard's father was a Baptist Minister who served on the Southern Baptist Theological Seminary and was a professor of Boyce Bible College. His mother was a school teacher. Hubbard grew up in Murray, Kentucky, obtained his Bachelor's at Georgetown and his law degree from the University of Louisville. He joined the Kentucky Young Democrats and was a member of the Kentucky National Guard. In 1967, Hubbard won a seat in the Kentucky Senate. Where he'd spar often with Julian Carroll.

Hubbard in the Kentucky Senate
Photo via the Kenton County Library

The surprising thing about the fact that Hubbard was not the activist that other Watergate babies were was because his election was of similar circumstances to those that were: taking on the old guard and winning. In fact, when Hubbard acknowledged victory after defeating Democratic Representative Frank Stubblefield in the '74 primary, he told supporters, "The people have voted their dissatisfaction with the 93rd Congress. The people were anxious for a change in Washington."

Hubbard did not seem particularly intimidating to Stubblefield when he first entered the race. In fact, he acknowledged years later that in winning, he "did what many Kentuckians thought was impossible." Stubblefield was not only the vice-chair of the House Agriculture Committee but chaired the influential Tobacco Subcommittee. But he was 67 and Hubbard charged that his representation of the First District was not up to par and specifically raised his high absenteeism on votes. Some interest groups, particularly labor and the United Miners agreed and backed Hubbard. Stubblefield retained the backing of most farm interests.

Hubbard with his sometimes nemesis, Governor Julian Carroll
Photo via the Kenton County Library

Stubblefield mopped up in the Eastern part of the 24 county district but Hubbard did the same out west, taking 60% in McCracken (Paducah). Out of 60,000 votes cast, Hubbard came on top by 624 for a 50.6-49.4% win. It was an exhilarating night for the Hubbard family as his brother Kyle narrowly prevailed in his primary in the state's Fourth District where an incumbent Republican Gene Snyder was seeking re-election.

Stubblefield asserted that "a lot of our vote did not go to the polls" but nonetheless conceded gracefully. Others weren't as generous with their God-speed. For a brief period, Hubbard required police protection as two callers contacted him to inform him that "you won't live long enough to be our next representative." In any case, Hubbard prevailed in the general election with 78%, losing only a single county at the far Eastern end of the district (Kyle conversely narrowly lost to Snyder). Until 1992, he'd never again have to sweat an election though his '88 primary opponent did give him a run for his money (literally) before Hubbard went on to capture 73%.

Hubbard went to Washington having won more than his Congressional seat. With help from another freshman, Paul Simon from across the border in Illinois, he became president of the large freshman class. Bill Goodling, another member of that large class (and one of only 17 Republicans), revealed another of Hubbard's secrets. Goodling had sent a letter to every fellow freshman. Only Hubbard responded. He kept in touch with the class. John Lawrence in his book on the Watergate class noted that Hubbard drove 300 miles to attend a fundraiser for another freshman, David Evans of Indiana.

Hubbard was assigned to both the Banking Committee and Merchant Marine and Fisheries and joined the Conservative Democratic Forum. His Presidential support score did not radically change with Jimmy Carter or Ronald Reagan. Beyond 1975 where he supported Gerald Ford on just 34% of votes, he never went above 60% or below 43%. His stances on issues were more malleable. A supporter of a Balanced Budget Amendment before it was cool, Hubbard withdrew his name in 1982 at the request of then-House Majority Leader Jim Wright. He also opposed the ERA. His record was such that Tip O'Neill once told him jokingly, "You vote so often with our Republican minority, why don't you just join the Republican Party?"

When it came to Reagan's request for an MX missile, *The New York Times* reported on how ferociously Hubbard was targeted. He was attending a statewide basketball tournament and, "When the semifinal game went into overtime, the police summoned Mr. Hubbard out of the stands for an emergency telephone call. It was, of course, President Reagan in the White House, wanting to present arguments for the MX."

Hubbard's electoral dominance at home did not mean the same would translate into other victories. An attempt to win the state's governorship and a major subcommittee chairmanship fell flat.

The bid for the Blue Grass State's governorship came in 1979 (the state's off year statewide elections spared him from having to surrender his House seat). It wasn't hard to see why Hubbard thought he could prevail – the Democrats had a fractured, five-person field of serious contenders. Carroll had ascended to the governorship after Ford was elected Senator but was barred Constitutionally from seeking re-election. That didn't stop Hubbard from making him his boogeyman. In accusing Carroll of running, "the most corrupt and vicious" administration in state history, Hubbard claimed he had prevailed on the Department of Justice to delay indictments until after the primary. But the presence of State Auditor George Atkins, who also hailed from Western Kentucky, complicated matters for Hubbard. Hubbard carried the First District but actually ran third in McCracken (Paducah), taking only a quarter of the vote. And he won little else statewide and ended with just 12%.

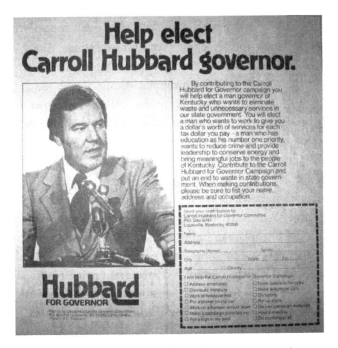

Photo courtesy of the West Kentucky Journal

Hubbard delved back into his Congressional duties but was stymied somewhat in his ability to move up. He had seniority to assume the chairmanship of the Economic Stabilization Committee of Banking but withdrew when it became clear that New Yorker John LaFalce, a fellow Watergate Baby albeit a notch below Hubbard on the panel, had sufficient backing to win.

For 2/3 of his House career, Hubbard faced a force far more potent than any possible Republican challenger or gubernatorial opponent: *The Louisville*

Courier. Kentucky's largest newspaper had once run a headline, "Turnover High on Congressman's Staff" and the relationship degenerated from there. *The Courier* profiled Hubbard as, "A man who cares little for the legislative work of Congress, devoting most of his time to guarding his public image. A man-who expects his aides, regardless of their positions, to produce mounds of mail to his constituents. A man who is so suspicious of his employees that, in at least a few cases, he has rifled wastebaskets and called to make sure they reported to work on time. A man who flies into tirades over matters as simple as a comma missing from a letter, who humiliates his employees in front of others and who sometimes fires people for minor infractions." There was even one story that he once berated a female receptionist for answering the phone with the greeting, "Good Morning," when it was really afternoon. Hubbard responded by calling a Congressman, "a sitting duck for wild charges by disgruntled, unhappy former employees and ambitious young reporters." Hubbard threatened legal action and the paper was forced to admit "we found we made some dumb mistakes with the statistics."

The Courier Journal did add feint praise. "All of the former aides agreed that he can be kind to favored staffers driving them home after a late night at work, paying them all very well, lending money to a new employee short of cash." Still, the bitterness continued through the duration of Hubbard's tenure in office.

Ditto with his poor relations with the state's leading Democrats. Hubbard's feud with Carroll was legendary but he also tangled with Ford over the restoration of Alben Barkley's birthplace in Paducah, contending the money should be used for deficit reduction. And he committed perhaps the most cardinal of all sins when he vowed at the outset of the 1990 Senate campaign to remain "neutral" in the race between junior Republican Senator Mitch McConnell and Louisville Mayor Harvey Sloane (McConnell prevailed by just 4%).

Hubbard was one of three Democrats who in the aftermath of the Robert Maplethorpe exhibit, signed a letter to President George H.W. Bush asking him to restrict funding for the NEA (Frank Annunzio of Illinois and Bill Sarpalius of Texas were the other two). But as he neared the end of his career, Hubbard began shifting, most notably on abortion rights when he began voting to overturn the gag order and restrictions on federal funding for abortions. In 1989, he vowed to oppose any attempt to eliminate Roe vs. Wade on the House floor, telling his colleagues, "I admit to you I have fully grown on this issue in the past years." He did the same on gun control, supporting a ban on semi-automatic weapons despite a furious lobbying campaign by the

NRA's 18,000 members followed by the Brady Bill two years later. But the savings and loan crisis was one critical area on which he didn't mature.

During the hearings conducted by Banking Committee Chair Henry Gonzales, "Hubbard displayed himself as at best tone-deaf and at worst complicit in the wrongdoing – or even more charitably, complicit with the complicitor."

First came his interaction with Federal regulator M. Danny Wall, whom Hubbard said he was "proud to call a friend." Hubbard had made a call to Wall months earlier inquiring about the sale of the Lincoln Thrift (Senators Alan Cranston and Dennis DeConcini made similar calls and underwent career-ending scrutiny for nearly two years) Wall had initially stated in an interview the purpose of Hubbard's call was to ensure "prompt consideration" of approval. Later, Wall changed his story to say that Hubbard was merely seeking a "status report."

Next, during banking Committee hearings, Hubbard accused another thrift regulator, Edwin Gray of "impugn(ing) the reputations of four long-time Senators who are not here to defend themselves." Hubbard at one point had contacted Gray regarding the First Federal Savings and Loan Association of Mayfield. When Hubbard told Gray that "your testimony may be flawed too," Gonzales ruled Hubbard out of order. Gray reciprocated just before Hubbard faced his last primary, telling *The Courier* that, "he did basically what he thought the industry wanted him…He was the antithesis of a person who seem to have the broad public interest at heart."

Locally, Hubbard worked on a gaseous diffusion plant West Paducah as well as the fair distribution of satellites. "Today," he said in 1987, "the number one issue here in Washington is aid to the contras in Nicaragua. But in portions of Western Kentucky, aid to satellite-dish owners is also important." He helped nix a bill requiring outside banks to have annual outside audits. And he urged an inquiry into a 1985 crash that killed 248 service members returning to Fort Stewart in his district, claiming, the government has not done all that it could to totally put this tragedy to rest."

In 1992, Hubbard appeared to have prospects for continuing in Congress indefinitely – he had faced no Republican opposition for the previous three cycles (he had dispatched a candidate running under the Populist banner with 87% in 1990). He even thought he could expend political capital to Eastern Kentucky by getting his wife Carol to seek a Congressional seat. His rationale may been that had she won, it most certainly would have been a feather in his cap as he strived toward a '95 gubernatorial bid. Instead, she lost. And keeping it in the family, so did he.

Photo via Getty Images

To say that defeat took Hubbard and Washington by storm is an understatement. Many thought his legendary reputation for signing and personalizing letters to constituents would itself have been enough to insulate him from defeat. In fact, one county clerk said just after the voting that, "I wouldn't have thought the president . . . could have beat Carroll Hubbard."

Hubbard did have an opponent in Tom Barlow but he was untested and in fact had been trounced by Hubbard in the 1986 primary. In fact, much of the attention in the days leading up to the May 30 primary was on at the other end of the state. The Congressman's wife of eight years was a school teacher and a former Miss Kentucky who hailed from the Seventh District. She had declared her intention to challenge fellow Democrat Chris Perkins in November 1990, just after he had come within an eyelash of defeat. Perkins's father was the venerable Carl Perkins who had chaired the Education and Labor Committee for many years. "Chris Perkins isn't the man his father was." Perkins announced he was leaving Congress in January 1992 and the district was merged with Republican Congressman Hal Rogers. Hubbard remained in the race and prepared for a cacophonous primary as her husband reached out to his banking committee allies and urged them to contribute to her race: she raised $300,000, a charge that State Senator Joe Doug Hays called, "obscene."

Meanwhile, Barlow was hitting Hubbard and *The Courier-Journal* followed, running a piece 10 days out about how Hubbard opposed nearly every Banking Committee amendment that would beef up security. As the check bouncing saga thickened, Hubbard denied that he had any overdrafts, until Carol did it for him without citing how many. When the official list was released on April 16, it became clear how many: 152. The timing could hardly have been worse – the primary was six weeks away.

Hubbard carried most of the turf in the central part of the district near the Indiana border, but with unimpressive margins and in many cases below 50%. He carried all but one county at the district's eastern end. Barlow carried every county but Fulton in the Western part of the state. Both men were from McCracken County but voters there were reeling against Congressional perks as much as anywhere - Barlow took 57% there (hearkening back to 1974 when it was Hubbard who prevailed so handily there over Stubblefield). That added up to a 48%-45% win for Barlow, a 3,000 vote win (a third candidate, Charles Banken, took 7%). Reminded following his concession that he could pocket the money in his campaign account, Hubbard replied, "I was caught by surprise tonight and I have not given any thought what I will do with the campaign funds." It was not an auspicious night for the Hubbard family. Carol took just 17%, finishing behind Hays who took 30% and Ned Pillersdorf who slipped past her by 133 votes. She did manage to carry seven counties.

Leaving did not come easy for Hubbard. As his term wound down, he conducted an interview with C-Span in which he said, "I may run again in 1994…There was a protest vote in Kentucky against Washington in May and I think the protest vote is still there even in October. We'll find out whether it's present on November 3rd across this nation." A senior committee staffer recalled him remaining in his personal office until long after the furniture had been taken out, at one point sitting on top of a wastepaper basket he had turned upside down. Hubbard did enter into the *Congressional Record* his gratitude for, the "benefit of a tremendous staff here in Washington and Western Kentucky."

Hubbard as he was preparing to leave office
Image via C-SPAN

After leaving office, Hubbard displayed why he epitomized the term, "mischief maker" and it came through a confluence of events – the banking scandal, Carol's Congressional campaign and his own shenanigans. For one, Hubbard had funneled money – as much as $50,000, from his campaign to Carol's. Another no-no: "Hubbard directed one of his employees to shred and throw away documents that had been subpoenaed" by a grand jury. "Prior to that," the publication continued, "Hubbard had staged a burglary at one of his offices to make it appear that his House Bank and campaign records had been stolen." Hubbard aides also charged that they were made to work on Carol's campaign. The Congressman also steered an endless amount of money from PAC's, particularly from the banking community.

In late 1993, Hubbard decided to become an FBI informant and create a sort of, "Abscam II" to investigate Libyan agents. His rational was that cooperating in various sting operations the Bureau wanted him to undertake would lessen the penalties when charges were filed. FBI agents even bestowed upon him a name – "Elmer Fudd." Hubbard later contended that he was an "FBI slave" and agents denied that plans for an "Abscam II" like scenario had ever been laid. But if Hubbard thought that leniency would be forthcoming, he was wrong. He was sentenced to three years in prison – prosecutors had sought more, with the Judge saying, "The success of our system depends on public confidence in public officials. You have obviously and seriously jeopardized that confidence." Carol was fined $27,000, given five years' probation and forfeited her teachers certificate. She died in 2015 at age 75.

By 2001, Carroll had done his time and sought to return to practicing law. The Kentucky Bar Association voted 16-0 against re-instating it but was overturned by the State Supreme Court. Hubbard remarried and opened a practice in Paducah.

Meanwhile, Carroll decided he could not rid himself of the political bug and mounted a comeback bid for a Kentucky Senate seat in 2006. His responase about how his would-be constituents would respond to his past: "They know I'm a felon." He came tantalizingly close, losing by just 81 votes out of 31,000 cast (repeat efforts in 2008 and '12 came up well short). But in a sign that time heels old wounds, Julian Carroll, himself back in the Senate chamber, campaigned for his former foe.

CHAPTER FORTY-SIX

Alexander a Gifted Public Servant but Hounded By Personal Woes that Ended Career

Introductory Quote: "I have a message for Democrats based on my baptism by political fire in Southern politics: Answer Representative Newt Gingrich's attacks upon our party or be prepared to lose again and again. Answer Gingrich or lose... The Republican strategy forged by Newt Gingrich, Lee Atwater and their political soul-mates across America is based upon the fundamental political notion that the people of this country, as we say in the South, 'don't have the sense God gave a goose.'" – Congressman Bill Alexander in a 1989 piece in *The New York Times* urging his party to not roll over and play dead against forthcoming Republican attacks.

Photo courtesy of the Museum of American History, Cabot Public Schools

For some time throughout his 24-years in Congress, Bill Alexander basked in the Arkansas tradition of serving long, accumulating seniority and holding prestigious leadership slots. Personal mistakes and a longstanding feeling among constituents that he had drifted put an to his career in the 1992 Democratic primary when he was stunned by a political novice who made his woes the issue. To add salt to the wound, the 31-year-old challenger, Blanche Lambert, was the daughter of a family friend and had once worked as a receptionist in Alexander's office.

Alexander was born in Memphis, Tennessee but attended school in Osceola, Arkansas. He served in the Army during the Korean War and attended the University of Arkansas but ultimately obtained his degree in Political Science and History from Southwestern at Memphis South. His law degree from Vanderbilt University followed. Alexander then did research for federal Judge Marion Boyd in Memphis and as hired by Memphis law firm of Montedonico, Boone, Gilliland, Heiskell & Loch before starting up a practice in Osceola, Arkansas.

In 1968, Alexander entered the Democratic Congressional primary to succeed retiring Congressman Ezekia "Took" Gathings. With seven candidates, including Jack Files, an aide to Senator William Fulbright, the primary was genuinely up for grabs. In a district 30% black, all candidates courted African-American voters. Alexander outdistanced his rivals with 38% in the primary and prevailed over Files 62%-38% in the runoff. The district contained Northeastern Arkansas which included suburbs of Memphis but also poor, impoverished agricultural dependent areas of the Mississippi Delta. Alexander expressed concern about the "cost price squeeze" and advocated a "brain bank."

Alexander was initially assigned to the House Agriculture Committee but in his third term, got to trade that in for the all prestigious Appropriations Committee. He sponsored the Guaranteed Commercial Operating Loan Program for agribusinesses, farmers, and ranchers along with legislation creating the National River Academy and the Mid-South Energy Project. He was a major proponent of ethanol and founded the Alternative Fuels Council.

Most of Alexander's agenda was making sure that his poor district wouldn't get further left behind. *The Commercial Appeal* in 1992 wrote that, "Alexander's office has been quick to announce countless federally funded water projects and sewer treatment grants that brought sanitary living conditions to countless Delta homes." The paper went on to say, "He can be so quick to announce one piece of progress or another that an industrial developer said agencies sometimes hesitate in letting Alexander in on negotiations for a project for fear he will jeopardize it by making a premature announcement." There were certainly a lot of press releases. *The Encyclopedia of Arkansas* wrote, "More than $30 billion in economic development resulted from (Alexander's) congressional initiatives.

In 1976, Alexander, complaining of, "a double standard for foreign countries," offered an amendment to a foreign aid appropriation to cut off aid to countries who have defaulted on repaying the U.S. for more than a year. It passed 229-189, though Otto Passman of Louisiana, famously known for opposing aid, said the product resulted from "an emotional thing at the end of a long day," and "was a good thing to demagogue on." The provision was removed in conference. That same year, when Congress banned postal rate increases for the forthcoming year, Alexander accused colleagues of, "passing the buck to the next Congress to solve the serious problems that persist in our Postal Service…It boils down to a question of who is going to decide what a pot is. Is it going to be the Congress or a few self-appointed people within the administration?"

With colleague Ed Bethune in 1979 attending the inauguration of a 32-year old Governor named Bill Clinton
Photo courtesy of the Museum of American History, Cabot Public Schools

When Ronald Reagan won the White House, Alexander found little to like on his domestic agenda. He opposed Reagan's tax cuts despite wide pressure within his constituents to back it. In 1985, when Congress was forced to accept the austerest of farm aid legislation, Alexander said, "our farmers are in a state of despair. They feel let down by their Government." When Congress was debating an override of Reagan's veto of a major trade bill in 1988, Alexander put his own spin on Will Rogers's prediction that "America would be the first nation to go to the poorhouse in a Cadillac. What he did not know," Alexander added, "was that Ronald Reagan would be driving the car, and instead of a Cadillac, it would be a Toyota."

Alexander battled the president on foreign matters as well. He opposed continued production of the MX missile and told colleagues of his discussion with Reagan as the House debated its authorization. Alexander asked Reagan why he doesn't propose a balanced budget to which he replied, "There was a silence on the other end of the line; the President obviously had not thought that he would be questioned about his plans for a balanced budget, and he said, 'You know, that is the most hypocritical question I've ever heard.' I said, "Mr. President, that is the most reasonable question that could be asked at a time when you are pursuing a credit card defense policy which, by your own definition and figures will leave the American people with an $185 billion deficit when you leave Washington and return to California." Alexander also accused the president of becoming "angry and profane" in that conversation.

Alexander viewed aid to Nicaragua as similarly misguided. Because much of the assistance went toward 62,120 belts and 53,526 boots, as noted by *The New York Times*, Alexander said, "We are not helping democracy in Central America. We are helping capitalism in Florida, the Cayman Islands and the Bahamas...The inventory sounds more like Imelda Marcos' closet than a revolutionary inventory."

Cuba was a different matter, if only because Alexander viewed the nation as pertinent to the prosperity of his rice growers. He cultivated Fidel Castro not only with multiple meetings but by scuba diving with him. His philosophy: "If a Kansas wheat farmer can sell wheat to the Soviet Union, why should an Arkansas rice farmer be forever forbidden from selling his rice to Cuba?"

Consistently, Alexander also was supportive of the Bush Administration's effort to bestow Most Favored Nation Status on China. Calling it, "not in the best interests of our nation to distance ourselves from the Chinese just as they are emerging from a 40-year transition from a feudal society ruled by emperors to a modern state governed by pluralism," adding, "Time is required for such sweeping revolutions."

Photo courtesy of the Museum of American History, Cabot Public Schools

After Jim Wright of Texas won the position of Majority Leader in 1976, he named Alexander a deputy whip. In 1980, he was a chief deputy whip which Alexander viewed as a high-level position that could mean great advancement in his district. He even began plotting to run for Majority Whip – the third ranking position in his caucus, in 1986 but, severe political problems back home forced him to pull the plug before that contest even took shape.

That year, Alexander was startled by what was by far his toughest opponent, State Senator Jim Woods and Wood's campaign consultant was Darrell Glascock who had gained notoriety for running a few key races. Alexander had encountered a massive amount of negative publicity for a military jet that he requested to fly himself and four other members of Congress to Brazil for a fact-finding mission. It not only turned out that Alexander was the only member who made the trip but that when it was over, he and his daughter were transported to Honduras for a vacation. The tab came to $56,364, Democrats refused to condone it and Wood's during the campaign called him, "an international jet-setter."

The Alexander-Woods primary was an all Democratic affair but Republicans got in on the action as well. Hoping to soften the eventual winner up for an unusually strong GOP candidate in the fall, state officials fielded a lottery in the First District promising two free worldwide plane tickets and $2,000 in spending money if they answered a survey. After the election, Alexander's campaign filed a complaint on the propriety of the lottery though admitted that some 150 of his own volunteers entered the survey.

For Alexander, the real scare came on primary night. Before any vote was tabulated, Alexander was expected to hold off Woods with room to spare but, after the 156,000 votes were cast and Alexander prevailed by just 7,000 out of 156,000 cast, a margin of 52-48%. Alexander carried Creighead (Jonesboro) by exactly 100 votes among 13,000 cast and his votes from the black community carried him through. Woods later acknowledged that, "My real problem was I couldn't raise enough money and I couldn't get people to take me seriously until the last two or three weeks."

Meantime, the discontent toward Alexander came through loud and clear and he stepped down as Whip. "I was planning a campaign to be Majority Whip of the House to provide even greater influence for Arkansas. You, the people of the 1st Congressional District, have sent me to work in a different direction. And believe me, I got the message." He vowed to go forward not as a "national Democrat but as an Arkansas Democrat."

Photo courtesy of the Museum of American History, Cabot Public Schools

The near-death scare resulted in a slight, though not super-noticeable shift right. For example, Alexander supported Bush's signature capital gains tax cut and the amendment banning desecration of the flag. While these positions were popular among his constituents, the Democratic leadership opposed them and it wasn't long before that Alexander had opposed high-profile legislation in similar circumstances (the Reagan tax cuts, etc.). But he was pro-choice and did support most of his party's other social initiatives.

In 1990, Alexander became a member of the Treasury, Postal Service and General Government Subcommittee of Appropriations ("I suppose I am fortunate in coming to this subcommittee at this time because it is a time when acceptance of the Postal Service by the general public has increased dramatically"). He immediately fought on behalf of residents of Nettleton, Arkansas to avoid its post office merging with Jonesboro and prevailed. He also advocated for a local stamp commemorating Elvis Presley, whom her felt was "likened unto the Messiah." That same year, he proposed an amendment halving funding for Radio Marti and lost big on the House floor.

Pursuing local interests still left Alexander time to stand up to a Democratic boogeyman – Newt Gingrich of Georgia. Gingrich had just won the position of House Minority Whip and was simultaneously going after Jim Wright for a book deal. But Gingrich had problems with his own book deal. Alexander had filed a complaint against Gingrich and labeled him, "a Congressional Jimmy Swaggart, who condemns sin while committing hypocrisy." After accusing the Ethics Committee of foot-dragging by not interviewing key players, Alexander used his own attorney to mount their own investigation. He authored a piece in *The New York Times* in which he gave two pieces of advice to fellow Democrats. "First, hold him to the same standards he demands of others." The other was simply to fight back and to promote that argument and he used his close call to illustrate it. "I speak from experience," he wrote. "Starting in 1968, I pursued for 18 years a policy of ignoring right-wing attacks upon me as a socialistic, big-spending apologist for communist causes. My policy was that people knew me, and they knew better. While this policy may have won me praise from a few editorial writers, by 1986 I found myself in the political fight of my life."

**Alexander (second from right) with Senator David Pryor, Chairman
Frank Coffman of the First Federal Bancshares of Arkansas at
Harrison, and Congressman John paul Hammerschmidt**
Photo courtesy of the Pryor Center for Arkansas Oral and Visual History

Alexander's Democratic colleagues respected his acumen enough so that, when the Conservative Opportunity Society was making they asked Alexander for his advice. His answer: "not to participate in the debates because it would dignify their presentation far beyond what it's entitled to." Instead, he let television stations of the respective member no when a speech was occurring so they could presumably run footage of him/her addressing a mostly empty chamber.

Alexander's pledge to get back to Arkansas issues seemed to be working as in 1988, later, Glascock challenged the incumbent himself in the primary but drew just 33% and Alexander was unopposed entirely in the general. 1990 was more difficult. Mike Gibson filed at the last minute and had backing from Sam Walton and Jack Stevens. He spent $500,000, mainly to tar Alexander for — This time, Alexander wouldn't be caught napping and he put on a full court press among voters. Gibson, well aware of Alexander's edge among African-Americans, stumped hard in that community. Gibson only carried five counties (two barely) but Alexander didn't romp in most of the others that he won. But it was enough to outpace Gibson 54-46%, a margin of 12%. The general was its usual non-affair and Alexander racked up 64%.

In a 1991 piece on Alexander's finances, *The New York Times* wrote that, "Since 1986, Mr. Alexander's liabilities have outpaced his assets. Congressional financial statements are imprecise, but Mr. Alexander's report shows liabilities of $865,000 to $1.9 million. He lists his assets at $171,000 to $491,000. He said he owes at least $348,000 in interest and principal to the two Arkansas banks." Alexander likened his personal crisis to that of "a farmer who didn't make a crop. You just work hard and make another one." Nor did he attempt to conceal its severity. "I was borrowing money from anybody who would lend it to me and I made a big mistake" and it went, "from Peter to pay Paul."

Alexander might have thought that because voters had overlooked his personal woes, even sometimes by the barest of margins, the controversy over the checks would evaporate. But he and other members underestimated the fuel that poured fire on the national uproar toward Congress.

Unlike other members, when news of the overdrafts came out, Alexander didn't try to foment or deny. Instead, his response was, "I've basically been broke for the last six years." Alexander had appeared to catch a break when Gibson declined to seek a rematch. But 31-year-old Blanche Lambert filled that void. It seemed an initial surprise. Lambert's dad had been a long-time family friend and she herself had been a receptionist in his office on several different occasions, which led Alexander to quip that, "I raised her right while she was working in my office." But the checks appeared to put on the table an opening that she couldn't resist. Sure enough, she told voters, "I can surely balance my checkbook." Alexander was then hit by reports, published by *The Arkansas Democrat* that he put $16,200 from his campaign account into, among other areas, his mortgage payment, which was legal but undoubtedly politically tone-deaf in a district as impoverished as the First.

As late as days before the primary, Alexander led Lincoln 43-38% and most analysts were contending that Lambert wasn't strong enough a match for Alexander and that he'd withstand her challenge. They were wrong by a longshot as the anti-Alexander sentiment again revealed itself to be severely underrated. Lambert unseated 61-39%, a margin of—and a win of 23 counties. Only Woodruff and Poinsette Counties came through for him.

After his loss, Alexander told reporters, "I wish her luck." He was contrite about his own difficulties: "I don't want to take anything away from her. She saw an opportunity and she seized it. But, I'm not blaming it on anyone else. I'm accepting full responsibility for what happened. It's not anyone else's fault." He also said, "I'm not a career politician; I'm a lawyer. I'll leave this to go to work and do something else."

He did indeed resume practicing law while becoming a partner in Advantage Associates, a Washington D.C. based lobbying firm composed of former colleagues of both parties.

CHAPTER FORTY-SEVEN

Anthony Left Office Office Just as Fellow Arkansan was Winning White House

Introductory Tidbit: Beryl Anthony often hosted hunting trips that doubled as fundraisers for the DCCC but he carefully guarded the privacy of those in attendance, even when he was no longer chair. The mantra of "what happens on hunting trips stays on hunting trips" was tested one day in 1991 on a quailhunt trip on an Arkansas farm. Frank Guarini, a Congressman from what *The Washington Post* called "the wilds of Jersey City," was an attendee and, apparently aiming his shotgun too low, grazed the tail of the owner's dog. Rumors about what happened circulated to colleagues and the Washington press and Anthony was hesitant to even comment. Ultimately, Tom Kenworthy, reporter for *The Washington Post* reporter read Anthony the story prior to printing. Meanwhile Guarini (who is profiled in chapter 29), said there were no hard feelings between he and the dog.

I f Arkansas Democrat Beryl Anthony was a Karen Carpenter fan, he might have had the song, "Top of the World," going through his head in early 1992. By mid-year, however, he found that his fortunes as an insider had worked against him back home to the point that he'd soon be out of a job.

Anthony's personal etiquette proved just the right formula to make it in politics. *CQ* once wrote that, "He can please a crowd of rural voters in East Tennessee with his homespun wisdom from Arkansas and also mix well with a group of well-heeled donors in West Palm Beach." Indeed, when he entered Congress, it was as a backbencher who positioned himself somewhat to the right of most in his caucus. In fact, when he first emerged from a hotly contested primary and runoff to win his Southwestern Arkansas Congressional seat in 1978, he was firmly pro-business who opposed the labor backed Humphrey-Hawkins legislation. 14-years later, Anthony had steadily emerged as a trusted ally of the Democratic leadership which he was actually a part of for several years. He had chaired the Democratic Congressional Campaign Committee (DCCC), designed to help other Democrats get elected during the 1990 cycle and on issues, was taking stands that put him on par with the national party. This included opposing the Balanced Budget Amendment and backing the "Brady Bill."

Despite this, there was no foreseeable scenario for Anthony's Congressional career to end. Then came the anti-incumbent mood that was amplified by disillusionment for his gun control vote and overdrafts at the House bank. All of those factors collided to cause Anthony's defeat in a June runoff which ironically came the year his fellow Arkansan, Governor Bill Clinton, won the White House. Had he remained, his stature would have likely soared as perhaps the most sought after House member on Capitol Hill.

An El Dorado native, Anthony's interest in politics was sparked while sitting in the House gallery during a trip to Washington as a boy. The usher pointed to a member she suspected would be going places and his name was John F. Kennedy of Massachusetts. Anthony recalled, "Kennedy went from the House to the Senate to the White House and it was during that period of time that a lot of people like me got caught up in government." Not that politics seemed a desire for Anthony. After he received both his undergraduate and law degrees from the University of Arkansas, he returned home "thinking I would come back into my family business. I stayed there for sixty days." That business was his family's enterprise, Anthony Forest Products that his father and three uncles were running but Anthony decided to practice law.

This opened more doors. Before long, he was appointed an assistant Attorney General and by 1971, elected prosecutor for five counties.

In 1962, meanwhile, Anthony married Shelia Foster, whom he met in Hope while trying to recruit her kids to pledge to his fraternity, Sigma Chi. Anthony recalls, "I got more interested in her although they did pledge." Foster's brother Vince Foster was a gifted lawyer and Deputy White House Counsel prior to his suicide during the first summer of the Clinton administration.

In 1978, Anthony decided to seek the Fourth District U.S. House seat that Ray Thornton was giving up to seek the open U.S. Senate seat. He announced his candidacy on his 40th birthday and began the race well-known in part of the district that he was already serving as prosecutor (his name recognition was also attributed to the business). No Republican had filed which meant that whichever Democratic contender took the nomination was certain to be a member of the next Congress. It was something of a mild surprise that the Democrat turned out to be Anthony.

Most of the major candidates shared similar ideological viewpoints which prompted one to joke when he got a flat tire that he and his rivals had so much in common that, "I was hoping one of them had done it so I could have something to criticize him about it." By running, what *CQ* cited as, "surprisingly well in the southwestern part of the district," Anthony secured a place in the runoff with 27%. First place went to Secretary of State Winston Bryant who took 33%. Bryant had unions behind him which allowed Anthony to label him a tool of labor during the runoff campaign. Bryant captured 79% in Hot Springs and a smattering of counties at the southeastern edge of the district and the two men battled to a draw in Pine Bluff. But Anthony won all but several other counties for a 52-48% win. No general election opponent meant the advantage of forging relationships and when he got to Washington, he was assigned to the Agriculture Committee and Science and Technology.

In office, Anthony was not only a "Boll Weevil" but a member of the Conservative Democratic Forum. He outright made the case that "I personally don't believe there is a lot of tolerance on the part of some Northeastern liberals when it comes to viewing our voting records." A UPI profile noted that "his 1980 voting rated him 22 on the 100-point 'liberal quotient' scale of Americans for Democratic Action." By 1988, his ADA score was 80 percent.

In his first term, Anthony could easily have been regarded as a backbencher who lacked a broad base of allies among leadership (Caucus Chair Gillis Long, a Louisianan was the exception). In fact, when he decided to vote for the

Reagan budget in 1981, he offered to resign from the Budget Committee but Chairman Jim Jones of Oklahoma did not accept it (Anthony had joined with fellow Democrats Bill Hefner of North Carolina and Bill Nelson of Florida in sponsoring a resolution in Budget advocating more defense spending which Jones supported).

The death of Connecticut Congressman Bill Cotter in 1981 was the impetus of Anthony's opportunity to rise to prominence in Democratic circles. Cotter sat on the prestigious Ways and Means Committee and his passing left a vacancy. Anthony went for it and had some big fish in his corner including Long and the panel's new chair, Dan Rostenkowski. He won the slot. Among those he beat out: future vice-presidential nominee Geraldine Ferraro and future Washington State Governor Mike Lowry. What did he have to do for the job? Zippo. "I had to pass no litmus test. There were no commitments asked and no commitments given."

In his early years on the panel, that was borne out as Anthony went in a direction contrary to liberal orthodoxy on a major issue: Social Security. In an effort to save the program, he proposed an increase in payroll taxes and a slight reduction in benefits beginning in the year 2000. The measure was advanced by the House Ways and Means Subcommittee on Social Security by a 7-4 vote. Later that month, Anthony supported a proposal by Texas Democrat Jake Pickle to rein in Social Security costs in part by raising the retirement age to 67 because "you just cannot increasing the tax rate to bail out Social Security." Folks living longer was also a factor.

During much of that time, Anthony was trying to make the Social Security Disability Program more user-friendly and he was at the forefront of writing legislation that would require the Reagan administration to enforce more literally provisions from language passed three years earlier. At a field hearing in Hot Springs, Arkansas (chaired by Pickle) Anthony charged the administration with using "a meat-ax approach and slashed checks to many persons actually disabled who deserve support under the program...When you have an administration that takes a mandate from the Congress but tries to enlarge upon that mandate in order to make their budget look better and expedites the hearings, and then changes the rules during the play of the game, it creates chaos. And, that is exactly what has happened." Represeenting a poor district, Anthony was very committed to fighting poverty. At one hearing, angered that White House Budget Director David Stockman was sugarcoating data on poverty, Anthony told him, "As usual, you come prepared to discuss your numbers and we come prepared to discuss our numbers."

Throughout much of his tenure, Anthony's focus was strongly parochial. In 1985, he and Kentucky Republican Larry Hopkins (another member of the class of '78) successfully sponsored legislation to require nerve gas to be demolished from chemical munitions at storage sites. Hopkins had been reacting to the Lexington-Blue Grass Army Depot but Anthony had the Pine Bluff Arsenal in the Fourth District in mind where "the Army stores thousands of agent tons of chemical munitions."

When Agriculture Secretary Clayton Yeutter unveiled a program for European rice subsidies, Anthony and Senator David Pryor cried foul, complaining to Yeutter that it would hurt rice growers in Arkansas. On land preservation, Anthony and the state's senior Senator, Dale Bumpers, tangled on how much wilderness area to designate. Bumpers wanted 117,000 while Anthony only favored 42,000. Both chambers passed their respective versions and Anthony led a delegation that included a hike and a press conference. Members then jumped in the pool and were photographed by the state's largest newspaper. The photo appearing on the front page created momentum which resulted in what Anthony calls "a compromise all the way."

With Republican Hal Daub of Nebraska, Anthony was able to secure a two percent increase in Medicare/Medicaid payment rates for rural hospitals. He would often go to the mat with Rostenkowski when he felt the chairman was shortchanging rural interests. Folks around the country noticed. Anthony won awards from the National Hospital Association and the Arkansas Hospital Association Legislator of the Year Award.

Image via C-SPAN

Issuewise, Anthony's proclivity for centrism hit its stride in 1989 when President George H.W. Bush was promoting his signature tax proposal – a cut in the capital gans. He was the recipient of serious wooing by both sides - Democrats wanted him to oppose the measure at the same time he seemed firmly ensconced as a member of the "Gang of Six," a group of six centrist Ways and Means Democrat led by Ed Jenkins of Georgia who favored a generous cut. Anthony's place in that gang was to the consternation of at least some liberals. The normally placid Don Pease of Ohio cited Anthony's status as DCCC head, stating, "Given the opposition of the Speaker, the Majority Leader and the Majority Whip, he has a responsibility to join the team." Anthony responded that, "My obligation is to live up to commitments and to represent my Congressional district. I got elected campaigning on capital gains." He also saw the issue as a way of broadening the tent ("We've got wealthy Democrats in this country too"). In the end, he cast his lot with Jenkins.

Anthony had been named head of the DCCC in 1986 (a major advocate was then Government Operations Committee Chair Jack Brooks of Texas) and held the post for two cycles. He came in amid great financial disarray from his predecessor, Tony Coelho of California and his first priority was restoring confidence and stability. Anthony often hosted hunting trips that doubled as fundraisers for the DCCC but he carefully guarded the privacy of those in attendance, even when he was no longer chair. The mantra of "what happens on hunting trips stays on hunting trips" was tested one day in 1991 on a quailhunt trip on an Arkansas farm. Frank Guarini, a Congressman from what *The Washington Post* called "the wilds of Jersey City," was an attendee and, apparently aiming his shotgun too low, grazed the tail of the owner's dog. Rumors about what happened circulated to colleagues and the Washington press and Anthony was hesitant to even comment. Ultimately, Tom Kenworthy, reporter for *The Washington Post* reporter read Anthony the story prior to printing.

In 1990, Anthony authored a letter to *The New York Times* bemoaning the high cost of Congressional Campaigns. "While the cold war may be over, we in Washington are locked in a campaign- spending arms race… While numerous proposals have been advanced to control campaign spending, there is only one sure way: spending caps. Until we limit the amount of money a campaign can spend, loopholes will be found for the wealthy to keep raising the stakes, and the rest will have to find ways to catch up… Without a cap our election process will continue to be nothing but an auction with victory going to the highest bidder."

While the party's nine-seat gain that November was generally hailed as a success, the advent of the Persian Gulf crisis boosted the fortunes of at least some vulnerable GOP incumbents. But Anthony's biggest near-miss might have been the survival of Newt Gingrich, the pugnacious Minority Whip from Georgia. Anthony had begun taking aim at Gingrich as early as 1985 when he referred to him as, "crazy" but Gingrich's '90 race against a businessman named David Worley had been totally under the radar so, when his too-close-to-call race on election night culminated with a 970 vote win, Anthony vowed to make him a number one target two years later.

Image courtesy of C-SPAN

In 1989, the resignations of Jim Wright and Coelho created a domino effect in the House leadership and Anthony went for the position of Majority Whip, the third ranking position in the Democratic Conference. He faced Budget Committee Chair William Gray of Pennsylvania and David Bonior of Michigan. He sought to quash perceptions that his candidacy was based on region. He told C-SPAN, "I am not running as a Southern candidate but at the same time, I think you have to acknowledge that you can have an imbalance in the leadership if you're not careful." There should also be a recognition among the Democratic caucus as to where the population is growing," observing that Pennsylvania and Michigan were poised to lose Congressional seats following the 1992 remap as much of the South was growing. But Anthony garnered just 30 votes, 104 votes behind Gray who won the position.

Back home, Anthony's re-elections were afterthoughts – he took 72% in 1990 and there was every expectation that he'd continue to post similar margins going forward. But a few things happened along the way. One was that he had supported the $30,000 Congressional raise. In actuality, one reason was because the package contained a provision eliminating honoraria when members gave speeches (his view was "it was better to get government money than it is to get whole pieces of money from the private sector"). But his support of the "Brady Bill" was really the vote that incurred the wrath of the NRA and it followed his earlier backing of a ban on cop-killer bullets.

Secretary of State Bill McCuen decided to try to take advantage of Anthony's woes and he announced plans to challenge him in a primary. Pine Bluff insurance agent Pat Pappas also entered the race. Shortly before the filing deadline, Anthony acknowledged that he had written 109 overdrafts at the House Bank and pronounced himself "embarrassed and truly sorry." But as the primary campaign went on, it was clear that Anthony was on the defensive and a week before the primary, he took "necessary leave" from the House to focus on the race.

On primary day, Anthony polled first but with an anemic 40%, well shy of the 50% needed to avert a runoff. Meanwhile, McCuen barely edged Pappas out for second place 31-30%. The runoff was two weeks away and it promised to be a slugfest. Clinton campaigned for and made phone calls on Anthony's behalf (his campaign even leased office space to him in the basement of its headquarters).

Though it was an understatement to say that McCuen was not particularly beloved by his own party, he used his trademark Harley Davidson and some hard hitting ads to resonate with apathetic voters. One featured, "Man in the Moon" dynamics lambasting the pay raise for being done "late one night when Washington slept." In another ad entitled, "Merry Christmas," McCuen charged Anthony with arresting a woman "for bouncing one $324 check for Christmas." Anthony claimed that the woman was a repeat offender. McCuen's hands weren't totally clean. He came under fire from the Federal Election Commission during primary season for not filing a campaign report, which he said was mailed on time.

Turnout dipped from the actual primary which typically did not bode well for an incumbent. Though Anthony carried Pine Bluff comfortably, McCuen edged him out by a handful of votes in Hot Springs. Anthony did well in the central portion of the district but McCuen carried enough of the other counties to eke out the win, 51-49%, a difference of 1,740 votes

(44,743-43,003). Most of the counties were within ten points either way but in a major sting to Anthony, Union County provided well more than the margin of difference as McCuen took 66%, though Anthony did best McCuen in his home county, Garland. He later called himself, "a perfect case in point. I thought I was doing fine in my district. I thought I was performng wonderful services. I was on a good committee. I was developing senoirity. And I had a good, striong legislativre record but I got caught up in a sea of change." Anthony also credited Ross Perot whose surge in polls was at its peak.

Anthony appeared on C-Span as his term neared an end and, when asked how he hoped to be remembered, he told host Brian Lamb that, "I would hope that my voters would respect me for the fact that I worked hard for them for 14 years, especially trying to bring infrastructure back to the district, to rebuild water systems (and) to try to put the fundamentals in place so that you can have economic growth and development."

After leaving office, Anthony became a partner in the prominent Washington D.C. law firm, Winston and Strawn where his first client was the American Hospital Association that was working with First Lady Hillary Rodham Clinton on health care reform. He spends a great deal of time hunting, fishing and listening to music, all of which he likes (save for opera) but especially country.

CHAPTER FORTY-EIGHT

Politically, Edwards was On an All-Time High Until Rubbergate

Introductory Tidbit: As a Congressman, Mickey Edwards was a stalwart conservative. He was also a stickler for both process and civility. His commitment to being nice was evident at a town meeting early in the Reagan administration when a constituent admonished him to, "do something about that Tip O'Neill. He's crazy." Edwards assured the woman that O'Neill wasn't "crazy. He's just as strong about his views as we are about ours. I'll bet the people at his town hall meetings in Massachusetts say to him, "That Mickey Edwards is crazy. Can't you do something about him!"

Photo courtesy of The Oklahoman

Of all of my subjects in this volume, Mickey Edwards's background may be the most sundry. He was a lawyer, advertising exec, publisher, and Congressman and professor. He edited *Private Practice Magazine* and was assistant editor of *The Oklahoma City Times*. The diversity in his background also carried through to his personality. As a member of Congress, he was not considered pugnacious but neither was he phlegmatic.

If Edwards was a fan of singer Rita Coolidge, the song that might apply to him as 1992 got underway was, "All Time High." The eight-term Oklahoma Republican was chair of the House Republican Planning and Research Committee and held the top GOP position on the influential Appropriations Foreign Assistance Subcommittee. With a combination of joviality, seriousness and respect for the institution, his respect among fellow members was second-to-none and besides tapping him for leadership roles, they looked to him for partisan strategy. Back home, he was as secure as can in a heavily Republican Oklahoma City based Congressional district was made even more so by redistricting. 386 overdrafts and the revelation of severe financial problems changed it all and by the end of the year, Edwards was a politician without an office.

The phrase "battle-tested" has different meaning to different people but by the time Edwards made it to Congress, it was definitely applicable to his career. He had not only come unexpectedly close to toppling a twenty-year incumbent in an awful year for his party but was also the survivor of two gun-shot wounds that had nearly claimed his life as a 19-year old.

Though Mickey Edwards would go through life as an Episcopalian, he was actually born Marvin Henry Edwards to a Jewish family in Cleveland. His father was the owner of Schiff's, a shoe store in the city. Edwards was a student at Oklahoma State University but would continue to help his dad. The shooting took place in 1956 as Edwards was preparing to leave for the evening. As he crossed the street, someone pointed a gun at him. In retrospect, Edwards said, "the thing I remember most is probably how stupid I was. If I was a normal intelligent human being, I would have handed over the money."

Edwards recovered from his wounds, obtained his degree, then became a reporter and editor for *The Oklahoma City Times*. For the next ten years, he alternated between public relations, the law and editing. The P.R. endeavor was for Beals Advertising Agency, the editing for *Private Practice Magazine* and a law practice took shape following the attainment of his J.D. in the midst of the two other vocations from Oklahoma City University Law School. But it was the next two years that set the stage for a forthcoming political career. Edwards was a legislative consultant for the Republican Steering Committee in Washington D.C., which gave him access to roughly 30 Republican officeholders. He soon decided he had a future among them.

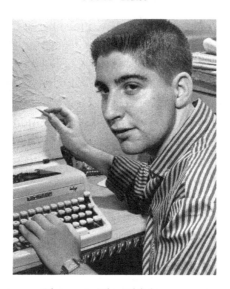

Photo via The Oklahoman

In 1974, Edwards mounted what seemed like a hapless a challenge to longtime Democratic incumbent John Jarman. It was the anti-Watergate election but Jarman was somewhat asleep at the wheel and, with an impressive get-out-the-vote operation, Edwards fell fewer than 4,000 votes shy of nipping him (52,107 votes to 48, 705). Jarman got the message. In early 1975, he switched parties and announced that he would retire when his term was up the following year. Edwards at that point was biding his time teaching journalism at OCU.

Many Republicans felt that Edwards' strong showing warranted him a second try for the seat but that view was not unanimous. One person opposed was G.T. Blankenship who wanted to run himself. He credibly dubbed himself a "middle-of-the road realist," as he had supported Nelson Rockefeller for president over Richard Nixon in 1968. Conversely, as '76 began Edwards was heartily supporting the more conservative Ronald Reagan over incumbent President Gerald Ford. *The Daily Oklahoman* endorsed Blakenship but Edwards had enough name recognition to squeak by 50-45%

Once again, Edwards was not the favorite going into the general election. Hospital administrator Tom Dunlap, who had prevailed in a hotly-contested runoff, was the Democratic nominee and he had at least some name recognition as the son of the Chancellor of Higher Education. The final margin was almost a mirror image of the '74 vote - just under 4,000 votes (78,651 votes to 74,752), but this time, Edwards was on the winning end. He was assigned to the Education and Labor Committee and Interior.

Until 1992, Edwards never sweated either primaries or general election. 1982 embodied that. Democrats controlled the process and wanted to make the Fifth a Republican vote-sink in order to shore up other areas. They drew Edwards a district that stretched to Kansas which led *Politics in America* to observe that, "the new boundaries require candidates to advertise in the Oklahoma City, Tulsa and Wichita Kansas media markets." Edwards could have faced another ambitious Republican in a primary but none took him on and he went on to rack up 67% in the general.

Initially, Edwards was a conservative's conservative (though he did have a mustache in his early years). He recalled in a C-Span interview as his tenure was nearing an end how, "When I was a child I had two pictures on my bedroom wall. One of them was Bobby Feller who was a pitcher for the Cleveland Indians. And one of them was Patrick Henry. I have felt strongly about the fact that this country is founded on some principles, separation of powers for example that give us the freedom and the opportunity that we have." Edwards authored a book, *Hazardous To Your Health*, on what he viewed as the dangers of national health insurance. Yet he did try to court unions and made clear that he had no tolerance for civil rights violations. Indeed, he accused the Justice Department of "foot-dragging" on a KKK related investigation.

Photo via The Oklahoman

In 1981, Edwards secured a seat on the House Appropriations Committee. He engaged in a rare bit of sniping in 1981 when he opposed Reagan (and GOP colleague Jack Kemp's) attempt to increase funding for the International Development Association (IDA) to $850 million from $520 million. Gutting an increase, Edwards rationed, was "a way to save the taxpayers $330 million without taking away a single education loan or a single food stamp." In committee, he told Kemp, "You can talk to me about strategy, about conference committees, about coalitions but there is no way you can defend the increase in funding for IDA in this bill." Kemp replied, "Let me say it frankly and candidly. there's not going to be a bill" if the Edwards amendment were adopted and Democrats bolted as a result. "We need their votes and they need ours." A Kemp compromise setting the budget at $750 million was ultimately adopted (Edwards supported Kemp for the GOP Presidential nomination in 1988).

In the mid-1980s, Edwards was very much in the idle of "Cold War" style debates, be it aid to the contras, nuclear weapon cutbacks or the proposed nuclear freeze. The nuclear freeze battle gave him an opportunity to prove his credentials as a strategist. He was chairing the American Conservative Union and when they began a "truth squad," he took part. "It isn't just coincidence that the A.C.U. is launching this program on the 41st anniversary of the Japanese attack on Pearl Harbor," he said. "We want every American to remember what happened the last time we were caught unprepared and we want Americans to vow that it will never happen again,"

When Congress again debated a freeze in 1985, Edwards invoked his own history. "30 years ago I was a teenager, and 30 years ago I was afraid of war. 30 years ago I knew that there was a danger of war with the Soviet Union and I knew there was a possibility that my friends and myself might die in that war. But the people who were teenagers 30 years ago and were afraid of war and were afraid they would never live to be adults, have lived to be adults. They have lived to be adults because we remained strong."

Photo via The Oklahoman

The issue of aid to the contras was more protracted and *The Daily Oklahoman* in 1988 said Edwards, "has been the Reagan administration's point man in the House on nearly every showdown over continued Contra funding." By the time the issue sunsetted, it had been a roughly five-year process that saw the normally cohesive Oklahoma delegation split. Edwards's Oklahoma colleague, Democrat Dave McCurdy, got in on the festivities to the point that *The Oklahoman* contended that one, "might say it will be a McCurdy-Edwards shoot-out at the OK Contra corral." If so, it probably ended a draw.

Edwards as early as 1983 was of the view that, "Dave has gotten himself a little out of the mainstream on this one." 1986 produced two different verdicts. When the vote was first held in March, McCurdy came on top 212-210. By June, Edwards and Ike Skelton, a Democrat from Missouri, settled on a three-tiered aid package. "The McCurdy language," he told colleagues, "does not provide one-dime of military assistance, not one nickel of military assistance, not one penny of military assist. It says. We'll think about it. Maybe we'll decide to do something about it in the future." Edwards/ Skelton made it through the chamber on a 221-209 vote (the backdrop was so dramatic that George O'Brien, a terminally ill Republican from Illinois, was on hand in the event his vote was needed). McCurdy had authored a proposal at that time that would have required Congress to approve the aid a second time which also cleared the chamber. But in 1988, the outcome was different. The House was taking up a new aid package for the contras and the vote was another cliffhanger but Reagan and Edwards went down 219-211.

Edwards could wax eloquently at times and the emotional 1984 House debate on aid to El Salvador was an example. He framed his speech in support of the measure around his request to secure only one minute of time in order to give other members a chance to speak. "What can one say in only one minute about an issue that is so vital to five million people willing to risk their lives for the right to live in a democracy? One minute is not such a short time, Mr. Chairman. One minute is all it took for a guerrilla bomb to kill a woman and two small children in San Miguel. One minute is all it took for each of the bombs that destroyed the electrical power and water supplies in one-third of El Salvador. One minute is all it took for a man or woman, threatened with beatings, with mutilation, with death, to cast a vote to help turn one more nation into a democracy. And one minute is all it will take for each of us to cast a vote that will help protect their democracy or destroy their dreams."

As the decade moved on, Edwards was still very conservative. His liberal score on both social and economic issues was zero in both 1989 and '90 (and 9 and 18% on economic). He opposed a minimum wage override, Family Leave legislation and an independent panel to hammer out Eastern Airlines, contending, "When no transportation emergency exists...the president and Congress have no role to play in labor disputes." But as loyal a Republican as Edwards was, he did have limits. While the term "respect for the institution," is overly used, most who watched him operate would agree that, when it came to Congress, his words were sincere. Edwards was a conservative who made no bones about it but at the end of the day, separation of powers loomed large. He saw the Line Item Veto as shortsighted on the basis of separating Executive/Congressional prerogatives. Edwards also displayed little patience for officials in GOP administrations whom he felt had poor bearings. Defense Secretary Casper Weinberger, he said, was "an absolute disaster" and a "serious political liability for the president." Budget Director Richard "Dick" Darman was another and Edwards had been chiding him for often overlooking Congress. As Darman was testifying on the Hill one day, Edwards opened his questioning with, "Hi, I'm Mickey Edwards. Pleased to meet you."

Edwards had long taken issue with plans by Republican strategists to nationalize Congress, claiming during Tip O'Neill's time that plans to morph Democratic candidates into him "are the dumbest things I've ever heard. They're not going to cause two people to vote for us." By 1990, Newt Gingrich was still flirting with a similar strategy but Edwards cited surveys that showed voters tended to be swayed more toward local issues.

If military terms applied, Edwards and Gingrich might have been in the same unit when it came to messaging, but not necessarily the same bunker. Gingrich liked to win battles through brazen rhetoric while Edwards saw the need to woo voters by ideas. Edwards explained his strategy: "While the noise and fury of a strategy and confrontation may be cathartic for frustrated Republicans, it serves only a limited usefulness politically." There seemed to be no limit for Edwards personally. Following the elections of 1988, colleagues elected him Republican Policy Chair, the fourth ranking position on the GOP rung and he had become top Republican on the Foreign Operations, Export Financing and Related Problems Subcommittee. In early 1989, when Wyoming Congressman Dick Cheney's appointment to the post of Defense Secretary created openings in the leadership team, Edwards was urged to seek the position of Minority Whip and many thought he had the vote to prevail. Edwards concluded that he was best suited for Policy and Gingrich narrowly captured the post.

**Edwards and staff at a retreat at the Congressional
Country Club in Bethesda, Maryland
Photo courtesy of Rick Moore**

A longtime Edwards confidante, Rick Moore, remembers that his first and foremost purpose was fidelity to his constituents. Moore began with Edwards as Organization Director for his 1984 re-election and his Field

Director immediately after and on his first day on the job, Edwards laid down a simple ground rule. "When someone walks through the door," he told Moore, "I don't want you to ask if they are an R (Republican) or a D (Democrat). I want you to ask them their address, and if they live in our district, I want you to take care of them!" As a boss, could Edwards be gruff on occasion? Sometimes but not intentionally. Moore recalls instances when he'd come off the House floor following a heated debate and "might come up as being cross." It wouldn't be long, however, before he'd apologize.

Edwards was the prototype of the small but well-known members of Congress who had severe money woes while in Congress and in his case, he was dirt-poor before he set foot in the chamber and dirt-poor when he left. The Capitol Hill magazine *Roll Call* in 1990 had found Edwards to be tied as the ninth poorest member of Congress and his divorce, child support payments and $60,000 in campaign debts were the culprit for his woes. By 1981, he had a fourth wife.

Edwards, 43, had met Lisa Reagan, 23 on a flight from Oklahoma City to Washington. She was not only a former Miss Oklahoma but a mezzo-soprano prominent in the Washington arts. The pair married within three months and had a child. That might suggest Edwards was a player but he wasn't. In fact, though Edwards and Reagan split up in 1990, both she and wife number three, Sue Lindley, publicly vouched for his character. Reagan said she waited until after Election Day to announce their separation because Edwards "is an honest, hard-working congressman who gives his constituents so much that that the emotional part of his life gets short-changed." Lindley said that, "While he may not be a one-woman man, he was definitely a one-woman-at-a-time man," calling him, "a great guy" and a wonderful father. In fact, Edwards actually married each of the women he dated which prompted Reagan to admonish him following their divorce with the plea: "Mickey, just date for a while. Don't get married."

If it was debateable that Edwards was "shortchanging" his personal life, it was crystal clear that he was doing the same with his finances. As the Congressionaal bank episode came to light, *The Washington Post* reported that he, "borrowed heavily to buy a $182,000 house in Vienna (Virginia), remodel their basement and purchase a car. They also made mortgage payments on a town house in Oklahoma City." Reagan later said, "We had loans out the kazoo." Perhaps unsurprisingly, when the worst abusers list was released, Edwards was one of three Republicans on it. With 386 overdrafts, the amount of checks in the red was $54,000 and he had exceeded his negative balance during 13 of the 39 months.

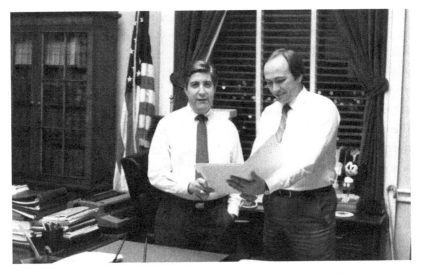

Edwards with a Field Director and longtime confidante, Rick Moore
Photo courtesy of Rick Moore

While Edwards initially held town meetings to do a mea culpa for the scandal (he cited "sloppy bookkeeping" and proclaimed himself, "stunned and embarrassed"), he soon went in a different direction. One assertion was that, "The House Bank never gave me full credit for my salary. They never put it into my account in the first place." He further professed that, "If they had just given me the same deposit everyone else got, I wouldn't have been even among the top 65." Edwards did appeal his place on the list to the House Ethics Committee but was rejected on a tie-vote. His response: "I stand here humiliated because the Ethics Committee was not willing to reconsider the definition of a net deposit."

Edwards tried to assuage the criticism by saying he, "didn't buy stock, didn't make investments, didn't buy houses and didn't buy drugs." That proved a tough road to hoe with many constituents. One, Charles Neal said, "It's sad that you believe your constituents will swallow this explanation." Indeed, a few officeholders from Edwards's own party called for his resignation. Instead, he moved forward and four candidates from his own party filed to challenge him, including State Senator Ernest Istook and restauranteur Bill Price who was initially expected to be his chief rival.

Edwards resisted calls to abandon his bid for another term and in announcing his intention to run, took his case to constituents. "If you feel I have been an unworthy public servant, that I have played you falsely and have been an embarrassment, I will not ask again for your vote and will not seek re-election." House Republicans, led by Gingrich, led a fundraising solicitation or him. But as the race neared an end, Edwards conceded that, "If my own mother had been alive, even she would not have voted for me. My son Patrick told me, 'Now you've really screwed up.'" *The New York Times* wrote, that with those lines, Edwards "sought an understanding chuckle from his audience at the recent luncheon. Instead, it left him standing gamely in an unforgiving silence." Still, he persisted, telling voters, "I've always been there when you needed me. Now I need you."

Voters didn't reciprocate. Edwards placed third in each of the district's counties and drew just 26% overall, failing to make the runoff (Istook and Price advanced and Istook won three weeks later). Addressing supporters with Patrick by his side, Edwards maintained that voters truly wanted to "clean house. They saw some new faces out there and they're not real happy with what's happening in Washington."

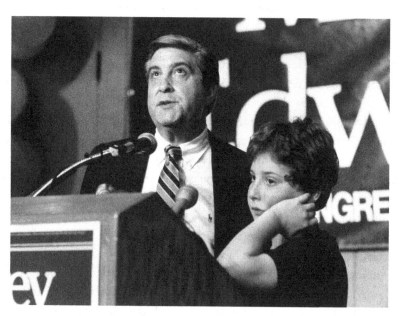

With his son Patrick beside him, Edwards concedes his primary
Photo via The Oklahoman

During the transition, Edwards reportedly prohibited his staff from making contact with Istook's people. After Congress, he ran the Aspen Institute and taught at Princeton University. In 2008, he published, *Reclaiming*

Conservatism: How a Great American Political Movement Got Lost - And How It Can Find Its Way Back. He often appears on C-Span and other programs relating to Congress and government at work. He notes that he and his wife are about to celebrate their 22nd anniversary.

In that C-Span interview as Edwards was leaving office, he hearkened back to his views about separation of powers and freedom and said, "That's why I ran for Congress. I ran because I believe strongly in those things. And I still do."

CHAPTER FORTY-NINE

Coleman Epitomized the Anti-Incumbent Feeling that Hit Congress in 1992

Introductory Quote: "I would have used the dog earlier." –Defeated Missouri Congressman Tom Coleman on what he might have done differently during his campaign. Coleman had used his beloved Molly in a late commercial.

Photo courtesy of the Collection of the U.S. House of Representatives

Missouri Republican Tom Coleman might have been the poster boy for the anti-incumbent fever that hit members of Congress like a bolt of lightening in 1992. A political wonder - some say miracle, when he first won his seat 16 years earlier at age 33, Coleman was a mild-mannered, hard-working, inoffensive incumbent without a whiff of scandal or bank overdraft. But his major electoral scare in 1990 transformed into complete vulnerability for '92 and he went on to lose his seat by a wide margin.

Coleman's inspiration for public service was a young, charismatic Democratic Senator from Massachusetts named John F. Kennedy. As a 17-year-old boy, Coleman and a few friends waited three hours for Kennedy's parade to pass through Kansas City. Another role model: John Lindsay. Coleman was already in graduate school in New York City when the aspiring Mayor was running but, he canvassed neighborhoods in the Village. One apartment contained the kitchen and living room and that image was one that stayed with him.

In 2019, Coleman explained his decision to pursue a career as a Republican. "From the (Kansas City) *Star* pages I read lengthy features on Kansas City's organized crime families, union corruption and their close association and political alliances with the state and local Democratic Party. I decided then that I would look to the only alternative available in which to pursue a political career, and that was with the GOP."

Coleman's early rise gave him the ingredients for a successful political career. Born in Kansas City, he earned his B.A, from William Jewell College, his Master's in Public Administration from NYU and his law degree from Washington University. At 26, he was an Assistant Attorney General of Missouri under future U.S. Senator John Danforth and after pursuing a campaign to become Clay County Clerk, decided to run for the Missouri House at age 29. No Republican had ever been elected from Clay County so it was noteworthy that Coleman took 58% to win the seat. He hung on with 54% in the Watergate year.

Four years after his election, Coleman decided to try for what even his allies knew was a long-shot bid for the Sixth Congressional District being vacated by the larger-than-life Democrat, Jerry Litton. Coleman was confident of his chances but, with three children and deep in the minority in the Missouri House, it was kind of an "up-or-out" mentality." It was up yet, to say his opponent, Morgan Maxfield self-destructed on the way to the general election would be a big understatement.

A wealthy realtor, Maxfield had spent $200,000 of his own money to secure a big primary win over rivals that included Pat Danner (who would unseat Coleman in '92) and two local legislators. But to say he self-destructed on the way to the general election would be a big understatement and Coleman, despite an inkling, was able to enjoy a front row seat. Coleman caught wind that Maxfield was not all he had claimed to be at the Republican National Convention which happened to be held in Kansas City. Coleman was issued a credential but as he recalls, it was in the "nosebleed section."

As he was surveying the floor, he got a glimpse of Maxfield and singer Pat Boone shaking hands on the floor. Coleman's initial thought was, "There's something wrong with this picture – I'm the nominee." At that point, "we knew he was a phony," and he was going to be exposed. Even Coleman could not have imagined what occurred in the ensuing months.

As if Maxfield's campaign were a paperback novel, his campaign chairman not only resigned one month before the election but in a subsequent press conference, called him a "pathological liar" (Coleman is clear that his campaign had nothing to do with that). The main reason was that Maxfield had professed to be single yet had a wife and two kids living in Texas where Maxfield had resided prior to 1969. In actuality, Maxfield and his wife had long-ago separated but it didn't matter because he had established an illustrative image as a quintessential bachelor, to the point that he was routinely profiled in *The Kansas City Star* and other papers. There was more to the story. Maxfield was not dirt poor as he had claimed and hadn't even come close to graduating from the Harvard Business School. This type of publicity couldn't save the most gifted of pols and Maxfield quickly dropped in the polls as a big loss became inevitable.

Coleman meanwhile simply put forth his platform, which included a Balanced Budget Amendment (a fairly novel concept at the time) and requiring impact statements for all spending bills. Coleman won with 59% and *The St. Louis Post Dispatch* best captured how the race got away with the post-election headline, "Maxfield Had Everything Going For Him While He Was Single." Perhaps thinking voters had short memories, Maxfield tried again in 1978 but his own party wouldn't dare give him more than 20% in its primary (he perished in a 1981 plane crash).

That year, Democrats tried to prove that Coleman was a fluke by putting up a former colleague and friend, State Senator Phil Snowden who still had nostalgia among residents from his days as a former football star at the University of Missouri. The two waged a civil campaign and Coleman proved his staying power by racking up 56%, carrying every county but Ray. In 1982, he faced State Representative Jim Russell who chaired the Commerce Committee. Russell's objective was to benefit from rural discontent with Reagan, whose presidency he labeled, "dupenomincs," but Coleman hung on with 55%. 1986 was not the easiest cycle as the farm crisis put Coleman on the defensive but he still dispatched Doug Hughes with 57%.

During his entire tenure, the overwhelming amount of Coleman's legislative energies focused on areas involving his two committees - Agriculture and Education and Labor and he promoted measures that strived for efficiency. In his first year, he made a contribution to a food stamps revision bill by proposing language that would prohibit any person convicted of food stamps fraud from taking advantage of the program for at least a year. Committee members rejected it 5-12.

The Sixth had an abundance of farms and Coleman's core philosophy was not easy to nail down. *Politics in America 1986* in fact intimated an epiphany, writing that "early in his career, he was most visible as a caustic critic of farm programs sponsored by Democrats. That Coleman is not heard very much anymore." It did not happen overnight and he often took pains to support the agenda of President Ronald Reagan while going to bat for his constituents, which wasn't always simultaneously achievable.

Coleman with his family during a re-election campaign
Photo courtesy of Tom Coleman

When the Reagan administration proposed cuts to food stamps programs, Coleman was not opposed on its face. "Let's keep the lid on, let's keep control over the program," he said, also expressing the view that "a mandate from the House to cut back this program and many others" existed. This was in contrary to other home-state Agriculture colleagues such as Harold

Volkmer, a Democrat, who contended that pain that could result. Nor was Coleman in the mood to do a flex bill as Kansas Democrat Dan Glickman had proposed, calling an annual review, 'a constructive and healthy thing...I just as soon come back each year." Talking the talk, Coleman proposed an amendment to fund the program with the proposed cuts for FY '82 but to revisit the issue again in '83. The committee rejected it but a compromise was eventually reached between members and White House Budget Director David Stockman.

When it became clear that the administration's policies were becoming a liability, Coleman had no problem calling them out. The 1985 farm bill was one area and Coleman contended, "The administration became almost irrelevant during our markup. I have felt from the start that the White House misunderstood the farm-credit situation and the severity of things going on out there...There are so many backs to the wall, people trying to survive that they don't spend a lot of time trying to figure if President Reagan or (Agriculture Secretary) Jack Block is to blame."

During the 1985 drought, Coleman partnered with Democratic Congressman and future Senate Majority Leader Tom Daschle of South Dakota to create a farm credit bill both sides could live with claiming, "We have not made this a political issue. We cannot afford to do so." To that end, he told colleagues, "...this is not just a rural bill. That is not just a farm bill. The people in the cities and in other areas of this country that may not produce the food certainly have a lot of their livelihood dependent upon the farm sector. Almost 23 million people in this country depend for their job directly or indirectly on agribusiness and agriculture. That is why we are reaching out to our urban colleagues, reaching across party lines today, to come up with a bipartisan support for a bill that is very necessary." Colleagues heard the message loud and clear but Reagan didn't. The House passed the legislation 318-103 but it fell victim to his veto pen.

One provision Coleman did get into the '85 farm law proved a savior to thousands of people in desperation. The rural development measure he sponsored with Democrat Glenn English of Oklahoma became known as Section 1440 of the '85 law and its goal was to stabilize farm-dependent communities on the verge of extinction from a battered economy. The program pumped money into Cooperative Extension Services already in place in eight farm-states to stop the outflow which impacted families and businesses alike. The publication, *Extension Responds To The Rural Crisis by the University of Missouri* wrote, "Year two was a transition from crisis intervention to prevention strategies," including task forces. The Rural Crisis Recovery Program Act of 1987 extended this and it was largely credited with overcoming the hardships of many.

Coleman in 1987 and 1990 legislation was the prime sponsor of a Rural Development Initiative that was designed to address the needs of economic development to rural areas via broad-band connections and incentives to locate and provide economic, social and psychological assistance to those needing it. It gave the Extension Service of USDA authority to improve employability and deal with stress management and became contained in a farm bill known as Section 1440, which also became the program's name. The Rural Development Administration was located in St. Joseph, Missouri, Coleman's district. The office shut down after Coleman's loss but he proudly notes that "27 years later, legislation is again being introduced to accomplish the same goals."

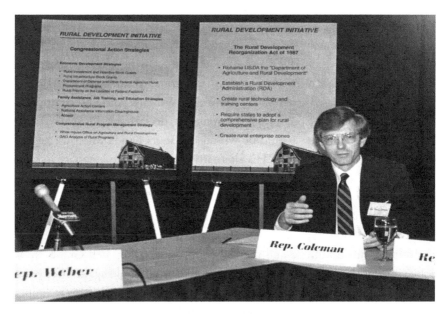

Unveiling the Rural Development Initiative
Photo courtesy of Tom Coleman

Beyond rural matters, Coleman was among the many Republicans ambivalent about the sweeping tax legislation Reagan had proposed and as the President prepared to meet Republicans that December, Coleman wasn't sure he could be mollified. "We love the president," he said, "but we've also sworn under oath to serve our districts, our consciences." He was assuaged enough that changes would be made by a House/Senate conference committee to support the measure.

Coleman's overall support score of the Reagan administration had its limits: 70% in 1981 but just 55% in 1982 (and 56% in '84).

In early 1991, Coleman got a boost heading into a difficult re-election campaign by becoming ranking member of the Agriculture Committee when President George H.W. Bush appointed Ed Madigan Secretary of Agriculture. Yet he may have arguably had more influence that year as ranking Republican on the Education and Labor Subcommittee on Postsecondary Education, a post he had held for nearly a decade.

From that perch, Coleman had long been active on student loan issues. In his early years, he felt the value of homes should not play a role in determining eligibility for loans. He also wanted retraining as opposed to grants for math and science teachers.

In what ultimately became a 16-month process beginning in 1991, Coleman was active on the committee's revision to the Higher Education Act of 1965 and waded into key areas with minimal results. On the issue of Pell Grants, he resisted attempts by Chairman William Ford and committee Democrats to make the program an entitlement, declaring it, "just absolutely incredible that Congress would be willing to tie its hands when we have a budget deficit of $350 billion." His alternative bill contained language to raise the amount of money provided under Pell but cutting the number of people eligible, which a spokesman, Craig Orfield labeled "economic reality."

For Coleman, this was not new – he had long expressed reservations about the direction of the program. In 1988, he had offered an amendment in both the subcommittee and the full committee to stop Pell Grants from achieving entitlement status. He lost both times as he would again three years later. It was deja-vu in 1991, after the subcommittee rebuffed his attempts to limit it by a vote of 9-12, Coleman took the matter to the full committee where it was again defeated. Other prominent Democrats in the House, including Bill Natcher of Kentucky, the Appropriations subcommittee chair with jurisdiction on higher education and Budget Chair Leon Panetta voiced similar reservations (Panetta cited violations of the 1990 budget agreement cap) and ultimately, that did not make its way into the final bill.

A similar direct loan program that had made its way into the bill was also a target and Coleman had ammunition from the Bush administration which opposed it. He did take part in efforts to compromise and at one point, advocated a pilot program. Committee Democrats nixed that as well. If Coleman had been allowed to take the reins himself, it seems that more of what he wanted could have been incorporated. Instead, they were constrained by what Charlie Kolb in *White House Daze: The Unmaming Domestic Policy in the Bush Years* illustrated as incompetence by Bush officials (most notably OMB Director Richard Darman) who dangled veto threats. The result was a direct loan demonstration program well beyond the size already proposed and disregard for the budget caps.

One law Coleman did have his name on was the Graduate Assistance in Areas of National Need program that gave support to graduate school students pursuing their doctorate.

That same year, Coleman and Democrat Bart Gordon of Tennessee introduced an amendment to the higher-ed bill that was a response to a "Prison U" piece that showcased prisoners receiving financial aid. Coleman incredulously posed the question, "How can we be rewarding prisoners first" and the amendment restricting it passed 351-69 but House-Senate negotiators could agree only on restricting it to those "condemned to death or serving life sentences." All-in-all, Coleman was happy with the final package and voted for it as did most every other House member.

Then came the issue of funding for the NEA. When a logjam ensued over federal funding of obscene exhibits arose (critics wanted to zero-out funding for the National Endowment for the Arts due to several obscene exhibits), Coleman negotiated a compromise with Montana Democrat Pat Williams to allow states more latitude with what they fund (increasing it from 20 percent to 27.5%) and he explained its nature on the House floor. "Our application procedures are tightened up. We require a detailed description by the grant applicant to tell what they want funded, and the NEA will know what in fact they are being asked to fund. The conditions of grant awards will continue so that an artist cannot change in midcourse that which he has already presented to the endowment as to what the project will be, and he cannot go off and change it in another direction without approval. They need to submit these interim reports, and also the money will not be given all up front, all at once, because we feel that by giving two thirds up front and one third after the completion of the project, we maintain some sort of control in the sense that the applicant will follow through with what they have been approved to do." It passed the House 349-76 and Coleman said the compromise signifies that, "you can work the system so the middle holds and the extremes don't have to prevail." Though the vote did "put the matter to rest" nationally, it might have contributed to his drop-off at home as folks would question him about why he was involved with funding smut. Another matter was his vote against the anti-flag burning amendment. Supporters were baffled but Coleman truly believed the issue was freedom of speech.

The NEA compromise was evident that Coleman was never one to "let the extremes prevail" and he was always malleable. He switched from previous Congresses in 1992 to back Family Leave legislation, though as early as 1986, he was one of three Republicans to support a watered-down substitute in committee. He was generally pro-life but voted to overturn the Bush administration's "gag rule" on abortion counseling at federally funded clinics. He was more pro-gun than not but supported the Brady Bill.

Coleman was also very congenial. He declined to vote to censure Massachusetts Democrat Barney Frank in 1990 and had many friends on the liberal spectrum. Wisconsin Republican Steve Gunderson came to Congress in 1980 and, serving with Coleman on both Agriculture and Education and Labor, observed that "we pursued parallel paths." Gunderson called his colleague, "one of the brighter minds. Just as much an academic and a parochial perspective for his district." As such, he was "willing to deal with the really complicated issue." English echoes that calling Coleman "a fellow who had a lot of common sense. You can reason with him more than almost anyone else. I think highly of Tom."

It wasn't often that Coleman had eye-popping re-election margins but, by 1990, he didn't appear to be in any kind of danger. That changed on election night when he held off Bob McClure, a retired truck driver who spent just $22,000 by the skin of his teeth – a 52-48% margin that came to just 5,863 votes out of 152,000 cast (78,956 to 73,093). McClure actually carried 13 of the district's 26 counties and tied in another. In 1988, conversely, Coleman lost just three counties and seven in his expensive '86 re-election. The day after, Coleman told *The Constitution Tribune*, "We were part of a national mood caught up in our area and in the state of Missouri. All in all, considering the general swing, we're happy to be re-elected." McClure's response: "I still have faith the election went the way it was supposed to, and praise the good Lord for all the good things he gives me, and hope and pray Mr. Coleman will do a good job and I certainly wish him well."

We can be Proud that He is Different from the Rest.

Paid for by Citizens for Coleman

A Coleman campaign mail piece
Photo courtesy of Tom Coleman

It's probably safe to say Democrats did not share that sentiment. They promptly targeted Coleman for 1992 and despite some saying to the contrary, he immediately recognized that he would have a true fight. He blamed the budget stalemate that had kept members in Washington for his close shave, verbalizing how, "The budget controversy that was on the TV news 30 days and nights was a tragi-comedy."

Coleman might have hoped that his ascension to ranking member on Agriculture might help him back home. Perhaps it did but not by nearly enough. The opponent who emerged from another crowded Democratic primary was Pat Danner, now a popular State Senator and an apostle of Jerry Litton.

Remap changed the district little - Bush had carried the new seat by just under 3,000 votes, only the slightest uptick from the 205 votes by which he had won the old Sixth in 1988. But the opponent who emerged from another crowded Democratic primary to take him on was a heavyweight: Pat Danner, now a popular State Senator and an apostle of Jerry Litton.

Danner hit Coleman for not doing much to prevent other states from sending their waste to Missouri. Coleman responded by accusing Danner of "taking cash for trash," and accepting contributions from folks eyeing to build an incinerator in Mercer County. Danner then went after Coleman for voting for a pay raise but Coleman pointed to the size of her wealth as "hypocritical of her to make an issue of congressional salaries when she has multiple millions in assets and doesn't know what it's like to live on a salary." He called Danner's record "the worst in the Missouri Senate."

One issue Coleman didn't need to touch personally was the House bank: he never had an account and thus had zero overdrafts. Danner substituted by raising the use of the Congressional franking privilege which she accused him of "abusing." For all of his problems with the Democrats, Coleman was not without pains on his right by two key interest groups. His votes on the gag rule and the Brady Bill earned him the ire of both anti-abortionists and the NRA and being in such a precarious electoral position, Coleman could not afford any more defections (Danner was both pro-life and gun). The NRA proceeded to launch what Coleman believes that in today's money would be a roughly $500,000 buy against him.

Perhaps knowing that his fate and Bush at the top of the ticket were linked, Coleman questioned the wisdom of Vice-President Dan Quayle, with whom he was elected in '76, remaining on the ticket. "I'm very concerned," Coleman said, "that George Bush doesn't have his act together campaign-wise." But the genesis of Coleman's problems was expressed by one who said, "Even people who go to Washington find Tom to be distant and aloof and not very accessible." *The Kansas City Star* did not feel that way as they stuck with the incumbent. Meanwhile, Coleman didn't have a campaign manager but Danner, the only mother/son duo to be serving in any legislature, were able to cover separate grounds.

Most frustrating to Coleman was that he appeared to be personally popular. A poll he conducted showed that 2/3 of voters approved of his job performance but that he actually trailed Danner by a percentage point. The problem was his incumbent status and nothing his campaign tried was able to move the needle. Frustrated, he asked his campaign late in the game to "humanize me" and they taped an ad with his dog Molly.

By Election Day, it was clear to just about everyone including Coleman that he would lose and the final margin was unambiguous - Danner won 55-45%, a margin of 29,000 votes out of 269,000 cast. She carried all but three counties. Coleman essentially conceded early: "I don't think it will be a Republican night in Missouri. Frankly, I don't think it's going to be a very good night for Tom Coleman. It's a Democratic landslide." But, Coleman verbalized his distaste for those weary of the political prospect. "Some people have lost faith. I haven't...I'm proud, I'm not bitter." Coleman said he hope's Danner, enjoys the $35,000 pay raise I'm giving her."

The Kansas City Star noted Danner "made plans the day after the election to attend a task force meeting on Trans World Airlines and its overhaul base in Kansas City North. Coleman, by contrast, flew home to Washington on the morning plane."

After leaving office, Coleman became Vice-President of Government Relations for BASF SE. He was an adjunct professor and advisor at Robert Wagner Graduate School of Public Service at New York University. In 2016, he was among the scores of Republican lawmakers who signed a letter refusing to back Donald Trump for president (he had backed his former colleague, John Kasich of Ohio during primary season). He is now prominent with the Serve America Movement (SAM) which advocates centrist Democrats, Republicans and Independent voters to form a new political party. By 2019, he was calling for the impeachment of the president.

CHAPTER FIFTY

Big Sky Country Featured Big Redistricting Matchup that Led to Marlenee's Demise

Introductory Quote: It's like "a pimple on the end of your nose. It's in the wrong place and it hurts." – Montana Congressman Ron Marlenee on the differences within his proposed Montana Wilderness legislation and that of Minnesota Democrat Bruce Vento.

Photo courtesy of the Collection of the U.S. House of Representatives

The pairing of any two Congressional incumbents via redistricting always becomes a major, widely watched affair but Montana's 1992 matchup between Republican Ron Marlenee and Democrat Pat Williams seemed a battle of the titans even before it became inevitable. The longevity alone of the eight-term Marlenee from eastern Montana and the seven-term Williams from the west was enough to generate suspense but the political and policy distinctions made it a true barnburner. In this case, the anti-abortion, pro-development minded Marlenee was pitted against the pro-choice, more wilderness protection minded Williams in what was then a fairly closely divided state. Add to the fact that it had been obvious as early as the summer 1989 that Montana would be losing a seat and it became perhaps the most anticipated Congressional race in a long, long time. When it was over, it was Marlenee on the short end of the stick.

Marlenee was born in Scoby, Montana, attended Montana State University and the University of Montana. Auctioneering became a passion and he learned the tricks of the trade in Mason City, Iowa at the Reisch School of Auctioneering. Later, he operated "Marlenee Big Sky Ranch."

In 1976, Marlenee opted to run for the Congressional seat held by Democrat John Melcher, a mission that seemed destined to fall short until Melcher announced he would be stepping down to try to succeed Mike Mansfield in the Senate (he won). The GOP primary was a five-way affair and John Cavan, the only officeholder of the bunch, was viewed as the initial front-runner due to his base being in Billings. Marlenee was able to match that with backing from farm organizations and it showed. Though Marlenee came out on top with 41% (Cavan got 30% and Math Dasinger 15%), the span of his win was remarkable – he lost only five counties throughout the geographically humungous state. In the general election, he faced State Senator Thomas Towe and started out a distinct underdog, who made his reputation by raising cain with the Montana Power Company as a State Senator. Marlenee campaigned on individual liberties and hit Towe's stance on gun control.

Election night was busy for Marlenee – he had one party in Billings, then flew to another in Great Falls (Billings had "gone all out" but "we owe it to our people in Great Falls to be there, too"). He'd be exhausted but euphoric. Marlenee carried all but three counties (losing two of them – Great Falls's Cascade and Big Horn by a hair), for a 55-45% win. He even took Yellowstone which was Towe's turf. He was assigned to the Agriculture Committee and Interior and Insular Affairs, two posts that fit his state like a glove. But because Marlenee came to Washington in a distinct minority, achieving his goals was a pipe-dream and he recalled that he and other-like minded colleagues were relegated, "to holding the line until the re-enforcements got there." That re-enforcement was Ronald Reagan.

It's time one
of us went to
Congress.

☆Ron Marlenee
One of us for U.S. Congress

Photo via the Great Falls Tribune

In some ways, Marlenee might be considered a westerner's westerner. A bulky, rugged looking-man, he was a rancher and auctioneer early in life who once in Congress, gained notoriety by driving a pick-up truck to work.

That also seemed to govern his style. At times, Marlenee whom *Politics in America* wrote, "sometimes loses his temper over issues that most other members see as routine," could be irreverent with his rhetoric. Washington D.C. he once said, had "a homicide rate so high its tourism promotion should issue every visitor a handgun." He labeled environmentalists, "prairie fairies" and referred to a 4.4 million California desert protection bill as a, "great California land grab." When Congress was considering an override of Bush's veto of the Family and Medical Leave Act, Marlenee's view was, "if you're working for a jerk who won't give you medical leave to take care of your family, quit your job and find another."

When Congress in 1985 debated a farm bill that contained a referendum that would codify production controls by the government in exchange for higher crop costs, Marlenee dismissed it as a "Hollywood-Hayden-Fonda-Willie Nelson-Harkin food referendum" (a number of celebrities along with Iowa's junior Senator, Tom Harkin, had been championing the idea). Marlenee then contended that many of his colleagues would "vote for the referendum because they have been propagandized by country singers (at the recent Farm Aid concert) and because they want to avoid a vote on which they themselves can be held responsible." Finally, when Indian reservations thought about imposing fees, *The Almanac of American Politics* noted Marlenee reminded them that he can "jerk the purse-strings very, very hard and very, very quickly."

Yet Marlenee could also display a gentle side. Though he often battled Interior Chair Mo Udall, he pushed back against critics who felt that Udall should resign when he was afflicted by Parkinson's Disease. Marlenee said he'd, "support Mr. Udall for as long as he chooses to come to Congress. I have the greatest respect for him." He had a similarly productive relationship with Washington Democrat and future House Speaker Tom Foley when he chaired Agriculture. Despite his public rhetoric, he often worked to try to find compromises for thorny issues and declined to join many Republican colleagues who voted to either censure or expel his Massachusetts colleague, Barney Frank. And longtime allies scoffed at the notion that Marlenee was, as his son-in-law, Peter Helland said, "an enemy of the environmentalists," noting he was the first person I knew who recycled back in the 80s. He loved the outdoors."

Many times, however, it was Marlenee's tone-deafness that came out. In 1987, he traveled to South Africa and responded to critics with, "We are not dealing with a Banana Republic." In 1988, when House Democrats put forth a second South Africa sanctions bill to complement the one that had been enacted two years earlier over Reagan's veto, Marlenee accused sponsors of "advocating a scorched-earth policy against a very Christian - and I emphasize Christian-nation which has been a longstanding friend." He maintained that new regulatory laws such as the American with Disability Act, which he voted against were "well intentioned" but "give people a headache." He was one of just eight Republicans to oppose initial passage of the Clean Air Act. He also opposed the 1990 budget summit conference report.

Earth to Ron . . . ?

"The threat of nuclear war is nonexistent."
— Rep. Ron Marlenee (R-Mont.)

Image courtesy of John Moore

After the 1989 Supreme Court decision affirmed the Constitutional right of American citizens to burn the flag, Marlenee was aghast. Invoking the men who raised the flag at Iwo Jima, he said said, "These six brave soldiers were symbolically shot in the back by five men in black robes. The treasonous nature of the decision on the bench should be remembered every time we say the Pledge of Allegiance, every time we sing the national anthem, every time we pass a national cemetery. Six brave men raised the flag. Five Supreme Court justices tore it down."

Sometimes, even Republican administrations weren't immune from Marlenee's malapropisms and discontent. "Agriculture is skidding toward disaster and this farm bill accelerates that skid. The wheat section of the bill is like skidding from loose gravel to glare ice." In 1989, Secretary of Agriculture Cayton Yeutter bore the brunt of discontent. "Mr. Speaker," Marlenee said on the House floor, "shall we call it an agricultural bill? Shall we call it the Kansas Plan? Shall we call it a consumer bill? Shall we call it a foreign giveaway? Shall we call it unilateral disarmament? Shall we call it George Bush's give to agricultural? No, I think we should call it the greatest disaster ever written, collectively put together by a trade representative posing as a Secretary of Agriculture. The Secretary of Agriculture Clayton Yeutter got it all wrong.

Producers said a bushel of wheat for a barrel of oil, not a bushel of oil for a gallon of gasoline."

Marlenee usually knew the buck stopped with his constituents and he wasn't skimpy about getting them their fair share. In 1983, he introduced a "sodbuster" bill that would codify their loan status from the federal government, a bill opposed by the National Association of Conservation Districts (they instead gave thumbs up to legislation championed by Senator William Armstrong of Colorado). Environmental interests wanted to deny benefits to "sodbuster's" who didn't undertake soil conservation measures and when the bill reached the Ag committee the following year, Marlenee called it, "the single greatest threat for bureaucratic abuse ever offered before this committee in the years I have served."

Subsidies were another area Marlenee was dead seat on preserving and in 1981, he viewed the Reagan administration's proposed farm bill as, "needlessly severe" due to its impact on wheat subsidies. Later, *The Almanac of American Politics* noted he was "the only Republican to support Iowan Dave Nagle's proposal to "put target prices on an upward trajectory again." Marlenee also viewed the heavy importation of beef and cattle from Europe to Canada as "backdoor brokering," and in turn, detrimental to United States imports and in 1986, he filed legislation to limit it coming to the United States. And in 1985, Marlenee pressed the case of maintaining airline service to rural areas. Mr. Speaker," he said on the House floor, "in 1978 the communities served by commuter and smaller airline services stood by Congress' efforts to deregulate the airline industry. We struck a bargain with those mostly rural communities to insure continuation of their service through the Essential Air Service Program for one full decade. We have three years left on that commitment and this body should not go back on that promise."

Yet that apparently had its limits. *Politics in America* also wrote that he "has not been much of a coalition builder on Interior or a strategist for Republican forces." He opposed a reauthorization of the Bureau of Land Management because it gutted "a balanced management policy" and also a 1985 move by Ohio Democrat John Seiberling to create an American Conservation Corps., instead proposing an amendment before Interior that would give the secretaries the latitude to do so (it was rejected). In the aftermath of the Chernobyl nuclear accident when members wanted to substantially raise the compensation limit for victims of a nuclear accident, the pro-nuclear Marlenee was concerned that the anti-nuclear phenomenon "appears to have put us under some kind of cloud." But Marlenee worked with Udall on a compromise involving both the proposed amount for the fund, which increased from $640 million to $6.5 million, along with the removal of other provisions that he deemed unacceptable. During a 1989 Interior Committee hearing, he contended that Democrats would, "be more comfortable if he Sierra Club occupied our (Republican) chairs on this side," to which senior Interior Democrat George Miller shot back, "that's for damn sure." His rating with the AFL-CIO was sometimes zero and his highest was 22% in 1982.

When Massachusetts Democrat and House Interior Oversight Committee Chair Ed Markey requested a hearing into nearly $9,000 for two Christmas parties thrown by Interior Secretary James Watt at Arlington National Cemetery "with checkbook in hand," Marlenee called it, "a totally hypocritical stance when this very Interior Committee spent around $36,000 for ... trips in 1981." The investigations, he said, "have maligned his commitment to public lands. And, worse, they have maligned his religious convictions. And, sadly, I ask you, are we now seeing an attempt to malign his integrity?"

As some told it, to know Marlenee was to love him. Wisconsin Republican Steve Gunderson served on Agriculture with him. Gunderson was far more centrist but called his colleague, "a really nice guy," who was "there for all the right reasons." He "brought the voice of Montana" to Congress and was not arrogant. He was "representative" of his state "but did it in an aw-shucks kind of way."

Marlenee's acerbicness could cause him problems come election time. While he mostly held his seat at ease, 1986 was different as farmer Buck O'Brien was nipping at his heels over the farm downturn, and was especially empathetic because he had suffered his own losses. Releasing his financial records, O'Brien contended he had been lucky. "But if I've been lucky, and I am losing money," he said, "I wouldn't want to see the returns of a farmer who hasn't been so lucky. We must demand a change in federal policies, a change in agriculture policies that allow producers to receive a price for their products, at the marketplace, that reflects the cost of production." Marlenee held O'Brien off just 53-47%. O'Brien was back for another round two years later but state Republicans were having their best year in two decades, winning a U.S. Senate seat and the governorship and Marlenee increased his percentage to 55%. In 1990, he shot up to 63% against token opposition.

Before those numbers were in, all eyes were on the marquee matchup that was inevitable for 1992. Reapportionment was going to be costing Montana one of its two House seats which meant that if Marlenee and Williams, wanted to remain in Congress, they would have to battle each other. Neither man relished the battle that lay ahead. Williams, who was junior to Marlenee only by one term, was entrenched in his district that took in the western part of the state and was as liberal as Marlenee conservative (interestingly, their offices in Washington were both doors apart in the Rayburn House Office Building). It also guaranteed that Big Sky Country would become big television country as buckets of outside money would be infiltrating the state from national interest groups in favor of one candidate or the other. That was a reason the first inclination of politicos on both sides was to entice one man or the other into the governor's race but neither man was interested, even when the seat became open by the retirement of GOP Governor Stan Stephens. But, because they had been colleagues – and friends for so long, Marlenee recalled, "I knew where he stood and he knew where I stood. The lines were pretty drawn and we liked that."

As 1992 finally got underway, both camps harbored scant hope that the state would be able to salvage both seats when the Supreme Court agreed to a case challenging the mathematical system of counting voters as politicians of all parties had filed an amicus brief urging them to do just that). The Court rejected that effort (the House could have increased its membership and Marlenee interestingly was the lone member of the House Interior Committee to oppose a referendum by the people of Puerto Rico to determine the island's future status as one plan would give the island a Congressional vote if passed).

Like a true-barnburner, the race offered ebbs and flows for both sides. In polls years out, Williams started out ahead, then Marlenee inched forward following the Gulf War. Most of the time though, both men were close but as October got underway, it was clear that Williams had at least a nominal edge.

Marlenee tried to turn the tables on Williams's attempt to find a compromise to the thorny NEA "sexually explicit performance including two 12-year-old girls as the main characters" and a homosexual film festival in San Francisco. The House check scandal was hardly a factor as both men had overdrafts. Marlenee's 20 was a third of Williams' 61, though there was disparity with the amount ($3,500 for Marlenee as oppose to $35,000 for Williams). But Marlenee was quick to add, "The House Bank operated under the control of the leadership which the Democrats have. They knew that there were problems with that bank a long time ago."

Marlenee, running under a slogan, "Ron: Putting Montanans First," contended that he has long been fighting for "liberty for all Montanans." In one debate, which was reasonably polite given the stakes, both candidates were asked why, given the long-running stalemate over the wilderness bill that "we shouldn't turn it over to the other 49 states?" Marlenee replied, "That was the problem. The other states wanted to solve our problem. They wanted to get in there…they essentially killed the Montana Wilderness bill compromise." He singled out Bruce Vento, a Minnesota Democrat who chaired a key Interior subcommittee that was advocating a hefty wilderness bill, maintained that, "The bill that Williams and Vento put out was an expansion of wilderness. We didn't want that in the state of Montana." Williams reply was that, "the work wasn't done, the shift-whistle hadn't blown…you should have stayed around and given us a hand."

While Marlenee and Williams argued over the issues, the race was devoid of personal attacks. It was no accident. While tensions are inevitable in such high-profile races, the two had worked well together in Congress (their offices were nearby) and Williams recalls both men "worked hard" to avoid gutter politics. Both camps "put the word out to our workers – don't say bad stuff about Pat and don't say anything bad about Ron." Williams considers Marlenee a friend to this day.

On Election Night, 1992
Photo via The Bozeman Daily Chronicle

The usually conservative *Billings Gazette* endorsed Williams but Marlenee held onto *The Great Falls Tribune*. On election night as Williams built up a lead, Marlenee told supporters, "If Pat Williams wins this race it will be with all of the PAC money he received. It will be the PAC money he bought in the state of Montana." Williams finally prevailed 50-47%, a margin of 203,711 votes to 189,570. Marlenee did take 53% in the Second Congressional District but Williams took 55% on his home turf. Williams racked up big margins in Missoula and Lewis and Clark in his area, yet also Big Horn in Marlenee's. The Republican won Flathead in the Second but, beyond that, only a smattering of small counties. Yellowstone County, which cast 55,000 votes and was in the Second, split down the middle and Williams prevailed by 371. Similarly, Gallatin the First preferred Williams 51-47%. The defeated Congressman told his assembled supporters, "You've not seen the last of Ron Marlenee. He's going to play, I hope, an important role in the direction that Montana takes." But when it came to the public eye, Montana had in fact seen the last of Ron Marlenee. While national Republicans had courted him for various comebacks, particularly challenging vulnerable Democratic Senator Max Baucus in 1996, Marlenee was comfortably retired in Scobey and elected not to.

CHAPTER FIFTY-ONE

Scientist Ritter Combined Precision and Idealism To Advocate Staunchly Anti-Communist Agenda

Introductory Quote: "I hope you have got your facts straight on Tabasco Sauce, and that you have checked with the Centers for Disease Control before you made those off-the-cuff remarks because you never know what is out there that can cause ill health." –Congressman Don Ritter rebutting Victor E. Schwartz, Executive Director of the Federal Interagency Council on Insurance during a 1983 hearing on compensating victims of exposure to hazardous waste. Schwartz questioned "who is to know where the cancer came from, whether it came from too much Tabasko Sauce or whether it came from the dump 20 miles away."

Photo courtesy of the U.S. House of Representatives Collection

E lections in Pennsylvania's Fifteenth Congressional District sometimes seem to surprise mid-senior incumbents. It's how Republican Don Ritter first won his job in 1978 and the manner in which he was shown the door 14 years later in this LeHigh Valley-Allentown anchored industrial district.

Throughout his Congressional tenure, Ritter not only made a name ingratiating himself with pro-freedom policies worldwide but many times led the way. Afghanistan, Granada and the former Soviet Union are prominent examples. Ritter was also a scientist in another life and few would doubt *The Morning Call's* 1988 contention that he "is seen as someone whose enthusiasm and scientific expertise are seldom matched in Congress."

Ritter's science profession made him a rare breed on Capitol Hill and his background made him a go-to person among members and staff on any forthcoming issues relevant to the topic. Born in Manhattan, he attended the Bronx High School of Science, earned his undergraduate in Metallurgical Engineering from Lehigh University and both his Master's and Ph.D in Physical Metallurgy and Materials Science from the Massachusetts Institute of Technology. Then, his life got really interesting. As his website noted, "Dr. Ritter had been a National Academy of Sciences (NAS) post-Doctoral 'Exchange Fellow' in the USSR in 1966-67, spoke fluent Russian and had extensive background in Russian culture and history." After his education concluded Ritter became an engineering consultant assistant professor at California State Polytechnic University. Eventually, science and Lehigh would combine to become a major part of Ritter's early career as he managed the development of the university's new research programs.

When Ritter decided to take on eight-term Democratic Congressman Fred Rooney in 1978, his initial chances for success seemed bleak. First, he had to secure the nomination which he did by prevailing in a six candidate field with 46%. But Ritter was able to tap into resentment from those who felt Rooney had been neglecting the district.

The fall campaign found Ritter facing a number of challenges. One was his dearth of name recognition which he sought to overcome with two creative techniques. Embarking on two walks through the district was one gimmick but turning an issue identified with Rooney against him was the other. The incumbent had long been a champion of Conrail but Ritter held press conferences near the old cars to illustrate their poor condition.

Election Day found Ritter aided by the unexpected strength of the GOP ticket, particularly gubernatorial nominee Richard Thornburgh who was surprising Democrat Pete Flaherty. Ritter won 53-47% and was assigned to, where else? The Science and Technology Committee (along with Banking, Finance and Urban Affairs).

It might have seemed like fortuitous timing if there could be such a thing for a calamity but, the Soviet invasion of Afghanistan occurred during Ritter's first year in office and it enabled him to lend his energy and expertise. In fact, *The Morning Call* wrote that, "During his first term, Ritter introduced 16 pieces of legislation, four of them aimed at the Soviet occupation of Afghanistan and the crackdown in Poland."

In time, Ritter would found the Congressional Task Force on Afghanistan and in 1984, visited the Kyber Pass in that nation to advise the rebels. The result was the Ritter-Tsongas (Paul of Massachusetts) resolution that paved the way for "material assistance," in terms of military support to the refugees. He and another Massachusetts Democrat Barney Frank had worked together on an issue closer to home: Afghanistan refugees. The pair sponsored a resolution expressing the sense of Congress that the administration should establish a process for screening Soviet defectors and prisoners of war (Ritter opposed both the expulsion and censure of Frank in 1990, a distinct minority among Republicans within the latter).

Later, Ritter was not afraid to heartily support aid the contras and he confronted many naysayers in doing so. Calling the Nicaraguans, "hard-core communists, serving as agents of the Soviets and Cubans," Ritter acknowledged the contras were "an imperfect body," but said, "they look like angels when compared to the communist Sandinistas." To state his case, he published editorials in major newspapers. In one such editorial that appeared in *The New York Times*, Ritter wrote of the impending Intelligence Authorization Act on the House floor. He called the vote, "one of the most important in this Congress, and if it goes the wrong way it could legitimize the 'Brezhnev Doctrine' here in our hemisphere..." Ritter went on to cite the "the home-court advantage" the United States had by virtue of the Monroe Doctrine. "But today the Soviet Union, by its actions in Cuba and through Cuba in Central and South America, is challenging our historic guarantee to protect Western Hemisphere nations against European interference "for the purpose of oppressing them or controlling in any other manner their destiny..."

Photo courtesy of C-SPAN

Ritter also had little use for the nuclear freeze that liberal colleagues were advocating. "In 1969, we got an ABM (antiballistic missile) treaty with the Soviets only after the House voted - narrowly - to authorize the building of an ABM system. We're asking with this resolution to freeze and then negotiate reductions. I ask, where is the incentive for the Soviets if we do that?"

Ritter was overjoyed in 1989 when the Eastern bloc began collapsing, proclaiming, "What's happening in Eastern Europe is nothing short of spectacular. But," he cautioned, "the hardcore totalitarians still have all the guns." That December, when President George H. W. Bush was preparing for a summit with Soviet President Mikhail Gorbachev, Ritter spoke realistically of what he expected would be accomplished; "I'm hoping for a good working relationship built on honesty and not hype - and that means both sides."

Ritter had a seat on the Helsinki Commission and by 1991 had become the top House Republican, an assignment that gave him the platform to carry out his agenda. Following the Soviet invasion of Lithuania, a very distraught Ritter organized a Commission hearing. He chided the uncertainty, predicting, "The scenario could get real grim. In the worst case, a renegade Soviet government could change its position on support for us in the Persian Gulf." He was bereft because, "The Soviet Union has come so far ... it's just painful realization that Gorbachev was reverting to Stalinism here. You wonder how far and deep it goes and how much of glasnost and perestroika is gone." Ritter also said Bush had to exercise more leadership. "I have yet to hear a strong comment from the president himself. He denies he is preoccupied (by the impending Gulf War), but he's got this (other) very critical issue right now." When a hearing was convened by Maryland Democrat Steny Hoyer, Ritter proposed stripping Mikhail Gorbachev of his Nobel Prize, which he acknowledged was "a strategy to hold Mr. Gorbachev's feet to the fire." A further sign of his commitment was his repeated authorship of resolutions designating June 14 as "Baltic Freedom Day."

When the Energy and Commerce Committee in 1983 approved legislation requiring a certain percentage of auto parts to be made in the United States, Ritter successfully tacked on a study on impact. Later in the decade, he was among the lawmakers that took aim – literally at a Toshiba boombox outside the Capitol when the company moved its submarine technology to the Soviet Union (sledgehammers and all). As such, he voted for the controversial Gephardt Amendment and against the Reagan administration's position to eliminate the two-month plant closing notification measure. He helped write the Leaking Underground Storage Tank program.

As a scientist, telecommunication issues were more than matter-of-fact for Ritter. He championed an Advanced Technology Program and wanted the National Bureau of Statistics to merge and become a part of National Institute of Standards and Technology (NIST).

In 1983, Ritter opposed legislation that put him on the receiving end of an unusually hostile letter from FCC chairman Mark Fowler who wrote, "There is no need for Congress to ban flat charges to protect universal telephone service...We fully intend to maintain the universality of telephone service under our plan." Fowler cited "demagogic statements." On high-definition television, Ritter and Science Chair George Brown (D-California) were able to get a bill earmarking funds and he introduced the High Definition Television Competitiveness Act (HDTV) of 1989 which he called "legislation to spur the modernization of our telecommunications." Another area on which he made his mark: a bill refusing to allow states to block caller id or ANI.

On social issues, almost no one would mistake Ritter for a liberal. He voted to sustain Bush's veto of a minimum wage increase, the Family Leave Act and the Civil Rights Act of 1990 while backing the Constitutional Amendment banning flag desecration. At a time when virtually no one was talking about global warming either pro or con, Ritter seemed to be questioning its existence and he linked it to a reauthorization package of PBS. Angered that the network did not air the "Greenhouse Conspiracy," he in 1986 circulated a letter calling for the Corporation for Public Broadcasting to investigate a possible political agenda by the network. "For a decade," he said, "the leftist view has dominated on PBS without any balance from the other side. This is wrong."

Ritter was, however, among a group of a bipartisan quartet of lawmakers who sponsored a renewal of the Clean Air Act of 1983 (the other lawmakers were Democrats John Dingell of Michigan, Jim Florio of New Jersey and Republican Norman Lent of New York). He successfully fought for the exclusion of diesel engine. Ritter had no problem requiring small businesses to reveal toxins that go into – (as future Senators Al Gore and Barbara Mikulski in part were trying to do in the aftermath of "Love Canal") but he was concerned about encroaching on the prerogative of the Executive Branch ("We should not in Congress be in the business of writing detailed regulations in legislation").

Ritter often expressed concern about excessive spending and in 1984, the Watchdogs of the Treasury, Inc., awarded him and five colleagues its "Golden Bulldog Awards." One project on which he expressed deep reservations over the Superconductor-Supercollider in 1987 ("fantastic pork") and he proposed funding be halted until a project site was determined. Locally, he was instrumental in a Basin Street underpass in Allentown and Rt. 33. Quality Valley USA.

Ritter introduced the Risk Analysis Research and Demonstration Act of 1980 (and in several succeeding Congresses) which would "direct the President to establish and direct a coordinated program for the improvement and use of risk analysis within Federal agencies through research, interagency coordination and the development of comparative risk strategies."

On a lighter note, Ritter enacted a resolution establishing the National Walking Act and the Birds of Prey Conservation Week. He was anti-smoking long before it was cool and prohibited it in his office.

Being a scientist to many of Ritter's colleagues, many of whom, as *The Morning Call* noted, were lawyers. A former aide told the paper, "People don't understand him because he's so intelligent. He also picks issues that are not sexy and it's hard to build a consensus. His staff has helped him learn how to play the political game."

Before 1992, Ritter's toughest opposition seemed to come from Allentown Mayor Ed Reibman in 1988 and he won 57-43%. Anti-incumbent 1990 was more routine, even after backlash to the overall budget process (he opposed the final agreement). Ritter made hey out of Social Security, contending Richard Orloski "cannot be trusted" and ticked up to 61%.

Despite a permeating and seemingly sustained anti-incumbent mood, Ritter seemed to be in similar shape for 1992. In fact, while not completely safe, nearly every observer viewed Ritter as favored to hold his job through election night. Instead, he had a fairly early election night loss.

Even if both parties recognized Ritter's predicament late, the incumbent sure did not. As early as the summer, he replaced his longtime campaign team. Paul McHale was no slouch. An Iraq War veteran and attorney, he was particularly adroit at getting his points across. Ritter explained his dilemma being in a box held "by four pincers: the weakness of the economy, the weakness of the president, the anti-incumbency mood, and McHale's ability to carry the mantle of change. They used different pincers to keep us in the box. How do you get out of the box is the question."

McHale meanwhile left no stone unturned, which included gradually branching out to rural areas of the district about six weeks out where he acknowledged he truly lacked name recognition. On election night, Ritter conceded early. Calling it, "a sad moment when something you worked very hard for does not come through," Ritter contended he, "worked tirelessly to serve the interests of the Lehigh Valley, and I've worked tirelessly to make the U.S. a better place to live." He also acknowledged getting, "nailed on a lot of features of incumbency."

As his term neared an end, Ritter conceded, "You develop a kind of momentum, and that builds as you remain in Washington longer. Then, when something like this happens, it all comes to a stop, and you end up focusing on matters closer to home."

After his retirement, Ritter continued his pursuit of global liberty and in 1996, founded the Afghanistan Foundation.

CHAPTER FIFTY-TWO

Bill Green an Endangered Specie as a New York City Republican Persevered for More Than a Decade

Photo courtesy of C-Span

For nearly 15 years, Bill Green, a Republican, represented a Manhattan district that voted Democratic for president by a bigger margin than any district in the nation held by the GOP, mostly without breaking a sweat. The amazing thing was that he held for a decade and a half which is one of the reasons s why, when his luck finally ran out in 1992, it was viewed as a minor upset.

Green would attribute his success in part to being "aggressive on behalf of the city in getting dough." But keeping a distance from the national party, particularly the administration of Ronald Reagan was key. So meticulous was he in maintain a ferociously independent record that he proudly brandished a letter in 1983 that Reagan had sent him thanking him for voting with him when "you could give it."

Green was born "Sedgwick William Green" to a securities trader in Manhattan and earned both his undergraduate and law degrees from Harvard. The nickname, "Swidge" was acquired in college in part by his signature when he was active on *The Harvard Crimson*. Green graduated magna cum laude. He served in the Army before becoming a law secretary to District Court Judge George T. Washington in Washington. He then served as joint counsel to the New York Joint Legislative Committee on Housing and Urban Development.

In 1964, Green sought a seat in the New York Assembly and won a five-way primary that included future State Senator and New York State Republican Chair Roy Goodman and the eleven-term incumbent, State Assemblyman John Brook, who placed last with 8% (Green captured the nomination with 41%). His ability to prevail in the general was most impressive. While Republicans in Manhattan were being mauled into extinction not just by Lyndon Johnson but Bobby Kennedy, Green eked to a three point victory over John Heimann. His 1965 and '66 re-elections (multiple remaps took place) were effortless.

Green attempted to make it to Congress ten years before he actually arrived. In 1968, local Republicans were urging him to challenge Democratic Congressman Ted Kupferman. Green acquiesced but Kupferman retired and Green faced opposition in the primary from someone with whom he was well acquainted – State Senator Whitney Seymour, Jr. Green took 46% but Seymour ended up winning the primary (he lost in the fall to Koch). Green spent the next six years as regional administrator of the federal Department of Housing and Urban Development but when Democrat Ed Koch won the Mayoralty in 1977, he set his sights on capturing the seat in the special election the following February.

Unsurprisingly, Green's 1978 win was considered a huge upset. The victory came against former Congresswoman Bella Abzug. But while Abzug's voting record fit most areas of the district, her style, led by her ubiquitous hats, was more contained. The scene: the city's Silk-Stocking district which *The New York Times* notes is, "so named because it includes some of Manhattan's toniest areas."

The Times summed up the state of the race near its end. "Since entering the race as a virtual unknown eight weeks ago, (Green) has faced the problem of gaining recognition while running against an opponent who needed no introduction to voters." About the only issue of substance the pair disagreed on was the controversial Westway project which Green favored and Abzug opposed. Both candidates stressed their legislative experience. But the convention that ultimately awarded Abzug the nomination was messy and resentment lingered (three ballots and a judge's intervention were required to iron it out).

Green had perhaps the one weapon that could overcome a dearth in polls – deep pockets. His family founded the Grand Union supermarkets that were abundant in the New York-New Jersey area and Green outspent Abzug 2-1. It was key. Abzug took 75% in the Lower East Side and Greenwich Village but turnout there was abysmal (overcoming apathy was key for both sides). When the votes were tallied, Green had denied Abzug a comeback by 1,161 votes out of 60,000 cast. When Green arrived in Washington, a number of overjoyed Republican colleagues, including Harold Hollenbeck of New Jersey, wore hats to welcome hill.

Though Green was elected in a 1978 special election, he was technically a freshmen with those elected in '76. He stands at the top row, far left of that class photo of House Republicans
Photo courtesy of Harold Hollenbeck

That fall, Green had to win a full term and he faced ex-City Councilman Carter Burden, who had been on the losing end of the rancorous convention battle with Abzug. The race could easily have been the battle of the heirs, as Burden's family was part of Vanderbilt and Whitney. Not surprisingly, both camps spent what Green termed a, "ridiculously astronomic" sum of money, though *CQ* noted that Green was hardly immune to spending because he "bought up all advertising space on city bus routes running through the district," no cheap feat in Manhattan. Democrats had hoped that Burden sharing a base with Green might sway crucial votes back to their fold but Green widened his margin From February prevailed 53-47%.

Votingwise, Green's political tightrope began nearly as soon as his upset win. He organized a PAC for centrists, MODRNPAC and backed his then-colleague, John Anderson for President in 1980 over Ronald Reagan and George H.W. Bush.

In October 1981, Green voted for a House budget Reagan threatened to veto, which passed 249-168. He called it, "a message to the budget cutters that the House does not want to see the 'safety net' cut to shreds." Green did vote for Reagan's signature tax cut but only after getting the White House to insert a provision for tax-exempt bonds for mass transit projects.

During Reagan's second term, Green's support of the president never hit 40%. In 1981, Green, along with Carl Pursell of Michigan became leaders of the "Gypsy Moth," a group of roughly 25 Northeastern/Midwest lawmakers who pressed or the restoration of spending cuts that they considered to be deleterious to their regions. In Green's case, it was more funding for mass transit, energy assistance and in times, AIDS funding and defense cuts would help fund it.

Green told *The New York Times* his, "consciousness-raising came earlier this year when I saw the President negotiating with Southern Democrats when they were demanding a $5 billion cut in the deficit before they'd go along with Gramm-Latta, and I suppose if the President had decided to achieve that $5 billion reduction by ending 2 percent rural electrification loans or cutting out peanut and tobacco subsidies or the Tenn-Tom water project, I wouldn't have minded as much. But instead he was doing it by cutting mass transit operating subsidies and taking away from the strategic petroleum reserve, which is more important to our part of the country." He was more accusatory when he said, "We always seem to be selling out Northeast interests and Midwest interests to pick up southern Democratic votes."

In October 1981, Green voted for a House budget Reagan threatened to veto, which passed 249-168. He called it, "a message to the budget cutters that the House does not want to see the 'safety net' cut to shreds." Green did vote for Reagan's signature tax cut but only after getting the White House to insert a provision for tax-exempt bonds for mass transit projects. In 1983, Green voted for the Democratic budget.

Like most New Yorkers of both parties, Green opposed the landmark 1986 tax package because it was "harmful to New Yorkers and bad for the city." He called the bill discriminatory of rentals because it would force higher rates, "removing the working poor from the tax rolls and, conversely, making sure that people and companies that make money pay taxes."

Green chaired the House-Senate Environmental and Energy Study Conference. Republican leaders helped Green as well. Appropriations seats are prized but Republican leaders gave Green one and by 1981, he was top Republican on the HUD subcommittee, which was critical to both New York and his interests.

When the interests of housing were pitted against others, Green sided with housing advocates every time even if he supported the other interests in principle. One example was on 1984 amendment to an Appropriations measure in which Colorado Democratic Congressman Tim Wirth proposed shifting $220 million from housing programs to the EPA. Wirth's amendment was adopted. Green did support clean air and in 1988, he authored a letter with Minnesota Democrat Bruce Vento urging Congress to pass the most strenuous possible legislation.

One issue on which Green was able to showcase his opposition with the Reagan administration was production of the MX missile. When Reagan unveiled the missile, known as the Dense Pack, Green's reaction was, "No matter how it is packaged, the MX missile program is a mistake militarily, socially and economically." Efforts to stop the missile in 1982 failed on a tie vote (26-26) in Appropriations and Green cited the deficit. The following year, MX passed the full House but Green was one of three Republicans to oppose it. In 1985, MX cleared a closely divided House (219-213) but Green was in the minority.

Green with a Democratic Congressman and fellow Manhattanite, Ted Weiss
Image courtesy of C-SPAN

Another issue on which Green was active was a test ban proposal, which he sponsored with Democratic Congressman Les AuCoin of Oregon. It cleared Appropriations 31-22 and passed the full House in spite of warnings that Reagan would veto the entire spending bill. To the astonishment of many, the amendment remained in the package and became law.

During Reagan's second term, Green's support of the president never hit 40% and departure from the party line continued into the Bush administration and it started with trying to influence the 1988 convention platform. "In 1919," he said, "it was a Republican Congress that proposed the 19th Amendment giving women the vote. It was the Republican Party that, in 1940, placed the ERA in its platform, four years before the Democrats."

Green supported the Family and Medical Leave override but not the minimum wage. In 1990, Green was a rare Republican who opposed both the Balanced Budget Amendment and the flag-burning prohibition amendment. On the latter, he said on the House floor, "We are here today to decide which to see injured, an occasional American flag or the Bill of Rights. The flag is the symbol of that for which America stands. The Bill of Rights is the substance of that for which America stands. Each year, vast numbers of American flags are manufactured. If a few of those are destroyed by zealots for various causes, what is the loss? But we have only one Bill of Rights. If today, for the first time in our Nation's 200-year history, we start on the course of weakening the Bill of Rights, where does that loss end?" And he ardently defended a woman's right to choose, sponsoring the Reproductive Health Equity Act.

Green has been a strong proponent of gutting the Hyde Amendment which since its enactment in 1975, famously prohibited the use of federal funds for abortions except when the mother's life was in danger. Though he saw the mathematic in practicality of getting rid of the amendment in 1988, he made clear "We're not going to standby in definitely on issues of this kind." On the floor, he said, "To force a woman who has been raped to carry to term a fetus which is the pregnancy of that rape is an act of horrible cruelty, second only to the rape itself." Green was similarly sanguine when the House upheld Bush's veto on providing federal funding to women seeking abortions as a result of rape and incest. "I fear, as a Republican, that President Bush may have stumbled on the one issue that could cost him re-election in 1992."

Stylistically, Green's lifestyle belied his wealth. *New York Magazine* in 1984 ran a piece which stated he traveled by subway, owned a 1969 Chevy and only owned a black and white television set without cable ("we didn't want to encourage the kids to watch more television than they already do"). "He considers politics a distraction from government which is his real work." *The Almanac of American Politics* said Green, "is not a natural glad hand or spellbinder and does not seem fascinated by the glitz as mesmerized so many others in the district."

Sitting on that subcommittee put Green in a position to earmark dollars galore to housing programs. Green wanted to be practical when it came to the space station. "If you want the space station, you can't use that account is cornucopia...Don't start the space station and then nimble it to death."

Throughout the entire 1980s, Green rarely sweated electorally against up'n'comers on the Manhattan political scene, which included a future New York City Public Advocate, Mark Green in 1980 and the Manhattan Borough President Andy Stein in '84. His race against Stein, which he won with a surprisingly comfortable 56%, was the most expensive – and by far the nastiest of his career and he tarred Stein as being in the pocket of the city's real estate developers.

Near the end of the campaign, *New York Magazine* said, "Green owns North of 59th Street and Stein owns south of 14th. In between is Stuyveasant Town and Peter Cooper Village, and that is probably be where the race is won or lost." Like Abzug, Stein was far from monolithically popular among Democrats and he in fact became quite damaged by a barrage of articles by *Town & Country Magazine*. But he used famed political consultant David Garth and had enough assets that the contest was initially expected to go down-to-the-wire.

Green raised issue of Stein's missed votes as an Assemblyman while Stein challenged Green to release his tax returns and intimated that his brother-in-law had squandered up to $40 million on a business venture. One example of the extent of the acrimony came when the author of that *New York Magazine* piece, Joe Klein asked if he thought Green was a dilettante, Green replied, "No, I think he's very skilled at grandstanding. I think he's got that down to a science."

The next three cycles spared Green of a serious challenge. His 59% against Fran Reiter in 1990 (the Liberal Party nominee who was tapped by Democratic leaders when Democrats failed to file a candidate at the deadline), only proved his continued durability in a district that, if anything, was becoming more Democratic. Then came 1992.

As big a Democratic year as it was, the results suggest Green would have held off Maloney had the 1980s boundaries been in effect. But the state's loss of three Congressional seats meant that the 15th had to expand (and become the 14th), and the areas it picked up were loath to support any Republican, much less one that wasn't particularly known. They included Astoria, Queens and Greenpoint, Brooklyn.

Maloney campaigned on Congress having too many millionaires and not enough women. She contended that "the biggest issue confronting this city is the economy and jobs. Bill Green voted consistently with the Reagan economic measures that have gutted the city." Green attacked Maloney's effectiveness on Council.

The two candidates traded leads all night – Maloney led, then Green inched ahead before Maloney jumped in front again and stayed there. Green carried Manhattan by fewer than 2,000 votes and that was about 90% of the district. But Queens and Brooklyn went to Maloney with 65% and 61% respectively, and that was enough to secure a 4,000 vote win.

In 1994, Green mounted a somewhat quixotic campaign to win the GOP nomination for governor of New York State

Green died of complications from cancer in 2002 two days before his 73rd birthday.

CHAPTER FIFTY-THREE

Whether A Republican Or Democrat, Ireland Served With Integrity

Florida is legendary for hosting spring training for baseball teams and in 1964, Boston Red Sox General manager Paul O'Connell decided to take local officials up on their offer and use Winter Haven, Florida for its practice. The Chain of Lakes Park was constructed for $425,000 and the Red Sox began getting ready for their season for the ensuing twenty-five years. Who were the community leaders most instrumental in convincing the Sox to practice in Florida? Winter Haven Mayor Dick Dantzler and future-Congressman Andy Ireland. Everything starts somewhere.

Photo courtesy of Andy Ireland

For 16 years, Polk County, Florida was represented by a very capable, congenial Democrat turned Republican named Andy Ireland and regardless of which party (his switch came in the midst of his fourth term), he fit his district like a comfortable shoe.

Ireland had an early background far removed from the fields of central Florida. He was reared in Cincinnati, the son of a beloved businessman and was educated at prep schools both locally and at Phillips Academy in Massachusetts. He earned his business degree from Yale University and took classes at Columbia University before finally, settling on an exclusive program offered only by a few institutions, including the Louisiana State University, School of Banking of the South.

For Ireland, returning to Cincinnati after completing his education was not an option as he prepared to start a career in the world of financial affairs. Why? Because of his father's prominence. As he explained, "I would never know if I got help for me or whether I got it because of my father." His plans at the time were to travel to California but that proved a little too far. So he headed straight for Florida.

First there was the Barnett National Bank but eventually, he was senior vice-president of the Broward National Bank in Fort Lauderdale. Within a few years, he was in the central Florida town of Winter Haven where he eventually became president of the First National Bank. The connections Ireland made served Ireland well as he got the political bug though it took a while for him to branch beyond locally. He was elected to the Winter Haven City Commission in 1966 and became close friends with the Speaker of the Florida House. In 1972, Governor Reuben Askew prevailed on Ireland to challenge an incumbent for a seat in the Florida State Senate. Ireland forced a runoff but lost by a small margin. But his many acquaintances would not let him wither on the vine and they pleaded with him to run for "something."

That something proved to be a Congressional seat in 1976 that longtime incumbent James Haley opted to vacate after 24 years in office and decreasing election percentages. The race to succeed him was a six-way primary where Ireland and State Representative Ray Mattox were the two candidates with the most widespread support.

During the campaign, Ireland put Mattox on the spot for not releasing details about his net worth. Shortly before the primary, Mattox did so, but only because he contended Ireland, "has made a sham of financial disclosure by using this subject to create a diversionary issue to cover up for his total lack of qualifications and experience." A runoff had been expected but Ireland's 51% proved enough to avoid one and he took 58% against State Representative Robert Johnson in November. Given his background, one might have expected Ireland to pursue interests in financial services but the committee assignments on which he was seated were Foreign Affairs and Small Business.

Ireland's district had awarded Ronald Reagan 58% in 1980 and, the Congressman's party label seemed to be the only thing that separated the two men. *CQ* noted that Ireland was among just nine Democrats to support all five of Reagan's controversial economic proposals. He described himself as a "hawk who has always believed that U.S. military superiority is our best chance for democracy and World Peace. However, I am also a fiscal conservative with a former banker's penchant for frugality." Indeed, his Americans for Democratic action scores could be zero in a given year but never more than 11%. His AFL-CIO score did not top 25% since he was a Democrat.

Photo courtesy of Andy Ireland

By 1984, Ireland was the top Democrat on the Small Business Subcommittee. But he was genuinely unhappy and on March 17, 1984, he announced that he was becoming a republican. He framed his decision thus: "In becoming a Republican after a lifetime as a Democrat, I do not see myself leaving the Democratic Party so much as I see the Democratic Party leaving me and our state and its values." House Speaker Tip O'Neill's response, besides, "Andy, you ruined my St. Patrick's Day Parade," was that he never voted with the party anyway, a viewpoint Ireland did little to dispute. "The House Democratic leadership," he said, "uses the Solid South to sustain itself but when it comes time for input they say, 'Go take a hike'" (O'Neill and Ireland nevertheless maintained a very jovial relationship).

Photo courtesy of Andy Ireland

Congressional scholar Norm Ornstein called Ireland, "the kind of guy you want in the House. He did not switch parties as a shallow, cold calculating move or as a springboard to higher office." Ireland subsequently informed his donors that he would return their contributions as a result of the switched but only one $50 contributor was interested.

Locally, some Democrats grumbled but Ireland's switch took just fine as he beat Democrat Patricia Glass 62-38%. The next two elections pitted him against David Higginbottom but instead, it was the challenger who plummeted to the bottom as Ireland scored his highest percentages as an opposed incumbent (he had been unopposed in 1978 and '82), grabbing 71% and 73%.

As a result of the switch, Ireland lost his Foreign Affairs post but his legislative portfolio seemed to gravitate toward Small Business anyway where he remained. He was assigned to Armed Services to compensate and a fair amount of his pedigree in any case was increasingly becoming geared toward matters concerning defense.

Excessive cost overruns was one and Ireland had little tolerance for governmental nonsense. When it was revealed that the government had a $100 billion in unused funds, Ireland introduced legislation eliminating it and was joined by Congressional heavyweights (Energy and Commerce Chair John Dingell was among his supporters).

At one point declaring, "The time has come to lay one of these guys down and set an example," Northrop Corp.'s was among Ireland's first targets. "Along with waste, fraud and abuse," he said, "we better start worrying about management crisis…This management is appalling."

In 1990, Ireland took aim at the $80 billion A-12 Avenger fighter jet in 1990 after learning McDonnell Douglas was at least a year behind schedule and $1 billion over budget. The investigation led to an Inspector General report and the early retirement of the chief of the Naval Air Systems Command at which point Ireland gloated about "a process ripe for abuse." He contended that, "Program managers are giving assurances about contractors' adherence to budgets based largely on the word of the contractors themselves.

Ireland had been championing the issue until the day he left office. Late in 1992, he delivered a floor speech in which he attacked a Senate provision of a Defense Authorization bill that would allow Defense to "pay old debts with new money," a practice he called, "inconsistent with the maintenance of integrity and discipline in accounting and finance at the Department of Defense," not to mention a violation of the Anti-Deficiency Act. "Surely," Ireland told colleagues, "if sufficient money remained in those accounts, DOD would use it. What is the problem? The answer to these questions is very simple. There can be only one reason why DOD is proposing section 1003. Those accounts are empty. The money is gone. In technical terms, those accounts are over-obligated. It's the same old story. DOD has bills to pay, and no money to pay them."

Photo courtesy of Andy Ireland

Given his history, Ireland would seem to have little in common with a nationally known liberal Democrat from Colorado but the two sponsored a proposal in early 1989 that would draw down the number of U.S. troops in Europe. While Ireland cited, "a substantial groundswell for this type of thing." It was opposed by the Pentagon as well as leading Defense oriented members of Congress, among them Armed Services Chair Les Aspin and the Senate's top committee Republican John Warner.

If there is one matter Ireland fought to the core regardless of party it was refusing to allow drilling off of the Florida coast, and on that, his work was bipartisan. In the mid-1980s, he took issue with Interior Secretary Donald Hodel's suggestion that drilling was safe. In July 1989, after Hodel's successor at Interior, Manuel Lujan seemed to imply that drilling was safer than the transporting of oil, Ireland introduced legislation with Miami Democrats Dante Fascell and Bill Lehman and Republican Bill Young to permanently ban exploration.

And of course there was citrus. Ireland represented citrus country and he did not take kindly to threats to either restrict imports or boycott grapefruits altogether. He took issue with the Overseas Private Investment Corporation (OPIC) when they wanted to install orange trees in Belize. In 1989, Korea was advocating a boycott (claiming without evidence that they contained Alar) and Ireland and his GOP colleague, Tom Lewis, arranged a meeting with the Korean Ambassador. Later, it was Japan which was refusing to honor its promised import quota. He, Lewis and GOP Senator Connie Mack fought to have February declared, "National Grapefruit Month." He also favored National Motorcycle Awareness Month.

Ireland genuinely looked for ways to ease to burdens among small businesses. He got through a White House conference on small business. He mandated that the Import-Export Bank award some contracts to small businesses. He fought cabinet-level status for the Small Business Administration and promoted the idea of loans of up to $10,000 for welfare recipients who aspired to open a business. Concern about impact on small businesses was one reason Ireland opposed the Family and Medical Leave Act. Still,

In Congress, Ireland was as well-liked by colleagues as his constituents. New York Democrat John LaFalce chaired Small Business when Ireland was ranking member and he has "nothing but good recollections about Andy." They agreed on many things and the rare areas of disagreement "didn't lend itself to partisanship." Miami Democrat Larry Smith called Ireland, "a very pleasant, non-confrontational Congressman," adding, "He was conservative, but not an ideologue."

Photo courtesy of Andy Ireland

By 1992, Ireland was the top Republican on the Small Business committee where he worked amicably with the panel's chairman, John LaFalce of New York. But that spring, he announced his decision to join the Hill's increasingly large exodus that year. It had not appeared that leaving was Ireland's intention at the beginning of the cycle. In the spring of 1991, he made a well-publicized move from his longtime abode in Winter Park to Manatee County because, he said, he feared Polk County would be split into two districts. At any rate, he addressed rumors by saying, "I don't have a secret agenda or a hidden agenda of any kind. I am enthusiastic about what's doing, and I feel very strongly - and I have all my life - that when you've done something and given it your all, sometimes it's important to move on."

Move on Ireland did though he still remained in the nation's capital. He set up a lobbying shop, Zeliff/Ireland with his a former New Hampshire Republican colleague, Bill Zeliff. But he also took up the circus. Rather, in 1993, Ireland became the head Capitol Hill lobbyist for Ringling Bros. and Barnum & Bailey Circus. It was a marriage made in heaven. It was noted that" Ringling Bros. helped his campaign...lending him showgirls and clowns for his fund-raising events at Washington's RFK Stadium." Plus, Ireland handwrote a resolution allowing "permitting 13 fice-ton elephants on the grounds of Congress celebrating the circus' 125th anniversary." Most importantly, Ireland is known to end all of his letters with, "May all your days be circus days."

CHAPTER FIFTY-FOUR

Obscure Early Done in by His Fifteen Minutes of Fame Relating to Bank Scandal

Introductory Quote: "I'm doing things that I think are very important for this district and this state. I'm not moving up in anything visible but that doesn't bother me." – Massachusetts Congressman Joe Early on his lack of notoriety in Congress.

Photo courtesy of The Worcester Gazette & Telegram

O f all of the members of Congress profiled for this volume, Joe Early may have been the one who toiled most in anonymity – but that was just the way he liked it. Unfortunately for Early, that was more than made up for during his final year in office when his role in the House Bank Scandal gave him unmitigated publicity. This led to his subsequent defeat from the seat which had fit him like a glove for eighteen years.

Early was a proud product of the Bay State's second largest city - Worcester and his heavy and emphatic pronunciation of the land often referred to as the "Heart of the Commonwealth" (Woo-stah) was all the assurance one needed to see how he personified his people. In fact, *Politics in America*, labeling him "a portly, rumpled cigar smoker," also observed that he "looks the part of a Massachusetts pol."

On his death in 2012, *The Boston Herald* summed up Early's legacy to a tee: "Early, the man who worked quietly in the House committee system for 17 years, was forced in his final year to defend himself." Decades earlier in 1989, Kenneth J. Moynihan who was a history professor at Worcester's Assumption College said, "I think he would have to make a colossal mistake to lose that seat." In 1992, those confluences came together for him to do just that.

Early was a microcosm of his district – Irish Catholic, the father of eight and pro-life. He lived most of his life in Worcester and graduated from the College of the Holy Cross in 1955, a year after he helped the school's basketball team, the Crusaders, win the National Invitational Tournament at Madison Square Garden as a co-captain. After graduation, Early joined the Navy and his early adulthood was spent as a teacher and basketball coach. At that time, he married Marilyn Powers and lived in a triple-decker.

Early sought a seat in the Massachusetts House at age 29 and won the primary over a friend, Bob Kneeland, by 15 votes. He eventually became vice-chair of the Committee on Ways and Means.

In 1974, longtime Democratic Congressman Harold Donohue opted to retire and Early entered the race to succeed him, at which time *The Worcester Telegram* labeled him, "No hoopla, no nothing." How accurate was that assertion? Just days before, Early informed *The Telegram* of his intention to run for Congress by hand-delivering a letter to a reporter and leaving.

Seven Democrats filed for the nomination and four seemed to have a serious chance: Early, Worchester School Committeeman Gerald D'Amico, ex-Worcester Mayor Paul Mullaney, and John Anderson. It was generally a friends and neighbors competition but Early won the majority of counties in the district, mostly with pluralities in the mid-30s. In Worcester, he had just 33% but it was by far the most populous area and his top competitors were also favorite-sons. In any case, it proved enough to win him the nomination with 32% (D'Amico edged out Mullaney for second place by 122 votes). Early faced David Lionett in the fall and, in a less Democratic environment, would likely have struggled immensely. As it was, Early fell slightly below 50% (49.8%) but outdistanced Lionett by 11%. Until 1992, he would never struggle again and was in fact unopposed in 1976. The 67% he grabbed in 1984 was his lowest margin.

In Congress, then Majority Leader Tip O'Neill helped Early gain a seat on the House Appropriations Committee. It was a position that while not only lucrative, would seem to make someone a quintessential insider. If folks expected that of Early, they would be sorely disappointed. He once said, "I'm more interested in the ombudsman part of this job. That's more important to me than re-election" and this showed in how he conducted his responsibilities.

Early dove deep into the confines of his committee but he was not a man about town - he rarely went through the perfunctory legislative mechanisms of speaking on the floor or co-sponsoring colleagues bills. Early acknowledged to *The Worcester Telegram & Gazette* that, "My style is that I've always been a loner" which extended to press conferences and stinginess about co-sponsoring legislation. In fact, in 1990 Early opened his first media briefing with members of the Massachusetts delegation to fight for a foreign takeover of a Worcester factory by reminding them that, "Most of you don't know who I am." This prompted *Politics in America* to observe that *The Boston Herald* "included a picture of Early with a full head of black hair, something that hasn't been seen in person in a few years." At its conclusion, Early told those gathered, "I assure you we won't have another one for another 28 years."

Be that as it may, when it came to fulfilling the obligatory Appropriator role of delivering the goods, Early excelled. Michael Sheehy was the legislative director for Early's legendary district neighbor, Edward Boland, and described his gift as: "There's an old saw around here about some members being show horses, and some members being workhorses. I think Mr. Early is a workhorse. Most of what he does you will never see - lobbying for and against amendments, particularly on the amendments he's working on. That's how he spends his time. That's not very visible from the press gallery." In fact, *Politics in America* wrote he "digs in with the persistence of a bulldog if the program cuts affects his district."

Photo courtesy of The Worcester Gazette & Telegram

One of those "goods" included securing NIH research grants for the University of Massachusetts Medical School in Worcester, which helped enhance the renowned reputation that the facility has long brought to the entire region. Funding for Tufts Veterinary School also yielded major dividends. Other local projects included an extra $50,000 for the Blackstone River Valley National Heritage Corridor and operating expenses for the Higgins Armory Museum.

An Appropriations staff member called Early, "a pretty aggressive guy as far as witnesses are concerned and he will ask the tough questions. If he thinks they're trying to pull the wool over his eyes, he'll go after them. I'd say he is more aggressive than most of the other members." One example came in 1989 when the Commerce Department was threatening to close weather stations around the country, one of which was based at Worcester Airport. Early confronted Secretary Robert Mosbacher at an Approps hearing and he agreed to spare the station.

Early was labeled "counterintuitive" and there were a few examples during his eighteen years in Congress to back that up. He voted against the impeachment of Judge Alcee Hastings from the bench, one of only seven to do so. He was one of just thirteen Democrats to oppose turning the Department of Environmental Protection into a cabinet agency.

The most infamous example might have been in 1989. While many members feared the almost certain recriminations of supporting a Congressional pay raise, Early took to the floor to defend it. In doing so he used an analogy most probably wouldn't have gone near. He said, "You have to look at the intrinsic worth of the job and you have to show leadership. A number of years ago in the House we didn't...and in the names of public opinion, sent Marines into Beirut. There were 244 Marines killed." *The Worcester Telegram & Gazette* cited "a stir in the galleries overlooking the House chamber" as a reaction. Except for his defense of routine budget matters, not many could recall the last time this Congressman of 15 years had taken the floor to fight for anything, never mind such a profoundly unpopular proposal.

There was no mistaking that Early's "counterintuitive" style transferred into his office. A famous tale had it that his personal secretary once complained to him that she was accustomed to being far busier in other offices than his and asked if he could rectify that by assigning her more work. Early's response: "type slower." He was a generous boss though and, during at least one period, Early spent the most money on salaries for the Bay State delegation staff.

Among his colleagues, Early was disinclined to sign co-sponsor forms which usually is a no-brainer for forging relationships. Yet he was there when it counted and was known as a nice, helpful person with a heart of gold. In his book *Mayor*, Ed Koch who was then a Congressman from New York, wrote about how he and Early were on a trip to Saudi Arabia when Koch arranged an early morning visit with members of the government in a less than savory area. Regardless of the potential danger the meeting posed, Early offered to accompany Koch to which the future New York Mayor said he would always be grateful (years later, Koch tried to return the favor by telling Early that he "looked thinner" but Early would have none of it. "Ed," he replied, "I have told everyone here that you are an honest man and only tell the truth. I weigh 250 pounds so, please don't tell me that I look thinner").

Early also took interest in cystic fibrosis and near the end of his tenure, sponsored annual Cystic Fibrosis Golf Tournaments. On his spare time, he could often be found at the racetrack.

Photo courtesy of The Worcester Gazette & Telegram

The late 1980s found Early under fire from his colleagues due to troubles that ultimately led to the end of his career. As Massachusetts Governor Michael Dukakis's campaign to secure his party's presidential nomination gained steam, Early, who was close to ex-Governor Ed King (the man Dukakis both lost to and later beat to win back the governor's mansion), privately warned members of Congress of Dukakis's deficiencies. These specifically related to economic issues. Early took heat in the process but as the Bay State's fiscal situation deteriorated, most realized that he had indeed been prescient.

The political challenges Early faced began early in 1991 when each Massachusetts Democrat had a big task ahead given that the state was slated to lose a House seat. A plan created rather early was to combine Worcester with the city of Lowell. Early lambasted this as "Boston pols [having] cannibalized Central Massachusetts" but it in fact came to fruition because the Democratic Congressman from Lowell, Chester Atkins, barely held his seat in 1990 and volunteered to be paired with Early's district. Early called this "unique. I've never heard of anything like this before." Late in the year, Early held what *The Boston Herald* labeled as an, "organizational tune-up meeting at the Worcester Centrum - a session that was attended by several thousand supporters."

Next came the House Banking matter. At the time that news of members' overdrafts first became public, Early shrugged off potential problems. As late as March 1992, when the Ethics Committee voted to make the "worst abusers" public, Early had little reason to be nervous. His impression was that the members with the most to fear had already been notified. He was wrong. The list revealed that Early overdrew his account 140 times, an amount which might not have been politically fatal in itself (some members held their seats having overdrawn far more). In this situation the "devil was in the details." Early's account exceeded its balance for 15 of the 39 months examined with the amount totaling $182,119. Early, who pronounced himself "shocked, embarrassed and disappointed," steadfastly maintained that, "I never wrote a bad check. I never thought I overdrew my account." He called, "public office...a public trust," and was adamant that, "I have not violated that trust." However, the checks were not his first brush with a testing of that trust. He came under scrutiny for the revelation that two of his children were given scholarships by members doing business before Approps.

This time, in words that struck many tone deaf, Early put forth the following explanation: "I am not a rich man. In a very real sense, I live paycheck to paycheck as do many other Americans." *The Boston Herald* had a field day with that one. "Poor Joe Early," they opined. "Maybe he does live paycheck to paycheck - but what a paycheck! How many of Early's constituents take home a weekly check in the neighborhood of $2,480? That's what Early's $129,000 annual congressional pay amounts to. So pardon us, if we have no tears to shed for the Worcester Democrat whose banking records will now become the subject of a further House investigation." *The Worcester Telegram* went even further, calling on Early to resign.

Had Early stopped there, he might have been okay. Whether it was the pressure or genuine frustration, he took to the House floor one day to lambaste the speaker, Ethics Committee, and seemingly everything in his midst. On Tom Foley, he said the speaker "has handled this as a disgrace," and didn't spare well-liked Majority Leader Richard Gephardt in saying he "has shown no leadership either…they go as a team." Early acknowledged in the midst of the campaign that, "My expression has caused me a little more trouble." He said the Ethics Committee, "…ran like rats. Like rats." In fact, the Committee considered whether to remove his name as a worst abuser but rejected it on a tie vote.

In the aftermath of the press fiasco, Early issued another acknowledgement. He said, "I have to explain the process. I have to P.R. my message better. I don't do a good job with that." To rectify that, he hired his first ever press secretary.

In what proved exasperating to candidates across the Bay State, redistricting was not completed until early July. When it was, the aggravation was hardly quelled. Not only was roughly half of the third new territory for Early, but it also stretched from Worcester to coastal communities near the Rhode Island border, an elongation that led many to deride it as, "the Ivy League district because it runs from Princeton to Dartmouth." Early's primary opponent, State Senator Gerard D'Amico, was harsher. The new third, he said, was "two peacocks in a pre-mating ritual dance, a peck here and peck there." Another candidate called it, "a snake that swallowed a mouse." The candidates were able to find their footing and the Democratic primary field, consisting of five fellow Democrats who challenged Early for the Democratic nod, included D'Amico. He had been second fiddle to Early eighteen years earlier in the race to succeed Donahue.

Not everyone wound up abandoning his or her Congressman. Labor unions displayed their appreciation to Early by giving him their backing. At times, Early was spared at least some part of the sniping as D'Amico and a third candidate in the race, Martin Healey, had only recently moved in from elsewhere. This prompted D'Amico to say, "You dropped in from wherever… looking for a congressional seat." Healey countered by citing D'Amico's close proximity to tempestuous State Senate President Billy Bulger in the statement: "When you called him your boss you didn't whisper in his ear, 'you're dangerous to women.'" D'Amico didn't let Early off the hook on abortion either, as one ad he ran portrayed him as "dangerous to women."

Against such split opposition, Early was able to win the primary with just 37%. The only incumbent who did worse in a primary that year and survived was his friend Austin Murphy of Pennsylvania. Early addressed supporters that night with unusual poignancy saying, "I never had the analysts and the pollsters in Washington and Boston, I've only had you people and that's the only poll I ever wanted. I love each and every one of you and you people like me. I never broke the public trust, I never will break the public trust. I go to the people and tell them what I'm going to do." State Senator Peter Blute prevailed over David Lionett in winning the GOP nod to face Early.

Unlike Nick Mavroules (Early's fellow Democrat from Peabody who came under indictment), most observers gave him a fighting chance to hold his seat and the race was judged as a tossup. Had it not been a redistricting year, Early may have been fine. However, seventeen towns were added and with such little visibility outside Worcester, their first introduction to him involved the problem checks. Blute also reminded voters that he believed Early was out of touch on other areas. Labeling him, "Tahiti Joe," one ad claimed he suffered from, "a terrible addiction: perkomania," and a Bart Simpson-sounding voice dismissed the criticism with, "Hey dude, no big deal." Early tried to counter him through outspending Blute by roughly half and running on his influence. When confronted about the prospect of defeat he responded, "Whatever happens, happens."

Many Democrats hoped – and Republicans privately fretted that Bill Clinton's expected romp in Massachusetts would allow Early a squeaker win. It didn't. Counting went into the morning hours. Worcester was hung up by a computer failure but Early soon concluded that any outstanding precincts would be insufficient to put him over the top. He delivered the news to steadfast backers at 1 a.m. stating, "I lost the election but I can accept that. Those things happen." Reflecting Democratic Governor Bill Clinton's win over incumbent President George H.W. Bush, Early added, "Again, it's just change." However, he conceded that, "It was a vote against Joe Early."

The city of Worcester came through for Early with 57%, though Blute won 51% in the county overall while Fall River gave him 59%. Blute, who made no secret that his strategy was to appeal to voters outside of his home town, told a reporter on Election Day that, "Many people we talk to said they've never seen Joe Early." It worked. Blute quipped, "In Attleboro they didn't count the votes, they weighed them."

Early's name lived on in public service. His son, Joe Early, Jr., has been Worcester's long time District Attorney since 2006.

CHAPTER FIFTY-FIVE

Mavroules's Devotion to District was as Legendary as His Legal Woes

**Introductory Quote: "Dad, that man should run for Mayor of Peabody." –
Gail Mavroules, daughter of future Congressman Nick Mavroules upon
meeting John F. Kennedy who was then a Senator from Massachusetts.**

Photo courtesy of the U.S. House of Representatives Collection

I t was a tale of two sides of Nick Mavroules. One was the "smooth, silver
haired lawmaker," as *The Herald* called him, the "for the people," and
"bread'n'butter" oriented public servant who made the system work and used
his plum Armed Services Committee position to keep defense jobs in the area.
The other was the convict, summed up by *The Herald* as, "Nicky Pockets."
Whatever the case, both traits converged to bring his career to a shattering
end and to make the often described "energizer bunny" a jailbird.

By every measure, Mavroules was the town of Peabody, Massachusetts. He was born in the mid-sized city, having graduated high school there and married his high school sweetheart. Rather than attend college, Mavroules went to work at a Sylvania Electronics Factory. He rose through the town, mounting an unsuccessful bid for Council in 1955 but succeeding three years later at age 29. Within nine years, Mavroules was Mayor and served in the position until he went to Congress a dozen years later. However, 1973 brought what *The Globe* called, "a close and acrimonious race" for re-election, one that Mavroules barely won. This proved to be a precursor for what brought his career to an end two decades later.

In 1978, Mavroules announced his plans to challenge fellow Democratic Congressman Michael Harrington in the primary. Harrington, seeing that his base eroded, retired and Mavroules was left to compete with James Smith, a State Senator who challenged Harrington. Mavroules, who was labeled the more moderate contender, edged Smith 44-35% and won the seat in November with relatively little trouble.

1980 was Mavroules's one tough contest prior to the '92 race. He was against prominent attorney Thomas Trimarco, a protégé of former Republican Governor John Volpe. Trimarco hoped to galvanize support among the district's large Italian-American population and to use Ronald Reagan's expected big win in the district to gain votes. He was initially given ammunition by rumblings about Mavroules' ethics, but the incumbent was cleared and he squeaked past Trimarco by just 8,000 votes. Trimarco tried again in 1982 but conditions veered back toward the Democrats. This time Mavroules would nab 58%. He gained a great deal of influence policy-wise within the body.

Mavroules's legacy in Congress was working to stop production of the MX missile. He had been immersed in the issue for several years. For two years in a row he came tantalizingly close to succeeding. Mavroules said the MX program represents a "build first, justify later mentality this nation can no longer afford." In 1985, having fallen short by nine votes the prior year, Mavroules led the attempt to cease funding for any missiles not already allocated. The debate, including procedural maneuvering, went on for seven hours before anti-MX forces lost by a 212-218 vote.

It was especially disconcerting to many that the compromise amendment was crafted by Wisconsin Democrat Les Aspin, the new Armed Services Chair whom Mavroules was good friends with. Mavroules made his reasoning known on the floor: "I oppose the system. I think it is a waste of money. The

MX missile probably would give you more fire power as part of the triad. If you honestly believe that 1,000 warheads on 100 MX missiles is going to take the greatest brunt from the Soviet Union, you are mistaken, because what they are going to do is build more missiles, and they can build them. Let us not kid ourselves. They will build more missiles, and they can aim them right at the MX missiles. The fact here is this: It is deterrent. Do we have a force? Do they recognize the fact that we can retaliate, and I think they do."

Later that year, Mavroules led an investigation into the bombing of an American barracks in Beirut, Lebanon that claimed the lives of 241 Marines. Committee members were furious that the higher-ups in the Marines were stonewalling the investigation. Adequate security was instilled as protection. Mavroules stated, "In view of the April bombing of the embassy and the intelligence reports they were receiving it was surprising that there hadn't been greater security measures. There was greater security at the embassy than there was at the compound. They could've had loaded weapons."

Beirut would not be Mavroules's only rendezvous with a Congressional investigation of a tragedy. In 1989, the Committee investigated the Navy response to the explosion aboard the U.S.S. Iowa that killed 21 sailors. Mavroules saw the correlation to the Beirut investigation in that officials were trying to assign blame without pursuing the truth. "If that were my son (who was killed) I'd be all over you like a hound dog. You wouldn't hear the end of it. And if that were your son, you'd be all over me." He later told the press, "Let me be very candid with you, I thought all the higher ups ran like scared rabbits, pointing the finger at someone else."

Only in Congress could a member who had been so ambivalent about association with Armed Services be a chairman-wannabe less than a decade later. Mavroules mounted a long-shot bid for the gavel of the panel in 1987. "Opposition to MX," he said, was a "significant factor," and Mavroules prided himself on being "the mainstream of the Democratic Party." Dennis Hertel of Michigan placed his name in nomination but ended last in a field of four and mustered just 35 votes. He became Chair of the Subcommittee on Readiness that year and in 1989 he took the helm of the Investigations panel.

Mavroules's other committee assignment was Small Business, to which he authored the Small Disadvantaged Business Act. Locally, Mavroules fought for renewable energy technology and the Salem Maritime National Historic Site. One of his son-in-laws said he was, "in awe of how many of the police officers, wait staff and regular people knew Nick and he knew them. He always treated them with the same respect as he did the Head of State."

For much of Mavroules's tenure, rumors percolated about serious ethical lapses. This hit fever pitch in 1988 when his son-in-law and probation officer, Andrew Gerakaris, was indicted on fourteen counts relating to his job (false record keeping, a shakedown for gratuities, etc.) For Mavroules himself, being legally tied in with illegalities would not come until the early 1990s.

By April of 1992, some were talking of Mavroules retiring but he was having none of it. "I am very much encouraged. I've gotten an enormous amount of tough publicity, and I've taken a lot of tough hits. But I've been able to ride it out." The good news was that neither redistricting nor the check bouncing scandal impacted him. The district's boundaries shifted less than any other in the state and he had but one single overdraft.

The bottom dropped as Mavroules was handed an 18-count indictment on charges that were a potpourri of small town government mischief. One involved Mavroules having linked the grant of a liquor store license to a $25,000 payment from the owners, Ralph and Bernard Kaplan. With it came the condition that they were to employ Mavroules' brother for $100/week. There was an allegation that Mavroules demanded $12,000 from the family of Michael Karahalis to relocate him from a federal prison in Florida to Connecticut. Other charges included: having accepted use of a cottage in Gloucester from developer Gerald Gouchberg for whom Mavroules intervened to save a condominium project, having taken two separate payments of $4,000 to approve the opening of a massage parlor, having accepted seven automobiles from Lynn auto dealer Bob Brest for free, and that he had failed to amend his Congressional disclosure form reflecting that (Mavroules did acknowledge the latter charge). It was also said that he demanded one-fifth interest in a Peabody bar be transferred to his nine-year old daughter. In handing down the indictments, U.S. Attorney John Pappalardo contended, "Congressman Mavroules used the power of his office to enrich himself."

Mavroules pled not guilty to the accusations just two and a half weeks before the primary, having called them, "absolutely a bunch of lies." His attorney, former Lieutenant Governor Francis Bellotti said the same and declared, "If they (the prosecution) seek indictments, in all likelihood, they will get them. That will be an accusation and nothing more." He accused the government of "selective" prosecution. The indictment forced Mavroules to surrender his subcommittee chairmanship, which turned out not even to be the most severe consequence.

Mavroules was already in the fight for his life in the Democratic primary against State Senator Barbara Hildt and the indictments naturally exacerbated his problems. Lucky for him, he had broad levels of support, particularly in urban areas. Alec Anderson was evocative of the affection Mavroules unleashed. "We're going to support Nick all the way," he declared, "He's done very much for this district, and all this (legal allegations) going back 20 years? Forget about it." Indeed, Mavroules contended his foes were trying to make hay of his legal woes and said, "If I didn't have the other problem, I can guarantee they would not be in this race."

Using "Stick with Nick" as his slogan, Mavroules told supporters as he opened his headquarters, "I'm not talking victory. I'm talking big victory." As the event neared, Mavroules was heard on audio saying, "I'm going to whip her ass." Hildt backers pounced but the challenger shrugged it off, saying that he meant to say, "I'm going to cut her grass." Days before the primary, Hildt released a poll showing her tied with Mavroules. The incumbent responded by unveiling endorsements from local officials on her home turf.

Abortion was a dominant issue with Hildt berating Mavroules for his opposition (she had firm backing from Emily's List). Mavroules, while not softening his opposition, maintained that he could not back the pending Freedom of Choice Act. "If that act goes through, it will be abortion on demand. I don't think that's what the American people want in this country."

There was a third candidate in the race, Eric Elbot but he was dogged all cycle long by accusations that he was a stalking horse for Mavroules. This was a charge that appeared to "bear fruit" when he demanded Mavroules receive equal time to rebut a Hildt charge at the end of a debate and when he appeared at the incumbent's election watch party on primary night and embraced him on stage. He received a mere 7%.

Though Mavroules started off behind on primary night, he ultimately came back to win by just over 669 votes – 45,516 votes to Hildt's 44,847 (47.6 to 47.1%.) *The Herald* reported "Mavroules rolled up big margins in the cities, taking his home base of Peabody 7,136 to 2,812 for Hildt; winning Salem, 4,963 to 2,442; and carrying Lynn, 5,244 to 2,225." He told supporters at 1 a.m. the win would mark, "one of three. We won this evening, we're going to win in November - and I promise you I'm going to clear my name." One voter, Dick Bradbury, summarized Mavroules's ability to prevail with the assertion. He said, "You can't beat Nick. He's done a lot for the working man." Hildt talked that evening about a recount but spokesman Michael Goldman dismissed that in saying, "Barbara won't do anything to prevent Nick beating a right-wing, George Bush regressive."

Republican State Senator Peter Torkilden captured the GOP nomination to face Mavroules for the fall. In the weeks leading up to the general election, *Congressional Quarterly* rated the direction each nationwide contest was headed in. While many Democratic incumbents landed in the "tossup" column, Mavroules was the only one who found himself in the "Leans Republican" column. That was not reactionary. Less than three weeks out, Mavroules fired his campaign manager and had just $15,000 on hand. Former Senator Paul Tsongas refused to stump for him, though current Senators Ted Kennedy and John Kerry did. Mavroules tried to get a gag order on talk about the upcoming trial. Days before the election, Mavroules declared having "made a lot of movement…We were struggling to put the organization together and get my message out." If true, it wasn't enough. Torkildsen carried the day 55-45%, a margin of 29,000 votes out of nearly 290,000 cast.

Shortly after leaving office, the trial commenced. The turning point came in April when the Judge, David Mazzone, rejected the defense motion to exclude a tape presented by Gerakaris, who was now Mavroules's former son-in-law. The tape was of him talking to Mavroules about accepting a $5,000 bribe (Deborah testified that he threatened to "take my father down"). A week later, Mavroules pled guilty to 15 counts. As he exited the courtroom, Mavroules didn't try to put a pretty face on its outcome. "It's not a happy day, let's face it. But I'll face up to it."

At sentencing, Mazzone told Mavroules, "This was not a minor violation; it was an abuse of public trust." The ultimate sentence was a $15,000 fine and 15-months in prison, carried out at the Federal Correctional Institution in Bradford, Pennsylvania.

After completing his sentence, Mavroules returned to Peabody and died in 2003 at the age of seventy-four.

CHAPTER FIFTY-SIX

Affable but Impervious: Kolter Often Prompted Head-Scratching for Misstatements, Fantasy-Like Pursuits and Judgement

Introductory Quote: "It's certainly not for intellectual stimulation." – California Congressman Doug Bosco on why members of Congress, including his Pennsylvania colleague Joe Kolter, opt for seats on the Public Works and Transportation panel.

Photo courtesy of The Beaver Times

J oe Kolter was, to put it mildly, an interesting man. Nice as can be and without question a man of the people, the Pennsylvania Democrat was not impervious to the shady workings of a politician that some of which, he soon found out, were illegal. His personal style sometimes made him the laughing stock of colleagues who questioned his intelligence and editorial boards back home. Though if his hand in the cookie jar was stereotypical of a pol, so was his pride in hailing from steel country. Championing the needs of his Western Pennsylvania district came first and few can say that he didn't succeed in building them up.

A *Pittsburgh Post Gazette* profile on members of Congress from Western Pennsylvania succinctly captured the essence of Kolter's style. It read, "Joe Kolter is an enigma. He sometimes says the most brilliant things and sometimes you wonder where he's coming from." *The Almanac of American Politics* called Kolter "a pleasant man given to malapropisms." Some of the following: I am "a political whore," "some of the people taking over defunct S & L's are people who have defuncted themselves," and the Nicaraguan contras were "controlled by a man named Uno (UNO was actually the acronym for the United Nicaraguan Opposition). In that same appearance, Kolter referred to the Sandinistas as "communists." The Washington Post stated in a profile during Kolter's 1982 campaign that, "He read everything during the debate. Opening remarks, closing remarks, even jibes and asides were carefully typed out. He was so chained to his script that one could almost hear the rattle of manacles when he moved. The sound of turning pages was clearly audible."

Kolter, of Croatian decent, was born across the border in McDonald, Ohio and graduated from Geneva College following his service in the Army during World War II. He later became an accountant. Kolter's political career began by winning a seat in the State House in 1968 where he quickly became a favorite of Democratic leaders and chaired the Transportation Committee. His first Congressional bid came in 1974 when he challenged ten-term incumbent Frank Clark in the Democratic primary where Clark prevailed 56-32%.

Kolter's second quest for a seat in Congress came out of circumstances few could have foreseen. Eugene Atkinson, with whom he had served in the Pennsylvania Legislature, had been elected to the Beaver County centered Fourth Congressional District as a Democrat in 1978 and seemed to have a hold on the seat for the foreseeable future. That changed in 1981 when Atkinson decided to become a Republican. He did so after voting for Ronald Reagan's tax cut following a surprise telephone conversation with the President on a Pittsburgh radio show. For the GOP, this was an effortless electoral gimme and they were determined to keep it. They used redistricting as a first step for doing so.

Even though Pennsylvania was to lose two Congressional seats, Republicans controlled the redistricting process and succeeded in giving Atkinson what they thought would be a safe district by removing Democratic heavy portions of Beaver County (*CQ* noted "the Democratic registration edge of 45,000 was cut in half"). Kolter was not deterred and in 1982, he entered the Democratic race to take him on and received a big boost when former Lieutenant Governor Ernest Kline demurred. He still faced four rivals for the nomination, the most serious being Beaver Falls Attorney Peter Steege. But Beaver County's Democratic Chair Don Donatella mobilized the district for Kolter, who prevailed with 46%.

At the time of his primary win, Kolter took advantage of a Pennsylvania law that allowed him to seek two offices at the same time. He initially ran for re-election to his State House seat and Congress but, under criticism from his rivals, dropped his bid to stay in Harrisburg when he won the Congressional nomination.

For the general, Kolter focused on Reaganomics. Exploiting its impact wasn't difficult because Beaver had an unemployment rate of 20.5%. The district became a battleground for national figures of both parties, including George Bush and Walter Mondale, who descended to boost their man. Atkinson's philosophy toward the impact of his party switch, as he expressed in a debate with Kolter was, "Maybe I will pay a political price, maybe I won't?" His first surmise proved more prescient. Despite Atkinson's campaign's claim that "the trend is in our direction," Kolter returned the district to its Democratic roots by winning 60-39%.

Exulting in victory on election night, 1982
Photo courtesy of The Beaver Times

It was only natural that Kolter was assigned to the Public Works and Transportation Committee and from that perch, he diligently fought for his district's interests. His philosophy was, "You cannot always accept 'no' for an answer." However, this did not always come without unwanted recognition. A 1987 spar with the chair of the Aviation Subcommittee, fellow Democrat Norm Mineta of California, was characteristic of this.

Mineta was known for opposition to specific projects outside the bill he composed and, during one mark-up, Kolter earned his scorn by referring to the "enhanced discretionary authority." He not only proposed a $200 million airport improvement measure but also invited colleagues to request their wants as part of the amendment. Obviously, this did not sit well with Mineta who spoke against it. The amendment was ultimately defeated.

Kolter and Mineta would meet one more time. He wanted to create an expressway, and brought Mineta to the area for a daylong visit to meet on the topic. One paper referred to this project as a "fantasy land."

By and large, Kolter succeeded in aiding the district and one project he took on was a bypass of Pennsylvania State Route 711 in Ligonier. In 1991, Kolter became chair of the Economic Development Subcommittee of Public Works.

On social issues, Kolter was fairly conservative. He backed the flag protection amendment and opposed abortion. On pocketbook issues such as a minimum wage increase, family and medical leave, etc., he was very progressive. He additionally proposed a bill to help folks who needed organ transplants.

Photo courtesy of The Beaver Times

A rare notoriety Kolter gained was sponsoring legislation that temporarily suspended aid to the contras. "Presently," he said on the House floor in 1987, "our nation is at a crossroads where emotions tend to run high. And while emotions are vital to what one may or may not support, they should not overshadow, read on, nor disguise the truth." But He embarrassed himself when, appearing on a broadcast, he referred to the Nicaraguan government as communists (Kolter blamed the mishap on the fact that he was a last minute substitute on the program).

Kolter opposed the use of force in Iraq in 1991. His rationale was, "I'm still worried about all the cuts in benefits and health care that vets from our earlier wars have suffered. Before we talk about war, I want Congress to make sure that if people come back less than whole, services will be there for them."

Kolter's first electoral danger sign came in 1990 when he beat Gordon Johnson, the teacher he dispatched with 70% two years before, by just 56-44%. This occurred shortly after *The Pittsburgh Post* story in which a number of colleagues were quoted. One called Kolter, "a nice guy, a decent human being... who works hard." Another said he was, "friendly and outgoing, not a national figure, but people in his district like him." An anonymous aide to a GOP Congressman was tougher. Kolter is, he said, "a well-intentioned man, but there's not a lot going on up there." To that, Kolter responded, "If I have a problem, it's because I'm not a 'yes' man. I'm not a team man. I don't want to be controlled by a party. I don't want to be controlled by any chairman of a committee. I don't want to be controlled by any caucus. I do what's best for my district." Whether his district appreciated it was about to be put to the ultimate test.

1992 was a redistricting year and some salivated that Kolter's district might be eliminated. Instead, the district survived at the cost of Kolter's elimination. It could be said, however, that he eliminated himself.

Roughly half the territory in the redrawn district was new to Kolter and he faced three opponents in the Democratic Party. One was Ron Klink, a former well-known Pittsburgh television station reporter. State Representatives Frank LaGratta and Mike Leon were also in the race and they tried emulating Kolter by seeking re-election at the same time. Kolter returned the favor by contributing a combined $10,000 to their primary opponents.

The first indication that Kolter would be undercut came when a tape recording of his strategy session at his New Brighton headquarters was leaked to *The Pittsburgh Press* in March. This was at a time when the lawmaker needed to put forth the most positive image. Unfortunately, the image it painted was anything but that of a choirboy.

On the tape, Kolter labeled himself, "a whore, I'm a political whore. And I'm going to play it to the hilt. That's what I'm going to be doing. Shaking hands and kissing everybody. I mean, I'm here to get elected." That view might have not been too out of line with the attitudes of most politicians, but it didn't stop there. "I'll be going to a lot of funeral homes," Kolter added. "Just walk in and if I faintly remember who these people are, just walk in, shed a little tear, sign my name and then take off." He apparently then referred to LaGrotta as "a Mafioso," an account that press aide Mike Short, who was with Kolter throughout his entire tenure, disputed. Short said his boss "never used that kind of language" and another aide, Chris Sainato, also had no recollection of the slur.

A former press aide, Sam Siple said the tape was made for "in-house" purposes that Kolter authorized. After all, by the time the tape made it in the hands of the newspaper, Siple was an ex-employee. He left Kolter's office of his own volition but amid some very questionable circumstances that in the end meant even more shady publicity for Kolter. The Congressman had left for two weeks to have surgery, but didn't inform him of either his situation or destination, which led Siple to complain of "being deceived about his whereabouts."

Then there were substance-oriented attacks. Kolter had infuriated labor by missing a vote extending unemployment benefits during his mysterious hiatus. This partly enabled the AFL-CIO to endorse Veon, a rare slap at an incumbent and no small potatoes in these parts. Kolter replied by citing friction with the AFL-CIO president in saying it was, "a personality thing" and, "He has a dislike of me." Kolter still continued to plead his case. At one labor event he told attendees, "Let me talk to my labor friends. I stood strong and I stood tall for you. I still do...To my brothers in the trades: Joe Kolter is your friend. I've been your friend for 24 years...and I'm not a quitter." He pointed to his many accomplishments and said, "All this I did under a Republican president. Imagine what I could do under a Democrat." When Klink hit Kolter in a candidate for declining to meet with steel workers in Washington D.C., Kolter cut him off by saying, "You're a liar, my friend. That's a lie. I never turned my back on any working people." LaGrotta got in on the discourse as well, stating, "Kolter's just an idiot but Veon is evil. He'll use government and power and citizens. I watch that every day. Kolter's not smart enough to do that."

Some surmised that such a fractured field might save Kolter but it didn't even come close. He was held to 19%, the worst showing for an incumbent member of Congress both in that year and since and he took third place. Klink came in on top with 45% and Veon grabbed 22%. Kolter's concession and the moments before was a demonstration of failing to look before he leaped. Prior to it being clear that he lost, he told his supporters, "We used to have people power. Now we have media power. I'm almost afraid to pick up a newspaper this evening to see if there's another bad story, another pack of lies by my opponent, that's picked up by the media." His supporters were even less forgiving. New Brighton Democratic chairwoman Trade Knox spoke bitterly of Veon's candidacy as a betrayal of Kolter. "This was the dirtiest campaign…I can't believe he did this to Joe. I just can't believe it." She expressed shock that "naïve people of this God-forsaken valley had acted as they did."

Kolter vowed on the spot to reclaim his seat in 1994 even though he had asserted during the campaign that he was seriously considering retiring that year if he completed his projects. Klink was unimpressed. "The people have spoken. Joe Kolter's style of politics is dead. It's gone. Joe Kolter talks about building roads, ('I built this bridge')' But where are we going on it? You don't have a job to drive to. He doesn't get it."

Then the boom hit. Kolter, who was spared a single overdraft at the House bank, was named along with his neighboring colleague Austin Murphy and Ways and Means Chair Dan Rostenkowski of Illinois, as being linked to the House Post Office scandal. In essence, postal officials were using stamp sales to give cash to House members or their campaigns. In May, the three lawmakers' records were subpoenaed. Kolter's spokesman addressed the allegations by saying, "He certainly doesn't know if staff did, but he said he did not do that." However Kolter, along with Rostenkowski and Murphy, refused to testify and invoked their Fifth Amendment rights.

That November, former aide Gerald W. Weaver II was indicted on accepting $2,800 in checks ostensibly used as stamps from the Post-Office over a two-year period. It is noted that he subsequently used the money to buy cocaine from a postal employee. Weaver pled not guilty and was released without bail. Kolter was close with House Postmaster Robert Rota who had allegedly been at the epicenter of the cash disguised as stamps.

By July 1993, Kolter was out of office and Rota was pleading guilty to providing what prosecutors referred to as, "largely untraceable source of illegal cash" to members. It soon became known that Rostenkowski was "Congressman A," while Kolter was "Congressman B." Over an intermittent period of five years, Kolter received about $11,000 from Rota under the guise of stamps. The reason for the hiatus was because, as *The Washington Post* told it, "Between 1987 and 1989, however, Kolter and Rota could not continue their practices, the grand jury said, because a new employee was working in the House Post Office. After that employee left, the two men resumed their business, the indictment said."

In October 1994 a federal grand jury returned charges against Kolter on five counts, the most serious of which was trading $11,000 for cash. There was more, though. Kolter disguised more than $33,000 of purchases from the House Stationary Store as related to his Congressional duties. In reality, *The Washington Post* reported that among the items purchased were: "more than 650 pieces of China and glassware worth a total of $21,000; 40 wristwatches and clocks worth $4,300; more than 30 Mont Blanc pens worth $3,300; about 30 pieces of luggage worth more than $2,000; and two gold necklaces worth almost $500."

Kolter initially vowed to fight the charges. In 1996, he pled guilty to only one count. On sentencing, Kolter told Judge Norma Holloway Johnson, "I regret my actions as they have caused pain and have been embarrassing to my family, loyal friends, colleagues and former constituents." To that the Judge replied, "One thing I cannot overlook is you have betrayed the public trust." She showed leniency and sentenced him to six months. Rota was given four months.

Kolter completed his sentence and resumed his life. He died in September 2019 at age 93 at which time Jerry Hodge, who ran his Beaver County office opined that, "I think he just got caught up in some stuff that was over his head. I hope folks will think more about the good things he did rather than the troubles he had at the end of his career."

CHAPTER FIFTY-SEVEN

Lacking Political Background
Extraordinary for Thomas Whose Abilities
Hailed from Central-Casting

Introductory Quote: This is a true example of one never knowing where their friends are. In the runup to the Persian Gulf War, Georgia Congressman Lindsay Thomas traveled to 1/230th Field Artillery Battalion of the 48th Infantry Brigade of the Georgia National Guard that was undergoing rigorous training at the National Trainin g Center in the Mojave Desert of California. Major Major Milton H. "Woody" Woodside, a former Thomas staffer, was among those in the unit. In a totally impromptu moment, Thomas crawled down into a covered fox hole under a 155 artillery piece and discovered a young soldier from his home town of Screven, Georgia. Thomas soon realized he had coached the boy in little league football on a team that his own son was part of.

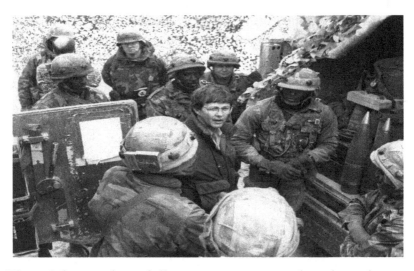

Thomas's favorite photo of all time – an impromptu taking during his visit with troops from Georgia at the Mohave Desert Training Center as they prepared for the Persian Gulf War. It hangs in the UGA Conference Room
Photo via the Richard B. Russell Library for Political
Research and Studies, University of Georgia

L indsay Thomas was one Representative who, as they say, had his head on straight. In a body filled with senor members with highly coveted positions, ten years is a rather short time to make an impression. Thomas was able to do just that. A moderate with central-casting political looks that include a ready-made smile, Thomas was able to use his bridge building skills to become a highly trusted member of Congress with friends on both sides of the aisle. He represented his coastal Georgia and Savannah area district capably and competently which meant voting with the Democratic leadership when possible but far from often enough to be labeled a national Democrat. That created an immensely successful formula that Thomas could have continued practicing indefinitely if he hadn't suddenly walked away at age 49 to pursue a far more high profile interest.

In a district as diverse as the First, Thomas's professional background covered a wide array of the turf itself. An English major at the University of Georgia (his grades were "average"), Thomas before running for Congress had been in the Georgia National Guard and achieved success as a stockbroker before returning to his family farm at age 29. In fact, for most people, leaving their career behind to return to farming might seem a reverse-penultimate part of life. But for Thomas, it gave him credibility to present himself as empathetic and well-versed to district interests when he was seeking the Congressional seat being left open by Bo Ginn, a fellow Democrat who was running for governor. The farm had been caught in the economic downturn of the prior decade and Thomas told *Georgia Trend Magazine* in 2001 that, if prices had remained up and I had been making money on the farm, I probably never would have run."

The initial frontrunner in the race was State Senator Charles Wessels of Savannah who boasted of support from the black community, partly resulting from the fact that as *CQ* noted, "His family bank, Southern Bank and Trust, made loans to African-Americans years before any other lending institution in the city could." But he was hurt by the presence of an African-American State House member, Bobby Hill. Thomas for his part formed an affinity with farmers by living on his family's 650-acre farm in the town of Screven and vowed to fight to see that farmers got their fair share in international trade. He also promoted defense cuts. He placed first with 27% and in a primary he was supposed to dominate, Weasels barely held on to the second spot, edging a rural State Senator, Rene Kemp by 256 votes. In an impressive feat, Thomas prevailed in every county in the runoff save for Chatham (Savannah), which gave him 61%.The general election was no contest.

Bob Hurt had worked for Ginn but Thomas brought him on board and named him Chief of Staff. Because Thomas was new to elected office, his first priority was serving as his "guide." Adjustment was required. Hurt recalls that while Thomas would dutifully adhere to his schedule, he would often get up and leave the office. When Hurt would question him, Thomas would reply, "I just can't stare at the concrete." Thomas was a hunter after all and so his forte was to run wild. Recreation would usually find him in the woods and occasionally, he'd ride around in his truck trying to get a signal to check on the office. After that, it would be back to hunting. Eventually, he adapted to the rigors of Congressional life.

**The Smurfs were immensely popular in 1982 and so was Lindsay Thomas
Photo via the Richard B. Russell Library for Political
Research and Studies, University of Georgia**

Thomas was immediately assigned to the Agriculture Committee and the Merchant Marine and Fisheries Committee and in fact, no two posts could possibly be better suited for the First. In Thomas's first year in office, he scored a coup usually seen in seasoned members. Impatient by the slow pace that members were prioritizing revising the tobacco program, he got the Agriculture Committee to host a field hearing in the district. In 1985, he proposed a plan to erase debt for farmers with a credit relief/debt consolidation plan that would offer loans of up to 90% to farmers "with a proven track record of first-class farming skills."

Representing a district that was predominantly rural, Thomas wanted the folks from those areas to know that they were not being left behind. He called tourism "under exploited," and urged international trade within the region. In a speech to the Georgian Southern College Conference on Rural Development, Thomas told attendees, "Many of the programs which have been the bulwark of rural America are targeted for cutbacks. Now is a crucial time for us to come up with a plan to survive, even prosper, in a time of travail." That was one reason Thomas could get so exasperated when outsiders didn't recognize his needs.

Thomas had worked hard to secure funding for the Eugene Talmadge Memorial Bridge in Savannah and when Reagan vetoed it, he responded by saying, "I don't know how the president has gotten away with this kind of appeal, calling this a budget-buster" (the veto was overridden). Thomas also opposed the landmark 1986 tax package.

Other local projects: fighting for aid following the Savannah River oil spill, getting an expansion of the Kings Bay Submarine Base, the Fort Stewart Hunter Army Airfield complex and keeping jobs in the district by fighting a merger of an FBI office in the district with one that was Atlanta-based. In later years, he sought to protect Georgia's dominance of the Vidalia onion by proposing the Federal Vidalia Onion Act of 1989 which would ward off "counterfeit" onions by imposing "penalties for selling or offering to sell as Vidalia onions those not of the Vidalia variety or not grown in the Vidalia onion production area."

With the Peanut Princess (top) and Molly Moo-Moo (bottom)
Photos via the Richard B. Russell Library for Political
Research and Studies, University of Georgia

In 1985, Thomas proposed legislation to put a moratorium on an egg-breaking machine manufactured by Egg King in California, citing the potential for salmonella poisoning or even death. The United Egg Producers (UEP), whom *The Washington Post* labeled "mad as wet hens," favored the amendment and the Agriculture Committee approved it but California Republican Robert Badham sought to kill it on the House floor (Egg Kings CEO Mike Maynard, resided in his district). Thomas fought it with all of his might. Speaking with uncharacteristic passion, he explained how, "Eggs are literally dumped into the machine along with traces of blood, chicken manure, dirt, rot and fragments of paper egg cartons…The issue here is that it is just a matter of time before someone gets seriously ill or perhaps dies from salmonella poisoning as a result of the use of this process that, follow me closely, was outlawed in 1970." Badham prevailed.

Unlike some Georgia colleagues, Thomas supported the Civil Rights Act of 1990 and voted to allow federal funding for victims of rape and incest. He backed Bush's capital gains tax request. But in an area dominated by small businesses, he could not back the Family and Medical Leave Act and usually opposed gun control measures. On defense matters, he supported the MX and contra aid but drew the line with the Strategic Defense Initiative (SDI). His concoction for the nuclear freeze movement was to "build-down." Mostly, however, he wanted to be as informed as possible. When Congress was considering Alaskan oil drilling, Thomas not only toured ANWR but camped there – for three straight nights. Officials were giddy: "Many people toured," they thought. "No one stayed."

At a Trident air base
Photo via the Richard B. Russell Library for Political
Research and Studies, University of Georgia

In 1989, Thomas, who once boasted of having, "just as many friends on one side of the aisle as the other," proved malleable enough to snag a seat on the plum House Appropriations Committee, usually impossible for a member who lacks good standing with the bulk of the caucus. In fact, he is proud of telling about frequently walking in to the GOP cloakroom and hearing members say, "There's Lindsay, again, working both sides of the aisle." That also extended to personal relationships.

Thomas, who had a reputation as a highly accomplished turkey caller, was instrumental in putting together the Congressional Sportsman's Caucus, the largest bipartisan organization in Congress. He was the caucus's first Vice-President (his friend, Pennsylvania Republican Richard Schulze was President). It focuses on conservation, hunting, fishermen and game and thrives in Congress to this day. Thomas's philosophy is, "Without land and habitat, the land would be converted...Wildlife sustains that natural environment and it's why I've always had an interest in preserving." Wildlife was long a part of Thomas's life. Besides archery and hunting, he boasts of cooking fried quail and gravy for my friends," noting he, "makes the best biscuits from scratch." Thomas also chaired the Forestry 2000 task force and the Sunbelt Caucus, the latter from which he worked on wetland issues. So devoted was Thomas to his surroundings that a trip to Eastern Europe as a member of the Appropriations Military Construction Subcommittee in 1989 was his first out of the country.

Thomas's 1990 re-election, which he had won with 71%, left him poised to make out just fine from redistricting and continue his quiet and faithful service. Instead, he dazzled nearly everyone by exiting the stage. One reason was his nine-year old daughter and Thomas explained that, "Anyone who offers for this job must be aware it makes a special requirement of you. It's very time-consuming if you do your job." A summation of the emotions both in Georgia and among colleagues (three of whom had gone hunting with him the weekend before and had nary a clue that he was planning to stand down), was captured by House Speaker Thomas Foley who said, "A fellow with that youth, intelligence and energy is going to be a real loss." But Thomas more than made up for it in his many wide-ranging endeavors.

Thomas arguably had bigger fish to fry.

**Thomas with his two pride and joys – his family and hunting
Photos via the Richard B. Russell Library for Political
Research and Studies, University of Georgia**

Atlanta had landed the 1996 Summer Olympics and Thomas had applied for the position of senior vice-president for external relations for the Atlanta Committee for the Olympic Games (ACOG) in part by reaching out to CEO Billy Payne. He thus announced that in order to maximize his concentration on the endeavor to the max, he would forego re-election. Thomas explained his reasoning to *The Atlanta Journal and Constitution* in 1995: "I got tired of being on the front lines all the time. I don't have a burning political ambition. In Congress, you usually only get to deal with the top level of issues. I wanted to be more hands-on, but I wasn't looking for headlines."

For an avid hunter, however, Thomas was no lame-duck. He continued doing the job until the lights in his office were literally out and maintained full schedule. That perplexed constituents who wondered why Thomas was so hard on the job when he wasn't standing for re-election. His answer: "For the same reason I came before – I care." Further evidence of his caring was his leftover campaign fund. Thomas had $40,000 in excess money and he donated most of it. Among the causes: churches, colleges, relief for the victims of the recent Flint River flood, the Boys Club. He also threw a party to express his appreciation to his numerous friends and volunteers. As a testimony to Thomas's goodwill, 700 people attended.

Thomas's next mission immediately following the Olympics was reinvigorating the ailing Georgia Chamber of Commerce and landing the job signified his proclivity for grabbing folks at hello. *Georgia Trend Magazine* wrote that at the time Thomas met officials, "Others were scheduled to be interviewed. None were" (the ever impish Thomas invokes Abe Lincoln's famous line, "You can fool some of the people all of the time." Once settled, Thomas's work was cut out for him – membership had declined and the Chamber lacked a focus. Thomas rectified that. *Georgia Trend Magazine* wrote he, "brought a new energy plus a strategy for growth and inclusion, a desire 'to bring everybody to the table.'" Recruitment meant traveling all across the state and resulted in an increased membership of 3,300 from 1,800. In turn, *Georgia Trend Magazine* placed him on the cover as the state's "Most Trusted CEO." As a takeoff of his success with the Talmadge Bridge, the headline was "Master Bridge Builder."

Next Thomas was Senior Vice-President of Governmental Relations for AGL Resources and today, he consults near his Georgia farm where, at 76, he still thrives.

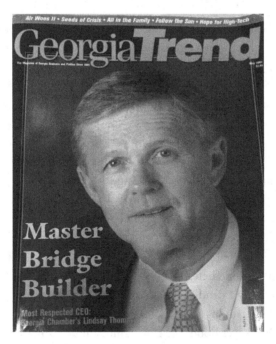

**Thomas was posted on the cover of Georgia Trend Magazine in 2001
for his success at reinvigorating the state's Chamber of Commerce
Image courtesy of Georgia Trend**

CHAPTER FIFTY-EIGHT

Hatcher, Ray and Barnard: Georgia's Turnover a Microcosm of Congress in 1992

Hatcher, Ray and Barnard
Top image courtesy of C-SPAN: Photos courtesy of the
U.S. House of Representatives Historic Collection

The state of Georgia proved a microcosm of the nationwide turnover of Congress in 1992. Six of the state's ten members – all Democrats, would not return for the 103rd and the departures were due to genuine retirements, redistricting and the check bouncing and other scandals that led to defeats of lawmakers in both the primary elections and the general. While all were political moderates and a handful among the most conservative of the "Boll Weevil" Democrats in the House, all were malleable enough to have durable appeal with their constituents who were nowhere near philosophical soul mates the national party.

While Congressional heavyweight Ed Jenkins of the Ninth Congressional District, "Bridge Builder" Lindsay Thomas of Savannah, and former "Dukes of Hazard" star Ben Jones of the Fourth are portrayed in other chapters given their outside roles, the stories of Charles Hatcher, Richard Ray and Doug Barnard are below.

Charles Hatcher

Image courtesy of C-SPAN

Unlike Lindsay Thomas who left in high standing and on his own terms, the equally obscure Hatcher was done in by mistakes. 819 highly publicized mistakes.

Hatcher was born in born in Doerun, Georgia in Colquitt County. He served in the Air Force for four years, then took his Bachelor's at Georgia Southern and his J.D. at the University of Georgia, after which he commenced law in Albany. Hatcher won a seat in the Georgia House of Representatives in 1972 and became close to Democratic Governor George Busbee. He also was an assistant floor leader.

In 1980, when the Second District's longtime Congressman, Dawson Mathis left the seat behind to challenge U.S. Senator Herman Talmadge in the Democratic primary for U.S. Senate, Hatcher ran for the seat. Six other Democrats entered the fray as well. While Hatcher won all but seven of the 27 counties and a clear first place primary win, his 38% was well short of the 50% needed to avoid a runoff. For the second spot, Mathis aide Julian Holland edged out broadcasting aide and Nashville (Georgia) Mayor Hanson Carter by 229 votes (both took 15%). The counties both men won were more aligned along the district's geographical lines but Hatcher beat Holland 53-47% and took 74% in the general. He was assigned to Agriculture (particularly the very parochial Agriculture Subcommittee on Tobacco and Peanuts) and Small Business, two areas that encompass the heart of the 2nd District.

Hatcher once described himself as an "obscure Congressman," and while it worked magic for him back home, he was not particularly helped in Congress, specifically as he tried to win a seat on the Appropriations Committee. But he knew early on exactly how to play the game. In his first year in office, Hatcher did not explicitly come out and say it but less than subtly linked his vote on the Reagan tax cuts to the administration's plans to phase out peanut subsidies. "They are savvy enough to know that I would really appreciate it. I'm smart enough to know that they would really appreciate my vote." He was appeased enough to support them.

It was on agriculture issues on which Hatcher truly left an impression. Thomas recalls being a freshman member of the Ag Committee and sitting through debates that lasted to the point that "the paint on the wall started to peel." To Thomas, some of the material was "arcane and downright boring," and he was struggling to follow a lot of it." But, "I could turn to Hatcher and he knew every detail." He was "disarmingly bright."

In 1982, Mattis was evidently not enjoying retirement and decided he wanted back to Congress. In an effort to convince former constituents that his allegiance was with them, Mathis swore off future statewide contests. He tried to appeal to African-Americas upset that Hatcher had sided with Reagan on the tax cuts. But much of the party apparatus was behind Hatcher and many farmers grumbled that Mathis had forfeited his legitimacy to return when he gave up his seniority for a risky Senate bid. Albany, from which around both men hailed, was expected to be decisive and Hatcher won it. Ditto with Valdasta. Mathis racked up decent margins in the rural areas but it was not enough and Hatcher won re-nomination 52-48%. It would mark his last tough race in either the primary or the general for the ensuing decade though ironically, the result would be among the factors that would sink him a decade later.

Hatcher was a pretty conservative Democrat with his presidential support scores in the early years of the Reagan administration sometimes exceeding his opposition. The Second was conservative at the national level but for Hatcher, general elections were a walk in the park including 1988 when his opponent, Ralph Hudgens, chided him as being out of touch because he rode in a Mercedes-Benz at the Pecan Festival (Hudgens's campaign manager had photographed him). Though Hatcher's 62% was a career low, that wasn't saying much. Redistricting notwithstanding, he was expected to have a pretty easy go in 1992. Then came "Rubbergate."

There was no nuancing the fact that Hatcher was among the worst abusers. Once the initial list of 24 worst was released (initially leaked by those who omitted the three Republicans), that was indeed confirmed. With 819 overdrafts, only five current or former members had overdrawn their account more. And though a few colleagues exceeded Hatcher's overdraft total of $273,360.94, Hatcher had overdrawn his salary for 35 of the 39-months profiled, the most of any member. Hatcher blamed medical bills, saying, "I'm not a wealthy person." He also said, "We were almost never informed of overdrafts. That's no excuse. I should not have allowed myself to participate on this system and for doing so I apologize to my constituents."

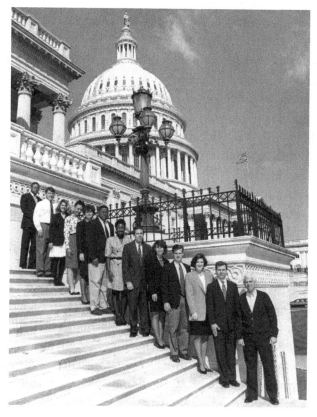

Hatcher with the men and women who worked for him
Photo via Richard B. Russell Library for Political
Research and Studies, University of Georgia

For Hatcher, the bad publicity could not have come at a worse time as redistricting was destined to dramatically change the shape of the Second. The initial, Democratic drawn map, would have suited Hatcher fine as *The Atlanta Journal and Constitution* noted it would have, "maintained its agricultural character," with the black population growing to 39%. But the Justice Department rejected it for "minimizing" African-American opportunities. Legislators rectified that and not to Hatcher's favor as the new Second became was 52% black, but also picked up urban areas such as portions of Columbus and Macon. Hatcher's response: "Instead of being 100 percent rural, is 70 to 75 percent rural, so I'm comfortable with it." But others were not comfortable with it and the result was that five folks filed to take Hatcher on in the Democratic primary, the most prominent of whom was 16-year legislator Sanford Bishop, an African-American. *Politics in America* wrote that Hatcher "charged that Bishops Columbus financial supporters were trying to buy a second seat" (the newly created Third district also took in portions of the city).

**Photo via the B. Russell Library for Political Research
and Studies, University of Georgia**

It was easy to spot what was at the apex of Hatcher's quest for survival: peanuts as Hatcher now chaired the all-important subcommittee and he constantly reminded voters of what his position meant. And some, such as Banker, illustrated the prevailing view of many for why he believed Hatcher would survive. "Charles has been good for the peanut farmers. It would take a pretty strong man to challenge him and I don't see anybody like that," before joking, "Heck, if you check back far enough, you might even find a mistake that I made some years back." Had it not been for redistricting, he most certainly would have.

Hatcher's real problem was the checks. His initial reasoning was that it, "provides a springboard for people to run, but it's certainly not the major issue. I think people have been satisfied by my voting record and my constituent services." While he was ultimately wrong, it wasn't by a mile. While campaigning, it was not uncommon for Hatcher to raise the issue of the checks himself.

With three weeks to go before the primary, Hatcher posted a very tepid lead over the pack and it was clear that a runoff would result. It did. Hatcher took 39%. Bishop followed with 22% and immediately earned backing from the three others contenders who failed to advance to the runoff.

Photo via Richard B. Russell Library for Political Research and Studies, University of Georgia

In the runoff, Hatcher called the contest "about regionalism, not race… whether southwest Georgia will continue to be represented by a congressman who is interested in agriculture or one controlled by an urban power…" He and allies professed that a loss would be devastating for the region. Bishop took the opposite tack. He labeled Hatcher's tenure a "disappointment" and hit him for backing the $35,000 pay raise. Meanwhile, African-American leaders, most notably Jesse Jackson, stumped for Bishop.

Hatcher won nearly every county in the Southern part of the district, in some cases with a majority. But he lost much of the Northern part and Bishop won big in his base, racking up 95% in Muscogee (Columbus) and 75% in Bibb (Macon). Again, Hatcher mopped up in the Southern part but it was not enough to offset Bishop in the north, a fact Hatcher referenced in a speech to supporters on primary night ("a few (rural) counties are still out, but it's probably not enough"). He predicted that, "Next year I'll probably be practicing law somewhere or teaching."

Meanwhile, Hatcher called the bank, an "evil perk that no longer exists. It was not a good system, and I wish I hadn't overdrawn even once." As to both the radically redrawn districts and the checks, Hatchr concluded, "I could have handled one or the other but not both." Whatever the case, both led to him neither being seen nor heard from again since he left office. In the years ahead, Hatcher became director of the Tobacco and Peanuts Division in the Consolidated Farm Service Agency which enabled him to continue advocating for a cause near and dear to his heart: peanut growers.

Richard Ray

Image courtesy of C-SPAN

The beginning of Richard's Ray political career was governed by venerable U.S. Senator Sam Nunn while the end culprit might have been Newt Gingrich or more accurately, the failed attempt by Georgia Democrats to exterminate his career. In the intervening period, Ray was a politician who marched to the beat of his own drummer. Largely obscure, he liked it that way but, hard work was his mantra (one loyal aide said "no one could outwork" Ray) and effectiveness was the result.

It's not unusual for close elections to mean future electoral repercussions but in the case of Ray, it was a razor-thin win by Gingrich that governed his own. Had the future House Speaker lost his 1990 election rather than prevailing over David Worley by 974 votes in his suburban Atlanta district, the map that was redrawn for the '92 cycle would have looked radically different, and probably would have enabled Ray to keep his seat for at least another term (though all bets would have been off for '94). But because Democratic leaders in both Washington and Georgia saw Gingrich's squeaker and the forthcoming remap as the opportunity to nuke Newt, Ray took on an abundance of new, Republican heavy territory from Gingrich's turf which, coupled with an anti-incumbent mood, turned him out of office.

Ray's linkage to such figures of national importance was ironic given that he was without question among the most obscure members of the Democratic caucus, if not the entire House. If anything, the little notoriety he had on the Hill may have resulted from his reputation as a demanding boss. He was even said to have forbade his employees from cursing. True as that was, however, it didn't detract from Ray's reputation as a man for generosity. Cindy Gillespie served him in a number of capacities for roughly seven years (including as Press Secretary and Armed Services Committee aide) and said "he expected you to work but was the first to support you when you needed support. Mr. Ray totally showed appreciation and was good to his employees." Among other things, this meant Christmas parties at Mount Vernon.

It is common in politics to find a career based on proximity to a well-known official and in Ray's case, it was the venerable Nunn. Ray was born in Fort Valley, Georgia and enlisted in the Navy following high school during World War II. He farmed for a while, then opened a pesticide business. In the 1960s, Ray was Mayor of Perry, the same town from where Sam Nunn hailed (Ray might have given him a start by naming him to a panel to study race relations).and served as president of the Georgia Municipal Association.

When Nunn won a U.S. Senate seat in 1972, Ray was by his side and would remain his right hand man for a decade as his administrative assistant.

Only when he decided to seek the House seat being vacated by Jack Brinkley in 1982 did he step down. He prevailed over Jim Cantrell with 63% in the primary and Tyron Elliot with an astounding 71%.

When Ray first embarked on his bid for Congress, he received just $250 from the national party. The reason: the apparatus had demanded that he be a stalwart supporter and he had no inclination – either personally or politically, to make that commitment.

Ray's voting record clearly made him a Georgia-centric representative. According to *The Almanac of American Politics*, his liberal score on economic issues was just 22% and just a third on social issues. That translated to opposing his party on numerous occasions. In 1986, Ray opposed the sweeping tax package negotiated by Reagan and congressional Democrats because he feared it would send small businesses, "into a tailspin."

Ray was notorious for taking photos and signing them
Photo via Richard B. Russell Library for Political
Research and Studies, University of Georgia

On social issues, he opposed the Eastern Strike Board, the minimum wage veto, and the Family and Medical Leave Act. But he did back the 1990 Civil Rights Act when three other Georgia Democrats (including Jenkins) did not. He was pro-life.

Ray's preference was quietly tending to his committee work - Armed Services and Small Business and on the former, he assiduously looked after Fort Benning and Robins Air Force Base. He also chaired the Defense Restoration Panel that looked at mechanisms for disposing of hazardous wastes and angered some environmentalists by expressing preference for a Worst Case First cleanup.

Aid to the Nicaraguan contras was one matter on which Ray deviated from his party. Ray genuinely cared about improving conditions and had led the first delegation into Nicaragua yet, when the protracted issue first came before the House in March of 1986, he was one of the genuine swing votes. In the end, he resisted furious Reagan administration entreaties and opposed the package. By June, however, he shifted. What happened? In the interim, Ray had visited both Contra leaders in Miami and families in the Honduras and he explained to colleagues his change of heart. "With the leaders, I came away from that meeting impressed with the UNO leadership and the mechanisms they have put in place to make sure that the civilians are in control of the military. I firmly believe that they are well on the way to becoming a government in exile." As to the families, "I came away absolutely convinced that we must give them military and humanitarian aid now." His vote was among the reasons the March defeat was narrowly reversed.

That first visit to Nicaragua brought about a Ray-instituted policy change involving the Air Force purchasing flight bomber jackets. As Gillespie explained, Ray was concerned that the Air Force wasn't giving priority to operations and maintenance-training or keeping planes and equipment in good repair. "They were prioritizing purchasing more planes over the nuts and bolts of maintenance, logistics and flying hours that needed to be able to engage in combat." This came to a head when the Air Force ran short of money and cut flying hours and furloughed the workers at the Air Force depots, including Robins in the district. What the Air Force didn't do was slow down procurements of new weapons systems which brought with it the $5 million contract for new jackets.

Ray did not oppose the bomber jackets but wanted to ensure protection for the workers and taking it on was aimed simply at "getting the Air Force to fund maintaining the systems they had and train pilots as a priority over buying new planes." Ray broached the matter diplomatically and when that didn't work, a stalemate resulted. Ray finally catapulted the dialogue by going into the Defense Authorization Act and inserting a provision prohibiting the Air Force from purchasing the jackets. That naturally got the attention of officials and a meeting was scheduled before long.

Air defense within the NATO bases was another issue Ray worked on. A visit to East Berlin through convinced him that U.S. bases in Europe couldn't rely simply on protection from ground defenses. He saw the air threats from the Soviets as equally important to the threat of ground invasion and felt the European bases were especially exposed. It took several years and Ray's trademark persistence but he eventually was able to get the military to submit a plan for NATO air defense and fund it.

Photo courtesy of Cynthia Gillespie

For Ray, constituent services was a high-point and as a practice, he was known for siding with his district even if it put him against the view of other Georgians. When Congressman Buddy Darden introduced an amendment to nix funding for the C17 (McDonnell Douglas was in his district), Ray and Congressman Roy Rowland were the lone Georgians who opposed it, though Ray was recovering from heart surgery and didn't actually vote. He and another Congressman from Georgia, Doug Barnard, voted against a measure that would curtail the military's immunity from environmental lawsuits. He favored a "soft landing" for forthcoming defense cuts.

Ray had a vintage style that meant rewarding those who worked hard. Gillespie was one such person, in ways she had neither sought nor expected. The first reward came the day after the 1982 campaign when Ray and Gillespie were meeting for the first time. Gillespie had loyally volunteered in his campaign office for months and, having been seated at the front of the headquarters, was on hand on election night when reporters wanted a victory statement. The Press Secretary at that point had essentially rendered his duties complete so Gillespie chose to read portions of the speech to the press. Ray had been en route to one of several campaign celebrations and heard the quotes on the radio, not having a clue who Gillespie was. When he learned she had been a part of his campaign for months, he offered her the job of press secretary in the district office simply because she had taken the initiative when it was required.

Eventually, Ray made Gillespie his Armed Services Committee aide and though there was "no more of a male world" than that post, he was not about to embrace gender stereotypes and that became clear during a classified committee markup. Ray would traditionally be unavailable to even the most pressing matters during that time but a senior executive at a major defense corporation was not accepting of that – he wanted to speak to the congressman and wouldn't settle for Gillespie. Days later, Ray finally told Gillespie to tell the Executive that speaking with Gillespie was his only option but, he still refused telling her, "You would not understand this." The Exec had been hoping to convey word of a classified system at Robins Air Force Base that was in danger of being cut as the mark-up got underway but, because of the Exec's recalcitrance in refusing to communicate this to Gillespie, this never came to light until the mark-up had ended. While Ray's office was able to rectify the matter by coordinating with Nunn who chaired the Senate Armed Services Committee, Ray was red with anger. He got the CEO on the phone and made clear "Gillespie is my person. You deal with her or you don't deal with this office." The message was taken and the Executive paid the price.

Ray also had a way of making his presence known among the committees on which he sat. Many members found watching the grass grow more appealing than sitting through hearings following asking their questions but not Ray who typically stayed until the end. The staff loved him.

In 1990, Ray won re-election 63-37%, even an after voting for the unpopular budget agreement. Two years prior, he was unopposed. 1992 would more than make up for that. The remap gave him five counties held by Gingrich which were fast-growing and hostile even to Democrats with a voting record like Ray's. But first he had to get past a primary from Worley, the man had come so close to toppling Gingrich. For most of primary night, it appeared that Ray would be forced into a runoff with Worley but he finally rallied and won outright with 51%. Then came the general.

Collins threw the incumbency card at Ray, particularly travel perks. He campaigned on "Sending A Working Man To Congress," despite the fact that his net worth was a pretty penny. Ray outspent Collins by roughly $900,000 but it couldn't change the trajectory of the race. Ray carried all of the counties at the Southern end of the district including Baldwin (Milledgeville), Muscogee (Columbus), and Upson (Thomaston) but most cast fewer than 7,000 votes. Moreover, Collins walloped his rival in the five counties at the Northern end of the district and those were heavily populated. And with a margin at or above 66% in three such counties, swept to victory districtwide 54-46%, a margin of 20,000 votes. President George H.W. Bush carried the district with 51% in a three-person race.

Ray died in 1999 after emergency surgery to repair a heart valve. Who but Nunn could possibly have delivered the eulogy? His words: "Richard Ray knew no limits on his own abilities and on his own responsibilities. He knew that he was placed on this earth to serve others. He took those talents he was given, and he multiplied them many times over. In the end, Richard's heart may have finally given out because he gave so much of it to all of us."

Doug Barnard

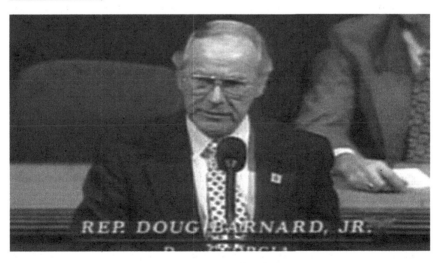

Image courtesy of C-SPAN

Doug Barnard's record in the House was by-and-large as close to the Republican as the Democratic mainstream and his outlook was too. Consider this. Barnard declined to attend a Democratic rally during the 1988 campaign, opting instead for an event where Oliver North was speaking. He was a founding member of the conservative leaning Boll Weevil's and toward the end of his career, had a voting record to the consternation of the left in both Georgia and Washington.

Barnard not only looked the part of the quintessential Southern Congressman but also the distinguished Southern gentleman. A banker, the Augusta Democrat hewed closely to his hometown throughout his entire 95-years and assiduously promoted its interests.

Barnard attended high school at the Academy of Richmond County and received his Bachelor's from Mercer University in 1942. He then enlisted in the U.S. Army where he served during World War 11 before returning to earn his J.D. from the Walter George School of Law.

Barnard's political involvement began as the Richmond County (Augusta) Democratic Committee in 1958. By 1963, he was Executive Secretary to Georgia Governor Carl Sanders, then became executive vice president of the Georgia Railroad Bank and Trust. Ironically, Barnard came to Washington with the man who had denied Sanders a comeback for the governorship, Jimmy Carter, the 39th Commander-in-Chief and a fellow Georgian who began his presidency at the same time. His tenure in Congress was made possible by the 1976 retirement of eight-term Democrat Robert Stephens, Jr. The seat was anchored in Augusta but encompassed Athens and even took in a portion of Gwinnett County.

The Democratic primary was a seven-person field. In round one, Barnard prevailed over Mike Padgett 27-21%, a former aide to another Georgia governor, Lester Maddox who had billed himself in those days as "the man to see." Both men hailed from Augusta and Barnard did take second-fiddle to Padgett in Richmond County but with 70% from Clarke (Athens), he managed to defeat Padgett by about 3,000 votes – 52-48% districtwide and was assured of victory in November by lack of a Republican opponent. He thus became the first Congressman from Augusta in 72 years. He took seats on the Banking Committee and Government Operations.

After the 1982 election, Barnard aimed for a seat on the Appropriations Committee but was foiled by Democratic leaders who wanted at least a semi-loyalist. Their backing went to Bill Boner of Tennessee who won the post. The disenchantment that leaders shared toward Barnard was mutual. He was so disillusioned with Tip O'Neill that in 1984 that he called on him to step down as Speaker and vowed instead to support Charles Stenholm of Texas who ultimately never ended up becoming a candidate. It did not however prevent him from serving as chair of the Government Operations Subcommittee on Commerce, Consumer and Monetary Affairs.

Banking was Barnard's niche and his obituary said he, "devoted much of his Congressional career to restructuring outdated regulations in order to expand American competitiveness in global markets, particularly after the European Union commenced modernization of its financial markets in 1990." His fellow '76er, Ed Jenkins of Gwinnett County called him "probably the most knowledgeable person about banking on the Banking Committee and there are about 50 members." His colleague, he added, was "very tenacious." Jeff Tassey was Barnard's top Banking Committee aide for seven years but, despite his boss's decades-long experience, he was not a sycophant for the industry. In Tassey's words, Barnard saw banks "as a bundle of services – it can be assembled and disassembled in different ways and his mission was, "I'm not trying to save banks. I'm trying to save banking."

Barnard's 15 minutes of fame resulted from a year-long probe by his subcommittee on the allegation of corruption within the IRS. While the subcommittee was a hampered by a law that allowed only tax writing committees in Congress to gain access to certain documents, it was thorough enough to receive contact from current and former IRS employees willing to spill the beans about alleged shenanigans.

It started after the IRS seized documents from Jordache Enterprises, essentially on a tip from executives of the just seized Guest? Incorporated, the Marciano family. But it appears to have been done out of a personal vendetta as the two companies were longtime competitors. Plus, the Marciano's had wooed the head of the L.A. criminal investigations unit essentially by wining and dining him. *The LA Times* reported, "The Barnard subcommittee compiled information on a wide variety of alleged abuses at the IRS, including alleged incidents involving IRS agents drinking on duty, using government expense accounts to pay for trips to visit mistresses, and reprisals by high-ranking officials against agents who complained of corrupt practices." The investigation also revealed what Barnard termed, "significant erosion," and Jordache was eventually found to be in the clear.

It was on cultural issues where Barnard might have lent credence to those who dubbed him a Democrat in name only. He opposed the Civil Rights Act of 1990, abortion and refused to override the minimum wage and Family

Leave Act. He also voted "no" on the Eastern Strike Board despite the fact that it was headquartered in Georgia.

After House Democrats rejected a capital gains tax cut (a proposal drawn up by Jenkins), Barnard mocked the national party as being out of touch. "The leadership and the party have just not gotten the national message. The country is moving to the center, and the party continues moving to the left. There are nine Democrats in the Georgia [House] delegation, and only one is really in synch with the party."

Whatever Barnard's impact in the financial services industry, Augusta was his pride and joy. He helped Saint Sebastian Way and got funds for the Riverwalk. The Uptown VA clinic bore his mark as well. Barnard, along with Ray, opposed a measure removing the immunity from the military for environmental violations.

Staffwise, Barnard's preference was to hire interns and promote them from within and Beverly Bell was exhibit a. She began as an intern and made her way to legislative correspondent and Chief of Staff during Barnard's last three years in Congress. She was also the envy of many on Capitol Hill. "So many people commented to me while he was in office and after he left office on how nice he was to them, how he always spoke to everyone," from the Speaker of the House to elevator operator. Tassey got the same feedback. He was once asked if Barnard was as nice to his staff as other Capitol employees and he replied, "even nicer." In what was certainly welcome to his employees, Barnard lived by his own creed: "You hire good people and you let them do their job." As such, Bell said he "didn't second-guess staff or say, 'I wish you had asked me.'" He never lost his temper either. And in the ultimate embodiment of Barnard as a father figure, Tassey recently recalled Barnard taught him "a lot of things someone else should have."

One of Barnard's attributes was to not make a ruckus about credit. Tassey calls his forte "focusing on substance" which means he was not "a press hound." That might not have always been to his benefit as, "People loved to dismiss him as a hick from Georgia but he turned the tables on them."

On lighter notes, Barnard's obituary cited "his great sense of humor and his constant search for a good practical joke." Like Ed Jenkins, Barnard was fairly short and when they gave addresses, many would jokingly call for him to "stand up." Tassey on the other hand was 6'2 and he recalls Barnard introducing him by joking, "I was as tall as he was when he started working for me."

Barnard turned 68 in 1990 and despite persistent rumors that he might retire, he declared his intention to go forward because "there's no good reason for me not to run." But he vowed to make it his last term, anticipating that, "after reapportionment, it will give everyone in the district" a chance for new blood.

That race proved far more difficult than Barnard had previously been accustomed. Barnard dispatched a primary rival, Scott Starling, who mocked his opposition to abortion and civil rights legislation renewals with 71% but the general was tough going. Jones had hoped to make inroads in the suburban-Atlanta Gwinnett County portion of the district which was growing and where Barnard wasn't as well known. This campaign was the year after the extent of the Savings and Loan crisis had come to light and Republican Sam Jones, announcing his challenge to Barnard early in the year, vowed to make it a major issue and delivered.

With $39,750 from S&L interests, Barnard ranked twelfth among House members in terms of campaign cash and Jones placed Barnard's name on billboards and castigated him for taking $20,000 to folks linked to S & L kingpin Charles Keating. Barnard played down his influence, questioning that, "If I'm such a friend to banks, why am I trying to get the Justice Department to prosecute white-collar crime in the banking industry? Sixty percent of all bank failures involve some criminal wrongdoing?" He contended that, "Go-go lenders, get-rich-quick developers and compliant appraisers are equally to blame for this alarming situation." He sought to turn the tables on Jones by calling out the GOP for accepting $100,000 from Keating and pledging to return $20,000 to the U.S. Treasury if they parted with it. But *The Atlanta Journal* noted that while Barnard, "collects substantial campaign contributions and speaking fees from bankers, he has taken pains to divest himself of business stock and other holdings."

Still, confronted with his first-ever tough race, Barnard knew more convincing was needed and he ramped up his "rusty" campaign apparatus and began running ads, one of which ended, "If they had listened to Doug Barnard, there would not be a savings and loan crisis." He campaigned in Gwinnett harder than ever before.

While Jones soundly won Gwinnett, polling 61%, Barnard racked up first place everywhere else by handsome margins, including 65% in Clarke (Athens) and 74% in Richmond (Augusta) to achieve what everyone was certain would be his last term with 58%.

Despite his early pronouncements, of a probable '92 retirement, Barnard kept many people guessing through 1991, claiming, "I was just so frustrated, exhausted and absolutely discouraged with the whole process." He finally announced his departure late in the year and the health of his wife was a factor.

Barnard at his 70th birthday celebration
Photo courtesy of Beverly Bell

Barnard made clear he was a proponent of fiscal soundness even through the end. "If I've got one mission left," he told *The Atlanta Constitution* as he prepared to leave office, "it will be to try to convince my friends how invidious this continuing build-up of national debt is and what it's going to do to our country down the road."

Barnard missed much of the final proceedings of the 102nd Congress – his last, due to open heart surgery. But in remarks inserted into the *Congressional Record*, he did not hold back expressing his disdain for the changing House climate. "I have been saddened to watch the deterioration of the House which has occurred during my time here," he said. "The worst aspect is that, for the most part, it has been a self-inflicted wound. For all its widely publicized faults, America still has the greatest system of government in the world. As Churchill said, many forms of government have been tried, and will be tried in this world of sin and well. No one pretends that democracy is perfect or all-wise. Indeed it has been said that democracy is the worst form of government except all those other forms that have been tried from time to time." He then put his own print on Sam Rayburn's famous, "Any jackass can tear down a barn" quip by saying "Sometimes, I think we have so many jackasses around here that the carpenters will never be allowed to make necessary repairs."

As for the money, Barnard initially said after leaving office, "I'm not in any hurry. I'm just going to leave it like this for a while." Toward the end of the year, however, he had a second heart and it was revealed that he was keeping most of the $250,000. His explanation: there wasn't one. It isn't, "anybody's business but mine. Frankly, I've made a decision and I'm paying about $70,000 in taxes on it. It's not that much money that's being left and it's my business and I just don't care to talk about it."

In his golden years, Barnard typified the trend of conservative Democrats by if not outright becoming Republican, certainly strenuously promoting the party's causes. In 1998, he chaired a group of Democrats backing the re-election of Republican U.S. Senator Paul Coverdell and in 2007, following the death of Congressman Charlie Norwood, he was an avid supporter of a Republican seeking to succeed him, Barry Fleming.

In retirement, Barnard taught Sunday school and served on various boards. He passed in 2018 at age 95, an occasion on which a close family acquaintant, John Bell remarked, "Everybody liked Doug Barnard and he made things happen. He was that kind of guy. You've got a project and he's gonna figure out how to make it happen. That guided his whole life." A highway in downtown Augusta bears his name.

CHAPTER FIFTY-NINE

Erdreich, Alabama's Second Jewish Congressman, a Fighter for Justice and Fairness His Entire Career

Introductory Tidbit: In 1982, Ben Erdreich was seeking to become only the second Jewish Congressman Alabama elected (the first had served more than a century before). While the campaign was largely devoid of overt derogatory references to his religion, there were a few covert incidents that Erdreich strongly suspected the campaign of his opponent, Albert Lee Smith was behind. . The Erdreich camp got wind of one when a supporter in Gardendale, AL, a conservative, white area of the district, received a call asking, "Don't you know Ben Erdreich is Jewish." Angered by it, she called into his campaign office and vowed to "take care of it" and alerted a neighborhood friend who had yet to receive a call. Sure enough, when the call came in, the friend was ready with a retort to the, "Don't you know Ben Erdreich is Jewish." It was, "Of course, he is one of the chosen people."

Photo courtesy of Ben Erdreich

While names like Martin Luther King, Jr., John Lewis and Rosa Parks transcend the struggle for civil rights, the movement could not have successfully been carried out without young, courageous non-black participants who risked their safety in the name of fighting for equality. Ben Erdreich was one such person. Alabama's second Jewish Congressman (the first had served one term, from 1853 to 1855), who two decades later would serve in the House of Representatives with Lewis, marched in Birmingham promoting equality for African-Americans.

Erdreich (ERD-RICH) did have a Yale education and initially practiced law in New York City. But having been born and reared in Birmingham, earning his law degree at the University of Alabama (where he edited the Law Review) and marrying a girl from the Yellowhammer State, he was without question an Alabaman to the core.

After law school, Erdreich served in the Army where he was sent to New York City and initially stayed there as his wife Ellen, who like him hailed from Birmingham, finished her education. The family was prominent enough that the 1965 wedding announcement was run in *The New York Times*. His first firm upon returning was Cooper, Mitch and Crawford where his father-in-law, Jerome "Buddy" Cooper, was the founding partner. Led by Buddy. Ellen's family was equally progressive. In 2018, she would write how during his time in Alabama, "Dad's labor law practice, unique in the South, changed lives by using the legal process to achieve equal pay for equal work. In a legally segregated society, Buddy dared bring white and black workers together in the same union halls, training programs and jobs." Buddy, who had once clerked for Supreme Court Justice Hugo Black (and served 44 months in the Navy during World War II), even advised President John F. Kennedy shortly before his assassination).

After Ben and Ellen returned south, Erdreich got his political feet wet by winning a seat in the Alabama legislature in 1970. With his Jefferson County colleague, Chriss Doss, he pushed through landmark clean air legislation.

In 1972, Erdreich might have hoped Alabama would revert to its habits of voting Democratic again and he announced his candidacy to take on four-term Republican Congressman John Buchanan. But Buchanan had insulated himself since his fluke win in '64 and Erdreich predictably lost 59-36%. In 1974, after his term in the legislature, he still landed on his feet. His new elected office: Jefferson County Commissioner of Public Welfare, a role *The Encyclopedia of Alabama* noted "Erdreich's popular programs included a 'meals on wheels' service and Eldergarden, a downtown recreational gathering for seniors." In 1981, Erdreich was among a number of county officials who traveled to Washington D.C. to protest the Reagan administration's proposed cuts to housing programs, which he decried as draconian. He told a Senate Banking, Housing and Urban Affairs subcommittee that, "we can't continue to deny low-income people of a basic need - that of adequate shelter."

Whether Erdreich knew it or not, he would soon be sitting on a dais very near the podium where he had testified, at least on the other side of the capitol. Erdreich decided to try again for Congress in 1982 when the Sixth District still did not appear to be easy territory for a Democrat to navigate. Not only would it award 59% to Ronald Reagan in 1984, but it had chosen him over fairly decent margins to Jimmy Carter, who grew up in next door Georgia, in 1976 and '80. But Congressman Albert Lee Smith, Jr., was a freshman Republican who had little time to insulate himself and redistricting had given the Sixth district more Democratic pockets of Birmingham. Smith also may have had segments of the Republican Party angry with him for his defeat of longtime GOP Congressman John Buchanan in the '80 GOP primary. 1982 was a better year for Democrats and Birmingham's 15% unemployment fueled Erdreich's cause.

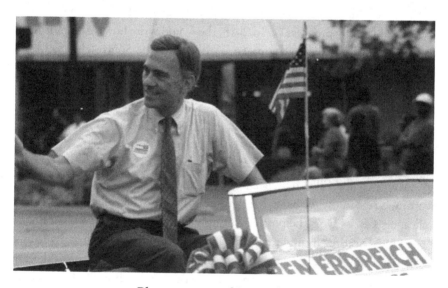

Photo courtesy of Ben Erdreich

Smith began the campaign ahead but Erdreich recalls conducting telephone calls and getting "positive results." In September, *The Birmingham Post Herald* conducted a poll showing Smith nicely ahead but also taking a surprisingly large number of African-American voters which was taken with a grain of salt. Republicans, citing the fact that Erdreich's father-in-law had been counsel for the United Mine Workers, the United Steelworkers and other unions, sought to tar Erdreich as too liberal.

While there were no major efforts to divide the electorate based on religion, the campaign was not devoid of a few tertiary incidents. The phone call eluded to above was one. Another was a leaflet circulated by a group asking residents of the 6th, "Do You Want a Jew for a Congressman?" The answer apparently was a yes as Erdreich edged the incumbent 53-45%. The jubilant Congressman-elect vowed to, "take a good dose of common sense to Washington and get this country on the move again."

In his Capitol Hill office
Photo courtesy of Ben Erdreich

CQ wrote Erdreich "quickly earned a reputation for methodical decision-making – an approach heralded by his supporters as conscientious but criticized by detractors as befitting a judge more than a politician." He also figured out the ingredient for success in a district where labor was important, but business was dominant. While Erdreich's labor scores were acceptable, Alan Ehrenhalt wrote in a 1985 political column that," There is little disagreement about how Ben Erdreich has become a political powerhouse. He has cultivated - Republicans would say co-opted, the Birmingham business community...Erdreich used his first term to put together a campaign network that read like a directory of the Birmingham corporate establishment. His finance committee included the chairman of the Alabama Gas Co. and the chief executive officer of the largest bank in the state. That said, he quietly but tenaciously championed good government, clean air and elements important to his state and district and his assignment on the Banking Committee gave him a perch to able look after Birmingham.

Birmingham was a city where steel had once been dominant and in his first year in office, Erdreich introduced the Unfair Foreign Competition Act. He fought against hostile takeovers and for the establishment of metal casting centers in Alabama over the Bush administration's opposition. Erdreich made his case by noting that, "over half of U.S. factories have closed since 1971, putting tens of thousands of Americans out of work." A compromise was worked out several months later.

In 1990, angered by a landfill near the town of Emelle that had been housing hazardous waste from as far away as Texas, Erdreich introduced a bill to require states to devise a 20-year plan to maintain landfills. U.S. Senator Richard Shelby, still a Democrat, sponsored a similar measure in the Senate and President Bush signed it near the end of the year. In 1988, Erdreich and two other colleagues found themselves on the losing end of Public Works Chair Glenn Anderson, and subsequently the House Rules Committee when projects they were advocating were stricken from a Transportation Appropriation Bill because they hadn't received prior approval but leaders found a maneuver to put them back in.

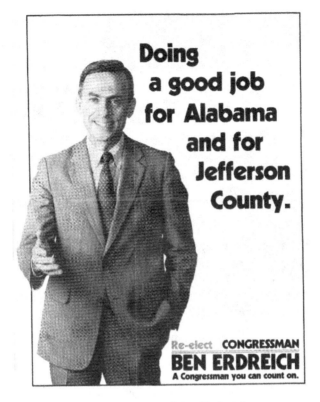

Photo courtesy of Ben Erdreich

On issues, Erdreich proved himself as true a moderate as they come. His Presidential support score was just 37% in 1983, but 49% in '89. He voted for the Equal Rights Amendment, resisted education cuts sought by the Reagan administration and spoke in favor of the Emergency Assistance Act. In future Congresses, Erdreich gave the substantial business interests in Birmingham a bone by opposing the two-month notification requirement for plant managers to give employees prior to closing, as well as compensation for workers who lost their jobs due to provisions in the Clean Air Act of 1990. But he backed the override of Bush's veto of both the minimum wage increase and the Family and Medical Leave Act. He backed the anti-flag burning amendment and opposed the Brady Bill. But Erdreich was solidly pro-choice and the only Alabaman to vote to restrict smoking on airplanes. Following nationwide uproar over a proposed pay-raise, Erdreich sponsored a bill barring members from increasing it in the middle of their term.

Photo courtesy of Ben Erdreich

In mid-1989, Erdreich became chairman of the Subcommittee on Policy and Research following the bribery conviction of New York Democrat Robert Garcia. With his colleague, Tom Carper of Delaware, Erdreich sponsored The National Flood and Erosion Insurance Mitigation Act of 1989. Four months after the catastrophic 1989 earthquake in San Francisco, Erdreich held a hearing that advocates hoped would culminate with a national earthquake insurance program (future House Speaker Nancy Pelosi, whose district was the epicenter of that quake, was instrumental in advocating for the hearing). The program would fall along similar lines as the flood insurance program. Erdreich was initially non-committal, in particular questioning whether California was the place to start, though did acknowledge the soundness of the flood insurance program, "both in terms of cost and preparedness."

Erdreich also sponsored a source-licensing bill, the Intellectual Property Rights Improvement Act and the National Child Search Assistance Act of 1990. His contribution to a 1990 housing overhaul was sponsoring an amendment that would extend the same criteria to mobile home buyers as first-time home owners seeking federal aid. As a member of the Select Committee on Aging, he took part in a hearing in Birmingham that his Senate counterparts had called on eldercare abuse. He told attendees that, "The House Subcommittee on Health and Long-Term Care, on which I sit, has found that about five percent of the Nation's elderly may be victims of abuse from moderate to severe. To put this another way, about one out of every twenty older Americans, or more than 1.5 million persons, may be victims of such abuse every year. Physical violence, negligence and financial abuse appear."

**Chairing a Banking subcommittee (ranking Republican
Doug Bereuter of Nebraska is to the left)
Photo courtesy of Ben Erdreich**

Beyond these pursuits, Erdreich dipped his toes into housing issues. In his final term in Congress, he sponsored the Family Education Assistance Act of 1992, the Resource Conservation and Recovery Financial Responsibility Improvement Act of 1992, the Federal Reserve Bank Branch Modernization Act and securing grants for biomedical training and exchange programs. He also introduced legislation requiring the Secretary of the Treasury to conduct a study regarding the insurance industry in the United States.

On a lighter note, Erdreich and President George H.W. Bush were on different sides of the aisle politically – and occasionally on the court in the House gym. Erdreich, who was on the touch football team at Yale, played paddle-ball against the President on occasion, and once teamed with Mississippi

Congressman Sonny Montgomery (Bush's teammate was a member of the White House staff). They bet $1 per–game but Bush won twice, 21-16 and again 21-15 (Erdreich could boast of getting "a few good ones" past Bush).

As a boss, Erdreich was wondrous. Anita Ray was both a Chief of Staff and campaign manager and recalls one word "service" governed his life's mission. Consequently, "there was only one question I was required to be able to positively respond in decision making: 'Is your decision just?'" Pat Kobor points out "he wasn't really a glad-hander or small-talker like many politicians. He was pleasant and polite always, and expected the same of his staff." To that end, "he did not care" for personal news or gossip. Kobor recalls a sense of empathy. Erdreich replied that he had just witnessed a Congressman from a well-known family delivering a speech shaking. "What must it be like for this guy to do this job with every eye on him, such heavy expectations," Erdreich thought, adding, "I look at him differently now." Hence, Kobor believes, "that ability to put himself in others' shoes is one of the qualities that made him a good Congressman."

After his initial win over Smith, Erdreich soon attained so much popularity that he became untouchable. His re-election with 60% in 1984 became 73% in '86 and in 1990, Republicans didn't even field a candidate against him. There was little question that he could hold his current seat indefinitely. Then, like with so many other incumbents, Erdreich was confronted by the realities of redistricting. Alabama was not losing a Congressional seat but was required to implement a minority-majority district and while the final shape was imponderable, it was a certainty that it would take in much of Birmingham. The delegation dickered over a plan acceptable to all of them. Finally, the legislature passed one and subsequently overrode GOP Governor Guy Hunt's veto and Erdreich's close friend and colleague, Claude Harris, began making moves to take him on in a primary. That plan ultimately proved unacceptable to the federal panel which had jurisdiction: they adopted a GOP drawn map that for Erdreich, was beyond intimidating: 85% white, wealthy and a place where Republican candidates were regularly awarded near-monolithic totals of its vote.

To Ellen Erdreich with best wishes, George Bush Barbara Bush

Photo courtesy of Ben Erdreich

Erdreich would not go down without a fight. The winner of a Republican runoff was Spencer Bachus, who had beaten GOP State Chair Marty Connors. Erdreich hit Bacchus on a sizable amount of missed votes as a member of the legislature while the challenger struck at votes on abortion, funding for the National Endowment for the Arts and other issues to back up his claim that Erdreich was liberal. Erdreich cited his support for a Balanced Budget Amendment and Line Item Veto while also pointing he cast 32 votes to lower spending for the legislative branch.

Erdreich carried the Tuscaloosa County portion of the district, newly added, with 63%, but it cast just 30,000 votes. Jefferson County (Birmingham) was at least 2/3 of the district and Bacchus carried it 54-45%. (Bachus also prevailed in Shelby County, another new and very Republican area added to the 6th District, with 62%). The new 6th district had eliminated most of the black voters, a reliable Democratic base, which earlier had comprised about 35% of the district, but after the new lines were drawn, that was reduced to 15%.

Bill Clinton failed to crack ¼ of the vote here (President Bush took 64% while Ross Perot grabbed the rest) pointedly demonstrating the Republican tilt of the newly drawn seat. Bachus won, but barely, with 52.4% of the vote to 45% for Erdreich. In fact, Erdreich recalls informing Bush of that statistic at the White House Christmas party and him replying, "I didn't think I did that well anywhere." *The Almanac of American Politics* called it, "amazing not that he lost but that he fought gamely and almost won."

Out of office, President Bill Clinton named Erdreich chairman of the federal Merit Systems Protection Board, a post he held for seven years. In recent years, Erdreich and his family run Metropolitan LLC, a major housing and commercial development firm in Birmingham, Alabama.

At a White House Christmas Party
Photo courtesy of Ben Erdreich

CHAPTER SIXTY

Huckaby, Tallon and Harris Fit Districts Like Gloves Until Voting Rights Act Mandated Black Majority Creations

"Introductory Quote: "I'm such a great guy, I thought I could win anyway." –Congressman Jerry Huckaby joking why he could win another term following the 1992 redistricting that substantially reduced the African-American population in his district. Many top Democrats in Washington had urged him to not even try.

Jerry Huckaby (top), Robin Tallon and Claude Harris
Top and botton left photo courtesy of the U.S.
House of Representatives Collection;
Right image courtesy of C-SPAN

1 992 yielded the election of a record African-Americans to the U.S. House, an exhilarating phenomenon in a region where opportunities had been full and far between since Reconstruction. One reason it had not taken place prior was that the U.S. Department of Justice did not enforce the creation of additional majority-African-American districts in states covered by the Voting Rights Act. That changed in 1992 and, in order for that to be accommodated, the lines required drawing significant numbers of minority Democratic areas out of existing districts that were held by popular and perpetually safe Democratic incumbents. Consequently, many of these lawmakers were forced to either retire or lost and they included Jerry Huckaby of Louisiana, Robin Tallon of South Carolina and Claude Harris of Alabama.

All three incumbents represented areas that were fairly, albeit not exclusively rural and all had served together on the House Agriculture Committee, though Harris moved to the exclusive Appropriations Committee at the start of his final term in 1991. Two of the three – Huckaby and Harris, fell victim to a process that was entirely controlled by their own party (Alabama did have a GOP Governor but legislative Democrats had veto-proof majorities). Tallon's fate on the other hand was left in the hands of a Republican governor and a Democratic legislature who found themselves unable to agree on a compromise, thereby leaving the matter to a court. It might not have made a difference.

Jerry Huckaby

Though Thomas Gerald "Jerry" Huckaby came to Washington as a giant killer, the fact is, the Congressional titan he had unseated had seen better days. In fact, by the time of his involuntary departure at the hands of Huckaby, Otto Passman's energy and peak of influence were so far removed that they were well outside the rearview mirror. But his bigger problem was now being compounded by major liabilities, chief among them a $1,700 reimbursement he was force to make to the federal government following a *Wall Street Journal* publication of travel improprieties. Plus, Passman came under scrutiny for a series of shipping contracts.

Huckaby was a 34-year-old political novice when he decided to challenge Passman, a fifteen-term incumbent, in the 1976 Democratic primary. Born in Hodge, he had earned his B.A. from Louisiana State University and his MBA from Georgia State. By this time, Huckaby was a husband to Suzanna

Woodard. He became a field electrical engineer for the Western Electric Company and remembers helping install a computer telephone switching center underground in the mountains of North Carolina which controlled the worldwide communications for the Pentagon. So primitive was the operation that it was a classified military site "like a James Bond type of thing" and a top secret clearance was required. By the early 1970s, Huckaby decided to go full-time into the dairy business from his farm in the town of Ringgold

Though Passman, among the House's most ardent foes of foreign aid, was looking vulnerable, the long string of heavyweights who had once been chomping at the bit to challenge him evidently decided they couldn't beat him and passed. Huckaby was not considered one of the heavyweights but he was not intimidated and went forward. Did many think he had lost his mind. Possibly, Huckaby recalls but, "I thought I could win." So did "Bubba" Henry, a personal friend and Speaker of the Louisiana House and he lent Huckaby early backing. "That gave me credibility and open doors." Meanwhile, Huckaby spent many hours in Shrevepo outside the district reviewing files of Congressional archives to locate aspects of Passman's voting record that might point to vulnerabilities.

As the primary approached, many still intimated that Huckaby would be an also-ran. *Congressional Quarterly* was one of them. The publication wrote, "some observers think he avoided major opposition this year because potential successors believed (Passman) would retire in two years and decided to wait." But they didn't account for Huckaby putting in $61,000 of his own money into the race.

Personal campaigning played a role in both campaigns - Huckaby did so vigorously while Passman, after years of relying on his long tenure to carry him through, stepped up his game. It was still expected to be enough for the incumbent but on primary day, Huckaby held Passman to a 76-vote win in his home parish of Ouichita and swamped him elsewhere, for a 53-47% win. The euphoric Huckaby campaign soon turned to sadness when Jim Leslie of Jim Leslie Associates, a firm with a record of producing come from behind wins, was gunned down as he returned from another election night celebration. One of Leslie's employees, Deno Seder, called it "somewhat analogous to a football team that loses its quarterback. Jim was the focal point of the agency. We all knew we'd have to work harder and work longer hours to make up for the loss."

In most instances in the South in those days, the winner of the Democratic primary would normally be guaranteed a seat in Congress as it was still monolithically Democratic. But the GOP was beginning to make inroads in Louisiana. Henson Moore had captured an open seat two years earlier and President Gerald Ford was campaigning hard to deny his Democratic opponent, Jimmy Carter, a victory in the state.

Republican had nominated an attractive businessman, Frank Spooner, to take on Huckaby and thanks in part to his own party circling the wagons, he did manage to close his initial deficit as the campaign went on. Spooner tried to gain hay by trying to tar him as a liberal Democrat and near the end of the campaign, *The Monroe News Star* said, "Spooner has attempted to make a campaign issue by saying that Huckaby will be at odds with a liberal Democrat Caucus in the House that can thwart any effectiveness Huckaby may have. Huckaby counters that he can be more effective as a legislator by being a member of the majority party in the House." Former Texas Governor John Connally and Ronald Reagan - who had carried Louisiana in his primary against Ford, stumped for Spooner. At the end of the day, Ford narrowly captured the 5th even while falling short statewide but Huckaby hung on to take the seat with 53%.

Huckaby knew immediately that he would have to prove himself and, for starters, He swore off voting against San Francisco Democrat Phil Burton for Majority Leader because "he's liberal." He vowed to fill his staff with locals but also folks who knew how Washington worked, as well as African-Americans. And with Passman having been lax in recent years, Huckaby saw being close to the people as a must. Telling a reporter, "I want to give people in the district more participation in government." His committee assignments – Agriculture and Interior, gave him a good perch from which to do that.

In 1978, Huckaby landed a spot on the Environment Action's "Dirty Dozen." Only four on the list were Democrats and Huckaby was the only freshman. He had no trouble dispatching that challenge and, until 1992, did the same with ease.

Huckaby's influence was felt as early as the second month of his second term and it came on an issue that would soon rivet the nation; the Alaska Lands Act. In February of 1979, Huckaby startled Congressional watchers by denying Morris K. "Mo" Udall a victory in the very committee he chaired as the House Interior Committee rejected Udall's Alaskan land proposal and voted in favor of one sponsored by Huckaby 23-20. In the halls of Congress, that was no fluke. Fellow Louisiana Democrat, John Breaux had managed to pass similar language out of the Merchant Marine Committee over that of a stronger bill put forth by Gerry Studds of Massachusetts. In Breaux's case, support from Michigan Congressman John Dingell, a titan on the Energy and Commerce Committee, seemed to add credence to its prospects.

**A handful of Southern Democrats met with President Ronald Reagan
and Vice-President George H.W. Bush including Huckaby (to the left
of the president) and Andy Ireland of Florida (next to Huckaby)
Photo courtesy of Andy Ireland**

The Huckaby substitute, referred to as an "oil and patch driven" measure, siphoned 44 million acres eligible for protection from the Udall bill, and would permit drilling in the Caribou after a seven-year study. It opened the Arctic Wildlife Range for drilling and would permit logging and mining in certain sites that Udall's bill would not. It had the strong support of Alaska's At-Large Republican Congressman, Don Young.

Udall accused supporters of Huckaby's language of favoring a park where tourists could "shoot a caribou every hour on the hour, and in one corner there would be a pizza parlor and a concession for a shoe factory." This gained the attention of the Carter administration. Domestic Policy Advisor Stuart Eizenstadt declared the provisions in the Huckaby-Breaux bills, "totally unacceptable to the president," and threatened a veto should it clear Congress. It didn't.

When the matter reached the House floor weeks later, debate was spirited. Huckaby in essence accused environmentalists of trying to grab as much as they can. "What it really amounts to, in last year's House-passed bill, the southern half of Misty Fjords was not a wilderness. The environmentalists found out that U.S. Borax wanted to actually develop a large commercial mine there, so this year this area has wilderness characteristics all of a sudden, so it should be a wilderness to preclude any development up there. And that is the bottom line of what is happening." He said the compromise, "truly represents the best possible balance that can be put together to preserve the environment and to develop Alaska in an orderly way in those areas where there are extremely high potentials for oil and gas and the seven major mineral finds in Alaska." At the end of the day, the House overwhelmingly adopted much of Udall's bill and that of Illinois Republican John Anderson (it became law in December of 1980).

Huckaby would again challenge Udall in the mid-1980s, albeit on a matter with far lower profile. The issue involved using disputed drilling revenues from gas and oil and Huckaby succeeded in passing a series of amendments out of Interior over his chairman's opposition, including one that would give a higher share of money to coastal states (Udall and other Democrats wanted to go as high as 37% while the Reagan administration only wanted 16 ½). Huckaby proposed 27% which he felt worked to Louisiana's benefit.

Huckaby (far left) with members of the Louisiana House delegation in 1985

Huckaby was not afraid to duke it out with wilderness groups years after the land bill and many times, that involved working with Young. When New York Democrat Bob Mrazek proposed repealing the timber harvest goal in the late 1980s, Huckaby and Young proposed an alternative that was rejected 18-22. When Interior Committee Democrats sought to preserve the Tongass forest in Alaska, Huckaby offered a compromise amendment that was supported by Young. And when House Democrats undertook a rewrite of wetlands legislation, Huckaby moved to exempt all current land from the proposed regulations and vowed to use the 1990 farm bill as "the vehicle to do it." He declared it, "ridiculous for a farmer to have to get a Section 404 (Clean Water Act) permit to dig a ditch on his land, when he's been ditching there for the last 40 years."

When Ronald Reagan captured the White House in 1980, Huckaby found himself siding with him appropriate because the new president was the ideological soulmate of many in the district. He voted for both the Republican substitute for FY 1982 and the rule —. But when it came to final passage, Huckaby conditioned it on White House support of the price support system for the 5th's abundant sugar growers and when the administration yielded, Huckaby provided the vote. And on a bill trimming the food stamp program, Huckaby opposed an amendment by fellow Democrat Dan Glickman to reduce the amount that would be cut and along with four colleagues, gave Republicans the margins necessary to prevail. As he explained to *The New York Times*, "The people in my district are 97 percent registered Democrats. But on a national level philosophically, most of the people in my district think more in tune with Republicans. It's just, they've been Democrats since the War between the States."

Be that as it may, Huckaby wasn't about to abandon the needs of his constituents. In 1981, he voted against a Reagan request to cut the growth of a dairy price support program. Nor was Huckaby about to jeopardize it for personal luxuries." How can we in good conscience make Cuts in food stamps and Welfare and at the same time increase the amount of money we spend here in Washington on these committees?"

Huckaby's increasing seniority would mean great things for his district. He chaired the House Agriculture Subcommittee on Cotton, Rice and Sugar and his ultimate legacy for his farmers was perhaps getting a price support program for cotton and rice growers. He was also instrumental in seeing the loosening of sugar imports.

**When President Reagan came to Monroe, Louisiana in 1984 to view the
flooding, he gave Huckaby a lift back to Washington on Air Force One
Photo courtesy of Jerry Huckaby**

Still, holding the gavel did not insulate Huckaby from challenges to his
interests. As the House debated the '90 farm bill, Huckaby was forced to
defend the cotton subsidies. "In 1985," he told colleagues, "we implemented a
new program called marketing loan for cotton. Since then, cotton production
has increased in the United States from a little more than 10 million bales
to almost 15 million bales per year. We have seen the price increase from less
than 50 cents a pound to almost 75 cents a pound, a dramatic increase."

In that same debate, Huckaby found himself strenuously arguing against
an amendment by New York Democrat Tom Downey and Ohio Republican
Bill Gradison to end sugar subsidies. "The price of sugar increased 6 percent.
But look at the price of soft drinks, 25 percent. Candy, 45 percent; cereal, a
whopping 93 percent increase. All of these products that are heavily sugar
dependent significantly increased during the 1980s, but not the price of sugar."

Other matters were important to his people. In 1987, following the
revelations of the Mississippi farmers gaining $1,015 million by setting up 15
corporations to qualify for a $50,000 per person "deficiency" payment, (which
became known as the "Mississippi Christmas Tree"), Huckaby made sure no
one could exceed $100,000. It came in an $80 billion deficit reduction bill, the
Omnibus Budget Reconciliation Act of 1987. Vermont Senator Pat Leahy urged

support, saying, "Without Huckaby, we're going to see something a heckuva lot stronger." That didn't mean, however, that it would automatically happen.

For more than two years, Huckaby pressured the Department of Agriculture to reverse the awarding of such exorbitant sums, even threatening to "enact legislation making all trusts and estates ineligible for payments, beginning retroactively with the 1989 crop year." He stepped up the pressure with the dawn of the Bush administration when Clayton Yeutter became Agriculture Secretary saying, "I feel strongly that the aforementioned operation violates both the spirit and letter of the law. It was clearly not the intent of Congress that such operations would qualify for such vast sums; if this operation does receive the reported 1.4 million dollars, it will only happen because USDA has failed to implement and enforce the law as intended by Congress." The matter eventually became a court case, DCP Farms vs. Yeutter and it went before a U.S. District Court. The money was vacated, then re-instated before finally, the "many, many hours negotiating a final product" bore fruit. "It defined what a person was and what an entity was and concluded that you can have only three entities. That meant that under the most elaborate scheme, one can only pass $150,000."

Image courtesy of CSPAN

Protecting the oil industry was another Huckaby cause. In an early South Africa sanctions bill in 1985, Huckaby was concerned about a provision by a fellow Democrat, Bob Wise of West Virginia that would have prohibited the awarding of energy-related leases to U.S. companies that continued doing business in South Africa. Huckaby compared Shell Oil "to offshore oil and gas drilling what IBM is to computers" but the committee roll call stripping the provision from the sanctions out was unsuccessful by two votes. Huckaby also had rural Louisiana on his mind after the 1992 Los Angeles riots. Members wanted to give federal aid their share of federal aid but Huckaby said people in his communities, "feel they have their own problems that need tending to."

Overhauling nuclear insurance was another issue that Huckaby saw as important to his constituency and in 1987 played a pivotal role in forging a compromise between those who favored using the compensation fund to pay lawyers and those who wanted every last cent to go to victims of nuclear accidents. An amendment Huckaby proposed would allow portions of the fund to go toward lawyers but of the limit was reached, it would came at the expense of the victims (Democrats Sam Gejdenson and Austin Murphy of Pennsylvania helped forge the compromise).

Another nuclear related issue required nearly all of Huckaby's tenure to come to fruition. The quest to establish an Emergency Response Program within the Nuclear Regulatory Commission began shortly after the accident at Three Mile Island in Pennsylvania. It's primary component was a data system "to be able to instantaneously transmit to NRC headquarters timely operating information for many commercial nuclear power reactors during an emergency." The measure appeared to get its due in 1988 when the measure made it to the House floor. Huckaby pressed his proposal by stating how "currently, the NRC communicates with nuclear powerplants by phone during an emergency. This has proven to be very slow and error prone. Faulty information can lead to loss of precious time and inaccurate advice by the NRC." He proudly emphasized that the cost would be "only $7 million." Ohio Democrat Dennis Eckart objected to the measure, in part because it "would preempt any state or locality from establishing its own electronic data system in the future." Huckaby responded that it would in no way infringe on states rights because those with existing laws would be grandfathered. In the end, members seemed to agree with Gejdenson who called it, "my preference (is) to have this system up and running 24 hours a day on a continuous basis." The measure cleared the chamber 341-77 but would be stymied in the Senate by another Ohioan, Howard Metzenbaum, who was thought to be acting at the behest of environmentalists. Not until 1991 did it finally become law.

As the years went by, Huckaby remained a knee-jerk centrist but began voting a tad to the left. For example, in 1989, he was one of roughly 30 members who switched to oppose the Dornan Amendment that prohibited federal funding for women seeking an abortion. That might have been one reason that he was successful in winning a seat on the Budget Committee, his second attempt (in 1985, he had argued that Louisiana lacked representation but Democratic leaders might have viewed him as too unpredictable). He became a close ally of Texas Democrat Charlie Stenholm, a leader of the "Boll Weevils." But he was also close with Leon Panetta, the California Democrat with whom he had come to Congress in 1976 and who was a leadership loyalist. This was due in part to Huckaby's welcoming, congenial demeanor.

1992 meant the drawing of a new Congressional map and while it was expected that a new African-American majority seat would be required, it was by no means a certainty that Huckaby would be the odd man out. One reason was that Democrats appeared to control all the cards and Huckaby was closest to the most powerful one of all, Governor Edwin Edwards. As early as June 1991, the Louisiana House all but codified Huckaby's safety when lawmakers passed a remap proposed by New Orleans Democrat Emile "Peppi" Bruneau, Jr., 77-24. But complicating the matter was that the Bayou State was losing a House seat and though, it was almost universally agreed that Republican Congressman Clyde Holloway had few cards to play, a second incumbent essentially had to lose in order to accommodate the VRA required district (Bruneau and others had maintained that creating such a district was no requirement). The Senate then passed its bill while the House essentially laughed it off, with House Speaker Pro-tem Sherman Copelin even proclaiming, "We're going to kill it," and producing a version of their own. That was fairly close to what ultimately made it into law. What happened next was major hop-scotch. The House approved a bill with no VRA district, then changed that when black lawmakers and Republicans complained.

The Sugarbeet Grower
FEBRUARY/1985

In early 1992, another proposal – known as the Huckaby plan, made its way through and the person with the most to lose in that scenario was Baton Rouge area Republican Richard Baker. When lines were finally drawn, Huckaby found himself with a double-whammy: one was that much of his turf was merged with another incumbent, Jim McCrery, a sophomore Republican. Two, the African-American percentage in the old 5th was reduced from 31% to 19%. Democrats in Washington told Huckaby he couldn't win and tried to talk him into retirement but he bravely went forward.

A week before the all-party primary, where getting 50% of the vote meant automatic victory, a poll had Huckaby leading McCrery by 11 points. The actual results told a different story. McCrery vaulted into first place with 44% while Huckaby only took 29% as a Democratic lawyer named Robert Thompson spent $22,000 but nonetheless grabbed 22%. Huckaby got decent margins out of his base but they were mostly lightly populated rural areas. McCrery meanwhile won Caddo and Bossier parishes big while Huckaby was relegated to third place in Ouachita (Monroe). U.S. Senator Bennett Johnston, called the 20 point swing, "incredible," adding, "That never used to happen." But for Huckaby, it was a dangerous harbinger for November.

With so much at stake, calling the November race vituperative was an understatement. For starters, Huckaby was hurt by the House bank scandal which found him with 88 overdrafts totaling $41,373. Huckaby cut a check for $1,780 to the American Heart Association, as that is what the overdraft fees of a commercial bank would add up to but McCrery was able to milk the publicity by boasting that he had zero overdrafts.

Next, the two argued about lifestyle. McCrery had introduced one of his main campaign themes on primary night when he brought up Huckaby's D.C. residence, contending, "He doesn't even live in the district anymore," That did not sit well in a debate when Huckaby replied McCrery, "attacked me for the fact that Sue and I live together in Washington...My wife and I have been married 29 years, and we have two wonderful children...He's 43 years old...He's been married one year, and he and his wife choose to live apart." McCrery yelled back, "All congressmen make sacrifices...If you did your job as well as I do mine, you'd make the same sort of sacrifice."

What Huckaby had been making at least a subterranean reference to in bringing up Huckaby's recent marriage was a story by a gay newspaper in Washington that sought to out McCrery. He denied it was true and Huckaby said, "I want to believe him."

In a Hail Mary, Huckaby vowed to appeal to constituents in any way possible. He pledged to not seek re-election in 1996 if the deficit wasn't cut in half by then. But the seeds were planted after the first-round and on Election Day, McCrery won the battle 63-37%, taking ¾ in Bossier and Caddo and 64% in Ouachita. It was the largest margin of defeat of the 24 incumbents turned out that day.

With Bill Clinton having won the presidency, Huckaby received serious mention as a possible Secretary of Agriculture. This came to pass and Huckaby immediately after took up lobbying. It was short and not so sweet as he candidly conceded, "I was never comfortable sitting on the other side of the table. I wasn't comfortable asking members like John Breaux to see such and such a person or Bob Livingston to go to such and such a reception." By this time, his wife Suzanna had become among the most highly covetred realtors in the nation – her sales over 30 years exceeded $1 billion and Jerry Huckaby became the firm's president. He then went to work with The Jefferson Group. He alternates between Louisiana and Florida today.

Robin Tallon

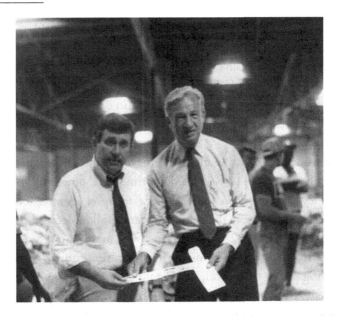

**Tallon with the President of Phillip Morris at the opening of the
South Carolina tobacco markets in Mullin, the biggest in the state
Photo courtesy of Robin Tallon**

Unlike past representatives from South Carolina's Sixth Congressional District Robin Tallon was as fastidious as they come. As far removed from the glare of Washington television camera as can be, Tallon's singular concern was providing his rural constituent a voice and he used his seat on the Agricultural Committee and Merchant Marine and Fisheries to ably advocate for their needs. And with a middle-of-the-road voting record that offered something for everyone, his constituents responded just fine come election time. So popular was Tallon that Francis Marion political scientist Neal Thigpen called Tallon, "what I like to call a ballot-box candidate. Voters like him. They can identify with him," adding, "Robin is consistently underestimated."

This was the Pee Dee and Grand Stan district. While it certainly leaned Republican at the national level, it was by no means universally so as Ronald Reagan took 57% in 1984 while George H.W. Bush got 56% four years later. In neither cycle did Tallon even break a sweat at the ballot box and in 1990 he was unopposed altogether.

For six years prior to 1980 the seat was represented by John Jenrette whose eccentricity enabled the "Capitol Steps." Before that, it was held by a segregationist named John McMillan who consistently thwarted voting-rights advancement for the District of Columbia. Tallon conversely could so squarely advance the concerns of the simple man in his district because he was one.

For starters, Tallon epitomized a small businessman. He enrolled at Florence University of South Carolina for a year but dropped out to open a clothing store named Robin's. It soon grew to a chain - fifteen stores in the Carolinas and Georgia and eventually, two top of the line POLO Franchise stores in premier malls called LeMasters (he also dabbled in real estate). This helped Tallon become a delegate to the White House Council on Small Business.

Tallon won a seat in the South Carolina House of Representatives in 1980 and was likely content to stay there a long time but, something happened at the federal level. Republican John Napier had upset Jenrette for the Sixth District Congressional seat that same year and Tallon decided to risk it all by challenging him in 1982. With backing from many party leaders, he took a near-majority in the four-candidate Democratic primary (47%) and an overwhelming one in the runoff, racking up 71%.

The general election focused on, among other things, Reaganomics. Napier carried Horry (Myrtle Beach), Florence and tiny Marlboro but Tallon took everything else, for a 53-47%, a difference of 6,000 votes. Napier passed on a rematch in 1982 and Republicans had to settle on Lois Eargle. Tallon won 60-39%. Tallon's electoral potential seemed unlimited – he took 76% in 1988 and was unopposed in 1990 altogether.

One reason Tallon proved so popular at home was because he was parochial. His Agriculture Committee seat, specifically the Peanuts and Tobacco Subcommittee was tantamount to delivering and his philosophy was, "The tobacco farmer in my district and elsewhere should be the point of reference for any government program, domestic or export." In his last term, he left Peanuts and Tobacco but only because he assumed a different gavel – the Subcommittee on Domestic Marketing, Consumer Relations and Nutrition.

Photo courtesy of Robin Tallon

Beyond Agriculture, Tallon went to the mat to save Myrtle Air Force Base, arguing to Defense Secretary Richard Cheney that the closure should be the Camp Parks facility in Oakland, California. He fought for a Hybrid striped bass project South Carolina, arguing it, "has the potential to become the Holly Farms of striped bass." He sponsored a beach erosion and hurricane protection study for the "Grand Strand" beaches, specifically the 37 mile stretch from Little River Inlet to Murrel's Inlet. As anti-smoking measures gained steam, Tallon opposed banning the sale of cigarettes in military commissaries. On a lighter note, Tallon introduced a resolution designating May 1991 as "Go Camping America Month."

On national issues, Tallon stuck with Democratic leaders more often than not. He did oppose federal funding of abortion at military facilities as well as the override of the Family Leave Act but backed the unsuccessful minimum wage override). He opposed the Balanced Budget Amendment and a flag burning amendment. He endorsed Medicare Parts A and B for all Americans, and verbalized why. "I can understand the first thing they want to see when you come into a hospital is the insurance card. But it shouldn't be that way." Calling the system, "totally out of control," Tallon spoke of the detriment to small business. "We have had town meetings and small business people come in and say they simply can't stay in business because of escalating health care costs. People are having to pay much higher deductibles and co- payments." And he backed the 1990 budget summit package.

The support Tallon gave to his House colleague, Richard Gephardt of Missouri in the 1988 presidential race, no doubt helped his standing with Congressional leaders. In fact, when his Republican friend and colleague in the legislature, Republican Congressman Arthur Ravanel, was flirting with switching to the Democratic side of the aisle, Tallon made that happen... almost. He arranged meetings with the Democratic leadership who promised Ravanel the coveted seat on the Merchant Marine Committee that had proven elusive in his own Conference. But Republican Chair Lee Atwater, a South Carolinian, got wind of the machinations and didn't want to be embarrassed seeing one of his own bolt. Ravanel got the seat and stayed a Republican, leaving talon somewhat chagrined.

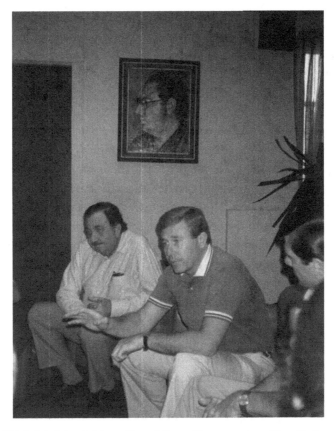

**With his friend, Texas Republican Congressman Tom DeLay
and Nicaraguan President Daniel Ortega in Managua (left)
Photo courtesy of Robin Tallon**

Tallon's one moment in the national spotlight was when he sought transparency into the 1985 Newfoundland crash, a request he was forced to keep making until the day he left office. The crash had killed 248 soldiers on a DC-8, including a constituent of Tallon's. While the conclusion reached was that ice on the wings had caused the crash, many found that explanation preposterous on its face and Tallon told one Judiciary Committee hearing the incident was either "ineptness or the best-contrived coverup...ever." In 1992, he held up a piece of what was believed to be the wreckage with an "explosive hole" that he claimed resulted from a bomb that was never pursued.

Tallon was equally harsh on government officials when Hurricane Hugo pummeled the coast of South Carolina in 1989. Calling the response, "botched," Tallon claimed, "They weren't in there fast enough," an assertion that was mild compared to his fellow Democrat, Senator Ernest "Fritz" Hollings, who called the responders, "as sorry a bunch of bureaucratic jackasses as I've worked with in my life").

Tallon often found himself on unusually shaky ground with some fellow Democrats in the Palmetto State delegation. For one, Jenrette kept Democrats on pins and needles about taking him on in the 1988 primary until just before the filing deadline until ultimately deciding against it (Tallon had k'oed a request by Jenrette to perform required community service at his office following his conviction). He tangled with the nearly universally beloved Butler Derrick and Hollings (the latter he had accused of having bungled relief for Hurricane Andrew). With his future career nearly certain to be in a state of flux post-1992 due to the need for a black majority district, Tallon at least entertained the thought of challenging Hollings in the primary. And, when it became obvious that an African-American majority district would have to be drawn, he toyed with the idea of taking on his fellow Democratic colleague, John Spratt (a joke had long circulated around South Carolina that the state had sent both the "smartest" Congressman to Washington (Spratt, a Rhodes Scholar) and the "dumbest" (Tallon who had left college). Very preliminary plans circulated by the legislature would have left Spratt the heavy favorite.

The deadlock between South Carolina GOP Governor Carroll Campbell and Democrats in the legislature over the new plan forced the filing deadline to be pushed back. When the court finally did issue its new plan, Tallon found himself with both good news and bad. The good news was that the new Sixth District contained 43% of his current turf. The bad news was that it was 61% black, meaning he'd have to do serious outreach against at least one prominent African-American politician.

Initially, Tallon vowed to go forward, stating, "I see this as an exciting opportunity to promote not only a better life for everyone, but to promote racial harmony." But days later, he withdrew, explaining, "This contest couldn't have done anything but further divide the races, cause racial disharmony and unrest. I don't want any part of it. It goes against everything I've worked for." An African-American State Senator, Jim Clyburn, won the primary and the subsequent general election to succeed him (he is still serving today). But with Democrat Bill Clinton having won the presidential election simultaneously, Tallon admitted his envy as he prepared to depart. "Jim Clyburn is going to be in an environment I was never fortunate enough to work in. I think it's going to be an exciting time, where we're going to make a lot of progress."

Tallon caused a bit of a stir in the year after he left office by violating a one-year ban on lobbying (the office he had paid a visit to was a visit to Clyburn's office). But beyond that, he made a career as a consultant with the Washington D.C. based consulting firm, Advantage Associates, which employed a bipartisan firm of ex-Democratic and Republican members of Congress. Bipartianship after all had always been Tallon's strong suit. Aside from counting like minded-Democrats such as Georgians Lindsay Thomas and Buddy Darden and Bill Sarpalius of Texas as his closest friends, perhaps his best pal on the GOP side was Tom DeLay, the arch-conservative fire-breathing Texan and well-known Democratic boogeyman

Claude Harris

Photo courtesy of the U.S. House of Representatives Collection

For constituents who seek a Congressman and not a publicity hound, Claude Harris is the kind of person folks dream of. The quiet, unassuming Democratic Representative from Alabama's Seventh Congressional District had a voting record that appealed to all sectors of the electorate and was devoted to the needs of his constituents in every way. The feeling became mutual - Harris took 67% and 71% in his two re-election bids. But by 1992, redistricting, specifically the VRA forced him to abandon his next campaign, a term that, had he won, he wouldn't have lived to complete.

Before going to Congress. Harris had been a Judge, a profession which prepared him well for his role in Congress, for he approached each issue with the sort of judiciousness required to perform his duties both fully informed and competently.

Harris grew up in the town of Bessemer, Alabama and took his Bachelor's and J.D. from the University of Alabama. He joined the Alabama National Guard as a Private and served in the District Attorney's office for eleven years, then became a Circuit Court Judge. Harris was absolutely devoted to his wife Barbara who, aside from being a loyal spouse, was also a partner on campaign matters: she handled his campaign finance reports. He then became a judge on Alabama's sixth circuit court, a position he held for eight years, including three as a presiding judge.

In 1986, when 7th district Congressman Richard Shelby, still a Democrat in those days, announced plans to run for the U.S. Senate, Harris entered the race to succeed him. Seven candidates entered the race though, the most serious in addition to Harris were District Attorney Billy Hill and Probate Judge William McKinley Branch. Harris, aided by 81% in Tuscaloosa, narrowly outpolled Hill but, taking 35% meant a runoff would ensue. Harris had support from the New South Coalition (NSC) headed by Birmingham Mayor Richard Arrington, which threw much support from black leaders his way. This time, Harris took 90% in Tuscaloosa

After the election, Harris sent 72 Alabama quails to House Speaker Jim Wright and House Judiciary Chairman Jack Brooks, both Texans. He ultimately was assigned to the Agriculture and Veterans Affairs Committees. In 1991, he was named to the Energy and Commerce, a prestigious assignment that was evidence of a capable balancing act between home state and partisan interests. All throughout his short tenure, he became the go-to person for many members who had questions about legislation on judicial or criminal justice matters.

Members who served with Harris made clear that Harris epitomized the term, model for probity. Fellow Alabama Democrat Glen Browder said as Harris prepared to leave office that, "If there was one word that you'd use that I think would ring a bell with those of us who served with him, it's 'straight arrow.' Claude was...the same when you saw him on the floor of the Congress or when you saw back here at a catfish fry in Alabama." One person after his death said, "Some people go to Congress dragging a load of self-importance behind them. Claude Harris pulled a U-Haul trailer. He was a man who valued horse sense over pretentiousness and people over politics."

Harris worked on the culling the infant mortality rate for Alabama, bringing the Metal Casting Center to the University of Alabama and securing veterans housing for members of the National Guard. He won money for a flood control project at Mound Hood State Park in the district and introduced the National Fire Mobilization Act to a bill to provide $100 million to rural communities that relied on volunteer firefighters (the capability of putting out forest fires was the primary concern).

Photo via Getty Images

Opposed a provision in the omnibus crime bill. His economic and social scores on the liberal Spectrum were almost next 54 to 46 conservative on economic and 52-47 unsocial in 1989. He voted for the emergency Eastern strike board, for overriding the minimum wage veto, the 1990 budget summit agreement and the Civil Rights Act as well as abortion money. But he also supported a balanced budget amendment and opposed the Family Medical Leave Act, the proposed two-month plant closing notification and severance pay for those who lost their jobs as a result of the Clean Air Act. He did back the controversial Gephardt Amendment.

Harris's Achilles Heel for a long and successful Congressional career was redistricting. Under a revision to the Voting Rights Act of 1992, Alabama was required to draw one African-American majority district. The negotiations were protracted and down-to-the-wire. Legislative Democrats passed a map which was vetoed by Republican Governor Guy Hunt. The Legislature overrode his veto. Ultimately, however, the Justice Department rejected that proposal and enacted a map that had already been drawn up found Harris in a district that would jump from 30% African-American, to 67%, making the odds of someone with his moderate voting record prevailing in a primary next to impossible. The date was March 28, ten days prior to the filing deadline.

Initially, Harris vowed to challenge his friend, colleague, and fellow Democrat Ben Erdreich in the Sixth district where Erdreich himself was reeling from his cozy Birmingham base being carved up to make way for the majority-minority district. But on April 3, he yielded to the political realities and announced his retirement. In doing so, he took a stab at the process which forced his political demise: "I regret that due to actions beyond my ability to influence or control, the 7th District has been destroyed. This purely partisan action had nothing to do with meeting the legitimate aspirations of black Alabamians to select one of their own to the Congress." Harris also noted that, "I wanted to get out of the way and let other people who may be thinking about running know what I was going to do before the deadline. I think that's only fair." A true gentleman to the end, Harris rented his Washington apartment to his successor, Democrat Earl Hilliard.

Months after he left office, Harris was nominated for the position of U.S. Attorney for the Northern District of Alabama (Birmingham) by President Clinton. It culminated a long game of suspense that saw Harris and —but had little time to savor it: he was diagnosed with lung cancer the following May. He died that October, nearly a year to the day after achieving the position at age 54.

Tragically, aside from the two Congressmen who died before the 102nd Congress ended, Harris was the first member of the large number of '92 departures to pass. Walter Braswell, his loyal aide was appointed to replace him as U.S. Attorney (Braswell himself succumbed to cancer at age 56). In a moment that had to have been considered bittersweet to say the least, Harris's second granddaughter was born just days before. His estate later sued for claims of asbestos.

Image via C-SPAN

Patterson Adroitly Held Very Republican South Carolina District Until Reality Caught Up

Introductory Tidbit: In a recent oral history project for the Library of Congress, Liz Patterson recounts the story of a visit to the office of House Speaker Jim Wright.in her early days in Congress. When he asked her about how the life of a Congresswoman was treating her, Patterson replied that she had "one complaint." She explained that, "all through orientation, and even now, you all don't seem to realize that there are women here." When Wright asked for an explanation, Patterson explained, "Well, every place I go, it's 'Fellas, let's get ready and do this.' 'Fellas, let's get ready and do this.' It just seems to me, you could have said something, 'colleagues,' or something besides 'fellas.'" At that point, Wright opened a dictionary and found the word "fellow." Of course, it's not male—"fellowship." His explanation: "So we really weren't talking you all down. We were including you. In this fellowship, we're all together." Patterson recalls, "I had to sort of smile and say, "Well, that's not quite how I take it, but thank you.'" But she added that Wright treated her very well as a member.

Photo via the Congressional Bio Guide

For six years, Democratic Congresswoman Liz Patterson carved a nice niche between her party and her very conservative constituency in the Fourth District of South Carolina and despite an initially precarious electoral position, it seemed as though her constituents had made the distinction between her voting record and party as well. In 1992, however, Patterson became one of the year's biggest upset victims as she was unseated by a hard-charging rabble-rousing lawyer in what became a harbinger of what would transpire throughout the South in 1994 and the ensuing years.

Patterson learned early lessons about straddling between the national party and Democrats in South Carolina. Her father, Olin Johnston, served as Governor and Senator of the Palmetto State and was sometimes at odds with Northern members on the issue of civil rights. In an uncanny occurrence that could only happen in states with politicians who routinely serve since the War of the Roses, both U.S. senators from South Carolina during Patterson's time in Congress, Strom Thurmond and Ernest "Fritz" Hollings, had faced Johnston in statewide elections. It was at that time that Hollings was exposed to Liz Patterson. While recalling Johnston, "beat the hell out of me, Liz worked in that campaign, and I found out then that she could make a talk." But on matters beyond civil rights, Johnston was firmly in the corner of the little people, often supporting Democratic social programs and generous benefits to the thousands of textile workers prevalent in his state. Patterson would emulate her father and make a hallmark of showing an impeccable devotion to people.

Patterson on the lap of her father, Governor and later Senator Olin Johnston (left) and with both her parents (right)
Photo courtesy of the Elizabeth J. Patterson Papers, South Carolina Political Collections, University of South Carolina

Patterson's early exposure to politics went well beyond the dining room table. Her mother was Olin's campaign manager who herself gave many a political stump speech and Margaret Chase Smith, the sole woman in the Senate at that time, was Liz's political role model. Patterson got her undergraduate degree from Columbia College. After a year of graduate school at the University of South Carolina, she earned a summer internship in Washington, DC as a recruiting officer for the Peace Corps which was in its infancy. She decided to forego her second year of graduate school to accept a job with VISTA (Volunteers In Service To America) in the office of public affairs. After the death of her father in 1965, she returned home to South Carolina to work for the Office of Economic Opportunity establishing Head Start offices. In 1970, she left her job with Head Start when she became pregnant with her first child which began a pattern of balancing her family and her career in public service. After the birth of her first son, she went on to work for the local Congressman whose seat she would one day hold, Jim Mann. She left Mann's office because, "that was about the time that my family decided that I needed another child, so it was about the time I had to stay home with children." But once she decided to seek elected office, she advanced relatively quickly.

Patterson's career began with a seat on the Spartanburg County Council and in keeping with the theme of her career, she was the first woman to hold that post. It's not that Patterson possessed any burning desire to run but, two men well connected with county politics offered to give her campaign $100 should she run. As Patterson recalled for the oral history project, "$100 to them was a lot of money, but it wasn't a whole lot of money for a campaign. So there were men who really supported me. "It was in that role (on County Council) that she "learned that you have to compromise, you have to work with other members"

One discovery Patterson made on County Council was that the state had a way of forcing unfunded mandates down to local governments. How did Patterson propose rectifying that? By running for a seat in the South Carolina Senate. It was 1978 and she was the only woman at the time. In fact, the male colleague with whom Patterson would be sharing an office openly wondered if, "she'll make us paint this office pink" (it was already pink). She initially chose to sit on the Education Committee as well as the Medical Affairs and Corrections & Penology committees. Eventually, she secured a spot on the Judiciary committee (even though her colleagues acknowledged she was not a lawyer). In her last term, took a seat on the mighty Senate Finance Committee.

In 1986, Patterson decided to throw her hat into the ring for the congressional seat being vacated by Carroll Campbell, a Republican who was running for governor. It was a heavily Republican district and Patterson's chances were all but discounted. Geography seemed to make her goal even more unattainable - Greenville encompassed more than half of the district and no member of Congress had hailed from outside of the county in 68 years. That record seemed poised to continue when Greenville Mayor William Workman won the GOP nomination. But there were major cliques in the race for that party's nomination.

Supporters of the other candidate in the Republican primary, airline pilot Ted Adams, had tagged Workman as beholden to "fat cats," and his supporters remained bitter after his defeat. Many were affiliated with the influential evangelical wing of the party. To circumvent that, Workman felt he couldn't lose by tying Patterson to the liberal agenda of her party, proclaiming that she "will go up there and be a friend and ally of the Tip O'Neills of the Congress." But Workman proved less than an ideal candidate. Meanwhile, Patterson encountered resistance, spoken and not because she was a mother. To counter that, her campaign ran an ad with shots of her kids going off to school, Patterson legislating in Columbia and, "the final shot (where) I was back home, sitting on the floor playing Scrabble with my children. So that commercial supposedly showed that I could be wife, mom, and legislator." Voters gave her the benefit and Patterson was elected 52-48%. Her victory made her the first South Carolina female (and to this date the only) to serve in Congress without succeeding her husband.

Campaigning with Jim Mann in her quest to win South Carolina's Fourth Congressional District in 1986
Photo courtesy of the Elizabeth J. Patterson Papers, South Carolina Political Collections, University of South Carolina

Former Democratic State Party Chair Frank Holleman later called the '86 race "one of the elections where the outcome was really a function of a person, and her personality." That became a hallmark throughout her service. During her 1990 re-election campaign, *The State* wrote of how, "In this bellwether community of Greenville County, Democrat Liz Patterson's greatest asset appears to be Liz Patterson. Voters like her not so much because of her record, which is conservative, but because she comes across as a genuinely decent, kind and caring person." At a 2015 testimonial, her former staffer, the Reverend Rob Brown told the story of how Patterson was running extremely late to a fundraising event but insisted on stopping at a nursing home to visit a constituent who had written her. Brown protested but Patterson responded, "It's never about money. It's always about people." That was a chip off the old block as Patterson told a 2017 oral history project how, "My dad never missed speaking to somebody. You know, if there was a crowd, he worked the whole crowd."

The truth is, some members of Congress were better about asking for money than others and Patterson fell firmly into the latter. "There was too much emphasis on raising money when I was here. I'm not good at it, for one thing," she confided in the oral history interview.

Patterson was one of two Democratic females in the class of '86. The other was Louise Slaughter, a Kentucky born Congresswoman from New York. Slaughter's Southern accent was distinct while Patterson's was not, leaving a number of folks to mistake Slaughter as the Congresswoman from South Carolina (the two were close friends). She was also helped by the fact that a number of colleagues had been well acquainted with her father, among them "Lindy" Boggs of Louisiana.

When it came time to select committees, Patterson made two choices. One – Veterans Affairs, was predictable (one in nine constituents were veterans and she had spoken about issues of importance to them often during her campaign). Her second choice shocked nearly everyone: Banking and Urban Affairs. The post had little power in those days but Patterson said she, 'was looking at what issue was right before us at that time – it was trade." But then somebody told her, "You know, it also does housing. And I was interested then in several issues dealing with housing. I felt more comfortable about going on that. Banker friends at home wanted me to go on the, wanted to have representation on that committee." One initiative she worked on with North Carolina Democrat David Price was early pre-payment of low income mortgages by developers.

A meaningful piece of legislation Patterson passed called for excess space at veteran facilities to be used for day care for the children of nurses & staff. The inception of the bill came from an administrator of a VA in North Carolina who had complained to Patterson that he was losing good employees due to the lack of options for their young children. Another concept she championed: full credits for veterans pursuing technical degrees at vocational schools.

Patterson, on Capitol Hill (left) was a member of the Banking Committee during her tenure in Congress (right) Photo courtesy of the Elizabeth J. Patterson Papers, South Carolina Political Collections, University of South Carolina

Not surprisingly, Patterson's voting record was near the conservative end of her party, though she did try to compile a "South Carolina first" record. She opposed overriding Bush's veto of both the 1989 minimum wage increase and the Family and Medical Leave Act, supported the anti-flag desecration amendment and refused to prohibit employers from hiring permanent replacement workers to take the place of strikers (the delegation was united on that one). She was one of a dozen Democrats to vote to censure Barney Frank but Frank liked her very much and gave her his blessing to do so beforehand (he did not want any fellow Democrats to pay a political price defending his bad judgements). She did vote to override President George H.W. Bush's veto of the Civil Rights Restoration Act. Patterson was an opponent of abortion but did have limits and federal funding for rape and incest victims were among them, as were allowing the procedure to be performed at military installations. Patterson also opted against the "gag rule," calling it unrealistic to tell a doctor "he doesn't have a right to counsel his patients."

On economic issues, Patterson supported Bush's proposed capital gains tax and was despondent when Congressional leaders of her own party lobbied against the Balanced Budget Amendment and ultimately were successful in killing it. "I'm really angry at all the pressure from special-interest groups and lobbyists. People were really twisting arms. It just wasn't the way it was supposed to be." She voted for the authorization of force against Iraq.

Patterson fought to limit textile imports, opposing Bush on his veto of the textile import restrictions legislation and even traveling to China, a nation that was responsible for the largest trade deficit. As her third term neared an end, she was named chair of the Congressional Textile Caucus. She was a fierce promoter of anti-drug legislation.

Patterson had a genuine interest in deficit reduction and she chaired the Conservative Democratic Forum's Task Force on Budget Reform. She was also a sponsor of the Budget Simplification and Reform Act.

Patterson's first re-election campaign in 1988 was arguably as tough – if not tougher, than even her '86 race. It became obvious that Bush would be polling Herculean numbers in the Fourth district and this time, the GOP would not be squandering its chances on an ill-advised nominee. It was actually the opposite.

Greenville Councilman and former Campbell aide Knox White was her opponent and Campbell was profuse, if not exorbitant in letting his former constituents know his feelings toward him. White hitched his fortunes to Bush's, saying, "I want to work with George Bush, not against him," and mentioned Patterson's backing of Dukakis, though Patterson had caused a stir within her delegation by skipping the Democratic National Convention in Atlanta that July.

Still, White's campaign manager, Bob Knight said "We want to be able to talk about issues. Does she represent us or would he represent us better?" Patterson called that, "a bumper-sticker mentality that twists complex issues into misleading and meaningless one-liners. But in Congress, I can tell you that bumper-stickers don't fly and rhetorical one-liners don't get critical legislation passed." She said in a debate that, "I go to vote as the people of the

Fourth District would have me vote." White claimed Patterson had not been sufficiently supportive of Reagan's defense budget.

On Election Day, Bush ran strong, taking 67% but, enough voters split tickets to enable her to run 20 points ahead of Dukakis, and she retained her seat 52-48%. Patterson's 4,000 vote edge for much of the night ballooned to 7,000 as Union reported late. After that brouhaha, no one on either side could have possibly predicted that Patterson would have it easy for 1990 but, circumstances made that happen as the candidate Republicans were most excited about, State Senator David Thomas bowed out suddenly during the Spring. That left the nomination to House Minority Leader Terry Haskins. Patterson may have earned kudos in this conservative turf by opposing the budget summit package and took 61%, even carrying Greenville for the first (and only) time in her career. Though she would never be perpetually safe, the expectation was that she had weathered the electoral storm for future campaigns. Her name was even mentioned as a possible contender for governor in 1994. But first she had to get past '92.

An analogy for Patterson's surprise '92 loss might be that she was jumped from behind. But in actuality, she might have missed several warning signs or failed to take an advantage of an opportunity to stop a few Inglis campaign incomings. One precursor to Patterson's danger might have come as early as April of that year when Inglis came fairly close to matching Patterson's cash on hand.

Inglis campaigned on a distinct anti-Congress theme. Patterson was a member of the "imperial Congress," and he tagged her as a part of the House Bank and Post Office scandals, even though she bounced zero checks and wasn't implicated in any scandal. He swore off PAC money. When Inglis first tried that theme, Patterson responded, "My comment is 'welcome aboard'" She spoke of reducing the deficit. The turning point might have come the weekend before the election when the Christian Coalition distributed 200,000 leaflets to churchgoers. They re-enforced this criticism with radio ads the Monday before the election. Still, Patterson appeared in virtually no danger. A poll released slightly more than a week out gave her a near majority – 49.4% with Inglis stuck at 30%.

While Patterson increased her margin in Union to 69%, her deficit in Greenville (42-58%) and her winning margin in Spartanburg (56-44%), decreased from prior elections which produced a 52-48% win for Inglis. Furman University political scientist Don Aiesi called the district, "the only place in America where Bush had any coattails." Patterson pronounced herself, "not surprised. I'm disappointed. I really, really believe that I was a public servant, that I was serving the people and doing the best of my ability." She also cited the dearth of representation from outside of Greenville prior to her own election, saying, "You always have to figure when you have a Republican from Greenville, it's going to be a very tough race." She also blamed Inglis's tactics and the Christian Coalition, saying, "I think he linked me with all the bad things in Congress when there was no connection. I thought the people knew me, but evidently the people saw all this and thought, 'Maybe he is right.'" Patterson told an oral history project a quarter of a century after her defeat that, "After the campaign, I went around to several of the churches and told them I was sorry they put that information out, and I tried to straighten them out on it, but they were pro-life, and didn't like anything that I had to say. I'd always point out to them, 'I have an adopted child. You think I don't believe in life?' It's crazy. It was a big issue."

Patterson also felt burned by Bush. "When I had met with the President on some votes," she recalled, "He assured me and other Democrats who helped on certain issues, 'Don't worry, I will not come to your district.'" He did not keep that word during the '92 cycle, stumping in the Fourth District and Inglis believes that swung the election.

But there were at least some signs that Patterson failed to seize opportunities to respond. In particular, Inglis hit her with criticisms and challenged her to a number of public opportunities to respond but she didn't.

In 1994, Patterson, who following her upset vowed to "take it one day at a time," aimed for a political comeback and won the Democratic nomination for Lieutenant Governor of South Carolina. But 1994 was not the year for Democrats to be making comebacks and Patterson lost to Bob Peeler, who sought notoriety via a 14-foot plastic cow, 50-45%. She began working at Converse College and completed a Master's degree in liberal arts with an emphasis in politics. She also taught political science for several years at Spartanburg Methodist College.

Patterson remained active in the Democratic Party for the rest of her life and is uniformly well-regarded as a trailblazer for South Carolina women. She died in 2018 at age 79.

CHAPTER SIXTY-TWO

Ben Jones Brought a Bit of "Cooter" to Capitol Hill

Introductory Quote: "If you ask Ben Jones what he had for breakfast this morning he won't say, 'Two ovals encased in an enamel-like covering.' He'll say he had eggs, and that's what I like about him. He'll say, 'Your mama died,' or 'Get your hand off my knee' - he's direct and he tells it like it is." – Georgia State Senator Lawrence "Bud" Stumbaugh on Ben Jones

Photo courtesy of the U.S. House of Representatives Collection

B en Jones might not be the most recognized name among political junkies and Congressional scholars but, mention Cooter Davenport and that's entirely different. An auto-mechanic on the long-running "Dukes of Hazard," Cooter became an icon for ordinary men in hillbilly country who were content to practice their vocation while serving as trustworthy confidantes to friends and townspeople. After "Dukes" went off the air, Jones saw an opportunity to put those traits to use in another way - public service. In 1988, he won a seat in the House from Georgia's Fourth Congressional District. It came on his second try and while Jones learned that solving the problems of the nation were far more complex than fixing the "General Lee," he throughout his four years in office displayed the same characteristics of accessibility and generosity to his colleagues and constituents that made him beloved in Hazard County, Georgia.

Jones's family stability belied the fact that he was a very troubled youth. Born in Portsmouth, Virginia, his dad was a railroad section chief and his mother a homemaker and someone who was happiest when she was singing (to her, "it was just like talking"). Jones was called "Buster" while his siblings were nicknamed Buck and Bubba (their actual names were Hubert, and James). He was an early lover of baseball and played for his local team – the Cardinals while in grammar school and recounts breaking the windshield of a townsman's '32 Chevy while hitting a ball.

The South was heavily segregated in those times but, Jones in his book, *Redneck Boy in the Promised Land: The Confessions of Crazy Cooter*, made clear that people at least in his locale would be hard-pressed to know it. "It always seemed to me that folks overlooked the fact that segregation was, in many ways very integrated. As much as the white power structure tried to separate the races, the fact remained that we were all around one another just about all the time: on the street, at work, and in the stores." Jones was still keenly aware of segregation and throughout life, would constantly be doing his part to right it. He and friends began conducting sit-ins at local eateries including Brady's Restaurant and the Tar Heel Sandwich Shop. Eventually and predictably, Jones got himself arrested. And this proved a further eye-opener. "In a cell with four bunks," he wrote, "there were twenty-two prisoners, singing and back-slapping like it was a pep rally. Among the arrested there was Father Clarence Parker, an Episcopal Priest. The kindly father was 82-years old."

By the late 1960s, Jones had been performing in a number of local acting roles. In 1969, on the tip of a friend, Jones moved to Atlanta to pursue additional roles. "It had a vitality and a freshness that I had not seen in many other places," and he used it to ends that would enable him to change the trajectory of his life. First, he got the part of the Giant in "Jack and the Beanstalk" at the Alliance Theater. He did everything from plays, commercials and movies." In 1972, he got a part in "Summer and Smoke," a film produced by the husband of actor Eva Marie Saint and appeared in "Smokey and the Bandit."

Life took rapid turns from there. First came Jones's epiphany that alcohol was not his salvation which came in 1977 – September 25, when he checked himself into a clinic. A year later, he was an actor on an internationally known television series that encapsulated the stereotypes of life in a small, rural deep southern county.

To say his life changed in a jiffy was an understatement. In 1975, Jones had auditioned for the subplot that became "The Dukes of Hazard," the first cast member to do so. Its success was expected to be non-existent and off the air in no time. Instead, the series lasted seven years and became an icon for generations.

Jones was cast as the role of "Cooter Davenport," the wily owner of "Cooter's Garage" in townsquare (a "Cooter" was a large freshwater turtle). His insignia might have been his routine greetings on the CB. The introduction: "Breaker one, Breaker one, I might be crazy but I ain't dumb, Craaaazy Cooter comin' atcha, come on." Crazy, he could be. Cooter once stole the Sheriff's patrol car and "borrowed" the President's limousine. But Cooter was harmless and in turn, beloved by fans and the Duke's for whom he routinely teamed with to use subterfuge for foil against the overzealous Sheriff Roscoe P. Coltrane and Boss Hogg.

Cooter took a slight absence during the second season of the Dukes when a dispute with producers over whether he should have a beard proved temporarily irreconcilable. The producers wanted it removed while Jones's responded, "I've got to feel right about doing this and I don't want to play a stereotype." That produced a stalemate which led to him briefly walking out, though a compromise was subsequently worked out.

Jones's favorite episode was entitled, "Nancy Lou," where his daughter returns to Hazzard County thinking his father had kicked his old barroom habits only to catch him in a brawl. Again, Jones brought a piece of himself to the episode. "Everyone knew what I had been like and what Cooter had been like so, it was easy to believe that we were once wild and settled down."

Jones became friends with a number of cast members, including Catherine Bach who played the legendary "Daisy Duke," later saying, "She had the best legs in the history of legs." Even as a member of Congress, Jones made clear that he could easily emulate Cooter, reminding people that, "What a lot of people don't know is that Cooter may have been a garage mechanic but he was also the smartest man in town. He could fix anything. And he was a loyal friend indeed to everyone."

The Dukes' successful run ended in 1985 but Jones had bigger fish to fry: elective office. Georgia's Fourth Congressional District had a freshman

Republican Congressman named Pat Swindall who was quickly becoming a master of self-destruction.

Jones labeled himself, "An old alkie actor who came out of nowhere to take on Ken and Barbie." Politically, he was "an old-fashioned Southern, moderate Democrat and I look at both sides of the issue. Pat doesn't." He vowed to make public education a focal point of his campaign. And of course, his candidacy invited predictable press with *The Atlanta Journal Constitution* running with the headline, "Dukes' actor might hazard a run at politics."

From the very beginning, Jones, like Cooter and the beard, decided that being anything other than authentic was not his shtick. He never thought to rewrite his past and, in admitted he had tried marijuana twice, joked that, "I could have said I was the guy who never exhaled." On another occasion, Jones admitted he, "had more bones in my closet than the Smithsonian Institution," but added, "My life is not a story about falling down but a story about getting up."

The race was hard fought throughout. Former President Gerald Ford stumped for Swindall. On Swindall's contention that Jones was spewing mud (Swindall did admit to being "far too thin-skinned to be a politician"), Jones replied, "He doesn't know the difference between being hit below the belt and being kicked in the rear."

On abortion, Jones said, "If I had my druthers, any abortion would take place in the first trimester" while Swindall said, "the circumstances under which a child is conceived is not really relevant to the real issue regarding abortion." They argued over Star Wars funding, and Swindall's votes to cut Social Security. Jones alleged a sweetheart deal on an issue of Swindall's new home and while the Congressman replied that, "what's relevant in this campaign is the federal budget, not my family's personal budget," events years down the road would prove Jones's query prescient.

Swindall had predicted he'd take the election with roughly 65%. The final margin was a little closer – he did hang on but by only 53-47%. Jones, who had actually attended an Atlanta Hawks basketball game early in the evening made clear when it was evident Swindall had won that his political career was only in its salad days. "My momma didn't raise no fool," he said. "We won something very important. We came within an eyelash of winning."

The entertainer declared early that he would go for a second act and seek to finish the job two years down the road. He did but the battle scars, as summed up by *The Atlanta Journal Constitution* near the campaign's end, were evident. "U.S. Rep. Pat Swindall," the paper wrote, "has compared campaigning for his 4ᵗʰ District seat to being in labor. Ben Jones, Mr. Swindall›s Democratic challenger, has likened it to fighting alligators and to getting a root canal. The national media has judged it No. 1 for viciousness."

In the primary, Attorney Nick Moraitakis ("Some people call me Dukakis") outspent Jones 2-1 but Jones, who had the backing of powerful Georgia House Speaker Tom Murphy, still prevailed with 62%. Swindall immediately issued him a congratulatory message with one big caveat. We can "focus on the significant issues about which we differ. Before we can focus on those issues, however…I'm asking you to obtain and release a copy of your complete driving records…criminal arrest records and your complete health records." This forced Jones to attest to his sobriety which he said he had since 1977. Swindall dredged up battery charges against Jones from when he shoved his wife from a long-ago second marriage but Jones blamed that on alcohol. Jones countere with ammunition on Swindall, specifically a 1980 traffic incident in which he had left the scene of a crime. He called Swindall, "painfully thin."

On the issues, Swindall gave Jones ammunition, particularly his call to turn a program for disadvantage children into a voucher system.

This time, Swindall had problems that he had been without in '88 and they would define the race. Swindall had arranged for an $850,000 loan from a businessman, Charles La Chasney to renovate his condo but little did he know that the businessman doing the biddingwas an IRS agent, Mike Mullaney who told Swindall that the cash was "drug money." Swindall promised to look the other way.

The events of October were clearly not what Swindall had had in mind. As the month began, he was calling for his own indictment so a speedy trial could commence and reveal his innocence before the voters made their own judgement. He almost got his wish. The indictment was issued October 17 and charged that Swindall had lied ten times to a grand jury the previous February. In an extraordinary action, Judge Robert Vining agreed to expedite the trial, scheduling jury selection for the following week. In an even further unheard of move, Swindall convinced the legal team of another defendant to switch trial dates so his matter could be adjudicated first and all sides agreed. A defiant and perhaps impervious Swindall summarized the episode by saying, "The whole thing sounds like a bad spy novel."

By this time, Jones was leading Swindall by 18 points, though he vowed it wouldn't alter his strategy. "I'm not going to assume anything. We are going to continue exactly the kind of campaign we've been running." He said Swindall's legal difficulties are "not something I've been talking about in the campaign, and I'm not going to make it part of the campaign now." He needn't have as Swindall succeeded in doing it for him.

One campaign ad that Swindall submitted intended to inform voters that he had taken and passed a polygraph exam backfired when the Judge was forced to dismiss the jury because at least one reported receiving campaign literature of the sort. Even when attempting to defuse his perilous situation, Swindall found himself on the defensive. When he suggested that Jones had advance knowledge of the LeChesney tapes, Jones responded by invoking Abe Lincoln: "The thing that kills the skunk is his own publicity."

The fact of the matter was that, the publicity surrounding Swindall coming so close to Election Day cemented the matter in voters' minds and when the vote was held, the outcome was not ambiguous. Jones trounced him 60-40%, carrying every county, even heavily Republican Rockford (though the margin was within 50 votes). Nationally, only six incumbents fell to challengers that day but Jones's margin was the widest. The euphoric Congressman-elect told his supporters, "The eagle has landed. We have struggled together, persevered together, endured together. And now we have prevailed together...You have done something that they said was impossible."

Swindall by contrast had been predicting "a miracle" as late as 9 p.m., but, when he finally conceded an hour later, he for once was able to accurately forecast one prophecy. "If I remember correctly, old Abraham Lincoln had a few losses. I guess if we've got to lose one, I'd rather lose tonight than at the trial. I've got more to worry about than politics" (to his credit, he lived up to his vow to facilitate a smooth transition for Jones and his staff). In June 1989, Swindall was convicted of perjury. He said he felt he had "been forgiven by God and my constituents," his 20 point loss evidently notwithstanding. But after countless appeals, he finally reported to prison in 1994.

Jones would serve two terms in Congress and during that time, walked a fine line between supporting his party and trying to please constituents in a district that had given President George H.W. Bush 59%. For starters, he won seats on the Public Works and Transportation Committee and Veterans Affairs. He was pro-choice, opposed school prayer and supported the minimum wage override and aid to the National Endowment for the Arts which were national Democratic priorities. He also backed a creation of an independent Eastern Airlines strike board that his suburban Atlanta Republican colleague and future opponent, Newt Gingrich, so vociferously opposed. But he supported the capital gains tax cut that Bush was making the centerpiece of his economic plan and, despite intensive lobbying, opposed the Family and Medical Leave Act. He voted to enact the controversial House pay raise but also voted with the majority in a divided House in backing an ethics package which prohibited, among other things, members accepting honoraria.

On international matters, Jones traveled to the Eastern bloc following the fall of the Berlin Wall, was a strong supporter of aiding the Nicaraguan contras and voted in favor of "temporary protected status" for dissidents from that nation, El Salvador, and China.

Locally, securing $23 million in improvements for Atlanta's MARTA train system was a big get. The line, he said, "runs parallel to one of the heaviest-traveled corridors in Atlanta, and this will help alleviate traffic congestion in one of the fastest-growing areas of" the district.

On issues, the notoriety Jones most achieved in Congress had to do with his outspoken opposition to the proposed amendment banning desecration of the American flag. The stance was risky. Jones knew that the amendment had wide support in his district but, he refused to be abandon his unease about enacting it. "Something that folks loathe almost as much as flag burners is politicians who demagogue, who wrap themselves in the flag for some partisan votes." He went on to say that if "we yield to the pond scum" that is burning a flag, America would be giving away much of the principles for which it so renowned.

Personality-wise, Jones was highly refreshing in Congress and routinely found himself a draw among a number of Democratic colleagues in districts that bore resemblance to Hazard County, Georgia. And despite not having a seat of his own, he was happy to do his part to make sure they returned. These members included Carroll Hubbard of Kentucky, Robin Tallon of South Carolina and Harley Staggers of West Virginia (he joked at one that, "I did talk to Uncle Jesse, and he said times are tough in Hazard County").

Lacking an opponent filled with skeletons in his closet, it was inherently obvious that Jones would face a far tougher road for a second term than his first ("Jones was elected, Swindall was unelected," Billy Thorne said). The party settled early on John Linder, a State Senator and dentist to take him on. A number of national Republicans, including, Vice-President Dan Quayle and Utah Senator Orrin Hatch made early visits to stump for Linder. *CQ* explained the narrative of the race by saying "Linder paints Jones as a slick actor hiding behind a down-home accent" and the flag bill was exhibit A. Linder also invoked his opponent's stardom, accusing Jones of being "kind of caught up with his celebrity status" who "seems to be raising more money for others than himself." Jones's retort: "The only thing me and Jane Fonda have in common is a desire to lose weight."

Then came 1992. To say that redistricting left Jones with few good choices was an understatement. His home was removed from the Fourth District but, more ominously, so were a number of black precincts that made running for re-election under those lines a dicey proposition, and in fact a Republican (Linder as a matter of fact), did end up winning the seat. Thus, Jones decided to aim for the 10th District which spanned from Gwinnett County in suburban Atlanta to Athens and Augusta, the latter in areas that his Democratic colleague, Doug Barnard, was leaving behind. But Jones's past to the nomination proved difficult for a number of reasons, not the least of which was the fact that he was facing a well-regarded State Senator, Don Johnson, who not only chaired the Appropriations Committee but had an influential role on the redistricting panel. As expected, he had widespread influence over how the lines would be drawn. Three other candidates were also in the race.

Johnson's modus operendi against Jones was to essentially tar him as an insider. He attacked him for the pay raise and for his vote against closing the House bank saying, "He went to Washington as 'Cooter,'" Jones said, "but came back to Georgia as Boss Hogg." Jones struck back by claiming Johnson was aware of corruption in the legislature. Johnson's ads were criticized even by fellow Democrats as over the top and Jones responded that, "Everybody knows when a guy's on the ropes he starts throwing low blows. People are tired of this negative stuff - they want to talk about jobs. Since Don has attacked me for voting as a Democrat, I'm starting to wonder whether he got in the wrong line at qualifying."

Unfortunately, despite polls showing Jones running 20-points ahead, in actuality, it was he who was on the ropes and *The Atlanta Journal* endorsed Johnson. When Johnson began primary night with a large lead, Jones initially hoped to force a runoff, saying, "If Johnson drops under 50 percent, that sound he hears is me sharpening my cleats." But as it became clear that wasn't going to happen, Jones conceded and told supporters, "We ran a high-road campaign, and I hope he understands that the people deserve better than someone who will do anything or say anything to get elected. The people have spoken, and I have accepted their verdict. I have had a great run for six years, and I thank the people of Georgia for the privilege of serving them." Johnson ultimately took 53% as Jones was relegated to just 30% and refused to extend his backing to the victor, claiming, "I lost because I refused to get down in the ditch with my opponent, who had one of the most relentless negative attacks in recent memory."

Two years later, Jones attempted a comeback but, it was the most inhospitable of places in the most inhospitable of years against the toughest possible opponent. The place was Georgia's Sixth District where Minority Whip Newt Gingrich was seeking re-election. Jones was under no illusions about the task at hand. "This is a mighty steep and a mighty long hill to climb," he told his supporters. "He's going to try to paint me somewhere to the left of Trotsky." Still, he was getting into the race because Gingrich, "poisoned the well of politics for his own purposes."

Jones put on a brave face throughout the campaign but by that time Gingrich, who had survived a number of near death scrapes in the Sixth, was trying to orchestrate a Republican takeover of the House. Jones nonetheless tried to caricaturize Gingrich's prior image and produced a short ad that *The Atlanta Journal and Constitution* commented, "looks and sounds like a music video, with jumpy editing and a hip-hop beat, and its verbal message is minimal. But the message Jones wanted to get out was unmistakable." A grew of people would chant, "Newt," then someone else, a "cooler," person as *The Journal* wrote would respond, "Not." Jones could be less subtle for his distaste of Gingrich, at one point stating, "Oh, f-- him and the horse he rode in on." One newspaper got in on the fortuitous pun-names opened the story with the headline, "Cooter Tries to Neuter the Newtster."

When Gingrich cancelled a scheduled debate to stump for a fellow Republican in Wisconsin. Jones in turn followed him to the "Badger" State and did a little "Badgering" of his own, calling Gingrich a "wuss" (Jones took part in the debate solo). It was not a Democratic-friendly year, however and Gingrich's "Contract With America" only fueled his popularity and enabled him to defeat Jones 64-36%.

Jones might have been out of office but for his Hazzard fans and cast members, no title was necessary for their affection. Catherine "Daisy Duke" Bach said for this book, "All of us on 'The Dukes' were so very proud of Ben's political career. He was always so caring and down to earth in his public life, just as he was on our show. When we did our first 'reunion' movie, 'Cooter' came back as the Congressman from Hazzard County. Ben was always so articulate about the things he cares about, and he is just as down to earth as 'Cooter' was."

Jones relocated to Virginia and made one more try for elective office in 2002, taking on freshman Republican Eric Cantor in fertilely Republican territory but failed to draw a third of the vote (he did carry Rappahannock). In later years, he had a stint in the movie, "Primary Colors." He has opened a number of stores, including "Cooter's Place," in Sperryville, Virginia and Tennessee. His life has clearly progressed by his motto, "When one door closes, another opens. It's only a question of how long you stand in the hallway."

Jones (top row, far right) with the Duke's cast members
Photo courtesy of Cooter's Place

CHAPTER SIXTY-THREE

Traxler's Love for Mackinac Island Was as Strong As Aiding Michigan Via Appropriations

Introductory Quote: "I told the commissioner, if you do nothing for me, I don't mind asking you to, but if you were to hold the first drawing in Bay City, I'd be grateful." – Bob Traxler in a 2008 oral history project recalling how he subtly convinced the new Michigan lottery commissioner to hold the first drawing in Traxler's hometown (Traxler was a founding father of the Michigan legislature).

Photos courtesy of Bob Traxler

Shortly before Bob Traxler won a U.S. House seat in a 1974 special election, a friend labeled him someone who likes to "talk, argue, scheme, drink line, and maneuver." Those very qualities might have been a secret to his success, not just in winning and nailing down a seat that had been a longtime GOP bastion, but of holding it with immense popularity for just shy of two decades.

Traxler was a consummate politician as they come, wheeling and dealing, securing high ranking committee assignments and bringing home the pork. He was also, as *Politics in America* called him "boisterous almost to the point of being clownish," and that's often an effective method when trying to disarm or win over critics. But those very same qualities and a deep understanding of his people not only gave his folks a voice in Washington but helped many projects turn into realities in his state.

Traxler was born in the rural town of Kawkawlin to a mailman and farmer and young Bob himself, as *The New York Times* pointed out, had "hoed beans and topped beets along with the rest of the commonfolk." But he described his life as, "kind of a Huckleberry Finn. We built rafts for the river, we swam in the river. We skated there and played hockey in the winter. It was an idyllic existence. Bay City was five miles away." More importantly, as he told Bill Ballenger in a Michigan State university Oral History Project, it gave me an insight into the farm community of Michigan."

After attending Bay City Junior College for two years, Traxler transferred to Michigan State University to finish his undergraduate work in Political Science with a History minor (he was in the Army at that time as well). When he first told his father of his plan to attend law school, his response was, "So you want to be a crook?" But he was quite successful, to the point that, not long after obtaining his J.D., from Detroit College of Law, he was an assistant Bay County prosecutor.

In 1962, Traxler was elected to the first of six terms in the Michigan House and any doubt that he would simply toil behind the scenes would be quickly evaporated when in just his first year, the capital press rated him the most effective legislator. Though Traxler recalled during the oral history project that, "I was in my caucus rather aggressive, impatient and keenly involved with policy issues," he was evidently doing something right because respect among his colleagues was evident and he concedes, "I sort of stirred up the cozy relationship that existed between Republicans and Democrats."

In his second term, Traxler would be Majority Floor Leader (Democrats had won the majority in '64). But Democrats suffered a big loss in 1966 and Traxler concedes that he might have instigated too much progressive legislation because when he asked one of his defeated members what went wrong he replied, "Bob, you did too damn much." Be that as it may, the show went on. Traxler would transfer to the Judiciary Committee and eventually become chair. *The New York Times* noted that as a State House member, Traxler wrote "or championed bills on drug law reform, no fault divorce, no-insurance, aid to church supported schools, the state lottery and the lifting of criminal penalties for alcoholism." He got a revision of the criminal code through the House (though not the Senate) and a Judicial Tenure Commission created. In 1972, he inserted legislation into a highway package funding "critical maintenance" money for bridges.

Bringing the lottery to the Wolverine State was undoubtedly Traxler's crown jewel and with adroit maneuvering becoming of a true political master, he used his proximity to House Speaker Bill Ryan to arrange to have the legislation routed to Judiciary, rather than Appropriations, where its chair, Dominic "The God Father" Jacobett wanted it (Traxler told Tim Skubick in 2017 that, "Jake was unhappy").

Traxler and other proponents of a lottery had been closely following New Jersey's progression with instituting a lottery and were very impressed (it had netted the Garden State $33 million in new revenue in a very short span). Michigan had serious infrastructure and education needs and Traxler contended, "It's either this or $60 million in new taxes." His partners were fellow State Representative Arthur Law of Pontiac and Senator Jonathan "The Fox" Bowman of Roseville, both Democrats and they kept winning over doubters by accentuating the positives. "Another possibility of keen interest," Traxler told *The Detroit News*, "is that if we can develop a lottery into a twice weekly affair, with 50-cent tickets, the state could muscle in on organized crime's chief money maker, the numbers game...we have to think in modern merchandising terms." That turned out to be a "Gambling Czar." The Czar was an idea that was opposed by some fellow Democrats but Traxler's rationale was, "I felt that with the huge amounts of money going to be involved here and knowing that people always seek money wherever it is. The ideal approach would be to have a single individual whom you could ask the question, how did this happen? Why did this happen? How did you allow it to happen?"

The lottery still had to clear Wolverine State voters but did so in a May referendum. Legislators also passed an "anticipation" bill codifying it and Republican Governor Bill Milliken, despite ambivalence, signed it into law. Traxler thereafter became known as, "Bingo Bob." With so much accomplished, it seemed like the right time to contemplate going to Washington.

When longtime Congressman James Harvey gave up his seat to become a federal judge in 1973, Traxler threw his hat into the ring to replace him. He would face James Sparling, a former Harvey aide and, perhaps more adversely consequential to him, a former Nixon aide as well. It seemed a daunting task – the Eighth District had not elected a Democrat since 1932. But Bay County (Bay City) had been added to the district in the '72 remap and it joined Saginaw as a big bastion for Democratic votes. Furthermore, the disillusionment of Watergate was hitting a crescendo and that became paramount to Traxler's strategy. The election, he said, was "a referendum on Nixon's priorities and moral leadership."

Inadvertently, Sparling may have intimated the same thing. Nixon, he said, should "get out of the White House, where he is isolated, and face the people." What better place, Sparling surmised, than the battleground Eighth? To his chagrin, Nixon took him up on the issue and by stumping in the "thumb," the president likely exacerbated the issue and Traxler was only too pleased as to help. A Sparling win, he said, would enable Nixon to, "come out on the front steps of the White House and blow a trumpet. He'll shout, 'All is well,' and then retire and we won't see him again" until his term ends. He urged folks to "send a message" to the president.

The Ripon Forum gave a summation of how bad things had degenerated for the GOP: "In Bad Axe, a solid GOP farm area, more than 350 persons including top GOP officials turned out in 20-degree weather at a dinner held to raise funds for Traxler's campaign. Local politicians said they could not recall such attendance at a Democratic gathering in this town of 3,000 during this century - not even during the depression of the 1930's."

When the day came, 116,000 voters cast ballots and Traxler emerged victorious by 3,445. Key was his 67% in Bay County and holding Sparling to a 386-vote win in Saginaw, where 43,000 folks voted. Sparling did top 60% in the three thumb counties. The Congressman-elect told jubilant supporters, "we're going to Washington with a message – throw the rascals out," adding, "If I was a Republican, I would not want the Nixon albatross around my neck in November."

Traxler's election got the attention of Vice President Gerald Ford, a fellow Wolverine who was also reeling from seeing his former reliably Republican seat fall into the Democratic column. On Traxler's win, Ford said, "The trend as I see it, at the moment at least, is for the Democratic Party to end up with a potentially overwhelming majority," which, as he gratuitously threw in, threw in "leads to further legislative dictatorship and I don't think that's good for the country." Traxler years later told the Oral History project, "I wouldn't want to do it again. It was totally a committed campaign physically, mentally." He wouldn't have to. Sparling filed again for November but the Watergate impact was on full display and he took just 43%. After that, Traxler was set.

Photo courtesy of Bob Traxler

By 1976, Traxler had cemented his hold on the district and took 59%. He was utterly safe thereafter and by the mid-1980s, was taking over 70%. Part of Traxler's gift at home was a genuine versatility which *The Times* illuminated: "He also seems to some to be quite ready to tailor himself and his manner to the audience he is with - using such terms as 'into this' and 'far out' with young people, for example, and 'right on' with blacks. This characteristic has caused some of his enemies to accuse him of demagogic leanings."

Traxler pronounced himself "opposed to an OPEC-like foreign sugar cartel that will surely come into existence if we allow the sugar beet grower to go out of business."

Traxler's big Congressional enchilada came via his appointment to the Appropriations Committee and he readily conceded in the oral history project that, "I took a leaf out of the Southerner's book. The Southerners believe that their purpose in Washington was to fill their carpetbag with as much gold for their districts as they could possibly carry. I felt that coming from a state that was always at a disadvantage in the apportionment of federal funds, that it was my responsibility as a Michigan member of the appropriations committee to do whatever I could to right what I perceived to be a great injustice.

Traxler was no media hound but an assiduous fighter for local interests. He sat on the Appropriations subcommittee on Agriculture and his background gave him much rapport to the needs of the farmers in the district (though Traxler didn't always carry the counties in the thumb).

Photo courtesy of Mlive Media Group

In 1979, he notified the Forest Chief that he was "completely opposed to proposals including the Northern portions of the Au Sable River in the Wild and Scenic Rivers Program." Stressing local control, Traxler tersely reminded Forest Chief John R. McGuire that the Wild and Scenic Legislation "did not propose that the only method of protecting this environment would be to have the federal government to take over every single foot of scenic area."

Traxler's parochialism made him popular at home, but it could sometimes be to the consternation of liberals in other parts of the country. He resisted the implementation of air bags in cars, and colleagues in 1979 complied by approving a voice-vote to a Transportation bill that prohibited funding but did allow continued studies on the issue. In 1981, he was the primary sponsor of legislation, along with Elwood Hillis, a Republican from Indiana, that would raise the standards for hydrocarbon initiatives from for hydrocarbons 3.4 grams per mile to 7 grams per mile, which Leslie Dach of the National Audubon Society called "a radical rewrite of the Clean Air Act."

In 1987, Traxler called for extending the Clean Air Act as is and without economic sanctions pending the adoption of new, more stringent provisions. He called the extension, "the only vehicle. It is inescapable." But lawmakers rejected an effort by fellow Appropriator John Murtha of Pennsylvania to extend it for two years.

When times were bad, Traxler wanted a cap on member salaries and used an emergency spending bill on jobs during a lame-duck session in late-1982 to advance it. Acknowledging that "there are prominent and very worthwhile organizations and media," that support higher pay for members, "I am compelled, in view of the dire economic circumstances in my state, 17% unemployed, to offer this amendment and to plead with the members to recognize that while the need may be there, the time is not here. The timing is very poor, and I would urge this body to defer the issue until the economy has made a recovery and keep faith with the less fortunate than we are, the unemployed in my state and in this nation." An initial 15% increase had cleared the chamber by a vote of 303-109 and Traxler introduced his amendment the next day maintaining the current numbers. Speaker Tip O'Neill cast the deciding vote and it failed 208-208.

Traxler's party support scores typically reached the 80s but there were exceptions. One was gun control which he generally voted against, including the Brady Bill. Traxler also generally voted pro-life but not monolithically so: he voted to override the Bush veto of the "gag rule." And he routinely opposed fast track trade measures, as is obligatory for a Michigan Democrat. In 1988, he mildly annoyed some Democrats when, following the presidential debate between George H.W. Bush and Michael Dukakis, Traxler said, "I'd give them both a 7.5."

In 1989, Traxler ascended to one of the most coveted perches on Capitol Hill – the "College of Cardinals," which meant that he was one of 13 men holding an Appropriations subcommittee gavel. In his case, it was the VA-HUD Appropriations Subcommittee and veteran facilities reaped huge benefits – a new VA hospitals in Detroit, a major expansion to the existing property in Ann Arbor and a veterans cemetery in Battle Creek. Shepherding funding for cleanup of the Rogue River endeared himself to his Detroit area colleagues and a $107 million food toxicology building at MSU, a project that took ten years to see through, endeared himself so much to colleagues that they wanted to name the building after him (he declined).

There was also a $45 million for a NASA research center in Saginaw, curious because, late in his career, Traxler displayed at least some financial hostility to NASA, particularly the space station. Perhaps it wasn't personal – there was an ongoing tug of war was between space and housing programs and Traxler seemed inclined to favor the latter. "The point of the matter," he said, "is, we don't have enough money. Programs are under great stress and strain and it's only going to get worse." Yet Traxler was unable to convince a majority of his colleagues to accept his viewpoint as attempts to strike funding for NASA failed two years in a row by almost identical, though not overwhelming votes.

In 1991, Traxler had initially appeared poised for a win when the subcommittee eliminated funding for the space station but the full House, following intense lobbying from the Bush administration and the space community, reversed it 240-173. Traxler had done a little lobbying himself as Richard Munson in the book, *The Cardinals of Capitol Hill* wrote, "the ebullient cardinal, a consummate inside player, frequently wrapped his arm around the shoulders of colleagues, a lobbying stance perfected by Lyndon Johnson." But unlike Johnson who was masterful for snatching victory from the draws of defeat, Traxler could not pull wins out of his hat.

The following year, subcommittee members actually rejected Traxler's entreaties to kill it 6-5 and the full chamber concurred. But at the end of the day, his championship of housing needs was not for naught. Despite the obvious crunch for dollars, Traxler in 1991 still managed to allocate $7.45 billion for six housing projects in Michigan alone.

Traxler did support reforming the retirement system for federal civil servants. "My fear is that the leaders are not knowledgeable about housing and will cut a bad deal. They'll do the deal for the sake of the politics."

Traxler was a workaholic and when asked about his hobbies, he responded, "I don't have time for any. Politics is my whole life." As he turned 60 in 1991, perhaps he was becoming introspective about changing that.

Photo courtesy of Mlive Media Group

Politically, Traxler was in sterling shape. Redistricting had initially been a concern and as Michigan was losing two seats, the plan Republican legislators submitted to the courts did combine the districts of Traxler and Flint area Congressman Dale Kildee, a fellow Democrat and very good friend with two years less seniority than Traxler. But when the court drew its map, Traxler's turf remained intact and his re-election would have been a walk in the park, even with the revelation that he had overdrafts at the House Bank. But few outside Traxler's circle knew he didn't want it.

Calling his job, "very stressful," Traxler announced his retirement on the House floor two weeks shy of the state's filing deadline. He told colleagues he, "no longer (has) the wherewithal to fight the great fight." Addressing the gridlock between a Democratic Congress and a Republican president, Traxler cited, "a sense of powerlessness. Like my constituents, I, too, am frustrated and angry. I am so deeply grieved by what I have seen happen to our country that I have, on several occasions, privately been driven to tears. It is as if I am hemorrhaging inside.

I can no longer endure the pain." On his pension rising if he stayed longer, Traxler replied "that is not compatible with my definition of quality of life." He said he wanted to retire "while I have a modicum of good health" and that, "If I don't do it now, I'm not doing it."

Colleagues were still stunned. Fellow Democrat Sander Levin, who had shared hotel rooms with Traxler as members of the legislature, told colleagues, "Bob had threatened retirement a number of times. We did not take it seriously, but this time he fooled us." Some speculated that he purposely waited for the culmination of redistricting to ensure that the district remained whole so that his Chief of Staff, John Hare, could succeed him. Instead, a Bay City legislator, Jim Barcia, won the Democratic nod and subsequently the seat.

Less than one month after his announcement, Traxler made national headlines the hard way: he was the victim of a mugging blocks from the capitol at 1:30 a.m., which left Traxler unconscious and with a severe head wound. *The Washington Post* noted that the valet of the Hyatt Hotel where Traxler had been spending the evening with friends had "warned the congressman to be careful, and Traxler jokingly threw up his arms." The robbers got away with $8.

In retirement, Republican Governor John Engler named Traxler to a seat on the Mackinac Island Park Commission and to the Board of Trustees at MSU. He died at age 88 in 2019. His Macomb County colleague, Congressman Dennis Hertel noted "my cousins live in Bob's old district in Deckerville in the thumb of Michigan where there were more cows than people. And they always said he was the only Democrat that Republicans in those rural counties supported. People knew he wanted to help them. Bob really passionately cared about helping people. He got things done on Appropriations and was fun to hang out with."

CHAPTER SIXTY-FOUR

Washington State Bid Adieu To Its Three GOP Members, All Respected Moderates, In 1992

Sid Morrison, Rod Chandler and John Miller

Washington State was not immune to the Congressional turnover that befell Congress in 1992 but, unlike most of the other states, the exodus was not bipartisan. Zero of the three Republicans in the Evergreen State's delegation returned for the 103rd Congress while the five Democrats did. One might say the departures from the House at least were voluntary. John Miller retired while Sid Morrison and Rod Chandler were stymied by their quests to become Governor and U.S. Senator respectively. Nevertheless, the three Republicans were defined by their almost obligatory proclivities for compromise, moderation and support for abortion rights and that is what helped them thrive throughout their multiple terms.

Sid Morrison

With seemingly no chance of escaping the GOPs "permanent minority," in the House, Sid Morrison gave up a safe seat to launch an uncertain bid for governor of Washington State. If the objective was keeping his political career alive, it wasn't a bad strategy. Morrison lost the primary by just 8,000 votes and may well have edged the ultimate winner, his former colleague Mike Lowry in the fall. Having fallen short, his political career was over but his integrity, legacy and record for his Central Washington district would be firmly intact.

Morrison was about as non-ideological as they come and as his campaign for governor got underway, he promoted himself by saying, "I love bringing people together and working out solutions" – fairly apropos for a man whose hero was Abraham Lincoln. Fittingly, he offended few during his twelve years in the other Washington and as a result, may have embodied the axiom, "you can't please all of the people all of the time." That came out front-and-center when he tried to forge numerous compromises based on the "give a little-take a little" principle from both sides on some of the most intractable issues in the Northwest, including the Northern spotted owl, the Hanford Nuclear Plant, the Columbia Gorge National Scenic Area and the Environmental Protection Act. These were matters where the differences between the two sides were as vast as Washington's Fourth Congressional District.

Morrison was a fruit grower who was devoted to his profession, so much so that in an interview with Washington State College long after his career had ended, he still contended that he was an "official" grower. He labeled his legislative endeavors in both Washington's, "political side trips."

Like so many residents of the once small and sleepy Eastern Washington, the Morrison family business passed from generation to generation. In this case, it was an apple and cherry farm founded by his grandfather. The middle of three children, young Sid would help harvest the crop. He served in the Army and initially began his higher education at Yakima Valley College. After one year, he transferred to Washington State College where he naturally pursued a degree in Horticulture. A proud Cougar who served on the Executive Council, this would set him on the path to his career as he later called his farming, "an extension of the classroom at WSC." He would operate and serve as president of Morrison Fruit Growers until he became a legislator. In 1955, he married the woman he had dated since the 9th grade, Marcella.

Morrison was elected to the Washington State House in 1966 and advanced to the Senate eight years later. He advocated for a state income tax.

Morrison as a freshman in the Washington House in 1966 and in 1973
Photos by Jeffers, Susan Parish Photograph
Collection, Washington State Archives

In 1980, Morrison decided that he might better serve his community by heading to, "the other Washington," and decided to challenge Democratic Congressman Mike McCormack. The incumbent had prided himself on holding a Republican district for ten years but both parties were anticipating that the nature of the year would make holding it a challenge. They were right. Morrison hit McCormack's record on defense. President Carter's concession before polls on the west coast had closed helped Morrison oust McCormack with 57% and in victory, the Congressman-elect said, "I'm just glad I can be part of the team Americans elected to get the economy straightened out." He won 69.8% in 1982 and exceeded 70% in his next four subsequent elections. Meanwhile, as Morrison "worked" Congress, Marcella would run the farm.

Initially, Morrison was one of only two Republicans in the Washington House delegation (Joel Pritchard was the other) but his relationship with Democrats was excellent. Tom Foley was his colleague in Spokane and on occasion, had Morrison stand in for him when he was unable to address agriculture groups, a true compliment. Lowry, at the time a very liberal colleague from Seattle, called Morrison "a wonderful man," and said, "I have never heard anyone say a bad word about him." His friendship with another Washington Democrat, Al Swift, was so sound that he voted for a campaign-finance bill Swift was sponsoring, "simply because of the flat-out respect I have for him." Morrison called his proclivity for finding common ground "a character-building experience" that stemmed from his experiences in the minority.

Committee-wise, Morrison took seats on Agriculture and Science, two posts that were very important to the district. At one point, he rejected a seat on the "A-level" Energy and Commerce Committee due to his increasing seniority.

Even as heavy Republican turf, the Fourth was not an easy district to navigate. One publication wrote, "The district's size means 400-mile driving days when Morrison visits the home front. Its remoteness requires a 7:30 p.m. Pasco-to-Seattle commuter flight, followed by an 11:30 red-eye flight in which Morrison must change planes in Atlanta on his return to the capital."

One trait that enabled Morrison to keep earning gargantuan like numbers each election year was that he offered something for everyone. Realizing that migrants were critical to his farm dependent district, Morrison worked with California Democrat Leon Panetta toward putting a foreign worker program in the immigration reform measure that House members were considering. It would allow undocumented citizens under contract to work in the country for 11 months to assist with the laborious chores of planting and growing fruits. Hispanic and labor interests did not embrace the measure either and Texas Democrat Henry Gonzalez, citing the lack of parameters for the rights of the migrants, labeled it a, "rent-a-slave program." The House adopted the measure 228-172 but leading GOP Senators were opposed. One was Alan Simpson of Wyoming who feared it could become, "an open-ended guest worker program." A compromise was not reached that session but 1986 brought new momentum. This time, under leadership from New York Democrat Charles Schumer, language was agreed upon. But Morrison said, "If any of the elements are discarded along the way, then all of the parts of the package come apart." Any problems came to pass and the bill was enacted.

One of Morrison's earliest accomplishments – not to mention a careful test of his navigation, was his work on the Washington Wilderness Act of 1984. He got in protection for the Lake Chelan-Sawtooth Wilderness. Morrison was also in the midst of an effort to what ultimately led to the creation of a 250,000-acre Columbia Gorge National Scenic Area in the Cascades. Local residents were against the proposal but Morrison viewed it as inevitable, which he explained to a constituent who queried him in Skamania County about simply saying no to the plan. Morrison's answer: "I suppose it would slow them down for about 30 seconds. I don't think this issue is going to go away…And I don't want to be left out of the action where the Gorge is concerned." One compromise was exempting 13 towns. It took the waning days of the Congressional session and furious opposition by Oregon Republican Congressmen Bob and Denny Smith (no relation) to get the bill passed and Washington's Republican Senator Slade Gorton had admitted how, "At times over the past few days, I didn't even give it a 50-50 chance. But final House passage was 290-91 and the Senate followed. Despite threats by the administration to veto the measure, the president ultimately signed it.

On the other end of the spectrum, Morrison did view the Endangered Species Act as needing revision and he was a tireless proponent of the Hanford Nuclear Reservation – advocacy which saw many statewide careers end. In fact, in 1982, the normally placid Morrison startled colleagues by vowing that Hanford could take in some nuclear power, calling his constituents "comfortable with nuclear energy." His caveat was, "I'm not saying we'll be the nuclear site of the world but" the ball should begin moving. That contention was put to the test with passage of The Nuclear Waste Act in 1982 which called for one eastern state and one western state to house a storage site. When the Reagan administration unveiled the three finalists for the Western sites in 1986 and Hanford was on it (the other two perspective sites were in Nevada and Texas), Morrison not only backtracked but spoke out against the proposal because research showed that the basalt rock under Hanford would crack under the heat of high-level nuclear waste.

For much of '86, it appeared that the Energy Department was fast tracking Hanford to be the site and Ben Rusche, director of the Office of Civilian Radioactive Waste Management, said Hanford was "the most distant site" as far as being away from high-populous areas. But when Rusche testified, Morrison and other Western members peppered him with appearing to abandon a plan to locate one in the East, telling him, "I believe this decision is not only unwise, but clearly violates the Nuclear Waste Policy Act of 1982. The act was a result of congressional effort to achieve an equitable, workable balance from a great diversity of interests…DOE's announcement has eroded this balance and jeopardized the outcome of the entire program." Morrison immediately called for a Hanford feasibility study ("If it's not right technically, I'll be among the first to say we don't want it here. If it is right, it will be here anyway").

By 1987, Morrison was pressing for quick resolution. The elongated timetable "leaves a big cloud of uncertainty for many years, and that cloud of uncertainty makes it difficult for communities like the Tri-Cities to attract businesses that may be sensitive about such things." He used the term, "dangling in the wind." That would end later that year at Nevada's expense as lack of seniority – and thereby influence, among that delegation ultimately gave them the gift they could have sooner done without, which prompted the state's new Senator, Harry Reid to call it the, "Screw Nevada law." Washington was off the hook.

So long as Hanford was conducting operations, Morrison would go to the mat for its interests. When the Bush administration in 1992 was contemplating replacing The Westinghouse Hanford Co. with a new contractor for the site, Morrison called it, "a declaration of war." His reasoning: "These workers have a great deal of experience and skill. The ERMC should in no way threaten these workers' wages, benefits or working conditions." And when the Bush administration threatened to cancel funding for the "Fast Flux Test Facility," (FFTF) Morrison searched for a way to save it if it could be privately funded. But in his final years in Congress, Morrison supported the DOE closing the Nuclear Reactor Site for six months pending a safety study that he and Senator Daniel Evans urged be conducted.

Another issue on which Morrison's negotiating skills was tested was timber interests vs. the Northern Spotted Owl. It began when the U.S. Fish and Wildlife Service put the Northern Spotted Owl on the endangered species list, a move that did not sit well with loggers whose loss of numerous jobs in the region (potentially as many as 28,000 by one estimate) would be guaranteed. The move called for 8.4 million acres of forest to be off-limits. Morrison introduced a compromise in 1990 which went nowhere and both sides became even more frustrated when the Bush administration responded to the decision by creating more uncertainty, leading Morrison to query, "I'd like to find out if we will get some direction or continue to be whipsawed back and forth between the federal courts and different branches of the administration." The matter remained at a standstill through Morrison's duration in Congress though the 1990 farm bill did give him an opportunity to help Washingtonians who might be displaced down the line as Morrison incorporated a provision providing retraining and other skills to impacted workers.

By his fourth term in the House, Morrison was ranking Republican on the House Agriculture Subcommittee on Forests and Family Farms and in 1988, Morrison won national attention on a matter that was literally a part of his back yard – Alar. This was a product used by Uniroyal that enhances the shininess of apples. But "60 Minutes" was about to run a piece linking Alar to cancer. Morrison asked Uniroyal to pull Alar off the market but they refused and saw their stock take a large tumble. He also favored irradiation and told an event that products such as pork won't have to be cooked until it's "an old army boot."

Social issues were the hallmark of Morrison's pragmatic streak. Early in his career in Congress, he supported the Equal Rights Amendment (ERA) and refused to vote for education cuts many Republicans were championing. Morrison voted to authorize money for protective services for the mentally ill. He supported abortion rights ("I trust the women of Washington. I trust them a whole lot more than I trust people like me") and in later years, he backed the Family and Medical Leave Act and refused to vote to either censure or reprimand his Democratic colleague, Barney Frank. He voted for legislation to ban cop-killer bullets that would penetrate Kevlar vests which caused the NRA to take ferocious aim at him when he mounted his campaign for governor. He signed on to the Dollars For Scholars Community Foundation Development Act, a bill sponsored by Republican Vin Weber that had bipartisan support.

Morrison stuck with President George H.W. Bush on his veto of the larger minimum wage increase Democrats were proposing (Washington's Fourth District has many businesses with fewer than ten people) and opposed the Civil Rights Act of 1990 until the Bush Administration and Democrats reached a compromise. He voted for Ed Madigan of Illinois over firebrand Newt Gingrich for the position of House Minority Whip.

There was another iconic presence in Morrison's world. Gretchen White, his aide since the legislative days, was called the eyes and ears not only of his office but of his entire political world. In a 1986 profile of Morrison, *The Seattle Post Intelligencer* referred to White as "tall, middle-aged, nasal-voiced woman (who) is one of Capitol Hill's toughest, most savvy aides." She was a former Republican operative.

After his friend, Democratic Governor Booth Gardner decided to forego a bid for a third term, Morrison threw his hat into the ring. Calling himself, "an outsider as far as the Olympia establishment is concerned," Morrison won hefty financing from agriculture related groups." His major primary opponent was Attorney General Ken Eikenberry.

Morrison attempted to throw a bone to Washington's heavily Democratic lean by calling it, "a progressive state and I don't intend to change that." This prompted one Republican to query that, "I wish I knew what in hell he stands for. Sid's so goddam squishy on the issues you can't smoke out how he feels about anything." Morrison responded that he was specific enough. On education, for example, his contention was, "You don't need 127 different points relating to the reform of education; you need the four or five most specific ones." A key platform was education and he received a standing ovation from teachers unions following one speech on which he called for raising salaries for new teachers.

Morrison's problem was geography. The "Cascade Curtain" was a curse that hampered all candidates east of the Cascades from capturing statewide office and ultimately, Morrison proved no different. Eikenberry's base was in Western Washington while Morrison ran exceedingly strong in the counties near his Congressional district. But, with the exception of Yakima, where he racked up 59%, none were population centers. What hurt him was that Spokane went to Eikenberry by nearly the entire margin that Morrison lost statewide, a margin of 8,000 votes, 22.3 to 21.7% in the all-party primary (258,553 to 250,418).

Despite acknowledging as the count neared conclusion that, "the appropriate thing for me is to step aside," enough animosity lingered that Morrison's wouldn't give Eikenberry or other Republicans his contributor list. That paid dividends when Lowry defeated Eikenberry in November. In evidence of the wide-regard for which he was held all across the spectrum, Morrison was selected by the non-partisan State Transportation Commission to serve as the Secretary of Transportation. He held the post for eight years and accomplished, as *Washington HistoryLink* noted, Morrison "tried to do away with the old hierarchy and give employees more decision-making power in order to reduce paperwork, to reduce the number of staff meetings required, and to increase the department's efficiency and employee work output with the reduction of bureaucracy. He got the agency started on new concepts like public-private partnerships and design-build contracts, built new ferries, and "set the stage" (Morrison) for additional funding from the Legislature.

Though he stepped down as Secretary in 2001, at age 85, he continues to make valuable contributions to areas involving energy.

Rod Chandler

Until 1992, Rod Chandler was the only Representative Washington's Eighth Congressional District ever had. It had been created a decade earlier when the Evergreen State had gained a new seat following the 1980 census and Chandler won it by a big margin amid Republican losses nationwide.

In many ways, Chandler was the quintessential person to win the district. His political heroes were Abraham Lincoln and former Oregon Governor Tom McCall, two celebrated leaders one-hundred years apart whose consensus-building creed was something that Chandler tried to emulate. Chandler explained his style in 1986. "I have deliberately not attempted a flash-in-the-pan, high-visibility presentation – that's not the way you build credibility around here. I don't hold a news conference on everything I do." He even once said that, "Pensions, employee benefits and insurance (which was an area he greatly pursued as a member of Ways and Means), those are not very often front-page, 30 minute newscast stories." Chandler's shunning of national publicity belied the fact that as a former newsman, his pretty good catch phrases could have mastered. When Congress debated a visa program, Chandler charged that the amendment "would even offend a slave driver" since it did "not even provide the skeletal labor protections that existed under the infamous bracero program." After Saddam Hussein invaded Iraq, Chandler said, "President Bush is not a gun-slinger, he is not a Rambo."

Like Tom McCall, Chandler had grown up in Oregon, the town of La Grande (his great-great-grand uncle was Zacharia Chandler, an abolitionist Senator from Michigan in the mid-1800s). There, the gift of a Kodak Brownie camera for Christmas as an eight year old produced a love for photography that would last a lifetime. Chandler enlisted in the National Guard at age 17 and, after Eastern Oregon College and the attainment of his M.Ed. from the University of Nevada, he moved to Washington State where he served as a reporter for KOMO-TV. In fact, an *AP* publication took note of his, "stylish and imposing 6-foot-4 with poise and polish honed in five years" at the station.

Gradually, Chandler began a civic involvement that began with the King County Metro Council. He won a seat in the Washington House and – By 1982, it was time to go to the other Washington.

Much of the action when the district was created was in the primary and Chandler was far from the favorite. That honor belonged to a colleague, Bob Eberle, who had a hand in drawing the district that coincidentally, took in all of the constituents he was currently representing in the legislature. But Eberle was joined by another hard-line conservative, King County Councilman Paul Barden. Chandler was a moderate and many Democrats, with sparsely contested primaries of their own, were motivated to cross over and support him. He won the all-party primary 27-20%. The general election against Mercer Island Mayor Beth Bland, who had taken 33%, was spirited, but not super-tight and Chandler dispatched her with 57% and won re-election by margins that increased each cycle until 1990.

On the night he was resoundingly capturing a third term with 65%, Chandler explained the secret of his success. "It's just a very good district for me - for any Republican. You can't be too terribly far to the right and you also won't do well as a liberal." Chandler generally kept that in mind during his ten years in the other Washington.

While Chandler's voting record did give those a little left-of-center constituents something to like, it was dependent on the issue at hand. On high profile business issues, he usually sided with the chamber – against overrides of President George H.W. Bush on the minimum wage, the Family and Medical Leave Act and the Civil Rights Act of 1990, the latter which had come to be seen as a quota bill. Where Chandler's liberal streak came was on social and freedom related issues – he was pro-choice even to the point of federal funding, backed the Brady Bill, opposed the Constitutional Amendment permitting school prayer and even surprised some as a rare Republican vote against the amendment banning flag burning. In his fourth month in office, Chandler was thrust into the debate on the "Baby Doe," situation in Bloomington, Indiana. The baby's parents had supposedly withheld life-saving treatment for the Down Syndrome inflicted baby. Chandler sponsored an AMA proposal with the objective of giving parents latitude of making decisions absent "privacy-violating intrusions" but his amendment was defeated 182-231.

In his first re-election campaign, Chandler found himself on the "Doomsday Dozen" list of the the Council for a Livable World who targeted he and 11 of his colleagues (mostly freshman) for defeat. Chandler was never in danger and not one on the list was unseated. In his second term, Chandler secured money from the EPA for studies to clean up dumps throughout various locations in his states.

1985 was the year Chandler arguably made his presence known in Congress. He probably never imagined he'd be publicly ambiguous toward issues involving a president of his party but he was out in the open in at least two areas. One was his concern over the federal deficit and that led Chandler and nine other GOP Congress to sign a letter to Reagan urging him to freeze both domestic and military spending in his FY '86 budget. "I wouldn't call it a demand. But we made it clear that unless defense spending is included in a comprehensive freeze, we're not playing ball - we're not even going onto the court... The trouble is, we could spend trillions of dollars on defense and, sure, we'd be real strong. But what good does it do to protect ourselves from the Soviets and lose to the deficit?'"

A rare issue on which Chandler made national headlines was aid to the Nicaraguan contras. Going into the vote, Chandler was uncomfortable with President Ronald Reagan's aid request because of the lack of diplomacy and he called it "probably one of the most difficult issues that I've ever faced as a decision-maker." Chandler's beef was not just with the administration but also House Speaker Tip O'Neill for refusing to entertain anything other than an all or nothing approach. `But he was furious at White House Communications Director Patrick J. Buchanan for the way he framed the debate. Chandler responded that, "It's not as stark, or as black and white as Mr. Buchanan made it."

Chandler did end up declaring his intention to vote "no" and just as the dispute seemed beyond intractable, he procured a major concession. Reagan agreed to impose a 90-day suspension of the aid, minus the $30 million for humanitarian purposes, which would be carried out via Executive Order. In the meantime, negotiations with the Nicaraguan government would begin. This was enough for Chandler to sell most of the holdouts in his party. Democrats on the other hand were not assuaged, despite the best effort of Chandler's partner on the matter, Dave McCurdy of Oklahoma, to produce something and the package went down 222-210. The issue came before the Congress again and the tally nearly mirrored the last vote – 211 to 209 only this time, the Reagan administration had prevailed. Chandler responded to naysayers by projecting that, "The likelihood of American troops (invading) Nicaragua is zero as long as President Reagan holds that office." There were a number of skirmishes when it came to contra votes in future Congresses but none approached the suspense of the previous scuttle.

There was a postscript to the matter. In 1990, Chandler was named one of 20 U.S. observers of the Nicaraguan election but was denied a visa along with other members. Ex-President Jimmy Carter intervened to allow him to take part.

Many of the causes Chandler sponsored were across the aisle. He had won a seat on the prestigious Ways and Means Committee in 1986, a natural given that he had chaired the panel in the State House and much of his crusades focused on tax issues. His partner on one, in 1987, was with Alabama Democrat Ronnie Flippo to eliminate penalties on pension withdrawals. "Let's make it legal to gain access to those funds and do so without that very destructive requirement of terminating a pension plan." A portability plan was with John McCain and a tax bill giving incentives to employers to offer health coverage to its workforce was offered with Arkansas Democratic Senator David Pryor. With Nancy Johnson of Connecticut, Chandler proposed legislation that would give firms with three to 25 people access to health care coverage by requiring employers to help them purchase it. Both co-chaired the House Republican Task Force and Minnesota Senator David Durenberger sponsored similar measure in that body. Another bill would eliminate penalties for both removing money from pension funds and taxes from revenue from a health fund aimed for employees retirement. The Education Savings Act of 1992 was Chandler's as was the Employee Investment Opportunity Act and the Employee Benefits Simplification Act. Finally, the Major League Baseball Equity Act "would force teams to put a portion of their revenues from broadcast contracts into a common pool."

Chandler was in no mood to forge a balance on the Gephardt Trade Amendment. In fact, he made his visceral distaste known about the retaliation against China in no uncertain term, comparing it to "a mindless Sherman tank bashing through a rose garden. It's sure to get out of control" (the amendment was projected to have a deleterious effect on the trade-dependent Pacific Northwest).

Chandler was fairly unrestrained (some say uncharacteristically) when House Minority Whip Newt Gingrich publicly opposed the Bush White House following the budget summit package that resulted in new taxes. Chandler had provided critical support for Gingrich in his cliffhanger vote to become Whip in 1989 and made clear that, "I voted for a guy who promised to bring the party together. If you can't be there as a leader you either resign or keep your mouth shut." In early 1992, zero overdrafts at the House bank did not stop him from taking the floor to declare that, "Regrettably, the U.S. Capitol has become our castle in the hill, the Potomac River our — that separates us from the people who elected us."

Chandler's something for everyone shtick seemed to be working and despite Democratic rumblings about taking him on, re-elections came easy. A well-funded challenge by David Giles in 1986 ended with Chandler racking up 65%. Giles stayed out in 1988 and Chandler dispatched his foe with 71%. But he returned in 1990 and Chandler must have thought that he would dispatch him with similar ease. Giles evidently thought the same thing as *The Seattle Post-Intelligencer* noted, just before the election that he had "little money, no campaign manager, no headquarters, no yard signs." The result was a little bit closer than either had anticipated but Chandler still won 56-44%.

Chandler had made it known as early as 1986 that he would like to stand for higher office – it was simply a question of when an opportunity would present itself. That opportunity came in 1992 when freshman U.S. Senator Brock Adams was preparing to seek a second term. Chandler had already been preparing to make the race but it got a shake-up when Adams, long-haunted by a string of sexual harassment allegations, exited the race in March of '92, leaving the Democratic nomination in a free-for-all.

Before reaching the eventual nominee, Chandler had to deal with a distraction that proved a major impediment to his winning the nomination. Leo Thorsness, a POW in Vietnam who had taken 47% against South Dakota Senator George McGovern in 1974, had since moved to Washington and was running to Chandler's right, so much so that *The Seattle Times* ran a headline saying, "Chandler Sheds His Easygoing Image."

In 1991, Chandler had taken tremendous heat from abortion rights advocates when he flirted with opposing legislation that would overturn the Bush administration's ban on "the gag rule" that prevented federally funded clinics from discussing abortion (a Planned Parenthood spokesperson responded by calling it "very distressing." Chandler ultimately supported the measure but it was still indicative of the high stakes nature of the primary. He had also told lumber workers fearful of losing their jobs to pending Northern spotted owl legislation that, "I am being attacked like *we* are being attacked. That bunch of liberals in Seattle are totally indifferent to you and your concerns."

**Chandler's love of the camera was instilled at age eight when
he received a Kodak Brownie camera for Christmas
Photo courtesy of Rod Chandler**

When Thorsness attacked Chandler for the amount of PAC money he was accepting, Chandler hearkened back to his contributions to the campaigns of Senators. He demanded to know, "Which Senators votes did you buy? Frankly, I think you have been hypocritical throughout the whole thing." The days before the primary had some pegging Chandler as a possible upset victim but he did hold off Thorsness 20-16% in the blanket-primary that featured both party candidates.

The candidate who emerged from the Democratic primary was State Senator Patty Murray, whom a male colleague had famously dubbed, "just a mom in tennis shoes." Chandler's downfall may have come at the end of what *The New York Times* called "an otherwise ordinary debate," with Murray when he opened a rebuttal with an old Roger Miller song: "Dang me, dang me. You ought to take a rope and hang me. Hang me from the nearest treeeee. Woman, would you weep for me." Murray's response was that he displayed, just "the attitude that brought me into this race, Rod." Chandler's campaign team was befuddled and his spokesperson simply said, "I can't explain it." It apparently didn't take Chandler long to realize that the line was costly as well.

He conceded it was, "a dumb thing to do. It was a mistake. I was trying to lighten it up a little bit...I miscalculated."

Murray displayed a rustiness on the trail that Chandler certainly could have taken advantage of in a more benign cycle and he did gain traction by exploiting it. But aside from the fact that Bill Clinton was stomping over George H.W. Bush in Washington State, 1992 was the "Year of the Woman," and voters were willing to give Murray a break. While polls just before the election appeared to show a dead heat, the final result wasn't as Murray won 54-46%. Chandler conceded two hours after polls closed, telling supporters, "There are still a lot of votes to be counted yet, but I can count, too." And with considerable class, he told his foe, "Patty, you got better as you went along. You can take a great deal of pride in the race you ran." He was less charitable to the state of the Republican Party. In late December 1992, he declared, "The Republican Party is like an airplane that just flew into the side of a mountain. We've got to piece it together from scratch. We got clobbered at the top of the ticket in 1974 and 1976 because of Watergate. But I'd say we are in worse trouble now" (Chandler could not have anticipated Republican-rich 1994).

After his loss, Chandler formed a lobbying partnership with Tom Downey, another Ways and Means veteran who had recently lost his bid for re-election bid in New York. He now lives in solitude in the west and devotes much of his time to photography.

John Miller

The man who declared himself "a John Miller Republican, not a Ronald Reagan Republican" was never quite predictable so when the four-term Congressman announced his departure in January of 1992, it was appropriate that it came as something of a surprise. Miller was just 54 and, despite a few tough scrapes at the ballot box, his suburban Seattle district was actually becoming more Republican in the district lines that would be used in the fall. Miller had even publicly expressed interest in a bid for the U.S. Senate, hardly the kind of talk for one planning on calling it a career. Yet it made perfect sense. He was battle weary and in such a precarious climate that would culminate with the defeat of Republican President George H.W. Bush, his re-election was by no means assured. Furthermore, Miller's desire to spend more time with his family and cease the long commutes to the other Washington

("You only have one chance to be a Dad and that's what I want to do") made it crystal clear where his priorities were.

Miller had a colorful background. His middle name was "Ripin," and he was a Jewish kid from New York City who attended Bucknell University and Yale Law School before heading West for seven interviews at Seattle law firms (he had mailed out hundreds of resumes). There was a story behind that which Kurt Stone in *The Jews of Capitol Hill* told. In fourth grade, Miller was "enchanted by a picture of 'rain forests and misty rain'" in Puget Sound and when it came time to seek an internship, that story reappeared in his mind. He soon landed a position at the Washington Attorney General's office but three years later, was picked up by the firm Johnson, Johnson and Inslee.

Eventually, Miller became a partner at Miller, Howell and Watson and was barely settled before taking on seemingly intractable battles. One was the Shorelines Management Act of 1971. Miller sought his Council seat as a reform candidate affiliated with a group CHECC (Choose an Effective City Council) in a non-partisan election in 1971. One motivation for his political entry was preventing the closing of the landmark and tourist heavy Pike Place Market and he grabbed 64%.

Miller was prominent in Seattle's environmental movement and actually founded the Washington Environmental Council with the man who would become his Democratic opponent for Congress in 1984, Brock Evans. With another ally Bruce Chapman, Miller was instrumental in the creation of the P-Patch Program that proved cutting edge for community gardening projects. His interest had been generated by a meeting during the '71 campaign with Darlyn Rundberg who had recently succeeded in convincing the Picardo brothers to let her use part of their Wedgwood farm for a community garden. Miller promised to lead the effort for Seattle to lease or purchase gardens should he win and the first garden the city leased was the Picardo farm in 1975. Thus, the "p" in P-Patch was for "Picardo" and Washington's *Historylink* reports that by 2017, 90 P-Patch gardens graced Seattle. Other Miller initiatives on Council: the elimination of the Alaska viaduct, opposing the entrance of the Washington Public Power supply system in a nuclear plant and advocating gay-rights.

1975 was a very tough year to be seeking re-election and the campaign was dominated by a 98 day Seattle City Light technician strike over a payraise (City Light was offering an 11 percent increase while the technicians union was demanding 15 percent.). Miller's backing of City Light sent unions into the camp of his Democratic opponent, Ling Eng Tuai and Miller edged him by just 1,412 votes out of 165,000 cast.

In 1977, Miller mounted a bid for Mayor of Seattle but garnered limited support and took just 7%. In 1980, he decided to try to become Washington's Attorney General as an Independent, an undertaking that initially had both Democrats and Republicans on pins and needles over which side he might take more votes from. But in a twist of circumstances, Miller was actually looked to as the savior of the spoiler label as the campaign neared an end.

The Democratic nominee, John Rosellini had found himself the target of a prolonged investigation by the Washington State Bar Association. In an extraordinary development that said much about Miller's respectability as it did about Democratic fears of getting shut out of the race, a group of prominent Democrats, including Seattle Mayor Charles Royer and Olympia Democatic Congressman Don Bonker, sent Rosellini a "Dear John" letter asking him to quit the race and endorse Miller, saying that the chances of the "partisan" Republican Ken Eikenberry prevailing were "unacceptable." Eikenberry refused to heed the warnings and prevail he did, albeit with a 46-38% plurality (Rosellini finished a poor third with 15%). Miller won King County by a nose and a number of other Western Washington counties but Eikenberry cleaned up in the rest of the state. Miller returned to practicing law and doing commentary for KIRO in Seattle but another opportunity for office was in sight.

In 1984, quintessential and highly respected moderate First District Congressman Joel Pritchard announced plans to run for Lieutenant Governor and Miller decided to seek the seat. He edged out State Senator Susan Emerson Gould in the September all-party primary along with four other Republicans who took mid-to-high single digits. Miller then prepared to do battle with Evans, now the head lobbyist for the Sierra Club who had been unopposed in the Democratic primary.

With similarities on social stances, the two aimed their fire at each other on fiscal matters. Miller backed a Balanced Budget amendment while Evans unveiled specific spending cuts. Miller supporters worried that voters would be swayed by what *CQ* labeled Evans's "propitious name." His surname was Evans, the same as Daniel Evans, the state's U.S. Senator and mega-popular governor while "Brock" was the named of a former Seattle area Congressman and Secretary of Transportation. Any confusion subsided and Miller prevailed by an unexpectedly large 56-44%.

When Miller came to Congress, he was deep in the minority and therefore wanted to carve a niche that could win bipartisan backing. George Weigel, a longtime confidante and part-time aide wrote in *National Review* on Miller's death, that he "suggested that he take up a cause that no one else found very interesting – the cause of Lithuania's persecuted Catholic human-rights and pro-democracy activists." It fit Miller like a glove - his grandparents had been Latvian immigrants. He thus founded the Lithuanian Religious Freedom Caucus whose mission was to improve conditions for pro-freedom members of the Jesuit. One such member, Father Tamkevicius Sigitas had been serving a 10-year prison sentence in Siberia for his activism in a resistance movement and Miller's intervention encouraged Mikhail Gorbachev to release him and others, including Alfonsas Svarinskas, and Nijole Sadunaite. Weigel refers to the threesome as "a clandestine Jesuit, a diocesan priest, and a clandestine nun." He also worked on Soviet Jewry.

Like Morrison and Chandler, Miller was a centrist who supported abortion rights. He backed a bill by Massachusetts Democrat Ted Kennedy and California Democrat Henry Waxman to encourage AIDS testing while maintaining privacy, contrary to the hard-line proposal of William Dannemeyer, a staunchly conservative Republican from California. When Congress took up reauthorization of the McKinney Homeless Assistance Act in 1990, Miller proposed language that 15% of funds go to homeless education in schools. His view was that education "cannot afford to wait."

In the 101st Congress, Miller backed the flag burning amendment and opposed the minimum wage hike over Bush's veto but did vote to override him on the Family and Medical Leave Act. On another matter: "He virulently opposed the congressional pay raise and gave the money to charity."

Miller opposed the Civil Rights Act of 1990 for reasons he explained on the House floor. "Imagine a business back in the year 1971, a fish processing company. Imagine that that business is a leader in minority hiring, that 52 percent of their unskilled positions are held by minorities. Imagine further that 24 percent of their skilled positions and management positions are held by minorities. Imagine further that the minority percentage of the population in the area is 10 percent. Then imagine that the government in 1971, in a class of plaintiffs, take this business to court and alleges and claims there is a presumption of discrimination because of the difference between the 52 percent figure for minorities in unskilled positions and the 24 percent in skilled positions, a presumption of discrimination in skilled position hiring. No individual acts of discrimination are alleged. While unfair hiring practices are alleged, there is no causal link stated between such hiring practices and the statistics. Imagine that this litigation goes on for 19 years, with millions of dollars of attorney's fees. Imagine finally that the Supreme Court says hey, wait a minute. Statistics without a causal link to unfair practices, that is not enough. You cannot say there is a presumption of discrimination, or otherwise we would end up with hiring by statistics. We would end up with quotas. Well, that is not imagination. That is the real thing. That is what happened to the Ward's Cove Packing Co. in my district." On the proponents, he said, "Of course, they say they do not want quotas, but because they allow a presumption of discrimination without a causal link between the statistics and the practices, and because of the unlimited damages, that is what is going to happen.

Miller was in no mood to stick with Bush when it came to renewing Most-Favored Nation Stauts (MFM) for China. "The president," he said, "has asked us to follow a trade policy with China that is divorced from morality." During the MFN debate, he proposed human rights principals any President would be required to follow when dealing with China.

After the 1988 election, Miller had a decision to make. He had just secured his seat on the Budget Committee and had to surrender one of his committee assignments. Many expected it would be Foreign Affairs. Instead, he deep-sixed Merchant Marine and Fisheries which was pertinent to Seattle. *Politics in America* wrote "Miller's decision to serve on Budget and keep his foreign policy soap box can be viewed in the broader context in which Miller apparently sees himself."

Miller was the recipient of unusually bad publicity following the sinking of the factory trawler, Aleutian Enterprise that killed nine in 1990 when revelations came that he had intervened to waive the limit of the number of people allowed on a trawler. That was ironic because two years earlier, Miller had teamed with Seattle Democrat Mike lowry to pass the Commercial Fishing Industry Vessel Safety Act to beef up inspection requirements. Miller offered to address the memorial service but an organizer said, "We politely told Congressman Miller's office that we didn't feel it would be very sensitive to the families of the victims if he said a few words." Another local issue Miller successfully took on was transporting Seattle's Sand Point Naval Air Station (better known as Magnusson Park) from federal to municipal control.

Miller's office provided good constituent service and *The Herald* spoke of his Saturday town meetings on his death. "At the two-hour mark, when they were supposed to wrap up, Miller would gather his staff and they'd continue meeting one-on-one with attendees, until dinner if necessary, so the Republican lawmaker could dig deeper into the details of their concerns." According to associates, Miller was also a man of great personal integrity. "During one re-election campaign, researchers discovered salacious material about his opponent. John refused to use it. He wanted the campaign to be about the issues, not his opponent's personal life."

None of Miller's three re-election campaigns were easy. In 1986, he staved off Washington Education Association Reese Lindquist just 51-49%, a difference of 5,272 votes. His margin in Kitsap County was just 65 votes but more populous King and Snohomish gave him slightly bigger majorities. His backing from the Sierra Club (not to mention his '84 opponent Evans) was likely critical. While he was up to 55% against Lindquist two years later, Miller like many members of Congress got tied down by the budget stalemate in 1990. Democrat Cynthia Sullivan, a King County Councilwoman, started way behind in cash but more than made up for with the budget brouhaha that was encompassing the other Washington. Miller's campaign spokesperson admitted that the protracted negotiations threatened to turn away 30% of GOP voters and Sullivan was able to begin a hard-hitting tv presence that hit the incumbent for, among other things, the S&L mess of which he had little to do. Miller retorted by going after her record on Council, specifically on spending. Election night was again a time of nail biting for Miller but he mostly stayed ahead and jokingly told supporters "it looks like another landslide." He conceded, "I've never had an easy campaign. If I did, I don't think I'd know what to do with it." The final margin was 52-48%, a difference of 8,000 votes. This time, Kitsap delivered Miller a double-digit margin but he only limped to victory in King and Snohomish.

Miller's decision to stand down for 1992 was made in early January and apparently was finalized during a trip to Croatia. When he began delivering the news to supporters, they implored him to not, "jump to a hasty decision because 'maybe you'll start to salivate and think you're God's gift to the state or the First Congressional District or whatever the office is.' But that hasn't overcome me." Instead, Miller said "It just became a decision between family, Puget Sound and unspecified other endeavors vs. D.C." He had a young son and, "eight years is enough."

Out of Congress, Miller and his Chief of Staff, Bruce agnew, founded the Cascadia Project at Discovery Institute, in part to deal with the ever-growing Northwest. In 2002, President George H.W. Bush named him Ambassador-at-large and director of the State Department's Office to Monitor and Combat Trafficking in Persons where Weigel in *The National Review* wrote on Miller's death that he, "wore himself out, physically and emotionally, traveling to such hellholes as the slums of Bangkok, where young girls and women were kidnapped or otherwise trapped into the global sex trade, talking to the victims, and learning how such atrocities could happen today." Miller conceded early on, "I had no idea of the dimensions of this problem. This has emerged as the primary human-rights issue in the 21st century."

Departing in 2006, Miller taught at George Washington and Yale University. He authored a novel, *The Man Who Could Be King* about George Washington that was published shortly before his death from cancer in 2017 at age 79.

Photo courtesy of the United States Department of State

Longtime Appropriator and Watergate Baby AuCoin's Career Halted by an Unsuccessful Senate Bid

Introductory Quote: "Sometimes, the establishment on the Hill reminds me of the court of Louis XIV." –Congressman Les AuCoin during his first year as a member of the House of Representatives.

Photo courtesy of the U.S. House of Representatives Historical Collection

L es AuCoin was one of those Jim Dandy politician who basked in idealism, talent and all of the other characteristics that make up political central casting. A prominent Democratic member of the Watergate class of 1974, he represented a suburban Oregon district that was not the easiest for a Democrat to hold down for 18 years but, while championing issues that were mostly bread-and-butter for Democratic constituents, he never strayed too far out and often gave centrists something to chew on. And had he not fallen just shy of a similarly entrenched Senate incumbent in 1992, AuCoin might have been able to do similar wonders in the upper chamber for years to come.

The Oregonian once wrote that AuCoin "makes it a point to appear perpetually cool, well-pressed and unruffled." A former journalist, he always had a good line or play on words in either a Congressional or political debate. And his background offered solid appeal to traditional liberals.

Born in Portland, AuCoin's parents separated when he was five and he, his mother Alice and younger brother Lee relocated to the town of Redmond. Les often had to play the role of caregiver to his brother Lee so Alice could work as a waitress to support them. But to hear AuCoin tell it, his background was even less savory. "I lived in a one-bedroom, wood-frame house with no foundation behind a Piggly Wiggly grocery store. And I always felt that I was from the wrong side of the tracks." If that was the case, he soon righted the track very quickly.

AuCoin played basketball in high school and upon graduation, enrolled in Portland State University, the first member of his family to go to college. Ultimately, he attained his degree from Pacific University and began a stint in the U.S. Army as a public relations specialist and much of his writing was published in Southern newspapers. He dabbled in journalism and public relations at his alma mater after graduation. A supporter of Senator Eugene McCarthy in 1968, AuCoin chaired his campaign in Washington County, Oregon and of course, the Beaver State was the only one to prefer the Minnesota Senator to his New York colleague, Robert F. Kennedy.

In 1970, David Frost left his seat in the Oregon House behind and AuCoin decided to pursue the seat. He was elected with 57% over E.G. Kyle and worked on business and job legislation. At the start of his second term, AuCoin displayed a young man in a hurry syndrome by throwing his hat in for Speaker. Richard Eymann beat him but the consolation prize wasn't bad: Majority leader. And two years later, a trip to Congress which might have been improbable had he been victorious. In the meantime, Eymann and AuCoin worked exceptionally well together.

AuCoin sought the Congressional seat in 1974 when moderate Republican incumbent Wendell Wyatt opted against seeking reelection. He consolidated support among Democrats. The First had never before sent a Democrat to Washington D.C., and Wyatt was furiously working to elect his prodigy, Diarmuid F. O'Scannlain, who naturally vowed to govern in the "Wendell Wyatt tradition." In any other year he might have succeeded as O'Scannlain was a moderate who directed the Department of Environmental Quality but '74 was the Watergate year. As *The Albany Democrat-Herald* wrote, AuCoin called his rival a tool of corporations while O'Scannlain called his foe a tool of labor

("That's the old tactic of pitting one group against the other"). While AuCoin embraced Democratic themes such as national health care and "foolhearty" Pentagon spending, he also tried to offer moderates something to chew on, such as "ending the reign of terror that has been visited on small businessmen" due to OSHA which he nonetheless favored. AuCoin won with 56%.

Administrative Assistant Bob Crane years later labeled AuCoin, "sort of your basic freshman-sophomore back-bencher finding his way around." He was assigned to the Banking Committee as well as Merchant Marine and Fisheries. On Banking, his main goal was to for formula fairness among regions, even if that was sometimes not to the utmost benefit to Oregon. Why? "My allegiance is to the West but I also belong to the United States" (the Northeast and Midwestern United States were often pitted against the South and West).

After the 1980 election, AuCoin was awarded a seat on the Appropriations Committee, a political miracle given that Democrats had to surrender a number of seats from the nationwide bloodbath they had taken in the midst of the Reagan Revolution. He requested seats on the Interior and Transportation subcommittees and after six years in Congress, many could say AuCoin arrived. The state's senior Republican Senator, Mark Hatfield, chaired the panel in the upper chamber and that meant a steady partnership. *The Oregonian* credited, "The Hatfield-AuCoin axis on the Appropriations Committees," for bringing, "a steady stream of federal money flowed to Oregon, culminating in funding for the Portland metro area's light-rail system."

Securing funding for parochial interests was an AuCoin priority and a big enchilada was a light rail system into Washington County (Salem), 75% of which became federally funded. A $500,000 grant for the Oregon Graduate Center for research on a thermomechanical process for making wood pulp was another accomplishment. Other endeavors: helping Crater Lake Lodge, build an Oregon Trail center outside Baker, buy nine new rescue helicopters to be based in Portland and building new MAX light-rail centers." He got a south jetty for Tillamook, a new Job Corps Center in Portland, and Coast Guard housing in Astoria. There was also, according to *The Encyclopedia of Oregon*, "the U.S. Fish and Wildlife Forensics Library in Ashland, the Seafood Consumer Research Center in Astoria, the Oregon Trail Center at Baker City, and the Lewis & Clark Visitors' Center at Fort Clatsop."

In his last six years in the House, AuCoin put increasing focus on Coast Guard issues and was able to re-allocate $1.9 billion from the Pentagon to the Coast Guard. In an attempt to save business for a Navy ship repair at

Portland's Swan Island repair facilities – in danger because it did not have a home port, AuCoin brought House Armed Services Chair Les Aspin for a tour (when Aspin had sided with the MX proponents only a few years earlier, AuCoin, who had backed him for the chairmanship had said, "frankly, it burns the hell out of us"). And when folks wanted to mine at Three Sisters Wilderness, AuCoin fought against it.

In 1986, AuCoin proposed an amendment in Appropriations that would zero funding for the controversial Hanford waste nuclear storage site. It was defeated by voice vote. That year he also proposed an amendment urging Japan to give its products a chance on the US market. It passed with just five dissenting votes.

In 1983, AuCoin won a seat on the Defense Subcommittee panel and as Robert David Johnson wrote in *Congress and the Cold War*, he opted for that dais "for very specific reasons," and as a main proponent of a nuclear freeze. AuCoin was part of a group that included increasingly senior and influential members such as Dick Gephardt, Tom Downey, Marty Russo and Mike Synar who, sensing that something would pass wanted to make it as narrow as possible. The measure reached the floor in May 1983. Many, among them Republican Congressman and future North Carolina Governor Jim Martin contended a freeze "takes a lot of the zing out of the anti-Reagan objectives of the freeze movement" but the House was unswayed and, after 53 hours of debate, cleared the chamber by a vote of 278-159.

AuCoin also viewed stopping or vastly limiting production of the MX missile (along with the B1 Bomber) as a major starting point toward achieving a freeze and that became a major part of his legacy. The MX was, "the Pearl Harbor of our missile fleet. We're telling the Russians: 'Here's my glass jaw. Come and hit me," and he called forthcoming debates, "the first test of whether Congress will respond to clear public feeling that they want less defense spending."

Reagan was seeking $625 million to begin the MX and AuCoin found an ally in New York Democrat Joe Addabbo. But in what AuCoin labeled, "The Treaty of Pennsylvania Avenue," a number of centrists, most notably Aspin, Norm Dicks of Washington and a guy named Al Gore of Tennessee, all of whom had expressed reservations about MX in the past, entered into negotiations with the administration which at the end of the day yielded big dividends for the president. This yielded many bruised feelings within the Democratic camp and AuCoin pronounced himself, "amazed at the Democrats who have entered into a bargain with the administration. The president gets the MX and Congress gets a statement of sincerity about arms control. If that's a bargain, I say to my colleagues, 'I'm pleased they're not negotiating with the Soviet Union.'"

On the floor, AuCoin worried about the long-term practicalities of cutting off a missile after its inception saying, "No strategic weapons system that has ever passed this stage of funding . . . has been permanently cancelled." Reagan's request cleared the House 239-186 and AuCoin said, "We can't bargain with Reagan. All the evidence tells us that under his administration, there will be no arms control. Period. It's wishful thinking to pretend otherwise."

At a ceremony for the MAX Light Rail Line in Gresham, Oregon
Photo via Steve Morgan

AuCoin's advocacy on this issue continued through the decade. In 1986, when Reagan wanted to back out of the parameters of the SALT II agreement, AuCoin responded that it "would be one of the bonehead plays of all time." The following year, AuCoin and Dicks authored an amendment in Appropriations which required Reagan to SALT appliance.

Wilderness issues were also at the core of AuCoin's legislative pedigree. In 1982, AuCoin fervently supported a wilderness bill, even chastising his GOP colleague from the state, Denny Smith, for suggesting that the bill was being rushed. Citing the number of public hearings held statewide on the subject,

AuCoin said, "If anyone in this chamber believes that the Oregon delegation has been somehow remiss in letting Oregonian speak out on this bill they are sadly mistaken... I think that 13 million acres figure for commercial lands and two million acres figure for wilderness is a reasonable proposition. It is at least reasonably enough to attract the interest of the two Republican senators from the state of Oregon and all of the Democrats in the House." But it was the end of the session and the bill died. Another version was enacted in 1984.

AuCoin had similar luck on banning drilling off the California coast. Along with Washington Democrat Don Bonker, he sponsored a proposal dealing with a Columbia Gorge River. The Republican senators from Washington and Oregon had their own version which was similar but Bonker-AuCoin was considered stronger. A compromise was worked out over the opposition of Oregon's two Republican Congressman that Reagan, despite his own reservations, enacted into law. He wasn't as successful on the issue of timber, AuCoin proposed a compromise but that for the most part withered on the vine.

Abortion might have been the crème'de la crème' of AuCoin's legacy Though he was a steadfast supporter of a woman's right to choose throughout his entire career, his vocalness and support of its affirmation became firmly on display in the late 1980s.

AuCoin saw the tide as beginning to turn in abortion rights direction after the Supreme Court decision of Webster. His first opportunity to impact policy came on an Appropriations spending bill for the District of Columbia and when virulent anti-abortion foe, Republican Robert Dornan of California, proposed a ban on federal funding for abortions in cases of rape and incest in the District. AuCoin gave an uncharacteristic saddle 'em up speech. He told House members on the floor that "a new political era begins right now. It is not a free political ride anymore... Those of us who defend a woman's freedom of choice are drawing a line in the sand today, a line of decency, a line of fair play, and a line of serious politics…If you vote for those amendments, you will be held accountable in ways you have never dreamed possible at ballot boxes all over this country. The pro-choice movement is mobilized. And from this day forward, it is going to take names and kick ankles" Colleagues got the message. Dornan's amendment went down 206-216, marking the first win for abortion rights supporters in ten years. With that, AuCoin tipped his strategic card by asserting that, "You seldom achieve quantum leaps in politics." President Bush vetoed the measure but by the numbers, the momentum was clearly in the hands of the pro-choice camp.

That might have been AuCoin's Congressional strategy as well. In 1988, *The Oregonian* quoted a Congressional aide as saying, "I perceive him as being a very smart politician...Les AuCoin is never going to get into anything that he is not going to win. He is not a risk-taker."

As such, AuCoin was not universally liberal. In 1983, he voted to raise the Social Security retirement age to 67. Mostly, however, those were the exceptions and he was a reliable vote for his party.

Initially, gun control was another area on which AuCoin departed from liberal orthodoxy. He opposed federal regulation throughout most of his tenure, attributing that to being from a community, "where you learn to shoot before you learn to read." But by 1991, he believed the NRA "absolutely out of touch with reality," and was ready to back the Brady Bill. Declaring that "crime control is gun control," he announced his change surrounded by law enforcement officers ("If anybody understands, it's the people behind me"), but it was a shot heard around the capitol. Brady Bill sponsor Chuck Schumer said his conversion "presages that, finally, the chokehold of the National Rifle Association over this Congress and this country is ended."

AuCoin opposed the Persian Gulf War but, proving that you can't take journalism away from the man, he spoke up for reporters who were under fire.

On occasion, AuCoin could put an heir of incredulousness into making a point. When California colleague Ed Roybal successfully had a nude statue removed from a federal building bearing his name, AuCoin asked, "Who in the hell elected Ed Roybal our Minister of Culture?"

AuCoin did have two difficult elections in the 1980s. The 1982 redistricting gave him more Republican enclaves and that year, a solid one for Democrats nationally, AuCoin was outspent by wealthy timber executive Bill Mushofsky and beat him just 54-46%. Two years later, Mushafsky was back with more support from his party. In a year that Reagan was carrying his district with 55%, AuCoin hung on 53-47%. It may have been his lowest margin, but the GOP got the message and never targeted him again. But soon, AuCoin found himself with a higher calling.

For years, Oregon Democrats have been trying to entice AuCoin into challenging one of the states to Republican Senators Mark Hatfield or Bob Packwood. In 1990, AuCoin said that he would never challenge Hatfield, an ally on environmental issues and a popular former governor who had built up a reservoir of goodwill throughout a more than 30-year career statewide. Packwood had longevity as well having served in the Senate since 1968. But despite favoring abortion rights, he lacked the beloved nature of Hatfield and it was an understatement to say that he and AuCoin were not friends. Packwood's seat came up in 1992 and AuCoin decided to take the plunge and from the get-go until its culmination, it became the most widely anticipated race in the nation. In his announcement, AuCoin invoked another Oregon Senator, Wayne Morse by vowing, "Principle above politics" (Packwood had unseated Morse in 1968). His campaign manager was Mary Beth Cahill who in 2004 would go on to run John Kerry's presidential campaign.

AuCoin-Packwood was immediately expected to be one of several marquee in the country and it didn't disappoint. But AuCoin in the spring received a major distraction that came within an inch of derailing him from even facing Packwood. That was news of the Congressional check bouncing scandal. When the scandal first broke, AuCoin had been told that he had 7 bad checks worth $500. But when the official list was made public, it ballooned to 83 checks, worth a combined value of $61,000.

Businessman Harry Lonsdale who had taken a surprisingly high 46% against Hatfield in 1990, had already been in seeking the Democratic nomination to face Packwood. The checks gave him carte blanche to go after Congress as an institution. "It's not just the checks," Lonsdale said. "It's the cover-up." AuCoin responded by calling Lonsdale "shifty."

As the primary approached, Lonsdale actually led AuCoin 39-36% and received assistance from a very unlikely source: Packwood himself. The Senator made no attempt to conceal the fact that he would rather face Lonsdale in his bid to win a fifth term than AuCoin and began slamming the Congressman for the checks. He very nearly got his wish. As primary night opened, AuCoin trailed Lonsdale and not before every vote was counted did he pull into the lead by 207 votes, which The Oregonian labeled equivalent to "a double-overtime Trail Blazers game." The final number came down to 40,000 absentees that remained to be counted and when that happened, AuCoin clinched the nomination by 330 votes (153,029 to 152,699).

Packwood was a tough campaigner. In 1964, the year of the Goldwater drubbing, he guided Oregon Republicans to a takeover of the House chamber – the only one in the nation that had shifted to GOP control that year. Naturally, the race was dirty. AuCoin opened one joint candidate debate by chiding Packwood for throwing out the first "negative shot of the campaign." Packwood responded with fire: "I wasn't going to let you have the first cheap shot, Les." Packwood chastised his rival for leaving the House and "throw(ing) over his seniority and what he could do for Oregon. If somebody was really concerned for the state of Oregon, would he leave his position of clout in the House to come to a junior position in the Senate? I think not." AuCoin had unveiled his rebuttal earlier in the campaign when he asked, "Which is best, a senior member of a small minority in the U.S. Senate, or a Democratic senator who has easy access to the Democratic White House?" In any case, Packwood, he said, was "Oregon's George Bush." But Packwood, with a long-history of being pro-choice and supportive of Israel was able to successfully blur the issues.

By the start of October, AuCoin, drained from the primary with Lonsdale, had little more than $200,000 on hand. Packwood had $3 million, a disparity AuCoin had sought to rectify just after his primary win had been certified in calling for a one million dollar spending limit. The Packwood campaign predictably rejected that proposition.

In the closing weeks of the campaign, Democrats became increasingly optimistic that the presidential coattails of Bill Clinton would put him over the top. Packwood, recognizing Clinton's broad appeal, began linking himself to some of his stances. Yet he also had to worry about backing from Hatfield who appeared on the fence (he finally reaffirmed his support for his colleague). The count was slow due to Portland and the race wasn't officially called until mid-Wednesday morning. Packwood had hung on 52-47%.

When AuCoin conceded the next morning, he praised the nation for adopting hope over fear in its election of Clinton. Telling his supporters, "We dared greatly and I would do it again in a minute," Au Coin declared himself, "a lucky man, not a defeated man, because of those 18 years of mutual trust." He then labeled himself "a formerly important person." Packwood, in declaring victory, announced that he'd be recommending AuCoin for the position of Secretary of the Interior and while the Board of Forestry gave him it's hearty backing, critics, including a handful of rural Democrats, contended that AuCoin's environmentalism had moved too far left. AuCoin withdrew his name.

Less than three weeks after the election, *The Oregonian* reported of harassment allegations against pack work by multiple women. The paper had known of the story for weeks before the election and decided not to run it. Away from Congress, AuCoin had a rendezvous with the classroom, lecturing at, among other places, Syracuse University. He is today a successful blogger and informant on issues of the day.

CHAPTER SIXTY-SIX

In Red Eutopia Idaho, Stallings a Rare Streak of Thriving Blue

Introductory Quote: "If I can't stick my neck out for something that is right, perhaps the office isn't worth it." –Idaho Congressman Richard Stallings on his decision to oppose Ronald Reagan's request to aid the Nicaraguan contras, a move quite unpopular with his constituency.

Photo courtesy of Richard Stallings

Near the end of Idaho Democrat Richard Stallings's tenure as Idaho's Second District Congressman, his wife Ranae quipped that he "liked swimming upstream." The remark was not in jest. Stallings was near completion of an improbable eight years of representing some of the most Republican terrain in the nation and was likely a prime motivation for his decision to go up or out in 1992 by mounting a bid for a U.S. Senate seat that despite the political hurdles, many viewed as his to lose.

"Rick" Stallings had every reason for pursuing a Senate seat. After squeaking out a victory against an ethically tarnished and perpetually controversial incumbent by 170 votes in 1984, he forged such strong relations

815

with his very conservative district that he won his last two terms with 63% and 64% respectively. A key reason: Stallings had a voting record that while giving all sides something to like, was geared more towards the right on high-profile issues such as abortion. With the somewhat tempestuous and unappealing Steve Symms up for re-election and Stallings having served half the state in Congress, 1992 was no better time to leap toward the Senate. Only Symms retired soon after and Stallings ended up facing the popular and handsome Mayor of Boise whose appeal proved greater than expected. As such, he could not salvage the seat and was forced into retirement.

Stallings's early background was in Utah. Born in Ogden, he received his B.S. from Weber State College and an M.A. in History from Utah State University. He then embarked on a teaching career, first history in Utah but eventually heading north to Ricks College in Idaho which became home. He chaired the History Department and stayed for 15-years prior to his run for Congress in 1984. All throughout his career, Stallings proved that you could not take the classroom out of the kid. *The Post Register* said the following of Stallings during his Senate campaign. "Even in a comfortable setting - a classroom packed with teachers and high school students – Rep. Richard Stallings is a man in a fight. He can be decisive on issues one moment, entertaining the next."

Prior to her 2014 passing, Stallings's wife Ranae was by his side in every sense
Photo courtesy of Richard Stallings

Prior to his election in Congress, Stallings essentially practiced politics without actually holding office, though not for lack of trying. He ran the campaign of Stan Kress who fell just shy of unseating Hansen and made two unsuccessful runs for a legislative seat. Even his election to Congress had come on his second attempt. Stallings had first challenged Republican George Hansen, an on-again-off-again incumbent (Hansen himself had given up the seat once to make a Senate race) in 1982. One thing that was not on-again-off-again was Hansen's knack for getting into ethical scraps and revelations had come out during that first campaign that a Texas businessman had given his wife a $50,000 loan but that he had left it off his tax return. In a strong year for Democrats nationally and even in Idaho, Stallings fell short with 48%. He immediately vowed to try again but, it's safe to say that the climate in 1984 wouldn't be half as hospitable. What was on Stallings's side, however, was Hansen's mounting legal woes. They were no small potatoes (he was convicted in April) and it made for a rodeo of a race.

There was a longstanding rule in Idaho, "Never bet against George." The selection of Geraldine Ferraro as Walter Mondale's Vice-Presidential nominee very nearly upheld that rule on Election Day. The Democratic ticket was already more anemic in Idaho's Second Congressional District than virtually anywhere in the nation and Hansen, even with his ideological rigidity, was not out of line with Idahoans on most issues. The long-running legal woes was really the elephant in the room and his contention that his supporters, "would vote for me if I were chained in the Bastille" was a boast no one could dare challenge as lacking credibility.

Hansen had long proclaimed himself, "some kind of a crusader against government abuses," and the tax problems of Ferraro's husband came along at a pretty opportune time. Hansen said, "It showed people there was some credibility to what I'd been saying." While Stallings conceded Ferraro's situation "clouds" the Hansen matter, he framed the issue as part of Hansen's overall culture which began with his pitch: "Give me your vote and George Hansen will never embarrass this great state again."

The two did agree to a single debate but Stallings resisted more due to Hansen's proclivities for backing out (Stallings spokesman Paul Pugmire said, "We will not be jerked around by this guy"). Hansen contended Stallings was bought by huge amounts of out-of-state money," including unions which were donating to him.

Early on election night, a victory did not look good and Magic Valley came in stronger than expected for Hansen. Only when Ada and Bannock reported near 2 a.m., did Stallings pull forward but even those returns made victory far from certain. When the remainder of scattered precincts reported, Stallings remained ahead, but by 67 votes. He addressed his apparent win by telling weary supporters, "It was a long night. It was a successful night...We did what we had to do. I would have liked a greater majority, but a majority of one is sufficient."

Not for Hansen. He claimed irregularities in an effort to overturn the loss. One was the methods Democrats used to transport voters to polling sites on the Fort Hill Indian Reservation, a charge Stallings viewed as nonsense. The slim margin ballooned to 170 votes (101,287 to 101,117) but Hansen did not fade away. In 1986, he asked his wife Connie to try to regain her husband's name by running for the seat but local Republicans were ready to move on. She finished third in the GOP primary.

Campaigning for a second term in 1986
Photo courtesy of Richard Stallings

Once he made it to Congress, Stallings's was assigned to the Agriculture Committee and Science, Space and Technology which would serve his constituents well. His first year in office coincided with a severe nationwide agriculture downturn and he asked folks to keep in mind the human toll. "Farm ownership goes much deeper than just owning a business. It is a whole identity, a way of life. What does a 50-year-old man do after losing a farm that's been in his family for three generations," he asked in 1985. "We're dealing with human beings here. That sometimes gets lost in all the statistics."

In Idaho, potatoes were no small matters and Stallings in his third term introduced the "Potato Research and Promotion Amendments of 1989." Barley was another big matter for Idaho's farmers. In 1990, when the Department of Agriculture sought reimbursement for "deficiency" payments that had been mistakenly awarded to the farmers, the delegation met with Agriculture Secretary Clayton Yeutter who turned down the request (he was interested in finding other means to aid them). Stallings subsequently introduced legislation to include the malting barley price from the required repayments.

Photo courtesy of Richard Stallings

Enhancing the greatness of the Idaho National Engineering Laboratory (INEL) was high on Stallings's plate. He urged Defense Secretary Dick Cheney to keep funding for the Specific Manufacturing Capabilities, a 460-person project tank armor project that he said fosters, "a critical, highly specialized technology and capability which is in danger of extinction" (it was on the list for elimination). The special IDLE Separation Project was another priority. He got funding into an Energy Appropriations bill to convert a nuclear facility into a center for brain tumor research. And he fought for construction of a federal minimum security prison in St. Antony.

With Democrat Wayne Owens of Utah (who also gambled on a failed Senate campaign in 1992), Stallings in 1990 fought the attempt by Sierra Pacific Resources to locate the Thousand Springs Power Plant in Nevada. Doing so, the deuce argued, would be deleterious to the air in their respective states. Sierra Pacific eventually pulled the plug on the project. Stallings also sponsored the Craters of the Moon National Park Act of 1989.

Photo courtesy of Richard Stallings

On national issues, Stallings opposed the Congressional pay raise, backed President George H.W. Bush on a capital gains tax cut and supported a Constitutional Amendment banning flag desecration. He did vote to override Bush's veto of a minimum wage increase but sustained him on Family and Medical Leave. He also backed striker replacement legislation and opposed the use of force in the Persian Gulf because he felt more time needed for sanctions to work. When Republicans criticized Stallings for the vote after the war concluded, Stallings responded that the troops that gave the ultimate sacrifice didn't do so for, "30 second ads."

Like most forms of gun control, Stallings opposed the Brady Bill. During debate, he told colleagues it "conflicts with traditions and lifestyle choices that have genuine value for those of us in the American West. These alone might not be grounds to oppose H.R. 7, particularly since I agree with the bill's goal of curbing the criminal misuse of handguns. But I do not believe the bill's mechanism would have any real impact. I do not believe it would make meaningful progress toward the goal. At the same time, and with all due respect to other interpretations, I do not think the bill is consistent with the original intent of the second amendment of our Constitution." Instead, he supported the less restrictive "Staggers Amendment" put forth by West

Virginia Democrat Harley Staggers to implement an instant computerized background check.

While there was no ambiguity in Stalling's opposition to abortion, loyalist Randy Stapilus observed when Stallings was well out of office that, "His position on abortion did not make him invulnerable to attacks from the left or right." He justified Governor Cecil Andrus's veto of an anti-abortion bill by contending it was too extreme. Stapilus wrote, "the Idaho Democratic Party had to take (Stallings's) position into account when drafting their party platform.

House Democratic leaders in Washington had to offer Stallings passes on difficult votes as well and he rationalized it by saying, "I think they recognize...that I can give them 100 percent of the votes for two years but that would be the end of it." Indeed, Thomas Foley, whom mid-way through Stallings's tenure became Speaker of the House, represented a conservative district across the border in Washington State and, himself having had to court very hostile territory early on, was empathetic to the perils Stallings faced. As such, Foley served as a mentor to Stallings throughout his career.

Campaigning for a second term in 1986
Photo courtesy of Richard Stallings

Stallings made a rare bit of national news in the summer of 1988 when three pro-life Minnesota delegates cast their votes for him during the roll call at the Democratic National Convention. Stallings had been on the convention floor when that occurred and his governor, Cecil Andrus, was sitting beside him. Andrus asked Stallings what was happening to which he replied, "Your guess is as good as mind." He declared himself "blown away."

At the time Stallings entered the Senate race, he cited a poll showing him dominating every region save for the Spokane market where his deficit was only about three points. Though the race remained a true tossup for much of the year, that was the high point.

For starters, Symms would not be his opponent. Whether it was a recognition that he would have a difficult time winning or a desire to leave public life, he announced his retirement in the summer of '91, contending, perhaps disingenuously that, "I've never lost an election. And if you look at the polls right now, they show that I would beat Stallings if I were to run again." Symms's parting words was pledging to keep Stallings out of the seat, asserting he would "not sit idly by while a left-leaning Democrat sells the Idaho electorate a bill of goods." He succeeded. Republicans after a spirited primary nominated Dirk Kempthorne, the popular former mayor of Boise.

Before Symms retired, Stallings had already raised $100,000 and national Democrats had promised him $2 million. When he exited the race, Stallings and fellow Democrats moved forward as if it had no impact on the trajectory of the race, a fact Stallings himself acknowledged as his term was about to wind down (he told a reporter, "I was focused totally on getting Symms out of the Senate"). Stallings's involvement in the House banking scandal was minor - eight returned checks but it added to Kempthorne's exploitation of the anti-incumbent mood. Stallings tarred Kempthorne for and those Stallings accused Kempthorne of a wishy-washy stance on NAFTA (Stallings firmly opposed both that treaty and Fast Track due to the potential ramifications on Idaho's sugar beat industry) and ran an ad attacking Kempthorne for raising taxes as Mayor. Kempthorne in turn accused Stallings of not sufficiently standing up to the federal government when it came to local control of water.

Photo courtesy of Richard Stallings

On some issues, Stallings tied himself with the stance of Idaho's former GOP Senator Jim McClure. Wilderness protection was among them and in a candidate forum, Stallings said Kempthorne "has got himself into a bit of a situation where he raises an issue, and then his campaign chairman agrees with me. I don't think Jim McClure was eager to say that Richard Stallings was right." Kempthorne's bottom line was that "the REAL Richard Stallings" is "only telling you what you want to hear."

Almost until Election Day, polls did show a tossup race with Kempthorne only stubbornly leading (45-41%). The final numbers weren't as pretty. As the incoming returns were looking bleak, Stallings implored his backers to "Remember '84!" But they would change little and Stallings phoned Kempthorne four hours after the polls had closed. He told supporters, "The people of Idaho have spoken, and I have a great deal of respect for the democratic system. Now, it's time to get some rest and return to my family." The final was 57-43% and Democrats blamed a laconic ad campaign from the national party.

In 1998, Mike Crapo, who had succeeded Stallings in the Second District in '92, was pursuing the Senate seat (Kempthorne declared "we never got Potomac Fever" and decided to run for Governor) and Stallings used it as an opportunity to reclaim his House seat. Local Democrats, now grasping at straws when it came to wins, were thrilled to have him back and awarded him the nomination. Though he faced a formidable foe in Idaho House Speaker Mike Simpson. Stallings was favored to reclaim the seat through Election Day with one GOP strategist proclaiming the day before that Simpson was "toast." But Simpson surprised folks by prevailing 52-45%. Stallings took his defeat with humor. When asked why he lost, he replied, "Because the other guy got more votes."

In retirement, Stallings became director of the Pocatello Neighborhood Housing Association and a U.S. nuclear waste negotiator. He took one more run at the Second District House seat in 2014 by challenging Simpson but once again, picked the wrong incumbent to go after in the wrong year.

CHAPTER SIXTY-SEVEN

Owens Exceptionalism Evident as a Role Model and a Democrat From Utah

Introductory Quote: "Hey, I've got Senator Ted Kennedy and Robert Redford on my boat!' And the voice came back, 'Yeah, I've got Richard Nixon and Spiro Agnew on my boat!'—which was a big joke." - Steve Owens, the son of Utah Congressman Wayne Owens recalling his father's attempt to enlist the help of other boaters when he, Kennedy and Redford got stuck on a sandbar.

Owens with the Congressional staff that truly loved him
Photo courtesy of Paul Warenski

Wayne Owens is evidence that childhood dreams can come true. His goal as a boy was to serve in Congress – he'd learn Congressional statistics, and during the election of 1948, would use chalk to write, "Harry Truman for President" on local sidewalks. Owens achieved his goal at a relatively early age of 35, remarkable for a state that was even somewhat hostile to Democrats in his time. But his attempt for durability was cut short by a penchant for taking leaps at statewide Senate races that, though credible at the time, was too much of a reach for a member of his party.

The town in which Owens hailed was Panguitch in rural Garfield County and he was the youngest of nine children. His father had lost his farm during the Depression and the family was so poor that Owens didn't have an indoor bathroom until he was a sophomore in high school. But he did have ambitions and he pursued them vicariously through politicians of the day. Besides his labors on behalf of Truman, there was Democratic Senate candidate, Congressman Walter Granger. In a 1992 *Deseret News* profile, Bob Bernick, Jr. wrote that Owens, "traveled the county, pushing Granger's candidacy over GOP Senator Arthur Watkins to anyone who would listen. 'Walt lost the race but he carried Garfield County.'"

Owens earned both his undergrad and his J.D. from the University of Utah, an institution he put himself through by washing dishes at Bryce Canyon Café. He also served a mission, including the presidency, for the Church of Jesus Christ of Latter-day Saints in France.

Owens had a pre-Congressional career that produced connections most aspirants would die for. He spent seven years as an administrative assistant to Democratic U.S. Senator Frank Moss and made such a good impression that Moss "lent" Owens to his colleague, Robert F Kennedy of New York. Kennedy had not declared as a presidential candidate but he and Owens grew close when the Senator vacationed with his family on the Colorado River. Before long, Kennedy was in the race and Owens was his Rocky Mountain Coordinator. While that quest came to a tragic end on June 6, 1968 with Kennedy's murder, Owens carried the torch in part by working for Edward Kennedy.

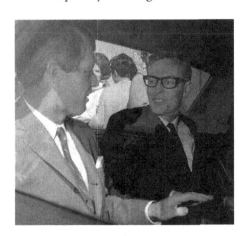

With Robert F. Kennedy, for whom he coordinated Western states in 1968

Owens's first run for Congress came in 1972 when he aimed for the Second Congressional District. Republican Sherman Lloyd had held the seat intermittently since 1960 but, despite being held to a six point victory margin in 1970, seemed poised to benefit from the expected Richard Nixon stampede over George McGovern. But in Owens, Lloyd faced an opponent of youth and zeal which he demonstrated by walking the entire 1,000 mile district, which *The Almanac of American Politics* observes went from Salt Lake City and Provo, "all the way to the Arizona border then." Owens was dubbed the "walking candidate," and recorded his experiences in a book, *The Diary of a Candidate*).

The immense energy paid off Owens not only unseated Lloyd but did so by a solid 11 point margin, 54-43%. How? Well, for starters, the circumstances weren't that adverse. Nixon did handily dispatch McGovern but Democrats were seizing control of the Salt Lake County Commission. That provided a cushion for Owens even as he lost the rural counties. He told supporters, "We are deeply grateful to an incredibly competent staff and 3,000 willing volunteers. We couldn't have even placed, let alone win without them…We are thrilled at the prospects of participating in Congress and pledge just as much energy in serving there as we have expended in getting there." Lloyd "closed my political career with no regrets and without rancor and extend to Mr. Owens my congratulations and good wishes." Time Magazine named him among their "Leaders for the Future."

He fulfilled a campaign promise by sharing his office expenses – including furniture purchases, etc., with his constituents. He fulfilled a campaign promise by sharing his office expenses – including furniture purchases, etc., with his constituents.

Owens's assignment to the House might have seemed like an ordinary, docile assignment when but the 1973-'74 period was anything but ordinary or docile. Watergate was brewing and after the Saturday Evening Massacre, of which Owens was informed by a reporter when he was on a fishing trip, he co-sponsored a motion making the impeachment hearings public, which the House approved 346-40. The result produced a national exposure to the gavel-to-gavel proceedings which riveted generations of all ages.

In late June of 1974, Owens authored a resolution to release 7,200 pages of impeachment material that had been examined. He had made it known that he was unmoved by John Doar's contention that he might have to forego portions of the investigation because he lacked the manpower and urged Doar to ask Congress "for another 20 lawyers" if that's what was required.

One of those charges was that the president had evaded his taxes but when that became a cause for impeachment, for Owens, that proved a bridge to far. His reasoning: "I believe Mr. Nixon knowingly underpaid his taxes...and knowingly had improvements made on his homes. But these offenses don't rise to the level of impeachability."

When the time for deliberations had ended, Owens had no compunction about having the president bear the consequences. As he delivered his statement to Judiciary, he said, "I believe that the impeachment and removal of this president...would be to the public benefit of my country. If we set the standards of impeachment which are too narrow, if we fail to impeach now with this evidence before us, we are saying to future presidents, 'You are not required to obey the law.' And we would...render impotent the impeachment power which the Constitution vested in Congress as the last resort to prevent serious abuses of power by any president." He voted for all four Articles. As the committee deliberated on Article Three, he told members, "Congress must say to future presidents that impeachment is automatic if the President stonewalls Congress and refuses to yield evidence."

Owens was in the midst of a Senate campaign that year to replace the seat's longtime occupant, Wallace Bennett which, had it succeeded, would have meant a Democratic flip of the seat.

For Owens, taking the leap from the House to the Senate after one term wasn't far-fetched at all. Having represented half the state, he entered the contest with a 30 point lead in polls. And as he geared up for his campaign, he acknowledged that despite being a frontrunner, "the pollsters say that can change if there is an issue that emotionally affects the people." In this instance, that issue proved to be Watergate.

The enormity of the scandal increased and as Bob Bernick wrote for *The Deseret News* two decades later, Owens recalled that, "Nixon wasn't the only politician whose career was maimed by Watergate...Mine was, too." For starters, the Watergate hearings forced Owens to remain in Washington through much of the summer, a critical phase for campaigning (his wife often had to play the candidate by standing in for him at county conventions). But the president's approvals weren't as anemic in Utah as other places and this was a rare instance of a potential backlash occurring.

The Republicans nominated Salt Lake City Mayor Jake Garn who equaled or exceeded Owens's name recognition because, as *The New York Times* noted, "the Salt Lake City television stations are picked up in Provo and Ogden, making Mr. Garn a familiar public figure in those cities." Owens recalls "an image was created of a young Ted Kennedy protege running for the Senate over the body of Richard Nixon. That hurt." What also didn't help was the tepid support he received from the most popular Democratic politician in the state, three-term Governor Cal Rampton. These impediments were thought to be at least somewhat neutralized by the presence of American Party nominee Bruce Bangerter, whose votes were projected to come entirely from Garn. Issuewise, Owens hewed firmly to articulating his party's strength such as inflation and a 4% grocery increase.

In the closing days of the campaign, Owens appeared to be slightly ahead. But President Gerald Ford traveled to Utah to stump for Garn and Utah was one of few places where, the Nixon pardon wasn't toxic. Perhaps even more influential: Ezra Taft Benson, President of the Church of Jesus Christ of Latter-day Saints came out for Garn, who ended up winning 50-45%. A harbinger for the loss was that Owens only prevailed in Salt Lake County by a microscopic margin and, other than mid-sized Carbon County, only managed to win a few small areas where few votes were to be had. With Frank Moss's defeat by Orrin Hatch two years later, no Democrat has since come closer than Owens to winning a Senate seat from the Beehive State.

In a fascinating post-script and a reminder that even the most high profile feuds dim with age, Owens struck up a long-distance friendship with Nixon. It stemmed from Owens's proposal to allow former presidents to remain active in government as a non-voting Congressional delegate and Owens recalled, "We had a wonderful conversation that lasted about an hour and a half. We talked about Watergate and the investigation."

For Owens, the next mission was a mission presidency – in Montreal, Canada for the Church of LDS. Kent Tingey started with Owens when he was president of Cooper missionaries, a group of about 250 who lived in Quebec. He calls Owens "very patient, very kind, very thoughtful, always honest and ethical and beloved by his staff...always driven to do the right thing for the right reason." Tingey, who became an executive assistant to Owens when he returned to Congress, said he possessed, "a great leadership ability who had this kind of magnetism that would draw people to him." He remembers often going to Owens's home in the Mount Royal section of Montreal late at night for applesauce pancakes. The group would many times be assembled until late and the next morning, would be sleeping but Owens without fail, would call them at 6 a.m.

In 1984, Owens decided to try for a second political act but this time went for the state level, governor. He had little trouble passing the Boyer Co., construction firm founder Kern Gardner for the Democratic nomination even though Gardner spent $300,000 of his own money and campaigned to Owens's right. The Republican he'd be facing, Norm Bangerter, was as tough as they come. Owens walked 525 miles from the Idaho to Arizona border – turf that spanned more than half a time zone, to attract publicity, though the trip also enabled him to meet rural Utahans. Education was a dominant theme. But Bangerter's name rec and the monstrous Republican edge in Ronald Reagan's best state proved too much and the fact that Owens was able to take 44% was probably satisfactory.

In 1986, Owens made it out of the political wilderness by regaining the House seat he had held more than a decade earlier. Incumbent Republican Congressman David Monson, as Bob Bernick wrote, "was considered by some too much of a light-weight to win re-election against the savvy Owens. The (GOP) leaders talked Monson out of running again, in part by promising him a nice job back in Utah (which the leaders never delivered on)." Owens meanwhile tried for a comeback. The district had more than a Republican lean but Democrats could always be reasonably competitive there and unlike Owens's first stint which contained much of rural Utah, it was now entirely based in Salt Lake County. The Republicans turned to Salt Lake County Commissioner Tom Shimizu in the primary (Shimizu had been interned in a Japanese camp as a boy but had since become president of a Mormon mission).

Owens brought in a number of former colleagues in high places, including Udall and soon-to-be Speaker Jim Wright) while Shimizu tied himself to Reagan. Owens attacked Shimizu for property taxes and raises for colleagues while opponents tried to turn his ties to Ted Kennedy in particular into a liability. Kennedy, who had spent a great deal of time with Owens on a personal level in Utah, actually asked how he could help and he replied, "Stay away." It likely wouldn't have mattered - Owens prevailed 55-44%, the same margin as in '72.

Paul Warenski worked on Owens's staff for two years during the second stint. He notes that although Owens returned to Congress as technically a sophomore, "he was held in pretty high stature by virtue of the fact many of the people with whom he had served during his first term were now in positions of power." Thus, he recalled "he knew everyone in the capitol and you could hardly walk 20 feet without running into people who would say, 'Hey Wayne.'"

It was on wilderness matters that Owens toiled the hardest and one issue that encompassed almost his entire second Congressional career was his legislation to bring back the gray wolf in Yellowstone National Park following completion of a two-year study and he had a strong ally in the Defenders of Wildlife. Not everyone was enamored.

Conducting a press conference with Utah Senator Orrin Hatch
Photo courtesy of the U.S. Senate website

Matt Durham was active on Owens' bid for governor of Utah in 1984 as a volunteer coordinator and had a paid position on the '86 Congressional race. He recalls that constituents who were ranchers and farmers wondered why a congressman from Utah was involving himself in a matter that impacted the states to its north while others warned him not to expand too much capitol on the matter. Owens responded by invoking a question he got from his son: "How can congressmen (from the other states) who don't know anything about what the parks need stop them (park managers) from taking care of Yellowstone?" Owens's answer was that, "There was no answer except, 'That's politics.' And that wasn't good enough."

Owens had a substantive response as well. "The wolf has a bum rap in this country," he declared in 1988. He has very bad press. But wolves do not attack people, and ordinarily do not attack domestic animals if they have a shot at wild animals. In fact, there is no documented case of a healthy wolf ever attacking a human being in the history of North America." The bill had been designed to quell objections from ranchers with a clause that would compensate them for animals lost. It created the Federal Wolf Recovery Committee. But when the U.S. Fish and Wildlife Service issued it's the plan required under the law to begin implementing the wolves reintro, it actually appeared designed to eliminate other wolves. For that, Owens called it, "a cowardly wolf in sheep's clothing," as well as, "a plan that turns the National Environmental Protection Act on its head and endangers the Endangered Species Act." He vowed it "would be fought legislatively. It will be fought politically." It wasn't until the Clinton administration that the Owens plan came to fruition, at which time the now ex-Congressman proclaimed himself, "proud as a papa wolf about to have pups."

America's Redrock Wilderness Act was less successful. It came after a national coalition of some of the most powerful environmental groups joined forces and produced a plan legislation that would preserve 9.4 million acres of the Red Rock Country. But despite attempts in each session of Congress by Owens and long after he had passed to enact the legislation, as well as a highly publicized Executive Order by President Bill Clinton in 1996 establishing the Grand Staircase-Escalante National Monument, the goal has proven elusive to this day.

Owens had long championed the Central Utah Project which Durham notes: "was an important piece of legislation to Utah. That's how the water from the Colorado River got to the farmers and ranchers." It was not a piece of cake. "Everybody wanted the appropriation," he recalled, "but not necessarily the conservation measures that Owens was advocating" (protecting stream flows and habitat). But Garn wanted it to succeed and Republicans generally went along because he was in the majority. "Had he not been there, it wouldn't have happened."

Owens's greatest contribution to his own people might have been The Radiation Exposure Compensation Act which he introduced with Utah's senior Senator, Orrin Hatch and worked out language with Massachusetts Democrat Barney Frank. That was to compensate "downtrodders" – Utahans who had been exposed to radiation following testing in Nevada. Speaking of Nevada, he pressed to have the Thousand Springs power plant killed because of its would-be close proximity to Utah. He also pushed hard for a land-trade bill that would have given land to the federal government for up to $200 million in federal aid. Though "tough parts" had been worked out, and Bangerter supported the measure, the bill died at the close of the 102nd Congress.

For a Democrat in such a GOP heavy district, Owens made no bones about maintaining a voting record overwhelmingly in opposition to Republican presidents. In his last four years in office, his support score of either Reagan or Bush failed to top 30%

It was Owens's liberalism on social and some high-profile foreign affairs matters that carried the most risk in Utah, specifically his opposition to the flag desecration amendment. But Owens had few qualms about supporting a seven day waiting period for the purchase of firearms which he explained on the House floor: "Mr. Chairman, I come from the West where the second amendment is held nearly scared and inviolate, but it is not inconsistent with that amendment to vote for the Brady Bill." While explaining that he preferred an instant background check, Owens noted it had been tried two years earlier by passage of the McCollum amendment and that it had failed." On abortion, Owens was more pro-life than not but he drew the line when rape, incest and the life of the mother was at stake.

In the run-up to the Gulf War, Owens and 45 colleagues sued George H.W. Bush, arguing that Congressional approval is required prior to any action involving force. He sponsored one amendment to prohibit assistance to Serbia and Montenegro. Owens did throw red meat to conservative voters on fiscal issues. During the '86 campaign, he indicated his support for the Gramm-Rudman spending law and reminded voters that he had voted to cut Nixon's budget during his first term in Congress. Going forward, he supported the Balanced Budget Amendment and a capital gains tax. And for small businesses, he advocated gutting Section 89— He wanted to extend the smoking ban that existed on commercial flights to military aircraft.

Republicans were initially optimistic about toppling Owens in 1990, particularly with former Congressman Dan Marriott's entrance into the race. But Marriott was upset by a wealthy businesswoman, Genevieve Atwood and though Bush did travel to Utah to do an appearance on her behalf, her fortunes tanked and Owens won another term with 58%.

Durham recalls that Owens's "politics rubbed a lot of Republicans the wrong way but they got along. He had a good relationship with Hatch as well as First District Congressman Jim Hansen, even though Hansen drew up a redistricting plan that was not politically favorable to Owens (a former Owens staffer, Kenley Brunsdale, had given Hansen a strong race in 1990).

Durham referred to him as, "easy to like, funny warm, self-deprecating." He also recalled his boss as, "always overextended which kind of frustrated his scheduler." But he had an uncanny ability to read the politics of the situation." He also was able to connect like no other. Durham worked for Owens even while going to school and could personally attest to his stature among the youth. "Wayne really had a gift for finding, motivating and inspiring talented young people. He always had a cadre of talented and gifted people around him." He was demanding but Durham never recalls him, "losing his temper with a staff person. On one occasion, he even recalls having a science related proposal, presenting it to the Congressman but having him reply that it basically wasn't ready for him to see. "But," Durham recalls, "he did it nicely."

Warenski also echoes Owens's energy, recalling that he not only contained, "a lot of energy but a good sense of humor and a fondness for stories." He calls him, "a good mentor," and acknowledges that, as a 23-year-old staffer, I didn't fully appreciate all that Wayne had accomplished." He cites working with him as "one of the greatest opportunities in my life to this day."

In mid-1991, Garn announced his retirement and Owens, despite having promised voters during his '86 House race to not again aim for any future Senate openings, could not resist the opportunity to try to succeed him. In such impregnably hostile territory, even one mistake could be fatal. So Owens was hurt immeasurably when it was revealed that he had 87 overdrafts at the House bank totaling $118,900, a number that by itself was problematic but even more so since he just missed landing a spot among the worst abusers.

The Republicans, after a bitter primary and somewhat against the expectations, nominated Robert Bennett over Joe Cannon 51-49%. In an irony that proved that truth can be stranger than fiction, Bennett had a direct connection to Watergate. His firm employed burglar Howard Hunt which steered Owens's dialogue toward, "Bob's past life." And just like 20 years earlier, there was even a break-in and charges by Owens that a "mole" had infiltrated not only his campaign headquarters but Cannon's during the primary.

The general was messy. Bennett tried to frame the race in the role of government terms. "I trust the people on the local level. Wayne trusts the people on the federal level first." Owens presented himself as, "a different kind of Democrat" and said the state "doesn't need another (Republican Senator) Orrin Hatch without hair." Owens hammered at Bennett's, "less than complete explanations" regarding Watergate. This may have backfired as Owen's single digit deficit seemed to widen with Bennett's hard hitting rebuttal. In truth, however, Owens was always swimming seriously upstream in conservative Utah from the outset and he lost 55-40%.

Owens had long been active in trying to foster peace in the Middle East, and he had both trust and credibility with both sides. In 1988, in violation of the state department policy, he went to Tunisia and had a private meeting with Yasser Arafat bearing a gift of snake-skin cowboy boots from Utah that Arafat received with great enthusiasm. Owens came up with the idea of a Middle East Development Bank that won the backing of Egypt and Israel but, as Owens told *The Deseret News*, Jordan and Saudi Arabia held out because, "there is real antipathy toward any economic cooperation where Israel is involved - no matter how indirectly," In the midst of the Gulf War when Iraqi launched scud-missiles were wreaking havoc, Owens ignored warnings and traveled to Jordan where he stayed at King Hussein's palace, "the safest place to be in all of Jordan." Following his departure from Congress, he would be in the region as often as once a month and was well known by staff. So it was appropriate, albeit tragic given his age, that he took his last breaths there.

It was in 2002 and Owens had traveled to Tel Aviv on a mission. One afternoon as the nine-nation trip was concluding, he decided to, "take one last walk along the Mediterranean beach in Tel Aviv — his favorite thing to do." Owens was later discovered unresponsive and pronounced dead of a heart attack. He was 65 years old.

After his death, it was Garn who perhaps paid him his highest compliment. Calling his former foe, "a good politician" he was quick to add, "that's a compliment. You've got a lot of people in both parties who are the grandstanders — always running to talk to the media and such — but Wayne was willing to stick to his political philosophy whether it was popular or not. He sincerely believed in what he was doing, and you have to respect that." Bangerter Chief of Staff Bud Scruggs called Owens, "a tremendous motivator, and he didn't do it with rah-rah speeches."

Warenski recalls being awestruck at Owens's funeral as there were representatives of both Israelis and the PLO. It fit, for Owens was among, "the people on the earth who had the unwavering trust of the Israelis and Palestinians. The peace process suffered badly when he died."

Image via C-SPAN

CHAPTER SIXTY-EIGHT

Jim Moody Emulated Frank Sinatra: He Did It His Way

Introductory Quote: "The House moves in fits and starts and lurches down the road to some uncertain destination. It makes for a lot of time spent...not all of which ends up producing results." - Jim Moody in 1984

Photo courtesy of the Collection of the U.S. House of Representatives

If Jim Moody was a Frank Sinatra fan, his signature song might be, "My Way." Outspoken and unpredictable, the Wisconsin Democrat was in no way out of touch, uninspiring or unappreciated but more than once, he could be befuddling and *The Almanac of American Politics* once wrote, "He has made loud foreign policy pronouncements, some of which have been politically embarrassing."

The five-term Congressman from Milwaukee was often eclipsed by better known members of both the Democratic caucus and his own delegation but had Moody not gambled his House seat on a spectacularly unsuccessful Senate run in 1992, he might have found his niche when Republicans won control two years later. Getting routinely outvoted wouldn't have been pleasant by any means but his flair for hardball and catch-phrase rhetoric would have made him a presence. Examples: those advocating cutting the budget of the National Endowment for the Arts due to obscene exhibits had a "Salman Rushdie mentality" and the 1990 budget summit compromise was a "Leona Helmsley budget" ("only little people pay taxes").

Moody was not iconoclastic or even out of his party is mainstream. It's where he went with a particular issue that sometimes led to head-scratching. One example was the Public Works bill that the committee was deliberating on in 1986. Moody proposed an amendment cutting "demonstration projects" in Congressional districts around the nation – the equivalent to taking candy from a baby as far as members were concerned. He was in turn outvoted 48-2 and one colleague told him the proposal "was as welcome as an illegitimate child at family reunions."

At first glance, Moody seems out of place with crusty, working-class Milwaukee. Born in Virginia, he attended Haverford College and earned his PhD in economics at Harvard University. But if Milwaukee is an ethnic city, Moody seemingly had a touch of every ethnicity and *The Journal Sentinel* said, "he spoke five languages - Greek, Spanish, Serbo-Croatian, Farsi and French." He had very few heirs and one source even speculated he'd "dress in tatters if someone did not force him into buying clothes."

Empathy was also vintage Moody because, having a father who worked for the American Red Cross and a mother who assisted refugees gave him exposure to the poorest of the poor. It also meant traveling the world – grade school was in Shanghai, high school in Athens, Greece and his work for CARE in Iran and Yugoslavia. In testimony before a Congressional committee decades later during the Serb/Croat conflict, Moody noted he had "been in literally every Republic on a number of occasions as well as every town and almost every village in that country." That was well before the Peace Corps where it was off to Bangladesh and Pakistan. Once back at stateside, he worked at the Peace Corps office in Washington D.C., the U.S. Agency for International Development and as an economist for the federal government.

One refreshing trait about Moody was that folks always know where he stood. After supporting the much-criticized pay raise in Congress, he offered the explanation, "I owe my honest assessment of every single issue - even one so subject to political posturing and pandering as this one has been."

In the early 1970s, Moody obtained his Ph.D in Economics from Berkeley College and, throughout his years in Congress, would tell members of the California delegation that the years he spent in the state made him feel like an honorary member. His move to the Badger State came when he was offered a position as a professor at the University of Wisconsin and politics came soonafter. In 1976, he won a seat in the State Assembly and the State Senate two years later. He championed trucking deregulation and a moratorium on the building of expressways.

In 1982, the retirement of a 28-year fixture, Henry Reuss, created an opening for the 5th Congressional district and Moody went for it. He was far from alone. Six other Democrats filed for the nomination and Moody's main rival appeared to be Fred Kessler who at age 42, had spent literally half his life in politics. Kessler had won a State Assembly seat at age 21 but, until resigning to try to take the 5th, had gone on to become a Milwaukee Circuit Court Judge. State Senator Warren Braun was the sole anti-abortion candidate in the race while Milwaukee Alderman Kevin O'Connor was supposedly being groomed to run for mayor via this race. A former Alderman, Orville Pitts was expected to dominate the African-American vote in the city but little else. A television newscaster named Marty Aronson was also in the race.

Photo via The Milwaukee Journal Sentinel

With the field such a donnybrook, someone needed a technique to stand out among the voters. In Moody's case, it was incessant door-knocking that had begun almost the moment Reuss had announced his departure a year earlier. *CQ* wrote just before the primary that, "his visits to 20,000 district households have all been preceded by a piece of mail announcing his arrival and followed by another note thanking the person he met." The other candidates knocked on doors as well but they could not match Moody, or his mother who was his campaign manager (Kessler brought along his mom sometimes too which created the "Battle of the Moms"). The visits accomplished their goal. On Moody's obituary, *The Journal Sentinel* wrote that when he and his brother attended, "a Milwaukee Brewers game, they hardly had time to watch the players. People in nearly every section knew Jim from his time door-knocking."

How up for grabs was the nomination? There were seven candidates and on primary night, all but one finished in the teens. With 18.4%, Moody finished 1,269 votes ahead of Kessler who took 17.1%. Pitts took a very surprising 16% (benefitting from turnout in the city's African-American wards where he had concentrated his media advertising), Brown 14%, Aronson 12% and O'Connor an anemic 11%. Pitts was angered that a number of his supporters were not permitted to vote for not having proper identification and briefly threatened a recount.

The nomination was Moody's and it seemed, so was the general election. Redistricting had added pockets of GOP enclaves – particularly four suburbs, but that said very little for this district – it was by far the safest for a Democrat in the Badger State and in any case, 1982 was not a year for the GOP to make a breakthrough. It wasn't for lack of trying. The GOP was high on Moody's colleague, State Senator Rod Johnston who urged folks to, "vote for the man, not the party." Most voters concluded they were one in the same and he was able to garner just 35%.

In such a lopsidedly Democratic district (Michael Dukakis took 64%), Moody never again sweated a general election though he did not always escape spirited primaries. In 1988, Matt Flynn held him to 58% Peter Taylor challenged him in 1990. Labeling the incumbent, "laid-back," Taylor said, "I don't think Jim Moody has been representing the interests of the people." Voters disagreed and Moody turned him back 78-22%.

Moody was assigned to the Interior and Insular Affairs Committee and Public Works and Transportation but, in 1987, following a vocal campaign, Moody secured a seat on the House Ways and Means Committee despite the misgivings of Chairman Dan Rostenkowski that he would not be a loyalist.

While calling Moody confrontational might be a stretch, one of his characteristics could be in-you-face rhetoric when he saw things as unjust. He had no problem calling the other side out for dishing out a raw deal and a speech on the House floor on vocational education was classic Moody. "Yesterday in Kentucky, President Reagan extolled the virtues of vocational education, yet he proposes a 39% reduction for fiscal year 1984 for vocational instruction, a $350 million dollar cut that would seriously impair the effectiveness of this program."

On kitchen table and many international issues, Moody was firmly ensconced with his party. Pro-choice and in favor of gay rights quite early, Moody and a handful of other members threatened legislation to fight Reagan's prohibition against aid for international family planning organizations that "promote" abortion. He joined Lindy Boggs of Louisiana to sponsor a bill studying hurdles that women who own businesses face ("I think it will be a more interesting world when both men and women are free to move across previously rigid borders").

Moody framed his view against the flag-burning amendment by telling colleagues about his recent visit to the suddenly free Bulgaria. "This country (the U.S.) is different, thank God. For 200 years, one of the basic foundations of our Republic has been free speech. Even when that speech is ignorant, childish, and even offensive as it is with flag burners. We have been through 200 years of civil rights turmoil, Vietnam War protests, debates, division, and even a wrenching Civil War. Never once in all of that time did we feel it was necessary to water down the Bill of Rights, and particularly the first amendment.

In 1987, Moody circulated a letter calling for the resignation of Elliott Abrams as Assistant Secretary of State for Inter-American Affairs due to his "various deceptions and his clear contempt for the Constitutional role of Congress in conducting foreign policy, It was signed by 125 colleagues. Moody routinely opposed contra aid. In 1990, Moody was outspoken on the need to cease aid to El Salvador.

Photo via The Milwaukee Journal Sentinel

In 1987, Moody and his colleagues, Tom Downey of New York and Bob Carr of Michigan took a nine-day trip to Siberia to inspect a "phased-array radar" site in Krasnoyarsk that the Reagan administration claimed was not in compliance with the Anti-Ballistic Missile Treaty. The conclusion they and scientists traveling with them reached was that there was no violation of ABM.

His erraticism came on other matters. He would often vote against water projects. In 1990, Moody, "with a heavy heart and mixed feelings," became a supporter of the Balanced Budget Amendment.

Moody had backed Florida Democrat Claude Pepper's ambitious catastrophic health care plan in 1988 against Rostenkowski, the only Ways and Means Democrat to do so. It was therefore not surprising that a little over a year later, Moody found disconcerting the stampede by members to repeal the catastrophic health coverage in the face of seniors angry over premium hikes. He called the move to do so "the epitome of the old adage that 'when you're being run out of town get out in front and make it look like a parade.' But this is not a parade that any of us should rush to join. The pressure to 'just get rid of this issue' is undeniable. To yield to it is wrong."

In arguing that, "the principal winners (of repeal) will be the wealthiest senior citizens in the country," Moody's view was essentially repeal and replace. "We should repeal catastrophic and enact a long-term care bill: A long-term care program will cost $60 billion a year, minimum. Proponents of repeal know this. Who do they think that they're kidding? If we are not going to hold fast on a $10 billion catastrophic coverage program, where are we going to find the courage to enact a $60 billion long-term care program?"

Not surprisingly, Moody plotted to take action. With Illinois Democrat Marty Russo, Moody was the prime sponsor of a single payer health care system and he cited a Congressional Budget office (CBO) report that 67 billion dollars could be saved by moving. Canada was a role model. There, he said at a Ways and Means panel, "they don't review every surgical decision on a case-by-case decision. The way it's done here, with tremendous overhead costs involved in doing that... they only pick out the outliers (of an entire doctor's record) very much the way the IRS does income tax. The computer spits out the outliers and they look at it. If a doctor is two standard deviations away from his peers, then they look at it."

Moody had flirted with undertaking a Senate bid in 1988 and was all in when he determined that he could not compete with the millionaire Milwaukee Bucks owner Herb Kohl who won the seats. In 1992, despite the fact that another millionaire for the Democratic nod, Chris- was in the race, he got in and stayed in. But he was also facing a very original State Senator by the name of Russ Feingold and the race became anybody's.

Money wasn't as much Moody's problem this time – he had $2 million compared to Checota's $3.6 million (Feingold had $600,000) and for a good part of the campaign, Moody was in the lead. The problem was tone. He and Checota eviscerated each other so brutally that pundits got turned off and voters followed. Income taxes were a main issue – Checota accused Moody of paying his late and following an arrest warrant while Moody said Checota did not pay his at all.

Moody ran an ad contrasting his progressivism with Checota's flaws. "While health-care executives made obscene profits, Jim Moody wrote a plan for national health insurance while some wealthy Americans paid no taxes. Jim Moody fought to cut taxes for working families."

By late August, all three candidates were within the margin of error in the low 20s. It seemed that everyone would be mocking the dueling duo and Feingold was no exception. One ad said, "While they've been discrediting each other, I've been issuing my 82-point plan to eliminate the federal deficit. And I've been talking to you voters…." Feingold contrasted his house in Middletown with his rivals. In Checota's case, a sign read, "Private. Dead end." With Moody, there was a photo of Moody's house in DC and a "brochure" of an abode in Jamaica" where the campaign could not afford to travel to take an authentic photo. By mid-August, Moody began taking aim at Feingold. Trying to paint himself as the true liberal, he said, "I didn't know progressives used an orthodoxy, and that we had litmus tests for what it takes to enter the club. I think Russ Feingold is taking a few differences with me and magnifying them…in order to avoid a third-place finish in this race."

Photo via The Milwaukee Journal Sentinel

Both Moody and Checota got the message and pulled their negative advertising but by that time, it was too late – Feingold had cultivated an image of "Mr. Clean" and voters responded in kind. Marquette Political Science Professor George Reedy put a colorful take on Feingold's surge. "Moody was calling Checota a bum. And Checota was calling Moody a bum. The public finally decided they understood each other, and they're both bums."

Realizing that he neither he nor Moody were going to win, Checota kicked the Congressman while he was down. In a debate, he told Wisconsinites that he'd truly like to be their Senator, then added, "If it can't be me, I believe that

Russ Feingold would better represent the people of Wisconsin." Voters agreed though his 70% showing was a true eyebrow raiser.

Feingold racked up 84% in Dane. Milwaukee was slightly kinder to Moody but not by much – he took just 25%, a stunning obliteration for a longtime officeholder from that part. The only pleasure of sorts Moody could take from the evening was that he finished 3,000 votes ahead of Checota though that was even qualified. Checota managed to carry three counties in the Northern part of the state. Moody took not-a-one. He was gracious. "Losing a campaign is a very humbling experience, but I have very positive memories and I don't have any regrets at all." He made it known that the wounds on his part had already healed, telling backers to, "Make sure Wisconsin has a new United States Senator - Russ Feingold. The state deserves better than it has had."

Immediately out of office, Moody was a deputy director of the preparation of newly-elected President Bill Clinton's forthcoming budget. Becaue its focus was remedying a dire fiscal situation with hard choicesm the blueprint was entitled, "Eat Your Broccoli First." Moody's overall post-Congressional career was a mixture of teaching (the University of Maryland and American University), and humanitarian (Vice-President of the U.N.'S International Fund for Agriculture Development). He also acted as an international election monitor. He died in 2019 at age 83.

CHAPTER SIXTY-NINE

"Mr. Jobs," Roe Yielded to No One When it Came to Jersey Infrastructure

Introductory Quote: "I'm not sure that we have enough room to locate the new NASA launch facility in the Meadowlands." – Congressman Robert Roe as he became chair of the House Science, Space and Technology Committee. Roe had made the remark in jest but it reflected his tireless efforts to bring infrastructure to New Jersey.

Photo courtesy of the Robert A. Roe Archive, David and Lorraine Cheng Library, William Paterson University

To his constituents, Bob Roe was a Representative always on hand and willing to listen. To his colleagues, no parochial project was too insubstantial, no consensus was too far apart to forge, and no ideology or party affiliation was ever a hindrance. To his state and nation, greatness was attainable via a hefty infrastructure that he was only to proud to foster.

For Roe, a Democrat who served in Congress 23 years, patience was not a virtue. Working endless hours was a hallmark and he was "very aggressive on legislation (and) very creative" to the point that the joke in Washington was "it's the Roe way or no way." Sometimes, his agenda and timing didn't always mesh with even those with whom he would normally be expected to be on the same page. At no time was that more illustrated than his abrupt retirement announcement shortly after the culmination of a redistricting process that sacrificed Democratic colleagues and gave him a safe seat. But his, "there's always a way to do this," as one staffer almost always came true.

Vice-President Walter Mondale dubbed Roe, "Mr. Jobs," and that proved his shtick throughout his whole career. It came via public works which Roe made sure was vigorous and properly funded at every level. Near the end of his career, Roe got to chair the panel that doled those projects out and the results were profound all across the nation. New Jersey was at the hallmark and he once famously said, "I'm not sure that we have enough room to locate the new NASA launch facility in the Meadowlands."

Roe was born to a postman in Wayne, New Jersey and during World War II, served as an Army groundsman with the Second Infantry in Europe. He was awarded a Bronze Star. He attended school in Oregon and Washington State, studying engineering and political science respectively and the underdeveloped and somewhat sleepy nature of those two fairly new states might have helped Roe forge an appreciation for the necessity of progress that would define his career.

Politically, Roe first sought a seat on the Wayne Township Committee and, proving the axiom that the third time's a charm, succeeded in winning on his third attempt. He eventually became Mayor.

In 1963, New Jersey Governor Richard J. Hughes named Roe Commissioner of Conservation of Economic Development and again, smart progress was the name of the game. In December 1965, he said, "...We can no longer afford the desecration of our environment in any respect. We must seek to achieve the full communion of our human and natural resources to combat the major environmental problems facing our state today. Our degree of success depends in a large measure on how we realistically appraise our objectives and goals to the resources at hand. If we devote our time and energies toward preserving, protecting, enhancing and developing these resources, we shall have come a long way toward achieving the society we seek..."

To that end, Roe helped make the now treasured Superfund a reality and launched the first study of a Pinelands preservation which became a much ballyhooed reality roughly a decade later. One of his initiatives was the New

Jersey Natural Lands Trust, written up as, "an organization that could accept land donations and ensure their protection in perpetuity by resisting the exercise of eminent domain by public agencies." The legislature enacted the proposal and it grew to having oversight of 26,000 acres of open space. The 1,117 acres of Skylands was purchased from Shelton College under Roe's direction ("I regard the preservation of this area of the state as essential and a foremost opportunity to meet the Green Acres objectives"). He helped make Teterboro Airport a reality and revitalized the state's once prospering oyster industry that had been destroyed a decade earlier by a shellfish disease called MSX.

Brian Hughes, the governor's son who later became Mercer County Executive called Roe, "the guy who could build a consensus. If it took one vote at a time, he would go after it one vote at a time. I think some of that he learned from my father. It doesn't happen much anymore but it can happen if there are grownups in the room."

With his boss, Governor Richard J. Hughes
Photo courtesy of the William Patterson
University Library Special Collections

When Democratic incumbent Charles Joelson was appointed to the New Jersey Superior Court in 1969, Roe was selected the nominee to replace him in a Passaic County based district where the major towns were Clifton,

Passaic, Paterson and Wayne. The GOP tapped Passaic Valley Sewerage Commissioner Gene Boyle who also owned a local restaurant that even Roe frequented ("I love the food here, but of course, I brought my food taster tonight," he quipped during the campaign). Boyle accused him for profiting off of a land deal while Roe spoke of a periodic withdrawal from Vietnam. The race was considered Roe's to lose and the unexpected landslide win by GOP gubernatorial candidate William Cahill almost caused him to do so, but he finally won by just 960 votes (67,188 to 66,128).

Roe was assigned to the Public Works and Transportation Committee where he forged a close relationship with another New Jerseyan, Jim Howard, who would one day rise to become chair. The pair was talking about traveling to Ireland together hours before Howard dropped dead of a heart attack in 1987. Roe plunged straight into the issue of trying to give residents a break from noise from jets and at the start of the next Congress, took a seat on the Science, Space and Technology Committee.

To get to that next Congress, Roe had to run for a full-term in 1970 and Assemblyman Alfred E. Fontanella charged hard at him. The challenger attacked the incumbent for doing little to stop the increasing drug epidemic while Roe attacked Fontanella on his record of taxes in the Assembly. But the impression Roe had formed with voters, while brief, was unflappable (one of his billboards labeled him, "Your Personal Representative") and Roe shot up to 63% and never faced a remotely tough race again.

By 1975, Roe chaired the Public Works Subcommittee on Economic Development. His earnestness for infrastructure improvement often led him to butt heads with presidents of both parties but many times, though not always, he came out on the winning end. His first accomplishment with national ramifications came during his third year in the House when he helped write Federal Water Pollution Control Act Amendments of 1972. Roe and most of his colleagues were astonished when President Nixon vetoed the bill weeks before Election Day but Congress overrode him.

In the midst of the 1975 recession, Roe sponsored a major anti-recession package that cleared the chamber 313-8. His closing argument was, "We would hope that the administration would...now see fit to place its support behind this measure for the last thing America needs in this hour of economic peril is a partisan tug-of-war." Roe called beliefs that it would cause inflation, "absurd" and President Gerald Ford signed the measure.

In at least his first decade in the Congress, 1977 was probably Roe's busiest year, though a big electoral defeat made it less than exhilarating. First, he shepherded yet another public works bill to passage. Roe had been angered by an amendment by Pennsylvania Senator John Heinz that would have revised the distribution formula for projects at the expense of the Garden State. Roe vowed to, "fight like hell against that Senate amendment," but Senators killed it on the floor. Roe also worked on reversing a 70-30% formula from the '76 jobs bill that had been intended to award construction jobs to communities with the highest levels of unemployment (the money ran out far quicker than anyone intended and many communities were left out). Henceforth, a minimum unemployment was set for the doling out of the grants.

In 1977, Roe decided to take advantage of the astounding unpopularity of Governor Brendan Byrne, a fellow Democrat. Byrne, whose enactment of an income tax provoked unmitigated anger, seemed poised to be relegated to going down as, "One-term Byrne." Roe called for a ballot initiative to decide the tax increase and a convention to find its replacement, saying, "If the people of New Jersey are to regain their confidence in our state government, they must have a larger voice in the decision-making." He spent $815,000 which *The New York Times* called, "nearly twice the amount raised by most major candidates in both races. Had the race been one-on-one, or even one-on-three, Roe most certainly would have defeated Byrne. But five serious candidates and eleven total (including his South Jersey colleague Jim Florio), helped Byrne prevail with a mere 30%, roughly 40,000 votes ahead of Roe who took 23%. Passaic came in big for its hometown boy (86%) and Morris and Sussex went for him as well. But Florio took much of south Jersey and Byrne was able to limp to the top of most of the other counties.

Roe tried for the governorship again in 1981 and this time, abandoned the big-money, instead relying on small donations. He adopted the slogan, "Give a Buck for Bob" and explained, "When you see the signs that say, 'This commercial paid for by friends of,' remember they're not being paid for by any friends; they're being paid by you!" Because Roe turned down public financing, his supporters resorted to what *The New York Times* described as, "organizing cake and cookie sales, film festivals on college campuses, a hayride, dances, horse races and $1 buffet lunches in a campaign for Governor that is unusual this year because it is old-fashioned." Bea O'Rourke, his field director gleefully quipped, "We're emphasizing the old techniques - get a friend, get a buck, make the system work. And I haven't had so much fun in years."

This time, the field was even more fractured than '77 – 13 candidates encompassing every part of the political spectrum. Florio was one of them and he managed to come out on top with 25%. Roe did well in north Jersey and even managed to eke out a win in populous Bergen County but did not even place in the top five in some southern counties. There would be no more statewide runs on Roe's horizon.

**Photo courtesy of the Robert A. Roe Archive, David and
Lorraine Cheng Library, William Paterson University**

1977 brought Roe more success on the legislative front. As Congress geared up to renew the expiring authorization of the 1972 Water Pollution Control Act, newly inaugurated President Jimmy Carter was infuriating members of both parties by proposing to cut funding for water project around the nation. Then Roe had to deal with an eight-month stalemate between House and Senate conferees as funding was nearing an end. But an early Christmas came in mid-December when an agreement was forged. As a result of Roe's stewardship, 98 water sewage-treatment facilities throughout New Jersey became a reality and the Garden State would be guaranteed $178,575,000 in each of four years beginning in Fiscal Year 1979 (and a slightly less amount in '78).

In 1980, Roe had a rare case of misfiring – badly. The Carter administration had an ambitious urban policy renewal agenda in the hopper, which potentially meant a $5 billion budget increase for the Economic Development Authority. Roe wanted $2 billion which Carter was not prepared to give. Finally, Carter agreed to Roe's demand but the election was looming and Republicans gambled that they'd win the election and decided not to act. That indeed happened and the now lame-duck administration was forced to settle for the same funding levels.

The 98th Congress (1983-'85) was without question the most frustrating for Roe because two major reauthorization packages failed to get implemented - his sweeping $800 million water reauthorization legislation and the Clean Water Act Reauthorization legislation. The water bill, which *The New York Times* called, "the first comprehensive public works bill in 16 years," had cleared Public Works 49-0 died primarily because the Senate refused to act. Among other things, it contained cost-sharing formulas, port funding, flood control, etc.

Photo courtesy of the Robert A. Roe Archive, David and Lorraine Cheng Library, William Paterson University

Roe and Howard made another push for the legislation in 1985 and reduced the cost of the bill by $9 million which the House cleared 340 to 83. This bill called for a loan program to eventually phase-out direct funding for sewage programs. They again faced a recalcitrant Senate but also the Reagan administration who wanted the phase-out to occur sooner. Roe's response was, "If we cut the bill one more penny we are destroying pollution control and the water supply of this country." Reagan did sign it in November '86 and Robert Dawson, Assistant Secretary of the Army for Civil Works called it, "a very historic moment."

Roe with New Jersey Senator, "Dollar Bill" Bradley
Photo courtesy of the Robert A. Roe Archive, David and
Lorraine Cheng Library, William Paterson University

Clean water extended into a third session of Congress. Though Roe in 1986 moved the bill to the floor by negotiating an end to a protracted battle with the New York City delegation over the amount of sewage New Jersey would accept, Reagan vetoed the measure. As soon as the 100th Congress convened, Roe began anew and contended during the debate that, "Clean water is life itself. There is nothing more important that we could do." The initial vote was 406-8 but a Reagan veto came at them again. This time, however, it was overridden.

Roe's position on Science put oversight of the 1986 Challenger disaster in his lap. He would not be holding the gavel of the full Science Committee until the following January but Don Fuqua of Florida was leaving to take a NASA related job and saw chairing the hearing a conflict of interest. During a series of hearings following the release of the (William) Rogers Commission Report on why the tragedy took place, Roe declared, "Because of its great success story, Congress has been too shy in finding fault with NASA. As the result of the Challenger accident, Congress and NASA must begin a new era, one in which Congress must apply the same strong oversight to NASA that it does to any other government agency." Roe admonished Rogers even in his opening statement to stick to the scopes and hit NASA Administrator James Fletcher.

Roe spoke of plans for astronaut safety, asking 'What kind of figure do we assign to a life?' We're going to take another serious look at this, an in-depth look at what we may be able to do to help astronauts (in accidents).We're going to be looking in our next oversight to that particular issue, as to how we put the system cost analysis-benefit ratio to the loss of human life."

In later years, Roe continued supporting space exploration and in 1987, helped thwart efforts to move money for the space station into programs for housing. Ditto in 1991 when he faced a determined effort by some influential Appropriators to kill it. He took the floor after a four-hour wait, Hosanna, hosanna. hosanna," he declared, resorting to the biblical term that means, "save, rescue." He continued: "You know, I came to Congress 22 years ago and I think we were talking about some pride and dreams. It is not just what we do as bean counters and lemmings, it is what the country is about. We would never have been able to fight Desert Storm if it had not been for advanced technology. It could not have been done. And we saved lives doing it."

During his stint on Science, Roe also advocated hard for construction of the Super Conductor Collider, even though New Jersey had no stake in it. The SSC, he said, "will enable the United States to regain its world leadership in high energy physics." Roe worked with proponents to ward off the quest for less money that could have potentially killed the project, particularly an effort by Missouri Congressman Jack Buechner to cut funding on the floor (Roe sponsored a compromise that was accepted).

Photos courtesy of the Robert A. Roe Archive, David and Lorraine Cheng Library, William Paterson University

After the 1990 election, Roe was comfortably ensconced at Science and the gavel at Public Works was not even a second thought. Though there was widespread concern over the leadership of the panel's aging chair, Glenn Anderson of California, Roe actually endorsed Anderson for the new Congress, one of only two Public Works Democrats to do so (Doug Applegate of Ohio was the other). Instead, the full caucus ousted Anderson and Roe decided to throw his hat into the ring. He faced competition from Norman Mineta of California but won 121-107 and credited the fact that, "Everybody I looked at, I think, either had a bridge or a highway or a railroad or something we worked with the on." He forged harmonious relations with his ranking Republican of the committee, John Paul Hammerschmidt of Arkansas.

That turned out to be the right spot at the right time and, unbeknownst to everyone including Roe himself, a last hurrah. His penultimate achievement in Congress undoubtedly came during that term as he shepherded to fruition the Intermixed Surface Transportation Efficiency Act (ISTEA or "Ice Tea"), a $150 billion piece of legislation that became known as the Highway Act of 1991.

The blueprint was entitled, "A Nickel for America" and the objective was to build 458 projects in colleague's districts throughout the nation, in part by a nickel gas tax. He called them "Congressional projects of national significance." Treasury Secretary Sam Skinner pegged them as unnecessary, in part contending that many of the projects "have not had rigorous evaluation; have little merit in terms of advancing new technology or concepts," etc.

In presenting his plan, Roe said, "The time to rebuild America is now. We must not allow our infrastructure to decay and collapse while user fee taxes paid by the American people are diverted to address other intended issues. If the nation is to be competitive in the global economy of the 21st century," Throughout the process, he made clear his disdain for "people who have made a career of being environmentalists" and fighting the act. Eventually, the nickel tax fell by the wayside but a comprehensive plan was enacted and President Bush eagerly signed ISTEA into law.

Again, Roe's mastery of the details made outfoxing him impossible. One colleague said, "He didn't just know it but he plunged into it. He "knew our bill, chapter and verse." Infrastructure needs continued even after and when technical corrections were needed to ISTEA in 1992, Roe inserted money for sound barriers in Paterson.

Roe's vociferously opposed abortion but, aside from that, his voting record was in perfect company with other liberals. He opposed raising the Social Security retirement age, favored passage of ERA and opposed military aid to Nicaragua. He was solidly aligned with labor.

**Photo courtesy of the Robert A. Roe Archive, David and
Lorraine Cheng Library, William Paterson University**

Roe was legendary for his simplistic lifestyle which was defined by his endless devotion to his work. Shortly after his death, Phil Beachem of *The Star-Ledger* wrote, "You never had to wonder where you would meet the congressman in Washington. He was usually in his office in a quiet corner of the Rayburn House Office Building preparing for the next meeting. Late-night meetings or grabbing a sandwich in the House cafeteria with federal workers were the norm."

During a farewell special order to retiring New Jersey members, fellow New Jersey Democrat Rob Andrews, a freshman, said Roe, "does not know what a recess or a vacation is. I sometimes think he does not know what a weekend means because he loved this job." Bill Clinger, a Pennsylvania Republican who served on Public Works with Roe for 14 years, declared in that special order that, "If there is harder working, more dedicated or more effective member of Congress the. Bob Roe, I do not know of him or her."

The same was evidently true for his staff though, it's not clear whether this was voluntary. voluntarily. A member of his subcommittee told *The New York Times* in 1977 subcommittee that Roe is, "quite a character as long as you like to work 18 hours a day," while adding, "He's totally conscientious and has a good sense of humor. He's probably the most technically and professionally qualified subchairman the House has ever had."

Sante Esposito was the Democratic counsel for Public Works during the drafting of ISTEA and he recalls "months when I did not see my family or house in daylight," adding, "the biggest challenge was finding a gas station" that was open at those hours. So intense was the process that one morning, Esposito needed to clear his head and told his secretary to tell Roe when he called that he had not yet arrived. He called again ten minutes later and the response was the same. Moments later, Esposito found a 6'4 intern hovering over him saying, "The chairman wants to see you." The intensity was such that, "we sometimes struggled to give him the best we should have because he wanted stuff yesterday." But Esposito is quick to call Roe, a "decent boss" for whom it was good working for.

While selfish is not a fitting label for Roe, one longtime confidante and employee recalls that accepting change was not easy. This individual tendered his resignation in part because he wanted to retire and in part to care for his ailing wife and Roe simply couldn't understand it. Tension between the two men eventually went away but it took a while. On another note, while he and Florio became good friends after the gubernatorial elections, Roe was known to constantly rib him about the '77 primary and costing him critical support (how Florio's support would have trickled down would have been speculative in any case).

Another Roe hallmark was his residence and Beachem noted that he lived for his entire tenure in Washington in "the Skyline Inn — a cheap and seedy hotel in one of Capitol Hill's less picturesque neighborhoods." For other attributes, Roe was known as a good dancer with had a dry sense of humor. On his death, *The Star-Ledger* wrote, "Roe was in a constant hurry and virtually any greeting would be met with the efficient reply 'likewise.' He was fond of cheddar cheese sandwiches on white bread with ketchup, which he would invariably follow with a cigarette."

Enactment of the highway coincided with the beginning of the redistricting process. With New Jersey losing one Congressional seat, nothing was certain save one thing: that Roe would not be the odd man out. Indeed, the priority of cartographers on both sides was to create a safe district for Roe and even when a judicial panel adopted the GOP plan, Roe's district was safe as can be. Only, he didn't want it.

Late in March, Roe announced that he would forego another term in the House. "After 23 years in Congress," he explained, "I want to spend more time at home in New Jersey. I want to be able to spend more quality time with friends and family...I simply want to pursue other endeavors of public and private sectors." There was panegyric shock but, in New Jersey it was not without anger. State Senator Ray Lesniak said, "We would have collapsed Roe's district and saved Frank Pallone and Bernie Dwyer." Mostly though, Roe was saluted for a career that "took him from the sewer to the highways and to the stars."

Photo courtesy of the Robert A. Roe Archive, David and Lorraine Cheng Library, William Paterson University

Even after retirement, Roe would be hard at work for New Jersey.

It was no secret that Roe was a drinker and, while never impacting his ability to perform his job duties, it did create needless problems for which he later in life paid some price. The summer he retired, he injured two when he crashed into a minivan in the town of Rockaway. Several years later, after New Jersey legislators voted to rename Route 23 after Roe, Mothers Against Drunk Driving and family members of the victims protested and Roe asked that the project be called off. Roe died at age 90 in 2014.

In retirement
Photo courtesy of the William Patterson
University Library Special Collections

CHAPTER SEVENTY

To Some, Scheuer was an SOB but to New Yorkers, "He was Our SOB"

Introductory Quote: "Power is the name of the game now. When I was a kid it was ice cream. When I got older, it was sex. Now I know its power. When you touch the power nerve, you'd better know what you're doing." –New York Congressman James Scheuer as he embarked on his bid to become New York City's Mayor in 1969.

Photo courtesy of the Collection of the U.S. House of Representatives

Throughout his lengthy political career, Jim Scheuer took Manhattan, the Bronx though, not Staten Island but Long Island too. Oh, and also Brooklyn and Queens. Dubbed, "the Flying Dutchman," an election, a defeat and two remaps allowed Scheuer to represent four of the five Boroughs and remain immensely popular. Ultimately, a third remap in 1992 proved to permanently slay the dragon as age, new boundaries would have been too much for him to bear.

If anything is certain in a Congress full of uncertainties, it's that Jim Scheuer would never win a popularity contest. Cantankerous, ornery and just plain difficult were some notable characteristics. Scheuer's reputation was personified at a New York delegation meeting when a colleague stood up and informed the others of Energy and Commerce Chair John Dingell's push to strip Scheuer of his post as head of the Consumer Protection and Finance Subcommittee. Harlem Democrat Charlie Rangel stood up and said that while, "Jim Scheuer may be an S.O.B, he's our S.O.B." Those difficulties didn't detract him, however, from a political record of deep compassion and trying to rid civil wrongs. At the top of his list: poverty, education inequities and racism. A *New York Magazine* profile cited Scheuer (shoy-ER) as, "a reserved man who appears more at ease in private conversations or with small groups than he does in crowds or large public gatherings. He is tall, soft-spoken, smokes pipes constantly and uses them effectively as political props." Every program has roots and, for Head Start, bilingual education, Scheuer played a pertinent role that could easily rank him as a founding father.

Scheuer earned a little fame early, learning to play the harmonica and becoming New York City's champion at age 13. His obituary noted that, "throughout his career he continued to entertain and impress his constituency and his peers with his ability to play anything from Bach to Sousa marches." Scheuer received his Bachelor's from Swarthmore College, an Industrial Relations degree from Harvard's Graduate School of Business Administration followed by his L.L.B. degree from Columbia University Law School in 1948, the same year he married and caught polio on his honeymoon (he would often be reliant on a cane as a result).

The path of Scheuer's career closely correlated with the nation's war and recovery. He was a flight instructor in the Army, an economist for the U.S. Foreign Economic Administration and a lawyer for the Office of Price Stabilization. By the 1950s, he had become a "package real estate developer," and president of the Renewal and Development Corporation of New York City. The RDC fostered lower income projects in major cities across the nation and San Juan, Puerto Rico (the Capitol Park in Washington D.C. was one of the projects and the first for Washington D.C.). As if he needed the exposure, the role proved a boon to Scheuer's portfolio. He was appointed to the State Special Task Force on Middle Income Housing by New York Governor Nelson Rockefeller and a similar post at the federal level by President John F. Kennedy.

Scheuer first sought elective office in 1962 when he challenged incumbent James Healey of the famed Charles Buckley machine in the Democratic primary for a seat based in the Southwest Bronx as a reformer. It was thought that the presence of two other candidates in the race would save Healey and it did, but only with a bare majority. Scheuer finished close behind with 43%. By 1964, he was back and had the reform mantle to himself, armed with the backing of Mayor Robert Wagner. It was a heavily Jewish district in, as *The New York Times* wrote, "a basically residential section whose north-south spine is the Grand Concourse. The fringes fall away to rat-infested slums with poor public services."

Healey's stroke following the '62 race impacted his ability to campaign but not his rhetorical jabs. He accused the pair of being partners in the biggest payroll heist since Brinks...Between them, they hand out more than $110,000 in tax money as rewards for political allies." Scheuer responded that what he has developed was, "a limited profit, moderate-rent housing project in Washington known for its beauty and pioneering in shattering segregated patterns of living, but I have no interest, direct or indirect, in any property in New York State." Scheuer ousted Healey 53-47% and had no trouble winning the general.

Calling unemployment "surely the prime threat to the integrity of the war on poverty,"

Scheuer used his seat on the Education and Labor Committee to pursue a plethora of activist legislation that was pertinent to lower-income citizens and his district. He sponsored a Presidential Commission on Negro History and Culture and proposed ending the "archaic" 1873 law that made acquiring contraceptives through the mail illegal. Not until 1971 did he succeed on the latter. He sponsored the Bilingual Education Act and broke a stalemate between the Johnson administration and Texas Senator Ralph Yarborough by mandating that the program would apply to all non-English speaking children, not simply those who speak Spanish. Eradicating drug use was another initiative and to accomplish it, he visited France and Turkey to learn their techniques.

In 1969, Scheuer decided he'd like to become Mayor of New York City and laid out $500,000 of his own money to aim for the Democratic nomination. His platform was essentially rebuilding. "We have a nation that is, in a very real sense, dying here. Our cities have lost their sense of comity. We have been unable to provide the essential facilities and services that a civilized nation provides for its own people. The war has sapped our resources and alienated the young and the poor." In part to prove his mettle, he authored, *To Walk The Streets Safely* Scheuer also hit Mayor John Lindsay's leadership. "It is not a cliché to say that the city is in a crisis. People are asking, is the city governable. The implication is scarifying, that we are destined to play out a drama of pre-ordained tragedy." He attacked Lindsay's "sloppiness, amateurism, the absence of normal thinking-through." One example that he told New York Magazine was the Ocean Hill-Brownsville melee: Lindsay "never thought to ask what happens when you say you're going to transfer this massive glob of power from one group to another." Zero-tolerance for anti-semitism was a theme he displayed prominently. He took just 39,000 votes and 5%, taking fifth place. Things would not get easier electorally for the foreseeable future.

1972 was a redistricting year. When he was pitted in a district mostly held by Mario Biaggi, Scheuer trained his sites on Jonathan Bingham, an ally and fellow reformer with whom he came to Congress in '64 and who hosted fundraisers for him. *The New York Times* described the district as, "an eyecatching configuration with 71 distinct corners that winds its improbable way from the Hutchinson River and Co-Op City all the way clown to the Harlem River and Yankee Stadium." A leaflet his campaign distributed read, "Some people say the right things. Jim Scheuer does them." He contrasted his role on Education and Labor with Bingham's more worldly interests. I think Jack would prefer to be Secretary of State or an ambassador and chairman of the Senate Foreign Relations Committee," he said in a debate. "Jack doesn't seem to be challenged by the urban problem… He's oriented to give Riverdale or Bel Air or Grosse Pointe, Mich., a very elegant and a very sophisticated and constructive representation, particularly in the field of foreign affairs, but I don't think he relates to this district in a meaningful way…" While conceding that foreign affairs "is, my adult life, I suppose," he sought to give his assurance that it, "has not prevented me from being actively interested and actively pursuing many items of legislation that directly affect the cities and districts such as the 22nd."

The New York Times spoke for many in citing the "uncommonly difficult choice" the GOP gerrymandered plan forced upon voters and that, "to have to pick one and sacrifice the other is a spectacular waste of legislative talent." *The Times* felt Bingham could "make a more distinctive contribution to the work of Congress" and enough voters agreed and he prevailed over Scheuer 55-45%.

At the time, Scheuer and allies viewed a comeback as improbable but, the indictment of Frank Brascoe for conspiracy to accept bribes changed the dynamics of the race in a Southeast Brooklyn/South Queens district. His

Democratic opponent was State Senator and Scheuer's ex-New York City rent official Leonard Yoswein but Scheuer spent $200,000 and won 53-47%. The district was Democratic but not by New York City standards. In 1980, Ronald Reagan actually carried it while four years later, Mondale won it by just 52-47% but, that didn't stop Scheuer from racking up 74 and 63% respectively.

Beginning in the first year of his return to Congress, Scheuer repeatedly introduced the Maternal and Child Health Bill. Scheuer was also active in the backbreaking clean air rewrites of both 1976 and '77. When Henry Waxman of California and Andy Maguire of New Jersey proposed eliminating the Class III requirement of the deterioration of air, Scheuer spoke of the common-sense soundness of it. "12 cities," he said, "did not meet or barely met the annual am'tlent nitrogen oxide, NOx standard in 1975. The Council on Environmental Quality found that the NO,.. standards for 1975 was exceeded by 66 percent in Los Angeles, by 33 percent in Chicago, and by 21 percent in New York City . .. The Waxman-Maguire amendment time schedule gives Detroit more than ample time to iron out any bugs that may still remain in the Volvo system." It won just 49 votes.

With two major airports being located in Queens (John F. Kennedy International and Laguardia), noise control was a paramount concern for Scheuer's constituents for much of his career. In 1979, he was angered by a parliamentary maneuver by Nevada Democratic Senator Howard Cannon that would defer the implementation of noise control beyond 1985. Scheuer called the maneuver "crumby, third-rate, sleazy."

While Scheuer now had a firm place electorally, his style would eventually nearly relegate him to an internal afterthought. Scheuer was fortunate to be able to reclaim his seniority on both Energy and Commerce and Science and Technology which meant getting the gavel of the Commerce Subcommittee on Consumer Protection and Finance. But come 1980, it would be worth next to nothing under the panel's titanic chairman, John Dingell.

To say that Scheuer got under Dingell's skin was an inherent understatement. Scheuer and other clean air advocates battled with Dingell forces over the stringency of the clean air reauthorization, including the implementation of airbags that Dingell's heavily automotive Detroit constituency had a hand in and, Scheuer believed Dingell's views on the matter were "irrational." Though Scheuer and his forces probably won the war on the airbag issue, Dingell eventually found Scheuer's turf to be a patient study in deferred gratification and sought to eliminate his gavel when he became chair of the full committee following that year's election. Dingell's argument was that the workload could not accommodate seven subcommittees but he also made clear his trump card was Scheuer's unpopularity among colleagues, claiming, "if I were held in that kind of esteem by my colleagues, I'd have the same apprehension he's feeling."

As the vote neared, Speaker Thomas P. "Tip" O'Neill intervened to broker a solution and Scheuer put on a full court press with committee members to save his spot and believed it was going his way, until, members codified Dingell's plans by a vote of 14-7. His reaction: "That's life. The chairman twisted a lot of arms." He believed he, "enraged him by standing up to him."

A New York colleague, Fred Richmond was not as magnanimous. He penned a letter to *The New York Times* criticizing the abolishment. He wrote, "There have been many explanations of why Jim Scheuer's colleagues on the Energy and Commerce Committee did not reconstitute his subcommittee. I believe it was in large part because he did his job too well on certain issues of consumer protection." Referring to airbags, Richmond wrote, "Apparently, there are some people who do not wish to encourage that kind of legislation in the future. Unfortunately, the American consumer will be the loser if that attitude prevails." He believed he, "enraged him by standing up to him."

Did Scheuer hide in a corner and sulk? Not a chance. He shifted his energy to the Science, Space and Technology Committee and would turn his efforts to holding the Reagan administration's feet to the fire on policies and personnel decisions that he considered anathema to soundness. In doing so, he had no problem verbally socking it to officials he viewed as bending the rules.

First, there was Rita Lavelle who allegedly sought to have EPA officials fired over their criticism of the agency's practices. When the Justice Department report found no wrongdoing, Scheuer responded that it "carries an aroma of freshly applied white paint." When the administration began purging EPA officials, which started with the reassignment of Inspector General Matthew Novick after he issued a critical report on the agency's financial records, Scheuer maintained he "was asked very nicely to walk the plank....A frightened administration, unable to stop the hemorrhaging, is now attempting to limit the bad news by killing off the messengers."

Anne Gorsuch, Reagan's EPA head and "ice queen." was another official for whom there was no love lost. "At best, EPA officials have been sloppy and incompetent. At worst, they may have knowingly looted Superfund." When Inspector General Matthew Novick and Assistant EPA head John Horton resigned in 1983 after writing a report critical of the administration's plan,

Scheuer rendered his opinion: "I have no doubt that his willingness to do his job properly, that is to uncover fraud and illegality at the Environmental Protection Agency, has had a direct bearing on this firing,." He called it "a crude attempt to stem the mushrooming scandal." Scheuer's solution was to make the EPA an independent agency but it went nowhere (he wanted to do the same with the National Oceanic and Atmospheric Administration (NOAA).

Beyond clean air, Scheuer was angered by the proposal to cut off funding for international planning services that mention abortion. Calling it, "a bizarre misapplication of United States power and influence," Scheuer said, "There is something offensive and unacceptable about the premise that a non-private organization, because it may be contributing to an affiliate abroad that carries on abortion counseling, may have its funds cut off." He was interested in world population and was named chair of a new committee examining the issue.

Scheuer rarely found anything to like with the Bush administration's policy on Israel. In 1991, his beef was that the administration had the latitude to use all but $1 billion in loan guarantees as leverage for future settlements. "Apparently, Mr. Speaker," Scheuer said on the House floor, "even that was not enough for this administration, which is obsessed with tying the loan guarantees to Israel's settlement policy." Scheuer called this, "grossly unfair because there is no such linkage when it comes to guaranteeing loans for Arab nations."

Legislative charcateristics aside, Scheuer was not considered one of the Hill's gentler bosses. In fact, his staff turnover rate was high. One colleague, a fellow member of Science, recalls attending meetings in Scheuer's office with the staff and witnessing his shabby treatment of his staff. He later approached him and ordered him to clean up his act or I won't continue coming to these meetings. Scheuer muttered something about that not being how he does things but did "calm down a little."

For Scheuer, being abrasive and compassionate were not mutually exclusive. A longtime aide, Michael Neibauer, cited his boss's anonymity with giving. "He contributed to local groups personally and never wanted any publicity about it. If a non-profit group needed help and it was legitimate, Scheuer would write a very generous check and he told me never to publicize it.

Another trait. It was once written that, "One of his techniques is to arrange two luncheons with various experts, and then to commute from one to the other to get the best of both."

In his last year in office, Scheuer proposed making trapping, or possessing "fur" a felony in the U.S.

Scheuer came out of the 1982 remap in tact, remarkable considering New York had to lose five districts. He ended up with a district that took in 60% Queens, a quarter of the Bronx and a portion of Nassau County, Long Island (including the Sound), a compendium of Jewish seniors and African-Americans and Hispanics. Well before 1992, it was clear that he would have to get mighty lucky to survive that one. Another remap was forthcoming and this time, New York would be losing three seats. Additionally, a majority-minority seat would have to be created. It had long been suspected that he would be combined with either Gary Ackerman or Bob Mrazek.

The House Bank scandal didn't help Scheuer, though given the lines and would-be opponent who had similar problems, the aggravation might have been tertiary. He wrote 140 bad checks and appeared on the Ethics Committee's 24 Worst abusers. However, after producing documentation that his commercial bank had held up a series of transactions, Scheuer convinced members to remove him from the list. But it would have been brutal nonetheless and Scheuer acknowledged as much. At 72 years of age, I must point out in all candor, that perspectives and priorities change. I would not be comfortable with a brand new congressional district, more than half of which is new to me...I would have been under relentless, merciless pressure to get to know the people out there."

The turf of Queens Congressman Gary Ackerman was merged with Scheuer, a prospect he probably relished as early as March. Ackerman just happened to be on the House Ethics Committee that was investigating the House Bank and Scheuer, and another New York Congressman Ackerman might have faced, Robert Mrazek on Long Island, happened to be among the worst abusers. The names were leaked to the press. Still, Scheuer acknowledged, "If I had been 10 years younger, I probably would have decided sure, let's go for it."

Scheuer's post-Congressional career was United States Director of the European Bank for Reconstruction and Development (EBRD). He died at age 85 in 2006.

CHAPTER SEVENTY-ONE

Hammerin Hank Nowak a Quiet Figure on the Hill but Earned Slam-Dunk Shots for Buffalo

Introductory Quote: "It is an important fabric that helps knit communities together and it teaches people character, discipline, co-operation, and sportsmanship." – Former Congressman Henry Nowak on the role of sports during his induction into the Buffalo Sports Hall of Fame in 1994.

Image courtesy of C-SPAN

If Henry Nowak's Congressional tenure was modeled after a song, it would be called, "Takin Care of Business" by Bachman-Turner Overdrive. The nine-term Democratic Congressman from Buffalo, New York made so few headlines in his 18-years in Congress that he often made *Roll Call's* "Obscure Caucus" and even close friends said he could at time appear distant. But he was content with delivering the goods to his district and New York State and his senior position on the Public Works and Transportation Committee gave him just the means to do so. In fact, when Nowak announced his retirement in 1992, *The Buffalo News* wrote that, "Only Newark, N.J., topped Buffalo as the city with the highest per capita in the United States after Nowak had been in the House for six years." And that was before he got a subcommittee chairmanship. Hard as that would be to overlook, Nowak's real greatness might have been on the basketball court.

Nowak never had to shuffle off to Buffalo – that was his home in every sense of the word. He grew up in a Polish-Catholic family —. Nowak entered Canisius College where he immediately began playing basketball on the school's team, the Golden Griffs. At 6'3, he quickly earned the nickname, "Hammerin Hank" *The Buffalo Sports Hall of Fame* wrote that, Nowak, "led the Griff's to their only three appearances in the NCAA basketball tournament, averaging 19.4 points in nine tourney games...When he graduated in 1957, he was Canisius College's all-time scoring leader. In three years as a starter he scored 1,449 points and averaged 18.6 points a game. Today, he still holds the first-place title in rebounding and third in all-time scoring." Nowak earned his degree in accounting, served in the Army, then entered the University of Buffalo to begin working toward his J.D.

Nowak had been courted by the NBA but declined. His rationale: "At that time, there wasn't the money in playing basketball that there is now. And, I decided that I could build a much more substantial career by attending law school at UB." Nowak became an Assistant Erie County D.A. at age 23 and found a mentor in Democratic Chairman Joseph Crangle. That helped him become Erie County Comptroller in 1965 and his popularity soared. Nowak told the *Am-Pol Eagle* that his goal upon winning the office was to "modernize our operations. Before I became comptroller, things were largely done by hand." He greatly admired Maine Senator and presidential candidate Ed Muskie during that time, calling him, "the most impressive public figure I ever met." He held the job until heading to Congress nine years later, an opening that resulted from the retirement of longtime incumbent Thaddeus Dulski. Nowak got the primary to himself and won the general election in a lopsidedly Democratic district 75-25%. None of his re-elections were ever on the board competition-wise and his last campaign, in 1990, was won with 78%.

Though Nowak was one of 75 "Watergate Babies," his style differed from that of many of his vocal reform-minded classmates, including fellow New Yorkers such as Steve Solarz and Tom Downey. Nowak was committed to serving the people which might have lent credence to those who viewed him as having risen up the political ladder. But in truth, his devotion to Western New York made him a billion dollar industry, because that's how much money he funneled into the communities that encompassed the Buffalo area over his 18 years in the House. In that vein, *The New York Times* labeled him, "noted for avoiding long speeches and focusing on local concerns." *The Buffalo*

News said his, "quiet, self-effacing style was sometimes mistaken for a lack of toughness." But he was not a grudge-holder and some who had opposed him made out just fine with their political wants.

Early in his Congressional career
Photo courtesy of the Collection of the U.S. House of Representatives

Rekindling the greatness for which Buffalo was renowned in the 19th Century was a major priority and Nowak saw the outer harbor as the logical link to do so. But so was the infrastructure and Nowak scored a coup during his first term by scoring funding for a Buffalo subway system. His contention was, "It's either a subway or a new highway. From the point of view of energy, the environment and the Buffalo economy, a light rail rapid-transit system looks like the answer." That viewpoint was nearly unanimously shared by New York's often incohesive 39-member delegation and Nowak's New York City colleague, then-Congressman (and future Mayor Ed Koch) summed up his persuasion: "It's not only that the proposal is meritorious but also that Henry Nowak advances it in a way that no one could refuse." The delegation was hardly united a year later when conferees on President Jimmy Carter's energy legislation were forced to consider the proposed Section 515. Put forth by fellow Democrat Dick Ottinger of Westchester, it would have mandated power companies to use a uniform rate in selling electricity, a prospect that

Nowak contended would cause "sudden and harsh dislocation" upstate by virtue of the layoffs that would result from the power companies inability to compete.

Koch's description of Nowak's persuasiveness was his preferred operandi even when his vision was not unanimous, or at times, when he was up against forces that his own people didn't think was worth the fight. One example came in 1981 when —— Another was a year later when, concerned at the number of jobs being lost to Buffalo's Northern neighbors as a result of deregulation, he asked the ICC to Canada.

Other successes: the Peace Bridge Expansion, the Erie Basin marina, the Elm-Oak arterial, the Lockport Expressway, a new Father Baker bridge, the Bird Island pier, money for the Cazenovia Creek flood control, a study of local water supply, and the downtown Buffalo pedestrian mall, to name a few. The New York State Barge Canal received 50% of it's funding through Nowak and 50% through New York State. Likewise, a $50 million center for national earthquake at the State University of Buffalo (again, the federal government put up $25 million and New York another 25).

Beyond bridges, Nowak was a strong advocate of a $200 million international trading center in West Buffalo near Front Park advanced by Peter and Robert Elia. By the time he left office, the Gateway Bridge was going over the Buffalo River even though some local officials had initially mocked the concept and the Peace Bridge was being enlarged for truckers. Nowak was a strong advocate of an international trading center in West Buffalo near Front Park and a $50 million center for national earthquake research at the State University of Buffalo (the federal government put up $25 million and New York another 25).

Nowak's chairmanship of the Public Works subcommittee on water resources, which he attained in 1987, gave him House jurisdiction over national water projects, which made him the go-to person for wants of every member. He was also able to do wonders for his own region. Nowak's commitment to bettering the quality of Western New York also extended to cleaning it up and he pressed the Army Corps of Engineers to do so for portions of Buffalo. He secured $11 million for a demonstration project to clean up Woodlawn Beach and turned the decrepit Fuhrmann Boulevard into a parkway. Linking North and South Buffalo was also a priority.

On occasion, Nowak could be thrust into minor disputes within the community. One related to the overabundant but now mostly empty grain elevators that still existed from Buffalo's bygone days as a grain mecca. Nowak envisioned using their parts for other means or gutting them entirely and asked the Army Corp of Engineers for help to do so. But folks were historically sentimental, led by Susan A. McCartney, president of the Preservation Coalition of Erie County cited, "a cult of grain elevator buffs who see them as esthetically important" and advocated for them remaining.

One area on which Nowak had his work cut out for him was saving the Economic Development Administration (EDA) from the limited government reaches of the Reagan administration. Nowak actually hoped to expand the program and prevailed.

Nowak also co-chaired the Great Lakes Task Force and when the Bush administration came to power, he urged them to honor funding for cleanup programs reserved for the Great Lakes which were overrun by toxin contaminants human and not. In fact, when zebra mussel were wreaking havoc after being discovered on the floor of the Great Lakes, Nowak said, "The history of the zebra mussel on the Great Lakes reads like bad science fiction." His success was mixed and the following year, he was still pressing for more dollars. The lack of them, he said, was "the essential problem," and by 1992, *The News* was reporting that 85% of the shoreline was still contaminated.

Nowak did secure $11 million for a demonstration project to clean up Woodlawn Beach and succeeded in turning the decrepit Fuhrmann Boulevard into a parkway. On a related matter, Nowak was active on anti-ocean dumping legislation of the 1980s and a water project authorization project which enabled him to make many friends among colleagues. He proposed the Water Resources Development Act of 1992. His crown jewel was a Buffalo waterfront where the paper reported, "plans are being made for a complex which will house and Aquarium like Baltimore's a Hands-On Science Museum like Toronto's a planetarium and an Environmental Research Center."

Nowak also sat on the Small Business Committee, a position with almost as much relevance to his constituency as Public Works. By his fourth term he chaired the Subcommittee on Tax Access to Equality Capital and Business Opportunities. That was at a time that the national recession was gripping his district hard (13.8% in early 1982), and Nowak tried to encourage area banks, particularly Chemical, to reduce interest rates. Nowak told small business people from his district that, "a healthy small business sector could be the greatest single solution to the nation's unemployment crisis. He got a nearly $2 million grant for residents of the Buffalo suburb of Lackawanna which had been ravaged by unemployment (the Bethlehem Steel Corporation Plant had shut down).

Pursuant to that, adaptation to technological changes was critical for workers and Nowak told *The Am-Pol Eagle* in 2018 how, "One thing about which I was especially concerned was modernizing our auto manufacturing operations in this area and making sure that our workers were trained to implement the manufacturing technology of the future, including robotics.... I was able to do this in a way that has played a major part in keeping General Motors providing thousands of jobs here in WNY (Western New York), an accomplishment of which I have always been very proud." Another proud achievement: the Small Business Secondary Market Improvements Act of 1984.

Nowak's presidential support score when Republicans controlled the White House wasn't as low as other Democrats from New York (typically the mid-30s), but wasn't particularly high. Nowak opposed abortion but didn't sign a 1989 letter authored by his neighbor, John LaFalce, urging Democratic National Committee Chair Ron Brown to remove an abortion rights plank from the Democratic plank. He opposed the flag-burning amendment as well as the 1992 Balanced Budget Amendment, the latter he said, because he feared it would lead to "judicial intervention (that could) tie up budgets, depress the economy and result in court-ordered budget priorities."

Still, about half a year into his tenure, Nowak said his greatest frustration, "has been the lack of cohesiveness in the general legislation - lack of a plan of action." Family sacrifices became evident as well and Nowak actually considered quitting at one point because of the time constraints (his family and school-age children returned to Buffalo in 1982 and Nowak joined them after weekly votes had concluded).

On a personal level, Nowak was devoted to his staff. At least several people who worked for him did so throughout his entire tenure and his Executive Assistant, E. Plumber Godby, was with him since his Comptroller days. Nowak in fact insisted the names of all of his staffers be published in *The Buffalo News* when he announced his retirement and when the paper failed to include three people, he contacted *The News* to tell them).

As early as December 1991, Nowak began informing colleagues that he was genuinely undecided about standing for a tenth term and people from throughout the community began lobbying him profusely to stay. Even the completion of New York's notoriously late redistricting did not force his hand and he expressed satisfaction that the Buffalo area seats were left in tack, though he did pick up new turf. But by that time, member after member, from New York as much as anywhere, began heading for the exits and Nowak, always with Buffalo in mind, felt Buffalo would be at a disadvantage down the line were he to stay on for another term or two, then retire as the new class was gaining seniority. In mid-June, Nowak finally decided to call it quits. He said, "I sought to match local needs with federal opportunities to help ameliorate these impacts and sustain our quality of life in Western New York. This has been the most gratifying part of my representation." He vowed to donate the $220,000 in his campaign treasury to charity.

After retiring, Nowak became a consultant to Ecology and Environment, Erie Basin and the Rapid Transit System. Meanwhile, the political baton has passed to Nowak's son, Hank, Jr., who in 2010 won a seat on the Erie County Supreme Court.

In an extraordinary tribute, *The Buffalo News* summed up Nowak's contribution to his people succinctly: "Nowak set the table for a banquet, but all the community wanted were scraps." Legacywise, he couldn't possibly have asked for more.

CHAPTER SEVENTY-TWO

Blunt and Bellicose, Peter Kostmayer
Lived by His Ideals

Introductory Tidbit: In 1988, Pennsylvania Congressman Peter Kostmayer presided over a House hearing examining the National Energy Strategy Act. Among the witnesses: actor Ted Danson who was testifying on behalf of the American Oceans Campaign. Kostmayer posed what he thought was a gimme to Danson, whether the gas tax should be raised. Instead, the bemused celebrity turned to his staff who beckoned him to, "Say yes." "Say yes?" Danson asks them.

Pennsylvania Congressman Peter Kostmayer was exhibit A on how Democrats held the House of Representatives for 40 years uninterrupted. Having won his seat at age 30 in a district that was very inhospitable to his party, Kostmayer combined fastidious courtship, hard work and shrewd instincts to actually manage to please some of the people some of the time. While he was unseated during the 1980 Republican wave, Kostmayer used those same skills to persevere by winning the seat back two years later, and hold it with relative ease until the uproar of 1992 again prevented him from doing so.

Being driven and punctilious with balancing his district demands did not mean being free of controversy. Kostmayer had a bluntness that could border on at best inartful and at worst crass which at times could make colleagues on both sides of the aisle ill at ease. One example for which he received huge notoriety was the 1988 Democratic National Convention when he proceeded to offer a piece of advice to Democratic Party activists. "We are not going to blow it this time. Just shut up, gays, women, environmentalists. Just shut up, and you will get everything you want after the election. In the meantime, just shut up so we can win." In the days ahead, Kostmayer apologized for using the term "shut-up," and joked, "I've gotten my foot almost out of my mouth."

Kostmayer's background made his election from this Bucks County district in Eastern Pennsylvania all the more unlikely. A Columbia University graduate, he had been a coordinator for the presidential campaign of George McGovern only four years before his own election to Congress. McGovern was getting soundly trounced in Bucks, as nationally (62-35%). Kostmayer then served as press secretary to Attorney General J. Shane Carter and a deputy press secretary under Democratic Governor Milton Shapp (his media experience had come as a writer for *The Trentonian*, a daily paper just over the border in New Jersey).

Kostmayer jumped into the race for the Democratic nomination for Congress at age 29 in 1976 when longtime GOP Congressman Ed Beister announced his retirement. His odds for winning were daunting and he had to first make it through a crowded primary, the leader of which appeared to be Joseph Pavlak, a Western Electric employee who seemed to have much of the Bucks organization behind him. But Kostmayer articulated his platform. On cutting defense, he wanted it done wisely calling it, "essential we remain number one." He favored restrictions on Saturday Night specials but felt "the education should be carried out by private groups." On abortion, "I would not support an amendment even though I have personal reservations." He won the primary with 46%.

The Republicans had a slightly more ideological primary and State Representative John Renninger narrowly outpolled his colleague, James Wright, Jr. But Renninger was the more conservative of the two and seemed to have trouble reaching Independents. A major part of Kostmayer's background was against overdevelopment. Counting went past midnight and Renninger initially refused to concede but, the morning after, Kostmayer told reporters how he pulled off the final margin of 1,312 votes out of 185,000 cast. "I was down by a 10,000 Republican voter registration lead in the district. I made substantial inroads among Republicans in Central Bucks. Our door-to-door campaign in Montgomery County kept the Republican edge down there. We did very well in Lower Bucks among Democrats. And I figure we took four out of every six independent votes."

Kostmayer was hardly situated in Washington before ethics became high on his plate and he was very unmoved by the fact that Joshua Eilberg and Daniel Flood were powerful members of the Pennsylvania delegation. He, along with other reform-minded junior Democrats Berkley Bedell of Iowa, Andy Maguire of New Jersey, and a neighboring Pennsylvania Congressman, Bob Edgar in fact called for an investigation ("It is our belief that the situation has developed to the point where formal inquiries on this matters are appropriate and necessary"). The group became armed with a few reform minded proposals and one would bar members from voting on the floor until their jail sentences were served and their fines paid. A second "required the Standards Committee to send to the House for action a resolution recommending expulsion of any representative convicted of a felony" within 30 days. The full caucus rejected that.

At home, Kostmayer's most-lasting impact was the 1978 kerfuffle over building a dam at Tocks Island Dam on the Delaware River and he came up with a concoction. Have that part of River (just above Trenton) designated part of the Wild and Scenic Program. Trenton's Congressman Frank Thompson labeled the maneuver a "back-door process," because it did not go through regular order, that being the Public Works Committee. As such, he tried to strike it on the House floor. But Kostmayer had commenced an Interior Committee hearing in New Hope that was chaired by the influential Phil Burton of California and Burton sided with opponents through the end. That was enough and a dam remains elusive to this day.

Kostmayer was active on the Alaska Land Bill," claiming, "The longer the oil is at the refinery the higher the price will climb." He tried to blunt opponents of the bill's contention that enactment could have a wide-reaching impact in the lower 48 by introducing an amendment clarifying that the act would only impact Alaska.

In 1978, few could have anticipated that an incumbent in such a precarious district would poll as well as any established member – 61%. Kostmayer did catch a critical break in late 1977 when the leading GOP candidate, popular State Senator Ed Howard decided to pass on challenging him and the eventual nominee, Bucks County Commissioner G. Roger Bowers had a few liabilities.

Bowers tried the Kostmayer is weak on defense shtick but to no avail and the size of the margin showed that Kostmayer had wooed many independents.

1980 was different. Republicans landed Upper Makefield Supervisor John Coyne, who was president of the George S. Coyne Chemical Corp., Inc., and unlike Bowers, he at least articulated the views of a centrist. Coyne nearly doubled Kostmayer spending and wrested the seat from the incumbent by 4,000 votes. Kostmayer declared himself, "an innocent victim of circumstances...The voters didn't reject Peter Kostmayer, but they did reject Jimmy Carter. We tried to make our substantial differences with the president known, but it didn't work...I think I was clearly caught up in a nationwide tide, a sweep by Governor Reagan. The only factors were Jimmy Carter and Ronald Reagan."

Kostmayer admitted defeat but hardly accepted it – in fact to watch him in action over the next two years one would think he still held office. Though he did find employment at the Congressional Management Foundation, he still continued helping former constituents who, whether mistakenly or otherwise, contacted him for help with federal agencies. He was obviously plotting a rematch and the economic doldrums of 1982 made a comeback attainable. Not to say it came easy. Unemployment created strong voter apathy which made either candidate getting a leg-up difficult. Plus, Reagan was personally popular in these parts which Kostmayer conceded and Coyne ruefully eluded, saying, "It's better running against a Carter-era Democrat than some fresh face." Kostmayer won his seat back by slightly more than 3,000 votes.

Coyne declined furious GOP entreaties to seek a rematch in 1984 and the party had to settle for veterans activist/labor consultant David Christian, whom they found a mere two weeks before the filing deadline. Naturally, this meant Christian trailed Kostmayer in fundraising. His slogan was, "Why gamble when you have something proven?" and Walter Mondale, the Democratic standard bearer for president, attended campaign kickoff. In a risky strategy for a district where Republicans outnumber Democrats by 27,000, Kostmayer pledged not to be a "water boy" for Reagan but he gave a nod to the affluence of Bucks by vowing to oppose any personal income tax hike. A key moment might have been when the state shut down a veterans outreach center in North Philadelphia that Christian operated. Counting was nip'n'tuck but again, Kostmayer proved his staying power. The final numbers gave him 112,648 votes to 108,696 and he declared, "Tonight is really not my victory, but a victory for the independent judgment of the thousands of independent men and women of this district."

Photo courtesy of C-SPAN

Kostmayer continued his activist bent. He proposed grants to promote the use of bicycle helmets by those under age 16. While others were simply proposing restricting an incinerator, Kostmayer proposed an outright moratorium until 2000. The House adopted a Kostmayer amendment mandating that at least twelve percent of the Energy Department contracts go to small businesses.

On foreign affairs, Kostmayer remained true to himself. In 1985, he voted with the majority of Foreign Affairs colleagues to fund Cambodian resistance leaders, declaring, "All of us feel the shadow of Vietnam in the committee room." He vowed to hold the administration's feet to the fire on aid to Central America. After Secretary of State George Shultz visited the Foreign Affairs Committee to seek Congressional authorization for contra funding, Kostmayer said, "If Congress refuses to reverse the cutoff of funds to the Contras, the administration's illegal war should come to an end in Nicaragua. But one never knows. Congress must make sure the administration does not use illegal means to fund an illegal war. Nor should we approve legal or overt funding which would allow the administration and its escalating rhetoric" to use it as a backdoor means to get involved.

At one point in the hearing, Kostmayer came to the defense of his New York colleague, Ted Weiss who compared the administration's tactics to those of Wisconsin Senator Joseph McCarthy in the 1950s. When Shultz protested angrily, Kostmayer replied, "It is you who began the escalation of rhetoric. You have raised the ante. There is a lot of red-baiting going on in the administration. You have a lot of nerve to come before this committee and criticize the members of this committee for being demagogues." When Shultz fired back that, "I thought I was here at the invitation of the committee but if you care to withdraw the invitation, I've got a lot of other things to do," Kostmayer's retort was classic indignance: "You are the secretary of state. There is nothing I can do about that."

Image courtesy of C-SPAN

Kostmayer was in the crosshairs of an effort to restrict funding for the National Endowment Arts (NEA) after a grotesque exhibit by the University of the District of Columbia, The Dinner Club. Kostmayer was dead set against the restriction and labeled it, "book burning in America, 1990." He maintained that, "Artists should be accountable only to themselves and their work. Artists in America should not be accountable, even to the American people. When we ask art and artists to be accountable to the public, we appeal to a kind of public common denominator." For that reason, he opposed an amendment by Virginia Republican Stan Parris to delete $1.6 million in funding for the University of the District of Columbia, which passed. His opponent, Audrey Zattick Schaller said his vote "shows a total disregard for the values of the people in the 8th Congressional District." But by the fall, voters were focused on other things and Kostmayer won with 57% (Parris coincidentally lost his seat).

Kostmayer got such a reputation that one day in the Spring of 1987, as he asked to be included in meeting of a quartet of Republican Senators visiting Nicaraguan President Daniel Ortega in Managua, Arizona Senator

John McCain initially vetoed his presence. McCain had no choice but to back down, however, when Ortega threatened to call the meeting off unless he was included.

In the 101st Congress Kostmayer chaired the Interior Committee Subcommittee on General Oversight and Investigations. *Politics in America* noted that as a member of the Foreign Affairs committee, "he has been known for baiting and challenging administration witnesses and he was no favorite among the Republican members of the committee."

Kostmayer's bluntness was not always reserved for domestic affairs. On Panama, he observed in 1988 that "the administration really doesn't know where it is going and to be honest, Congress doesn't either." He opposed the start of the Gulf War, saying he wasn't "prepared to send my constituents to the gulf to fight for cheap gas."

Nor was Kostmayer's incessant energy always appreciated by colleagues of his own party. When Larry LaRocco came to Congress in 1991, the Idaho Democrat received assurances from Kostmayer that he would always be consulted before Kostmayer introduced wilderness protection legislation that impacted Idaho. But later in the year, Kostmayer proposed a measure.

Kostmayer was also a ferocious advocate of a robust Family Planning program. He had proposed a $300 million Family Planning amendment to a 1989 Foreign Operations bill but the vocal anti-abortion Chris Smith and Henry Hyde were opposed. When the Smith Amendment went to the floor, Kostmayer offered his own language saying that it could be enacted to the extent that this is consistent with U.S. law." Because Roe v. Wade was the law of the land in the United States, it could not be circumvented. It was rejected 163-229. Smith and Hyde tried a similar maneuver was tried in 1991 but it fell 234 to 188 and Kostmayer's response was ""Let that be a message for 1992."

In 1991, Kostmayer won a seat on the powerful Energy and Commerce Committee, an assignment so prestigious that most members typically surrender most of their other assignments. Not Kostmayer. He remained on Interior, Foreign Affairs and (he did part with his gavel).

During his 1988 re-election campaign, Kostmayer was forced somewhat on the defensive by the "shut-up" gaffe. His opponent, ex-State Senator Edward Howard said, "I call on Peter Kostmayer today to reveal precisely what he thinks gays, women and environmentalists should shut up about before the election that cannot be revealed until after the election. Anyone who would tell a reporter that his party's strategy should be to conceal the truth from the voters has obviously become a total political animal and has great need of an early retirement from Washington politics." Kostmayer responded by, "stand(ing) by my statement. I think the American people are fed up with special interest groups. If the Democratic Party has a chance to win, we need a common agenda based on the fundamental issues." When speakers at the republican National Convention cited Kostmayer's sentiment, he responded by saying, "I always appreciate any mention at the Republican convention. I'm delighted." Whether "shut up" was a misstatement or the truth, it caused him no harm. He won re-election in the fall with 57%.

After that, it seemed that Kostmayer could hold his seat for the foreseeable future. Though Pennsylvania was losing two House seats after the 1990 census, a certainty was that Kostmayer could not be dislodged as a result – merging Bucks County in with another district was geographically impossible. But the Congressional check bouncing scandal – and with it the focus on lawmakers' perks, could not be overcome.

Kostmayer was the prototype of getting in front of a scandal before it defines you. Almost from the moment Rubbergate made the public eye – and before the lawmaker himself knew the full extent of his own involvement. In a sense, he had no choice as USA Today ran his picture.

When it was revealed that Kostmayer had 50 overdrafts, he announced that he would be donating a $750 - $15 per check, to three in-district charities (the Bucks County Opportunity Council, A Woman's Place, a shelter for abused women; and the American Red Cross Homeless Shelter in Bristol). In doing so, he would forfeit a charitable deduction on his own tax return. He was contrite: "The recent investigation revealed serious management failures at the House Bank. But I take full responsibility for my overdrafts. It was my account and I should have been more careful." Kostmayer proceeded to go even further than just checks to rehabilitate the image– he declined to take a tax deduction on his charitable contributions and even ceased using the Congressional pharmacy.

But Republicans were not about to let the issue get away and, to Kostmayer's chagrin, neither were the voters. As if being unable to catch a break, neither was even his ex-wife. To face him, the GOP nominated Jim Greenwood, a very moderate state senator.

All have heard the expression of running for office as if their ten points down but two weeks before Election Day, Kostmayer found himself ten points up but essentially expected to lose. In fact, he gathered his staff and told them to prepare for defeat. He was right and the final margin was unambiguous. 244,000 vote were cast and Kostmayer was unseated by 15,000, 52-46%.

This was one district where the Democratic tide of the year didn't benefit Kostmayer: Bill Clinton only carried the Eighth by a single percentage point. A day later, he acknowledged, "the anti-incumbent trend was a very strong factor; we were just swept under by the tide....People were angry and they wanted a change." The checks, he said, "came to symbolize the public's anger." Kostmayer was the Democratic lawmaker with the fewest overdrafts whose defeat could be linked to the scandal (Arizona Republican Jay Rhodes, with 32, had the fewest overall).

He became President of Zero Population Growth. Kostmayer aimed for a political comeback in 2002 making a run for the State Senate but fell short 53-47%. He then moved to Manhattan where he has served as President of the Citizens Committee for New York City since 2005.

CHAPTER SEVENTY-THREE

Donnelly Epitomized the Working Class South Boston District He so Ably Represented

Introductory Quote: Mr. Chairman, I have great personal and professional respect for the three authors of this amendment. I have worked closely with them over the years. But let me paraphrase what Ted Koppel said to the Governor of my State this time last year: 'Fellows, you just don't get it, do you?'" – Congressman Brian Donnelly regarding Ways and Means

Photo courtesy of the Collection of the U.S. House of Representatives

Massachusetts Democrat Brian Donnelly was another of those many mid-senior members who could have ascended to major strides once many of their senior colleagues had retired. Instead, his abrupt retirement announcement in March 1992 right amidst the plethora of other departures effectively killed that advancement. Yet as the dust settled and Democrats would lose control of Congress two years down the road anyway, Donnelly's colleagues could hardly have quibble with the decision in retrospect.

Donnelly was the embodiment of the most Irish district in America – himself Irish Catholic, working-class, somewhat conservative on social issues, and beyond family oriented. He was also a fighter. One example. Dismayed by what he viewed as the House Democratic leadership's half-hearted negotiation strategy during the budget summit negotiations, Donnelly said,"Where I come from in Boston politics, when someone hits you, you hit back," he said. "Down here (in Washington D.C), the (Democratic) party takes some hits and they negotiate. I wasn't raised that way."

When Donnelly jolted everyone with that announcement, *The Boston Herald* opined that, "In a congressional delegation bristling with titanic egos, two Kennedys and several colleagues who never met a TV camera they didn't like, Donnelly was often overlooked. He didn't mind." On that note, Rachel Cohen of *The Boston Herald* paid him a tribute. "Can't remember his ever putting in an appearance on 'Nightline' or getting a sound bite on the network evening news. Can't remember his being the subject of major scandal, either - not sexual indiscretion or bribery violations. No, Brian Donnelly just got on the plane to Washington every week and did the job of representing his district in a workmanlike manner, never losing sight of the fact that most of his constituents were just working stiffs, like his Dorchester neighbors and the folks he grew up with." This was in some ways remarkable given that a fair number of endeavors he pursued were of high profile and far-reaching nature at home and abroad.

Donnelly's background was all South Boston. He attended high school there – Catholic Memorial High School and earned his degree from Boston University where he played football. And coached after. He remained in his boyhood home throughout his Congressional years. In 1972, he won a seat in the Massachusetts House in the same class that future Congressional colleagues who did thrive by the limelight – Barney Frank and Ed Markey, were part of.

Six years later, Donnelly ran to succeed longtime Congressional fixture Jimmy Burke and the real race was in the primary. Patrick Henry McCarthy had garnered 43% against Burke in the '76 primary but that seemed more a reflection of the incumbent's increasing infirmity as he was advancing into his 70s. State Representative James Sheets was the other dominant figure in the race and he put a herculean effort into door-to-door. Boston Councilman Patrick McDonough and a prominent 27-year-old attorney, Margaret Dinneen, were credible candidates as well though that didn't necessarily translate into on the ground support.

McCarthy had once been a staffer for Southie's venerable Congressman Joe Moakley. He used Al Shea. But aside from residual distaste among regulars for his challenge to Burke, he was hurt by his California connection. Donnelly meanwhile displayed his regular guy persona: "The people here are looking for someone who can help them economically, to get the money to send the kids to Boston College and to buy the second car."

Donnelly declared himself, "a great believer in headquarters," saying, "it gives people something to hook onto." But it also gave the capacity to build an advantage in a campaign and having ten throughout the relatively compact district enabled him to do just that. By taking a near majority in Plymouth, Donnelly took the nomination with 43% (McCarthy had 20% and Sheets 17%). He faced no major party opposition in November to win the right to represent what was the most Irish district in America. As such, Irish issues encompassed much of his legislative pedigree.

First, there was getting situated. The Donnelly's and Tip O'Neill had a long history in Boston politics. In the 1940s, as a ward man, O'Neill opposed Donnelly's uncle for a local office and, three decades later, when Donnelly made it to Washington, O'Neill apologized "for what I did to your uncle." Donnelly replied: "and thanks for trying to keep me from getting here." Yet O'Neill became Donnelly's biggest booster in Congress and Donnelly in turn angrily sought to keep him in favor with more conservative members of his caucus who often talked about a revolt.

At first, Donnelly got a brutal reminder that O'Neill lived by his legendary story about how "people like to be asked." Upon coming to Washington, he automatically assumed O'Neill would take care of him committee-wise. When Donnelly asked the Speaker, he was told that he hadn't asked. By the start of his second term, Donnelly learned his lesson and O'Neill saw to it that he got a very plum assignment: a seat on Ways and Means.

Donnelly's most lasting legacy was without question the euphemistic Donnelly Visas. They came to be in 1986 when Donnelly authored an amendment to the Immigration Reform and Control Act to assist Irelanders who were down on their luck in their homeland. Future Senate Minority Leader Chuck Schumer was also instrumental and Ted Kennedy pushed it through in the Senate and President Ronald Reagan, himself a proud Irishman, signed it into law. The New York Times wrote that, "Out of the first 10,000 visas issued to 36 different nationalities, 4,161 went to the Irish." On the 25th anniversary of the Act's implementation, *Irish Central* wrote, "Because of the Donnelly Visa, at least 20,000 Irish people were able to embark upon a new life in the US. Some stayed there, raised families, and partook of the American Dream. Others returned to Ireland and, using their American education and skills, contributed mightily to the rise of the Celtic Tiger."

Donnelly's committed to human rights extended around the world. When three Baltic state's split from the Soviet Union, Donnelly introduced the Emergency Baltic States Immigration Relief Act of 1991 to provide special temporary protected status for certain nationals of the Baltic States. He also championed a solution to a problem debated three decades later. That "aliens" who die while serving under U.S. forces in hostile operations be considered American citizens.

Image courtesy of C-SPAN

When Boston colleague Doris Bunte, a colleague of Donnelly's when both served in the Mass House, let him know of a woman giving birth in an elderly housing unit, Donnelly introduced legislation creating "age specific" housing. "I don't think mixing old people and the mentally ill young together in housing is good policy. Nobody told us this was happening. And I think I understand why. The policy defies all rules of common sense."

When Congress enacted the Catastrophic Health Insurance bill in 1988, lawmakers thought they had a winner. But the virulent backlash that accompanied the rising costs (Dan Rostenkowski was chased by an angry pack of seniors from his car) extinguished that and it was Donnelly who sponsored the resolution repealing it. His first attempt to do so failed in Ways and Means. By fall, however, the appetite to repeal the measure was unmistakable and Donnelly led it. He told his colleagues, "I personally support all of these benefits. They are good benefits. They are needed benefits." But a case of reality reared its ugly head. "The last thing that the elderly people in this country want us to do to them is to try to trick them. Let us tell them the truth. We made a commitment to go back to square one, to look at the needs, to listen to the people that we are going to ask to finance the program. Now we are coming through the back door adding, in a patchwork quilt, additional good coverages, with no way to pay for them other than on the backs of beneficiaries who rejected that same proposal just half an hour ago." He cited the drug benefit which had increased stratospherically from the initially projected $5 billion cost to $12 billion. The co-payment," he said, "starts out at $4 a month; it goes to $6 a month; it goes to $12 a month; it is a never-ending road. The administrative costs are outrageous." A further contention was that it, "has no support among the people we purport to help" and members agreed: the vote to repeal was 360 to 66 (the Senate vote was unanimous).

As the House debated the use of force in the Persian Gulf, Donnelly took the floor. "Let me disabuse everybody here that this is an international coalition. Yes, my friends, it is an international coalition when they vote in the United Nations. But when they have to put their sons and daughters on the line to restore the legitimate Government of Kuwait, where are they?"

Declaring his intention to "make a clean break," Donnelly surprised nearly everyone by announcing that he'd be stepping down at the end of the term. The time away from his family was a root reason. "From the outside," he said, "this looks like the greatest job in America but it can be a grind...The bottom line is, I'm here and they're 400 miles away."

Donnelly explained his philosophy and it started with his family. For much of his tenure, Donnelly rented an apartment near Capitol Hill for $600 a month but both of his children had been born since he first took his oath. "I can no longer reconcile spending just a few hours every weekend with my kids, going from airport to airport and missing their childhoods." Shortly before his announcement, the check overdraft scandal had come to public fruition and Donnelly did not know whether he was impacted but he tamped down speculation that it factored in his decision. "I'm not leaving because of any check thing. I was perceived as, frankly, unbeatable," before quickly adding, "but I don't want to sound arrogant." Donnelly had said that if he did end up on "some check list," who do I turn myself in to?" When the official list came out, Donnelly did have 70 overdrafts, but fewer than five members of the Bay State delegation.

Donnelly had also faced another complication – redistricting. The Bay State was losing one House seat and while Donnelly by no means as expected to get the short end of the stick (the knives were really out for Chet Atkins), Donnelly's decision to step down spared his other colleagues from elimination.

At the end of the day, frustration was key to Donnelly leaving as he told *The New York Times*, "I just want to go back to Boston." He told *The Boston Herald* days later, later said, "It got to the point where I couldn't even sit out on my front porch and have a beer. People would spot me and come running up: 'Hey, I've got a kid tryin' to get a job on the T, can ya help him?'…It was like a parade out there sometimes."

The election of a Democratic President Bill Clinton, would give Donnelly an opportunity to continue his public service as he was named Ambassador to Trinidad and Tobago.

In 1998, Donnelly did try to make a return to elective office – for governor of Massachusetts. But he through his hat into the ring late and was hampered in the Democratic primary by revelations that the football career he had boasted about in college was non-existent. Donnelly might have turned off some by easing off his longstanding opposition to abortion. "I am who I am, I was raised a certain way. I have very strong personal and religious feelings about abortion. But I'm not going to put that on the people of the Commonwealth. I will defend the right of a woman to choose." As for a tax cut, Donnelly said he wanted it targeted toward the folks who need it most. "Those are the people who gain the least during the good times and suffer the most during an economic downturn. Fairness must be the basic overriding principle of any tax cut." Like a true working class man, he vowed to live off his savings as he went forward with his bid. Still, he conceded, "It's an uphill fight for Brian Donnelly," and though his home area came through (he took 30% in Plymouth and 27% in Norfolk) he placed third statewide with just 17%.

Donnelly is now comfortably retired and living on Cape Cod.

CHAPTER SEVENTY-FOUR

Hopkins a Stalwart Conservative from Kentucky Bluegrass Country

Introductory Quote: "America doesn't have on it green eyeshadow. It has on its helmet." –Kentucky Congressman Larry Hopkins prior to the launch of the Persian Gulf war.

Photo via the Kenton County Library

For a somewhat accidental Congressman, Kentucky Republican Larry Hopkins made a tremendous impact in a variety of areas during his 14 years in Congress, including leading role in the most influential Pentagon measure of the 1980s. While his quest to become governor of the Blue Grass

State was spectacularly unsuccessful, Hopkins could point to having provided capable representation and solid accomplishments for his Lexington-area constituents.

By birth, Hopkins was a Michigan boy. Born in Detroit, he came to Kentucky as a youngster and not only attended public schools there but Murray State University. After serving in the Marines, he became a stockbroker and settled in Lexington. Hopkins's political career began with his appointment as the Fayette County Clerk but, a 1969 bid for county commission ended in defeat. He rebounded two years later by winning a seat in the State House and by 1977, was winning re-election with 76%.

By 1978, the Sixth District's three-term Democratic Congressman, John Breckinridge, was expected to cruise to another term but, he was upset in the primary by State Senator Tom Easterly. Easterly. Mary Louise Foust had been the Republican nominee but she was considered a sacrificial lamb and withdrew. Officials turned to Hopkins who mounted a world-class campaign. Advertising was a key area – Hopkins was on the air during the summer while it took Easterly until October to do the same. Easterly had a high ranking position with the state's AFL-CIO, but that was not a particular plus here and Hopkins didn't hesitate to make the association. He also spoke of not spending more than is taken in.

Hopkins won six counties and Easterly ten but Fayette came through for the Republican with 63%, for a 51-46% victory win overall. He vowed to be frugal with government spending. Noting that he had been the only legislator to oppose that year's state budget, Hopkins looked to experiences in that body. "You hear them whisper up there (in Frankfort) that you don't vote against the budget because they'll use the things in the budget to beat you the next time. If I'm the only member of Congress to vote against deficit spending, that's what I'm going to do. I've never been an advocate of the 'go along to get along' syndrome."

Politics in America wrote that, "The sixth District is Kentucky as the rest of the nation pictures it. Horses, tobacco and whiskey are the mainstays of its culture ad economy." By taking places on the Agriculture and Armed Services Committees, Hopkins was very much attuned to representing its interests and his re-election margins reflected it. Though he was held into the 50s in 1980 and '82, he was never seriously challenged for the duration of his tenure.

Hopkins with his legislative assistant, Martha Gerhardstein
Photo via the Kenton County Library

Hopkins's voting record was fairly conservative but not monolithically so – he did vote in 1983 for ratification of the Equal Rights Amendment (ERA). But on spending, he did live up to his vow to be was stingy. In 1982, he opposed the Clinch River Reactor project in next door Tennessee. Noting that the estimates had catapulted from $700 million to $8.8 billion, he called the project, "a budget buster in the classic sense. When we are facing a federal deficit looming as large as $200 billion, this is simply unacceptable."

One matter on which Hopkins was stingy was U.S. troops in Lebanon. In September 1983, Hopkins visited the troops the administration had already stationed there but, upon his return, essentially told UPI the situation was futile. "I would like to see us get out of there, but that does not mean right away. That (withdrawal) would be followed by the slaughter of thousands and thousands of people in Lebanon. I think a lot rests on the current cease-fire…'What if they kill 800 Marines? What if they sink a ship? What do you do then? Then you have a situation you don't like to think about it." Hopkins's thoughts were eerily prescient. Two months later, 241 Marines were killed during an explosion at the U.S. barracks in Beirut.

Hopkins's crown jewel during his 14 years in Congress was a military restructuring. Predictably, the concept was initially given a cold reception, which he responded by calling "a substantial frontal assault orchestrated by opponents at the Pentagon who are determined to maintain the status quo." Other heavyweights shared Hopkins's view with Senators Sam Nunn and Barry Goldwater writing, "If we leave it up to the Pentagon, there will be no change. The Constitution gives Congress the power —and the duty, to make rules for the government and the regulation of that land and Naval forces. We must exercise that power and that duty." That resulted in The Goldwater-Nichols Act which 383-27. Reagan signed it into law in June of '86.

If there was one hill on which Hopkins would die on, it was that of nerve gas. The Army had stored 70,000 M55 nerve gas rockets ("igloos") at the Lexington-Blue Grass Depot. Because they were not likely to be used, there was talk about building an incinerator to burn them, which pumped fear into local residents given that the gas was classified as deadly. Hopkins agreed. "These old rockets are no threat to any enemies of the United States. They're nothing but a threat to our own people. Terrorism is on the rise in our country. You don't need a Phi Beta Kappa key to figure out what could happen if a terrorist got into one of those igloos." As time went on, Hopkins was angered by repeated postponements of the environmental impact report. His solution was to have the nerve gas it shipped elsewhere and by 1990, an 18-month delay was placed on the project which Hopkins said again showed the need for the Army to do a new environmental study that "fully accounts for any changes made in risk calculations."

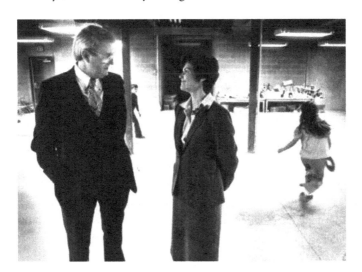

Photo via the Kenton County Library

Another Hopkins passion: killing the LHX, a $42 billion Light Helicopter program. When his amendment to strike funding was adopted, Hopkins replied, "Members agreed with me that we don't need and can't afford the most expensive conventional weapons system in the Army's 200-year history." The Army did not respond in kind and the internationally syndicated publication, *The Army Times* labeled Hopkins, "our prime candidate for Villain/Congressman of the Year." Still, House/Senate negotiators codified that cut in the final spending agreement. Hopkins was also the only Republican to back liberal California Democrat Ron Dellums's attempt to kill the MX rail-mobile version.

As far as domestic interests, Hopkins's most lasting impact was on preserving tobacco subsidies, a must in the Bluegrass State. In 1981, Wisconsin Republican Tom Petri proposed the Tobacco Deregulation Act which would repeal the loan program. Hopkins naturally opposed it but conceded that, "five years from now, tobacco growers will be operating under a totally different federal tobacco program, and they should prepare for some changes." By 1990, it was Rhode Island Republican Ronald Machtley pressing the subsidy ban.

Hopkins tried to help his farmers by limiting imports but colleagues felt it smacked of protectionism and refused to go along. He was more successful urging a five-month extension in the marketing quota for burley leaf farmers and the 1990 budget summit agreement that contained the language gave him a victory anyone would take prior to launching a statewide campaign.

Locally, Hopkins secured money for a six lane widening project of Interstate 75 in Fayette and Scott counties. He co-sponsored legislation that would classify the Red River as part of the Wild and Scenic River System. But when Congress was trying to include the financing of a Falmouth Dam into a water projects measure, Hopkins bemoaned the process. "Tying a load of items together in a single package is a genuine problem in Congress. Many times there are both good and bad things in such bills, but you get to vote only one way. Personally, I'd be glad when possible and feasible to take the items one at a time and not try to hide behind an omnibus bill." Hopkins's amendment killing the dam earned the wrath of his neighboring GOP colleague, Gene Snyder, who backed it. He was unsuccessful in his quest to stop the closing of the Lexington-Blue Grass Army Depot.

Hopkins's ardent conservatism by no means made him an automatic vote for his party. In 1986, he found himself furiously in the crosshairs over President Reagan's request to aid the Nicaraguan contras. Hopkins had been among the dozen or so Republicans genuinely undecided about that vote until literally the last moments. In March, he and many of those same Congressmen who were uncertain of how they'd vote all sided against the administration which resulted in a narrow defeat (222-210). But June was make or break and the pressure was on.

The Council for Inter-American Security ran ads urging Hopkins to back the measure and Reagan, needing every vote, contacted him in his office. He told *The Lexington-Herald Leader* that he reached his decision during that call. He had been staring at a picture of his son Josh and he told Reagan that, "I don't want to find myself making a vote that causes Josh - or anybody else's Josh - to get his head blown off because I made a wrong decision." Hopkins explained that, "When I got that commitment from the president that he had the staying power to see this thing through, that's when I decided...I told him I'm not interested in escalation, I'm interested in stopping it. He said that was his goal." This time, the margin from the March vote was nearly identical but in the opposite direction and Reagan's request passed 221-209.

Even home-state Republicans were not immune from an occasional chastising. In 1989, he criticized home-state GOP Senator Mitch McConnell's call to shoot down aircraft carrying drug smugglers as "goofy" and "irresponsible." But as another governor's race approached, that didn't make Republicans less likely to back him.

Hopkins had been urged to consider throwing his hat into the ring for governor in both 1983 and 1987 but had no interest. In '87, he even led in some straw polls yet passed. By 1990, Hopkins was more seriously eyeing the '91 race but, as the calendar moved forward, was noticeably dawdling. But President George H.W. Bush made a big push for him to run and he acquiesced (a jog with the president didn't hurt). Even so, Hopkins did not appear elated even into the campaign. In February of 1991, he told Republicans, "I want to make this very clear. If you can find a candidate who can do the job better than Larry Hopkins, not only should you vote for him, you should work for him."

Hopkins with Kentucky Chief Justice Bob Stephens
Photo via the Kenton County Library

Many in the party took Hopkins up on that. While state and national Republicans hoped that Hopkins to waltz to the nomination, Larry Forgy had other ideas. Forgy had been the party's nominee for governor in 1987 and had taken 35%. Forgy even had the backing of Eric Deters, the Fourth District GOP chair who had been named to the post by a Hopkins colleague and supporter, Congressman Jim Bunning. Forgy, endorsed by Pat Robertson, vowed to reject contributions of more than $300 and spoke of doubling farm income. Hopkins attacked Forgy for a draft deferment but Forgy returned fire by telling voters that Hopkins had touted himself as a Korean War veteran but did not actually enlist in the Marines until 1954 (Hopkins said he joined "in the latter part of the Korean War conflict" and that the war technically was ongoing until 1955. They argued over competency testing for teachers (Hopkins backed it, Forgy did not). The result was a true horse-race to which Kentuckians are accustomed as Hopkins pulled it out 81,526 to 79,581 votes, a difference of 1,955 votes.

The Democrat Hopkins was facing was Lieutenant Governor Brereton Jones who prevailed in his own acrimonious primary. Hopkins accused him of having "sold-out" to win union backing. But he had money – $4 million to $2 million and the division that plagued Hopkins during primary season continued into the general. For one, Hopkins and his running-mate, Eugene Goss, disagreed on both Right-To-Work and the environment. Hopkins also alarmed female voters by coming out in favor of jailing women who had illegal abortions should Roe v. Wade one day be overturned.

Trailing in the polls. Hopkins on October 22, declared "our campaign is starting now," but, in actuality, most Republicans had already written him off. He ran a "Mr. Fred" commercial that featured a talking horse attacking Jones, which included hitting him for failing to release his tax returns. That galvanized few and on Election Day, Jones galloped to victory 65-35%, a margin that exceeded both camp's expectations. He carried every county in the Sixth District. Hopkins won a single county in Northern Kentucky (Lewis) and a smattering near the southern end of the state but nothing else.

Hopkins conceded gracefully, telling supporters, "This is going to a tough time for our next governor. We ought to all help the new governor help this state." Jones meanwhile resisted calls, even when pressed by reporters, to salute his rival for running a spirited race. Hopkins acknowledges that beyond waiting too long to enter the campaign, "We should have gotten started earlier. We were going against a guy who had been running for five years." The vituperative nature of the primary, he said, also proved counterproductive.

There was salt on the wound to follow. The banking scandal was out and about and it was discovered that Hopkins had 32 overdrafts. But in truth, popular Lexington Mayor Scotty Baesler had indicated plans to challenge Hopkins for re-election and that would have seriously tied Hopkins down. Two days after Baesler entered, Hopkins bowed out, saying he had neither the "energy or enthusiasm" for another campaign now. He shed further light on his decision. "Right up till Christmas I would say that we were running for Congress. During the holidays…maybe Christmas Day or the day right after Christmas, we just decided that after 15 campaigns in 22 years and going to Pittsburgh (to change planes) 100 times a year was not what we wanted to do again this coming year." Baesler was not a factor. "Had it not been him," he said, "it would have been others who are waiting in the wings out there.

At that time, Hopkins had more money in his campaign account ($660,682) than all but two members who would be departing Congress in 1992 and that was of course the last year that members could convert that money to personal use.

CHAPTER SEVENTY-FIVE

Weber and Sikorski the Minnesota Twins of the House Banking Scandal

Introductory Quote: "You bounce enough checks and it doesn't matter if your Sir Lancelot, you're going to be gone." – Steve Schier, Carleton College Political Science professor in 1992 as the enormity Rubbergate took its course.

Photos courtesy of C-SPAN

No one would ever call Vin Weber and Gerry Sikorski two peas in a pod. One is a liberal Democrat and the other was an equally conservative Republican. The only thing the pair had in common, aside from their Roman Catholicism, is that they seemed to be among the brightest stars of Minnesota politics in their respective parties. In fact, to say that Weber and Sikorski exuded the term political wunderkind understate the natural abilities of both men. But the trajectories for both men were eroded by revelations of their roles in the House Bank scandal in the spring of 1992 and, politically at least, it proved career-enders for each.

At the time of Rubbergate, Sikorski had been receiving serious mention as a potential challenger to Republican U.S. Senator David Durenberger in 1994 while Weber, a member of the House Republican leadership, was thought to be in contention for the second or third ranking position in the conference. Because their careers dimmed after the revelations, they faded. His prominence was such that it was not uncommon to see him on a Sunday morning talk show articulating the GOP position on the issue of the day.

At first glance, Weber's checking woes were substantially less severe than Sikorski's. With 125 checks returned, the amount of his overdrafts came out to $47,987. With 697 overdrafts on the other hand, Sikorski had the ninth highest numerical number in the House, though the $119,966.67 that he was in the red wasn't anywhere near the monetary amount of some other colleagues. High as the numbers were, Weber might have been able to salvage his political career had he tried but he decided otherwise. Sikorski did try but was likely doomed from the start.

Gerry Sikorski

Shortly after taking office as a Congressman, Sikorski was riding with a New York Times reporter in his hometown of Stillwater. He compared his new role to, "like the two paths in the woods: I've taken a path, but I haven't gone so far that I still don't see the other path. I hope I don't lose that path." But after ten years in the nation's capitol, he evidently got lost in the woods.

To call Sikorski a political natural drastically understated the word. An indefatigable campaigner, he captured a seat in the Minnesota State Senate at age 28 and ascended to the position of Majority Whip four years later (his specialty became issues concerning children and battered women). Sikorski had a rusty background. Born in the farm town of Breckinridge on the North Dakota border, his father worked on a railroad and bartender while his mother was a waitress. Sikorski graduated Summa Cum Laude from the University of Minnesota, then obtained his J.D. from the UM Law School.

Along the way, Sikorski did experience one minor setback when he tried for an open Congressional seat being vacated by Republican Al Quie, who was winning the governor's chair. His Republican opponent was Secretary of State Allan Erdahl. But aside from running in a politically adverse district in a year that was among the worst in history for Minnesota Democrats, some would-be constituents might have thought Sikorski was trying for a leap prematurely. Sikorski tried to show versatility by playing up his agriculture background but, when he came out for tax cuts, Erdahl replied, "The candidates might sound alike, but one of them's been a Republican a lot longer than the other one has been." Accordingly, Erdahl prevailed in every county for a 56-42% win but Sikorski came close in the district's two most populous counties, Washington and Winona.

Four years later was a different story. Redistricting had made the district more Democratic and the Reagan recession was causing voters to revert to their roots. And with just one county from the district he currently represented in the new district, Erdahl wasn't even supposed to be the Republican nominee. He had actually tried for the First District but lost the nomination to Tom Hagedorn. But when Erdahl took up GOP entreaties to run in the Sixth District, he gave Sikorski a surprisingly strong run. Sikorski distributed maps to district households reminding voters of the trek Erdahl took to move from his old turf to the new district. This time, Sikorski wrested the seat from Erdahl by 3,512 votes out of 215,000 cast.

Almost immediately, Sikorski began lobbying for a seat on the Energy and Commerce Committee, and with help from fellow Minnesotan Marty Sabo who sat on the Democratic Steering Committee, he became one of six freshman to land a seat. He immediately became an ally of erstwhile Californian Henry Waxman of California, whom he came to regard as a mentor. Ironically, John Dingell, the powerful chairman Sikorski thought he could woo for support with their mutual heritage ("The Polish connection doesn't hurt") became a semi-adversary. In fact, Politics in America wrote, "There are those who oppose Dingell on clean air but go out of his way to placate him on other issues. Not Sikorski."

Waxman helped Sikorski introduced an amendment banning burning of non-combustible items and batteries.

Sikorski saw acid-rain as, "the powder-keg environmental problem of the decade." Keynoting a convention, he said, "every day more than 176,750 tons of sulfur dioxide and nitrogen oxide—the equivalent of 4,144 fully loaded freight cars—are shot into the skies of America." He and Waxman sponsored the National Acid Rain Deposition Act. It required a ten million ton reduction in Sulphur dioxins (a fairly lofty goal considering that 22.5 million tons were emitted in 1980) and a nationwide tax on scrubbers to allow the rest of the country to share the burden. Perhaps even more lofty was prospects for its passage. The Canadian government, angered that their nation was absorbing pollution from its southern neighbors, implored action but Dingell was widespread against it and it died by a single vote in committee.

In 1986, when a U.S.-Canadian consortium vowed to invest in a method, Sikorski, who had re-introduced his measure, replied, "We already know how to clean up acid rain and we don't need to spend more taxpayers' money to find some new Buck Rogers technology." It wasn't until 1990 that movement took place when he and Massachusetts Republican Silvio Conte sponsored legislation.

Another priority, electric cars, also took four Congresses to come to fruition. Lawmakers defeated his proposal for a nationwide utility tax but he and New York Republican Bill Green successfully included a requirement that automobile manufacturers provide an eight year, 80,000 warranty for catalytic converters. The margin was 229-190.

Even after the law was implemented, Sikorski had work to do. For one, he saw Vice-President Dan Quayle as trying to undercut it. "Many Americans," he said, "think that Dan Quayle's purpose is to provide jokes for Johnny Carson and Arsenio Hall and, frankly, many Americans would sleep better believing that to be true. Unfortunately, on clean air and kids' health, he seems to have made the transition from irrelevant to dangerous. Recent efforts to dilute the clean air laws of the land have Dan Quayle's fingerprints all over them."

Beyond that, there was more policy to be had.

A Sikorski amendment to a 1987 Commerce Committee markup would mandate victims nuclear insurance be prioritized by courts before legal fees. He explained, "It simply states that in the event of a nuclear accident, victims will be compensated before lawyers. If there are sufficient funds to compensate the victims, then the court may award attorneys' fees from the balance." It cleared committee but was essentially circumvented and rendered moot by another amendment by Texas Democrat Ralph Hall the following day. The full House eventually got to settle the matter but lawmakers defeated Sikorski's measure was rejected 183-230.

Informing the public about chemicals was another hefty endeavor Sikorski undertook. The idea emanated from a catastrophe in Bhopal, India that claimed the lives of thousands of children but, American towns were not immune to potential for harm (a *New York Times* profile had detailed a river town in Louisiana that had massive deficiencies). Especially disturbing to Sikorski was that the public was made aware of only five percent of the chemicals released and in 1991, he unveiled the Community Right to Know Act. Its name belied the fact that it was truly far-reaching. Applying to businesses with more than ten people, not only did the proposal mandate informing the public which chemicals were being used but it also required plans for chemical reductions. Calling it, "a philosophical leap of faith," Sikorski called it, "kind of a heartfelt belief that people in communities have an absolute, fundamental right to know what goes into the air their kids breathe, the water they drink and the ground they play on."

In response to the deaths and injuries by electric garage door openers, Sikorski introduced the Automatic Garage Door opener Safety Act. At least

55 children nationwide were among the dead, including some who had been crushed or suffocated by a falling door. Sikorski said that, "Without a fail-safe device, parents can be fooled into believing their garage-door opener is operating safely, when the reverse mechanism is actually defective. With fifty-five dead kids, we can't just shrug our shoulders…turning that friendly open garage door of home to a fearsome death trap." The Door Operator and Remote Controls Manufacturers Association opposed the measure.

After a 1987 accident in the town of Mounds View, Minnesota Sikorski fought for gas pipeline safety.

Sikorski's wife suffered from multiple sclerosis which led him to promote legislation aiding victims. On the mounting troubles of Attorney General Ed Meese, he said, "The American people have good reason to be disheartened, perhaps even angered by these failures…Mr. Meese is not some middle-level functionary; he holds a very important position in this government and his personal history should make him extraordinarily sensitive to disclosure issues…the ethics buck stops at his desk." And his then-opposition to abortion made him strive to exempt contraceptives from a proposed public liability law. Sikorski also sat on the Post Office and Civil Services Committee and the Select Committee on —

As talk of advancement accelerated, Sikorski was urged to challenge Republican Senator Rudy Boschwitz in 1990 but opted to stay put. At that point, most viewed him as a sure bet to run for the seat of Minnesota's other Republican Senator, Durenberger when his seat expired in 1994. But Sikorski faced looming troubles and that was years before rubbergate entered the scene.

At the outset of the scandal, both men did themselves few favors by opposing full disclosure or giving other details (conversely, other member of the delegation with minimal involvement in the scandal opened up at once) at which point he said, "All we can do is go around and tell it to people and be as open as we can").

In 1988, Sikorski was hit by stories detailing allegations by staff members about his rigorous job requirements. *The Washington Post* reported "Former aides also took care of his dry-cleaning; looked after his house and dogs when he and his family were away; arranged his personal trips; occasionally did his Christmas shopping; and drove his young daughter to and from school." One high ranking member of Sikorski's staff, Ione Yates said this began as early as his first term in Congress, adding, "You were never asked, 'Would you do this as a favor to me?' You were told…I just got tired of feeling like a piece of property." Sikorski acknowledged his temper but took issue with the transgressions, saying,

"No one was ever asked to, requested to, or authorized to do any of those things." The Ethics Committee mounted an investigation into the matter but dismissed it in 1990. Sikorski would not be so lucky with Rubbergate.

When Sikorski learned that he had such a high place on the list of check writers, he began by releasing a statement calling the revelations, "embarrassing," and "painful...Despite the fact that we were told that holding checks was standard operating procedure and despite the fact that no taxpayers' money was involved, we should have known better." He immediately returned to Minnesota, "talking to everyone who wants to talk to me," the first of which was done in a 16-hour day. His wife went farther, "We should not have been so casual and careless with our personal account. ... Over the coming months, all we can do is explain the facts, be completely open, and have faith that the people of Minnesota will understand."

Sikorski pressed forward but, so did a Democratic State Representative, Alice Johnson. Her rationale: "People no longer trust him, people are questioning his credibility." Sikorski further eroded his base when he abandoned his long-held pro-life stance and affirmed that he favored a woman's right to an abortion. That earned him the enmity of the Minnesota Citizens Concerned for Life (MCCL). "I should have been much more attentive to the House overdraft perk. For the disappointment I brought to you, to my party, I'm sorry." Delegates apparently forgave him as he retained the party's endorsement but, he was not home free. An ambitious, pro-life legislator named Tad Jude announced plans to challenge Sikorski in the September primary.

The Sikorski camp had a first-rate get out the vote (GOTV) operation. Jude forces meanwhile were hoping for crossover votes from Independents and Republicans. The two-men see-sawed for much of the night before Jude finally called Sikorski to concede at 1 a.m., five hours after the polls closed. The difference was 2,051 votes, 49-46%. Many Democrats might have hoped Sikorski was now home-free for November but that was hardly the case at all. Republicans had nominated Rod Grams, a former news caster on KMSP-TV who drew comparisons to the character Ted Baxter on "Mary Tyler Moore."

There was a third-party candidate in the race, Dean Barkley who had the Independence Party backing. Sikorski backers had hoped that Barkley would dilute the anti-Sikorski votes from Grams but what they weren't gambling on was that he would himself prove a candidate with legs (indeed, Sikorski in his concession statement credited Barkley with "the best Independent campaign I have ever seen"). Barkley won the backing of *The Star Tribune* and *The St. Pioneer Press* which undoubtedly helped sway disaffected Democrats, not just

Independents to his side. Meanwhile, Sikorski was not helped by revelations that he was among the top ten frankers in the House.

By Election Day, most pundits were rating the contest as a tossup but most in Washington thought Sikorski's fate was sealed. The returns confirmed that and they were brutal. Sikorski was abandoned by 2/3 of voters as Grams won the seat 44-33%. Barkley took an impressive 16% and another Independent candidate affiliated with Ross Perot grabbed an additional 5%.

Sikorski, addressing his tearful supporters, said, "You know, I've been truly blessed. For that time in my life I loved to go to work every day, because I was doing exactly what I wanted to do, for exactly who I wanted to do it for...The voters of the Sixth District today decided to make a change. I respect and honor the democratic decision of the people of the Sixth District, who've I've had the pleasure to serve for the past 10 years." Alluding to Democrat Bill Clinton's election as president, he said, "Tonight, America embraced the future, and so do I."

As he prepared to leave office, Sikorski told *The Star Tribune* he "packed about 20 years of Congressional life into 10," adding, "There are some laws that my name is attached to that I'm real proud of." He was picked up with the prestigious Washington law firm, Holland and Knight. Before Grams died in 2013, Sikorski said he considered him a friend. On the other hand, "I won't comment on the jerk who ran against me in the primary."

Though having been unseated by scandal, Sikorski wound down his tenure on the Hill with a little light(s). He and his daughter joined Speaker Tom Foley and Minnesota Senator Paul Wellstone for the Capitol tree lighting in December 1992
Photo via Getty Images

Vin Weber

Weber was a Congressman at age 28 and he displayed himself to be the same kind of political wunderkind as Sikorski, only in a behind-the-scenes sort of way. This meant cutting his teeth for fellow Republicans, a task that suited Weber just fine. Born in the town of Slayton, his family ran the influential Murray County Herald.

He attended the University of Minnesota though didn't graduate. He snagged a post as delegate to the Republican National Convention at age 20, before going to work on the Congressional campaign of GOP Congressional candidate Tom Hagedorn in 1974. It was a horrendous Republican year nationally but Hagedorn won and Weber became his press secretary. He repeated that with Rudy Boschwitz, who was elected Minnesota's U.S. Senator in 1978 (having taken a break in the interim to act as the co-publisher of Murray County newspapers).

These connections seemed to nicely position Weber for a 1980 challenge to Democratic Congressman Richard Nolan, a three-term incumbent who had a shaky hold on an increasingly right-trending district. But Nolan retired and the Democratic nomination went to Nolan's aide, Richard Baumann who formally organized for the Farmer's Union. Weber meanwhile required ten tries in order to capture the GOP convention nod. But in a year that was turning sharply against Democrats, Baumann would have needed everything to go right and his willingness to make exceptions for abortion turned voters off even in some heavily Democratic areas (Weber managed to carry St. Cloud). He won 53-47% and a majority of counties.

Despite bemoaning government "meddling" in agriculture matters in what was a very farm oriented district, Weber prevailed. The freshman Congressman would not be the only man with the Weber surname in the House: Ed Weber was winning a House seat from Toledo but would lose after one-term. Fortunately, Vin Weber's tenure would last a little longer and as his Ohio colleague was losing, he warded off a determined challenge from State Senator Jim Nichols 54-46%. He was assigned to the Budget and Small Business Committees.

On policy, Weber was a staunch conservative, and early on inclined to support Reagan on most, though not all matters). It was on style that he transcended his class, he embraced Reagan's call for "bold, pastel colored differences" with the Democrats.

A then-little known New York Congressman named Jack Kemp was among his closest friends and allies and the pair, along with their colleague from Illinois, Henry Hyde, put forth legislation in 1985 stating a "finding" of Congress that life begins at conception (Weber was so pro-life that in 1990, he reportedly voted for Democratic Governor Rudy Perpich over the Republican nominee, Arne Carlson). In 1986, he, Kemp, Gingrich and others circulated a letter urging aid to the contras, arguing that without it, the Nicaraguans, through the auspices of the Sandinistas, "will soon be helping their brothers in arms in Libya and Iran to achieve their stated goal of defeating Israel." In 1988 as Kemp sought the presidency, Weber was his tight end, becoming among his most ardent Congressional backers.

Like a number of his primarily junior colleagues, Weber was frustrated by what he viewed as the GOPs perpetual minority status and with other aggressive members of the Conservative Opportunity Society (among them future Speaker Newt Gingrich of Georgia), set out to remedy it. But as one publication wrote, "In a group that likes to ponder the march of history and proposed Grand ideas Weber stands out as a hard-headed pragmatist more concerned with sound strategy that was ideological debating points." He thus became coordinator of what *CQ* referred to as "parliamentary acrobatics." Weber was angered when Tip O'Neill ordered people to pan around the chamber to showcase the renegades addressing a nearly empty chamber, calling it, "a sham what they were doing, and we just can't stand for that." Weber responded that, "What we want is a debate before the American people." While high-profile Democrats like House Majority Leader Jim Wright of Texas called the group, "as phony as a $3 bill," and Pat Schroeder of Colorado, expressed her hope that "it's just kind of a passing folly." Not a chance - they were just getting started. And they didn't stop there. The Society published, *A House of Ill Repute.*

Weber also wanted to make sure his own party was out in front of messaging and when Kansas Senator Robert Dole ascended to the position of Senate Majority Leader, Weber made clear that stronger leadership was required in order for Republicans to grasp the future. "Our problem with Dole is that he's very much a minority-mindset Senator. Senate Republicans have done a poor job of advocating the kind of agenda that is going to attract people to our party for a generational commitment...The central question for the Republican Party now is how do we cement the loyalty of voters under 40 years old, The big division in the Republican Party today is not between left and right, it's between people who want to make the Republican Party a majority party and people who are locked into a minority party mindset."

Weber was among the many Congressman in both parties who asked the President to fire Secretary of State George Shultz, calling him, "a real liability for the President and the administration with Congress." The Secretary, he said, "has so pre-empted decision-making on foreign policy, his sins have been transferred to the President."

Weber opposed Reagan on the Clinch River Funding, taking the line that, "A truly market-oriented approach should reject massive, long-term subsidization of any one energy technology." He also opposed production of the Midgetman because another weaponry, the MX, was at an all time high and Weber, along with an odd coalition of liberals and conservatives (including Massachusetts Democrats Barney Frank and Ed Markey) did not see the necessity of two. When the Bush White House did indeed opt to fund both, Weber was stupefied. "The membership of the House has been begging the White House not to spend as much money on defense, and I don't think you solve that problem by saying, 'Okay, we're going to build two missiles instead of one.'"

One issue on which Weber ad no moral qualms about deviating from Reagan was on the issue of economic sanctions against South Africa and he did so in early-1985 well before it became clear the GOP Senate would eventually confront him (he and Gingrich had also urged Reagan to scrap a trip to Bitburg, a Nazi cemetery in Germany, calling it, "morally wrong"). Weber explained, "We younger conservatives grew up in the 60's with a clear impression of national consensus favoring racial justice. We cannot afford to be burdened by an old conservative image, whether true or not, that this party provides a haven for racism."

Gray showed his appreciation by holding a major hearing on farm issues in Worthington in Weber's district which an aide called, "a coup." Democrats were not happy and tried, unsuccessfully to get Gray to call it off.

The farm crisis of the mid-1980s forced Weber top at least re-evaluate his ways and as he began promoting (or not refusing) at least some government intervention to help his people, he explained that it wasn't a fundamental shift. Rather, "I've always thought of myself as a practical politician. My district is facing an economic crisis, and government has to help people facing economic crisis. When people in my district were doing better, I guess I didn't think so much about that." Weber had long opposed the cutting of dairy subsidies but now was joining with liberals such as Tom Daschle of South Dakota who was sponsoring Emergency Farm aid legislation. Taking the floor in February 1985, Weber addressed critics. "The point that I want to make, particularly to Members on my side of the aisle that have some concerns about what they view as a 'bailout' for people who got themselves into difficulty, is that that is just simply not the case. Granted, we had in the 1970's many people who speculated in agriculture, who made some bad decisions. I can tell you, most of those people are no longer in agriculture. We are talking today about good, efficient, honest producers who are in trouble regardless of what our friends at the Office of Management and Budget say, through no fault of their own." Reagan vetoed it against Weber's admonition.

In 1986, the perception that Weber was part of the problem with regard to the farm crisis and an unusually strong challenger gave him the race of his life. David Johnson was a Republican farmer from the town of Hector who switched parties to challenge Weber (noting that he was original a Democrat, he chirped, "The prodigal son has come home to the DFL,"). He accused the incumbent of doing an "about face" on the farm crisis, hit him for not having a seat on the Agriculture Committee, and released a poll showing Weber with just a 45% re-elect. In fact, when tendonitis caused Weber to limp through the district during the campaign, one Democrat surmised, "It must be because he's not used to going home every weekend." Weber played up the party switch as opportunistic. "As late as last August, (Johnson) was telling party officials that he was a conservative Republican. Someone who changes parties just because there's an opening and he wants to run for office, he has to be suspect."

At one point during the campaign, Weber was blindsided by the disappearance of $32,000 (his treasurer was subsequently fired). He spent $750,272 on the race. Counting was close and with 60% counted, Weber said, "I'd be fooling you to say we're in high spirits right now." With 94% counted, Weber's lead was just 3,000 votes though it doubled when the last few precincts reported. The final total was 100,049 to 94,048). It wasn't until 4.a.m that he learned with certainty that he had won.

As a way of acknowledging that he recognized that fences needed to be tending to back home, Weber sought and received a post on the House Appropriations Committee. By 1988, most was forgiven as Weber won his fifth term with 58%. He took 62% in anti-incumbent 1990 and seemed poised to do so by a similar margin in '92. Like so many of his colleagues, Rubbergate put a damper on that.

Initially, Weber, like the other Republicans who wanted the extent of the scandal to be uncovered, was initially giddy about the repercussions. "Having us in the position of defending the Ethics Committee while Democrats defend the Speaker serves us well politically." But when the extent of his own problems became known, Weber addressed them by proclaiming himself, "ready to take my medicine. I'm a big boy. I can handle that." He initially sought to tamp the fires by reminding constituents in a press release that, "I was among the first to admit not having covered all checks, and I am among the first to disclose details on my account."

As the months went forward, Weber evidently reached the conclusion that "taking his medicine" meant opting out altogether and in April 1992, he stunned many by calling it quits altogether.

Weber was prepared to explain his decision to call it quits as a family matter but he told reporters that was vetoed by his wife ("I don't want you to say that anymore because it gives people the impression that I'm trying to talk you out of this"). Weber said, "The truth was I didn't want to do it," then proceeded to invoke his past life in candidate recruitment. "The most important element in the campaign," he said, "is a properly motivated candidate…If I didn't have the proper motivation to seek reelection in a year like this one, it was the wrong thing to do."

CHAPTER SEVENTY-SIX

McEwen's Career Encompassed the Highs and Lows of a Congressman

**Introductory Quote: "It looks like a junior Chamber of Commerce." –
House Majority Leader Jim Wright in 1981 on the large number of young
Republicans in the freshman class.**

Photo courtesy of Bob McEwen

Bob McEwen possessed all the ingredients for a sky's the limit political career. Elected to the Ohio House at age 24 and the U.S. House at 30, McEwen was being talked about as a Senate or gubernatorial candidate well before the end of his first decade. His smile which politically speaking, came straight from central casting, didn't hurt either. That talk culminated in 1992 following McEwen's involvement in the House banking scandal which led to his defeat in a seat that, while drastically changed by redistricting, was still fairly fertile Republican territory.

In two sentences in separate articles, *The Akron Beacon Journal* might have inadvertently summed up the paradox of McEwen's triumph and downfall. It once labeled McEwen, "ebullient, fast-talking and charismatic." And as he was fighting for his political life, the paper called it "almost eerie how quickly Bob McEwen has gone from being the perfect profile of the invulnerable congressional incumbent to the perfect profile of an endangered incumbent."

Through his Congressional years, home for McEwen was the small, southwestern Ohio town of Hillsborough and he left only to obtain his degree from the University of Florida. He got his law degree of Ohio State University College of Law in 1974, the same year he won his State House seat where he worked on a flood-prone creek and getting rid of the Ohio lottery. When he wasn't performing his legislative duties, McEwen was practicing real estate in town.

In 1980, the district's longtime, immensely respected Republican incumbent, William Harsha was stepping down and McEwen went for the seat. Trying to claim Harsha's mantra was not hard – McEwen had directed two of his campaigns (Harsha declined to endorse because he had an affiliation to a few other candidates). McEwen faced six other Republicans including Clermont County Transit Board Chairman Jim Christy, with whom he shared a geographic base. Ohio League of Young Republican Club Chairman James Murray was another heavyweight in the race and labeled McEwen a political "chameleon," but he won the primary with 45%.

The general election was not at all daunting. Minister and psychiatrist Ted Strickland had lost the two prior elections to Harsha by wide margins and chided McEwen's "simple solutions" for intricate problems grappling the nation. While McEwen was not an incumbent, 1980 was the wrong year to be a Democrat in this part of Ohio. In actuality, McEwen's 55-45% win, while solid, was not particularly overwhelming and he did lose Chillicothe and Portsmouth. The seat was nonetheless his and, with posts on the Public Works and Veterans Affairs Committees and a voting record that was solidly conservative, his appeal to the district was unquestioned.

Early in his tenure, Bob McEwen of Ohio might have been confused with Robert McEwen, who represented upstate New York for nearly two decades. Their styles could not have been more different as McEwen the New Yorker was a soft-spoken, quintessential moderate while McEwen the Ohioan was aligned with the right-of-center wing of his party who gained distinction by pointing out disdain for the system under Democratic control. Yet both were tenacious boosters of their districts.

On Public Works, McEwen became the advocate of infrastructure, particularly as it involved the federally dependent Southern Ohio. One example came in 1985 when he felt the House was not adequately funding a plant in Piketon. He urged colleagues to shun "incessant nay-saying and irresponsible hypothesizing." He tried in vain to find ways for a centrifuge uranium enrichment plant in Piketon to remain open despite being on the U.S. Energy Department's list or closure. With Akron Democrat John Seiberling, they argued to Energy Secretary John Herrington that more than $3 billion had been committed to the project and threatened to haul him before Congress for hearings. Eventually, more than 400 employees were laid off and McEwen and Seiberling could do little more than lead the fight to retrain them. Then he led the fight for a Strategic Defense Initiative (SDI) plant at Piketon.

McEwen also complained that the revenue sharing formula employed by the federal government was not helpful to his neck of the woods and with colleagues from both parties, aimed to get the aviation trust fund removed from the budget, a priority for astute pork-barrelers. Near the end of his tenure, he was able to secure money for two badly needed interstate highways and sponsored a bill authorizing ten national cemeteries, including one that went to Cleveland.

McEwen learned early that being a junior member of the minority wouldn't always impede his effectiveness. One example was his quest for a Greenup Lock and Dam on the Ohio River. A formula in a dam-bridge program allowed the construction of just two dams every two years. Greenup was number 24 in the queue which meant a 48-year wait. That changed at a Public Works markup when McEwen filed an amendment to strike line two (the proposed Auburn Dam in California) and insert line 24 (Greenup). The presence of Auburn's chief advocate, Doug Bosco of California, on Public Works, made McEwen's work cut out for him, particularly since Bosco was a Democrat. When the amendment came up, Public Works Chair Jim Howard of New Jersey whom McEwen liked very much, recognized him but, McEwen, not wanting to draw attention to the maneuver, declined to speak on the project. At that point, Bosco was in the midst of a conversation and when Howard asked for an objection, Bosco simply looked up and resumed talking. Howard then said loudly, "Is there any request for recognition" but Bosco was too immersed to realize what was happening. Howard finally banged the gavel down and ruled the amendment adopted.

The Rt. 32 Appalachia Highway System was another endeavor. In the 1960s, Ohio's Republican Governor John Rhodes had negotiated a funding formula so that the federal government would pay for 90% of its upkeep while Ohio would only be responsible for ten percent. Critics derided it as "Rhode's Road to Nowhere," and Democratic Governor John Gilligan nixed that formula in the 1970s. He got a four-lane Rt. 32 built. McEwen and Kentucky Democratic Congressman Chris Perkins promoted a highway between Columbus, Ohio and Lexington, Kentucky with the logic that it would shorten the commute and ease traffic between the two cities.

McEwen saw big dividends from a fight McEwen interjected himself in between Ohio and Clermont County officials that people were puzzled as to why ("you have no dog in this fight, Bob"). The county wanted to draw water out Harsha Lake of the East Fork but the state interpreted literally a provision that water was not to be taken from a lake. McEwen made noise about solving the problem and the next day, the (Department of) Natural Resources people drove into the parking lot "with their tires squealing." McEwen filed legislation to ease the prohibition and ultimately, an accommodation was reached that allowed the water to be transferred to the County Commission. In 2013, the water treatment plant was named for McEwen.

On other matters, McEwen in 1985 garnered rare national attention when he fought efforts to deport Tsui Chi Hsii, a Chinese man who had been nicknamed, "Charlie's Two Shoes," by U.S. Marines who essentially adopted him during World War II when he was a ten-year-old boy (they could not pronounce his name, hence the "two-shoes"). Chi Hsii had come to the U.S in 1983 but had overstayed his visa. The case came down to the wire but the saga had a happy ending when he was granted citizenship in 2000.

Votingwise, McEwen was solidly anti-abortion and opposed the 1990 Civil Rights Restoration Act. There was little difference stylistically. *Politics in America* wrote how "in the waning hours of any legislative day...you may see McEwen playing the trusty sidekick, Sancho Panza to Bob Dornan of California, both tilting at the attest liberal windmill."

If there was one McEwen creed, it was as a freedom fighter. During the Gulf War, he took CNN to task for its frequent airing of Saddam Hussein remarks. Doing so, he said, was offering, "the demented dictator a mouthpiece to more than 100 nations." He tried to remove the policy banning assassinations of foreign leaders and chided the Bush administration for shooting down Iraqi planes targeting Kurdish opposition protesters. But after the war, McEwen scoffed at giving money to Kuwait, arguing, "There are plenty of petro-dollars there to do that. They don't need our help."

West Virginia & Regional History Center

With Actor Danny Thomas
Photo courtesy of the West Virginia & Regional History Center

In 1991, McEwen bemoaned a Soviet aid package because it lacked provisions for accountability. "Now, not only are we going to give $700 million in cash, we can take anything that America possesses and give to them free with no accountability under any circumstances. Now, rest assured if this amendment is allowed to pass this afternoon, I swear, I guarantee, we are going to be sending trucks to the Soviet Union to transport food, rest assured; not to your local hospital board, not to a fire department, not to a police department. We are going to be sending it to the Soviet Union so they can build aircraft."

McEwen had always displayed a staunch anti-communist bent and as such, was among those who met with the national security team at the home of President George H.W. Bush in Kennebunkport, Maine to plot advancement as Poland moved toward freedom. He sponsored the National

Strategy Act that meant a crucial realigning of the chain of command during the 1991 Persian Gulf War. True to form, on a trip to Moscow in 1991, told a reporter, "If you love freedom and believe in democracy, this has to be the greatest time in the history of man to be alive."

McEwen's first flirtation with higher office came as early as 1986 when he explored the possibility of running for governor. But it was most serious during the 1988 cycle as he actually announced his candidacy to challenge Democratic Senator Howard Metzenbaum. By early 1987, 29 of the state's 39 Republican state legislators had endorsed his bid and he ran television ads putting his name out to greater Ohio. His message was to wrap himself in Reaganomics and he contended, "It's never been this good for your parents; it never was this good for your grandparents; and the 1980s are going to be the best decade in this country in 50 years, second only to the 1990s." But Cleveland Mayor George Voinovich had the momentum fairly early (even McEwen's Cincinnati colleague, Bill Gradison, backed Voinovich) and in December 1987, McEwen announced that he was staying put. He explained that a contentious primary would damage the odds of beating Metzenbaum, which didn't come close to happening anyway (the incumbent brushed aside Voinovich with 57%).

Voinovich and McEwen again butted heads temporarily as the 1990 governor's race took shape and Voinovich tried to settle a potential primary with his old foe by offering McEwen the Lieutenant Governor's slot. McEwen rebuffed it ("I made it clear from the start I wasn't interested"). One person who did not rebuff Voinovich's overture was McEwen's colleague, Mike DeWine and the ticket was elected.

As 1992 got underway, a number of Republicans were pushing McEwen to take on U.S. Senator John Glenn. But House Republicans had awarded him a seat on the prestigious Rules Committee and he opted to continue his career there. Beyond that term, however, he was thwarted from doing so by a double dose of bad luck: redistricting and the House bank.

Ohio was losing two House seats as a result of reapportionment and with split control of the process, both parties agreed that each party would surrender a seat. But the haggling went on so long that the filing deadline was pushed back. Not surprisingly, 74-year old thirteen termer Clarence Miller became the GOP casualty but, even though his district was carved up four different ways, he refused to go quietly. Instead, after pondering his options, he opted to challenge McEwen where 40 percent of his constituents lived (the two battled over three other counties that had shifted from Miller to

McEwen following the 1982 remap). The battle proved more generational than ideological. Miller, often described as "courtly," was old school while McEwen embraced many of the same tactics that were gradually fueled the Republican ascendancy. But the race soon exceeded personality.

For months prior to the filing deadline, the bank scandal was percolating and McEwen steadfastly denied any involvement. He even blamed a "right-wing clique" in his party for drawing out the issue, including his colleague from Southern Ohio, future House Speaker John Boehner. When it was revealed that he had 166 overdrafts, he blamed the management of the bank, saying, "Whoever was in charge owes America and Congress an apology. It has done serious harm to many decent people." He added, "I'm blaming the Sergeant-at-Arms more than anything. . . . Anyone who knew this vulnerability existed should be blamed." Miller was unmoved by McEwen's laying the feet of mismanagement in the Democrats lap. His response: "I have dealt with that bank for many years. If the bank was so bad and mismanaged, why don't I have a problem?"

For McEwen, the timing could not have been worse. The primary was just six weeks away and though Miller initially downplayed the issue ("I would like to see the check problem quieted down"), he then proceeded to hammer McEwen running an ad claiming the score of overdrafts was 166-0.

There were many other issues pertinent to the campaign and Miller's physical stamina was chief among them. At 74, many wondered whether he was up to continued service in Congress. McEwen labeled the contest about "the strongest voice in the 1990s," and once said that how, "At age 42, I'm not ready for a rest home yet." Whether the remark was made in jest or not, Miller cried foul but inadvertently, might have been lending credence to the speculation. Having scheduled a press conference after slipping on a bar of soap in the shower weeks before the primary, many expected that Miller was going to announce his departure. Instead, he lambasted McEwen not just for the checks, but for frequent travel and ranking 19th among House members for contributions from the Savings and Loan industry.

Primary night began with McEwen a good 2,000 votes ahead but as Miller's portion of the new district reported, it dwindled to just 269 votes. Miller did not go quietly. McEwen's margin was certified at 286 votes out of 67,000 cast but Miller alleged irregularities and refused to concede. Specifically, he contended that Highland County, where McEwen happened to live, was last to report and delivered him the election. Miller pursued litigation for nearly three months after the primary before finally dropping it in late August due to lack of money, halfway between the primary and the general.

Meanwhile, McEwen faced a familiar foe: Strickland but, despite a divisive battle and a more slightly Democratic presence in the district (which still didn't say much), was still hardly on the radar screens of national Democrats. By mid-October, the race seemed to be headed into true tossup status but the surmisal was that the Republican lean would limp McEwen across the finish line. Money and campaign resources were obvious reasons. McEwen, however, might have failed to heed the warning until too late.

Roll Call wrote that while McEwen was blanketing the district, "Strickland is a viable presence to the traveler only in a few areas of his home county of Scioto (although Scioto is the largest county in the district)." The publication also wrote that one McEwen campaign ad was played 32 times in one day. Yet Strickland was doing a fairly good job of tying McEwen to an unpopular Congress. He criticized him for backing a $40,000 pay raise and for accepting honoraria when Congress was in session and voting (in particular, he pointed to $3,000 McEwen had collected when the House was voting on a transportation bill). Strickland also appealed to this rural district by opposing most gun control even though McEwen relentlessly tried to convince voters that the opposite was true.

Vice-President Dan Quayle, Jack Kemp and Pat Buchanan stumped for McEwen who told voters, "I can honestly tell you that I have always tried to do the right thing, often when it's been unpopular, and I have never forgotten where I came from." Many voters remained unsure, however, and Miller was among them. He clarified that indecision less than a month before the election by endorsing Strickland. It was a far cry from McEwen's primary night utterance that, "trusting that the results hold, we look forward to the support that Clarence's endorsement is sure to bring."

A look at the numbers show that, had the district not been reconfigured, McEwen would have held the seat. He won the western counties handily, including prevailing over Strickland by 10,000 votes out of only 22,000 cast in Warren County near suburban Cincinnati. But the further east removed from McEwen's base and the Southern ends, Strickland did well. The challenger prevailed in Pike County narrowly but his margins in Lawrence and Scioto with 58% and Athens with 65%. That resulted in an incredibly narrow 122,720 to 119,252 election, a 50.7%-49.3%. *The Almanac of American Politics* called McEwen's loss "stinging" given that Bush won the district while losing Ohio, albeit with a plurality, a view a dejected McEwen might have shared by seeking solace by taking a drive alone the next day and could not be found. He felt the addition of one more precinct from his old district would have reversed the loss.

Other McEwen supporters placed the blame solely at Miller's feet, with one supporter complaining that if Miller had told "his people to vote for Bob," that would have made the difference. But a Republican consultant put the most evident spin on the one-time rising star's loss: "He got hurt by that and the character issue and integrity. The loss didn't have anything to do with a great campaign by Ted Strickland. McEwen could have been beat by L'il Abner, there was such an anti-McEwen vote."

Unexpectedly, the new year would offer McEwen a second chance at political life. Gradison was offered a job with the Health Insurance Association of America and decided to accept it shortly after the new session of Congress convened in January. Much of the district contained areas that had been in the old Sixth District (the rest took in suburban Cincinnati) and McEwen initially said, "I'd be lying if I said a lot of people hadn't asked me to run." He decided to do just that but, it turn out, not everyone was thrilled at the prospect of a return. Rob Portman was one of them. The prominent, well-connected Cincinnati attorney and one-time Bush White House official entered the race armed with endorsements from Gradison, among others.

McEwen conceded personal shortcomings during the campaign, saying, "I felt I could never admit a mistake," and that, in his brief time on the outside looking in, "I have learned a great deal." Portman prevailed 36-30% with wealthy homebuilder Jay Buchert taking 26%. McEwen was gracious in defeat saying Portman would make a "fine Congressman." *Congressional Quarterly* noted that McEwen, "stung by his second loss," said, "I don't anticipate running for office again. I've enjoyed my time in public life, and we look forward to the next step." In his case, the next step was developing an enterprise that meant motivational speaking all over the country.

In 2005, McEwen found motivation to return to Congress. Portman resigned to accept a post with the Bush administration and McEwen decided, "it's time to roll up our sleeves and get back into the fray," and jumped into the race to succeed him. Four serious candidates were seeking the GOP nod including Hamilton County Commissioner Pat DeWine, the son of U.S. Senator and McEwen's former House colleague, Mike DeWine.

Many Republicans questioned the wisdom of McEwen's bid but his response was, "You like to do things that you feel that you're skilled at and I care very deeply about our country and the questions that we're facing, both internationally and domestically over the next few years, are things that I feel Ohio can use a strong voice on," McEwen's challenge was expressed by an Ohio Republican still in Congress who said, "A lot of people don't know who Bob McEwen is."

McEwen could still count on old friends such as Kemp and Ed Meese but, having been off the grid so long, McEwen had lost his swagger even among anti-abortionists and by now, it was Jean Schmidt, a State Representative and leader in the Right-to-Life Community who had momentum. McEwen carried five of the seven counties, including Scioto and Pike by large margins. But Schmidt took Hamilton (Cincinnati) and her home of Clermont for a 31-26% win.

The following year, Schmidt was up for a full term and, having made a reference to "cowards" that many thought had been directed to Pennsylvania's Jack Murtha. The two debated the war with McEwen expressing the view that U.S. troops should start winding down their mission but Schmidt favoring staying the course. Unfortunately for McEwen, GOP voters opted to stay the course as Schmidt again prevailed, 48-42%. Though out of office, his current contribution to America is motivational speaking.

CHAPTER SEVENTY-SEVEN

Classic Insider Lowery Nonetheless Articulated Needs of San Diegans

Introductory Quote: Lowery-"The biblical idea of repentance is more than just being sorry. It also requires a commitment to change the way you live and reform the mistakes of the past." –Bill Lowery apologizing for his role in the House overdraft scandal.

Photo courtesy of the Collection of the U.S. House of Representatives

I f any member of Congress could be labeled the quintessential, yet underrated insider, Bill Lowery would top the list. A political golden boy in San Diego, Lowery had the connections, affability and skill to make it as big as anyone in the minority. Yet Lowery was a man about town in the nation's capitol and his associations, misdeeds and some have said, taking his eye off the ball, clearly led to his downfall in 1992.

It seems that, most of Lowery's political life was guided by the name Wilson. The son of a hardware store owner, Lowery had served as the national youth Director for President Gerald Ford's 1976 campaign and the Ford family didn't forget it. Locally, Lowery was a San Diego Councilman when Pete Wilson, the Mayor of San Diego, scooped him up and asked him to become a deputy Mayor. The city had a Republican Congressman named Bob Wilson at that time and his retirement in 1980, 28-years after his election with Richard Nixon on the vice-presidential ticket, meant a clarion generational shift with Lowery the obvious beneficiary. He immediately announced his candidacy for the La Jolla, Mission Bey and San Diego based Congressional seat.

So well-groomed was Lowery in local GOP circles that party-bigwigs were reportedly waiting for a seat to open for him to seek and Lowery himself said he had a "clue" that Wilson would soon be stepping down. Naturally, Pete Wilson heartily backed him though that did not mean the nomination was his for the asking.

In the primary, Lowery faced Dan McKinnon, whose father had proceeded Bob Wilson in Congress as a Democrat. He owned KSON so was personally wealthy and put up billboards calling himself "a longtime Reagan supporter." Lowery had backing from Ford and top officials at the National Republican Committee which prompted McKinnon to complain about "a case of politicians perpetuating other politicians in office." McKinnon started primary night ahead but Lowery overtook him and prevailed 52-46%

In the fall, Lowery faced another Wilson – another Bob Wilson in fact. This person was a Democratic State Senator whom prognosticators actually considered the frontrunner. But his hopes of keeping the seat in the Wilson name were extinguished not only by the district's Republican leanings, but by the fact that with another Californian, Ronald Reagan leading the ticket, 1980 would be such an exceptional Republican year. Lowery prevailed 53-43%.

Lowery's Congressional battles, and in some cases the circumstances that forced him out of Congress, could be a tale of neighboring colleagues who made it to Congress against considerable odds. His election meant a rivalry with Duncan Hunter, another young Reagan Robot who had defeated an unsuspecting Democratic incumbent in a monumental upset that same year. Both coveted a seat on the Armed Services panel but Lowery won it.

In 1982, Lowery sought a seat on the Appropriations Committee and seemed to have the inside track when Bobbi Fielder, a GOP Congresswoman from the L.A. suburbs and a similar upset winner from the class of '80, threw her hat into the ring. The result was that neither Californian got the post.

That did not repeat itself two years later and this time, it was Lowery's for the asking. One of his assignments was the Military Subcommittee and by his final term in Congress, he was the panel's top Republican.

Lowery's pedigree was decidedly local. He focused on increasing housing for military facilities, securing funding for the San Diego trolley, the Otay Mesa border crossing and a sewage plant to guard against waste from Tijuana. In 1985, Reagan signed into law a Lowery sponsored bill – the Interstate Cost Estimate, which provided funding to complete Highway 52.

Following the much-publicized death of two eight-year old boys from abandoned land mines in San Diego, Lowery fought for funding for their removals. He worked to reignite the area's struggling ship building industry and during consideration of the 1986 tax law, he advocated temporarily exempting Gaslamp Quarter developers because it would harm their efforts to restore a historic site. He also advocated protecting the least bell's vireo, a songbird on the endangered species list.

While Lowery's voting record was conservative, he was not an ideologue and in fact worked well with Democrats, particularly when it came to California issues. One was drilling off the coast which he strongly opposed and held the Reagan administration's feet to the fire when they appeared to go wayward (Wilson and California Democrats Vic Fazio, Leon Panetta and Mel Levine were his most vocal partners). At one point in 1984, a "preliminary agreement" was reached but it was skimpy and the following year when no moratorium was issued, language was incorporated that would force Interior Secretary Donald Hodel to meet with a Congressional committee from California every 60 days to discuss the issue.

At that time, talks between the California delegation and the administration were ongoing but Lowery vowed that if they went nowhere in 1985, there would be a "fight with every ounce of energy we have." Near the end of the year, Appropriators gave California a surprise jolt by voting 27-26 to block a moratorium (two Massachusetts members were supposedly swayed by a Hodel promise to exclude drilling off that state's coast). The following July, however, Lowery and his California colleagues got at least something when an agreement was reached to halt drilling for Lease Sale 91 until 1989 when a new administration would take over.

It wasn't simply the drilling off California's coast that Lowery fought and the year that new administration did come in, he got unexpected leverage from an international catastrophe. Ohio Republican Ralph Regula, a member of Appropriations, wanted to eliminate the moratorium on drilling off the

Alaska coast but the Exxon-Valdez oil spill changed the mindset. That incident, Lowery said, has "proven our contention that the spill cleanup technology is not there." On other open space matters, Lowery opposed Mel Levine's California Desert Protection Act but worked with Panetta to establish the Monterey Bay National Marine Sanctuary.

During the early 1980s recession, Lowery authored a tax credit for the jobless who aspired to continue their education. He was a strong supporter of the space program and amid a tug of war between Appropriators who were arguing over whether money should go for space or housing, sponsored an amendment with Texas Democrat Jim Chapman to restore $1.9 billion that the committee had cut just days earlier. The amendment passed 240 to 173 after which Lowery said, "There was simply not the feeling in Congress to concede America's leadership in space."

Perhaps being an insider meant Lowery was respected on both sides of the aisle. Levine, a Democrat from Los Angeles, worked with him on a number of coastal issues, labeled him "very collaborative and very easy to work with." Another L.A. Democrat, Howard Berman called him, "quite willing to cut deals with Democrats to get things done, good to work with."

One area on which Lowery did not compromise was his opposition to abortion and for that reason, he seemed to be the choice of the pro-life movement to succeed Wilson in the Senate when he was elected governor in 1990 and got to name his own successor. But that was just after Lowery's tepid re-election and any talk of him as a serious contender fizzled.

Lowery had been plagued by insider-related controversy since the middle of his twelve-year tenure. In mid-1985, Common Cause called out Lowery for promising anyone "private" access to him and other Washington bigwigs if they contributed $1,000 to the Congressional Leadership Council. This earned the enmity of Common Cause who accused him of "parceling out his representation in $1,000 chunks." Lowery's response was that he regularly holds "town hall meetings that anyone could come to for free. No one has to pay a dime to come to those."

Lowery's association with Savings and Loans in particular gave him a much closer re-election than expected. Initially, psychiatrist Dan Kripke hardly seemed intimidating. Lowery had beaten him with 68% in 1986 and 66% in '88 and a similarly effortless campaign this time seemed on the horizon. Early in the '86 race, Kripke had tried to gum up publicity from Lowery's campaign headquarters opening above an adult bookstore ("an awful place for a congressional campaign"). Lowery replied by calling the race "the sleaziest campaign I've ever seen. I thought he was an educated man." His opinion probably changed after 1990.

In the aftermath of Charles Keating, Savings and Loans had become a pariah and a study by Common Cause found that the $85,088 Lowery had received from S&L's exceeded that of any other member of Congress. That invited more scrutiny. Don Dixon, owner of the now-defunct Vernon Savings and Loan, had hosted several events for Lowery at his house where sexual activity took place. Lowery did return $16,000 but was slow to realize he faced trouble and resisted Kripke's call to debate. The challenger meanwhile promised to give $1,000 to a homeless shelter every time Lowery did debate. Kripke hit Lowery for his pro-life stance and vowed to, "stand up to corruption, even if the odds are great."

Beyond that, there was the general anti-incumbency mood that was as prevalent in San Diego as anywhere. Former San Diego Mayor Roger Hedgecock had started a PAC called (DRIP – Don't Re-elect Incumbent Politicians) and t worked to some extent as two local state legislators were unseated. Lowery narrowly avoided being another. In fact, only the presence of a Peace and freedom candidate who took 7%, most likely at Kripke's expense, prevented the forcing of Lowery into political oblivion, at least for 1990. Lowery hung on 49-44%, a margin of 12,000 votes as his mentor Wilson was winning the governorship. Kripke essentially declared victory by virtue of the fact that he held Lowery t under 50%.

Initially, this San Diegan charged ahead vowing to play closer attention to his people. He conducted focus groups and acknowledged to *The L.A. Times* that, "We allowed (Kripke) to define me in the most extreme and dishonest fashion possible, and by not responding to it, that was the only picture some people got." Kripke shot back that, "Bill Lowery's main problem is Bill Lowery. He's lucky more people haven't heard the Bill Lowery story." In any case, Lowery admitted, "We got a wake-up call in November, and believe me, we're paying attention. There was a message, and it's been heard."

Late 1991 forward produced a drip-drip, drip for Lowery's future. First came the release of a redistricting plan which created a safe Republican district in North San Diego where Lowery was inclined to run. Only, so was Randy "Duke" Cunningham who had upset a scandal-tarred Democratic incumbent, Jim Bates the previous year. Leading Republicans, including Wilson, tried to get Cunningham to run elsewhere but after appearing to consider it, declared that he was in the race to stay.

Then came the House Bank scandal. Initially, Lowery claimed to have a "handful" of overdrafts returned. When the official list was released, the "handful" turned out to be 301 overdrafts worth $104,000. The overdrafts escalated the rhetoric not only with Cunningham (who had a single overdraft) that he proved had been erroneously cashed, but also with Hunter, who with 399 overdrafts worth $129,000 had a sum hire than Lowery's. Hunter was seeking re-election which prompted Lowery to ask, "Is he asking for Duncan Hunter to be defeated or to resign? What does he say about Hunter's checks?" Cunningham's response was a somewhat disingenuous, "I haven't been following Duncan's thing. I've been worrying about my own race. Duncan is Duncan's own guy, and my fight is against Bill Lowery, and that's what I'm doing." He said Lowery "must have meant a Jolly Green Giant handful." Hunter also responded in kind. "The in thing to do now is to appear weeping before the press to try to draw on public sympathy."

What Hunter was referring to was Lowery's mea culpa, a press conference in which he labeled himself "a victim of sloppiness in my personal finances...I accept responsibility for my actions. I am sorry for bouncing checks at the House bank, and I apologize for any pain or embarrassment I have caused this country, which I love so much." His wife Katie chimed in: "I wrote a lot of checks and when Bill was in San Diego I didn't always get through to him - there might have been something pressing with one of the kids - and I didn't always tell him what I had done." Lowery proceeded to introduce reform legislation.

In mid-April, Lowery abruptly quit his re-election and in doing so, took thinly veiled jabs at his Republican colleagues who pressed for the names of full disclosure. "Somehow, this belief that you can throw a grenade and control where the explosion occurs is nonsense. It makes you wonder why they ran for Congress in the first place." Indeed, as he began calling supporters, he expressed relief of leaving the firing squad, by saying, "Free at last. Free at last. Thank God, I'm free at last." Because Lowery's departure came after the filing deadline, his name remained on the ballot and he received 12% of the vote.

In an interview with *The LA Times* as he prepared to leave office, Lowery declared himself, "a little nostalgic on the House floor as I managed the military construction appropriations bill for the last time, but I'm ready to have a private life. I'm ready to move on after 15 years in public office."

Arguably, Lowery's insider status continued well after his years in Congress. One of Lowery's closest friends in Congress was Jerry Lewis, a fellow Republican from Southern California who in 2005 became chair of

Appropriations. The following year, *Rolling Stone Magazine* published an article that cited a direct correlation -"If you want an earmark from Lewis, you have to hire Lowery," says Melanie Sloan of Citizens for Responsibility and Ethics in Washington. "There's a direct exchange." Lowery disputed that and very little damage, if any, to his reputation took place. He remains a highly accomplished attorney in the nation's capitol to this day.

CHAPTER SEVENTY-EIGHT

Olin of Virginia -The Man Who 'Couldn't Be Pigeonholed

Introductory Quote: "I would say that Jim Olin has his own agenda." –John Miller of the Virginia State Dairymen's Association. The line appeared to not be meant as either a compliment nor insult but rather an accurate description of the Congressman from Virginia's method of deliberating.

Photo courtesy of James Olin

Shortly after he announced his retirement, *The Roanoke Times* wrote, "Talking to Jim Olin isn't like talking to other politicians. He speaks in short, dry, declarative sentences, salted with 'hell' and 'dam'...He comes to the point, says it, and moves on. Perhaps it's just his background as a business executive, or his engineer's precision, or maybe it's just him." An example of the Roanoke, Virginia Democrats earthiness: during his 1985 amendment to cut back on dairy subsidies, he explained on the House floor that, "I do not think the dairy farmers want to be jerked around with fancy special policies that involve payoffs of one type or another." Whatever the case, *The Times* also cited how Olin's, "dry manner and Father-Knows-Best appearance" paid dividends in a district that was very politically adverse, and that was indisputable.

It's kind of a rarity for a politician from this area but Olin not only was born someplace else but held elective office somewhere else, albeit briefly and nearly 30 years before. His birthplace was Chicago, he grew up in Kenilworth and excelled in high school as both the student body president and right guard on the football team. Olin earned a full scholarship to Deep Springs College in California and took his Bachelors in Electrical Engineering from Cornell University in New York. World War II was ongoing at this point and Olin found a bride, Phyllis, joined the Army and was sent to Alaska. He became a test engineer for General Electric Company in Erie, Pennsylvania, then was sent to Schenectady, New York.

In the 1950s, Olin acquired the political bug and won election as Town Supervisor of Rotterdam, New York. Unfortunately for Olin, his boss did not get the political bug and told him that he could no longer pursue both endeavors. Olin wisely chose to continue at GE and throughout the ensuing 25-years, received no less than five promotions, including as a division general manager and vice-president. By the end of his career, he was in Virginia.

In 1982, Olin stepped down from GE and launched a new adventure, a true challenge few expected he'd achieve. It was a run for the open Sixth Congressional District as a Democrat. Olin won the challenge and mounted one of the biggest upsets of campaign in a year that saw many so-called fluke Democratic candidates outrun their GOP rivals. It's not hard to see why. No Democrat had held the Sixth district since 1952 and the GOP seemed to have a golden boy to succeed Butler in Republican State Senator Ray Garland. But a funny thing happened on the way to Garland's coronation: he was denied the nomination to State Delegate Kevin Miller, an unabashed Reaganite and accountant whose backing extended to the Jerry Falwell wing of the GOP. The nomination was awarded via convention and after Garland fell 23 votes shy on the first ballot, Miller was able to gradually win support from some of his other rivals and prevail on the fourth ballot.

Garland's loss changed the trajectory of the race, both geographically and politically. With the former, Roanoke was the population center (40% of the population) and where Olin was expected to run strongest while Miller was from the Northern end of the district. Miller's decision to place his campaign headquarters in Roanoke signified that he recognized its importance and he garnered the backing of the Chamber of Commerce and Butler. But while his arch conservatism was no handicap with GOP voters, it proved to be a turnoff with Independents. Olin stressed his business background and in a period of a deep recession, called for a repeal of the third year of the Reagan tax cuts. But he had African-American support and, having dealt with unions at GE, was on good terms with members as well.

Miller crushed in Augusta and Rockingham (Harrisonburg) and the middle counties were close but Olin won the three Southern counties of the state comfortably, including Roanoke, to win the seat by 1,655 votes. On victory, Olin said, "In running the campaign, I heard thousands and thousands of people who needed help. Mr. Olin, they'd say. I've been out of work for two years..."

Photos courtesy of James Olin

With such a small margin for error in a district that, politically, was not on his side, Olin knew that he could not ignore his constituents if he was going to have durability. His committee assignments, Agriculture and Small Business were strong fits and he was visible during the avian flu outbreak and sponsored an annual economic conference in the district.

Indeed, his formula was put to the test in 1984 against heavy Republican crosswinds. Reagan would be taking 66% of the vote and this time, the GOP apparently realized their mistake from two years earlier and gave the moderate Garland the nomination. Only his rhetoric was not so moderate. To him the Democratic Party was a "busted-out $2 whore." This and other indignancies led *The Roanoke Times* to run an editorial that said, "Come Back Home, Ray Garland." Olin won by 14,000 votes with just under 54%.

Olin might not have been a card-carrying member of the moderate wing but he was, without question a moderate sympathizer who had something for everyone. For conservatives, he supported the Balanced Budget Amendment and the anti-flag desecration amendment while voting against family and medical leave legislation and motor voter. In the liberal direction, he was pro-choice, supported ERA, the minimum wage over Bush's veto, creation of the Eastern Airlines independent strike board, banning companies from permanently replacing strikers, the Civil Rights Act of 1990 and the budget summit package that included taxing the rich. Two votes that stood out: opposing Americans with Disability, one of five Democrats to do so as well as the authorization of force in the Persian Gulf.

Photo courtesy of James Olin

In 1985, Olin sponsored an amendment with House Minority Leader Robert Michel that would trim the dairy price support system 50 cents at the beginning of each year provided it reached 10 billion pounds each year. The Reagan administration backed the proposal. As he took the floor, Olin swatted critics argument that this was not meant to be a death knell for the industry. "First of all, we are going to continue the Government purchases of dairy surplus. The purpose of the surplus is to stabilize the dairy industry, not to provide income for the dairymen. They make their own income." Olin sought to reassure colleagues that, "On each January 1, we would take a look at the projected surplus. In the first year, if the projected surplus is 10 billion pounds or more, we would lower the price support 50 cents. In subsequent years, if it is over 5 billion pounds, we would lower the price support 50 cents. We would keep on doing that until we get down to the point where it is only marginally profitable to sell milk manufactured products to the Government."

The amendment was rejected 266-144 but more consequently for Olin, drew the ire of House Majority Whip Tony Coelho who contended that, "The Olin-Michel proposal would prefer to put people into bankruptcy and to eliminate dairy farmers." That more than anything else likely impeded Olin's ability to secure his choice assignments. Three times he aimed to win a slot on the Budget Committee, citing his business pedigree, and three times he failed. A more junior Virginian, L.F. Payne of the Fifth District got the slot and Olin's theory was that, "L.F. isn't as frightening to the leadership. He's got such a nice way about him." Attempts to win an Intelligence Committee post also went nowhere.

Photo courtesy of James Olin

Olin's crusade against overly generous dairy subsidies was consistent with his views on other subsidies. When cattleman sought reparations for losses from what they considered bad planning, Olin was concerned about the precedent it would set, believing, "Cattlemen have never been among those who feed at the public trough."

With votes that would potentially alienate a large segment of the electorate, Olin saw consultation with his people as his ticket back to Washington. The proposed 10-mile Roanoke River Parkway was one area and like a true engineer, he weighed the facts carefully, including at one point requesting a study before jumping on board. He was on the scene when labor unions were concerned about job losses following Norfolk Southern made known its interest in taking over Conrail.

The Commonwealth was one of 16 states that lacked an official veterans home and Olin attempted to rectify that by having one placed in, where else? Roanoke. Congress had to approve this project even though Olin assured his colleagues that, "it would not cost the federal government a dime," because the Department of Interior had given Virginia the land as a park. He got funding for a Roanoke Valley visitors' center on the Blue Ridge Parkway, flood control projects for Roanoke River and Buena Vista and a new Lynchburg bridge. He **spearheaded** efforts to —fair cost on an equitable basis.

Olin sponsored ten wilderness projects and in 1988, Reagan signed one sponsored by Olin and Frederickburg Democrat Rick Boucher that added 25,000 acres in Virginia to the Natural Wilderness System. At times, big business interests such as Westvaco did not like these proposals but Olin wouldn't bat an eye. Jim Loesell recalls Westvaco would be amazed because they "would say no and a congressman would dare do otherwise…The Chamber of Commerce lobbyist told me, 'but Congressman Olin didn't check with us on this.' Literally. That represented a new way of doing business."

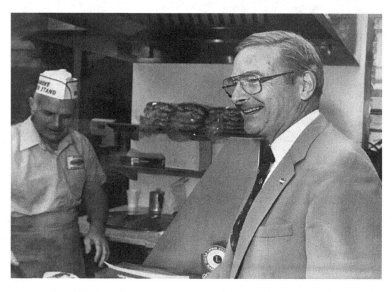

As a Congressman, staying close to the people was vintage Olin
Photo courtesy of James Olin

Securing many of these projects often required cooperation from Appropriators and Olin concedes, "I tried not to incur the wrath of Appropriations Committee members, especially with flood projects. I made sure I didn't cast that vote that would give them trouble."

Olin had a touch and go relationship with the environmental community. During the writing of the 1990 farm bill, Olin drew their ire when he temporarily supported a measure by his Ag colleagues, Charlie Stenholm of Texas and Pat Roberts of Kansas that would eliminate a reference to biological alternatives for soil. An agreement was reached. That same year, Greenpeace called a pesticides bill Olin sponsored, "ridiculously weak" but once again, a compromise was formed.

On other issues, Olin and the environmental community were simpatico. He promoted the Waste Materials Management Act and wrote a letter to the editor to explain it. The bill, he said, "has received a good deal of attention because of the provisions addressing the Kim-Stan landfill situation in Selma. As you may know, the bill would require each state to draw up a 20-year plan for taking care of its own trash before it could export trash to another state. The bill would accomplish many other worthy goals as well. One of the most significant is its recycling provisions."

After the 1984 election, Olin was never seriously challenged. His 1990 opponent was an openly racist motel security guard who wistfully spoke of the days of yore. "In South Africa," he explained, "its whites over blacks. Here, it's getting to be blacks over whites." That didn't go over well in a state that elected the first African-American Governor in the nation since Reconstruction (though the 6th, having given Marshall Coleman 54% over Doug Wilder, had little to do with it).

Photo courtesy of James Olin

By late 1991, Olin was wrapping up his first decade in the House and a Roanoke Valley Poll revealed that, with a 73 percent job approval, he could have continued for the foreseeable future. But that December, he decided that he was, "looking for something constructive to do," and announced his retirement. "At the end of next year," he explained," I'll be almost 73, believe it or not, I'll have been working for more than 49 years. There are many things Phyllis and I want to do while we are still able which are not possible with the rigorous demands of the congressional job." One potential Republican candidate, Delegate Phoebe Orebaugh, offered a surmisal that Olin had long since decided to call it quits, saying he otherwise, "wouldn't dare have cast the votes he did. I'm referring to his vote against the war and on labor relations." But his votes – and retirement for that matter, seem consistent with his style. As he prepared to retire, *The Roanoke Times* wrote, "Olin has cut across the conventional political grain. He has cut across the conventional congressional grain with his methodical speaking style, his disinclination to seek the limelight - and his preference for developing expertise in specific technical areas of legislative interest over striking poses on hot-button issues."

After Olin moved on, the Sixth District became illustrative of the area as a black hole for Democrats. In a race that was considered a tossup, Republican Bob Goodlatte overwhelmed Steve Musselwhite with 61% (Olin had backed a former aide for the nomination).

In 1994, Olin raised eyebrows somewhat by endorsing Sylvia Clute over incumbent Democratic Senator Charles "Chuck" Robb in 1994. It wasn't personal, simply more reflective of Robb's personal difficulties. "I guess I think the senator may find it very, very difficult to handle criticism that will come to him in the campaign, therefore the Democratic Party may be better off to have a different candidate." Olin did say, "I'm not going to elaborate on the various problems he might have."

Olin died in 2006 at age 86.

CHAPTER SEVENTY-NINE

Until Redistricting, Staggers Continued the Public Service Family Tradition

Introductory Quote: "I saw in the newspaper that 3,000 people are standing in line for food here in Parkersburg. (West Virginia). Alan is the type of Congressman (who) when he sees 3,000 people in line, he feels special and wants to get in the front of that line." – Congressman Harley Staggers on his rival and fellow Democratic colleague, Alan Mollohan during a 1992 matchup necessitated by the Mountain State's loss of a Congressional seat via redistricting.

Photo courtesy of Harley Staggers

F or nearly four years, as soon as it became apparent that West Virginia would be losing one of its four House seats, an intriguing parlor game of musical chairs took placed over who would end up on the short end of the stick. Much to his chagrin, that dubious honor went to Harley Staggers, a five-term Democratic Congressman whose legendary name had been a hallmark of the district for all but two years since his father, Harley Staggers, Sr., won the seat in 1948 and Staggers, like his father, was a true bread and butter Democrat. Gun control was a notable – and rare departure as he famously opposed the Brady Bill. In fact, the amendment he offered was viewed as a much weaker alternative to the entire package.

Harley, Sr., would use the seniority system to become chair of the powerful Commerce Committee in the late 1970s. He was already a Congressman when the boy who would be known as "Bucky" to colleagues was born in the nation's capitol in 1951. How did Staggers acquire the nickname? With four older sisters, he was typically referred to as "boy" and his parents came to the conclusion that a better nickname was necessary. "An old classmate of my father had referred to him as 'Bucky' because of the way he would buck the line in football. When he saw my parents and used the old nickname, my parents gave it to me." Stagger's mother told him they discussed calling him, "Rocky," but "she was afraid it would encourage me to throw rocks."

"Bucky" received his undergraduate degree from Harvard University and J.D., from West Virginia University School of Law. Shortly thereafter, he was an assistant Attorney General. By 1980, he was comfortably situated in a law practice in the town of Keyser when Harley Sr., opted to step down in 1980. His hope of Bucky succeeding him eventually materialized but took a detour or two.

Ray Formanek, Jr., of the AP said that while Staggers's law colleagues in were urging him to make the race, he, "hesitated about getting in." In the end, "reporters played a large role in his becoming involved by their constant calls asking if he was going to run." His main opponent was State Senator Pat Hamilton who was Vice-Chair of the Senate Labor Committee. Delegate Joe Caudle and two minor candidates were running as well. Staggers faced criticism for being subterranean which led many to believe he was relying on his name. In fact, Harley, Sr., exerted a much effort on his behalf. Hamilton benefitted from union support and the fact that his base was around Morgantown, the district's largest city. With roughly 80% of precincts reporting, Staggers led by roughly 1,700 votes but the outstanding areas - Greenbrier and Monroe Counties, decisively favored Hamilton who ultimately prevailed by 1,248 votes out of 66,000 cast between the two, 42-41%. Caudle took just 13%.

Thanks to two unexpected elections, however, Staggers landed on his feet and eventually, in Congress. The first was a State Senate seat that had come open shortly after the primary and he won it with 57% and became chair of the Agriculture Committee. That same year, Cleve Benedict had won the Congressional seat over Hamilton but as a Republican, he really wasn't supposed to. Two years later, Benedict saw the handwriting on the wall and decided to go up or out (he challenged the state's revered Senator Robert Byrd and failed to win a third of the vote). Staggers won the nomination to succeed him unopposed and faced a millionaire who spent $500,000 on his campaign. *CQ* noted that Staggers "spent much of the time offering homilies about his love for West Virginia." That turned out to be a better strategy – he won every county and only three, Morgan, Grant and Upshur were even close.

Staggers was assigned to the Committees on Agriculture, Judiciary and Veterans Affairs and was a decidedly centrist Democrat. In his first term, he took on Energy and Commerce Chairman John Dingell by opposing his amendment to transfer the National Institute for Occupational Safety and Health to the National Institute of Health (Occupational Safety employed 250 in Morgantown in the district and Staggers was not assuaged by Dingell's assurances that there would not be a transfer). Another reason for his opposition was that, "the mandate of the mission of the NIOSH is incompatible with the mission of NIH." While "NIH does pure research, after-the-fact analysis...NIOSH is preventative in nature." He said, "Frankly speaking, the Dingell amendment is unacceptable to the Second Congressional District of West Virginia and it should be opposed by all members concerned with the health of American workers, those workers in our nation's coal mines as well as others." Members agreed and Staggers' side prevailed.

Staggers was pro-life and opposed capital punishment to the point that he attempted unsuccessfully to have provisions stricken from the 1990 crime legislation. He called it "ironic that the House is attempting to attach a death penalty to a bill that's ultimate purpose is to save lives" but his proposal failed 103-322. Staggers backed the anti-flag burning amendment but was was solid with his party on other issues, including overrides of President George H.W. Bush's vetoes of a higher minimum wage, Family and Medical Leave and the Civil Rights Act of 1990. He favored national health legislation.

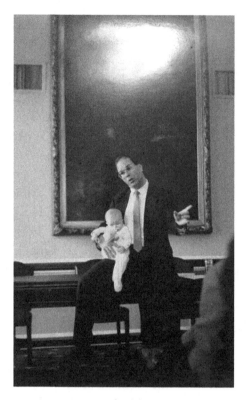

With his daughter during his first months in Congress
Photo courtesy of Harley Staggers

In 1990, Staggers proposed legislation that would ban landfills within three miles of the Potomac River (those that had been operating by April of that year would be grandfathered). The Metropolitan Washington Council of Governments announced its opposition.

Staggers' proposals on veterans issues often attracted support from ideologies spanning the House spectrum. The Veterans' Home Loan Mortgage Indemnity Act of 1989 attracted 38 co-sponsors, liberal and conservative. Keeping VA Hospitals open throughout the state was also high on his plate.

With a constituency almost totally rural, Staggers worked those issues hard. In 1989, he proposed the Rural Economic Sustainability Act as well as the Rural Water and Waste Water Management Consolidation Act of 1989

In 1991, Staggers famously opposed the Brady Bill put forth by fellow Democrats Charles Schmer of New York and Edward Feighan of Ohio. His solution was an instant background check, and he proposed that as an alternative to Brady. To him, the Brady Bill was "an emotionally charged paper tiger designed to make one think that they are doing something to prevent criminals from buying handguns through licensed gun dealers." Yet in reality, it was "anything but substantive….Emotional issues are hard to deal with, and there are no real simple answers. A seven-day waiting period is a simplistic answer. In the same logic, if we would wait, say, seven days to purchase cocaine, we could solve the drug problem. The same logic is that if in fact we said to journalists, 'Wait seven days before you file your stories, we would have no libel suits. Now I assume that if we could wait seven days, the same logic, for our second amendment rights, the same logic would say we can wait seven days for our first amendment rights. Obviously that is not right, and we would not accept that." Schumer responded by calling Staggers's bill, "a ruse, it's a sham, it's a fake.' The duo had a testy exchange on "The Today Show" and colleagues ultimately agreed with Schumer's view - the Staggers Amendment failed 234-193.

Staggers' stance did not impact friendships. Feighan called him, "a great guy…thoughtful and decent," and "someone I respected a great deal." He played an integral role on both the House Democratic baseball and basketball teams and for a few years, pulled together a team of the best players from both parties to travel to West Virginia to compete against a high school All-Star team.

The one other instance Staggers faced groans from within was his 1990 sponsorship of legislation to "reform" the Legal Services Corporation's Migrant Legal Action Program. Democrat Charlie Stenholm of Texas and Republican Bill McCollum of Florida had been the bill's original sponsors and legal aid supporters felt it would undermine the program's stability. Staggers, who had opposed the measure two years before, argued the opposite. "Having always been an advocate for the Legal Services program," Staggers declared, "I am interested in seeing it be as strong a program as possible, meeting the needs of the economically underprivileged across the country."

Two controversial aspect of the proposal raised the wraths of liberal colleagues. One would require the Legal Services Corporation (LSC) to reimburse the defendant's legal fees if they lost. The second would make it difficult for agribusiness employees (particularly farm workers) to sue through LSC. Another provision would prohibit the organization from representing drug dealers evicted from public housing.

One reason Staggers had opposed McCollum/Stenholm in the previous Congress was because "I had serious reservations about some of the provisions, and because I lacked confidence in the Board of Directors at the Legal Services Corporation which would have implemented these reforms. This year significant improvements have been made in the package" which included a new board. Liberal colleagues did not share that view. In his written testimony against the bill, Michigan Democrat William Ford, chairman of the Education and Labor Committee was unhappy. "The proposed 'reform' amendments," he said, "relating to the Legal Services Corporation undermine the legal protections created and agreed to in the AWPA. These so called 'reforms' would subject injured workers to a number of procedural requirements that are not applicable to any other potential class of litigants."

Since capturing the seat with 64%, Staggers' re-election margins were all over the place. He took 56% in 1984 against a rival with very audacious ideas not designed to win over colleagues ("requiring Congress to sit five days a week during political campaigns" and fining members $100 a day for House votes missed). Staggers took 64% in 1986, was unopposed altogether in '88 but received just 55% in 1990.

The latter showing was somewhat of a surprise but, perhaps it shouldn't have been given anti-incumbent atmosphere and the star power of his rival. That race could have been known as one between two jocks – the baseball/basketball player vs. the football star. Republican nominee Oliver Luck played for the Houston Oilers and was a quarterback at West Virginia University and while outraised by Staggers, he spent enough money to stay competitive. Harley, Sr., taped an ad but, with statewide elections one-sided (Senator Jay Rockefeller was winning re-election in a rout), turnout was low and so was Staggers' margin. Nevertheless, *The Bluefield Telegraph* ran a headline was, "Stagger's Doesn't Need Luck To Win." That would not be the case for 1992.

An eight percent population loss left it clear that West Virginia would be losing one of its four seats long before 1992. Still, as the cycle got underway, the consensus was that Nick Joe Rahall, an eight-termer would be the odd man out in the redistricting puzzle. It was easy to see why – Rahall had barely squeaked by in his '90 race, had encountered bad publicity from a series of drunk driving incidents and seemed to have the fewest amount of allies in the legislature. That scenario was complicated when Third District Congressman Bob Wise accused Staggers of reneging on a deal that would have placed Rahall's home in his district (Staggers denied a deal existed). A stalemate dragged on for months and when the final lines were drawn, Staggers' district was the one carved up. After weighing his options, he opted to challenge Alan Mollohan, a classmate in a district that contained the panhandle and only 20% of his current territory.

It was a race against Congressional kin. Mollohan's dad had represented the seat for four years in the 1950s and 14 between 1968 and 1982. When he retired, Alan won the seat with ease.

The campaign was not tame. Mollohan had compiled 12 overdrafts worth $26,000 and Staggers, who had zero, mocked him relentlessly. One ad, accompanied by band music –called him, "Mollohan the Rubberman, nothing in common with the common man..." Staggers also hit his rival for voting in favor of a 1989 pay raise (which Staggers had opposed), using a taxpayer funded car phone and a corporate plane ride back to the district. Mollohan refuted by calling Staggers out for $29,000 on air travel.

Influence was another point of argument. Mollohan sat on the Appropriations Committee and boasted of the projects he helped secure. He also emphasized that he "sit(s) on the subcommittee that funds NASA" and all three West Virginia based projects were in the district. Staggers replied that the man responsible for that funding was Byrd and he held up a year-old press release claiming Mollohan had given Byrd the credit at the time. Likewise, he claimed Mollohan didn't have "one red cent" of money inserted into a recent highway bill. In one debate, Staggers said, "Alan has refused to be held accountable for his record," while Mollohan accused Staggers of using "vague generalities and badly distort(ing)" his record.

Staggers' overall philosophy in an economic downturn was, "We need to do away with trickle down and have percolate up."

Mollohan did take criticism from some in his district for his lack of visibility but by-and-large, the current portion of his old district that remained stayed loyal and he won most counties with 2/3 or even 3/4. This compensated for Staggers easily holding his turf in the eastern portion of the district and the result was a Mollohan 62-38% rout. All in all, it was a rough year for Staggers – Harley, Sr., had passed the previous August. Staggers resumed practicing law in Keyser where he remains today.

The Staggers family commitment to public service continues. In 2006, Bucky's sister Margaret Ann won a seat in the West Virginia State House. Emulating him, her first bid for office was narrowly unsuccessful but she didn't let defeat deter her and tried again.

CHAPTER EIGHTY

In Thy Name of The Father: Perkins' Hubris from Fabled Name Sent His Career Back to Earth

Introductory Quote: "You can't hardly go to the bathroom without him handing you the toilet paper." – Pikesville attorney Larry Webster on the increased visibility of Seventh District Kentucky Congressman Chris Perkins following his near re-election defeat in 1990.

Photo via the Kenton County Library

At some point after succeeding his larger-than-life father, the late Congressman Carl Perkins, Carl C. "Chris" Perkins, Jr., declared he, "wanted to be a Congressman for the rest of [his] life." At age 30, he seemed destined to have his wish fulfilled. A series of missteps and arguably taking his "eye off the ball" sent Perkins crashing down to Earth. He ultimately retired just eight years later at the age of thirty-eight.

Perkins' problems were twofold. He suffered from endless comparisons to his widely revered father and particularly fell under the assumption that the late man's greatness would inevitably translate to his own. A bigger problem was his own hubris; a ho-hum, if not amateurish, style along with a failure to recognize that he was not infallible in politics and life.

Very few people aside from Perkins's political opponents questioned his capabilities. On certain issues it's hard to think what he could have done to more adequately represent his Eastern Kentucky district. His downfall was personal faux pas coupled with a lackadaisical attitude.

and redistricting.

Carl Perkins, Sr., had what *TDN* labeled, "a folksy, bumpkin-like manner that charmed voters and disarmed political foes." By showering his impoverished Appalachian district with grants, Perkins became a man of the people who cruised back to Washington cycle after cycle for 36 years before succumbing to a heart attack in April of 1984 at age 69. A lifetime seat was now open but aspiring politicians deferred to Chris Perkins who took the nomination unanimously. He won 76% of the votes in the general election. At age 30, Perkins was by no means the youngest Congressman in history but he might have been a little young for a job that requires such commitment and seriousness. He was assigned to his father's stomping ground – Education and Labor as well as Science, Space and Technology and he seemed destined for unlimited potential.

Perkins's charmed early life began literally at birth. He was born in the nation's capitol when his dad had already served five years in Congress and began traveling the district with him at age four. He pursued his undergraduate studies in Economics from Davidson College and his law degree from the University of Louisville. He began practicing law and had a celebrated speaking style. In 1980 at age 26, he won a seat in the Kentucky House, probably to some degree on his famous name. Once in the door, however, Perkins had to prove that he could read and write and he worked hard, particularly on nursing home regulation and energy assistance issues. His only drawback perhaps was his personal style. As *The Lexington Herald-Leader* noted, "Some legislators resented Perkins' habit of wearing flannel shirts to work and putting his feet on his House desk." Still, his childhood goal was to make it to Congress and the opportunity tragically came about by his father's untimely passing.

Early in his Congressional tenure Perkins stated, "The differences between my father and myself may be more a matter of style, I think, than substance at times. I think we believed in a lot of the same sorts of programs." As for his own goals, he expressed hope that, "When it's all over, I hope people say, hey, he did what he thought was right. That would be the one thing."

He started off strong. Like his father, he fought for black lung benefits and won $40 million in flood control for the district as well as money for school aid. In 1989, Education and Labor cleared his language that would have raised the minimum wage 40 cents an hour over a four year period. "While I oppose any acid rain legislation, I believe that the flexibility allowed in this proposal will be less harmful to the coal industry than some other proposals offered by my colleagues in the House and Senate." He fought Bush's move to trim the Appalachian Regional Commission.

On local issues, Perkins advocated for a highway from Prestonburg to Paintsville, U.S. 119 over Bent Mountain, widening a section of U.S. 23, a Kentucky Wilderness Bill. He took an interest in graduation rate reporting and eradicating black lung disease, the latter a distinct control in coal mining country.

Protecting his father's legacy was also paramount. When Republicans proposed gutting the Perkins grant, Chris replied it "would make it virtually impossible for low-income students to get a higher education. Higher education is not just for the more affluent middle-and upper-class youth in this land." Aside from the high-profile issues, it was becoming increasingly evident to all that Perkins and his father were night-and-day.

When some discontent reached the forefront in 1990, Perkins told *The Lexington Herald-Leader*, "What you see is what you've got. I'm myself. I don't put on airs. I'm just me. A lot of people don't understand that...That has nothing to do with how you do your job...just as soon be anonymous. I don't hunger for people to look at me and say 'Oh, there's Congressman Perkins.' What I hunger for is to be able to get within the system and manipulate that system in a fashion that accomplishes concrete results. That's what enthralls me."

By the time Perkins won his third term there was a sense that the "what you see is what you get" was not mutual. For one, he bought a house in Lexington, which was outside the 7th's boundaries. One Democrat mocked how long it took his office to respond to mail and that he was even lax pounding the pavement in the district (a political term for working the district). Some dismissed it as simply being his style with one confessing, "Chris is not very fast to respond. I don't think he's had the personal touch with people his father had."

Perkins may have suffered trying to live up to his father's reputation, but he wasn't even coming close to reaching "Uncle Carl's" image. In 1983, Perkins held three people at gunpoint though the charges were dismissed and apparently forgotten by the people. That however, was not the case with his personal lifestyle. First came his marital situation as *Politics in America* told readers that in 1987, "he had divorced his wife, remarried and fathered a child in the space of three months."

Then there was hoopla at a 1988 Democratic retreat in Greenbriar, West Virginia. As was told by the author of *Hill Rat*, a book about Texas Congressman Ron Coleman, "Perkins had a party animal image second-to-none." Coleman slept in the room next door and his then-girlfriend Amy stated that Perkins's girlfriend "was making animal noises all night," and added that though photos were taken, "I'd be rich if I had a video camera." Another publication wrote, "Talk of the incident and of his drinking prompted two senior Democrats to sit Chris down for some fatherly advice," and it was reported as time went on that Perkins was "settling down." This wasn't all of the scrutiny that Perkins had to bear, though. The issue of his finances was very much a big deal.

Perkins defaulted on a $19,000 loan, failed to repay property taxes on a Scott County farm ("I didn't know I had those bills"), and during his divorce, said he required $23,000 per month to live.

Perkins was re-elected over Pike County Circuit Judge Will Scott 59-41% in 1988, not a danger sign in and of itself but a warning that voters were starting to notice his antics (he had won 80% in 1986). However, he failed to heed that warning because in 1990 he was nearly thrust into political oblivion. He was not considered particularly vulnerable even with the mounting publicity. Though if any fences needed tending it was expected that they would be disposed of in the primary, not the general. His primary opponent was Jerry Cecil who derided Perkins as out of touch ("When he votes against drug testing someone who is flying a plane, that doesn't represent me in any way"). Perkins won 68-32%.

Scott was happy to pick up where Cecil left off. He came up with great attention-getting techniques. *The Lexington Herald-Leader* said he "parachuted out of an airplane, took a boat trip down the Big Sandy River and drove a team of mules up Ky. 15 to draw attention to issues."

Scott romped in the northern portion of the district and held a 5,000 vote lead with 3/5 counted on election night (he ended up carrying nine of the district's 23 counties.) Only when the rest of the district reported did

Perkins edge him out by just 1,977 votes (61,330 to 59, 377.) He ran behind Democratic Senate candidate Harvey Sloane who hailed from the far away town of Louisville.

The closeness of the race stunned both parties. Perkins, like many incumbents, blamed the federal budget stalemate for the razor-tight margin. "One of the great disadvantages I had was that I only got to campaign a week. Prior to this, I didn't have a good feel because I didn't have an opportunity to spend enough time in the district." Perkins also shrugged it off in saying, "Hell, we won. Elections are pass-fail. We passed." In the opinions of many, this embodied the very laissez faire refusal to "smell the roses" attitude that generated such apathy. Meanwhile, Republican National Committee co-chair Ed Rollins offered an apology for turning down Scott's prior request for national help. In the days following the election, Scott sought to overturn Perkins's slim margin and formally conceded two weeks later.

Within a month, it was clear that Democrats were not going to be lulled again into false complacency as far as Perkins was concerned. Word ensued that Carol Hubbard, the wife of First District Congressman Carroll Hubbard, would run against him in the 1992 primary. Hubbard's base was at the other end of the state, an issue she solved by moving back to where she was raised. When Perkins was first informed of Hubbard's plans he thought it was a joke. She was quite serious, though, and contended that, "Eastern Kentucky hasn't had good representation since 1984. Chris Perkins isn't the man his father was, and I think my old neighbors and Eastern Kentucky deserve the same quality representation as the other six congressional districts."

It wasn't clear that everyone was abandoning Perkins. By mid-1991, leading Democrats were holding fundraisers for him. Meanwhile he seemed to have learned that, as *The Almanac of American Politics* wrote, he "certainly seems to have come close to squandering a precious political inheritance." Ally and friend State Senator Kelsey Friend noted, "The last race made a better congressman of him. He learned a lot."

Bigger problems loomed, some of which were out of his control. The Commonwealth was going to lose one of its seven House seats and when the dust settled, the home of Republican Hal Rogers was placed with Perkins. Around the same time, news of the House Bank broke. As one press account told it, "some members admitted having written bad checks on the House bank, while Perkins at first denied writing any. Later, he said he would have to research the issue, then refused to answer questions about it."

Shortly after the first of the year, Perkins decided to call it a career. In his announcement at the Knott County Courthouse he said, "Serving in Congress takes a great toll on one's life and, in turn, on the family, I have witnessed this cost personally and have decided, with the full support of my wife and family, to forgo this career and move onto other pursuits." Redistricting was a factor. "The {new} 5th District is a politically marginal district now for both parties. The most important aspect of the job, serving the constituents of the 5th District, will have to be sacrificed for the sake of a continuous fund-raising campaign effort. Each and every race will be hotly contested as the state parties pull the district back and forth." Going forward, he pledged to find new "personal business pursuits." The comparisons to his father continued to get parting shots. Democratic Party Chair Grady Stumbo said his move to Lexington was, "a tragic mistake …He should never have moved out of the region. His home should have been Hindman. It was good enough for his father." Supporter Ron Daley was more blunt in saying, "None of us want to let Carl D. go."

A parting shot also grabbed Perkins's financial woes. Just around the time he was calling it quits, news came about that 514 overdrafts at the House Bank worth $565,650.95 were returned. Because Perkins exceeded his next months' salary for 14 of the 39 months profiled, the eyebrow-raising sum ranked him among the 22 "worst abusers" category that was created (his highest negative balance was a $41,200 check.)

The full extent of Perkins' problems went on full display after he left office. In 1994, he was indicted on three counts including conspiring to make false statements, bank fraud, and violating the false statements statute. He was subsequently sentenced to two months in prison.

While Perkins would never again hold public office, he regained some degree of public trust. By way of the ministry and following enrollment in the Louisville Seminary, Perkins was given a pulpit at a Presbyterian church in Ezel, Kentucky. One example of his preaching: "My friends, the Gospel is not about power and status. The Gospel shows us that God picks up the earthly notions of what is powerful and glorious and honorable and turns them upside down."

As for his own heritage: "I'm proud to be Carl Perkins' son. He was my father. He was my teacher. He raised me and shaped me."

CHAPTER EIGHTY-ONE

Hayes of Illinois the First Member Implicated In Rubbergate to Fall

Introductory Quote: "I do not have a problem delineating justice from injustice or right from wrong." Unfortunately for him, when he faced re-election amid the House check bouncing scandal, voters did have a problem delineating it as Hayes was unseated.

Photo courtesy of the U.S. House of Representatives Collection

The infamous House check bouncing scandal was responsible for ending roughly two dozen careers in the House of Representatives. The very first to fall – at least electorally — was Charlie Hayes of Illinois, whose demise came days after his place on the list of the worst abusers was revealed. The notoriety that the Chicago Democrat received as a result of the affair was a stark contradiction to the fact that he was among the least ubiquitous members of the House, certainly as compared with his neighbor, the virulent, anti-Semitic Gus Savage, who lost his seat the same day.

It was observed by many that Hayes's stint in Congress was a "second career." His papers cite him as the first trade union leader to be elected to Congress, and his election came at age 65, following the election of the seat's current occupant, Harold Washington, as the city's Mayor in 1983. Hayes actually had an association with Congress nearly a quarter-of-a-century before actually becoming a member. The year was 1959 and Hayes was hauled before the House Un-American Activities Committee.

The irony of Hayes hailing proudly from the Chicago establishment was that he was born near the farthest point in the state from the big city – the Southern Illinois town of Cairo, which *The Almanac of American Politics* observed, is "closer to Mississippi than Chicago."

Hayes's father was a farm laborer and, after graduating from an all-black high school, the future Congressman was hired as a tree planter by the Civilian Conservation Corps (CCC). He then got a job as a machine operator for E.L. Bruce Hardwood Flooring Co., and shortly thereafter became acclimated with the aspect of his career for which he would become ubiquitous: labor and its mechanics. First, he founded a carpentry local – 1424 of the United Brotherhood of Carpenters and Joiners of America and served as president.

Hayes's journey to Chicago and going stardom in labor interceded in 1942 when a family connection helped him gain employment at a Wilson & Co. meatpacking plant. Hayes satisfied his constituency by making the chapter a member of the United Packinghouse Workers of America and his 3,500 colleagues responded by electing him president. They got what they paid for as he ferociously went about fighting for rights for increased quality of life matters including increased wages, due process, and justice. The first cause was fighting segregation in plants. His constituency then rose to 35,000 as he became district director for District One. Hayes was instrumental in moving the District One headquarters.

For Hayes, politics, labor, and civil rights were all deeply intertwined throughout his career. The Charlie A. Hayes Papers said he "recruited and mentored more minority and women leaders, including labor leader and women's rights and civil rights activist, the Rev. Addie Wyatt, who worked under Hayes as a field representative and program coordinator." Worker wages dominated the agenda. He invoked the Fifth Amendment and denounced Communism (his union colleagues subsequently asked him to resign as a result, but he didn't). Civil rights also loomed large as Hayes was instrumental in the formation of several organizations designed to accelerate opportunities for African-American union members, which included raising money for the equality struggles undertaken by Dr. Martin Luther King, Jr. in the south. He was active in the National Coalition of Black Trade Unionists and Jesse Jackson's Operation PUSH in 1971.

Following the merger of the Packing House and meat-cutters union, Hayes became international vice president of the United Food and Commercial Workers Local. The Union merged with the Retail Clerks Association Union, and it became the United Food and Commercial Workers Union. Then came Congress.

Hayes had been a fundraiser for Chicago's First District Congressssman Harold Washington, and his profound organization abilities impressed him greatly. When he won Chicago's Mayoralty in 1983, Washington gave Hayes the ultimate compliment by deciding he'd be worthy of filling his shoes and made it clear that he favored him as his successor. Hayes did not clear the field - six other candidates competed for the Democratic nod, but Hayes did prevail 45-32% over including radio commentator Lutrelle "Lu" Palmer and civil rights Al Raby (curiously, two State legislators finished at the back of the pack). In a district as one-sided as the First, that was tantamount to the election. At 65 years old, Hayes was heading to Washington D.C.

Despite his longtime association with the new Mayor, Hayes emphasized that he was his own person. Of Washington, he said, "I'm not going to be a mouthpiece for him. If I can just do what he did when he was (in Congress), just do my own thing as a representative, I'll be all right."

What Hayes was a mouthpiece for was the economically disadvantaged of his district and, on that, he fit his South Side district like a glove. His name was always at the top when it came to opposition to the Conservative Coalition and he was not ambiguous about sharing his antipathy toward the Reagan administration priorities of working people which he chided as, "a callous disregard for the dreams and aspirations of millions of poor and disadvantaged children and young adults." Well before Reagan faced the voters for a second term, Hayes said, "We must replace him with a chief executive who is committed to solving the problems of poor people. We've got to put America back on the track of greatness."

While domestic issues were his forte, Hayes was vocal when it came to the South African government. Early in his tenure, he was arrested outside the South African Embassy for protesting apartheid, to which Hayes said, "These acts should force the South African government to stop oppressing, jailing, and killing its black citizens who are only seeking justice."

Apropos for a labor leader, the issues of jobs and increasing wages ranked high on Hayes's agenda. What better place to pursue those endeavors than the Education and Labor Committee to which he was assigned. His issues were opportunity for youths and local wage earners. His prime legislation was the Dropout Prevention and Re-Entry Act, a $500 million jobs program for state and local governments. The text said the bill would, "create "programs to identify potential dropouts and prevent them from dropping out; (2) programs to identify dropouts and encourage them to reenter school; and (3) model systems for collecting and reporting information on dropouts to local school officials." Hayes's contention: "The greatest security our Nation can have is to have our children properly educated." He introduced a $5 billion jobs program. With Republican Senator Arlen Specter of Pennsylvania, Hayes introduced the School Dropout Demonstration Assistance Act of 1987, which would authorize $50 million for demonstration programs of dropout prevention, persuasion and reentry. A similar effort in the previous Congress had been thwarted by an unlikely source: the U.S. Catholic Conference, which feared that funding would be used to promote abortions or birth control. Hayes's legislative director Howard Woolfson conceded the backlash caught, "its sponsors by surprise. That wasn't even considered, whether kids would be counseled to get abortions or not." Nevertheless, those issues were worked out.

The Quality of Life Action Act would have mandated every adult willing and able to work to be granted a right to a choice for employment. It also mandated that those able to work "have the right to an adequate standard of living." The bill languished in Education and Labor and died at the end of the session. Hayes also lobbied to locate the Black Higher Education Center in the nation's capital. He unveiled an Economic Bill of Rights and a Community Ratepayer Act, the latter which garnered 17 co-sponsors, some of whom were Republicans.

Hayes also wanted to ensure that the 1978 Humphrey-Hawkins Act was being implemented with maximal exertion and his Income and Jobs Action Act of 1985 would require more of a focus to be on unemployment to "focus attention and find solutions to the problem of unemployment and stop acting as though the problem does not exist."

With his Indiana colleague, Jim Jontz (right) and a dairy farmer
Photo courtesy of Calumet Regional Archives, Indiana University, Northwest

Hayes discovered the link between internal politics and realizing the third time is a charm in his quest to win a seat on the Post Office Committee. What was particularly stinging about his rejection on two prior occasions was that the post had gone to more junior colleagues with Hayes claiming he had enough votes "until they got behind closed doors." Only the tragic death of Texas Democrat Mickey Leland opened a slot, as well as a subcommittee chairmanship for Hayes on the panel in mid-1989. It was the Subcommittee on Postal, Personnel, and Modernization. One issue the committee dealt with was anti-pornography in the U.S. mail and Hayes declared it "would put teeth into the current statutes regarding the mailing of pornographic materials. Mailers would certainly think twice before arbitrarily mailing their materials to those households."

Unlike Savage, Hayes's record on Israel was not hostile, though he did oppose the relocation of the U.S. embassy to Jerusalem.

Prior to the bank scandal, Hayes had nary an electoral worry in the world. Hayes went unopposed in the primary and, even in a monolithically Democratic district, beat Republican Babette Peyton by a margin of 94-6% in 1990.

Had it not been for redistricting, which added more suburban (and white) territory to the First District, Hayes might have held off Rush, though that was not a certainty as the challenger did carry eight of the district's twelve African American wards. Working to his detriment, however, was the district's population loss coupled with the fact that Illinois had lost two seats, due to reapportionment, meant that Hayes had to grab many new would-be constituents. The addition of Oak Lawn, Morgan Park and Beverly were predominantly white, and voters there were not enchanted with the status quo. The new district came out to 69% African American, but now 25% white.

Hayes also attracted challenger, who ultimately turned out to be top tier. While Hayes had been organizing unions, Rush had been organizing Black panthers, as he was one in the 1960s. In fact, he founded the Illinois Black Panthers chapter in the 1960s. By the 80s, Rush settled down and had not only become an Alderman, but an ally of the regular order Democrats. Another Alderman, Anna Langford entered the race as well.

Rush made clear that his quest to unseat Hayes was not personal. "Charlie Hayes is a guy who has made a lot of significant contributions to the civil rights movement and the labor movement. I tip my hat to him. He was one of my heroes. But he doesn't have the fire in the belly we need." Rush painted Hayes as "a captive of the perks and privileges of Congress," but Hayes scoffed at Rush's notions that he was ineffective. "To say that a person can just go (to Congress) and change it all - it doesn't work that way. And I'm not going to mislead people and say it does."

Then the banking scandal enveloped, and for Hayes, it could not have come at a worse time.

The House Ethics panel had voted to reveal the names of the 24 worst abusers. Not only was Hayes on the list, but with 716 overdrafts, his account was in excess of his next month's salary for 15 of the 39 months examined. He tried to be circumspect. "If it had cost the government money or the taxpayer money, it would be an issue. I covered any overdraft and I owe no money to anyone." On another occasion, he said, "I want it clearly understood: I'm not a criminal, and I don't want to be treated like this." Rush's response was that, "Charlie Hayes' record in Congress is like his record of 700 overdrawn checks: insufficient ideas, insufficient commitment, insufficient action, insufficient funds."

The counting went well into the night, but Rush clung to a stubborn 42-39% lead for most of it. That's where the race ended as Rush won by 4,000 votes. Langford, who had dropped out, received 11%. Before the results were final, Hayes spokesman Jim Andrews spoke of "a witch hunt," to claim, "A man's 52-year career in the labor movement and Congress was reduced to a 72-hour feeding frenzy."

A few weeks after his defeat, Hayes took the floor of the House to denounce the track that the banking investigation had taken. He began by declaring himself, "very dismayed that I have to take this precious time to rise to address such an issue at a time when this Nation is truly falling apart. People are suffering because of poverty, homelessness, unemployment, and the lack of education and health care. Children in my district dodge bullets as they walk to and from school, elementary children are offered drugs every day, people that are homeless are forced to live outside when hundreds of useful homes are boarded up, many senior citizens fear leaving their homes be- cause of the dramatic increase in violent crime, and thousands of people line up to apply for jobs when only a few can realistically be hired. These are the issues that ought to be legislated, yet the leadership, on both sides of the aisle, have chosen a different path."

"Even before I could adequately respond, I had been tried and convicted by the press. There was basically no time to develop any damage control on the issue, and it cost me my reelection bid." He did add, "I have moved past my anger and bit."

Rush, with some credence but also, perhaps, a shade unfairly, predicted that, "Two years from now, they're going to marvel at what a congressman can do and is supposed to do." He does still hold the seat to this day. A dejected Hayes completed his term and retired to Chicago.

The Charles A. Hayes Post Office was dedicated on Chicago's South Side in 1996. Shortly thereafter, Hayes was diagnosed with lung cancer and succumbed to the disease in 1997 at age 79.

CHAPTER EIGHTY-TWO

Bustamante's Legal Woes Put Abrupt Brakes on a Potentially Long Albeit Undistinguished Career

Introductory Quote: "Cheques calientes." – Republican Henry Bonilla during his 1992 challenge to Congressman Al Bustamante, who had been hampered by, among other things, overdrafts at the House Bank.

Photo courtesy of the Collection of the U.S. House of Representatives

In 1992, all 27 Congressmen from Texas sought new terms. Only Albert Bustamante was denied one. Through Election Day, the four-term Democrat was locked in a race with Republican Henry Bonilla that was considered possible to go either way, so, it was a genuine shock when he found himself on the losing end of a 21-point deficit — the second worst drubbing of any incumbent defeated in a general election. Yet like so many other colleagues who departed that year, Bustamante's woes were almost entirely self-inflicted.

Throughout October of '92, three Democratic Texans, Charlie Wilson of East Texas, Ron Coleman of El Paso and Bustamante were in races that were viewed as tossups. Wilson and Coleman, somewhat against the expectations, survived. Bustamante did not.

The 23rd District of Texas stretched from Bexar County, ricocheting north just below Midland, all the way to Webb County in Laredo. Redistricting in the 1980s had aided Bustamante by removing parts of Val Verde County and, ultimately, produced a district that was nearly 56% Hispanic. Monolithically Democratic, the 23rd was not as George H. W. Bush actually led Michael Dukakis 50-49% in 1988, but the culture was such that a Democrat really had to screw-up big-time in order to be shown the door. Enter Bustamante. A protracted legal investigation, involvement with the House Bank and other poor judgements contributed to his ouster by the novice Bonilla.

Bustamante was a lifelong product of the district. Born in Asherton, Texas to a migrant, he was the eldest of eleven children. The family had severe financial hardships that required him to pick crops and berries. It also meant that he wouldn't start school until age nine, and thus did not know or learn English until that time.

Bustamante entered the Army as a paratrooper, eventually received his education at Sul Ross State College, and became a junior high school teacher and a basketball coach. Then it was like metaphorically going from rags to riches as Bustamante went to work for a Congressman, the legendary Henry Gozalez. Few congressmen can claim to have been fired by a future colleague but, in the case of Bustamante, that was exactly the case. His termination happened three years later when Bustamante was seeking a seat on the Bexar County Commissioner against longtime Commissioner Albert Pena Jr., a veteran of the Mexican-American civil rights movement who himself had been an ally of Gonzalez before the pair had a falling out. In a 1996 oral history project, Pena said, "I believe that he could have stopped him, but he didn't want to. He didn't stop him...that is what defeated me." Bustamante forced Pena into a runoff and beat him. Pena, decades later, said a prime reason was, "because he could raise money and I couldn't." After holding the seat for six years, Bustamante captured the post of Bexar County Judge in 1978.

In 1984, Bustamante decided to challenge a seemingly secure eight-term incumbent and fellow Democrat, Abraham "Chick" Kazen. Bustamante got the endorsement of San Antonio Mayor, Henry Cisneros, and ex-Governor, Dolph Briscoe, while Gonzalez and other members of the Texas delegation stuck with Kazen. Fortuitously, primary day was May 5 and Bustamante urged voters to, "Help me on Cinco de Mayo to declare our independence from an old political family who has control the destiny of this area." While Gonzalez and most other members of the delegation stuck with the incumbent, voters did not. Bustamante won a lopsided 59-37% victory and told euphoric supporters, "We put together a coalition of business people, labor people, Albert Bustamante people from all walks of life." No Republican had filed for the seat, which meant that with his win, he was automatically a member-elect (the gap did mean he'd be "looking for a job until January"). He was appointed to seats on Armed Services and Government Operations.

In Congress, Bustamante proved himself capable of going after colleagues, both Democrat and Republican. One incident came when Texas Republican Senator Phil Gramm pre-empted him in announcing a grant for Asherton. Bustamante accused him of "Gramm-standing" and accused the Defense Department of purposely holding back publicizing it in order for Gramm to get a head-start. During his first year in office, when House Armed Services Committee Les Aspin supported the MX missile, Bustamante was profoundly disturbed. He had supported Aspin in his hard-fought bid to win the position and pronounced himself sorry to have done so.

Additionally, sore feelings between he and Gonzalez died hard when Bustamante, in 1990, accused Gonzaez of gutting a $9.2 million appropriation for San Antonio Missions National al Historical Park. Gonzalez, who sat on the conference committee ironing out the differences between the House and Senate passed bills, responded that his former employee was "hallucinating," and that he had long been working on the project, ("Why would I wreck something I started years ago?"). Bustamante said, "I know (Gonzalez) doesn't like me, and that's fine. But I don't think you have to hurt the people of San Antonio. The most important thing is to get the funding for the people of San Antonio, and Bentsen got that funding," referring to the state's senior Senator, Lloyd Bentsen.

Bustamante was among the members who were seriously wooed on the vote to send aid to the Nicaraguan contras. Contending, "there will be no peace in Central America until internal reform is forced," on the ruling Sandinistas, he yielded to the pressure. His reasoning was that, "I came away convinced we need to continue to pressure the Sandinistas."

Other Reagan administration priorities were too much and, in 1987, Bustamante led the fight against the Special Isotope Separation (SIS) plant that had been proposed in Idaho on the grounds of safety (he had a very high-profile partner in Massachusetts Senator Ted Kennedy). "Basically this reactor has been living on the edge of a major disaster for over 30 years." Bustamante proposed an amendment to a defense authorization bill that would limit funding saying, "When funding essential activities to keep our Armed Forces ready is difficult, we cannot justify building an expensive facility we do not need." Though the amendment failed, funding for the Isotope was postponed.

Bustamante opposed the resolution authorizing war against Iraq but sponsored a series of bills that would extend the health care needs of troops, including amending the National Defense Authorization Act to extend a scheduled increase in the annual deductible for the Civilian Health and Medical Program of the Uniformed Services (CHAMPUS), as well as proposing that the scheduled sunsetting of mental health provisions for returning troops be postponed. He wanted the Impact Aid program studied for military dependents on Indian land in districts near bases and put forth the United States-Mexico Border Environmental Zone Protection Act. Another frequent cause: sponsoring the designation of Mays in certain years as, "Karate Kids Just Say No to Drugs Month."

During debate on the Civil Rights Act of 1990, Bustamante cited his own experiences. "It is no fun to be run out of restaurants, out of barber shops, to be denied employment simply because you are a Mexican or a wetback or a Mescin or whatever other title they used to use for us or to live in segregated housing or to go to segregated schools. It is the most humiliating experience. It tears at your heart. It brings you down as a person. Mr. Chairman, we should not have that in America."

In 1987, colleagues chose Bustamante to lead the Congressional Hispanic Caucus. He rounded up support for embattled fellow, Texan Jim Wright, in his futile attempt to salvage his Speakership in 1989. Yet Bustamante would soon become embattled himself.

In 1990, it came to light that the FBI was investigating Bustamante's friend, businessman Eddie "Bingo King" Garcia. The inquiry did nothing to dent Bustamante at the polls – he had a Republican opponent for the first time in four cycles but dispatched him with 64%. But the beat went on. At one point during the saga, Bustamante even claimed the investigation was politically motivated because he had supported Hispanic agents in a civil rights lawsuit. "This is what the FBI has sunk to. They have been looking for anyone to say anything damaging about me."

One reason Bustamante was not considered to be in especially horrendous shape until late in his campaign was because the allegations first presented themselves in 1990, yet he survived with 64%. '92 was different. For one, his woes deteriorated. Two, an anti-incumbent mood penetrated the nation like never before and, in Henry Bonilla, Bustamante found himself with a deft enough challenger able to exploit it. Pursuant to that, Bustamante was also confronted with other woes, and the House Bank scandal topped the list. Though the incumbent's 30 overdrafts were a relatively paltry number, Bonilla deftly exploited it by running ads notifying residents of his "cheques calientes" for "hot checks."

Probably more hurtful was his purchase of a $618,000 home in Dominion, a neighborhood not only outside the district, but a stance that was counter to residents of the district of whom Bustamante had said as President Bush broke his "no new taxes," pledge that, "The average person in my district doesn't pay income taxes." Gramm got in on the anti-Bustamante festivities as well, dispatching his regional director, Ed Hodges, to assist.

The campaign was long and the rhetoric bordered on vituperative. Bonilla's wife was Deborah Knapp, an anchor at KENS-TV who took a leave of absence to stump for her husband (she used the Bonilla name), but Bustamante charged the station with using its computers to assist the campaign, and credibility was lent when another anchor attempted to host a fundraiser for him. This caused Bustamante to run an ad showing a Bonilla lookalike putting a coin in a newspaper machine and taking out all of the papers, as well as stealing towels from a hotel. Bonilla's spokesman, Frank Guerra, used the opportunity to jab their rival, saying, "Albert knows a lot about hotels with all of his junkets." Bustamante's Treasurer said the ad was, "supposed to be amusing. It's not supposed to be taken literally," but it underscored the intense acrimony between the two men. Bustamante hoped to benefit from the presence of Lena Guerrero, who was seeking a seat on the powerful Texas Railroad Commission, but she was not without her own substantial baggage: she had inflated her resume. Meanwhile, Bonilla rarely mentioned his GOP affiliation and Bustamante hit him for opposing an increase in the minimum wage, saying he calls him an, "eunuch for the plantation owners." Bustamante tried to play up his effectiveness by reminding voters of the job-related contracts he had secured for the district, including Sterling Foods and Northrup Corp for an Air Force training plant. He also saw strength in numbers.

The sparring got so bad that *The San Antonio Express News* opined shortly before Election Day that, "Thankfully, those of us not in District 23 don't have to sort this out and make a decision that won't embarrass us the rest of our lives." Either way, voters had to make a decision, and, at the end of the day, they conclusively decided that ethics trumped the advantages of incumbency. And for Bustamante, that meant a thumping. Bonilla unseated him by 35,000, a margin of 59-39%, and carried Bexar with a resounding 81%. He even narrowly outpolled the incumbent in El Paso. Bustamante did carry Webb with 63%, and its smaller surrounding counties, as well as a smattering of counties at the Northern portion of the district, but fell far short in Val Verde, which had ironically been placed in the district in order to help him. Contending that, "Bexar County proved to be my graveyard," Bustamante told supporters on conceding that, "I guess I'll go pull weeds in my garden. I'm going to do OK.'" That proved to be wishful thinking.

Just seven weeks after his term ended, a federal jury indicted Bustamante on ten counts in violation of the Racketeer Influenced and Corrupt Organizations Act (RICO). The indictments charged that in total, Bustamante accepted $344,000. The most serious count was that he accepted $35,000 for steering a contract to the Falcon Food Services, Inc, in order to help win a contract at Lackland Air Force. Another count was that the law firm where Rebecca Bustamante worked, which specialized in tax delinquency matters and just happened to be one of the most influential in Texas, was used as the go-between to forward the Congressman some of the money. Rebecca was charged with seven. The other eight counts involved bribery.

On the witness stand, Falcon Foods President Al Aleman testified on Bustamante's behalf, telling jurors that he simply asked Bustamante for help obtaining the contract and that no favors were asked or delivered. The jury didn't buy it and, while Bustamante was acquitted on convicted eight counts, he was convicted on the two most serious (Rebecca was acquitted on all). When sentencing came, the Judge did Bustamante a favor. He could have received up to 20-years in prison but was given only 3 ½.

In presenting his closing arguments to the jury, Albert Bustamante rose to become one of the most powerful men in our country - a United States Congressman. But, the same set of laws applies to him. He told jurors the "deception, dishonesty and corruption...shakes the very foundation of our democracy." *The Galveston Daily News* wrote that Bustamante "visibly wavered" when the verdicts were waved. "But he regained himself and leaned over and kissed his wife, Rebecca, on the cheek when she was found innocent of the seven counts on which she was charged."

Bustamante was released from prison in 1998, at which time his homecoming included a mariachi band. Bustamante's son John tried to win his dad's seat in Congress in 2012 but lost the primary to Pete Gallego.

CHAPTER EIGHTY-THREE

Atkins's Star-Quality, Once Unstoppable, Withered Away from Alienations and Weaknesses

Introductory Quote: "At a time when we worry about bringing the international criminal Saddam Hussein to justice for his atrocities, we wink and blink and nod at Pol Pot who put to death over a million of his countrymen." -Chet Atkins

Chet Atkins the politician (left) greets Chet Atkins the singer (right)
Photo via Getty Images

The most famous Chet Atkins was a famous guitarist dubbed "The Country Gentleman" from Tennessee. In Massachusetts, Chester G. "Chet" Atkins was a political natural and exceptionally talented state party chair who once in Congress, filled his district with goodies via his seat on the powerful Appropriations Committee. But the meteoric force that launched his political career came crashing down in 1992 at age 44 as the anti-incumbent wave, the House Bank scandal and Atkins' own weaknesses, cost him his seat by a resounding margin – the same year the guitarist wowed 4,000 people in nearby Springfield. But perhaps the biggest blows to his career was self-inflicted. In recent years, Atkins had distanced himself from and even alienated both people and groups with whom he had spent years forging critical alliances.

It seems every Massachusetts Congressman is affiliated with one specific town - Joe Early was Worcester, Nick Mavroules Peabody and Ed Markey Malton. For Atkins, it was Concord. Though he was born in Geneva, Switzerland to "die-hard Stevenson Democrats," he spent his boyhood in Concord and attended the town's high schools before going off to Antioch College in Ohio. That, and the antiwar movement that he was a part of, sparked his political interest.

In 1968, Atkins ran a Congressional campaign in Ohio before deciding that he wanted to be part of the process himself. The opportunity presented itself just two years later, far sooner than he likely thought conceivable. Back in Massachusetts by then, Atkins decided to mount a bid for a State House seat being vacated by John McGlennon. It was not easy.

For starters, Atkins recalls, "It had always been a Republican seat since there had been a Republican party around the time of the Civil War." Plus, Democrats already had a heavyweight contender, Jerry Bush who had been assistant Labor Secretary in the Kennedy administration. In a 1993 oral history interview, Atkins recalled that 33 of the 35 committee members were aligned with Bush and said, "people just assumed that he would win, that he would get the Democratic nomination hands down." But Atkins proved indefatigable. He knocked on every door in some communities twice and won, then beat businessman George Rohan in the general, even as Republican Governor John Volpe was winning re-election.

Atkins took his oath the youngest member of that body and recalled his "rude awakening." He explained that, "What I found was a politics that was dominated by patronage, a politics that was very much personal for the politicians, personal struggles over jobs and power, and power rather than a larger fight over ideas and principles...I was very much a kind of angry young man who really didn't have much contact with the leadership, fought against them on a number of things."

Atkins might have figured that if he were going to be swimming against the grain, he might as well hold a higher position. Two years after embarking on such a hard fought fight to win, Atkins risked it all by undertaking a bid for the state Senate and again won. He repeated that feat in 1974 and *The Lowell Sun* explained how in the primary, "he ran against a former corrections officer from Marlboro, who berated Atkins for his liberal positions and received undue coverage in the Marlboro Enterprise. Atkins still beat him soundly, even in Marlboro's blue collar wards that many thought would have had nothing to do with the young Yankee liberal from the suburbs." Finally, however, the fights yielded dividends as he became chair of the Public Services Committee. In the ensuing years, Atkins had become close to State Senate President Billy Bulger and saw the fruits of that relationship blossom when he was named chair of the Ways and Means Committee.

Atkins's opportunity to go to Washington came in 1984 when Democratic incumbent Jim Shannon left the Fifth District behind to again succeed Paul Tsongas, who was retiring from the Senate (Tsongas had held the seat previously for two terms). The Fifth was working class territory consisting primarily of Lawrence, Lowell and Framingham.

Even with the entry of State Senator Phil Shea, Atkins's path to capturing the nomination seemed clear. But Shea mounted an energetic campaign of contrasts. *Congressional Quarterly* framed the race as one between a "blue-blood" against an "Ordinary Joe." Shea, who hailed from a working-class Lowell neighborhood called, "The Scrabble," was to the right of Atkins on most social issues, including abortion. But he had a populist flair, backed a nuclear freeze and challenged Atkins to not accept PAC money and pledge to resign from Congress if he did. His goal was to hold down Atkins's margin in Lawrence and he had a grand operation to try to do so. But many of the well-known pols favored Atkins, including Fourth District Congressman Barney Frank. By primary day, the race was considered a dead-heat but Atkins prevailed 53-47% (Shea was a good sport – he showed up at Atkins's headquarters and endorsed him on the spot).

The general election against Phillip Hyatt was similarly tough. The 5th was no Democratic bastion – Massachusetts native Michael Dukakis failed to carry it in his 1988 presidential campaign. Hyatt had been a leader in the enactment of the tax-cutting Proposition 2 ½ in 1978 and was currently lobbying for Citizens for America. He hoped to benefit from Ronald Reagan's expectation of doing relatively well in Massachusetts (he carried it). Again, Atkins won 53-47% and with the help of Speaker Thomas P. "Tip" O'Neill, became the only freshman Democrat to be appointed to the Budget Committee. Meanwhile, Atkins continued to chair the Democratic State Committee.

Congressional Quarterly labeled Atkins, "a reserved New England Yankee with a dash of hard-charging Massachusetts pol, a skilled legislative deal-cutter occasionally willing to paddle against his party's flow." But by the end of his career, *The Almanac of American Politics* wrote: "Atkins seems to have run out his strength; he has turned on political benefactors, antagonized constituents, and fought back with low blow tactics." Those confluence of factors might explain Atkins's opinion of his time in Congress: "I found Washington to be a stimulating environment for the first six years. The last two years were really a miserable time."

The highlight of Atkins's tenure might have come as he was beginning his third term when he proved his political chops by winning the seat on the House Appropriations Committee left vacant by Second District Congressman Ed Boland. Most noteworthy was his competition: Joe Kennedy II, a junior colleague. To win, Atkins overcame ferocious lobbying not just by Kennedy but from his uncle, Senator Edward Kennedy. But that intervention might have backfired as at least one powerful member of the New England delegation, Rules Committee Joe Moakley of South Boston was irked by his tactics. Kennedy had initially led the balloting 8-6, with 3 votes for Connecticut Democrat Bruce Morrison, who was thereby eliminated. That sent the race to a second ballot and Atkins edged Kennedy 9-8.

One of Atkins's first missions was to hold newly elected President George H.W. Bush's feet to the fire as far as Boston Harbor. Bush had famously derided the Harbor for its high pollution in his campaign against Massachusetts Governor Michael Dukakis ('Now, as holder of our highest national office, he has ignored this problem by failing to commit federal resources to the...cleanup effort." Atkins pressed for $20 million in spending for cleanup and got it. Other endeavors on Appropriations: increased funds for Lowell National Historic Park, the Boot Mills Office Complex and the Wang Laboratories. He is particularly proud of, "the work that I did on the expansion of the Great Meadows National Wildlife Refuge and Walden Woods and the Concord-Sudbury-Assabet River basin," the latter which was a study that would potentially pave the way for three rivers in the 5th to become incorporated into the wild and scenic rivers program.

Atkins fought to keep Fort Devens open. Bemoaning the slow pace of choosing between Massachusetts and Arizona, he said, "At some point, you say what do you want? What's the only thing they have at Fort Huachuca that we don't have here? They can play golf 12 months a year there." On another occasion, he alleged politics. "It's not unreasonable to look at the fact that Nov. 6 is Election Day in both Massachusetts and Arizona. All of a sudden they postpone the date (for the beginning of the realignment) until right after the start..." Efforts to keep the Fort open ultimately failed.

As U.S. troops went to Saudi Arabia amid the uncertainties of war in 1990, Atkins urged energy conservation.

Another Atkins crusade was Atkins a vicious anti-smoking drive that sought to obliterate the tobacco industry and was one of 35 Congressman – 21 Democrats and 14 Republicans, who went on the attack. Atkins accused the U.S. government of "exporting death," by urging, and in some cases bullying, Asia to take tobacco "at the expense of citrus products, beef, leather, rice and hi-tech equipment…When we have a drug our own government says is addictive and is killing us and we are spreading that drug overseas." He said, "If we are as sensitive as we are about the health of American consumers, this certainly looks like an outrageous double standard."

One area that Atkins did not successfully navigate was the issue of the Cambodia (the 5th was home to a large number of Cambodians). Atkins had angered many by his call to normalize his relations with Vietnam. However, there were major qualifiers to that stance. Though many wanted to end the U.S. embargo, Atkins was worried about including the Khmer Rouge. Having once called that faction, "the most genocidal people on the face of the earth," Atkins hardly was ready to depart from that view in 1990 when he asserted that, "One single clear and continuing theme in United States policy to Cambodia has been our insistence on the inclusion of the Khmer Rouge in the interim Government. That is really quite astonishing. It sent an enormous signal to the Cambodian people that the killing fields could very easily happen again." Testifying at a Foreign Affairs Committee hearing in 1991, he seemed to double down by asking that the Khmer Rouge be not part of a U.N. initiated settlement. "Rhetorically, we revile the Khmer Rouge," he said, "but in practice we answer to a larger geopolitical imperative in Southeast Asia…which suggests that the Khmer Rouge will be used as a foil for Vietnam." That brought an angry rebuke from New York Democrat Stephen Solarz who asked him if he had read the report andunderstood the matter at hand.

As the Bay State's spending woes exacerbated, Atkins proposed a way for the state to save $500 million.

At first, Atkins bemoaned interest in serving on Ethics, telling colleagues, "Let this cup pass from my lips." But whether it was the bullying or convincing, he was prevailed to accept just as the panel was taking up potentially the most sensitive investigation in Congress: that of Speaker Jim Wright. And if Atkins did not have uniform recognition before his appointment, he sure would come April of '89 when he and another Democrat, Bernard Dwyer of New Jersey, voted with the committee Republicans on a key plank: agreeing that George Mallick, a Fort Worth businessman who had contributed $145,000 to Wright, had a direct interest on upcoming banking legislation. He had focused on a report Mallick prepared for Wright. "Each and every one of those recommendations would, if adopted, substantially increase the net worth of Mr. George Mallick. How do we explain that there was not a direct interest in legislation?"

For both Atkins and Dwyer, it was a shot heard around the Hill. One Democrat summed up the feelings of colleagues by saying, "You can't bitch that it's a Republican plot. You've got two reputable Democrats who went along." Another Democrat noted, "Atkins and Dwyer are not showing their faces around here." But as the Speaker prepared to resign, Atkins told *The Lowell Sun*, he never felt "singled out by my colleagues, isolated," or "threatened."

At the end of the day, ex-Speaker Tip O'Neill told Wright that, "I would have told you not to put him on the Ethics Panel but you never asked me." Incidentally, Atkins apparently had enough of high profile investigations. A year later, as the panel looked into alleged wrongdoing by Massachusetts Democrat Barney Frank, Atkins recused himself, stating his longtime friendship. He might have had the time in any case. Back in Massachusetts, another election was coming up and Atkins found him hard pressed not only by the state's woeful economic conditions, but by a well-funded State Representative named John MacGovern.

MacGovern revealed his formula early on. "Not only are most voters of Massachusetts anti-Dukakis," he said, "but increasingly anti-Democratic establishment. And Chet Atkins personifies that establishment more than anyone in the state." A co-founder of the Dartmouth Review, *CQ* called MacGovern's campaign consultant Todd Domke, "known for making a lot of a little." For one, Vice-President Dan Quayle stumped for him. MacGovern campaigned hard, telling supporters at one appearance, "Two centuries ago, an embattled farmer fired a shot heard around the world. Two weeks from now, embattled taxpayers can fire Chester Atkins and that firing can be heard around the country." But many voters cited Atkins's penchant for bringing home the bacon as a reason for keeping him and *The Lowell Sun* noted the incumbent "delivered several strategically timed federal grant awards in the last week of the election." It made just enough of an impression.

After trailing with almost half the vote counted, Atkins prevailed 52-48%, a margin of 9,000 votes out of 212,000 cast (110,232 to 101,017 votes) and the smallest margin of any incumbent in the delegation. He took Lawrence by just 744 votes but Framingham by close to 5,000. MacGovern called it, "a considerable accomplishment to be taking on the chairman of the Democratic Party in Massachusetts...with enormous resources at his disposal...in a race that we have very nearly won. I look at it as the thimble is half full." That assessment evidently brought Atkins's concurrence. That very night coincided with Republican William Weld winning the governorship and Atkins announced on the spot that he would relinquish the Democratic Party Chair. He recognized, "The Democratic Party has a lot of rethinking to do" and said wistfully, "There's only so much punishment one individual can take." His campaign was in debt $33,000. But that might not have been the only consideration.

Redistricting was around the corner and it was untidy as can be. From the moment it became clear that Massachusetts would lose a seat, it was obvious that Akins was the member with the biggest target on his back. By the beginning of 1992, uncertainty reigned supreme. As early as September of '91, Atkins had startled many Bay State Democrats by volunteering to be paired with Early, the Worcester Democrat. State Senator Walter Boverni, who happened to be co-chairing the redistricting panel, explained Atkins's logic. "Chester realizes that it's obvious. All he's looking for is a fair chance. He knows that west has to move east, and east has to move west, and he's in the middle." But as *The Boston Herald* observed, "There is no love lost between the incumbent Democrats, who collided in 1988 when Early managed Rep. Joseph P. Kennedy's bid for a seat on the Appropriations Committee in the House."

For a time, it appeared Atkins would get his wish as one draft submitted by Democrats would put Worcester and Lowell in the same district while removing Framingham, the latter which was contrary to Atkins's wishes. He also said he wanted Lawrence and Lowell gone, which earned him little love from *The Lawrence Eagle Tribune*.

By the end of March, a Supreme Court case had been heard and it was still unclear whether Massachusetts would be spared the loss of a Congressional seat but Brian Donnelly of Dorchester called it quits, which at the very least spared an incumbent from getting sacrificed. But ironing out the lines was a different matter.

When the list of those with overdrafts was revealed, Atkins had 127. This was not particularly large number - the monetary total was $15,410 (multiple members had overdrafts that totaled in the hundreds of thousands) but it did lend credence to critics that said Congress needed reform. And coming on the heels of an election, the publicity was something Atkins could ill afford.

It took until July for the new lines to be released and the good news for Atkins was that when they were, he did not have to face another incumbent.

SCOTT CRASS

But that would be the only piece of good news. Not only did Lowell and Lawrence remain in the district but Framingham was gone. And Atkins had a major primary against Marty Meehan, the First Assistant District Attorney for Middlesex County. Ironically, Meehan had been quoted by *The Lowell Sun* on election night '90 as saying, "Lowell has a record of rewarding members of Congress who produce for the district." He surely hoped Atkins would not run an ad quoting him.

As Atkins announced his candidacy for another term, he vowed to "create a new national economic direction that will produce jobs for the country and the Fifth Congressional district…this district is going to need a strong advocate to bring back jobs."

Most of the Democratic heavyweights stuck with Atkins. Tsongas conceded, "Chet is more calculating than what people up here are used to … and he plays closer to the vest, giving people a level of discomfort, so they're not exactly sure what they're dealing with." But Tsongas nonetheless endorsed him.

Atkins campaign spokesmen Patrick Halley noted he'd, "readily concede that if this were a popularity contest simply, Chet Atkins would not win. But when it comes to the question of effectiveness, Chet wins hands down." Meehan, he said, has "blamed Chet for everything from people having to pay income taxes to the fact that it gets dark at night." But Meehan wasn't grasping at straws for a good part of the blame. Atkins did have the issue of the checks and the Congressional pay raise that he had supported in 1989. Atkins retorted by championing his effectiveness. One ad said, "It's not that I like the guy – it's just that need him." But on primary day, voters rejected that viewpoint by a landslide.

The result was an unambiguous 65-35% win for Meehan. Atkins conceded gracefully: "Let me say to the voters of the 5th District, 'Thank you for letting me serve'…To Mr. Meehan, I say congratulations and I'll be voting Democratic in November." In the oral history project conducted the following year, Atkins made clear that the remap was the most virulent culprit. "I lost a lot of my strongest communities, Weston, Lincoln, Framingham, and this added a lot of new territory that was far more conservative such as Billerica, Tewksbury, and some of the other communities up there…" After leaving office, he told the oral history project that, "I guess some of the ironies and the curiosities of my career is that I've been both an insider but never a real insider…" That was prescient indeed but a realization that was clearly years too late.

CHAPTER EIGHTY-FOUR

Rhodes the Son Not As Ubiquitous As His Father But A Master at Legislating

Introductory Quote: Yes, peace came to Vietnam. It was the peace of repression, of poverty, of imprisonment, of death, of slavery." –Arizona Congressman Jay Rhodes, a Vietnam veteran, as the House debated aid to the contras.

Photo courtesy of the U.S. House of Representatives Collection

J ay Rhodes was an example of even the most seemingly-safe Republicans getting swept up in the anti-incumbent mood. A three-term Arizona Republican, Rhodes had one of the most golden names in booth GOP and Grand Canyon State politics. His father was John Rhodes, Sr., who represented most of the same First Congressional District Jay held from 1953 until his retirement thirty years later. The elder Rhodes was elevated to his colleagues as House Minority Leader and played a major role near the end of the Nixon presidency in convincing him to resign.

For a man with such a prominent name, John Jacob "Jay" Rhodes operated in a manner that was quite nonchalant - his goal was to work hard and end stalemates on issues of complexity. Rotund and quiet, Rhodes was operated in a manner that was congenial and able. He graduated from Yale University and the University of Arizona Law School and during the Vietnam War was an Army Captain. He was both Republican chair and president of the Mesa Board of Education and in 1982 was elected statewide to the board of the Central Arizona Water Conservation District. His run for Congress came when John McCain decided to move up to the Senate. In such a heavily Republican district, the action was entirely in the primary and Rhodes's main competitor was Ray Russell. He prevailed 44-37%.

Rhodes sat on the Interior and Insular Affairs Committee and while he and the panel's chair, fellow Arizona Democrat Morris K. "Mo" Udall did not always see eye-to-eye, they legislated a great deal together for Arizona's interests. Udall chaired the House Interior Committee on which Rhodes sat and often tangled over thorny issues impacting the region. The first with significance came early in his first year during the Central Arizona Project reauthorization. The U.S. Bureau of Reclamation wanted to add the Cliff Dam to the Grand Canyon dams that would be built and it was opposed by environmental organizations because, as one member said, "it would have destroyed a substantial segment of critical riparian habitat on the Verde River." The negotiations were exhausting – fellow Republican Jim Kolbe estimated that the delegation and their staffs spent 13 hours over five days with various environmental interests and in the end, Rhodes sided with them and against the dam. As Rhodes took the House fooor, he stated, "The product we bring to the House floor today is an accommodation which, though we each may not be totally satisfied, we nonetheless now unite behind and make a joint commitment to implement." He said, "What we have accomplished here is to keep together the Arizona water partnership. It is a partnership of Arizona water interests and local governments with the Federal Government."

In 1988, Rhodes was with Udall – and against California's George Miller, on a government land swap that exchanged 118,000 of acres in Phoenix for Florida wetlands. Miller had called the deal a "bargain-basement price" and proposed an alternative in the Interior Committee calling for an independent examiner but it garnered just three votes. In 1990, Rhodes led a proposed Arizona Wilderness Act to compromise with Udall and other members of the delegation in 1990 (though not Republican Bob Stump of Flagstaff who objected to the exhorbitant designations) and it cleared the House 356-45.

Rhodes played a role in the Salt River Pima-Maricopa Indian Community Water Rights Settlement Act of 1988 which merited remedies for with Indian claims impacting five Western states with large tribes, including Arizona.

In 1991, Rhodes introduced a measure that would level the flow of the Glen Canyon Dam which he called a necessity in order to meet the Grand Canyon's interests. That met opposition from an unlikely combo – Miller, who was now acting-chair of Interior (Udall was preparingto leave the House due to the increasing effects of Parkinson's Disease) and the Bush White House. Miller's beef was that Arizonans would foot the bill regardless of whether they used the Canyon or not which Rhodes didn't deny. His retort was, "Obviously the name of the game in this town is to get somebody else to pay your way" but it was "a question of fairness" (the administration's issue was separation between the branches of government).

Near the end of the 102nd Congress, Rhodes labored for passage of a measure to protect the Grand Canyon, which was part of a 39 western state interior project. While the bill cleared the House, it fell victim to procedural roadblocks by California Republican Senator John Seymour over issues related to his state. Rhodes probably wasn't thinking at that point that he wouldn't be returning to Congress but the happenstances that be took their toll and it started with deep unease among the GOP base.

On most national domestic issues, Rhodes was a stalwart conservative. He was firmly in the camp of NASA advocates when a dispute between housing and space advocates hit Appropriators. While pro-housing forces prevailed in committee, the matter reached the House floor where Rhodes called the question one of "who makes policy or this country? I think each one of us would say, 'The Congress of the United States makes policy for this country.' I think this bill would indicate that there is a qualifier on that answer. The Congress of the United States makes policy for this country except when the Appropriations Committee disagrees with the policy." Fiscally, Rhodes hewed to the right as well and one example was the abolisdhment of Social Security payroll taxes.

The dismay that conservatives had toward Rhodes appeared to spiral in 1988 when he called for the resignation of Arizona's embattled GOP Governor Evan Mecham. His reasoning was the report, "brings us to a climax — gives us an opportunity now to say to the governor, 'Spare us from the rest of this. Do as President Nixon did and let us get about the business of our state as President Nixon did with the business of our country.'" The following year, Rhodes backed moderate Ed Madigan of Illinois in the race for House

Minority Whip that Gingrich ultimately won 89-87. He also backed the controversial House pay raise. The irony was that Rhodes was somewhat stingy with federal spending. He viewed the proposed Steamtown USA Park in Pennsylvania as a doozy of a juggernaut, saying, "It appalls me that it's going to cost $6 million a year to operate the park."

The harbinger of weakness among GOP voters came in 1990 when Rhodes held off a primary challenge just 62-38%. He was unopposed in November but further anger the right by supporting the budget summit package which contained tax increases.

The House Bank investigation revealed that Rhodes had 32 overdrafts, not an overpowering number given what some of his colleagues had but well more than the two for "small amounts" he had first reported. But Rhodes was the only Arizonan to have overdrafts and the state seemed to be ground-zero for the Ross Perot citizen-oriented vengeance toward Washington that was building at the same time. His view was that, "my name has been tarnished unfairly" and the Sergeant-At-Arms failed to contact him beyond the initial two.

Rhodes's re-election woes were fought in two battles, neither of which particularly ended well. Redistrictinmg had appeared to strengthen him – the Republican lean of the First increased. His problem, as CQ noted, was that, "the most conservative Republicans in East Mesa and Chandler have been replaced by more moderate voters in West Mesa, Tempe, Chandler and parts of Phoenix." That and the bnank scandal invited a fractious primary from his right. Four Republicans challenged him in the primary, with the most hefty being State Representatives Stan Barnes and Bill Mundell. Rhodes took a fox guarding the hen-house mentality against his two rivals, invoking the well-publicized scandals that had plagued Phoenix. "Were you satisfied with the way the Legislature was handled in the last few years? These two guys are part of the problem. What makes them think they would suddenly become more effective congressmen?"

When the votes were counted, 2/3 of Republican voters had deserted Rhodes but, the multi-field of candidates enabled to hang on 33%-30% over Barnes (15,601 to 14,194) while Mundell took 24%. Barnes may well have defeated Rhodes had it not been for reports by his ex-wife of infidelity with a statehouse staffer (he denied it). A showing like that would leave any incumbent quaking in their boots for November but the original feeling was that Rhodes wouldn't have much difficulty winning in November. Rhodes may have shared that opinion. On primary night when he was still neck and neck with Barnes, Rhodes acknowledged that, "anti-incumbency has clearly been a factor," but added, "I don't think it's going to be enough to bring me down to defeat."

Democrats nominated Sam Coppersmith, an aide to former Phoenix Mayor Sam Coppersmith. He ran as a centrist Democrat, favoring a Balanced Budget Amendment and a Line Item veto and labeled Rhodes's position on abortion "so extreme that it only makes sense that he wants to be the right-to-life poster boy." Coppersmith also vowed to clean up Congress, including seeking staff reductions and tagged Rhodes "an incumbent who bounced checks, who voted himself a pay raise and who abused the frank. He's someone who simply doesn't understand the challenges facing the district and is not capable of providing leadership." Rhodes in turn attacked Coppersmith's reform mantra, saying, "If you're interested in changing Congress, the thing for you not to do is send to Washington a Democrat who is patterned after the mold of people who are leading Congress."

Rhodes led an active retirement. He was heavily involved with the U.S. Association of Former Members of Congress and served as its president. Near the end of his life, Rhodes was "not happy that my party" was gaining a reputation for being "the party of no." He traveled to Afghanistan and the Ukraine to monitor their elections. Rhodes died in 2011 of complications he had suffered in an automobile accident three months earlier at age 67.

Rhodes presides over the House on "Former Members Day"
Image courtesy of C-SPAN

CHAPTER EIGHTY-FIVE

Reapportionment Pitted Bruce, Nagle and McMillan Against Colleagues

Introductory Tidbit: Maryland Congressman Tom McMillen literally spoke history. It was 1991 and the Persian Gulf War was nearing a surprisingly quick end. McMillen had been working out in the House gym and relaxing in the sauna was President George H.W. Bush who often frequented the Hill to visit some of his friends still serving in Congress. When McMillen saw the television reports that Iraqi President Saddam Hussein had surrendered, he asked the Secret Service if Bush had been informed. They replied "no" and granted him permission to go into the sauna to tell him. The president replied, Tom - that is truly great news and thanks for letting me know." Recounting that story to The Baltimore Sun after Bush died in 2018, McMillen said, "I've wondered how often someone has the opportunity to tell a president that a war is over."

Terry Bruce (D-Illinois), David Nagle (D-Iowa) and
Tom McMillan (D-Maryland) lost their seats to other
incumbents as a result of the 1992 redistricting
Images courtesy of C-SPAN

"Geography is destiny." Those words were spoken by Illinois Congressman Terry Bruce following his loss to a colleague, Glenn Poshard, in the March 1992 Democratic primary. Bruce was hardly alone.

1992 saw a number of Congressional incumbents leave office either by their own volition or scandal but, redistricting was the cause of demise for a number of others. A handful saw the new boundaries created – either by their state legislatures or a court and decided the odds of the new lines were too great to overcome. Others put on a brave face and went forward. A few, including a trio of mid-junior Democrats including Bruce, David Nagle of Iowa and Tom McMillen of Maryland, were pitted against other incumbents and lost, thus seeing their careers come to unceremonious ends (interestingly, all three served together on the Science, Space and Technology Committee).

Terry Bruce

Four-term Congressman Bruce was an example of the sky being the limit had it not been for redistricting as politics was in his blood. Just 26 when he won a seat in the Illinois Senate, Bruce was a natural who might well have had decades more to serve had reapportionment not reared its ugly head. His knack for walking the lines between competing liberal interests, while painstaking, was also laudable and he accomplished a great deal for the region he was so much a part.

Bruce is a faithful son of Southern Illinois. To this day, the small community of Olney, Illinois (the white squirrel capital), has been the only hometown he has ever known and the UI system was his only source of higher education, having awarded him his Bachelor's and J.D. While attending school, Bruce was a research analyst on farm issues for the U.S. Department of Labor and managed the legislative campaign of Phil Benefied who was defeated for re-election. He had also been an assistant to one of his Congressional predecessors, Democratic Congressman George Shipley. Bruce first ran for the legislature when incumbent Phil Broyles opted to retire and as he campaigned, his wife and small daughters often handed cookies to voters.

In the legislature, Bruce used geography to make his presence known. He and downstate colleagues were upset that Chicago had a stranglehold on the chamber and he and seven colleagues decided to do something about it. *CQ* noted "the downstate Senators blocked the leadership's choice for Senate President until their demands were met, including Bruce's elevation to assistant leader." On issues, he focused on the state's freedom of information act and collective bargaining for teachers but also saw 300 bills with his name become law.

Bruce was re-elected three times but in 1978, aimed for the U.S. House seat being vacated by Shipley. He was facing Dan Crane, the brother of suburban Chicago Congressman Phil Crane who, with another brother David challenging a Democratic incumbent in Indiana, had acquired the nickname in some circles, "the Kennedys of the Cornfield." Crane and Bruce argued over Social Security and the two sounded the year's increasing popular conservative themes while Bruce protested his excessive spending. He spent more than $350,000 which *The Decatur Daily Review* wrote, "is believed to be a record for a downstate Illinois congressional race." Bruce lost, though not badly, 54-46% (David prevented a trifecta by losing his race). Still, he evidently viewed Crane as secure enough that he instead decided to concentrate on his Senate duties (he did not have to give up his seat to run for Congress).

Then came the revelation in 1983 that Crane had engaged in sexual relations with a 17-year old Congressional page. The district had also been redrawn since the '78 election to exclude four counties that were GOP friendly while grabbing left-leaning Champaign. Bruce decided to try again for Congress and faced a five-way primary in an 18-county district. He presented himself as someone with "a record of a doer, of experience in action…It's easy to oppose everything. But the tough work of government is not opposing everything, but of getting things done." His main rival in the Democratic primary was Crane's 1982 opponent, attorney John Gwinn.

Bruce faced angry opposition from the Champaign County National Organization of Women who ran to his left called him, "an enemy of the Equal Rights Amendment." By carrying all of the counties in the Southern portion of the district, Bruce won with 37%. Gwinn won much of the rest, including Champaign where turnout was off the charts for Gary Hart who was seeking the Democratic Presidential nomination, and ended with 31%.

Crane had said at the outset that he didn't care which of his rivals emerged to take him on – "You could put all four in a brown paper bag and you'd see the same liberal rhetoric." But Bruce was the one with the political chops and he knew how to use them.

For all of Crane's problems, Bruce struggled to unseat him. Liberals weren't ecstatic that he was carrying their banner and, contending as early as primary night that he'd, "work very hard to mend bridges wherever they need mending," he had to reassure that wing that he'd be in their corner. At the same time, he criticized Crane for not passing a single bill, for being inattentive to issues concerning seniors and for failing to advance the cleanup of the dump at Greenup, often called the worst in Illinois. Near the end, Bruce forces accused Crane's campaign of selective editing by running an ad and leaving out Bruce saying, "No one should go to Washington and say, 'I'm proud to be a big spender.'" Around that time, his own ads began raising the ethics issue, calling Crane, "the only Illinois congressman to be censured."

With a big Republican year on the horizon, one well-placed Democrat offered he view that, "The only question is whether Reagan's coattails will be long enough to pull in Dan Crane. If Terry wins, he'll have to beat Reagan and Dan Crane." Whether that strategist accounted for Congressman Paul Simon beating U.S. Senator Charles Percy was not clear but Simon ran well in Southern Illinois from where he hailed and that made conditions salvageable for the rest of the ticket. In the end, Bruce only won five counties but Crane's margin in Danville and Coles (his home) was just two percent while Champaign came through for Bruce with 65% and he dislodged the incumbent 52-48%.

In Washington, Bruce was assigned to the Agriculture Committee, Education and Labor and Science, Space and Technology, all of which were well suited for the district. Agriculture was a perfect fit. Bruce owned a farm in Olney - 25 acres of tillable, 5 acres of hay ground and 10 acres of woods. His federal earnings were below $500 a year but to avoid even the appearance of a conflict of interest, he donated the proceeds to his church. At the start of his second term, he was named to the plum Energy and Commerce Committee.

Bruce was a major player on the Clean Air Act, specifically taking part in a group of nine that aimed to forge what appeared to be an intractable dispute between the panel's full chair, John Dingell of Michigan and his arch-rival, Henry Waxman of California. Given the district he represented, it was no surprise that Bruce got a taste of passions on both sides of the issue. Environmentalists, including his local Sierra Club, angrily rebuffed his efforts to forge a compromise and Bruce acknowledged he was in a no-win situation. "The environmentalists want me to be their champion," he said. "But no one wants to come back to his district and hear industry say, 'Hey, we're shutting down or laying off because of some new clean air law.'"

Throughout the whole clean air reauthorization, Bruce had no problem calling things as he saw it and, if that meant going after the powerful Dingell, so be it. In 1989, he and his Republican colleague, Ed Madigan of a neighboring district, chided Dingell for failing to adequately address their regional cost-sharing concerns. Bruce had introduced his own legislation that sought a balance. By May of 1990, Bruce had emerged as a key negotiator in at

SCOTT CRASS

least several areas that was making up the Clean Air Act of 1990. One was an amendment with Ohio Republican Mike Oxley to reduce the depletion of the ozone layer, which involved last-minute negotiations with sponsors of a similar amendment, Jim Bates of California and Sherwood Boehlert of New York that went to 5:45 a.m. the morning it was to be considered. It would aid companies such as Fedders Air Conditioning in Effingham, Illinois by phasing-out CFCs (chlorofluorocarbons) as opposed to doing it in a one fell swoop.

Photos courtesy of Terry Bruce

One thing environmentalists were happy about was Bruce helping to spearhead Archer Daniels Midland Co.'s plan to increase ethanol production in areas that included the corn rich 19th.

Another initiative was regulating commercials during children's programming and Bruce with a number of Commerce colleagues from both parties sponsored the Children's Television Act Which, thanks to a Reagan veto in 1988, took a few cycles to implement. Speaking on behalf of the measure as the Subcommittee on Telecommunication and Finance considered it the following year, Bruce said, "the road to deregulation under former President Reagan was usually bumpy but often beneficial, at least at first. However, as Congress and the administration drove toward deregulation, we oftentimes took wrong turns, and that is the case with the FCC's decision to deregulate television for children."

Bruce also sponsored the Food Quality Protection Act of 1991 and the Clean Coal Technology Efficiency Act of 1991. When Congress considered the nationwide base-closing recommendations, Bruce took issue with the commission's mechanism for deciding what bases would close. "The whole tone of the commission was based on manipulating data, changing ratings, fudging dollar figures and misleading both Congress and the public."

Trade was an area on which Bruce was perpetually leery and as Congress prepared to increase trade with Mexico (eventually becoming known as NAFTA), Bruce had no problem calling it a bad idea. Why? "My political assessment is that we're better off not to mess with GATT," and he introduced legislation calling for impact studies. Bruce also displayed hostility to trading with Japan, in part because he didn't see them as playing fairly. When the Bush administration wanted to sell six FSX planes to Japan, Bruce sponsored legislation to prevent it from going through. It passed but the 262-155 margin by which it cleared the House was far short of the margin to override a certain Bush veto. In the midst of his 1992 re-election campaign, he introduced a "get-touch" resolution aimed at Japan. He took part in trying to bring the Chicago & Northwestern Railway strike to a close and as he prepared to leave the House, his longtime colleague and friend said he "demonstrated extraordinary leadership in bringing that strike to a fair conclusion." Helping to bring a biotech research facility to UI was also something for which he was proud.

On social issues, Bruce had a liberal voting record, though not monolithically so (he was generally pro-life and opposed federal funding for rape and incest victims). But he did vote to override President George H.W. Bush's veto of a minimum wage increase and opposed the flag burning amendment. In 1991, Bruce had a ready retort for then-minority Whip Best Gingrich who was bemoaning the fact that three months was a long time to wait for Democrats to produce a balanced budget. Bruce replied that, "Four months was a long time to wait," for those trying to claim unemployment benefits. Mostly though, his vote was dependent on his district's interest.

Photo courtesy of Terry Bruce

After his first win, Bruce's next three actions were effortless - he won with 66, 64% and 66% respectively and the seat seemed safe as long as he wanted it. His downfall was that the 19th district wasn't going to be the 19th district much longer. Redistricting was going to cost Illinois two seats come 1992 and with a Democratic legislature and Republican Governor unable to agree on how to redraw the lines, the matter went before a panel of judges. Thus, Bruce became one of the surprise casualties from the map that resulted.

An initial Democratic plan would have left him safe and, even when the courts ended up drawing a map, he still has a district from which to run. The boundaries of the new 19th district were obscene. It ran from the Springfield suburbs down much of the state's Eastern side to the Kentucky border, annexing Macon County (Decatur) that was held by Durbin and Jackson County (Carbondale) where his two-term Democratic colleague and friend, Glenn Poshard was from. Poshard's turf had been sliced four ways but decided just before the filing deadline to mount a seemingly uphill bid to salvage his career.

Poshard to this day wishes there had been another way. "Terry was a good Congressman," he recalls, "and I think it caught him as unaware as it did me." In those kind of circumstances, it surprised no one that the campaign began as a race between two allies but quickly disintegrated into a slugfest.

For starters, Bruce pointed to "a record of accomplishment that Glenn Poshard just can't point to," but Poshard retorted, "I've had several of my bills wrapped inside other bills that have passed and he knows that." Bruce reminded audiences of his "100 percent voting record with organized labor." Poshard, conversely, "voted against organized labor one out of four times he voted." Bruce also hit Poshard's vote for the 1990 budget summit agreement that he opposed, contending they led to higher gasoline and telephone taxes ("You need to drive to work and everyone uses the phone"). Poshard's response was that the package contained child care subsidies that was needed for parents in areas with low income such as this. Bruce meanwhile crowed of getting a defense grant for Wagner Castings Co in Decatur.

Happy Holidays

- 1991 -

The Bruce family wishes you good health and happiness We hope to see you often in the coming year.

Terry   Charlotte
Emily   Ellen

Photo courtesy of Terry Bruce

Not only did Bruce dwarf Poshard in territory from their current districts but, through his Commerce seat, had a great deal more money on hand. Poshard at one point had $60 in his account. Just before the primary, Bruce had spent $300,000 compared to just $80,000 for Poshard, who responded by saying, "I don't worry about how much (he) is spending. We made our choice. He decided to take PAC money; I didn't." It seemed that in the year of Ross Perot, Poshard had a style of populism that voters found far more effective and he prevailed by an unexpectedly large 62-38% margin. Bruce won nearly every county in his old district 2-1 but Poshard exceeded 90% in many of the counties he was representing, which Bruce alluded to in his concession saying, "We couldn't crack the south (end of the district)." He called the loss "the awful part because I don't know what to do. I haven't lost a race before (as an incumbent)." The stroke of Bruce's father the weekend before made the loss especially sobering.

Once his term ended, Bruce needn't had to fret over being away from his friends because the position he accepted gave him great access to his former colleagues. He would be the lobbyist for the Midwest office of Ameritech Corp. In 1996, Bruce became CEO of the Illinois Eastern Community Colleges, a post he held for 23 years prior to his retirement in 2019.

David Nagle

Photo courtesy of David Nagle

The contest in Iowa's Second Congressional District was known as the, "Nagle-Nussle Tussle" and save for the At-Large Montana matchup between Democrat and Republican incumbents Pat Williams and Ron Marlenee, the pairing of Democrat Dave Nagle and Republican Jim Nussle had been a foregone conclusion longer than any of the redistricting battles that ultimately materialized. It also had one of the more surprising outcomes.

Iowa was among the early states to complete the redistricting process, in March of 1991. This was somewhat extraordinary for a state with a governor of one party and a legislature of another where a Congressional seat would be relinquished. A major reason for the ease was probably that both sides wanted a "fair-fight," and by merging Nagle, a fairly liberal three-term Democrat with Nussle, a very conservative freshman incumbent, that goal was certainly met. Nagle himself conceded following passage of the plan that, "you can do better, you can do worse. It's a fair plan" (he amended that in later years to say "God couldn't have won were he a Democrat").

From the time the new lines were unveiled until about the weekend before Election Day, the race was considered Nagle's to lose. He had run unopposed in 1990 while Nussle had surprised Democrat Eric Tabor for an open seat in the next-door Second District by a mere 1,600 votes, primarily because Tabor's family had been caught in a late breaking scandal involving absentee ballots. Furthermore, Nussle was viewed as a little right-of-center in a new district where Michael Dukakis would have received 55%. When one considered that 56% of the new district contained Nagle's constituents and just 35% Nussle's, the Democrat seemed to have it made. Yet Nussle was determined to make his presence known in Congress and succeeded.

When the House Banking scandal came to the forefront, Nussle wore a paper bag on the floor of the House to chide the veil of secrecy by not releasing the names ("it's time to take off the mask"). Nussle was admonished by the presiding House Speaker but it allowed him to bask in notoriety most members (particularly freshmen) could only dream. His membership of the "Gang of Seven," group of freshman Republicans that included future House Speaker John Boehner and future U.S. Senator Rick Santorum, enabled him to establish a niche as at least an ostensible reformer and his campaign treasury became flooded with nationwide donations.

Nagle, on the other hand had been a staunch defender of House Speaker Jim Wright in 1989 and had resisted the popular opinion in the House to subpoena the bank records of members, ("public opinion be damned,") an utterance that won praise from local newspapers but invited a devastating ad from Nussle.

Nagle was a political natural and it was easy to see why – it was practically in his blood. He "got hooked on it" via a friend during the 1956 presidential election. Despite the fact that Iowa was still a heavily Republican state, Nagle, then 13, supported Adlai Stevenson over President Dwight Eisenhower. His epiphany came during the 1964 presidential campaign. As he relayed to *The Gazette* 28 years later, "I listened to this discussion for about 35 minutes, and I remember raising my hand, and they called on me and I said, 'Why don't we rent a bus' and someone said that was a good idea, and I said to myself, 'I'm smart enough to be in this league.'"

Nagle was born in the town of Grinell, Iowa and attained his Bachelor's and J.D. from the University of Northern Iowa (it was State College of Iowa at the time). He commenced a practice in the town of Evansdale, then rose up to city attorney before becoming an the assistant county attorney for Black Hawk County. On its face, his time as chairman of the Iowa Democratic Party was not the most auspicious for the party – Republican Terry Branstad was governor. Nagle, however, arguably matched or even outdid the GOP as far as victories. The year Branstad was elected, Democrats won control of both chambers of the legislature and two statewide elections – Lieutenant Governor and Treasurer. 1984 saw the double-digit win of Tom Harkin for

U.S. Senator and the fifth highest showing in the country for presidential nominee Walter Mondale.

Nagle's most triumphant moment as chair was clearly the preservation of Iowa's influence come caucus-time and that required politicking, lawsuits and much political skill. If an award existed, he would easily be the recipient of an MVP in the fight to preserve Iowa's status as the first presidential caucus in the nation, a fight that continued at least through the 2012 presidential cycle.

The saga arguably began in 1980 when a commission headed by North Carolina Governor Jim Hunt assembled to look into to preserving Iowa and New Hampshire's impact on the presidential nominating process while also condensing it. The Commission recommended setting the calendar beyond the two states at 13 weeks and while Iowa would always be first and New Hampshire second, the Granite State was required to have an eight-day start on whichever state went next. The problem for 1984 arose when Vermont scheduling its "beauty pageant" the same day as New Hampshire, a development the Hunt Commission had initially not even considered a possibility because it was non-binding. To remedy that, New Hampshire moved the date of its own primary to February 27, just a day after Iowans were scheduled to caucus.

To Nagle and others in the Hawkeye State, this was a no-no as the odds of having influence with New Hampshire polls opening literally hours after the returns were counted in Iowa would be non-existent. This was confirmed by at least one respected member of the national press who told Nagle that, should he have to choose between broadcasting from Iowa or New Hampshire, he would choose the latter.

At a hastily convened state committee meeting, a measure was adopted to move Iowa's caucus to February 20 if New Hampshire didn't budge which is indeed what happened. But not before a lawsuit was heard mandating Iowa return to the 27th. A judge dismissed that because campaigning by the candidates was well underway but the Democratic National Committee was still looking into reprisals. In fact, as late as April, it wasn't even certain that the DNC was going to seat the Iowa delegation at the National Convention in San Francisco in July, or even provide hotel rooms. Nagle promised if that happened, "we'll stay in an adjacent community and commute to San Francisco." In this instance, all's well ended well.

In 1986, Nagle decided to seek the open Third District Congressional seat being vacated by Republican Cooper Evans. The main areas were Cedar Falls, Waterloo, Marshalltown and Iowa City where the University of Iowa was located. He had certainly accumulated many chits throughout his time as chair but still had to fight his way through the primary against House Majority Leader Lowell Norland who seemed the frontrunner. Differences on the issues were few but style was night-and-day. Nagle promised, "I can be more aggressive on behalf of the state than Lowell and I think that's what the state needs. The state has to adopt the characteristic of fighting. I've been involved in political battles and I've been successful." In contrast to past Congressman, Nagle vowed to, "not be the sort of laid-back, traditional, sit-in-the-back-row kind of person the district has been in love with before." Norland's base was near the Minnesota border and he claimed an ability to attract rural voters and Republicans. He had more money on hand but Nagle had endorsements and prevailed 50-43%.

Then came November. On paper, it seemed that a Nagle win in the general election would be a political miracle as no Democrat had held the seat since 1934 – and that was for but a single term. The farm crisis clearly played a role but so did a gaffe from his opponent that garnered him immense ridicule. John McIntee had penned a letter to President Reagan that suggested farmers keep their crops outdoors during the winter months, a suggestion that predictably garnered serious derision among farmers. The witty Nagle responded by telling audiences, "I know what it is to pick corn, and most of all, I know when to pick corn." Nagle accompanied that ribbing with a pledge from House Majority Leader Tom Foley to place him on the House Agriculture Committee and defeated McIntee 55-45%.

Two years later, Republicans put up a verbally stable candidate but Nagle had been hard at work on the hustings – on at least one occasion more than key allies thought he should be. Monfort was a meat-packing plant owned by ConAg with many employees in the district and at one point during the year threatened to ship jobs overseas. Allies in labor had warned Nagle not to intervene but he didn't listen, and "had a heck of a confrontation." He hauled representatives from ConAg into his office and promised to be "very difficult to deal with under these circumstances." That was all they needed to hear as two days later, Nagle received word that the workers were getting a new contract. He took an eye-popping 63%. It was no wonder Republicans couldn't find a breathing body to take him on two years later.

**Nagle delivering a response to Ronald Reagan's
Saturday Morning Rdaio Address
Photo courtesy of Dave Nagle**

Nagle put maximal exertion into serving his district (*The Gazette* called him, "hyperactive"). That did not always sit well with colleagues, particularly very senior ones. Foley did come through with the Agriculture assignment but Kika de la Garza of Texas, likely wished he hadn't, at least initially.

De la Garza was the full committee chair and Nagle's initiatives might have gotten under his skin. One was saving the Farm Credit System. According to Nagle, there was a reason it reached that point. "Everyone had a plan and no one had the same plan." Nagle had learned in a transition meeting with Evans that the System was broke and in order to begin pumping back at least some life, it would be loaned $600 million instead of $5 billion. Nagle brought the matter to Speaker Jim Wright who reviewed it and immediately called de la Garza to his office. Handing him the memo, Wright ordered him to have it reported within two weeks. When de la Garza replied that it would be virtually impossible, Wright told him if it's not done, "we're probably not going to have time to get any of your legislation through the House." While De la Garza suddenly acquiesced, there was a final wrinkle. In reviewing the conference report, Nagle's staffer Susan Keith noticed that the chairman had excluded a Texas bank from the reforms. As Nagle looked back later, he recalled, "If I wasn't already in trouble, he sure as hell wasn't going to be happy" with him with this twist. The result was that when it came time to negotiate the farm bill in a House-Senate conference committee, De la Garza left Nagle off – one of just three of the panel's 27 Democrats to not make the cut. Be that as it may, Nagle had rectified a stubborn long-term problem in a matter of months, prompting a senior Democrat on Agriculture, Charlie Rose of North Carolina, to one day call Nagle "my Moses."

There were signs of a thaw in the relationship as the years went on as de la Garza did place Nagle on a drought conference committee. Whether the thaw continued in perpetuity is a different question. Still, shortly after Nagle was defeated, *The Gazette* wrote, "Taking their lead from the chairman…many of the staffers complained that he unnecessarily delayed hearings by badgering witnesses and proposing numerous amendments." Thaty view might have extended across party lines as Nagle was also viewed as having frequently "badgered" Agriculture secretary Ed Madigan. Nagle Staffer Tom Raftis acknowledged his boss "rubbed some people the wrong way" but that it was a central factor to his effectiveness. Indeed, that same *Gazette* article quoted Mike Hall, a noted foreign-agricultural trade consultants in Washington, as calling Nagle's loss, "really a shame. Those people don't know what he's done for them. They couldn't."

Beyond that incident, Nagle's style did little to diminish his effectiveness. With help from Majority Leader Richard Gephardt, Nagle won funding for the Avenue of the Saints, which emanated from St. Louis, Gephardt's hometown, to St. Paul.

Nagle was a reliable liberal. He opposed the Balanced Budget Amendment, contending it would "devastate Iowa, cause a national economic depression and fundamentally alter the constitutional balance between our three branches of government." He also combined an Iowacentric focus with national/international issues that were not always mutually exclusive.

One was providing the food aid to the Soviet Union which would benefit Iowa farmers and he showcased his ability to bring together disparate groups who had common goals. He told high school students that, "If we do help them and we do give them a chance and we do see that they have adequate food, the demilitarization, economic reform and political reform can probably continue" and he wrote a bill to do just that. Convincing the Bush administration was another story as they did not initially view food aid as a priority, which Nagle called "incredible. What we have here is the equivalent of a grain embargo." Convincing colleagues on either side of the aisle wasn't a walk in the park either.

Photo courtesy of David Nagle

Initially, House Majority Whip David Bonior refused to whip (count votes) on the package because he wanted Bush to introduce a domestic stimulus package first. Nagle's reaction; "If Bush wasn't going to introduce a stimulus for America, he sure as hell wasn't going to" propose one for Russia. Still, one person who was not opposed to an aid package was Speaker Tom Foley and he asked Nagle to lead the effort.

With Democrats divided, Nagle needed Republican votes and the man tasked with producing them was Minority Whip Newt Gingrich of Georgia and Gingrich was reporting to Nagle that each day, Republican support was eroding. Ever the quick strategist, Nagle reached out to the candidates seeking the Democratic nomination for president convincing them that, "Bush will either do it or if you win the presidency, you'll have to do it." That pitch got everybody but California Governor Jerry Brown on board. Nagle also assembled a coalition of roughly 125 interest groups to conduct a ferocious lobbying effort, groups with priorities so disparate that *The Christian Science Monitor* wrote many "seldom are found working on the same side of issues on Capitol Hill." The Freedom for Russia and Emerging Eurasian Democracies and Open Markets Support Act of 1992 passed on August 6 by a vote of 255-162. Like many Congressional signing ceremonies, Nagle, albeit proud of his work, did not attend. He was content with the effort he had put forth behind the scenes.

Defending Iowa's interests often meant castigating the Bush administration and increasing the use of ethanol was a key area. Nagle authored the Relying on Ethanol for America Program Act which had three co-sponsors across the aisle (Leach, Republican Pat Robert of Kansas and Democrat Lane Evans of Illinois) and worked on assisting Archer Midland with ethanol from corn and blamed "regulatory roadblock," when Archer was forced to abandon the mission due to difficulties with the administration. At roughly the same time, the administration was blocking a pork sale which Nagle also found loathsome. He told the Iowa City Area Chamber of Commerce, "It was almost as if the Bush administration had set its sights on Iowa and decided that they were going to deal us a couple of major body blows." It was no surprise that in 1990, Nagle's presidential support score was just 20%. He also authored the Soybean Graduated Equity Loan Program Act of 1990.

In addition to Agriculture, Nagle managed to win a seat on the Science, Space and Technology Committee in the face of unusually fierce competition. The space shuttle Challenger disaster had occurred almost a year to the day early and many junior members sought the assignment due to the oversight that would be occurring. Nagle won a post in part due t the prominence of the University of Iowa Physics Department where legendary space scientist James Van Allen was based. The committee was where the bureaucracy of NASA was often in his wrath even though he was a firm backer of their missions. Disturbed by what he viewed as sweetheart deals by the Bush administration, Nagle wanted accountability when it came to awarding contracts for space programs. "This has such a curious history, we ought to ensure that we have competition." He opposed the Advanced Shuttle Rocket Motor. His crusades led Bill Nelson, a Florida colleague who once undertook a mission to space to playfully label Nagle a "pitbull." From that panel, Nagle also opposed Pennsylvania Republican Robert Walker's amendment mandating that operators of government contracts certify that their workplace was "drug-free." Nagle said it would create a "police state."

On most issues, Nagle was a traditional lunch-pail Democrat, solidly pro-choice and labor and backing most of the party's priorities (family leave in 1990 was an exception). In one of Capitol Hill's strangest but not unheard of alliances, Nagle teamed up with arch-conservative and the very pro-defense Republican Robert Dornan to place a one-year moratorium on the Depressed Trajectory (low-flying) Ballistic Missile, so long as the Soviet Union did the same. They were grouped together by Robert Sherman who formerly had worked with Congressional Democrats promoting a nuclear freeze and Nagle's philosophy, as he said later was, "whoever fires second is lost." Lawmakers agreed 262-160.

Depending on what side one was on, Nagle either shined or stunk during the Wright affair. He argued that members who were advocates of getting the matter behind them is "outweighed by the recognition that the Speaker has a right to a hearing. It's in the hands of the lawyers and the process has to play itself out." As the saga transpired, he hosted meetings with other members in undisclosed settings and it was at one, on May 17, that most attendees concluded, as one put it, that no one in the inner circle realized he was in that much danger" (Wright announced his resignation ten days later).

Then came the match-up – the Nagle-Nussle tussle. Nagle certainly had the geographic advantage on paper but Johnson (Iowa City) and Marshall Counties were removed from the district and they were Democratic areas that were precious. On the other hand, four counties that Nussle had lost in 1990 had been dropped from the new lines. In short, the wisdom was that only a galvanizing issue could win the seat for Nussle. Congressional reform proved to be that issue.

One was Congressional mailings - Nagle ranked 6th in the entire House on franking and Nussle was 169th. Nagle himself had only four overdrafts totaling $605 but Nussle hit him with the insider label "The fact that Dave Nagle initially claimed that he didn't even use the House bank and then had to admit to bounced checks raises legitimate questions of honesty and credibility." Nagle did trash the insider label but decried the "vicious character assassination and personal attacks" that he was subjected to.

Nussle took a narrow lead on Election night and while Democrats expressed hope that Bill Clinton, who was running strong in the district, might pull Nagle through, he did not. Iowa had been voting heavily against a proposed ERA amendment and that clearly worked to Nussle's benefit (it also helped pull another Republican incumbent left for dead, Jim Ross Lightfoot, across the finish line). The final margin was a 2,970 vote win for Nussle, 134,536 to 131, 570, which came out to 50-49%. Nagle, calling Nussle, "the apparent winner," conceded just after midnight, three hours after polls had closed. It certainly was not a race of class. At a press conference the day after the election, Nussle gave his defeated rival the salutation, "Ex-Congressman Nagle," even though his term wouldn't end until the coming January. Roger Runningen, who had served as press secretary to Secretary Madigan responded to Nagle's defeat with, "Good, and that's for the record."

Nagle, who had told supporters as he was conceding that, "I'll see you down the road," wasn't long into his involuntary retirement when he decided he'd like a rematch two years later. Initially, Nussle appeared to be in, what *The Wall Street Journal* called "deep political trouble" for holding up aid following the devastating Midwest floods of 1993, so much so that well into '94, his was among only a handful of GOP held seats rated a "tossup." Nagle did his best to grab the edge and in early summer, did lead within the margin of error. In one debate, he painted Nussle as, "the most partisan member in the House of Representatives." And attacked him for fostering "gridlock…When you block health-care reform … government hasn't been listening," Still, Nagle was out of office and that greatly hampered his ability to raise money and eventually, this race, like many others, got caught in the partisan trend of the year, which ultimately meant Nussle roared to re-election 56-42%.

After leaving office, the publicity Nagle endured was not always favorable. As he flirted with a political comeback, he was arrested for intoxication and sentenced to a half-way house (a sentence he called "absolutely appropriate"). At that time, he said, "Three of the greatest days in my life were the day I married (current wife) Deb, the day I adopted (8-year-old son) Matt and the day I got stopped this last time, because this stop the last time forced me to confront this." There would be another occasion but Nagle has had his sobriety for over a decade.

Nagle was in the midst of seeking to challenge Nussle again in 2002 he lost the primary and resumed his behind the scenes role. The end of the decade found him again continuing to defending Iowa's first in the nation primary against state's that wanted to "frontload." He now practices law in Waterloo.

Tom McMillen

**McMillen testifies at a Congressional committee (left) and with future
Vice-President Al Gore (right), one of among eight members of Congress
with whom McMillen briefly purchased an island in the Caribbean
Photos courtesy of the University of Maryland**

Most politicians acquire fame when they come to Washington. Tom
McMillen did so before he even finished high school. Having graced the
cover of *Sports Illustrated* in his senior year and an Olympian shortly thereafter
followed by a successful college basketball player and member of the NBA,
McMillen might have had the most celebrated teenage years and 20s of
virtually any future Congressman. The fame did not stop when he became a
member of Congress. At 6'5, McMillen is believed to be the tallest member
of Congress ever and his website points out that "at 6 feet 11 inches, he is
two feet taller than Maryland Senator Barbara Mikulski, who is believed to
be the shortest representative ever." Unlike other Democratic colleagues from
Maryland, however, McMillen did not tower over the redistricting process
and that proved his downfall in 1992.

Philosophically, McMillen's classification as a "raging moderate" was
absolutely credible. His stance on issues weren't always hand-in-hand with
liberals but, they seemed to suit his constituents fine.

Marylanders don't always take kindly to outsiders but McMillen's early
years in Elmira, New York were mitigated by his ties to the area via his time
at the University of Maryland and as an NBA star for the Washington Bullets.
And that McMillen ended up at Maryland at all did not come without drama
and an immense family tug of war.

The family had resided in Mansfield, Pennsylvania and McMillen was already a star basketball player at his high school who had been appointed to the President's Council on Physical Fitness and Sports, the youngest person to this day to sit on that highly coveted panel. He swears that the only "B" he earned resulted from an anti-war teacher seeing his picture in *The Washington Post* with Richard Nixon.

By the time college selection came rolling around, McMillen's brother wanted him to follow in his footsteps by going to Maryland where he had played basketball, another brother wanted him to attend Carolina while his sister was urging him to study at her alma mater, the University of Pennsylvania. As if that weren't enough pressure, the coach at the University of Virginia had formerly taken the reins of a team in McMillen's hometown. As decision-time neared, McMillen remembers "the coach of Virginia was sitting in my house the night before. Dean Smith from North Carolina was calling from Europe every hour. It was pure chaos" (Smith had been seeking him out since the ninth grade). McMillen chose Maryland on the day registration was closing and never looked back ("It turned out okay").

UM had a new coach that year, Lefty Driesell and he and McMillen led that first season to a 16-0 showing. McMillen's stardom in fact led to a through the roof demand for tickets that ultimately was rectified by creation of a University television station, WMAL. His teammates respect was immense – they called him, "Senator." McMillen's major was Chemistry which, proved challenging for pursuing his extracurriculars. Still, he recalled, "Lefty would tolerate me because I had labs in the afternoon and I would often show up late for practice." Once he achieved his B.S., McMillen was awarded a Rhodes Scholar and went on to Oxford for his Master's in administration.

The it "turned out okay" was certainly debatable in September of 1972. McMillen was part of the U.S. Olympic team competing in Munich, Germany and they seemed poise to keep the gold medal in American hands until geo-politics intervened. The U.S. team had chipped away at a ten-point deficit to trail by just one with three seconds on the clock. U.S. member Doug Collins was fouled by a Soviet player and proceeded to take his free shots, one of which landed in the basket. Collins then took the second shot and the Soviets called time out which appeared to be too late given that the ball was in the air. With Collins having made the shot, that seemed to be the game until, as McMillen recalled to *The Wall Street Journal*, the Soviet time-out was ruled valid and a German announcer told the audience and the world, "Ze game is not over, put three seconds on ze clock." The Soviets now had another shot but missed and very few could dispute that the game was over. Only the Soviets tried – and succeeded.

Again, Olympic officials claimed a clock malfunction, another shot was given to the Soviets and again, the ball went through the net. The game was declared in favor of the Soviets but, feeling cheated, the U.S. team declined to accept the Silver medal. McMillen recalled, "The terrible irony is that the Germans had taken great pains to erase every trace of the 1936 Olympics in Berlin, which had been a showcase for Hitler. A few days before the games we had visited Dachau, one of the sites of the concentration camps."

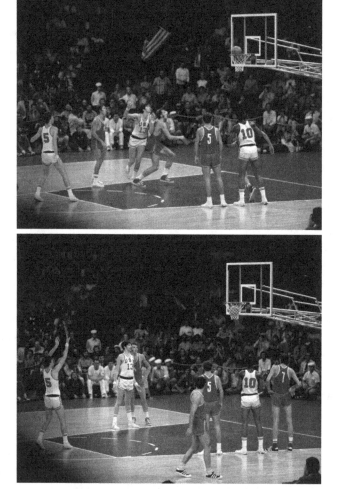

Photos courtesy of the International Olympic Committee (IOC)

Near the 44th anniversary of Olympics '72, McMillen expressed to *The Baltimore Sun* that the result was preordained. "When you have 18-year-old kids playing against pros and the world getting better, it was only a matter of time." As if past is prologue, McMillen noted, "the cheating still gets back to the same old issues. There is a lot of commonality cycle to cycle."

After Maryland, McMillen was drafted by the Buffalo Braves and the Virginia Squires but he opted for the Braves. He played 11 years for the Atlanta Hawks, a team owned by Ted Turner. By the mid-1980s, he was getting the Congressional bug and he asked Turner to trade him to Washington and this proved one instance of something actually going as planned. McMillen managed to be traded for Randy Wittman that he labe "the first political trade in sports."

In 1986, Maryland's Fourth Congressional district came open when 14-year GOP incumbent Marjorie Holt announced her plans to retire and McMillen decided to run for the seat. He squeaked into office by 428 votes (65,071 to 64,643).

The cliffhanger at the ballot box made perfect sense. Beyond the fact that the Fourth had been held by Holt, it had given Reagan 59% in 1984. Plus, Neall was not some random candidate. As a member of the state House of Delegates for twelve years, he had risen to become Minority Leader and pushed through pension regulation. McMillen, he said, was a "carpetbagger."

Election night was nip'n'tuck. Prince Georges County gave McMillen a solid 71% and Howard 56% but they were only slivers of the district. Anne Arundel County was the population heft and Neall grabbed 55%. When the votes were in, McMillen told his supporters they had secured a "triple overtime victory" and "I want you to know that in every team I've been associated with, we have a great record in overtime."

Like a true basketball player in somewhat unfriendly territory, McMillen's popularity at home was in part fueled by operating in center court. He was solidly pro-choice but, unlike the majority of his party, backed the Balanced Budget Amendment and the Bush capital gains cut. To prove you can't take the boy out of basketball, he proposed legislation with Senator Bill Bradley of New Jersey (the other Rhodes Scholar/NBA player in Congress) and New York Congressman Ed Towns entitled the Student Right to Know Act. It required each higher education institution to report how many students awarded scholarships for a respective sport actually obtain their degrees. His reasoning: "Our young people must understand that athletics alone will not sustain a life."

McMillen also conducted hearings on the integrity of the NCAA and in 1990, introduced The Collegiate Athletic Reform Act Act. Fueled by anger over NBC being given the rights to cover Notre Dame games, McMillen's bill provided a five year exemption for football and basketball from federal anti-trust laws in order to restructure, which meant, among other things, establishment of a Board of Presidents. Throughout this time, his voting attendance was nearly spot on – by 1991 he cast 2,050 consecutive votes which led *The Baltimore Sun* to call him, "the Cal Ripken Jr. of the Maryland Congressional delegation."

On the Gulf War, McMillen supported the Solarz/Michel resolution giving the president the authorization to use force against Iraq. "There is no evidence indicating that sanctions will succeed in achieving this goal. Once we extend the deadline, the force of sanctions will be lessened, as Saddam will demobilize his military, conserving his resources and precious spare parts for the next deadline...Certainly Iraq will be hurt if sanctions are extended, but the economic dislocation to the free world of extending the deadline will be astronomical." McMillen did say he was, "praying that Hussein will back off before the deadline." Opinion was obviously mixed and, "my town meetings on the Gulf War vote had turned into shouting matches, and I knew I would get grief from my constituents for my vote." That prompted him to ignore an early morning call from the White House shortly after the vote from Bush thanking him (the call was placed from Camp Spring in his district). The two did later manage to connect.

With two years to learn the ropes of his district, McMillen rebounded like a good basketball player in 1988, winning a second term with 68%. 1990 saw slippage but his 59% came against a more credible foe, Robert Duckworth, and after backing the unpopular budget summit package. After that election, he got a committee assignment he needed to raise cash (mostly in the form of PACs) for the battles ahead: a seat on Energy and Commerce from which he sponsored the Medicare EKG Payment Restoration Act of 1991. McMillen did accept honoraria but gave every cent to charity.

Then came redistricting. Had McMillen run in anything remotely resembling his current turf in 1992, he would have probably scored a three pointer in winning re-election. Only the recalcitrance of a governor of McMillen's own party, William Donald Schaefer, who insisted on protecting the seat of Republican Helen Delich Bentley, caused his career to go out of bounds.

Unlike Illinois and Iowa, Maryland was not losing a Congressional seat. The challenge was drawing a required second minority-majority seat when all eight incumbents would be seeking re-election. McMillen was the early target and fellow Democrats Steny Hoyer and Ben Cardin, in tandem with most of the delegation, circulated a plan that would defeat him and spare Bentley, which McMillen called, "backroom dealings." They ultimately succeeded but, with the playing field so heavily aligned against him, the surprise was not that he lost but that he came so close to hanging on.

McMillen had a powerful ally in Senate President Mike Miller and initially got the plan of his dreams in the Senate. The map that body passed 33-9 would have made his district more Democratic by siphoning off a small portion of Anne Arundel (coincidentally heavily GOP precincts) while carving up Baltimore County into five. The latter did not go over well with Baltimorans who booed him at a public redistricting forum. It also put the tensions with his fellow Democrats out into the open. When McMillen accused Cardin of trying to sell out Baltimore to defeat him, Hoyer and another Maryland Democrat, Beverly Byron, struck back, with Hoyer calling it, "unfortunate Tom chose to go to the papers on this, particularly when I think he was inaccurate in his representation."

The euphoria over passage of the Senate plan proved, alas, too short. House of Delegates Speaker Clayton Mitchell, Jr., objected and with GOP support, steered through the body a plan 89-13 that would pare McMillen against Bentley in a district that would decidedly favor the Republican.

Uncertainty reigned in the days ahead. The Governor's Advisory Commission came back with a recommendation that Schaefer called, "very unfair" and McMillen did little to help his cause when he questioned "how much longer a woman of Mrs. Bentley's age (she would be 69) will remain in Congress." More so, Bentley allies were energized. A last ditch effort was made by Miller to give McMillen Cecil County but Mitchell objected because his hometown of Crofton was split. After the map cleared, McMillen said, "The process was designed more for political protection than what's good for the state." It was easy to see why. 57% of the new district was in the First District currently represented by Republican Wayne Gilchrest.

Considering all of his options, McMillen toyed with running in the new black-majority 4th district but quickly drew fire from African-American leaders and other Democrats. He decided to challenge Gilchrest, an iconoclastic high-school teacher who prided himself on his pick-up.

McMillen did have a primary and State Representative Samuel Johnson II in particular hoped his solid base on the Eastern Shore could make a dent in McMillen (another legislator, John Astle, was in the race as well). While the 55% McMillen ended up with was not a slam dunk, it was only March, early enough for him to put all of his resources toward November.

The advantage of McMillen's height seemed to extend to his fundraising - he outspent Gilchrest 4-1 and one publication labeled him, "flash and cash." But Gilchrest was not impervious to the ways of Washington. He sent out districtwide mailings after bemoaning the process and reversing himself on term limits.

The Baltimore Sun reported that the Gilchrest campaign, capitalizing on McMillen's overseas trips, portrayed McMillan as, "a slick jet-setter awash in special-interest money from political action committees." One memorable ad showed, "More sushi, Mr. McMillen...Box of Saltwater taffy, Mr. Gilchrest?" Gilchrest's wife accused McMillan of hiring a private detective to spy on the family and McMillen, referring to the vituperative tone of the race said, "Wayne started it. Anybody who watched me in the NBA knows if I'm punched, I punch back." But some critical interest groups, including the Sierra Club, were sidingwith Gilchrest.

The day of the vote, McMillen got 58% on the turf he was previously representing, a 16,000 vote margin while Gilchrest got a 25,000 vote and 60% margin on the Eastern shore, where voters listened to his plea to elect, "one of us." That was ballgame. The final numbers were Gilchrest 120, 084 to McMillen's 112, 771 or 52-48%. On an otherwise exhilarating evening for Democrats, McMillen essentially amalgamated the two portions of his professional life in conceding defeat. "I've been a competitor all my life. And when you give 100 percent you have to feel good about it...I'm just sorry I couldn't be part of the Clinton-Gore team by being in Congress."

In fact, McMillen would deliver for Clinton-Gore in a bigger and arguably bigger role. In early 1993, Clinton named McMillen chair of the Presidential Commission which he viewed as going full circle because, when Nixon appointed him, he was not only a kid but a junior member of the commission. This role made Clinton very accessible. He was on the Maryland Board of Regents for seven years and is now President and CEO of LEAD1 Association, which represents the athletic directors and programs of the Football Bowl Subdivision.

CHAPTER EIGHTY-SIX

For One Brief Shining Moment: Cox and Horn Confounded Experts by Winning but Adverse Remap Prevented Them From Replicating it

Introductory Quote: "I don't think it has tainted me yet. Maybe you get in one term here without being accused of selling out to the process." –Freshman Illinois Congressman John Cox on his desire to reform the House

Photos courtesy of the U.S. House of Representatives Collection

In a year of immense turnover, two freshman Democratic incumbents lost their bids for re-election in 1992. While the initial wins of John Cox of Illinois and Joan Kelly Horn of Missouri two years earlier were pegged as flukes (Cox's was in fact a massive upset few saw coming), both got caught up not by the anti-incumbent fervor that swept the nation, but by the politics of reapportionment which went against both in big ways. Despite these very adverse circumstances, both Cox and Horn seemed to be at least slight favorites in their re-elections at varying points in the campaign, including as late most of October which made it likely that had either lawmaker gotten a slightly better hand, both may well have been seated in the 103rd Congress and served alongside a Democratic President.

John Cox

Cox brought bold idealism to the district - opposition to the death penalty, a determination to right the federal budget deficit even if it meant raising taxes, and an overall staunch resolve to do what was right consequences be darned. In his sole term, even adversaries would have to agree that he practiced what he preached.

Cox was the first Democratic Representative of the 16th District of Illinois since 1850 when Abraham Lincoln was still practicing law at the other end of the state in Springfield. In 1912, the district did turn to a Progressive, William Hinebaugh but only for a single term. By 1990, Rockford had also been trending in the Democrats direction, having opted for Charles Box as Mayor a year earlier and many of his consultants eagerly began assisting Cox.

The 16th district of Illinois was on the Wisconsin border and Cox himself was born in the state, in Hazel Green. He graduated from the University of Wisconsin and earned his law degree from John Marshall Law School. Cox was a veteran serving in the Army during Vietnam after and taught at Loras College. His most recent position before running for Congress was as the Jo Daviess District Attorney and his anti-capital punishment stance led him to promise to resign rather than carry out the death penalty (he was never put in that conundrum).

In 1990, the current Republican occupant, Lynn Martin, opted to challenge U.S. Senator Paul Simon for re-election (and lost nearly 2-1) and Cox entered the Democratic primary race to earn what seemed to be the right to lose in the November general election. But even the primary was no foregone conclusion.

Even though Cox was Jo Daviess County State's Attorney, he only won a low turnout primary with a very small plurality, 33-31% over teacher and school board member Stephen J. Eytalis and 25% for Dixon Mayor James Dixon. Eytalis's base in Winnebego, the most populous of the eight counties, made him a force to be reckoned with and he did carry his home turf but Cox was clearly aided by *The Chicago Tribune* who tapped him, "for his years of responsible public service in municipal and county offices." State Representative John Hallock won the Republican primary 54-46%, an unexpectedly narrow margin over restauranter Donald Manzullo, who relied on zealous support from anti-abortion organizations (he was strongly pro-life and homeschooled his kids).

After that, the district's rigidness for conservatism suggested that Hallock would not have been out of line for measuring drapes in his Congressional office. Except that a little thing called ethics and scrupulousness would prevent him from ever having a Congressional office.

As the year went on, Hallock encountered at least twin bouts of devastating publicity and it's hard to know which proved more damaging. One was a very messy divorce while the other was the revelation that he had been ticketed for driving 107 mph, a charge he initially denied by saying that his automobile could not detect a speech that exceeded 85 mph (he eventually pled guilty to driving 95 mph which brought along a $300 fine).

Even with Hallock's faux-pas, few thought he was anything other than at least a decent favorite to win. He thought he could make up for any ground Cox had shaven off by mocking his rivals own platform, which included trimming down the federal budget to pay for the S&L debacle and taking money from the Social Security trust fund to address problems of big cities. That led Hallock to accuse Cox of wanting to throw money at, "Washington, Detroit and New York City" and the candidate recalls driving around the district to see billboard after billboard with his name connected to tax hikes. While it did turn out that Hallock had to answer for his own votes to raise taxes in the legislature, he still tarred Cox's spending proposals as out of the mainstream saying, "I personally believe that my view is the same as most of the people in the district. He has advocated five tax increases so far. I don't believe people in the 16th District are making that request."

By September, Cox commissioned a poll that showed his deficit at only seven points with both men under 50%. To make up ground, he was urged to go negative and respond by invoking Hallock's personal woes. The Democratic Congressional Campaign Committee (DCCC) even composed an ad attacking Hallock. Cox studied the ad and discovered that it contained distortions and told the staffer that he would not be running it (the man hung up). Instead, Cox pounded themes home with precision. Tapping a theme that would later work so well for another newbie who made Illinois his home state, Barack Obama, Cox questioned whether experience was truly a plus. "I suggest to people that it is the experienced legislators serving in Washington today, working with the experienced members of the administration, that have gotten us into the mess,"

The view that Cox couldn't win evaporated on election night when Cox thumped Hallock with a solid 55-45% victory. Cox had 56% in Winnebago and 64% in Jo Daviess and carried seven of the district's eight counties, falling short only in Lee. The 500 supporters who gathered with him on election night were ecstatic. Cox was as well. "Tonight proves that hard work and telling the truth, and telling them where you stand on the issues leads you to victory," before also adding that it was, "more than a victory of a political candidate. It is a victory of volunteers and staff."

One factor Cox felt aided him was the fact that Rockford was the population center and Jo Daviess hugged the Iowa border. That might have given him an affinity with the manynon-Rockfordites. Also, while it is unlikely that the climate that was generally against Republican lawmakers that year could have been enough for Cox to prevail, he had that on his side as well. Only later was it realized that Hallock was complacent, perhaps somewhat understandably given the district's partisan bent but also to the point of being cocky. Campaign signs with his name that had been given to him to personally distribute to supporters were found in the trunk of his pickup.

In Congress, Cox got right to work for his constituents. He opened three district offices and won seats on the Government Operations Committee and Banking, Finance and Urban Affairs. His record was generally liberal but, aside from questioning the spending associated with some legislation (such as a 1992 jobs bill in Banking that he voted to "get out in the open"), he backed the Balanced Budget Amendment, NAFTA and term limits.

The fearlessness he displayed on the trail even extended to the halls of Congress, and that meant intimidating very powerful colleagues who were part of the system. When Congress came under heavy fire for ethics, Cox was outspoken about the need for reform. Saying many members make it to Congress by resorting to, "a campaign process that is obnoxious and totally unacceptable to me," Cox quoted House Speaker Tom Foley as calling it, "risky business to get into. 'My opinion is that the structural problems around here are so bad, let's take the risk.'" This did little to hurt him back home. *The Chicago Tribune* called Cox "one of the most thoughtful and conscientious members of the Illinois delegation." And Cox's activism did not rub all of the big fish in Washington the wrong way. Ways and Means Chair and fellow Illinoisan Dan Rostenkowski genuinely liked him. Cox called him Dan (which brought guffaws from colleagues who thought protocol meant they address him as, "Mr. Chairman") and actually asked him to speak against legislation Rostenkowski was shepherding through the House floor. It turned out that Rostenkowski actually opposed the measure and was simply doing perfunctory bidding for leadership on the House floor, and he was more than happy to give Cox five minutes to argue against it. Rostenkowski ended up voting for the measure but colleagues were awe-struck about what Cox had accomplished.

Cox had made his arrival in Washington and for future years, political stardom awaited. All he had to do was stay there. Rostenkowski liked to align his panel with loyalists and he needed to fill the void being left behind by Marty Russo, another Chicago-area lawmaker and remap casualty who had lost in the March primary. Beyond that, U.S. Senator Paul Simon had told Cox that when his term was up in 1996, he was likely to retire and he his wife Jeanne would publicly endorse Cox. The kicker was that he had to hold his House seat until then. Enter 1992.

In 1991, state Democrats devised plan that would have preserved the base of every Democratic incumbent except the aging Frank Annunzio. Given the geography of the 16th, Cox could not have been able to count on re-election in perpetuity, but his vulnerability in such a GOP stronghold would have been substantially eased. But Republicans had ideas of their own and their plan was enacted by the court. It moved a sizable portion of deep-red McHenry County that had been represented by arch-conservative Republican Phil Crane into the new district. Adding insult to injury, the new map removed areas that Cox had worked hard to cultivate, such as Whiteside County which was trending Democratic (it was placed in safe Democrat Lane Evans's district but might have made a difference for him given his perilously close shaves in the late 1990s). The expectation was that Cox would face Jack Schaffer, a moderate and well-respected member of the legislature in November but Manzullo again stunned everyone by upsetting him for the nomination. Cox proposed his own economic blueprint which called for a gasoline tax hike of 25-cents a gallon.

Cox hung onto Winnebago 51-49% and was able to count on a big margin in Jo Davies (57%) but took just 35% in McHenry. Manzullo won 56-44%. Cox told upset supporters, "We leave here tonight sad of course but recognizing the good that we did. We really challenged people." Two days after the election, *Rockford Star* political editor Chuck Sweeny opined that, "Cox never answered Manzullo clearly. Instead, he ran a series of grainy, obscure ads in which he talked regally of his high principles. What I wanted to know was why I needed to have my gasoline taxes raised a quarter of a gallon. And his commercials didn't tell me."

Cox flirted with attempting a comeback but wisely decided that 1994 was not the year for a Democrat in a politically adverse district. He continued practicing law. Meanwhile, Democratic leaders, very respectful of what he accomplished, tapped Cox to speak to incoming freshmen.

Cox was introspective on his loss. He told *The Star*, "I ran the type of campaign I wanted to run. I behaves like the kind of person I said I would in Congress and I have no regrets." Cox's press secretary Mary Ann Pressman was even more blunt in her assessments. "Two years ago," she said, "when John ran for office, he said, 'I'm going to go out there and tell it like it is and I may end up being a one-term Congressman. It's that's the way it is, so be it.' I guess the 16th District is not interested in hearing it like it is."

Joan Kelly Horn

Horn knew she was on the bubble ever since her 54-vote victory over two-term Republican incumbent Jack Buechner (Beek-ner) was confirmed a good month after the election, and was a mid-upset in that most analysts expected Buechner to retain his seat (as the polls opened, she thought "we had a chance"). As such, she was rated the most vulnerable incumbent for almost the entire two-years in which she served in Congress.

Horn was a professional political consultant whose firm worked on the campaign of Democratic Congressman Robert Young, whose 1986 re-election loss to Buechner set the stage for her 1990 challenge to him (she had actually flirted with doing so in 1988 but party leaders preferred another candidate, Bob Feigenbaum, who went on to lose to the incumbent spectacularly – 67-33%. But she has held non-elected jobs at the St. Louis Housing Authority and the St. Louis County Office of Community Development. She also chaired the Missouri Women's Political Caucus and the Freedom of Choice Council where she was steadfast in promoting abortion rights. When she decided to mount a bid against Buechner, most expected it would do wonders for her political resume but little for her Congressional ambitions. They were wrong.

Advertising was in Horn's blood – literally as her father was an executive. She grew up in University City and graduated from Visitation Academy. She was in the midst of taking classes at St. Louis University when she dropped out to get married and eventually, have six-kids. In the 1970s, she returned to the University of Missouri and earned both her Bachelors and masters in Political Science.

Horn fended off two rivals, including an anti-abortion Democrat, with 65%. The general election was infinitely tougher. The race was messy and Horn deployed creativity that reflected her talents as an ad consultant. She labeled Buechner "the Pinocchio of the Potomac." She ran an ad showing pigs playing in the mud for his "trips to the public trough." "More sushi, Mr. Buechner." Another ad opened with the words, 'Oh Jack, Paris is so beautiful," to inform listeners that Buechner was taking his girlfriend to Paris on the taxpayers dime. "No, honey. I'm not missing anything important. Just some silly old savings and loan votes" (Buechner replied that he had attended the Helsinki Commission Human Rights Conference and missed "preliminary" S&L votes because he was robbed in the France capital).

As a divorced mother of six, Horn assured the working-class that she knew what it was like to struggle. Voters did not here most of these ads for much of the campaign. Instead, her campaign made the strategic decision of waiting until the final 10-days to air them, judgement *The St. Louis Post-Dispatch* said, "took some discipline...To afford that, Horn said, she had only a small field operation and scrimped on some other costs."

There were other openings, albeit smaller. Horn produced a letter from a would-be constituent from Maryland Heights which showed Buechner appearing to contradict himself on his support for the Stealth Bomber. In one correspondence, Buechner had vowed to "continue full funding" while in the other, he promised to "carefully review this program..." Horn also was critical of Buechner for lackluster efforts to have radioactive waste removed from Lambert Field. Meanwhile, Horn did not highlight the abortion issue because a fair number of voters in St. Charles County were Catholics who were staunchly pro-life.

Horn garnered the enthusiastic backing of *The St. Louis Post Dispatch*: "Two-term incumbent Jack Buechner has told voters to ignore rhetoric and look at the record. But his record shows a sad lack of support for family issues, badly needed cuts in defense spending, abortion, health care and civil rights. His Democratic opponent, Joan Kelly Horn, would be a newcomer to public office, but she has a long record of interest and involvement in public affairs and concern for Americans who too often were neglected during the Reagan years. Voters who favor policies that will help reverse the trends of the 1980s should elect Joan Kelly Horn." Buechner gave Horn major ammunition when he agreed to support the budget summit pan that Congressional negotiators had worked out. That went hand-in-hand with an earlier vote for a Congressional pay raise and one Horn radio ad slammed him for that and backing, a budget that raises the taxes on working people" and "to cut your Medicare you depend on." Buechner not only did little to rebut this, but, curiously, in an anti-incumbent year, he reminded voters of his lengthy legislative portfolio and that Horn lacked, "elective or appointive government experience of any kind." One of the few times he mentioned Horn was to accuse her of distorting his record saying, "Joan Horn talks a lot about ethics; maybe it's time she practiced some."

In fundraising, Buechner led Horn by a sizable margin. The day before Election Day, he predicted that he'd hold off Horn 62-38%. It didn't take long for the counting to get under way to prove that he had miscalculated.

The result was a true nailbiter. Horn led most of the count, including 51-49% with 58% reporting and, when every single vote was tabulated, Horn stayed ahead, but by a mere 52 votes (94,300-94,248). It was inevitable that a recount would take place and Horn vowed to supporters, "we're not going to pop any champagne bottles until the recount is in." On how she was able to achieve the outcome: "There may be some anti-incumbency feeling out there, but I think we said some things about ethics, about performance, being on the job, representing the people paying your salary, about jobs and working people." The recount narrowed the margin somewhat – to 48 votes, and by mid-December, it grew to a landslide 54 votes, at which time Horn said, "We are pleased that one more step - I should say the final step - is out of the way." Buechner talked about trying to force another election but, in late January, abandoned those efforts due to lack of cash. Meanwhile, Bush had told Buechner that he "felt personally responsible for your loss" presumably referring to his budget summit vote. In a race that close, that was no doubt the pivotal factor.

In office, Horn concentrated on local issues and her committee assignments that left her well positioned to deliver. They included Public Works and Transportation and Science, Space and Technology along with Select Children, Youth and Family Services). Harriet Woods, a former statewide candidate, praised Horn for getting, "a running start by focusing on the right kinds of issues and the right kinds of committees, rather than spreading herself around too thinly and trying to make herself lovable." But personality did count. *The Post-Dispatch* said that others have used to describe Horn were "conscientious," "diligent" and "cautious" describe Horn.

Protecting McDonnell Douglas Corp., a major St. Louis employer topped her list and she got $75 million earmarked to a defense bill for worker retraining in the event of job loss, which seemed very likely when the Navy's A-12 was cancelled. She fought for a light rail appropriation for the city and to preserve the pensions of TWA workers. Near the end of the term, she was able to get the Page Avenue extension into Creve Coeur Park by way of a pipeline bill. Horn wanted to "open the federal government to people" and she met with social service agency heads. She made herself accessible and visible to her constituents, often visiting post offices to meet them.

At the same time, Horn made good on her campaign pledge to donate her pay raise to charities (which bizarrely had been attacked by Republicans for being illegal under Missouri law), in this case to the Salvation Army in St. Charles County and Alternatives to Living in Violent Environments.

Horn knew that she was on borrowed time at the moment she was sworn into office but, she probably couldn't have expected that it would be harder on allies were undermining her. But 1992 was a redistricting year and prior to Buechner's loss, he, Dick Gephardt and Bill Clay, who represented the other two St. Louis precincts, had devised a remap that was palatable to all three. Horn's victory upset the apple cart. Gephardt, who in 1990, had posted a less than astronomical re-election margin, was thinking about running for president in the future and did not want to have to struggle on his home turf. Clay represented the solidly Democratic 1st District but, it had to pick up turf due to the loss of population and Clay didn't really like to campaign to boot. Horn's presence was more of an aggravation. It's not that her team didn't try. At one point, her husband presented a map that she felt could suit the political realities of all three (she wanted to pick up more of St. Louis) and Horn got most of the female Democratic members if the Missouri legislature to sign a letter urging that she be accommodated but, to no avail. The result was that Horn surrendered a number of reliably Democratic precincts to Gephardt and thus entered the race of her life.

The GOP had a spirited primary to take on Horn and State House Minority Leader beat George H. "Bert" Walker III, the cousin of the sitting president. Talent won 58-32% and entered the fall campaign with a devoted contingent of "Religious Right," activists, primarily those who opposed abortion.

The general campaign did not lack for visibility – Horn and Talent debated roughly a dozen times. And though pigs were absent from the airwaves this time, it was no less dirty. Talent tried to tar Horn with being a part of the unpopular Congress but her response was, "Having been there just

22 months, I really don't think I have to take responsibility for the excesses of the past." While Horn reminded voters she was not part of the "funny business that had been plaguing Washington," Talent made political hay out of one ongoing debate that may have stuck: support for a Balanced Budget Amendment that Horn was for before she was against. When Talent charged in a debate that Horn either, "changed her mind or somebody changed it for her." Horn vowed "to make it very clear to Mr. Talent that no one makes up my mind for me but myself." Instead, she credited the language amendment for her change of heart and noted that she did back another version. But what gave Talent's charge more resonance was that she had initially co-sponsored the legislation.

On other issues, Horn spoke of "family friendly policies" and tarred her rival not only for his abortion opposition but for being against "right-to-die" legislation in the legislature. In the closing days of the campaign, the NRA ran ads targeting Horn, primarily for her support of the Brady Bill. After the election, she called the tactic, "very frustrating, because you feel totally helpless against it...You don't really know what it is, or where it's coming from." One fundraiser she had featured "Peter, Paul and Mary."

Like 1990, Horn started out ahead on election night but this time, fell behind as the count went on. After about five hours with the clock at midnight, she sent supporters home, telling them, "I don't want you to stay all night; the numbers don't look good...I don't know how we'll pull it out." She carried St. Charles 50-47% but lost St. Louis 51-47% and Talent won by 9,000 votes, 50%-48% (157,594-148,728).

In 1996, Horn thought she could rewrite history and unseat Talent, by then, also a two-term incumbent as Buechner had been but, by that point, the district was unquestionably Republican and she lost 61-36%.

Horn continues to teach at Washington University and take involvement in causes dear to her heart.

In 1990, the only other Democrats whose wins were more stunning than Cox and Horn's were Bill Orton of Utah and Dick Swett of New Hampshire. They lived to survive another term though eventually, they too saw the partisan leans of their districts sweep them up. In reality, the climate of 1994 would almost certainly had sent Cox and Horn to the exits. But they would have served two terms instead of one and, they would have served under a Democratic president. An overzealous redistricting precluded that from happening but, it doesn't take away the fact that, though their service was brief, their service was great.

CHAPTER EIGHTY-SEVEN

Riggs and Nichols Rare Freshman Republicans To Be Shown The Door In '92 – And Under Distinct Circumstances

Introductory Quote: "Much of life is in our mental attitude. If you think great things might happen, they do. If you question them ever happening, they won't!" –Dick Nichols who was referred to as an "incurable optimist" throughout his life.

Riggs and Nichols were the only Republican frosh elected in
1990 who failed to return to Congress two years later
Photos courtesy of the U.S. House of Representatives Collection

Just as two Democrats elected to the House in 1990 laid down their seats after one term (see prior chapter), so also was the case with their GOP counterparts. Dick Nichols of Kansas and Frank Riggs of California.

Riggs was the only member of the reform minded "Gang of Seven" to lose re-election in 1992. That had to have stung both himself and his colleagues but, fortunately for Riggs, his time on the outside looking in wasn't long.

Two years later, he became the only one of the 110 members who had left the House in 1992 to return. Riggs picked up exactly where he left office only this time, he found himself in the much more enviable position of serving in the majority.

That Riggs was even a member of the 102nd Congress was seen as a fluke. All through the fall of 1990 when he was seeking to topple four-term Democrat Doug Bosco, he was given virtually no shot of prevailing. The district was heavily Democratic and Bosco was fairly popular. Instead, Riggs earned himself a say in some pretty heavy-duty debates. One of his first votes was on whether to send Americans to war and one of his last was impeaching a Commander-in-Chief.

Bosco had long been caught in the middle of the battles between the Hatfields and McCoys of the First Congressional District – the hard-core environmentalists and timber interests and once expressed the fine line he was walking by quipping, "Everyone likes trees. Some like them vertically and others like them horizontally." His inability to please both sides led to the presence of an unusually strong Peace and Freedom candidate, Darlene Comingore, who was poised to siphon votes from Bosco's left but not nearly enough to deny him re-election. The second factor was the emergence of the Savings and Loan scandal and Bosco's link to two of them. Riggs accused his rival of "consorting with scoundrels but Bosco had led Riggs by intimidating margins as recently as a week before the vote. Another factor was the budget stalemate that forced Bosco and his colleagues to remain in Washington until ten days before voting and Democratic Congressional Campaign Chair Beryl Anthony acknowledged Bosco pleading to get done because his campaign was "in very serious jeopardy."

On Election Day, these confluence of factors caused Riggs to sneak by Bosco. With 52% of precincts reporting, Riggs led by three points, 45-42% before Democratic areas helped Bosco close the gap, but not enough. The difference was 3,000 votes, 43-42% as Comingore polled an unexpectedly high 15%, a margin so close that Bosco did not concede (by telegram) until the Thursday after the election. He acknowledged that, "It is safe to say there is a very active liberal community throughout the North Coast and their disaffection with me wasn't a secret." His ultimate vote for the package may have been the final nail in the coffin – it contained a tax on wine that was anathema to parts of the district. Bosco did carry Humboldt County but by a microscopic margin and besides Lake, managed to eke out a win everywhere else. Mendocino County was evocative of Riggs's predicament.

Riggs garnered just 40% but with Carmingore grabbing 21%, the incumbent was relegated to just 38%.

Just as Riggs's win was unconventional for his district as a Republican, so was his profile for the district. Born in Louisville, Kentucky, he moved to San Rafael, California at age 17. He served in the U.S. Army as a military police officer and earned his degree from Golden Gate College. When he finished, he became a police officer in Santa Barnara and later further up the coast in Sonoma, followed by an FBI agent (his wife was a fellow officer). Riggs then left the force to open a real estate firm. When he decided to run for Congress, his only political experience was a stint on the Windsor School Board.

The glory of the office belonged to Riggs but so did the distinction of being perhaps the most marked-man in the House. In his first weeks in office, he stunned many by being one of just three House Republicans to oppose the authorization of force against Iraq, a decision he kept close to the vest until the last possible moment as he gathered any last bit of information. "under these delicate circumstances, I'd probably be better advised to commit my thoughts and feelings in a *Congressional Record* and a personal letter to the president." In that letter to the president, Riggs explained that "I had to vote my conscience and beliefs."

While the district's numerous anti-war contingent hailed Riggs's vote, Democratic leaders were circumspect. Jim Wolner predicted his "true colors (as a Republican") would come out. It took in some cases years and his Congressional hiatus but his bona-fides After calling the Congressional pay raise "obscene," he reversed himself upon taking office and decided to accept it, at least until he could pay his campaign debts. At the time of his election, he was pro-choice and voted to overturn the "gag" rule. He also vowed to decline timber related contributions, stating accepting it might, "diminish my credibility and compromise my ability to resolve the ongoing controversies with respect to both those issues on the North Coast."

Riggs was a stalwart Republican in the minority in that he did what members in the majority party do: he railed against the majority. One example was a one minute speech he delivered as the House leadership Mr. Speaker, if the Republicans ran the House, we would not even be thinking about going home next week for adjournment until we had enacted an economic growth package... because we realize on this side of the aisle that it is pure hypocrisy and very, very mean-spirited politics to extend unemployment insurance benefits without enacting an economic growth package that would create jobs for those folks when their extended unemployment insurance benefits expire.

I wonder if my colleagues on the Democratic side of the aisle intend for those folks to remain permanently on welfare.

In the wake of the bank scandal, Riggs saw reform as a way to cultivate voters and became a member of the "Gang of Seven." But he was embarrassed by the revelation that he had three bad checks and the local press took him to task. "When it's other members of Congress bouncing checks, it's because they're crooks and bums who ought to be thrown out of office. But when Frank Riggs bounces checks, it's the House bank's fault." His bid for a second term was quickly approaching.

Riggs worked with Rick Santorum of Pennsylvania (left) and John Boehner of Ohio (right) who would eventually achieve national recognition
Photo courtesy of the Library of Congress Prints and
Photographs Division Washington, D.C.

Had Bosco had his way, he would have been the person to take Riggs out. He was preparing to do so until it was revealed that he had 124 overdrafts at the House Bank. Instead, the nominee went to Dan Hamburg, a former member of the Mendocino County Board of Supervisors. There was a Peace and Freedom candidate on the ballot but it became obvious early on that he would not be nearly as strong as Carmingore two years earlier. Hamburg won 48-45%. The morning after the election Spencer Abraham, at the time a top aide for the National Republican Congressional Committee (NRCC) singled the seat out as one where Bush's anemic 1/3 of the vote in the district made an uphill slog mission impossible for Riggs. "I don't think he lost that," he told reporters. "I think the district made it real hard." His departure was felt by Republicans from coast to coast. Bill Paxon and Susan Molinari of New York later called his loss "the biggest disappointment on election night" and said "we want Frank back." But it wasn't a given that he'd run in 1994 and in fact he appeared to pass until just ten minutes before the filing deadline. On his reversal he said, "I have unfinished business back there."

Riggs accused Hamburg of environmental extremism, instead saying, "I say jobs first, not earth first." Hamburg took Mendocino and Sonoma by the barest of margins – 20 and 56 votes respectively, but Riggs won by bigger margins everywhere else to reclaim his job 53-47%. Riggs was assigned to the plum Appropriations Committee on his return engagement which, even at a time his party was pitching fiscal leanness, couldn't hurt his attempt to convert a few votes in this swing district. He also became a stalwart "Contract With America" supporter.

By 1996, the national climate again left Riggs in grave trouble and the unpopularity of House Speaker Newt Gingrich was a prime reason (the Capitol Hill newspaper *Roll Call* in analyzing his vulnerability joked Riggs was "already preparing for a '98 rematch"). His opponent was Michela Alioto, the granddaughter of a colorful former San Francisco Mayor. Alioto, 27, had been paralyzed from a skiing accident" as a teen. But she had fallacies as a candidate, chiefly not remembering towns in the district, not having voted in four previous elections and having moved from the district from San Francisco and had not paid taxes.

Riggs had the noose of Gingrich around his neck and tried to walk a fine line ("he helped me raise money but he knows that I have to be an independent voice for a very independent-minded district"). Riggs did declare that, "I agree wholeheartedly with Newt Gingrich that the best thing we can do for our children and grandchildren is to balance the federal budget and replace the welfare system with an opportunity society that rewards hard work and self-reliance."

Riggs was named to the "Dirty Dozen," and Steven Krefting of the Sierra Club said the organization, "believe(s) that Frank Riggs has one of the worst environment voting records in the House." But he was assigned to sponsor the pre-election minimum wage bill that cleared Congress and was signed by President Clinton, a perfect way to trumpet his moderation.

The nationally known murder of Polly Ann Klass in Petaluma in the district took a role in the campaign. Alioto opposed capital punishment and the Riggs campaign Polly's father asked the Riggs campaign to cease.

When the votes were counted, Riggs won every county but Mendocino for a 50-44% win and credited the win to "a lot of hard work over the last two years." He said residents "want and need stability and continuity of representation in Washington."

Riggs sensed that his days were clearly numbered. State Senator Mike Thompson, whom the Democrats had tried to recruit to oppose him in '96, indicated that he'd make a bid and Riggs began toying with a run against Democratic Senator Barbara Boxer. He announced his candidacy in February on a platform "to repair and rebuild the moral fabric of American society. We have balanced the budget and eliminated the federal deficit. Now we need to address the moral deficit. We must teach our children that there is nothing more important than personal morality, that the truth matters and character counts." Her evidently viewed abortion as an impediment to morality as he had done a complete 180 on the issue. Crediting his son's enrollment in a Catholic school, Riggs declared himself newly pro-life.

While Riggs's supporters included John Doolittle, one of the most conservative members of the House, his entry date gave him little time to blunt the head start of two rivals, one very rich (car magnate Darrell Issa) and another with a strong political footing (Treasurer Matt Fong). Consequently, Riggs withdrew in April stating, "The time has come to admit the obvious. My late entry into the race has made it exceedingly difficult, if not impossible, to be competitive with my Republican primary opponents." Riggs still managed 5% in June's primary and nearly 300,000 votes.

Riggs closed his career by voting to impeach President Bill Clinton on a count of perjury under oath. Undecided almost until the end (just like the Gulf War vote), Riggs's view was that," The truth was on trial. This vote showed we are a nation of laws and not a nation of kings."

Riggs eventually relocated to Arizona and tried his hand at politics there. He won a multi-candidate primary for Superintendent of Public instruction by 259 votes but lost to Democrat Kathy Hoffman 52-48% in November.

Dick Nichols of Kansas was the only other Republican elected in 1990 who failed to win a second term and unlike Riggs, the culprit in his case was not the partisan dynamics of his district but the fact that in the aftermath of the remap, he no longer even had a district.

Another distinction with Riggs was that Nichols was not a novice politician and the race that finished him off came in the primary in a safe Republican district rather than the general election. But the duration of his tenure upon his election was expected to be equally short, mostly because of the reapportionment that was going to be costing Kansas one of its five House seats. It was almost a foregone conclusion that the seat to go would be Nichols whose central Kansas turf was easy to parcel out among its neighbors. That's exactly what happened.

Nichols was a pro-choice and pro-business Republican. His biggest notoriety in life might have come in 1986 when he was in New York City observing the 100th anniversary of the Statue of Liberty, having donated money for its restoration. As Nichols and his wife were riding the Staten Island ferry, they were mugged by a homeless refugee and sustained injuries that required hospitalization. The Nichols's were visited by New York Mayor Ed Koch who joked Nichols "spent more time consoling me." Johnny Carson invited him to appear on "The Tonight Show" as a result.

Nichols's early years were commensurate with that of a Western Kansas youth. Born in Fort Scott, Kansas, he served his country as an ensign in the Navy during World War II, then went to Kansas State University. Calling college, "a diversified maze of subjects and materials," Nichols had a hard time settling on a major but finally chose Agricultural Economics and Technical Journalism (those around him say he was the Wildcat's biggest fan throughout life). While Nichols was information counsel to the Kansas State Board of Agriculture, banking proved his professional cup of tea. He became President of the Home State Bank in 1986 and President of the Kansas Bankers Association. In 1986, Nichols sought to become GOP Chair for Kansas. He told *The McPherson Sentinel* on his 50th anniversary in banking that he was like a kid before Christmas when he spotted an ATM machine in Spain and "I saw how it worked and I told my associates, we've got to get us some of those ATM. Technology started gradual, but it's developed pretty dramatically at times. We had some old, cumbersome processes."

Nichols's opportunity to run came in 1990 when six-term Republican Congressman Robert Whittaker announced his retirement. The main population centers in the district were Emporia, McPherson (Nichols's hometown) and Pittsburg. Whittaker alluded to the future redistricting as a factor in getting out but his frustration for the long-suffering minority also played in. The district was heavily Republican so it was clear that the winner of the primary could start measuring drapes in his/her Congressional office.

Predictably, the field was a six-person donnybrook and most of the candidates were nearly half Nichols's age. Shelia Bair was the longtime legal counsel for U.S. Senator Bob Dole who himself had served part of the district when he was a Congressman. Doyle Talkington was the governmental affairs liaison for the National Pork Producers Council and Ed Roitz was a former State Senator. Farmer Kent Hodges and teacher Bill Otto were also in the race.

Nichols benefitted from his connections across the district but also from the fact that he wasn't much of a target of the other candidates. His philosophy: "We don't need people in government who say, 'Spend less,' then turn around and spend the most... The campaign required Nichols to borrow $150,000 of his money though he also raised roughly that same amount from friends. He campaigned on a platform of balancing the budget, term limits and deficit/debt reduction.

Nichols carried only the three western counties in the sprawling district but by big enough margins to squeak past Baer by fewer than 700 votes, a margin of 29-28%. It was while giving a radio interview nearly five hours after the polls closed that Nichols was told Baer had conceded. The race was so tight that Connie Nichols compared it to the birth of a baby. "We were pacing back and forth – we wanted to deliver a candidate to you. And we've just gone the full nine months." He beat the Democratic nominee, ex-State Senator George Wingert with 59% in the fall.

In a one-minute 1991 speech on the House floor, Nichols lamented the relative prosperity of the 1980s and said, "The tax policy of the 1980's was a key factor in U.S. economic growth during the past decade. It did not simply benefit the rich at the expense of the poor, but, rather provided a better way of life for all classes of Americans." With that in mind, Nichols introduced legislation to repeal the luxury excise tax that had been part of the controversial 1990 budget summit package. Reminding the House that Beech Aircraft manufactures boats, Nichols said, "The purpose of my bill is not to protect the rich. It is to restore and preserve the jobs of working men and women in this country who produce these goods and revitalize the industry they work in which have been severely and negatively impacted.... The purchase of these items may be a luxury to the purchasers, but to the men and women producing these goods their jobs and salaries are a necessity. It is not fair to punish working men and women who produce goods simply because they produce goods Congress labels as luxuries."

Nichols's single term coincided with the exposure of the many perks that enraged ordinary citizens. "Late one night, I walked along East Capitol

Street in the mist with Connie. We stopped, marveling at the Capitol at night looking up at that gleaming alabaster dome in the dark, with the intense spotlights on it. And I felt the greatness of America, and of the challenge facing me, and the privilege to serve my country, and I was choked with emotion. After being in Congress 15 months. I'm still choked with emotion, but, for a different reason. The abuses of power, the arrogance of Members, and the disgrace of Congress give us all reason to choke with emotion. Somehow, the idealism and the struggle and the desire to make this country great has bogged down in the muck and the mud of politics. Somehow, Congress has lost touch."

One way for Congress to get back in touch was a Balanced Budget Amendment and as Congress prepared to vote, he told the chamber that he had left his wife's bedside in Kansas following breast cancer surgery with her blessing because, "Connie and I decided I should come back to Washington to speak for the people of my State because this issue, more than any other, symbolizes the reason I decided to run for Congress and the frustration of the people of Kansas."

Nichols opposed Wichita Democrat Dan Glickman's attempt to create the Flint Hills National Monument in his district, fearing overreach. "While I fully support developing the land privately," he said, "there is no role for the Federal Government in this project. The people of my district, in a survey with over 15,000 votes returned, actually oppose this by more than a 2-to-1 margin. The surrounding landowners do not want Uncle Sam taking their land at some point in the future as he surely would. The National Park Service does not want the land, and the Federal Government cannot afford to maintain the parks it already owns."

As a person, Nichols was known for his inherently sunny disposition. He calls himself "an incurable optimist" which those close to him could attest to. His second wife Linda once said he could get into an elevator with a stranger and have that person practically eating out of the palm of his hand. She said "On one of our first dates, we drove to where he liked to park and it was full so he said 'no problem, I'll drive around the block and we'll come back and it will be available,' and it was. I thought he was so naive with his positive nature." Nichols would have to be positive given what lay ahead.

Almost immediately upon winning the election, it became the least concealed secret in Kansas that Nichols was in for a short tenure. The state's population loss had come from the more rural part of the state and with control of Kansas state government divided between the parties, it was assumed that the most junior member would be the one to be sacrificed. That is sure enough what happened though Nichols put up a hell of a fight.

The new map placed McPherson with fellow Republican Pat Roberts, a senior Republican member of the Agriculture Committee who was entrenched in the sprawling Western Kansas first district. Much of the other communities from the Fifth landed in the Second Congressional District that was held by Democrat Jim Slattery. Nichols never toyed with challenging Roberts and found another Democrat Dan Glickman of Wichita, a more enticing target. Though Glickman's re-election margins rivaled those of Roberts, he was tarnished by 105 overdrafts at the House bank and with support from national Republicans, Nichols went for the challenge. State Senator Eric Yost had other plans and with support from Wichita's vocal anti-abortion activists, he entered as well. Complicating Nichols's efforts was the candidacy of Richard LaMunyon who like Nichols was pro-choice.

Of the 11 counties in the district, Nichols carried five but, with the exception of Harvey, all were relatively small. Yost carried five of his own including Sedgwick which contains Wichita and cast 38,000 votes and won there with close to a majority (LaMunyon eked out Kingman County). Districtwide, Yost prevailed 45-34%, then lost to Glickman 51-42% in the fall. Nichols was content. He told *The Wichita Eagle*, "I had two years. I went in endorsing the idea of citizen legislatures, where people come from private business or industry or farms, serve a period of time, and then come home...I suppose if I mulled it over repeatedly, you could get very depressed about it. But actually it was a competitive election and a fair election, and I had some recognized disadvantages and some hurdles that were pretty high."

Once his term in Congress ended, Nichols would have little time for mulling anything over. Nichols Kansas Bankers Association and as commanding general of the Kansas Cavalry, a state economic development agency which focused on recruiting businesses. Retirement was not exactly stress free. Connie Nichols died of breast cancer in 1992 and a son preceded him in death as well. Nichols remarried Linda Hupp in 1996 and died of respiratory failure in March 2019 at age 92.

In 2007, Nichols told *The McPherson Sentinel* he "was once described as Jimmy Stewart in disguise. It (Congress) was what I expected — a very gripping, all-consuming 24 hours a day job. I always had a thought that this is a great nation that helped me enjoy a great life. I felt I owed some public service and I believed in basic American values."

Nichols died in 2019 at age 92.

CHAPTER EIGHTY-EIGHT

Citizen James Was Happy To Leave Congress After Two Terms – On His Own Terms

Introductory Quote: "Hey! What am I doing here? Talking to myself?" –House Ways and Means Chair Dan Rostenkowski when freshman Congressman Bill James interrupted a conversation with another member and dragged that person away.

Photo courtesy of Florida Memory

Craig James was without question the biggest upset House winner in 1988 and four years later, among the most surprising retirements. In between, he worked hard to shrug off the "accidental Congressman" label, succeeded in overcoming a very stiff challenge for a second term and along the way, compiled an unpolished style but voting record that appealed to all sides. Perfectly fitting for someone who was a registered Democrat until just before deciding to run.

While no one could dispute that James's win was due to ten-term Democratic incumbent Bill Chappell's ethical embattlement, the fact is, it wouldn't have materialized had the Republican uptick in voters been any slower. As it was, his 791 vote margin over Chappell was hotly contested.

James was born in Augusta, Georgia along with his twin brother, Gregory. He attended the University of Florida but received his B.S. from Stetson University before receiving a J.D. from the same institution. He served in the National Guard and U.S. Army Reserve. DeLand, Florida became his hometown and with Greg, purchased a fern farm in that town. He also started a general law practice though it would be a mistake to tag him a general lawyer. He was indefatigable and *The Orlando Sentinel* wrote "he once threw himself onto a courtroom floor to re-enact the stomping a client had suffered."

The motivation for James to seek a seat in Congress came from his law partner, James Clayton but, when he announced that he'd be taking on Chappell in Florida's Fourth District, few noticed. Chappell after all was a powerhouse in the region. As Chair of the Appropriations Subcommittee on Defense, he was responsible for lucrative contracts. That also proved his downfall as Chappell became the target of an investigation of a Pentagon procurement bid-rigging scandal.

The district was comprised of Flagler, Putnam and St. Johns Counties and parts of Clay and DuVal. He faced two fellow Republicans in the primary and cleared the 50% needed to avoid a runoff by a handful of votes. James ran an ad labeling Chappell "an embarrassment." His name didn't hurt. "You've heard of Craig James the football player? No connection. But he's a good football player, and I'll be a good congressman."

Most folks on both sides believed Chappell's ethics by itself would not have been fatal even with George H.W. Bush winning big districtwide (he took 63%) and they were likely correct. James himself admitted weeks out "the only reason I have a chance at all is the monumental issue that man created all by himself." The 5'7 James was also dwarfed by Chappell's fundraising edge and his budget was tight. Going into the vote, James did not think he would prevail. What no one expected was the surge in GOP registered voters. By Election Day 1988, the Republican registration had increased nearly five percent from 1984, to 39.6%. That was exactly the margin of error but even that wasn't apparent until the absentee ballots reported. When the actual machine votes had been tallied, Chappell had led but both sides held their powder until the absentees were tallied. They typically lean Republican and when the counting finally ceased two days later (there was a holdup in DuVal),

James was in front by 727, losing only Putnam. Suspecting the closeness of the margin he implored his folks "If you have to hire a special team to guard the ballots, do that." It wasn't paranoia. Chappell contested the election for weeks.

In particular, Chappell took aim at "irregularities" from Flagler County, a charge James dismissed as "utter nonsense" and urged Chappell to end his career with "dignity." The Florida Supreme Court temporarily granted Chappell's request to bar Flagler officials to certify their election returns, but only in order to give Chappell more time to make his case. In getting to work on his response, James joked, "I'm back into the practice of law whether I like it or not. I take one final case — my own." When the Court ruled in mid-December that Flagler officials had "substantially complied," James was officially Congressman-elect. He would be working out of Washington D.C., a city he had visited only twice in his prior 47 years. Unbeknownst to virtually anyone, Chappell at that point had been seriously ill with cancer that would claim his life less than three months after leaving office, leading many to question why he even sought another term. Incidentally, the Republican surge was felt around the state. Republican Cliff Stearns rivaled James for biggest "upset" status by stunning Florida House Speaker Jon Mills to win the seat Democratic Congressman Buddy MacKay left behind to seek a Senate seat. Statewide, MacKay led until the absentees put Republican Congressman Connie Mack in front. He was assigned to the Judiciary and Veterans Affairs committees.

Getting acquainted with Capitol Hill was an adjustment – for James as well as his colleagues. As a free-wheeling lawyer, he was not accustomed to being constrained by legislative protocol. Near his first six months in office, *The Orlando Sentinel* wrote "bombastic, feisty, and half-mad are some of the descriptions bandied about by detractors on the Hill."

One method for James to earn these adjectives was taking on the perks common within the institution. James, who never used the House gym or took a foreign trip, was not shy about saying Congress "is not supposed to be a professional office" and took steps nearly from day one to make that happen. One of the first orders on James's docket was rejecting a pay-raise because," as a freshman Congressman, I think that would interfere with what I have said and what I want to accomplish my first two years…" Months later, James proposed a Constitutional Amendment limiting members to two terms. Calling Congress, "a closed society," James said, "We must change the self-serving attitudes of our Congress. We must demand responsive, representative members of Congress. Until we do that, we will continue to have bad government." Many in the Republican side were less than enamored with the proposal including Minority Whip Newt Gingrich of Georgia and Conference Secretary Vin Weber but James found it amusing that the plank was included in the GOPs "Contract With America" that Gingrich spearheaded in 1994 as the party took the majority. Back home, James, who had conducted 80 town meetings to make himself known, built up a moderate portfolio. He fought against offshore drilling and when federal officials wanted to house a new VA facility near Florida's coast, James successfully convince them that hurricanes would be an albatross.

James found himself top Republican on the Judiciary Subcommittee on Administrative Law and Government Relations. The chairman of that committee was Massachusetts Democrat Barney Frank, himself known for a biting temperament, but with whom James worked well. Frank had called James "hard-working and conscientious," and defended him against the perceived impropriety of not disclosing the conflicts with the Legal Services Corporation (LSC), joking to other committee members, "Don't make eye contact with Mr. James." James returned the favor in 1990 when he refused to vote to expel Frank as other conservatives had in the summer of 1990.

James had been put on the defensive for participating in a hearing during the 1990 reauthorization of LSC for not disclosing interest in the fern farm but that appeared to be a rookie mistake as opposed to an attempt to gain an upper hand and he ultimately recused himself from final negotiations "out of the simple reason that they were going to make a mountain out of a molehill."

One molehill that at times did become a mountainous climb James did oppose abortion and that's where many saw his vulnerability as he came up for a second term, particularly after a much derided gaffe where he questioned a woman's fitness to decide whether to have an abortion because an early pregnancy "is probably the most confusing point of any woman's life regardless of her economic or social status." His highly touted opponent would be wealthy grocery store and gas station owner Reid Hughes, who also operated Hughes Oil Co., and James's freshman status and a cool $400,000 of his own money Hughes was kicking in was enough to put James near the most vulnerable chart (*Roll Call* called his support "soft").

By the time the campaign closed, Hughes had outspent the incumbent by $300,000. James focused on his efforts to reform and said, "I don't want to be the only bum thrown out." Hughes viewed James's criticism of PACs as a farce because James was now accepting them ("you lie down with the dogs, you get up with the fleas"). James rebutted assertions that he vowed to swear off PACs, saying none had been sent his way during the '88 race because no one thought he had a chance. Jim Duran, his campaign manager called him, "the most anti-incumbent incumbent in Washington."

James viewed Hughes's business as his feet of clay and he accused Hughes Oil of causing environmental damage by maintaining leaky gasoline tanks and one ad went, "Leaky gas tanks. Higher gas taxes. That's Reid Hughes." Hughes claimed his company had sold the stations in questions years earlier and called James's contentions "a lie...It's a scare tactic by a desperate opponent."

The two also tussled over abortion. James did back abortions in cases of rape, incest and when the life of the mother was in danger but Hughes hit him for voting against federal funding (James claimed the bill didn't adequately define rape). But the issue, a major factor in GOP Governor Bob Martinez's loss to Lawton Chiles, largely fizzled here despite Hughes's strong backing from women's groups. Hughes still called James "an extremist, not just on his voting record, but for his off-the-wall nutty statements."

The venom of the ads hit a fever pitch when Hughes ran a spot criticizing James's 1973 representation of the Green Valley School that had been raided by the state for mistreatment of emotionally disturbed children. The ad omitted key facts about the timing of James's involvement and James at one point threatened a libel suit. After the election, Hughes admitted "backlash" and said he would "probably not" have done it in hindsight. James struck back with an ad that said, "Oil millionaire Reid Hughes is using his oil money to spread lies about Craig James." *The Sentinel* said James "has represented his district well enough to warrant his re-election on Tuesday." Hughes got assistance from actor Robert Redford and Crosby, Stills and Nash.

As Election Day approached, polls showed differing stories with one neck and neck and another showing a more solid James lead. The surprise for both candidates on Election Day was that James kept his job with 56%. He called it "a landslide mandate," particularly since he wasn't entirely sure a win was in the bag ("I expected to win, but I wasn't sure, quite frankly").

In his second term, James's legal background found himself siding with Democrats on a few civil rights and crime measures. He backed the Civil Rights Act of 1990 over Bush's veto and did not agree with kids being forced to turn state's evidence (essentially ratting out others they knew committed crimes in order to gain leniency). The following year, he supported the Brady Bill, opposing the watered-down bill by Harley Staggers and opposed efforts by fellow Floridian Bill McCollum to recommit the bill. While he had supported McCollum's call for an instant check system the previous year, he now believed in a more stringent check. "Neither (bill) is perfect, as I think the proponents of each will concede, but both are well-intentioned. The real question is which will work better over the short term. The real question is which will work better over the short term...I do not think that the so-called instant-check hotline will be operating effectively in six months. From what I have heard and read, two to eight years is a better estimate of what it will take to fully computerize the criminal records of this nation." He voted for Ohio Democrat Dennis Eckart's amendment to cut funding for the Superconducting Super Collider (SSC). Legislatively, he proposed removing the President's authority to grant debt forgiveness to foreign countries and his seven co-sponsors spanned the legislative gamut (liberal and moderate Democrats and conservative Republicans).

On nearly every other issue that pitted Democrats against Republicans, James voted a solidly conservative line and after the conclusion of the Gulf War, resisted calls to establish international court military tribunals for Iraqis accused of atrocities (his worry was that U.S. soldiers might wrongfully be accused). At a Judiciary Committee International Law, Immigration and Refugee Subcommittee Hearing, James queried a General. "I take it that what you are suggesting is that, if you could make it a matter of general jurisdiction, then indeed, anyone that could allege that there were war crimes against any of the parties involved in the (Allied) coalition and would have a trial based perhaps on the legitimacy of the allegations. In other words, the negligence of our bombing may be an issue. The acts of any of our specific officers or generals may indeed be an issue."

The feathers James had ruffled showed no signs of dissipating in his second term and the attention naturally attracted notice among staffers as well. A 1992 survey of Capitol Hill aides for *The Washingtonian* asked which legislators they'd most like to see leave Congress. James placed eight. *The Sentinel* summarized it: One person called him a "screamer" (though James to this day denies having raised his voice at a single person including his own staff) while another derided him as "a know-it-all." James's response: "I made a lot of people mad because I have consistently taken a strong stand against waste and congressmen's proclivity to squander money." Unbeknownst to virtually anyone, the staffers would soon be getting their wish.

James proved he meant what he said about despising career politicians. In May 1992, seemingly out of nowhere, James announced that he would stand for a third term. The main culprit was guilt by association with the scandals enveloping the Hill, which James had no role in (zero bounced checks, declining use of the House gym, etc.). He refused to have my "reputation tarnished by the acts of others. If one does not have his good name, he has nothing." Taking a shot at the House leadership, James said, "The crisis facing this country regarding health care reform and economic recovery - including a balanced budget amendment - needs my full time and attention. But Congress is deadlocked in partisan bickering due to the mismanagement of the House by the majority party." He added, I've got to be able to look at myself in the mirror and say, 'Craig, can you believe that you're going to make a difference with these issues?' I doubted I could say that…"

James said he had been thinking about calling it a career – albeit a brief one, over the past month and years later recalled he was "tired of begging for money, tired of fundraising and asking people who couldn't afford it (to contribute) in order to run." He was also guided somewhat by redistricting which moved his district south. While confident he could win, he was realistic about what he could really accomplish and asked, "Win what?" In hindsight, James maintains he "enjoyed being there," but did not relish campaigning non-stop.

James rejoined his law firm which eventually became James/Zimmerman and like a true citizen politician, was nary seen nor heard from again. He retired in 2016.

CHAPTER EIGHTY-NINE

Cincinnati's Luken A One-Term Wonder

Introductory Tidbit: In December 1979, tragedy struck Cincinnati as 11 fans of the British rock group, "The Who," were killed during a stampede in an attempt to get first-come, first-serve seats at the city's Riverfront Coliseum. Ten years later almost to the day, the city's Mayor Charlie Luken, a self-dubbed, "frustrated rock star," announced that he'd like to see the group return. It wasn't to be, at least for that era. Luken and the Queen City had to wait 30 years after he expressed his wish as not until April 2019 did "The Who" finally return to the vicinity, though the concert's official performance was Highland Heights, Kentucky just outside the city limits.

Image via C-SPAN

I n a year as politically atypical as 1992, the departure from Congress by freshmen Democrat Charles Luken might not have been atypical at all. But the method for which he made that departure known certainly was and it baffled colleagues and constituents alike. After all, most members do not quit after having been re-nominated for another term, particularly when they lack an opponent of the other party (only an Independent was on the ballot). Luken, quite simply, never got Potomac Fever and was not afraid to leave it behind in the most quirky of ways – he save the announcement for his 19th wedding anniversary and it was a complete surprise to his wife.

Given the razor-tight margin by which he won the seat two years earlier, Luken's position had to be the envy of any member who ever had to fight to solidify a seat. Furthermore, while it is not unusual for politicians to bemoan the time the job takes them from their families, few actually retire for that reason.

When he won the Cincinnati based seat in 1990, voters needed no introduction to the Luken name. His father, Thomas Luken had been its occupant consecutively since 1976 and had also held the Queen City's other seat for much of 1974 before losing the general election to Bill Gradison, who continued serving alongside both Lukens. An uncle, Jim, was a Bobby Kennedy associate who played a large role in helping him nab Jimmy Hoffa in the 1950s (and later the Queen City's Mayor).

The elder Luken, by no means a "Boll Weevil" Democrat, had a voting record that was rather conservative for a Democrat north of the Mason-Dixon Line. In particular, he was an opponent of abortion and tangled with clean air advocates to the point of exasperation as legislation to make it more stringent was being considered. He was also impetuous and known for throwing phones in his office. Charlie Luken was at least a couple of degrees cooler as *The Almanac* called him "more humorous and personable than his irascible father."

Charlie attended Cincinnati schools and received his Bachelor's in Economics from the University of Notre Dame. Central Indiana wasn't that far away but, Luken decided to return home to attend law school at the Cincinnati College of Law. He commenced a law practice then was elected to the City Council. By 1984, he was Mayor at a salary of $39,500. Well before the Brady Bill, Luken sponsored a 15 day waiting period for handgun purchases in the city. The NRA opposed it but Council passed it 7-2. He proposed lights over Riverfront Stadium, saying, "I think it would be an excellent addition to the downtown skyline, and I think it would enhance the image of the city."

Tom Luken announced that he would not stand for re-election in 1990, on one hand tired but also irritated that voters were confusing him with an Ohio colleague, Donald "Buz" Lukens, who had been battling headlines for having sex with a 16-year-old Capitol Hill intern.

Charlie, a former Cincinnati Councilman who was currently serving as Mayor, was a natural to succeed him. That was enough for other Democrats to yield to him and he won the primary unopposed. Republicans were not about to give him that luxury.

The GOP nominee was J. Kenneth Blackwell, one of two African-American Republicans with a serious chance to win a seat in the House for the first time since the 1930s (the other was Gary Franks of Connecticut). Blackwell was someone with whom Luken was well acquainted if not personal friends, having himself served on council and as Mayor before Luken dislodged him by virtue of getting the highest number of votes among all council candidates. By the time national Republicans persuaded Blackwell to enter the race, he was serving as an assistant to Housing and Urban Development Secretary Jack Kemp.

Blackwell campaigned as a conservative's conservative. He boasted of having kept *Playboy* off Cincinnati's TV and called for a "leaner and meaner" federal government. When Blackwell labeled Luken a "tax-and-spend liberal" during a debate, Luken reminded him that once upon a time, "you were the fifth vote on council that made me mayor and you cited my conservatism when you did it." Both candidates opposed the final budget summit package with Luken saying, "Unless there is a spending discipline in Congress, raising taxes is futile" (President George H.W. Bush still campaigned for Blackwell). Luken benefitted as a chip off the old block and *The Almanac of American Politics* speculated after the campaign that his dad's "seat on Energy and Commerce can't have hurt his son's fundraising efforts."

As Election Day neared, some pundits were predicting that Blackwell would win his election while Franks would come up short. Instead, the opposite happened, albeit not by much. In fact, so close was the outcome that Luken at one point thought he would lose and Blackwell did not admit defeat until 2:28 a.m., some seven hours after the polls had closed. Luken detailed the vote-counting odyssey to his supporters. "My dad phoned in the results from the Board of Elections. When it got to be a thousand votes (difference) with 50% of the votes in, I got nervous and told somebody I didn't think we would win." Luken grabbed 57% in Cincy proper while Blackwell won 52% outside the city. The final margin was 83,932 for Luken and 80,362 for Blackwell, a 51-49% margin. Blackwell congratulated his on-again-off-again foe "on a hard-fought contest and I think he knows I will be ready and willing to work with him. We have lost an election but we have not lost our dream." Luken meanwhile exhaled: "The first thing a new congressman does is go on vacation with his wife and three children."

Luken was placed on the Banking, Housing and Urban Affairs Committee and Government Operations. On one of his first votes, he opted to support the resolution authorizing the use of force against Iraq. His record on fiscal matters was stingy, backing the Balanced Budget Amendment and earning the ire of some Democrats in the normally cohesive delegation when he joined Buckeye State Republicans John Boehner and Mike Oxley in calling for a rescission of previously approved 642 projects, some of which were earmarked for Ohio. Luken freely admitted that some "weren't too happy" but it was "a bread-and butter issue for me."

Another quality of life issue was noise control in the town of Dehli near the busy Northern Kentucky/Greater Cincinnati Airport and as a result, he opposed a U.S. Postal Service express mail hub there. Procter & Gamble was based in the city and Luken looked after their interests. He and Gradison tried to expedite the review process for the anti-fat drug olestra by the Food and When Fifth-Third Star Bank made noises about acquiring Star-Banc Corp, Luken requested a federal investigation and secured a commitment from the U.S. Justice Department to "carefully scrutinize" any merger. When Kentucky Democratic Senator Wendell Ford toyed with luring the U.S. Food and Drug Administration district office and National Forensic Chemistry Center from Cincinnati to the Bluegrass State, Luken objected.

Internally, Luken was a fan of good government and joined the bipartisan "Young Turks" to press the case for reform against their leadership's wishes. He called "outrageous" an $80 million franking appropriation that lawmakers approved and advocated for ratification of the 27th Amendment to the Constitution that would bar a pay raise from taking effect until the convening of the following session of Congress. Doing so, he believed, would put Congress, "more in touch with the voters."

It was at the end of June, nearly four weeks after Ohio's primary that Luken made his bombshell announcement to step aside at the end of the term. The lack of comity was one reason. "Partisanship on both sides of the aisle prevents us from acting in the national interest," he said. "The Congress is not productive. Much of my time is wasted on partisanship, in which I have no interest." Then Luken revealed that family concerns was much behind the reason, and he purposely saved revealing the decision to his wife for their 19th anniversary. While acknowledging the present was, "peculiar," Luken rationalized his thinking. "My children are young; they seem to get a year older and 3 inches taller every time I look at them. Marcia and I talked about it, and you know, my dad started in Congress at 50 and I'm only 40." He said that he had been thinking about abandoning his campaign several weeks before he made it official.

When he retired from office, Luken began offering commentary for the city's NBC affiliate, WLWT. But he was motivated to seek a comeback in 1999 and he aimed for a job without a demanding commute – the City Council. One rationale: "I have never seen the kind of chaos and disorganization that you can see if you watch a council meeting on TV." In Cincinnati, at that time all candidates for council run as a blanket slate and the candidate who gets with the highest votes becomes mayor. It was a mild stunner when Luken deposed the incumbent, Todd Portune, from first place and Luken himself said that at the outset of the campaign, "I didn't think it was possible." His 20-year old daughter Lauren said, "I think this is where he belongs." But with the glory came the challenges – and in some cases, the bloodshed.

Luken was forced to govern under fire in 2001 when a Cincinnati police officer shot and killed Timothy Thomas, a 19-year old unarmed black man. It was the fifth such shooting of an African-American and the result was demonstrations that, over four days, led to 65 injuries and window breaking at City Hall. Luken declared a city-wide curfew. "I think the black citizens are tired and scared, I think the white citizens are tired and scared. There's gunfire going on here like you might hear in Beirut. It's dangerous and it's getting more dangerous…I'm not asking anyone not to be frustrated, but to just realize in the short-term someone could get hurt."

By 2001, voters slammed the lid on the highest vote system for Mayor and instead called for the top two highest primary vote-getters to advance to a runoff. By pure happenstance, that primary was held September 11, 2001. The race was fought largely around racial lines and Luken's handling of the April situation was a dominant issue. Luken ran behind an African-American Councilman Courtis Fuller, receiving 38%, a daunting sign given that Fuller had well over a majority – 54%. But on Election Day, he rebounded by solidifying much of the opposition vote and kept his job 55-45%.

When Luken's term as Mayor ended in late 2005, he joined the law firm of Calfee, Halter & Griswold LLP where he continues to serve as a senior counselor.

Members of the U.S. House of Representatives Who Left Office Following the 1992 Election					
State/Member	**District #**	**Party**	**Year Elected**	**Age**	**Reason for Departure**
Alabama					
Bill Dickinson	2	R	1964	67	Retirement
Ben Erdreich	6	D	1982	54	General Defeat
Claude Harris	7	D	1986	52	Retirement
Arizona					
Jay Rhodes	1	R	1986	49	General Defeat
Arkansas					
Bill Alexander	1	D	1968	58	Primary Defeat
John Paul Hammerschmidt	3	R	1966	70	Retirement
Beryl Anthony	4	D	1978	54	Primary Defeat
California					
Frank Riggs	1	R	1992	40	General Defeat
Barbara Boxer	6	D	1982	52	Won Senate Race
Tom Campbell	12	R	1988	40	Lost Senate Race
Robert Lagomarsino	19	R	1974	66	Primary Defeat
Edward Roybal	25	D	1962	76	Retirement
Mel Levine	27	D	1982	49	Lost Senate Race
Mervyn Dymally	31	D	1980	66	Retirement
Glenn Anderson	32	D	1968	79	Retirement
William Dannemeyer	39	R	1978	63	Lost Senate Race
Bill Lowery	41	R	1992	45	Retirement
Colorado					
Ben Nighthorse Campbell	3	D	1986	59	Won Senate Race
Delaware					
Tom Carper	At-large	D	1982	45	Won Governorship

Florida					
Charles Bennett	3	D	1948	82	Retirement
Craig James	4	R	1988	51	Retirement
Andy Ireland	11	R	1976	62	Retirement
Larry Smith	20	D	1982	51	Retirement
William Lehman	18	D	1972	79	Retirement
Dante Fascell	19	D	1954	75	Retirement
Georgia					
Lindsay Thomas	1	D	1982	49	Retirement
Charles Hatcher	2	D	1980	53	Primary Defeat
Richard Ray	3	D	1982	65	General Defeat
Ben Jones	4	D	1988	51	Primary Defeat
Ed Jenkins	9	D	1976	59	Retirement
Doug Barnard	10	D	1976	70	Retirement
Idaho					
Richard Stallings	2	D	1984	52	Lost Senate Race
Illinois					
Charles Hayes	1	D	1983	74	Primary Defeat
Gus Savage	2	D	1980	67	Primary Defeat
Marty Russo	3	D	1974	48	Primary Defeat
Frank Annunzio	11	D	1964	77	Retirement
John Cox	16	D	1990	43	General Defeat
Terry Bruce	19	D	1984	48	Primary Defeat
Indiana					
Jim Johntz	5	D	1986	41	General Defeat
Iowa					
David Nagle	3	D	1986	49	General Defeat
Kansas					
Dick Nichols	5	R	1990	66	Primary Defeat

Kentucky					
Carroll Hubbard	1	D	1974	55	Primary Defeat
Larry Hopkins	6	R	1978	59	Retirement
Chris Perkins	7	D	1984	38	Retirement
Louisiana					
Jerry Huckaby	5	D	1976	51	General Defeat
Clyde Hollway	7	R	1986	49	General Defeat
Maryland					
Tom McMillen	4	D	1986	40	General Defeat
Beverly Byron	6	D	1978	60	Primary Defeat
Massachusetts					
Joe Early	3	D	1974	59	General Defeat
Chester G. Atkins	5	D	1984	44	Primary Defeat
Nick Mavroules	6	D	1978	63	General Defeat
Brian Donnelly	11	D	1978	46	Retirement
Michigan					
Carl Pursell	2	R	1976	60	Retirement
Howard Wolpe	3	D	1978	53	Retirement
Robert Traxler	7	D	1974	61	Retirement
Guy Vander Jagt	10	R	1966	61	Primary Defeat
Robert W. Davis	11	R	1978	60	Retirement
Dennis Hertel	14	D	1980	44	Retirement
William Broomfield	18	R	1956	70	Retirement
Minnesota					
Vin Weber	2	R	1980	42	Retirement
Gerry Sikorski	6	D	1982	44	General Defeat
Missouri					
Joan Kelly Horn	2	D	1990	56	General Defeat
Tom Coleman	6	R	1976	49	General Defeat

Montana					
Ron Marlenee	At-large	R	1976	57	General Defeat
New Jersey					
Bernard Dwyer	6	D	1980	71	Retirement
Matthew Rinaldo	7	R	1972	61	Retirement
Robert Roe	8	D	1969	68	Retirement
Frank Guarini	14	D	1978	68	Retirement
New York					
Thomas Downey	2	D	1974	43	General Defeat
Robert Mrazek	3	D	1982	47	Retirement
Norman Lent	4	R	1970	61	Retirement
Ray McGrath	5	R	1980	50	Retirement
Jim Scheuer	8	D	1964/74	72	Retirement
Stephen Solarz	13	D	1974	52	Primary Defeat
Bill Green	15	D	1992	63	General Defeat
Ted Weiss	17	D	1976	65	Death
David Martin	26	R	1980	48	Retirement
Matthew McHugh	28	D	1974	54	Retirement
Frank Horton	29	R	1962	73	Retirement
Henry Nowak	33	D	1974	57	Retirement
North Carolina					
Walter Jones	1	D	1966	79	Retirement/Death
North Dakota					
Byron Dorgan	At-large	R	1980	50	Won Senate Seat
Ohio					
Charles Luken	1	D	1990	43	Retirement
Bob McEwen	6	R	1980	42	General Defeat
Clarence Miller	10	R	1966	75	Primary Defeat
Dennis Eckart	11	D	1980	42	Retirement
Donald Pease	13	D	1976	61	Retirement
Chalmers Wylie	15	R	1966	72	Retirement

Edward Feighan	19	D	1982	45	Retirement
Mary Rose Oakar	20	D	1976	52	General Defeat
Oklahoma					
Mickey Edwards	5	R	1976	55	Primary Defeat
Oregon					
Les AuCorin	1	D	1974	50	Lost Senate Race
Pennsylvania					
Joe Kolter	4	D	1982	66	Primary Defeat
Richard Schultze	5	R	1974	63	Retirement
Gus Yatron	6	D	1968	65	Retirement
Peter Kostmayer	8	D	1976	46	General Defeat
Lawrence Coughlin	13	R	1968	63	Retirement
Don Ritter	15	R	1978	52	General Defeat
Joseph Gaydos	20	D	1968	66	Retirement
South Carolina					
Elizabeth Patterson	4	D	1986	53	General Defeat
Robin Tallon	6	D	1982	46	Retirement
Texas					
Albert Bustamante	23	D	1984	57	General Defeat
Utah					
Wayne Owens	2	D	1972/86	55	Lost Senate Race
Virginia					
Jim Olin	6	D	1982	72	Retirement
George Allen	7	R	1991	40	Retirement
Washington					
John Miller	1	R	1984	54	Retirement
Sid Morrison	4	R	1980	59	Lost Governor's Race
Rod Chandler	8	R	1982	50	Lost Senate Race

West Virginia					
Harley Staggers	2	D	1982	41	Primary Defeat
Wisconsin					
Jim Moody	5	D	1982	57	Lost Senate Race

ACKNOWLEDGEMENTS

Tom Albert
Congressman Beryl Anthony
Evan Anderson-Braude
Bill Andresen
Lucia Annunzio
Catherine Bach
David Batdorf
State Representative Pat Bauer
The Beaver Times
Beverly Bell
James Bennett
Congressman Howard Berman
Matthew Boyer
Boone County (Arkansas) Library
John Spoor Broome Library, California State University, Channel Islands
Congressman Terry Bruce
George H.W. Bush Presidential Library and Museum
Congresswoman Beverly Byron
Congressman Rod Chandler
David and Lorraine Cheng Library, William Paterson University of New Jersey
Kay Christiansen
Dan Clarke
The Cleveland Public Library
Congressman Bill Clinger
Congressman Tom Coleman
C-SPAN
Sandra Diamond
Congressman Tom Downey
Tori Martin Duskas
Matt Durham
Congressman Dennis Eckart
Congressman Mickey Edwards
Congressman Glenn English

Congressman Ben Erdreich

Sante Esposito

Congressman Edward Feighan

Mike Finley

Gerald R. Ford Presidential Library and Museum

Scott Frey

Bernie Friedman

Cindy Gillespie

William Goold

Jim Gottlieb

Congressman Bill Gradison

Congressman Frank Guarini

Congressman Steve Gunderson

Tim Hagan

John Hammerschmidt, Jr.

Rob Hartwell

Professor Otto Hetzel

Congressman Dennis Hertel

Congressman Hal Hollenbeck

Congresswoman Joan Kelly Horn

Nancy Horton

Steven Horton

Lorraine Howerton

Congressman Jerry Huckaby

Bob Hurt

Congressman Earl Hutto

International Olympic Committee (IOC)

Congressman Andy Ireland

Congressman Craig James

Congressman Ben Jones

J.Y. Joyner Library, East Carolina University

State Representative Shelia Klinker

Patricia Klem Kobor

Congressman John LaFalce

Keith Laughlin

Kenton County (Kentucky) Library

Kheel Center, Catherwood Library, Cornell University

Congressman Mel Levine

Livingston County (Missouri) Library
Jim Margolis
Congressman Bob McEwen
Congressman Ray McGrath
Congressman Matthew McHugh
Kathleen Tynan McLaughlin
Amy Miller-Jackson
John Moore
Rick Moore
Congressman Sid Morrison
Christopher Klose
Dan Kripke
Michael Lewan
Milwaukee Journal Sentinel
National Institute for the Deaf at Rochester Institute of Technology
Congressman David Nagle
Debbie Nagle
Congresswoman Mary Rose Oakar
Office of Art and Archives, House of Representatives
The Oklahoman
James Olin
Brian O'Malley
Scott Paul
Jeanne Pease
Jennifer Pease
Congressman Glenn Poshard
Curtis Prim
The David and Barbara Pryor Center for Arkansas Oral and Visual History
Anita Lacy Ray
Rockford (Illinois) Public Library
Linda Roderick
Royal Oak (Michigan) Public Library
Michael Rosenberg
Edward Roybal Foundation
Mark Ruge
Congressman Marty Russo
Gary Russell
Saint Peters University Archives

Paul Schlegel
Paul Schlesinger
Nancy Schulze
Congressman Richard Schulze
Michael Scrivner
Seton Hall University Library Archives and Special Collections Center
Congressman Larry Smith
Sammy Smith
Marc Smolonsky
Congressman Harley Staggers
Cogressman Charles Stenholm
George Stephanopoulos
Clay Swanzy
Congressman Robin Tallon
Jeff Tassey
Dennis Teti
Congressman Lindsay Thomas
Congressman Jill Long Thompson
Congressman Bob Traxler
Mary Lee Jontz Turk
University of Illinois at Chicago Library, Special Collections and University Archives
Donald Upson
Barbara VanVoorst
Washington State Archives
Congressman Henry Waxman
Stephen Weiss
Jackie Miller Williams
Congressman Pat Williams
Brad Wylie
Yakima Valley Libraries
Charles E. Young Research Library, UCLA

Sources

Bill Alexander
The Almanac of American Politics, 1992 and 1994; Politics in America; Ourcampaigns.com
CQ (December 6, 1968); The New York Times (March 5, 1976); The New York Times (September 11, 1976); CQ (December 19, 1981); CQ (February 11, 1984); Congressional Record (March 27, 1985); The New York Times (By Steven V. Roberts, October 9, 1985); CQ (May 31, 1986); CQ (By Janet Hooks and Jacqueline Calmes, July 12, 1986) ; The Encyclopedia of Arkansas; The New York Times (By Bill Alexander, April 25, 1989); The Commercial Appeal (By Joan I. Duffy, May 25, 1990); The Chicago Tribune (By Steve Daley, June 3, 1990); CQ (June 23, 1990); CQ (October 18, 1990); The New York Times (July 19, 1991)The Commercial Appeal; The Encyclopedia of Arkansas

Glenn Anderson
The Almanac of American Politics; Politics in America; Our Campaigns; The New York Times (By Peter Hart, August 15, 1965); The Desert Sun (November 9, 1966); The Washington Post (By Carole Shifrin, August 2, 1979); The New York Times (By Irvin Molotsky, November 8, 1979); Congressional Record (December 20, 1979); The New York Times (AP, January 19, 1984); Congressional Record (April 30, 1984); The Daily Breeze (By Marcus Stern, August 14, 1984); The LA Times (By Bill Stall and George Hatch, December 18, 1990)
The Daily Breeze (December 9, 1991); Congressional Record (July 29, 1992); The Daily Breeze (December 10, 1992); The LA Times (By Myrna Oliver, December 14,1994); The Long Beach Press Telegram (By James Carroll, December 14, 1994); Glenn Anderson: Conscience of California (By Myron Roberts and Harold Garvin)

Beryl Anthony
The Almanac of American Politics; Politics in America; Our Campaigns; The Washington Post (By Steve Sothern, April 25, 1989); Bluefield Daily Telegraph (Thursday, February 24, 1983); Joint Hearing of the Committee on

Social Security on Ways and Means (March 24, 1984); Disposal of Chemical Munitions: Hearing Before the Investigations ..., Volume 5 By United States. Congress. House. Committee on (March 13, 1985); The New York Times (By Da, September 23, 1992); C-Span

Frank Annunzio
CQ (1970); CQ (1980); UPI (By Bud Newman, February 13, 1987); The Fair Credit Billing Act Amendments of 1975 Heaing (October 23, 1975); The Chicago Tribune (October 18, 1987);
The Chicago Sun Times (By Jerome Idaszak, September 12, 1986); The Chicago Tribune (UPI, October 29, 1987); The LA Times (AP, June 3, 1988); CQ(June 25, 1988); The Washington Post By Kathleen Day, July 28, 1989); Chicago Magazine (By David Jackson, August 1990); Reader (By Bryan Miller, October 18, 1990); The Washington Post (By David Broder, October 22, 1990); The Chicago Tribune (By William Grady, April 9, 2001); The Chicago Sun-Times (By Steve Neal, By April 11, 2001); The New York Times (By Irvin Molotsky, April 17, 2001); S & L Hell: The People and the Politics Behind the $1 Trillion Savings and Loan Scandal (By Kathleen Day)

Chet Atkins
The Almanac of American Politics; Politics in America; Our Campaigns;Congressional Quarterly; CQ (September 1, 1984); CQ (By Janet Hook, December 10, 1988); The Worchester Telegram and Gazette (By Gerald S. Cohen, April 18, 1989); The Worcester Telegram and Gazette (By Gerald Cohen, May 18, 1989); The Lowell Sun (June 3, 1989); The Worcester Telegram & Gazette (By Amy Bayer, July 12, 1989); Worcester Telegram & Gazette (January 9, 1990); The Worcester Telegram & Gazette (September 29, 1990); The Lowell Sun (By Jules Crittenden, October 26, 1990); The Lowell Sun (November 7, 1990); The Washington Post (By Mary McGrory, April 11, 1991); The Boston Herald (December 12, 1991); The New York Times (By Barbara Crossette, December 21, 1991); The Boston Herald (By Robert Connolly, January 8, 1992); The Boston Herald (By Eric Fehrnstrom, September 12, 1992); Concord Oral History Program (November 8, 1993); Tip O'Neill and the Democratic Century (Bu John Farrell); Concord Oral History Program (November 8, 1993); Corporate Corruption: The Abuse of Power (By Marshall Barron Clinard); The United States and Cambodia, 1969-2000: A Troubled Relationship (By Kenton Clymer)

Les AuCoin

The Almanac of American Politics, 1992; Politics in America, 1990; The Washington Post (By Margot Hornblower, May 25, 1983); The Sacramento Bee (By Lee Rennert, March 27, 1985); Congressional Record (June 25, 1986); CQ (Overview, 1986); The Oregonian (By Foster Church, October 17, 1988); CQ (August 5, 1989); The LA Times (Don Phillips, December 10, 1989) The Oregonian (By Jeff Mapes, April 19, 1992); The Oregonian (March 19, 1991); The Oregonian (March 30, 1991); The Oregonian (May 22, 1992); The Oregonian (June 23, 1992); The Oregonian (August 2, 1992); The Oregonian (September 13, 1992);

The Oregonian (October 18, 1992); The Oregonian (By Jeff Mapes, October 22, 1992);

The Oregonian (By Jeff Mapes, November 5, 1992); Coalitions & Political Movements: The Lessons of the Nuclear Freeze (edited by Thomas R. Rochon and David S. Meyer); Congress.gov

Doug Barnard

The Almanac of American Politics; Politics in America; The Atlanta-Journal Constitution (By Scott Thurston, 1987); The New York Times (By Nathaniel C. Nash, July 26, 1989); The Atlanta Journal and The Atlanta Constitution (By Mike Christensen, July 31, 1989); The Atlanta Journal and The Atlanta Constitution (September 29, 1989); The Atlanta Journal (October 15, 1989); The Atlanta Journal (By Charles Walston, September 25, 1990); AP (By David Pace, February 8, 1994); The Macon Telegraph (June 3, 1999) ; The LA Times (By Robert A. Rosenblatt, January 13, 1990); The Augusta Chronicle (February 26, 2007); WRDW (By Celia Palermo, January 12, 2018)

Charles Bennett

The Almanac of American Politics; Politics in America; House.gov; CQ (1951); The New York Times (January 10, 1953); The Miami Herald (April 23, 1985); CQ (January 10, 1987); The St. Petersburg Times (AP, June 6, 1991); The Tampa Tribune (June 8, 1992); The St. Petersburg Times (By Rebecca H. Patterson, October 24, 1992); The Miami Herald (November 2, 1992); Florida Times Union (November 11, 1998); The New York Times (By Sewell Chan, September 23, 2010); The Florida Times Union (By Jessie-Lynne Kerr, December 13, 2010); CQ (By Nadine Cohodas and Diane Grabat); In the Smaller Scope of Conscience: The Struggle for National Repatriation ...(By C. Timothy McKeown)

William Broomfield

The Almanac of American Politics, 1990 and 1992; Politics in America, 1992; The Daily Tribune (November 7, 1956); UPI (August 6, 1982) 5/5/1983; The Miami Herald (By Davis Hess, July 31, 1983); The Michigan Daily (January 8, 1987); Congressional Record (May 10, 1983); The New York Times (By Hedrick Smith, September 22, 1983); The Christian Science Monitor (By Julia Malone, November 2, 1983); The Michigan Daily (January 8, 1987); The New York Times (By Linda Greenhouse, March 12, 1987); USA Today (September 22, 1987); UPI NewsTrack (September 23, 1987); By John Gizzi, March 5, 2019)

Terry Bruce

The Herald and Review (March 5, 1984); The Decatur Herald and Review (November 7, 1984)

The Journal Gazette (March 21, 1984); The Journal Gazette (October 11, 1984); The Journal Gazette (November 8, 1984); CQ (January 5, 1985); The NYT (AP, April 19, 1989)

Energy and Commerce hearing transcript (April 6, 1989); The Journal News (June 8, 1989)

By Michael Weisskopf (February 4, 1990); The Herald & Review (By Dave Moore, March 7, 1992) ; The Journal Register (By Jenni Davis, March 16, 1992); The Herald & Review (June 6, 1992)

Albert Bustamante

Del Rio News Herald, May 6, 1984; The Washington Post (By Edward Walsh, June 26, 1986);

The New York Times (By Keith Schneider, October 7, 1988); The Bulletin of the Atomic Scientists (By Dan Reicher and Jason Salzman, November 26, 1988); Congressional Record (August 3, 1990); The San Antonio Express-News (By Gary Martin; October 31, 1990); UPI Archives (September. 21, 1991); CQ (By Ceci Connolly, October 10, 1992);

San Antonio Express News (By Bruce Davidson, October 28, 1992); The San Antonio Express News (By David Anthony Richelieu, November 1, 1992); The Dallas Morning News (AP, July 25, 1993); https://library.uta.edu/tejanovoices/xml/CMAS_015.xml

Beverly Byron

The Almanac of American Politics, 1990 and 1992; Politics in America, 1990 and 1992; House.gov; The Library of Congress Oral History Project; The New York Times (By Lynn Rosellini, July 16, 1981); The New York Times (By Richard Halloran, December 22, 1987); CQ (1987); CQ (1989); CQ (1990); The Washington Post (By Timothy Flynn, June 29, 1989); The Baltimore Sun (December 30, 1990); The Baltimore Sun (March 27, 1991); The Baltimore Sun (By Tom Bowman, May 13, 1991); The Washington Post (January 18, 1992); The Baltimore Sun (By Tom Bowman and James M. Coram, March 4, 1992); The Frederick Post (By Glen Burns and Dan McMahon, November 4, 1992); The Frederick News Post (By Don DeArmon, January 8, 2017)

Rod Chandler

The Almanac of American Politics, 1990 and 1992; Politics in America, 1990 and 1992;
UPI (June 28, 1984); CQ (1986); The Seattle Times (By Ross Anderson, March 1, 1985); The Seattle Times (By Eric Pryne, March 13, 1986); The Seattle Post-Intelligencer (July 8, 1986); The Seattle Times (By Eric Pryne, September 21, 1986); The New York Times (By Leonard Sloane, June 22, 1987); The Seattle Post-Intelligencer (February 12, 1990); The Seattle Post-Intelligencer (November 3, 1990); The New York Times (By Timothy Egan, October 19, 1992); RodChandlerPhotagraphy.zenfolio.com

Tom Coleman

The St. Louis Post Dispatch (By Linda Lockhart, November 4, 1976); CQ (By Harrison Donnelly, May 16, 1981); The New York Times (By Steven V. Roberts, May 13, 1981); The Washington Post (By Ward Sinclair, October 1, 1985); UPI (December 16, 1985); CQ (1985 – Overview); The Chillicothe Constitution Tribune (By Karen DeWitt, November 7, 1990); CQ (1991 Overview); The Kansas City Star (July 25, 1992); The Kansas City Star (September 29, 1992); The Kansas City Star (October 23, 1992); The Kansas City Star (By J.D. Moore, October 29 1992); The Kansas City Star (J.D. Moore, Jr., November 4, 1992); The Kansas City Star (By J.D. Moore, November 9, 1992); CQ(1992 overview); The Daily Caller (March 2019); Extension Responds To The Rural Crisis by the University of Missouri (By James Summer, the University of Missouri, 1990); UPI (By Ira Allen, Fe

Larry Coughlin

Politics in America, 1990 and 1992; The New York Times (By Richard L. Berke, November 28, 1991; The New York Times (April 3, 1971); CQ (June 28, 1975); Congressional Record (March 2, 1977); The New York Times (By Seth S. King, September 13, 1981); Congressional Record (December 14, 1982); Congressional Record (May 23, 1984); CQ (October 13, 1984); The Philadelphia Inquirer (March 22, 1986); The Philadelphia Inquirer (October 11, 1986); The Morning Call (October 31, 1986); The Philadelphia Daily News (By Reginald Stuart, September 7, 1989); The Morning Call (February 1, 1991); The Morning Call (November 20, 1991)
The Daily News (2001)

John Cox

The Almanac of American Politics, 1992 and 1994; Politics in America, 1992 and 1994
By Judith Barra-Austin; The Rockford Star (By Chuck Sweeny, November 7, 1990); The Rockford Star (By Ray Quintanilla, November 4, 1992)

Robert W. Davis

The Almanac of American Politics, 1992 and 1994; Politics in America 1986, 1990 and 1992; The Washington Post (By Lloyd Grove, February 7, 1985); The Detroit Free Press (April 26, 1992); The Detroit Free Press (Maryanne George and Patricia Montemurri, May 5, 1992); AP October 19, 2009; The Downfall Dictionary; People

Bill Dickinson

The Almanac of American Politics, 1990 and 1992; Politics in America, 1992; Ourcampaigns.com; The Anniston Star (March 31, 1965); The New York Daily News (UPI, April 29, 1965); Benton Harbor News Palladium Archives (April 29, 1965); CQ (May 26, 1979); The Annison Star (January 5, 1985); CQ (1985 wrapup); CQ (1989); CQ (1990); The Anniston Star (By Robert B. McNeil, October 2, 1987); The Anniston Star (By Robert B. McNeil, January 24, 1988); The New York Times (By Susan F. Rasky, July 13, 1988); The Anniston Star (By Robert McNeil, July 15, 1988); The Anniston Star (February 7, 1989); Congressional Quarterly (By John Cranford, June 9, 1990); The Montgomery Advertiser (August 30, 1990); The Montgomery Advertiser (November 7, 1990); The Huntsville Times (AP, March 10, 1992);

Roll Call (By Karen Foerster, March 12, 1992); The Mercury News (April 1, 1992);The Washington Post (By Phillip Rawls, April 2, 2008)

Brian Donnelly
Ourcampaigns.com; The Boston Globe (By Norm Lockman, Globe Staff, October 14, 1978); Congressional Record (October 4, 1989); The Boston Herald (Andrew Miga, March 25, 1992); The Boston Herald (By Andrew Miga, March 29, 1992); The Boston Herald (February 4, 1998); South Coast Today (By Martin Finucane, February 4, 1998); South Coast Today (By Martin Finucane, February 4, 1998); Tip O'Neill and the Democratic Century (By John Farrell); Govtrack

Tom Downey
The Almanac of American Politics, 1990 and 1992; Politics in America, 1992; Ourcampaigns.com; Newsday (By Robert Fresco, February 4, 1974); Newsday (By Robert Fresco, November 6, 1974); The New York Times (By George Vecsey, November 7, 1974); The New York Times (By Martin Tolchin, February 10, 1975); The New York Times (By Pranay Gupte, December 7, 1975); The New York Times (By John Finney, March 29, 1976); CQ (1975); CQ (October 9, 1976); The New York Times (By Irwin Molotsky, May 7, 1978); The New York Times (By Edward C. Burks, January 28, 1979); The SALT II Treaty Hearings (September 6, 7, 10, 11 and 12, 1979); The New York Times (By Steven Roberts, May 1, 1981); CQ (1981); The Congressional Record (October 24, 1983); CQ (1983); The San Diego Union (March 6, 1985); CQ (March 9, 1985); CQ (By Pat Towell, with Nadine Cohodas and Steve Pressman, March 23, 1985); The New York Times (By Steven V. Roberts, July 12, 1985); The LA Times (By Paul Houston, September 27, 1985); The New York Times (By Martin Tolchin, June 29, 1988); New York Magazine (December 18, 1989); CQ (1990); CQ (1992); Newsday (By Jack Sirica, April 17, 1992); Congressional Record (June 25, 1992); The New York Times (By Josh Barbanel, October 31, 1992); Newsday (By Charles V. Zehren and William B. Falk, November 4, 1992); Newsday (By November 4, 1992); Newsday (Sidney C. Schaer, November 5, 1992); Newsday (By Paul Vitello, November 5, 1992); The New York Times (By Alison Mitchell, November 8, 1992); CQ Overview (1992); Debate Over Child Care, 1969-1990: A Sociohistorical Analysis (By Abbie Gordon Klein); Niscanen Venter (By Joshua McCabe, September 18, 2017); The Great Book of Washington

DC Sports Lists (By Len Shapiro and Andy Pollin); Pat Schroeder: A Woman of the House (By Joan A. Lowy); Brookings (By Tom Downey, June 1, 2001);

Bernard Dwyer

The Courier News (November 4, 1957); The New York Times (December 29, 1977); The Review (By Jim Powers, June 5, 1980); UPI NewsTrack (October 6, 1980); The Courier News (November 5, 1980); The Record (By Jon Shure, February 24, 1985); The New York Times (By Tom Wicker, April 18, 1989); The Star-Ledger (July 30, 1989); The Star Ledger (By Lenny Melisurgo, May 27, 1990); The Asbury Park Press (By Mark Magyar, November 7, 1990); The Home News (By Romel J. Hernandez, November 7, 1990);The Star-Ledger (November 5, 1998)

Joe Early

The Almanac of American Politics, 1992 and 1994; Politics in America, 1986, 1992 and 1994;
Worcester Telegram & Gazette (April 2, 1989); Worcester Telegram & Gazette (October 18, 1989); The Worcester Telegram & Gazette (June 25, 1991); The Boston Herald (By Robert Connolly, January 8, 1992); Worcester Telegram & Gazette (January 14, 1992); The Boston Herald (By Ralph Ranalli and Joe Sciacca); The Worcester Telegram and Gazette (By John J. Monahan, March 16, 1992); Congressional Quarterly (March 21, 1992); The Lowell Sun (AP, June 1, 1992); The Worcester Telegram & Gazette (July 10, 1992); Congressional Record (September 17, 1992); The Boston Globe (By Peter J. Howe, November 5, 1992); The Boston Globe (Toni Locy, November 4, 1992); The Washington Post (By Matt Schudel November 9, 2012)

Dennis Eckart

The Almanac of American Politics, 1990 and 1992; Politics in America, 1986 and 1992; CQ (1980); The Washington Post (By David Marines, January 29, 1984); The New York Times (April 30, 1984); The New York Times (By Phillip Shabecoff, May 4, 1984); The New York Times (By Phillip Shabecoff, September 19, 1984); The Washington Post (By Cass Peterson, June 26, 1985); The Akron Beacon Journal (April 30, 1985); The New York Times (By State's News Service, August 11, 1985); CQ (1986 Overview); The Akron Beacon Journal (February 4, 1987); The LA Times (By Rudy Abramson, May 11, 1990); The Akron Beacon Journal (January 29 1990); The New York Times (By Matthew Wald, May 14, 1991); The New York Times (By Roberto Suro, May

24, 1992); The L.A. Times (June 24, 1992); The Plain Dealer (June 27, 1992); Tunnel Visions: The Rise and Fall of the Superconducting Super Collider (By Michael Riordan, Lillian Hoddeson, Adrienne W. Kolb); The Environmental Case (By Judith A. Layzer); Mr. Chairman (By William Lehman)

Mickey Edwards
The Almanac of American Politics; Politics in America, 1986 and 1992; The Encyclopedia of Oklahoma; AP (December 12, 1982); The Daily Oklahoman (Oklahoma Wire Service, July 28, 1983); The Congressional Record (March 27 1985); The LA Times (By Doyle McManus, June 26, 1986); The Tulsa World (February 25, 1990); The New York Times (By Susan F. Rasky, March 8, 1990); The Daily Oklahoman (By Chris Casteel, March 19, 1990); The Daily Oklahoman (March 23, 1990); The Tulsa World (November 6, 1990); The Tulsa World (March 18, 1992); The Oklahoman (By David Zizzo, June 7, 1992); The New York Times (By Clifford Krauss, August 25, 1992) Published: Fri, March 25, 1988 12:00 AM
The Daily Oklahoman - March 18, 199

Ben Erdreich
The Almanac of American Politics, 1990, 1992 and 1994); Politics in America, 1986; The Encyclopedia of Alabama; The New York Times (AP, April 22, 1981); The Anniston Star (November 3, 1982); Billboard (June 21, 1986); CQ (June 28, 1986); CQ (May 20, 1988); CQ (June 25, 1988); CQ Overview, 1988); The San Jose Mercury News (By Carl Cannon, February 11, 1990); The Times Picayune (By Edgar Poe, March 17, 1990); Birmingham News (October 5, 1992); The Huntsville Times (AP, October 25, 1992); The Huntsville Times (AP, October 29, 1992); The Press-Register (November 4, 1992); The Birmingham News (By Michael Brumas, October 3, 1994); The Birmingham News (March 1, 2000); https://www.aging.senate.gov/imo/media/doc/publications/6291991.pdf

Dante Fascell
The Almanac of American Politics, 1990 and 1992; Politics in America, 1992; The New York Times (By Bernard Gwertznian, November 20, 1971); The New York Times (Benjamin Welles, Apil 16, 1972; The Washington Post (By David Rouda, March 2, 1977);
CQ (1974); The New York Times (June 4, 1980); The New York Times (November 25, 1980);

The New York Times (By Steven V. Roberts, April 26, 1981); The New York Times (AP, August 11, 1982); The New York Times (By Martin Tolchin, May 10, 1983); The New York Times (By Bernard Weinraub, May 19, 1983); The LA Times (By Lee May and Douglas Jehl, August 1, 1985); The Orlando Sentinel (1986); Miami New Times (By John Lantigua, August 20, 1998); The Miami Herald (By Rupert Cornwell, December 3, 1998); The New York Times (By Larry Rohter, May 28, 1992); Roll Call (May 28, 1992); The Miami Herald (By Michael Putney, September 2, 2014)

Ed Feighan
The Almanac of American Politics, 1990 and 1992; Politics in America, 1992; The Akron Beacon Journal (October 5, 1977); The New York Times (William K. Stevens, October 9, 1977); The Daily Reporter (November 9, 1977); The Elyira Chronicle-Telegram (May 22, 1982); The Washington Post (By Bill Peterson, May 25, 1982); The Akron Beacon Journal (September 16, 1986); The Washington Post (By Tom Kenworthy September 16, 1988); The Dayton Daily News (December 13, 1989); The New York Times (July 25, 1990); The Akron Beacon Journal (October 29, 1990); CQ (1990); The Plain Dealer (March 17, 1992); The Plain Dealer (April 1, 1992); The Akron Beacon Journal (April 1, 1992); Congressional Record (September 30, 1992); The Cleveland Plain Dealer (By Thomas Brazaitis, December 20, 1992)

Joe Gaydos
The Almanac of American Politics, 1990 and 1992; Politics in America, 1986 and 1992; Congressional Record (August 27, 1980); Congressional Record (December 9, 1981); The Pittsburgh Post-Gazette (February 23, 1983); CQ (By Janet Hook, April 22, 1989); The Pittsburgh Post Gazette (January 16, 1992);

Bill Green
The Almanac of American Politics, 1990 and 1992; Politics in America, 1990; The Jews of Capitol Hill (By Kurt Sone); The New York Times (By Glenn Fowler, February 13, 1978); CQ (February 18, 1978); CQ (October 23, 1978); The New York Times (By Martin Tolchin, October 7, 1981); The New York Times (Editorial, November 1, 1981); The New York Times (By Richard Halloran, November 23, 1982); The New York Times (By Richard Halloran, December 3, 1982); New York Magazine (By Joe Klein, January 23, 1984); New York Magazine (By Joe Klein, October 29, 1984); The New

York Times (By Sarah Lyall, October 25, 1992); The New York Times (By Ian Fisher, May 10, 1994); The New York Times (2002); The Deficit and the Public Interest: The Search for Responsible Budgeting in the 1980s (By Joseph White and Aaron Wildavsky)

Frank Guarini
The Almanac of American Politics, 1992; Politics in America, 1992; Our Campaigns; The New York Times (June 7, 1985); The Washington Post (By Tom Kenworthy, Bruce Brown and Ralph Gaillard Jr. (February 14, 1990); The Chicago Tribune (January 16, 1991, By Michael Arndt)
The New York Times (By Maurice Carroll, April 19, 1985); CQ (1988 overview)
America: Who Really Pays the Taxes? (By Donald L. Barlett)
The Atlanta Journal and Constitution (By Kenneth Harney, April 21, 1991); Congressional Record (October 1, 1992) NJ.com (By Patrick Villanova, November 20, 2017)

John Paul Hammerschmidt
The Almanac of American Politics, 1990 and 1992; Politics in America, 1986 and 1992
Boone County Headlight (By Bill Simmons, November 7, 1974); UPI (October 5, 1980); CQ (1984); The Daily Oklahoman (AP, October 9, 1986); AP (March 23, 1989); The Tulsa World (AP, September 13, 1989); The Star-Ledger (By Guy T. Baehr, March 14, 1991); The New York Times (AP, April 10, 1991); The New York Times (By Richard L. Berke, July 26, 1991); The St. Louis Post-Dispatch (William Buckley column, November 3, 1991); The Washington Times (March 3, 1992); USA Today (Judith Barra, March 27, 1992); The New York Times (By Adam Clymer, April 5, 1992); The Tulsa World (By John Klein, October 22, 1992); the David and Barbara Pryor Center for Arkansas Oral and Visual History, University of Arkansas; Arkansas Memories Project, John Paul Hammerschmidt Interview (March 30, 2009); The New York Times (By Sam Roberts, April 2, 2015); Northwest Arkansas Democrat and Gazette (By Doug Thompson, May 5, 2015)

Charles Hatcher
Congressional Quarterly (July 26, 1980)
The Almanac of American Politics, 1990, 1992 and 1994; Politics in America, 1986, 1992 and 1994; The Atlanta Journal and The Atlanta Constitution - November

3, 1988 ; The Atlanta Journal and The Atlanta Constitution - August 31, 1991; The Atlanta Journal and The Atlanta Constitution (By Jeanne Cummings, September 8, 1991); The Atlanta Journal and The Atlanta Constitution (January 22, 1992); The Atlanta Journal Constitution (March 15, 1992); The Atlanta Journal Constitution (By Bill Montgomery, July 11, 1992); The Atlanta Journal and The Atlanta Constitution - August 5, 1992; The Atlanta Journal and The Atlanta Constitution - August 8, 1992; The Atlanta Journal and The Atlanta Constitution (By Bill Montgomery, August 10, 1992)
The Atlanta Journal Constitution (By Bill Montgomery, August 12, 1992)

Dennis Hertel
Politics in America, 1990 and 1992; The Detroit Free Press (August 6, 1980); Congressional Quarterly (October 14, 1980, November 1, 1980, January 3, 1981); The Ironwood Daily Globe (November 5, 1980); UPI (By Elmer Lammy, February 4, 1982); UPI (September 11, 1982); The New York Times (By Bill Keller, June 26, 1985); The San Diego Union, (By Marcus Stern, June 26, 1985); The New York Times (By James Clarity and Warren Weaver, Jr., December 5, 1985); The Times Union (April 30, 1987); The Providence Journal (By Peter Lord, June 30, 1987);
USA Today (By Jerry Moskal, February 12, 1988); The Detroit Free Press (March 15, 1988); USA Today (June 14, 1990); Green Bay Press Gazette (Gannett News Services, June 15, 1990);
The Detroit Free Press (April 11, 1991); The Detroit Free Press (April 13, 1991); The Detroit Free Press (April 2, 1992); USA Today (April 10, 1992)
June 28, 1990; The Watertown Daily Times (1992)

Joan Kelly Horn
The Almanac of American Politics, 1992 and 1994; Politics in America, 1992 and 1994
Women In Congress; The Chicago Tribune (March 6, 1990); The Chicago Tribune (By Rick Pearson, October 3, 1990); The St. Louis Post-Dispatch (October 21, 1990); The St. Louis Post-Dispatch (By Mark Schlinkmann, with Roger Koenig, October 25, 1990); The St. Louis Post-Dispatch (By Mark Schlinkmann, November 7, 1990); The St. Louis Post-Dispatch (December 22, 1990); The St. Louis Post-Dispatch (February 2, 1991); The St. Louis Post-Dispatch (October 14, 1992); The St. Louis Post-Dispatch (By Mark Schlinkmann, October 31, 1992); The St. Louis Post-Dispatch (By Mark Schlinkmann, November 4, 1992); The St. Louis Post-Dispatch (By Bob Adams, November 13, 1992)

Larry Hopkins

CQ (By Charles Mahtesian, April 27, 1991); The Louisville Courier-Journal (January 1, 1992)

Frank Horton

CQ (December 7, 1962); The Almanac of American Politics, 1982, 1990 and 1992; Politics in America, 1986 and 1992; Congressional Record (July 9, 1965); Congressional Record (September 15, 1965); Silver City Press (By Carl Craft, September 24, 1971); The New York Times (January 30, 1973); The New York Times (By John Finney, March 20, 1973); Democrat and Chronicle from Rochester (September 2, 1976); Congressional Record (March 24, 1980); The New York Times (By John Herbers, March 25, 1981); The New York Times (By David Burnham, May 15, 1985); The Post-Standard (December 12, 1986); Frank Horton: Twenty-Five Years in the United States Congress: 1962 to 1987 (By James Fleming); The Post Standard (By Jonathan D. Salant, December 12, 1987); CQ (By Richard Cowan, May 14, 1988); The Post Standard (Patrick Lakamp, October 28, 1988); The Post Standard (February 3, 1989); The Watertown Daily Times (By Alan Emory, February 5, 1989); CQ (1989); The Heritage Foundation (April 26, 1990); The Watertown Daily Times (March 20, 1990); The Post Standard (By Jonathan Saliant, June 14, 1990); The Post Standard (Jonathan D. Salant, June 30, 1990); Syracuse Herald-Journal (July 23, 1990); The Post Standard (By Jonathan Salant, January 15, 1991); The Watertown Daily Times (By Alan Emory, June 4, 1992); The Post-Standard (June 16, 1992); The Watertown Daily Times (August 15, 1992); The Watertown Daily Times (July 11, 2003); The Washington Post (By Matt Schudel, September 1, 2004); Beyond FTS2000: A Program for Change (By Bernard J. Bennington and Judy Chamberlain)

Carroll Hubbard

The Almanac of American Politics, 1992 and 1994; Politics in America, 1986 and 1992;
The Courier Journal (May 29, 1974); CQ (1974); The Courier Journal (September 24, 1981);
CQ (May 26, 1979); Lexington Herald-Leader (November 12, 1989); The Courier Journal (November 20, 1989); CQ (April 14, 1990); The Courier Journal (April 17, 1990); Lexington Herald-Leader (December 5, 1990); Congressional Record (June 11, 1990); The Courier-Journal (May 17, 1992); The Courier Journal (May 21, 1992); The Courier Journal (May 28, 1992);

The Savings and Loan Crisis: Lessons from a Regulatory Failure (edited by James R. Barth, S. Trimbath, Glenn Yago); The Deficit and the Public Interest: The Search for Responsible Budgeting in the 1980s (By Joseph White and Aaron Wildavsky)

Jerry Huckaby
The Almanac of American Politics, 1992 and 1994; Politics in America, 1986 and 1992; CQ (By Matt Pincus, August 7, 1976); The Biloxi Herald (August 16, 1976); The Monroe News Star (By Tom Walker, October 29, 1976); The Monroe News Star (By Tom Walker, By November 16, 1976); The New York Times (June 5, 1978); The New York Times (By Seth King, April 26, 1979); Congressional Record (May 16, 1979); The New York Times (May 17, 1979); The New York Times (By Steven V. Roberts, March 29, 1981); The New York Times (By Hedrick Smith, May 5, 1981); The New York Times (By Steven Roberts, May 13, 1981); The New York Times (By Seth King, June 27, 1981); Congressional Record (May 10, 1988); The Advocate (Joan McKinney, March 20, 1990); State Times (By Bill McMahon, Capitol News Bureau, June 19, 1991; The Advocate (March 30, 1992); The Advocate (May 4, 1992); Congressional Record (July 24, 1990); The Times Picayune (May 31, 1992); The Advocate (By Joan McKinney, October 12, 1992); The Advocate (October 17, 1992; The Life and Times of Morris K. Udall (By Donald Carson and James W. Johnson)

Andy Ireland
The Baltimore Sun (Knight-Ridder, November 4, 1995)

Ed Jenkins
The Almanac of American Politics, 1990 and 1992; Politics in America, 1986 and 1992; The Atlanta Journal (By Calvin Lawrence, October 20, 1985); The Atlanta Journal (Scott Shepard, July 11, 1987); CQ (By David Cloud, November 14, 1987)

Ben Jones
The Atlanta Journal and The Atlanta Constitution (May 7, 1986); The Atlanta Journal and Constitution (By Hal Strauss, May 10, 1986); The Atlanta Journal Constitution (By Ann Cowles, October 13, 1986); The Atlanta Journal and Constitution (By Ann Cowles, October 22, 1986); The Atlanta Journal and Constitution (By Amy Wallace (August 4, 1988); The Washington

Post (By Morris S. Thompson, October 18, 1988); The Atlanta Journal and Constitution (By Amy Wallace and Cynthia Durcanin, November 9, 1988); The Atlanta Journal and Constitution (By Scott Shephard, December 19, 1988); The Atlanta Journal and Constitution (By Susan Laccetti, May 1, 1990); The New York Times (By Robin Toner, June 17, 1990); AP (By Mike Robinson, June 22, 1990); The Atlanta Journal and The Atlanta Constitution (By Rebecca McCarthy, July 19, 1992); The Atlanta Journal and The Atlanta Constitution (By Rebecca McCarthy, July 22, 1992); The Atlanta Journal and The Atlanta Constitution (July 23, 1992); The Atlanta Journal and The Atlanta Constitution (September 4, 1992) ; The Atlanta Journal Constitution (March 3, 1994); The Atlanta Journal and The Atlanta Constitution (October 5, 1994); The Atlanta Journal and The Atlanta Constitution (October 26, 1994); Redneck Boy in the Promise Land: Confessions of Crazy Cooter (By Ben Jones); The Atlanta Journal Constitution (By Deborah Ann Matthews, November 5, 1986)

Walter Jones
The Almanac of American Politics, 1990 and 1992; Politics in America; The New York Times (April 30, 1987); The Chicago Tribune (May 12, 1989); The Charlotte Observer (By Bill Arthur, July 10, 1989); Congressional Record (November 8, 1989); The Greensboro News and Record (January 24, 1990); The Charlotte Observer (AP, November 4, 1990); The Charlotte Observer (By Rob Christensen, October 5, 1991); Mother Jones (By Robert Dreyfuss, January/February 2006 issue); Titanic: Destination Disaster : The Legends and the Reality (By John P. Eaton, Charles A. Haas)

Jim Jontz
The Almanac of American Politics, 1990 and 1992; Politics in America, 1990 and 1992; The Courier journal (November 8, 1974); The Louisville Courier (By Patrick Siddons, January 12, 1975); Groundwater Protection Through Farm Legislation in the 101st Congress (By Judy Campbell Bird and Janet Edmond); CQ (October 11, 1986); The Indianapolis Star (November 5, 1986); The Post Tribune (April 20, 1987) The Washington Post (By John Lancaster, September 25, 1989); CQ (By David Cloud, April 28, 1990); CQ (By David Cloud, May 19, 1990); CQ (By David Cloud, June 2, 1990); The Times (July 19, 1990); The Post Tribune (By Rich James, August 29, 1990); The Times (September 14, 1990); The Post Tribune (By Rich James, September 30, 1990); The Times (October 16, 1990); The Post Tribune

(November 11, 1990); USA Today (March 6, 1991); USA Today (April 10, 1991); The Congressional Record (June 25, 1991); The Post Bulletin (By Lonnie Kemp, July 25, 1991); The Indianapolis Star (October 30, 1994); The South Bend Tribune (By Jack Colwell, November 5, 1994); High Country News (By Tony Davis, September 2, 1996); By Ray Boomhower

Joe Kolter
CQ (May 8, 1982); CQ (1982); Congressional Record (January 7, 1987)
The Post Gazette (March 12, 1990); Pittsburgh Post-Gazette (By Lee Bowman, January 13, 1991); Kittanning Leader (March 4, 1992); The Altoona Mirror (AP, March 9, 1992)
The Pittsburgh Post Gazette (April 16, 1992); The New Castle News (By John K. Manna, April 25, 1992); The Pittsburgh Post Gazette (April 29, 1992); The Pittsburgh Post Gazette (April 30, 1992);CQ (By Charles Mahtesian, April 18, 1992); The Chicago Tribune (By CQ, May 24, 1992); The LA Times (By Ronald J. Ostrow, November 25, 1992); The Chicago Tribune (By Michael Tackett and Christopher Drew, July 20, 1993); CQ (1993 Overview); The Washington Post (By Toni Locy, October 19, 1994); The New York Times (AP, August 1, 1996); The Times (By J.D. Prose, September 13, 2019)

Peter Kostmayer
The Bucks County Courier (November 3, 1976); The Daily Intelligencer (November 6, 1980); The New York Times (By Hedrick Smith, October 5, 1982); Philadelphia Daily News (By By John F. Morison, November 7, 1984); The Washington Post (By Rowland, Evans and Robert Novak, September 7, 1987); The Morning Call (By Hal Marcowitz, August 19, 1988); The Morning Call (By Hal Marcowitz, August 29, 1990); The Washington Post (By Amanda Spake, January 12, 1992); CQ (February 22, 1992); The Morning Call (By Pete Leffler, April 17, 1992); The Morning Call (By Hal Marcovitz, November 5, 1992); Lost Rights: The Destruction of American Liberty (By James Bovard)

Robert Lagomarsino
The Santa Cruz Sentinel (March 5, 1974); The Lompoc Record (May 21, 1976); The Congressional Record (March 5, 1980); CQ (1983, overview); The New York Times (By Leslie H. Gelb, June 27, 1986); The Congressional Record (November 17, 1983); The Congressional Record (August 3, 1989); CQ (1989, Overview); The LA Times (By Kenneth Weiss, July 1, 1990); The

LA Times (By Kenneth Weiss, November 7, 1990); The LA Times (By Tina Daunt, June 4, 1992); The LA Times (June 5, 1992); The New York Times (By Robert Reinhold, November 5, 1992); The LA Times (December, 1992); The LA Times (By Darryl Kelley, November 29, 1998); The Robert J. Lagomarsino Collection – The Online Archive of California; the Robert J. Lagomarsino Oral History (with Sallie Yates); A Unique Relationship: The United States and the Republic of China Under the Taiwan Relations Act (edited by Ramon Hawley Myers); NPS.gov (By Yvonne Menard, March 1, 2005); Citations – Ventura County Bar Association (By Kathleen J. Smith, June 2017)

William Lehman

The Almanac of American Politics, 1990 and 1992; Politics in America, 1990 and 1992; CQ Overview (1983); The New York Times (AP, March 2, 1983); The New York Times (By Bernard Gwertzman, March 8, 1984); The Miami Herald, (November 22, 1984); The New York Times (February 6, 1986); The New York Times (By Martin Tolchin, March 9, 1987)
The Miami Herald (By Geoffrey Tomb, July 11, 1983); The Sun Sentinel (B William E. Gibson, May 17, 1989); Congressional Record (March 5, 1992); The Jews of Capitol Hill

Norman Lent

The Almanac of American Politics, 1990 and 1992; Politics in America, 1986, 1990 and 1992; CQ (October 2, 1970); UPI (August 10, 1984); CQ (1984); CQ (1987)'The New York Times (By Martin Tolchin, January 24, 1968); The New York Times (By Martin Tolchin, January 31, 1968); The New York Times (By James Clarity, February 21, 1968); The New York Times (By Syney Schanberg, January 30, 1969); The New York Times (By David C. Berliner, March 12, 1972); The New York Times (By Martin Tolchin, February 29, 1976); The New York Times (March 9, 1976); UPI (Patricia Koza, June 11, 1981); UPI (Author: Juan J. Walte, June 24, 1981); The New York Times (By James Barron, July 19, 1981); UPI (By Michael Cohen, May 26, 1982); The New York Times (By Irvin Molotsky, April 2, 1984); The Washington Post (By Cass Peterson, August 11, 1984); Elyira Chronicle-Telegram (Oct); CQ (1984 Overview); The New York Times (January 6, 1985); The New York Times (Letter To The Editor, September 5, 1985); Knickerbocker News (October 9, 1986); AP (By Christopher Callahan, June 10, 1987); CQ (1987 Overview); The New York Times (By Allan R. Gold, October. 12, 1989); The New York Times (By John Rather, August 26, 1990); The New York Times

(By Keith Bradsher, June 24, 1992); The News (AP, July 24, 1992); Newsday (By Sid Cassese, June 13, 2012)

Mel Levine

The Almanac of American Politics, 1990 and 1992; Politics in America, 1986 and 1992; The Los Angeles Times (June 4, 1980); The St. Louis Dispatch (April 10, 1984); The LA Times (By Keav Davidson, March 10, 1985); The LA Times (By Michael Fairley, April 27, 1985);

The LA Times (By Richard Straus, May 18, 1986); The New York Times (Editorial, August 4, 1986); The New York Times (By John H. Cushman, Jr., November 23, 1986); The New York Times (By Philip Shabecoff, July 22, 1987); The Washington Post (August 4, 1987); Congressional Record (October 18, 1990); The LA Times (By Jonathan Weber, January 29, 1991); The LA Times (By Barry M. Horstman, February 25, 1991); The San Diego Union Tribune (By Gerry Braun; March 15, 1992); The LA Times (By Bill Stall and Tracy Wilkinson, March 31, 1992); The San Diego Union Tribune (By Mark Z. Barabak, March 25, 1992; The New York Times (April 17, 1992); The LA Times (By Douglas P. Shuit, May 14, 1992); The Washington Post (By Howard Kurtz, June 7, 1992); The LA Times (By Glenn F. Bunting, December 30, 1992); Running as a Woman: Gender and Power in American Politics (By Linda Witt, Glenna Matthews, Karen M. Paget); Israel: Israel in the International Arena (edited by Efraim Karshins); A Fragile Relationship: The United States and China since 1972 (By Harry Harding)

Bill Lowery

The Almanac of American Politics, 1990 and 1992; Politics in America, 1990 and 1992; The San Diego Union (July 17, 1986); The San Diego Union (July 24, 1986); The San Jose Mercury News (July 25, 1986);

Charles Luken

The Almanac of American Politics, 1992 and 1994; Politics in America, 1992; Ourcampaigns.com; The Cincinnati Post - March 28, 1992; The Columbus Dispatch (AP, February 22, 1988); The Columbus Dispatch (April 8, 1988); The Columbus Dispatch (By Mike Harden, November 17, 1989); The Cincinnati Post (By Sharon Moloney, October 29, 1990); The Cincinnati Enquirer (November 7, 1990; The Cincinnati Post (June 8, 1991); The Cincinnati Post (June 27, 1991); The Cincinnati Post (By Adam Condo, May 5, 1992); The Cincinnati Post (By Sharon Moloney, June 30, 1992); The

Dayton Daily News (June 30, 1992); The Cincinnati Enquirer (By Howard Wilkinson, November 3, 1999); City Beat (By George Flannery, June 5, 2001); CNN (April 11, 2001)

Ron Marlenee

The Almanac of American Politics, 1990 and 1992; Politics in America, 1990 and 1992; CQ (April 30, 1986); The Hackensack Record (May 22, 1986); CQ (March 19, 1988); The Bozeman Daily Chronicle (By Scott Williams, AP, November 4, 1992)

David Martin

The Almanac of American Politics, 1990 and 1992; Politics in America, 1990 and 1992; The New York Times (By Edward A. Gargan, September 12, 1984; The Watertown Daily Times (February 28, 1988); The Watertown Daily Times (June 15, 1989); The Watertown Daily Times (December 8, 1989); The Watertown Daily News (By Alan Emory, September 11, 1990); The Watertown Daily News (By Marsha J. Davis, January 19, 1990); Congressional Quarterly (September 15, 1990); The New York Times (January 6, 1993); By Gordon Block, Times Staff Writer 2014

Nick Mavroules

The Almanac of American Politics, 1992 and 1994; Politics in America, 1986, 1992 and 1994
The Washington Post (By Margaret Shapiro and Fred Hiatt, December 21, 1983) ; The Daily Press (By Robert Becker, February 12, 1990); The Boston Herald (By David Armstrong and Shelley Murphy, August 28, 1992); The New York Times (AP, August 29, 1992); The Lowell Sun (August 31, 1992); The Worcester Telegram and Gazette (August 31, 1992); CQ (By Ceci Connolly, September 5, 1992); The Boston Herald (September 11, 1992); The Boston Herald (September 17, 1992); Justia U.S. Law (February 17, 1993); The Boston Herald (April 7, 1993); UPI (By Ken Cafarell, June 29, 1993); The Boston Herald (June 30, 1993); The Congressional Record (January 21, 2004)

Bob McEwen

The Almanac of American Politics, 1992 and 1994; Politics in America, 1986 and 1992; CQ (May 24, 1980); The Columbus Dispatch (March 23, 1987); The Columbus Dispatch (March 5, 1991); The Columbus Dispatch (September 6, 1991); The Dayton Daily News (By Adrianne Flynn, April 17,

1992); The Columbus Dispatch (By Roger K. Lowe, Dispatch Washington Bureau, May 31, 1992); The Columbus Dispatch (By Roger K. Lowe, June 4, 1992); Roll Call (October 18, 1992); The Dayton Daily News (By Martin Gottlieb, March 5, 1993); Roll Call (2005)

Ray McGrath

The Almanac of American Politics, 1990 and 1992; Politics in America, 1986 and 1992; Congressional Quarterly (October 1980); The New York Times (By Frank Lynn, Ocober 24, 1982); CQ (1985); The Chicago Tribune (Bill Neikirk and Lea Donosky, September 29, 1985); AP (By Jim Luther, November 26, 1985); The New York Times (By David E. Rosenbaum, November 27, 1985); AP (By Eileen Putman, December 13, 1985); The New York Times (By Lindsey Gruson, June 10, 1992); The New York Times (By State News, June 28, 1992); The Washington Post (By Peter Carlson, October 17, 1993); Bargaining Under Federalism: Contemporary New York (By Sarah F. Liebschutz)

Matt McHugh

The Almanac of American Politics, 1990 and 1992; Politics in America; ourcampaigns.com;CQ (January 4, 1975); CQ (1979); CQ (October 11, 1980); CQ (1981); CQ (October 22, 1983);
CQ (By Carroll Doherty, August 25, 1990); The New York Times (By Bernard Gwertzman, February 25, 1978); The New York Times (By Martin Tolchin, April 27, 1983); The Turkey and the Eagle: The Struggle for America's Global Role (By Caleb S. Rossiter); The Washington Post (October 28, 1989); The Syracuse Herald-Journal (By Lillie Wilson, May 5, 1992); The Post Standard (Eric Lichtblau, April 6, 1987); The Post-Standard (December 24, 1987); The New York Times (May 10, 1992); The Washington Post (By Kenneth J. Cooper, May 5, 1992) Deciding to Intervene: The Reagan Doctrine and American Foreign Policy (By James M. Scott); Author: Steve Gerstel, January 4, 1984; USA Today (By John Machacek, October 3, 1990); USA Today (By John Machacek, April 23, 1991); The New York Times (By Adam Clymer, June 21, 1991); The Syracuse Herald-Journal (April 1, 1993)

Tom McMillen

The Almanac of American Politics, 1990, 1992 and 1994; Politics in America; Our Campaigns;
UPI (By Myriam Marquez, November 6, 1986); The Baltimore Sun (June 14, 1991); The Baltimore Evening Sun (By Josie Karp, July 26, 1991); The

Baltimore Sun (By John Fairhall, August 30, 1991); The Baltimore Sun (William Thompson, September 25, 1991; The Baltimore Sun (October 6, 1991); The Baltimore Sun (October 12, 1991); The Baltimore Sun (By Liz Atwood, October 9, 1992); The Baltimore Sun (By William Thompson and Tom Bowman, October 25, 1992); The Baltimore Sun (By William Thompson and Tom Bowman, November 4, 1992); Interview with Andy Ockershausen (Transcribed by Janice Ockershausen (January 25, 2018); The Baltimore Sun Gazette (December 6, 2018)

Clarence Miller

Politics in America; The Almanac of American Politics, 1992; CQ (1976 overview);
Athens Messenger (November 9, 1966); Congressional Quarterly (December 16, 1966);
Congressional Record (June 16, 1976); The Congressional Record (September 23, 1992)
The Columbus Dispatch (December 29, 1991); The Cincinnati Post (By Adam Condo, May 16, 1992); The Columbus Dispatch (Roger K. Lowe, May 31, 1992)

John Miller

The Almanac of American Politics, 1990 and 1992; Politics in America, 1990 and 1992; Ourcampaigns.com; The Jews of Capitol Hill (By Kurt Stone); Walla-Walla Union Bulletin (October 31, 1980); The Seattle Post-Intelligencer (April 2, 1987); The Seattle Times (By Eric Pryne, April 29, 1987); The Seattle Times (July 12, 1990); The Seattle Times (July 19, 1990); The Seattle Times (July 29, 1990); The Seattle Post Intelligencer (By Neil Modie, November 7, 1990); The Seattle Post Intelligencer (Rebecca Boren, P-I Reporter, By January 18, 1992); Washington History Link (By David Wilma, October 16, 2001); The Discovery Institute (September 5, 2003); The Herald (By Jerry Kornfield, October 15, 2017); The National Journal (By George Weigel, October 2017); Historylink.org (By Rita Cipalla, November 8, 2018)

Jim Moody

The Almanac of American Politics, 1990 and 1992, By Michael Barone); Politics in America, 1986 and 1992; Civil Strife in Yugoslavia: The United States Response : Hearing ...(February 21, 1991); Milwaukee Journal Sentinal (By Sophie Carson, March 27, 2019); Raising Hell for Justive (By David Obey)

Sid Morrison

The Almanac of American Politics, 1990 and 1992, By Michael Barone); Politics in America, 1986 and 1992; Walla-Walla Union Bulletin (November 5, 1980); The New York Times (By Robert Pear, July 30, 1984); The Reno Gazette Journal (December 20, 1984); The Seattle Post Intelligencer (By Joel Connelly, May 4, 1986); The LA Times (By Bob Secter, August 1, 1986); The Seattle Post Intelligencer (October 17, 1986); UPI (By Ethan Rarick, June 22, 1990); Kitsap Sun (March 24, 1992); The Kitsap Sun (April 16, 1992); Seattle Post Intelligencer (By Joel Connelly, May 20, 1992); Reno Gazette Journal (By Dennis Myers, July 21, 2011); Defending Wild Washington: A Citizen's Action Guide (By Edward A. Whitesell); Immigration Reform and Perishable Crop Agriculture: Compliance Or Circumvention? (By Monica L. Heppel and Sandra L. Amendola); Katie Floyd, Cahnrs and WSU Extension Marketing, News, and Educational Communications Intern

Robert Mrazek

The Almanac of American Politics, 1990 and '92); Politics in America, 1986 and 1992; Our Campaigns; UPI (June 3, 1987) ; The New York Times (By Jane Perlez, October 21, 1982);
The LA Times (By Nina Easton, August 4, 1988); The Washington Post (By Dan Morgan, June 28, 1990); The New York Times (By Frank Linn, March 17, 1991); The New York Times (By Kevin Sack, June 6, 1991); New York Magazine (July 7, 1991); The New York Times (By Barbara Gamarekian, July 25, 1991); The New York Times (By Michael Specter, March 16, 1992); The New York Times (By Robert Pear, March 20, 1992); The New York Times (By Michael Specter, April 8, 1992); Congressional Quarterly (By Jeffrey L. Katz and Ines Pinto Alicea); Nitrate Won't Wait: A History of Film Preservation in the United States
(By Anthony Slide); Roll Call (April 13, 2016); The Asylumist (October 25, 2017)

David Nagle

Politics in America, 1992; The Almanac of American Politics, 1992 and 1994; Ourcampaigns.com; CQ (May 1986); The Des Moines Register (By David Yepsen, May 29, 1986); CQ (By David Cloud, May 27, 1989); The Gazette (By Lyle Muller, January 14, 1992); The Gazette (June 11, 1992); The Washington Times (By William J. Eaton, June 13, 1992); CQ (1992); The Gazette (By David Lynch, November 8, 1992); The Gazette (By David Lynch, October 10, 1994); Telegraph Herald (Dubuque, IA) - September 5, 1997

Dick Nichols

Politics in America, 1992; The Almanac of American Politics, 1992 and 1994; Ourcampaigns.com; CQ (July 27, 1990); The McPherson Sentinel (August 9, 1990); The Press Democrat (January 13, 1991); The Congressional Record (June 10, 1991); The Congressional Record (June 1, 1992); The McPherson Sentinel (By Jim Misunas, June 30, 2007)
The Wichita Eagle (By Stan Finger, March 9, 2019)

Henry Nowak

Politics in America, 1986 and 1992; The Almanac of American Politics, 1992; The New York Times (By Martin Tolchin, July 21, 1975); The New York Times (By Martin Tolchin, February 1976); The New York Times (November 13, 1977); The New York Times (By Jane Perlez, February 4, 1983); The New York Times (August 19, 1984); The New York Times (August 15, 1986); The Buffalo News (By Robert J. McCarthy, January 29, 1989); The Buffalo News (March 16, 1989); The Buffalo News (April 1, 1989); The Watertown Daily Times (May 3, 1990); The Buffalo News (By Jerry Zremski, March 20, 1992); The Buffalo News (By Douglas Turner, June 17, 1992); The Buffalo News – Editorial (June 17, 1992); The Buffalo News (By Douglas Turner, June 22, 1992); The Am-Pol Eagle (By Glenn Gramigna); Heavy Traffic: Deregulation, Trade, and Transformation in North American Trucking (By Daniel Madar)

Mary Rose Oakar

The Almanac of American Politics, 1992 and 1994; Politics in America, 1986, 1992 and 1994; The New York Times (By Bernard Gwertzman, November 5, 1977); Congressional Record (May 27, 1982); The New York Times (By Bernard Weintraub, June 18, 1982); UPI (August 18, 1985); The Seattle Post-Intelligencer (May 28, 1986); The New York Times (March 28, 1987); Akron Beacon Journal (By William Hershey, December 5, 1988); Akron Beacon Journal (September 1, 1989); Congressional Record (October 11, 1990); The Plain Dealer (By Tom Diemer, November 24, 1991); Congressional Quarterly (March 27, 1992); The New York Times (By Adam Clymer, May 27, 1992); The New York Times (March 31, 1992); The Plain Dealer (By Jonathan Riskind, May 31, 1992); The Plain Dealer (By Keith C. Epstein, October 11, 1992); The Plain Dealer, (By Steve Luttner, October 14, 1992); The Plain Dealer (By Michelle Ruess, November 8, 1992); The Plain Dealer (By Michelle Ruess, May 23, 1993); CleveScene (By Mark Naymik, April 2, 1999)

Jim Olin

The Almanac of American Politics, 1990 and 1992; Politics in America; Our Campaigns; CQ (October 9, 1982); The Washington Post (By Celestine Bohlen, November 4, 1982); CQ (September 27, 1985); The Roanoke Times (By Dwayne Yancey, December 26, 1991)
The Roanoke Times, (July 14, 1990) ; The Richmond Times-Dispatch (UPI, March 1, 1989); The Roanoke Times (February 11, 1990); The Roanoke Times (April 9, 1990); The Roanoke Times (By Greg Edwards, April 26, 1990); The Roanoke Times, (August 3, 1990); The Roanoke Times (By David Reed, AP, November 5, 1991); The Roanoke Times (By Dwayne Yancey, December 17, 1991); The Roanoke Times (By Dwayne Yancey, December 26, 1991); The Roanoke Times (February 12, 1994); Jim Olin Obituary; The Roanoke Times (Editorial, May 16, 2018)

Wayne Owens

The Salt Lake City Tribune (November 8, 1972); The New York Times (By James M. Naughton, April 28, 1974); The Daily Independent Journal 9July 30, 1974); The New York Times (By Jon Nordheimer, November 6, 1974); CQ (October 11, 1986); CQ (By Joseph A. Davis, March 19. 1988); CQ (1988); CQ (February 25, 1989); The Deseret News, (April 7, 1989); The LA Times (July 9, 1989); The Deseret News (February 7, 1991); The Chicago Tribune (By James Coates, May 26, 1991; The Deseret News (By Bob Bernick, June 14, 1992); The Salt Lake City Tribune (By Jim Woolf, October 10, 1992); The Salt Lake Tribune (By Dawn House and Shelia R. McCann, October 12, 1992); The Deseret News (Bob Bernick Jr., Political Editor, Oct 31, 1992); The Desseret News (By Lee Davidson, October 1, 1993); The Desseret News (By Lee Davidson, December 19 and 20, 2002); Utahpolicy.com (By Bob Bernick, 2014); The Wayne Owens Papers

Don Pease

The Almanac of American Politics, 1990 and 1992; Politics in America, 1992; Ourcampaigns.com; The Washington Post (By Susanna McDee, November 11, 1977); The New York Times (By John De St. Jerre, April 9, 1978); The New York Times (By Jonathan Fuerbringer, June 13, 1984); The Akron Beacon Journal (January 31, 1985); The Akron Beacon Journal (By William Hershey, May 25, 1986); The Columbus Dispatch (By R. Chris Burnett, July 20, 1986); The New York Times (By Jonathan Fuerbringer, March 13, 1987); The New York Times (By Jonathan Fuerbringer, June 13, 1984); The

Columbus Dispatch (By R. Chris Burnet, June 14, 1987); The Columbus Dispatch (R. Chris Burnett, July 13, 1986); CQ (1989); The Multinational Monitor (December 1990); The Akron Beacon Journal (October 1, 1991)

Chris Perkins
The Almanac of American Politics, 1990 and 1992; Politics in America, 1990 and 1992; The Lexington Herald-Leader (By Michael York, January 4, 1985); The Lexington Herald-Leader (By Lee Mueller, August 26, 1985); The Lexington Herald-Leader (June 17, 1988); The Lexington Herald-Leader (June 14, 1989); The Lexington Herald-Leader (January 20, 1990); The Lexington Herald Leader (By Mary Ann Roser, April 15, 1990); The Lexington Herald-Leader (By Lee Mueller, November 7, 1990); The Kentucky Post (November 9, 1990)
The Lexington Hearld-Ledger (By Mary Ann Roser, December 29, 1991); The Lexington Herald-Ledger (By Mary Ann Roser and Lee Muelle, January 23, 1992); TDN (Staff, January 8, 2005)

Liz Patterson
The Almanac of American Politics, 1990 and 1992; Politics in America, 1992; The State, (July 31, 1988); The Herald-Journal (September 7, 1988); The Herald Journal (October 18, 1988); The State (By Kathy Kadane, July 25, 1989); The State (By Lee Bandy, July 15, 1991); The Herald-Journal (May 30, 1992; The Herald-Journal (June 12, 1992)
The Herald-Journal (October 18, 1992); The Herald-Journal (October 23, 1992);
The Herald-Journal (November 4, 1992); The State (November 5, 1992); The Herald-Journal (By Felecia Kitzmiller, August 28, 2014

Carl Pursell
The Almanac of American Politics, 1992; Politics in America, 1986 and 1992; CQ (1986 Overview)
http://www.nwitimes.com/uncategorized/russo-s-barbados-trip-blasted-on-tv/article_8bc4fb43-1ca0-596e-9334-669ec3ece50c.html
Carl Pursell, Oral History Interview, 1998 - Digital Commons @ EMU commons.emich.edu/cgi/viewcontent.cgi?article=1021&context=oral_histories
The New York Times (By Jane Perlez, May 11, 1982); The New York Times (By Steven V. Roberts, June 8, 1982); The New York Times (March 2, 1983);

The Chicago Tribune (By Bill Neikirk and Lea Donosky, September 29, 1985); The Washington Post (By Mike McIntyre, March 4, 1987); Michigan Daily (By Vince Wilk, November 9, 1988); AP (June 7, 1990); The LA Times (By William Eaton, December 4, 1990); Detroit Free Press (March 25, 1992); Newsweek (By Floyd Sanholtz with Ann McDaniel and Thomas DeFranke, October 15, 1990; The Washington Post (Saturday, June 13, 2009); Congressional Record (2009); Roll Call (2009)
Reforming the US Corporate Tax (By Gary Clyde Hufbauer); Agenda for Empowerment: Readings in American Government and the Policy Process (edited by Stuart M. Butler)

Matthew Rinaldo

The Almanac of American Politics, 1990 and 1992; Politics in America, 1992 Ourcampaigns.com; The New York Times (By Ronald Sullivan, February 10, 1970); The New York Times (By Ronald Sullivan, February 10, 1972); The New York Times (April 2, 1972); The New York Times (May 21, 1972); The New York Times (By David C. Berliner, October 21, 1973); Congressional Record (July 10, 1974); The Christian Science Monitor (By Ed Townsend, October 15, 1980); The Courier News (November 5, 1980); The New York Times (By Joseph F. Sullivan, October 18, 1982); The Courier News (By Gabriel H. Gluck, November 3, 1982); CQ (1983 Overview); UPI NewsTrack (October 26, 1983); The Record (By Robert Kravitz, March 21, 1985); Subcommittee on Telecommunications Hearing (September 30, 1987); The New York Times (State News Services, February 21, 1988); UPI (By Norman D. Sandler, July 11, 1988); USA Today (March 28, 1989) ; The Star-Ledger (May 25, 1989); Congressional Quarterly (By Allyson Pytte, June 30, 1990);The Courier-News (September 12, 1992); The New York Times (By Jerry Gray, October 17, 1992); The Record (New Jersey) - April 9, 1993 ; The Star-Ledger (By Carly Rothman, October 16, 2008)

Don Ritter

The Almanac of American Politics, 1992; Politics in America, 1990; CQ (1987 Overview);
The Philadelphia Inquirer (By Carl Cannon, March 13, 1983); UPI (Author: Charles J. Abbott, June 21, 1983); The New York Times (By David Shribman, August 5, 1983);
The Morning Call (By Katherine Reinhard, September 14, 1984); The Chicago Tribune (By Terry Atlas, February 28, 1985); The Morning Call (October 13,

1988); The Morning Call (By Scott Higham, October 19, 1988); The Morning Call (By Pete Leffler, December 1, 1989); The Morning Call (By Rosa Salter, January 14, 1991); The New York Times (By David Binder, January 18, 1991); The Morning Call, (By Bob Wittman, December 27, 1992); Trade Warriors: States, Firms, and Strategic-Trade Policy in High-Technology Competition (By Marc L. Busch); Metropolitan Area Networks Newsletter (By Paul Polishuk); Hazardous Substance Victim's Compensation Legislation: Hearing Before the Subcommittee on Commerce, Transportation and Tourism (By United States. Congress. House. Committee on Energy and Commerce. Subcommittee on Commerce, Transportation, and Tourism, June 29, 1983)

Jay Rhodes

The Almanac of American Politics, 1992; Politics in America, 1990; Ourcampaigns.com; The Congressional Record (June 24, 1987); The Sierra Club Canyon Echo, Grand Canyon Chapter (August 1987); The Arizona Daily Star (February 10, 1991); The Arizona Daily Star (September 9, 1992); The Arizona Daily Star (By Ellen Gamerman, October 7, 1992)

Robert Roe

The Almanac of American Politics, 1990 and 1992; Politics in America, 1986 and 1992; CQ (November 1969); The New York Times (By Martin Gansberg, October 8, 1970); The New York Times (By Edward Burks, February 13, 1977); The New York Times (By Joseph Sullivan, February 22, 1977); The New York Times (By Edward Burks); The New York Times (By Martin Waldron, June 4, 1977); The New York Times (By Edward C. Burks, December 19, 1977); The New York Times (By Joseph Sullivan, Aril 28, 1981); The New York Times (By Phillip Shabecoff, July 24, 1985); LA Times (AP, June 10, 1986); UPI June 11, 1986); CQ (By Steve Blakely and John Crawford, June 14, 1986); A (March 30, 1992); (Politickernj (By Max Pizarro, July 14, 2014); The Star Ledger (By Scott Orr, July 16, 2014); The Star Ledger (By Phillip Beachem, July 18, 2014)

Edward Roybal

The Almanac of American Politics, 1990 and 1992; Politics in America, 1990 and 1992; CR (October 14, 1978); CQ (1990 Overview); Mo-The Life and Times of Morris K. Udall; Los Angeles Transformed: Fletcher Bowron's Urban Reform Revival, 1938-1953 (By Tom Sitton); Jet (February 25, 1960); The Washington Post (By Charles Babcock, October 14, 1978); UPI NewsTrack

(April 1, 1981); The New York Times (By Robert Pear, December 18, 1982); MacNeil Lehrer Transcript (May 30, 1984); The New York Times (By Robert Pear, October 13, 1986); The New York Times (By Linda Greenhouse, June 12, 1986); The LA Times (By Glenn Bunting, December 23, 1991); The LA Times (By Terry McDermott, January 15, 1999); The LA Times (By Antonio Olivo, July 27, 1999); PeoplesWorld (By Rosalio Munoz, Novmber 2, 2005) Pioneering Minority Representation: Edward Roybal and the Los Angeles City Council, 1949-1962 (By Katherine Underwood); Race and politics (By Leland T. Saito, (Asian –Americans, Whites and Latinos in an LA Suburb); Kennethburt.com (May 11, 2013)

Marty Russo

The Almanac of American Politics; Politics in America; President Carter: The White House Years (By Stuart E. Eizenstat); Harvey Star Tribune (By Stephanie Rusnak, November 7, 1974); CQ (By Ann Pelham, May 5, 1979); CQ (By Pamela Fessler, May 4, 1985)' CQ (By Joan Biskupic, February 9, 1991); The Chicago Tribune (By Martin Locin, March 17, 1991); The Chicago Tribune (By Thomas Hardy, January 31, 1992); The Chicago Tribune (By Steve Johnson, February 19, 1992); The Chicago Tribune (By Thomas Hardy, February 26 1992); UPI (March 17, 1992); The Chicago Sun Times (By Tom Brune, March 18, 1992); CQ (By Bob Benenson, March 7, 1992); By David Moberg (

Jim Scheuer

The Almanac of American Politics; Politics in America; Our Campaigns; CQ (May 22, 1964 and June 5, 1964); The New York Times (October 29, 1964); CQ (1965); New York Magazine (By Fred Ferretti, March 3, 1969); The New York Times (By Paul Montgomery, January 15, 1972); The New York Times (By Joseph Lelyveld, April 25, 1972); The New York Times (Op/Ed, June 12, 1972); The New York Times (June 14, 1972); The New York Times (By Irvin Molotsky, November 8, 1979); The Washington Post (By Margot Hornblower, January 28, 1981); The New York Times (By Irvin Molotsky, Jan. 29, 1981); The New York Times (February 6, 1981)

Richard Schulze

The Almanac of American Politics, 1984, 1990 and 1992; Politics in America, 1992; CQ (February 4. 1978); The Washington Post (By Ward Sinclair, October 7, 1979); The Washington Post (By David Broder, July 27, 1981); LA Times (October 6, 1989)

The Morning Call (October 31, 1991); The Philadelphia Inquirer (March 17, 1992)

Gerry Sikorsi and Vin Weber

The Almanac of American Politics, 1984, 1990 and 1992; Politics in America, 1992; CQ (October 11, 1978); CQ(October 11, 1980); CQ (January 3, 1981); The New York Times (By David Shribman, April 24, 1983); The New York Times (By Martin Tolchin, May 10, 1983); Open vault from WBGH (July 24, 1983); The New York Times (By Steven Marcus, November 7, 1983); The Washington Post (January 29, 1984); The New York Times (By Steven V. Roberts, May 15, 1984); The New York Times (By Hedrick Smith, July 28, 1985; The New York Times (By Neil Lewis, August 16, 1985); The New York Times (By Susan F. Rasky, September 15, 1985); The Star Tribune: Newspaper of the Twin Cities (January 9, 1986); The New York Times (By Steven V. Robert, February 10, 1986); The Chicago Tribune (By Casey Burko, March 9, 1986); The Star-Tribune (By Steve Berg, March 13, 1986); The New York Times (By Robert Pear, March 20, 1986);The Star Tribune: Newspaper of the Twin Cities (April 20, 1986); The Star Tribune: Newspaper of the Twin Cities (May 18, 1986); The Star Tribune (By Richard Meryhew, November 5, 1986); The Star Tribune (By Cliff Haas, July 19, 1987); The Washington Post (By Erin Pianin, May 21, 1988); CQ (April 22, 1989); Knight-Ridder (By Mark Thompson, April 27, 1989); The New York Times (By Leonard Sloane, September 15, 1990); CQ (1990 Overview); The LA Times (By Michael Ross, March 23, 1991); The New York Times (March 24, 1991); The Star Tribune (April 18, 1991); The St. Paul Pioneer Press (March 13, 1992); The Chicago Tribune (By Jan Beck, March 19, 1992); Newsweek (March 28, 1992); The New York Times (By Clifford Krause, April 16, 1992); The Star Tribune (August 25, 1992); The St. Paul Pioneer Press (April 4, 1992); The Washington Post (By Edward Walsh, April 19, 1992); The Minneapolis Star Tribune (By Mike Kaszuba and Chris Ison, September 16, 1992); The St. Paul Pioneer Press (By Steven Thomma, November 5, 1992); The Star Tribune (By Clifford Haas, December 20, 1992); The Age of Missing Information (By Bill McKibben);

Larry Smith

The Almanac of American Politics, 1990 and 1992; Politics in America, 1986 and 1990; The Miami Herald (August 17, 1982); CQ (By Phil Becker, August 21, 1982); The New York Times (By Bernard Gwertzman, February 11, 1984);

The New York Times (By Joel Brinkley, May 27, 1984); Congressional Record (1984); The Sun Sentinel (By Renee Krause, May 15, 1985); The Christian Science Monitor (By George Moffett III, May 28, 1985); The New York Times (By Bernard Gwertzman, September 13, 1985); CQ (1985 Overview); The Jewish Floridian of South Florida (October 10, 1986); St. Petersburg Times (December 17, 1987); The Jewish Floridian of South Broward (By Howard Rosenberg, May 6, 1988); The Miami Herald (November 8, 1988); The Sun Sentinel (By Ken Cummins, February 26, 1989); The Miami Herald (By David Hess and Brenda Flory, Washington Bureau, June 22, 1990); The Miami Herald (August 9, 1990); The New York Times (By Michael R. Gordon, September 27, 1990); The Congressional Record (June 6, 1991); The Washington Post (By John M. Goshko, February 25, 1992); The Washington Report (By Andrew I. Killgore, June 1992); The Miami Herald (By Peter Slevin and Eston Melton, September 8, 1992); Roll Call (By Stacy Mason); The New York Times (AP, August 3, 1993); The Tampa Tribune (By Lisa Ocker, October 6, 1993); The Miami Herald (By Ronnie Greene, February 24, 1995)
The Sun Sentinel (By Kathy Hensley Trumbull,)
The Washington Post (1991)

Stephen Solarz

The Almanac of American Politics 1990 and 1992; Politics in America, 1986 and 1992; The Washington Post (By Don Oberdorfer, September 5, 1980); The LA Times (By Sara Fritz, April 4, 1985); The LA Times (By Don Shannon, May 1, 1985); The New York Times (By Neil A. Lewis, August 16, 1985); CQ (1985 – Overview); The New York Times (By Jonathan Fuerbinger, June 6, 1985); The New York Times (By Stephen J. Solarz, February 25, 1989); Congressional Record (January 1, 1991; The Washington Post (By Lois Romano and Tom Kenworthy, May 29, 1991); The New York Times (By Lindsey Gruson, March 16, 1992); The Chicago Tribune (April 1992); Stephen J. Solarz: Journeys to War and Peace (By Stephen J. Solarz); The United States and Cambodia, 1969-2000: A Troubled Relationship (By Kenton Clymer)

Harley Staggers

The Almanac of American Politics; Politics in America; Congressional Record (November 17, 1983); The New York Times (By Wayne King and Warren Weaver Jr., April 16, 1986); Congressional Record (June 23, 1990); The

Richmond Times Dispatch (July 12, 1990); Congressional Quarterly (July 20, 1990); The Bluefield Telegraph (AP, November 7, 1990); Legal Services Corporation Reauthorization: Hearing Before the Subcommittee (By United States. Congress. House. Committee, March 13, 1991); The New York Times (By Gwen Ifill, May 8, 1991); The Washington Post (By Tom Kenworthy, May 9, 1991); Congressional Quarterly (April,1992); The Cumberland Times (May 13, 1992)

Richard Stallings
The Almanac of American Politics, 1990 and 1992; Politics in America, 1990 and 1992; The Washington Post (By James Schwartz, September 1, 1984); Walla Walla Union (September 23, 1984); The Lewiston Tribune (AP, March 1, 1990); AP (By Quade Kenyon, August 7, 1991); The Lewiston Tribune (AP, June 17, 1992); The Post Register (October 4, 1992); Congressional Quarterly (October 24, 1992); The Post Register (By Stephen Stuebner, November 4, 1992); The Post Register (By Tony December 27, 1992)

Robin Tallon
The State (AP, November 9, 1988); The Item (By Bruce Smith, September 30, 1989); The State (March 3, 1990); The State (AP, November 1991); The State (By Lee Bandy, January 5, 1992

Lindsay Thomas
The Almanac of American Politics, 1990 and 1992; Politics in America, 1986, 1990 and 1992; Ourcampaigns.com; The Washington Post (By Ward Sinclair, December 2, 1985); The Atlanta Journal and Atlanta Constitution (January 9, 1992); The Atlanta Journal and Atlanta Constitution (January 15, 1992); Georgia Trend Magazine (By Ed- 2001)

Bob Traxler
The Detroit Free Press (By Roger Lane, December 26, 1971); Benton Harbor News Palladium Archives (February 25, 1972); Congressional Quarterly (April 16 and 23, 1974); The New York Times (By William K. Stevens, April 18, 1974); Ripon Forum (May 1, 1974); CQ (1981 Overview); UPI (By Edward Roby, December 24, 1981); CQ (December 15, 1982); The Chicago Tribune (By David Broder, October 23, 1988); CQ (Overview, 1992); The Detroit Free Press (May 1, 1992); The Washington Post (By Brian Mooar and Gabriel Escobar May 29, 1992); Michigan Political History Society Oral

History Project (With Bill Ballenger, May 14, 2008); My Bay City (By Tim Skubick, August 17, 2017)
Ironwood Globe (

Guy Vander Jagt

The Almanac of American Politics; Politics in America; Ourcampaigns.com; Harper's Magazine (By John Corry, 1971); The Washington Post (By E.J. Dionne Jr., November 2, 1990)

Ted Weiss

Politics in America; The Almanac of American Politics, 1990 and 1992; Ourcampaigns.com;
The Jews of Capitol Hill (By Kurt Stone); The New York Times (By Clayton Knowles, June 29, 1966); The New York Times (By Maurice Carroll, July 2, 1966); The New York Times (By Clayton Knowles, September 26, 1966); The New York Times (By Maurice Carroll, January 21, 1970); The New York Times (By Edward Ranzal, January 28, 1972); The New York Times (By Mary Breasted, February 9, 1976); The New York Times (By Edward Ranzal, May 14, 1976); The New York Times (September 22, 1976); The New York Times (December 6, 1976); The New York Times (March 24, 1977); The Christian Science Monitor (By Christina Ravashicric, February 5, 1982); The New York Times (By Frank Lynn, April 4, 1982); Columbia Spectator Archive (November 11, 1983); AP (By Mike Shanahan, February 28, 1985); The New York Times (By Michael Oreskes, June 28, 1986); The New York Times (By Phillip Boffey, October 7, 1987); The Washington Post (By Spencer Rich, October 9, 1987); The Washington Post (By Paula Yost, July 12, 1989); The New York Times (By Robin Toner, July 13, 1989); The Chicago Tribune (By Elaine Povich, September 13, 1989); The LA Times (By William J. Eaton, October 13, 1989); The Daily Oklahoman (December 21, 1989); The LA Times (By Shawn Pogatchnik and Allan Parachini, December 17, 1989); CQ (1990); The New York Times (By Philip J. Hilts, November 15, 1990); The New York Times (By Lindsey Gruson, July 11, 1991); The New York Times (By Todd Purdum, September 24, 1992); Congressional Record (September 30, 1992); Time Magazine (By Ed Magnuson, June 24, 2001);

Howard Wolpe

The Almanac of American Politics; Politics in America; CQ (2/24/87); The New York Times (By Jonathan Fuerbringer, June 6, 1985); The New York

Times (By Stephen V. Roberts, September 13, 1986); The Jewish Telegraphic Agency (1987); The Detroit Free Press (March 31, 1992); The Battle Creek Enquirer (By Gazette Staff, December 13, 1992)
Newsreel.org (January 2006, Onlined Version); The Kalamazoo Gazette (Gazette Staff, October 27, 2011); The Wilson Center (By Steve McDonald, October 28, 2011); Paying Attention to Foreign Affairs: How Public Opinion Affects Presidential ...(By Thomas Knecht)

Chalmers Wylie

The Almanac of American Politics; Politics in America; CQ (December 16, 1966); Congressional Record (June 25, 1986); The New York Times (By David Stout, August 15 1998); The New York Times (By Marjorie Hunter, September 22, 1971); CQ (1971); The Columbus Dispatch (By Ray Crumbley, February 28, 1990); The Columbus Dispatch (August 21, 1990); The Columbus Dispatch (March 17, 1990); The Columbus Dispatch (By George Embley, September 11 1991); The Columbus Dispatch (September 15, 1991); The Columbus Dispatch (By Mike Curtin and Roger K. Lowe, March 31, 1992); The Columbus Dispatch (November 1, 1992); The Lexington Herald-Leader (By Ken Fireman, June 27, 1986); The Columbus Dispatch, (March 22, 1987); The Dover Times Reporter (March 21, 1987); The New York Times (By Nathaniel C. Nash, August 4, 1987); The New York Times (By Stephen Labaton, December 15, 1991); Congressional Record (September 22, 1992)

Chapter One

The Capital Times, (October 3, 1991); USA Today (BY Bob Minzesheimer and Richard Wolf, October 3, 1991); USA Today (BY Bob Minzesheimer and Richard Wolf, October 3, 1991); The Washington Post (By Tom Kenworthy and Eric Pianin, October 4, 1991); The Capital Times (AP, October 10, 1991); CQ (By Janet Hook, March 7, 1992); The Plain Dealer (March 13, 1992); CQ (By Phil Kuntz with Pat Towell, Janet Hook and Thomas Galvin, March 14, 1992); The New York Times (By Jeffrey Schmalz, March 16, 1992); CQ (By Jeffrey Katz and Ines Pinto Alicea, March 21, 1992); The Washington Post (By Michael Ross and Sara Fritz, March 20, 1992); Bloomberg (By Paula Dwyer, March 30, 1992)
Criticism of the House Bank Is Overdrawn
By Thomas S. Foley

Printed in the United States
By Bookmasters